Charlie
Auness

Charlie
Munro 55

p 35-43

TORTS AND COMPENSATION

PERSONAL ACCOUNTABILITY AND SOCIAL RESPONSIBILITY FOR INJURY

Fourth Edition

By

Dan B. Dobbs

Professor of Law
University of Arizona

Paul T. Hayden

Professor of Law
Loyola Law School, Los Angeles

AMERICAN CASEBOOK SERIES®

WEST GROUP

ST. PAUL, MINN., 2001

American Casebook Series, and the West Group symbol
are registered trademarks used herein under license.

COPYRIGHT © 1985, 1993 WEST PUBLISHING CO.
COPYRIGHT © 1997, 2001 By WEST GROUP
                610 Opperman Drive
                P.O. Box 64526
                St. Paul, MN 55164–0526
                1–800–328–9352

ISBN 0–314–25095-6

 TEXT IS PRINTED ON 10% POST CONSUMER RECYCLED PAPER

2nd Reprint — 2003

In thanks to and in memory of those lawyers, scholars, and students, living and dead, who have taught me most in tort law: Robert A. Leflar, Tom Pryor, Robert G. Byrd, Page Keeton, Wex Malone, and most of all, my students. —D.B.D.

To Diane, without whom my accomplishments would be fewer and far less meaningful, and in memory of my parents, Charlie and Grace, who gave me a good start.   —P.T.H.

*

Preface to the Fourth Edition

In the preface to the Third Edition, we emphasized the continuing development of tort law and our effort to present in this book both the changing and unchanging nature of that law. This edition reflects new developments in cases, topics, and academic contributions to tort law. The user will find more than 25 new main cases new to this edition and more than 30 new case abstracts, in addition to many new case citations. A few of the cases new to this edition antedate the third edition, but no less than twelve were decided in 2000.

We want to add that some important changes that have influenced this edition were not changes in the law. First, times change and students reflect cultural attitudes and preoccupations. Second, we ourselves learn from experience in teaching the materials– both our own experience and that of other teachers who have generously made suggestions or engaged us in discussion about particular items. This edition's changes reflect the influence of changed times and added experience.

Recent legal changes include these:

Lawyers and state and federal administrators have been increasingly involved in problems of nursing home liability for mismanagement and harm to patients. We have added a substantial new section on nursing home liability, with sidelights on the larger topic of elder abuse and the role of administrative law compared to tort law. Other new health care materials involve managed care and some new ideas about informed consent, in particular the suggestion that patients may be entitled to get the health care provider's record of success and failure.

Products liability has heavily engaged practicing and academic lawyers (not to mention judges) for decades. The new Products Restatement reflects changed attitudes and issues. The privity issue largely disappeared in personal injury cases some time ago. The issue of liability for unknowable risks has shriveled and shrunk. Liability for inadequate warnings accordingly loom larger, as does the proof of defect issue. These are among the legal changes we've tried to reflect there, along with citations to the final version of the Products Restatement.

Another new Restatement is the Restatement of Apportionment. That Restatement deals both with apportionment of responsibility between plaintiffs and defendants and with apportionment among the defendants themselves–in other words, with comparative responsibility and with what we have traditionally called contribution and indemnity. Some of the problems tackled by that Restatement are quite difficult and some of its provisions have generated a degree of controversy. This edition reflects the issues and the Restatement itself both in the chapters on comparative responsibility and in the chapter on apportionment among defendants.

Prompted by the Restatement and by an interesting article, we have re-introduced and expanded coverage of an old idea–that in some cases the plaintiff has "no duty" to protect herself and hence cannot be charged with comparative fault if she fails to do so in certain circumstances.

The march of immunities as the general solution to almost everything and with complete absolution for faulty conduct that causes injuries is a phenomenon that has not been adequately noted in the literature of torts, but one that is much reflected in this book at a time when political figures can argue in the same breath for both accountability and immunity.

Less obvious to casual observers of tort law are problems of integrating tort law with its neighbors. As in earlier editions, this book tries to introduce to first year students some of the non-tort ways of dealing with injury through administrative law (nursing home regulation, workers' compensation, social security disability). Contract, criminal law, and property concepts also play their part. Some of the new materials in this edition deal with this borderland of tort and other solutions.

Suggestions from teachers who use this book and our own experience resulted in another major change in this edition. We have added a new Chapter 1 to introduce some of the considerations that go into tort liability–justice, social policy (such as deterrence), and process concerns. Concerned that some students start law school with fixed opinions that get in the way of learning, we have also tried to use this chapter to let students directly confront the claim that tort plaintiffs are simply greedy people who want something for nothing by showing them a few damages cases.

New materials do not necessarily make a good book and we have tried at all times to keep the main goal in sight–to teach students, to challenge them, and to provide everyone involved with a good time in the process. An email from a worried student at another school leads us to add that we select and edit cases to provide opportunities for analysis and to strengthen skills in reading, interpretation, evaluation, and synthesis of legal materials. Students using this book should not see their job as merely listing a collection of elusive (and illusive) majority rules. They should realize that we have selected cases and written notes with the purpose of sharpening intellectual skills and the understanding of legal process.

On the topic of case selection, we should add that we attempt to use cases that reflect both our times and the factual setting in which injury occurs. A good many real-life tort cases are most unpleasant, involving murderous parolees, spouse-beaters, child abusers, or horrible medical injuries. Although legal principles might be distilled from old cases and in less varied settings, tort law is about living people with real injuries and our cases verbally (but not graphically) reflect some of these.

As with other editions, this one focuses primarily on personal injury torts. That focus includes, most centrally, common law tort solutions. Yet, most injuries in America are redressed through alternative means, such as workers' compensation, social security, or private insurance. A picture of injury law, therefore, includes those topics and they remain a part of the fourth edition.

Yet not all tort law is about personal injury. Indeed, some of the biggest growth in tort law in the late 20th century is found in areas involving economic torts such as interference with contract. Even so, the economic tort materials provided in this book are limited to core rules. They cannot take the place of appropriate advanced courses that cover defamation, misrepresentation, intellectual property, interference with contract, employment law and the like. The materials in this book provide an introduction to those topics that suffices to help students recognize that tort law is not exclusively injury law and perhaps to help them decide on advanced elective courses.

Apart from new materials and ideas, we have added a few charts or diagrams. We have also divided some chapters into shorter units so that they will be less daunting. Most omissions of citations go unmarked. We cite a few cases in our notes but, as in earlier editions, we try to avoid mere case collections. We hope that these styles and formats will help make this book readable and contribute to its value as a teaching tool.

Editing and Abbreviations

We've discovered that some students are not familiar with the use of ellipses to indicate omission, so we make this explanation. The opinions of appellate judges almost always include a good deal of matter on procedural points. They may also include discussions of many arguments made by lawyers that are not relevant to the issue we are developing in this book. They almost always include many citations to cases as precedent or example. Finally, some opinions are extremely repetitive. All this can make for very long opinions, sometimes many times the length of the edited case we present here. We mark our omissions in the main cases by ellipses – three dotes for omissions internal to a sentence, four for omissions that go to the end of the sentence or beyond.

To save space and improve readability, we also omit almost all citations the judge makes to other cases. Finally, as another space-saving device, we sometimes summarize some portions of cases in our words. When we do this in a main case, we put our words in square brackets and omit the judge's words.

The case abstracts in this book are different. They are our own summaries of a point in the full case, somewhat similar to briefs the student writes. In these abstracts, usually only one long paragraph, we use quotation marks if we quote the judge, but in the absence of quotations we have no need for ellipses or brackets since the abstract is merely our summary.

There are some standard works on torts that we cite from time to time. A major work in six volumes, now being published in a third edition, is Fowler V. Harper, Fleming James, Jr., and Oscar S. Gray, The Law of Torts (2d ed. 1986) and some volumes in the third edition. We cite this work as Harper, James, and Gray. A second work is Dan B. Dobbs, The Law of Torts (2000), a one-volume work. It is cited as Dobbs on Torts.

The Restatements of Torts in various editions are the product of the American Law Institute. They attempt to state a black-letter rule about most traditional tort issues. Students may find them difficult to parse, but they have had an enormous effect on tort law. The newest Restatements are designated as the Restatement Third of Torts with subtitles to indicate the particular area covered, for instance, the Restatement Third of Torts: Products Liability. We'll often refer to these Restatements by their subtitle–The Restatements of Products Liability, the Restatement of Apportionment, the Restatement of Unfair Competition.

—DAN B. DOBBS
PAUL T. HAYDEN

Tucson, Arizona
Los Angeles, California
February, 2001

Acknowledgements

For her excellent and much-needed help, I would like to thank especially Barbara Butler who served as my principal research assistant and editor in preparing this edition. When the inevitable crunch came, Abbe Goncharsky, Susan Myers, and Karen Pollins pitched in to provide further research and editing for some chapters. Davon May provided perfect support in preparing the manuscript. Finally, thanks to Loretta Taylor for her long-suffering personal support. –D.B.D.

Many thanks to my colleagues Larry Helfer, David Leonard and Dan Selmi for their helpful suggestions on this edition. I received excellent research assistance from Henry A. Kim and Dorothy Gibbons-White. For top-notch proofreading and cheerful help on many fronts, thanks to Ann Palmer. I could not have completed work on this book without the generous support of Loyola Law School. Last but not least, my sincere gratitude goes out to my family: Diane, Olivia, Dorothy and Rose, for their patience and flexibility. — P.T.H.

*

Summary of Contents

Table of Contents

TOPIC B.   THE SCHEME OF NEGLIGENT WRONGS

Subtopic 1.   The Prima Facie Case

Subchapter A.   The Fault Basis of Liability

Subchapter B.   Duty and Breach

Page

Table of Cases

The principal cases are in bold type. Cases cited or discussed in the text are roman type. References are to pages. Cases cited in principal cases and within other quoted materials are not included.

*

TORTS AND COMPENSATION

PERSONAL ACCOUNTABILITY AND SOCIAL RESPONSIBILITY FOR INJURY

Fourth Edition

*

Part I

A FIRST LOOK AT TORTS

Chapter 1

TORT LAW: AIMS, APPROACHES, AND PROCESSES

§ 1. WHAT IS TORT LAW?

Tort as wrongdoing. Torts are wrongs recognized by law as grounds for a lawsuit. These wrongs include an intentional punch in the nose and also a negligent car wreck. They include medical malpractice and some environmental pollution. The list of tortious wrongs is very long. All torts involve conduct that falls below some legal standard. In almost all cases, the defendant is in some sense at fault, either because he intends harm or because he takes unreasonable risks of harm.

Harm required. In all tort cases, the defendant's wrong results in a harm to another person (or corporation) that the law is willing to say constitutes a legal injury. The injured person is said to have a "cause of action," that is, a claim against the person who committed the tort. This claim can be pursued in court. Most of the cases in this book involve some kind of physical injury or threat of physical injury. Some torts, however, involve harm that is purely commercial and others involve intangible harm such as harm to reputation.

Torts, crimes, and contracts. A breach of contract is often grounds for a lawsuit, but a breach of contract is often not considered to be a tort at all. It must ordinarily be redressed under the rules for contracts, not the rules for torts. Some torts are also crimes. A punch in the nose is a tort called battery, but it may also be a crime. Sometimes a defendant who attacked the plaintiff is prosecuted criminally and is also held liable to the plaintiff for the tort. The two fields of law often overlap. However, they are not identical. Some acts that cause no harm at all to individuals might be crimes but not torts. Conversely, some acts cause harm and are torts but are not crimes. That is because criminal law aims at vindicating public interests, while tort law aims at vindicating individual rights and redressing private harms.

Non-tort systems. Physical injuries inflicted by one person upon another are commonly addressed by tort law, but there are alternatives. Toward the end of this book, several chapters consider alternatives such

2

as workers' compensation systems, which require employers to buy insurance and to pay for all on-the-job injuries even when the employer is not at fault. This is important for tort lawyers and also for those who wish to understand the way society deals with injuries. However, for now we are going to concentrate on the way tort law deals with injuries.

Common questions in tort law. Much of the law of torts is concerned with three questions: (1) What conduct counts as tortious or wrongful? (2) Did the conduct cause the kind of harm the law will recognize? (3) What defenses can be raised against liability if the defendant has committed a tort? The answer to these questions turns in part on why we have tort law and what its aims are. Before we look at those, however, we can get a better idea of what tort law *is* by looking briefly at what it *does* and what it aims to do.

§ 2.   THE AIMS AND APPROACHES IN TORT LAW–JUSTICE AND POLICY, COMPENSATION AND DETERRENCE

a.   Some Broad (and Conflicting) Aims

DAN B. DOBBS, THE LAW OF TORTS
§§ 8–11 & § 13

Copyright © 2000 by Westgroup.

[Section 8]

Justice, Policy, and Process Aims of Tort Law

... *Morality or corrective justice.* Particular aims of tort law are usually erected under one of two large systems of thought. The first bases tort law on moral responsibility or corrective justice. It attempts to hold defendants liable for harms they wrongfully caused and no others. Good social effects may result when courts act to right the wrongs done by defendants, but in this system of thought that is not the point of imposing liability. Liability is imposed instead when and only when it is "right" to do so.

Social utility or policy. The second large system of thought reverses the emphasis; it bases tort law on social policy or a good-for-all-of-us view. Social policy may coincide with justice in particular cases, but the dominant concern is not justice to the individual; it is to provide a system of rules that, overall, works toward the good of society.

Process. One kind of utility or social policy is inward looking. Rules must be made with the legal process itself in mind. They must be the kind of rules judges and juries can understand and apply in a practical way, and they must not leave too much to the judge's or the jury's discretion. These and a host of similar considerations focus on the litigation process itself as a good to be preserved rather than on the abstract ideal of justice or social utility.

Potential conflicts. The first two ways of looking at tort law are usually regarded as antithetical to each other. Although justice and policy often point to the same result, they do not always do so, and when they do not, one of these views must prevail or both must be compromised. The legal process view might also conflict with the aims of justice or those of policy.

Suppose a city, facing a raging and spreading fire, attempts to create a firebreak by blowing up a row of houses. Because time is critical, the city insists upon doing so before the plaintiff, who owns one of the houses, can remove his furniture. When the whole thing is over, the plaintiff claims damages from the city for the value of the furniture he could have saved. The city has acted for the good of its residents generally, but the plaintiff is the one who pays the costs. If the city's action is to be judged by a standard of social policy, some jurists might say the city should not be liable. On the other hand, if it is judged by corrective justice standards, the city should pay for the damage it did. Otherwise, the city would get the advantage of its action (whatever that advantage might be) but would pay none of the costs. There are more subtle examples, but this one is enough to suggest the potential conflict between a decision based upon (supposed) social policy and one based upon justice to the individual.

[Section 9]

Ideas of Corrective Justice

... *Fault and corrective justice*. Tort law imposes liability upon defendants for conduct the law treats as wrong. In most instances, the conduct adjudged as wrong can be viewed as morally faulty conduct: it is intentional misconduct or at least unreasonably risky conduct likely to cause harm to others. In these cases, tort law seems to be commensurate with corrective justice ideals. The defendant's fault is a wrong that has harmed the plaintiff in some recognizable way; tort liability, by requiring the wrongdoer to compensate the plaintiff, can put the accounts right between the parties.

Conversely, it can be argued that in a corrective justice scheme, it would be wrong to impose liability upon a defendant who is not at fault in causing the plaintiff's harm. Society may wish to compensate injured people by the use of public funds, but it cannot justly force one innocent individual to compensate another.

These views emphasize individual accountability for fault, accompanied by individual freedom to act without fault. They are consistent with an ideal of social responsibility for victims, however; they do not speak against government compensation for victims when the defendant is not at fault, only against compensation by the faultless defendant.

Strict liability and corrective justice. When tort law imposes liability without fault, does it go beyond the principle of corrective justice? At least *some* strict liability seems commensurate with corrective justice. For example, suppose a long-standing custom in our neighborhood permits any neighbor to borrow garden equipment from any other neighbor, but the custom is equally strong that if the equipment is damaged or lost while in the borrower's possession, the borrower must make the loss good. Suppose I borrow your lawnmower and without my fault it is damaged when a truck backs over it in my driveway. A rule that imposes liability upon me would be a strict liability rule because I was not at fault. Even so, liability seems to accord with corrective justice so long as you and I both know of the custom.

Uniting the potential for gains and losses. Some thinkers have advocated a general regime of strict liability on the ground that strict liability is a morally based system and therefore within the principle of corrective justice. One idea behind this view is that when I make choices about my conduct, I am entitled to the gains that may result from that conduct (including my personal pleasure), so I should also take responsibility for the losses. If I choose to hang-glide off the mountainside, either for personal pleasure or as part of a demonstration that brings me profit, then I should pay any damages I do when I cannot control the glider and land on your vegetable garden or your cat. This line of thought works best when an active person causes harm to a person or thing at rest. When two hang-gliders (or car drivers) crash into each other without fault, it is much harder to work out a system of strict liability that is also based on corrective justice.

[Paragraphs on strict liability for nonreciprocal risks and strict liability dictated by community standards are omitted.]

Fault again. Although innovative thinkers have sought to justify strict liability within a corrective justice framework, many of the cases they consider seem to entail special kinds of fault, for example, fault as judged by the fairness of imposing non-reciprocal risks or as judged by deviations from community-accepted norms. Whatever is to be said of strict liability theories of corrective justice, the great majority of tort cases turn on some kind of perception that the defendant is at fault in a significant way. At least for those cases, tort law begins with corrective justice ideals, even if those ideals may be modified by pragmatic, process, or policy considerations in particular cases.

[Section 10]

Compensation, Risk Distribution, Fault

... *Risk distribution or loss spreading.* ... [S]ome commentators have argued that tort liability should be strict or expansive in order to secure compensation for more injured persons. Some defendants if not all were seen as good "risk distributors" who should be liable for any harms they cause regardless of fault because they can "distribute" the costs of paying compensation. This means that some defendants, such as products manufacturers, could pay compensation for injuries they cause and then recoup some or all of those costs by raising the price of products. In this view, each individual purchaser of the products will pay a tiny fraction of the costs of injuries inflicted by those products and the injured person will not be compelled to bear the entire cost alone. Loss would thus cause less social dislocation. At the same time, an enterprise would be forced to internalize losses typically generated by the business itself.

Limited acceptance of risk distribution arguments. The common law of tort has not in fact generally adopted views that compensation is more important than corrective justice or that liability should be strict. Distribution arguments and strict liability have gone hand in hand, but only in a few kinds of cases. They have not supplanted fault as the most common basis for tort liability.

Moral and policy reasons for limiting compensation to cases of fault. Since compensation *is* indeed important and one of the goals of tort law, why is it that courts do not adopt strict liability across the board and order compensation in every case in which the defendant causes harm? The most obvious possibility is that judges feel heavily committed to a system of corrective justice and turn to social policy only when they feel social policy and corrective justice coincide at least in part. It is also possible, however, that in spite of social policy favoring compensation, other social policies counsel only limited compensation through the tort system.

First, the role of judges in framing schemes of distribution is doubtful. The risk distribution arguments may be sound, but sometimes may better be addressed to legislatures. In fact, some legislation in effect adopts such arguments. Workers' compensation statutes, for example, impose strict liability upon employers when workers are injured on the job. The cost or loss is distributed in part to workers themselves, whose wages might be higher but for the employer's cost of insuring against their injury. Part of it is distributed to customers who buy the employer's products or services. Second, an invariable award of compensation that must be paid by a defendant may eliminate any deterrent effect that the award would have if it were confined to cases of fault. Third, the tort system is an extremely expensive system to operate. If compensation is the most important goal, the tort system is a poor way to accomplish it because other means are cheaper. . . .

[Section 11]

Fostering Freedom, Deterring Unsafe Conduct;
Economic Analysis

Deterrence. Courts and writers almost always recognize that another aim of tort law is to deter certain kinds of conduct by imposing liability when that conduct causes harm. The idea of deterrence is not so much that an individual, having been held liable for a tort, would thereafter conduct himself better. It is rather the idea that all persons, recognizing potential tort liability, would tend to avoid conduct that could lead to tort liability. They might sometimes engage in the conduct in question, but only if they would get more out of it than the tort liability would cost. Some critics believe that tort law fails to provide systematic deterrence.

Deterrence in corrective justice and social policy systems. Both corrective justice and social policy goals can agree that deterrence is acceptable, but the two approaches might call for deterring quite different conduct. If you focus on conduct that is wrongful in the sense of being unjust to an individual, you might regard any given act as wrongful even though it is economically useful in society. If you focus on social policy, you might want to forgive defendants who cause harms by their socially useful activities....

Economic analysis. As the example suggests, one particular kind of social policy consideration is the economic one. If economics is defined broadly enough to include a consideration of all human wants and desires, then perhaps all social policies are in a sense economic policies.

For instance, economic analysis of the personal injury part of tort law might attempt to suggest rules for finding the right balance between the number of injuries and the freedom of defendants to act. People in general ought to be free to build buildings, including cheaper ones, if they do so carefully; the law wants to protect their freedom and indeed encourage the enterprise because economically sound decisions are indeed good for the community as a whole. So one line of economic thought suggests that in deciding [liability of a builder whose carefully-constructed building collapses and causes harm] the costs of injury should be weighed, but so should the social (economic) utility of the cheaper building. This line of thought in fact accords with a great many decisions in the courts that do not mention economics at all. Depending on how much the builder saved and how high the injury costs were, this line of thought might lead a court to deny any recovery against the builder....

Note

Considerations of costs and utilities are often identified with the drive for efficiency, meaning the greatest net good for the community. Efficiency in turn is contrasted with fairness or justice.

[Section 13]

Process Values in Tort Law

... Process values are values we attach to the legal process itself, in particular, the process of deciding disputes. Jury trial rights, discussed later, are one part of the dispute resolution process, but there are others. Many process values are represented in procedural codes and in constitutional prescriptions. Due process is a prized right even if it is not precisely formulated: we should hold the trial before the verdict; each party should be entitled to know what the other claims; disputing parties must be able to present their side of the dispute.

Adopting, formulating, and applying tort rules. . . . A judge might justly award damages to an injured plaintiff even if there were no rules at all, but the process of adjudication would then itself be suspect and in a sense unjust. So rules adopted must be rules that can be seen, understood, and applied, at least by the professionals involved in litigation. Judges striving to formulate or apply tort rules attempt to meet this modest concern for the litigation process itself.

Process goals. No authoritative list of process values guides judges, so lawyers can argue that any given rule is undesirable because it does not appropriately respect process concerns. Broadly phrased, the legal process should be designed not only to get good results in accord with justice and policy, but also to leave participants with a sense of humane participation in the process. That might include the felt need to tell one's side of the story and relate a sense of injustice. It might also include a sense that justice is not only done but seen to be done. There is also a practical side to process. Rules should be structured to permit efficient decision making—no litigant should be compelled to spend weeks getting a decision that can be made as well in a day.

Loose rule formulation that diminishes judicial accountability. . . . If rules are too abstract, they may fail to constrain the judge or the jury. They may instead effectively permit the decision makers to do as they like. . . . A rule that merely told people "be good" has at least two process defects. First, it fails to point to evidence a lawyer could adduce or arguments she could make. Second, the rule is so undefined that it fails to constrain the judge in appropriate ways. If too many rules were like this, the judge's decision would be a ukase of a judicial czar, not an adjudication of facts and law. The judges' rational explanations of what they do is usually the only effective check on them. If their decisions are not subject to professional scrutiny because the rules are so uncertain that anything goes, judges are likely to become in time more arbitrary and ultimately less just.

Tight rule formulation that eliminates needed flexibility. Conversely, however, precise rules may constrain the decision makers too much, leaving no room for justly deciding the individual's case which is at the heart of our concept of justice. A rule that says "be good" violates the process interest in understandable, reasonably precise rules. At the other extreme, a rule that says "never, ever, drive more than 40 miles per hour in this zone" may leave too little flexibility for the case of the driver rushing his child to the emergency room.

Rules guiding lawyers' investigation and arguments. Although some rules are actually read and understood by the people whose conduct they regulate, many tort rules are not. Rules often attempt to reflect the way people should behave even if they have not read the statutes and the cases. Thus, many tort rules are mainly read and understood by lawyers. Judges formulating tort rules must have in mind that lawyers use rules in very practical ways, to know what arguments and what facts are relevant so that investigation can proceed accordingly. . . .

Rules failing to specify provable facts. Rules also detract from good process when they call for facts that cannot be proved with reasonable confidence or proved within a reasonable length of time. Suppose that it is normally a tort to touch someone who has not consented to a touching, but that it is not a tort to touch someone who has consented to it. If the plaintiff plays in a game of tag or football, consent seems apparent even if it is not expressed. If judges were to say that anyone touching the plaintiff is liable unless the plaintiff actually, subjectively consents to the touching, the rule would not point to evidence that can be reached by the defendant's lawyer, since no one can produce evidence about the plaintiff's state of mind except so far as it is outwardly or objectively expressed. That might or might not lead to unjust results, but it leads to process concerns because we would not be very sure of our basis for judging the question of subjective consent if we are not permitted to consider the outward signs. . . .

Note

Many writers have addressed the goals or methods of tort law. Major contributions and differing views about justice vs. deterrence (or moral vs. economic analysis) are discussed in Gary T. Schwartz, *Mixed Theories of Tort Law: Affirming Both Deterrence and Corrective Justice*, 75 Tex. L. Rev. 1801 (1997). There is also an admirably succinct summary in William E. Nelson, *From Fairness to Efficiency: the Transformation of Tort Law in New York*, 1920–1980, 47 Buff. L. Rev. 117 (1999). David A. Fischer, *Successive Causes and the Enigma of Duplicated Harm,* 66 Tenn. L. Rev. 1127 (1999) concludes that when courts are forced to choose between the goals of fairness and efficiency, they have opted for fairness. The materials in this book may help you determine for yourself whether that conclusion is correct.

b. *Applying Some Approaches*

A great deal can be said about approaches to tort law or its goals, but for those without experience in reading actual cases and encountering actual tort problems, the goals are so abstract that they almost elude the grasp. The best approach may be to keep the goals or approaches in mind while reading cases. In many instances the different approaches will lead to the same outcome. When they do not, the differences are worth thinking about. To leave this topic with a sense of how some of these approaches might differ and a sense of different judicial styles as well, consider the following hypothetical case and the approaches taken by the three judges.

PROSSER v. KEETON

143 Unrep. Case 1113.

ALLEN, J., stated the facts for the court: Prosser was the owner of a valuable watch. It was stolen on or about April 1 by a person then unknown, but later discovered to be one Thurlow. Thurlow, in possession of the stolen watch, represented to Keeton that the watch was Thurlow's and that, because his mother was ill, he needed to sell it to raise funds. Thurlow and Keeton were both members of the same church and knew each other slightly. Keeton, because of this connection, reasonably believed that Thurlow was indeed the owner and he paid Thurlow $500 for the watch, a sum which approximated its real value. Thurlow immediately disappeared. About a month later, however, Prosser saw Keeton wearing the watch and identified it by a secret mark on the back. There is no question about the identification and Prosser demanded its return. Keeton argued that as he had paid for it, he would not return it. The trial judge held that Keeton, though in good faith, was a converter and liable to return the watch or pay its reasonable value. Keeton appeals.

ALLEN, J. The thief obviously did not obtain title to the watch. (It would be absurd to say that Prosser could not sue the thief if he had discovered the theft immediately.) If the thief did not have title, how could he transfer the title he did not have? Obviously he could not do so. And if the thief could not transfer title, then Keeton did not get title from the thief. It is true that Keeton paid money, but that can hardly go to show that the thief could suddenly convey a title he did not have. Since Keeton obtained no title, he has no right to the watch and he is a converter, liable to Prosser.

BATEMAN, J. A rule of law should work justice between the parties. Neither Prosser nor Keeton were guilty of wrongdoing, but as the thief has disappeared, one or the other must bear the loss. Purchasers are generally in no position to determine the true ownership of watches and this purchaser in particular had every reason to believe that the thief was honest. Watch owners, though undoubtedly victims of theft, are in better position to guard against theft than purchasers are to discover it. Justice therefore requires us to hold that the purchaser, Keeton, takes good title by operation of law.

COMPTON, J. The law may give the good faith purchaser title if there is an apt reason of policy for doing so, and this is true even if the thief could not give title. There is no reason of justice to make Prosser bear the loss. It has not been established by evidence that Prosser in particular or watch owners in general can protect themselves from thieves any better than purchasers can. Justice does not help us put the loss on either Prosser or Keeton. However, social policy, which transcends the question of justice between two individuals, does speak to this issue. Social policy in an enterprise society demands that exchange of goods be fostered. If every buyer had to investigate the provenance of the goods he or she purchased, the process of production and the satisfaction of human needs and wants would be made much more costly if it was not stopped altogether. Social policy, therefore, requires us to hold that Keeton should be given title to the watch by operation of the law.

Notes

1. *Formal styles of legal reasoning.* Judge Allen's reasoning might be described as "formal," or less flatteringly, as "conceptual" or "mechanical." Does Allen appeal either to justice or to policy?

2. *Justice and morality.* If a lawyer today were asked to mount an argument against formalistic reasoning, the answer might well be something like this: "Formalistic reasoning takes the eye off the ball. The real problems for which courts were instituted are justice and social policy." Judge Bateman's decision in *Prosser v. Keeton* emphasized justice, and concluded that it was "just" for the owner to bear the risk of theft rather than the purchaser. Might she have argued instead that it is unjust to deprive an owner of property by force or theft? This would have put her in accord with Judge Allen. Is her opinion more likely to be predictable and "correct" than Judge Allen's?

3. *Policy.* When the demands of justice conflict with demands of policy, which should prevail? If ideas of justice can be manipulated in an argument maybe ideas of policy can be, too. Is there any policy argument in favor of holding Keeton liable?

4. Suppose someone says to you: "Why should the courts bother with such a small case? After all, it is just a watch. People shouldn't burden the courts with small claims like this." Do you find any responses in considerations of justice? Of social policy?

§ 3. IMPLEMENTING TORT LAW PURPOSES WITH DAMAGES AWARDS

In a few cases the remedy for a tort is an injunction. That is, the court will order the defendant to cease committing a tort like a nuisance or a continuing contamination of the plaintiff's land. In the overwhelming majority of injury cases, however, the remedy is compensatory damages, an award of money to compensate for the tort committed by the defendant.

HOLDEN v. WAL–MART STORES, INC.

Supreme Court of Nebraska, 2000.
259 Neb. 78, 608 N.W.2d 187.

CONNOLLY, J. . . .

The appellant, Debra J. Holden, fell after stepping in a hole in the parking lot of a store owned by the appellee, Wal–Mart Stores, Inc. Holden subsequently underwent knee replacement surgery and sustained medical bills of at least $25,000. . . .

In July 1992, Holden was injured after she fell in the parking lot of a Wal-Mart in Scottsbluff, Nebraska. Prior to the fall, Holden had been issued a handicapped parking permit dated June 2, 1992, because prior problems with her knees and feet made it difficult for her to walk distances. On the day of the fall, Holden parked in a handicapped parking space at Wal–Mart. When she pulled into the stall, she did not notice any holes in the surface of the parking lot. After she got out of her van and was walking toward the rear of it, she fell and experienced immediate pain, the worst of which was in her right knee. After she composed herself, she saw that the cause of the fall was that her foot had twisted in a hole. Following the fall, Holden went to the emergency room. Holden subsequently underwent knee replacement surgery and brought the instant action against Wal–Mart seeking damages....

[Dr. Diane Gilles, an orthopedic surgeon, testified about Holden's earlier knee problems, but also testified] that if Holden had not fallen, she probably could have waited between 5 to 10 years before requiring a total knee replacement. Gilles also testified that prior to the fall, Holden had an 87–percent lower extremity impairment and a 35–percent whole person impairment and that after the fall, this increased to a 97–percent lower extremity impairment and 39–percent whole person impairment. Gilles' charges for treatment related to the fall were $646.75.

The record reflects that Holden first saw Dr. Mark Alan McFerran, another orthopedic surgeon, on January 10, 1994. McFerran subsequently performed a total knee replacement and placed Holden on maximum medical improvement in May 1995.... McFerran also testified that he thought the fall at Wal–Mart hastened the need for Holden to have her knee replaced.

The total of McFerran's charges was $24,707.91. McFerran testified that the hardware involved in the knee replacement has a lifespan of 15 to 20 years, after which Holden would require another replacement costing between $40,000 and $50,000, barring complications. Holden presented evidence regarding the pain she experienced after the fall and her need for assistance due to the fall.

The jury returned a verdict finding 40 percent negligence on the part of Holden and 60 percent negligence on the part of Wal–Mart. The jury determined total damages to be $6,000. As a result, Holden recovered $3,600....

[On appeal Holden contended] that the jury erred in its computation of damages, arguing that the jury made a mistake.

"An award of damages may be set aside as excessive or inadequate when, and not unless, it is so excessive or inadequate as to be the result of passion, prejudice, mistake, or some other means not apparent in the record.... If an award of damages shocks the conscience, it necessarily follows that the award was the result of passion, prejudice, mistake, or some other means not apparent in the record."

We conclude that the award in the instant case was not the result of a mistake.... Evidence was presented at trial regarding Holden's previous problems with her right knee, and there was conflicting evidence regarding the effect of the fall on this preexisting condition. Holden testified regarding the additional pain and difficulties the fall caused, and her physicians indicated that the fall sped up the need for her to have knee replacement surgery. However, there was also evidence that Holden had been having similar knee pain causing difficulty in her life prior to the fall. However, she did not report the additional pain in several following appointments with her physicians. The evidence was strong that Holden would, at some point, have undergone knee replacement surgery regardless of the fall. However, when she might have done so was unclear.

[T]he jury could have reached any number of factual conclusions. A jury is entitled to determine what portion of a claimed injury was proximately caused by the incident and what portion of the medical bills was reasonably required. The jury in this case could have determined that the fall was the proximate cause of only a small portion of Holden's damages. The evidence for such a determination is apparent from the record, and we will not disturb that determination on appeal. . . .

Affirmed.

Notes

1.　*Liability.* Most cases in this book will be considering whether the defendant should be liable to the plaintiff at all. In this case and the next, assume that the judge and jury, considering the detailed testimony not available to us, properly imposed liability. That will permit us to focus on the question of appropriate compensation.

2.　*The jury damages award.* Did the jury get the award about right or was the award too low because it was less than the plaintiff's actual medical expense? Actually, you might consider whether we have facts sufficient to permit us to judge either way.

3.　*Judge and jury.* The appellate judges seem to recognize an important role for the jury, yet also seem to say that the judges will reject the jury's verdict in some cases. Can you say when judges will do that? Is *Holden* more about process values than about, say, appropriate deterrence or exact compensation?

4.　*Compensatory damages elements.* The injured person has the burden of proving damages. If he offers adequate proof, he can recover any (1) lost wages or lost earning capacity, (2) medical and other expense, and (3) pain and suffering endured. This may include mental or emotional pain. In many cases those elements have a future dimension. If so, the plaintiff can recover for reasonably proven future losses. The award, if any, is subject to some adjustments. For instance, adjustments may be made to account for delay in payment, for inflation and other items. We leave aside those more technical details for now. The gist of the damages rules is that the defendant has wrongfully reduced the plaintiff's net assets, tangible and intangible, and should be required to restore them. Is this consistent with some or all of the broad goals of tort law?

5.　*Punitive damages.* In a very few cases, juries are permitted to award punitive damages in addition to compensatory damages. Punitive damages are awarded against those wrongdoers who act maliciously or wilfully or wantonly in causing injury. They are intended to provide a measure of added deterrence and perhaps some punishment for the wrongdoer's serious misconduct.

6. *Attorney fees costs to the plaintiff.* One of the most important institutional rules covering most litigation is that a losing party is not required to pay the winning party's attorney fees. The almost universal system of litigation finance is that plaintiffs' attorneys are paid by contingent fees. They are paid nothing if they lose, a percentage of the recovery if they win. The percentage may vary from around 25% to 40%, sometimes higher. The percentage may sound high, but bearing in mind the lawyer's investment of time and effort and the fact that the lawyer will be paid nothing in some cases, the percentage fees are often quite reasonable.

7. *Criticisms of damages.* You may have heard or read many criticisms of tort law–that it is out of control, that Americans litigate trivial matters, that they are greedy, and that they seek something for nothing. No doubt greed shows up in law suits as well as in corporate board rooms and elsewhere. However, it is important to know that the studies available do *not* support the claim that litigation by individuals has increased or that juries often run amok. A recent study is Deborah Jones Merritt and Kathryn Ann Barry, *Is the Tort System in Crisis? New Empirical Evidence,* 60 OHIO ST. L.J. 315 (1999). Studies *do* show that corporate and business litigation has increased, however. We'll see more details about this in a later chapter.

8. *A case example.* You might want to be cautious about forming judgments about all tort law based upon anecdotes or media presentations rather than an understanding of the whole system. One case that grabbed media attention and comes in for vituperative comment involved a large judgment for a woman who was burned by scalding coffee handed her by McDonald's. Sitting in the car, she held the container between her legs to take the top off and the coffee spilled. It was hot enough to inflict third degree burns–which covered her groin and genital area. Third degree burns can burn entirely though the skin and vessels and all the way to the bone. She was hospitalized, underwent skin grafts, had excruciating pain, and was permanently disfigured. She asked McDonald's to pay her $11,000 hospital bills, but McDonald's refused. She hired an attorney who demanded $90,000 in damages, but McDonald's refused that, too. The attorney then filed a suit and discovered that McDonald's intentionally kept its coffee hot enough to inflict third degree burns and in fact had known of at least 700 people who had been burned by its scalding coffee. He now demanded more and punitive damages, to boot. The jury awarded the plaintiff $200,000 in compensatory damages, reduced to $160,000 because it considered that she was partly at fault. The jury then added a whopping sum as punitive damages because McDonald's was reckless or even malicious. The jury's verdict for that was $2.7 million, a large sum meant to deter such misconduct. Even so it only represented about two days' of McDonald's revenues from coffee sales. The judge reduced the punitive award to $480,000, for a total award of $640,000. Media and web commentators present a different picture. They often leave out the fact that most of the award was for deterrence, not compensation, that it was reduced as part of the ordinary mechanisms of tort law (the judge's review) and that the coffee was not merely "hot," but capable of great harm, which it in fact caused quite needlessly. You can read comments

on the web in essence saying that "an old woman" spilled coffee on herself and got something for nothing, omitting to note that the jury reduced the compensatory damages by $40,000 for the plaintiff's supposed fault in spilling the coffee, and perhaps betraying a contempt for "old women." You'll want to judge for yourself, but as professionals we should decide on the basis of more facts than appear in the popular media. For these facts and others, and also for the media portrayals, you can find a summary of the McDonald's case in Mark B. Greenlee, *Kramer v. Java World: Images, Issues, and Idols in the Debate over Tort Reform,* 26 CAP. U. L. REV. 701 (1997).

9. *Pain and suffering.* One difficulty in assessing proper compensation is that for many of us, our main assets are not in the form of money or property but in the form of good health and freedom from pain. Although pain is not quantifiable, freedom from pain has economic value. We can see that in the expenditures people make to gain pleasure and avoid pain. You could also imagine that someone offered you money for the right to break your leg. If you would accept such an awful offer at all, you would almost certainly demand even more money if the break would entail pain. The amount of money you would demand to suffer pain is not the measure of a tortfeasor's liability (he is only liable for reasonable compensation, not what you would demand). Even so, if freedom from pain is an intangible asset, pain inflicted by a defendant represents a real loss and should be compensated somehow.

10. *Estimating damages.* How does the jury know what about to award for pain and suffering? Remember that twelve jurors must agree on an award. If jurors are randomly chosen, does that tend to guarantee that awards are likely to represent the community's sense of an appropriate award on the facts of the particular case? Remember, too, that the jury is not merely reading an abbreviated media account but is instead seeing all the witnesses and learning of all the harms actually done.

11. Mr. Cho, with a medical appointment, asked Buckner to move his truck, which was blocking Cho's car. Buckner refused. Cho then honked at Buckner. This seems to have triggered Buckner's response: he kicked Mr. Cho in the head, knocking him down. When Mrs. Cho came out, Buckner knocked her down, kicked her down a second time, then hit her in the chest, causing a third fall. Mrs. Cho had medical bills of more than $8,600, Mr. Cho of more than $1,300. If we are the jury, what amount do we award the Chos as compensatory damages? *Norfolk Beverage Co., Inc. v. Cho,* 259 Va. 348, 525 S.E.2d 287 (2000).

ESTEVEZ v. UNITED STATES

United States District Court for the Southern District of New York, 1999.
72 F.Supp.2d 205.

SCHEINDLIN, DISTRICT JUDGE.

[In October, members of the Estevez family were injured in a collision with a postal truck for which the defendant was responsible. In a trial without a jury, the judge found that the postal driver was negligent. The court then considered damages. Joseph was two years old at the time. Only portions of the court's opinion dealing with his damages are included here.]

[Joseph] was transferred to the pediatric intensive care unit of Montefiore Medical Center, where he remained hospitalized for approximately five weeks. During that time he underwent the following surgical procedures: (1) exploratory laparotomy, bowel resection (removal of 8 cm. of the intestine), and repair of perforations in the bowel wall; and (2) aortic endartectomy (removing a clot from the artery), thrombectomy (removing a clot from the vein) and patch angioplasty. During this last procedure a Gortex patch was permanently placed on his aorta. The first surgery was due to a perforation of a section of the small intestine, an abdominal wall hernia and a tear or fracture of the lower pole of the right kidney. The second surgery was due to an intimal tear, which is a tear to the inner lining of the aorta. [Later, an additional 8 cm. of intestine were removed. Later still, Joseph underwent a spinal fusion at L2–L3. All the operations resulted from injuries caused by the accident.]

In addition to these surgical procedures, Joseph sustained the following injuries or underwent the following treatment: (1) he wore a special spinal fracture brace (a "TLSO" brace) for seven weeks for a compression fracture at L2–L3; (2) he was placed on high blood pressure medication as a result of renal injuries until May, 1997; (3) he was intubated with an endotracheal breathing tube for a brief period of time; (4) he was forced to utilize a nasogastric feeding tube for a brief period of time and (4) he has a foot drop (unable to flex his foot) in his right lower extremity. As a result of this last injury he has received physical therapy from the time of the accident to the present.

The parties agree that Joseph has incurred $138,000 in past hospital and medical costs.... [The court awarded only $88,000 that was not covered by no-fault insurance. The court also awarded $500,000 for Joseph's pain and suffering up to trial.]

With respect to future risks resulting from these injuries, Dr. Spigland testified that Joseph is at high risk for the development of intestinal adhesions, which can lead to intestinal obstructions. Such adhesions can be painful and can be treated either through surgery or through the use of a nasogastric feeding tube and intravenous fluids. He is also at risk of suffering an infection of the Gortex patch or of developing pseudoaneurysms of the aorta. Finally, he will be at risk of developing an infection of the lining of the heart, known as endocarditis. Dr. Spigland believed this last risk was preventable through prophylactic treatment (antibiotics prior to any bloody procedure) and early diagnosis.

The Government agrees, based on the testimony of its expert, Dr. Spigland, that Joseph will require an annual cardiology consultation and an annual echocardiogram. Because Joseph's life expectancy is 67.5 years, the Government concludes that he will have 13 annual examinations as a child (through age 17) and 55 annual examinations as an adult (through age 72). The cost of a cardiac consult for a child is $250 and for an adult is $330. The cost of an echocardiogram for a child is $850 and for an adult is $963. The total cost of these procedures is $85,415.

Joseph's treating physician, Dr. Leonard Seimon, testified that Joseph needs a scannergram and x-ray of his leg every 18 months during the next five years at a cost of approximately $350 per scan and $250 per office visit. This would result in additional expenses of $1,800.

There is some dispute over the future cost of treatment for the foot drop. There is little doubt that at a minimum Joseph would require an orthotic shoe insert. Each insert costs approximately $1,000. During his growing years, until age 16 or 12 more years, he would require a new orthotic each year, amounting to $12,000. During his remaining life span, ages 16–72, or 56 years, he would require a new orthotic every two years, amounting to $28,000. Another possible treatment is continued physical therapy. There is testimony in the record that each session costs $75 and that Joseph has been receiving therapy three times a week, at a weekly cost of $225. The Government argues that he will only require therapy through the end of 1999 at a projected cost of $5,850. Plaintiff, in turn, argues that Joseph will continue to need physical therapy for a longer period of time. At the rate of $75 per session times 3 sessions per week, the annual cost of physical therapy is $11,700. The final dispute is whether Joseph will need tendon lengthening surgery to treat his foot drop. There was no testimony in the record as to the cost for that surgery.

Joseph is entitled to an award for future medical expenses. Based on the totality of the evidence in the record, Joseph is awarded a total of $220,815 in future medical expenses. That award includes the following components: $85,415 for annual cardiology consultations and annual echocardiograms; $1,800 for scannergram's and leg x-rays during the next 5 years; $40,000 for orthotic devices; and $93,600 for physical therapy, assuming that Joseph will need 8 more years of physical therapy. No amount is awarded for any tendon lengthening surgery as no cost estimate was provided for that procedure. An award might also be appropriate for surgery or hospitalization due to abdominal adhesions because Dr. Spigland testified that Joseph was at high risk for developing this condition. However, because there was no figure provided for either surgery or hospitalization, any award would be unduly speculative.

[The court here considered in detail the testimony concerning the foot drop condition and its possible treatment.] I conclude, based on the totality of the evidence, that Joseph's conditions of foot drop, leg length discrepancy and abnormal gait are permanent. I further conclude that he will benefit from continued physical therapy until he is fully grown, namely for an additional 12 to 16 years.

Joseph is entitled to an award for future pain and suffering. The setting of any such award is by definition speculative.... I conclude based on my review of the evidence, and on cases submitted both by the plaintiff and the Government, that an appropriate award for future pain and suffering is $750,000. I reach this conclusion based on the totality of Joseph's medical problems and his long life expectancy. As noted earlier, Joseph's life expectancy is 67.5 years. This award, then, provides little more than $10,000 per year for a permanent limp and leg shortening, a damaged spine, potential abdominal adhesions, risk of infection of the Gortex patch, and the continued discomfort of medical monitoring and associated procedures.

Joseph requests an award for future lost earnings. He claims that as a person with a disability, his earning capacity is diminished compared to people who have no disability. He relies on the testimony of Andrew Gluck, who performed a vocational economic assessment. Mr. Gluck testified based on his observations of Joseph, his meeting with Joseph's mother, and his review of the medical records.

Mr. Gluck made several assumptions. First, he assumed that Joseph has a permanent non-severe disability. Second, given the education of Joseph's parents, he assumed that Joseph is likely to obtain a college degree. He next assumed, based on statistical tables made available by the United States Government, that disabled males with a college degree are statistically likely to earn $10,000 less per year than non-disabled males. More specifically, he testified that a non-disabled college graduate can expect to earn an annual salary of $64,610, whereas a disabled college graduate can only expect to earn an annual salary of $54,526. Finally, he concluded that occupationally disabled people have a shorter work life expectancy than non-disabled people. He testified that on average occupationally disabled people work 6.67 years less than those who have no disability. . . .

I agree with the Government that there is no principled way to conclude that Joseph's earning power, given the credible assumption, that he will graduate college, will be any less than that of a healthy person who is a college graduate. Nonetheless, I disagree with the Government with respect to work life expectancy. Based on all of the evidence in the record, I conclude that Joseph has a less than average work life expectancy. I accept Mr. Gluck's testimony that a person with Joseph's complex of medical problems . . . is less likely to work as long or as continuously as a healthy person. According to Mr. Gluck's testimony a non-severely disabled person has a 6.67 year reduced work life expectancy based on reduced job opportunities, limitations on activities of daily living, continuous medical problems, and earlier retirement. Given the $64,610 average annual salary of a 45–year old college educated male, I conclude that Joseph is entitled to a future lost earnings award of $432,887 ($64,610 x 6.7 years).

Joseph is therefore entitled to a total award of $1,993,902. [Of this, 25% is allocated to attorney fees. There were future reductions based on the fact that some of the damages would not actually occur until sometime in the future. The total adjusted award was $1,511,052.]

Notes

1. In many of the cases we will see, the courts are concerned mainly with determining the justice or policy of the case and with formulating legal rules accordingly. In *Estevez,* the judge is a trial judge sitting as a jury, not an appellate judge. He is less concerned with formulating rules and more concerned with finding facts, just as a jury would be.

2. If the exact amount of loss is uncertain because losses cannot be precisely quantified, should recovery be denied? Or should the tortfeasor have to live with the best estimates we can make?

3. The tort in *Estevez* is "negligence." Negligence has a special meaning in tort law that we will explore at length later. We can state a good approximation right now, however. Negligence means conduct that inflicts an unreasonable risk of harm upon others. Perhaps the defendant's negligence was quite minor, a short distraction while driving, for example. Yet compensatory damages are not punishment for fault and for that reason are not proportionate to fault. Compensatory damages are intended to be exactly proportionate to the plaintiff's actual injury, so if minor fault causes great harm, the defendant must compensate for that harm. Bear in mind, though, that no damages at all are awarded unless the defendant has wrongfully caused the injury. Consider whether awarding damages disproportionate to fault but proportionate to harm done is consistent with any of the aims of tort law.

4. *Loss sharing.* We've just said that the plaintiff's compensatory damages are measured by her losses and not by the degree of the defendant's fault. But that does not mean that the defendant will pay all the damages assessed. Sometimes damages liability is shared. If there are two or more tortfeasors, for example, each may bear some portion of the liability. Even if only one tortfeasor has caused the plaintiff's harm, the plaintiff herself may be partly at fault. In that case, the plaintiff will share some of the loss or even in some instances may lose her claim entirely. The problems of loss sharing present big challenges to tort law. Can we achieve appropriate fairness, efficiency, or deterrence if losses are shared? Professional development of this problem must wait for coverage later, but you should be aware now that a defendant's liability is often reduced by sharing that liability with the plaintiff or other tortfeasors.

Chapter 2

READING TORTS CASES: TRIAL PROCEDURES

§ 1. LOOKING FOR FACTS, RULES, AND REASONS

Reading cases to understand principles and predict law. This course proceeds in part by presenting real cases that involved individual human beings as plaintiffs, defendants, lawyers and judges. The "cases" in this book are actually the explanations given by judges for the legal decisions they make. By reading them carefully, good lawyers can learn the governing principles. They can also begin to predict what other important rules could develop from these principles. Along with this skill, they can learn to understand issues, to distinguish seemingly similar cases, and to find similarities in cases that are seemingly different. Why are these skills important? One reason is that these are skills needed to make professional estimates about likely results if a client must sue or defend. Another is that they are skills needed to construct sound and persuasive legal arguments to courts.

Rules. Case reading is easier if you have some idea what to look for. You are certainly looking for rules or principles that might help resolve similar disputes later on. Sometimes a judge earmarks a rule so you can identify the rule just by reading the judge's statement of it. More often, you must interpret what you read. Few judges attempt to state all the conditions and qualifications that go with a rule. Instead, they are likely to state only the portion of the rule that is at issue in the case. So you must always try to read the judge's statements about rules in the context of the issue presented.

Reasoning. The rules in most judicial decisions are interpreted in part by following the judge's reasoning. Ideally, the judge's reasoning explains why the rule exists (or why the judge is creating the rule) and how it applies to the case. What the judge emphasizes in reasoning about the rule tells you a great deal about what the rule is and what its limits might be.

Facts. The facts of a case are likely to influence the judge in selecting appropriate rules. For instance, the rule appropriate to liability

20

of a teenager for harms he does might be not be appropriate for liability
of a four-year-old. Facts are also likely to influence the way the judge
reasons and states the rules. If the case is about a four-year-old who
causes harm, the judge's observations about the liability of children may
really be observations about the liability of very young children. This will
require interpretation on your part, and it means that you must understand the facts in the case very well indeed.

Process and issues. Reading cases well requires attention to the
issues in the case. The issues are shaped partly by the parties' assertions
and partly by the legal procedures that raise those issues. The allocation
of power between judge and jury is a major process element in many tort
cases. Suppose: (1) The issue is whether the judge should dismiss the
plaintiff's claim without letting a jury decide it, and that the judge lets
the jury decide. (2) The jury decides for the defendant. (3) The judge
upholds the jury's verdict. Process values explain this sequence. In item
(1), the judge is not saying that the plaintiff should win merely because
the judge refuses to dismiss the case. The judge is saying instead that the
decision on the particular issue and the particular facts should be made
by the jury, not by the judge. So the jury's verdict either way will be
upheld on those particular facts. In other cases, judges will take the case
from the jury, allocating power to themselves instead of the jury. The
appropriate sphere of judge and jury is often the basic concern in
applying legal rules, so a reader of cases must pay attention to the
process and issue.

Application of rules. Although rules found in yesterday's cases will
help resolve today's disputes, they usually will not do so simply or
directly. You will find you must reason about how the rule is to be
applied in your client's situation. You will also find that any given rule
must ordinarily be made to work effectively with other rules.

Rules point lawyers to evidence required and arguments available.
Frequently, the rules in yesterday's cases do not actually resolve today's
disputes at all. Instead, their most important function is to point to
evidence that lawyers will need to gather for a trial and to arguments
lawyers will need to construct in presenting a claim or in defending it.

§ 2. PROCEDURES AT TRIAL

The cases you read are usually the decisions of appeals court judges.
Less often they are decisions of trial court judges who occasionally decide
to provide a written explanation of their decisions. The judges are
usually addressing the facts that are shown by a transcript of the trial.
Since all decisions about tort law are made in deciding some procedural
point, it is necessary to have a basic idea what the trial procedure is like.

Trial procedure can be complicated, but the basic plan of a trial is
very simple. It is designed to resolve two kinds of disputes. The first kind
of dispute is about the facts, about what happened. Almost all trials
involve at least some factual dispute. The second kind of dispute is about

the law. Most trials also involve disputes about law as well as disputes about fact.

It may be helpful to imagine a very simple kind of case in which the plaintiff contends that the defendant struck him. Defendant denies this completely. How does this get to court and what happens there?

1. *Complaint*. Plaintiff's lawyer, having investigated the facts, writes up a document called a complaint or petition. This document states the facts as claimed by the client. This document is formally filed with the court (in the court clerk's office) and a copy is served on (delivered to) the defendant, often by an officer of the court such as the sheriff or the federal marshal.

2. *Answer*. The defendant, within the time allowed, must file some sort of paper taking a position on the complaint. Very often it is an "answer." An answer usually simply disputes the factual claims of the plaintiff. For example, if plaintiff's complaint states "Defendant struck the plaintiff in the face," the defendant might answer saying she denies that she struck the plaintiff. This reveals what is at dispute between the parties–a dispute about the facts (not the law). Because the dispute is about the facts, the parties will gather evidence for presentation at trial. If that evidence shows different versions of the facts (as forecast in the complaint and answer) the jury will ultimately resolve the factual controversy.

3. *Selection of a jury*. When the case comes up for trial, prospective jurors are questioned by the judge and perhaps by the lawyers to determine whether they are biased about issues in the case or about one of the parties. Lawyers may "strike" or eliminate some prospects. Of those who remain, 12 (or sometimes six or eight) are then "put in the box" as jurors for the particular case.

4. *Opening statements*. At this point the judge will ask the plaintiff's lawyer to state the case for the plaintiff. This is not an argument but a preliminary view of the testimony the plaintiff will put on. The defendant's lawyer makes a similar opening statement.

5. *Plaintiff's case*. The plaintiff's attorney then calls the first witnesses. By asking questions, the lawyer elicits answers that establish what the witness knows about the facts relevant to the case. After each witness is questioned by the plaintiff's lawyer, the defendant's lawyer has an opportunity to cross-examine the witness, by asking questions that may put the matters in a different light, or may give them a different emphasis, or may show that the witness was mistaken, lying, or biased. The two examinations of the witness thus can give the jury a basis for judging how much the witness really knew and how credible the witness might be.

6. *Defendant's case*. When all of the plaintiff's witnesses have been examined and cross-examined, the defendant puts on witnesses who give the defense side of the story. These witnesses, answering questions on the defense counsel's examination, often give a different factual picture

from that given by the plaintiff's witnesses. After each witness is examined, the plaintiff's counsel cross-examines.

7. *Closing arguments.* Plaintiff's lawyer, then defendant's lawyer, then plaintiff's lawyer in rebuttal, make closing arguments to the jury. These are arguments, not statements of fact. They are aimed at persuading the jury on the basis of the testimony that one side or the other should be believed.

8. *Instructions to the jury.* At this point (or sometimes before closing arguments) the judge instructs or "charges" the jury. These instructions tell the jury the relevant law. The judge decides what instructions to give, but the lawyers for each side first suggest instructions that favor their positions and theories–a crucially important strategic juncture of the trial. The judge tells the jury to decide what the facts are and then to apply the legal rules given in the instructions. Thus, a judge might instruct the jury that if it finds that the defendant intentionally struck the plaintiff with intent to harm, it should bring in a verdict for the plaintiff. Notice that this leaves the fact-finding to the jury and the legal rules to the judge.

§ 3.   PROCEDURES RAISING LEGAL ISSUES

The preceding paragraphs emphasized the factual disputes of the parties and the order of trial. Most cases also involve arguments about what the legal rules are, or how they should apply to the particular case. The issues are raised by several different procedural devices, which will appear in most of the tort cases in this book. The appeals courts never simply agree or disagree with the outcome or result of the trial. Instead, appeals courts always apply legal rules to determine whether the trial judge erred on some particular motion, admission of evidence, or instruction to the jury. The scope of the issue and hence the scope of a rule in a given case often depends upon the procedure used to raise the legal issue.

We summarize the main procedures that raise legal issues on appeal so you can read them in one place and also so you can sticky tab this page and look back at them as you encounter them in cases. In the appendix following this section, we narrate a hypothetical case so you can see the procedures being applied.

a.   *The Motion to Dismiss or Demurrer*

If the defendant believes that the plaintiff's complaint does not state facts that show a good legal claim, the appropriate response is to file a motion to dismiss the complaint. The effect of this motion is to say to the judge, "Take all the facts stated in the complaint as if they were proved; even so, they do not show a valid legal claim."

Since the facts alleged are temporarily assumed to be true for purpose of considering this motion, there is no factual dispute. The issue raised is one of law, for the judge to decide, not the jury. Suppose plaintiff's lawyer wrote up, filed and served a complaint stating that defendant had frowned at the plaintiff. Frowning is not a tort, so defendant's motion to dismiss would be sustained.

Conceivably the plaintiff's complaint would be rewritten or amended to add important allegations. This would usually be permitted. However, in most cases in this casebook, the issue is on appeal for the very reason that the plaintiff *cannot* add any provable facts that will help.

If the judge sustains the defendant's motion to dismiss, that usually decides the whole case. The rule that can be derived is that the facts stated by the plaintiff do not show a tort, or, more specifically, frowning is not a tort.

Notice that the motion to dismiss comes at a very early stage of the case–before the answer is filed or along with the answer. In other words, it comes before any time has been invested in developing proof or calling a jury.

If the motion to dismiss or demurrer is denied, or if the plaintiff amends the complaint to state a good claim, the case will proceed and defendant will file an answer or motion for summary judgment. However, defendant may still win the final round, since at the end of the trial he may appeal the trial judge's denial of the motion to dismiss.

b. *The Motion for Summary Judgment*

The motion to dismiss assumes all the facts stated in the complaint are true and argues that, even so, the complaint fails to show a good legal claim. The summary judgment motion, on the other hand, is based on (a) a showing of new facts in addition to those stated in the complaint, and perhaps in contradiction to them; (b) a showing that there is no real dispute about these new facts; plus (c) a showing that on these new facts, the law compels judgment for the moving party. The summary judgment motion is almost always made by the defendant asserting that given the undisputed facts the legal rules do not permit the plaintiff to win.

Where do these new facts necessary for summary judgment come from? Usually from the process of discovery, in which sworn testimony or admissions of the parties and witnesses can be taken out of court, and relevant documents exchanged.

Summary judgment determines the law suit without a jury. It is appropriate only if there is no room for dispute about facts. Suppose the parties go through discovery and the plaintiff states "he hit me," while the defendant states, "I did not." The defendant may have added a new "fact" in his testimony that he did not hit the plaintiff. However, he cannot get summary judgment because that fact is directly disputed by the plaintiff. It will be for the jury to decide which party is speaking truthfully.

c. *Objections to Evidence and Offers of Evidence*

Evidence that is not relevant to help prove any element involved in the case should be excluded by the judge, especially if the evidence is likely to mislead the jury or to be "prejudicial." However, the attorneys have to carry the initiative to raise this point, as they do with every other point in the trial. Thus if the plaintiff offers evidence and the defendant makes no objection, the defendant will not be permitted to complain later on.

A trial judge's admission of evidence over objection, or her refusal to admit evidence because of objection, raises legal issues. The judge's ruling in effect takes a conscious or unconscious position on those issues. The most common issue about evidence is whether it is relevant to any legal issue in the case, and to answer this, one needs to know what the legal issues and legal rules are. Thus rulings on admission of evidence are often rulings based on a specific principle of law.

Example. Suppose a plaintiff claims he suffers severe mental distress and becomes ill as a result of seeing defendant beat a dog across the street. Defendant objects to this evidence. The evidence would be relevant if it tends to show a tort to the plaintiff. Under a rule generally recognized by courts, this is not a tort to the plaintiff. For that reason this evidence should be excluded. The trial judge probably will not express her reasons in ruling on the evidence. However, a ruling that excludes this evidence tends to imply a rule of law.

d.   Motion for Directed Verdict

This motion is usually made at the end of the plaintiff's proof and renewed at the end of all the evidence given on both sides. The motion for directed verdict asserts that the proof offered by the plaintiff is legally insufficient to warrant a jury's verdict for the plaintiff. (More rarely, a plaintiff might move for directed verdict, but such a motion is seldom granted in view of the plaintiff's burden of proof.)

The judge considers the evidence in the light most favorable to the plaintiff. That is, the judge takes into account all the reasonable inferences the jury would be allowed to draw from the testimony. Considering all the evidence in this light, the judge will grant the motion for a directed verdict if a jury of reasonable persons could not differ on the evidence, or if the facts taken in this favorable light do not establish any legal claims. The standard can be stated in other ways, but the basic idea is that the judge is not to take over the jury's role. So a directed verdict should be denied if there is room for reasonable jurors to disagree. This almost always involves some interaction of fact and law–do the facts, taken in a light favorable to the plaintiff, establish the elements required by law?

A motion for directed verdict is somewhat similar to both a motion to dismiss and to a summary judgment motion, but it is based on the *evidence produced in full at the trial*, not on general allegations of the complaint and not on the claim that the facts are undisputed.

e.   Proposed Instructions and Objections to Them

Instructions are the trial judge's statements of law to the jury. They tell the jury what it must consider and what facts must be found to exist before the plaintiff can recover, or what facts must be found before a defense applies. Instructions must accurately state the law, and must not mislead the jury or mis-emphasize some element. Lawyers must actively object to instructions they feel are incorrect statements of law, or propose instructions of their own. Lawyers, especially defense lawyers, usually do both.

Since an instruction is supposed to represent a correct statement of the law, and one on which the jury will act, an erroneous statement of the law would be ground for appeal. On well-settled matters there are few erroneous statements. But most litigated cases contain some element that is special and unusual, which is why the cases are litigated. Because of unique elements in each case, there are almost always some issues of law that are not settled. If these issues of law are not dealt with by motions to dismiss, summary judgment, or directed verdict, there will be an instruction on these issues, and the lawyers will have an opportunity to state their positions on these issues, by objecting to instructions given or by proposing their own. The substantive legal issue raised by an instruction, then, is whether it correctly states the law.

f. Motion N.O.V.

The motion N.O.V. is a virtual renewal of the motion for directed verdict. (N.O.V. is for the Latin *non obstante veredicto*, meaning notwithstanding the verdict.) The motion asserts that the evidence is not legally sufficient to justify a jury verdict for the plaintiff. A judge who is unwilling to grant a directed verdict before the jury reaches its decision may grant an N.O.V. after the verdict is reported. There may be several reasons for this. For example, the judge may firmly believe the jury will find for the defendant even without a directed verdict. Or the judge may believe that the jury will come in with a verdict for the plaintiff, but that it will be small and reasonable. Afterwards, when the N.O.V. is presented, the judge may have some second thoughts.

The legal issue presented by the N.O.V. is the legal sufficiency of the evidence. It should be granted on proof that would warrant the grant of a directed verdict motion.

g. Motion for New Trial

The parties are entitled not only to a trial but one that is carried out without any serious legal error. If an error was committed in the trial and the judge now recognizes this, there is the possibility that the error influenced the jury. If this seems to be a strong possibility, a new trial should be granted.

A second kind of new trial motion is unique. This asks the judge to grant a new trial, not because of error, but because the verdict is against the weight of the evidence or because the damages award was unconscionably high (or possibly unconscionably low). These motions really ask the judge to use something like discretion. The judge cannot substitute herself for the jury and make the ultimate decision in the case merely because she differs from the jury about what is right. Still, the judge does have considerable power to grant a *new trial*. If a new trial is granted, a new jury will hear the evidence. This may be done in many states because the first jury's verdict is against the weight of the evidence (though not legally wrong), or because the damages award was excessive. Judges do not often grant such motions.

Appendix: A Narrative Case with Procedural Rulings

A Complaint and Answer

Rosa Light makes an appointment with an attorney, Lawton. Careful questioning by Lawton develops the story summarized here: "Two months ago, when I was about 8 months pregnant, I was at a dance with Bill Burton. He got angry with me because I danced with his brother, who is a terrible flirt. Anyway, Bill hit me in the stomach. Two or three weeks after that I had the baby. I had no permanent bad effects from the blow and the baby had no obvious injury, but I want to sue Bill. Can I?"

Lawton writes up a complaint for Rosa, asserting that Bill had committed a battery against her. Lawton also writes up a complaint on behalf of the child, Adrian. This complaint alleges the same facts, and in addition says in part: "On information and belief it is alleged that the plaintiff Adrian Light felt the blow and suffered pain from it."

The complaint is then filed in the office of the clerk of the Superior Court and a copy is served on (or handed to) Bill. Bill's lawyer gets a different story. Bill says in substance: "I did try to pull my brother away from Rosa and when I did she came flying at me, trying to scratch me. I held her at arm's length—well, maybe I had to push a little—but didn't hit her in the stomach or anywhere else."

Bill's lawyer, Atwood, files a paper which combines two documents: First, he files an "answer," in which he says Bill denies the facts alleged; Bill did not hit Rosa at all. This is extended to say that to the extent Bill touched Rosa at all, it was in justifiable self defense. This answer raises factual issues to be decided by the trier of fact.

The Defendant Demurs or Moves to Dismiss

Atwood also includes in the papers a motion known as a *demurrer* at common law and as a *motion to dismiss* in federal rule types of procedural systems. The paper asks the court to dismiss the claim of the child, Adrian, on the ground that even if the facts claimed by Rosa and Adrian were true, no law supports any claim by the child.

Judge Yacashin Ponders and Decides

The *Light* file comes to Judge Rebecca Yacashin in the usual course of her work as a Superior Court Judge. Her first reaction is that the motion to dismiss the child's claim should be granted, since the facts alleged in the complaint do not appear to her to show a battery to the child, though undoubtedly the complaint states facts showing a battery to the mother. On second thought, she recognizes that the case is novel and she is loath to dismiss it without study. She therefore has the clerk send a formal note to each lawyer asking that each submit a brief or memorandum within ten days, stating arguments for or against the motion, together with any pertinent cases. The memorandum submitted by Atwood on Bill's behalf argues: "An unborn child is not a person to whom a tort can be committed." Judge Yacashin considers this argument and the cases cited on both sides and concludes it did not represent the law. Accordingly, she signs a formal order denying the motion to dismiss. This was mailed to each lawyer.

Defense Planning: Discovery

"Does this mean we'll have to have a trial?" Bill asks. "Maybe," Atwood says, "but not necessarily. We could take depositions of witnesses and of the plaintiff, and maybe we could get some helpful stuff, maybe even an admission that the baby wasn't hurt. If we could get the plaintiff to admit that the baby wasn't hurt, we could file a motion for summary judgment, because I believe that if the baby wasn't hurt or at least offended, there wasn't any battery, even if the baby is a person who can sue for a tort before her birth."

Bill says, "But they won't admit that. They already said in their complaint that the baby felt pain." "You are right, but maybe we can do something even better. Maybe we can file an affidavit of a doctor saying that the baby felt nothing. Affidavits can't be used at trial as proof, but they can be used to show there is no real dispute about the facts. If the plaintiffs can't deny the affidavit by an affidavit of their own, the judge will have to say there is no dispute about the facts for a jury to decide, and that means she'll have to decide on the law."

The Defense Motion for Summary Judgment and Judge Yacashin's Ruling

Atwood is able to get an affidavit, but it is not quite so good as he had hoped. The doctor gave an affidavit saying that the child might have felt a blow, but could not differentiate it from many other movements or feelings, or attribute it to a human being. Atwood files this affidavit along with his motion for summary judgment.

A jury trial in another case is completed about 3:00 one afternoon in Judge Yacashin's court and no other case is scheduled. She begins working through other files in her office and encounters the summary judgment motion in *Light v. Burton*. "I've already ruled that the baby, though not born at the time, is a person who could be victimized by a tort," she reflects. "But it is true that there is no battery if the plaintiff is not hurt or offended." She reads the affidavit from the defendant's doctor. "So the baby could not tell the blow was from a human source or distinguish it from other discomforts." The plaintiff, however, has filed a counter-affidavit from another doctor saying that, while it was true that before birth the baby could not distinguish one blow from another, it would feel pain as an unpleasant sensation if the blow was hard enough.

Judge Yacashin would be glad to get rid of the case, but she concludes that the defendant's affidavit does not really establish a fact helpful to the defendant. She writes a brief statement of her reasons for denying the summary judgment motion as follows:

> "The defendant's affidavit establishes that the baby could not distinguish this harm from other harms, but it does not establish that there is no harm. The plaintiff's complaint alleges, and her affidavit supports, the idea that the baby before birth could and did feel unpleasant sensations as the result of the blow, if there was a blow. The facts shown by the defendant and left undisputed by the plaintiff do not warrant judgment in his favor, since I hold that the child's feelings would constitute 'harm' under the law of battery. The case will have to go to trial, therefore, on the factual issues raised by the complaint and answer."

Pre-trial, Trial, and Admission of Evidence

Months later, after a pre-trial conference in which the judge attempts to get issues clarified and to encourage settlement, the case is scheduled for the actual trial and a jury is impaneled.

Rosa Light's attorney, Lawton, begins putting on his case. After Rosa has testified to the main events stated in her complaint, Lawton asks:

Q. What happened after Bill Burton hit you?

A. He pulled his brother by the arm outside.

Q. What did you do?

A. I went to the window and watched while Bill beat his brother up. Then I got sick.

At this point Atwood stands up and says, "We object, Your Honor. This testimony should be stricken and the jury cautioned." Judge Yacashin says, "Overruled. Go on Mr. Lawton."

Motions for Directed Verdict

The trial proceeds in normal fashion. The plaintiff's witnesses are examined and cross-examined. When the plaintiff's case is completed, the defendant's attorney approaches the bench. "We move for a directed verdict as to the infant plaintiff, Your Honor," Atwood says in a voice the jury could not hear. "The plaintiff has failed to prove an essential element of her case: harm or offense. There is no offense without consciousness. As to harm, the Restatement Second of Torts requires 'physical impairment of the condition of another's body, or physical pain or illness.' [§ 15]. There is no testimony even remotely supporting the idea that there was physical pain or illness. We do not think the Supreme Court of this state would accept a passing discomfort as 'harm,' and this is the most the testimony would support." Lawton answers: "Doctor Veillicht testified, Your Honor, that the child in the womb could feel a blow like that attributed to the defendant and would feel it as a

negative thing, pain in the sense that the baby would try to avoid it."
Judge Yacashin: "I'm going to deny the motion and instruct the jury as
to the definition of harm."

After Judge Yacashin denies the motion for directed verdict, the
defendant proceeds to introduce his evidence, and again witnesses are
examined and cross-examined. When the defendant completes his proof,
Atwood again moves for directed verdict and it is again denied.

Closing Arguments and Instructions to the Jury

The lawyers then give their closing arguments, summarizing the
evidence favorable to each side and discounting evidence against them,
each trying to persuade the jury that his client was telling the truth. In
addition, Lawton talks considerably about the importance of damages.
Atwood urges the jury to keep things in perspective.

After the closing arguments, there is a recess for lunch. Judge
Yacashin asks the lawyers to meet with her in chambers before resuming
the afternoon session. In chambers, she reminds them that they had
previously submitted proposed instructions to the jury, had also previously seen the instructions she expected to give, and had made their
"record" of objections and requests about those instructions.

"Now the evidence always takes a few unexpected turns," she adds,
"and I think I had better add a couple of instructions. One instruction
should deal with the mental distress on the part of Rosa Light and
caution the jury not to award any damages for distress at the sight of the
brothers fighting, but that they may award damages, if they find a
battery, for all mental distress resulting from the battery." She shows
the lawyers her proposed draft instruction, written along the lines just
indicated. They have no objections.

Then Judge Yacashin goes on. "I've been worried about the question
of harm to the fetus. There is no evidence of any pathological harm. As
you know, Mr. Atwood, I refused to grant your motion for directed
verdict, which you made on the ground that there was no harm as a
matter of law. The only definition of harm we've seen here is the
Restatement's definition and our Supreme Court often follows the Restatement. So I think there may be enough evidence to get to the jury on
this, but I do think we need a very careful statement to the jury. Does
either of you have a proposed instruction?"

"I do not, Your Honor; whatever you think will suit us," Lawton
says.

"I do have one," Atwood says, and he passes copies. (He had asked
his associate to draft one during the lunch hour.) His proposed instruction would tell the jury that before the infant plaintiff could recover, it
would be necessary to find that harm was done and that harm would
require either an identifiable physical symptom or sign, or some identifiable medical condition, and that it could not be a transitory feeling.

"We would object to that, of course," Lawton comments.

"Yes, I think that's maybe too strong," the judge says, "but maybe something along those lines." She begins writing on the instruction proposed by Atwood and comes up with this:

"You are instructed as to the infant plaintiff there can be a recovery only if there is a battery as the Court has already defined that term to you. As to the infant plaintiff, this will require, in addition to an intentional unpermitted blow by the defendant, that the infant plaintiff has suffered harm. Harm is defined to include any physical impairment of the body, physical pain, or illness. It is not necessary that there be any permanent ill-effects, but on the other hand a trivial and transitory feeling on the part of the fetus would not constitute harm for this purpose."

Lawton objects to the last clause, and his objection is written down as part of the record. Atwood objects to the instruction so far as it fails to require some identifiable medical condition or the pain of a conscious, living being. This objection is also noted. The judge and lawyers then return to the courtroom for the remainder of the trial.

The Jury's Verdict

Judge Yacashin duly instructs the jury, which then adjourns to the privacy of the jury room. For the lawyers it is a waiting time. Because the case does not involve large damages claims, and because both lawyers feel the jurors would not have widely differing ideas about the facts, they think the jury will return within a relatively short time. Atwood and Lawton go to the courthouse basement and buy a coffee, then sit with it in a hall outside the courtroom until the bailiff announces that the jury is coming in. The bailiff has also notified Judge Yacashin, who takes the bench. The lawyers go to their tables and the jury files in.

"Have you reached a verdict?" Judge Yacashin asks.

"We have, Your Honor," the foreman says.

"Please hand it to the bailiff." The bailiff hands the paper to the judge. The form has been provided by the judge and filled in or crossed out by the jury. " 'We the jury,' " Judge Yacashin reads out loud, " 'find for the plaintiff Rosa Light in the sum of $10,000 and for the plaintiff Adrian Light in the sum of $5,000.' Is this your verdict?"

"It is, Your Honor."

Judge Yacashin thanks the jurors for their services, explains their obligation to return for further jury duty at a later date, discharges them, and adjourns the court.

NOV and New Trial Motions and the Final Judgment

One motion, or pair of motions, remains to be asserted by the defendant's lawyer, Atwood. He files a written motion two days later, in two parts. The first part moves for "Judgment N.O.V.—a judgment notwithstanding the verdict. The second part moves in the alternative for a new trial for errors committed in the trial, and especially the error in the instruction on the battery to the child.

Judge Yacashin denies the motions and enters a judgment on the verdict. The judgment is usually the last formal order. It is signed by the judge and reflects the jury's verdict. Here it provides that the plaintiff Rosa should have and recover from the defendant $10,000 and that the plaintiff Adrian should have and recover from the defendant $5,000.

Getting to the Appeal

These are the kinds of events that have occurred before the appeal. At this point the appeal process takes over. Here Atwood files notice of appeal, and in the course of the next few months provides the Appellate Court with excerpts from the trial record and files a brief arguing that the trial judge committed error in a number of respects. You can test yourself by determining what specific rulings or actions by the judge might constitute grounds for appeal. You can check the footnote for an answer.[1]

The Appellate Court Decides

Having seen Atwood's brief for the appellant, Lawton files a brief for the appellee. The Appellate Court schedules oral arguments for some months later and after those are heard, the judges of the appellate court and their law clerks research the law further. They hold conferences about the case and draft an opinion. The various judges comment on the proposed opinion and finally they all agree on a final draft. This is then formally announced and a copy is sent to the lawyers. It is then published in "advance sheets" such as the Northwestern Reporter Second Series, and finally in an official state volume. This kind of "opinion" or formal explanation of the court's decision, is the "case" with which law study begins, in an effort to isolate principles and rules, and to learn how arguments can be constructed to persuade judges.

REFERENCES: KENNEY HEGLAND, INTRODUCTION TO THE STUDY AND PRACTICE OF LAW (NUTSHELL SERIES 2000).

---

1. Each of the procedural devices listed above is the basis for this appeal. The judge, Atwood argues, should have granted the motion to dismiss, the summary judgment, and the directed verdict motion; she should have instructed the jury as Atwood requested, and should not have admitted the evidence to which he objected. Each of these arguments is supported by propositions of law, for which Atwood argues in his appellate brief.

Part II

FAULT–BASED LIABILITY FOR PHYSICAL HARMS TO PERSONS AND PROPERTY

Topic A

DIRECT INTENTIONAL WRONGS

Chapter 3

ESTABLISHING A CLAIM FOR INTENTIONAL TORT TO PERSON OR PROPERTY

§ 1. BATTERY

The plaintiff must prove certain things in any given tort claim. When the plaintiff has produced evidence of those elements, the plaintiff has made out a "prima facie case"—a case good "on the face of it" or at first look. When the plaintiff makes out a prima facie case, the judge will not direct a verdict for the defendant. Instead, the judge will allow the jury to decide the issues. The plaintiff has the burden of proving the elements necessary. The defendant may offer defenses, but this won't be necessary if the plaintiff fails to produce enough proof to make out the prima facie case.

a. Requiring Fault

VAN CAMP v. McAFOOS

Supreme Court of Iowa, 1968.
261 Iowa 1124, 156 N.W.2d 878.

BECKER, JUSTICE.

This case comes to us on appeal from trial court's action in sustaining defendant's motion to dismiss. We are therefore limited to what can be gleaned from the pleadings.

In Division I of her petition plaintiff sues Mark McAfoos alleging in pertinent part, "That at said time and place defendant Mark McAfoos was operating a tricycle on said public sidewalk, and drove the tricycle into the rear of the plaintiff without warning, striking the right leg of the plaintiff thereby causing an injury to the Achilles' tendon of that leg.

"That as a direct and proximate cause of the defendant's action, plaintiff's tendon was injured and subsequently required surgery...." [In another part of the petition the plaintiff alleged that Mark was three years, one month old.]

35

The trial court sustained the motion to dismiss as to Division I stating in part, "It is not alleged that the defendant was negligent. It is not alleged that the action of the defendant was willful or wrongful in any manner. Under these circumstances it is difficult to see how the Division as now set out states any basis upon which the plaintiff could recover."

The question presented is, did plaintiff plead a cause of action....

I.   Plaintiff's sole assignment of error as to Division I is "The trial court erred in failing to recognize categories of tort liability other than negligence, in evaluating the pleading in plaintiff's first division."

... She stands firmly on the proposition that invasion of her person is in itself a wrong and she need plead no more. We do not agree.... In essence plaintiff urges a person has a right not to be injuriously touched or struck as she lawfully uses a public sidewalk. She was injuriously struck by Mark. Therefore Mark is liable. She argues that no more need be pleaded. It follows that no more need be proved in order to justify submission of the case. Plaintiff's posture satisfies us she would have us impose liability without fault. We are not prepared to extend this concept to childish acts (by children).

II.   Plaintiff's reply brief states "If the absence of a single word or conclusory label remains the *sine qua non* of pleading a valid cause of action, we have restored today's jurisprudence to the specious procedural formalism of the 18th Century common courts."

The trial court's ruling was not a return to legal formalism. Plaintiff makes it abundantly clear she insists on a right to recovery by proof of an accident caused by another, independent of fault or wrong doing. Where an essential element of the cause of action is missing, the question is not what may be shown under the pleading but whether a cause of action has been pled.

... Intentionally wrongful or negligently wrongful use of the tricycle is neither pled nor can it be made out from the bare allegation defendant "operated a tricycle on said public sidewalk and drove the tricycle into the rear of the plaintiff without warning." ...

III.   Plaintiff cites many cases from other jurisdictions holding a child of tender years may be liable *in tort*; *Garratt v. Dailey*, 46 Wash. 2d 197, 279 P.2d 1091. All of the foregoing cases involve the fault concept. Many turn on the question of whether the child could be guilty of the fault charged but each case has fault as one of the essential elements of liability. We need not disagree with those authorities. Whatever her motive, plaintiff has chosen to plead in such a way as to avoid bringing herself within the scope of those cases....

Affirmed.

Notes

1. The court held, in omitted portions of the opinion, that Mark's parents were not liable because they had not been shown to be at fault, either.

2. Casebook editors may select cases and materials with more than one purpose in mind. At any given point, several themes may be in progress. *McAfoos* displays both a substantive and a procedural theme. The substantive or tort law theme has to do with the basis or grounds of liability. The procedural theme has to do with how legal issues are raised in court. Most cases in this book will raise one or more points that bear analysis and further thought. Notes like these should help you develop that analysis or furnish related information.

Substantive Issues

3. *Historical strict liability.* From the early days of tort law, about the 13th century until perhaps as late as the 18th century, anyone who acted affirmatively and directly (like Mark McAfoos) might be held liable for harm done, even though he was not at fault. In these cases the plaintiff used a form for suing called *Trespass* and he would win unless the defendant had some special defense, called justification or excuse. An example of a defense would be self-defense. If the harm caused was indirect, on the other hand, the defendant was not responsible unless he was at fault in some way. If Mark McAfoos had left his tricycle on the walk and the plaintiff had bumped into it in the dark, this would have been an indirect harm and even in the early English law Mark would not have been liable without fault. Cases of indirect harm required the plaintiff in that period to select a Form of Action for suing called *Trespass on the Case*, or just *Case*.

4. *The rules today.* In the light of this history, how would you interpret the *McAfoos* case? Does it implicitly or expressly reject the older dichotomy between direct and indirect harm? Is fault required in all cases?

5. *What is fault?* What would it take to show fault in *McAfoos*? Suppose Mark said he ran into Ms. Van Camp on purpose because he wanted to hear her get mad. •••

6. *Evaluation.* How does the rule or principle in *McAfoos* stack up against the aims of tort law? Consider whether it attempts to do justice and whether it reflects appropriate standards of deterring wrongdoing. You can answer such questions only when you have a firm grasp of the rule itself and know its scope. Evaluation is important to lawyers. It is one process by which lawyers become sure they have grasped the rule and its implications. It is also a process by which lawyers begin to formulate legal arguments. Evaluating rules and principles is an important part of good lawyering.

7. *Grasping a principle. McAfoos* involved a child on a tricycle. But the principle or reason behind the case might apply to many other situations. One function of a lawyer is to recognize the possibility of applying the principle of a case to a new set of facts. Try it:

—H becomes angry with his wife, W, and repeatedly hits her with his fist, breaking her jaw and bruising her face. W required medical attention.

Would the principle or idea in *McAfoos* either establish or exclude liability? No
See Douglas D. Scherer, *Tort Remedies for Victims of Domestic Abuse*, 43 S.
C. L. REV. 543 (1992).

—The defendant's yard has a tree near the sidewalk. The tree appears
to be sound and healthy, but in fact it is rotten and it blows over in a wind.
It strikes a passerby. Louisiana, a state which retains much of the "civil
law" derived from European Codes, might impose liability under its code
even though the owner did not intend for the tree to fall and had no
reasonable way to avoid it. See *Loescher v. Parr*, 324 So.2d 441 (La.1975).
Can you predict from *McAfoos* what the Iowa court or some other common
law court would hold? Not Res.

Procedural Issues

8. Cases today are begun by a complaint or petition, a document
that states the main facts on which the plaintiff relies. If the facts are in
dispute, the jury decides what the facts were. In *McAfoos*, the parties
seemed to disagree over the legal rules rather than the facts. Did you
notice the procedural device used to resolve this difference?

b. Elements of Battery

"[T]he least touching of another in anger is a battery.... If any of
them use violence against the other, to force his way in a rude
inordinate manner, it is a battery...."—*Cole v. Turner*, 6 Mod. Rep.
149, 90 Eng. Rep. 958 (Nisi Prius 1704).

SNYDER v. TURK

Court of Appeals of Ohio, 1993.
90 Ohio App.3d 18, 627 N.E.2d 1053.

RICHARD K. WILSON, JUDGE....

[Defendant was a surgeon performing a gall-bladder operation. The
procedure did not go well. Evidence would permit these findings: The
defendant became frustrated with the operation itself and with the
plaintiff, a scrub nurse in the operating room. Defendant's perception
was that the plaintiff was making mistakes and complicating an already
difficult procedure. The defendant finally became so exasperated when
the plaintiff handed him an instrument he considered inappropriate that
he grabbed her shoulder and pulled her face down toward the surgical
opening, saying. "Can't you see where I'm working? I'm working in a
hole. I need long instruments."]

The parties agree that a "battery" is defined as an intentional,
unconsented-to contact with another. The appellee contends that there is
no liability for the commission of a battery absent proof of an intent to
inflict personal injury. Dr. Turk further contends that the directed
verdict was properly granted on the battery liability issue because of the
absence of evidence that he intended to inflict personal injury....

"A person is subject to liability for battery when he acts intending to
cause a harmful or offensive contact, and when a harmful contact

results. Contact which is offensive to a reasonable sense of personal dignity is offensive contact. . . .

A motion for a directed verdict assumes the truth of the evidence supporting the facts essential to the claim after giving the nonmovant the benefit of all reasonable inferences from the evidence and refers the application of a reasonable-minds test to such evidence. It is in the nature of a demurrer to the evidence.

Applying the above test we believe that reasonable minds could conclude that Dr. Turk intended to commit an offensive contact. The first assignment of error is sustained.

COHEN v. SMITH

Appellate Court of Illinois, 1995.
269 Ill.App.3d 1087, 207 Ill.Dec. 873, 648 N.E.2d 329.

Justice Chapman delivered the opinion of the court:

Patricia Cohen was admitted to St. Joseph Memorial Hospital ("Hospital") to deliver her baby. After an examination, Cohen was informed that it would be necessary for her to have a cesarean section. Cohen and her husband allegedly informed her physician, who in turn advised the Hospital staff, that the couple's religious beliefs prohibited Cohen from being seen unclothed by a male. Cohen's doctor assured her husband that their religious convictions would be respected.

During Cohen's cesarean section, Roger Smith, a male nurse on staff at the Hospital, allegedly observed and touched Cohen's naked body. Cohen and her husband filed suit against Nurse Smith and the Hospital. The trial court allowed defendants' motions to dismiss. We reverse.

In reviewing a motion to dismiss for failure to state a cause of action, the court must view all well-pleaded facts in the light most favorable to the plaintiff. A trial court may dismiss a cause of action for failing to state a cause of action, based solely on the pleadings, only if it is clearly apparent that no set of alleged facts can be proven which will entitle a plaintiff to recovery. . . .

The Restatement (Second) of Torts provides that an actor commits a battery if: "(a) he acts intending to cause a harmful or offensive contact with the person of the other or a third person, or an imminent apprehension of such a contact, and (b) a harmful [or offensive][1] contact with the person of the other directly or indirectly results." (Restatement (Second) of Torts, § 13 (1965).) Liability for battery emphasizes the plaintiff's lack of consent to the touching. "Offensive contact" is said to occur when the contact "offends a reasonable sense of personal dignity."

Historically, battery was first and foremost a systematic substitution for private retribution. (W. Prosser & Keeton, Torts § 9, at 41 (5th ed. 1984) (Prosser).) Protecting personal integrity has always been viewed as

---

1. The editors of this casebook inserted the bracketed phrase. It appears in Restate- ment § 18, not § 13, which the court is quoting.–Eds.

an important basis for battery. "Consequently, the defendant is liable not only for contacts which do actual physical harm, but also for those relatively trivial ones which are merely offensive and insulting." This application of battery to remedy offensive and insulting conduct is deeply ingrained in our legal history. As early as 1784, a Pennsylvania defendant was prosecuted for striking the cane of a French ambassador. The court furthered the distinction between harmful offensive batteries and nonharmful offensive batteries: "As to the assault, this is, perhaps, one of that kind, in which the insult is more to be considered than the actual damage; for, though no great bodily pain is suffered by a blow on the palm of the hand, or the skirt of the coat, yet these are clearly within the definition of assault and battery, and among gentlemen too often induce duelling and terminate in murder." (Respublica v. De Longchamps (Pa.1784), 1 Dall. 111, 1 L.Ed. 59, in Gregory, Kalven, & Epstein, Cases & Materials on Torts 904–905 (1977).)....

Although most people in modern society have come to accept the necessity of being seen unclothed and being touched by members of the opposite sex during medical treatment, the plaintiffs had not accepted these procedures and, according to their complaint, had informed defendants of their convictions. This case is similar to cases involving Jehovah's Witnesses who were unwilling to accept blood transfusions because of religious convictions. Although most people do not share the Jehovah's Witnesses' beliefs about blood transfusions, our society, and our courts, accept their right to have that belief. Similarly, the courts have consistently recognized individuals' rights to refuse medical treatment even if such a refusal would result in an increased likelihood of the individual's death.

A person's right to refuse or accept medical care is not one to be interfered with lightly. As Justice Cardozo stated, "Every human being of adult years and sound mind has a right to determine what shall be done with his own body; and a surgeon who performs an operation without his patient's consent commits an assault, for which he is liable in damages."

Accepting as true the plaintiffs' allegations that they informed defendants of their religious beliefs and that defendants persisted in treating Patricia Cohen as they would have treated a patient without those beliefs, we conclude that the trial court erred in dismissing both the battery and the intentional infliction of emotional distress counts.

Notes

1. Under the Restatement rule quoted in *Cohen,* must the plaintiff prove an intent to harm in order to prove a battery? Must the plaintiff prove an actual harm such as pain or a bruise? See if you can support a yes or no answer.

2. *The object of intent.* What must be the object of the defendant's intent? To harm the plaintiff? To offend? To touch? All three? Try to see if

Snyder supports a rule about this. Suppose the defendant hugs her husband in an ordinary way but, surprisingly, this breaks a vertebrae. Is this a battery, because contact was intended and it turned out to be harmful? You might try writing a three-sentence argument, more or less in the form of a syllogism, in which the first sentence or premise states, with exceptions not relevant, that fault is required to establish liability in tort.

3. In the light of the rules stated or applied in *Cohen,* how should the following cases be resolved?

a. Karen Whitley was standing in front of her locker at school when LeGault shoved her. The shove caused no physical harm. LeGault argued that she was not liable because (1) no harm was done by her shove and (2) no intent to harm was proven. *Whitley v. Andersen,* 37 Colo.App. 486, 551 P.2d 1083 (Colo.Ct.App.1976).

b. The plaintiff's employer was engaged in teasing and horseplay with an automobile condenser that had been electrically charged, giving employees a mild shock. He shocked the plaintiff, who was trying to avoid it. The plaintiff, quite unexpectedly, developed a serious nerve problem that required surgery. *Caudle v. Betts,* 512 So.2d 389 (La.1987).

c. The defendant was a judge and the plaintiff's employer. Against the plaintiff's wishes, the defendant kissed the plaintiff. *Johnson v. Ramsey County,* 424 N.W.2d 800 (Minn.App.1988).

4. Suppose the defendant has a good motive–he administers medical treatment over the plaintiff's objection. E.g., *Roberson v. Provident House,* 576 So.2d 992 (La.1991).

5. *Autonomy.* The quotation preceding *Cohen* suggests that at one time the law was interested only in protecting against violent or angry acts. The *Cohen* case makes it clear that no such limit applies today. Is this because we want to prevent duels? Or because we want to respect the plaintiff's personal autonomy?

6. *Act.* The defendant must commit some "act." What if defendant's arm strikes the plaintiff when defendant is jostled in a crowd? What if his arm moves reflexively or out of control in a seizure?

7. *Bodily contact.* Neither harm nor offense would be sufficient without bodily contact. Does this require that the defendant's body directly touch the plaintiff's body? Imagine a defendant who fires a bullet into the plaintiff's body and seeks to escape liability for battery on the ground that there was no touching. Try reasoning from the purposes of battery law. Given those purposes, would courts treat the bullet as a touching? Now consider a defendant who shakes the limb of a tree on which the plaintiff is sitting, but does not touch the plaintiff. A modern classic case on this point is *Fisher v. Carrousel Motor Hotel, Inc.,* 424 S.W.2d 627 (Tex.1967). The plaintiff, Fisher, was a mathematician attending a meeting on telemetry equipment. He and the others at the meeting adjourned for lunch in the defendant's hotel. As the plaintiff was about to be served, he was approached by the manager, who "snatched the plate from Fisher's hand and shouted that he, a Negro, could not be served in the club." The court said: "[T]he intentional grabbing of plaintiff's plate constituted a battery. The intentional snatching

of an object from one's hand is as clearly an offensive invasion of his person as would be an actual contact with the body."

LEICHTMAN v. WLW JACOR COMMUNICATIONS, INC.

Court of Appeals of Ohio, 1994.
92 Ohio App.3d 232, 634 N.E.2d 697.

... Leichtman claims to be "a nationally known" antismoking advocate. Leichtman alleges that, on the date of the Great American Smokeout, he was invited to appear on the WLW Bill Cunningham radio talk show to discuss the harmful effects of smoking and breathing secondary smoke. He also alleges that, while he was in the studio, Furman, another WLW talk-show host, lit a cigar and repeatedly blew smoke in Leichtman's face "for the purpose of causing physical discomfort, humiliation and distress." ...

Leichtman contends that Furman's intentional act constituted a battery. . . .

In determining if a person is liable for a battery, the Supreme Court has adopted the rule that "[c]ontact which is offensive to a reasonable sense of personal dignity is offensive contact." It has defined "offensive" to mean "disagreeable or nauseating or painful because of outrage to taste and sensibilities or affronting insultingness." Furthermore, tobacco smoke, as "particulate matter," has the physical properties capable of making contact.

As alleged in Leichtman's complaint, when Furman intentionally blew cigar smoke in Leichtman's face, under Ohio common law, he committed a battery. No matter how trivial the incident, a battery is actionable, even if damages are only one dollar. The rationale is explained by Roscoe Pound in his essay "Liability": "[I]n civilized society men must be able to assume that others will do them no intentional injury—that others will commit no intentioned aggressions upon them." Pound, An Introduction to the Philosophy of Law (1922) 169. . . .

We do not ... adopt or lend credence to the theory of a "smoker's battery," which imposes liability if there is substantial certainty that exhaled smoke will predictably contact a nonsmoker. . . .

... Concerning Cunningham, at common law, one who is present and encourages or incites commission of a battery by words can be equally liable as a principal. . . .

With regard to WLW, an employer is not legally responsible for the intentional torts of its employees that do not facilitate or promote its business. . . .

Arguably, trivial cases are responsible for an avalanche of lawsuits in the courts. They delay cases that are important to individuals and corporations and that involve important social issues. The result is justice denied to litigants and their counsel who must wait for their day in court. However, absent circumstances that warrant sanctions for frivolous appeals ... we refuse to limit one's right to sue. Section 16, Article I, Ohio Constitution states, "All courts shall be open, and every person, for an injury done him in his land, goods, person, or reputation, shall have remedy by due course of law, and shall have justice administered without denial or delay."

... [W]e reverse that portion of the trial court's order that dismissed the battery claim in the second count of the complaint. This cause is remanded for further proceedings consistent with law on that claim only.

Notes

1. *Bodily contact.* If being touched by smoke is bodily contact that will support a battery claim, what about being touched by light waves or sound waves? Your noisy neighbor bombards you with loud music every night. Could this be a battery?

2. *Damages.* What kind of damages should the plaintiff recover, if any, when the contact is merely offensive and not harmful? Courts have traditionally permitted juries to award substantial damages even though the plaintiff has no pecuniary loss. The award is not limited to nominal damages, and it might reach hundreds and even thousands of dollars. See DAN DOBBS, THE LAW OF REMEDIES § 7.3 (2) (1993). In your considered opinion, is this a good idea? In addition to compensatory damages, courts may allow punitive damages against an intentional tortfeasor who is guilty of "malice" or wanton misconduct.

c. Re-focusing on Intent

The meaning of intent. What does "intent" mean? Does it mean purpose or desire, for example a purpose to harm or offend? Or could "intent" include a certainty that harm will result even when there is no purpose to cause harm? Consider the next case.

GARRATT v. DAILEY

Supreme Court of Washington, 1955.
46 Wn.2d 197, 279 P.2d 1091.

HILL, JUSTICE....

Brian Dailey (age five years, nine months) was visiting with Naomi Garratt, an adult and a sister of the plaintiff, Ruth Garratt, likewise an adult, in the back yard of the plaintiff's home, on July 16, 1951. It is plaintiff's contention that she came out into the back yard to talk with Naomi and that, as she started to sit down in a wood and canvas lawn chair, Brian deliberately pulled it out from under her. The only one of the three persons present so testifying was Naomi Garratt. (Ruth Garratt, the plaintiff, did not testify as to how or why she fell.)

The trial court, unwilling to accept this testimony, adopted instead Brian Dailey's version of what happened, and made the following findings:

"III. . . . [T]hat while Naomi Garratt and Brian Dailey were in the back yard the plaintiff, Ruth Garratt, came out of her house into the back yard. Some time subsequent thereto defendant, Brian Dailey, picked up a lightly built wood and canvas lawn chair which was then and there located in the back yard of the above described premises, moved it sideways a few feet and seated himself therein, at which time he discovered the plaintiff, Ruth Garratt, about to sit down at the place where the lawn chair had formerly been, at which time he hurriedly got up from the chair and attempted to move it toward Ruth Garratt to aid her in sitting down in the chair; that due to the defendant's small size and lack of dexterity he was unable to get the lawn chair under the plaintiff in time to prevent her from falling to the ground. That plaintiff fell to the ground and sustained a fracture of her hip, and other injuries and damages as hereinafter set forth.

"IV. That the preponderance of the evidence in this case establishes that when the defendant, Brian Dailey, moved the chair in question *he did not have any wilful or unlawful purpose* in doing so; that *he did not have any intent to injure the plaintiff, or any intent to bring about any unauthorized or offensive contact with her person* or any object appurtenant thereto; that the circumstances which immediately preceded the fall of the plaintiff established that the defendant, *Brian Dailey, did not have purpose, intent or design to perform a prank or to effect an assault and battery upon the person of the plaintiff.*" (Italics ours, for a purpose hereinafter indicated.)

It is conceded that Ruth Garratt's fall resulted in a fractured hip and other painful and serious injuries. To obviate the necessity of a retrial in the event this court determines that she was entitled to a judgment against Brian Dailey, the amount of her damage was found to be $11,000. Plaintiff appeals from a judgment dismissing the action and asks for the entry of a judgment in that amount or a new trial.

The authorities generally, but with certain notable exceptions, state that when a minor has committed a tort with force he is liable to be proceeded against as any other person would be.

In our analysis of the applicable law, we start with the basic premise that Brian, whether five or fifty-five, must have committed some wrongful act before he could be liable for appellant's injuries. . . .

It is urged that Brian's action in moving the chair constituted a battery. A definition (not all-inclusive but sufficient for our purpose) of a battery is the intentional infliction of a harmful bodily contact upon another. The rule that determines liability for battery is given in 1 RESTATEMENT TORTS, 29, § 13, as:

"An act which, directly or indirectly, is the legal cause of a harmful contact with another's person makes the actor liable to the other, if "(a) the act is done with the intention of bringing about a harmful or offensive contact...."

... In the comment on clause (a), the Restatement says:

"Character of actor's intentions. In order that an act may be done with the intention of bringing about a harmful or offensive contact ..., the act must be done for the purpose of causing the contact ... or with knowledge on the part of the actor that such contact ... is substantially certain to be produced." See, also, Prosser on Torts 41, § 8.

We have here the conceded volitional act of Brian, i.e., the moving of a chair. Had the plaintiff proved to the satisfaction of the trial court that Brian moved the chair while she was in the act of sitting down, Brian's action would patently have been for the purpose or with the intent of causing the plaintiff's bodily contact with the ground, and she would be entitled to a judgment against him for the resulting damages.

The plaintiff based her case on that theory, and the trial court held that she failed in her proof and accepted Brian's version of the facts rather than that given by the eyewitness who testified for the plaintiff. After the trial court determined that the plaintiff had not established her theory of a battery (i.e., that Brian had pulled the chair out from under the plaintiff while she was in the act of sitting down), it then became concerned with whether a battery was established under the facts as it found them to be.

In this connection, we quote another portion of the comment on the "Character of actor's intention," relating to a clause (a) of the rule of the Restatement heretofore set forth:

"It is not enough that the act itself is intentionally done and this, even though the actor realizes or should realize that it contains a very grave risk of bringing about the contact or apprehension. Such realization may make the actor's conduct negligent or even reckless but unless he realizes that to a substantial certainty, the contact or apprehension will result, the actor has not that intention which is necessary to make him liable under the rule stated in this section."

A battery would be established if, in addition to plaintiff's fall, it was proved that, when Brian moved the chair, he knew with substantial certainty that the plaintiff would attempt to sit down where the chair had been. If Brian had any of the intents which the trial court found, in the italicized portions of the findings of fact quoted above, that he did not have, he would of course have had the knowledge to which we have referred. The mere absence of any intent to injure the plaintiff or to play a prank on her or to embarrass her, or to commit an assault and battery on her would not absolve him from liability if in fact he had such knowledge.

Without such knowledge, there would be nothing wrongful about Brian's act in moving the chair and, there being no wrongful act, there would be no liability.

While a finding that Brian had no such knowledge can be inferred from the findings made, we believe that before the plaintiff's action in such a case should be dismissed there should be no question but that the trial court had passed upon that issue; hence, the case should be remanded for clarifications of the findings to specifically cover the question of Brian's knowledge, because intent could be inferred therefrom. If the court finds that he had such knowledge the necessary intent will be established and the plaintiff will be entitled to recover, even though there was no purpose to injure or embarrass the plaintiff. If Brian did not have such knowledge, there was no wrongful act by him and the basic premise of liability on the theory of a battery was not established.

It will be noted that the law of battery as we have discussed it is the law applicable to adults, and no significance has been attached to the fact that Brian was a child less than six years of age when the alleged battery occurred. The only circumstance where Brian's age is of any consequence is in determining what he knew, and there his experience, capacity, and understanding are of course material. . . .

The cause is remanded for clarification, with instructions to make definite findings on the issue of whether Brian Dailey knew with substantial certainty that the plaintiff would attempt to sit down where the chair which he moved had been, and to change the judgment if the findings warrant it. . . .

Notes

1. On remand, the trial court found that the plaintiff was in the act of sitting down when Brian moved the chair, and that Brian knew this. On the basis of the substantial certainty test, the judge found for the plaintiff. This was affirmed on the second appeal, *Garratt v. Dailey*, 49 Wn.2d 499, 304 P.2d 681 (1956).

2. What is the definition of intent accepted by the *Garratt* court? Defendant hates the plaintiff, sees him at a distance and hurls a stone, hoping to hit the plaintiff but believing that success is extremely unlikely. The stone does in fact hit the plaintiff, however. Is this a battery? Is the intent involved the same intent on which Brian Dailey was held liable?

3. *Intent, negligence.* Legal fault usually takes the form of intent or the form of negligence. Negligence is a large subject, to be considered beginning in Chapter 5. In general, negligence is conduct that creates an unreasonable risk of harm. Driving too fast would be an example. Can you distinguish between *Garratt v. Dailey* intent on the one hand and negligence on the other? Test it out: Defendant became highly intoxicated and drove his car on the wrong side of the highway, causing a head-on collision that seriously injured the plaintiff. *Garratt v. Dailey* intent, or negligence? What about

fumes from a manufacturing plant, molecules of which are overwhelmingly likely to hit someone, though not necessarily likely to do harm?

4. *Recklessness, wanton misconduct, wilfulness.* Wilful or wanton conduct is "a course of action which shows actual or deliberate intent to harm or which, if the course of action is not intentional, shows an utter indifference to or conscious disregard for a person's own safety or the safety or property of others. [It is] a hybrid between acts considered negligent and behavior found to be intentionally tortious." *Pfister v. Shusta,* 167 Ill.2d 417, 212 Ill.Dec. 668, 657 N.E.2d 1013 (1995). Recklessness is defined in much the same way. Courts sometimes distinguish recklessness or wanton misconduct from intent or negligence because of certain rules of damages or because of different statutes of limitation. Conduct that falls short of intentional wrongdoing, for example, may still be reckless or wanton so that punitive damages would be justified.

DAVIS v. WHITE, 18 B.R. 246 (Bkrtcy.Va.1982). "On the day of the shooting Davis and his brother, Marvin W. Davis, were washing cars in front of their mother's house on Fairmount Avenue in Richmond, Virginia. At the same time White, a neighbor who lives less than one block away on the same street, was having a conversation with William Tipton (Tipton). In that conversation White and Tipton continued an argument which had begun approximately one week earlier. White had obtained a gun in anticipation of seeing Tipton. White was carrying the pistol in a container on his motorcycle and pulled it out of the container during the course of that argument. When White pulled the gun Tipton mounted his motorcycle and sped away. White shot at Tipton as Tipton passed within twenty-five feet of Davis. He missed Tipton and the bullet hit Davis in the stomach. White fled the scene." Davis recovered a judgment against White. Thereafter, White filed a petition in bankruptcy. Under the bankruptcy law, this will permit White to be "discharged" or freed of all liability except for willful, deliberate or intentional injuries. In the trial court, *held*, the injury is intentional and White cannot be discharged in bankruptcy.

White committed the wrongful act when he shot at Tipton. The act was intentional and it produced an injury although not to the person White intended to injure. White's action cannot be excused solely because he missed his intended victim and instead hit someone else. The injury is not required to be directed against the victim, but includes any entity or other than the intended victim. Under the doctrine of transferred intent one who intends a battery is liable for that battery when he unexpectedly hits a stranger instead of the intended victim. W. Prosser, *The Law of Torts,* 33 (4th ed. 1971). If one intentionally commits an assault or battery at another and by mistake strikes a third person, he is guilty of an assault and battery of the third person if "[d]efendant's intention, in such a case, is to strike an unlawful blow, to injure some person by his act, and it is not essential that the injury be to the one intended.

Note

The transferred intent doctrine is well accepted whenever it is discussed. Is it sound? Why not say that, as to Davis, White was merely negligent or reckless?

WALKER v. KELLY

Circuit Court of Connecticut, 1973.
6 Conn.Cir. 715, 314 A.2d 785.

DEARINGTON, JUDGE.

The plaintiff, on behalf of himself and his minor son, Michael Walker, hereinafter referred to as Michael, brought this action against the defendants, parents of Sharon Kelly, their minor daughter. The plaintiff alleges that Sharon wilfully and maliciously assaulted Michael, causing a laceration over his right eye. The defendants in their answer deny the alleged assault and in a special defense allege that Sharon was five years of age and incapable of acting deliberately, wilfully and maliciously.

The action was brought under § 52–572 of the General Statutes, the pertinent part of which provided that the parents of any unemancipated minor who wilfully or maliciously caused injury to any person shall be liable with such minor for such injury to an amount not exceeding $750 if such minor would have been liable if he had been an adult.[2]

The finding, which the plaintiff did not move to correct, recites as follows: Michael and Sharon lived on the same street. Michael was eight years of age and Sharon was five. At the time, Michael was riding his bicycle on the street and Sharon was on the street with other children. On more than one occasion Michael rode his bicycle close to Sharon, and it appeared to her and other children that Michael was trying to run her over. One of the older children, Robert Blinn, twelve years old, told Sharon to throw a rock at Michael's bicycle. Sharon threw a rock, intending to hit Michael's bicycle, which at that time was moving fifteen or twenty feet away on the opposite side of the street. The rock struck Michael on the forehead, causing a laceration that required medical treatment.

The court concluded that (1) Sharon did not intend to strike Michael; (2) Sharon was too young and immature to appreciate the risk involved in throwing a rock at Michael's bicycle; (3) Michael's injury was not inflicted wilfully or maliciously.

The plaintiff has assigned error as follows: (1) The court erred in failing to find that Sharon intended to strike Michael; (2) a child of five years of age may be held responsible for acts of violence; (3) Sharon's testimony indicated that she acted wilfully and maliciously. . . .

---

2. The amount has since been raised to $5,000.—eds.

It appears from the certified transcript of the evidence that Sharon testified on direct examination when asked to relate what happened: "A.—Well, I was trying to go over to Lisa Blinn's house and Michael was trying to run me over with the bike and so I picked up a rock and I threw it. I meant to hit him in the fingers but by mistake, I hit him in the head. Q.—Before you threw the rock, Sharon, do you remember Bobby Blinn saying anything? A.—He said that aim . . . 'Throw the rock, but aim for the fingers.' Q.—Did you mean to hit Michael with the rock at all? A.—No." Thus, we have conflicting testimony from the witness. No further interrogation on this subject was pursued either on direct examination or cross-examination. . . .

Where there is conflicting evidence in the testimony of a witness, it is a function of the trier to accept the testimony which is believed. "[T]he trier is the final judge of the credibility of witnesses and of the weight to be accorded their testimony. . . ." It cannot be said that the court erred in its finding in that it accepted part of the testimony of Sharon and rejected other portions where the evidence was conflicting. The trial court is in a far better position than an appellate court to evaluate the testimony—from observation of a witness, from the surrounding circumstances, and from a consideration of the entire evidence. Especially is this so where, as here, the witness is of tender years. The court's conclusion that Sharon did not intend to strike Michael was warranted on the facts found.

. . . [T]he statute provides that the injury, if damages are recoverable, must result from a wilful or malicious act. Ordinarily, tort liability attaches regardless of age where the nature of the act is such that children of a like age would realize its injurious consequences. "However, where a tort requires a particular state of mind, and an infant because of his age or mental capacity, is incapable of forming such state of mind, he cannot be found guilty of the tort. Accordingly, although an infant of quite tender years may be held liable where the only intention necessary to the commission of a tort is the intention to perform the physical act in question . . . such an infant cannot be held liable where malice is the gist of the tort and he is too young to formulate the necessary malicious intention. . . ." The statutory requirement is that the act must be done "wilfully or maliciously" if recovery is to be successful. "A wilful or malicious injury is one caused by design. Willfulness and malice alike import intent. . . . [Its] characteristic element is the design to injure, either actually entertained or to be implied from the conduct and circumstances." . . . It is evident from the finding that the court considered the surrounding circumstances and the ages of those involved and that it concluded that Sharon did not wilfully or maliciously intend to injure Michael. Since this conclusion is logically supported by the finding, it must stand.

There is no error.

JACOBS, JUDGE (concurring).

I join the opinion of the court based on the finding that Sharon, a five-year-old child, did not intend to strike Michael and that Michael's injury was not inflicted wilfully or maliciously. . . .

There is, however, a statement in the record before us which reads as follows: "To find the defendants' child liable for such an act would be to impose upon a child of five years a standard of conduct and maturity of judgment not reasonably to be expected of children of such tender age." This statement, which appears in the trial court's memorandum of decision, is an incorrect statement of the law and one which we cannot and should not overlook. . . .

Notes

1. Suppose (a) Sharon had been an adult; or (b) Sharon had intended to hit the bike but not the boy. Under the first supposition would she have been wilful? Under the second would she have had *Garratt v. Dailey* intent?

2. Does the court here interpret the statutory term "wilfully" to mean something more than an intent of the kind required in common law battery?

Parental Liability

3. *Respondeat superior.* There is a very general rule that certain employers are liable for the torts of their employees committed in the scope of employment. For example the telephone company is liable if its driver, on the way to connect a telephone, negligently runs into a car owned by the plaintiff. This liability of the "master" for torts of the "servant" is called vicarious liability or *respondeat superior* liability, and it is limited to cases in which the employee is in a general way engaged in the job. Vicarious liability is explored further in Chapter 20 but it can be taken here as a very general rule.

4. *Parents' vicarious liability.* Parents are not generally vicariously liable for acts of the child, unless, of course, the parent is an employer using the child as a "servant," as where the parent operates a store and the child is making deliveries as part of the enterprise.

5. *Parents' fault.* In the absence of statute, then, parents' liability for the acts of the child must be founded not on vicarious liability but on the parents' own fault. Suppose parents tell a child, "Throw a rock at that boy." If the child threw it and injured the boy would the parent be liable? If so, why? Suppose a parent merely refused to exercise control over a child who constantly committed acts of violence against others?

6. *Statutes.* A number of states impose liability upon parents for certain limited acts of their children, often acts that are wilful, or acts that are directed against certain persons. These statutes vary slightly in their exact content, but most often they limit the parents' liability to a relatively small sum such as $750 or $500. California, however, permits parental liability up to $10,000 for wilful misconduct of a minor and up to $30,000 under some circumstances when the minor causes injury by discharge of a firearm. WEST'S ANN. CAL. CIV. CODE §§ 1714.1, 1714.3. How suitable is it to hold parents liable for acts of the child?

Child Liability

7. As recognized in *Walker*, there is a very general view that minors are liable for their torts. An older view, still sometimes referred to, was that children under seven were "conclusively presumed to be incapable of harmful intent." Several states still follow this "rule of sevens."

8. What solutions are available for dealing with the problem of child-produced harms? Notice that the child's age would be relevant to show that he could not form an adequate intent to touch, to offend or to harm. Should we say as a matter of law that a child of four cannot harbor an intent to strike a babysitter in a harmful or offensive way, or is it a matter of assessing the intent in the particular case? *Bailey v. C.S.,* 12 S.W.3d 159 (Tex.App.2000) (4–year-old hit babysitter in the throat, crushing larynx). What about holding a child liable for intended harms, but not for intended offense? This was approved in *Horton v. Reaves*, 186 Colo. 149, 526 P.2d 304 (1974).

POLMATIER v. RUSS

Supreme Court of Connecticut, 1988.
206 Conn. 229, 537 A.2d 468.

GLASS, JUSTICE.

... On the afternoon of November 20, 1976, the defendant and his two month old daughter visited the home of Arthur Polmatier, his father-in-law. Polmatier lived in East Windsor with his wife, Dorothy, the plaintiff, and their eleven year old son, Robert. During the early evening Robert noticed a disturbance in the living room where he saw the defendant astride Polmatier on a couch beating him on the head with a beer bottle. Robert heard Polmatier exclaim, "Norm, you're killing me!" and ran to get help. Thereafter, the defendant went into Polmatier's bedroom where he took a box of 30–30 caliber ammunition from the bottom drawer of a dresser and went to his brother-in-law's bedroom where he took a 30–30 caliber Winchester rifle from the closet. He then returned to the living room and shot Polmatier twice, causing his death. . . .

The defendant was taken to a local hospital and was later transferred to Norwich Hospital. While in custody he was confined in Norwich Hospital or the Whiting Forensic Institute. The defendant was charged with the crime of murder ... but was found not guilty by reason of insanity. . . . Dr. Walter Borden, a psychiatrist, testified at both the criminal and this civil proceeding regarding the defendant's sanity. . . . He concluded that the defendant was legally insane and could not form a rational choice but that he could make a schizophrenic or crazy choice. He was not in a fugue state. The trial court found that at the time of the homicide the defendant was insane.

The substitute complaint for the wrongful death of Polmatier alleged in the first count that the death resulted from an assault, beating and shooting by the defendant, and included a second count for exemplary damages and a third count based on negligence. . . .

The majority of jurisdictions that have considered this issue have held insane persons liable for their intentional torts. See 4 Restatement (Second), Torts § 895J. The majority rule has been applied to cases involving intentional homicide. . . .

A leading case is Seals v. Snow, 123 Kan. 88, 254 P. 348 (1927).[In that case, the Kansas Supreme Courts said:] "The great weight of authority is that an insane person is civilly liable for his torts. This liability has been based on a number of grounds, one that where one of two innocent persons must suffer a loss, it should be borne by the one who occasioned it. Another, that public policy requires the enforcement of such liability in order that relatives of the insane person shall be led to restrain him and that tort-feasors shall not simulate or pretend insanity to defend their wrongful acts causing damage to others, and that if he was not liable there would be no redress for injuries, and we might have the anomaly of an insane person having abundant wealth depriving another of his rights without compensation."

. . . The defendant argues that for an act to be done with the requisite intent, the act must be an external manifestation of the actor's will. . . . The defendant argues that if his "activities were the external manifestations of irrational and uncontrollable thought disorders these activities cannot be acts for purposes of establishing liability for assault and battery." We disagree.

. . . Comment b . . . in pertinent part "A muscular reaction is always an act unless it is a purely reflexive reaction in which the mind and will have no share." Although the trial court found that the defendant could not form a rational choice, it did find that he could make a schizophrenic or crazy choice. Moreover, a rational choice is not required since "[a]n insane person may have an intent to invade the interests of another, even though his reasons and motives for forming that intention may be entirely irrational." . . .

We recognize that the defendant made conflicting statements about the incident when discussing the homicide. At the hospital on the evening of the homicide the defendant told a police officer that his father-in-law was a heavy drinker and that he used the beer bottle for that reason. He stated he wanted to make his father-in-law suffer for his bad habits and so that he would realize the wrong that he had done. He also told the police officer that he was a supreme being and had the power to rule the destiny of the world and could make his bed fly out of the window. When interviewed by Dr. Borden, the defendant stated that he believed that his father-in-law was a spy for the red Chinese and that he believed his father-in-law was not only going to kill him, but going to harm his infant child so that he killed his father-in-law in self-defense. The explanations given by the defendant for committing the homicide are similar to the illustration of irrational reasons and motives given in comment c to § 895J of the Restatement. . . .

Under these circumstances we are persuaded that the defendant's behavior at the time of the beating and shooting of Polmatier constituted an "act" within the meaning of comment b, § 2, of the Restatement....

As discussed above, the defendant gave the police and Borden several reasons why he killed Polmatier. Under comment c to § 895J of the Restatement, it is not necessary for a defendant's reasons and motives for forming his intention to be rational in order for him to have the intent to invade the interests of another. Considering his statements to the police and to Borden that he intended to punish Polmatier and to kill him, we are persuaded that the defendant intended to beat and shoot him. Because the defendant was found not guilty by reason of insanity, it is uncontested in this civil action that he was incapable of forming the intent necessary for criminal responsibility for Polmatier's death. Under General Statutes § 52–555, the wrongful death statute, however, intent is not an essential element of the cause of action.

There is no error.

Notes

1. *Majority rule*. *Polmatier* states the usual American view that the defendant's insanity is not, in itself, an excuse from tort liability.

2. *Role of fault*. Should we regard this as an exception to the principle that liability is based upon the defendant's fault? Or is it merely that fault is defined by an objective standard, not by the plaintiff's subjective capacities? Should liability be based upon moral fault of the defendant and his responsibility for that fault? Or should it be based on compensation for the victim?

3. *Common law*. Canada, like the United States, is a common law country in which most tort law is made by judicial decision in concrete cases. Canadian case law, like American, refuses any blanket immunity for insane persons. The question is whether the defendant had the requisite intent; if he did, the fact that it arose from insanity is not relevant. Sparse English authority seems to agree.

4. *Civil law*. The civil law, as contrasted with the common law, begins with general principles formally stated in codes of law. Civil law courts of course decide particular cases, but they begin analysis by considering a Code provision. Civil law, rooted in Roman jurisprudence, is the dominant legal system in Europe, Central and South America, and elsewhere outside the Anglo–American legal communities. It is also an important heritage in Louisiana by way of the French connection and in the Southwest by way of the Spanish connection. The traditional civil law held that a mentally unsound person "cannot commit a fault." This can be seen today in the German Civil Code § 827, excluding civil responsibility for one who is unable to exercise free will, except where he brought on temporary disability by use of alcohol or similar means. But civil law countries today are divided. In Mexico, the Código Civil para el Distrito Federal § 1911 provides that the incompetent person is liable unless some other person such as a guardian is liable. ("El incapaz que cause daño debe repararlo, salvo que la responsabili-

dad recaiga en las personas de él encargadas, conforme lo dispuesto en [otros artículos]."")

5. *Options.* If you were writing a statute to resolve the problem of injury caused by insane persons, would you want to consider any other options besides liability or non-liability? Crime victims' compensation statutes have been enacted in many states. Under these statutes the state may create a fund for the partial compensation of crime victims, at least where the criminal himself is not made to pay. See Charlene Smith, *Victim Compensation: Hard Questions and Suggested Remedies*, 17 RUTGERS L. J. 51 (1985). Would this be a good solution for the problem represented by *Polmatier*?

6. *Bases for general rule.* What are the bases for the general rule that refuses to shield insane persons? First consider whether they are persuasive. Could you convince some judges to reject them? Second, consider the nature of the reasons. Are they arguments about justice or about policy?

WHITE v. MUNIZ

Supreme Court of Colorado, 2000.
999 P.2d 814.

JUSTICE KOURLIS delivered the Opinion of the Court. . . .

In October of 1993, Barbara White placed her eighty-three year-old grandmother, Helen Everly, in an assisted living facility, the Beatrice Hover Personal Care Center. Within a few days of admission, Everly started exhibiting erratic behavior. She became agitated easily, and occasionally acted aggressively toward others. [A physician concluded that she had progressive dementia, loss of memory, impulse control and judgment, a degenerative dementia of the Alzheimer type.]

On November 21, 1993, the caregiver in charge of Everly's wing asked Sherry Lynn Muniz, a shift supervisor at Hover, to change Everly's adult diaper. The caregiver informed Muniz that Everly was not cooperating in that effort. This did not surprise Muniz because she knew that Everly sometimes acted obstinately. Indeed, initially Everly refused to allow Muniz to change her diaper, but eventually Muniz thought that Everly relented. However, as Muniz reached toward the diaper, Everly struck Muniz on the jaw and ordered her out of the room.

[Muniz sued Everly and White as her representative for assault and battery. After the evidence was presented, the trial judge instructed the jury in part as follows.]

> The fact that a person may suffer from Dementia, Alzheimer type, does not prevent a finding that she acted intentionally. You may find that she acted intentionally if she intended to do what she did, even though her reasons and motives were entirely irrational. However, she must have appreciated the offensiveness of her conduct.

Muniz's counsel objected to the last sentence of the instruction, claiming that it misstated the law. [The jury found for Everly and White. The Court of Appeals held the instruction to be error and reversed.]

The question we here address is whether an intentional tort requires some proof that the tortfeasor not only intended to contact another person, but also intended that the contact be harmful or offensive to the other person.

State courts and legal commentators generally agree that an intentional tort requires some proof that the tortfeasor intended harm or offense. See W. Page Keeton et al., Prosser and Keeton on the Law of Torts § 8 (5th ed.1984); Dan B. Dobbs, The Law of Torts § 30 (2000). According to the Restatement (Second) of Torts [§ 13],

> (1) An actor is subject to liability to another for battery if
>
> > (a) he acts intending to cause a harmful or offensive contact with the person of the other or a third person, or an imminent apprehension of such a contact, and
> >
> > (b) an offensive [or harmful] contact with the person of the other directly or indirectly results....

[Historically,] the actor had to understand that his contact would be harmful or offensive. See Keeton, supra, § 8; Dobbs, supra, § 29. The actor need not have intended, however, the harm that actually resulted from his action. Thus, if a slight punch to the victim resulted in traumatic injuries, the actor would be liable for all the damages resulting from the battery even if he only intended to knock the wind out of the victim.

Juries may find it difficult to determine the mental state of an actor, but they may rely on circumstantial evidence in reaching their conclusion. No person can pinpoint the thoughts in the mind of another, but a jury can examine the facts to conclude what another must have been thinking. For example, a person of reasonable intelligence knows with substantial certainty that a stone thrown into a crowd will strike someone and result in an offensive or harmful contact to that person. Hence, if an actor of average intelligence performs such an act, the jury can determine that the actor had the requisite intent to cause a harmful or offensive contact, even though the actor denies having such thoughts.

More recently, some courts around the nation have abandoned this dual intent requirement in an intentional tort setting, that being an intent to contact and an intent that the contact be harmful or offensive, and have required only that the tortfeasor intend a contact with another that results in a harmful or offensive touching. Under this view, a victim need only prove that a voluntary movement by the tortfeasor resulted in a contact which a reasonable person would find offensive or to which the victim did not consent. These courts would find intent in contact to the back of a friend that results in a severe, unexpected injury even though the actor did not intend the contact to be harmful or offensive. The actor thus could be held liable for battery because a reasonable person would find an injury offensive or harmful, irrespective of the intent of the actor to harm or offend....

Because Colorado law requires a dual intent, we apply here the Restatement's definition of the term. As a result, we reject the arguments of Muniz and find that the trial court delivered an adequate instruction to the jury.

Operating in accordance with this instruction, the jury had to find that Everly appreciated the offensiveness of her conduct in order to be liable for the intentional tort of battery. It necessarily had to consider her mental capabilities in making such a finding, including her age, infirmity, education, skill, or any other characteristic as to which the jury had evidence. We presume that the jury "looked into the mind of Everly," and reasoned that Everly did not possess the necessary intent to commit an assault or a battery.

A jury can, of course, find a mentally deficient person liable for an intentional tort, but in order to do so, the jury must find that the actor intended offensive or harmful consequences. As a result, insanity is not a defense to an intentional tort according to the ordinary use of that term, but is a characteristic, like infancy, that may make it more difficult to prove the intent element of battery. Our decision today does not create a special rule for the elderly, but applies Colorado's intent requirement in the context of a woman suffering the effects of Alzheimer's. . . .

[Jury verdict reinstated.]

REFERENCES: DOBBS ON TORTS §§ 24, 28–31 (2000); HARPER, JAMES AND GRAY ON TORTS § 3.3 (3d ed. 1996).

§ 2. ASSAULT

Elements of Assault

"Assault" has a technical meaning in tort law. Newspapers may use the term as a euphemism for sexual battery. Even judges, particularly in older cases, may use the term assault to mean a battery. Used as a technical term, however, assault refers to an act by the defendant that puts the plaintiff in apprehension of an imminent bodily touching that would be harmful or offensive. The defendant must intend his act. Beyond that, the defendant must also intend either (a) to put the plaintiff in apprehension of a touching that would count as a harmful or offensive under the battery rules, or (b) must intend some other trespassory tort, such as battery itself. No actual touching is required.

Defendant threw a bottle at the plaintiff, who was not far away. The plaintiff ducked and the bottle missed. If the defendant intended to miss the plaintiff but to put her in apprehension of an imminent offensive or harmful contact, he has committed an assault, provided the plaintiff was actually under such an apprehension. What if the defendant intended actually to hit the plaintiff? That is also an assault, again provided that the plaintiff was in apprehension of an imminent offensive or harmful contact.

DICKENS v. PURYEAR

Supreme Court of North Carolina, 1981.
302 N.C. 437, 276 S.E.2d 325.

Exum, Justice.

Plaintiff's complaint is cast as a claim for intentional infliction of mental distress. It was filed more than one year but less than three years after the incidents complained of occurred.... Defendants' motions for summary judgment were allowed on the ground that plaintiff's claim was for assault and battery; therefore it was barred by the one-year statute of limitations applicable to assault and battery.

The facts brought out at the hearing on summary judgment may be briefly summarized: For a time preceding the incidents in question plaintiff Dickens, a thirty-one year old man, shared sex, alcohol and marijuana with defendants' daughter, a seventeen year old high school student. On 2 April 1975 defendants ... lured plaintiff into rural Johnston County, North Carolina. Upon plaintiff's arrival defendant Earl Puryear, after identifying himself, ... pointed a pistol between plaintiff's eyes and shouted "Ya'll come on out." Four men wearing ski masks and armed with nightsticks then approached from behind plaintiff and beat him into semi-consciousness. They handcuffed plaintiff to a piece of farm machinery and resumed striking him with nightsticks. Defendant Earl Puryear, while brandishing a knife and cutting plaintiff's hair, threatened plaintiff with castration. During four or five interruptions of the beating defendant Earl Puryear and the others, within plaintiff's hearing, discussed and took votes on whether plaintiff should be killed or castrated. Finally, after some two hours and the conclusion of a final conference, the beatings ceased. Defendant Earl Puryear told plaintiff to go home, pull his telephone off the wall, pack his clothes, and leave the state of North Carolina; otherwise he would be killed. Plaintiff was then set free.

Plaintiff filed his complaint on 31 March 1978. It alleges that defendants on the occasion just described intentionally inflicted mental distress upon him. He further alleges that as a result of defendants' acts plaintiff has suffered "severe and permanent mental and emotional distress, and physical injury to his nerves and nervous system." He alleges that he is unable to sleep, afraid he may be killed, suffering from chronic diarrhea and a gum disorder, unable effectively to perform his job, and that he has lost $1000 per month income.... Judge Braswell ... concluded that plaintiff's claim was barred by G.S. 1–54(3), the one-year statute of limitations applicable to assault and battery....

[T]he Court of Appeals concluded that the complaint's factual allegations and the factual showing at the hearing on summary judgment support only a claim for assault and battery. The claim was therefore, barred by the one-year period of limitations applicable to assault and battery. Plaintiff, on the other hand, argues that the factual showing on the motion supports a claim for intentional infliction of mental distress—a claim which is governed by the three-year period of limitations. At least, plaintiff argues, his factual showing is such that it cannot be said as a matter of law that he will be unable to prove such a claim at trial. We agree with plaintiff's position.

North Carolina follows common law principles governing assault and battery. An assault is an offer to show violence to another without striking him, and a battery is the carrying of the threat into effect by the infliction of a blow. The interest protected by the action for battery is freedom from intentional and unpermitted contact with one's person; the interest protected by the action for assault is freedom from apprehension of a harmful or offensive contact with one's person. The apprehension created must be one of an immediate harmful or offensive contact, as distinguished from contact in the future. . . .

Common law principles of assault and battery as enunciated in North Carolina law are also found in the Restatement (Second) of Torts (1965) (hereinafter "the Restatement"). As noted in § 29(1) of the Restatement, "[t]o make the actor liable for an assault he must put the other in apprehension of an *imminent* contact." (Emphasis supplied.) The comment to § 29(1) states: "The apprehension created must be one of imminent contact, as distinguished from any contact in the future. 'Imminent' does not mean immediate, in the sense of instantaneous contact. . . . It means rather that there will be no significant delay." Similarly, § 31 of the Restatement provides that "[w]ords do not make the actor liable for assault unless together with other acts or circumstances they put the other in reasonable apprehension of an *imminent* harmful or offensive contact with his person." (Emphasis supplied.) The comment to § 31 provides, in pertinent part:

"a. Ordinarily mere words, unaccompanied by some act apparently intended to carry the threat into execution, do not put the other in apprehension of an imminent bodily contact, and so cannot make the actor liable for an assault under the rule stated in § 21 [the section which defines an assault]. For this reason *it is commonly said in the decisions that mere words do not constitute an assault,* or that some overt act is required. *This is true even though the mental discomfort caused by a threat of serious future harm on the part of one who has the apparent intention and ability to carry out his threat may be far more emotionally disturbing than many of the attempts to inflict minor bodily contacts which are actionable as assaults. Any remedy for words which are abusive or insulting or which create emotional distress by threats for the future, is to be found under §§ 46 and 47 [those sections dealing with the interest in freedom from emotional distress].*

"1.   A, known to be a resolute and desperate character, *threatens to waylay B on his way home on a lonely road on a dark night. A is not liable to B for an assault under the rule stated in § 21. A may, however, be liable to B for the infliction of severe emotional distress by extreme and outrageous conduct*, under the rule stated in § 46." (Emphasis supplied.)

. . . Thus threats for the future are actionable, if at all, not as assaults but as intentional inflictions of mental distress. . . .

Although plaintiff labels his claim one for intentional infliction of mental distress we agree with the Court of Appeals that "[t]he nature of action is not determined by what either party calls it. . . ." The nature of the action is determined "by the issues arising on the pleading and by the relief sought," and by the facts which, at trial, are proved or which, on motion for summary judgment, are forecast by the evidentiary showing.

Here much of the factual showing at the hearing related to assaults and batteries committed by defendants against plaintiff. The physical beatings and the cutting of plaintiff's hair constituted batteries. The threats of castration and death, being threats which created apprehension of immediate harmful or offensive contact, were assaults. Plaintiff's recovery for injuries, mental or physical, caused by these actions would be barred by the one-year statute of limitations.

The evidentiary showing on the summary judgment motion does, however, indicate that defendant Earl Puryear threatened plaintiff with death in the future unless plaintiff went home, pulled his telephone off the wall, packed his clothes, and left the state. The Court of Appeals characterized this threat as being "an immediate threat of harmful and offensive contact. It was a present threat of harm to plaintiff. . . ."

We disagree with the Court of Appeals' characterization of this threat. The threat was not one of imminent, or immediate, harm. It was a threat for the future apparently intended to and which allegedly did inflict serious mental distress; therefore it is actionable, if at all, as an intentional infliction of mental distress.

Having concluded, therefore, that the factual showing on the motions for summary judgment was sufficient to indicate that plaintiff may be able to prove at trial a claim for intentional infliction of mental distress, we hold that summary judgment for defendants based upon the one-year statute of limitations was error and we remand the matter for further proceedings against defendant Earl Puryear not inconsistent with this opinion. . . .

Notes

1. *Summary judgment.* Summary judgment is granted where there is no material issue of fact and the only issue is one of law. The sequence of procedure in *Dickens* is typical. After the complaint was filed, the defendants engaged in "discovery," a procedure for taking testimony of witnesses under oath, but before trial and not in court. The testimony was transcribed and the resulting "deposition" filed with the court. The defendant can then move for summary judgment. If the deposition and any formal admissions of the parties reveal disputes about significant facts, the case must go on to the

trial stage for resolution by a jury. If there is no material factual dispute, however, the judge can grant the motion for summary judgment on the legal dispute.

2. What happens to the *Dickens* case after the Supreme Court of North Carolina remands it?

3. Dabbs holds Purtle's cat over the edge of Dabbs' roof. "Purtle," he says, "I'm going to drop your cat now and we can see how many lives it has." As Dabbs knows, Purtle loves his cat. Is Dabbs' action an assault? What rule determines the answer?

4. Dabbs calls Purtle, his next door neighbor, and says: "I'm coming over right now and I'm going to beat you up." Dabbs slams down the phone, but becomes absorbed in a TV program and never leaves the house. Is it an assault? What rule would determine the answer?

5. *Free Access to Clinics Act.* The federal Free Access to Clinic Entrances Act (FACE), 18 U.S.C.A. § 248, creates a civil claim against anyone who by threat, force, or physical obstruction intentionally injures, intimidates, or interferes with a person seeking to obtain or provide "reproductive health services." Dr. Lucero alleged that Father David Trosch appeared on the Geraldo Show, a television program. Trosch allegedly indicated that it would not be murder to kill doctors who performed abortions. Dr. Lucero performed abortions and was also on the same show. Trosch answered the question "would you kill him?" by saying "He is a mass murderer and should be dead." In Birmingham, where Lucero practices, Trosch made similar statements. Would Trosch's words count as a common law assault? Would they be actionable under the statute? *Lucero v. Trosch,* 904 F.Supp. 1336 (S.D.Ala.1995); *Lucero v. Trosch,* 928 F.Supp. 1124 (S.D. Ala. 1996).

6. *Stalkers.* Statutes in a number of states create a claim against stalkers who follow or stalk someone. The stalkers almost always seem to be men and their victims women. The California statute creates a statutory tort called stalking based on a pattern of conduct the "intent of which was to follow, alarm, or harass the plaintiff," with resulting reasonable fear by the plaintiff for herself or an immediate family member. In addition, the defendant must either make a credible threat or violate a restraining order. CAL. CIV. CODE § 1708.7.

7. *Casual language about assault.* Sometimes courts have said that "[e]very battery necessarily involves an assault." *McGlone v. Hauger,* 56 Ind.App. 243, 104 N.E. 116 (1914). Can this be an accurate formulation? To test it, suppose the defendant struck a sleeping plaintiff with a baseball bat. Do you have a firm conclusion? It takes a good deal of knowledge and lawyerly experience to know when judges' remarks should be taken literally and when they should be taken as only a general approximation of the rule or as only remarks addressed to the particular facts of the case under consideration.

8. *Damages.* The plaintiff suing for assault can recover damages of the same kind recoverable for battery.

———

CULLISON v. MEDLEY, 570 N.E.2d 27 (Ind.1991). Defendants apparently believed that plaintiff had been "bothering" a young woman in their family. The plaintiff claimed they entered his home at night after he had gone to bed. While accusing the plaintiff of being a "pervert" and berating him generally, one of the defendants kept grabbing at a gun strapped to his thigh, as if to shoot the plaintiff. *Held*, such facts are sufficient to show assault for which mental distress damages could be recovered.

The Use of Words in Putative Assaults

(a) *Words alone.* Courts have sometimes said that words alone cannot count as an assault. It is almost impossible to imagine words alone, divorced from any act at all. Suppose someone stands perfectly still at the entrance to a dark alley. He is masked and holding a gun. He says: "I am now going to shoot you dead." Surely this could be reasonably understood as a threat of imminent bodily harm. Maybe "words alone" is another shorthand or inaccurate statement. Perhaps it means that the plaintiff must reasonably apprehend an immediate touching and that in most cases words alone will not suffice to create such an apprehension.

(b) *Words negating intent to effect immediate touching.* Sometimes acts seem threatening but the threat is countered by words. The defendant draws back his arm as if to strike, but at the same time he is saying "If the police officer were not here, I'd punch your nose." The words clearly mean he is *not* going to punch your nose. If there are no facts to make it reasonable to believe that the defendant will strike you in spite of the police officer's presence, this does not look like an assault.

(c) *Words offering a choice of tortious alternatives.* Suppose the defendant in a menacing way says "I won't beat you to a pulp if you give me your basketball tickets; otherwise you are going to be pretty bloody."

ALTEIRI v. COLASSO

Supreme Court of Connecticut, 1975.
168 Conn. 329, 362 A.2d 798.

Loiselle, Associate Justice.

This action is one for battery brought by a minor, the plaintiff Richard Alteiri, to recover for injuries he suffered, and by his mother, the named plaintiff, to recover for expenses incurred. The complaint alleges that while the minor plaintiff was playing in the back yard of a home at which he was visiting, the defendant threw a rock, stone or other missile into the yard and struck the minor plaintiff in the eye and "[a]s a result of said battery by the defendant, the plaintiff Richard Alteiri suffered severe, painful and permanent injuries." . . .

[The defendant asserted that the plaintiff's complaint actually alleged the commission of a negligent act, and that the one-year statute of limitations for negligence actions had run prior to the filing of the complaint. The complaint had been filed within the three-year statute of limitations for battery.]

Six interrogatories were submitted to the jury. Two interrogatories were answered in the affirmative as follows: "On April 2,1966, did the defendant John Colasso, throw a stone which struck the plaintiff, Richard Alteiri, in the right eye?" Answer: "Yes." "[W]as that stone thrown by John Colasso with the intent to scare any person other than Richard Alteiri?" Answer: "Yes." The jury answered "No" to four other questions concerning whether the defendant had intended to strike either the minor plaintiff or any other person and whether he had thrown the stone either negligently or wantonly and recklessly. A plaintiff's verdict was returned. The defendant had appealed from the judgment rendered. . . .

The jury specifically found, as evidenced by their answers to the interrogatories, that the conduct of the defendant was neither negligent nor reckless and wanton but that it was intentional. Consequently, the Statute of Limitations relied upon by the defendant . . . § 52–584, by its terms does not apply to this action; rather General Statutes § 52–577 which limits actions founded upon a tort to be brought within three years from the date of the act or omission complained of would govern. . . . The issue to be determined on this appeal is whether a jury upon finding that the defendant threw the stone with the intent to scare someone other than the one who was struck by the stone can legally and logically return a verdict for the plaintiffs for a wilful battery. . . .

It is not essential that the precise injury which was done be the one intended. 1 Cooley, Torts (4th Ed.). § 98. An act designed to cause bodily injury to a particular person is actionable as a battery not only by the person intended by the actor to be injured but also by another who is in fact so injured.

This principle of "transferred intent" applies as well to the action of assault. And where one intended merely an assault, if bodily injury results to one other than the person whom the actor intended to put in apprehension of bodily harm, it is battery actionable by the injured person.

The defendant claims that comment b to subsection 2 of § 16 of the Restatement (Second) indicates that subsection 2 applies only to negligent acts where a person not intended to be injured is injured. The comment states in pertinent part that "[i]t is not necessary that the actor know or have reason even to suspect that the other is in the vicinity of the third person whom the actor intends to affect, therefore, that he should recognize that his act, though directed against a third person, involves a risk of causing bodily harm to the other so that the act would be negligent toward him." It is clear that the gist of this comment is that the actor need not know or suspect the presence of the third party, that is, need not be negligent.

It follows that the jury could logically and legally return a plaintiff's verdict for wilful battery, and that the court in accepting that verdict and denying the defendant's motion [for judgment N.O.V.] was not in error.

Notes

1. Assault, like battery, requires intent. The meaning of intent is the same as in battery cases—either a purpose or substantial certainty.

2. *Transferred intent.* Can you now state two versions of "transferred intent"?

3. Defendant sneaks up behind A with intent to beat his head with a board. B sees this and deflects the blow so that A is not touched, but A turns in time to see the blow coming toward him and is put in apprehension. What legal claims can be successfully asserted?

4. In light of the wide principle of "transferred intent" should we restate the *object* of intent required to establish an intentional tort? Prosser took the view that transferred intent originated with the old writ or form of action called *Trespass.* This writ was "the progenitor not only of battery, but also of assault, false imprisonment, trespass to land and trespass to chattels; and it seems fairly clear that when the defendant intends any one of the five, his intent will be 'transferred' to make him liable for any of the five, provided the harm is direct and immediate." WILLIAM PROSSER, TORTS 33 (4th ed. 1971).

5. *Liability for all damages.* It is said that the defendant who is guilty of an intentional tort, at least if it involves conscious wrongdoing, is liable for all damages caused, not merely those intended or foreseeable. We will call this the extended liability principle. That principle will actually explain most transferred intent cases, as where the defendant intends an assault and puts the plaintiff in apprehension, and then accidentally causes a harmful touching as well. See Osborne M. Reynolds, Jr., *Transferred Intent: Should its "Curious Survival" Continue?,* 50 OKLA. L. REV. 529 (1997). No doubt there is a limit somewhere. Still, stating the rule in terms of extended liability is probably less likely to produce error than stating it in terms of transferred intent.

§ 3. FALSE IMPRISONMENT

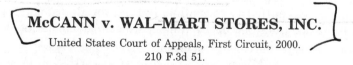

McCANN v. WAL–MART STORES, INC.
United States Court of Appeals, First Circuit, 2000.
210 F.3d 51.

This case involves a claim for false imprisonment. On December 11, 1996, Debra McCann and two of her children—Jillian, then 16, and Jonathan, then 12—were shopping at the Wal–Mart store in Bangor, Maine. . . . [T]he McCanns went to a register and paid for their purchases. One of their receipts was time stamped at 10:10 p.m.

As the McCanns were leaving the store, two Wal–Mart employees, Jean Taylor and Karla Hughes, stepped out in front of the McCanns' shopping cart, blocking their path to the exit. Taylor may have actually put her hand on the cart. The employees told Debra McCann that the children were not allowed in the store because they had been caught stealing on a prior occasion. In fact, the employees were mistaken; the son of a different family had been caught shoplifting in the store about two weeks before, and Taylor and Hughes confused the two families.

Despite Debra McCann's protestations, Taylor said that they had the records, that the police were being called, and that the McCanns "had to go with her." Debra McCann testified that she did not resist Taylor's direction because she believed that she had to go with Taylor and that the police were coming. Taylor and Hughes then brought the McCanns past the registers in the store to an area near the store exit. Taylor stood near the McCanns while Hughes purportedly went to call the police. During this time, Debra McCann tried to show Taylor her identification, but Taylor refused to look at it. . . .

Although Wal–Mart's employees had said they were calling the police, they actually called a store security officer who would be able to identify the earlier shoplifter. Eventually, the security officer, Rhonda Bickmore, arrived at the store and informed Hughes that the McCanns were not the family whose son had been caught shoplifting. Hughes then acknowledged her mistake to the McCanns, and the McCanns left the store at approximately 11:15 p.m. . . .

The jury awarded the McCanns $20,000 in compensatory damages on their claim that they were falsely imprisoned in the Wal–Mart store by Wal–Mart employees. Wal–Mart has now appealed. . . .

Although nuances vary from state to state, the gist of the common law tort is conduct by the actor which is intended to, and does in fact, "confine" another "within boundaries fixed by the actor" where, in addition, the victim is either "conscious of the confinement or is harmed by it." . . .

While "confinement" can be imposed by physical barriers or physical force, much less will do–although how much less becomes cloudy at the margins. It is generally settled that mere threats of physical force can suffice, and it is also settled . . . that the threats may be implicit as well as explicit, and that confinement can also be based on a false assertion of legal authority to confine. Indeed, the Restatement provides that confinement may occur by other unspecified means of "duress." . . .

The evidence, taken favorably to the McCanns, showed that Wal–Mart employees . . . told the McCanns that they had to come with the Wal–Mart employees and that Wal–Mart was calling the police, and then stood guard over the McCanns while waiting for a security guard to arrive. The direction to the McCanns, the reference to the police, and the continued presence of the Wal–Mart employees (who at one point told Jonathan McCann that he could not leave to go to the bathroom) were enough to induce reasonable people to believe either that they would be restrained physically if they sought to leave, or that the store was claiming lawful authority to confine them until the police arrived, or both.

Wal-Mart asserts that under Maine law, the jury had to find "actual, physical restraint," a phrase it takes from [Knowlton v. Ross, 114 Me. 18, 95 A. 281 (1915)]. While there is no complete definition of false imprisonment by Maine's highest court, this is a good example of taking language out of context. In Knowlton, the wife of a man who owed a hotel for past bills entered the hotel office and was allegedly told that she would go to jail if she did not pay the bill. . . . The court noted that the defendants did not ask Mrs. Knowlton into the room (another guest had sent for her), did not touch her, and did not tell her she could not leave. The court also said that any threat of jail to Mrs. Knowlton was only "evidence of an intention to imprison at some future time." In context, the reference to the necessity of "actual, physical restraint" is best understood as a reminder that a plaintiff must be actually confined– which Mrs. Knowlton was not.

Taking too literally the phrase "actual, physical restraint" would put Maine law broadly at odds with not only the Restatement but with a practically uniform body of common law in other states that accepts the mere threat of physical force, or a claim of lawful authority to restrain, as enough to satisfy the confinement requirement for false imprisonment (assuming always that the victim submits). It is true that in a diversity case, we are bound by Maine law, as Wal–Mart reminds us; but we are not required to treat a descriptive phrase as a general rule or attribute to elderly Maine cases an entirely improbable breadth. . . .

Affirmed.

Notes

1. *Elements.* "False imprisonment occurs when a person confines another intentionally without lawful privilege and against his consent within a limited area for any appreciable time, however short." *Bennett v. Ohio Dept. of Rehab. and Correction*, 60 Ohio St.3d 107, 573 N.E.2d 633 (1991). In addition, it is usually said that the plaintiff must have been aware of the confinement at the time or else must have sustained actual harm. Notice that bad motive is not one of the elements, only intent.

2. *Exclusion.* Confinement implies limited range of movement and it is not enough to exclude the plaintiff from some place such as a bar or restaurant. However, discriminatory exclusion of the plaintiff may violate civil rights laws. Suppose you are prevented from leaving Taiwan. Is that false imprisonment? *Shen v. Leo A. Daly Co.*, 222 F.3d 472 (8th Cir. 2000).

3. *Confinement by physical barrier or force.* Suppose the plaintiff is locked in a room but knows of a safe and reasonable means of escape. Is she confined? Suppose the defendant refuses to stop a moving car, the doors of which are not locked. Is his passenger confined?

4. *Confinement by threats or duress. (a) Threats or demands.* When the claim is confinement by explicit or implicit threat or duress, factual details

are critical. Suppose that in *McCann* the store guards had not mentioned police but had said, "You must wait until our supervisor arrives." Suppose instead that they had said "if you leave, we'll see that you are prosecuted." What if a female employee is surrounded by six burly men who accuse her of theft? You can think of many variations. The central issue is whether the facts show confinement. *(b) Assertion of authority.* Submission to an officer's assertion of arrest under colorable legal authority is sufficient to show confinement. *(c) Duress of goods.* The defendant grabs the plaintiff's wallet and refuses to return it. Plaintiff wishes to leave but doesn't want to leave without her wallet. Is this an implicit threat that results in confinement?

5. Paul is a cantankerous old man in a nursing home. Busy nurses and nurses' aides are constantly aggravated by him and he gets in their way. For their convenience, they give him unnecessary sedatives along with his regular and needed medication. The effect is that he will sit quietly for hours without disturbing anyone. Is this false imprisonment?

6. *Damages.* False imprisonment is a trespassory tort, so the plaintiff can recover damages even if she sustains no actual harm. Actual harm is required, however, to support a claim where the plaintiff was not aware of the confinement at the time it took place. The Restatement supposes a case in which defendant locks a baby in a bank vault with a time lock. The baby is not conscious of confinement but suffers actual harm, so that a recovery is permitted. RESTATEMENT SECOND OF TORTS § 42 (1965) and *Illustration 3.*

7. *Transferred intent.* Could you intend a battery and accomplish a false imprisonment?

8. *Privileges.* When an officer of the law improperly arrests a person, the tort is usually called false arrest. The rules requiring confinement are the same, but the officer, and sometimes others, may have defenses. A proper arrest based upon warrant or probable cause is of course not a tort. Privileges and affirmative defenses are considered in Chapter 4.

§ 4. TORTS TO PROPERTY

Many torts may involve intentional invasions of property interests. One might, for example, be defrauded in a way that causes loss of property. Only three torts, however, involve direct application of force and thus furnish substantial analogy to personal injury cases such as those involved in battery or false imprisonment. These torts are trespass to land, conversion of chattels, and trespass to chattels.

a. Trespass to Land

1. Trespass to land usually requires an intentional entry upon land of another. This might be accomplished by personal entry or by causing an object to enter the land, as by firing a bullet or throwing a stone or driving a car onto the land. The right of the landowner extends downward beneath the surface and to at least a reasonable height above ground, so that if one were to dig beneath the surface or fly very close to the ground this would also constitute a trespass. In one situation intentional *entry* is not required. This occurs when one unintentionally

enters, as where a car goes out of control without fault, and then refuses to leave. The refusal to leave is now considered a trespass.

2. *Intent.* Intent includes either purpose to enter or substantial certainty that entry will take place. The object of the intent need not be "to trespass," however. It is enough that the defendant intended to enter the land. He does not escape liability merely because he reasonably believes he is on his own land or because he reasonably believes he has a right to be there. Prosser thought that since trespass to land is a trespassory tort, the rules of transferred intent would apply.

3. *Damages without harm.* In trespassory torts, the defendant is liable for damages even if no physical or economic harm is done. If physical harm is inflicted, the defendant is liable for damages measured either by the cost of repairing damage or by the diminution in the value of the premises resulting from the tort, depending on circumstances. See 1 DAN DOBBS, LAW OF REMEDIES § 5.1 (1993). Parasitic damages may also be recovered as in any other trespassory tort: the trespasser whose bawdy songs upset the placid home life may be liable for mental distress.

4. *Punitive damages without harm.* Similarly, punitive damages may be awarded if the trespass is deliberate or "malicious." In *Jacque v. Steenberg Homes, Inc.,* 209 Wis.2d 605, 563 N.W.2d 154 (1997) the defendant wished to deliver a mobile home by hauling it across the plaintiff's fields. The plaintiff refused permission, but the assistant manager instructed his workers to cut a path and drive it across the plaintiff's land. The jury found no actual damages but awarded $100,000 punitive damages. Courts frequently say that punitive damages cannot be awarded unless the plaintiff first shows actual loss or damages. No such loss was shown in *Jacque,* but the court said that "in the case of intentional trespass to land, the nominal damage award represents the recognition that, although immeasurable in mere dollars, actual harm has occurred." It thus held the punitive award proper.

5. *Extended liability.* The trespasser is liable for damages inflicted even if he never intended harm and could not foresee it. Suppose the defendant knows he is trespassing on a farm, and throws his cigarette into what appears to be a puddle of water. The "water" is really gasoline leaked from a tractor, and it spreads a fire that burns down the farmer's barn. The extended liability rule makes the trespasser liable for loss of the barn.

6. *Limiting extended liability.* There are almost certainly limits to this rule. It might not apply fairly to trespassers who reasonably believe they are rightfully on the land, for example. Beyond that, it may be that the extended damages for which the trespasser is liable are those that are somehow related to security of possession. Suppose that while trespassing, the defendant sees the landowner commit murder. He reports the murder and the landowner is convicted and subjected to a life sentence. The extended liability rule does not suggest that the trespasser is liable for the murderer's imprisonment merely because the trespass provided the information essential to conviction. Cf. *Food Lion, Inc. v.*

Capital Cities/ABC, Inc., 194 F.3d 505 (4th Cir.1999) (trespassing journalists not liable for publishing truth they obtained while trespassing).

7. *Trespass as interference with possession.* Trespass is theoretically an invasion of one's right to possession, not to ownership. The distinction is seldom important, since owners usually have the right to possession as well. However, it is possible that one who possesses the land, perhaps even adversely to the owner, has a right against the trespasser for disturbance of that possession. Similarly, one who is in possession rightfully—under a lease, say—has a right to sue for trespass. If the trespass invades possession and also does permanent damage, the owner may also have an action, but this would be for actual damages done to the owner's reversionary right. Since this is not very "direct," it might be considered non-trespassory, but the point is of little importance today. However, the rule that trespass protects possession still has some importance to indicate that this particular claim cannot be made for the protection of non-possessory interests such as those in easements or right-of-ways.

8. An unidentified cat perches atop a fence that divides the Plunkett property from the Durfee property. The cat sets up an intolerable caterwauling in the middle of the night and Durfee hurls a shoe at the cat from her side of the line. The cat dodges and continues its serenade, but the shoe falls on Plunkett's property. Do these facts make a prima facie case of trespass?

9. John Dangle took off from a mountain point in a hang-glider. He passed over Pergolesi's land at a height of 250 feet. Shortly thereafter a shotgun blast from an unidentified source ripped holes in the glider's surfaces and Dangle lost control. He landed safely in Burger's back yard. No damage was done to Burger's property. Is Dangle a trespasser as to either Pergolesi or Burger?

b. *Conversion of Chattels—Trover*

Dubbs steals Pedrick's watch. This is a conversion and Dubbs is a converter. He has, as it is said, "converted the watch to his own use," by exercising substantial "dominion" over it. In such a case Pedrick can sue for the value of the watch at the time and place of the taking. In the earlier common law the form of action used to redress this conversion was known as *Trover,* and this is the word under which conversion cases are usually indexed even today.

1. *Intent.* Conversion is an intentional tort. The defendant must intend to exercise substantial dominion over the chattel. But, as in the case of trespass to land, there is no requirement that the defendant be conscious of wrongdoing. One who takes another's watch in the honest belief that it is her own is still a converter if the dominion thus exercised is sufficiently substantial. Should the transferred intent doctrine apply anyway?

2. *How conversion is accomplished.* A simple theft is a conversion, but substantial dominion over another's property may take place in

other ways. In each case suppose the defendant believes he has a right to deal with the property, but he is reasonably mistaken:

(a) Defendant decides to burn his copy of a torts casebook and throws it in the fire. By mistake he got the plaintiff's copy instead.

(b) Defendant restaurant holds a coat checked by A and also one checked by B. By mistake defendant gives B's coat to A, who disappears and is never found. B's coat is far more valuable than A's.

(c) Defendant, honestly believing that Turvey has the right to sell a watch, buys it from him. The watch in fact was stolen from plaintiff.

All these cases are cases of conversion. Notice in each case the defendant might be wholly innocent. Nevertheless, he has exercised substantial dominion over the property of the plaintiff and intended to do so.

One of the more difficult issues is what constitutes such dominion. It is clear that dominion is exercised in all the above cases, and also where the property is substantially damaged by the defendant. But in other cases defendant merely takes the property for a short period of time, as in the case of a joyride. If he takes a car for a joyride and it is destroyed in the process, he is no doubt liable. But suppose he takes it and returns it. Is this a conversion? These facts and many variations on them raise questions of degree which cannot be resolved firmly on principle. The American Law Institute concludes that it is all a matter of how serious the interference is. Since a finding of conversion will mean that the defendant pays the full value of the chattel, the ALI concluded that the interference should be serious enough to justify imposing such liability and that a number of factors were important including:

(a) extent and duration of control;

(b) the defendant's intent to assert a right to the property;

(c) the defendant's good faith;

(d) the harm done; and

(e) expense or inconvenience caused.

See RESTATEMENT SECOND OF TORTS § 222A (1965).

3. *What property may be converted.* The traditional common law rule was that conversion would lie only for tangible personal property. Thus neither land nor intangible property such as paper money or promissory notes could be converted. The rules today seem more liberal. One can convert shares of stock or bonds and other documents which are strongly identified with the right itself. Suppose a thief steals a retailer's account books, which show how much each customer owes. Has he converted the accounts themselves so that he is liable for everything customers owed the retailer? Or has he converted the books only?

What if a patient undergoes a course of treatments by a physician, who withdraws blood or blood cells at least ostensibly in the course of treatment and (a) sells one unit of blood to a blood bank and (b) uses another unit to develop a unique line of cells that are commercially valuable for making an important drug. Along with others in the venture, but not with the patient or with the patient's knowledge, he patents the products in order to reap the commercial gains. Is the doctor guilty of conversion anywhere along the line? Is the blood property? The California Supreme Court has held that the use of blood cells to develop a cell-line as a commercial product is NOT a conversion. The court seemed to say that the patient lacked a property interest in his own body tissues once they were removed, but its main concern was not to hinder development of socially useful medical treatments. *Moore v. Regents of the University of California*, 51 Cal.3d 120, 271 Cal.Rptr. 146, 793 P.2d 479 (1990). The court did say, however, that the physician was under a fiduciary duty to disclose some of the facts to the patient. Rejection of the conversion claim probably means that the plaintiff's recovery would not equal the commercial value of the product drawn from his body.

4. *Serial conversions.* Dubbs steals Pedrick's watch, then sells the watch to Byer. Dubbs is a converter and so is Byer, since both have exercised substantial dominion and have intended to do so. Pedrick could sue either or both, though he could collect only once.

5. *Bona fide purchasers.* Byer in the preceding illustration is liable even if she buys in good faith, that is, even if she is a bona fide purchaser for value and without notice of Pedrick's rights. The theory is that Byer cannot purchase from Dubbs any more than Dubbs has. Dubbs has no title and thus cannot transfer title to Byer.

There is one special wrinkle in this rule. If Dubbs does not steal the watch but tricks Pedrick into selling it to him, then Dubbs *does* get title. Since Dubbs got it by a trick or fraud, Pedrick could go to court and have the sale avoided; he could get his watch back because of Dubbs' fraud. However, he is not *required* to do this. He may do nothing at all and keep the money Dubbs paid him. At any rate, until Pedrick does go to court, Dubbs has title to the watch. This means that Dubbs could transfer title to someone else, including Byer. In this kind of case Byer would obtain good title and would *not* be a converter if she were a bona fide purchaser for value and without notice of Pedrick's rights. On the other hand, if Byer knew of the fraud practiced on Pedrick, and bought the watch anyway, she would also be a converter, along with Dubbs.

6. *The Uniform Commercial Code.* A comprehensive statute enacted in almost all states regulates many commercial dealings. One provision of the code covers this kind of case: Orwell takes his bike to the Merchant Bike Shop for repair. The bike shop repairs the bike but before Orwell returns, sells it to Dalzell. Under the rules stated above, Dalzell would be liable, since Merchant had no title to pass. The UCC, however, provides that if goods are entrusted to the possession of a merchant who deals in goods of that kind, the merchant has the legal power to transfer all the rights of the "entrustor." Is Dalzell is liable or not? Suppose Orwell had stolen the bike, then taken it to Merchant for repair. Would Dalzell be liable?

7. *Remedies*. The usual remedy for conversion is damages, measured by the value of the chattel at the time of conversion. At times, however, the value of the chattel fluctuates in the market, as in the case of shares of stock or commodities. The plaintiff, who has lost her property, may be forced to replace it in a rising market. If so, the time of conversion rule would be unfair. Some courts have accordingly permitted the plaintiff to recover the highest market value of the chattel that occurs within a reasonable time for replacement. The plaintiff might, instead of seeking value of the chattel, seek "replevin" or "claim and delivery," that is, an actual return of the chattel itself. This might also be possible in some instances through an injunction suit brought in equity.

> REFERENCES: See generally, DOBBS ON TORTS §§ 61–67 (2000); HARPER, JAMES & GRAY, LAW OF TORTS, Chapter 2 (3d ed. 1996).

c. *Trespass to Chattels*

Trespass to chattels involves some intermeddling with a chattel of another person, and at times even dispossession, but something short of a conversion. As in the case of conversion itself, it is much a matter of degree. Liability is imposed only if the possessor of the chattel suffers dispossession or lost use, or if the chattel or the possessor is harmed. See RESTATEMENT SECOND OF TORTS § 218 (1965). Liability is based on actual damage, however, not on the market value of the chattel.

Is there a trespass to chattel, a conversion, or no tort at all in the following cases?

> (a) Defendant pets the plaintiff's dog although the plaintiff has repeatedly told him not to do so. The dog is not harmed.

> (b) Defendant leans against the plaintiff's car.

> (c) Defendant takes the car for a joyride against the plaintiff's will, and puts the dog in the front seat with him.

> (d) Defendant, angered at the dog's barking, kicks the dog, then pushes the car over a cliff, causing substantial damages.

A law clerk to a firm, believing one of the lawyers is engaged in improper billing, secretly removes documents relating to that lawyer, makes photocopies, and secretly returns them. Is the law clerk guilty of conversion? Of trespass to chattels? See *Poff v. Hayes,* 763 So.2d 234 (Ala. 2000).

Trespass to chattels has traditionally involved the plaintiff's tangible chattel. However, recent cases have held that clogging a company's email or computer systems with large amounts of unwanted email or other electronic interference can count as a trespass to chattels. See, e.g., *CompuServe Inc. v. Cyber Promotions, Inc.,* 962 F.Supp. 1015 (S.D.Oh. 1997).

§ 5. FORCIBLE HARMS AS CIVIL RIGHTS VIOLATIONS

This section introduces civil rights claims brought under statutes or under the Constitution for direct invasions of the person, analogous to the direct invasions seen in the trespassory cases like battery, assault, and false imprisonment. Other kinds of civil rights claims, such as those based on job discrimination, are not included here. Some of those can be found in Chapter 32.

42 U.S.C.A. § 1983

Every person who, under color of any statute, ordinance, regulation, custom, or usage, of any State or Territory or the District of Columbia, subjects, or causes to be subjected, any citizen of the United States or other persons within the jurisdiction thereof to the deprivation of any rights, privileges, or immunities secured by the Constitution and laws, shall be liable to the party injured in an action at law, suit in equity, or other proper proceeding for redress.

Notes

1. This statute, which was passed by the Congress as one of several civil rights statutes following the Civil War, is usually known by its section number in the present code—"1983."

2. Notice that the statute creates a federal cause of action–one governed by federal law. Although the plaintiff may sue in either federal or state court, state courts must follow precedent set by federal courts in interpreting the statute and the rights it protects.

3. What elements must the plaintiff prove to establish the § 1983 action? Try to glean these from the statute itself.

YANG v. HARDIN

United States Court of Appeals, Seventh Circuit, 1994.
37 F.3d 282.

BAUER, CIRCUIT JUDGE....

On January 8, 1991, at approximately 11:00 p.m., Mike Yang, co-owner of a south-side shoe store, received a call from his alarm company notifying him that the store had been burglarized. Yang called his brother, Myung and an employee, Bob. The defendants, uniformed police officers employed by the Chicago Police Department, had already arrived at the store when Yang got there. While Yang and his employee and brother busied themselves with repairing the shattered front display window, Officer Hardin prepared a police report by the front door of the store, adjacent to the broken window. Officer Brown entered the store to investigate.... Believing that Officer Brown had stolen some merchandise, Yang approached the officer and requested that the merchandise be returned. At first, Officer Brown denied that he had taken any merchandise. But after a discussion that escalated into an argument, Officer Brown reached into his jacket and pulled out a pair of "L.A. Raiders" shorts and threw them at Yang. Officers Brown and Hardin then proceeded to enter their police car to drive away. When Yang followed, Officer Brown shoved Yang. Throughout the confrontation, Officer Hardin stood by the passenger door of the squad car. He did not speak or intervene in any manner despite Yang's repeated requests for Officer Hardin to call the police sergeant.

In an attempt to prevent Officer Brown from leaving, Yang held onto the driver's side door of the squad car to keep it open so that Officer Brown could not drive off. However, Officer Brown drove anyway, with the driver's side door ajar and Yang hanging onto the car. Officer Brown drove fast and recklessly in a zig-zagging pattern, braking and accelerating, in an attempt to throw Yang off. Officer Brown also repeatedly struck Yang in the ribs with his left elbow. Yang asserts that he was unable to let go of the car without being run over. Throughout the drive, Officer Hardin sat in the passenger seat. Officer Hardin did not say anything or in any way attempt to intervene. The squad car traveled, with Yang hanging on, more than two full city blocks until two men on the side-walk saw what was happening and ran out to the street to stop the police car. Yang let go when the car stopped. Officer Brown then got out of the car and punched Yang in the face, knocking him to the ground. Meanwhile, Yang's brother, who had run after the squad car, arrived at the scene. Officer Brown knocked Myung Yang to the ground.

Throughout these events, Officer Hardin did not call the sergeant or attempt to stop Officer Brown in any way. However, as the Yang brothers lay in the street, Officer Hardin got out of the passenger seat of the squad car, drew his gun, pointed it at the brothers and shouted obscenities at them. The Yangs froze. Officers Hardin and Brown got back in the police car and drove away.

[The officers were convicted of criminal offenses and Yang filed this action in federal court under § 1983, also claiming state-law torts. The trial court found against Brown and assessed damages at more than $229,000, including lost income, injury, and punitive damages.] Attorney's fees against Officer Brown pursuant to 42 U.S.C.§ 1988 were also awarded. The district court concluded that, as a matter of law, Officer Hardin was not liable for violating section 1983, nor for the state common law claims. Yang appeals.

Liability under § 1983 requires proof of two essential elements: that the conduct complained of (1) "was committed by a person acting under color of state law" and (2) "deprived a person of rights, privileges, or immunities secured by the Constitution or laws of the United States." In the present case there is no dispute that Yang has proved the first element. [The officers] were on duty, wearing Chicago police uniforms, driving a marked squad car and were investigating a crime when the incident occurred. The crux of this case is whether Officer Hardin's failure to intervene deprived Yang of his liberty rights under the Due Process Clause of the Fourteenth Amendment and his rights under the Fourth Amendment to be free from unreasonable seizure. See Mathis v. Parks, 741 F.Supp. 567, 570 (E.D.N.C.1990) (Fourth Amendment seizure occurs when government actors restrain liberty of citizen by means of physical force or show of authority).

... "[O]ne who is given a badge of authority of a police officer may not ignore the duty imposed by his office and fail to stop other officers who summarily punish a third person in his presence or otherwise within his knowledge." This responsibility to intervene applies equally to supervisory and nonsupervisory officers. An officer who is present and fails to intervene to prevent other law enforcement officers from infringing the constitutional rights of citizens is liable under § 1983 if that officer had reason to know: (1) that excessive force was being used, (2) that a citizen has been unjustifiably arrested, or (3) that any constitutional violation has been committed by a law enforcement official; and the officer had a realistic opportunity to intervene to prevent the harm from occurring.

The district court orally ruled in favor of Officer Hardin. The court found that the facts alleged by Yang did not demonstrate the availability of a reasonable time for Officer Hardin to intervene, or a reasonable likelihood of successful intervention. This finding is clearly erroneous.... At a minimum Officer Hardin could have called for a backup, called for help, or at least cautioned Officer Brown to stop. In fact, Officer Hardin should have arrested Officer Brown....

[The court also concluded that Hardin was guilty of common law false imprisonment and assault. Reversed for determination of damages against Hardin.]

Notes

1. *§ 1983.* A § 1983 tort requires the plaintiff to establish that someone, usually an official, acted under color of state law and also that the action deprived the plaintiff of a federal right. Although the federal right involved might be based on some other federal statute, most often it has been based on the federal constitution itself.

2. *Constitutional provisions.* Three constitutional provisions are frequently invoked in the physical attack cases: (a) The 14th Amendment's due process clause, guaranteeing the citizen against loss of rights in life, liberty, and property without due process of law; (b) the Fourth Amendment, guaranteeing the citizen against unreasonable searches or seizures; and (c) the Eighth Amendment, prohibiting cruel and unusual punishments for crimes. Did Officer Hardin violate any of these? Suppose the FBI instructs its sniper that "any armed adult observed in the vicinity of the Weaver cabin could and should be killed." The sniper then kills a person in the cabin who is offering no threat. Does this violate any of the constitutional provisions? *Harris v. Roderick,* 126 F.3d 1189 (9th Cir.1997).

3. *Common law torts and § 1983.* (a) Many § 1983 claims also constitute common law torts under state law. It is not uncommon to see § 1983 used to redress claims that appear to be batteries, assaults and false arrests and imprisonments. There are even § 1983 cases that seems to involve something like conversion and trespass to land.

(b) In most cases, the plaintiff can sue under § 1983 even though he could just as well claim under state tort law. See *Zinermon v. Burch,* 494 U.S. 113, 110 S.Ct. 975, 108 L.Ed.2d 100 (1990). As a practical matter, plaintiffs often support their claims by pointing both to common law theories like battery and to constitutional torts.

(c) The plaintiff can usually claim both federal rights violations and common law torts in the same suit. That suit can be brought in either federal or state court and in either case both federal and common law theories can be pursued.

4. *Color of law.* This phrase in § 1983 means the exercise of power "possessed by virtue of state law and made possible only because [of] the authority of state law...." See *West v. Atkins,* 487 U.S. 42, 108 S.Ct. 2250, 101 L.Ed.2d 40 (1988) (doctor hired by state to provide medical services at prison acted under color of law in providing allegedly inadequate treatment). This definition is sufficiently broad to include some acts of off-duty officers. It also includes acts of private persons who conspire with state officials and acts of private persons who pursue a state-enforced "custom or usage" that violates federal rights—segregation, for example. See *Adickes v. S.H. Kress & Co.,* 398 U.S. 144, 90 S.Ct. 1598, 26 L.Ed.2d 142 (1970).

5. *Liability of public entities.* The officer (or private person) who violates the plaintiff's federal rights under color of state law is personally liable. If the officer acts on behalf of a local public entity such as a city, the city may be held as well. However, cities are liable under § 1983 only under special conditions that can be considered later. States—as distinguished from cities and individual officers—are simply not liable under § 1983 at all.

6. *Practical value of § 1983.* Why sue under § 1983 rather than on simple common law torts? Reasons may include: (1) A § 1983 claim permits suit in federal court; a state tort claim ordinarily would not. A federal forum might be desirable in some cases because the judge seems more favorable or because the juries are drawn from a wider area and have a different demographic composition. (2) A § 1983 claim permits the prevailing plaintiff to recover reasonable attorney's fees. The rule for ordinary tort cases is usually the opposite, and each person pays his or her own attorney. In tort cases the practice is for the plaintiff's attorney to take a contingent fee, ranging from about one-fourth to one-half of the plaintiff's judgment. (3) A § 1983 claim might sometimes avoid defenses or immunities that would defeat a common law claim.

GRAHAM v. CONNOR, 490 U.S. 386, 109 S.Ct. 1865, 104 L.Ed.2d 443 (1989). The plaintiff was a diabetic who hurried into a convenience store to purchase orange juice to counteract an insulin reaction he felt coming on. Lines at the counter made him fearful that it would take too long, so he left almost immediately to search elsewhere. A police officer saw him enter and almost immediately come out. The officer became suspicious and after following the plaintiff for a distance pulled him over. The "sugar reaction" was explained to the officer, but he went to his car to call for backup. Graham got out of his car and ran around it twice, then passed out. Backup arrived, Graham was rolled over on the side-walk and his hands cuffed behind him. Graham came to and asked officers to check his wallet for his diabetes card, but they told him to shut up. After inflicting some other indignities they threw him head-first into the police car and refused to let him have orange juice a friend brought. In the Supreme Court, *held:* (1) the specific provisions of the Fourth Amendment rather than the general concept of due process provides the constitutional standard that governs "a free citizen's claim that law enforcement officials used excessive force in the course of making an arrest, investigatory stop, or other seizure of his person." (2) Subjective tests based on malice or good faith have no application. The test is the one specified in the Fourth Amendment, reasonableness. (3) Reasonableness would be judged objectively, through the eyes of a reasonable person at the scene. This would allow for errors made in emergent circumstances, but would not allow an officer to escape the consequences of unreasonable force merely because he did not act maliciously. Conversely, the officer's evil motives do not make the use of force actionable if it is otherwise reasonable. Consequently, a rule that protected the officers acting in good faith was error.

COUNTY OF SACRAMENTO v. LEWIS, 523 U.S. 833, 118 S.Ct. 1708, 140 L.Ed.2d 1043 (1998). A county sheriff's officer observed a motorcycle approaching at high speed. He yelled to its 18–year-old operator to stop, then attempted to position his car to block the motorcy-cle. The operator evaded the car. The officer then pursued with siren and emergency lights, reaching speeds of 100 m.p.h. in a residential neigh-borhood. The motorcycle eventually tipped over and the officer, only 100 feet behind it, skidded into the 16–year-old passenger, knocking him 70 feet and inflicting massive injuries, from which he died. This is a civil rights suit against the county for his death. *Held:* (1) No one contends that this was a search. It is not a seizure, which occurs only when there is a governmental termination of freedom of movement through means intentionally applied. The Fourth Amendment with its reasonableness language does not apply. (2) The case must be analyzed under the 14th Amendment's due process clause. Abuse of governmental power violates due process rights only when it shocks the conscience. "[T]he Constitu-tion does not guarantee due care on the part of state officials; liability for negligently inflicted harm is categorically beneath the threshold of constitutional due process." Although "deliberate indifference" may shock the conscience in some settings, as where the plaintiff is held in custody by governmental agents, where time to decide is limited, intent to injure is required. No intent to injure is claimed here. The officer's alleged recklessness is thus insufficient to show a due process violation.

HUDSON v. McMILLIAN, 503 U.S. 1, 112 S.Ct. 995, 117 L.Ed.2d 156 (1992). The plaintiff, a prisoner, claimed that guards beat him in violation of the Eighth Amendment's prohibition against cruel and unusual punishment. In the Supreme Court, *held:* (1) Application of unreasonable force to a prisoner does not violate the Eighth Amendment. By its terms, that amendment is violated only by application of cruel or unusual punishment. (2) But the test of liability is not whether the injury was minor or major. Although not every push or shove is actionable, prison officials are liable for sadistic or malicious use of force against inmates regardless of the amount of injury. "Otherwise, the Eighth Amendment would permit any physical punishment, no matter how diabolic or inhuman, inflicting less than some arbitrary quantity of injury." Justice Thomas dissented. He argued that a serious injury is always required in Eighth Amendment cases.

Note

Many prisoners bring Eighth Amendment suits. Some issues are parallel to common law tort issues but their analysis and argument may take a different form. The plaintiff must argue in the language of the Eighth Amendment that he suffered "punishment" and that it was cruel or unusual. In *Robins v. Meecham,* 60 F.3d 1436 (9th Cir.1995) a prison guard fired bird shot at one prisoner but it ricocheted and struck a different prisoner. The court said the issue was not transferred intent but whether the Eighth Amendment protects all victims of cruel and unusual punishment or only those against whom the guard directs his acts. The answer was "all." A guard's unprovoked attack would count as a battery, but would it count as "punishment" and hence as cruel and unusual punishment? See *Pelfrey v. Chambers*, 43 F.3d 1034 (6th Cir.1995).

Chapter 4

DEFENSES TO INTENTIONAL TORTS—PRIVILEGES

The defenses encountered in this chapter are for the most part purely affirmative defenses. That is, the defendant must affirmatively raise these defenses, usually by answer to the complaint, and the proof must affirmatively convince the jury that the facts supporting the defense are established. To put it differently, the plaintiff had the burden of proving the elements of the prima facie case but the defendant has the burden of proving affirmative defenses. Although all of the defenses or "privileges" are important and raise serious issues, some of them will be summarized briefly in text and left to courses in criminal law for further exploration.

§ 1. PROTECTING AGAINST THE APPARENT MISCONDUCT OF THE PLAINTIFF

a. Self–Defense

1. *Rule.* One is privileged to use reasonable force to defend against harmful or offensive bodily contact and against confinement. This privilege depends on apparent necessity of self-defense, not on actual reality. Thus if the defendant reasonably, but mistakenly believes she is attacked, she is privileged to use reasonable force to forestall the attack or minimize its effects.

2. *Reasonable deadly force?* What is reasonable force in self defense will vary with the facts. But can you say that deadly force is never reasonable? The general rule is that the defendant's privilege extends only so far as reasonably necessary to prevent the harm and, if the harm threatened is not itself death or serious bodily harm, then the defendant may not use force likely to cause death or serious bodily harm.

3. *Retreat.* The defendant who is attacked is not required to retreat or otherwise avoid the need for self-defense. When the defendant is sexually attacked, or attacked by force likely to cause death or serious bodily harm, she is privileged to respond with such deadly force of her own so long as it is reasonable. Some states require reasonable retreat

before deadly force is used unless the defendant is in her own dwelling. See RESTATEMENT SECOND OF TORTS § 65 (1965); HARPER, JAMES & GRAY, LAW OF TORTS § 3.11 (3d ed. 1996). Others make no such requirement. DOBBS ON TORTS § 71 (2000).

4. *Excessive Force.* The privilege covers only reasonable force. Any excessive force is unprivileged and the defendant is liable for it. Likewise, the defendant may not take the occasion to retaliate or to continue a "defense" after the fight is over. What is excessive force is a matter of degree and depends very much on the facts of each case. Suppose Pearson attacks Doolittle by punching him in the nose. Doolittle, reasonably perceiving that other blows may follow, proceeds to knock Pearson down, straddle his chest, and beat him for five minutes. Is this excessive force? What if Doolittle honestly believes such force is required to subdue Pearson, but his belief is unreasonable–is the excess slapping a battery, or merely a negligent tort?

5. *Provocation.* Provocation is not sufficient to raise the self defense privilege. Insults and arguments, for example, do not justify a physical attack by the insulted defendant. Distinguish acts that create the reasonable appearance of an attack from mere provocation.

6. *Resistance to unlawful arrest.* The privilege of self-defense permits one to resist false imprisonment as well as assaults and batteries. Should the privilege cover a right to resist an unlawful arrest? In *White v. Morris*, 345 So.2d 461 (La.1977), an officer demanded identification of some boys in a parking lot. One of them refused in no uncertain terms. The officer then attempted to make an arrest. The boy broke free, was grabbed again and this time struck the officer in the face, breaking his jaw. The officer sued. The court upheld the "centuries old common-law right to resist an unlawful arrest." The cases go both ways. See DOBBS ON TORTS § 73 (2000). What arguments on each side?

7. *Assault and imprisonment in self-defense.* The Restatement specifically recognizes that one may be privileged, given appropriate facts, to commit what otherwise would be an assault or a false imprisonment in self-defense. See RESTATEMENT SECOND OF TORTS § 67 (1965). One point of special interest is the rule in § 70 that the defendant may be privileged to put the plaintiff in apprehension of a harmful or offensive bodily contact even though the contact itself would not be privileged. Would this authorize defendant to point a gun at the plaintiff to forestall a punch in the nose, even though the defendant would not be privileged to fire it?

b. *Defense of Third Persons*

At one time, privilege to defend third persons was limited to permit only defense of family and servants. This seems to have little support today and in general one may defend others on the same basis that he may defend himself. Suppose defendant sees A striking B. Believing that B is attacked, defendant seizes A and delivers a stunning blow. B then runs off. It turns out that A was a police officer attempting to carry out a lawful arrest which B was resisting. Some courts have held that the defendant is liable for battery to the officer. Others have held that the privilege covers even this case. The Restatement Second of Torts § 76 has followed this latter view.

c. *Arrest and Detention*

GREAT ATLANTIC & PACIFIC TEA CO. v. PAUL

Supreme Court of Maryland, 1970.
256 Md. 643, 261 A.2d 731.

DIGGES, JUDGE....

Still in a convalescent state Mr. Paul ... went shopping at his local A & P store in Hillcrest Heights, Maryland, on December 20, 1967. So recent had been his heart attack that this was one of the first times he had ventured out in his automobile. The Hillcrest Heights store was a typical supermarket with check-out counters in the front.... On this occasion, due to heavy crowds in the store, Mr. Paul left his cart at the end of one aisle and slowly proceeded to examine carefully the labels of various articles of food to make sure they complied with his strict post-cardiac diet. Having examined and selected a particular item he would then return to his cart, deposit the goods and go in search of other merchandise.

[Parker, an assistant manager, watched Paul and concluded he had put a can of tick spray in his coat with intent to steal. Parker confronted Paul. The two men gave quite different versions of what happened. Paul testified that Parker grabbed him and forced him to march to the manager's office, where he was searched without discovery of any tick spray.] There was testimony that word of this incident spread throughout Paul's neighborhood.... Paul testified that the incident aggravated his heart condition causing him physical pain and suffering, as well as personal humiliation.

[The jury awarded Paul $10,000 in compensatory and $30,000 in punitive damages.] The jury by its verdict chose to believe Paul's version of the occurrence, and appellant realizes this aspect of the case is final. It insists, however, that mistakes of law requiring reversal have been made by the trial judge....

Appellant ... claims error was committed in the false imprisonment phase of the case.... The necessary elements of a case for false imprisonment are a deprivation of the liberty of another without his consent and without legal justification....

Appellant urges that Maryland should adopt the rule expressed in Restatement (Second) of Torts, Sec. 120 A (1965) "One who reasonably believes that another has tortiously taken a chattel upon his premises, or has failed to make due cash payment for a chattel purchased or services rendered there, is privileged, without arresting the other, to detain him on the premises for the time necessary for a reasonable investigation of the facts." Appellant cites several jurisdictions which have adopted this qualified privilege. It offered an instruction substantially embodying the Restatement language at the trial level, and it is refusal to instruct the jury in accordance with this rule that it assigns as error. It urges strenuously that probable cause should be a defense in this limited situation, detailing the growing problem of shoplifting in this country. It states that the modern self-service style of retail selling makes the shopkeeper powerless to protect his goods unless Section 120 A is adopted in substance. . . .

Whatever technical distinction there may be between an "arrest" and a "detention" the test whether legal justification existed in a particular case has been judged by the principles applicable to the law of arrest. A shopkeeper under these principles has only the rights of a private person. In Maryland a private person has authority to arrest without a warrant only when a) there is a felony being committed in his presence or when a felony has in fact been committed whether or not in his presence, and the arrester has reasonable ground (probable cause) to believe the person he arrests has committed it; or b) a misdemeanor is being committed in the presence or view of the arrester which amounts to a breach of the peace. Breach of the peace signifies disorderly, dangerous conduct disruptive of public peace and it is clear that the usual shoplifting incident does not fit within this category. Since most shoplifters steal inexpensive items, the only crime they are generally guilty of is petit larceny, a misdemeanor. Thus a private person has no power to arrest them, and probable cause to believe they committed the crime is in fact not a defense. . . . There is a narrow exception to the general rules of arrest stated above. Any property owner, including a storekeeper, has a common law privilege to detain against his will any person he believes has tortiously taken his property. This privilege can be exercised only to prevent theft or to recapture property, and does not extend to detention for the purpose of punishment. This common law right is exercised at the shopkeeper's peril, however, and if the person detained does not unlawfully have any of the arrester's property in his possession, the arrester is liable for false imprisonment. [The Maryland legislature had enacted a statute which substantially embodied the rule of section 120 A, but the judiciary found it unconstitutional due to titling defects. The legislature declined to reenact the statute.] . . . In view of this resolution by the Legislature we do not believe we should remake the law in this area even if we were inclined to do so. . . .

Having stated all the foregoing, we do not think that even if 120 A of Restatement (Second) had been the law of Maryland it would have aided appellant in this case. There was sufficient evidence for the jury to find that the manner and method of the detention here was not within the privilege "necessary for a reasonable investigation of the facts." But the reasonableness of the detention does not become an issue unless it is first shown that the person invoking the privilege "reasonably believes that another has tortiously taken a chattel upon his premises." Parker testified he did not see Paul place any merchandise in his coat and did not check the shelf to see if the "missing" item had been returned, although if he had, these activities would not have necessarily constituted probable cause. He further testified he stopped Paul in an aisle before Paul had given any indication of leaving the store, even though customers could not pay for any item until they reached the check-out counters at the front of the store. In a self-service store we think no probable cause (which, for the purpose of this opinion, we assume is equivalent to "reasonable belief" under 120 A) for detention exists until the suspected person actually attempts to leave without paying, unless he manifests control over the property in such a way that his intention to steal is unequivocal. Construing all the evidence in a light most favorable to the defendant, there is no showing of probable cause here. . . .

Judgment affirmed. Costs to be paid by appellant.

Notes

1. The privilege recognized by the Restatement's § 120 A is a privilege to detain for investigation for a short time, until police can arrive for example. *Guijosa v. Wal–Mart Stores, Inc.,* 6 P.3d 583 (Wash. App. 2000). It does not include a privilege to hold longer than necessary for investigation or for any other purpose. Why did the Maryland Court refuse to recognize this privilege?

2. Police officers are privileged to make an arrest under a warrant that appears to be authorized and on the basis of "probable cause" or reasonable grounds to believe that a felony has been committed by the arrested person. A private person is similarly privileged, but if he was mistaken about the actual existence of a crime the privilege would afford no protection to the private person. The private person could not ordinarily effect an arrest for a misdemeanor that was not a breach of the peace.

3. The common law rules authorizing arrest for felony and misdemeanor are summarized in the Restatement Second of Torts §§ 112–139 (1965). See also DOBBS ON TORTS § 83 (2000); HARPER, JAMES & GRAY, THE LAW OF TORTS § 3.17 & 3.18 (3d ed.1996 & Supps.). Statutes may play a large role today. The law of arrest is especially important in the field of criminal law. The details are left for courses dealing with that subject matter.

d. Defense and Repossession of Property

KATKO v. BRINEY

Supreme Court of Iowa, 1971.
183 N.W.2d 657.

MOORE, CHIEF JUSTICE.

[Defendant Bertha Briney inherited an unoccupied farm house. For ten years there were a series of housebreaking events, with damage to this property. She and her husband boarded up the windows and posted no trespass signs and eventually they set up a shotgun trap in one of the rooms. The gun was rigged to an old iron bed, barrel pointed at the door.

A wire ran from the doorknob to the trigger. It was pointed to hit the legs of an intruder. Mr. Briney admitted he was "mad and tired of being tormented," but said he did not intend to injure anyone. There was no warning of the gun. The plaintiff and one McDonough had been to the house before. They were looking for old bottles and jars. They broke into the house, and plaintiff started to enter the bedroom. The shotgun went off, and much of his right leg, including part of the tibia, was blown away. He spent 40 days in the hospital. The jury found for the plaintiff in the sum of $20,000 actual damages and $10,000 punitive damages.]
. . .

Plaintiff testified he knew he had no right to break and enter the house with intent to steal bottles and fruit jars therefrom. He further testified he had entered a plea of guilty to larceny in the nighttime of property of less than $20 value from a private building. He stated he had been fined $50 and costs and paroled during good behavior from a 60–day jail sentence. . . .

The main thrust of defendants' defense in the trial court and on this appeal is that "the law permits use of a spring gun in a dwelling or warehouse for the purpose of preventing the unlawful entry of a burglar or thief". . . .

Instruction 6 stated: "An owner of premises is prohibited from willfully or intentionally injuring a trespasser by means of force that either takes life or inflicts great bodily injury; and therefore a person owning a premise is prohibited from setting out 'spring guns' and like dangerous devices which will likely take life or inflict great bodily injury, for the purpose of harming trespassers. The fact that the trespasser may be acting in violation of the law does not change the rule. The only time when such conduct of setting a 'spring gun' or a like dangerous device is justified would be when the trespasser was committing a felony of violence or a felony punishable by death, or where the trespasser was endangering human life by his act."

The overwhelming weight of authority, both textbook and case law, supports the trial court's statement of the applicable principles of law.

Restatement of Torts, section 85, page 180, states: "The value of human life and limb, not only to the individual concerned but also to society, so outweighs the interest of a possessor of land in excluding from it those whom he is not willing to admit thereto that a possessor of land has . . . no privilege to use force intended or likely to cause death or serious harm against another whom the possessor sees about to enter his premises or meddle with his chattel, unless the intrusion threatens death or serious bodily harm to the occupiers or users of the premises. . . . A possessor of land cannot do indirectly and by a mechanical device that which, were he present, he could not do immediately and in person." . . .

Affirmed.

Notes

1. Would the case have been different if the trespasser had been entering the defendants' bedroom?

2. Would you favor a rule that permitted spring guns if there were a large, clear warning sign? How about electrified fences or trained attack dogs? In deciding how to structure a rule on this subject, should you consider the possibility that a child or a police officer with a warrant might enter and be killed or grievously wounded if deadly force were permissible?

BROWN v. MARTINEZ

Supreme Court of New Mexico, 1961.
68 N.M. 271, 361 P.2d 152.

MOISE, JUSTICE.

Appellants, being father and son, appeal from a judgment dismissing their claim for damages against appellee growing out of injuries suffered by the son when he was shot in the left leg while engaged with several other boys in a watermelon stealing escapade on appellee's property. It is sufficient to point out that on the night of September 18, 1954, appellant, a 15–year old boy, and two other boys visited appellee's garden patch adjacent to the road for the purpose of stealing melons. About 8:30 or 9:00 P.M., the next night, being September 19, 1954, appellant with several other boys again went to the farm of appellee for the purpose of stealing watermelons. While two of the boys entered the melon patch, appellant went to the southeast corner of the property and was in the highway right of way close to the fence when appellee hearing the boys in the patch came out of his house with a rifle in his hand, called to the boys to get out, and seeing the two boys running toward the southwest corner of the property fired the gun toward the southeast to scare them, the bullet striking appellant in the back of the left leg, half way between the ankle and the knee, breaking the bones and coming out of the front of the leg. . . .

Our examination of the authorities convinces us that the question of the reasonableness of resort to firearms to prevent a trespass or to prevent commission of an unlawful act not amounting to a felony is one of law for the court, and that such conduct is not excusable.

Dean Prosser in his Handbook of the Law of Torts, states the rule thus:

"The reasonableness of the force used is usually a question of fact for the jury. But as in the case of self-defense, the law has marked out certain limitations. The force used must be of a kind appropriate to the defense of the property. A push in the right direction may be proper where a slap in the face is not. *And, since the law has always placed a higher value upon human safety than upon mere rights in property, it is the accepted rule that there is no privilege to use any force calculated to cause death or serious bodily injury where only the property is threatened.* The defendant may use the force reasonably necessary to overcome resistance and expel the intruder, and if in the process his own safety is threatened, he may defend himself, and even kill if necessary but in the first instance a mere trespass does not justify such an act." (Emphasis ours.)

There is no suggestion in the proof here that appellee in any way felt his safety was threatened. Accordingly, under the facts as proven and found, the appellee acted improperly and is liable for injuries caused in using a gun in the manner he did, and with such unfortunate consequences, in order to drive away trespassers on his property, or to protect his watermelons, or to scare the intruders.

It follows from what has been said that the cause must be reversed and remanded with instructions that the court set aside its order of dismissal; determine appellants' damages; and otherwise proceed in a manner not inconsistent herewith.

It is so ordered.

Notes

1. Did the defendant do any unprivileged act? Does the law of transferred intent help the plaintiff here?

2. *Recapture of chattels.* Defending possession is one thing; using force to regain possession is something else. If a thief runs out of a store with a valuable electronic calculator, the store detective is privileged to recapture it if he does so immediately or in hot pursuit. Once possession has been lost, however, the detective cannot forcibly recapture it from him a week later. The store instead will be forced to sue or to invoke criminal processes. Similarly, one cannot use force in the repossession of consumer goods such as automobiles, even though the buyer is in default. The car seller may repossess the car from the defaulting buyer only if he can do so peaceably; indeed, the buyer may defend his possession with reasonable force.

3. *Repossession of land.* Many courts, operating under statutes, invoke similar rules when the owner of land has lost or given up possession: he must seek recovery in the courts, not by use of force, even by the use of reasonable force. The cases are divided, however, and some permit the owner with right to possession to use force, limited always to reasonable force. See DOBBS ON TORTS § 80 (2000).

e. Discipline

Some states refuse to permit children to sue their parents for torts. See Chapter 12. Where children are permitted to sue parents, parents still enjoy a privilege to discipline children, and to use force and confinement to do so. The limits of this force are ill-defined. The Restatement says parents may use the force they reasonably believe necessary. See RESTATEMENT SECOND OF TORTS § 147 (1965).

People who are not the parents of a child but who are in charge of the child also enjoy a similar privilege. Teachers and school bus drivers are the most obvious surrogates to claim the privilege. It may be that the teacher would not enjoy the same latitude for punishment that courts would recognize in a parent. Suppose a child is spanked by her parent for misbehavior and again by her teacher for additional misbehavior. Apart from local school board regulations affecting corporal punishment, what factors should a court consider in determining whether either the parent or the teacher is liable in tort?

Military discipline is now almost entirely governed by the Uniform Code of Military Justice and dealt with by actions within the military.

REFERENCES: DOBBS ON TORTS §§ 93–94 (2000); HARPER, JAMES & GRAY, LAW OF TORTS § 3.20 (3d ed. 1996).

f. Observing Privileges

Many common law privileges have the effect of resolving the issues in the case into matters of reasonableness and degree. In self-defense, the issue is frequently whether the defendant reasonably believed that defense was necessary and then whether he used the amount of force reasonable to cope with the apparent threat. In the case of schoolroom punishment, teachers, being privileged to inflict some punishment, are liable only if they go too far. In false imprisonment cases a defendant might be privileged to detain for investigation for a short time, but not for long. All such cases involve matters of reasonableness and hence matters of degree.

Notice how those cases differ from cases in which a defendant commits a "kissing battery"—he kissed the plaintiff, a stranger, or touched the plaintiff in a private place. This is an offensive battery and it is no defense to say the touching did not last long, that the force used was minimal, or that the injury was not great. Thus in common law actions, there are cases in which "degree" is not important, and other cases in which, because the issue of privilege is injected, degree becomes quite significant.

What do you think about the following cases—is the victim's right a categorical one regardless of the amount of force or harm, or would you expect courts to consider questions of reasonableness and degree?

(A) A police officer while on duty casually kicks the outstretched legs of a beggar seated on the sidewalk. He is not harmed, the force is minimal and the officer's malice is not great.

(B) A school teacher paddles a child because the child has stuck bubble gum on the class pet, a cat. The paddling consists of five moderate blows with a ping-pong paddle. The child cries but is not otherwise hurt.

§ 2. THE SPECIAL CASE OF CONSENT

Austin cooked a continental dinner for a new acquaintance, Berwyn, served in candlelight and accompanied by excellent French wines. After dinner the couple sat on the sofa listening to *Traviata* and sipping Benedictine and Brandy. The moment came, as it must in every scene of this sort, in which Austin drew closer and with parted lips looked in Berwyn's eyes. A kiss was imparted and Austin's hand caressed Berwyn's neck. Suddenly, to the surprise of everyone, there was a snap as a vertebra in Berwyn's neck broke.

This vignette illustrates several problems about the surprisingly complex "defense" of consent, but also suggests some common sense answers to some of those problems.

1. Berwyn testified: "I never consented to be touched at all, and in fact I was revolted at the idea." If the trier of fact believes this testimony, does it show there was no consent?

2. Was there anything to show there *was* consent?

3. Berwyn's lawyer argued to the trial judge: "Berwyn certainly did not consent to a broken vertebra even if there was consent to a kiss." What do you think of this argument?

4. Is consent really a "defense"? What practical matter would turn on the answer to this?

5. Common sense answers to these questions should suggest several legal principles. Could you state them?

NOTE: RELATIONSHIP OF PARTIES

In real cases lawyers would want to know a great deal more about the facts. Maybe Austin can take it that consent is given by silence in some relationships but not in others. Maybe in some cases a person has no capacity to consent and the actor knows it. Suppose you are sedated and while sedated give "consent" to an operation. If the doctor knows you are heavily sedated should the doctor believe you have manifested consent? Do you lack capacity to consent to acts with people who have great power over you? Suppose an employer asks an employee to engage in a sexual relationship. Does the employee have capacity to consent? Can the employer reasonably believe that consent is freely given if the employee expressly agrees?

"A position of relative weakness can, in some circumstances, interfere with the freedom of a person's will. Our notion of consent must, therefore, be modified to appreciate the power relationships between the parties." *Norberg v. Wynrib*, 92 D.L.R. 4th 449 (Can. 1992).

REAVIS v. SLOMINSKI, 250 Neb. 711, 551 N.W.2d 528 (1996). Reavis worked for Slominski as his dental clinic. They had sexual intercourse at times between about 1973 and 1975. From 1975 to 1988 Reavis was not working for Slominski. She resumed work for him in 1988 with the understanding that he would "leave her alone." They had no intercourse until after an office New Year's Eve party in 1991. According to Reavis, both were "somewhat intoxicated." Her testimony was that when they were alone Slominski locked the door and began kissing her. She pushed Slominski away and told him no. Slominski laughed and said, " 'You know you want it.' "Reavis said, " 'Oh, hell,' "and then walked down the hall toward Slominski's office and "threw [her] sweater off." Reavis testified that she felt there was nothing she could do because Slominski would just laugh at her. In the office, Reavis admonished Slominski and said, " 'You know you should not be doing this.' "Reavis felt that if she did not comply, she would lose her job. She said that she numbed her mind and body during the sexual intercourse, but that the physical contact was hurting her "very bad." Slominski's defense was that the intercourse was consented to. Reavis argued in the alternative that her words and acts did not amount to consent but that if they did her consent was ineffective because she suffered from an abnormal inability to refuse sexual intercourse as a result of childhood sexual abuse. The jury found in favor of Reavis on her battery claim.

Held, in a plurality opinion, remanded for new trial. Consent is not effective if a person lacks capacity to give consent. But the trial court erroneously refused to instruct the jury: (a) Incapacity of an adult plaintiff renders her consent ineffective only if her condition substantially impairs her capacity to understand and weigh the harm and risks of harm against the benefits flowing from the proposed conduct. (b) The plaintiff's incapacity does not render her consent ineffective unless the defendant has knowledge of that incapacity.

Notes

1. Four judges wrote concurring or dissenting opinions or both on various issues this case.

2. Is it correct to say that for the *Reavis* court, incapacity is governed by the apparent consent rules?

3. What about the separate issue of duress? Should employers be permitted to claim that employees who are dependent for a job, wage increase, or promotion, have consented to sexual intercourse?

4. Incapacity of an adult is usually established only by showing that the adult could not manage his own affairs, or, in consent cases, that he did not understand the nature and character of his act. On that test, does the evidence show that Reavis was legally incompetent to give consent?

5. Federal statutes against employment discrimination in effect forbid sexual harassment of employees. Dr. Slominski's conduct might count as a violation of those statutes, which are usually considered in advanced courses. You should be aware, however, that the damages award under those statutes may be less attractive to the plaintiff in some instances than the common law award. In addition, if Reavis had sued under those statutes, an issue similar to the consent issue might be raised: courts would ask whether Dr. Slominski's advances were "welcome" or not.

6. Some state statutes forbid all sexual contact between mental health professionals and their patients. Under these statutes, the patient's consent

is not legally effective to bar a claim against the therapist. If that is a good legal rule, should it apply as well in employer cases?

ASHCRAFT v. KING, 228 Cal.App.3d 604, 278 Cal.Rptr. 900 (1991). In 1983, a 16–year-old woman consented to an operation on condition that any blood transfusions required would be made only from family-donated blood. The family donated blood for this purpose, but this blood was not used. Instead, the transfusions used blood from the general supplies on hand at the hospital. The blood was infected with the HIV and after the operation the patient tested positive for AIDS. The reasons for the patient's insistence on family-donated blood were not clear. *Held*, the patient states a claim for battery, since the transfusions exceeded the consent given.

KENNEDY v. PARROTT, 243 N.C. 355, 90 S.E.2d 754 (1956). The plaintiff consented to an appendectomy by the defendant, Dr. Parrott. During the operation, the doctor found some enlarged cysts on her left ovary and punctured them. After the operation, the plaintiff developed phlebitis in her leg. She sued the doctor for battery on the theory that the phlebitis was proximately caused by the unauthorized extension of the appendectomy. She testified that Dr. Parrott told her that while he was puncturing the cysts, he had cut a blood vessel, causing her to develop blood clots. The trial judge entered a nonsuit for the defendant at the conclusion of the plaintiff's testimony. *Held*, affirmed. "[Some] courts, though adhering to the fetish of consent, express or implied, realize that 'The law should encourage self-reliant surgeons to whom patients may safely entrust their bodies, and not men who may be tempted to shirk from duty for fear of a lawsuit.'

"In major internal operations, both the patient and the surgeon know that the exact condition of the patient cannot be finally and definitely diagnosed until after the patient is completely anesthetized and the incision has been made. In such case the consent—in the absence of proof to the contrary—will be construed as general in nature and the surgeon may extend the operation to remedy any abnormal or diseased condition in the area of the original incision whenever he, in the exercise of his sound professional judgment, determines that correct surgical procedure dictates and requires such extension of the operation originally contemplated. This rule applies when the patient is at the time incapable of giving consent, and no one with authority to consent for him is immediately available."

Notes

1. Is *Kennedy v. Parrott* correct? What if the doctor knew or should have known that cysts were often found on such occasions, but did not mention this to the patient ahead of time? What if the plaintiff consented to an operation by Dr. A, but it was performed by Dr. B? In *Perna v. Pirozzi*, 92

N.J. 446, 457 A.2d 431 (1983) the New Jersey Court said this would be a battery.

2. *Medical "informed consent" cases.* A common case involves "informed consent." In this situation the patient expresses consent to a named operation, but is not informed about its nature or material risks. The doctor says, "You must have your thyroid out," but does not explain that there is a risk that the patient will lose her voice. You can view this as a case of battery on the theory that consent was ineffective because it was the product of the patient's mistake or possibly misleading conduct by the doctor. Most courts now deal with this as a problem of negligence. Consequently informed consent problems are considered in the chapter on medical malpractice.

3. *Substituted consent.* In a *Kennedy* situation to what extent should hospital personnel try to obtain the consent of relatives? Could this override the patient's own wishes? A woman undergoes a cesarean section with her fourth child. Her blood does not clot adequately and she requires transfusions to save her life, but she refuses them because of religious beliefs. Her mother and her spiritual advisor, both of whom are present, support her decision. Her husband, from whom she is separated, favors the transfusion. The woman herself is mentally competent. No evidence shows whether the husband could care for the children. Should a court issue an order permitting the transfusion over the woman's objection? Which facts, among those recited here, are most important to a decision? *In re Dubreuil*, 629 So.2d 819 (Fla.1993).

4. *Standards for substituted consent.* Substituted consent is almost a sub-specialty in itself. When someone is appointed as guardian for a person who is incompetent to give or withhold consent, should the guardian make the decision (a) on the best interests of the patient or (b) on the basis of what the patient herself would do if she were competent?

5. *Who is an incompetent?* People who are not able to manage their own affairs are usually legally incompetent. What about people who cannot manage their own affairs but who can understand the nature and effect of a proposed operation—should the doctor be required to obtain their consent or should the doctor look for a family member? In *Miller v. Rhode Island Hospital*, 625 A.2d 778 (R.I.1993) the plaintiff had consumed many, many drinks when he was in an automobile collision. The trauma team at the emergency room, fearing internal bleeding, insisted on performing a peritoneal lavage—circulating fluid inside the abdomen, so the fluid can be examined for signs of bleeding. The plaintiff objected and the doctors strapped him to a gurney and anesthetized him, then made the incision and performed the lavage. The plaintiff sued for battery. The court thought that competence to consent (or refuse consent) should be measured by the plaintiff's ability to understand the condition, nature and effect of the proposed treatment or its rejection.

6. *Consent of minors.* It is generally assumed that minors may consent to a number of touchings appropriate to their age. Probably two eight-year-olds can effectively consent to a football game in which touching is inevitable. Older minors can consent to more serious touchings, such as routine medical attention. The hospital emergency room that administers first aid to a 16-year-old with a broken arm is presumably protected from any claim of

battery if the teenager consents. But there are special cases that do raise special problems in the consent of minors, more or less as follows.

7. *Consent to major surgery.* There are few cases involving a minor's consent to major surgery that do not involve an urgent need. Suppose a 17–year-old asks a doctor to perform cosmetic surgery on his nose. Should the right to consent or refuse consent lie with his parents? What if the operation is a risky one that could cause death or serious debility?

8. *Consent to abortions.* The Supreme Court has held that states may not regulate a woman's right to control her own body, and that this means she is free to have at least certain first-trimester abortions without restriction. See *Roe v. Wade*, 410 U.S. 113, 93 S.Ct. 705, 35 L.Ed.2d 147 (1973). This right extends even to minor women, so that the states are not free to prescribe a blanket restriction of abortions to consenting minors. The Court refused to overrule *Roe v. Wade* in *Planned Parenthood of Southeastern Pa. v. Casey*, 505 U.S. 833, 112 S.Ct. 2791, 120 L.Ed.2d 674 (1992).

9. *Consent to intercourse.* An adult's consent to intercourse is effective to preclude any claim for battery, so long as the consent was not secured by fraud or some other tort. But statutes impose criminal liability for sexual conduct with a minor; the minor's consent is ineffective and provides no defense. Sometimes these statutes have been invoked to impose tort as well as criminal liability. Is it inconsistent to say a minor may consent to an abortion but not to sexual conduct?

10. *Consent to crime.* A and B agree to have an illegal boxing match. Each is injured. Some courts have said that the consent to illegal acts is ineffective. Under this rule, A and B could sue each other for battery, on the ground that one cannot consent to a crime. On the other hand, when it seemed to suit their purposes, courts readily switched to the rule that no one can found a cause of action on an illegal act. Under this view, courts would sometimes bar the victim who participated in crime. E.g., *Castronovo v. Murawsky*, 3 Ill.App.2d 168, 120 N.E.2d 871 (1954) (victim died, allegedly as the result of illegal and wholly negligent abortion, no recovery).

The Restatement rejects any flat view that consent is ineffective; it provides that consent IS generally effective and neither A nor B is liable to the other. In spite of this general rule, however, the Restatement also takes the position that a statute might make some act a crime for the very reason that the victims all too often are induced to consent by pressures against which the legislature wishes to protect, and that in such a case the expression of consent is ineffective. Suppose a statute makes it unlawful to hire a child under 15 for work near industrial machinery. Should the child's consent be a bar? What about consent to take illegal drugs? To incest? See RESTATEMENT SECOND OF TORTS § 892C (1979).

11. *Consent to other torts.* Would you expect the plaintiff's apparent consent to bar her claim for false imprisonment? Trespass to land?

———

DOE v. JOHNSON, 817 F.Supp. 1382 (W.D.Mich.1993). Plaintiff Jane Doe alleged: Earvin Johnson, Jr. transmitted human immunodeficiency virus (HIV) to her through consensual sexual contact. Johnson knew or should have known that he had a high risk of being infected with HIV because of his promiscuous lifestyle. Nevertheless, he did not warn Doe of this high risk or inform her that he did in fact have HIV. Nor did he use a condom. Doe suffers from HIV now and will develop AIDS. On motion to dismiss the battery claim, *held*, motion denied. One who knows he has a venereal disease and knows that his sexual partner does not know of his infection, commits a battery by having sexual intercourse.

Notes

1.   Where the defendant knows he has a sexually transmitted disease but neither warns his sexual partner nor provides any protection, several cases have imposed liability. E.g., *Hogan v. Tavzel,* 660 So.2d 350 (Fla.App. 1995) (genital warts not revealed). What if the defendant neither knows nor has reason to know he is infected with a sexually-transmitted disease, and infects his partner. Does her consent to intercourse bar a battery claim? See, e.g., *McPherson v. McPherson,* 712 A.2d 1043 (Me.1998). In *Doe v. Johnson,* can you say that the defendant had the intent to touch in a harmful or offensive way? Remember to distinguish intent from negligence.

2.   *Mistake or misrepresentation of collateral facts.* If the plaintiff manifests consent only because she relies upon the defendant's misrepresentation or her own mistake of facts, can we say that the consent is always nullified and the plaintiff is always permitted to recover? No. The rule is traditionally expressed by saying that the plaintiff's mistake (whether the result of misrepresentation or merely known to the defendant) must be about the "nature" of the transaction consented to. Thus mistakes about collateral matters such as price or timing do not nullify the consent. See. DOBBS ON TORTS § 100 (2000).

3.   In *Desnick v. American Broadcasting Companies, Inc.,* 44 F.3d 1345 (7th Cir.1995), Judge Posner set up a series of examples to distinguish between mistakes that vitiate consent and those that do not:

> The Restatement gives the example of a man who obtains consent to sexual intercourse by promising a woman $100, yet (unbeknownst to her, of course) he pays her with a counterfeit bill and intended to do so from the start. The man is not guilty of battery, even though unconsented-to sexual intercourse is a battery. Yet we know that to conceal the fact that one has a venereal disease transforms "consensual" intercourse into battery. Seduction, standardly effected by false promises of love, is not rape; intercourse under the pretense of rendering medical or psychiatric treatment is, at least in most states. It certainly is battery. Trespass presents close parallels. If a homeowner opens his door to a purported meter reader who is in fact nothing of the sort–just a busybody curious about the interior of the home–the homeowner's consent to his entry is not a defense to a suit for trespass. And likewise if a competitor gained entry to a business firm's premises posing as a customer but in fact hoping to steal the firm's trade secrets.

How to distinguish the two classes of case–the seducer from the medical impersonator, the restaurant critic from the meter-reader impersonator? The answer can have nothing to do with fraud; there is fraud in all the cases. It has to do with the interest that the torts in question, battery and trespass, protect. The one protects the inviolability of the person, the other the inviolability of the person's property. The woman who is seduced wants to have sex with her seducer, and the restaurant owner wants to have customers. The woman who is victimized by the medical impersonator has no desire to have sex with her doctor; she wants medical treatment. And the homeowner victimized by the phony meter reader does not want strangers in his house unless they have authorized service functions. The dealer's objection to the customer who claims falsely to have a lower price from a competing dealer is not to the physical presence of the customer, but to the fraud that he is trying to perpetuate.

4.   If Judge Posner were deciding *Ashcraft v. King*, supra, would he say that the plaintiff wanted the operation and therefore that her consent was valid even though based on a mistaken belief that the blood would come from her family?

Problem

Payton v. Donner

Lisa Payton suffered from an abscessed tooth. Before the source of her pain was discovered, doctors prescribed painkiller drugs. She gradually became addicted. When supplies dried up from normal medical sources she found Dr. William Donner, a medical doctor in his seventies, who was willing to prescribe for her claimed "pain." He also provided her ordinary medical treatment, referring her to a specialist on one occasion and ordering X-rays on another. After providing the drugs to Payton for many months, Donner forced her to admit that she was addicted. Thereafter, he refused to give her the drugs unless she would engage in sexual touchings. Although she resisted this for a while, she was unable to find other sources and eventually agreed to the exchange of sexual contact for the drugs.

A police investigation eventually broke up this arrangement. Payton underwent treatment for her addiction and is now drug-free. However, she suffers remorse and shame. She would have been free of her addiction sooner if Donner had properly referred her to a rehabilitation center. She may have medical expenses resulting from her addiction and from her relationship with Dr. Donner.

You represent Lisa Payton. Can you establish a prima facie case based on materials covered so far in the course? You can forecast that Donner will attempt to defend on the ground of consent. Do you think you can mount an argument based on legal rules or policies to overcome that defense?

REFERENCE: DOBBS ON TORTS §§ 95–106 (2000); HARPER, JAMES & GRAY, THE LAW OF TORTS § 3.10 (3d ed. 1996).

§ 3. PRIVILEGES NOT BASED ON PLAINTIFF'S CONDUCT

The "privileges" seen so far have been grounded largely in the plaintiff's conduct or apparent conduct. We now see privileges created by courts for reasons of policy.

(1) Arrests and searches. As you would expect, officers are privileged to enter land to execute a search or arrest warrant. But they are not privileged to invite the news media to cover their heroics, see *Wilson v. Layne*, 526 U.S. 603, 119 S.Ct. 1692, 143 L.Ed.2d 818 (1999) (sustaining claim for civil rights violation). And, except in Florida, the news media have no independent privilege to enter to cover news in the absence of the landowner's consent. See DOBBS ON TORTS § 96 (2000).

(2) Public rights. A user of a public utility or common carrier has the "privilege" to enter appropriate portions of the premises; in other words, the utility cannot deny the right of the public generally to patronize it. See RESTATEMENT SECOND OF TORTS § 191 (1965). This much was common law. Since the 1960s federal and some state statutes, known as public accommodations laws, have required that places open generally to the public cannot exclude would-be patrons on the basis of such considerations as race or gender. See 42 U.S.C.A. § 2000a. This might be expressed by saying not only that one has a right to patronize, say, a restaurant, but also that one is privileged to enter for that purpose and cannot be held as a trespasser. Another privilege of this kind is the privilege to enter land to reclaim goods of one's own, as for example, goods washed up on the plaintiff's land. Finally, very limited authority supports a privilege to exercise free speech rights by entering shopping center malls open to the public and campaigning on public issues there. See *Robins v. Pruneyard Shopping Center*, 23 Cal.3d 899, 592 P.2d 341, 153 Cal.Rptr. 854 (1979).

Perhaps the most interesting privileges are those of public and private necessity.

SUROCCO v. GEARY

Supreme Court of California, 1853.
3 Cal. 69.

MURRAY, CHIEF JUSTICE, delivered the opinion of the Court.

This was an action, commenced in the court below, to recover damages for blowing up and destroying the plaintiffs' house and property, during the fire of the 24th of December, 1849.

Geary, at that time Alcalde of San Francisco, justified, on the ground that he had the authority, by virtue of his office, to destroy said building, and also that it had been blown up by him to stop the progress of the conflagration then raging.

It was in proof, that the fire passed over and burned beyond the building of the plaintiffs', and that at the time said building was destroyed, they were engaged in removing their property, and could, had they not been prevented, have succeeded in removing more, if not all of their goods.

The cause was tried by the court sitting as a jury, and a verdict rendered for the plaintiffs, from which the defendant prosecutes this appeal under the Practice Act of 1850.

The only question for our consideration is, whether the person who tears down or destroys the house of another, in good faith, and under apparent necessity, during the time of a conflagration, for the purpose of saving the buildings adjacent, and stopping its progress, can be held personally liable in an action by the owner of the property destroyed. . . .

The right to destroy property, to prevent the spread of a conflagration, has been traced to the highest law of necessity, and the natural rights of man, independent of society or civil government. "It is referred by moralists and jurists to the same great principle which justifies the exclusive appropriation of a plank in a shipwreck, though the life of another be sacrificed; with the throwing overboard goods in a tempest, for the safety of a vessel; with the trespassing upon the lands of another, to escape death by an enemy. It rests upon the maxim, Necessitas inducit privilegium quod jura privata."

The common law adopts the principles of the natural law, and places the justification of an act otherwise tortious precisely on the same ground of necessity.

This principle has been familiarly recognized by the books from the time of the saltpetre case, and the instances of tearing down houses to prevent a conflagration, or to raise bulwarks for the defense of a city, are made use of as illustrations, rather than as abstract cases, in which its exercise is permitted. At such times, the individual rights of property give way to the higher laws of impending necessity.

A house on fire, or those in its immediate vicinity, which serve to communicate the flames, becomes a nuisance, which it is lawful to abate, and the private rights of the individual yield to the considerations of general convenience, and the interests of society. Were it otherwise, one stubborn person might involve a whole city in ruin, by refusing to allow the destruction of a building which would cut off the flames and check the progress of the fire, and that, too, when it was perfectly evident that his building must be consumed. . . .

The counsel for the respondent has asked, who is to judge of the necessity of the destruction of property?

This must, in some instances, be a difficult matter to determine. The necessity of blowing up a house may not exist, or be as apparent to the owner, whose judgment is clouded by interests, and the hope of saving his property, as to others. In all such cases the conduct of the individual must be regulated by his own judgment as to the exigencies of the case. If a building should be torn down without apparent or actual necessity, the parties concerned would undoubtedly be liable in an action of trespass. But in every case the necessity must be clearly shown. It is true, many cases of hardship may grow out of this rule, and property may often in such cases be destroyed, without necessity, by irresponsible persons, but this difficulty would not be obviated by making the parties responsible in every case, whether the necessity existed or not.

The legislature of the State possess the power to regulate this subject by providing the manner in which buildings may be destroyed, and the mode in which compensation shall be made; and it is to be hoped that something will be done to obviate the difficulty, and prevent the happening of such events as those supposed by the respondent's counsel.

In the absence of any legislation on the subject, we are compelled to fall back upon the rules of the common law.

The evidence in this case clearly establishes the fact, that the blowing up of the house was necessary, as it would have been consumed had it been left standing. The plaintiffs cannot recover for the value of the goods which they might have saved; they were as much subject to the necessities of the occasion as the house in which they were situate; and if in such cases a party was held liable, it would too frequently happen, that the delay caused by the removal of the goods would render the destruction of the house useless.

The court below clearly erred as to the law applicable to the facts of this case. The testimony will not warrant a verdict against the defendant.

Judgment reversed.

WEGNER v. MILWAUKEE MUTUAL INS. CO.

Supreme Court of Minnesota, 1991.
479 N.W.2d 38.

TOMLJANOVICH, JUSTICE.

... Around 6:30 p.m. on August 27, 1986, Minneapolis police were staking out an address in Northeast Minneapolis in the hope of apprehending two suspected felons who were believed to be coming to that address to sell stolen narcotics. The suspects arrived at the address with the stolen narcotics. Before arrests could be made, however, the suspects spotted the police and fled in their car at a high rate of speed with the police in pursuit. Eventually, the suspects abandoned their vehicle, separated and fled on foot. The police exchanged gunfire with one suspect as he fled. This suspect later entered the house of Harriet G. Wegner (Wegner) and hid in the front closet. Wegner's granddaughter, who was living at the house, and her fiance then fled the premises and notified the police.

The police immediately surrounded the house and shortly thereafter called an "Operation 100" around 7:00 p.m. The term "Operation 100" refers to the calling of the Minneapolis Police Department's Emergency Response Unit (ERU) to the scene. The ERU, commonly thought of as a

"SWAT" team, consists of personnel specially trained to deal with barricaded suspects, hostage-taking, or similar high-risk situations. Throughout the standoff, the police used a bullhorn and telephone in an attempt to communicate with the suspect. The police, receiving no response, continued efforts to establish contact with the suspect until around 10:00 p.m. At that time the police decided, according to ERU procedure, to take the next step in a barricaded suspect situation, which was to deliver chemical munitions. The police fired at least 25 rounds of chemical munitions or "tear gas" into the house in an attempt to expel the suspect. The police delivered the tear gas to every level of the house, breaking virtually every window in the process. In addition to the tear gas, the police cast three concussion or "flash-bang" grenades into the house to confuse the suspect. The police then entered the home and apprehended the suspect crawling out of a basement window. The tear gas and flash-bang grenades caused extensive damage to the Wegner house. . . .

Wegner commenced an action against both the City of Minneapolis and Milwaukee Mutual to recover the remaining damages. In conjunction with a trespass claim against the City, Wegner asserted that the police department's actions constituted a compensable taking under Minn. Const. art. I, § 13. [The lower courts held that any "taking" of property was justified and non-compensable under the doctrine of public necessity.]

Article I, section 13, of the Minnesota Constitution provides: "Private property shall not be taken, destroyed or damaged for public use without just compensation, first paid or secured." This provision "imposes a condition on the exercise of the state's inherent supremacy over private property rights." This type of constitutional inhibition "was designed to bar Government from forcing some people alone to bear public burdens which, in all fairness and justice, should be borne by the public as a whole."

The purpose of the damage clause is to ensure that private landowners are compensated, not only for physical invasion of their property, but also damages caused by the state where no physical invasion has occurred. A more significant restriction on recovery under this provision is the requirement that the taking or damaging must be for a public use. What constitutes a public use under this provision is a judicial question which this court historically construes broadly.

The City contends there was no taking for a public use because the actions of the police constituted a legitimate exercise of the police power. The police power in its nature is indefinable. However, simply labeling the actions of the police as an exercise of the police power "cannot justify the disregard of the constitutional inhibitions."

. . . This action is based on the plain meaning of the language of Minn. Const. art I, § 13, which requires compensation when property is damaged for a public use. Consequently, the issue in this case is not the reasonableness of the use of chemical munitions to extricate the barricaded suspect but rather whether the exercise of the city's admittedly legitimate police power resulted in a "taking." ...

The Constitution itself is the authorization for compensation for the destruction of property and is a waiver of governmental immunity for the taking, damaging or destruction of property for public use .....

... It is undisputed the police intentionally fired tear gas and concussion grenades into the Wegner house. Similarly, it is clear that the damage inflicted by the police in the course of capturing a dangerous suspect was for a public use within the meaning of the constitution.

[T]he court of appeals placed heavy reliance on the Georgia Intermediate Court of Appeals case of McCoy v. Sanders, 113 Ga.App. 565, 148 S.E.2d 902 (1966). The McCoy court held the draining of a pond by the police while searching for a murder victim's body was a proper exercise of the police power not requiring compensation under the Georgia Constitution.... The Georgia courts ... interpret the damage provision of their constitution as limited to those situations where there is physical interference with the property "in connection with an improvement for public use." This court never has held that the takings provision of Minn. Const. art. I, § 13 is to be applied in such a limited way.

We hold that where an innocent third party's property is damaged by the police in the course of apprehending a suspect, that property is damaged within the meaning of the constitution.

We briefly address the application of the doctrine of public necessity to these facts. The Restatement (Second) of Torts § 196 describes the doctrine as follows: One is privileged to enter land in the possession of another if it is, or if the actor reasonably believes it to be, necessary for the purpose of averting an imminent public disaster....

Although the court of appeals found there to be a "taking" under Minn. Const. art. I, § 13, the court ruled the "taking" was noncompensable based on the doctrine of public necessity. We do not agree. Once a "taking" is found, compensation is required by operation of law. Thus, if the doctrine of public necessity were to apply to a given fact situation, no taking could be found under Minn. Const. art. I, § 13.

We are not inclined to allow the city to defend its actions on the grounds of public necessity under the facts of this case. We believe the better rule, in situations where an innocent third party's property is taken, damaged or destroyed by the police in the course of apprehending a suspect, is for the municipality to compensate the innocent party for the resulting damages. The policy considerations in this case center around the basic notions of fairness and justice. At its most basic level, the issue is whether it is fair to allocate the entire risk of loss to an innocent homeowner for the good of the public. We do not believe the imposition of such a burden on the innocent citizens of this state would square with the underlying principles of our system of justice. Therefore, the City must reimburse Wegner for the losses sustained.

As a final note, we hold that the individual police officers, who were acting in the public interest, cannot be held personally liable. Instead, the citizens of the City should all bear the cost of the benefit conferred.

The judgments of the courts below are reversed and the cause remanded for trial on the issue of damages.

Notes

1. The central idea of justice behind the constitutional provisions is that individuals should not be forced to bear public burdens alone. If the public benefits from a burden it imposes upon others, it should pay. See *Armstrong v. United States*, 364 U.S. 40, 80 S.Ct. 1563, 4 L.Ed.2d 1554 (1960). Similar ideas have been advanced to justify imposing tort liability upon government.

2. If it is right to say that government should be required to pay when it forces an individual citizen to produce a benefit for the public, is the principle rightly applied in *Wegner*? In *Customer Company v. City of Sacramento*, 10 Cal.4th 368, 895 P.2d 900, 41 Cal.Rptr.2d 658 (1995) the California Court, on facts somewhat like those in *Wegner,* held that the city was not liable for damage done by police in apprehending an armed suspect, saying that compensation was required only in connection with a public improvement. As a matter of principle, which view is preferable, that the public should pay for the benefits it receives at the expense of individuals? Or that the public should not pay?

3. How far would the *Wegner* principle go? Suppose government forces all children to be vaccinated. This is for the good of everyone and the only way to stop disease. However, in rare cases the vaccinated child will suffer a serious reaction that may cause brain damage or even death even though no one is at fault. If a child is injured in such a case, should she be permitted to recover from the government on the ground that the government exacted a benefit for society as a whole by forcing the child accept the risks of the vaccination? In *Lapierre v. Attorney–General of Quebec*, 16 D.L.R.4th 554 (Can. 1985) the court rejected the claim that the government should be liable for injuries from compulsory vaccination. Distinguish: (a) government intentionally imposes harm, as in *Wegner*; (b) government intentionally imposes a *risk* that is not substantially certain to injure any particular or identifiable persons.

4. Compare *Wegner* to *Surocco*. Might *Surocco* be justified today on the ground that fire insurance is commonly purchased by all landowners and that it is a cheap and efficient way of dealing with the loss by fire? Why might that be cheaper than torts suits?

PLOOF v. PUTNAM, 81 Vt. 471, 71 A. 188 (1908). The defendant owned an island in Lake Champlain. The plaintiff, with his wife and two children, were sailing a sloop on the lake when a violent tempest arose. To avoid destruction of the sloop and injury to himself and his family, the plaintiff moored the boat at the defendant's dock. The defendant, through his servant, unmoored the boat. The sloop and its contents were destroyed and the people in it injured. The plaintiff claimed that unmooring the sloop was a trespass to it and that the defendant had a duty to permit the sloop to remain moored there. *Held,* for the plaintiff. "There are many cases in the books which hold that necessity ... will justify entries upon land and interferences with personal property that would otherwise have been trespasses.... If one have a way over the land of another for his beasts to pass, and the beasts, being properly driven, feed the grass by morsels in passing, or run out of the way and are promptly pursued and brought back, trespass will not lie. A traveler on a highway who finds it obstructed from a sudden and temporary cause may pass upon the adjoining land without becoming a trespasser because of the necessity. An entry upon land to save goods which are in danger of being lost or destroyed by water or fire is not a trespass.... One may sacrifice the personal property of another to save his life or the lives of his fellows.... It is clear that an entry upon the land of another may be justified by necessity for mooring the sloop."

VINCENT v. LAKE ERIE TRANSPORTATION CO.

Supreme Court of Minnesota, 1910.
109 Minn. 456, 124 N.W. 221.

O'BRIEN, J. The steamship Reynolds, owned by the defendant, was for the purpose of discharging her cargo on November 27, 1905, moored to plaintiff's dock in Duluth. While the unloading of the boat was taking place a storm from the northeast developed, which at about 10 o'clock P.M., when the unloading was completed, had so grown in violence that the wind was then moving at 50 miles per hour and continued to increase during the night. There is some evidence that one, and perhaps two, boats were able to enter the harbor that night, but it is plain that navigation was practically suspended from the hour mentioned until the morning of the 29th when the storm abated, and during that time no master would have been justified in attempting to navigate his vessel, if he could avoid doing so. After the discharge of the cargo the Reynolds signaled for a tug to tow her from the dock, but none could be obtained because of the severity of the storm. If the lines holding the ship to the dock had been cast off, she would doubtless have drifted away; but, instead, the lines were kept fast, and as soon as one parted or chafed it was replaced, sometimes with a larger one. The vessel lay upon the outside of the dock, her bow to the east, the wind and waves striking her starboard quarter with such force that she was constantly being lifted and thrown against the dock, resulting in its damage as found by the jury, to the amount of $500.

We are satisfied that the character of the storm was such that it would have been highly imprudent for the master of the Reynolds to have attempted to leave the dock or to have permitted his vessel to drift away from it.... Nothing more was demanded of them than ordinary prudence and care, and the record in this case fully sustains the contention of the appellant that, in holding the vessel fast to the dock, those in charge of her exercised good judgment and prudent seamanship. . . .

The appellant contends by ample assignments of error that, because its conduct during the storm was rendered necessary by prudence and good seamanship under conditions over which it had no control, it cannot be held liable for any injury resulting to the property of others, and claims that the jury should have been so instructed. An analysis of the charge given by the trial court is not necessary, as in our opinion the only question for the jury was the amount of damages which the plaintiffs were entitled to recover, and no complaint is made upon that score.

The situation was one in which the ordinary rules regulating property rights were suspended by forces beyond human control, and if, without the direct intervention of some act by the one sought to be held liable the property of another was injured, such injury must be attributed to the act of God, and not to the wrongful act of the person sought to be charged. If during the storm the Reynolds had entered the harbor, and while there had become disabled and been thrown against the plaintiffs' dock, the plaintiffs could not have recovered. Again, if while attempting to hold fast to the dock the lines had parted, without any negligence, and the vessel carried against some other boat or dock in the harbor, there would be no liability upon her owner. But here those in charge of the vessel deliberately and by their direct efforts held her in such a position that the damage to the dock resulted, and, having thus preserved the ship at the expense of the dock, it seems to us that her owners are responsible to the dock owners to the extent of the injury inflicted. . . .

In Ploof v. Putnam, 71 Atl. 188, the Supreme Court of Vermont held that where, under stress of weather, a vessel was without permission moored to a private dock at an island in Lake Champlain owned by the defendant, the plaintiff was not guilty of trespass, and that the defendant was responsible in damages because his representative upon the island unmoored the vessel, permitting it to drift upon the shore, with resultant injuries to it. If, in that case, the vessel had been permitted to remain, and the dock had suffered an injury, we believe the shipowner would have been held liable for the injury done.

Theologians hold that a starving man may, without moral guilt, take what is necessary to sustain life; but it could hardly be said that the obligation would not be upon such person to pay the value of the property so taken when he became able to do so. And so public necessity, in times of war or peace, may require the taking of private property for public purposes; but under our system of jurisprudence compensation must be made.

Let us imagine in this case that for the better mooring of the vessel those in charge of her had appropriated a valuable cable lying upon the dock. No matter how justifiable such appropriation might have been, it would not be claimed that, because of the overwhelming necessity of the situation, the owner of the cable could not recover its value.

This is not a case where life or property was menaced by any object or thing belonging to the plaintiff, the destruction of which became necessary to prevent the threatened disaster. Nor is it a case where, because of the act of God, or unavoidable accident, the infliction of the injury was beyond the control of the defendant, but is one where the defendant prudently and advisedly availed itself of the plaintiffs' property for the purpose of preserving its own more valuable property and the plaintiffs are entitled to compensation for the injury done.

Order affirmed.

LEWIS, J. I dissent.... In my judgment, if the boat was lawfully in position at the time the storm broke, and the master could not, in the exercise of due care, have left that position without subjecting his vessel to the hazards of the storm, then the damage to the dock, caused by the pounding of the boat, was the result of an inevitable accident....

I am of the opinion that one who constructs a dock to the navigable line of waters, and enters into contractual relations with the owner of a vessel to moor at the same, takes the risk of damage to his dock by a boat caught there by a storm, which event could not have been avoided in the exercise of due care, and further, that the legal status of the parties in such a case is not changed by renewal of cables to keep the boat from being cast adrift at the mercy of the tempest.

Notes

1. Is *Vincent* contrary to *Van Camp v. McAfoos*? After all, the court here recognizes that the captain was not at fault, yet liability is imposed. What if a bystander, not the captain, had renewed the lines, acting only out of good will, to save the ship. Would the bystander be liable?

2. The driver of a school bus with twenty children on board is coming down a mountain road. On her left is a sheer precipice. On her right is solid rock. As the bus picks up speed, a car coming up the hill traveling very fast appears in the bus' lane. It is now clear that the driver must act. If she stays where she is, a collision will ensue. If she turns left, she will take the children over the cliff. She can turn right before gaining any more speed, but if she does so she will certainly strike two children waiting at the bus stop. This would kill the two children or seriously maim them, but it will probably save most of those on the bus. On the rationale of *Vincent* would the driver be liable for the deaths of the two children? Professor George Christie, in *The Defense of Necessity Considered from the Legal and Moral Points of View*, 48 DUKE L.J. 975 (1999) analyzes the positions of a number of philosophers. He himself thinks that an intentional killing to save a greater number of lives is not privileged.

3. Presumably the shipowner and dock owner made some consensual arrangement about the use of the dock. If the shipowner had the right to

continued use of the dock under that arrangement, can it be said that by renewing the lines he took any benefit he was not entitled to?

4. Comparing *Vincent* and *Ploof,* can you outline the different legal effects or degrees of protection a privilege might have?

REFERENCES: DOBBS ON TORTS §§ 107–109 (2000); HARPER, JAMES & GRAY, LAW OF TORTS § 1.22 (1996).

Topic B

THE SCHEME OF NEGLIGENT WRONGS

Chapter 5

THE PRIMA FACIE CASE
FOR NEGLIGENCE

SUBCHAPTER A. THE FAULT
BASIS OF LIABILITY

§ 1. NEGLIGENCE AND FAULT

OLIVER W. HOLMES, THE COMMON LAW

(1881 Howe ed. 1963 pp. 76–78).

The general principle of our law is that loss from accident must lie where it falls, and this principle is not affected by the fact that a human being is the instrument of misfortune. But relatively to a given human being anything is accident which he could not fairly have been expected to contemplate as possible, and therefore to avoid. In the language of the late Chief Justice Nelson of New York: "No case or principle can be found, or if found can be maintained, subjecting an individual to liability for an act done without fault on his part. . . . All the cases concede that an injury arising from inevitable accident, or, which in law or reason is the same thing, from an act that ordinary human care and foresight are unable to guard against, is but the misfortune of the sufferer, and lays no foundation for legal responsibility." . . .

A man need not, it is true, do this or that act,—the term act implies a choice,—but he must act somehow. Furthermore, the public generally profits by individual activity. As action cannot be avoided, and tends to the public good, there is obviously no policy in throwing the hazard of what is at once desirable and inevitable upon the actor.

The state might conceivably make itself a mutual insurance company against accidents, and distribute the burden of its citizens' mishaps among its members. There might be a pension for paralytics, and state aid for those who suffered in person or estate from tempest or wild beasts. As between individuals it might adopt the mutual insurance principle *pro tanto*, and divide damages when both were in fault, as in the *rusticum judicium* of the admiralty, or it might throw all loss upon the actor irrespective of fault. The state does none of these things, however, and the prevailing view is that its cumbrous and expensive machinery ought not to be set in motion unless some clear benefit is to be derived from disturbing the status quo. State interference is an evil, where it cannot be shown to be a good. Universal insurance, if desired, can be better and more cheaply accomplished by private enterprise. The undertaking to redistribute losses simply on the ground that they resulted from the defendant's act would not only be open to these objections, but, as it is hoped the preceding discussion has shown, to the still graver one of offending the sense of justice. Unless my act is of a nature to threaten others, unless under the circumstances a prudent man would have foreseen the possibility of harm, it is no more justifiable to make me indemnify my neighbor against the consequences, than to make me do the same thing if I had fallen upon him in a fit, or to compel me to insure him against lightning.

Note

Is Holmes saying that liability is to be imposed only when the defendant is at fault? Tort law recognizes two basic kinds of fault. One revolves around intended invasions. The other revolves around negligence, meaning unreasonably risky conduct that causes harm.

Do you think Holmes was right in implying that liability could only be based upon fault? That we could not as a society properly agree to assist those who are injured without fault?

If we accept Holmes' statements, we still have issues to explore. Suppose liability is based only upon fault (as it usually is). Should liability then always be imposed upon a negligent person whose negligent conduct causes harm? Should liability be commensurate with his negligence or fault? What do we really mean by saying the defendant's conduct caused harm? These are among the difficult questions that will arise as we attempt to appraise negligence.

§ 2. INSTITUTIONS AND ELEMENTS OF NEGLIGENCE

a. *Some Institutions of Negligence Practice*

Intentional torts were defined in highly structured ways. In effect, the law of intentional torts prohibited specific acts like intentional touchings or intentional confinement of another person. The tort broadly called negligence is not defined by naming specific forbidden acts. Instead, negligence may be any conduct that creates an unreasonable risk of harm to others. It is actionable as a tort when that risk comes to fruition in actual harm. Before we explore the detailed meanings of negligence, we must recognize several important legal institutions or problems that condition negligence law. These are in no sense merely a general background; they are practices we must have in mind when we try to understand what it really means to impose liability for negligence.

(1) Litigation finance–the attorney fee. As we know from Chapter 1, each party must pay his or her own attorney. This has led to the contingent fee, under which the plaintiff may retain an attorney without payment of any fee unless the plaintiff wins the case. If the plaintiff wins, the attorney will share in the recovery, usually between 25% to 50%. In large time-consuming cases, large awards for pain and suffering or for punitive damages are required if an attorney is to take the case, for otherwise the attorney won't be paid enough to make the case economically feasible, or if the plaintiff fully paid the lawyer, she would not have enough to cover medical expenses and lost earnings.

(2) Liability insurance. Although liability insurance for automobiles may be compulsory, the policy limit–the sum available to pay for injuries–is likely to be too low to cover serious injury.

(3) The role of settlement. The number of personal injury trials is small. However, the number of personal injuries is large. The volume of routine negligence claims in, say, auto accidents, is vast. Almost all injury claims are settled without trial. To come up with a reasonable estimate of a case's settlement value, lawyers for each side must determine what facts will be proved if the case goes to court and what legal rules will affect the outcome. Accordingly, lawyers must know the rules and also how they are likely to be applied in court. Although lawyers approach the cases as adversaries, they must make neutral, balanced judgments about how the case will appear to the judge and jury. The lawyer who relies on a rule that represents injustice or bad policy may find that the judge will reject the rule or that the jury will find a way not to apply it. Accordingly, lawyers and students must make careful evaluation of the rules announced in cases.

b. Assessing Responsibility

So far as tort law is built on fault such as negligence, it clearly attempts to assess responsibility for one's actions. On closer inspection, assessing fault turns out to be a difficult, time-consuming, and expensive task. The assessment of responsibility is a major task for negligence law. It includes these elements:

(1) Fault. Intentionally harming another person is surely fault. But what is negligence? What about driving a car at 70 m.p.h.? Should we examine motives, states of mind, or merely external conduct? What if the defendant is in a hurry? Or does not understand the risk?

(2) Causation. One who causes no harm is not legally responsible, no matter how bad his act. Imagine that defendant drives 90 m.p.h., but does not strike anyone. Plaintiff is offended, but not harmed. This will not suffice in the case of negligence, since actual damages is an element of the plaintiff's case. In some cases causation will be quite doubtful. What if a doctor negligently delays treating the patient and the patient dies? Do we know that the patient would have lived if the doctor had not delayed?

(3) Fixing the scope of responsibility. One is not legally responsible for every harm that occurs because of one's negligence, though the rule might be otherwise with intentional torts. Suppose Jim, who has promised to baby sit at 7:00 p.m., is negligent in coming late. The parents, concluding that Jim would soon be there, leave the child alone. While the child is alone, he burns himself. Jim is undoubtedly negligent and responsible for something. In a sense he has caused the harm, since if he had not been late, the child would not have been burned. The law may well decide, however, that the injury was not within the scope of Jim's responsibility.

(4) A duty to take responsibility. In many instances it will be possible to find that a defendant has failed to behave reasonably, that his conduct has caused harm, and that the harm caused is the very kind that was risked by his negligent conduct. Yet not every problem is the defendant's responsibility. Suppose you know your neighbor fails to watch his toddler and consequently that there is a risk the child will run into the street and be injured. You *could* watch the child when you are not busy, but perhaps you should be free to decide that for yourself. If so, we will say you are under no duty to the child, even if a reasonable person would have tried to avoid injury to him.

Using these four elements of assessing fault, can we actually accomplish any of the diverse goals of tort law–justice or appropriate deterrence, for example? Chapters 5–8 are much concerned with such issues.

c. The General Formula for Negligence Cases

Drawing on the kinds the issues just discussed, courts have developed a general formula for the negligence claim. The plaintiff must allege and prove facts establishing five elements:

(1) The defendant owed plaintiff a legal duty;

(2) The defendant, by behaving negligently, breached that duty;

(3) The plaintiff suffered actual damage;

(4) The defendant's negligence was an actual cause of this damage; and

(5) The defendant's negligence was a "proximate cause" of this damage.

Different courts may state these required elements in slightly different ways, but the differences are matters of style, not substance. All courts require the plaintiff to sustain the burden of proving each of the five elements. All courts also agree that if the plaintiff fails to meet the burden of proving any one of them, the plaintiff cannot recover. In the following materials, we explore each of these elements in turn.

SUBCHAPTER B.   DUTY AND BREACH

§ 3. THE GENERAL DUTY OF CARE

The duty owed by all people generally—the standard of care they owe—is to exercise the care that would be exercised by a reasonable and prudent person under the same or similar circumstances to avoid or minimize risks of harm to others. Since no one tries to avoid risks that cannot be identified or harms that cannot be foreseen as a possibility, the reasonable person exercises care only about the kinds of harm that are foreseeable to reasonable people and risks that are sufficiently great to require precaution.–DOBBS ON TORTS § 117 (2000).

The New Jersey Supreme Court described the prudent person standard in this language: "The standard of care ordinarily imposed by negligence law is well established. To act non-negligently is to take reasonable precautions to prevent the occurrence of foreseeable harm to others. What precautions are 'reasonable' depends upon the risk of harm involved and the practicability of preventing it." *Weinberg v. Dinger*, 106 N.J. 469, 524 A.2d 366, 374 (N.J. 1987). Similarly, Justice Mosk recently emphasized: "foreseeability ... includes whatever is likely enough in the setting of modern life that a reasonably thoughtful [person] would take account of it in guiding practical conduct.... [W]hat is required to be foreseeable is the general character of the event or harm ... [and] not its precise nature or manner of occurrence." *Sharon P. v. Arman, Ltd.*, 21 Cal.4th 1181, 1203, 989 P.2d 121, 91 Cal.Rptr.2d 35 (1999) ((quoting earlier authority) (Mosk, J., dissenting).

a. The Due Care or Prudent Person Standard

STEWART v. MOTTS

Supreme Court of Pennsylvania, 1995.
539 Pa. 596, 654 A.2d 535.

MONTEMURO, JUSTICE. . . .

The sole issue presented before us is whether there exists a higher standard of "extraordinary care" for the use of dangerous instrumentalities over and above the standard of "reasonable care" such that the trial court erred for failing to give an instruction to the jury that the Appellee should have used a "high degree of care" in handling gasoline. Because we believe that there is but one standard of care, the standard of "reasonable care", we affirm.

The pertinent facts of this case are simple and were ably stated by the trial court:

On July 15, 1987, Plaintiff, Jonathon Stewart, stopped at Defendant, Martin Motts' auto repair shop and offered assistance to the Defendant in repairing an automobile fuel tank. In an effort to start and move the car with the gasoline tank unattached, the Plaintiff suggested and then proceeded to pour gasoline into the carburetor. The Defendant was to turn the ignition key at a given moment. While the exact sequence of events was contested, the tragic result was that the car backfired, caused an explosion and resulted in Plaintiff suffering severe burns to his upper body.

[In Stewart's suit against Motts, the plaintiff asked the judge to instruct the jury in part "that gasoline due to its inflammability, is a very dangerous substance if not properly handled.... With an appreciation of such danger, and under conditions where its existence reasonably should have been known, there follows a high degree of care which circumscribes the conduct of everyone about the danger...." The judge refused to so instruct and the jury returned a verdict for the defendant.]

We begin our discussion by reaffirming the principle that there is but one standard of care to be applied to negligence actions involving dangerous instrumentalities in this Commonwealth. This standard of care is "reasonable care" as well stated in the Restatement (Second) of Torts: "The care required is always reasonable care. The standard never varies, but the care which it is reasonable to require of the actor varies with the danger involved in his act and is proportionate to it. The greater the danger, the greater the care which must be exercised...." Restatement (Second) of Torts § 298 comment b (1965)....

Properly read, our cases involving dangerous agencies reaffirm these well accepted principles found in the Restatement. In Konchar v. Cebular, 333 Pa. 499, 3 A.2d 913 (1939) ... we recognized that the question of the plaintiff's contributory negligence was to be determined using the reasonable care standard in light of the particular circumstances of the case. One such circumstance, we acknowledged, was that gasoline, a dangerous substance, was involved requiring that the reasonably prudent person exercise a higher degree of care under these circumstances. Taken in context, our statement that the plaintiff was under a "high duty of care" did nothing more than reaffirm the general principle that the care employed by a reasonable man must be proportionate to the danger of the activity.

[The court reviewed other cases and concluded:] We do not believe that these cases created a heightened or extraordinary standard of care above and beyond the standard of reasonable care for handling dangerous agencies. When we referred to a "higher degree of care" in these cases, we were not creating a second tier of "extraordinary care" over and above ordinary or reasonable care. Instead, we were simply recognizing the general principle that under the reasonable care standard, the level of care must be proportionate to the danger involved. Our use of the language "higher degree of care" merely stated the common sense conclusion that the use of a dangerous agency would require the reasonably prudent person to exercise more care....

In summation, this Commonwealth recognizes only one standard of care in negligence actions involving dangerous instrumentalities—the standard of reasonable care under the circumstances. It is well established by our case law that the reasonable man must exercise care in proportion to the danger involved in his act.

With these principles in mind we must next examine the jury instructions in this case. The trial judge explained to the jury that negligence is "the absence of ordinary care which a reasonably prudent person would exercise in the circumstances here presented." The trial judge further explained: "It is for you to determine how a reasonably prudent person would act in those circumstances. Ordinary care is the care a reasonably prudent person would use under the circumstances presented in this case. It is the duty of every person to use ordinary care not only for his own safety and the protection of his property, but also to avoid serious injury to others. What constitutes ordinary care varies according to the particular circumstances and conditions existing then and there. The amount of care required by law must be in keeping with the degree of danger involved. . . .

We find that this charge, when read as a whole, adequately instructed the jury. The charge informed the jury that the proper standard of care was "reasonable" or "ordinary" care under the circumstances in accordance with the law of this Commonwealth. The charge properly instructed the jury that the level of care required changed with the circumstances. The charge also informed the jury that the level of care required increased proportionately with the level of danger in the activity. We find nothing in this charge that is confusing, misleading, or unclear. From these instructions, the jury had the tools to examine the circumstances of the case and determine that the defendant was required to exercise a "higher degree of care" in using the dangerous agency of gasoline. . . .

For the reasons set forth above, we affirm the order of the Superior Court.

Notes

1. The orthodox views are stated in *Stewart:* (a) the standard of care remains the same under all circumstances, but (b) if danger is high, the reasonable person will ordinarily exercise care greater than if danger is low. E.g., *Butler v. Acme Markets, Inc.,* 177 N.J.Super. 279, 426 A.2d 521 (1981), *aff'd* 89 N.J. 270, 445 A.2d 1141 (1982). The standard, however, remains the same whether danger is high or low. It is the care that would be exercised by a reasonable person under the circumstances, although that care is presumably greater when danger is greater.

2. Courts do not always observe the distinction just stated. Instead of saying that the single standard may require greater care when danger is greater, they sometimes say instead that the standard itself is higher and requires extraordinary care when danger is great. See *Wood v. Groh,* 7 P.3d 1163 (Kan. 2000); DOBBS ON TORTS § 128, at 303 (2000).

3. In *Purtle v. Shelton,* 251 Ark. 519, 474 S.W.2d 123, 47 A.L.R.3d 609 (1971), the plaintiff was injured in a hunting accident and offered an instruction that defendant should have used a "high degree of care commensurate with the dangers involved. . . ." The trial judge refused. The Supreme Court of Arkansas affirmed, saying that "the duty enunciated in an instruction should be ordinary care under the circumstances, and the contention that the circumstances dictate a high degree of caution should be left to arguments of counsel." How should counsel's argument be framed?

LYONS v. MIDNIGHT SUN TRANSP. SERVS. INC.

Supreme Court of Alaska, 1996.
928 P.2d 1202.

PER CURIAM.

Esther Hunter–Lyons was killed when her Volkswagen van was struck broadside by a truck driven by David Jette and owned by Midnight Sun Transportation Services, Inc. When the accident occurred, Jette was driving south in the right-hand lane of Arctic Boulevard in Anchorage. Hunter–Lyons pulled out of a parking lot in front of him. [Jette braked and tried to steer around Hunter–Lyons, but his truck collided with her car and she was killed. There was disputed evidence that Jette was speeding and that his maneuver to avoid striking Hunter–Lyons was inadequate.]

Over Lyons's objection, the jury was given an instruction on the sudden emergency doctrine. [The instruction read in part: "In an emergency, a person is not expected or required to use the same judgment and care that is required in calmer and more deliberate moments. If, in an emergency, a person acts as a reasonably careful person would act in a similar emergency, there is no negligence even though afterwards it might appear that a different course of action would have been better and safer."]

The jury found that Jette, in fact, had been negligent, but his negligence was not a legal cause of the accident. Lyons appeals, arguing that the court should not have given the jury the sudden emergency instruction.

The sudden emergency doctrine is a rule of law which states that a person confronted with a sudden and unexpected peril, not resulting from that person's own negligence, is not expected to exercise the same judgment and prudence the law requires of a person in calmer and more deliberate moments. The person confronted with the imminent peril must, however, act as a reasonable person would under the same conditions. . . .

We find that Lyons has little cause to complain of the sudden emergency instruction because the jury decided the issue in his favor. . . . Although the jury found Jette to have been negligent, it also found that this negligence was not the legal cause of the accident. Duty, breach of duty, causation, and harm are the separate and distinct elements of a negligence claim, all of which must be proven before a defendant can be held liable for the plaintiff's injuries. The sudden emergency instruction addresses only the standard of care imposed on all people to act as a reasonable person would under the circumstances. The instruction could not have infected the jury's finding that Jette was not the legal cause of Ms. Hunter–Lyons's death. . . .

Although any possible error resulting from the use of the sudden emergency instruction was rendered harmless by the jury finding that

Jette's negligence was not a legal cause of the accident, we take this opportunity to disapprove of the instruction's further use. It adds nothing to the established law that the duty of care, which all must exercise, is to act reasonably under the circumstances. The instruction is potentially confusing. Although we cannot say that the instruction is never appropriate, we discourage its employment. In support of this admonition, we offer the following background. . . .

Although not inherently inconsistent with modern methods of apportioning liability, the sudden emergency instruction has, nevertheless, come under criticism, and some states have limited or abolished it. Reasoning that because the standard of care is expressed in terms of a reasonable person under the circumstances, several courts have concluded that the instruction is wholly redundant. Mississippi eliminated the instruction in Knapp v. Stanford, 392 So.2d 196 (Miss.1980), because the court believed the instruction only served to obfuscate the operation of the comparative negligence statute, and was often interpreted as requiring a higher standard of proof for a finding of negligence. . . . Montana's supreme court, in Simonson v. White, 220 Mont. 14, 713 P.2d 983 (1986), found no reason to give the sudden emergency instruction in an automobile accident case stating that the instruction adds nothing to the applicable law in any negligence case, that a driver must exercise due care under the circumstances, and that it tends to leave jurors with the impression that an emergency somehow excuses the driver from the ordinary standard of care. . . .

We believe that the sudden emergency instruction is a generally useless appendage to the law of negligence. With or without an emergency, the standard of care a person must exercise is still that of a reasonable person under the circumstances. With or without the instruction, parties are still entitled to present evidence at trial which will establish what the circumstances were, and are also entitled to argue to the jury that they acted as a reasonable person would have in light of those circumstances. Thus, barring circumstances that we cannot at the moment hypothesize, a sudden emergency instruction serves no positive function. Further, the instruction may cause confusion by appearing to imply that one party is less blameworthy than the other. Therefore, we hold that it should not be used unless a court finds that the particular and peculiar facts of a case warrant more explanation of the standard of care than is generally required.

* * *

Notes

1. Does the standard of care change when the defendant is confronted with a sudden, unforeseeable emergency not of his own making?

2. Several courts, like Alaska, have now said that the idea behind the emergency instruction is adequately covered by the instruction defining the reasonable care standard and that the separate emergency instruction

should not be given. See DOBBS ON TORTS § 131 (2000). In such a jurisdiction, the trial judge must refuse to give the defendant's proffered emergency instruction. What should the judge do about the plaintiff's proffered instruction on commensurate care or care in keeping with the danger? Put more broadly, how exactly would you compare or contrast *Lyons* and *Stewart*?

3. Following up the ideas about how the standard of care should affect jury instructions, consider whether a lawyer could make a principled objection to an instruction that told the jury "The defendant is not liable for an unavoidable accident." See *Reinhart v. Young,* 906 S.W.2d 471 (Tex.1995).

4. In jurisdictions that reject the emergency instruction, is the *fact* that defendant acted in an unforeseeable emergency still relevant? If you represented the defendant, would you consider such a fact in determining what sum to offer in settlement? Would the emergency be any part of your closing argument to the jury?

5. A driver's car stalls at a light. He motions drivers behind him to go around. Some do, but several drivers must instead come to a quick stop because of traffic in the other lane. The defendant was the fourth driver compelled to come to a quick stop, but he was unable to do so without first crashing into the line of cars. In a state that continues to approve the emergency instruction in principle, should the instruction be given on these facts? *Beyer v. Todd,* 601 N.W.2d 35 (Iowa 1999).

6. Allen drives at a speed within the speed limit in a residential area. A number of children are playing soccer on a vacant lot. They appear to range in age from about 6 to about 15. Allen does not slow down. Baker, an 8–year old, runs into the street after the ball, and Allen is unable to stop in time. He would have avoided impact had he driven 5 miles per hour slower. What is the standard of care? Should the judge give any special instruction?

————

SHEPHERD v. GARDNER WHOLESALE, INC., 288 Ala. 43, 256 So.2d 877 (1972). Plaintiff Roxie Shepherd tripped over a raised concrete slab in the sidewalk in front of defendant's business. Shepherd suffered from cataracts, leaving her with 20/100 vision in one eye and 20/80 in the other. "[A] person with impaired vision is not required to see what a person with normal vision can see. Such would be impossible, and one is not guilty of negligence by using the public sidewalks with the physical inability to see what a person with normal vision can see. A person laboring under a physical disability such as defective vision is not required to exercise a higher degree of care to avoid injury than is required of a person under no disability. Ordinary care in the case of such a person is such care as an ordinarily prudent person with a like infirmity would have exercised under the same or similar circumstances."

ROBERTS v. STATE OF LOUISIANA, 396 So.2d 566 (La.App. 1981). Plaintiff Roberts, a 75–year old man, was injured when knocked down in a hallway by Burson, a blind 25–year old man who operated a concession stand in a U.S. Post Office. Plaintiff claimed that Burson "traversed the area from his concession stand to the men's bathroom in a negligent manner," specifically pointing to Burson's "failure to use his cane even though he had it with him in his concession stand." The trial court dismissed plaintiff's suit. *Held*, affirmed. Quoting the Prosser hornbook: "As to his physical characteristics, the reasonable man may be said to be identical with the actor. The man who is blind ... is entitled to live in the world and to have allowance made by others for his disability, and he cannot be required to do the impossible by conforming to physical standards which he cannot meet.... At the same time, the conduct of the handicapped individual must be reasonable in the light of the knowledge of his infirmity, which is treated merely as one of the circumstances under which he acts.... [H]e must take the precautions, be they more or less, which the ordinary reasonable man would take if he were blind." Applying this standard to the facts, Burson did not breach this duty in relying on "his facial sense" rather than using a cane for a short trip to the bathroom in a familiar, and crowded, place.

Notes

1. *Shepherd* and *Roberts* reflect the rule on the role of physical impairments, disabilities, or limitations in setting the standard of care in negligence cases. Accord, RESTATEMENT SECOND OF TORTS § 283C (1965). What if the general rule were otherwise? For example, what if an actor's physical limitations were not taken into account in setting the standard of care to which courts would hold him?

2. Suppose, instead of having a physical infirmity, the actor has strength and agility not possessed by normal persons, or that the actor's reaction time is exceptionally good. How would you express the standard of care owed by such a person? How might *Shepherd* and *Roberts* contribute to your analysis?

3. What about the standard of care owed *to* persons with physical disabilities? In *Payne v. North Carolina Dept. of Human Resources*, 95 N.C.App. 309, 382 S.E.2d 449 (1989) a teacher in the state's school for the deaf was allegedly negligent in failing to instruct or supervise a student, who, as a result, suffered injury while working on a hydraulic lift. The plaintiff argued that the teacher owed a "greater than normal" duty of care because of the student's hearing impairment. The court held that the standard "remains that of the exercise of ordinary prudence," although it agreed that the "amount of care due a student increases with the student's immaturity, inexperience, and relevant physical limitations."

4. *Intoxication.* What is to be done about an intoxicated person? Suppose one is wildly intoxicated, but drives in a perfect way. Injury results, though the driving is flawless. Presumably the law should not attempt to judge the ultimate worth or character of persons, but should judge conduct instead. The general rule is that an intoxicated person owes the same care as a sober person, and that if his overt conduct would be negligence in a sober person, it is also negligence in a drunken one. What can be made of this? Can it be reconciled with the rule that one considers physical impairments as

one of the circumstances? Is it possible that in the case of voluntary intoxication the risk is taken when intoxicants are consumed rather than later, when the driver speeds?

5. *Memory.* The Restatement says you must exercise the memory of a reasonable person in recognizing a risk. If you knew an intersection was dangerous because vegetation obstructed vision there, you would be expected to remember that fact and slow down accordingly, if an ordinary prudent person would remember it. RESTATEMENT SECOND OF TORTS § 289 (1965).

CREASY v. RUSK

Supreme Court of Indiana, 2000.
730 N.E.2d 659.

SULLIVAN, JUSTICE. . . .

In July, 1992, Lloyd Rusk's wife admitted Rusk to the Brethren Healthcare Center ("BHC") because he suffered from memory loss and confusion and Rusk's wife was unable to care for him. Rusk's primary diagnosis was Alzheimer's disease. Over the course of three years at BHC, Rusk experienced periods of anxiousness, confusion, depression, disorientation, and agitation. Rusk often resisted when staff members attempted to remove him from prohibited areas of the facility. On several occasions, Rusk was belligerent with both staff and other residents. In particular, Rusk was often combative, agitated, and aggressive and would hit staff members when they tried to care for him. . . .

On May 16, 1995, Creasy and another certified nursing assistant, Linda Davis, were working through their routine of putting Rusk and other residents to bed. Creasy knew that Rusk had been "very agitated and combative that evening." By Creasy's account:

[Davis] was helping me put Mr. Rusk to bed. She was holding his wrists to keep him from hitting us and I was trying to get his legs to put him to bed. He was hitting and kicking wildly. During this time, he kicked me several times in my left knee and hip area. My lower back popped and I yelled out with pain from my lower back and left knee.

. . . Rusk moved for summary judgment and the trial court granted his motion. Creasy appealed. The Court of Appeals reversed, holding "that a person's mental capacity, whether that person is a child or an adult, must be factored [into] the determination of whether a legal duty exists." . . .

[T]he generally accepted rule in jurisdictions other than Indiana is that mental disability does not excuse a person from liability for "conduct which does not conform to the standard of a reasonable man under like circumstances." Restatement (Second) of Torts § 283B; accord Restatement (Third) of Torts § 9(c) (Discussion Draft Apr. 5, 1999) ("Unless the actor is a child, the actor's mental or emotional disability is not considered in determining whether conduct is negligent."). People with mental disabilities are commonly held liable for their intentional and negligent torts. No allowance is made for lack of intelligence, ignorance, excitability, or proneness to accident. See Restatement (Second) of Torts § 283B cmt. c.

Legal scholars and authorities recognize that it is "impossible to ascribe either the volition implicit in an intentional tort, the departure from the standard of a 'reasonable' person which defines an act of ordinary negligence, or indeed any concept of 'fault' at all to one who . . . is by definition unable to control his [or her] own actions through any exercise of reason." Anicet v. Gant, 580 So.2d 273, 275 (Fla.Dist.Ct.App. 1991) (citations omitted). Rather, the Restatement rule holding people with mental disabilities liable for their torts was founded upon public policy considerations.

The public policy reasons most often cited for holding individuals with mental disabilities to a standard of reasonable care in negligence claims include the following.

(1) Allocates losses between two innocent parties to the one who caused or occasioned the loss. . . .

(2) Provides incentive to those responsible for people with disabilities and interested in their estates to prevent harm and "restrain" those who are potentially dangerous. . . .

(3) Removes inducements for alleged tortfeasors to fake a mental disability in order to escape liability. . . .

(4) Avoids administrative problems involved in courts and juries attempting to identify and assess the significance of an actor's disability. As a practical matter, it is arguably too difficult to account for or draw any "satisfactory line between mental deficiency and those variations of temperament, intellect, and emotional balance."

(5) Forces persons with disabilities to pay for the damage they do if they "are to live in the world." A discussion draft for the Restatement (Third) of Torts rephrases this policy rationale and concludes: "[I]f a person is suffering from a mental disorder so serious as to make it likely that the person will engage in substandard conduct that threatens the safety of others, there can be doubts as to whether this person should be allowed to engage in the normal range of society's activities; given these doubts, there is nothing especially harsh in at least holding the person responsible for the harms the person may cause by substandard conduct." Restatement (Third) of Torts § 9 cmt. e (Discussion Draft April 5, 1999). . . .

Since the 1970s, Indiana law has strongly reflected policies to deinstitutionalize people with disabilities and integrate them into the least restrictive environment. National policy changes have led the way for some of Indiana's enactments in that several federal acts either guarantee the civil rights of people with disabilities or condition state aid upon state compliance with desegregation and integrationist practices. See, e.g., Individuals with Disabilities Education Act, 20 U.S.C. § 1400 et seq. (1994) (requiring that children with disabilities receive a free appropriate public education in the least restrictive environment in states that accept allocated funds) (originally enacted in 1975 as the Education for All Handicapped Children Act, P.L. 94–142 (amending the state education grant program under the 1970 Education for the Handicapped Act, P.L. 91–230; requiring states to provide a free appropriate public education to all children with disabilities in order to receive state grant funds)); Americans with Disabilities Act, 42 U.S.C. § 12132 (1994), and implementing regulation 28 C.F.R. § 35.130(d) (1999) (providing that a public entity shall administer services, programs, and activities in the most integrated setting appropriate to the needs of qualified individuals with disabilities); Fair Housing Act, 42 U.S.C. § 3604 (1994) (prohibiting discrimination based on "handicap" in the sale or rental of a dwelling).

These legislative developments reflect ... a determination that people with disabilities should be treated in the same way as nondisabled persons.

[T]he Restatement rule may very well have been grounded in a policy determination that persons with mental disabilities should be institutionalized or otherwise confined rather than "live in the world." It is clear from our recitation of state and federal legislative and regulatory developments that contemporary public policy has rejected institutionalization and confinement for a "strong professional consensus in favor of ... community treatment ... and integration into the least restrictive ... environment." ... We observe that it is a matter of some irony that public policies favoring the opposite ends—institutionalization and confinement on the one hand and community treatment and integration into the least restrictive environment on the other–should nevertheless yield the same common law rule: that the general duty of care imposed on adults with mental disabilities is the same as that for adults without mental disabilities.

... We hold that a person with mental disabilities is generally held to the same standard of care as that of a reasonable person under the same circumstances without regard to the alleged tortfeasor's capacity to control or understand the consequences of his or her actions.

[The court held, however, that one employed to take care of a patient known to be combative because of Alzheimer's disease, has no complaint for injuries sustained in doing so. As to such a caretaker the duty of care is a one-way street, from caretaker to patient, not the other way around. Hence Rusk was not liable on these facts.]

Notes

1. Sometimes courts speak of insanity as a "defense," but it seems clear that the underlying issue is about the standard of care. The view of the Restatement Second of Torts § 283B (1965), and probably the prevailing orthodoxy, is that neither insanity nor mental deficiency relieves the actor

from liability, and that his conduct must conform to the general standard of care of a reasonable person under similar external circumstances.

2.   Low intelligence and other mental or psychological limitations are treated the same way. Durfee is a sane man of low intelligence. He has never connected the danger of fire with his storage of rags, newspapers and paint thinner in his garage. A fire originates in his garage and spreads to his neighbor's house. The jury will be instructed that Durfee is held to the care of a reasonable and prudent person. He does not escape liability because he did "the best he could do," or because he behaved as well as others of similar intelligence.

3.   *Contributory negligence.* The common law called a plaintiff's negligence "contributory negligence" and held that it barred the plaintiff's recovery completely. In most states today, contributory negligence of a plaintiff operates to reduce the plaintiff's recovery of damages, but does not necessarily bar all recovery. Contributory negligence is the failure to exercise due care for one's *own* safety and thus differs slightly from negligence, which is failure to use ordinary care for the safety of others. The difference is a slight one in many respects and the usual assumption is that the standard of care is the same, whether the issue is one of negligence or one of contributory negligence. RESTATEMENT THIRD OF TORTS, APPORTIONMENT OF LIABILITY § 3, cmt. a (2000). Some thinkers say that the objective standard of reasonable care should not apply to the plaintiff's conduct–in other words, should not apply to the contributory negligence issue. Can you formulate an argument for or against this view? Some of the cases that hold a mentally deficient person to a subjective standard seem to be in reality cases in which the defendant's duty (as a caretaker, for example) is to protect the plaintiff from his harms resulting from his own disability. *Jankee v. Clark County,* 235 Wis.2d 700, 612 N.W.2d 297 (2000), over dissents, came down squarely in favor of the objective reasonable person standard.

4.   Are the rules of liability for insane and mentally deficient persons based upon justice? Deterrence?

5.   What is to be done about a person with superior knowledge or mental ability, who can appreciate and act on some risk which reasonable and prudent persons, not having the special knowledge, would ignore?

6.   On liability of mentally disabled see DOBBS ON TORTS §§ 120–121 (2000); HARPER, JAMES & GRAY, LAW OF TORTS § 16.7 (1986 & Supps.).

––––––

HILL v. SPARKS, 546 S.W.2d 473 (Mo.App.1976). Wayne Sparks was an operator of earth-moving machinery and had several seasons experience with a machine known as an earth scraper. At an exhibit of such machines he drove one, instructing his sister to stand on a ladder on the machine. It hit a mound of dirt and, because of its large rubber tires, bounced back. Sparks' sister was thrown forward in front of the left wheel and was run over before Sparks could stop the machine. She died almost instantly. This is an action for her death. "[Sparks], as an operator, with several seasons experience with earth scrapers, was familiar with the propensities of such machines.... He had heard decedent's husband, upon observing a boy riding on the scraper ladder during the demonstration, tell a Liberty Equipment employee to get the boy off the scraper because if he fell he would fall right under the wheel. Despite his knowledge and experience, appellant directed his sister to ride as a passenger on the ladder while he operated the machine.... 'The standard of the reasonable man requires only a minimum of attention, perception, memory, knowledge, intelligence, and judgment in order to recognize the existence of the risk. If the actor has in fact more than the minimum of these qualities, he is required to exercise the superior qualities that he has in a manner reasonable under the circumstances.' 2 Restatement of Torts (2d),§ 289.... The evidence in this case presented an issue submissible to the jury of whether ... appellant met the requisite standard of care.''

ROBINSON v. LINDSAY

Supreme Court of Washington, 1979.
92 Wn.2d 410, 598 P.2d 392.

UTTER, CHIEF JUSTICE.

An action seeking damages for personal injuries was brought on behalf of Kelly Robinson who lost full use of a thumb in a snowmobile accident when she was 11 years of age. The petitioner, Billy Anderson, 13 years of age at the time of the accident, was the driver of the snowmobile. After a jury verdict in favor of Anderson, the trial court ordered a new trial.

The single issue on appeal is whether a minor operating a snowmobile is to be held to an adult standard of care. The trial court failed to instruct the jury as to that standard and ordered a new trial because it believed the jury should have been so instructed. We agree and affirm the order granting a new trial.

The trial court instructed the jury under WPI 10.05 that:

> In considering the claimed negligence of a child, you are instructed that it is the duty of a child to exercise the same care that a reasonably careful child of the same age, intelligence, maturity, training and experience would exercise under the same or similar circumstances.

Respondent properly excepted to the giving of this instruction and to the court's failure to give an adult standard of care....

The current law in this state is fairly reflected in WPI 10.05, given in this case. In the past we have always compared a child's conduct to that expected of a reasonably careful child of the same age, intelligence, maturity, training and experience. This case is the first to consider the question of a child's liability for injuries sustained as a result of his or her operation of a motorized vehicle or participation in an inherently dangerous activity.

Courts in other jurisdictions have created an exception to the special child standard because of the apparent injustice that would occur if a child who caused injury while engaged in certain dangerous activities were permitted to defend himself by saying that other children similarly situated would not have exercised a degree of care higher than his, and he is, therefore, not liable for his tort. Some courts have couched the exception in terms of children engaging in an activity which is normally one for adults only. See, e.g., Dellwo v. Pearson, 259 Minn. 452, 107 N.W.2d 859 (1961) (operation of a motorboat). We believe a better rationale is that when the activity a child engages in is inherently dangerous, as is the operation of powerful mechanized vehicles, the child should be held to an adult standard of care.

Such a rule protects the need of children to be children but at the same time discourages immature individuals from engaging in inherently dangerous activities. Children will still be free to enjoy traditional childhood activities without being held to an adult standard of care. Although accidents sometimes occur as the result of such activities, they are not activities generally considered capable of resulting in "grave danger to others and to the minor himself if the care used in the course of the activity drops below that care which the reasonable and prudent adult would use ..." Daniels v. Evans, 107 N.H. 407, 408, 224 A.2d 63, 64 (1966).

Other courts adopting the adult standard of care for children engaged in adult activities have emphasized the hazards to the public if the rule is otherwise. We agree with the Minnesota Supreme Court's language in its decision in Dellwo v. Pearson, supra, 259 Minn. at 457–58, 107 N.W.2d at 863:

> Certainly in the circumstances of modern life, where vehicles moved by powerful motors are readily available and frequently operated by immature individuals, we should be skeptical of a rule that would allow motor vehicles to be operated to the hazard of the public with less than the normal minimum degree of care and competence.

Dellwo applied the adult standard to a 12–year-old defendant operating a motor boat. Other jurisdictions have applied the adult standard to minors engaged in analogous activities. [The court cited cases in which the minor had been operating a tractor, a motorcycle, a minibike and an automobile.]

The operation of a snowmobile likewise requires adult care and competence. Currently 2.2 million snowmobiles are in operation in the United States. Studies show that collisions and other snowmobile accidents claim hundreds of casualties each year and that the incidence of accidents is particularly high among inexperienced operators.

At the time of the accident, the 13–year-old petitioner had operated snowmobiles for about 2 years. When the injury occurred, petitioner was operating a 30–horsepower snowmobile at speeds of 10–20 miles per hour. The record indicates that the machine itself was capable of 65 miles per hour. Because petitioner was operating a powerful motorized vehicle, he should be held to the standard of care and conduct expected of an adult.

The order granting a new trial is affirmed.

Notes

1. *General rule for children. Robinson* reflects the general rule: a child sued for negligence is held to the standard of care of a reasonably careful child of the same age, intelligence and experience. DOBBS ON TORTS § 124 (2000). Is this purely subjective?

2. *Support for the general rule.* What is the basis for the general rule? If it is unfair to hold a child to a standard he could not meet, is it not equally unfair to do the same to a mentally-disabled adult?

3. *Tests for the adult standard.* Is it possible that neither the "inherently dangerous" test nor the "adult activity" test captures the essence of the result courts are seeking? Suppose an adult is watching a child drive a car on a farm road and is struck when the child hits the gas pedal instead of the brake. Would you want to know whether the adult knew the driver was a child? If he did know, would it be reasonable to demand and expect an adult standard of care, even if the activity is "inherently dangerous" or "adult"? This issue will arise again in the next chapter. What is your opinion at this point? Should children be held only to the child standard when they are engaged in "carefree" activities appropriate to their development but to the adult standard when they engage in dangerous activities? See Caroline Forell, *Reassessing the Negligence Standard of Care for Minors*, 15 N.M. L. REV. 485 (1985).

4. *Application of the adult standard.* Alaska extended the adult standard to cover a 14–year-old's decision to permit another minor to drive the car with deadly results. *Ardinger v. Hummell*, 982 P.2d 727 (Alaska 1999). Meager authority has imposed the adult standard when a minor uses firearms. See *Goss v. Allen*, 70 N.J. 442, 360 A.2d 388 (1976). Otherwise, courts have imposed the adult standard almost exclusively in cases of motorized activity of a minor. So a 12–year-old might be held to an adult standard while operating a motor boat, but a 17–year-old held only to a child standard while operating a bicycle. In *Strait v. Crary*, 173 Wis.2d 377, 496 N.W.2d 634 (App. 1992), a 16–year-old drinking passenger attempted to climb out the window of a moving truck. He fell out and suffered a broken leg. The court used the child standard in determining whether he was guilty of contributory negligence.

5. *Trial problems.* (a) Prior to *Robinson*, the adult standard had not been applied to children in Washington. What made the lawyers think of raising that issue? (b) Why did the judge first refuse to tell the jury that children might be held to an adult standard and then, after the trial was over, hold that his earlier ruling was wrong? Did he simply change his mind or was there a calculated risk involved?

6. *The rule of sevens.* A few courts still say that minors over 14 are presumed capable of negligence, those between seven and fourteen presumed

incapable of it, and those below seven are incapable of negligence as a matter of law.

7. *Very young children.* The rule of sevens is not so common now, but most states hold that children of very young years, three and under, are simply incapable of negligence. See Oscar S. Gray, *The Standard of Care for Children Revisited*, 45 Mo. L. Rev. 597 (1980).

Suppose a four-year-old child plays with matches and sets the plaintiff's house afire, causing damage and injury. The plaintiff sues the child. If you represent the child and want to attempt a defense on the theory that the child is not capable of negligence at all, how would you raise this issue procedurally? Suppose a six-year-old boy runs alongside a moving train, trying to catch it, falls, and has his legs severed. Is he incapable of contributory negligence as a matter of law? Presumed incapable? Or merely subject to the subjective child standard of care? Which choice leaves it to a jury to decide? *Honeycutt v. City of Wichita*, 247 Kan. 250, 796 P.2d 549 (1990) (summarizing the current views and adopting the child standard).

b. *Specification of Duties—Negligence as a Matter of Law*

MARSHALL v. SOUTHERN RAILWAY CO., 233 N.C. 38, 62 S.E.2d 489 (1950). Plaintiff was driving at night on a paved road about 30 feet wide. Defendant's railroad trestle above the road was supported by large timbers, which narrowed the road to about 15 feet under the trestle. As plaintiff approached this, a car came toward him with bright lights on and plaintiff ran into the trestle supports. The trial judge sustained defendant's motion for nonsuit at the end of the plaintiff's evidence. *Held*, affirmed. "[I]t is manifest from the evidence that plaintiff failed to exercise due care at the time and under the circumstances of his injury. . . . It is a general rule of law, even in the absence of statutory requirement, that the operator of a motor vehicle must exercise ordinary care, that is, that degree of care which an ordinarily prudent person would exercise under similar circumstances. And in the exercise of such duty it is incumbent upon the operator of a motor vehicle to keep a reasonably careful lookout and to keep same under such control at night as to be able to stop within the range of his lights."

Note

Is the court here saying that plaintiff was guilty of contributory negligence "as a matter of law," that is, that there is no room for reasonable jurors to differ about this conclusion? Or is it saying that there is a rule of law that one must be able to stop within the range of one's lights, whether or not a reasonable person would be able to do so? What's the difference?

CHAFFIN v. BRAME

Supreme Court of North Carolina, 1951.
233 N.C. 377, 64 S.E.2d 276.

ERVIN, JUSTICE.

[Plaintiff was driving about 40 miles an hour at night on a paved highway 18 feet wide. A car approached driven by one Garland, who refused to dim his headlights. Plaintiff, blinded by the lights, ran into a truck left unlighted and blocking the entire right lane. Plaintiff sued the person responsible for the truck, who argued that the plaintiff was guilty of contributory negligence as a matter of law. The trial court, however, permitted the case to go to the jury, which returned a verdict for the plaintiff.] To sustain his position, the defendant invokes the long line of cases beginning with Weston v. Southern R. Co., 194 N.C. 210, 139 S.E. 237, and ending with Marshall v. Southern R. Co., 233 N.C. 38, 62 S.E.2d 489, declaring either expressly or impliedly that "it is negligence as a matter of law to drive an automobile along a public highway in the dark at such a speed that it can not be stopped within the distance that objects can be seen ahead of it."

. . . "Few tasks in trial law are more troublesome than that of applying the rule suggested by the foregoing quotation to the facts in particular cases. The difficulty is much enhanced by a tendency of the bench and bar to regard it as a rule of thumb rather than as an effort to express in convenient formula for ready application to a recurring factual situation the basic principle that a person must exercise ordinary care to avoid injury when he undertakes to drive a motor vehicle upon a public highway at night. The rule was phrased to enforce the concept of the law that an injured person ought not to be permitted to shift from himself to another a loss resulting in part at least from his own refusal or failure to see that which is obvious. But it was not designed to require infallibility of the nocturnal motorist, or to preclude him from recovery of compensation for an injury occasioned by collision with an unlighted obstruction whose presence on the highway is not disclosed by his own headlights or by any other available lights. When all is said, each case must be decided according to its own peculiar state of facts. This is true because the true and ultimate test is this: What would a reasonably prudent person have done under the circumstances as they presented themselves to the plaintiff?"

It thus appears that the cases invoked by the defendant enunciate no mere shibboleth. They simply apply to the factual situations involved in them the fundamental truth that the law charges every person with the duty of exercising ordinary care for his own safety. . . .

When the plaintiff's evidence is taken in the light most favorable to him, it reasonably warrants these inferences: The plaintiff was keeping a proper lookout and driving at a reasonable speed as he traveled southward along Route 18. On being partially and temporarily blinded by the glaring lights of Garland's approaching automobile, the plaintiff reduced the speed of his car, and proceeded with extreme caution. The plaintiff exercised due care in adopting this course of action instead of bringing his car to a complete stop because he reasonably assumed that Garland would seasonably dim his headlights in obedience to the law, and thus restore to the plaintiff his full normal vision. The plaintiff had no reason whatever to anticipate or expect that the defendant's truck had been left standing on the traveled portion of the highway ahead of him without lights or warning signals until his car came within 30 feet of it. He did everything possible to avert the collision just as soon as the truck became visible.

This being true, we cannot hold that the plaintiff was guilty of contributory negligence as a matter of law. . . .

There is in law no error.

Notes

1. In many cases, a court will conclude, on the particular facts of the case, that the plaintiff (or sometimes the defendant) was negligent "as a matter of law." This phrase means that the court concludes, on the facts, that reasonable persons could not find otherwise and accordingly directs a verdict for the opposing party on this issue. There are other cases, fewer in number, in which the court, having reached such a conclusion on the facts of the case, generalizes it and states it as a legal rule for all cases. Notice how the court in *Marshall v. Southern Railway Co.* states the range-of-lights rule.

2. Almost all rules of this kind have come to grief, or have caused it. Holmes once took the view that it was contributory negligence not to stop, look and listen at a railroad crossing and that, if vision was impaired, one might be expected to get out of the car and walk to the edge of the track to assess the danger. *Baltimore & Ohio Railroad v. Goodman*, 275 U.S. 66, 48 S.Ct. 24, 72 L.Ed. 167 (1927). Cardozo was later able gently to push this decision aside, pointing to some of the injustices that could result. "Illustrations such as these," he said, "bear witness to the need for caution in framing standards of behavior that amount to rules of law. The need is the more urgent when there is no background of experience out of which the standards have emerged. They are then, not the natural flowering of behavior in its customary forms, but rules artificially developed and imposed from without." *Pokora v. Wabash Railway*, 292 U.S. 98, 54 S.Ct. 580, 78 L.Ed. 1149 (1934).

3. Is there a pattern in *Marshall* and *Chaffin* on the one hand and *Goodman* and *Pokora* on the other?

MARTIN v. HERZOG, 228 N.Y. 164, 126 N.E. 814 (1920). Defendant, driving at night, crossed over the center line on a curve and struck a buggy occupied by decedent, causing his death. In a wrongful death action the defendant contended that decedent was negligent in driving without lights. A statute provided in part: "Every vehicle on wheels whether stationary or in motion, while upon any public street ... shall have attached thereto a light or lights to be visible from the front and from the rear from one hour after sunset to one hour before sunrise.... A person violating the provisions of this section shall be guilty of a misdemeanor punishable by a fine not to exceed ten dollars." The trial judge charged the jury that decedent's violation of the statute could be considered as evidence of contributory negligence but not as negligence in itself. The jury found for the plaintiff. The Appellate Division reversed for new trial. In the Court of Appeals, by Cardozo, J., held, the Appellate Division is affirmed. "We think the unexcused omission of the statutory signals is more than some evidence of negligence. It is negligence in itself.... Yet the jurors were instructed in effect that they were at liberty in their discretion to treat the omission of lights either as innocent or as culpable. They were allowed to 'consider the default as lightly or gravely' as they would. They might as well have been told that they could use a like discretion in holding a master at fault for the omission of a safety appliance prescribed by positive law for the protection of a workman. Jurors have no dispensing power, by which they may relax the duty that one traveler on the highway owes under the statute to another."

Notes

1. The position taken by Cardozo in this case is the one followed generally by most courts, namely, that violation of statutes is, subject to some qualifications, "negligence per se."

2. Generally, courts will apply the rule to city ordinances and even to administrative regulations as well as to state statutes.

3. How should the trial judge instruct the jury under the negligence per se rule?

TEDLA v. ELLMAN

Court of Appeals of New York, 1939.
280 N.Y. 124, 19 N.E.2d 987.

LEHMAN, JUDGE.

While walking along a highway, Anna Tedla and her brother, John Bachek, were struck by a passing automobile, operated by the defendant Ellman. She was injured and Bachek was killed. Bachek was a deaf-mute. His occupation was collecting and selling junk. His sister, Mrs. Tedla, was engaged in the same occupation. They often picked up junk at the incinerator of the village of Islip. At the time of the accident they were walking along "Sunrise Highway" and wheeling baby carriages containing junk and wood which they had picked up at the incinerator. It was about six o'clock, or a little earlier, on a Sunday evening in December. Darkness had already set in. Bachek was carrying a lighted lantern, or, at least, there is testimony to that effect. The jury found that the accident was due solely to the negligence of the operator of the automobile. The defendants do not, upon this appeal, challenge the finding of negligence on the part of the operator. They maintain, however, that Mrs. Tedla and her brother were guilty of contributory negligence as matter of law.

     . . . The Vehicle and Traffic Law (Consol. Laws, c. 71) provides that " . . . such pedestrians shall keep to the left of the center line thereof . . . , so as to permit all vehicles passing them in either direction to pass on their right. . . ." Mrs. Tedla and her brother did not observe the statutory rule, and at the time of the accident were proceeding in easterly direction on the east bound or right-handed roadway. . . . The trial judge left to the jury the question whether failure to observe the statutory rule was a proximate cause of the accident. . . .

     The plaintiffs showed by the testimony of a State policeman that "there were very few cars going east" at the time of the accident, but that going west there was "very heavy Sunday night traffic." Until the recent adoption of the new statutory rule for pedestrians, ordinary prudence would have dictated that pedestrians should not expose themselves to the danger of walking along the roadway upon which the "very heavy Sunday night traffic" was proceeding when they could walk in comparative safety along a roadway used by very few cars. It is said that now, by force of the statutory rule, pedestrians are guilty of contributory negligence as a matter of law when they use the center of the road. . . . A general rule of conduct–specifically, a rule of the road–may accomplish its intended purpose under usual conditions, but, when the unusual occurs, strict observance may defeat the purpose of the rule and produce catastrophic results.

     Negligence is failure to exercise the care required by law. Where a statute defines the standard of care and the safeguards required to meet a recognized danger, then, as we have said, no other measure may be applied in determining whether a person has carried out the duty of care imposed by law. Failure to observe the standard imposed by statute is negligence, as matter of law. On the other hand, where a statutory general rule of conduct fixes no definite standard of care which would under all circumstances tend to protect life, limb or property but merely codifies or supplements a common-law rule, which has always been subject to limitations and exceptions; or where the statutory rule of conduct regulates conflicting rights and obligations in manner calculated to promote public convenience and safety, then the statute, in the absence of clear language to the contrary, should not be construed as intended to wipe out the limitations and exceptions which judicial decisions have attached to the common-law duty; nor should it be construed as an inflexible command that the general rule of conduct intended to prevent accidents must be followed even under conditions when observance might cause accidents. We may assume reasonably that the Legislature directed pedestrians to keep to the left of the center of the road because that would cause them to face traffic approaching in that lane and would enable them to care for their own safety better than if the traffic approached them from the rear. We cannot assume reasonably that the Legislature intended that a statute enacted for the preservation of the life and limb of pedestrians must be observed when observance would subject them to more imminent danger.

Notes

1.   If the common law rules of "negligence as a matter of law" are too rigid, as *Chaffin* suggested, are statutory rules of "negligence per se" any less so?

2.   There are several ways to import flexibility in the administration of statutory rules, some of which are considered in the materials that follow. What was Judge Lehman's technique? Did he convince you that a deaf person is safer walking with his back to a small amount of traffic than he is walking with his eyes on a large amount of oncoming traffic?

3.   Notice that Judge Lehman approached the issue by construing the statute and asking what the Legislature intended. Is this necessary? Look at the statute quoted in *Martin v. Herzog*. Does it say anything about tort suits at all? If not, why is it relevant?

IMPSON v. STRUCTURAL METALS, INC.

Supreme Court of Texas, 1972.
487 S.W.2d 694.

GREENHILL, JUSTICE.

[The driver of defendant's truck attempted to pass a car within 100 feet of an intersection; the car turned left into the intersection and was struck by the truck. This is an action for injury to some passengers in the car and death of another. A statute prohibits passing within 100 feet of an intersection. The trial judge held that, the jury having found that the defendant passed within 100 feet of the intersection, negligence was established as a matter of law. Accordingly he entered judgment for the plaintiffs. The Texas Court of Appeal held that since defendant had offered some excuses, the negligence issue had to be submitted to the jury. The plaintiffs bring this appeal.]

[T]he problem here is to decide what excuses or justifications are legally acceptable. In *Phoenix*, the excuse was a tire blowout. In *Hammer*, it was that because of the wet streets, the defendant's bus unavoidably skidded out of control. In *Christy*, the contention was that it was simply impossible for the truck driver to stop within the prescribed distance from the railroad track. In none of these cases has this court addressed itself to the legal sufficiency of the excuse.

The Restatement of Torts, Second (1965), deals with this problem in a new section, 288A. It states that an excused violation of a legislative enactment is not negligence. While the section expressly says that the list of excusable situations given is not intended to be exclusive, it lists five categories. They are:

> "(a) the violation is reasonable because of the actor's incapacity;

> "(b) he neither knows nor should know of the occasion for compliance;

> "(c) he is unable after reasonable diligence or care to comply;

> "(d) he is confronted by an emergency not due to his own misconduct;

> "(e) compliance would involve a greater risk of harm to the actor or to others."

Under category (a), "incapacity," could come cases where the violator was too young, or did not have the mental capacity, to be charged with negligence. It might include a blind man who unknowingly walks a red light (though he may be contributorily negligent for other reasons), or a driver who is rendered physically incapable because of a heart attack. Under category (b) could come cases where a night driver has a tail light go out unexpectedly and without his knowledge. Under category (c), "unable after reasonable diligence or care to comply," could come cases involving impossibility, as in Christy v. Blades. Under category (d), "emergency not due to his own misconduct," could come cases in which there is an unexpected failure in the steering or braking system; a blowout of a tire which is reasonably thought to be in good condition; a sudden confrontation with blinding dust or smoke on the highway. It could include driving on the left side of the highway to avoid striking a darting child, and similar situations. Finally, the illustration given by the Restatement for category (e), "greater risk of harm," is one in which the law requires people to walk facing traffic, but due to particular circumstances, it would involve greater risk to walk upon that side. The above are intended merely as illustrations of a principle and are recognized to be dictum here. But we do approve of the general treatment of legally acceptable excuses as set out in the Restatement, Second.

[The defendant sought to excuse its violation of the statute by pointing to evidence that the driver had forgotten the existence of the intersection in question; that the sign marking the intersection was small; that there were no lines in the road to indicate "no passing"; and that he was watching the car ahead, which was partly off the road on the right, rather than watching for the intersection sign.]

All of the above matters fall within the realm of ordinary care,–or lack of care. The driver made his move deliberately, with knowledge of the law and with at least notice of the presence of the highway intersection. There was no impossibility, no reason for any particular hurry, no emergency, and no incapacity. The problem of greater risk of harm is not involved. If there was an emergency, it was only after the statutory violation had begun, and was due in large part to his own deliberate conduct.

In view of the evidence offered, the trial court correctly determined that there was no evidence offered of any legally acceptable excuse or justification. It was, in law, an unexcused violation. The finding, therefore, that the driver violated the statute intended as a safety measure and the finding of proximate cause entitled the plaintiffs to a judgment.

[On motion for rehearing the court remanded the case solely for consideration of certain issues about damages.]

Notes

1. In a number of extreme cases courts that ordinarily recognize the per se rule have held that statutory violation was excused. This has been the holding, for example, where the statute required good brakes, but the brakes suddenly failed without the driver's fault.

2. If excuses are limited to those formulated by the Restatement, might the effect be a kind of strict liability? On the other hand, if excuses are not limited, is the negligence per se rule in effect scuttled? In *Alarid v. Vanier*, 50 Cal.2d 617, 327 P.2d 897 (1958) the court said: "In our opinion the correct test is whether the person who has violated a statute has sustained the burden of showing that he did what might reasonably be expected of a person of ordinary prudence, acting under similar circumstances, who desired to comply with the law." What effect, if any, does such an approach give to the statute?

RUDES v. GOTTSCHALK

Supreme Court of Texas, 1959.
159 Tex. 552, 324 S.W.2d 201.

NORVELL, JUSTICE. . . .

[Gottschalk, an eight-year-old boy, was struck by a car as he attempted to cross a controlled access expressway. A statute provided that "every pedestrian" was required to yield the right of way except in a crosswalk. The jury found Gottschalk was not in a crosswalk. On this basis, the trial judge concluded he was negligent per se and denied all recovery.]

It is well settled that where common-law negligence as distinguished from negligence per se is involved, the minor is judged by the standard of a child and not that of an adult.

While defendant does not dispute the rule above set forth, he insists that a different rule applies to cases of negligence per se. Here the legislative regulation governing the crossing of highways in places other than crosswalks was obviously intended to guard against a general class of harm which included the unfortunate occurrence disclosed by the record before us and was undoubtedly designed for the protection of motorists using the expressway as well as those crossing the same.

Fundamentally, however, the application of proscriptions contained in criminal statutes as standards for determining tort liability stems from the judicial action of civil courts. The statute here does not expressly provide for the fixing of civil liability in a negligence action. Actions expressly provided for by statute are to be distinguished from actions based upon the doctrine of negligence per se. In the latter type of action, the civil courts may and often do consider acts or omissions as negligent because of criminal regulations against them, although such acts or omissions would not be considered negligent under the ordinarily prudent man test. In the usual negligence per se case, however, we are concerned with alleged conduct which would be considered substandard even in the absence of statute. We adopt the statutory test rather than that of the ordinarily prudent man as the more accurate one to determine negligence because the legislature, by reason of its organization and investigating processes, is generally in a better position to establish such tests than are the judicial tribunals. But this does not mean that the criminal statute is always accepted as a test of negligence by the civil courts under all circumstances. We have applied tests and standards taken from criminal statutes, even though such provisions are too indefinite for criminal proscriptions, and even when the statute may be wholly invalid as a criminal regulation because of a failure to comply with a procedural condition precedent. Clinkscales v. Carver, 22 Cal. 2d 72, 136 P.2d 777.

As the power of adopting or rejecting standards rests with the civil courts, we may accept or reject the criminal statute or use such part thereof as may be deemed appropriate for our purpose. We have applied standards set forth in criminal statutes even to those persons who are expressly excepted from criminal responsibility thereunder. And even while accepting a statutory standard of negligence in lieu of that of the ordinarily prudent man, we still retain the test of foreseeability of harm before liability is imposed under the doctrine of negligence per se.

We agree with the Court of Civil Appeals in holding that the conduct of a child is not to be judged by the standard of an adult simply because statutory negligence (negligence per se) is involved rather than common-law negligence. This holding is undoubtedly in accord with the overwhelming weight of authority in the United States.... [S]ome courts apply the general rule concerning a child's standard of care while others inquire by interrogatory or instruction into the child's capacity to understand and comply with the statute.... The general rule of a child's standard of care is, however, more compatible with the Texas practice and would be less likely to confuse a jury in a case submitted upon special issues.

Contributory negligence on the part of a child, like that of an adult, may appear as a matter of law.... It may be further said that at either end of the age bracket of childhood there exists a zone where under the particular facts of a case, it could well be said that reasonable minds could not differ but that the particular child, as a matter of law, must be held incapable of contributory negligence, or, on the other hand, held to the adult standard of the ordinarily prudent man. The age of the child in this case lies within the classic common-law brackets of seven and fourteen. The record does not compel the adoption of the adult standard on the theory that reasonable minds cannot differ as to the child's intelligence and discretion. The issue was for the jury and the Court of Civil Appeals correctly so held.

[Remanded for new trial.]

Notes

1. *Bases for ignoring the statutory standard.* The broader point in *Rudes* continues the theme begun with *Tedla v. Ellman* and *Impson v. Structural Metals.* Can you now state three distinct grounds for avoiding the negligence per se doctrine?

2. *Rejecting excuses.* If courts can adopt or reject the statutory standard when the statute does not address tort liability, could they also hold that all excuses would be rejected? Would that be strict liability? See Dobbs on Torts § 141 (2000).

3. *Child's standard in negligence per se cases.* A narrower point in *Rudes* addresses the minor's duties under statutes. Is the court saying that the child standard of care always prevails over the statutory standard ? In *Bauman v. Crawford*, 104 Wash. 2d 241, 704 P.2d 1181 (1985), the court said: "We hold that a minor's violation of a statute does not constitute proof of negligence per se, but may, in proper cases, be introduced as evidence of a minor's negligence." In *Rudes* the child was on foot; in *Bauman* he was riding a bicycle at night without a light. These are not exotic activities for children. Why would holding children to the statutory standard be such a bad idea?

4. *Common law negligence.* Be sure to notice that the plaintiff can claim negligence on ordinary common law principles even if the statute has no effect. That is, the standard of care "defaults" back to the reasonable and prudent person standard where the statute is held not to supplant it.

5. If the court is free to use some statutory standards and reject others, should there be some principles governing this choice or should the court be free to ignore the statutory standard when it feels like it?

6. "[T]he defendant in most negligence per se cases already owes the plaintiff a pre-existing common law duty to act as a reasonably prudent person, so that the statute's role is merely to define more precisely what conduct breaches that duty." *Perry v. S.N.*, 973 S.W.2d 301(Tex.1998). When the statute creates a wholly new obligation and does not in itself purport to create a new cause of action, courts tend to give the statute no tort law effect at all. That was the case in *Perry*, where the statute required people to report known cases of child abuse. Since no common law obligation of this sort existed, and the statute did not purport to create a new cause of action, the court denied recovery to children whose abuse might have been avoided if a timely report had been made.

7. *Invalid statutes.* What if a statute setting a standard of care is invalid because of a purely formal defect in its passage? Is this a good ground for refusing to use its standard in a tort case?

8. *Obscure or irrational statutes*. Alaska has said that the trial judge could refuse the negligence per se instruction in "highly unusual cases," because of "obscure, oblique or irrational" statutory provisions, and also where the statutory standard merely duplicates the common law standard. *Osborne v. Russell*, 669 P.2d 550 (Alaska 1983). Is this a good ground for refusing to use its standard in a tort case?

9. *Licensing statutes*. Should courts adopt licensing statutes as standards of care? In *Talley v. Danek Medical, Inc.*, 179 F.3d 154 (4th Cir.1999) the defendant manufactured a medical device without obtaining required approval of the Food and Drug Administration. A surgeon used the device on the plaintiff's spine, allegedly to her injury. The court held that the defendant's failure to obtain required approval before marketing a medical device would not be negligence per se. Perhaps the most famous case on this topic is *Brown v. Shyne*, 242 N.Y. 176, 151 N.E. 197, 44 A.L.R. 1407 (1926). The plaintiff alleged that the defendant held himself out to practice medicine, that his treatments paralyzed her, and that he had no license to practice medicine. The New York Court of Appeals held that the plaintiff could not get to the jury on this allegation but would instead be required to allege and prove negligence by ordinary means. A few cases apply the negligence per se rule to particular licensing statutes, or find limited exceptions. Do you think *Talley* and *Brown* were rightly decided?

WRIGHT v. BROWN

Supreme Court of Connecticut, 1975.
167 Conn. 464, 356 A.2d 176.

BOGDANSKI, ASSOCIATE JUSTICE....

The complaint alleged that a dog owned by the defendant Brown attacked and injured the plaintiff; that less than fourteen days prior to this incident, the same dog had attacked another person resulting in the quarantine of the dog by the defendant dog warden; that the dog warden released the dog prior to the expiration of the fourteen-day quarantine period required by§ 22–358 of the General Statutes; that as a result of that premature release, the dog was placed in a situation where it attacked the plaintiff. The second and fifth counts of the complaint were based on negligence, alleging that the dog warden and the town failed to comply with the standard of conduct required by§ 22–358. . . .

The dog warden and the town demurred to the complaint as follows: (a) to the second [and fifth] count "on the grounds that any purported violation of . . . [§ 22–358] would not constitute negligence since the plaintiff was not within the class of persons which that statute was designed to protect." . . .

The trial court concluded that § 22–358 was enacted to provide a period of quarantine to determine whether a person bitten by a dog required the administration of a rabies vaccine and "to protect members of the community from being bitten by diseased dogs." The court then concluded that the plaintiff was not within the class of person protected by § 22–358 since she had not alleged that she was bitten by a diseased dog. [Accordingly, the trial judge sustained the demurrer of the dog warden and the town and dismissed the case as to them.]

The purpose of the quarantine requirement in § 22–358 is readily ascertainable from the meaning of that word. "Quarantine" means to isolate as a precaution against contagious disease or a detainment to prevent exposure of others to disease. While the specific concern of the legislature may have been to protect the victim of a dog bite from the threat of rabies, that restricted purpose is not expressed in the language of § 22–358. Nowhere is the control of rabies mentioned. The intent expressed in the language of the statute is the controlling factor. The trial court correctly concluded that § 22–358 was intended not only to protect persons bitten by a dog from the threat of rabies, but also to protect the general public from contact with diseased dogs.

"Where a statute is designed to protect persons against injury, one who has, as a result of its violation, suffered such an injury as the statute was intended to guard against has a good ground of recovery." That principle of the law sets forth two conditions which must coexist before statutory negligence can be actionable. First, the plaintiff must be within the class of persons protected by the statute. Second, the injury must be of the type which the statute was intended to prevent.

If we apply these principles to the purpose of § 22–358, it becomes clear that the class of persons protected is not limited; rather the statute was intended to protect the general public or, as stated by the trial court, "members of the community."

Since the demurrer to the second and fifth counts was addressed only to the class of persons protected by § 22–358, and since the plaintiff, as a member of the general public, is within that class, the demurrer should not have been sustained on that ground.

Although we have concluded that the second and fifth counts are not insufficient for the reason specified in the defendant's demurrer, we are not to be understood as holding that those counts can successfully withstand a claim that the plaintiff's injuries were not of the type which § 22–358 was intended to prevent. The second and fifth counts allege only that the plaintiff was attacked and injured by a dog that was prematurely released from quarantine. That allegation does not claim an injury of the type § 22–358 was intended to prevent. . . .

———

HAVER v. HINSON, 385 So.2d 605 (Miss.1980). Hinson drove her car to the Havers' house, where she pulled over and parked on the left hand side of the street and immediately in front of the Haver residence. Mrs. Haver came over to chat. She was accompanied by a small child, Elizabeth. After a few minutes Hinson drove off after looking in all directions. She heard a thud after she had driven a few feet, stopped the car and found the child underneath, wedged against the exhaust pipe and seriously injured. In an action on behalf of the child, the Havers argued that "Hinson was negligent per se in driving and parking on the wrong side of the street in contravention of Mississippi Code Annotated section 63–3–601 (1972). We disagree, because violation of a safety statute constitutes negligence per se only where (1) the plaintiff is a member of the class sought to be protected by the statute, and (2) the resultant harm is of the type sought to be prevented by the passage of the statute We think it clear that the class sought to be protected by Section 63–3–601 includes only pedestrians and drivers who act in reliance upon the orderly flow of traffic dictated by the statute.... The risk of an accident of this sort would have been no less likely if Hinson had rounded the block and parked facing in the 'appropriate' direction."

Notes

1.   The Restatement Second of Torts §§ 286, 288 (1965) provides that violation of a statute is not negligence per se unless the person injured is within the class the statute aimed at protecting and the harm done was of the kind that the statute aimed to protect against. The same rule has been applied where the defendant violates a court order rather than a statute. In *Stafford v. United Farm Workers of America*, 33 Cal.3d 319, 188 Cal.Rptr. 600, 656 P.2d 564 (1983) a court order, issued in a labor dispute, prohibited the union from blocking access to a tomato field. A striker's truck did partially block access in a way that created a traffic hazard. The plaintiff was injured in a collision with the truck. Applying the "type of harm" and "class of person" analysis, would you think the court order set a standard of conduct governing this case?

2.   Was the court correct in *Wright v. Brown* in holding that the plaintiff was within the class of persons the statute was designed to protect? How is one to know?

3.   *Judicial adoption theory of statutes and the class of person and harm rules. Must* the court consider legislative purpose to protect a certain class of persons or to protect against a certain type of harm? If the court is free to adopt the standard as one that reflects what reasonable people would do, what difference does it make that the legislature wrote the statute narrowly? To think about this, suppose the statute provides that heavy machinery used at construction sites must automatically make back-up noises when in reverse gear, and that the statute is for the protection of workers at the job site. If the machine in violation of the statute backs over an unsuspecting student of architecture, on the premises to be shown how a building is constructed, he has no negligence per se claim. Cf. RESTATEMENT SECOND OF TORTS§ 286, Illustration 1 (1965). Yet the contractor violated the statute. It would have cost him no more to have complied with it for the purpose of protecting everyone than for the purpose of protecting workers on the job. Besides this, the legislature might have thought back-up beepers were needed "because of danger to workers," without really intending to exclude the possibility of saving other persons as well. These things might suggest that the class of person/class of risk rule should not be used to limit liability. But they might also suggest that the courts should use very large classifica-

tions, or, conceivably, that statutory violations should be treated in all cases as merely evidence of negligence.

4. The principles stated in *Wright v. Brown* are generally accepted. A great many cases, however, obtain results more or less consistent with those principles by holding that violation of a statute must be a significant cause of the plaintiff's harm—or in the language of the law, a "proximate" or "legal" cause of the harm. In many instances this appears to work out to about the same notion that is involved in a class of person/kind of harm analysis seen in *Wright*. The proximate cause cases are taken up in Chapter 8.

5. *The evidence of negligence rule.* Some states use a rule that makes violation of statute some evidence of negligence that may be considered by the jury but refuse to tell the jury that violation is in itself negligence. See, e.g., REV. CODE WASH. § 5.40.050; *Kalata v. Anheuser–Busch Companies, Inc.*, 144 Ill.2d 425, 435, 581 N.E.2d 656, 661, 163 Ill.Dec. 502, 507 (1991). This would be the statutory parallel to cases like *Chaffin v. Brame*, supra.

6. *Presumption rules.* Some other states reject the per se terminology and say that violation of a statute creates a presumption of negligence. In those states, the defendant can rebut the presumption by showing an appropriate justification or excuse for his actions. In those states, the language is different but the effect is similar to the per se rule.

7. *Statutes creating a cause of action.* The negligence per se issue arises when statutes say nothing explicit about tort liability but provide for criminal or administrative enforcement. Some quite different statutes expressly provide for tort liability. The civil rights statute, 42 U.S.C.A. § 1983 is like this. If a statute provides for tort liability, then the statute controls unless it is unconstitutional. In that case, tort liability is determined by the terms of the statute. In a few cases, legislatures pass statutes that seem to imply but do not expressly state that tort liability is intended. In that case, courts may find that the statute creates an *implied* right of action to be determined by the statute's terms. If so, the court would not be free to reject the statutory liability. How does that differ from the kind of statute that raises the negligence per se issue?

Problem

Lind v. Maigret

Driving his car on a mountain highway, Maigret hit a fog bank and slowed. A large boulder rolled down the hillside and struck the rear of Maigret's car from the side. The impact spun Maigret's car around. Maigret did not react skillfully. He went into a state of shock when he felt the impact, gripping the steering wheel and closing his eyes. When his car came to a stop, the engine was stalled. He was unable to start it. The car was projecting across most of one lane of traffic in fairly thick fog. At this point it was hit by a truck driven by Lind. That impact caused serious injury to Lind. A statute provided that "no person shall stop, park, or leave standing any vehicle, whether attended or unattended, upon the roadway."

Lind has proposed negligence per se instructions to the judge, who asks you, as Maigret's counsel, whether you have any objections or views on the subject. What is your position based on authority in this section?

Chapter 6

NEGLIGENCE: THE BREACH OR NEGLIGENCE ELEMENT OF THE NEGLIGENCE CASE

§ 1. BREACH: ASSESSING REASONABLE CARE BY ASSESSING RISKS AND COSTS

Once the court determines that the defendant owed the plaintiff a duty—usually the duty of reasonable care—the question is whether the defendant breached that duty by failing to exercise the care required. The defendant who breaches the duty of care is negligent.

Negligence is conduct that imposes unreasonable risks of harm. The risk of harm is unreasonable when a reasonable and prudent person would foresee that harm might result and would avoid conduct that creates the risk. Conduct may include a failure to act if action is required, but a mere state of mind is not conduct. If the defendant daydreams but drives properly in all respects, he might be careless in the lay sense, but he is not legally negligent. Negligence entails overt behavior that creates risks a reasonable person would avoid. Analysis of unreasonable risk leads us to consider, among other things, the alternative conduct that might be available to the actor.

Problem

Brown v. Stiel

The Stiel Company, a construction contractor, decided to build a building for its own use. It provided an architect with the basic design elements, and plans were drawn which Stiel then followed in building. Stiel chose a design in which the major structural components were steel. It rejected a design based on poured concrete in favor of steel beams because the steel beam construction was, in the particular situation, much cheaper and quicker. However, as Stiel knew, the kind of steel beam construction

137

proposed generally caused or was associated with accidents which caused death or serious injury. Statistics indicated that for a building the size of Stiel's, three workers or others would be killed or paralyzed or otherwise seriously injured. The concrete building also involved predictable injuries; but, for a building this size, the prediction for such injury was that only one person would be injured. Stiel nevertheless chose the riskier steel construction because of time and cost differences.

There was a collapse of some steel beams and John White, an employee of Stiel who had done steel work for many years, fell to the ground and suffered a broken back and permanent paralysis from the neck down. The same collapse dropped a steel beam on Billy Brown, a delivery person for a nearby deli. Billy Brown was on the premises bringing an order for the supervising architect when the beam fell. Brown lost a leg as a result of the building's collapse.

Notes

1. Did Stiel Co. commit an intentional tort? Consider whether this case differs from a case in which A throws a brick from the roof of a building into a crowd below.

2. Suppose a court holds that no intentional tort is shown in this problem. Even so, maybe Stiel ought to pay for the harm done as a matter of justice or social policy. If certain costs are more or less inevitable in a business, maybe those costs should be regarded as a cost that business should bear as a part of its overhead. If a construction company expects that its own construction vehicles will periodically collide and sustain damage, it will budget for this cost and charge sufficient amounts to cover this cost as well as all others. Should the same be done when it comes to human costs?

3. Workers' compensation statutes proceed upon the theory that work-connected injuries may generally be regarded as a part of the employer's cost of doing business–the human "breakage," analogous to broken plates in a restaurant. Since such losses are more or less inevitable in a statistical sense, the employer simply budgets for them–charging sufficiently for its work to cover the costs.

4. Is there any justification for holding Stiel liable to White for workers' compensation but not holding Stiel liable to Brown?

5. Assuming that Brown cannot recover workers' compensation from Stiel because he was not an employee, and that he cannot recover from the deli because the statute did not cover businesses with very few employees, would Brown nevertheless have an action under common law tort theory? Consider the introductory comments about negligence as well as the cases that follow.

INDIANA CONSOLIDATED INSURANCE CO. v. MATHEW

Court of Appeals of Indiana, Third District, 1980.
402 N.E.2d 1000.

HOFFMAN, JUDGE.

Appellant Indiana Consolidated Insurance Company seeks review of the finding that Robert D. Mathew (Mathew) did not act in a negligent manner so as to be liable for damages done to his brother's garage when a Toro riding lawnmower that Mathew was starting caught fire. Appellant insured the garage and premises under a homeowner's insurance policy and is pursuing this claim against Mathew by virtue of its subrogation rights.[1]

[T]he facts favorable to Mathew disclose that on May 1, 1976 Mathew's brother was out of town for the weekend. The two brothers lived across the street from each other and took turns mowing both lawns. In the late afternoon Mathew decided to mow both lawns and went to his brother's garage where a twelve horsepower Toro riding lawnmower was stored. The mower was approximately eight years old, was kept in good mechanical condition, and had required only minor tune-ups and belt replacements for the rotary mower assembly. Mathew pulled the mower away from the side wall of the garage and after checking the gas gauge filled the lawnmower approximately three-fourths full with gasoline using a funnel. He then went back across the street to his home for approximately twenty minutes. Upon returning to the garage Mathew started the lawnmower. However, he noticed a flame in the engine area under the hood and immediately shut the engine off. He opened the hood and saw a flame four to five inches tall under the gas tank. Using some clean towels Mathew tried to snuff out the flame but was unsuccessful. He could find no other means to extinguish the fire. The flames continued to grow and the machine began spewing gasoline, so he ran to his home to call the fire department. He returned to find the garage totally engulfed in flames.

At trial Mathew testified that he was afraid to try to push the flaming machine outside the garage for fear that the tank would explode in his face.

Indiana Consolidated brought this action against Mathew alleging that he breached a duty owed to his brother to exercise due care in starting the lawnmower and therefore stands liable for the damages resulting from his negligence. After a bench trial the court below entered the following finding, to-wit:

> The Court having heretofore taken this matter under advisement and having considered the evidence introduced in the trial of this cause and being sufficiently advised, now enters Findings as follows: The Court now finds ... that there is no evidence of negligence on the part of the defendant, Robert D. Mathew, and that the plaintiff should take nothing by its complaint.

> IT IS THEREFORE ORDERED, ADJUDGED AND DECREED BY THE COURT that the plaintiff, Indiana Consolidated Insurance Company, take nothing by its complaint; and Judgment is entered

---

1. [Editors' note.] A fire insurer or collision insurer who pays its insured's loss "stands in the shoes" of the insured for the purpose of suing any tortfeasor whose tortious acts caused the loss.

for and on behalf of the defendant, Robert D. Mathew. Costs of this action are taxed to the plaintiff.

On appeal appellant contends that the judgment is contrary to law because Mathew was negligent in filling the gas tank, in starting the mower in an enclosed area, and in failing to push the flaming mower out of the garage. The standard by which Mathew's conduct is to be measured is whether he exercised the duty to use due care in operating the mower that an ordinary prudent man would exercise under the same or similar circumstances.

The record amply supports the finding that Mathew did not act in a negligent manner in filling the gas tank. He testified that he did so carefully, with the use of a funnel. He did not fill the tank full, and he was adamant in his belief that he did not spill any gasoline. He hypothesized that even had any gas been spilled it would have evaporated in the cool air during the twenty-minute period before he started the mower. Appellant is merely asking this Court to reweigh the evidence in regard to any gasoline spillage due to Mathew's admission on cross-examination that he could have spilled some fuel. The trier of fact resolved this issue in favor of Mathew, finding that he exercised due care in fueling the mower, and it must remain undisturbed upon appeal. Appellant is again reminded that any conflicts in testimony when appeal from a negative judgment is taken must be resolved in favor of the appellee.

Appellant's contention that Mathew should be held liable for the act of negligently starting the mower inside the garage is also without merit. It cannot seriously be contended that the evidence shows that Mathew acted other than a reasonably prudent man in pulling the mower out into an open area of the garage and starting it. The mower was a riding type that was of considerable weight and size. Garages are designed to permit the starting of motorized vehicles such as automobiles and are commonly used for such purpose. That this particular mower would catch fire at this particular time was not reasonably foreseeable. As one is not required to anticipate that which is unlikely to happen, the trial court did not err in determining that Mathew was not negligent in starting the mower inside the garage.

Appellant's further allegation that Mathew negligently failed to push the flaming mower out of the garage area is refuted by the evidence that the machine was spewing gasoline and that he was afraid for his safety should the tank explode. Mathew therefore chose to leave and summon help from the local fire department. One who is confronted with a sudden emergency not of his own making is not chargeable with negligence if he acts according to his best judgment. The sudden emergency doctrine requires the person so confronted to do that which an ordinary prudent man would do under like circumstances. Mathew's course of action can be deemed an exercise of ordinary prudence. The law values human life above property. Greater risk of one's person is justified to save life than is reasonable in protecting property. If Mathew had tried to push the riding mower ten feet into an open area the machine might have exploded and caused much graver damage to his person than was suffered by the destruction of the garage. Contrary to appellant's position several jurisdictions have ruled that one may be deemed negligent in voluntarily risking life or serious injury for the purpose of saving mere property. . . .

The judgment is not contrary to law and is therefore affirmed.

Affirmed.

Notes

1. Precisely what permitted the trial court to find the defendant was not negligent? Does the emergency doctrine play a part here?

2. What factors are important in determining negligence?

STINNETT v. BUCHELE

Court of Appeals of Kentucky, 1980.
598 S.W.2d 469.

BREETZ, JUDGE.

This is a tort action filed by an employee against his employer for injuries sustained during the course and scope of his employment. The lower court granted summary judgment to the employer on the ground that there was no showing that the injury was caused by the negligence of the employer. We affirm.

The accident which gave rise to this suit was also the subject of a workmen's compensation claim. The Workmen's Compensation Board denied benefits because the employee, being employed in agriculture, was exempt from the coverage of the Workmen's Compensation Act. We have today, by separate and non-published opinion, affirmed the board in that regard. . . .

Earl S. Buchele is a practicing physician in Hardinsburg, Kentucky. He hired Alvin Stinnett as a farm laborer in January 1976. In September of that year Mr. Stinnett undertook to repair the roof on a barn located at one of Dr. Buchele's farms known as the Cloverport Farm. The repairs were to consist of nailing down the edges of the roof that had been loosened by the wind and painting the roof with a coating. Stinnett was severely injured when he fell from the roof while applying the coating with a paint roller.

Stinnett urges in his brief to this court that Dr. Buchele was negligent for failing to comply with occupational and health regulations and also for his failure to provide a safe place to work. Dr. Buchele denies both of those assertions, and, additionally, argues that Stinnett was contributorily negligent as a matter of law. We do not reach the issue of contributory negligence. . . .

Nor do we find any evidence to be submitted to the jury that Dr. Buchele was negligent in failing to provide Stinnett with a safe place to work. We agree with Stinnett when he states that Dr. Buchele had the obligation to furnish him:

> ... a place reasonably safe having regard for the character of work and reasonably safe tools and appliances for doing the work. The measure of duty is to exercise ordinary or reasonable care to do so. The standard is the care exercised by prudent employers in similar circumstances.

We also agree with the sentence immediately preceding the quotation from that same opinion: "An employer's obligation to its employee is not the frequently impossible duty of furnishing absolutely safe instrumentalities or place to work."

Although we may consider that painting a barn roof is dangerous work, we cannot say that Dr. Buchele can be held liable for failing to provide a safe place to work solely because he asked Stinnett to work on the roof. We hold, therefore, that there was no showing of any negligence on the part of Dr. Buchele arising solely out of the fact that he had asked Stinnett to paint the barn roof.

Stinnett next argues ... that a reasonable and prudent employer would have provided safety devices of some kind even though not required to by force of statute or regulation and that the question whether Dr. Buchele measured up to the standards of an ordinarily careful and prudent employer is one for the jury.... The liability of the employer:

> ... rests upon the assumption that the employer has a better and more comprehensive knowledge than the employees, and ceases to be applicable where the employees' means of knowledge of the dangers to be incurred is equal to that of the employer. 53 Am. Jur. 2d, Master and Servant, § 160.

Stinnett had been in the painting business with his brother-in-law for two years before he began working for Dr. Buchele. Although the record is not clear whether Stinnett, his brother-in-law or both did the painting, they did paint a church steeple and an undetermined number of barn roofs. On occasion safety belts and safety nets had been used while painting the barn roofs. Stinnett was injured on a Sunday. Dr. Buchele was not present and he did not know that Stinnett was going to work on the barn roof on that particular day. Dr. Buchele had, however, purchased the material that Stinnett was applying to the roof when he fell. Stinnett did not ask Dr. Buchele to procure a safety net nor did he check to see if one was available. He admitted he could have used a safety rope around his waist but he did not think any were available....

In short, we find no evidence of negligence on the part of Dr. Buchele to submit to a jury.

Notes

1. *Workers' compensation*. Although workers' compensation statutes have been adopted everywhere, they do not include all workers within their benefits. Statutes may exclude agricultural employees, domestic employees and casual employees, for example. One special case is that of the worker on interstate railroads. Under the Federal Employers Liability Act, 45 U.S.C.A. §§ 51 et. seq., called FELA, these workers have expanded tort rights, but no workers' compensation. Workers not covered by compensation laws must, like Mr. Stinnett, seek recovery under the tort system.

2. Does this case have anything to do with apportionment of responsibility between two negligent persons?

3. Even if Dr. Buchele was not at fault and this was simply an accident, Mr. Stinnett was still injured. Persons in this position may not be able to work at all and may have substantial medical needs. Apart from human sympathy, is there any reason to consider this as a social problem rather than as Mr. Stinnett's individual problem?

4. If there are social problems represented in injury cases and society ought to respond in some fashion, does that indicate that Dr. Buchele as an individual ought to bear any of Mr. Stinnett's loss?

5. If Dr. Buchele was at fault there might be good warrant for holding him responsible and making him shoulder the loss. *Was* he at fault? Surely it is foreseeable that one might fall from the roof if no safety gear is provided. Why is the defendant not then held negligent? Why is this not at least a jury question?

———

HALEK v. UNITED STATES, 178 F.3d 481 (7th Cir.1999). A mesh cage around the defendant's elevator pulley protected mechanics working on the elevator from getting caught in the pulley. The cage was not removable, but it had an open side. Attempting to retrieve a fallen bolt, which could have been done safely if the cage could have been removed, the plaintiff mechanic fell and his hand was caught in the moving pulley with most serious harms resulting. POSNER, C.J.: "Some hazards are so perspicuous that their mere existence is an adequate warning and thus discharges the landowner's duty of care.... [T]he obviousness of a risk may make the likelihood of its materializing so slight that there is no need to try to eliminate the risk." Nevertheless, the trial judge's finding of negligence was not clearly erroneous because the danger may not have been warning enough to eliminate any significant risk of injury.

BERNIER v. BOSTON EDISON CO.

Supreme Judicial Court of Massachusetts, 1980.
380 Mass. 372, 403 N.E.2d 391.

KAPLAN, JUSTICE.

About 2:30 p.m., May 24, 1972, the plaintiffs Arthur Bernier, Jr., and Patricia J. Kasputys, then eighteen and fifteen years old, were let out of school and, after going to Kasputys's house, sauntered to an ice cream parlor on Massachusetts Avenue in Lexington Center, one of the town's major shopping areas. A half hour later, Alice Ramsdell entered her 1968 Buick Skylark automobile parked, pointed east, on the south side of Massachusetts Avenue (which here runs west-east), in the last metered space about fifteen to twenty feet short of where the avenue meets Muzzey Street, a one-way street beginning at the avenue and running south. No traffic signals were posted at the junction with Muzzey Street.

As Ramsdell started her car, she noted, checking her rear-view and side-view mirrors, that there was a car—later identified as a Cadillac convertible driven by John Boireau—some seventy-five feet behind her. She wanted to make a right turn on Muzzey Street. Just before pulling out, Ramsdell observed that the Cadillac was much closer to her than before. Boireau, too, wished to turn right onto Muzzey Street. As there were no cars ahead of her before the intersection, Ramsdell thought she could make the turn before the Cadillac interfered.

As Ramsdell was pulling left slightly away from the curb, Boireau passed her traveling (as he said) about five miles an hour. Whether Ramsdell's car then "bolted" out and struck Boireau's car as he was negotiating the right turn, or Boireau turned into Ramsdell's car as the two attempted to make the turn, was the subject of conflicting testimony. So, too, the estimates of Ramsdell's speed on impact with Boireau varied from five to thirty miles an hour. Both drivers said they recognized the trouble and braked, but not before a minor collision occurred some ten to fifteen feet into the Muzzey Street intersection, Boireau's right front fender being slightly dented by contact with Ramsdell's left front fender.

What might have been a commonplace collision turned into a complicated accident. On impact, Ramsdell, a woman of sixty-nine, hit her head against her steering wheel and suffered a bloody nose. She testified she "lost complete control of that car." Dazed, she unknowingly let her foot slip from the power brake to the gas pedal. In the result, after veering right around Boireau's car and perhaps slowing slightly, she accelerated across the remaining twenty feet of Muzzey Street, bounced to the south sidewalk, about nine feet wide, of Massachusetts Avenue, and moved about fifty-five feet down the sidewalk. On this passage the car scraped the front of a camera store, hit and levelled a parking meter, struck and damaged extensively the right rear section of a Chevrolet Chevelle automobile (the third parked car beyond Muzzey Street), knocked down an electric light pole owned by the defendant Boston Edison Company (Edison), and struck the plaintiffs who had left the ice cream parlor and were walking side by side west, into the face of the oncoming car. There was much confusion at trial whether, after hitting the meter and car, Ramsdell first hit the pole and then the plaintiffs, or first the plaintiffs and then the pole, but no one denied she hit all three. The car came to a stop two to three feet over the stump of the pole with its left wheels in the gutter and its right wheels on the sidewalk, and in contact with the Chevelle.

The electric light pole, when hit, fell away from Ramsdell's car toward the east, struck a Volkswagen automobile parked along Massachusetts Avenue (the fourth car from Muzzey Street), and came down across the legs of Bernier. Boireau was able with help to lift the pole off Bernier. Bernier's thighs and left shin bone were broken, the latter break causing a permanently shortened left leg; and he had other related injuries. Kasputys lay within two feet of the pole further in from the curb than Bernier. There was no eyewitness testimony that she had been struck by the pole. She was unconscious and vomiting. She suffered a skull fracture on the right side of her head where pieces of metal and length of wire were found imbedded, and developed permanent pain in her left lower leg.

[Bernier and Kasputys sued Ramsdell, Boireau, and Edison. The claims against Edison alleged that it had negligently designed, selected, constructed and maintained the pole. The jury found against Ramsdell and Edison. Edison appeals.]

1. *Negligence issues.* [T]he gravamen of the plaintiffs' case, as it appeared at trial, was that Edison had failed through negligence to design a pole that was accommodated reasonably to foreseeable vehicular impacts so as to avoid pedestrian injuries, and that the continued use of the pole created an unreasonable risk of such injuries.

As designer or codesigner of the pole and in control of its maintenance, Edison "must anticipate the environment in which its product will be used, and it must design against the reasonably foreseeable risk attending the product's use in that setting." Certainly the evidence showed that a risk of automobiles colliding with Edison poles—in particular No. 6 poles—was not only foreseeable but well known to the company. About 100 to 120 Edison poles a year were knocked down in such collisions in Edison's "Northeast Service Center" which included Lexington. . . . A so-called "knock down truck" worked steadily replacing downed poles in the district and installing new ones, and there were estimates by employees that in their years of field work they had replaced "thousands" of Edison poles. One employee said he had been personally involved in replacing at least a hundred poles of the type involved in the accident at bar.

As in the case of vehicles, design should take into account "foreseeable participation in collisions." And for the speeds to be encountered and consequences entailed in collisions, one analyzes the whole "setting." This was a busy shopping area with heavy pedestrian and vehicular traffic.

... Edison installed this No. 6 pole on February 3, 1949. It was of reinforced concrete, twenty-six feet nine inches in height, and ran from an eight inch base to a 5–3/8 inch top diameter. Four anchor bolts held it to a base that extended 4–2/3 feet below the surface. The pole was hollow, allowing for feeder wires to come from an underground cable up to the luminaire. Implanted in the concrete shaft were six vertical steel rods, each .375 (3/8) inch thick. Total weight of the pole and luminaire structure was 1,200 pounds.

What precautions were taken in the design to guard against the risk of pedestrian injury through collapse of a No. 6 pole upon impact by a vehicle? According to the evidence, the problem was not seriously adverted to.... Overall, the major considerations in Edison's design of poles (including their materials) seemed to be cost, adaptability to Edison's existing system of power supply and connecting apparatus, and capacity of Edison employees to install the poles safely.[2]

... To begin with, since injuries might be serious (as the present case indeed indicated), the likelihood of accidents need not be high to warrant careful consideration of safety features.

The plaintiffs' major witness concerning design safety was Howard Simpson, who had a doctorate in engineering and practiced as a consulting structural engineer. His qualifications as an expert on the strength of reinforced concrete were unchallenged. In his opinion, the concrete of the thickness specified for No. 6 poles lacked "ductility," the quality which would allow a pole, when struck by a car, to absorb part of the impact and bend without breaking. No. 6 would shatter when hit with sufficient force; indeed, one of the Edison supervisors testified about No. 6 that the concrete "all crumbles at the point of impact." As the exposed steel rods could not then support the weight of the pole, it would fall. As to the force sufficient to break No. 6 in this fashion, Simpson testified that the pole would succumb to a 1968 Buick Skylark with a passenger, spare tire, and full gas tank going as slowly as six m.p.h. A medium-sized truck weighing 10,000 pounds could level No. 6 when traveling at 1.5 m.p.h.

Simpson went on to say that the strength of the pole could have been substantially improved by using steel rods of larger diameter or by placing steel "hoops" or "spirals" perpendicular to those vertical rods. In his opinion the latter device would have enabled the pole to withstand the impact of the Buick at 11 m.p.h.—an important advance, as a car going 9 m.p.h. has an energy considerably greater than that at 6 m.p.h.

---

2. It is fair to mention, however, that one engineer thought metal poles might have been passed over because they would tend to become electrified when downed and subject pedestrians to shock. Another thought pedestrian safety was adequately handled by having a reputable manufacturer fabricate the poles. There was some indication that Edison did not install so-called "breakaway" poles in areas such as Lexington Center because of danger to pedestrians.

Such hoops and spirals had been in use since the early 1900's in columns for buildings. Simpson calculated the cost per pole of the hoops at $5.75 and the spirals at $17.50.

We should add here that there was evidence from Edison employees of the existence of other pole-types, possibly of greater strength, that would at least have warranted comparison by Edison with the No. 6 pole in respect to safety values. Various metal poles (aluminum and steel) might have deserved such study. Edison's own No. 26, of prestressed concrete, designed in 1968, might have been an improvement....

Edison argues that a finding of negligence here left it in the grip of a "polycentric" problem. If it chose to protect pedestrians by using stronger poles, motorists might be more seriously injured when they hit poles which did not break. If it chose to protect motorists, pedestrians would claim recovery when poles fell on them. No designer or owner, Edison added, is required to make or use a product wholly accident-free. There is some disingenuousness in this argument as the evidence shows Edison paid scant attention in the design of the No. 6 pole to the safety either of motorists or pedestrians. But we think there is nothing in the argument to relieve Edison of a duty to take precautions against knock-downs by cars, and it would seem reasonable for Edison to consider pedestrian safety with particular seriousness. Persons in a car are protected by a metal and glass shield sometimes three times as heavy as the pole's entire weight; pedestrians are exposed. Whether drivers are hurt any less by impact at similar speeds with poles that topple than with poles that bend rather than fall is unknown to us and apparently to Edison as well. To be sure, many more cars will hit poles than poles will hit pedestrians, but a six m.p.h. threshold for cars, and less for trucks, seems little protection indeed.

... Here the jury could rationally find negligence of design and maintenance. They could find that the vehicular speed at which No. 6 would topple was grievously low, creating an unacceptable risk of grave injury to persons at the scene (who in shopping areas such as Lexington Center might be numerous). The impact resistance of the pole could have been improved by relatively minor alterations available at the time and not inconveniencing Edison or the public, or possibly by the use of another type of pole with greater resistance. "In balancing all the pertinent factors, the jury made a judgment as to the social acceptability of the design...."

... Judgments affirmed.

Notes

1. What factors are important to the court's belief that negligence was proved?

2. Do you have a good idea just how risky it was to use these poles? How much benefit was there in using these poles? To whom did the benefit, if any, flow? Suppose falling poles will cause one pedestrian injury per year

in Boston, on the order of a broken leg, and sturdier poles will cause two fractured skulls per year in Boston when motorists collide. What if the motorist injuries are caused in part by fault on the part of the motorist but the pedestrian injuries all involve non-faulty pedestrians?

3. The defendant's manhole cover sat high in its metal rim because dirt had accumulated under it. The plaintiff fell and suffered injury because of the slight rise. Is it relevant to any issue in the case that defendant's meter reader read the meter beneath the cover once a month? *Banks v. New Orleans Sewerage and Water Bd.,* 728 So.2d 527 (La.App.1999).

4. Is fault easy to assess here? Should we apportion some responsibility to Boston Edison, some to Mrs. Ramsdell? If the negligent actors are liable only for a portion of the harm, does that dilute the deterrent effect?

——————

GIANT FOOD, INC. v. MITCHELL, 334 Md. 633, 640 A.2d 1134 (1994). Plaintiff was shopping in the defendant's store. The defendant's employee, spotting an apparent shoplifter, pursued him. The seeming shoplifter fled, knocking down the plaintiff in the process of his escape. The plaintiff claimed that the store owner was negligent in pursuing the shoplifter because it was reasonably foreseeable that the fleeing shoplifter would run into the store's customers. *Held,* as a matter of law, the attempted recovery of property here did not expose invitees to unreasonable risk of harm. The fact that injury was foreseeable does not by itself show negligence. Rather, the "degree of risk of harm to invitees must be weighed against the privilege" to protect one's property.

PARSONS v. CROWN DISPOSAL CO., 15 Cal.4th 456, 936 P.2d 70, 63 Cal.Rptr.2d 291 (1997). The plaintiff was riding a horse. He was thrown when the defendant's garbage truck, operating in a normal manner, startled the horse with loud noises. *Held,* summary judgment for defendant affirmed. The social value of the interest the defendant is seeking to advance is the chief factor to consider. There is no reason to doubt that garbage collection activity is a vital public service and a matter of high social utility. A defendant is not negligent merely because he uses a machine that produces noises necessary to its regular operation, even though fright of horses might be foreseeable.

Note

In thinking about the preceding cases (and others), distinguish among these questions: (1) Does the court state an appropriate factor in determining liability? (2) Does the court state the test or factor fully and technically or does it state the gist only? (3) Did the court apply the test appropriately to the facts? Could you accept the court's opinion as an adequate statement of principle and still think it was wrongly applied?

UNITED STATES v. CARROLL TOWING CO.

United States Court of Appeals, Second Circuit, 1947.
159 F.2d 169.

L. HAND, CIRCUIT JUDGE.

[Proceedings in admiralty involving several different entities interested in the collision and sinking of a barge, the Anna C. Connors owned the barge, which was loaded with flour. Grace Line employees, operating the Carroll Towing Company tug, negligently caused the Anna C to break adrift. She was carried by wind and tide against a tanker, whose propeller broke a hole in her bottom. Connors' bargee was not on board, and the damage was not reported to anyone. Had there been a bargee there, the Grace Line employees, who had pumps available, could have saved the Anna C; as it was, she careened, dumped her cargo of flour, and sank. The court first held that Grace Line and Carroll Towing were liable, and then considered whether the absence of a bargee on board the Anna C was negligence that reduced recovery to Connors.]

It appears from the foregoing review that there is no general rule to determine when the absence of a bargee or other attendant will make the owner of the barge liable for injuries to other vessels if she breaks away from her moorings.... It becomes apparent why there can be no such general rule, when we consider the grounds for such a liability. Since there are occasions when every vessel will break from her moorings, and since, if she does, she becomes a menace to those about her; the owner's duty, as in other similar situations, to provide against resulting injuries is a function of three variables: (1) The probability that she will break away; (2) the gravity of the resulting injury, if she does; (3) the burden of adequate precautions. Possibly it serves to bring this notion into relief to state it in algebraic terms: if the probability be called P; the injury, L; and the burden, B; liability depends upon whether B is less than L multiplied by P: i.e., whether $B < PL$. Applied to the situation at bar, the likelihood that a barge will break from her fasts and the damage she will do, vary with the place and time; for example, if a storm threatens, the danger is greater; so it is, if she is in a crowded harbor where moored barges are constantly being shifted about. On the other hand, the barge must not be the bargee's prison, even though he lives aboard; he must go ashore at times.... In the case at bar the bargee left at five o'clock in the afternoon of January 3rd, and the flotilla broke away at about two o'clock in the afternoon of the following day, twenty-one hours afterwards. The bargee had been away all the time, and we hold that his fabricated story was affirmative evidence that he had no excuse for his absence. At the locus in quo—especially during the short January days and in the full tide of war activity—barges were being constantly "drilled" in and out. Certainly it was not beyond reasonable expectation that, with the inevitable haste and bustle, the work might not be done with adequate care. In such circumstances we hold—and it is all that we do hold—that it was a fair requirement that the Conners Company should have a bargee aboard (unless he had some excuse for his absence), during the working hours of daylight.

Notes

1. According to Judge Hand, which if any of the following factors are important in determining a defendant's negligence? (a) the cost of making the defendant's activity safer; (b) the social usefulness of the activity; (c) the probability of any harm from the activity; (d) the likely amount of harm if any harm results.

2. Notice that the party asserting negligence first identifies some specific act of negligence, by pointing to what the defendant did or did not do and identifying some specific safer conduct that might have been pursued. If the alternative conduct was safer, the court will want to know how much safer and something about its costs. What was the specific alternative conduct Judge Hand was considering in *Carroll Towing*?

3. Suppose that, by not having a bargee on board at all times, the barge would break loose and cause damage to itself or others about once a year, and that the average damage was $25,000. Suppose also that the cost of keeping a bargee on board at all times to prevent this would be an average of $30,000 a year. Judge Hand seems to say this would be a case of no negligence, and Judge Posner says this is correct because the function of the fault system is to impose liability rules that will bring about "efficient" or cost-justified rules of safety. A rule that required the barge owner to spend $30,000 to save $25,000 would be inefficient and not cost-justified. See Richard A. Posner, *A Theory of Negligence*, 1 J. Leg. Studies 29, 32 (1972).

4. Consider the hypothetical variation of *Carroll Towing* given in note 3. Where does probability come in? It is built into the "average." Suppose that the probability is that the barge without a full-time bargee will break loose once every *other* year with the damage of $25,000. The probability of harm is reduced, and this will be reflected in a new average—$12,500 instead of $25,000. Try working this out the other way—by supposing that the barge will break loose *twice* a year. Would it then be negligent not to have a full-time bargee?

5. In the light of this kind of thinking, reconsider the *Brown v. Stiel* problem.

6. Judge Hand says in *Carroll Towing* that "the owner's duty ... is a function of three variables...." Does it seem to you that he is really assuming a duty of reasonable care and then addressing the question of negligence?

NOTE: APPLYING THE RISK–UTILITY FORMULA

1. *Estimating risks*. Everything we do carries *some* risk. In applying the Hand formula, how do we know the degree of risk attributable to the defendant's activity? One answer might be that Hand was not proposing a formula into which actual numbers could be substituted for the "algebra." Instead, Hand might have been proposing only a model,

an indication about the nature of the decision or estimate we need to make. Do the cases preceding *Carroll Towing* suggest that courts were estimating comparative risks of the defendant's conduct and some supposedly safer alternative?

2. *Estimating costs or benefits.* How do you *know* how much a safety precaution would cost or how much the activity benefits people? Almost any activity has *some* benefit and almost any safety precaution has *some* costs. It is much easier to reduce costs and benefits to numbers than it is to do the same for risks. That is so because many costs can be identified in dollar-numbers. Benefits can also be identified in dollar-numbers by asking about the earnings, savings, or increase in capital value effected by the activity. Do the cases preceding *Carroll Towing* suggest that courts were estimating costs or benefits of the defendant's conduct compared to some supposedly safer alternative?

3. *The forgotten gopher hole.* As you leave your house one morning, on the way to try a tort case, you observe that a burrowing animal has dug a hole in your yard, very close to the sidewalk. Recognizing that the hole is a risk to anyone who might step off the sidewalk, you make a mental note to fill the hole or barricade it as soon as you get home. At the end of a long, hard day before a hostile jury, an irascible judge, and an unappreciative client, you have forgotten the hole. You plop in front of the television. In the meantime, the plaintiff, a neighbor on his way to bring you a misdelivered copy of *Torts Illustrated*, steps off the sidewalk in the dark, and breaks his ankle as he falls in the hole. Are you negligent? Does *Carroll Towing Co.* help you decide?

4. *The putative memory requirement.* Courts sometimes hold the actor to memory of dangerous conditions of which he had knowledge in the recent past, even though the ordinary prudent person will no doubt sometimes forget. See Mark Grady, *Why Are People Negligent? Technology, Non Durable Precautions, and the Medical Malpractice Explosion*, 82 Nw. U. L. Rev. 293 (1988); but cf. Restatement Second of Torts § 289 (1965) (memory of the reasonable person is required). Would such a rule help decide the case of the gopher hole? Could it possibly be consistent with the *Carroll Towing* formula?

5. *Costs of memory.* An engineer fails to blow a whistle at a crossing, and a collision with a car results. Blowing a whistle is cost-free, so it sounds as if the *Carroll Towing* formula could readily be applied: there is at least some risk in failing to sound the whistle and it costs nothing to do it; therefore, failure to do it is negligent. But from the railroad's point of view, the actual cost of preventing the engineer's inattention might be very high indeed. The railroad might be required to design a computer-controlled system to make the whistle blow, or to pay for a second engineer to help remind the first that whistles are important. This cost might be very great indeed. See Izhak Englard, *The System Builders: A Critical Appraisal of Modern American Tort Theory*, 9 J. Leg. Studies 27 (1980). How would lawyers, judges, and juries ever really know how much the costs would be?

6. *Costs of information.* The actor only needs to consider those risks that would be taken into account by a reasonable person. This is why courts discuss whether harm is "foreseeable"; they limit liability to cases in which the actor can recognize a risk or danger. Suppose the railroad above could reduce the speed of its trains by five miles an hour and thereby save an average of $25,000 a year in injury costs. Suppose this would cost the railroad only $10,000. It will be more efficient in this case to reduce the speed. But suppose the railroad does not know this and cannot find out without spending a great deal of money to make a study. Suppose the railroad doesn't even realize that it could find out? Information about the existence and degree of risk is itself an item of cost. Can you apply the *Carroll Towing* formula to such a case?

7. *Variable probabilities and costs.* Look back at *Indiana Consolidated Ins. Co. v. Mathew.* What if leaving the burning mower in the garage created a 90% probability of fire damage to the garage of about $10,000 and no more, but a 5% probability of fire totally destroying the house at a loss of $100,000, a 4% probability of a fire spread that would cause losses of more than a million dollars and a 1% probability of no harm. Does it seem preposterous to say that the jury should somehow factor all this in to its negligence decision?

8. What is the proper scope of *Carroll Towing*'s risk-utility formula? Professor Latin points out that many routine cases involve nothing more than mistake and momentary inattention. Howard Latin, *"Good" Warnings, Bad Products, and Cognitive Limitations,* 41 U.C.L.A. L. Rev. 1193 (1994). If he is right, and if normative rules should be based upon realistic assessment behavioral patterns, should *Carroll Towing*'s formula be discarded for routine automobile accidents? Where does the formula work best?

NOTE: EVALUATING THE RISK–UTILITY ASSESSMENT

1. *What values?* What values or tort goals does the risk-utility assessment foster? Since everything we do carries some degree of risk, one argument for a risk-utility assessment is that it provides deterrence in the "right" amount. Relatedly, it maximizes community resources, for the community is richer if its members do not spend $10 to save someone else $5.

2. Although economically oriented lawyers often like the risk-utility formula as Hand expressed it in *Carroll Towing,* there has been a strong current of objection to it so far as it emphasizes wealth or money. One approach says that basic liberties–freedom of action and security– are primary and take precedence over considerations of wealth. Under this approach, security from harm would be weighed against freedom of action, one basic liberty against another, but losses of liberty would not be offset by increases in wealth. See Gregory C. Keating, *Reasonableness and Rationality in Negligence Theory,* 48 Stan. L. Rev. 311, 383 (1996). But don't losses or gains in wealth–costs or benefits under the *Carroll Towing* formula–represent freedom of action?

3. *Alternatives to the risk-utility formula?* If you reject a weighing of risks and utilities, costs and benefits, how could you judge whether the defendant is negligent? Consider: Juries could judge (1) intuitively in a conclusory fashion, "it seems negligent to me"; (2) solely by statutory prescriptions such as speed limits; (3) by hard-and-fast rules developed by judicial prescriptions, like the rule that you are always negligent if you drive so that you cannot stop within the range of your vision; (4) by custom of the community or the business involved; (5) by a moral rule that imposes liability if the defendant did anything more risky than he would have done to prevent the same harm to himself or his own property. How does the *Carroll Towing* formula stack up among the alternatives?

4. Is the risk-utility assessment a matter of policy or a matter of justice? If policy, what policy?

5. On the risk-utility balance generally see DOBBS ON TORTS §§ 144– 146 (2000).

§ 2. ASSESSING RESPONSIBILITY WHEN MORE THAN ONE PERSON IS NEGLIGENT

Cases in the last section make it clear that unreasonably risky conduct of several persons may work together to cause harm to the plaintiff. In fact, most tort cases probably involve at least two tortfeasors who contribute to the harm done. To analyze and evaluate such cases properly, we need to understand as clearly as possible that liability of one person does not necessarily exclude liability of another. Equally, we need to understand how responsibility is apportioned–that is, who will pay what for damages caused. We deal with more advanced issues about this topic later on. For now, we can set out the structure of apportionment you should have in mind as we begin to read negligence cases.

In considering the rules set out in this section, you might want to have in mind a case like *Bernier v. Boston Edison Co.*, covered in the last section. Suppose that the jury found Mrs. Ramsdell to be chargeable with 20% of the fault and Boston Edison with 80%.

(1) Comparative fault. If Mrs. Ramsdell had been injured and sued Boston Edison, the rules in most states would allow her to recover, but with her damages reduced in proportion to her fault. The plaintiff's recovery is not ordinarily reduced to reflect her fault when the defendant is guilty of an intentional tort, but they are nowadays generally reduced in negligence and strict liability cases. The idea is that each faulty party must bear his or her share of the losses. The defendant's liability is correspondingly reduced so that he pays less than all of the plaintiff's damages. In some cases, the plaintiff actually recovers nothing at all, even though the defendant is also negligent in a substantial way.

(2) Apportionment among defendants. What would happen in the suits by Bernier and Kasputys against Boston Edison and Ramsdell if those defendants were chargeable with 80% and 20% of the fault respectively? Since both are negligent, it looks as if both should share in payments to the plaintiff. Ideally, then, Boston Edison would pay 80% of the damages for Bernier's permanently shortened leg and Kasputys' permanent pain and other injuries. Correspondingly, Ramsdell would pay 20% of those damages. Tort law recognizes this ideal by adopting one of two systems to accomplish it. One of these systems, called the joint and several liability system, also tries to accommodate some other ideals.

(3) Joint and Several Liability. "Joint and several liability" sounds mysterious. Joint and several liability means that the plaintiff can enforce her tort claim against either tortfeasor. She can actually obtain a judgment against both, but she cannot collect more than her full damages. Although it looks as if Kasputys had very substantial damages indeed, let's suppose for convenience that her damages came to $10,000. Under the rule of joint and several liability, the plaintiff might enforce that judgment entirely against either Boston Edison or against Ramsdell. But that is not the end of the story.

(4) Contribution. If Boston Edison paid the entire judgment of $10,000, it would be paying more than its fair share of the damages relative to Ramsdell. Under the joint and several liability system, most states would allow Boston Edison to obtain *contribution* from Ramsdell so as to make its payments proportional to its fault. Under today's rules, if Ramsdell's fault were 20% of the whole and Boston Edison's fault were 80%, Boston Edison should recover contribution from Ramsdell equal to 20% of the damages or $2,000. What is the net cost to Boston Edison after recovery of contribution? Do the rules of joint and several liability plus the rules of contribution carry out the goals of tort law?

Example of Joint and Several Liability With Contribution

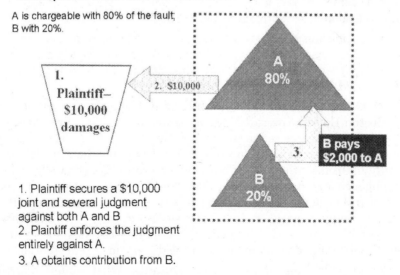

A is chargeable with 80% of the fault; B with 20%.

1.
Plaintiff—
$10,000
damages

2. $10,000

A
80%

3.   B pays $2,000 to A

B
20%

1. Plaintiff secures a $10,000 joint and several judgment against both A and B
2. Plaintiff enforces the judgment entirely against A.
3. A obtains contribution from B.

In the diagram, the plaintiff is not at fault and recovers all her losses resulting from the injury. Defendant A, although initially liable for all the losses, eventually recoups contribution from B. The net result is that A, who is chargeable with 80% of the fault, ultimately pays 80% of the plaintiff's damages and B, with 20% of the fault, pays 20%. The principle applies, of course, without regard to the amount of the damages.

(5) Insolvent or immune tortfeasors. Suppose hypothetically that Mrs. Ramsdell had no insurance and no personal assets from which Kasputys could collect a judgment. Or suppose that Mrs. Ramsdell for some reason was immune to tort liability. (As bad as it sounds, it is true that some wrongdoers are free to commit torts without any liability.) On these suppositions, the joint and several liability rule means that the plaintiff would recover her damages from Boston Edison but that as a practical matter Boston Edison could not recover contribution, either because Mrs. Ramsdell had an immunity or because she had no assets with which to pay contribution. The joint and several liability system, then, in effect requires the solvent tortfeasor, Boston Edison, to pick up and pay the insolvent, uninsured, or immune tortfeasor's share. In such a case, the law's ideal–payment proportioned to fault–is not achieved. What other important goal is being accommodated by the joint and several liability system?

(6) Several liability and comparative fault apportionment among tortfeasors. An alternative scheme of apportionment has been enacted in a substantial number of states. We'll call it several liability, proportionate share liability, or comparative fault liability. In the several or proportionate share systems, the trier of fact makes a comparative fault apportionment of liability. This several liability system differs from joint liability in that no tortfeasor is liable for more than his proportionate share. On our hypothetical assumptions about *Bernier*, the plaintiffs there would collect only 80% of their damages from Boston Edison in a several liability system, because Boston Edison's fault was only 80% of the whole set of faults. Thus contribution is not needed. The plaintiff would have to take her chances on collecting the remaining 20% from Mrs. Ramsdell. If Mrs. Ramsdell for any reason could not pay, the plaintiffs would bear 20% of their own losses.

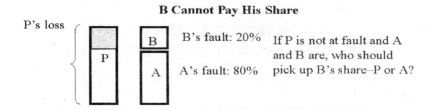

B Cannot Pay His Share

P's loss

B — B's fault: 20%

A — A's fault: 80%

If P is not at fault and A and B are, who should pick up B's share–P or A?

(7) Evaluating the two systems for apportioning loss. When tortfeasor A is fully insured and tortfeasor B has neither insurance nor assets, which system is more consistent with tort goals, the joint and several liability system or the comparative apportionment system?

(8) Recapping. This is a lot of specialized information to absorb at one time. Maybe the best recap is to try your hand at applying the rules for sharing damages liabilities. Suppose:

(a) Patricia, a single mother often up at night with her child, is sleepy while driving to work. Dunn, driving a truck, attempts to cross the street in front of Patricia. Patricia was probably slow in hitting her brakes. She broadsided Dunn's truck. Dunn wasn't injured but Patricia was. The jury finds that Dunn's fault was 90%, Patricia's 10% and that her damages come to $10,000. What amount of money must Dunn (or his liability insurance company) pay under the rules followed in most states?

(b) Agatha and Bert are each driving a car. Both are negligent and they collide in a city intersection. The force of the collision causes Bert to lose control. Consequently, his car strikes a pedestrian, Paul. Paul's injury results in medical expense, loss of wages, and pain. The jury assesses his damages at $100,000 and finds that Agatha's negligence was 75% of the whole, while Bert's was only 25%. (i) In a joint and several liability system, suppose that both Agatha and Bert are insured for liability or otherwise able to pay, but Paul enforces the judgment solely against Bert. What does Bert pay and what contribution rights does he have? (ii) If Agatha is insolvent and uninsured, what is Bert's position in a joint and several liability system? (iii) in a several liability with comparative fault apportionment?

§ 3. PROVING AND EVALUATING CONDUCT

The plaintiff must prove each element of the case by a preponderance of the evidence, that is, by the greater weight of the evidence. Negligence, for example, must be shown to be more probable than not. The trier of facts, in other words, must reasonably believe that the probability of negligence exceeds one-half. See David Kaye, *Probability Theory Meets Res Ipsa Loquitor*, 77 MICH. L. REV. 1456, 1467 (1979).

a. *Proving Conduct*

GIFT v. PALMER

Supreme Court of Pennsylvania, 1958.
392 Pa. 628, 141 A.2d 408.

BELL, JUSTICE.

[Action by Robert Gift for injury. The trial judge entered a nonsuit, the effect of which is similar to a directed verdict for defendant.]

The evidence is very meager. Defendant was driving east along Mt. Oliver Street in Pittsburgh. There was no direct evidence of how the accident (which happened in the middle of the block) occurred. Five minutes before the accident, Mrs. Jesse (a neighbor), who was a block away, saw Robert Gift, aged 3, and his sister Jeanne, sitting on their front doorstep playing with two little girls.

Robert's mother testified that a couple of days after the accident, defendant came to see her and said that he told her, "coming up our street he said that he felt something hit his front bumper and he had thought it was a stone and kept going until he looked in his rear view mirror and he saw my son lying in the street. . . . Then he stopped and picked him up." The day was clear, the street was 30 feet wide with trolley tracks in the middle, and no cars were parked on the south side. Although the law is clearly settled by countless cases, it seems necessary for us to repeat certain well established pertinent principles. A child three years old cannot be guilty of contributory negligence. The mere happening of an accident is not evidence of negligence. Plaintiff must prove by a fair preponderance of the evidence that the defendant was negligent and that his negligence was the proximate cause of the accident. Negligence is the want of due care which a reasonable man would exercise under the circumstances. Conduct is negligent only if the harmful consequences thereof could reasonably have been foreseen and prevented by the exercise of reasonable care. . . .

In Finnin v. Neubert, 378 Pa. 40, 105 A.2d 77, 78, supra, this Court directed a nonsuit under the following evidence: When defendant's automobile was about half-way through the intersection of the two streets, his wife yelled to him, "Look out for that kid and then the next thing I knew I then saw his feet were up in front of the windshield." Defendant never saw the plaintiff, who was 11 years old (and who was so badly injured that he could not remember any details of the accident), until his automobile hit him. The accident happened in broad daylight.

In the instant case there was no eye witness to the accident; there was no evidence of the speed of defendant's automobile; there was no evidence where Robert Gift was just prior to the accident; there was no evidence where he was at the time of the accident, when he bumped into the front fender of defendant's car; there was no evidence of facts or circumstances showing as the only reasonable conclusion that defendant could have seen Robert was in a place of danger and was likely to run into or be struck by his automobile and that defendant could have, by the exercise of reasonable care, stopped his automobile in time to avoid the accident.

Deep sympathy for this boy does not justify a Court finding negligence where no negligence was proved.

Judgment of nonsuit Affirmed.

Notes

1. A directed verdict is literally a direction to the jury to sign a verdict for the defendant. In some states the procedure is to "nonsuit" the plaintiff instead, but the effect is much the same.

2. In *Gift* there was *some* proof, but the judge took the case from the jury anyway. Why? Could reasonable persons find the defendant negligent? The problem in *Gift* has to do with the absence of proof about specific conduct. Could a reasonable person listen to the proof in *Gift* and state exactly how the defendant should have altered his conduct to make it safer? Was he driving too fast? Did he fail to keep a proper lookout?

UPCHURCH v. ROTENBERRY

Supreme Court of Mississippi, 2000.
761 So.2d 199.

PITTMAN, PRESIDING JUSTICE, for the Court....

On the night of October 5, 1992, the decedent, Timothy Adam Upchurch, was riding in the passenger seat of Teresa Rotenberry's car while Rotenberry was driving. Adam was the only passenger in the car. The car was traveling west on Highway 182 in Oktibbeha County, Mississippi when Rotenberry lost control of her vehicle. Upchurch claims Teresa left the road suddenly without warning, causing injuries and damages to the decedent that resulted in his death. [The plaintiff sued for wrongful death of her son. The jury found for the defendant. The plaintiff moved for judgment n.o.v. The trial court overruled the motion and this appeal followed.]

[There were no eyewitnesses except Rotenberry. One expert, Rosenhan, however, testified from evidence at the scene that Rotenberry's vehicle traveled in a straight line from the point it left the road to the point it hit the tree 160 feet away, that there were no scuff or skid marks, and that the vehicle's speed when it hit the tree was 60 mph.]

The speed the vehicle was traveling when it struck the tree, as well as, whether the vehicle left any marks either on the roadway or the area between leaving the road and striking the tree is ... disputed in this case. Rotenberry's expert, Thomas Shaeffer, testified that there were tire marks which began on the road and proceeded off the road, through the grass, and down toward the tree. Shaeffer identified these marks as yaw marks. Shaeffer defines yaw marks as a mark a tire makes when it is still rotating but not traveling in the direction that it is oriented....

On direct examination, Shaeffer testified that the car was traveling approximately 25 to 35 mph when it hit the tree. However, on cross examination, Shaeffer testified that the car was going 42 to 50 mph when it made impact with the tree.

Rotenberry introduced into evidence photographs to corroborate the conclusions of Shaeffer....

Shaeffer also testified that he observed small pebbles wedged between the rim and tire on both the front left and rear left wheels of the vehicle. This is additional evidence that the vehicle made an extreme right hand turn. All of the evidence presented at trial by Shaeffer was consistent with the vehicle making an evasive maneuver to the right in order to avoid an object on the roadway. Shaeffer's final determination was that the car struck the tree and flipped over on its top, which undoubtedly caused additional damage to the vehicle.

Rotenberry testified as an adverse witness. Throughout the discovery proceedings and at the trial itself, Rotenberry testified that she could not remember the events leading up to the accident including a two-day period just prior to the accident. However, on November 13, 1992 (about 5 weeks after the accident), Rotenberry did sign a written statement detailing the accident. In this statement, Rotenberry testified that a large animal, either a deer or a dog, ran across the road and into her lane ultimately causing her to leave the road. . . .

In her brief, Upchurch raises the issue that Kirk Rosenhan, plaintiff's expert, testified that he smelled alcohol on the defendant at the accident scene. However, on direct [cross?] examination of Rosenhan the following exchange occurred.

Q. Did you get close to Teresa Rotenberry?

A. Not really.

Q. Did you get close enough to smell her?

A. No, I didn't.

Q. Did you smell any odor of intoxicant on her?

A. Uh, not on her. . . .

On redirect examination after an overnight recess, Rosenhan changed his testimony to say that he had not been specific as to the driver of the vehicle the day before and that he did smell alcohol on the driver the night of the accident. The above exchange, however, makes it clear that Rosenhan was perfectly specific on direct examination in denying that he smelled alcohol on Rotenberry at the scene of the accident. It is noteworthy that Rosenhan did testify on direct examination that he smelled alcohol in the area. Also, the presence of beer in the car is not disputed in the facts of this case.

Larry Guyton, a trooper with the Mississippi Highway Patrol, also testified for the plaintiff. Officer Guyton testified that he arrived on the scene after Rotenberry had been taken away by ambulance. Officer Guyton spoke to Rotenberry by telephone in her hospital room two days after the accident, October 7th, and again on October 8th. Rotenberry was able to remember the accident at this point. She appeared alert during the conversation. Officer Guyton testified that Rotenberry told him that she was traveling westbound on Highway 182 near Starkville when she saw an animal coming into her lane from the opposite side of the road. She swerved to the right to avoid hitting the animal. In Officer Guyton's opinion, Rotenberry appeared to be telling him the truth.

Further, Officer Guyton testified on direct examination that Rotenberry told him that she had two beers earlier in the evening at a place called "The Landing" on Highway 182 near Starkville. On cross examination, however, Officer Guyton testified that Rotenberry did not tell him about drinking beer or about being at The Landing. He just asked her how the accident occurred, and she told him. Further, he stated that he did not put anything in his accident report concerning drinking or about being at The Landing. He continued by testifying that Rotenberry had not told him anything different than what was in his report. . . .

. . . [T]his Court concludes that reasonable and fairminded jury members could reach different conclusions. Consequently, the jury verdict stands, and the motion for JNOV is denied.

This Court will not intrude into the realm of the jury by determining the credibility of a witness and making findings of fact. The jury is the judge of the weight of the evidence and the credibility of the witnesses. Through her statement and the testimony of other witnesses, Rotenberry offered evidence explaining the events of that tragic night. The jury considered this evidence, weighed it, and found in favor of Rotenberry. . . .

This Court has been even more specific regarding the realm of the jury concerning the credibility of witnesses in stating:

> The demeanor or bearing, the tone of voice, the attitude and appearance of the witnesses, all are primarily for inspection and review by the jury. The jury not only has the right and duty to determine the truth or falsity of the witnesses, but also has the right to evaluate and determine what portions of the testimony of any witness it will accept or reject; therefore, unless it is clear to this Court that the verdict is contrary to the overwhelming weight of the credible testimony, this court will not set aside the verdict of a jury.

. . . According to its duty, the jury concluded that Rotenberry acted reasonably in swerving to the right to avoid an animal and that she did not have time to avoid a tree which lay only 160 feet (or slightly over 53 yards) from where Rotenberry left the road. The jury makes such fact determinations, not this Court. . . .

> The resolution of disputed facts such as this is a duty that devolves upon the jury sitting as finders of fact. They are charged with listening to the witnesses, observing their demeanor, and coming to their own conclusions of which evidence they find more credible. Our system of jurisprudence has determined that citizen jurors, employing their native intelligence and collective life experiences, are best qualified to make those judgments. Absent some clear indication that the jurors in a particular case somehow ignored that duty, neither the trial court, nor this Court reviewing the record on appeal, are permitted to interfere in the conclusions reached by these jurors.

Notes

The Process of Determining Fault

1. Lawyers often find it difficult to obtain facts necessary for an assessment of fault. One reason is that injuries are often caused by tiny

miscalculations, hard for the actor to appreciate and almost impossible for a jury to understand at a later date. For instance, a car traveling at 50 m.p.h. travels about 75 feet per second. The time for drivers to react to an emergency, such as a child darting into the road, varies considerably. About half of all drivers take nearly a second to respond, but some take two seconds. See LEON ROBERTSON, INJURIES, CAUSES, CONTROL STRATEGIES AND PUBLIC POLICY 42 (1983). If a driver hits a child 100 feet from the point of observation, a reaction time for hitting the brakes of one second might have been sufficient to avoid the impact, but a reaction time of two seconds would not. Or again, what about the fact that a driver may lose part of her field of vision as she gets older—and with no way to be aware of this? Studies seem to indicate that loss of visual field is commonly associated with auto injuries, yet the topic does not come up in the cases. See *id.* at 62.

2.   A second problem in obtaining facts for making a judgment about fault lies with the accuracy of testimony. A very considerable body of information indicates that witnesses are generally inaccurate in a number of particulars. Part of this lies in perception of events, which is especially difficult if they occur quickly, only once, and with violence or stress. See ELIZABETH LOFTUS, EYEWITNESS TESTIMONY (1979).

3.   A social scientist studying the process of settling tort claims in automobile accident cases has said that, in practice, evaluation of claims consists chiefly in discovering traffic violations and that though "formal tort law" concerns issues of duty, foreseeability, reasonable care and a "fine weighing" of negligence, in most auto cases a traffic violation is the central issue. H. ROSS, SETTLED OUT OF COURT 20 (1980). If this is so, is it merely a result of the negligence per se rule? Does it make it any more or any less important to find out exactly what the conduct was?

4.   As some of these paragraphs show, the process of determining fault in tort cases is difficult at best. This leads to the idea that if you try to deal with vehicle safety after injury has occurred, you must look for fault, but that if you try to prevent accidents before they occur, you might try to change the environment. For example, roads may be better designed or signals more visible. Another approach to automobile safety left the tort system altogether. This sought to require auto makers to provide safer automobiles. This approach required regulations to be issued by the National Highway Traffic Safety Administration. Current opinion indicates that, so far, this approach has not been very successful. See JERRY MASHAW & DAVID HARFST, THE STRUGGLE FOR AUTO SAFETY (1990). Does that leave us to rely upon uncertain estimates of fault?

The Credibility Rule

5.   Credibility of witnesses is almost always a question for the jury, and almost never a question for the judge. Standard instructions tell the juries to determine credibility of witnesses for themselves, considering factors such as the witnesses' demeanor and other factors mentioned in *Upchurch.* See, e.g., ILL. PATTERN JURY INSTRUCTIONS-CIVIL § 2.01 (3d Ed. 1992).

6.   *Lawyers' roles.* What is the role of the lawyers in this? Would you expect simply to gather favorable witnesses together, put their testimony on and quit? What else *could* you do?

7. *Credibility and directed verdicts.* Given the credibility rule, should the plaintiff be entitled to a directed verdict in her favor if the defendant puts on no evidence at all, or if his evidence does not contradict the plaintiff's? In *Dorn v. Leibowitz*, 387 Pa. 335, 127 A.2d 734 (1956), a pedestrian testified she crossed with the light, and was struck by a truck after she had taken five steps into the crosswalk. The defendant offered no testimony except that of a police officer, who did not contradict the plaintiff in any substantial way. The court held that the plaintiff was not entitled to a directed verdict or "binding instructions" in her favor, since her credibility was for the jury even though she was not contradicted. Some courts take the view that if the plaintiff offers testimony that is not only uncontradicted, but is clear and self-consistent, a directed verdict for the party having the burden of proof—usually the plaintiff—is permissible. See FLEMING JAMES & GEOFFREY HAZARD, CIVIL PROCEDURE 348 (3d ed. 1985). But, as one may readily imagine, there are few cases that meet such requirements.

———

FORSYTH v. JOSEPH, 80 N.M. 27, 450 P.2d 627 (App. 1968). Decedent was an occupant of a car struck by the Villa truck. The trial court found Villa to be negligent, partly because of excessive speed. There was evidence that Villa skidded 129 feet before the impact. *Held*, affirmed. "The speed limit was 55 miles per hour. The court found he was exceeding this speed and was traveling at the rate of 55 miles per hour at the point of impact. These findings are supported by the evidence. Even Villa testified that his speed 'at the point of impact' was 55 miles per hour. In addition thereto, we have the skid marks to which reference is above made, the force of the impact which knocked the Joseph vehicle about 20 or 25 feet and spun it about 90 degrees, and the continued momentum of Villa's vehicle, which carried it through the fence and into the open field where it came to a rest."

Notes

1. Circumstantial evidence–which is to say evidence of one fact that permits an inference of another fact–is often the most important evidence in tort cases. Almost all negligence cases involve at least some factual inferences. The inference may, of course, assist the defendant rather than the plaintiff. What inference would you draw if the proof showed defendant stopped her car in 33 feet?

2. Perhaps Villa did not literally mean he was traveling 55 at the point of impact. What else might he have meant? What is the responsibility of the lawyer about such a matter? Notice that Villa's admission was considered against him.

3. *Judge and jury.* Questions of fact and questions of credibility are for the jury to decide. What about *inferences* of fact, such as those involved in *Forsyth*? The answer is that the jury is also the decision maker as to inferences, provided there is room for reasonable persons to draw or reject those inferences. Judges may sometimes declare that any given inference is

one that reasonable people cannot draw on the facts of the case. If there are conflicting inferences possible, however, or if some reasonable persons would draw an inference of fact and others not, the jury must decide the matter.

4. *Evidence to assist in drawing inferences.* In many instances one might reject an inference of fact simply for lack of knowledge. Suppose the evidence is that the defendant left skid marks of 137 feet, and that his car was at a complete stop at the end of the marks. Do you know how fast he was going? What evidence could be introduced to assist a judge or jury in drawing an inference about speed?

NOTE: WITNESSES' OPINIONS AS TO FACTS AND FACTUAL INFERENCES

1. *Non-expert opinion.* Witnesses are not usually permitted to give opinions on "ultimate" issues that are reserved for jury decision in the case. For example, a witness would not be permitted to testify, "In my opinion, the defendant was negligent." The witness is required instead to state facts within his knowledge, for instance, "I saw the defendant run the red light." A few statements that might be classed as opinions are permitted, however, as a kind of shorthand or summing up of direct experience. An eyewitness may be permitted to estimate speed, distance, or intoxication, for example. It would be difficult to express any more accurately the facts on which it is based, and juries are likely to understand that the impression or estimate is no more than that.

The opinion rule reinforces the lawyer's active role in litigation. The lawyer must investigate, or obtain an investigation that produces detailed and convincing facts, and must maintain the initiative in the courtroom by presenting these facts effectively.

2. *Expert opinion.* Experts are usually allowed to give expert opinion or conclusions within the field of their expertise, provided the testimony is likely to be helpful to the jury on an issue in the case. For example, an orthopedic surgeon, examining a plaintiff who has tingling in the fingers and pain in the shoulder and neck, may infer that the patient suffers from some impingement on a nerve in the 6–7 cervical interspace of the neck. Although the surgeon may explain to the jury how she inferred the existence of an impingement, it would not be helpful to recapitulate large segments of a medical education.

For this and similar reasons, expert opinion often seems the most or only practical method of establishing certain facts, and it is usually admitted on medical issues. In the same way, investigating officers are usually allowed to give opinions about speed, distance, direction, and point of impact from evidence at the scene of a motor vehicle collision. See, e.g., *New Prospect Drilling Co. v. First Commercial Trust, N.A.,* 332 Ark. 466, 966 S.W.2d 233 (1998). But even this simple kind of testimony may be excluded if it is not helpful to the jury or the jury can readily determine the issue by interpreting the facts for themselves. See *Brugh v. Peterson*, 183 Neb. 190, 159 N.W.2d 321, 29 A.L.R.3d 236 (1968); *Johnson v. Yates*, 31 N.C.App. 358, 229 S.E.2d 309 (1976).

Expert opinion testimony raises serious issues. One very common problem is that experts often differ. One expert may testify that in her opinion the plaintiff suffers a serious paralysis that is irremediable, while another may testify that in his opinion the plaintiff is not injured at all or, if injured, will recover speedily. Juries have little basis for resolving such conflicts of opinion except on the basis of a feeling that one expert is more impressive than another–which perhaps suggests one of the reasons why courts are reluctant about opinion testimony in the first place.

A second problem with expert testimony is that the witness may not in fact be an expert at all with respect to his particular testimony; or that the expert may be an expert in some sense but still offer an opinion that is only speculation.

Another problem with expert testimony is that it may overwhelm the jury. Experts are often prestigious by reason of their professional status, and some are more or less professional witnesses whose presence and demeanor may be highly impressive. The seemingly independent status of the expert witness may suggest a disinterested appraisal, which may lend this testimony even more weight in the jury's mind, though in fact some experts become quite partisan.

Note

Should be we skeptical about our ability to resolve disputes by judging negligence? Chance plays a big role in determining whether you will recover if you are injured. As *Upchurch* shows, there may be no witness to the event other than the defendant himself; the evidence may be conflicting; and witnesses on your side may be unappealing personalities and disliked by jurors, while witnesses on the other side may be pleasant and convincing.

b. *Evaluating Conduct*

Problem

Kibler v. Maddux

You have been retained by the parents of Tommy Kibler, 4 years of age, to bring suit for Tommy's injuries. On January 6, Linda Rodriguez called Mrs. Kibler and invited Tommy to come play with her son, also 4, at her house. It was rainy and Mrs. Kibler dressed him in a slicker and took him to the Rodriguez home about 2:30. She asked Mrs. Rodriguez to call when she was ready for Tommy to come home, saying she would pick him up rather than let him cross the street alone. She had trained him to wait for her at the curb. About 4:00 Mrs. Rodriguez called and told Mrs. Kibler she would dress Tommy in his slicker and take him to the curb where Mrs. Kibler would meet him. It was anticipated that Mrs. Kibler would arrive slightly before or at the same time as Tommy, but she slipped and fell on her slippery sidewalk and walked rather slowly and painfully. Tommy arrived at the curb and waited for his mother, looking in the direction she was to come from.

In the meantime Irene Maddux was proceeding north on Spruce Street driving her car. She arrived at the crest of a slope and at that point she could see Tommy standing at the curb in his yellow slicker about 400–500 yards away. She proceeded on towards that point, driving at 20 m.p.h. because of the rain, slippery roads and gathering dusk. She watched Tommy constantly as she approached. When she reached a point she thinks was about 15 feet from Tommy, he suddenly ran out in front of her. It later became clear that he had waited somewhat longer for his mother than he expected to, and that when he saw her coming, he ran toward her. Maddux hit the brakes and also swerved to the right, but her left front fender struck Tommy and knocked him about 30 feet, causing some considerable injury.

Both sides have taken depositions and all the facts stated above are established. Defendant Maddux has moved for summary judgment on the basis of these admitted or established facts. How do you evaluate your case? What arguments can you make?

Notes

1.   In thinking about this problem, compare the case of *Gift v. Palmer, supra*. In that case the problem was that no specific act or omission was established by the plaintiff's proof, so that it was not possible to evaluate the defendant's conduct and state how it should have been safer. In *Kibler v. Maddux*, we have a good deal more information about the conduct of the defendant. What, then, is the problem for the plaintiff's attorney?

2.   In many cases, as in *Kibler*, it is possible to point to more than one act or omission that might constitute negligence. On occasion lawyers fail to perceive their best claims of negligence and argue only the most obvious. Suppose the trial judge decided to hold a brief oral argument on the defendant's motion for summary judgment, and you have an opportunity to state in what respects Ms. Maddux could be found negligent by the trier. Would your primary argument be that she was driving too fast considering the weather?

3.   Courts are reluctant to decide negligence cases on summary judgment motions. Why is this? "An inherently normative issue ... is not generally susceptible to summary judgment: the evidence requires that a jury balance the [safety precautions] against the nature and extent of the risk." *Little v. Liquid Air Corp.*, 952 F.2d 841 (5th Cir.1992). In other words, juries are often called upon to decide not merely bare facts but also to make normative evaluations of the conduct involved.

––––––

DISTRICT OF COLUMBIA v. SHANNON, 696 A.2d 1359 (D.C.App. 1997). The plaintiff was a child using a slide maintained on a playground by the District of Columbia. The side rails on the slide had open ends. The plaintiff put her thumb in the open end at the top. Her thumb was ripped out of her hand, apparently as she slid down the slide. It could not be reattached. The child settled with the slide manufacturer but pursued her claim against the District for its share of liability if any. *Held,* judgment for the plaintiff affirmed. If the appropriate care is within the realm of common knowledge and everyday experience, the plaintiff need not introduce expert testimony to establish the right amount of care. These facts presented a situation within the realm of common knowledge and experience. Hence it could rightly go to the jury without expert testimony to establish the kind of care required of playground maintainers.

JOHN Q. HAMMONS INC. v. POLETIS, 954 P.2d 1353 (Wyo.1998). A guest in defendant's motel took hold of the towel bar in the bath tub. It pulled out of the wall and he fell, suffering a back injury. Parts of the tile and wall came out with the bar and revealed the wall to be moldy and soft or putty-like. The jury found for the plaintiff. *Held,* affirmed. "Here, there was no expert testimony indicating the type of material behind the tiles or how long it would take to become crumbly and rotted. Even so, the jury could reasonably infer, based on common knowledge and ordinary human experience, that moisture had to have been accumulating behind the tiles for more than a short time for the wall to assume that appearance." It could have inferred further that defendant would have found and fixed the condition if it had been exercising reasonable care.

THOMA v. CRACKER BARREL OLD COUNTRY STORE, INC.

District Court of Appeal of Florida, First District, 1995.
649 So.2d 277.

KAHN, JUDGE . . . .

After eating breakfast at the Cracker Barrel, Thoma took three or four steps away from her table when her left foot slid out from under her, causing her to fall. The fall occurred in a common aisle, near the passage from the kitchen to the restaurant. When Thoma got up, she noticed an area 1 foot by 2 feet containing drops of clear liquid. She claims to have slipped on this liquid. Thoma was in the restaurant about thirty minutes before her accident. During that time, she saw no one drop anything on the floor in the area where she fell. [In Thoma's suit against the restaurant, the trial court granted defendant's motion for summary judgment.]

Mr. Leonard McNeal was the only known witness to the fall. He arrived at breakfast about 15 minutes before the accident. His seat was some 12 to 15 feet away from where Thoma fell. McNeal described the area as "a normal area where waitresses would frequently go in and out (the kitchen) door." McNeal felt sure he saw waitresses carrying beverage pitchers in that area. He did not see any Cracker Barrel customers carrying drinks in the area, nor did he see anyone drop or spill anything.

Cracker Barrel's manager, Mr. Charlie Gray, inspected the area of the fall and saw no foreign substance whatever on the floor. According to Mr. Gray, the Cracker Barrel is not a buffet restaurant and he would not expect customers to get up and walk around with food or drinks.

To recover for injuries incurred in a slip and fall accident, the plaintiff must show that the premises owner either created a dangerous condition or had actual or constructive knowledge of a dangerous condition. Notice of a dangerous condition may be established by circumstantial evidence, such as evidence leading to an inference that a substance has been on the floor for a sufficient length of time such that in the exercise of reasonable care the condition should have become known to the premises owner.

We have recently reversed a defense summary judgment in a similar case, Gonzalez v. Tallahassee Medical Center, Inc., 629 So.2d 945 (Fla. 1st DCA 1993). In that case, Gonzalez slipped and fell on a liquid substance that looked like water, but could have been "syrup or Sprite." Her grandson testified that ... the fall occurred near a soda drink dispenser set out for customer use and in an area where the cashier had a clear view. The grandson was in the cafeteria ten to fifteen minutes before the accident and did not hear or see anyone spill a liquid in the area of the fall. While we declined to speculate on what a jury might do with those facts, we held that inferences arose which "could establish the length of time the dangerous condition had been present on the floor, a critical element in proving that appellee, through the exercise of ordinary care, should have known of the condition."

In the present case, Thoma and McNeal took their breakfast at a location near where Thoma eventually fell. Despite their proximity, neither Thoma nor McNeal saw anyone drop or spill anything. The area of the fall was in clear view of Cracker Barrel employees, since they traversed it regularly on their way in and out of the kitchen. If a jury were to believe Thoma's description of the liquid as covering an area 1 foot by 2 feet, it might also be convinced that Cracker Barrel employees, in the exercise of due diligence, should have noticed the liquid before the accident. No one except Cracker Barrel employees were seen to carry food or beverage in the area of the fall, and the manager of the restaurant would not have expected customers to move around carrying food or drinks.

Cracker Barrel notes that "common sense" suggests "a plethora" of reasonable inferences other than the inferences urged by appellants. We certainly agree with this observation, but take issue with the suggestion that the existence of other possible inferences requires affirmance of the summary judgment in favor of Cracker Barrel. It will be for a jury to determine whether a preponderance of the evidence supports the inferences suggested by Thoma.

Reversed and Remanded.

Notes

1. In some slip-and-fall cases the plaintiff is able to show that the defendant was negligent in creating the dangerous condition, by spilling a slippery substance, for example. In other cases the defendant might be negligent in its method of merchandising, as where a grocery store's bins of fresh vegetables are likely to result in small slippery vegetables on the floor when customers shuffle through the lettuce or beans. See generally JOSEPH PAGE, PREMISES LIABILITY 143 (1988).

2. When the plaintiff cannot prove that the defendant itself negligently caused the slippery condition, the plaintiff can attempt to prove that the defendant was negligent in failing to discover and remove the condition.

3. One prominent problem in these cases is factual. What factual inference can be drawn from evidence that frozen okra on the floor had completely melted and become soft and slippery when the plaintiff fell? What inference from the evidence that the floor was swept only ten minutes earlier?

4. The main focus of this segment of the book is the evaluation of conduct. If we infer that the okra has been on the floor for an hour, we are left with the problem of evaluating the defendant's conduct. In some cases you might doubt whether courts or juries really have any way of saying that a reasonable and prudent store operator would have discovered a clear liquid on the floor within 15 minutes. Consider the risk-utility test. Can it be applied in evaluating the restaurant's conduct in *Thoma?* Could you evaluate the conduct as negligent or not by considering the consumer's reasonable expectations instead?

———

DUNCAN v. CORBETTA, 178 A.D.2d 459, 577 N.Y.S.2d 129 (1991). "The plaintiff William C. Duncan was injured when he began to descend a wooden exterior stairway at the defendant's residence and the top step collapsed. The court erred by precluding the plaintiffs' expert from testifying that it was common practice to use pressure-treated lumber in the construction of such stairways, even though the nonpressure-treated lumber used was permissible under the applicable building code. Proof of a general custom and usage is admissible because it tends to establish a standard by which ordinary care may be judged even where an ordinance prescribes certain minimum safety requirements which the custom exceeds. However, no significant prejudice resulted from the error. The plaintiffs failed to establish that the defendant had a role in the design or construction of the stairway." Judgment for defendant affirmed.

Notes

1. *General rule.* Evidence that the defendant violated customary safety precautions of the relevant community is usually sufficient to get the plaintiff to the jury.

2. *Customary statutory violations.* In *Duncan v. Corbetta* the court was willing to say that a defendant who complied with all the safety require-

ments of a statute might still be negligent if he failed to follow a safety custom. What if a litigant who failed to comply with a statute or ordinance wants to introduce evidence that the law is customarily violated, that is, that custom tends to show that violation is reasonable conduct? Judges generally disfavor such a use of custom evidence. See e.g., *Robinson v. District of Columbia,* 580 A.2d 1255 (D.C.App.1990) (rejecting party's argument that it was reasonable to disobey traffic law by jaywalking outside the marked crosswalk, as allegedly shown by "common practice of pedestrians at the location of the accident").

3. *What custom proves.* Existence of a safety custom might conceivably prove a number of different things. It might, for example, prove that harm was foreseeable, which is to say that the activity was recognizably risky; it might prove that the defendant knew or should have known of the risk; and it might prove that the risk was an "unreasonable" one unless the customary precaution is taken, or at least that it was unreasonable in the opinion of the community in general. Even if it proved none of these things, however, it might prove at least one thing, namely that a safety precaution was feasible.

4. *Custom involving different industry or activity.* Design of public bridges follows certain safety customs. Suppose a private landowner constructs a bridge on her own property but does not follow the safety customs that control the design of public bridges. The plaintiff, who is traveling the landowner's bridge by invitation, suffers property damage when the bridge collapses and his truck overturns. Can the landowner argue that evidence of the custom for public bridges should be excluded? *Simon's Feed Store, Inc. v. Leslein,* 478 N.W.2d 598 (Iowa 1991). What if the plaintiff can show that one other private bridge owner in the neighborhood built his bridge in accordance with design standards of public bridges?

5. *Custom other than safety custom.* What if the custom is well-established and even widespread, but there is no evidence whether the custom arose from safety considerations or from convenience? In *Levine v. Russell Blaine Co.,* 273 N.Y. 386, 7 N.E.2d 673 (1937), the plaintiff injured her hand on a rough, bristly rope for which defendant was responsible. There was an infection and later the arm had to be amputated. The plaintiff sought to introduce evidence that by custom the rope supplied should have been a smooth one. The court said:

> A smoother rope might have advantages other than greater safety. Its customary use might be due to these advantages, and might not show a general recognition that risk of injury would arise from use of a rougher rope. Proof of such custom or practice would then be insufficient, standing alone, to show negligence ... but the chain of proof might, in this case, have been completed if evidence of customary use of a different rope had been supplemented by expert evidence explaining how and why one kind of rope may cause a foreseeable risk of injury which others customarily avoid.

McCOMISH v. DeSOI, 42 N.J. 274, 200 A.2d 116 (1964). One of the defendants, Beloit, was employed to build a paper-making machine for a paper company. The machine was two blocks long and two stories high and required the movement of a large section during the paper-making process. Beloit designed an "A" sling to accomplish this purpose. The A sling was made of cables held together by clips. One of the clips slipped while this sling was being hoisted by a crane, and the whole A sling assembly collapsed, killing McComish and injuring one Toman. In actions against various defendants involved, the plaintiffs put on the evidence of Steward, a consulting engineer. He testified that the clips used were the wrong size, insufficient in number and improperly spaced along the cables they were securing. This was based in part on safety manuals or codes put out by various private companies (American Tiger Wire Rope) and by government agencies (U.S. Army Corps of Engineers). None of these had the force of law but were admitted by the trial judge. A jury found for the plaintiffs for $160,000 and $16,500. The Appellate Division concluded that the safety manuals should not have been admitted because they were hearsay. In the Supreme Court, *held*, although the cases are divided on this point, the safety codes were rightly admitted into evidence. "The basic test ... is whether reasonable care was exercised in the construction and assembly of the A sling. That is the standard to be used and departure or deviation therefrom is negligence. In applying the standard reasonable men recognize that what is usually done may be evidence of what ought to be done. And so the law permits the methods, practices or rules experienced men generally accept and follow to be shown as an aid to the jury in comparing the conduct of the alleged tortfeasor with the required norm of reasonable prudence. It is not suggested that the safety practices are of themselves the absolute measure of due care. They are simply evidence of 'how to' assemble the sling as commonly practiced by those who have experience in doing it."

Note

The objection to admission of safety manuals or industry-wide standards in written form is that they are hearsay. This is a technical concept usually explored in the course on evidence. Roughly it refers to second-hand evidence and it is objectionable because the plaintiff is not tendering a witness who can be cross-examined on the issue. Most jurisdictions traditionally sustained the objection to safety manuals and similar codes, unless they were enacted into law. Since 1975, the federal courts have been governed by a liberalized set of evidence rules, under which certain hearsay evidence may be admitted. A number of states have now also admitted such evidence. If the hearsay objection is overcome, is the evidence relevant and proper, perhaps as a reflection of custom?

Some safety codes prepared by trade associations or industry groups have been adopted by statute or ordinance. Many city ordinances, for example, adopt a building or electrical code prepared by industry. In such a case, the privately prepared safety code takes on the force of a statute or ordinance and is not only admissible but may set the standard of care.

In a jurisdiction that rejects the safety manual evidence, what would you do if you represented the plaintiffs in *McComish*?

THE T.J. HOOPER

United States Court of Appeals, Second Circuit, 1932.
60 F.2d 737.

L. HAND, CIRCUIT JUDGE.

The barges No. 17 and No. 30, belonging to the Northern Barge Company, had lifted cargoes of coal at Norfolk, Virginia, for New York in March, 1928. They were towed by two tugs of the petitioner, the "Montrose" and the "Hooper," and were lost off the Jersey Coast on March tenth, in an easterly gale. The cargo owners sued the barges under the contracts of carriage; the owner of the barges sued the tugs under the towing contract, both for its own loss and as bailee of the cargoes; the owner of the tug filed a petition to limit its liability. All the suits were joined and heard together, and the judge found that all the vessels were unseaworthy; the tugs, because they did not carry radio receiving sets by which they could have seasonably got warnings of a change in the weather which should have caused them to seek shelter in the Delaware Breakwater en route. He therefore entered an interlocutory decree holding each tug and barge jointly liable to each cargo owner, and each tug for half damages for the loss of its barge. The petitioner appealed, and the barge owner appealed and filed assignments of error. . . .

[Radio broadcasts gave forecasts of coming heavy weather. Reasonable masters would have put in at a safe harbor had they received the broadcasts. The masters of these tugs did not receive the broadcasts] because their private radio receiving sets, which were on board, were not in working order. These belonged to them personally, and were partly a toy, partly a part of the equipment, but neither furnished by the owner, nor supervised by it. It is not fair to say that there was a general custom among coastwise carriers so to equip their tugs. One line alone did it; as for the rest, they relied upon their crews, so far as they can be said to have relied at all. An adequate receiving set suitable for a coastwise tug can now be got at small cost and is reasonably reliable if kept up; obviously it is a source of great protection to their tows. Twice every day they can receive these predictions, based upon the widest possible information, available to every vessel within two or three hundred miles and more. Such a set is the ears of the tug to catch the spoken word, just as the master's binoculars are her eyes to see a storm signal ashore. Whatever may be said as to other vessels, tugs towing heavy coal laden barges, strung out for half a mile, have little power to maneuver, and do not, as this case proves, expose themselves to weather which would not turn back stauncher craft. They can have at hand protection against dangers of which they can learn in no other way.

Is it then a final answer that the business had not yet generally adopted receiving sets? There are, no doubt, cases where courts seem to make the general practice of the calling the standard of proper diligence; we have indeed given some currency to the notion ourselves. Indeed in most cases reasonable prudence is in fact common prudence; but strictly it is never its measure; a whole calling may have unduly lagged in the adoption of new and available devices. It never may set its own tests, however persuasive be its usages. Courts must in the end say what is required; there are precautions so imperative that even their universal disregard will not excuse their omission. But here there was no custom at all as to receiving sets; some had them, some did not; the most that can be urged is that they had not yet become general. Certainly in such a case we need not pause; when some have thought a device necessary, at least we may say that they were right, and the others too slack.... [H]ad [the tugs] been properly equipped, they would have got the Arlington reports. The injury was a direct consequence of this unseaworthiness.

Decree affirmed.

Notes

1. In *Texas & Pacific Railway v. Behymer*, 189 U.S. 468, 23 S.Ct. 622, 47 L.Ed. 905 (1903), Justice Holmes said: "What is usually done may be evidence of what ought to be done, but what ought to be done is fixed by a standard of reasonable prudence, whether it usually is complied with or not." These cases express the general rule.

2. Earlier decisions sometimes held that (a) evidence of custom was wholly inadmissible; or (b) on the contrary, custom represented the sole standard of care. As *The T.J. Hooper* would suggest, these older rules are largely obsolete. However, some courts are still cautious about admitting custom evidence, lest the jury treat it as a standard of care. *Jones v. Jitney Jungle Stores of America, Inc.*, 730 So.2d 555 (Miss.1998).

3. If you have reservations about the risk-utility rule of *Carroll Towing Co.*, how about using custom as the standard of care and the test of negligence?

4. Professor Epstein points to a distinction: (a) Some custom is the defendant's custom only; the plaintiff has no knowledge of it and has not agreed to have his safety governed by it. (b) Some other custom followed by the defendant is custom of which the plaintiff is aware; the plaintiff has, at least implicitly, accepted it as the standard. Roughly speaking, the first case involves strangers, that is, people who have no contract or other special relationship. The second case involves people who have some consensual arrangement with each other. Epstein thinks that in one of these cases the defendant's acts in accordance with custom ought to be conclusive evidence of due care. Which is the better case for that position? See Richard Epstein, *The Path to the T.J. Hooper: The Theory and History of Custom in the Law of Tort*, 21 J. Leg. Studies 1 (1992).

§ 4. PROVING UNSPECIFIED NEGLIGENCE: THE SPECIAL CASE OF RES IPSA LOQUITUR

"Some circumstantial evidence is very strong, as when you find a trout in the milk." H.D. Thoreau, Journal, *November 11, 1850* (B. Torrey, ed. 1906).

a.　*Origins and Basic Features*

BYRNE v. BOADLE

2 H. & C. 722, 159 Eng. Rep. 299 (Exch. 1863).

[Plaintiff gave evidence that he was walking in Scotland Road when he lost all recollection. Witnesses testified that a barrel of flour fell on him. The defendant's shop was adjacent and the barrel appeared to have fallen or to have been dropped from the shop. The trial judge "nonsuited" the plaintiff, taking the view that the plaintiff had put on no evidence of negligence. The plaintiff's attorney then sought review in a higher court by obtaining a "rule nisi to enter the verdict for the plaintiff...." What follows includes a portion of the argument by Charles Russell for the defendant before Barons Channell, Bramwell, Pigott and Chief Baron Pollock of the Exchequer Court.]

Charles Russell now showed cause. First, there was no evidence to connect the defendant or his servants with the occurrence.... Surmise ought not to be substituted for strict proof when it is sought to fix a defendant with serious liability. The plaintiff should establish his case by affirmative evidence.

Secondly, assuming the facts to be brought home to the defendant or his servants, these facts do not disclose any evidence for the jury of negligence. The plaintiff was bound to give affirmative proof of negligence. But there was not a scintilla of evidence, unless the occurrence is of itself evidence of negligence. There was not even evidence that the barrel was being lowered by a jigger-hoist as alleged in the declaration. [POLLOCK, C.B. There are certain cases of which it may be said res ipsa loquitur, and this seems one of them. In some cases the Courts have held that the mere fact of the accident having occurred is evidence of negligence, as, for instance, in the case of railway collisions.] On examination of the authorities, that doctrine would seem to be confined to the case of a collision between two trains upon the same line, and both being the property and under the management of the same Company. Such was the case of Skinner v. The London, Brighton and South Coast Railway Company (5 Exch. 787), where the train in which the plaintiff was ran into another train which had stopped a short distance from a station, in consequence of a luggage train before it having broken down. In that case there must have been negligence, or the accident could not have happened. Other cases cited in the textbooks, in support of the doctrine of presumptive negligence, when examined, will be found not to do so. Amongst them is Carpue v. The London and Brighton Railway Company (5 Q.B. 747), but there, in addition to proof of the occurrence, the plaintiff gave affirmative evidence of negligence, by showing that the rails were somewhat deranged at the spot where the accident took place, and that the train was proceeding at a speed which, considering the state of the rails, was hazardous.... Later cases have qualified the doctrine of presumptive negligence. In Cotton v. Wood (8 C.B.N.S. 568), it was held that a Judge is not justified in leaving the case to the jury where the plaintiff's evidence is equally consistent with the absence as with the existence of negligence in the defendant. In Hammack v. White (11 C.B.N.S. 588, 594), Erle, J., said that he was of opinion "that the plaintiff in a case of this sort was not entitled to have the case left to the jury unless he gives some affirmative evidence that there has been negligence on the part of the defendant." [Pollock, C.B. If he meant that to apply to all cases, I must say, with great respect, that I entirely differ from him. He must refer to the mere nature of the accident in that particular case. Bramwell, B. No doubt, the presumption of negligence is not raised in every case of injury from accident, but in some it is. We must judge of the facts in a reasonable way; and regarding them in that light we know that these accidents do not take place without a cause, and in general that cause is negligence.] The law will not presume that a man is guilty of a wrong. It is consistent with the facts proved that the defendant's servants were using the utmost care and the best appliances to lower the barrel with safety. Then why should the fact that accidents of this nature are sometimes caused by negligence raise any presumption against the defendant? There are many accidents from which no presumption of negligence can arise. [Bramwell, B. Looking at the matter in a reasonable way it comes to this–an injury is done to the plaintiff, who has no means of knowing whether it was the result of negligence; the defendant, who knows how it was caused, does not think fit to tell the jury.] Unless a plaintiff gives some evidence which ought to be submitted to the jury, the defendant is not bound to offer any defense. This plaintiff cannot, by a defective proof of his case, compel the defendant to give evidence in explanation. [Pollock, C.B. I have frequently observed that a defendant has a right to remain silent unless a prima facie case is established against him. But here the question is whether the plaintiff has not shewn such a case.] In a case of this nature, in which the sympathies of a jury are with the plaintiff, it would be dangerous to allow presumption to be substituted for affirmative proof of negligence.

Littler appeared to support the rule, but was not called upon to argue.

Pollock, C.B. We are all of opinion that the rule must be absolute to enter the verdict for the plaintiff. The learned counsel was quite right in saying that there are many accidents from which no presumption of negligence can arise, but I think it would be wrong to lay down as a rule that in no case can presumption of negligence arise from the fact of an accident. Suppose in this case the barrel had rolled out of the warehouse and fallen on the plaintiff, how could he possibly ascertain from what cause it occurred? It is the duty of persons who keep barrels in a warehouse to take care that they do not roll out, and I think that such a case would, beyond all doubt, afford prima facie evidence of negligence. A barrel could not roll out of a warehouse without some negligence, and to say that a plaintiff who is injured by it must call witnesses from the warehouse to prove negligence seems to me preposterous. [The other Barons concurred.]

Notes

1.   Consider how res ipsa loquitur evidence differs from ordinary circumstantial evidence. Using *Byrne* as a model, can you state exactly what *Byrne* has permitted that has not been permitted in earlier decisions?

2.   The judges in *Byrne*, which is more or less the original res ipsa loquitur case, repeatedly recurred to the common sense interpretation of the facts before them–the accident, they felt, "spoke for itself," and what it said was that the defendant must have been negligent. Suppose you are driving behind a large truck and trailer; the spare tire somehow comes out of the cradle beneath the trailer and crashes through your windshield, causing you injury. Is that enough to show negligence? *McDougald v. Perry,* 716 So.2d 783 (Fla.1998).

3.   Are there principles or at least guidelines about when this unusual doctrine applies?

––––––

VALLEY PROPERTIES LIMITED PARTNERSHIP v. STEADMAN'S HARDWARE, INC., 251 Mont. 242, 824 P.2d 250 (1992). Defendant rented space in the plaintiff's warehouse. The defendant's space was completely separate and defendant had the only keys. The electrical wiring was quite old. A fire started in the defendant's rented area and eventually consumed the entire warehouse. The plaintiff sued for the destruction of its warehouse. The plaintiff was unable to point to specific acts of negligence by the defendant, but argued res ipsa loquitur. *Held,* the trial court correctly refused to give instructions on the doctrine. "This Court has stated the doctrine of res ipsa loquitur in the following terms: (1) It may be inferred that harm suffered by the plaintiff is caused by negligence of the defendant when (a) the event is of a kind which ordinarily does not occur in the absence of negligence; (b) other responsible causes, including the conduct of the plaintiff and third persons, are sufficiently eliminated by the evidence; and (c) the indicated negligence is within the scope of the defendant's duty to the plaintiff. Under the facts of the present case, the doctrine is not applicable. A fire in a warehouse, of unknown origin, may occur in the absence of negligence. Further, the evidence did not clearly eliminate causes, such as a malfunction in the electrical system, which were not chargeable to the occupants of the warehouse."

EATON v. EATON, 119 N.J. 628, 575 A.2d 858 (1990). Sandra Eaton and her adult daughter Donna were traveling in a car at night in clear, dry weather. Police found the car overturned, with heavy damage on the passenger side. Sandra was seriously injured and later died; Donna sustained only minor injuries. Donna insisted that her mother had been driving, and that the accident had occurred when she swerved to avoid a head-on collision with a dark-colored Chevrolet Nova. Before her death from injuries, Sandra told the police that Donna was driving the car at the time of the accident. The investigating police officer concluded that the daughter's story was unbelievable, and cited her for careless driving. Plaintiff Gerald Eaton, Sandra's husband and Donna's father, sued Donna for negligently causing Sandra's death. The jury returned a verdict for Donna, finding that she was driving the car but was not negligent. Plaintiff's lawyer had not requested a res ipsa loquitur instruction at trial, but claimed on appeal that the trial court's failure to so instruct was plain error requiring remand for a new trial. The New Jersey Supreme Court agreed, holding that res ipsa applied. "Under the rule of res ipsa loquitur, a jury may draw a permissible inference of negligence from the circumstances surrounding certain accidents.... Application of the rule depends on satisfaction of three conditions: (1) the accident which produced a person's injury was one which ordinarily does not happen unless someone was negligent, (2) the instrumentality or agent which caused the accident was under the exclusive control of the defendant, and (3) the circumstances indicated that the untoward event was not caused or contributed to by any act or neglect on the part of the injured person. When the rule applies, it permits an inference of negligence that can satisfy the plaintiff's burden of proof, thereby enabling the plaintiff to survive a motion to dismiss at the close of his or her case. The inference, however, does not shift the burden of proof. As we said in *Lorenc*, '[t]he facts are said to provide circumstantial evidence of negligence to be weighed, but not necessarily to be accepted as sufficient; they afford a basis for an inference of want of due care which the jury may, but need not, draw. Even in the absence of explanation by the defendant, the jury may properly conclude that the inference should not be drawn or that the facts are not adequate to sustain the plaintiff's ultimate burden of showing, to the degree required, the origin of the accident in the negligence of the defendant."

Notes

1. To invoke res ipsa loquitur, the plaintiff must show that negligence is more probable than not, or as commonly expressed, that the event does not ordinarily occur without negligence of someone. But how do we know the probabilities? The answer is that in some cases, judges believe juries lack sufficient knowledge or experience to conclude that negligence is more probable than not. In such instances, judges direct verdicts for the defendant. E.g., *Scott v. James*, 731 A.2d 399 (D.C.App.1999) (stressing jury's lack of knowledge of chemistry). In situations like *Byrne v. Boadle*, however, judges believe that common knowledge and general experience of jurors permit them to think that, more likely than not, the defendant was negligent.

2. *Valley Properties* reflects the elements of res ipsa as set forth in RESTATEMENT SECOND OF TORTS § 328D. Are the requirements materially different from those set forth in *Eaton*? Expect variation in local verbalization of the rules, but always consider the possibility that a different verbalization may be intended to express substantially the same rules the Restatement uses. In *Reese v. Board of Directors of Mem. Hospital of Laramie*

County, 955 P.2d 425 (Wyo.1998), the court seemed to say that res ipsa could not be applied unless negligence was the only possible inference. Taken literally, would such a rule be rational? If not, maybe we should take the rule as a defective statement of the court's intent.

3. As we know, the usual standard of care is the reasonable person standard. However, in some situations, the standard is much less demanding and the defendant breaches his duty to the plaintiff only if the defendant is chargeable with gross negligence or reckless misconduct. These situations are considered in Chapter 10. Suppose that in *Byrne v. Boadle* the plaintiff, without invitation, had walked into the defendant's place of business just for a look around and had been hit by the barrel. If the defendant's duty under those circumstances was only to avoid gross negligence, would res ipsa loquitur take the plaintiff to the jury? See *Maiden v. Rozwood,* 461 Mich. 109, 597 N.W.2d 817 (1999). Does the answer turn upon a specific rule of law or upon assessment of the evidence in each case?

NOTE: PROCEDURAL INCIDENTS AND EFFECTS OF RES IPSA LOQUITUR

1. *Sufficiency of evidence issue.* As *Eaton* notes, the application of res ipsa loquitur means that, on the negligence issue, the plaintiff will survive a motion for directed verdict and get to the jury, which can then decide the case either way.

2. *Instructing on res ipsa.* If the plaintiff has adduced evidence from which the jury could conclude that the elements of res ipsa loquitur are present, then trial judges commonly give a res ipsa loquitur instruction to the jury. The instruction "merely tells the jury that if they do find the existence of these elements then they may draw the inference of negligence," not that they must do so. *K-Mart Corp. v. Gipson,* 563 N.E.2d 667, 670 (Ind.App.1990). Is an instruction necessary or desirable? In *Grajales-Romero v. American Airlines, Inc.,* 194 F.3d 288 (1st Cir. 1999), the court upheld the jury's verdict for the plaintiff because evidence made out a res ipsa loquitur case even though the judge had not instructed the jury on that doctrine.

3. *Permissible inference effect.* Most courts hold that res ipsa creates a permissible inference that the jury may draw if it sees fit. This is reflected in *Eaton* and in the instruction just quoted. Even if the defendant introduces no evidence at all, the jury may reject the inference and bring in a verdict for the defendant. This may be expressed by saying that the inference of negligence in a res ipsa case is merely "permissible" and that it does not shift the burden of persuasion.

4. *Abnormally strong inferences of negligence.* To say that the inference of negligence is merely permitted, not required, is to say that the plaintiff who makes out a permissible inference case would not be entitled to a directed verdict. But could there be cases so strong that the permissible inference becomes a mandatory inference so that the trial

judge would direct a verdict after all? In *De Leon Lopez v. Corporacion Insular de Seguros*, 931 F.2d 116 (1st Cir.1991), two women gave birth to twins in the University Hospital at Puerto Rico Medical Center. The hospital somehow switched one twin from each set, so that each mother went home with two children, but only with one of her own. The mistake was discovered after a year and a half. The court thought that occasions for directing a verdict for the plaintiff were "hen's-teeth rare," the court nevertheless permitted a directed verdict for the plaintiff in this case.

5. *The presumption effect.* A small number of courts say that res ipsa loquitur is *not* merely a common sense assessment of evidence which permits an inference of fault, but that, instead, it creates a "presumption" of negligence. The term "presumption" can be used loosely or can have technical meanings, explored in the course in evidence. Courts usually enforce one of two possible effects when a presumption of negligence applies:

(a) The jury is told that, once the presumption applies, the defendant has the burden of showing he is *not* negligent; OR

(b) The judge will direct a verdict for the plaintiff unless the defendant produces some evidence that he was not negligent. CAL. EVID. CODE § 646(b) is an example; it defines res ipsa as "a presumption affecting the burden of producing evidence." (How *much* evidence the defendant must produce is another disputed matter.)

The presumption in (a) is sometimes said to shift the burden of persuasion. The presumption in (b) is sometimes said to shift the burden of production (meaning production of evidence), or the burden of going forward with evidence. See, describing presumptions and their effects, DOBBS ON TORTS § 152 (2000). How would you compare or contrast the permissible inference approach to res ipsa?

6. *Rebuttal by defendant.* Suppose the defendant does in fact offer proof about his conduct. What does this do to the res ipsa loquitur inference? Can the plaintiff still get to the jury? Suppose in *Byrne* the defendant had proved that a trucker loading the flour had negligently dropped it. Suppose instead that the defendant proved it did everything normally, exercised all precautions about the flour storage and cannot understand why the injury took place? Would the results be different under these two versions of the defendant's proof?

b. Attributing the Fault to Defendant Rather Than Others

GILES v. CITY OF NEW HAVEN

Supreme Court of Connecticut, 1994.
228 Conn. 441, 636 A.2d 1335.

KATZ, ASSOCIATE JUSTICE.

The defendant Otis Elevator Company (defendant) appeals from the Appellate Court's determination that the trial court should not have granted the defendant's motion for a directed verdict in an action by the plaintiff, an elevator operator, to recover for the defendant's negligent failure to inspect, maintain and repair an elevator compensation chain that caused the plaintiff to sustain personal injuries. The Appellate Court concluded that the plaintiff had presented sufficient evidence to warrant presentation of the question of negligence under the doctrine of res ipsa loquitur to the jury. We affirm the judgment of the Appellate Court. . . .

[T]he Appellate Court reviewed the record and concluded that the trial court could reasonably have considered the following facts in deciding whether the doctrine of res ipsa loquitur applied. "For fourteen years, the plaintiff was an elevator operator for one of three elevators in the Powell Building in New Haven. On the date her injuries were sustained, the elevator she was operating was ascending from the first floor to the twelfth floor when its compensation chain became hooked on a rail bracket located on the wall of the elevator shaft. The plaintiff was not able to control the movement of the chain from the interior of the cab. Once hooked, the chain then tightened up and broke free from two bolts securing it to the underside of the cab. The cab began to shudder and shake, and the plaintiff struck her head and shoulder against the walls of the cab. The chain then fell to the bottom of the elevator shaft with a loud crash, which frightened the plaintiff. Upon hearing the crash, the plaintiff, fearing for her safety, reversed the direction of the elevator as it was approaching the twelfth floor. She directed the elevator to the nearest floor, the eleventh, where she jumped from the cab sustaining additional injuries. At the time the plaintiff received her injuries, the defendant had a longstanding exclusive contract with the building owner to maintain and inspect the elevator and its component parts. The elevator was installed by the defendant approximately sixty-one years before the accident. . . .

"[William] Hendry, [the defendant's district maintenance supervisor] testified that the normal sway of a compensation chain is approximately one to two inches, and in order for the chain to get hooked on a rail bracket it must sway at least eighteen inches. He further testified that for the chain to sway eighteen inches there must be some misoperation of the elevator, such as rapid reversals of direction. . . . [Plaintiff testified] that the crash of the compensation chain as it hit the bottom of the elevator shaft occurred before she reversed the direction of the cab."

. . .

Before the Appellate Court the parties agreed that . . . the accident would not have occurred unless someone had been negligent. The parties were, however, in disagreement about whether the plaintiff had made a case for the jury with respect to the second and third conditions of the doctrine, namely, control of the elevator by the defendant and the absence of responsibility for the accident on the part of the plaintiff.

The defendant challenges the application of the res ipsa loquitur doctrine to this case because in its view the plaintiff failed to demonstrate that the defendant had exclusive control over the elevator. Specifically, the defendant argues that because plaintiff operated the elevator and controlled its movement and its chain's sway, she could not benefit from the doctrine notwithstanding defendant's own duty to maintain and inspect the elevator and to warn of any dangerous propensity. We disagree. . . .

[I]n describing the extent of the defendant's control of the use of the instrumentality [that caused the event], we have never held that any use whatsoever of the instrumentality by the plaintiff would automatically preclude application of res ipsa loquitur. So restrictive an interpretation would substantially undermine the efficacy of the doctrine. Rather, our previous discussions of use were meant to reflect the idea of management and control, factors that help to limit the application of the res ipsa loquitur doctrine to those situations in which the defendant's negligence was more probably than not the cause of the plaintiff's injuries. The plaintiff's actual use of the instrument, therefore does not, in and of itself bar application of the doctrine.

The growing trend in res ipsa loquitur jurisprudence is not to apply the "control" condition in such a way that renders it "a fixed, mechanical and rigid rule. 'Control,' if it is not to be pernicious and misleading, must be a very flexible term. It may be enough that the defendant has the right or power of control, and the opportunity to exercise it. . . . It is enough that the defendant is under a duty which he cannot delegate to another. . . ." W. Prosser & W. Keeton, supra, § 39, p. 250.

"The point of requiring control by the defendant is, as indicated by Prosser, to provide the basis for an inference that whatever negligence was involved may properly be charged to the defendant. . . ."

In many jurisdictions, courts now deemphasize the role of exclusive control as a condition of res ipsa loquitur, even though their earlier decisions included such a requirement. "Exclusive control is merely one way of proving a defendant's responsibility. 'He may be responsible, and the inference may be drawn against him, where he shares the control with another.' Restatement (Second) of Torts § 328D, comment g. . . ." If the jury could reasonably find that defendant's control was sufficient to warrant an inference that the defendant was more likely responsible for the incident than someone else, even in the absence of proof of absolute exclusivity and control over the instrumentality by the defendant, the trial court must allow the jury to draw that inference.

. . . In this case, the parties agree that the defendant was in control of the maintenance and repair of the elevator and its parts, and that the operation of the elevator by the operator was tantamount to its use. The defendant, however, seeks to distinguish the components of the elevator from their mechanical function by arguing that, although it controlled the elevator chain, it did not control the chain's sway. Although by operating the elevator the plaintiff may have diminished the exclusivity of the defendant's control, a jury could find that her conduct did not strip the defendant of control or responsibility for the chain and its condition, which resulted in the excessive sway. . . .

Although Hendry explained that there was no reason to inspect the compensation chain and that he believed the accident had been caused by multiple rapid direction reversals, the plaintiff was not required to prove the absence of such reversals in order to avail herself of the res ipsa loquitur inference.

[The court found, finally, that Connecticut's adoption of comparative negligence compels the conclusion that res ipsa can apply to a case even where the plaintiff's negligence contributed to the injury, citing cases from seven other states which have also so held.]

The Appellate Court properly upheld the plaintiff's claim that the trial court should not have granted the defendant's motion for a directed verdict. Pursuant to the doctrine of res ipsa loquitur as we have refined its conditions in this opinion, the plaintiff was entitled to have a jury consider her claim that the defendant's negligence was the cause of her personal injuries.

The judgment of the Appellate Court is affirmed.

Notes

1. *The control rule. Giles* reflects a contemporary view of the control rule. In this view, "control" is only one way of establishing the important point that the negligence was probably that of the defendant, not that of someone else. It is enough if, more likely than not, there was negligence on the part of the defendant. See *Harder v. F.C. Clinton, Inc.,* 948 P.2d 298 (Okla.1997); *Errico v. LaMountain,* 713 A.2d 791, 796 (R.I.1998).

2. At one time, however, the control rule was taken quite literally. In *Kilgore v. Shepard Co.,* 52 R.I. 151, 158 A. 720 (1932), the plaintiff sat down on a chair in defendant's store. It collapsed and she was injured. The court rejected this res ipsa loquitur on the ground that the defendant was not in exclusive control of the chair, the plaintiff herself being in "control" when she sat upon it. In line with *Giles* and the preceding note, courts today apply res ipsa to cases of injury resulting from taking a seat on chairs, bar stools and even bleachers. E.g., *Trujeque v. Service Merchandise Co.,* 117 N.M. 388, 872 P.2d 361 (1994).

3. *Slip and fall cases.* Courts reject use of res ipsa loquitur to show negligence in slip and fall cases. Should they reach that result because (a) the plaintiff rather than the defendant is in control or (b) because evidence of a substance on the floor does not make the defendant's negligence more probable than not?

4. *Instrumentalities accessible to the public.* When, as in *Giles,* an instrumentality is more or less accessible to the public, numerous persons may have interfered with the instrumentality, so the defendant is not literally in exclusive control. Nevertheless, *Giles* is not alone in invoking res ipsa loquitur in public accessibility cases. On the other hand, New York has invoked the control rule to defeat res ipsa loquitur in the case of a plaintiff who was thrown to the ground when his shoe was caught in an escalator. *Ebanks v. New York City Transit Authority,* 70 N.Y.2d 621, 518 N.Y.S.2d 776, 512 N.E.2d 297 (1987).

5. *Exploding bottle cases*. Under a liberal formulation of the control requirement, the plaintiff might show that any fault in the case was attributable to the defendant merely by excluding other causes. Suppose the plaintiff buys a soft drink from a grocery, takes it home and suffers an injury when the bottle "explodes." The bottler obviously was not in control at the time of injury. Nor do we know when the negligence was likely to have occurred. The grocer or a customer might well have dropped the bottle, causing a chip for which the bottler is not responsible. In a leading case, *Escola v. Coca Cola Bottling Co.*, 24 Cal.2d 453, 150 P.2d 436 (1944), the California Supreme Court held that the plaintiff could use res ipsa loquitur by showing that the defendant had control at the time of the probable negligence, and that this could be shown by excluding the negligence of others. Thus the plaintiff might show that the bottle had not been subjected to any unusual treatment in the grocery store, and on making such proof would be permitted to use res ipsa loquitur. As the New York Court of Appeals put it in a non-bottling case, "the exclusive control requirement is thus subordinated to its general purpose, that of indicating that it *probably* was the defendant's negligence which caused the accident." *Corcoran v. Banner Super Market, Inc.*, 19 N.Y.2d 425, 280 N.Y.S.2d 385, 227 N.E.2d 304 (1967).

6. *Run-away car cases*. Another illustrative line of cases involves a car that rolls downhill some time after it has been parked. If the driver has left the area it is possible that someone has interfered with the car, by taking it out of gear or releasing the brake, for example. Even if the driver is in the vicinity it is possible that there is a mechanical failure that caused the car to roll. What is the most probable explanation—that someone interfered with the car or that the defendant negligently parked it? The courts usually let this go to the jury on res ipsa loquitur, even though it is obvious that defendant is not in control at the time of the injury. What added facts might be important either to the judge in deciding whether to let the case go to the jury or to the jury in deciding whether defendant was probably negligent?

7. *Eliminating the plaintiff's fault*. Courts have often said that the plaintiff must show that she herself was not at fault or did not contribute to the injury. In retrospect, this looks like a specific instance of the control rule and shares its purpose. If so, then the real point is to show that the fault was at least in part attributable to the defendant. If this is right, the control rule and its subsidiary rule about plaintiff-fault merely point to evidence that will be important but not conclusive. Is *Giles* consistent with this view?

8. Some courts apparently assume that the plaintiff-fault rule was a rule of contributory negligence. These courts have concluded that, with the advent of comparative fault, under which any contributory negligence will reduce but not bar the plaintiff's claim, the plaintiff-fault limit on res ipsa should be abolished or modified. E.g., *Cox v. May Dept. Store Co.*, 183 Ariz. 361, 903 P.2d 1119 (App. 1995).

9. *The special problem of multiple actors*. The plaintiff proves his automobile was struck by defendant's and that he, plaintiff, was injured. Is this a res ipsa loquitur case? When there are two moving vehicles there seems no basis for deciding that the driver of one is more likely at fault than the other, or so the cases say. Is the case any different if the plaintiff is not

one of the drivers but is instead a pedestrian injured by flying debris from a collision between A and B? The traditional answer has been no. See Fleming James, *Proof of Breach in Negligence Cases*, 37 VA. L. REV. 179, 209–212 (1951).

A few cases have allowed res ipsa loquitur against multiple defendants who exercise "joint control" over the instrumentality of harm. It may be that in some of these cases, the inference is that defendant A either caused harm by direct action or by his failure to control defendant B. Some of the complications in these cases are considered in Chapter 11, § 2, in connection with res ipsa loquitur as it is used in medical malpractice cases.

c. *Is Negligence More Probable Than Not?*

WARREN v. JEFFRIES

Supreme Court of North Carolina, 1965.
263 N.C. 531, 139 S.E.2d 718.

PER CURIAM.

Terry Lee Enoch, a 6–year old child, was injured when a wheel of defendant's Chevrolet automobile ran over his body, and from these injuries he died. Plaintiff instituted this action to recover for his alleged wrongful death. From judgment of involuntary nonsuit entered at the close of plaintiff's evidence, plaintiff appeals.

Plaintiff's evidence, taken as true for the purposes of this appeal, discloses these facts:

Defendant drove to Terry's home to see Terry's father and parked his car in the yard. Terry's father was not at home and defendant went in the house and waited for his return. The car was left standing on an incline. During the time there were in and around the house about a dozen children, including Terry; their ages ranged from 18 months to 20 years. The car remained parked for about an hour prior to the accident, and during this interval no one had gone to the car or touched it for any purpose. One of the children needed shoe polish and defendant gave Terry's mother the keys to his automobile so she could drive it to a store for the polish. She and five children, including Terry, started to the car. It was raining and Terry didn't want to wear his glasses; he gave them to his mother and she went back in the house to put them up. The five children (eldest, 20 years) got in the rear seat of the car; it was a 4–door sedan, and none of them got in the front seat. They did not touch any of the control mechanisms of the car. Terry was the last to get in and when he "closed the door something clicked in the front and … the car started rolling" backwards in the direction of a large ditch. One of the older children opened the door and told the others to jump out. All jumped out, Terry first. When he jumped out he fell, and the front wheel ran over his chest.

The mother's graphic description of her son is so typical of an alert and active little boy that it is worthy of preservation. "He was full of fun at all times, he never was still unless he was asleep, he was either laughing or playing or doing something to let you know he was around. One thing I remember, the lady I worked for give (sic) him a little puppy and he was crazy about this little dog. . . ."

Plaintiff alleges defendant was negligent in that (1) he failed to set the hand brake, (2) failed to engage the transmission, and (3) neglected to maintain adequate brakes as required by G.S. § 20–124. There is no evidence as to the condition of the brakes, whether the hand brake had been set, or whether the car was in gear. Apparently the car was not examined after the accident. What caused it to make a "clicking" sound and begin rolling backwards is pure speculation. The doctrine of *res ipsa loquitur* is not applicable. *Lane* v. *Dorney*, 252 N.C. 90, 113 S.E.2d 33; *Springs* v. Doll, 197 N.C. 240, 148 S.E. 251.

Affirmed.

Notes

1. Testimony, which the jury could believe, excluded the possibility of tampering by the children. Why, then, isn't *Warren v. Jeffries* a res ipsa case like any other case of a car inexplicably going off the road? Is there an explanation for the accident that would *not* involve negligence of the defendant?

2. Would it have helped the plaintiff to put on evidence that the car was examined immediately after the accident by a qualified mechanic and that the examination revealed nothing throwing light on the occurrence? Did the court in effect draw an inference against the plaintiff for failure to introduce some such testimony?

3. Consider *Howard v. Wal–Mart Stores, Inc.,* 160 F.3d 358 (7th Cir.1998). In that case, Judge Posner discussed a hypothetical case in which the plaintiff was struck by a bus. At that location, 51% of all buses are owned by company A and 49% by company B. Does the plaintiff make out a case against A by showing these facts plus negligence and causation? "If the 51/49 statistic is the plaintiff's only evidence, and he does not show that it was infeasible for him to obtain any additional evidence, the inference to be drawn is not that there is a 51 percent probability that it was a bus owned by A that hit the plaintiff. It is that the plaintiff either investigated and discovered that the bus was actually owned by B (and B might not have been negligent and so not liable even if a cause of the accident, or might be judgment-proof and so not worth suing), or that he simply has not bothered to conduct an investigation. If the first alternative is true, he should of course lose; and since it may be true, the probability that the plaintiff was hit by a bus owned by A is less than 51 percent and the plaintiff has failed to carry his burden of proof. If the second alternative is true–the plaintiff just hasn't conducted an investigation–he still should lose. A court shouldn't be required to expend its scarce resources of time and effort on a case until the plaintiff has conducted a sufficient investigation to make reasonably clear that an expenditure of public resources is likely to yield a significant social benefit. This principle is implicit in the law's decision to place the burden of producing evidence on the plaintiff rather than on the defendant."

4. *Absent evidence.* In some cases, the defendant or his witnesses appear to have extensive knowledge of relevant facts, but never offer any testimony about them. Courts sometimes permit the trier of fact to draw inferences against the defendant in this situation. The trier may be permitted to find that the evidence was not produced because it would have been adverse to the defendant, and then may be permitted to treat the case as if adverse evidence had in fact appeared. Is *Warren* a case in which the adverse inference was drawn against the *plaintiff* for failure to put on proof?

WIDMYER v. SOUTHEAST SKYWAYS, INC.

Supreme Court of Alaska, 1978.
584 P.2d 1.

BOOCHEVER, CHIEF JUSTICE.

[This is a suit for the wrongful death of passengers who were killed, along with the pilot, when a Southeast Skyways plane crashed in False Bay at Chichagof Island, Alaska. The plane had left Juneau in good weather. It traveled for a ways parallel to another plane, piloted by Bernhardt. Both encountered a heavy snow squall. When both were flying at an altitude of 50–100 feet, the Skyways craft turned right and Bernhardt then lost sight of it. Later Charles and Esther Kaze saw the Skyways craft near their cabin; it crashed a few seconds later, with no change in the audible pitch of the motor beforehand. The Kazes found the wreckage in vertical, nosedown position in tidal water just off the island. An accident reconstruction expert testified for the plaintiffs that in his opinion, the crash was due to a stall/spin and was the result of pilot error. He also concluded the pilot was in violation of Visual Flight Rules of the Federal Aviation Administration. Bernhardt testified that in his opinion the Skyways pilot was looking for Chichagof Beach, encountered trees and was forced to pull up sharply, which stalled the aircraft.]

[Skyways contended bad weather was the problem. Its testimony showed that there was severe turbulence in the crash area at the time. Experts gave the opinion that he encountered a snow squall, attempted to land and was struck by a gust.]

[At trial, the plaintiff requested an instruction informing the jury that they could draw an inference of negligence if, from all the evidence, negligence was found to be more probable than not. The trial judge refused this instruction and instead charged that the mere happening of an accident, of itself, did not warrant finding negligence. The jury then brought in a verdict for the defendant and the plaintiff appeals.]

Although there is a split of authority on whether the doctrine is applicable to cases in which the plaintiff introduces specific evidence of negligence, Alaska does not preclude use of the doctrine unless the specific acts furnish a "complete explanation" of the accident. We have declined to apply *res ipsa loquitur* in an air crash case when the injured plaintiff, the only passenger, testified to specific acts of the pilot prior to the crash. We stated:

... if the evidence discloses the circumstances of the accident to the extent that there is nothing left to infer, then the doctrine of *res ipsa loquitur*, which is founded upon inference, is no longer needed.

... Of note is the fact that in the Alaska cases which have applied this "complete explanation" standard regarding evidence of specific acts of negligence, there has been direct, rather than circumstantial evidence: in each case, a witness directly involved at the time of the occurrence had been available to testify.... We do not find that in the present case in which heavy reliance was placed by both parties on inferences of expert witnesses, that a complete *factual* explanation was offered. There were matters of considerable uncertainty, including the exact path of the plane from the Admiralty to the Chichagof side of the Chatham Strait and the precise sequence of events which occurred immediately prior to the crash. In an accident in which there are no survivors to testify and no other direct evidence of the cause, we do not believe that plaintiffs should be precluded from utilizing the doctrine of *res ipsa loquitur* because they have offered a possible explanation to the jury.

The second preliminary issue involves the question of superior knowledge. The superior court specifically noted Skyways' lack of superior knowledge as to the cause of the crash in denying a *res ipsa loquitur* instruction. In this case, neither party possessed superior knowledge: both were equally ignorant of the facts which occurred immediately prior to the crash.

A pre-statehood federal case, discussed this issue and applied *res ipsa loquitur* in a wrongful death case in which plaintiffs' deceased were lost in an airplane which disappeared without a trace on a flight from Yakutat, Alaska to Seattle, Washington. The court stated:

> An examination of the authorities in support of the rule ... [precluding the application of the doctrine where plaintiff's knowledge is equal to that of the defendant] ... discloses that it is applied to cases where the plaintiff has equal knowledge or where knowledge of the cause is equally accessible to the plaintiff—not to cases in which there is an equality of ignorance as in the instant case....

Skyways cites no Alaska case specifically requiring superior knowledge on a defendant's part as to the immediate cause of a crash before *res ipsa loquitur* may be invoked. There are no compelling reasons to apply such a rule to an aircraft accident in which there are no survivors and in which the parties place heavy reliance upon expert testimony. Moreover, while the carrier may not have superior knowledge as to the specific circumstances at the time of the crash, it has superior knowledge as to the characteristics of the particular airplane involved, its maintenance, the training and instruction of its pilots and its general operating procedure under varying conditions.

We now return to analysis of the three traditional prerequisites to the applicability of *res ipsa loquitur*: an accident that normally does not happen without negligence; exclusive control of the instrumentality by the defendant; and absence of voluntary action or contribution by the plaintiff.

The requirements are, in essence, "foundation facts," which must be established before invoking the doctrine.

> Since it is not the mere fact of injury itself, but the circumstances surrounding the injury, which justify the application of the doctrine, the applicability of the doctrine must depend on the peculiar facts and circumstances of each case. (footnotes omitted)

If the requirement of no plaintiff contribution is strictly applied, no *res ipsa loquitur* instruction could be given where the plaintiff lacks sufficient evidence, or any evidence, upon which to prove a negative. Yet, such an instruction was given in *Haasman* v. *Pacific Alaska Air Express,* the airplane disappeared without a trace. We believe that there must be some evidence upon which a jury could find plaintiff contribution before a *res ipsa loquitur* instruction can be denied for this reason. In the face of a silent record, the conclusion that a passenger did not interfere with the operation of an aircraft is much more compelling than the conclusion that he did interfere.

While it is clear that *res ipsa loquitur* is applicable in general to aviation cases, it is not necessarily applicable to every such case since the specific circumstances will vary. Weather may impinge upon the first prerequisite for *res ipsa loquitur* in that it may contribute to a set of circumstances in which it is not more likely than not that the crash was caused by the defendants' negligence. Again, the totality of the circumstances must be considered in each factual setting.

Cases involving in-flight injuries to passengers as a result of bumps, lurches or jerks of an aircraft in turbulence do not give rise to the application of the doctrine. In cases involving crashes, some courts, in applying *res ipsa loquitur*, have specifically noted the absence of evidence of weather as a causative factor.

To require a plaintiff to show that a crash was not caused by weather, as a prerequisite to the application of *res ipsa loquitur*, presents the problems inherent in proving a negative. Again, a strict application of this requirement would have disallowed the *res ipsa loquitur* instruction in Haasman, where the plane disappeared without a trace. We will not require a plaintiff to negate the possibility of weather as a cause of an airplane crash in order to obtain the benefit of a *res ipsa loquitur* instruction.

The general safety record of air travel and the present state of air technology compel us to conclude that air crashes do not normally occur absent negligence even in inclement weather. In *Alaska Airlines, Inc.* v. *Sweat,* 568 P.2d 916, 925 (Alaska 1977), we stated:

> [A]ir travel may no longer be regarded as inherently dangerous and ... flights aboard certified carriers do not involve an unreasonable risk of harm.

Thus, under the circumstances of this case, we find no reason to preclude the applicability of the doctrine of *res ipsa loquitur*. We find the lack of an instruction on the doctrine to be error.

Notes

1. *Specific evidence of negligence*. When the evidence presents a "complete explanation" for the accident, courts refuse to apply res ipsa. See, e.g., *Dover Elevator Co. v. Swann*, 334 Md. 231, 638 A.2d 762 (1994) (res ipsa inapplicable where plaintiff's expert witness purported to provide a complete explanation of the cause of an elevator accident). Why was there no complete explanation in *Widmyer*? If a plaintiff uncovers, through investigation, a complete explanation of what instrumentality caused the harm and how, should the plaintiff be upset that he does not have to rely on res ipsa loquitur?

2. *Probability*. The orthodox view is that in the early days of flight, there was little safety at all and a crash did not indicate negligence was probable; but that with safety advances, a crash of a plane, at least in good weather, does permit one to believe that negligence was the probable explanation. If this is right in principle, is it right in a case like *Widmyer* where bad weather almost certainly played a large part in the crash? Perhaps a more important question is this: how does anyone really know what the probability of fault is in air crashes? In *Hailey v. Otis Elevator Co.*, 636 A.2d 426 (D.C.App.1994), the plaintiff fell when the escalator on which she was riding gave a little bump or jerk. The court thought that there was no "common knowledge that moving escalators do not normally act in the manner described ... much less that such motions are 'ordinarily' the result of negligence." Is it fair to say that we know more about probability in air crashes than in escalator injuries?

3. *Stating the probability rule*. The plaintiff's proposed instruction in *Widmyer* would have invoked res ipsa loquitur if the jury found "it is more probable than not" that negligence played a part in the crash. The court, on the other hand, seems to justify res ipsa where the "accident ... normally does not happen without negligence...." Are these two statements of the rule the same?

4. *Defendant's superior knowledge*. Sometimes courts say that res ipsa loquitur does not apply unless the defendant has superior knowledge. But if res ipsa is a matter of assessing the probability that defendant is negligent, is special knowledge by the defendant really necessary? Suppose the defendant runs off the road in a car, injures the plaintiff and has amnesia. The plaintiff, on the other hand, remembers everything in perfect, horror-stricken detail. No res ipsa?

Problem

Chang v. Grey's Department Stores, Inc., et al.

Janice Chang ascended the escalator in Grey's Department Store when her jacket lodged between the escalator's moving handrail and stationery guide. This caused her to be thrown down violently and dragged to the top of the escalator, resulting in serious physical injuries. Before the accident, Chang noticed nothing unusual about the escalator. Her jacket was not unusual and she was riding the escalator in a normal manner. She did not see how her jacket became caught under the handrail.

Grey's Department store owns the escalator, but contracts with Presley Elevator Co. to maintain it. Just two weeks prior to the accident, Presley had inspected the escalator and had found no maintenance was required.

You represent Chang and wish to recover against Grey's or Presley, or both. Do you have a res ipsa loquitur case? Or must you do further investigation? What lines of investigation, if any, would you pursue?

REFERENCES ON RES IPSA LOQUITUR: DOBBS ON TORTS §§ 154–161 (2000); HARPER, JAMES AND GRAY, THE LAW OF TORTS §§ 19.5–19.12 (2d Ed. 1986 & Supps.).

Chapter 7

HARM AND CAUSATION IN FACT

§ 1. ACTUAL HARM

The third element of a negligence prima facie case is that the plaintiff must suffer legally cognizable harm, frequently referred to as actual damages. The plaintiff who proves that the defendant's conduct was negligent, but fails to show what actual damage resulted from it, will lose the case.

COPELAND v. COMPTON

Missouri Court of Appeals, Southern District, Division Two, 1996.
914 S.W.2d 378.

SHRUM, CHIEF JUDGE.

Joe and Tracy Copeland (Plaintiffs) appeal from an adverse judgment entered pursuant to a jury verdict in their damage suit against Amy Nelson (Defendant) for her alleged negligent operation of an automobile.

. . . Plaintiffs charge that there was a complete absence of probative facts to support the jury's verdict that defendant was not liable and, consequently, the trial court erred and abused its discretion in denying their motion for a new trial on that basis. . . . We affirm.

. . . Plaintiffs insist that Defendant conceded "liability" when her counsel made certain statements in the jury's presence to the effect that "fault" was not a significant issue in the case. They also point to trial testimony which tends to show that Defendant negligently operated her automobile. The flaw in Plaintiff's position is their failure to recognize the breadth of the meaning associated with the term "liability."

"In any action for negligence, the plaintiff must establish that (1) the defendant had a duty to the plaintiff; (2) the defendant failed to perform that duty; and (3) the defendant's breach was the proximate cause of the plaintiff's injury." Martin v. City of Washington, 848 S.W.2d 487, 493 (Mo. Banc 1993). . . . Liability is the conclusion when there is a duty, breach and causal connection between the conduct of the defendant and the resulting injury to the plaintiff.

In this case, if Defendant conceded anything it was "negligence," i.e., duty and breach; not liability—the whole prima facie case. However, we need not decide if "negligence" was admitted since Plaintiffs apparently assert that the alleged concession of these two elements made a jury finding against them impermissible, any other issues notwithstanding. This is obviously not so, since a plaintiff with a negligence claim must also prove the element of causation and damages.

. . . Joe claimed that injuries to his neck and back resulted from his collision with Defendant. However, evidence of similar ailments which predated the accident as well as statements made by Joe following the collision contradicted the testimony offered by Plaintiffs.

In 1972, Joe fractured his back in a bicycle accident, and that injury resulted in chronic and severe neck, head, and back pain. At that time (1972), Joe was obese and continued to be overweight throughout his adult life. At one point prior to 1992, his weight reached 336 pounds, although he was only 5'5" tall. Joe was involved in no fewer than three automobile accidents which predated his collision with Defendant, in 1979, 1980, and 1987. In all three he was treated for either neck or back pain, or both, as a result of the accidents. Joe testified that he had no complaints of pain at the scene of the accident in question. Joe also admitted that he lied about his medical condition to a doctor he saw in connection with an on-the-job injury he sustained after the collision with Defendant.

We conclude that this record contains probative facts to support a jury verdict for Defendant. The jury was entitled to believe that Joe's injuries did not directly result from Defendant's negligence.

. . . If the negligence causes no actual damages to plaintiff, defendant is entitled to a verdict. . . .

We affirm the judgment of the trial court.

CROW, JUDGE, concurring in result.

I concur in the result, but would dispose of Plaintiff's contention that the verdict was unsupported by substantial evidence, or any evidence, on a more fundamental ground.

Inasmuch as Plaintiffs had the burden of proof, the verdict for Defendant required no evidentiary support whatever. A defendant denying liability for a plaintiff's alleged injury need not introduce any evidence to support a verdict in the defendant's favor. Consequently, Plaintiff's hypothesis that the verdict was unsupported by substantial evidence or by any evidence presents nothing for appellate review.

I agree with the rest of the principal opinion.

Notes

1. What counts as legally cognizable harm? A woman takes her beloved pet Chow Chow to a pet hospital for the "limited purpose of grooming and clipping." Instead, the dog was castrated due to the negligence of the veterinarian. Affirming a directed verdict for defendants, the court said that there was no proof that the dog was worth less money because of the castration, and thus the plaintiff failed to prove any damages. Her plea for "at least nominal damages" failed since, said the court, "damages are an element of the cause of action for negligence." *Ponder v. Angel Animal Hospital, Inc.*, 762 S.W.2d 846 (Mo.App.1988).

2. An early case involved a plaintiff who was a passenger on an interurban streetcar. He was put off the train because he had failed to purchase a ticket. He sued the railway company for negligence, claiming it breached a duty to carry him from Fall River to Newport. The Supreme Judicial Court of Massachusetts had little trouble in affirming a defense verdict: "[I]f no injury was caused by this [negligence] to this plaintiff; if he suffered no damage whatever from the defendant's negligence, then he would not be entitled to recover. Although there has been negligence in the performance of a legal duty, yet it is only those who have suffered damage therefrom that may maintain an action therefor." *Sullivan v. Old Colony St. Railway Co.*, 200 Mass. 303, 86 N.E. 511 (1908).

3. *Origins of the actual damage element.* Where the writ of *Trespass* was used at common law, as in battery, assault, false imprisonment and trespass to land, the plaintiff was not required to prove damages. Where the writ of *Case* was used, the plaintiff was required to prove actual damages. Negligence claims were initially based upon the writ of *Case*, and the requirement of actual damage has continued to apply, no doubt because it filters out relatively minor claims. On the *Trespass-Case* distinction and the development of negligence law, see DOBBS ON TORTS §§ 14, 42, 110 & 111 (2000).

4. *Damages recoverable in a personal injury case.* Recall the elements of damages from Chapter 1–past and future medical expenses, loss of wages or earning capacity, pain and suffering (including emotional harm), and damages for any other specifically-identifiable harm, such as special expenses necessary to travel for medical care. Punitive damages are generally *not* recoverable unless actual damages are established and then only if the defendant has a bad state of mind variously described as wilful, wanton, reckless, or malicious.

5. Most damages issues arise in connection with difficult issues of proof or measurement, and must be left to courses in trial practice and remedies. Some key issues are further addressed in Chapter 23.

§ 2. CAUSE IN FACT

The fourth element of a negligence prima facie case is cause in fact or actual cause. The plaintiff must prove, not only that she suffered legally recognized harm, but that the harm was in fact caused by the defendant. Cause in fact is a very simple concept in the great number of cases. Defendant drives negligently and strikes a pedestrian. This knocks the pedestrian down and breaks her leg. The defendant's conduct is, commonsensically, a cause in fact of the harm done. If defendant had not behaved in a negligent manner—if he had behaved non-negligently—the pedestrian would not have been injured. This is expressed as a "but-for" rule: but-for defendant's conduct, the pedestrian would have avoided injury. When this statement can be shown to be true, cause in fact or actual cause has been proven.

Fact or policy? Probably the mainstream, orthodox thinking is that the actual cause issue is truly a factual issue in the sense that it does not entail policy decisions. We might have more confidence in our judgment about causation in some cases than in others, but it is nevertheless a judgment about the *fact* of causation, not a value judgment or a policy decision. See ARNO BECHT & FRANK MILLER, THE TEST OF FACTUAL CAUSATION (1961). Yet considerations of policy or justice definitely seem to dictate some outcomes on the cause in fact issue. A good discussion is David A. Fischer, *Causation in Fact in Omission Cases,* 1992 UTAH L. REV. 1335. Try to judge for yourself whether the cases in this section deal with neutral, factual issues, or whether they deal with policy judgments about what the defendant's legal responsibility *should* be.

Other elements of proof. Keep in mind that actual cause is only one of several elements that the plaintiff must prove in order to win. Even when the plaintiff has proved that the defendant owed a duty of due care, that he breached this duty and that the negligence caused proven damages, the plaintiff will not have won. She must go further and prove that the relationship between the defendant's wrongdoing and the plaintiff's harm is legally significant. In other words, she must convince the judge and the trier that the defendant not only caused harm in fact but that as a matter of principle or policy he should be liable for it. This last is a concept to be investigated in the next section, not here. But lawyers must always remember that a decision favorable to the plaintiff on the actual cause issue does not mean that the plaintiff will win the case. A decision against the plaintiff on the cause in fact issue, on the other hand, will bar the plaintiff's claim altogether, since cause in fact is one of the indispensable elements necessary to sustain the claim.

a. *The But-for Test of Causation*

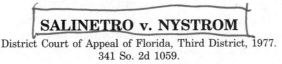

SALINETRO v. NYSTROM

District Court of Appeal of Florida, Third District, 1977.
341 So. 2d 1059.

[Anna Salinetro was in an auto accident and underwent a medical examination in connection with back injuries sustained. Dr. Nystrom made x-rays of her lower back and her abdominal areas.]

PER CURIAM.

Although unknown to her, Anna was approximately four-six weeks pregnant at the time; however, neither Dr. Nystrom nor his receptionist or his x-ray technician inquired whether or not she was pregnant or the date of her last menstrual period. Thereafter, upon suspecting she was pregnant, on December 12 Anna visited her gynecologist, Dr. Emilio Aldereguia, who, after running some tests, confirmed her pregnancy. In January Dr. Aldereguia learned that Dr. Nystrom had taken x-rays of Anna's pelvis and advised her to terminate her pregnancy because of possible damage to the fetus by the x-rays. Anna underwent a therapeutic abortion and the pathology report stated that the fetus was dead at the time of the abortion. Thereafter, Anna filed the instant lawsuit against Dr. Nystrom for medical malpractice. . . .

After the presentation of all the evidence on Anna's behalf, Dr. Nystrom moved for a directed verdict on the ground she failed to make a prima facie case of medical malpractice. The trial judge granted the motion and entered judgment for Dr. Nystrom. . . .

Assuming arguendo that Dr. Nystrom's conduct fell below the standard of care in failing to inquire of Anna whether she was pregnant or not on the date of her last menstrual period, this omission was not the cause of her injury. Anna herself testified that even if asked about being pregnant, she would have answered in the negative. Anna further testified to the effect that being a few days late with her menstrual period was not unusual and did not indicate to her that she may have been pregnant at the time she went to Dr. Nystrom; that six days prior thereto she had visited Dr. Aldereguia, and he had found no evidence that she was pregnant. We further note that simply because Anna was late with her menstrual period would not in and of itself mean that she was pregnant because further tests were required to ascertain whether she was pregnant. Thus, this point is without merit.

Notes

1. The defendant gets into her car and backs out of the driveway without looking in her rear-view mirror. Her husband was squatting behind the car at the rear bumper. Not knowing he was there, she backed into him. According to the reasoning in *Salinetro*, was her negligence in failing to look in the rear view mirror a cause of the injury? *Jordan v. Jordan*, 220 Va. 160, 257 S.E.2d 761 (1979).

2. A statute requires minors to complete a safety training course before hunting with firearms. Three boys, A, B, and C, go hunting without having taken the required course. A's gun accidentally discharges and the shot permanently paralyzes B. A is assuredly liable to the extent of his assets or insurance. What about C? Cf. *Cullip v. Domann*, 266 Kan. 550, 972 P.2d 776 (1999).

3. *But-for as a hypothetical or counterfactual test.* The but-for test is a hypothetical or counterfactual test; it asks what would have happened if the defendant had not been negligent. It thus requires the judge or jury to imagine an alternate scenario that never happened. Do you see any problems with this?

4. Consider the alternate scenario the court advanced in *Salinetro*. Is it the only alternative or is there any scenario under which the baby might have been saved? On the broad question whether such "counterfactuals" can work well, one writer cautions against an excess of either "bravado or dread," but agrees that counterfactuals like the but-for test must be used with care. See Robert N. Strassfeld, *If . . . : Counterfactuals in the Law*, 60 GEO. WASH. L.REV. 339 (1992).

5. *Res ipsa loquitur and but-for cause.* Does res ipsa loquitur always assist the plaintiff on causal as well as on negligence issues? Suppose a surgeon leaves sponges in the plaintiff's abdomen after an operation and this is regarded as a res ipsa loquitur case. This causes some harm, for which the surgeon would then be liable. But suppose the plaintiff claims the sponges caused stomach cancer. Will there be a causal issue that will require proof even though this is a res ipsa loquitur case?

b. Problems With and Alternatives to But-for Tests

NOTE: LIABILITY OF TWO OR MORE PERSONS

1. *Two persons causing a single injury.* Recall that two or more persons may be held liable for the plaintiff's injury. That liability may be either (a) joint and several liability with possible contribution, or (b) proportionate fault liability. When contribution is based on the relative fault of the tortfeasors, both these systems are forms of a fault apportionment approach. We'll call them fault apportionment rules for convenience. Do these fault apportionment rules fit with the but-for rule? Suppose A negligently runs into a horse and then negligently leaves the carcass on the highway where it might cause a second accident. B then negligently runs into the carcass, causing injury to his passenger, P. But-for A's negligence, the second collision would not have occurred, as there would have been no horse on the road. But-for B's negligence, the second collision would not have occurred because he would have stopped or taken evasive action to avoid hitting it. Both A and B are but-for causes of the plaintiff's single injury and both are subject to liability. The only question left in such a case is which fault apportionment rule to use, joint and several liability or proportionate fault liability.

2. *Causing separate injuries.* In paragraph 1, the injury was a single injury caused by two sets of negligent conduct. The but-for rule showed us that both sets of conduct were causal. In some cases, however, tortfeasor A may cause a broken arm while B causes a broken leg. So far as the two injuries are separate, each will be liable for the injury he caused and no more. In such a case, fault apportionment rules are not needed or used because liability can be apportioned by causation. That means that each tortfeasor is liable for harms he caused, no more, no less.

3. *Glancing back.* Before we go on, glance back at the two preceding paragraphs to see how simple they really are. If an indivisible injury is caused in fact by two or more persons, we cannot apportion liability by

causation. We must use some form of fault apportionment. But converse-ly if we can say that A caused only a broken arm and B only a broken leg, we can simply apportion liability to causes. A is liable only for the broken arm because he caused that harm and no other.

4. *Some defendants not a but-for cause of all injury.* Now suppose that C, a doctor, negligently makes both injuries worse, so that each break takes a week longer to heal than necessary. Can you work out (a) who is causally responsible for the broken arm and its delayed healing? (b) how joint and several liability would apply or not to the claims arising from the broken arm? Here is a start: A is a but-for cause of the broken arm. He is likewise a but-for cause of the delayed healing, isn't he? The doctor, C, is not a but-for cause of the broken arm but is a but-for cause of the added harm. How would joint and several liability work?

5. *Liability without but-for causation.* Under some circumstances a defendant is liable for harm to the plaintiff even though the defendant's negligent or illegal conduct was not a but-for cause of the harm. This is the case with *respondeat superior* liability: the telephone company is liable for its driver's on-the-job negligent driving that causes the plaintiff's injury. Such liability is not based upon the telephone company's negligence at all, but on the idea that, as a matter of policy, it should be liable for its employee's harmful torts. The same idea applies to partners in some circumstances, each being liable for the other's act. Analogously, those who act in a conspiracy or "in concert" to cause harm are all liable for the harm caused, even though only one of the conspirators is a direct cause of harm. At least one person must be a but-for cause of harm in such cases. If he is, the others are liable because they are deemed responsible for his acts.

6. These paragraphs show that two or more persons can be but-for causes and thus liable in some degree for the same harm. (The amount of liability depends upon whether the state follows joint and several liability or proportionate shares liability.) What is to be said about but-for cause if the independent acts of either A or B would be sufficient to cause harm even if the other had not acted at all?

LANDERS v. EAST TEXAS SALT WATER DISPOSAL CO.

Supreme Court of Texas, 1952.
151 Tex. 251, 248 S.W.2d 731.

CALVERT, JUSTICE.

[Plaintiff owned a small lake, which he had cleaned and stocked with fish at considerable expense. He alleged that on or about April 1 the pipe lines of the East Texas Salt Water Disposal Company broke and some 10 to 15 thousand barrels of salt water flowed over his land and into the lake, killing the fish and causing other damages. He alleged that the other defendant, Sun Oil Company, on or about the same day also caused large quantities of salt water and also oil to flow into his lake, killing the fish. He alleged that each defendant was negligent.]

Did the plaintiff in his pleading allege facts which, if established by evidence, made the defendants jointly and severally liable for plaintiff's damages? From the face of the petition it appears that there was no concert of action nor unity of design between the defendants in the commission of their alleged tortious acts, an absence said by the court in the case of Sun Oil Co. v. Robicheaux, Tex. Com. App., 23 S.W.2d 713, 715, to be determinative of the non-existence of joint liability. In that case the rule was thus stated:

"The rule is well established in this state, and supported by almost universal authority, that an action at law for damages for torts cannot be maintained against several defendants jointly, when each acted independently of the others and there was no concert or unity of design between them. In such a case the tort of each defendant is several when committed, and it does not become joint because afterwards its consequences, united with the consequences of several other torts committed by other persons in producing damages. Under such circumstances, each tortfeasor is liable only for the part of the injury or damages caused by his own wrong; that is, where a person contributes to an injury along with others, he must respond in damages, but if he acts independently, and not in concert of action with other persons in causing such injury, he is liable only for the damages which directly and proximately result from his own act, and the fact that it may be difficult to define the damages caused by the wrongful act of each person who independently contributed to the final result does not affect the rule." . . . .

The rule of the *Robicheaux* case, strictly followed, has made it impossible for a plaintiff, though gravely injured, to secure relief in the nature of damages through a joint and several judgment by joining in one suit as defendants all wrongdoers whose independent tortious acts have joined in producing an injury to the plaintiff, which, although theoretically divisible, as a practical matter and realistically considered is in fact but a single indivisible injury. As interpreted by the Courts of Civil Appeals the rule also denies to a plaintiff the right to proceed to judgment and satisfaction against the wrongdoers separately because in such a suit he cannot discharge the burden of proving with sufficient certainty, under pertinent rules of damages, the portion of the injury attributable to each defendant. . . . In other words, our courts seem to have embraced the philosophy, inherent in this class of decisions, that it is better that the injured party lose all of his damages than that any of several wrongdoers should pay more of the damages than he individually and separately caused. If such has been the law, from the standpoint of justice it should not have been; if it is the law now, it will not be hereafter. The case of Sun Oil Co. v. Robicheaux is overruled. Where the tortious acts of two or more wrongdoers join to produce an indivisible injury, that is, an injury which from its nature cannot be apportioned with reasonable certainty to the individual wrongdoers, all of the wrongdoers will be held jointly and severally liable for the entire damages and the injured party may proceed to judgment against any one separately or against all in one suit....

There is, of course, no joint liability for damages for the loss of trees and grass killed by the salt water escaping from the pipe line owned by East Texas Salt Water Disposal Company before such water entered the lake....

ANDERSON v. MINNEAPOLIS, ST. PAUL & SAULT STE. MARIE RAILWAY

Supreme Court of Minnesota, 1920.
146 Minn. 430, 179 N.W. 45.

LEES, C....

[Plaintiff's property was burned by a fire in October 1918. Plaintiff's proof tended to show that the fire was one set by defendant's engine in August, which smoldered until, in October, it swept east and burned the plaintiff's place. Defendant, however, offered proof tending to show that there were other fires sweeping east towards plaintiff's property and that these fires might have originated from other and perhaps non-negligent causes. The trial judge instructed in part: "If you find that other fires not set by one of the defendant's engines mingled with one that was set by one of the defendant's engines, there may be difficulty in determining whether you should find that the fire set by the engine was a material or substantial element in causing plaintiff's damage. If it was, the defendant is liable; otherwise, it is not...." The jury, so charged, found for the plaintiff.]

The following proposition is stated in defendant's brief and relied on for a reversal:

"If plaintiff's property was damaged by a number of fires combining, one being the fire pleaded, and the others being to no responsible origin, but of such sufficient or superior force that they would have produced the damage to plaintiff's property, regardless of the fire pleaded, then defendant was not liable."

This proposition is based upon Cook v. M., St. P. & S.S.M. Ry. Co., 98 Wis. 624, 74 N.W. 561, 40 L.R.A. 457, 67 Am. St. Rep. 830.... The Supreme Court of Michigan has referred to it as good law. The Supreme Court of Idaho says the opinion is logical and well reasoned, but the discussion is in a large measure theoretical and academic. Judge Thompson, in his work on Negligence (volume 1, § 739), says that the conclusion reached is so clearly wrong as not to deserve discussion. If the Cook Case merely decides that one who negligently sets a fire is not liable if another's property is damaged, unless it is made to appear that the fire was a material element in the destruction of the property, there can be no question about the soundness of the decision. But if it decides that if such fire combines with another of no responsible origin, and after the union of the two fires they destroy the property and either fire independently of the other would have destroyed it, then, irrespective of whether the first fire was or was not a material factor in the destruction of the property, there is no liability, we are not prepared to adopt the doctrine as the law of this state. If a fire set by the engine of one railroad company unites with a fire set by the engine of another company, there is joint and several liability, even though either fire would have destroyed plaintiff's property. But if the doctrine of the Cook Case is applied, and one of the fires is of unknown origin, there is no liability. G. S. 1913, § 4426, leaves no room for the application of a rule which would relieve a railroad company from liability under such circumstances. Moreover, the reasoning of the court in McClellan v. St. P., M. & M. Ry. Co., 58 Minn. 104, 59 N.W. 978, leads to the conclusion that, regardless of the statute, there would be liability in such a case. We therefore hold that the trial court did not err in refusing to instruct the jury in accordance with the rule laid down in the Cook Case. In the foregoing discussion we have assumed, although it is doubtful, that the evidence was such that a foundation was laid for the application of the rule, if it was otherwise applicable.

Notes

1.   Apply the but-for test to *Anderson*. Must you conclude that neither fire was an actual cause of the harm done to the plaintiff's property? But-for the defendant's fire, would the plaintiff have avoided harm?

2.   Apply the but-for test to *Landers*. How does that test work if you believe the two bodies of salt water entered the plaintiff's lake at the same time? How does it work if you believe that one body of salt water reached the lake first?

3.   *"Duplicative" causation*. Professor Richard Wright works out a modified and more complicated version of the but-for rule. Applying his rule, he draws a distinction between "preempted cause" and "duplicative cause." If each of the two fires in *Anderson* was sufficient to burn the plaintiff's property and would have done so regardless of the other fire, the two fires are "duplicative" causes. Professor Wright thinks cause should be defined in such a way that we would recognize the defendant's fire as a cause even if some other fire would have burned the property anyway, and applies the same idea to all duplicative cause cases. See Richard Wright, *Causation in Tort Law*, 73 Cal. L. Rev. 1735 (1985). Wright recognizes, however, that a straight but-for rule would not get this result.

4.   *"Preemptive" causation*. Professor Wright's "preempted cause" category is illustrated by a case in which one tortfeasor poisons the victim's tea. Just as the victim puts the tea to his lips, the other tortfeasor shoots him dead. Death would have followed from the poison even if the second tortfeasor had fired no shot at all, just as one fire would have burned the plaintiff's property even if no other fire had existed. But the two cases are not alike under Professor Wright's test. The victim died of a gunshot wound, not poison. The poisoner is not a cause. Is this *Landers*?

5. *Substantial factor.* In *Anderson* the court approved a jury instruction that allowed the jury to find actual causation if the defendant's fire was a "material or substantial element" in the harm done. Where the but-for test seems to produce clearly wrong results, as in the duplicative cause cases, the substantial factor test has been widely accepted. "[I]f two or more causes concur to bring about an event, then cause-in-fact is established by the 'substantial factor' test. . . . [W]hen either the 'but for' or 'substantial factor' test [is] satisfied, a party has established that the other party's conduct was the cause-in fact of an injury." *Busta v. Columbus Hospital Corp.*, 276 Mont. 342, 916 P.2d 122, 135 (Mont. 1996). California has seemingly adopted the substantial factor test for ALL cause in fact cases, not merely those involving two or more independent causes. *Mitchell v. Gonzales*, 54 Cal.3d 1041, 1 Cal.Rptr.2d 913, 819 P.2d 872 (1991). Is this a good idea? Does the substantial factor test call for a neutral, factual judgment or a judgment about policy, justice, or principle? Is substantial factor even a test or measure of anything at all?

6. *Indivisible injury.* A and B, each acting negligently, separately cause injury to the plaintiff. As a practical matter, the plaintiff cannot show how much of the injury was caused by A and how much by B. Under traditional rules, A and B are jointly and severally liable. Does this work when a large number of defendants contribute to harm? Suppose the plaintiff was exposed at work to various identified products of 55 different defendants, that toxins from these products entered his body, and "that each toxin that entered his body was a substantial factor in bringing about, prolonging, or aggravating" cancer. Would such facts sufficiently show causation? See *Bockrath v. Aldrich Chem. Co., Inc.*, 21 Cal.4th 71, 980 P.2d 398, 86 Cal.Rptr.2d 846 (1999). If your answer is "yes," what exactly is left to be decided in the case, if anything?

7. *Indivisible injury in several liability systems.* A negligently struck the plaintiff's stopped truck. The plaintiff suffered injury the extent of which was unknown but real. Several hours later, B negligently struck the plaintiff's stopped truck. The plaintiff was further injured. By the time the doctors could see the plaintiff, they could not say how much of the injury was due to A's impact and how much due to B's. We know how this would be handled under the traditional indivisible injury rule. How should it be handled in states that have abolished joint and several liability in favor of a several or proportionate share liability? *Piner v. Superior Court,* 192 Ariz. 182, 962 P.2d 909 (1998); *Gross v. Lyons,* 763 So.2d 276 (Fla. 2000).

8. *Divisible vs. indivisible injury.* Suppose two defendants separately release toxins that reach a lake and together destroy all plant and animal life in it, but that defendant A's toxins killed plant life only and defendant B's toxins killed animal life only. Would we need to know the relative fault of A and B? Now suppose that the events occurred as in *Landers,* except that we learn these additional facts: (1) tortfeasor A released twice as much salt water as B, but (2) B, though releasing less, was far more negligent than A. Did both cause an indivisible injury? Or did one in fact cause less harm than the other?

Problem

Tillo v. Thompson

Darlene Tillo gave birth to a child, Desiree, who was unusually large. Darlene Tillo suffered gestational diabetes. This, along with Desiree's size, contributed to a difficult delivery. Tillo's obstetrician, Dr. Josephine Kendrick, was negligent in estimating Desiree's size and in employing improper surgical procedures during delivery. As a result of Kendrick's negligence, Desiree suffered trauma in delivery and hypoxia, insufficient blood supply to cells and tissues. These conditions would or did cause brain damage and severe retardation.

Immediately after birth, Desiree was seen by a pediatrician, Dr. Eagle. Dr. Eagle was negligent in dealing with two conditions Desiree suffered, hyperbilirubinemia and excessively high hematocrit levels. Either of these conditions could ultimately cause damage to the brain and severe retardation unless it was properly treated. The conditions were not properly treated. Desiree is permanently and severely retarded. Care and treatment costs for her lifetime, not to mention other damages, will be very high.

Rules of law (including rules of causation) are often most important not because they dictate the final outcome but because they tell lawyers what kind of evidence to look for and what kind of arguments may be acceptable. You represent Dr. Eagle. What questions would you ask of him or of experts that would help clarify causal issues?

c. Proof: What Was Caused?

DILLON v. TWIN STATE GAS & ELECTRIC CO.

Supreme Court of New Hampshire, 1932.
85 N.H. 449, 163 A. 111.

[The defendant utility maintained uninsulated wires across a bridge. The bridge was constructed with steel girders rising on the sides and boys "habitually" climbed these and sat atop the horizontal girders at or near the level of the uninsulated wires. The decedent, a 14–year old boy, was on the top of a horizontal girder, leaned outward, lost his balance, and grabbed the defendant's electrical wire to save himself from falling. By chance, the wire carried high voltage current and he was electrocuted. The defendant moved for a directed verdict, which was denied. The jury could not agree on a verdict. The trial judge then transferred the case to the Supreme Court of New Hampshire on the defendant's exception to the denial of its motion for a directed verdict.]

ALLEN, J. . . .

If but for the current in the wires he would have fallen down on the floor of the bridge or into the river, he would without doubt have been either killed or seriously injured. Although he died from electrocution, yet, if by reason of his preceding loss of balance he was bound to fall except for the intervention of the current, he either did not have long to live or was to be maimed. In such an outcome of his loss of balance, the defendant deprived him, not of a life of normal expectancy, but of one too short to be given pecuniary allowance, in one alternative, and not of normal, but of limited, earning capacity, in the other.

If it were found that he would have thus fallen with death probably resulting, the defendant would not be liable, unless for conscious suffering found to have been sustained from the shock. In that situation his life or earning capacity had no value. To constitute actionable negligence there must be damage, and damage is limited to those elements the statute prescribes.

If it should be found that but for the current he would have fallen with serious injury, then the loss of life or earning capacity resulting from the electrocution would be measured by its value in such injured condition. Evidence that he would be crippled would be taken into account in the same manner as though he had already been crippled.

His probable future but for the current thus bears on liability as well as damages. Whether the shock from the current threw him back on the girder or whether he would have recovered his balance, with or without the aid of the wire he took hold of, if it had not been charged, are issues of fact, as to which the evidence as it stands may lead to different conclusion.

Exception overruled.

Notes

1. Are there limits to the principle in *Dillon*? See David W. Robertson, *The Common Sense of Cause in Fact*, 75 Tex. L. Rev. 1765, 1798 (1997); David A. Fischer, *Successive Causes and the Enigma of Duplicated Harm,* 66 Tenn. L. Rev. 1127 (1999) (detailed analysis of duplicative causes).

2. Richie Kilmer was 20 years old when he died by carbon monoxide poisoning from a gas furnace in leased premises for which the defendants were responsible. Kilmer had been born with hemophilia, a condition that required him to receive drugs or blood factors to help his blood coagulate. As a result of these treatments, he had tested HIV positive. A medical expert testified that "no one knows" the prognosis, that for several reasons Kilmer was in a statistically better protected group than the average person who had tested positive, that he was about to be evaluated for treatments with new drugs and might have lived until a cure for AIDs was found. This testimony was held admissible. *Kilmer v. Browning*, 806 S.W.2d 75 (Mo.App. 1991). Should the defendant have raised the *Dillon* rule? Do you think it is tactically easy to assert that defense to a jury? The jury brought in a verdict of $300,000. Do you think they took into account what the judge had in mind in *Dillon*?

SUMMERS v. TICE

Supreme Court of California, 1948.
33 Cal.2d 80, 199 P.2d 1.

CARTER, JUSTICE.

Each of the two defendants appeals from a judgment against them in an action for personal injuries. Pursuant to stipulation the appeals have been consolidated.

Plaintiff's action was against both defendants for an injury to his right eye and face as the result of being struck by bird shot discharged from a shotgun. The case was tried by the court without a jury and the court found that on November 20, 1945, plaintiff and the two defendants were hunting quail on the open range. Each of the defendants was armed with a 12 gauge shotgun loaded with shells containing 7-1/2 size shot.... The view of defendants with reference to plaintiff was unobstructed and they knew his location. Defendant Tice flushed a quail which rose in flight to a ten foot elevation and flew between plaintiff and defendants. Both defendants shot at the quail, shooting in plaintiff's direction. At that time defendants were 75 yards from plaintiff. One shot struck plaintiff in his eye and another in his upper lip. Finally it was found by the court that as the direct result of the shooting by defendants the shots struck plaintiff as above mentioned and that defendants were negligent in so shooting and plaintiff was not contributorily negligent....

The one shot that entered plaintiff's eye was the major factor in assessing damages and that shot could not have come from the gun of both defendants. It was from one or the other only.

It has been held that where a group of persons are on a hunting party, or otherwise engaged in the use of firearms, and two of them are negligent in firing in the direction of a third person who is injured thereby, both of those so firing are liable for the injury suffered by the third person, although the negligence of only one of them could have caused the injury. Both drivers have been held liable for the negligence of one where they engaged in a racing contest causing an injury to a third person. These cases speak of the action of defendants as being in concert as the ground of decision, yet it would seem they are straining that concept and the more reasonable basis appears in Oliver v. Miles, supra. There two persons were hunting together. Both shot at some partridges and in so doing shot across the highway injuring plaintiff who was traveling on it. The court stated they were acting in concert and thus both were liable. The court then stated: "We think that ... each is liable for the resulting injury to the boy, although no one can say definitely who actually shot him. *To hold otherwise would be to exonerate both from liability, although each was negligent, and the injury resulted from such negligence.*" ...

When we consider the relative position of the parties and the results that would flow if plaintiff was required to pin the injury on one of the defendants only, a requirement that the burden of proof on that subject be shifted to defendants becomes manifest. They are both wrongdoers negligent toward plaintiff. They brought about a situation where the negligence of one of them injured the plaintiff, hence it should rest with them each to absolve himself if he can. The injured party has been placed by defendants in the unfair position of pointing to which defendant caused the harm. If one can escape the other may also and plaintiff is remediless. Ordinarily defendants are in a far better position to offer evidence to determine what one caused the injury. . . .

Cases are cited for the proposition that where two or more tortfeasors acting independently of each other cause an injury to plaintiff, they are not joint tortfeasors and plaintiff must establish the portion of the damage caused by each, even though it is impossible to prove the portion of the injury caused by each. In view of the foregoing discussion it is apparent that defendants in cases like the present one may be treated as liable on the same basis as joint tortfeasors, and hence the last cited cases are distinguishable inasmuch as they involve independent tortfeasors.

In addition to that, however, it should be pointed out that the same reasons of policy and justice [which] shift the burden to each of defendants to absolve himself if he can—relieving the wronged person of the duty of apportioning the injury to a particular defendant—apply here where we are concerned with whether plaintiff is required to supply evidence for the apportionment of damages. If defendants are independent tortfeasors and thus each liable for the damage caused by him alone, and, at least, where the matter of apportionment is incapable of proof, the innocent wronged party should not be deprived of his right to redress. The wrongdoers should be left to work out between themselves any apportionment. Some of the cited cases refer to the difficulty of apportioning the burden of damages between the independent tortfeasors, and say that where factually a correct division cannot be made, the trier of fact may make it the best it can, which would be more or less a guess, stressing the factor that the wrongdoers are not in a position to complain of uncertainty. . . .

The judgment is Affirmed.

Notes

1. One tortfeasor caused the harm. What did the other tortfeasor cause?

2. In *State v. CTL Distribution, Inc.,* 715 So.2d 262 (Fla.Ct.App.1998), one or more truckers spilled a hazardous substance when making deliveries of that substance at a certain business. The state environmental agency sued the seven truckers who delivered the substance. It proved that one of them, CTL, had once spilled the substance and argued that *Summers v. Tice* would authorize liability for all seven. How would you rule if you were the judge?

3. In *Canada v. McCarthy,* 567 N.W.2d 496 (Minn.1997), a two-year-old child suffered from lead poisoning before July. After July the defendant

subjected her to additional lead exposure that enhanced the injury but the plaintiff cannot prove the amount of the enhancement. If *Summers* is appealing when two defendants are negligent, would it apply by analogy to a single defendant aggravating an existing injury? Would a court go further and hold the defendant liable if there was a good likelihood that the defendant caused no harm at all? See the next two cases.

WOLLEN v. DEPAUL HEALTH CENTER

Supreme Court of Missouri, 1992.
828 S.W.2d 681.

[Mr. Wollen died from gastric cancer. In this suit, his widow claims that the defendants involved in medical treatment negligently failed to diagnose or test and that had they correctly tested or treated, Mr. Wollen would have had a 30% chance of survival and cure. The trial judge dismissed for failure to state a claim.]

BENTON, JUDGE.

[The allegations are not sufficient to show that the defendants' alleged negligence was a cause of Mr. Wollen's death.] On the other hand there are compelling reasons for granting compensation in this type of cause of action. The traditional yes-no view of the world in causation theory does not match the 'maybe' view of the world found in probability, statistics, and everyday life. To both the statistician and the patient seeking care from a doctor, there is no meaningful difference between a 50.001% and a 49.999% chance of recovery.

Medical science has given patients real chances to recover, sometimes only a small chance, but still a chance, in circumstances that used to be hopeless. When patients go to doctors with serious illnesses, they expect to have those chances that medical science has provided. To the individual patient, if the doctor's negligence destroys the chance of recovery, it is irrelevant what that chance originally was. . . .

A patient with cancer, like Mr. Wollen, would pay to have a choice between three unmarked doors—behind two of which were death, with life the third option. A physician who deprived a patient of this opportunity, even though only a one-third chance, would have caused her real harm. In light of this reality, the patient does suffer a harm when the doctor fails to diagnose or adequately treat a serious injury or disease. The harm suffered is not, however, the loss of life or limb. The harm is the loss of the chance of recovery. While, in the end, damages can only be expressed by multiplying the value of a lost life or limb by the chance of recovery lost, the proper place for such an inquiry is in the damages stage rather than in the liability/causation determination. Therefore, rather than adopting a theory of proportional causation, this Court chooses to recognize a cause of action for lost chance of recovery in medical malpractice cases.

[Vacated and remanded.]

FENNELL v. SOUTHERN MARYLAND HOSP. CENTER, INC.

Court of Appeals of Maryland, 1990.
320 Md. 776, 580 A.2d 206.

CHASANOW, JUDGE. . . .

[Cora Fennell suffered a severe headache in the early hours of the morning. Her husband took her to the emergency room. Doctors thought there was a neurosurgical emergency, perhaps an intracranial bleed. A CT Scan was performed, probably about 3:30 in the morning. Mrs. Fennell was admitted to the hospital at 4:00 and a little later to the intensive care unit. She "arrested" at 7:40 and was found to be brain dead, but maintained on life support for another day until she "arrested" again and was pronounced dead. From 4:00 a.m. when she was admitted until just before brain death, she was not seen by any physician. The CT Scan, however, had ruled out a bleed and suggested an inflammatory process. In fact, autopsy showed she had been suffering from meningitis.]

Dr. Bach stated that the CT Scan taken at approximately 3:30 a.m. revealed brain swelling and that proper medical treatment required that a lumbar puncture be completed within one-half hour thereafter. He further stated that had decedent been diagnosed and treated in accordance with the appropriate standard of care, she would have had a 40% chance of survival. He concluded that the failure to follow-up the CT Scan with a lumbar puncture and the failure to immediately and aggressively reduce the swelling of the brain that was detected by the CT Scan were violations of the standard of care, and that as a result, the progress of the disease was irreversible. In effect, Dr. Bach established that decedent had a 40% chance of surviving the meningitis, but that the chance was lost as a result of the Hospital's negligence. [The Fennells asserted the claim that the patient would have had if she had lived.]

. . . Courts adopting the relaxed causation/new cause of action approach continue to award "all or nothing" damages, and when the plaintiff establishes a "substantial possibility" that the doctor's negligence caused the death, there is full recovery. The result is that relaxing the rules of causation merely improves the plaintiff's odds of receiving all rather than nothing.

The relaxed causation approach in medical malpractice cases has often been attributed to dictum in Hicks v. United States, 368 F.2d 626 (4th Cir.1966), where Judge Sobeloff writing for the Court stated:

"When a defendant's negligent action or inaction has effectively terminated a person's chance of survival, it does not lie in the defendant's mouth to raise conjectures as to the measure of the chances that he has put beyond the possibility of realization. If there was any substantial possibility of survival and the defendant has destroyed it, he is answerable. . . .

We are unwilling to relax traditional rules of causation and create a new tort allowing full recovery for causing death by causing a loss of less than 50% chance of survival. In order to demonstrate proximate cause, the burden is on the plaintiff to prove by a preponderance of the evidence that "it is more probable than not that defendant's act caused his injury." ...

Appellants urge this Court to adopt the loss of chance/damages approach first suggested by Professor King in his law review article King, Causation, Valuation and Chance in Personal Injury Torts Involving Pre-existing Conditions and Future Consequences, 90 Yale L.J. 1353 (1981).

In Cooper v. Hartman, supra, this Court described the damage approach as leaving "the traditional rules of causation intact," but treating "the loss of a chance as a way of approaching damages." The Court quoted a passage from Professor King's law review article which, by coincidence, describes the same "chance of survival" percentage shown in the instant case:

> "To illustrate, consider a patient who suffers a heart attack and dies as a result. Assume that the defendant-physician negligently misdiagnosed the patient's condition, but that the patient would have had only a 40% chance of survival even with a timely diagnosis and proper care. Regardless of whether it could be said that the defendant caused the decedent's death, he caused the loss of a chance, and that chance-interest should be completely redressed in its own right. Under the proposed rule, the plaintiff's compensation for the loss of the victim's chance of surviving the heart attack would be 40% of the compensable value of the victim's life had he survived. ...

Judge McAuliffe, in his concurring opinion in Weimer, supra, outlined the damage approach: "[A] claim under that theory does not involve the creation of a new tort, but rather involves a redefinition of damages involved in the claim. Traditional principles of law relating to duty, breach, causation, and burden of proof remain the same—what changes is the acceptance of the concept that damages may be recovered for the loss of a chance of survival where that chance is substantial and can be identified and quantified (and thus valued) without resort to conjecture or speculation." ...

A good argument can be made that damages ought to be recoverable when, due to a doctor's negligence, a patient loses a substantial, though less than probable, chance of survival. There are also some arguments against expanding damages in medical malpractice cases to include damages for loss of chance of survival.

Because loss of chance recovery is based on statistical probabilities, it might be appropriate to examine the statistical probabilities of achieving a "just" result with loss of chance damages. In Brennwald, Proving Causation in "Loss of a Chance" Cases: A Proportional Approach, 34 Cath.U.L.Rev. 747, 779 n. 254 (1985), the author, citing Orloff and

Stedinger's article, A Framework for Evaluating the Preponderance-of-the-Evidence Standard, 131 U.Pa.L.Rev. 1159 (1983), attempted to analyze statistically the errors produced using traditional tort recovery as compared to the errors produced by loss of chance recovery.

To compare the two rules, assume a hypothetical group of 99 cancer patients, each of whom would have had a 33 1/3% chance of survival. Each received negligent medical care, and all 99 died. Traditional tort law would deny recovery in all 99 cases because each patient had less than a 50% chance of recovery and the probable cause of death was the pre-existing cancer not the negligence. Statistically, had all 99 received proper treatment, 33 would have lived and 66 would have died; so the traditional rule would have statistically produced 33 errors by denying recovery to all 99.

The loss of chance rule would allow all 99 patients to recover, but each would recover 33 1/3% of the normal value of the case. Again, with proper care 33 patients would have survived. Thus, the 33 patients who statistically would have survived with proper care would receive only one-third of the appropriate recovery, while the 66 patients who died as a result of the pre-existing condition, not the negligence, would be overcompensated by one-third. The loss of chance rule would have produced errors in all 99 cases.

Re-defining loss of chance of survival as a new form of damages so that the compensable injury is not the death, but is the loss of chance of survival itself, may really be an exercise in semantics. Loss of chance of survival in itself is not compensable unless and until death ensues. Thus, it would seem that the true injury is the death.

While we should not award damages if there is no injury, the logical extension of the loss of chance damages theory arguably should allow loss of chance damages for negligence, even when the patient miraculously recovers....

Since loss of chance damages are only permitted when the patient dies, it is also arguable that, when we strip away the rhetoric, damages are really being awarded for the possibility that the negligence was a cause of the death. Maryland law clearly does not allow damages based on mere possibilities.

Another factor weighing against adoption of a loss of chance damages approach is its practical application in civil jury trials. Probabilities and statistical evidence comprise a substantial portion of the evidence submitted to the trier of fact in loss of chance actions. This evidence will generally be in the form of opinions based on statistics that show chance of survival of other individuals similarly situated to the victim. The use of statistics in trials is subject to criticism as being unreliable, misleading, easily manipulated, and confusing to a jury. When large damage awards will be based on the statistical chance of survival before the negligent treatment, minus the statistical chance of survival after the negligent treatment, times the value of the lost life, we can imagine the bewildering sets of numbers with which the jury will be confronted, as well as the difficulties juries will have in assessing the comparative reliability of the divergent statistical evidence offered by each side.

Traditional tort law is based on probabilities. If a patient had a 49% chance of dying from an injury or disease and if the patient was negligently treated and dies, full recovery will be permitted because, absent the negligence, it was more likely than not that the patient would have survived. Based on the 51% probability of surviving the injury or disease, we exclude the injury or disease as the cause of death. Damages are not reduced by the fact that there was a strong possibility that the patient would have died absent the negligence. Conversely, if the patient had a 51% chance of dying from an injury or disease, and was negligently treated and died, it was probably the pre-existing medical condition, not the negligence, that killed the patient, and there is no recovery. Damages must be proven by a preponderance of the evidence. Damages are not proven when it is more likely than not that death was caused by the antecedent disease or injury rather than the negligence of the physician.

When urged to adopt new theories of causation and/or new elements of tort damages, this Court should be "concerned with the substantial expansion of tortfeasor liability and the accompanying societal costs that will be imposed by this new cause of action.". . . .

The legislature is better able to ascertain the reasons for the increase in malpractice claims, and what, if any, remedial action is necessary. . . . Recognition of this new form of medical malpractice damages for loss of a chance would undoubtedly cause an increase in medical malpractice litigation, as well as result in an increase in medical malpractice insurance costs.

[Affirmed. Dissents and concurring opinions omitted.]

Notes

1. Both *Wollen* and *Fennell* involve some technical problems under wrongful death or survival statutes. Those problems may be significant in interpreting the scope of the courts' holdings, but they are peripheral to the issues in this section and are not reflected in the edited versions given here.

2. *The preponderance test.* Remember that the plaintiff must prove each element of her case by a preponderance of the evidence. This means the "greater weight" of the evidence or more likely than not. If this is put in numbers, it means that the plaintiff must persuade the trier that the probabilities are greater than 50% that each element is established. Look at *Wollen* with this in mind. Did the plaintiff prove that, more likely than not, death resulted from the defendant's negligence?

3. *Relaxed causation tests.* Some courts, either by their words or their deeds, have eased the plaintiff's burden of proof in cases like *Wollen* and *Fennell*. The reasoning is sometimes a little vague. Perhaps these cases are consistent with the view that the doctor's negligence concurs with the preexisting condition to produce a single indivisible injury. Unless there is some sound basis for attributing an identifiable portion of the injury to the

preexisting condition, the doctor thus becomes liable for the entire harm so long as his negligence is a substantial factor in the injury. E.g., *Hamil v. Bashline,* 481 Pa. 256, 392 A.2d 1280 (1978). These cases appear to permit a jury to award full damages, but not all of them actually involve evidence showing that the patient had a quantified chance below the .50+ level.

4. *Inference of causation.* Outside the medical or scientific cases, courts often relax causal rules in a different way. For instance, if the defendant negligently constructs stairs that are too steep and negligently fails to light them, it will be difficult to say with certainty that everyone who falls on the stairs did so because of the negligent construction or lighting. Yet in such cases courts are inclined to say that the jury can infer causation. See *Zuchowicz v. United States,* 140 F.3d 381, 390–391 (2d Cir.1998) (Calabresi, J.) ; David A. Fischer, *Causation in Fact in Omission Cases,* 1992 UTAH L. REV. 1335; Wex S. Malone, *Ruminations on Cause in Fact,* 9 STAN. L. REV. 60 (1958). If the jury finds causation, then full damages can be recovered.

5. *Duty to try analysis.* A similar but more striking approach appeared in *Gardner v. National Bulk Carriers,* Inc., 310 F.2d 284, 91 A.L.R.2d 1023 (4th Cir. 1962). Gardner, a seaman on board a ship at sea, was called to stand watch at 11:30, but he could not be found. He had last been seen five or six hours earlier. The ship notified the Coast Guard but did not attempt to return to those areas of the sea where, at any time during the five hours, he might have fallen overboard. In a suit for Gardner's death, the defendant argued that actual cause had not been shown, since a search probably could not have found a man who had gone overboard hours earlier. But the Fourth Circuit held that since the duty of the captain was to make every reasonable effort. "It was less than a duty to rescue him, but it was a positive duty to make a sincere attempt at rescue.... [C]ausation is proved if the master's omission destroys the reasonable possibility of rescue." The court apparently envisioned full liability for the seaman's death.

6. *Quantified value-of-the-chance approach.* Under a second theory, causal rules are not changed. Instead, the defendant's duty of care is broad enough not merely to protect the plaintiff against injury or loss of life, but also to protect the plaintiff against loss of substantial *chances.* If the *chance* of survival was 40% and the defendant's negligence more likely than not eliminated that chance, then the defendant would be liable for the loss he has caused–the chance. In damages, this is presumably 40% of the damages for which the defendant would be liable if he caused death. The plaintiff may still lose, of course, if the chance and its loss is not established by evidence. On this see *Alberts v. Schultz,* 126 N.M. 807, 975 P.2d 1279 (N.M. 1999).

7. *Unquantified value-of-the-chance approach.* In *Smith v. State,* 676 So.2d 543 (La.1996), the Louisiana Supreme Court recognized that loss of a less-than-even chance of survival was a distinct injury, but insisted that the loss could not be calculated by applying a discount based on the percentage chance of survival. Instead, Justice Lemmon's opinion left it to the jury to make a subjective valuation of the lost chance. The plaintiff must prove that he had a chance and that part of it was lost. The plaintiff must also provide evidence about the value of the chance, but evidently is not required to produce evidence in percentage terms.

8. *Supporting value of the chance approach.* The value-of-the-chance theory has gained substantial support in recent years, primarily as a result of Professor King's article cited in *Fennell.* A recent example is *Jorgenson v. Vener,* 613 N.W.2d 50 (S.D.2000); see DOBBS ON TORTS § 178 (2000).

9. *Rejecting value-of-the-chance approach.* A number of courts, including those in the District of Columbia, California, Florida, Texas, and Tennessee, have expressly rejected the lost-chance theory. Michigan does so by statute. Recent case examples are *Grant v. American Nat'l Red Cross,* 745 A.2d 316 (D.C.App.2000) and *Jones v. Owings,* 318 S.C. 72, 456 S.E.2d 371, 374 (S.C. 1995). The latter claimed that loss-of-chance recovery "is contrary to the most basic standards of proof which undergird the tort system." Some courts seem to have confused the calculation of damages for loss of a chance with comparative fault reductions.

10. *Merits of the approaches.* Consider the relative merits of the various approaches. Are you convinced by the *Fennell* court's example of 99 cases? The example seems to trace ultimately to Neil Orloff & Jerry Stedinger, *A Framework for Evaluating the Preponderance-of-the-Evidence Standard,* 131 U.PA.L.REV. 1159 (1983) by way of Stephen F. Brennwald, Comment, *Proving Causation in "Loss of a Chance" Cases: A Proportional Approach,* 34 CATH. U.L.REV. 747 (1985). Orloff and Stedinger, however, did not draw the conclusion drawn by the majority. Instead they emphasized that although the value of the chance (or expected value) rule might produce *more* errors in some sense, the preponderance of the evidence rule produced *larger* errors. Both the number and the size of the errors produced were important in evaluating the rule, so they thought that the appropriate rule might vary from one kind of case to another. Mr. Brennwald, seemed even less impressed with the number of errors analysis. He thought chances should be recognized as valuable interests. Is this the picture the *Fennell* Court conveyed?

11. Judge Posner has written approvingly of the loss-of-chance recovery in dictum, saying, "This basis for an award of damages is not accepted in all jurisdictions, but it is gaining ground and it is in our view basically sound. . . . It recognizes the inescapably probabilistic character of many injuries. It is essential in order to avoid undercompensation and thus (in the absence of punitive damages) underdeterrence, though to avoid the opposite evils of overcompensation and overdeterrence it must be applied across the board, that is, to high-probability as well as to low-probability cases. If the patient in our example was entitled to 25 percent of his full damages because he had only a 25 percent chance of survival, he should be entitled to 75 percent of his damages if he had a 75 percent chance of survival—not 100 percent of his damages on the theory that by establishing a 75 percent chance he proved injury by a preponderance of the evidence. He proves injury in both cases, but in both cases the injury is merely probabilistic and must be discounted accordingly." *Doll v. Brown,* 75 F.3d 1200, 1206 (7th Cir.1996). See also John Makdisi, *Proportional Liability: A Comprehensive Rule to Apportion Tort Damages Based Probability,* 67 N.C.L. REV. 1063 (1989) (supporting general use of lost chance or probabilistic causation). How would this change the "normal" rules of causation? How would juries determine these percentages?

12. In *McMullen v. Ohio State University Hospitals,* 88 Ohio St.3d 332, 725 N.E.2d 1117 (2000), the defendant's negligence hastened the decedent's death. That much was almost certain. There was testimony, however, that the plaintiff would not have lived more than a month anyway, and perhaps on that basis the trial court applied a value of the chance rule, reducing damages. The Supreme Court of Ohio held that this was error because it was almost "certain" that the defendants had caused the death. Should the defendants have been arguing not diminished chance but the rule in *Dillon?*

13. *Deterrence.* Which rule (if any) seems to provide the most appropriate deterrence? Take a look at the hypothetical facts and table below.

Three Cancer Patients

Each patient has a 1/3 or 33.33% chance of survival if properly treated. The defendant negligently treats each one and all three die. In each case, damages for wrongful death would have been $100,000 if the negligence is treated as a cause of the harm. We cannot in fact know which one would have lived had proper treatment been provided, but the overwhelming likelihood is that one would have lived. An omniscient trier of fact would know which one (line four).

	Recovery	Total Liability
Traditional rule	$0.0	$0.0
Relaxed causation	$100,000 each	$300,000
Lost chance	$33,333.33 each	$100,000
Omniscient Trier	$100,000 to one estate	$100,000

14. Do you think that value-of-the-chance would create limitless tort cases? Courts could say that certain actors, like physicians, owe a duty to maximize the value of the plaintiff's chances but that others do not. If an actor owed no duty to maximize chances, he would be held liable only under traditional causal rules. If he owed a duty to maximize chances, he would be held for the value of less-than-likely lost chances. Courts have so far applied value of the chance reasoning mainly to physician-patient cases. See *Hardy v. Southwestern Bell Tel. Co.,* 910 P.2d 1024 (Okl.1996) (refusing to extend loss-of-chance theory "beyond the established boundary of medical malpractice"). Is there anything special about the relation of doctor and patient that suggests a duty to maximize the patient's chances?

15. On value of the chance generally, see DOBBS, ON TORTS §§ 178 & 179 (2000).

⌐ALEXANDER v. SCHEID, 726 N.E.2d 272 (Ind.2000). The plaintiff's physician ordered an X-ray. The radiologist reported that it showed a "density . . . in the upper lobe" of her lung and concluded that "comparison with old films would be of value." In breach of the standard of care, the defendant did not follow up on this information. The mass grew but was not discovered until the plaintiff went to another doctor months later. By this time she was suffering from advanced cancer that had metastasized. The probability of her long-term survival was significantly reduced because of the delay. The trial court granted the defendant's motion for summary judgment and the Court of Appeals affirmed. In the Supreme Court of Indiana, *held,* reversed and remanded. "We think that loss of chance is better understood as a description of the injury than as either a term for a separate cause of action or a surrogate for the causation element of a negligence claim. If a plaintiff seeks recovery specifically for what the plaintiff alleges the doctor to have caused, i.e., a decrease in the patient's probability of recovery, rather than for the ultimate outcome, causation is no longer debatable. Rather, the problem becomes one of identification and valuation or quantification of that injury. . . . A number of jurisdictions allow recovery for negligence that has 'increased the risk of harm,' even where the full ramifications of the defendant's actions are not yet known. . . . More specifically, many jurisdictions have recognized a decrease in life expectancy as a cognizable injury. . . . [W]e hold that JoAnn may maintain a cause of action in negligence for this increased risk of harm, which may be described as a decreased life expectancy or the diminished probability of long-term survival. Here, we also have an injury that often accompanies a delay in diagnosis–the invasion of healthy tissue by a tumor or other growth. Accordingly, this case does not present the issue whether a plaintiff must have incurred some physical injury as a result of the defendant's negligence in order to recover for an increased risk of harm. Some courts have concluded, particularly in the loss of chance context, that the loss must be 'substantial' before it is compensable. We see no obvious method of quantifying that test. Because we measure damages by probabilizing the injury, the likelihood that plaintiffs will bring claims for trivial reductions in chance of recovery seems small. If, in the future, we face a volume of insignificant claims, perhaps such a rule will become necessary. For now, we are content to rely on basic economics to deter resort to the courts to redress remote probabilities or insubstantial diminutions in the likelihood of recovery."

Note

Professor King concludes that the courts are divided on whether to apply the loss of chance approach to future consequences that may not in fact ever occur. Joseph H. King, Jr., *"Reduction of Likelihood" Reformulation And Other Retrofitting of The Loss-of-A–Chance Doctrine,* 28 U. Mem. L. Rev. 491 (1998).

A NOTE ON MASS EXPOSURE AND TOXIC TORTS CAUSATION

1. Toxic torts cases often raise issues similar to those involved in the medical value-of-the-chance cases. These torts involve exposure of

individuals, often large numbers of individuals, to harmful biological or chemical substances. Examples include environmental exposure to contaminated air or water, sometimes from operations of ongoing industry, sometimes from hazardous waste disposal sites. Sometimes exposure to toxic material clearly causes the plaintiff's harm, as where the asbestos worker gets the special form of asbestos cancer, mesothelioma. Other toxic tort cases may be much more complex. For this note, imagine such a case:

> A landfill or toxic waste disposal site in which many producers of such waste contribute their different wastes in sealed containers. Over a period of time some containers leak and contaminate the soil. Eventually the contamination passes into a water supply and many persons drink it.

2. *Some causal difficulties.* Suppose that contributors to the landfill are legally liable if their contributions cause the plaintiffs harm. Then consider the "causal" difficulties for the plaintiff. (1) Did any given defendant contribute to the landfill and if so, did its container leak? (2) If the defendant's container leaked, did any of the substance therein have the capacity to cause harms of the type the plaintiffs complain of? (3) Were the plaintiffs exposed to the substance—did it actually reach the plaintiffs' drinking water, for example? (4) If the plaintiffs were exposed, did the harms they suffer result from the exposure or from other sources? Since many toxic tort cases involve a long latency period between exposure and disease, sometimes twenty years, the plaintiffs may have grave difficulty in mounting ordinary proof of causation.

3. *Epidemiological proof.* In many of these cases the plaintiff must attempt to provide major scientific evidence based in clinical tests, animal studies and epidemiological evidence. Epidemiological evidence is statistical evidence connecting disease with exposure. Proof of this kind does not address the question whether the plaintiff was exposed to the toxin. It addresses the question whether, upon exposure the toxin was capable of and actually did cause the harm.

4. *Value of the chance and epidemiological proof.* If the epidemiological or statistical proof shows that one exposed to the defendant's toxic wastes has a 20% greater likelihood of cancer than the general population and if the plaintiff actually had cancer after exposure, should the plaintiff be permitted to recover 20% of his damages under a value-of-the-chance type rule? Suppose 51 plaintiffs drank contaminated water but their relative chances of cancer were different because they drew on wells at different distances from the source and thus were subjected to different levels of exposure. Suppose the closest plaintiff had a 51% chance of cancer from her exposure and each succeeding plaintiff had 1% less chance than the one before so that the last one had only a 1% chance. If each plaintiff then actually suffered cancer after exposure and each had the same damages, what result under the traditional rule? Under value of the chance?

5. *Limiting the defendant's total liability to proportional cause limits*. One possibility for this situation is that the defendant's total liability should be limited to the total damages times the likelihood that the defendant caused them. For example, if each of our plaintiffs has $1 million in damages, the total harm from all cancers in the group would be $51 million. But the odds are that the defendant caused only 26% (the average probability of causation for all plaintiffs as a group). If the defendant's liability is limited to 26% x 51 million, its liability should be about $13 million. The defendant in such a case would have no just complaint at the use of proportional or probabilistic cause to fix damages, since that is probably the amount of liability it would have if full information about cause were available; the full information would merely give us a more accurate picture about *who* was injured. But if the defendant has no complaint in such a case, how would you divide the $13 million among the claimants? See Daniel Farber, *Toxic Causation*, 71 Minn. L. Rev. 1219, 1249 (1987).

AN END NOTE

Causation in fact has proven to be a difficult topic. From a moral or normative point of view, would it be wrong to hold a defendant liable when he has committed negligent acts but, fortuitously, has not caused harm? From the point of view of deterring unsafe conduct, would liability without causation be a good idea? See Margaret A. Berger, *Eliminating General Causation: Notes Towards a New Theory of Justice and Toxic Torts*, 97 Colum. L. Rev. 2117 (1997). Consider this possible rule for liability without proof of causation: The defendant is liable without proof that his conduct caused legal harm if, but only if

       (1) the defendant has acted negligently; and

       (2) the negligence created an identifiable risk; and

       (3) the plaintiff was one of the persons subjected to that risk; and

       (4) the plaintiff actually suffered harm of the kind risked by the defendant.

REFERENCES: On actual cause generally, see DOBBS ON TORTS §§ 166–179 (2000); David W. Robertson, The Common Sense of Cause in Fact, 75 TEX. L. REV. 1765, 1780 (1997); HARPER, JAMES & GRAY, THE LAW OF TORTS § 20.2 (3d ed. 1995). Besides articles cited in this section, see also the philosophically oriented symposium, *Causation in the Law of Torts*, 63 CHI-KENT L. REV. 397 (1987).

Chapter 8

NEGLIGENCE: THE SCOPE OF RISK OR "PROXIMATE CAUSE" REQUIREMENT

§ 1. THE PRINCIPLE: SCOPE OF RISK

The fifth and final element of the prima facie case in the negligence action is *legal or "proximate" cause*. Proximate cause determinations involve case-specific inquiries into whether the defendant should be held legally responsible to the plaintiff. Even when the defendant was negligent and in fact caused harm to the plaintiff, courts may refuse to impose liability when the harm was outside the risks created by the defendant's negligence. This idea is conventionally summed up by saying that the defendant's negligence, though a cause in fact, was not foreseeable or not a proximate cause of the harm.

Why would it be either just or good policy to hold that a defendant is not liable for harm he has negligently caused? Suppose that the defendant is Dr. Dayden, a surgeon who performed a vasectomy operation upon Mr. Fallow some years ago. Because the vasectomy was negligently performed, Mr. Fallow sired a child, William. William, when he reached the age of six, set fire to the plaintiff's garage. The plaintiff has now sued William, Mr. Fallow, and Dr. Dayden. The plaintiff can show that Dr. Dayden negligently performed the vasectomy and that his negligence in fact was one of the causes of William's conception and birth. The plaintiff can also show that since his garage would not have been burned but for William's existence, Dr. Dayden's negligence in the vasectomy operation was a cause in fact of that harm.

Probably all lawyers would agree that the surgeon is not liable for the burning of the garage. The reasons for this outcome may be expressed in different ways. Many judicial opinions are likely to emphasize "causation," the attenuated causal link between the surgeon's negligence and the harm ultimately done by William. Yet while causation is often the conventional locution, the underlying idea seems to be more precise and more principled: Liability for negligence is liability for the unreasonable risks the defendant created, not for reasonable risks or for those that were unforeseeable.

However judges express themselves on proximate cause issues, ask yourself in each case whether the reason for relieving the defendant of liability was merely one of practicality or policy. Or is it a moral reason, grounded in justice of limiting liability to harms for unreasonable risks?

MEDCALF v. WASHINGTON HEIGHTS CONDOMINIUM ASS'N, INC.

Appellate Court of Connecticut, 2000.
57 Conn.App. 12, 747 A.2d 532.

MIHALAKOS, J. . . .

[T]he plaintiff and a friend, Deborah Michelson, arrived at 1633 Washington Boulevard in Stamford at approximately 9 p.m. to visit a friend, Tracy Skiades. The defendant Washington Heights Condominium Association, Inc., is a Connecticut corporation comprised of the unit owners of the premises. The defendant Professional Property Management Company, Inc., is the managing agent in control of the operation, management and repair of the premises.

The plaintiff parked her car in the street level parking lot and walked to the lobby doors. The lighting in the parking lot was dim. She picked up the intercom outside the lobby and called Skiades. The intercom was answered by Skiades' brother-in-law, who told Skiades that the plaintiff was downstairs. Skiades then attempted to let the plaintiff into the lobby by using the electronic buzzer system. The system failed to work, and Skiades told the plaintiff that she would come down and let her in. Before Skiades could admit her, the plaintiff was attacked by a man, later identified as Kenneth Strickler. She suffered injuries as a result of the attack.

The jury, in response to interrogatories presented to it, returned a verdict for the plaintiff on only the following count of the complaint: "[failure to] maintain the building telephone security intercom communication system in working order so as to allow the plaintiff, and other persons entering the building, to contact others within the building; and for those persons within the building to electronically open the front lobby doors."

The defendants claim that the court improperly denied their motion for a directed verdict. We agree. . . .

The second component [of a negligence action] is proximate cause. "Proximate cause establishes a reasonable connection between an act or omission of a defendant and the harm suffered by a plaintiff." "The Connecticut Supreme Court has defined proximate cause as [a]n actual cause that is a substantial factor in the resulting harm. . . . The substantial factor test reflects the inquiry fundamental to all proximate cause questions, that is, whether the harm which occurred was of the same general nature as the foreseeable risk created by the defendant's negligence." Proximate cause is a question of fact to be decided by the trier of fact, but it becomes a question of law when the mind of a fair and reasonable person could reach only one conclusion. "Lines must be drawn determining how far down the causal continuum individuals will be held liable for the consequences of their actions.... This line is labeled proximate cause." ...

The defendants could not have reasonably foreseen that a malfunctioning intercom system might provide a substantial incentive or inducement for the commission of a violent criminal assault on their property by one stranger upon another.

We rule that, as a matter of law, the jury could not reasonably have found that the assault on the plaintiff and the resultant injury were within the foreseeable scope of risk created by the defendants' failure to maintain the intercom system. Therefore, the plaintiff failed to establish the necessary causal relationship.

The judgment is reversed and the case is remanded with direction to render judgment for the defendants.

Notes

1. Notice what the *Medcalf* court identifies as the fundamental inquiry in all proximate cause questions.

2. The claim in *Medcalf* seems to be that if the buzzer had worked properly, the plaintiff would have been admitted when she rang and would thus have avoided the attack. On that assumption, is it clear that the the defendant is a but-for cause of the plaintiff's harm and that the issue in *Medcalf* is not about causation in this sense?

3. We have been careful in this book to state the cause in fact element separately from the proximate cause or foreseeability element. However, many courts conflate the two by saying that the term proximate cause includes both cause in fact and foreseeability components. The two ways of speaking can be represented in a table as follows:

Elements of the Negligence Case

Analytical Version	**Conflated Version**
Duty	Duty
Breach (negligence)	Breach (negligence)
Actual Harm	Actual Harm
Cause in Fact	Proximate Cause [consisting of
Proximate Cause (foreseeability	both cause in fact and
etc.)	foreseeability etc.]

A glance at the two ways of stating the issues will show that they cover the same ground. However, judges using the system of statement in the right-hand column may talk about proximate cause without being clear whether they mean the cause in fact component or the foreseeability component. To avoid confusion, we will continue use the term proximate cause to refer to the second component alone, one that has nothing to do with cause in fact.

4. *Formulations of the principle.* Take a few minutes to consider the idea that the harm that occurred to the plaintiff must be of the "same general nature as the foreseeable risk created by the defendant's negligence." Evaluate the following as alternative statements of the idea. (1) Liability must be rejected unless a reasonable person would have reasonably foreseen and avoided harm of the same general kind actually suffered by the plaintiff. (2) The defendant who negligently creates a risk to the plaintiff is subject to liability when that risk or a similar one results in harm, but not when some entirely different risk eventuates in entirely different harm.

5. *Applying the rule in Medcalf.* Look at the facts in *Medcalf* itself. Ask yourself what kind of harm or risk the defendant negligently created. Some kind of risk or foreseeable harm makes us think the defendant was negligent. Was it the harm that transpired? A similar case is *Benaquista v. Municipal Housing Authority*, 622 N.Y.S.2d 129, 212 A.D.2d 860 (App. Div. 1995) where the defendant failed to maintain an intercom and the apartment owner was injured walking downstairs to admit a visitor.

6. *Other examples.* Try the idea on some other facts.

(a) Defendant negligently pollutes a bay with oil. One risk is that it will cling to docks and have to be cleaned off. Fire is not a foreseeable risk, however, because everyone involved reasonably believes that the oil cannot catch fire on the cold waters of the bay. Their belief, though reasonable, proved wrong and by a fluke, the oil caught fire and burned the plaintiff's docks. If the scope of risk rule enunciated and applied in *Medcalf* controls here, can the plaintiff recover? *Overseas Tankship (U.K.) Ltd. v. Morts Dock & Eng'g Co. Ltd. (The Wagon Mound),* [1961] A.C. 388 (Privy Council 1961).

(b) Last year, the plaintiff received a blood transfusion. Blood was supplied by the defendant blood bank, ABO. Neither ABO nor any one else at that time knew that blood could carry an obscure disease, tortosis, much less any way to test for it. However, ABO and other blood banks knew that blood could carry a devastating disease, contractosis and that blood could readily be tested for that disease. No such test was made. The blood received by the plaintiff carried tortosis, from which the plaintiff now suffers. If ABO had screened the blood for contractosis, it would have found signs of that disease and would have rejected the blood for that reason. If ABO was negligent in not screening for contractosis is it liable to the plaintiff for tortosis?

(c) Defendant installed a fire alarm system in a customer's premises, but negligently managed the system and negligently transmitted a false fire alarm. A fire engine was a dispatched to deal with the supposed fire. The engine's brakes failed because of the city's negligent maintenance and the engine crashed into a tree, causing injuries to the firefighters. The defendant argued that the brake failure "introduced a risk not merely of a different degree, but of a different kind." Is the defendant liable to the firefighters? *Lodge v. Arett Sales Corp.,* 246 Conn. 563, 717 A.2d 215 (1998).

7. *Policy or justice: the risk rule or not.* Maybe the scope of risk rule in *Medcalf* is wrong. It relieves a faulty defendant at the expense of the innocent plaintiff, doesn't it? For this reason, older cases sometimes held that the defendant would be liable, even for unforeseeable harms, so long as

they were "direct" and no new tort by someone else intervened. This view is rarely applied today.

8. *Policy or justice: justification for the risk rule.* If the scope of risk rule is right, what exactly is its justification? Consider: (1) The rule is purely pragmatic. Liability must stop somewhere. The but for causation test would leave people exposed to continuous liability as long as they lived. (2) The risk rule is just or at least logical. If liability is imposed only for negligence and negligence creates only a risk of harm A, then liability should be limited to harm A. Any other result would be a species of strict liability, that is, liability for harms as to which the defendant created no unreasonable risks. See DOBBS ON TORTS § 181 (2000).

PALSGRAF v. LONG ISLAND RAILROAD CO.

Court of Appeals of New York, 1928.
248 N.Y. 339, 162 N.E. 99.

CARDOZO, C.J. Plaintiff was standing on a platform of defendant's railroad after buying a ticket to go to Rockaway Beach. A train stopped at the station, bound for another place. Two men ran forward to catch it. One of the men reached the platform of the car without mishap, though the train was already moving. The other man, carrying a package, jumped aboard the car, but seemed unsteady as if about to fall. A guard on the car, who had held the door open, reached forward to help him in, and another guard on the platform pushed him from behind. In this act, the package was dislodged, and fell upon the rails. It was a package of small size, about fifteen inches long, and was covered by a newspaper. In fact it contained fireworks, but there was nothing in its appearance to give notice of its contents. The fireworks when they fell exploded. The shock of the explosion threw down some scales at the other end of the platform many feet away. The scales struck the plaintiff, causing injuries for which she sues. [The case was submitted to a jury, which returned a verdict for the plaintiff. The Appellate Division affirmed the judgment for the plaintiff.]

The conduct of the defendant's guard, if a wrong in its relation to the holder of package, was not a wrong in its relation to the plaintiff, standing far away. Relatively to her it was not negligence at all. Nothing in the situation gave notice that the falling package had in it the potency of peril to persons thus removed. Negligence is not actionable unless it involves the invasion of a legally protected interest, the violation of a right. "Proof of negligence in the air, so to speak, will not do." "Negligence is the absence of care, according to the circumstances." The plaintiff, as she stood upon the platform of the station, might claim to be protected against intentional invasion of her bodily security. Such invasion is not charged. She might claim to be protected against unintentional invasion by conduct involving in the thought of reasonable men an unreasonable hazard that such invasion would ensue. These, from the point of view of the law, were the bounds of her immunity, with perhaps some rare exceptions.... If no hazard was apparent to the eye of ordinary vigilance, an act innocent and harmless, at least to outward seeming, with reference to her, did not take to itself the quality of a tort because it happened to be a wrong, though apparently not one involving the risk of bodily insecurity, with reference to some one else. . . .

The risk reasonably to be perceived defines the duty to be obeyed, and risk imports relation; it is risk to another or to others within the range of apprehension. This does not mean, of course, that one who launches a destructive force is always relieved of liability, if the force, though known to be destructive pursues an unexpected path. "It was not necessary that the defendant should have had notice of the particular method in which an accident would occur, if the possibility of an accident was clear to the ordinarily prudent eye." Some acts, such as shooting are so imminently dangerous to any one who may come within reach of the missile however unexpectedly, as to impose a duty of provision not far from that of an insurer. Even today, and much oftener in earlier stages of law, one acts sometimes at one's peril. Under this head, it may be, fall certain cases of what is known as transferred intent, an act willfully dangerous to A resulting by misadventure in injury to B. Talmage v. Smith, 101 Mich. 370, 374, 59 N.W. 656, 45 Am. St. Rep. 414. These cases aside, wrong is defined in terms of the natural or probable, at least when unintentional. The range of reasonable apprehension is at times a question for the court, and at times, if varying inferences are possible, a question for the jury. Here, by concession, there was nothing in the situation to suggest to the most cautious mind that the parcel wrapped in newspaper would spread wreckage through the station. If the guard had thrown it down knowingly and willfully, he would not have threatened the plaintiff's safety, so far as appearances could warn him. His conduct would not have involved, even then, an unreasonable probability of invasion of her bodily security. Liability can be no greater where the act is inadvertent. . . .

The law of causation, remote or proximate, is thus foreign to the case before us. The question of liability is always anterior to the question of the measure of the consequences that go with liability. If there is no tort to be redressed, there is no occasion to consider what damage might be recovered if there were a finding of a tort. We may assume, without deciding, that negligence, not at large or in the abstract, but in relation to the plaintiff, would entail liability for any and all consequences, however novel or extraordinary. There is room for argument that a distinction is to be drawn according to the diversity of interests invaded by the act, as where conduct negligent in that it threatens an insignificant invasion of an interest in property results in an unforeseeable invasion of an interest of another order, as, e.g., one of bodily security. Perhaps other distinctions may be necessary. We do not go into the question now. The consequences to be followed must first be rooted in a wrong.

The judgment of the Appellate Division and that of the Trial Term should be reversed, and the complaint dismissed, with costs in all courts.

ANDREWS, J. (dissenting.) . . .

[1: Duty runs to the world at large and negligence toward one is negligence to all]

The result we shall reach depends upon our theory as to the nature of negligence. Is it a relative concept—the breach of some duty owing to a particular person or to particular persons? Or where there is an act which unreasonably threatens the safety of others, is the doer liable for all its proximate consequences, even where they result in injury to one who would generally be thought to be outside the radius of danger? This is not a mere dispute as to words. We might not believe that to the average mind the dropping of the bundle would seem to involve the probability of harm to the plaintiff standing many feet away whatever might be the case as to the owner or to one so near as to be likely to be struck by its fall. If, however, we adopt the second hypothesis, we have to inquire only as to the relation between cause and effect. We deal in terms of proximate cause, not of negligence. . . .

But we are told that "there is no negligence unless there is in the particular case a legal duty to take care, and this duty must be one which is owed to the plaintiff himself and not merely to others." Salmond Torts (6th Ed.) 24. This I think too narrow a conception. Where there is the unreasonable act, and some right that may be affected there is negligence whether damage does or does not result. That is immaterial. Should we drive down Broadway at a reckless speed, we are negligent whether we strike an approaching car or miss it by an inch. The act itself is wrongful. It is a wrong not only to those who happen to be within the radius of danger, but to all who might have been there—a wrong to the public at large. . . .

It may well be that there is no such thing as negligence in the abstract. "Proof of negligence in the air, so to speak, will not do." In an empty world negligence would not exist. It does involve a relationship between man and his fellows, but not merely a relationship between man and those whom he might reasonably expect his act would injure; rather, a relationship between him and those whom he does in fact injure. If his act has a tendency to harm some one, it harms him a mile away as surely as it does those on the scene. . . .

In the well-known Polemis Case, [1921] 3 K.B. 560, Scrutton, L.J., said that the dropping of a plank was negligent, for it might injure "workman or cargo or ship." Because of either possibility, the owner of the vessel was to be made good for his loss. The act being wrongful, the doer was liable for its proximate results. . . .

The proposition is this: Every one owes to the world at large the duty of refraining from those acts that may unreasonably threaten the safety of others. Such an act occurs . . . Unreasonable risk being taken, its consequences are not confined to those who might probably be hurt. . . .

[2: Liability is limited by proximate cause, not by defining the scope of duty or negligence]

The right to recover damages rests on additional considerations. The plaintiff's rights must be injured, and this injury must be caused by the negligence. We build a dam, but are negligent as to its foundations. Breaking, it injures property down stream. We are not liable if all this happened because of some reason other than the insecure foundation. But, when injuries do result from our unlawful act, we are liable for the consequences. It does not matter that they are unusual, unexpected, unforeseen, and unforeseeable. But there is one limitation. The damages must be so connected with the negligence that the latter may be said to be the proximate cause of the former.

[3: Proximate cause is determined by several factors, not by the scope of the defendant's negligence]

These two words have never been given an inclusive definition. What is a cause in a legal sense, still more what is a proximate cause, depend in each case upon many considerations, as does the existence of negligence itself. Any philosophical doctrine of causation does not help us. A boy throws a stone into a pond. The ripples spread. The water level rises. The history of that pond is altered to all eternity. It will be altered by other causes also. Yet it will be forever the resultant of all causes combined. Each one will have an influence. How great only omniscience can say. You may speak of a chain, or, if you please, a net. An analogy is of little aid. Each cause brings about future events. Without each the future would not be the same. Each is proximate in the sense it is essential. But that is not what we mean by the word. Nor on the other hand do we mean sole cause. There is no such thing.

Should analogy be thought helpful, however, I prefer that of a stream. The spring, starting on its journey, is joined by tributary after tributary. The river, reaching the ocean, comes from a hundred sources. No man may say whence any drop of water is derived. Yet for a time distinction may be possible. Into the clear creek, brown swamp water flows from the left. Later, from the right comes water stained by its clay bed. The three may remain for a space, sharply divided. But at last inevitably no trace of separation remains. They are so commingled that all distinction is lost.

As we have said, we cannot trace the effect of an act to the end, if end there is. Again, however, we may trace it part of the way. A murder at Serajevo may be the necessary antecedent to an assassination in London twenty years hence. An overturned lantern may burn all Chicago. We may follow the fire from the shed to the last building. We rightly say the fire started by the lantern caused its destruction.

A cause, but not the proximate cause. What we do mean by the word "proximate" is that, because of convenience, of public policy, of a rough sense of justice, the law arbitrarily declines to trace a series of events beyond a certain point. This is not logic. It is practical politics. Take our rule as to fires. Sparks from my burning haystack set on fire my house and my neighbor's. I may recover from a negligent railroad. He may not. Yet the wrongful act as directly harmed the one as the other. We may regret the line was drawn just where it was, but drawn somewhere it had to be. We said the act of the railroad was not the proximate cause of our neighbor's fire. Cause it surely was. The words we used were simply indicative of our notions of public policy. Other courts think differently. But somewhere they reach the point where they cannot say the stream comes from any one source. . . .

There are some hints that may help us. The proximate cause, involved as it may be with many other causes, must be, at the least, something without which the event would not happen. The court must ask itself whether there was a natural and continuous sequence between cause and effect. Was the one a substantial factor in producing the other? Was there a direct connection between them, without too many intervening causes? Is the effect of cause on result not too attenuated? Is the cause likely, in the usual judgment of mankind, to produce the result? Or, by the exercise of prudent foresight, could the result be foreseen? Is the result too remote from the cause, and here we consider remoteness in time and space. . . . Clearly we must so consider, for the greater the distance either in time or space, the more surely do other causes intervene to affect the result. When a lantern is overturned, the firing of a shed is a fairly direct consequence. Many things contribute to the spread of the conflagration—the force of the wind, the direction and width of streets, the character of intervening structures, other factors. We draw an uncertain and wavering line, but draw it we must as best we can. . . .

Once again, it is all a question of fair judgment, always keeping in mind the fact that we endeavor to make a rule in each case that will be practical and in keeping with the general understanding of mankind. . . .

. . . In fairness he would make good every injury flowing from his negligence. Not because of tenderness toward him we say he need not answer for all that follows his wrong. We look back to the catastrophe, the fire kindled by the spark, or the explosion. We trace the consequences, not indefinitely, but to a certain point. And to aid us in fixing that point we ask what might ordinarily be expected to follow the fire or the explosion.

This last suggestion is the factor which must determine the case before us. The act upon which defendant's liability rests is knocking an apparently harmless package onto the platform. The act was negligent. For its proximate consequences the defendant is liable. If its contents were broken, to the owner; if it fell upon and crushed a passenger's foot, then to him; if it exploded and injured one in the immediate vicinity, to him also. . . . Mrs. Palsgraf was standing some distance away. How far cannot be told from the record—apparently 25 or 30 feet, perhaps less. Except for the explosion, she would not have been injured. We are told by the appellant in his brief, "It cannot be denied that the explosion was the direct cause of the plaintiff's injuries." So it was a substantial factor in producing the result—there was here a natural and continuous sequence—direct connection. The only intervening cause was that, instead of blowing her to the ground, the concussion smashed the weighing machine which in turn fell upon her. There was no remoteness in time, little in space. And surely, given such an explosion as here, it needed no great foresight to predict that the natural result would be to injure one on the platform at no greater distance from its scene than was the plaintiff. Just how no one might be able to predict. Whether by flying fragments, by broken glass, by wreckage of machines or structures no one could say. But injury in some form was most probable.

Under these circumstances I cannot say as a matter of law that the plaintiff's injuries were not the proximate result of the negligence. That is all we have before us. The court refused to so charge. No request was made to submit the matter to the jury as a question of fact, even would that have been proper upon the record before us.

Notes

1.   Reading *Palsgraf* and *Medcalf* together, we can say that the defendant is liable only for harms within the scope of the risks he negligently created. More specifically, that the defendant is liable only (a) for types of injuries risked by his negligence and (b) to classes of persons risked by his negligence. In terms of foreseeability, the statement would be that the defendant is not liable unless a reasonable person should have foreseen injuries of the same general type that occurred and the general class of person who would suffer them.

2.   To what class of persons should the guard have foreseen injury in *Palsgraf*? Was Mrs. Palsgraf within that class?

3.   *"Foreseeability."* If a reasonable person would foresee no harm to anyone as a result of his actions we do not reach the proximate cause issue. Why not?

4.   *Cardozo's duty/negligence locution compared to proximate cause language.* In *Palsgraf,* Cardozo did not invoke the concept of proximate cause. Instead, he concluded that "Relatively to her it was not negligence at all," because no harm to her was foreseeable. Although expressed in terms of duty or negligence, the rule is identical to one that asserts the defendant's conduct is not a proximate cause when the defendant could not foresee harm to persons situated like the plaintiff.

5.   *Andrews: rejecting the duty/negligence locution.* Judge Andrews, dissenting, tried to establish two points. First, he argued that a person who is negligent to *any* class of persons is negligent to everyone who is in fact injured. He rejected Cardozo's effort to deal with the issue as one of duty or negligence. Instead, for Andrews, the issue became one of proximate cause.

6.   *Andrews: The limited role of foreseeability in proximate cause determinations.* Andrews' second point was that proximate cause was *not* a matter of foreseeability alone. For Andrews, proximate cause was a matter of

a host of factors. Since it was not foreseeability alone that determined proximate cause for Andrews, he would not allow the railroad to escape liability for its supposed negligence merely because no reasonable person would expect the package to cause harm to someone a distance away.

7. *Duty vs. negligence vs. proximate cause.* Cardozo explained his views both by saying that the railroad was not negligent toward Mrs. Palsgraf but also by implying that the railroad owed her no duty of care. Sometimes courts conclude that defendants owed no duty, or only a limited duty of care for reasons that have little or nothing to do with foreseeability. For instance, we'll see that occupants of land frequently owe only the most limited duties of care to trespassers and others. Rules of limited duty in this sense are made by judges (not juries) and they do not require any judgments about foreseeability in the particular case. Cardozo's view, however, seems to depend entirely on foreseeability of harm to the plaintiff. That is a matter that must necessarily be determined on the facts of each case. Consequently, when the question is about the scope of the risk, the question is usually one for the jury so long as reasonable people could differ. Why did Cardozo, then, refuse to permit a jury to decide foreseeability in *Palsgraf*?

8. When courts are concerned with the scope of risk question, they have generally adopted Andrews' proximate cause locution but Cardozo's foreseeability test. The result is that decisions on proximate cause today almost always emphasize foreseeability in some form as a limitation on liability. Only a few cases continue to reflect some affinity with Andrews' view that liability could be imposed for types of harm or to classes of person who were not reasonably foreseeable victims. See *Petition of Kinsman Transit Co.*, 338 F.2d 708 (2d Cir.1964); *Bowen v. Lumbermens Mutual Casualty Co.*, 183 Wis.2d 627, 517 N.W.2d 432 (1994).

NOTE: THE RESCUE DOCTRINE

One important pattern of cases may or may not involve an exception to the person-within-the-risk rule of *Palsgraf*. Defendant negligently creates a risk to A. B, who was not subject to the risk or who escaped it, attempts to rescue A and is hurt in the process. Defendant, having created a risk to A, is liable to him. Is he also liable to B? *Palsgraf* might lead one to answer that he is not, or that the issue would turn on whether rescue would be foreseeable at the time defendant was guilty of negligence. Judge Cardozo's own answer, however, was otherwise.

In *Wagner v. International Railway*, 232 N.Y. 176, 133 N.E. 437 (1921) the railway permitted passengers to stand in between the cars while the train was moving over a high trestle. One of them fell off as the train rounded a curve. The plaintiff attempted to climb down to locate the victim, who was his cousin. In the course of this attempt, the plaintiff himself was injured. Cardozo, speaking in his Delphic manner, held that the railway was liable to the rescuer. "Danger invites rescue," he said, suggesting, perhaps, that rescue is foreseeable or is foreseeable as a matter of law. But he added a few sentences later: "The wrongdoer may not have foreseen the coming of a deliverer. He is accountable as if he had." The latter statement might be read as rejecting any criterion of foreseeability, or it might be read to mean only that a reasonable person would have foreseen rescue, whether the defendant subjectively foresaw it or not. Whatever he meant, the cases have generally agreed that the rescuer can recover from the defendant whose negligence prompts the rescue. The rule includes cases in which the defendant negligently injures or endangers himself and the plaintiff is injured in attempting a rescue. See *Sears v. Morrison,* 76 Cal.App.4th 577, 90 Cal.Rptr.2d 528 (Cal.App.1999). The "rescue doctrine" that emerges affects comparative negligence as well as scope of risk.

Try applying the rescue doctrine to these cases: (A) Dorothy Lambert was in an accident, allegedly caused by a tortfeasor's negligence. Her husband, over a block away in an office, heard of the accident; he rushed out to reach his wife, slipped on a patch of ice, and was injured. Is the tortfeasor liable to the husband as a rescuer? *Lambert v. Parrish,* 492 N.E.2d 289 (Ind.1986). (B) Defendant ran over a small child. Police officers came to the scene. One gave aid to the child while the second helped in controlling a crowd and the child's hysterical parent. While so engaged, the second officer collapsed and suffered a fatal heart attack. Is the defendant liable to the officer's survivors or estate because the officer was a rescuer? *Snellenberger v. Rodriguez,* 760 S.W.2d 237 (Tex.1988).

NOTE: VIOLATION OF STATUTE
AND "PROXIMATE CAUSE"

In most states violation of statute is "negligence per se," but this rule is conditioned upon a finding that the statute was designed to protect against the kind of harm that occurred and also to protect the class of persons of which the plaintiff is a member. RESTATEMENT SECOND OF TORTS § 288 (1965).

A well-known and very clear example of this is *Larrimore v. American National Insurance Co.*, 184 Okla. 614, 89 P.2d 340 (1939). A statute forbade laying out poisons. The defendant provided a rat poison to its tenant, a coffee shop. The coffee shop put the poison near the coffee burner. The plaintiff was injured when she lit the burner, because the poison, which contained phosphorous, exploded. The trial judge, as trier of fact, found for the defendant. The Supreme Court of Oklahoma affirmed, commenting:

> It is not enough for a plaintiff to show that the defendant neglected a duty imposed by statute. He must go further and show that his injury was caused by his exposure to a hazard from which it was the purpose of the statute to protect him. . . . Those only to whom [the statutory] duty is due and who have sustained injuries of the character its discharge was designed to prevent can maintain actions for its breach.

The court is stating the fundamental scope of risk rule as applied to a statutory liability, isn't it?

§ 2. ASSESSING THE SCOPE OF THE RISK

a. Is Harm Outside the Scope of the Risk Because of the Manner in Which It Occurs?

HUGHES v. LORD ADVOCATE

[1963] A.C. 837 (H.L.).

[Post Office employees were working on an underground telephone cable in Edinburgh, Scotland. At 5:00 they took a tea break, leaving unguarded an open manhole, covered with a tent and surrounded by kerosene lanterns. Two boys, 8 and 10 years old, found the unguarded site, tied one of the lanterns to a rope they found, and descended into the manhole. They came back up without mishap, but once back on top, they knocked or dropped the lantern into the hole. The accepted reconstruction of what happened next was that the lantern broke and that, quite unforeseeably, some of the kerosene vaporized. This gaseous form of the kerosene came into contact with the flame of the lantern and there was a large explosion, followed by a raging fire. Hughes, the eight year old, fell into the manhole as a result of the explosion and suffered severe burns, some of them on his fingers as he tried to climb out by holding to the heated metal ladder. He brought an action against the Lord Advocate of Scotland, as representative of the Post Office. The courts of Scotland held in favor of the Lord Advocate on the grounds that though burns were foreseeable, the vaporization of the kerosene and the explosion were not.]

LORD REID. . . . I am satisfied that the Post Office workmen were in fault in leaving this open manhole unattended and it is clear that if they had done as they ought to have done this accident would not have happened. It cannot be said that they owed no duty to the appellant. But it has been held that the appellant cannot recover damages. . . .

Of course, the pursuer has to prove that the defender's fault caused the accident, and there could be a case where the intrusion of a new and unexpected factor could be regarded as the cause of the accident rather than the fault of the defender. But that is not this case. The cause of this accident was a known source of danger, the lamp, but it behaved in an unpredictable way. The explanation of the accident which has been accepted, and which I would not seek to question, is that, when the lamp fell down the manhole and was broken, some paraffin escaped, and enough was vaporized to create an explosive mixture which was detonated by the naked light of the lamp. The experts agree that no one would have expected that to happen: it was so unlikely as to be unforeseeable. The explosion caused the boy to fall into the manhole: whether his injuries were directly caused by the explosion or aggravated by the fire which started in the manhole is not at all clear. The essential step in the respondent's argument is that the explosion was the real cause of the injuries and that the explosion was unforeseeable. [Lord Reid here considered the judgment of Lord Thankerton in an earlier case.] If that means that the mere fact that the way in which the accident happened could not be anticipated is enough to exclude liability although there was a breach of duty and that breach of duty in fact caused damage of a kind that could have been anticipated, then I am afraid that I cannot agree with Lord Thankerton. . . . This accident was caused by a known source of danger, but caused in a way which could not have been foreseen, and, in my judgment, that affords no defense. I would therefore allow the appeal.

LORD GUEST. . . . In dismissing the appellant's claim the Lord Ordinary and the majority of the judges of the First Division reached the conclusion that the accident which happened was not reasonably foreseeable. . . . Concentration has been placed in the courts below on the explosion which, it was said, could not have been foreseen because it was caused in a unique fashion by the paraffin forming into vapour and being ignited by the naked flame of the wick. But this, in my opinion, is to concentrate on what is really a non-essential element. . . .

[B]ecause the explosion was the agent which caused the burning and was unforeseeable, therefore the accident, according to them, was not reasonably foreseeable. In my opinion, this reasoning is fallacious. An explosion is only one way in which burning can be caused. Burning can also be caused by the contact between liquid paraffin and a naked flame. In the one case paraffin vapour and in the other case liquid paraffin is ignited by fire. I cannot see that these are two different types of accident. They are both burning accidents and in both cases the injuries would be burning injuries. Upon this view the explosion was an immaterial event in the chain of causation. It was simply one way which burning might be caused by the potentially dangerous paraffin lamp. . . .

LORD PEARCE. . . . Did the explosion create an accident and damage of a different type from the misadventure and damage that could be foreseen? In my judgment it did not. The accident was but a variant of the foreseeable. . . . [It] would be, I think, too narrow a view to hold that those who created the risk of fire are excused from the liability for the damage by fire because it came by way of explosive combustion. The resulting damage, though severe, was not greater than or different in kind from that which might have been produced had the lamp spilled and produced a more normal conflagration in the hold.

I would therefore allow the appeal.

DOUGHTY v. TURNER MANUFACTURING CO., LIMITED, [1964] 1 Q.B. 518 (C.A. 1963). Defendant's manufacturing process involved use of two vats of molten liquid maintained at 800 degrees centigrade, into which metal parts were immersed. Covers made of asbestos and cement were set beside the vat, to be put on as needed to conserve heat. Such covers had been used in this process in England and in the United States for over 20 years. A worker knocked one of the covers into the molten liquid. The cover sank without causing a splash. After one or two minutes the molten liquid erupted and injured the plaintiff, who was standing nearby. Thereafter experiments indicated that a compound of asbestos and cement would undergo a chemical change when subjected to temperatures over 500 degrees centigrade, so that hydrogen and oxygen in the material would combine to form water. The water at this temperature would turn to steam and produce an explosion or eruption. The trial judge held in favor of the plaintiff, finding negligence on the part of the worker in knocking the cover into the vat. *Held*, appeal allowed, judgment for defendants. LORD PEARCE: "The evidence showed that splashes caused by sudden immersion . . . were a foreseeable danger which should be carefully avoided. The falling cover might have ejected the liquid by a splash, and in the result it did eject the liquid, though in a more dramatic fashion." Therefore, the plaintiff's counsel argued, the accident was "merely a variant of foreseeable accidents by splashing. . . . [I]t would be quite unrealistic to describe this accident as a variant of the perils from splashing. The cause of the accident, to quote Lord Reid's words, was 'the intrusion of a new and unexpected factor.' There was an eruption due to chemical changes underneath the surface of the liquid as opposed to a splash caused by displacement from bodies falling on to its surface. In my judgment, the reasoning in Hughes v. Lord Advocate cannot be extended far enough to cover this case." HARMON, L.J. "In my opinion the damage here was of an entirely different kind from the foreseeable splash." DIPLOCK, L.J.: "The first risk . . . is that if [the cover] is allowed to drop on to the hot liquid in the bath with sufficient momentum it may cause the liquid to splash on to persons. . . . The second risk is that if it becomes immersed in a liquid the temperature of which exceeds 500 degrees centigrade, it will disintegrate and cause an under-surface explosion which will eject the liquid. . . . There is no room today for mystique in the law of negligence. It is the application of common morality and common sense to the activities of the common man." The plaintiff's attorney relied on Hughes v. Lord Advocate where the plaintiff's burns were more serious than they would have been expected to be. "But they were the direct consequence of the defendant's breach of duty and of the same kind as could reasonably have been foreseen, although of unforeseen gravity. But in the present case the defendants' duty owed to the plaintiff in relation to the only foreseeable risk, that is of splashing, was to take reasonable care to avoid knocking the cover into the liquid or allowing it to slip in such a way as to cause a splash which would injure the plaintiff. Failure to avoid knocking it into the liquid . . . was of itself no breach of duty to the plaintiff."

HAMMERSTEIN v. JEAN DEVELOPMENT WEST, 111 Nev. 1471, 907 P.2d 975 (1995). Plaintiff, about 70 years of age, was a guest at defendant's hotel. As the hotel knew, he was a diabetic. Walking stairs was bad for him, but there were no rooms on the ground floor and besides there was an elevator. In the early morning hours a fire alarm went off. Elevators were locked and plaintiff had to walk down from the fourth floor. In doing so he twisted his ankle. Much later, on returning to his room, he found a blister on his foot. This eventually became a gangrenous infection probably because of his diabetes which interferes with circulation in the lower extremities. There was in fact no fire and the fire alarm system had gone off without a fire on numerous occasions but had never been corrected. *Held,* summary judgment for defendant was error. "It should have been foreseeable to Nevada Landing that if its fire alarm system was unreasonably faulty, harm to a certain type of plaintiff, i.e., one of its guests, could result. Also, this particular variety of harm, injuring an ankle or foot on the way down a stairwell, is a foreseeable variety of harm in this circumstance. The extent of the infection on Hammerstein's leg may not have been foreseeable, but the underlying injury should have been."

MELLON MORTGAGE CO. v. HOLDER, 5 S.W.3d 654 (Tex.1999). A police officer stopped the plaintiff, a woman, for an alleged traffic violation. He took her insurance and identification cards and told her to follow his squad car. He drove several blocks to the defendant's parking garage and there sexually assaulted the plaintiff in the squad car. The defendant knew of crimes in its garage, so crimes there were foreseeable to it. It took no significant steps to exclude improper entrance or otherwise minimize the crimes. *Held*, judgment for defendant. "It is not unreasonable to conclude that Mellon could foresee that an employee or some other person who frequents the garage could be the victim of a violent crime in the garage. . . . Holder, however, was not a member of this class nor any other that Mellon could have reasonably foreseen would be the victim of a criminal act in its garage." She was pulled over blocks from the scene and there was no reason to suspect that such a victim would be taken to the garage.

b. Is Harm Outside the Scope of the Risk Because Its Extent Is Unforeseeable?

NOTE: THIN SKULL CASES

The term "thin skull" or "eggshell skull" is widely used in tort law in reference to some variant on the following facts. Defendant negligently strikes the plaintiff. The blow is such that a normal person would suffer only slight injury, such as a bruise. The plaintiff, however, has an unusually thin skull, a fact the defendant does not know. As a result of the minor blow, the plaintiff suffers terrible injuries. If the defendant is in fact guilty of tort—that is, if he was negligent or guilty of intentional harm—then the fact that the harm was much worse than anyone would have expected does not limit his liability. This is the thin skull rule. It is often generalized by saying that the defendant "takes the plaintiff as he finds her," that is, with whatever extra damages the plaintiff might have because the plaintiff has a "thin skull," or is pregnant, or suffers hemophilia or is otherwise pre-disposed to suffer more.

A leading case is *McCahill v. New York Transportation Co.*, 201 N.Y. 221, 94 N.E. 616 (1911). There the defendant ran into the plaintiff, who suffered a broken thigh. In the hospital he began to suffer delirium tremens, from which he died. This results only because of pre-existing alcoholic condition. The defendant took the plaintiff as it found him and was held liable. Does *Dillon v. Twin States Electric Co.*, *supra* Chapter 7, suggest any partial defense here?

The thin skull cases do not impose liability without fault. The defendant's act must have been one that would cause some harm to a normal person, or the defendant must have been at fault because he knew or should have known of the plaintiff's susceptible condition. The thin skull rule merely holds that the defendant does not escape liability for the unforeseeable personal reactions of the plaintiff, once negligence or intentional fault is established.

NOTE: THE FIRE CASES

A classic case involving the spread of fire was *Smith v. London and South Western Railway*, L.R. 6 C.P. 14 (1870). The defendant railroad was responsible for a fire which started along its right of way, possibly in some grass clippings it had left there. The fire spread from the right of way and grass cuttings, crossed a hedge, a stubble-field and a road, and then burned the plaintiff's cottage. One of the judges, Chief Baron Kelly, quoted a finding that "no reasonable man would have foreseen the fire would consume the hedge and pass across a stubble-field, and so get to the plaintiff's cottage at the distance of 200 yards from the railway, crossing a road in its passage." The Chief Baron agreed with the finding, but added: "I do not feel that that is a true test of the liability.... It may be that they did not anticipate, and were not bound to anticipate, that the plaintiff's cottage would be burnt.... But I think the law is that ... the defendants were bound to provide against all circumstances which might result from [the grass clippings] and were responsible for all the natural consequences of it." The other judges agreed. Two of their comments are especially worth noticing. Channell, B., said:

> [B]ut when it has been once determined that there is evidence of negligence, the person guilty of it is equally liable for its consequences whether he could have foreseen them or not.

This statement led some courts to believe that foreseeability simply wasn't important in determining proximate cause limitations. To see why that interpretation was an error, look at this statement by one of the other judges in the case:

> If a man fires a gun across a road where he may reasonably anticipate that persons will be passing, and hits someone, he is guilty of negligence, and liable for the injury he has caused; but if he fires in his own wood, where he cannot reasonably anticipate that any one will be, he is not liable to any one whom he shoots, which shews that what a person may reasonably anticipate is important in considering whether he has been negligent; but if a person fires across a road when it is dangerous to do so and kills a man who is in the receipt of a large income, he will be liable for the whole damage,

however great, that may have resulted to his family, and cannot set
up that he could not have reasonably expected to have injured any
one but a labourer.

Standard doctrine has it that when the defendant's conduct otherwise
qualifies as a proximate or legal cause of the plaintiff's harm, the
defendant does not escape liability merely because the harm was more
extensive than anyone foresaw or could have foreseen. See RESTATEMENT
SECOND OF TORTS § 435(1) (1965). This simple rule might explain both the
thin skull and the fire cases in a way consistent with *Palsgraf/Medcalf.*

c. Is Harm Outside the Scope of the Risk Because It Results Most Directly from an Acts of an Intervening Person or Force?

NOTE: SCOPE OF RISK AND NATURAL AND CONTINUOUS SEQUENCE

Imagine this case: Tortfeasor A leaves an unlighted excavation in
the sidewalk. Tortfeasor B negligently jostles the plaintiff, who is caused
to fall into the excavation.

"The proximate cause of an injury is that which, in a natural and
continuous sequence, unbroken by any efficient intervening cause, produces an injury, and without which the injury would not have occurred."

These words and others very similar have been used in literally
hundreds of American cases. They have done quite a bit to obscure
issues and principles. For one thing, courts have recognized repeatedly
and we ourselves have seen that there may be many tortfeasors are all
liable and thus all proximate causes. When judges speak of "the"
proximate cause rather than "a" proximate cause, they may be pushed
to an unconscious bias against finding both tortfeasors liable.

When tortfeasors act in sequence, the first tortfeasor often argues
that the second tortfeasor is an "intervening cause" that "supersedes"
his liability entirely. Courts often use metaphorical rather than principled language here: a superseding cause breaks the causal chain.

The emphasis on intervening causes and causal chains has obscured
the more fundamental scope-of-risk principle. Under that principle, an
intervening act of some second tortfeasor should relieve the first tortfeasor of liability when the resulting harm is outside the scope of the risk
negligently created by the first tortfeasor. But equally, an intervening
act that is part of the risk the first defendant created should definitely
not relieve the first defendant. In other words, an "intervening cause
that lies within the scope of the foreseeable risk, or has a reasonable
connection to it, is not a superseding cause." *Fancyboy v. Alaska Village
Elec. Coop., Inc.*, 984 P.2d 1128 (Alaska 1999).

Look back at *Medcalf*. The plaintiff's injury resulted directly from
the act of her attacker, an intervening tortfeasor, not the landlord who
negligently left the buzzer in disrepair. The *Medcalf* court made no
special point about intervening actors and didn't need to. Instead it went

directly to the general principle–defendants should be liable for risks or harms they negligently created but not others. But in intervening cause cases, many courts make no direct mention of the general scope of risk principle. They instead put the weight of their discussion on intervening causes. Are they talking the language of intervening cause but in fact carrying out the scope of risk principle? Lets look.

WATSON v. KENTUCKY & INDIANA BRIDGE & RAILROAD, 137 Ky. 619, 126 S.W. 146 (1910). Defendant railroad negligently derailed a gasoline tank car and it sprung a leak. A man named Duerr threw a match into the area; an explosion resulted, causing the plaintiff injury. *Held*, if Duerr acted "for the purpose of causing the explosion," the railroad would not be liable. "[I]f the intervening agency is something so unexpected or extraordinary as that [the railroad] could not or ought not to have anticipated it, he will not be liable, and certainly he is not bound to anticipate the criminal acts of others by which damage is inflicted and hence is not liable therefor."

Notes

1.   A view common in the 19th and early 20th century was that the deliberate infliction of harm by a "moral being," who was adequately informed, free to act, and able to choose, would "supersede" the negligence of the first actor. This was thought of as somehow negating the causal connection between the first actor's conduct and the harm. See H.L.A. HART & A.M. HONORE, CAUSATION IN THE LAW 129 (1962).

Sometimes the idea was expressed in extreme form by saying that the last human wrongdoer or last culpable human will was the proximate cause to the exclusion of others. See, reviewing the history of proximate cause thinking, Patrick J. Kelley, *Proximate Cause in Negligence Law: History, Theory, and the Present Darkness*, 60 Wash. U. L. Q. 49, 78–81 (1991) (finding, however, cases inconsistent with this view).

In *Britton v. Wooten*, 817 S.W.2d 443 (Ky.1991) the court that decided *Watson* repudiated it, saying that if the defendant negligently created the increased risk of fire or its spread the defendant could be held responsible.

2.   In *Concord Florida, Inc. v. Lewin*, 341 So.2d 242 (Fla.App.1976) plaintiffs were injured in the defendant's cafeteria when an arsonist threw gasoline on the floor and set the place ablaze. The arsonist fled. The plaintiffs recovered against the defendant, who had been negligent in failing to designate fire escapes and in otherwise violating the fire code. To the court, the arsonist's intentional, culpable act was not a superseding cause. Would the burned plaintiffs have recovered anything at all if the arsonist had been regarded as the sole proximate cause?

3.   In *Hines v. Garrett*, 131 Va. 125, 108 S.E. 690 (1921) the defendant railroad went past the plaintiff's station without stopping. The plaintiff was required to get off and walk back through an area which, as the railroad knew, was especially dangerous. Criminals in the dangerous area did in fact attack the plaintiff. She sued the railroad. The court imposed liability. Here is what is said: "We do not wish to be understood as questioning the general

proposition that no responsibility for a wrong attaches whenever an independent act of a third person intervenes.... [But] this proposition does not apply where the very negligence alleged consists of exposing the injured party to the act causing the injury."

4.   A landlord leasing apartments to women fails to control access to the landlord's copy of keys to the apartments and fails to maintain records of access. Someone used the landlord's keys to gain entrance to the plaintiff's apartment. The intruder raped the plaintiff. In the plaintiff's suit against the landlord, the defendant argued that the intruder was a superseding cause. The court said, quoting the Restatement Second of Torts § 449, cmt. b: "[t]he happening of the very event the likelihood of which makes the actor's conduct negligent and so subjects the actor to liability cannot relieve him from liability." *Tenney v. Atlantic Assocs.*, 594 N.W.2d 11 (Iowa 1999). Was the court accepting, or rejecting the defendant's argument?

5.   A strange decision is *Doe v. Linder Construction Co.*, 845 S.W.2d 173 (Tenn.1992). The defendant developer of a planned unit development retained copies of keys to the plaintiff's unit, with labels. He negligently allowed two workers on the premises access to the keys and they used them to enter the unit and rape the plaintiff. In the plaintiff's suit against the developer, the trial court granted summary judgment for defendants on the ground that the criminal act of the rapists was an independent intervening act that broke the causal chain. The Supreme Court of Tennessee affirmed. "[T]he acts of rape were criminal acts of which the defendants had no warning and which they had no reason to believe would occur.... [I]f the injury was not reasonably foreseeable, then the criminal act of the third party would be a superseding, intervening cause of the harm, relieving the [defendants] from liability." What *do* you foresee as a danger if you leave a woman's house key available for any worker at a large construction project? The *Linder* decision was roundly attacked in Leslie Bender, *Is Tort Law Male?: Foreseeability Analysis and Property Managers' Liability for Third Party Rapes of Residents*, 69 CHI.-KENT L. REV. 313 (1993).

6.   *Suicide.* A jailer puts a pre-trial detainee into an unobserved cell but fails to take his belt as required by regulations. The detainee hangs himself with the belt. Can the jailer avoid liability on the ground that the detainee's own wilful act was a superseding cause of harm or death? *Hickey v. Zezulka*, 439 Mich. 408, 487 N.W.2d 106 (1992). Should the answer depend on whether the jailer knows that the prisoner is a suicide risk? See *Murdock v. City of Keene*, 137 N.H. 70, 623 A.2d 755 (1993). Can you build an argument from *Hines* or *Concord* in notes 2 and 3 above?

DERDIARIAN v. FELIX CONTRACTING CORP.

Court of Appeals of New York, 1980.
51 N.Y.2d 308, 434 N.Y.S.2d 166, 414 N.E.2d 666.

COOKE, CHIEF JUDGE.

[Defendant Felix Contracting Corp. was installing an underground gas main, and for this purpose had excavated most of the eastbound lane of traffic. Felix engaged Bayside Pipe Coaters to seal the mains. Bayside had a kettle of liquid enamel, boiling to 400 degrees at the job site.

Derdiarian worked for Bayside and was in charge of the kettle. Against Derdiarian's wishes, Felix insisted that he set up the kettle on the west side of the excavation, that is, facing the oncoming, eastbound traffic. Felix protected against this oncoming traffic by a single wooden horse barricade and by use of a single flagman.

[James Dickens was driving eastbound on Oak Street when he suffered a seizure and lost consciousness. Dickens was under treatment for epilepsy and had neglected to take his medication at the proper time. His car crashed through a single wooden horse-type barricade and struck the plaintiff, throwing him into the air. He was "splattered over his face, head and body with 400 degree boiling hot liquid enamel from a kettle struck by the automobile. . . . Although plaintiff's body ignited into a fire ball, he miraculously survived the incident."

[The jury found in favor of the plaintiff against Dickens, against Felix and against Consolidated Edison. The Appellate Division affirmed. Only the claim against Felix is involved here.]

To support his claim of an unsafe work site, plaintiff called as a witness Lawrence Lawton, an expert in traffic safety. According to Lawton, the usual and accepted method of safeguarding the workers is to erect a barrier around the excavation. Such a barrier, consisting of a truck, a piece of heavy equipment or a pile of dirt, would keep a car out of the excavation and protect workers from oncoming traffic. The expert testified that the barrier should cover the entire width of the excavation. He also stated that there should have been two flagmen present, rather than one, and that warning signs should have been posted advising motorists that there was only one lane of traffic and that there was a flagman ahead.

Following receipt of the evidence, the trial court charged the jury, among other things, that it could consider, as some evidence of negligence, the violation of a Mount Vernon ordinance. The ordinance imposed upon a construction "permittee" certain safety duties. Defendant Felix now argues that plaintiff was injured in a freakish accident, brought about solely by defendant Dickens' negligence, and therefore there was no causal link, as a matter of law, between Felix' breach of duty and plaintiff's injuries.

The concept of proximate cause, or more appropriately legal cause, has proven to be an elusive one, incapable of being precisely defined to cover all situations. This is, in part, because the concept stems from policy considerations that serve to place manageable limits upon the liability that flows from negligent conduct. Depending upon the nature of the case, a variety of factors may be relevant in assessing legal cause. Given the unique nature of the inquiry in each case, it is for the finder of fact to determine legal cause, once the court has been satisfied that a prima facie case has been established To carry the burden of proving a prima facie case, the plaintiff must generally show that the defendant's negligence was a substantial cause of the events which produced the injury. Plaintiff need not demonstrate, however, that the precise manner in which the accident happened, or the extent of injuries, was foreseeable (Restatement, Torts 2d, § 435, subd. 2).

Where the acts of a third person intervene between the defendant's conduct and the plaintiff's injury, the causal connection is not automatically severed. In such a case, liability turns upon whether the intervening act is a normal or foreseeable consequence of the situation created by the defendant's negligence. If the intervening act is extraordinary under the circumstances, not foreseeable in the normal course of events, or independent of or far removed from the defendant's conduct, it may well be a superseding act which breaks the causal nexus. Because questions concerning what is foreseeable and what is normal may be the subject of varying inferences, as is the question of negligence itself, these issues generally are for the fact finder to resolve.

There are certain instances, to be sure, where only one conclusion may be drawn from the established facts and where the question of legal cause may be decided as a matter of law. Those cases generally involve independent intervening acts which operate upon but do not flow from the original negligence. Thus, for instance, we have held that where an automobile lessor negligently supplies a car with a defective trunk lid, it is not liable to the lessee who, while stopped to repair the trunk, was injured by the negligent driving of a third party. (Ventricelli v. Kinney System Rent A Car), [45 N.Y.2d 950, 411 N.Y.S.2d 555, 383 N.E.2d 1149 (1978)]. Although the renter's negligence undoubtedly served to place the injured party at the site of the accident, the intervening act was divorced from and not the foreseeable risk associated with the original negligence. And the injuries were different in kind than those which would have normally been expected from a defective trunk. In short, the negligence of the renter merely furnished the occasion for an unrelated act to cause injuries not ordinarily anticipated.

By contrast, in the present case, we cannot say as a matter of law that defendant Dickens' negligence was a superseding cause which interrupted the link between Felix's negligence and plaintiff's injuries. From the evidence in the record, the jury could have found that Felix negligently failed to safeguard the excavation site. A prime hazard associated with such dereliction is the possibility that a driver will negligently enter the work site and cause injury to a worker. That the driver was negligent, or even reckless, does not insulate Felix from liability. Nor is it decisive that the driver lost control of the vehicle through a negligent failure to take medication, rather than a driving mistake. The precise manner of the event need not be anticipated. The finder of fact could have concluded that the foreseeable, normal and natural result of the risk created by Felix was the injury of a worker by a car entering the improperly protected work area. An intervening act may not serve as a superseding cause, and relieve an actor of responsibility, where the risk of the intervening act occurring is the very same risk which renders the actor negligent.

[Affirmed].

Notes

1. Is *Derdiarian* consistent with the scope of the risk principle? The defendant could foresee some kind of harm from a motor vehicle entering the excavation and that is what happened. The precise manner in which the injury came about, as we know from *Hughes,* does not necessarily matter.

2. Does the manner in which the injury came about ever matter? Suppose on facts like *Derdiarian* the injury occurs because an airplane crashes into the excavation. Try working that out under a scope of risk analysis.

3. Many, many cases use foreseeability in some fashion when there are intervening causes, but, like this one, often speak of foreseeability of the intervening cause itself rather than foreseeability of the general result. Is this the risk rule coupled with a tendency to describe the risk by describing the mechanism that brings the risk about?

4. In *Quirke v. City of Harvey,* 266 Ill.App.3d 664, 639 N.E.2d 1355, 203 Ill.Dec. 536 (1994), James Lewis had been fired by the electric company. He climbed a power pole maintained by his former employer and threatened to electrocute himself with the 34,000 volt charge it carried. It was around 1:00 a.m. At the police chief's direction, the company cut the power. This put out street lights and traffic signals. The plaintiff was injured several blocks away in an intersection collision that allegedly occurred in part because the streets were dark and the traffic signal was out. As to the electric company, *held,* summary judgment for defendant affirmed. The power outage was "a condition not a cause," and the negligence of the drivers was an unforeseeable superseding cause. Think about this a minute. In what way was the defendant negligent at all if it created no risks of injury in connection with inoperable stop lights?

5. In *Charles v. Lavergne,* 412 So.2d 726 (La.App.1982), the plaintiff and a crew of workers were splicing a new electric cable to an old one on a pole near a highway. To permit this, a long length of cable lay across the road and was attached to the pole on which the plaintiff was working. Defendant drove his truck loaded with 48,000 pounds of rice across the cable. The cable bounded off the pavement and became entangled in the rear axle. This pulled the cable taut and broke the pole, causing the plaintiff to fall to the ground. He suffered injuries to his back, neck, leg and arm. The trial judge gave judgment for the defendant on the ground that he was under a duty to slow down "to avoid striking the workers" and that "this duty did not encompass the particular risk of the cable becoming entangled in the axle of the truck and causing the pole to break and throw the plaintiff to the ground." On appeal this was affirmed. "[W]e do not believe that the risk and harm caused in this case were within the scope of the protection afforded by the breach of any duty by the defendant." Is this inconsistent with *Derdiarian*? Would the Louisiana Court have reached a different result if it had characterized the duty as the New York Court did in *Derdiarian*? "A prime hazard," the New York Court said there, was "that a driver will negligently enter the work site and cause injury to a worker."

SHEEHAN v. CITY OF NEW YORK

Court of Appeals of New York, 1976.
40 N.Y.2d 496, 387 N.Y.S.2d 92, 354 N.E.2d 832.

FUCHSBERG, J. [Sheehan drove a bus operated by Manhattan and Bronx Surface Transit Operating Authority, driving east on 138th Street in New York City. He stopped at the intersection with Jackson Avenue to permit passengers to board or alight. He did not pull over into the far right area near the curb, which was the designated bus stop, but stopped instead in the driving lane. This violated traffic regulations. While he was so stopped, a sanitation truck operated by the City of New York plowed into the bus. The driver of this vehicle testified that his brakes failed and this seems to be undisputed. One of the injured persons was a bus passenger, Novak, who is a plaintiff here. A jury found for Novak against both the City, as owner of the sanitation truck, and the Transit Authority, as owner of the bus. The trial judge set aside the verdict against the Transit Authority and assessed damages entirely against the City and the driver of the sanitation truck. The Appellate Division reversed and reinstated the verdicts.]

Assuming the designated stop was available for the bus's use, if it had in fact stopped there and, having discharged or boarded its passengers, pulled back into the traveling lane before proceeding across the intersection, it would, properly, have been in exactly the same position at which it found itself when it was hit. Or, if observing no prospective passengers in the stop and having none who wished to alight at that corner, the bus driver had decided not to go through the proper practice of pulling in and out of the stop, but, preparatory to crossing, had merely stopped in the traveling lane at the corner before doing so, his bus would have been in precisely the same position. In short, the bus at the time of the accident appears merely to have been at one point in the street where it had a right to be (the traveling lane) rather than at another point in the street where it had a right to be (the bus stop). The result of the sanitation truck's brake failure would have been no different, if, perchance, a pedestrian or a vehicle other than the bus had been using the street at the point at that time and had instead become the target of the truck's faulty brakes.

Unlike the situation in O'Neill v. City of Port Jervis, 253 N.Y. 423,171 N.E. 694, where defendant's active obstruction of a street compelled the injured party to detour to a place of danger, or that in Commisso v. Meeker, 8 N.Y.2d 109, 202 N.Y.S.2d 287, 168 N.E.2d 365, where the partial blocking of a two-lane noncity highway took place at an hour of the night when heavy traffic was to be expected, no act of the bus in the case before us caused the sanitation truck to be any place other than where it was. We conclude, therefore, as a matter of law, that the conceded negligence of the sanitation truck was the sole proximate cause of the injuries and that the continued presence of the bus in the traveling lane at the time it was struck merely furnished the condition or occasion for the occurrence of the event rather than one of its causes. This is especially so in the light of the fact that the absence or presence of prima facie proof of proximate cause was not dependent on pure logic alone but was rather to be determined by the trial court "upon mixed considerations of logic, common sense, justice, policy and precedent."

In addition, it appears quite clear that, if the bus's stop in the traveled lane could, on any view of the circumstances here, be regarded as a proximate cause of the accident, the failure of the truck's brakes might have been an independent, supervening cause. Though, where either of two independent acts of negligence may be found to be concurring, that is, direct causes of an accident, the perpetrator of either or both may be found responsible for the whole harm incurred [ ], when such an intervening cause "interrupts the natural sequence of events, turns aside their course, prevents the natural and probable result of the original act or omission, and produces a different result that could not have been reasonably anticipated," it will prevent a recovery on account of the act or omission of the original wrongdoer.

Novak's complaint against MABSTOA and Sheehan should therefore have been dismissed before the cases went to the jury. . . .

Notes

1. A judicial opinion may or may not reflect a judge's subjective motivations or the process by which he or she reached a conclusion. But it should express a rational basis for the conclusion which can be tested against arguments and ultimately operate as a principle to govern other like cases. Proximate cause issues are notoriously difficult and perhaps here more than elsewhere one must distrust mere language.

2. Does Judge Fuchsberg's statement imply that the bus operator is not liable because the bus driver did not cause "the sanitation truck to be any place other than where it was?" If so, would this mean that *Derdiarian* and *Sheehan* are in conflict, so that *Derdiarian* has in effect overruled *Sheehan*? Does that strike you as likely?

3. Does Judge Fuchsberg make it clear why a brake failure is an intervening cause that prevents recovery against the bus company? Surely brake failure is no less foreseeable than an epileptic's failure to take his medicine in *Derdiarian*. Is the result in *Sheehan*–that a bus is struck from behind while stopped in a driving lane–not within the risk?

4. One easily forgotten point: there is no proximate cause issue unless the defendant is first shown to be negligent. Since Judge Fuchsberg was talking about proximate cause, he must have been assuming that the bus driver was negligent and created some risk. But what risk could that be if it did not include being struck from behind?

VENTRICELLI v. KINNEY SYSTEM RENT A CAR, INC.

Court of Appeals of New York, 1978.
45 N.Y.2d 950, 411 N.Y.S.2d 555, 383 N.E.2d 1149, modified
46 N.Y.2d 770, 413 N.Y.S.2d 655, 386 N.E.2d 263.

[Defendant Kinney leased plaintiff a car with a defective trunk lid that did not close satisfactorily. Kinney unsuccessfully attempted a repair. While the car was parked on Mott Street, the plaintiff and a passenger were attempting to slam the lid shut. One Maldonado was parked several car lengths behind the plaintiff. His car suddenly "jumped ahead" and ran into the plaintiff. The jury awarded plaintiff $550,000 for his injuries. The Appellate Division reversed and dismissed as to Kinney.]

MEMORANDUM.

Order of the Appellate Division affirmed, with costs. Proximate cause and foreseeability are relative terms, "nothing more than a convenient formula for disposing of the case" (Prosser, Law of Torts [4th ed.], § 43, p. 267). In writing of the "orbit of the duty," Chief Judge Cardozo said "[t]he range of reasonable apprehension is at times a question for the court, and at times, if varying inferences are possible, a question for the jury." (Palsgraf v. Long Is. R.R. Co., 248 N.Y. 339, 345, 162 N.E. 99, 101). So it is with proximate cause and foreseeability.

Although the negligence of the automobile renter, defendant Kinney, is manifest, and was, of course, a "cause" of the accident, it was not the proximate cause. "What we do mean by the word 'proximate' is that, because of convenience, of public policy, of a rough sense of justice, the law arbitrarily declines to trace a series of events beyond a certain point." (Palsgraf v. Long Is. R.R. Co., 248 N.Y. 339, 352, 162 N.E. 99, 103, supra [Andrews, J., dissenting]). The immediately effective cause of plaintiff's injuries was the negligence of Maldonado, the driver of the second car, in striking plaintiff while he was standing behind his parked automobile. That Kinney's negligence in providing an automobile with a defective trunk lid would result in plaintiff's repeated attempts to close the lid was reasonably foreseeable. Not "foreseeble," however, was the collision between vehicles both parked a brief interval before the accident. Plaintiff was standing in a relatively "safe" place, a parking space, not in an actively traveled lane. He might well have been there independent of any negligence of Kinney, as, for example, if he were loading or unloading the trunk. Under these circumstances, to hold the accident a foreseeable consequence of Kinney's negligence is to stretch the concept of foreseeability beyond acceptable limits (see Prosser, Law of Torts [4th ed.], pp. 267–270; Restatement, Torts 2d, § 435, subd. 2).

FUCHSBERG, JUDGE (dissenting)....

Ample was the proof that, to the knowledge of the rental company, the trunk door on the automobile it furnished to the plaintiff had a penchant for flying open so as to obstruct the operator's view while the vehicle was moving. Given these facts, it was not only foreseeable, but a most reasonable rather than a remote expectation, that a driver confronted by such an emergency would alight and promptly proceed to the rear of the car to attempt to secure the lid manually so that he might continue on his way without further danger to others and himself. The seemingly ineluctable consequence was to expose the driver to the danger of being struck by another vehicle while he was positioned behind the trunk. On these facts, it could readily be found, as the jury apparently did here, that the choice between the alternatives—the danger from the obstruction of the driver's view from the vehicle and the danger of being struck while engaged in the act of removing the danger—was thrust on the plaintiff by Kinney's negligence. Of course, whether in making the choice he did plaintiff himself was negligent similarly raised a factual issue within the province of the jury. . . .

MARSHALL v. NUGENT

United States Court of Appeals, First Circuit, 1955.
222 F.2d 604.

Magruder, J.

[Plaintiff was a passenger in Harriman's car. There was ice and hard-packed snow on the highway. As Harriman topped a hill, he saw a truck coming toward him, partly in his lane. Harriman went off the road. The driver stopped to help pull the car back on the road. This effort partly blocked the road again, so the plaintiff walked toward the top of the hill to flag any approaching motorists. Before he could reach the top, Nugent drove over the hill, saw the truck blocking the road, and attempted to avoid it. He skidded into the plaintiff, Marshall. The plaintiff sued both Nugent and the truck driver. The jury found against the truck driver, who appeals urging that he was not a proximate cause.]

To say that the situation created by the defendant's culpable acts constituted "merely a condition," not a cause of plaintiff's harm, is to indulge in mere verbiage, which does not solve the question at issue, but is simply a way of stating the conclusion, arrived at from other considerations, that the causal relation between the defendant's act and the plaintiff's injury is not strong enough to warrant holding the defendant legally responsible for the injury.

The adjective "proximate," as commonly used in this connection, is perhaps misleading, since to establish liability it is not necessarily true that the defendant's culpable act must be shown to have been the next or immediate cause of the plaintiff's injury. . . .

. . . [S]peaking in general terms, the effort of the courts has been, in the development of this doctrine of proximate causation, to confine the liability of a negligent actor to those harmful consequences which result from the operation of the risk, or of a risk, the foreseeability of which rendered the defendant's conduct negligent.

Of course, putting the inquiry in these terms does not furnish a formula which automatically decides each of an infinite variety of cases. Flexibility is still preserved by the further need of defining the risk, or risks, either narrowly, or more broadly, as seems appropriate and just in the special type of case.

Regarding motor vehicle accidents in particular, one should contemplate a variety of risks which are created by negligent driving. There may be injuries resulting from a direct collision between the carelessly driven car and another vehicle. But such direct collision may be avoided, yet the plaintiff may fall and injure himself in frantically racing out of the way of the errant car.... Or the plaintiff may faint from intense excitement stimulated by the near collision, and in falling sustain a fractured skull.... This bundle of risks could be enlarged indefinitely with a little imagination. In a traffic mix-up due to negligence, before the disturbed waters have become placid and normal again, the unfolding of events between the culpable act and the plaintiff's eventual injury may be bizarre indeed; yet the defendant may be liable for the result. In such a situation, it would be impossible for a person in the defendant's position to predict in advance just how his negligent act would work out to another's injury. Yet this in itself is no bar to recovery.

When an issue of proximate cause arises in a borderline case, as not infrequently happens, we leave it to the jury with appropriate instructions....

Exercising that judgment on the facts in the case at bar, we have to conclude that the district court committed no error in refusing to direct a verdict for the defendant Socony on the issue of proximate cause....

Plaintiff Marshall was a passenger in the oncoming Chevrolet car, and thus was one of the persons whose bodily safety was primarily endangered by the negligence of Prince, as might have been found by the jury, in "cutting the corner" with the Socony truck in the circumstances above related. In that view, Prince's negligence constituted an irretrievable breach of duty to the plaintiff. Though this particular act of negligence was over and done with when the truck pulled up alongside of the stalled Chevrolet without having actually collided with it, still the consequences of such past negligence were in the bosom of time, as yet unrevealed.

If the Chevrolet had been pulled back onto the highway, and Harriman and Marshall, having got in it again, had resumed their journey and had had a collision with another car five miles down the road in which Marshall suffered bodily injuries, it could truly be said that such subsequent injury to Marshall was a consequence in fact of the earlier delay caused by the defendant's negligence, in the sense that but for such delay the Chevrolet car would not have been at the fatal intersection at the moment the other car ran into it. But on such assumed state of facts, the courts would no doubt conclude, "as a matter of law," that Prince's earlier negligence in cutting the corner was not the "proximate cause" of this later injury received by the plaintiff. That would be because the extra risks to which such negligence by Prince had subjected the passengers in the Chevrolet car were obviously entirely over; the situation had been stabilized and become normal, and, so far as one could foresee, whatever subsequent risks the Chevrolet might have to encounter in its resumed journey were simply the inseparable risks, no more and no less, that were incident to the Chevrolet's being out on the highway at all. But in the case at bar, the circumstances under which Marshall received the personal injuries complained of presented no such clear-cut situation. . . .

Notes

1. A phrase once used was "termination of the risk." In *Pittsburg Reduction Co. v. Horton*, 87 Ark. 576, 113 S.W. 647 (1908), a boy named Copple found explosive dynamite caps that the defendant had negligently left in a place where children could be expected to pick them up. Copple kept them at home and his mother knew of them. A week later he traded them to a 13–year-old boy, Jack Horton. Horton lost a hand while playing with them. The court thought that Mrs. Copple's knowing tolerance of the shells "broke the causal connection" and that the defendant which had negligently scattered them around for the children to find would not be liable. "Charlie Copple's parents having permitted him to retain possession of the caps, his further acts in regard to them must be attributable to their permission and were wholly independent of the original negligence of appellants." Commentators have suggested that this is an example of a "terminated risk." Defendant's conduct created a risk but the risk so created was no longer existent. How do you have to describe the risk if this view is taken? Is the termination of risk idea consistent with the risk principle?

2. The termination of risk idea emphasizes that the plaintiff had reached a position of "apparent safety." In *Horton* this would be because one could presumably believe that a mother, having actually discovered the caps, would confiscate them or otherwise provide for safety. But this was not because somehow the defendant's fault had terminated; the defendant had no reason to think the caps had been put in the protective custody of the mother.

3. But if *Horton* is wrong, liability must end somewhere. What would you suggest?

4. Defendant had sexual relations with the plaintiff's wife, W. Defendant infected W with a venereal disease. W, not knowing that defendant was diseased, had sexual relations with her husband and infected him. He sues defendant. Could defendant have foreseen that W's sexual partner would be infected? Would it matter under *Horton* if W discovered her infection before she infected her husband? See *Mussivand v. David*, 45 Ohio St.3d 314, 544 N.E.2d 265 (1989) (involving similar allegations).

5. Can the law of intervening cause be understood as a rational attempt to provide appropriate safety incentives? If the second tortfeasor, confronted with a danger initiated by the first, can effectively provide safety, the law of negligence should encourage him to do so. This may be especially so if he can do so "cost effectively." By eliminating the joint liability of the

original tortfeasor and by putting the entire burden on the second tortfeasor, the law puts incentive for safety on the second. Cf. Mark Grady, *Proximate Cause and the Law of Negligence*, 69 Iowa L. Rev.. 363, 415 ff. (1984). This, of course, minimizes the incentive of the first tortfeasor. Why not use joint and several liability, coupled with punitive damages or provisions for indemnity?

6. Defendant leaves keys in his car. The car is stolen by a group of teenaged boys. Several hours and a hundred miles later, the driver runs down a pedestrian. The pedestrian, unable to locate or collect from the boys, sues the defendant. Is the defendant negligent in leaving the keys in the car? If so, should the theft by the boys supersede the defendant's liability? What elements are most important here? The intended, intervening criminal act? The scope of the risk created by one leaving the keys in the car? The "termination" of the risk?

————

ANAYA v. SUPERIOR COURT, 78 Cal.App.4th 971, 93 Cal.Rptr.2d 228 (2000). "Anaya and Vides allege that their 11–year-old daughter, Norma Vides, was with them when their car collided with a Los Angeles City trash truck that was stopped in the number two lane of a road. Injured in the crash, Norma was airlifted by City helicopter; the helicopter crashed and Norma died. Anaya and Vides sued City of Los Angeles and the individual drivers of the trash truck, Ralph Diaz and Gabriel Lara, for, inter alia, wrongful death." The trial judge sustained a demurrer to the complaint. On review, *held*, the demurrer should have been overruled. "An actor may be liable if the actor's negligence is a substantial factor in causing an injury, and the actor is not relieved of liability because of the intervening act of a third person if such act was reasonably foreseeable at the time of the original negligent conduct. 'The foreseeability required is of the risk of harm, not of the particular intervening act.' . . . It has long been the rule that a tortfeasor responsible for the original accident is also liable for injuries or death occurring during the course of medical treatment to treat injuries suffered in that accident. . . . Obviously, if the original tortfeasor is liable for injuries or death suffered during course of the treatment of injuries suffered in the accident, the original tortfeasor is liable for injuries or death suffered during transportation of the victim to a medical facility for treatment of the injuries resulting from the accident. . . ."

————

NOTE: INTERVENING FORCES OF NATURE

In some instances, the defendant is negligent but an intervening force of nature, such as a violent storm, flood, or lightning is the immediate cause of harm. Suppose the defendant maintains a sign on his property that is poorly constructed and might blow into a pedestrian in a good wind. An extraordinary wind, the likes of which has never been seen in this locale, blows the sign loose and into a passing car, causing damage. Is this an intervening cause problem? The Restatement provides that the defendant can escape liability if the harm done is different from the harm that was risked by the defendant's conduct in the first place. RESTATEMENT SECOND OF TORTS § 451 (1965).

Note

Is this in substance a statement of the result one would obtain applying the risk rule? Why is a separate statement of it needed?

§ 3. THE LAWYER'S ROLE AND THE FUTURE OF PROXIMATE CAUSE ANALYSIS

The cases mostly embrace the scope of risk principle by emphasizing foreseeability, yet often employ the diction of intervening cause and "causal" significance. Within a single state you can find wide variation in language and perhaps conception. A few states have applied a hindsight rule rather than a foreseeability rule, imposing liability even for unforeseeable consequences that, in hindsight, do not seem abnormal, or, more commonly, considering hindsight as one factor in the ultimate determination under Restatement Second § 435(2). E.g., *Lynch v. Scheininger,* 162 N.J. 209, 744 A.2d 113 (2000). In some, maybe even all states, you can find courts applying seemingly contradictory tests. See, summarizing the different lines of authority in Oklahoma, *Hardware Mutual Ins. Co. v. Lukken*, 372 F.2d 8 (10th Cir.1967) (authorities supporting liability for all directly caused harms, others supporting foreseeability or scope of risk limits).

The courts' use of causal language to apply a scope of risk principle that has little to do with causation makes the lawyer's task difficult but serves to emphasize the importance of advocacy in these cases.

Consider the following general kinds of argumentation in the legal cause situation:

(1) Argumentation From Principle or Policy.

A lawyer can argue that the risk principle is, or should be, accepted, and that, once it is, the injury to the plaintiff is (or is not) within the risk. The lawyer can argue in terms of policy rather than principle–defendants should be liable for all the harms, the foreseeability of which made their conduct negligent, and by the same token should be liable for no more. What do the countering arguments look like?

(2) Argumentation From Fact–Pattern Rules.

Lawyers can often describe what courts actually do with a given set of facts, as a kind of "rule" for that set of facts. For instance, courts are pretty well agreed about the rescue situation. In this sense there is a "rule" for rescue cases that does not depend on whether the court uses the language of foreseeability, the language of risk, or the language of remote causation. Since these rules do not seem closely related to any general principle, it is possible that the decisions in such cases are motivated by factors we cannot readily grasp and that the supposed rules will change when a new fact is injected. Perhaps the rescue cases really only apply to certain kinds of rescue or certain kinds of rescuers, for example. In this sense the "rules" in rescue cases may be more uncertain that we might like, but, descriptively speaking, they are still "rules" in the sense that they predict what courts will do in most of the cases. A lawyer can thus argue the "rule" in rescue cases without adopting any position at all about the risk principle.

Fact patterns are not pre-ordained. The lawyer gathers facts by asking questions. Asking different questions will result in gathering facts differently. Additionally, once the lawyer "has" the facts, he or she may ethically characterize and categorize those facts in a number of different ways. You could review the cases in this chapter and find many descriptions and groupings. Some fact patterns leap to the eye—fire cases, automobile cases, or thin skull cases, for example. But these categories of fact may not be the most relevant. Might there be a factual category like this: *"Cases in which plaintiff is injured attempting to minimize or escape from a risk negligently caused by the defendant?"* The lawyer adept at finding and describing cases often can find "rules" in his or her favor, not in the language of the courts but in their composite results. A lawyer might write an argument in a brief like this:

"The courts of this state have consistently held that, when the plaintiff is injured in an attempt to rescue a person injured by the defendant's negligence, the defendant is liable. [Citations.] Our courts have also held without dissent that when the plaintiff is injured attempting to avoid a risk of harm created by the defendant's negligence, the defendant is equally liable."

(3) Argumentation From Comparison and Contrast.

Grouping of cases in more or less factual categories involves sophisticated lawyer skill in argument. Another use of the facts in cases that requires skill is the argument from analogy or disanalogy. Using this technique, the lawyer relies less on groupings of cases to suggest a "rule" for "rescue" or "car theft" or "suicide" cases. Instead, the lawyer attempts to identify special elements for comparison or contrast, analogy or disanalogy.

Legal cause is not easy to understand, much less easy to master. Working out the arguments in particular cases is perhaps the best method of working on the topic. In working out arguments for each side in the following problem what additional facts do you need, if any? If you wish to know more facts, be sure you can state why they are relevant.

Problem

Wolfe v. Gramlich, Inc.

Your client, Gramlich Corp., is being sued by Louis Wolfe on a negligence theory. The following facts are not disputed. Gramlich, as part of its business, maintained a large tank for storing tar. It negligently allowed the tar to spill over, so that it flowed from its premises onto an area where plaintiff, a 9–year old boy, and other children often played.

One day, plaintiff walked into the tar to such depth that his feet were covered up to his ankles. When he returned to his house, his parents saw the tar on his feet and began to remove it by taking the child into the middle of the back yard and using a solvent which is regarded as a safe product for removing tar from skin. While the parents were so engaged, a second child ran into their yard and unexpectedly exploded a cap from a cap-pistol, creating a spark that ignited the fumes from the solvent and resulted in serious burns to plaintiff's legs.

Gramlich's general counsel believes that it might be able to move for summary judgment on the ground that its actions, even if negligent, were not a proximate cause of Wolfe's injuries. She has asked you, as outside counsel, to advise her on the strengths and weaknesses of such a motion.

AN END NOTE:
THE FUTURE OF PROXIMATE CAUSE OR
SCOPE OF RISK ANALYSIS

Proximate cause rules arose before the system of joint and several liability with contribution was fully developed and before the advent of comparative fault systems. As we will begin to see in the next chapter, comparative fault systems are capable of apportioning liability among many tortfeasors, imposing greater liability upon those who are more at fault. Proximate cause rules, on the other hand, are all-or-nothing rules. In the intervening cause situation, the first actor may escape liability altogether, while the second bears the whole burden. That is surely as appropriate as it ever was when it is clear that the second defendant created an entirely new and different risk. When the judge merely feels that the second actor is much more at fault, it may be that proximate cause/superseding cause analyses are counterproductive and that comparative fault rules, with each tortfeasor liable for some portion of the damages, may provide the best solution, at least in doubtful cases. This is a point to bear in mind as we look at comparative fault apportionment of responsibility.

REFERENCES: On legal or proximate cause generally see DOBBS ON TORTS §§ 180–197 (2000); HARPER, JAMES & GRAY, THE LAW OF TORTS §§ 20.4–20.6 (3d ed. 1995); C. MORRIS & C. MORRIS, TORTS, 158–201 (2d Ed. 1980).

SUBTOPIC 2.   DEFENSES
Chapter 9

DEFENSES

A plaintiff who proves every element of a prima facie case for negligence will survive a directed verdict and get to the jury. Nevertheless, her recovery may be defeated or reduced if the defendant mounts a successful affirmative defense. The defendant has the burden of proving affirmative defenses. This chapter examines the major affirmative defenses–plaintiff fault, the various forms of traditional assumed risk doctrine, statutes of limitation, and the usually unsuccessful defense that the defendant complied with some statutory standard. Some of these defenses have changed over the years, but in their traditional forms, the defendant has the burden of proof on each of these defenses.

The defenses covered in this chapter are those traditionally recognized by general common law rules. Legislatures may create other narrow defenses for particular cases. Such defenses must be found in local statutes. Many other impediments that are not necessarily affirmative defenses at all may bar or limit recovery. Among these are rules that reduce or eliminate a defendant's duty of care and those that provide for complete immunity from tort liability. In addition, procedural impediments applied to particular claims like medical malpractice may vastly reduce the number of successful suits. Finally, among the partial defenses enacted by some legislatures are damages caps, limiting liability in particular cases. All of these appear in later chapters.

SUBCHAPTER A.
CONTRIBUTORY/COMPARATIVE NEGLIGENCE

§ 1. CONTRIBUTORY NEGLIGENCE: THE COMMON LAW RULE

BUTTERFIELD v. FORRESTER

11 East. 59, 103 Eng. Rep. 926 (1809).

This was an action on the case for obstructing a highway, by means of which obstruction the plaintiff, who was riding along the road, was thrown down with his horse, and injured, & c. At the trial before Bayley J. at Derby, it appeared that the defendant, for the purpose of making some repairs to his house, which was close by the road side at one end of the town, had put up a pole across this part of the road, a free passage being left by another branch or street in the same direction. That the plaintiff left a public house not far distant from the place in question at 8 o'clock in the evening in August, when they were just beginning to light candles, but while there was light enough left to discern the obstruction at 100 yards distance: and the witness, who proved this, said that if the plaintiff had not been riding very hard he might have observed and avoided it: the plaintiff however, who was riding violently, did not observe it, but rode against it, and fell with his horse and was much hurt in consequence of the accident; and there was no evidence of his being intoxicated at the time. On this evidence Bayley J. directed the jury, that if a person riding with reasonable and ordinary care could have seen and avoided the obstruction; and if they were satisfied that the plaintiff was riding along the street extremely hard, and without ordinary care, they should find a verdict for the defendant: which they accordingly did. [The plaintiff sought a "rule" which would have granted him a new trial.]

BAYLEY, J. The plaintiff was proved to be riding as fast as his horse could go, and this was through the streets of Derby. If he had used ordinary care he must have seen the obstruction; so that the accident appeared to happen entirely from his own fault.

LORD ELLENBOROUGH, C.J. A party is not to cast himself upon an obstruction which has been made by the fault of another, and avail himself of it, if he do not himself use common and ordinary caution to be in the right. In cases of persons riding upon what is considered to be the wrong side of the road, that would not authorize another purposely to ride up against them. One person being in fault will not dispense with another's using ordinary care for himself. Two things must concur to support this action, an obstruction in the road by the fault of the defendant, and no want of ordinary care to avoid it on the part of the plaintiff. [The new trial was refused.]

Notes

1. After *Butterfield v. Forrester*, the courts developed the rule of contributory negligence as a complete, all-or-nothing defense. Even relatively minor failure of the plaintiff to exercise ordinary care for her own safety would completely bar recovery. This remained true even if the defendant's negligence was extreme, so long as it fell short of a reckless or wanton act.

2. It is important, for reasons that will later become apparent, to identify the several grounds on which the result in *Butterfield v. Forrester* might be justified.

(a) *The fault principle*. If liability is to be based upon fault and the defendant mulcted because his fault causes harm, then should the same fault principle compel the faulty plaintiff to lose his case entirely?

(b) *Proximate cause*. Could *Butterfield v. Forrester* be understood as applying some view of proximate cause in which the plaintiff is treated as a superseding cause? Test this idea. Imagine that a child, standing near the obstruction, had been injured when the horse fell. Would the defendant, if negligent, have been liable for that?

(c) *Negligence*. Granted that the defendant owed the plaintiff a duty of care, was that duty breached? Formulate an argument that the defendant's conduct was not negligent at all. Try to draw on specific cases or hypotheticals for a principle or general idea that furthers the defendant's argument.

3. Why do you think the contributory negligence rule developed in such a stringent fashion? Rules often develop from social and economic needs or assumptions. But sometimes a rule develops from a conceptual failure, that is, because legal professionals are unable at the moment to put together a coherent or logical idea about what a rule ought to be. Does the contributory negligence rule reflect social or economic standards or merely a conceptual failure?

4. In several situations courts found reasons not to apply the contributory negligence defense. When an exception applied, the plaintiff made a full recovery in spite of her own fault. It was still an all-or-nothing system, but when an exception applied it was "all" rather than "nothing" for the plaintiff. We will look at these exceptions and how they fare under modern comparative negligence law in § 3 below.

§ 2.　CONTRIBUTORY NEGLIGENCE: ADOPTING COMPARATIVE FAULT RULES TO PERMIT RECOVERY

NEW YORK MCKINNEY'S CIV. PRAC. LAW § 1411

In any action to recover damages for personal injury, injury to property, or wrongful death, the culpable conduct attributable to the claimant or to the decedent, including contributory negligence or assumption of risk, shall not bar recovery, but the amount of damages otherwise recoverable shall be diminished in the proportion which the culpable conduct attributable to the claimant or decedent bears to the culpable conduct which caused the damages.

WISCONSIN STAT. ANN. 895.045

(1) Contributory negligence does not bar recovery in an action by any person or the person's legal representative to recover damages for negligence resulting in death or in injury to person or property, if that negligence was not greater than the negligence of the person against whom recovery is sought, but any damages allowed shall be diminished in the proportion to the amount of negligence attributed to the person recovering. . . .

———

BRITTAIN v. BOOTH, 601 P.2d 532 (Wyo.1979). Plaintiff, 16 years of age, worked for Hartsook, who was installing an underground tank. Plaintiff went into the excavation, which, as he knew, was not sloped or shored up. It caved in on him and he suffered severe back injuries requiring the fusion of four vertebrae in his lower back. He is partly disabled and will probably have future surgery. His medical expense alone had come to $7,800 at the time of the trial. The jury found the defendant, a supervisory employee, negligent in sending or permitting plaintiff to go into the excavation, fixing his negligence at 51%; it found the plaintiff guilty of 49% of the negligence and fixed total damages at $10,000. A judgment was entered for the plaintiff for $5,100. On plaintiff's appeal, complaining that the verdict was inadequate, held, affirmed. The jury could find the plaintiff guilty of contributory negligence. A reasonable person would recognize the danger, whether the particular plaintiff did so or not. The jury is the proper body to decide the appropriate amount of damages.

Notes

1. *Types of comparative negligence systems.* The comparative negligence system set up under the New York statute is usually called a pure comparative fault system. The system set up under the Wisconsin statute is usually called a modified system. In some states using a modified system, the plaintiff is barred if his fault is equal to defendant's; in others only if it is "more than" the defendant's.

2. *Adoption of comparative negligence.* The Federal Employers' Liability Act (FELA), 45 U.S.C.A. § 53 was promulgated in 1906 to facilitate claims against interstate railroads by workers injured on the job. It adopted a comparative negligence system as one of its major provisions. Another federal statute, the Jones Act, applied the FELA rules to seafaring workers. Only a handful of states adopted comparative fault systems until a wave of change occurred after the late 1960s. In some states, legislatures adopted comparative fault; in others, the courts did so. When change came through legislation, the modified system most often resulted. When change came through judicial action, pure comparative negligence was most often adopted. E.g., *Li v. Yellow Cab Co. of California*, 13 Cal.3d 804, 119 Cal.Rptr. 858, 532 P.2d 1226 (1975). By 2000, only Alabama, North Carolina, Maryland, Virginia, and the District of Columbia held out against the change.

3. When the plaintiff's fault was an absolute bar to recovery, some cases judged the plaintiff's contributory fault more leniently than they judged the defendant's fault. With the advent of comparative fault apportionment of responsibility, this approach may be difficult to justify. The Restatement of Apportionment now asserts that negligence of the plaintiff and negligence of the defendant are judged under the same standard. See RESTATEMENT OF THE LAW OF TORTS: APPORTIONMENT OF LIABILITY § 3 (2000). The fact that the plaintiff's fault imposed risks only upon herself and not upon others, however, may be relevant in assessing percentage responsibility. Perhaps it would also be relevant to proximate cause.

4. *Apportionment of responsibility.* How much fault is attributable to each party? If the evidence permits reasonable people to differ, this is a "fact" question, not a question of law. Attribution of fault percentages is necessarily a rough approximation even though it is expressed in mathematical terms. The jury is usually told, in effect, to treat all the fault in the case as 100% and to then find the percentage of fault attributable to each person. In some cases the jury is charged to reduce the damages in accordance with the percentage of fault attributable to each party; in others the jury is asked to answer special interrogatories fixing the damages of each party and the negligence of each, leaving the judge to make the computation.

5. *Computation.* What will each party recover under the following findings?

> A and B, each driving a car, collide head on and each is injured. The jury finds A's damages to be $100,000 and B's damages (asserted in a compulsory counterclaim) to be $50,000. A is guilty of 60% of the negligence and B is guilty of 40%. What if B has no damages at all?

6. *Multiple parties.* Almost every automobile injury case involves injuries to two or more persons, as in the example above. A great many involve claims against two or more persons as concurrent tortfeasors. These obviously become more complicated. The basic apportionment of liability remains the same, however. If A is guilty of 10% of the negligence and B and C are guilty of 45% and 45% respectively, A's damages will be reduced by 10%.

7. Some of the more complex problems arise from multi-party claims and when one or more parties are insolvent, or inadequately insured, or where one or more have settled out of the case. These problems must be left for more specialized study, though a few of them are considered in Chapter 23 on problems of litigating tort cases.

WASSELL v. ADAMS

United States Court of Appeals, Seventh Circuit, 1989.
865 F.2d 849.

POSNER, CIRCUIT JUDGE.

The plaintiff, born Susan Marisconish, grew up on Macaroni Street in a small town in a poor coal-mining region of Pennsylvania–a town so small and obscure that it has no name. She was the ninth of ten children, and as a child was sexually abused by her stepfather. After graduating from high school she worked briefly as a nurse's aide, then became engaged to Michael Wassell, also from Pennsylvania. Michael joined the Navy in 1985 and was sent to Great Lakes Naval Training Station, just north of Chicago, for basic training. He and Susan had decided to get married as soon as he completed basic training. The graduation was scheduled for a Friday. Susan, who by now was 21 years old, traveled to Chicago with Michael's parents for the graduation. The three checked into a double room at the Ron–Ric motel, near the base. . . . The Ron–Ric is a small and inexpensive motel that caters to the families of sailors at the Great Lakes Naval Training Station a few blocks to the east. The motel has 14 rooms and charges a maximum of $36 a night for a double room. The motel was owned by Wilbur and Florena Adams, the defendants in the case.

Four blocks to the west of the Ron–Ric motel is a high-crime area: murder, prostitution, robbery, drugs–the works. The Adamses occasionally warned women guests not to walk alone in the neighborhood at night. They did not warn the Wassells or Susan. [The plaintiff stayed on in the motel after the Wassels left; she was to look for an apartment because Michael was to be stationed there permanently.] She spent most of Sunday in her room reading the newspaper and watching television. In the evening she went to look at an apartment. Upon returning to her room at the motel, she locked the door, fastened the chain, and went to bed. She fell into a deep sleep, from which she was awakened by a knock on the door. She turned on a light and saw by the clock built into the television set that it was 1:00 a.m. She went to the door and looked through the peephole but saw no one. Next to the door was a pane of clear glass. She did not look through it. The door had two locks plus a chain. She unlocked the door and opened it all the way, thinking that Michael had come from the base and, not wanting to wake her, was en route to the Adamses' apartment to fetch a key to the room. It was not Michael at the door. It was a respectably dressed black man whom Susan had never seen before. He asked for "Cindy" (maybe "Sidney," she thought later). She told him there was no Cindy there. Then he asked for a glass of water. She went to the bathroom, which was at the other end of the room . . . to fetch the glass of water. When she came out of the bathroom, the man was sitting at the table in the room. (The room had a screen door as well as a solid door, but the screen door had not been latched.) He took the water but said it wasn't cold enough. He also said he had no money, and Susan remarked that she had $20 in her car. The man went into the bathroom to get a colder glass of water. Susan began to get nervous. She was standing between the bathroom and the door of her room. She hid her purse, which contained her car keys and $800 in cash that Michael had given her. There was no telephone in the room. There was an alarm attached to the television set, which would be activated if someone tried to remove the set, but she had not been told and did not know about the alarm, although a notice of the alarm was posted by the set. The parking lot on which the motel rooms opened was brightly lit by floodlights.

A few tense minutes passed after the man entered the bathroom. He poked his head out of the doorway and asked Susan to join him in the bathroom, he wanted to show her something. She refused. After a while he emerged from the bathroom–naked from the waist down. Susan fled from the room, and beat on the door of the adjacent room. There was no response. The man ran after her and grabbed her. She screamed, but no one appeared. The motel had no security guard; the Adamses lived in a basement apartment at the other end of the motel and did not hear her screams.

The man covered Susan's mouth and dragged her back to her room. There he gagged her with a wash cloth. He raped her at least twice (once anally). These outrages occupied more than an hour. Eventually Susan persuaded the rapist to take a shower with her. After the shower, she managed to get out of the bathroom before he did, dress, and flee in her car. To save herself after the rapes, she had tried to convince him that she liked him, and had succeeded at least to the extent that his guard was down. The Adamses' lawyer tried halfheartedly to show that she had consented to the rapes, but backed off from this position in closing argument.

The rapist was never prosecuted; a suspect was caught but Susan was too upset to identify him. There had been a rape at the motel several years previously (a sailor had opened the door of his room to two men who said they were "the management," and the men raped his wife). There had also been a robbery, and an incident in which an intruder kicked in the door to one of the rooms. These were the only serious crimes committed during the seven years that the Adamses owned the motel.

Susan married Michael, but the rape had induced post-trauma stress that has, according to her testimony and that of a psychologist testifying as her expert witness, blighted her life. She brought this suit against the Adamses on January 21, 1986. It is a diversity suit that charges the Adamses with negligence in failing to warn Susan or take other precautions to protect her against the assault. The substantive issues are governed by the law of Illinois. A jury composed of four women and three men found that the Adamses had indeed been negligent and that their negligence had been a proximate cause of the assault, and the jury assessed Susan's damages at $850,000, which was the figure her lawyer had requested in closing argument. But in addition the jury found that Susan had been negligent too—and indeed that her negligence had been 97 percent to blame for the attack and the Adamses' only 3 percent.... [T]he jury awarded Susan only $25,500 in damages. This happens to be approximately the midpoint of the psychologist's estimate–$20,000 to $30,000–of the expense of the therapy that the psychologist believes Susan may need for her post-traumatic stress....

Susan Wassell's counsel argues that the jury's verdict "reflected a chastened, hardened, urban mentality—that lurking behind every door is evil and danger, even if the guest is from a small town unfamiliar with the area." He takes umbrage at the defendants' argument that Susan's "antennae" should have been alerted when she didn't see anyone through the peephole. He rejects the metaphor, remarking unexceptionably that human beings do not have antennae and that this case is not a Kafka story about a person who turned into an insect (i.e., is not The Metamorphosis). He points out that a person awakened from a deep sleep is not apt to be thinking clearly and that once Susan opened the door the fat was in the fire–if she had slammed the door in the rapist's face he might have kicked the door in, as had happened once before at this motel, although she didn't know that at the time. The Adamses' counsel argued to the jury (perhaps with the wisdom of hindsight) that Susan's "tragic mistake" was failing to flee when the man entered the bathroom. Susan's counsel insists that Susan was not negligent at all but that, if she was, she was at most 5 percent responsible for the catastrophe, which, he argues, could have been averted costlessly by a simple warning from the Adamses. To this the Adamses' counsel replies absurdly that a warning would have been costly—it might have scared guests away! The loss of business from telling the truth is not a social loss; it is a social gain. . . .

The old common law rule barring the contributorily negligent plaintiff from recovering any damages came eventually to seem too harsh. That is why it has been changed in most jurisdictions, including Illinois. It was harsh, all right, at least if one focuses narrowly on the plight of individual plaintiffs, but it was also simple and therefore cheap to administer. The same cannot be said for comparative negligence, which far from being simple requires a formless, unguided inquiry, because there is no methodology for comparing the causal contributions of the plaintiff's and of the defendant's negligence to the plaintiff's injury. In this case, either the plaintiff or the defendants could have avoided that injury. It is hard to say more, but the statute requires more—yet without giving the finder of facts any guidance as to how to make the apportionment.

We have suggested in previous cases that one way to make sense of comparative negligence is to assume that the required comparison is between the respective costs to the plaintiff and to the defendant of avoiding the injury. If each could have avoided it at the same cost, they are each 50 percent responsible for it. According to this method of comparing negligence, the jury found that Susan could have avoided the attack at a cost of less than one thirty-second the cost to the Adamses. Is this possible?

It is careless to open a motel or hotel door in the middle of the night without trying to find out who is knocking. Still, people aren't at their most alert when they are awakened in the middle of the night, and it wasn't crazy for Susan to assume that Michael had returned without telling her, even though he had said he would be spending the night at the base. So it cannot be assumed that the cost . . . to the reasonable person who found himself or herself in her position . . . –was zero, or even that it was slight. As innkeepers (in the increasingly quaint legal term), the Adamses had a duty to exercise a high degree of care to protect their guests from assaults on the motel premises. And the cost to the Adamses of warning all their female guests of the dangers of the neighborhood would have been negligible. Surely a warning to Susan would not have cost the Adamses 32 times the cost to her of schooling herself to greater vigilance.

But this analysis is incomplete. It is unlikely that a warning would have averted the attack. Susan testified that she thought the man who had knocked on the door was her fiance. Thinking this, she would have opened the door no matter how dangerous she believed the neighborhood to be. The warning that was not given might have deterred her from walking alone in the neighborhood. But that was not the pertinent danger. Of course, if the Adamses had told her not to open her door in the middle of the night under any circumstances without carefully ascertaining who was trying to enter the room, this would have been a pertinent warning and might have had an effect. But it is absurd to think that hoteliers are required to give so obvious a warning, any more than they must warn guests not to stick their fingers into the electrical outlets. Everyone, or at least the average person, knows better than to open his or her door to a stranger in the middle of the night. The problem was not that Susan thought that she should open her bedroom door in the middle of the night to anyone who knocked, but that she wasn't thinking clearly. A warning would not have availed against a temporary, sleep-induced lapse.

Giving the jury every benefit of the doubt, ... we must assume that the jury was not so muddle-headed as to believe that the Adamses' negligence consisted in failing to give a futile warning. Rather, we must assume that the jury thought the Adamses' negligence consisted in failing to have a security guard, or telephones in each room, or alarms designed to protect the motel's patrons rather than just the owners' television sets. (The Adamses did, however, have an informal agreement with the local police that the police would cruise through the parking lot of the Ron–Ric whenever they drove down the street at night—and this was maybe three or four times a night.) The only one of these omitted precautions for which there is a cost figure in the record was the security guard. A guard would have cost $50 a night. That is almost $20,000 a year. This is not an enormous number. The plaintiff suggests that it would have been even lower because the guard would have been needed only on busy nights. But the evidence was in conflict on whether the Sunday night after a Friday graduation, which is the night that Susan was attacked, was a busy night. And the need for a security guard would seem to be greater, the less busy rather than the busier the motel; if there had been someone in the room adjacent to Susan's, she might have been saved from her ordeal. In any event the cost of the security guard, whether on all nights or just on busy nights–or just on unbusy nights– might be much greater than the monetary equivalent of the greater vigilance on the part of Susan that would have averted the attack....

If we were the trier of fact, persuaded that both parties were negligent and forced to guess about the relative costs to the plaintiff and to the defendants of averting the assault, we would assess the defendants' share at more than 3 percent. But we are not the trier of fact, and are authorized to upset the jury's apportionment only if persuaded that the trial judge abused his discretion in determining that the jury's verdict was not against the clear weight of the evidence. We are not so persuaded. It seems probably wrong to us, but we have suggested an interpretation of the evidence under which the verdict was consistent with the evidence and the law. And that is enough to require us to uphold the district judge's refusal to set aside the verdict.

Affirmed.

Notes

1. It may be difficult to reach the central issue decided by the *Wassell* court. The facts themselves are likely to generate strong feelings of anger, sympathy and frustration that somehow the victim is blamed for the outrage of another. On the other hand, some readers may feel that it is by no means clear that the defendant motel owners were themselves negligent. Such feelings are important but they should not obscure the issue addressed by the court, that of comparative fault. Remember also that the court was reviewing a jury apportionment of fault between the plaintiff and the defendant motel owners; neither the appeals court nor the jury was assessing the culpability of the rapist.

2. Should the plaintiff's fault be considered at all in a case not involving reciprocal risk-taking?

3. Judge Posner is attempting to apply a kind of *Carroll Towing* approach to comparative fault. When we first looked at *Carroll Towing*, we considered whether the risk-utility formula worked well in all kinds of cases or only in some. The same question arises with comparative fault. Another question is whether the *Carroll Towing* formula should apply to ANY comparative or contributory negligence issue.

4. Do you estimate the amount of negligence and contributory negligence by comparing costs of non-negligent conduct for each party? That is the approach Judge Posner took. What percentages of negligence on the part of each party would he find if each could have avoided the harm by expending $100?

5. To use the *Carroll Towing*/Posner approach, do you need to know exactly what it was that the plaintiff and defendant each did that was negligent? Is that why it is relevant to know whether the defendant was at fault for failing to give a warning (cost free) or failing to have a security guard?

6. Judge Posner seems to think the plaintiff herself would have had "costs" in avoiding the injury. What could he have in mind? Could they be reasonably quantified?

7.   In a fraud and misrepresentation case against a lawyer–certainly a different kind of case from *Wassell*–Judge Posner had this to say about contributory negligence:

> Due care is the care that is optimal given that the other party is exercising due care. It is not the higher level of care that would be optimal if potential tort victims were required to assume that the rest of the world was negligent. A pedestrian is not required to exercise a level of care (e.g., wearing a helmet or a shin guard) that would be optimal if there were no sanctions against reckless driving. Otherwise drivers would be encouraged to drive recklessly, and knowing this pedestrians would be encouraged to wear helmets and shin guards. The result would be a shift from a superior method of accident avoidance (not driving recklessly) to an inferior one (pedestrian armor) . . . . . . The law normally does not require duplicative precautions unless one is likely to fail or the consequences of failure . . . would be catastrophic.

Greycas, Inc. v. Proud, 826 F.2d 1560, 1566 (7th Cir.1987). How does this kind of analysis work, if at all, in a case like *Wassell*?

8.   Maine has a comparative negligence rule radically different from most. Instead of requiring the jury to reduce the plaintiff's damages in proportion to the plaintiff's relative fault, the statute requires the jury to make a reduction it considers to be equitable and just. In. *Pelletier v. Fort Kent Golf Club,* 662 A.2d 220 (Me.1995) the jury found that the defendant was more negligent than the plaintiff and that the plaintiff suffered $250,000 in damages. Yet the award was only $40,000. The court held this was within the jury's discretion. It is obvious that the jury could not have made its reduction on the basis of proportional fault, since on that basis the plaintiff would have recovered something more than $125,000. If the verdict was not based on any legal rule, what might have motivated to the jury?

9.   If you think *Pelletier* is just, or at least just enough, would it be equally permissible to let a jury find the defendant chargeable with 55% of the fault but liable for 99% of the plaintiff's damages? Do you think the *Wassell* jury would have brought in a different verdict under the Maine statute?

RESTATEMENT THIRD OF TORTS, APPORTIONMENT OF LIABILITY[1]
(2000).

§ 8.   FACTORS FOR ASSIGNING SHARES OF RESPONSIBILITY

Factors for assigning percentages of responsibility to each person whose legal responsibility has been established include

(a) the nature of the person's risk-creating conduct, including any awareness or indifference with respect to the risks

---

1. Citations in the Restatement's comments are omitted.

created by the conduct and any intent with respect to the harm created by the conduct; and

(b) the strength of the causal connection between the person's risk-creating conduct and the harm.

a. Assigning shares of responsibility. The factfinder assigns comparative percentages of "responsibility" to parties and other relevant persons whose negligence or other legally culpable conduct was a legal cause of the plaintiff's injury. The factfinder does not assign percentages of "fault," "negligence," or "causation."

"Responsibility" is a general and neutral term. Assigning shares of "fault" or "negligence" can be misleading because some causes of action are not based on negligence or fault. Assigning shares of "causation" wrongly suggests that indivisible injuries jointly caused by two or more actors can be divided on the basis of causation. Assigning shares of "culpability" could be misleading if it were not made clear that "culpability" refers to "legal culpability," which may include strict liability.

Of course, it is not possible to precisely compare conduct that falls into different categories, such as intentional conduct, negligent conduct, and conduct governed by strict liability, because the various theories of recovery are incommensurate. However, courts routinely compare seemingly incommensurate values, such as when they balance safety and productivity in negligence or products liability law. "Assigning shares of responsibility" may be a less confusing phrase because it suggests that the factfinder, after considering the relevant factors, assigns shares of responsibility rather than compares incommensurate quantities. Nevertheless, the term "comparative responsibility" is used pervasively by courts and legislatures to describe percentage-allocation systems.

b. Causation and scope of liability. Conduct is relevant for determining percentage shares of responsibility only when it caused the harm and when the harm is within the scope of the person's liability.

c. Factors in assigning shares of responsibility. The relevant factors for assigning percentages of responsibility include the nature of each person's risk-creating conduct and the comparative strength of the causal connection between each person's risk-creating conduct and the harm. The nature of each person's risk-creating conduct includes such things as how unreasonable the conduct was under the circumstances, the extent to which the conduct failed to meet the applicable legal standard, the circumstances surrounding the conduct, each person's abilities and disabilities, and each person's awareness, intent, or indifference with respect to the risks. The comparative strength of the causal connection between the conduct and the harm depends on how attenuated the causal connection is, the timing of each person's conduct in causing the harm, and a comparison of the risks created by the conduct and the actual harm suffered by the plaintiff.

One or more of these factors may be relevant for assigning percentages of responsibility, even though they may not be a necessary element proving a particular claim or defense. However, these factors are irrelevant even to apportionment if there is no causal connection between the referenced conduct and the plaintiff's injuries. See Comment b. It should be noted that the mental-state factors in this Section may be considered for apportioning responsibility even if they are not themselves causally connected to the plaintiff's injury, as long as the risk-creating conduct to which they refer is causally connected to the injury.

Note

Is the Restatement correct in inviting the trier to consider mental states of the parties and the strength of causal connections as well as the unjustified risks they created?

OUELLETTE v. CARDE, 612 A.2d 687 (R.I.1992). In a closed garage, Carde attempted to work under a car he had raised on jacks. While he was trying to work loose the muffler, the car fell, the gas tank punctured and ten gallons of gas ran onto the floor of the garage. Carde was partly pinned, but he was able to reach a phone and call a friend for help. The friend, who is the plaintiff here, came to his rescue, but when she activated the electric garage door opener, the gasoline ignited and she was badly burned. She sued Carde. Carde asked for a comparative negligence instruction, which the trial court denied. The jury found for the plaintiff without reduction in damages. *Held*, affirmed. "The rescue doctrine is a rule of law holding that one who sees a person in imminent danger caused by the negligence of another cannot be charged with contributory negligence" unless the rescuer acted recklessly. "The comparative negligence doctrine does not fully protect the rescue doctrine's underlying policy of promoting rescue," therefore the defendant is not entitled to have the jury consider the rescuer/plaintiff's fault in assessing damages.

GOVICH v. NORTH AMERICAN SYSTEMS, INC., 112 N.M. 226, 814 P.2d 94 (1991). Daniel Govich is hearing impaired. His dog alerts him to daily noises like telephone rings or knocks at the door. Returning home from dinner with his mother, he found smoke billowing from the house. When the dog did not respond to his calls, he entered the house to rescue the dog. His mother, Roane, in turn entered to rescue him. The dog was not saved. Daniel and Roane sue the defendant, alleging a defective coffee maker caused the fire and claiming for their injuries, emotional distress, and lost wages. *Held*, reversing a partial summary judgment for defendants: (1) under the rescue doctrine of *Wagner v. International Ry.*, the defendant owed a duty of care to Daniel and Roane, each of whom was a rescuer. (2) However, after the advent of comparative negligence in New Mexico, the allocation of fault between the negligent plaintiff/rescuer and the negligent defendant must be left to the jury.

NOTE: RES IPSA LOQUITUR IN COMPARATIVE FAULT SYSTEMS

(1) Goodbye to the control rule? Res ipsa loquitur was created and grew under the all-or-nothing system. In fact, as noted in Chapter 6, one supposed rule of res ipsa loquitur was that the plaintiff was required to show that the injury was not due to her own fault. The most logical interpretation of this rule is that it was merely an instance of the control rule. The defendant would not be in exclusive control of the instrumentality if the plaintiff was, even in part, a cause of the her own harm. However, courts have sometimes interpreted the rule to bar the application of res ipsa when the plaintiff was guilty of contributory fault. Interpreting the rule in this way, a growing number of courts have said that adoption of comparative fault has eliminated the rule against applying res ipsa loquitur when the plaintiff is at fault. Instead, the plaintiff's fault, if any, will reduce her recovery, but will not bar use of res ipsa loquitur. Even so, might the plaintiff's control over the instrumentality in a particular case be so significant that the res ipsa inference simply cannot be drawn?

(2) Apportioning the unknown fault in res ipsa loquitur cases. How is apportionment of fault to proceed in a res ipsa case involving a plaintiff's comparative negligence? The Connecticut court in *Giles v. City of New Haven,* 228 Conn. 441, 636 A.2d 1335 (1994) said that the judge, after determining that the requirements of res ipsa were sufficiently met to send the case to the jury on that theory, "should thereafter instruct the jury to compare the negligence of the plaintiff, if any, with that of the defendant to decide what percentages to attribute to each party." How is the jury to assign a percentage of fault to each when the defendant's negligence is not known? Is *res ipsa loquitur* simply not well suited to the proportional system of comparative fault?

§ 3. TRADITIONAL EXCEPTIONS TO THE CONTRIBUTORY NEGLIGENCE BAR IN A COMPARATIVE FAULT REGIME

a. *Last Clear Chance or Discovered Peril*

In the traditional system that barred all recovery for contributory negligence, courts allowed the negligent plaintiff a full recovery when the plaintiff was left in a helpless position by his own negligence and the defendant, who had the last clear chance to avoid injury, negligently inflicted it anyway. *See* RESTATEMENT SECOND OF TORTS §§ 479, 480 (1965).

The doctrine first appeared in *Davies v. Mann,* 10 M. & W. 547, 152 Eng. Rep. 588 (Exch. 1842). In that case the plaintiff had left his ass fettered in the road eating grass. The defendant negligently drove a team and wagon down the hill and ran over the animal, which, being fettered, was unable to move. The court held that the plaintiff's contributory negligence was no defense. Baron Parke said that "unless [the plaintiff] might, by the exercise of ordinary care, have avoided the consequences of the defendant's negligence, he is entitled to recover," stressing that if the rule were otherwise, "a man might justify the driving over goods left on a public highway, or even a man lying asleep there. . . ."

The last clear chance doctrine held that if the defendant discovered or should have discovered the plaintiff's peril, and could reasonably have avoided it, the plaintiff's earlier negligence would neither bar nor reduce the plaintiff's recovery. A slightly less generous version, called the discovered peril doctrine, applied these rules only if the defendant actually did discover the plaintiff's peril. The plaintiff could not invoke these doctrines unless the plaintiff was helpless; if he could extricate himself from danger at any time, the defendant did not have the last chance to avoid injury and the negligent plaintiff would be barred entirely.

A number of early cases involved railroad injuries. The clearly-negligent plaintiff is asleep or drunk on the tracks or in a stalled car. The defendant runs its train over him or into his car. If the defendant negligently failed to keep a lookout, or to blow a whistle, or to stop, then the defendant was held fully liable despite plaintiff's contributory negligence.

Those courts that retain the traditional bar of contributory negligence must still occasionally face last clear chance arguments. E.g., *Westbrook v. Washington Gas & Light Co.*, 748 A.2d 437 (D.C.App.2000) (holding that the doctrine did not apply on the facts). In states that have adopted comparative fault systems, however, the last clear chance and discovered peril doctrines have been discarded, mostly on the grounds that they were attempts to aid the plaintiff in a harsh system and not needed once comparative fault rules apply. HENRY WOODS & BETH DEERE, COMPARATIVE FAULT § 8.3 (3d ed. 1996).

If the doctrine was correct in a contributory negligence system, should it be retained in a modified comparative fault system where the plaintiff's contributory negligence can still operate as a complete bar to recovery when it is equal to or greater than the defendant's? Would the fact that the defendant had the last chance still be relevant in determining relative fault? On both points see DOBBS ON TORTS § 207 (2000).

b. *Defendant's Reckless or Intentional Misconduct*

Contributory negligence was historically no defense to an intentional tort. By extension of this idea, courts also held that contributory negligence was no defense to wilful, wanton or reckless torts, defined as involving "utter indifference to or conscious disregard for the safety of others." Such torts border on intentional wrongdoing because they involve a bad state of mind, as well as risky conduct. Under this rule the plaintiff charged with contributory negligence was allowed a full recovery against a reckless or wanton defendant.

Once comparative negligence rules are adopted, should courts discard the old rule and simply let the jury apportion fault between plaintiff and defendant, even when the defendant is guilty of reckless conduct? When he is guilty of an intentional tort?

The Restatement Third of Torts, Apportionment of Liability § 1 calls for application of comparative fault rules to all claims for personal injury, death, and harms to tangible property. That includes suits against an intentional tortfeasor. At the same time, the Restatement of Apportionment takes no position on the question whether a plaintiff's comparative fault reduces recovery against an intentional tortfeasor. Id., cmt. c.

Should comparative fault have a role in either of these cases?

Case 1. Defendant strikes the plaintiff. When sued, he argues that the plaintiff was guilty of contributory negligence because she provoked the attack.

Case 2. A negligently provides B with keys to A's car, knowing that B is dangerous, in a rage at P, and might attack her. B intentionally runs down P. After P recovers fully against A, A seeks contribution from B.

c. *Plaintiff's Illegal Activity*

BARKER v. KALLASH, 63 N.Y.2d 19, 479 N.Y.S.2d 201, 468 N.E.2d 39 (1984). The plaintiff, 15 years old, was making a pipe bomb from a pipe filled with powder he said was from firecrackers sold by a nine-year-old defendant. It exploded, he was injured and sued the 9–year-old, his parents and everyone else in sight. *Held*, no recovery. A distinction must be drawn between lawful activities regulated by statute, in which case violation of the statute is negligence or contributory negligence under the rule in *Martin v. Herzog*, and those activities that are prohibited. When "the plaintiff's injury is a direct result of his knowing and intentional participation in a criminal act he cannot seek compensation for the loss, if the criminal act is judged to be so serious an offense as to warrant denial of recovery.... Thus a burglar who breaks his leg while descending the cellar stairs, due to the failure of the owner to replace a missing step cannot recover compensation from his victims." Though plaintiff could not be criminally convicted, he does not escape this rule. He "was not a toddler. And building a bomb is not such an inherently innocuous activity that it can reasonably be presumed to be a legally permissible act by an average 15 year old." Nor does the comparative negligence statute relieve the plaintiff here. In referring to "culpable conduct" the statute does not allow a recovery here with diminution of damages. The rule that bars the plaintiff here is not the contributory negligence rule but a rule of public policy that courts should not aid one who engages in a substantial violation of law. Two judges dissented.

Notes

1. In *Zysk v. Zysk*, 239 Va. 32, 404 S.E.2d 721 (1990) the plaintiff alleged that before she married the defendant, she engaged in consensual

sexual intercourse with him, that he knew at the time he was infected with herpes and she did not; that he neither warned her nor took steps to protect her, and that she became infected as a result. She permanently separated from him and sought damages for injury, economic loss, and emotional distress. The court, considering the intercourse to be illegal under Virginia's fornication statute, held that this was not a case of proportional recovery, with damages reduced to reflect the plaintiff's fault. Instead the plaintiff was denied recovery altogether as one who "consents to and participates in an immoral or illegal act."

2. *Barker* and *Zysk* reflect the widely-held view that when a plaintiff's negligence action is based in whole or part on his own illegal conduct, his claim is entirely barred. An equally-held corollary rule is that where both plaintiff and defendant have participated in illegal activity which is the basis for the plaintiff's action, plaintiff's claim is also barred entirely. This rule was applied in *Orzel v. Scott Drug Co.*, 449 Mich. 550, 537 N.W.2d 208 (1995), to bar a plaintiff's negligence claim against a pharmacy where the plaintiff had obtained prescription drugs without a valid prescription. Some states have statutes on this subject. For example, in Ohio, tort recovery is not available to any person who has been "convicted of or has pleaded guilty to a felony, or to a misdemeanor that is an offense of violence, arising out of criminal conduct that was a proximate cause of the injury ... for which relief is claimed." OHIO REV. CODE § 2307.60.

3. But some authorities differ. In *Flanagan v. Baker*, 35 Mass.App.Ct. 444, 621 N.E.2d 1190 (1993), the court thought the persons who allegedly furnished the means for a teenager's crime should not be shielded from possible liability when the welfare of the general public is potentially threatened by such misconduct.

4. The illegal activity rule is not in any event applied across the board to all illegal activities. Speeding is illegal. Do you think New York or Virginia would bar all suits by speeding plaintiffs? Or merely consider their speeding on the issue of comparative fault? What about a felon who has robbed a hapless old woman in the subway station and is negligently shot by a police officer?

§ 4. CAUSATION AND COMPARATIVE FAULT

a. *Negligence or Fault Not a Cause in Fact or Proximate Cause*

(1) Plaintiff's non-causal fault. Both the cause in fact and the legal cause rules can apply to the plaintiff's side of the case as well as to the defendant's. The plaintiff may recover full damages if her contributory negligence was not a cause in fact or a proximate cause of her own harm. Suppose the plaintiff is driving negligently because she is not keeping a good lookout on the road ahead. The defendant's car strikes the plaintiff's car from the rear. Quite likely the plaintiff's bad lookout was not a cause in fact of the collision or injury. If not, her poor lookout does not reduce her damages any more than it would make her liable for the defendant's injuries.

If the plaintiff's fault is a cause in fact of her harm (along with the defendant's fault), it is still possible that the plaintiff's fault will be disregarded because the injury suffered was not within the risk created by her fault. Consider: a houseguest negligently blunders onto a dark patio. He is negligent because he is unfamiliar with the place and he might easily trip or fall into the swimming pool. Instead he is struck by his host's runaway car which crashes through the back gate. See Dan B. Dobbs, *Accountability and Comparative Fault*, 47 LA. L. REV. 939 (1987).

(2) Defendant's non-causal fault. Under the ordinary rules of negligence law, the negligent defendant escapes legal liability if his conduct is not a cause in fact of the plaintiff's harm. He likewise escapes liability if his conduct is not a proximate or legal cause of the plaintiff's harm. This rule does not change with the adoption of comparative fault. Again, as traditionally applied, causal rules invoke an all-or-nothing system. We do not merely reduce damages when the defendant's conduct is not a cause of the harm; instead, we dismiss the claim.

(3) Plaintiff's fault as a superseding cause. In *Boltax v. Joy Day Camp*, 67 N.Y.2d 617, 499 N.Y.S.2d 660, 490 N.E.2d 527 (1986) a man 20 years of age dove into a swimming pool on property owned by one defendant and leased to another. The plaintiff was a trespasser, who knew the dangers of diving, knew the water levels at each part of the pool, and "yet chose to dive head first from the lifeguard chair into shallow water." The court denied recovery altogether. The plaintiff's knowing act "was an unforeseeable superseding event that absolves defendants of liability...." No mention was made of comparative negligence.

In *Exxon Company, U.S.A. v. Sofec, Inc.*, 517 U.S. 830, 116 S.Ct. 1813, 135 L.Ed.2d 113 (1996), an Exxon tanker broke away from moorings owned by one defendant and operated by another. The captain managed to get the tanker safely past a number of perils nearby and safely out to sea. But once he reached safety, he neglected to get a fix on his position and he ran aground. The ship was substantially destroyed. Exxon claimed that the owner and operator of the moorings were responsible for the breakaway. The Court held that even if that were so, the captain's negligence in failing to fix his position once he had reached a position of relative safety was a superseding cause. So Exxon could recover nothing, even though admiralty law, which governed the case, uses pure comparative fault to divide damages.

Is it right to apply superseding cause rules to a plaintiff's own negligence? As we observed in Chapter 8, the all-or-nothing regime of proximate cause analysis may be inappropriate in many cases that can best be handled by apportioning responsibility according to comparative fault. At the very least, caution is required before invoking proximate cause rules to exclude all recovery when comparative fault rules offer a sound basis for apportionment. See *Torres v. El Paso Elec. Co.*, 127 N.M. 729, 987 P.2d 386 (N.M. 1999); DOBBS ON TORTS § 196 (2000). See, considering the various purposes that "superseding cause" and similar rules might have in excluding the plaintiff's recovery altogether, Paul T. Hayden, *Butterfield Rides Again: Plaintiff's Negligence as Superseding or Sole Proximate Cause in Systems of Pure Comparative Responsibility,* 33 LOYOLA L.A. L. REV. 887 (2000).

(4) *A mini-problem.* Under the old regime a court could say the plaintiff was at fault, or that the defendant's conduct was not an actual or legal cause of the plaintiff's harm. The result would be the same whichever view the court took. With the adoption of comparative fault, you really need to know whether you are talking about fault or causation because the effects can now be quite different. Consider the following case:

> Porter was electrocuted while working on school property and the plaintiff sues for his death. The school, in violation of a city ordinance which had adopted the National Electrical Code, used a two-wire, no-ground system. This created a risk that if there were any electrical leakage, anyone working with the electrical system might be seriously injured or even electrocuted. A three-wire system as required by the code, however, would have provided a ground and hence safety. Porter was using an electrical tool while working on the property and he was in fact electrocuted. However, he was using an extension cord he had made himself and from which he had removed the grounding prong. Thus, had the school properly provided a ground wire, Porter would not have avoided injury, since his plug would not have been connected to the ground.

Are there arguments against the position that the school's negligence is not a but-for cause of the harm? If so, is this a case for comparative fault apportionment rather than an exclusion of all liability?

b. Causal Apportionment and Comparative Negligence (Minimizing Damages)

The avoidable consequences or minimizing damages rule traditionally required the plaintiff to minimize her damages by reasonable efforts and expenses. If a plaintiff whose foot was bruised by the defendant's negligence could avoid loss of the foot by taking antibiotics, she might be expected to do so. If she unreasonably refused and lost the foot as a result, she would not be allowed to recover for loss of the foot, although of course she would be permitted to recover for the bruise.

This is not a rule of comparative fault. Instead, it simply excluded all recovery for a particular item of harm when the court concluded either that the defendant was not a but-for cause of that harm or that the harm was outside the scope of the risk negligently created by the defendant. When the plaintiff failed to take the prescribed antibiotics, some courts might treat the loss of her foot as if it were caused entirely by the plaintiff's fault. Such courts would not compare fault of the plaintiff in failing to take antibiotics with fault of the defendant in causing the injury in the first place. Instead, they would simply exclude liability for loss of the foot.

Automatic exclusion of all recovery in the foot example looks wrong because the defendant in that case is clearly a but-for cause of the foot's loss and because the foot's loss also seems to be within the scope of the risk the defendant created. Perhaps with cases like this in mind, the Restatement specifically follows some statutes by converting avoidable consequences or minimizing damages cases to comparative fault cases. The plaintiff in the foot case would no doubt be at fault in failing to take prescribed antibiotics and in computing damages, that fault would be compared with the defendant's fault. RESTATEMENT THIRD OF TORTS, APPORTIONMENT OF LIABILITY, § 3, cmt. b.

Are there cases, though, in which the defendant should not be liable at all for some items of harm, or should we factor all proximate and actual cause concerns into a comparative fault judgment?

REFERENCES: Contributory and comparative negligence generally: DOBBS ON TORTS §§ 198–210 (2000); Comparative negligence: VICTOR SCHWARTZ, COMPARATIVE NEGLIGENCE (3d Ed. 1994); HENRY WOODS & BETH DEERE, COMPARATIVE FAULT (3d Ed. 1996 & Supp.); ARTHUR BEST et al., COMPARATIVE NEGLIGENCE (1992 and Later Dates, 3 Vols.).

§ 5. ALLOCATING ALL RESPONSIBILITY TO DEFENDANT

a. *Allocating Responsibility to Protect the Plaintiff from Plaintiff's Own Fault*

BEXIGA v. HAVIR MANUFACTURING CORP.

Supreme Court of New Jersey, 1972.
60 N.J. 402, 290 A.2d 281.

PROCTOR, J.

This is a products liability case. Plaintiff John Bexiga, Jr., a minor, was operating a power punch press for his employer, Regina Corporation (Regina), when his right hand was crushed by the ram of the machine, resulting in the loss of fingers and deformity of his hand. His father, John Bexiga, Sr., brought this suit against Havir Manufacturing Corporation (Havir), the manufacturer of the machine. . . . The trial court dismissed the action at the close of the plaintiffs' case. The Appellate Division affirmed. . . .

The particular operation John, Jr. was directed to do required him to place round metal discs, about three inches in diameter, one at a time by hand on top of the die. Once the disc was placed on the die it was held there by the machine itself. He would then depress the foot pedal activating the machine and causing the ram to descend about five inches and punch two holes in the disc. After this operation the ram would ascend and the equipment on the press would remove the metal disc and blow the trimmings away so that the die would be clean for the next cycle. It was estimated by John, Jr. that one cycle as described above would take approximately 10 seconds and that he had completed about

270 cycles during the 40 minutes he operated the machine. He described the accident as follows:

> Well, I put the round piece of metal on the die and the metal didn't go right to the place. I was taking my hand off the machine and I noticed that a piece of metal wasn't in place so I went right back to correct it, but at the same time, my foot had gone to the pedal, so I tried to take my hand off and jerk my foot off too and it was too late. My hand had gotten cut on the punch, the ram.

Plaintiffs' expert, Andrew Gass, a mechanical engineer, testified the punch press amounted to a "booby trap" because there were no safety devices in its basic design and none were installed prior to the accident. . . .

Gass described two "basic types" of protective safety devices both of which were known in the industry at the time of the manufacture and sale. One was a push-button device with the buttons so spaced as to require the operator to place both hands on them away from the die areas to set the machine in motion. The other device was a guardrail or gate to prevent the operator's hands from entering the area between the ram and die when the machine was activated. These and other safety devices were available from companies specializing in safety equipment. . . .

Because of our disposition of the case it is necessary to consider defendant's contention that John, Jr. was contributorily negligent as a matter of law. Neither court below decided this issue. . . . [I]n negligence cases the defense has been held to be unavailable where considerations of policy and justice dictate. . . . We think this case presents a situation where the interests of justice dictate that contributory negligence be unavailable as a defense to either the negligence or strict liability claims.

The asserted negligence of plaintiff—placing his hand under the ram while at the same time depressing the foot pedal—was the very eventuality the safety devices were designed to guard against. It would be anomalous to hold that defendant has a duty to install safety devices but a breach of that duty results in no liability for the very injury the duty was meant to protect against. We hold that under the facts presented to us in this case the defense of contributory negligence is unavailable.

The judgment of the Appellate Division is reversed and the cause is remanded for a new trial.

McNAMARA v. HONEYMAN, 406 Mass. 43, 546 N.E.2d 139 (1989). Decedent, who was mentally ill, hanged herself while confined in a state hospital and died from the injuries sustained on that occasion. In a suit for her death, the trial judge rendered a judgment in favor of the plaintiffs against the Commonwealth. "Mentally ill people who are capable of forming an intent and who actually do intend an act that causes damage will be held liable for that damage. It follows that a mentally ill person can be comparatively negligent in some circumstances. . . . We join a number of courts in holding there can be no comparative negligence where the defendant's duty of care includes preventing the self-abusive or self-destructive acts that caused the injury.... To allow the defense of comparative negligence in these circumstances would render meaningless the duty of the hospital to act reasonably in protecting the patient against self-harm."

Notes

1. Should the principle in *Bexiga* apply after adoption of comparative fault?

2. On facts similar to *McNamara*, courts are quite willing to ignore the plaintiff's contributory negligence. E.g., *Hickey v. Zezulka*, 439 Mich. 408, 487 N.W.2d 106 (1992); cf. *Creasy v. Rusk,* 730 N.E.2d 659 (Ind.2000) (institutionalized Alzheimer's patient owed no duty of care to caretakers). Is *Bexiga* right in applying that idea to a rather different situation?

3. These cases can be understood as holding that when the defendant undertakes to protect the plaintiff from her own fault, or when the law imposes such a duty, the entire responsibility for care by definition falls upon the defendant and the plaintiff's fault cannot be held against her. That is logical enough, but when should the law impose such a duty if it is not one voluntarily undertaken by the defendant?

4. *Statutes.* Statutes sometimes impose a duty upon the defendant to protect plaintiffs who are vulnerable or disabled. Minor workers in dangerous occupations may be so protected by statutes. Similarly, a statute that requires school buses to remain stopped until school children have crossed the road is a recognition that the children may not exercise care to protect themselves when they cross. The school bus driver who violates such a statute may be denied the right to raise contributory negligence of the child as a defense. See *Van Gaasbeck v. Webatuck Central School District Number 1,* 21 N.Y.2d 239, 287 N.Y.S.2d 77, 234 N.E.2d 243 (1967). As a matter of requiring the enterprise to bear responsibility for all injuries, workers' compensation statutes also reject the contributory negligence defense when a worker is injured on the job, although this is balanced by limiting his award to specified benefits.

5. Apart from statute, when should courts impose a *Bexiga* duty upon the defendant? One characteristic that unites these cases is that the defendant imposes a risk upon the plaintiff, but that the plaintiff's fault imposes no similar risk upon the defendant. In other words, the risks are not reciprocal or mutual. Contrast the ordinary automobile collision case in which each driver is acting negligently, thus creating risks to others as well as to himself. Should the rule in *Bexiga* ever apply to such cases?

6. Maybe *Bexiga* and similar cases suggest that the plaintiff's vulnerability rightly plays a part in determining responsibility, but only in certain cases. The plaintiff's disability or vulnerability might be especially important if (1) the defendant knows of the plaintiff's disability which prevents or inhibits the plaintiff's care for himself; and (2) the plaintiff's risky conduct endangers himself but not others. Consider the following cases.

Case 1. A mentally disabled adult, John Clay, works for a farmer, Johnson. Johnson took Clay as a foster child, an arrangement made with the welfare department. Johnson put him to work with machinery on the farm, and explained his duties, but did not explain the dangers. Clay put his hand in a grinder and it was severely injured. A reasonable person would have perceived the risk and would not have put a hand in the grinder. Clay did not adequately perceive the risk because of his mental limitations. In Clay's suit against Johnson the defense was contributory negligence.

Case 2. Kincheloe, a child of 12, is driving a car on a rural road. His neighbor, Davis, was driving in excess of the speed limit in the opposite direction, approaching Kincheloe. He recognized Kincheloe and knew he was inclined to take his father's car and pull dangerous stunts. Nevertheless, Davis did not slow down. Kincheloe pulled over in Davis' lane, and Davis was unable to avoid collision because of his speed. Both Davis and Kincheloe were injured. In Kincheloe's claim against Davis, contributory negligence of Kincheloe was pleaded as a defense.

Case 3. Paulin, a mentally disabled adult, walked down a rural road in the pre-dawn hours. He walked on the right side and wore dark clothes. Dalrymple was driving in the same direction. As he neared Paulin, a car came from the opposite direction and Dalrymple dimmed his lights. He never saw Paulin until the last minute. He struck Paulin, who was seriously injured. Contributory negligence was the defense in Paulin's claim against Dalrymple.

Case 4. Perez and Dittman were both speeding as they traveled south on a public highway. Perez, who was 13, attempted to pass Dittman on a curve. At the same time Dittman lost control and began to skid over to his left. The two cars collided at this point. Each driver was injured. Contributory negligence is pleaded.

7. These examples suggest that you might agree with the principle in *Bexiga*, but might think that application of the principle to concrete cases is more debatable.

8. On the problem of allocating risks entirely to the defendant or the defendant's special duty to protect the plaintiff from her own fault, see DOBBS ON TORTS § 200 (2000).

b. *Rejecting Comparative Fault Reductions to Protect Plaintiff Entitlements*

LEROY FIBRE CO. v. CHICAGO, M. & ST. P. RY.

United States Supreme Court, 1914.
232 U.S. 340, 34 S.Ct. 415, 58 L.Ed. 631.

[The plaintiff owned land abutting the defendant's railroad. He stacked flax on the land for use in his manufacturing business. He alleged that the railroad negligently emitted sparks and coals that set fire to and destroyed the flax. The closest stacks were about 75 feet from the tracks. The defendant argued that the plaintiff was contributorily negligent in stacking the combustible flax so near the railroad. The jury, charged on the contributory negligence defense, found for the defendant.]

Mr. Justice McKenna delivered the opinion of the court:

That one's uses of his property may be subject to the servitude of the wrongful use by another of his property seems an anomaly. It upsets the presumptions of law, and takes from him the assumption, and the freedom which comes from the assumption, that the other will obey the law, not violate it. It casts upon him the duty of not only using his own property so as not to injure another, but so to use his own property that it may not be injured by the wrongs of another. . . .

The legal conception of property is of rights. When you attempt to limit them by wrongs, you venture a solecism. If you declare a right is subject to a wrong, you confound the meaning of both. It is difficult to deal with the opposing contention. There are some principles that have axiomatic character. The tangibility of property is in its uses, and that the uses by one owner of his property may be limited by the wrongful use of another owner of his is a contradiction. . . .

[The Court held that the contributory negligence defense presented no question for the jury.]

So ordered.

Mr. Justice Holmes, partially concurring. . . .

[A]s a general proposition people are entitled to assume that their neighbors will conform to the law; that a negligent tort is unlawful in as full a sense as a malicious one, and therefore that they are entitled to assume that their neighbors will not be negligent. . . .

If a man stacked his flax so near to a railroad that it obviously was likely to be set fire to by a well-managed train, I should say that he could not throw the loss upon the railroad by the oscillating result of an inquiry by the jury whether the road had used due care.

Notes

1. Put the shoe on the other foot. Suppose the flax caught fire and the fire foreseeably spread to burn down the shelter for abused children next door. Would the flax owner have no responsibility? If he does have responsibility to the shelter but not for any share of his own loss is something wrong? Or should we say that risks that threaten oneself are quite different from those that threaten others?

2. One way to look at this problem is to recognize that property law, emphasizing the owner's right to use property as she pleases, is sometimes at odds with negligence law, which emphasizes the safety of conduct and judges safety case by case after the event has occurred. Both approaches represent important values in our culture. How should we determine which prevails? William Powers, Jr., *Border Wars,* 72 Tex. L. Rev. 1209 (1994). See also Restatement Third of Torts, Apportionment of Liability § 3, cmt. d (2000).

3. The plaintiff purchases a home adjacent to a fairway on the defendant's golf course. Duffers and others slice balls into the plaintiff's yard, sometimes breaking a window and always endangering anyone in the yard. In the plaintiff's suit for property damage or personal injury from a zinging golf ball, can the golfers (or the golf course) defend by asserting the plaintiff's contributory fault? *Hennessey v. Pyne,* 694 A.2d 691 (R.I.1997).

4. Some cases ignore the property right and assume that the law of contributory negligence or similar defensive doctrines should bar the plaintiff. *DeAmiches v. Popczun,* 35 Ohio St.2d 180, 299 N.E.2d 265 (1973) the plaintiff was returning to her rented home in icy weather. She knew landlord-defendant had failed to repair a hole. She could not see the hole under snow. In trying to avoid it, she slipped and fell. On the assumption that the defendant was negligent, the court nevertheless rejected liability, blaming the plaintiff instead.

5. Some of the discourse on this topic is framed in terms of the plaintiff's rights or entitlements. The plaintiff may be entitled to use her property even if in doing so she is in danger of harm by the defendant's negligence. Similarly, the plaintiff might have entitlements not grounded in tangible property. She might be entitled to, say, use the public streets although they are dangerous or shop for groceries at night although rape or robbery is an ever present possibility. If she had such an entitlement, then under *LeRoy Fibre* she could not be charged with contributory negligence merely because she shopped at night. But how should courts go about deciding whether people do have such entitlements?

6. The entitlement idea can also be expressed by saying that because the plaintiff has an entitlement, she is under "no duty" to use reasonable care to protect herself. If she had no duty to protect herself by the use of reasonable care, she could not be charged with contributory negligence in failing to do so. The no duty language is infelicitous in one respect, since "duty" refers to an obligation enforceable by suit. The point of using no duty language, however, is to draw attention to a parallel set of rules that relieve defendants of liability for negligent conduct. For instance, we will see in the next chapter that landowners frequently do not owe a duty of reasonable care to trespassers. That means the landowner is free to be negligent toward trespassers. The idea of a plaintiff no duty rule is that the same approach should be taken to protect the rights or entitlements of the plaintiff.

7. Professor Ellen Bublick has argued forcefully for a "citizen no-duty" rule that would prevent all defendants from raising defenses of a rape victim's comparative fault. One basis for this position is that courts should "refuse to reinforce and legitimate the distressing reality of female fear and restriction." Ellen M. Bublick, *Citizen No-duty Rules: Rape Victims and Comparative Fault,* 99 Colum. L. Rev. 1413 (1999).

8. How should courts decide what entitlements a plaintiff has beyond those arising from ownership of tangible property? Can we identify any principle? Consider *Lynch v. Scheininger,* 162 N.J. 209, 744 A.2d 113 (2000). Mrs. Lynch was attended during a 1984 pregnancy by Dr. Scheininger, who failed to diagnose and treat her for Rh immunization, a well-known problem that results when the mother's blood is negative and the baby's is positive. As a result the baby was stillborn, but worse, the resulting change in the

mother's body meant that if she had another child, that child would have severe abnormalities. Mrs. Lynch did have another child and it suffered serious problems. She sued Dr. Scheininger. If Mrs. Lynch learned of this risk after the 1984 stillbirth but intentionally conceived a child later on, is she to be charged with contributory negligence or failure to minimize damages? Or does she, on analogy to *LeRoy Fibre*, have an entitlement to bear children even if it is risky?

Entitlements in Advance vs. Reasonable Judgments About Contributory Fault

9. Do we need entitlements decided in advance like those in the *LeRoy Fibre* case? Or, as argued by Professor Bublick, in the case of rape victims? Do you think it would suffice instead to judge contributory fault case by case in light of the plaintiff's rights and legitimate interests? For example, couldn't we rely upon courts to hold as a matter of ordinary analysis of contributory fault that a women is definitely not guilty of contributory fault merely because she shops late at night? Ellen M. Bublick, *Citizen No-duty Rules: Rape Victims and Comparative Fault,* 99 COLUM. L. REV. 1413, 1432–33 (1999) states that courts have found it unreasonable for a woman to go out at night to hail a cab, to walk to her car in a hotel parking lot, to fail to lock her door immediately, to double check door locks, or to assure herself that all windows are locked. Bublick says a woman has likewise been found unreasonable for permitting a salesman to enter her home or drinking alcohol with an older or streetwise man. If you think these decisions make judges untrustworthy when it comes to deciding issues of contributory fault, would you expect them to be more trustworthy in formulating entitlements in advance?

10. Does reciprocity of risk matter in determining contributory fault? Notice that in *LeRoy Fibre* and in the plaintiff-rape-victim cases, the plaintiff's fault, if any, is not fault that creates any unreasonable risk whatever to the defendant. Would that make those cases better for entitlements or no-duty rules than, say, a plaintiff who is speeding to reach a hospital in an emergency?

11. On the question of entitlements in advance vs. adjudication of particular cases, consider also *O'Brien v. Isaacs,* 17 Wis.2d 261, 116 N.W.2d 246 (1962). The plaintiff parked his car in the defendant's parking lot and left the keys with the attendant. When he returned to get it, the lot was closed. No instructions told him how to retrieve the car, so he took a bus home. The next day he appeared to pick up his car, but the defendant then demanded payment of an additional dollar for the overnight parking. The plaintiff's patience was at an end; he refused and rented a car until he was able to repossess his car by judicial proceedings. In these proceedings, the defendant argued that the plaintiff had failed to minimize damages, since he could have avoided the delay and rental car costs by paying $1. The court rejected the defendant's argument, saying that the defendant was essentially contending that plaintiff should have paid him a dollar to prevent him from committing a tort. Was the court creating a rule-of-law entitlement or was it adjudicating reasonableness of the plaintiff's behavior in the particular case in light of his rights and interests?

SUBCHAPTER B. ASSUMPTION OF THE RISK

§ 6. CONTRACTUAL ASSUMED RISK

BOYLE v. REVICI, 961 F.2d 1060 (2d Cir.1992). Cecelia Zyjewski was diagnosed by several physicians as having cancer. They all recommended immediate surgery. However, she consulted Dr. Revici, who purported to treat cancer, but not by any method accepted by the medical profession and not by surgery. Instead, he administered medications. He expressly told her that his medications were not approved by the FDA and that he could offer no guarantees. She also understood that his therapy was non-standard. Nevertheless she put herself in his care. Her condition deteriorated quickly and within a year, Zyjewski died. The trial court submitted the case to the jury on comparative fault instructions and the jury found for the plaintiff, but reduced damages for the Zyjewski's comparative fault. Even after reduction, the verdict came to over $1.3 million. The defendant appealed, arguing that the plaintiff was barred by an express assumption of the risk. *Held*, the jury should have been instructed on express assumption of the risk; it may find that Zyjewski expressly assumed the risk and is barred from recovery even though there was no written document at all.

TUNKL v. REGENTS OF UNIVERSITY OF CALIFORNIA, 60 Cal.2d 92, 32 Cal.Rptr. 33, 383 P.2d 441, 6 A.L.R.3d 693 (1963). Tunkl brought this action for injuries received allegedly as a result of the negligence of the hospital operated by defendant. Tunkl was admitted to the hospital on condition that he execute a release, absolving the defendants "from any and all liability for the negligent or wrongful acts or omissions of its employees...." The validity of this release was submitted to the jury, which found it to be valid and the trial court entered judgment for the defendants. *Held*, reversed. "While obviously no public policy opposes private, voluntary transactions in which one party, for a consideration, agrees to shoulder a risk which the law would otherwise have placed upon the other party, the above circumstances pose a different situation. In this situation the releasing party does not really acquiesce voluntarily in the contractual shifting of the risk, nor can we be reasonably certain that he receives an adequate consideration for the transfer. Since the service is one which each member of the public, presently or potentially, may find essential to him, he faces, despite his economic inability to do so, the prospect of a compulsory assumption of the risk of another's negligence.... From the observance of simple standards of due care in the driving of a car to the performance of the high standards of hospital practice, the individual citizen must be completely dependent upon the responsibility of others.... We cannot lightly accept a sought immunity from careless failure to provide the hospital service upon which many must depend."

CIOFALO v. VIC TANNEY GYMS, INC., 10 N.Y.2d 294, 220 N.Y.S.2d 962, 177 N.E.2d 925 (1961). Plaintiff fell at or near the edge of the swimming pool at defendant's gym. In her negligence action the defendant moved for summary judgment on the basis of an agreement in the plaintiff's membership contract that she agreed to assume full responsibility for any injuries which might occur, including injuries due to defendant's negligence. The trial judge granted summary judgment for the defendant. *Held*, affirmed. Exculpatory clauses are closely scrutinized and in some cases will not be given effect, as where such clauses are asserted by common carriers or public utilities or by employers as conditions of employment. And there must be "express language" before defendant will be exempted from liability. But here the language is clear and there is no special legal relationship or overriding public interest which requires the court to discard the contract provision.

JONES v. DRESSEL, 623 P.2d 370 (Colo.1981). Under a written contract, Jones was entitled to use defendant's facilities for sky-diving, including a plane from which the jumps were made. Jones suffered serious injuries when the plane crashed shortly after takeoff. He sued, alleging simple negligence and also willful and wanton misconduct. The defendant moved for summary judgment as to the simple negligence claim on the basis of an exculpatory clause in the contract which exempted it from liability for all liability arising out of injury "while upon the premises or aircraft of the Corporation or while participating in any of the activities contemplated by this Agreement, whether such loss, damage, or injury results from the negligence of the Corporation." Jones asserted that the contract limitation was invalid because the contract was one of adhesion and because the exculpatory clause was invalid in any event. *Held*, the contract and the exculpatory clause is valid. (1) This is not an adhesion contract, even if offered on a take it or leave it basis, since the record does not show a disparity in bargaining power or that the goods could not be obtained elsewhere. (2) An exculpatory agreement will not protect from wilful or wanton negligence. Whether it protects against ordinary negligence depends upon several factors. In this case the contract was not affected with the public interest as it was in *Tunkl*; the contract was fairly entered into; and it unambiguously expressed the parties' intent. The plaintiff is thus barred by the exculpatory clause.

Notes

1. Courts may require that a contract relieving one party of liability for negligence be clear, unambiguous, or even conspicuous. Otherwise, however, a contract under which one party assumes the risk of another's negligence is valid in the absence of a public policy to the contrary. See RESTATEMENT THIRD OF TORTS, APPORTIONMENT OF LIABILITY § 2. Do the cases above, taken together, sufficiently indicate when public policy would permit or reject contractual assumptions of the risk?

2. When the defendant is the only person who can provide reasonable safety, should he be permitted to shift the responsibility to another by contract?

3. Suppose a school district or a non-profit soccer club refuses to permit a student or members to participate in its sports program unless the student and parents sign an assumed risk or release agreement. Would that be effective to bar a claim for a student's negligently caused sports injury? See *Wagenblast v. Odessa School District No. 105–157–166J,* 110 Wash.2d 845, 758 P.2d 968 (1988); *Zivich v. Mentor Soccer Club,* Inc., 82 Ohio St.3d 367, 696 N.E.2d 201 (1998).

§ 7. IMPLIED ASSUMPTION OF THE RISK–COMPARATIVE FAULT OR CONTRACTUAL LIMITATION ON LIABILITY?

The plaintiff's assumption of the risk was a traditional complete defense to her tort claim. Analysis revealed, however, that courts seemed to mean quite different things by the term. Courts sometimes seemed to mean that (1) the plaintiff consented to the defendant's conduct by valid contract, express or implied; or (2) the plaintiff was guilty of an "unreasonable" assumption of the risk which seemed equivalent to contributory negligence; or (3) the defendant breached no duty to the plaintiff, either because of the consent or because courts concluded on policy grounds that the defendant was under no duty or that he was not negligent. This is confusing, but it means that you could drop the term "assumed risk" altogether. The defendant's arguments can be one of those named above and they cover the entire ground that was traditionally covered by assumed risk. That leaves us two problems. First, some courts continue to talk the language of assumed risk. Second, when they do so, it may be difficult to determine whether they are referring to a contractual agreement for shifting responsibility from the defendant to the plaintiff, or to contributory negligence or to something else. The problem is even more difficult when the court relies upon implied assumption of the risk, that is, when the parties have not expressly contracted about it.

DAN B. DOBBS
THE LAW OF TORTS
§ 214 (2000).

Most agreements in everyday life are tacit, not expressed. No logical reason prevents parties from tacitly or impliedly consenting or agreeing to a shift of responsibility to the plaintiff. The traditional assumed risk rules found such tacit consent when the plaintiff, knowing of the risk and appreciating its quality, voluntarily chose to confront it. . . .

As Prosser pointed out, the driver of an automobile cannot reasonably believe that the jaywalking plaintiff is consenting to the driver's negligence. The jaywalker assuredly confronts a known risk and does so voluntarily, but voluntary confrontation of the risk does not communicate any release of the driver from the duties of ordinary care. Instead, the jaywalker is simply negligent. His negligence is to be judged under comparative fault rules. . . .

BETTS v. CRAWFORD, 965 P.2d 680 (Wyo.1998). The plaintiff worked for the defendants as a housekeeper for several hours a week.

She occasionally had to pick up children's items on the stairs. One day she when was carrying bundled sheets to be laundered, she tripped over some items left on the stairs, fell down the stairs, and suffered serious injuries. The defendants asked the trial judge to instruct that "A servant assumes all of the risks and dangers pertaining to his employment which are known to him, or discoverable by the exercise of ordinary care ... even though said risks are directly attributable to his master's negligence...." The trial court rejected this and instead instructed the jury that homeowners must use reasonable care to avoid injury to those permitted on the premises, that an employer had a duty to furnish a safe place to work, that all persons owed a duty of ordinary care, and that comparative fault applied. The jury found for the plaintiff, reducing her damages 15% for her own fault. The defendants' appeal, claiming error in failing to give the assumed risk instruction. *Held,* judgment for plaintiff affirmed. "[T]here is no distinction between contributory negligence and assumption of risk when raised as a defense to an established breach of duty." Assumed risk is now merged into the comparative negligence system.

CREWS v. HOLLENBACH

Maryland Court of Appeals, 2000.
358 Md. 627, 751 A.2d 481.

HARRELL, JUDGE....

[Hollenbach, working for Honcho & Sons, Inc., excavated land that had been marked to indicate the location of gas lines.] Despite Byers' markers, Hollenbach struck a buried natural gas line owned by Washington Gas. The strike created a leak in the line. Neither Hollenbach nor anyone at the scene immediately contacted anyone regarding the leak, and natural gas released freely into the air and ground for a period of time. Two hours later, a resident, located approximately one mile from the leak, recognized the smell of gas in the air and notified the fire department. The governmental authorities evacuated the surrounding neighborhood. Washington Gas was contacted and dispatched a repair crew to the scene of the leak. Mr. Crews, a Washington Gas employee for over twenty years, was the foreman in charge of the crew. Upon arrival at the scene, Mr. Crews and his co-employees commenced the process of dissipating the gas that had permeated the ground. While he and his crew were engaged in closing off the leak, the gas ignited and an explosion occurred. Mr. Crews was injured severely. The cause of the spark that ignited the gas was unknown, but no allegation was made that Respondents were the cause of the ignition source....

[Crews sued Hollenbach and his employer and others engaged in the project. The trial judge gave summary judgment for defendants on the ground that Crews had assumed the risk. The intermediate court affirmed. Those decisions are now before Maryland's highest court.]

Assumption of the risk serves as a complete bar to a plaintiff's recovery. The defense is grounded on the theory that a plaintiff who voluntarily consents, either expressly or impliedly, to exposure to a known risk cannot later sue for damages incurred from exposure to that risk. In defining the defense of assumption of the risk, we have stated that:

> [the defense] rests upon an intentional and voluntary exposure to a known danger and, therefore, consent on the part of the plaintiff to relieve the defendant of an obligation of conduct toward him and to take his chances from harm from a particular risk. . . .

Our task in a conventional assumption of the risk analysis is to determine whether the plaintiff 1) had knowledge of the risk of danger; 2) appreciated the risk; and 3) voluntarily exposed himself or herself to that risk. In deciding whether a plaintiff had knowledge and appreciation of a particular risk, we apply an objective standard. We will not be swayed by a plaintiff's subjective denial that he or she did not comprehend the extent of a clearly obvious danger. The question of whether a plaintiff knew and understood the risk in a case is generally one for the trier of fact, but if a person of normal intelligence, in the same position as the plaintiff, would clearly have comprehended the danger, the question is one for the court. . . .

Mr. Crews plainly knew of the risks inherent in working on the gas leak on 23 March 1996. At his 21 April 1998 deposition, Mr. Crews admitted that he was aware of the heavy smell of gas near the gas leak. In response to a question asking whether there was a point when he recognized the smell of gas to be so heavy that he knew it was dangerous, Mr. Crews responded, "Well, we always are taught that any type of gas leak or odor is always dangerous." . . .

As we stated above, "[i]n determining whether a plaintiff had . . . appreciation of the risk, [the] plaintiff will not be heard to say that he did not comprehend a risk which must have been obvious to him." . . .

Mr. Crews's deposition statements support our conclusion that he appreciated the specific risks involved in using a backhoe to excavate near the gas leak, a possible ignition source. At his deposition, Mr. Crews acknowledged his understanding that the gas leak could lead to an explosion. Immediately following the excerpt quoted above, which Petitioner offered to show that Mr. Crews "had no idea that being in close proximity to a leaking gas pipe with a backhoe could cause an explosion" the following exchange occurred in the deposition:

Q. How about if you get into close proximity of the pipe or touch the pipe with your backhoe?

* * *

A. I'm not saying it won't, but I never knew it to do that before. But anything can set [the gas] off, [sparks] from gravels or rocks that hit together, hitting metal. That could set it off.

Q. For instance, the metal bucket of your backhoe striking a rock as you were digging—

A. That's correct.

Q. —you knew that that could create a spark?

A. We knew that.

Q. And you knew that if the spark occurs, you could have a fire and an explosion, correct?

A. That's correct, but as I said before, that it have to be worked, regardless....

Our cases illustrate that if a person was compelled to act and had no freedom of choice regarding whether to act, we will not say, as a matter of law, that he or she acted voluntarily....

[W]e conclude that Mr. Crews voluntarily assumed the risk in the present case. Petitioners contend that Mr. Crews was compelled by the exigency of the facts in this case to repair the leak to prevent serious harm to the people and property of the surrounding neighborhood. They argue that Mr. Crews was "faced with the choice of either abandoning the leak and staying in safety, or approaching the pipe and going into danger." Petitioners reason that opting not to act was not a reasonable alternative under the circumstances, therefore he was compelled to address the gas leak.... Although commending Mr. Crews's apparent initiative here, we cannot find in this record any evidence that he was forced to make those efforts or what the larger implications may have been had he not acted....

[T]he danger Mr. Crews encountered on Trillium Lane in Bowie on 23 April 1996 is the very danger that he accepted the risk of confronting when he became an employee of Washington Gas some twenty years earlier. In his own words, he accepted that responsibility when he was hired. Thus, the aspect of his job duties that involved fixing gas leaks, a clearly dangerous endeavor, and which he continued to confront for more than twenty years, constitutes a voluntary assumption of "those risks which might reasonably be expected to exist" on 23 April 1996 in Bowie. It seems to us, on this record, that the risk that led to Mr. Crews's injuries was reasonably identifiable and inherent in his job both when he was first hired and on 23 April 1996. Accordingly, we find no error of law in the Circuit Court's grant of summary judgment, on this record, in favor of Respondents.

Notes

1. Was Mr. Crews negligent in holding a dangerous job? Did he contract with the defendant to give up his right to reasonable care? Did the defendant create the risk in reliance upon Crews waiving his rights?

2. *Crews* reflects a highly traditional approach to assumed risk. The Restatement Third of Torts, Apportionment of Liability § 2 provides that a valid contract, even an implied contract, can absolve a person from liability. Otherwise, the Restatement treats assumed risk as merely one version of contributory fault to be handled under comparative negligence rules. Some

comparative negligence statutes provide the same. How would *Crews* be handled under the Restatement or *Betts v. Crawford*?

3. Suppose that the negligent persons who caused the gas leak and failed to report it had then contracted with Mr. Crews to come repair it. In that case, would it be fair to say that Crews was impliedly contracting to face the risks inherent in the dangerous situation? Where the plaintiff is retained by, or for the specific purpose of aiding the negligent defendant deal with a known danger, courts hold that the plaintiff has contractually assumed the risk. For example, those hired to care for combative Alzeimer's patients persons have no claim when they are injured by such a patient. *Creasy v. Rusk,* 730 N.E.2d 659 (Ind.2000). The negligent defendants in *Crews* did not retain Crews to deal with the dangers they had negligently created. Should that matter in determining whether Crews contracted or consented to relieve them of liability?

4. Suppose the defendants in *Crews* refused to excavate until Mr. Crews came from the gas company to instruct them and that Mr. Crews was injured while standing near the pipe giving instructions. In that case, you can think the defendant relied upon Mr. Crews' willingness to face the obvious risk. Is that a better or a worse case for finding consent or an implied contract to assume the risk?

5. *The broad traditional assumed risk.* Although the *Crews* court states that assumed risk is a bar because the plaintiff consented, the analysis does not focus on the reality of contract or consent but upon the plaintiff's subjective knowledge of the specific risk and the plaintiff's voluntary encounter with that known risk. Notice that these elements do not necessarily show that the plaintiff was contracting to relieve the defendants of liability. They do not even show contributory negligence, do they?

6. Traditional assumed risk doctrine narrowed the doctrine (or recognized plaintiff entitlements) by insisting that the plaintiff's assumption of the risk was ineffective unless it was voluntary and also based upon subjective knowledge of the specific risk that caused harm. Mr. Crews voluntarily accepted unavoidable risks of working with gas. Did he voluntarily accept risks that someone would negligently increase those normal risks?

§ 8. ASSUMED RISK AS LIMITED DUTY OR NO DEFENDANT NEGLIGENCE

SIRAGUSA v. SWEDISH HOSPITAL, 60 Wn.2d 310, 373 P.2d 767 (1962). Plaintiff was a nurse in defendant hospital. She was working at a washbasin in a patient's room, when the door to the room opened and swung toward her. On the back of the door was a large hook, the tip of which pointed out. This struck her in the back and she was injured. At the close of the evidence, the trial court granted a motion equivalent to a directed verdict, on the grounds that as a matter of law the plaintiff had assumed the risk. *Held,* reversed and remanded. "Where the dangers are ordinarily incident to the work, though it is said that the servant 'assumes' these, the true analysis is that the master is under no duty to protect the servant with regard to such risks and any injuries, therefore, are not due to the master's negligence.... To bar recovery when the employee is acting reasonably in exposing himself to a known and appreciated risk is to indulge in the unrealistic and rigid presumption that, in so exposing himself, the employee 'assents' to relieve his employer from his responsibility to furnish a safe place in which to work. Such a presumption has no basis in experience, and is not founded upon any current social policy.... We now hold that if an employer negligently fails in this duty [to furnish a safe place in which to work], he may not assert, as a defense to an action based upon such a breach of duty, that the injured employee is barred from recovery merely because he was aware or should have known of the dangerous condition negligently created or maintained. However, if the employee's voluntary exposure to the risk is unreasonable under the circumstances, he will be barred from recovery because of his contributory negligence."

SUNDAY v. STRATTON CORP., 136 Vt. 293, 390 A.2d 398 (1978). Plaintiff, about 21 years old, was a paying patron at the defendant's ski resort. Although the evidence was that the defendant provided a very smooth novice trail, on which the plaintiff skied, his ski struck a small bush within the trail. The bush was concealed by snow. The plaintiff's injuries resulted in permanent quadriplegia and he recovered a verdict and judgment of one and one-half million dollars. *Held*, affirmed.

"There is no claim advanced here, nor could there be, that plaintiff expressly assumed any risk. The claim is that the brush was an inherent danger of the sport. This is the equivalent of, and better put as, a claim that defendant owed plaintiff no duty with respect thereto, sometimes referred to as 'primary' assumption of risk. 'In case of injury resulting from such a risk, the servant is denied a recovery, not because he has assumed the risk, but because the master has not been guilty of a breach of duty.' Cast in this terminology, any chance of conflict between a comparative negligence statute and the defense of primary assumption of risk as an absolute bar to recovery becomes nonexistent. Where primary assumption of risk exists, there is no liability to the plaintiff, because there is no negligence on the part of the defendant to begin with; the danger to plaintiff is not one which defendant is required to extinguish or warn about; having no duty to begin with, there is no breach of duty to constitute negligence....

"While skiers fall, as a matter of common knowledge, that does not make every fall a danger inherent in the sport. If the fall is due to no breach of duty on the part of the defendant, its risk is assumed in the primary sense, and there can be no recovery. But where the evidence indicates existence or assumption of duty and its breach, that risk is not one 'assumed' by the plaintiff. What he then 'assumes' is not the risk of injury, but the use of reasonable care on the part of the defendant. The motion for directed verdict was correctly denied."

BJORK v. MASON, 77 Cal.App.4th 544, 92 Cal.Rptr.2d 49 (2000). The defendant took some boys to a lake for water skiing and innertubing. He used his boat, his rope, and his innertubes. When he sped up (in violation of a no-wake zone limit) the rope pulling a tube snapped and whipped back into the eye of the innertube rider, who brought this action. *Held*, (1) the rider assumed all the risks inherent in the sport, including some degree of negligence of the driver, but (2) he did not assume the risk of dangers not inherent in the sport, specifically dangers arising from the defendant's defective equipment and frayed ropes.

Notes

1. *Determining which form of "assumed risk" applies.* How can you determine in a particular case whether the old "assumed risk" should be treated as contributory fault (with damages reduction) or as a fact showing no-duty/no-negligence? Suppose plaintiff and defendant are rural neighbors, far from medical help. Plaintiff's spouse or partner is injured and needs immediate medical attention, but plaintiff's car is not available. Defendant's car could be used, but it is in a mechanical condition dangerous to the driver. Should defendant refuse permission to use the car? If he explains the risks and permits its use, but its bad condition causes an injury to the plaintiff, would the plaintiff be entitled to recover, with a reduction for contributory fault? Or would the plaintiff be denied all recovery?

2. *California cases.* California agrees with other states that some of the old assumed risk cases should now be dealt with under comparative negligence, while others should be regarded as no duty, no negligence, or contractual assumed risk cases. As in other states, the plaintiff has no claim at all if the defendant has violated no duty. In *Knight v. Jewett*, 3 Cal.4th 296, 11 Cal.Rptr.2d 2, 834 P.2d 696 (1992), the court said: "In cases involving 'primary assumption of risk'—where, by virtue of the nature of the activity and the parties' relationship to the activity, the defendant owes no legal duty to protect the plaintiff from the particular risk of harm that caused the injury—the doctrine continues to operate as a complete bar to the plaintiff's recovery. In cases involving 'secondary assumption of risk'—where the defendant does owe a duty of care to the plaintiff, but the plaintiff proceeds to encounter a known risk imposed by the defendant's breach of duty—the doctrine is merged into the comparative fault scheme."

3. In The Shepard's Fold Church of God it has long been the habit for worshipers to run or "trot" down the aisle "under the Spirit of the Lord." It is also the habit of other worshipers to kneel in the aisle and pray. What risks does a worshiper assume while praying in the aisle? *Bass v. Aetna Insurance Co.*, 370 So.2d 511 (La.1979). Are we talking about contract-consent or contributory fault or a duty limited by the the court?

TURCOTTE v. FELL

Court of Appeals of New York, 1986.
68 N.Y.2d 432, 502 N.E.2d 964, 510 N.Y.S.2d 49.

[Plaintiff, a renowned jockey who had won the Triple Crown on Secretariat, was riding in a race. He was thrown from his horse when it clipped the heels of another horse. He suffered severe injuries resulting in paraplegia. In this action he sues another jockey, Fell and some other defendants. He claims Fell was negligent under common law standards and also in violating rules of the New York Racing and Wagering Board regulating foul riding. Fell allegedly rode his horse so as to "cross and weave ... into the path of the horse ridden by plaintiff, impeding plaintiff in his path, and further defendant, Jeffrey Fell, caused his horse to jostle and strike the horse ridden by plaintiff without any fault on the part of plaintiff or his horse...." The Board's rules prohibited these forms of "foul riding."

[The trial court granted Fell's motion for summary judgment, "holding that Turcotte, by engaging in the sport of horseracing, relieved other participants of any duty of reasonable care with respect to known dangers." There were other defendants whose presence is not relevant here. The Appellate Division affirmed the grant of summary judgment.]

... [W]hile the determination of the existence of a duty and the concomitant scope of that duty involve a consideration not only of the wrongfulness of the defendant's action or inaction, they also necessitate an examination of plaintiff's reasonable expectations of the care owed him by others. This is particularly true in professional sporting contests, which by their nature involve an elevated degree of danger. If a participant makes an informed estimate of the risks involved in the activity and willingly undertakes them, then there can be no liability if he is injured as a result of those risks.

Traditionally, the participant's conduct was conveniently analyzed in terms of the defensive doctrine of assumption of risk. With the enactment of the comparative negligence statute, however, assumption of risk is no longer an absolute defense (see, CPLR 1411). Thus, it has become necessary, and quite proper, when measuring a defendant's duty to a plaintiff to consider the risks assumed by the plaintiff. The shift in analysis is proper because the "doctrine (of assumption of risk) deserves no separate existence (except for express assumption of risk) and is simply a confusing way of stating certain no-duty rules" (James, Assumption of Risk: Unhappy Reincarnation, 78 Yale L.J. 185, 187–188). Accordingly, the analysis of care owed to plaintiff in the professional sporting event by a coparticipant and by the proprietor of the facility in which it takes place must be evaluated by considering the risks plaintiff assumed when he elected to participate in the event and how those assumed risks qualified defendants' duty to him.

The risk assumed has been defined a number of ways but in its most basic sense it "means that the plaintiff, in advance, has given his * * * consent to relieve the defendant of an obligation of conduct toward him, and to take his chances of injury from a known risk arising from what the defendant is to do or leave undone. The situation is then the same as where the plaintiff consents to the infliction of what would otherwise be an intentional tort, except that the consent is to run the risk of unintended injury * * * The result is that the defendant is relieved of legal duty to the plaintiff; and being under no duty, he cannot be charged with negligence" (Prosser and Keeton, Torts § 68, at 480–481 (5th ed.); 4 Harper, James & Gray, Torts § 21.0 et seq. (2d ed.)....

Defendant's duty under such circumstances is a duty to exercise care to make the conditions as safe as they appear to be. If the risks of the activity are fully comprehended or perfectly obvious, plaintiff has consented to them and defendant has performed its duty. Plaintiff's "consent" is not constructive consent; it is actual consent implied from the act of the electing to participate in the activity When thus analyzed and applied, assumption of risk is not an absolute defense but a measure of the defendant's duty of care and thus survives the enactment of the comparative fault statute.

. . . It would be a rare thing, indeed, if the election of a professional athlete to participate in a sport at which he makes his living could be said to be involuntary. Plaintiff's participation certainly was not involuntary in this case and thus we are concerned only with the scope of his consent.

. . . Some "of the restraints of civilization must accompany every athlete onto the playing field." Thus, the rule is qualified to the extent that participants do not consent to acts which are reckless or intentional.

. . . The question of whether the consent was an informed one includes consideration of the participant's knowledge and experience in the activity generally. Manifestly a professional athlete is more aware of the dangers of the activity, and presumably more willing to accept them in exchange for a salary, than is an amateur.

. . . Turcotte conceded that there is a fine line between what is lawful and unlawful in the movement of a horse on the track during a race and that when and where a horse can lawfully change its position is a matter of judgment. Such dangers are inherent in the sport. Because they are recognized as such by plaintiff, the courts below properly held that he consented to relieve defendant Jeffrey Fell of the legal duty to use reasonable care to avoid crossing into his lane of travel.

Plaintiffs nonetheless contend that Fell's alleged violation of 9 NYCRR 4035.2, which prohibits foul riding, is sufficient to sustain their complaint. They assert that the rule is a safety rule and that a participant does not accept or consent to the violation of the rules of a game even though the violation is foreseeable . . .

The rules of the sport, however, do not necessarily limit the scope of the professional's consent. Although the foul riding rule is a safety measure, it is not by its terms absolute for it establishes a spectrum of conduct and penalties, depending on whether the violation is careless or willful and whether the contact was the result of mutual fault. As the rule recognizes, bumping and jostling are normal incidents of the sport. They are not, as were the blows in Nabozny and Hackbart, flagrant infractions unrelated to the normal method of playing the game and done without any competitive purpose. Plaintiff does not claim that Fell intentionally or recklessly bumped him, he claims only that as a result of carelessness, Fell failed to control his mount as the horses raced for the lead and a preferred position on the track. While a participant's "consent" to join in a sporting activity is not a waiver of all rules infractions, nonetheless a professional clearly understands the usual incidents of competition resulting from carelessness, particularly those which result from the customarily accepted method of playing the sport, and accepts them. They are within the known, apparent and foreseeable dangers of the sport and not actionable and thus plaintiffs' complaint against defendant Fell was properly dismissed.

[The motion for summary judgment in favor of the defendants was properly sustained.]

GAUVIN v. CLARK, 404 Mass. 450, 537 N.E.2d 94 (1989). The plaintiff and defendant were on opposing teams in a college hockey game. The plaintiff was injured when the defendant "butt-ended" the plaintiff in the abdomen in violation of a safety rule known and understood by all parties. The plaintiff required surgery and lost his spleen. The jury found a rule violation but also found that the defendant had not acted wilfully, wantonly, or recklessly. "Some jurisdictions explain the limitation on liability in sports competitions to cases of reckless conduct in terms of the doctrine of assumption of the risk. The Legislature has abolished the defense of assumption of the risk in Massachusetts, however. Because the doctrine has been abolished, "the focus of the analysis in [sport cases] has shifted entirely to the defendant's duty under the circumstances and should no longer be discussed in terms of the plaintiff's assumption of the risk." Thus, in setting out the standard of care, we discuss the policy in terms of the duty. "The majority of jurisdictions which have considered this issue have concluded that personal injury cases arising out of an athletic event must be predicated on reckless disregard of safety. We adopt this standard. Allowing the imposition of liability in cases of reckless disregard of safety diminishes the need for players to seek retaliation during the game or future games. Precluding the imposition of liability in cases of negligence without reckless misconduct furthers the policy that "[v]igorous and active participation in sporting events should not be chilled by the threat of litigation." Although the defendant violated a safety rule, the jury found that he was not reckless. *Held*, Judgment for defendant affirmed.

Notes

1. *Statutory treatment of assumed risk as comparative fault.* Notice that New York's comparative negligence statute (printed in § 2 above) treats contributory negligence and assumed risk alike. Why, then, doesn't the plaintiff's "assumed risk" simply reduce his damages in *Turcotte*?

2. *Changing the duty in sports and games cases.* A number of courts have now said that in sports and games cases the defendant owes only the duty to avoid reckless or wanton injury, instead of saying that plaintiff always assumes the risk of ordinary negligence. Although this seems to be

the dominant trend, a number of other courts continue to adhere to the negligence standard for sports activities. SEE DOBBS ON TORTS § 215 (2000).

3. *Special statutes.* State legislatures sometimes enact special statutes intended to protect some particular group of defendants. For instance: "A person who takes part in the sport of skiing accepts as a matter of law the dangers inherent in that sport insofar as they are obvious and necessary." N.M. STAT. § 24–15–10 (B). A number of statutes contain similar provisions. Suppose you are injured skiing on the defendant's slopes because the operator has left a dangerous, pointed stake just covered by the snow. Have you assumed the risk that the defendant has been negligent in this way? In other words, is the defendant's negligence an inherent risk of the sport? If not, then does the statute only mean that the defendant is not liable without negligence?

4. Hunting wild turkeys requires the hunter to emulate the female turkey, calling softly to the male, which is then expected to approach with such steady intent that the hunter can shoot him. What risks does such a hunter assume? *Hendricks v. Broderick*, 284 N.W.2d 209 (Iowa 1979).

5. *Assuming the risk of other misconduct.* If the duty of a participant in a game is only to avoid wanton, reckless, or intentional misconduct, would the same rule apply to other activities in which participants might overreact in the heat of the moment? Would a criminal mugger, for instance, "assume the risk" that the police officer might shoot him when lesser force would be more appropriate? New York allowed the mugger to recover in *McCummings v. New York City Transit Authority*, 81 N.Y.2d 923, 613 N.E.2d 559, 597 N.Y.S.2d 653 (1993). Can you square this with the limited duty (or assumed risk) in *Turcotte*? Can you square it with the rule of the same court that a criminal cannot recover for injury sustained as a direct result of a criminal act? *Barker v. Kallash*, 63 N.Y.2d 19, 479 N.Y.S.2d 201, 468 N.E.2d 39 (1984) (in § 3 above).

REFERENCES: DOBBS ON TORTS §§ 211–215 (2000); HARPER, JAMES & GRAY, THE LAW OF TORTS § 21.0 (1986 & Supps.).

SUBCHAPTER C. LIMITATION OF ACTIONS

§ 9. STATUTES OF LIMITATION

Statutes of limitation are not peculiar to tort law. Almost every kind of claim must be brought within a period of time specified by statutes of limitation. If the claim is brought later, it is barred by the statute, even though it is otherwise a legitimate claim. The traditional statute of limitations serves at least two distinct purposes. One is to bar "stale" claims, the presentation of which might be unfair or costly because evidence is lost or subtly altered with time. A second is to permit both personal and business planning and to avoid the economic burden that would be involved if defendants and their insurance companies had to carry indefinitely a reserve for liability that might never be imposed. The time limit for tort claims may vary depending on the tort. The period is often short in cases of libel or slander, but in cases of personal injury the statute in most instances will allow the plaintiff several years in which to bring his action. Once the action is properly brought, the statute of limitations has no other function. It does not, for example, require *trial* by any certain time, only the commencement of the action.

The traditional analysis of statutes requires the action to be brought within the statutory period after the claim "accrues." The tort claim often accrues at a readily definable moment, as when the defendant drives his automobile into the plaintiff. But suppose the defendant negligently built a house 20 years ago and as a result of his negligence the house collapsed last year, injuring its occupants. Would their claim be barred by a two-year statute of limitations? Or does the claim accrue only when injury occurs? The traditional answer to this question is that since negligence that causes no harm is not actionable until injury occurs, the cause of action only accrues when that injury results. Thus the statute of limitations would begin to "run" when occupants of the house are injured, and they will have two years from that time in which to bring their action.

CRUMPTON v. HUMANA, INC.

Supreme Court of New Mexico, 1983.
99 N.M. 562, 661 P.2d 54.

H. VERN PAYNE, C.J.

This is a frivolous appeal. We also note that there is a strong indication in the record that counsel for the appellant ineptly and perhaps negligently handled his client's case. Counsel for the appellant failed to file suit before the applicable statute of limitations had run. We are disappointed when members of our State Bar betray the trust and confidence of their clients by engaging in careless and unprofessional practice.

On February 8, 1979, Wanda Crumpton underwent surgery at Llano Estacado Medical Center in Hobbs. She alleged that she sustained injuries to her neck and legs when an attending nurse attempted to lower her hospital bed on February 11, 1979. Her suit was filed more than three years later on February 15, 1982. The trial court granted a motion for summary judgment on the ground that the suit was barred by the three-year statute of limitations....

Crumpton argues that her injury was not ascertainable until some time after the accident occurred. Further, she contends that the statute of limitations should have been tolled during the time the parties were negotiating.

These arguments are entirely without merit. In her deposition, Crumpton plainly testified that her injuries occurred on February 11, 1979. She also testified that she is still having problems in her shoulders, legs and sides which she attributed to the February 11, 1979 incident. Crumpton offers no evidence to contradict the fact that the alleged negligent act and injury occurred simultaneously on February 11, 1979.

In our view, the fact that she had continuing treatments and hospitalizations after the injury does not necessarily make the date of the injury unascertainable.

... [T]he statute of limitations commences running from the date of injury or the date of the alleged malpractice. ...

Crumpton cites no authority for her argument that the statute of limitations should be tolled during the time when the parties were negotiating a settlement. The record indicates that defendants did not fraudulently lead Crumpton to believe that the case would be settled at some future date. In fact, the record indicates that in May 1981, defendants sent Crumpton a letter wherein defendants made a final offer for a compromise settlement of the case.

Accordingly, we affirm the trial court's grant of summary judgment against Crumpton. Because we determine this appeal to be frivolous and entirely without merit, costs and attorneys fees are to be borne by appellants.

Notes

1. Attorneys responsible for failure to file a meritorious suit in time are subject to liability to the client for malpractice. What would you do to be sure you never filed a late claim, answer, or motion? Sometimes the client is late in consulting an attorney. Why would a client delay?

2. Suppose the defendant's insurance adjuster tells the plaintiff's attorney: "I'm sure we can come to an agreement. Don't file your claim and we will work this out." The plaintiff's attorney does not file and the statute runs. The adjuster then says, "Sorry, I can't settle, because the statute has run." The plaintiff's attorney then files a tort claim and the defendant pleads the statute of limitations. Is this a case in which the defendant is "estopped" to use the statute?

SHEARIN v. LLOYD, 246 N.C. 363, 98 S.E.2d 508 (1957). Defendant, a surgeon, performed an operation to remove plaintiff's appendix in July, 1951. Plaintiff returned for checkups, complaining of pain near the incision. Defendant repeatedly told the plaintiff he would be all right and that it would take time "to heal up and get tough." In November, 1952, the defendant admitted that something was wrong. X-rays showed a "sponge" had been left in the abdomen. This was removed in November, 1952, but in December "a knot" in the incision "rose up and bursted." Defendant dressed this, but another knot occurred in January, 1953, and another in May. In the fall of 1953 defendant told plaintiff he was doing all he could to kill the infection but that plaintiff needed another operation. Plaintiff then ended his relations with the defendant and commenced this action for negligence in November, 1955. There was a three-year statute of limitations. The trial judge granted defendant's motion for non-suit. *Held*, affirmed. A cause of action accrues so as to start the running of the statute of limitations as soon as the right to institute an action arises. "It is inescapable that plaintiff's cause of action accrued on July 20, 1951, when defendant closed the incision without first removing the lappack.... Defendant's failure thereafter to detect or discover his own negligence in this respect did not affect the basis of his liability therefor."

Notes

1. The *Shearin* case reflects the rule generally followed at the time it was decided. In a sense the rule was "logical." The idea was that the statute of limitations must begin running when the plaintiff can sue on a claim, since, if he can sue, the claim must have "accrued." Legally speaking, a plaintiff injured like the plaintiff in *Shearin* could sue on his claim when the incision was closed. Factually speaking, he could not do so, but that inability was not the result of any legal rule, only of his own ignorance. Thus, legally, he could sue at that time and the claim must have accrued.

2. These results are obviously harsh, and beginning in the 1960s a number of states changed the rule. North Carolina itself changed the rule by statute. N.C. GEN. STAT. § 1–52(16). Many changed it by judicial decision. They adopted instead the "discovery rule." The discovery rule holds that the statute begins to run when the plaintiff discovered, or should reasonably have discovered, the injury. This rule treats the cause of action as accruing when in *fact* the plaintiff could reasonably sue. This avoids the harsh result of *Shearin*, but it substitutes a good deal of uncertainty, since discovery will depend upon the highly individualized facts of each case. It also injects a normative issue—when plaintiff *should* have discovered the injury or its cause.

3. *Continuous treatment.* Some authority supports a rule that delays the start of the statute of limitations until the medical treatment for which the patient consulted the physician has been concluded. Is this a good idea? Why not when treatment for the harm caused by negligence has been concluded? Or when negligence itself ceases?

4. What result would you expect if the doctor deliberately conceals negligent treatment from the patient?

SCHIELE v. HOBART CORP.

Supreme Court of Oregon, 1978.
284 Or. 483, 587 P.2d 1010.

HOLMAN, JUSTICE.

[Plaintiff, a meat wrapper, developed serious lung problems, allegedly from using defendant's machine. The trial court gave summary judgment for defendant on the ground that the two-year statute of limitations had run.]

[P]laintiff began work as a meat wrapper at Fred Meyer in Portland, Oregon, in November of 1948. She worked in that capacity from 1948 through March of 1974. In May or June of 1972 Fred Meyer purchased and installed defendant Hobart's meat wrapping machine which allegedly incorporated defendant Dayton Electric's ventilator. The machine used a hot wire to cut the polyvinyl chloride meat wrapping film allegedly manufactured by defendant Borden Chemical. In December of 1972 plaintiff began using the new meat wrapping machine during a considerable part of her work day. Prior to this time, plaintiff had been in good health. Soon after beginning use of the machine, she began to experience a variety of health problems, more specifically, nausea, dizziness, choking, coughing, and difficulty catching her breath. Almost from the outset, plaintiff associated these problems with the fumes which the machine generated as its hot wire cut the polyvinyl chloride meat wrapping film.

Between January of 1973 and October of 1973, plaintiff's condition worsened. Her choking and coughing increased. She began to cough at night and experienced pain in her lungs. In the summer of that year she began to cough up quantities of white sputum at night. While at work she experienced coughing spells six to eight times a day which forced her to walk out to a breezeway to get air. She complained about the problems to her employer's manager but nothing was done.

Between October of 1973 and January of 1974, plaintiff's condition continued to deteriorate. She experienced fatigue, shortness of breath, and a burning sensation in her eyes, in addition to the symptoms previously described. To facilitate breathing at night, plaintiff elevated her head with two or three pillows.

In January of 1974, plaintiff noted that her lungs were more sore than usual. During the latter part of January and the first part of February 1974, the pain became almost constant. Plaintiff put in her last day at work on March 12, 1974. Almost immediately thereafter she was hospitalized for pulmonary pneumonia. After testing and x-rays during March 1974, plaintiff's doctors informed her on or about April 15, 1974, that her illness was possibly due to her exposure to polyvinyl chloride fumes on the job.

Plaintiff filed her complaint in this action on March 8, 1976. . . .

Plaintiff contends that the statute of limitations did not begin to run until plaintiff was informed by a physician of the nature of her disease or injury and its possible cause. Since this did not occur until April of 1974 she argues that her March 8, 1976 filing fell within the limitation period. Defendants argue that the limitation period began to run when plaintiff first became aware of her symptoms and their cause. Since she first associated her symptoms with the fumes prior to March 8, 1974, defendants believe the two-year limitation period had expired by the time plaintiff initiated her action.

[The court here discusses earlier decisions involving long exposure to silica dust.]

These cases stand for the proposition that the statute of limitations on claims involving negligent infliction of an occupational disease does not begin to run until the plaintiff knows, or as a reasonably prudent person should know, that he has the condition for which his action is brought and that defendant has caused it. Plaintiff's actionable condition in this case is alleged to be her *permanent injuries*. However, it still remains to be determined exactly what type of knowledge plaintiff must have before it should be said that she knew or should have known of her condition. Plaintiff argues that the statute of limitations did not begin to run until her physician diagnosed her disease and identified its source. We agree that the acquisition of such information from a physician would undoubtedly start the period running. However, we reject plaintiff's contention that nothing short of a positive diagnosis by a physician will have this effect. A plaintiff whose condition has not yet been diagnosed by a physician can have or, in the exercise of reasonable care, could have access to information which requires or would require a reasonable person to conclude she is being seriously or permanently injured.

On the other hand, we reject defendants' claim that knowledge of symptoms and their causal relationship to defendants' actions in and of itself initiates the running of the statute. We do not believe the legislature intended that the statute be applied in a manner which would require one to file an action for temporary sickness or discomfort or risk the loss of a right of action for permanent injury.

The statute of limitations begins to run when a reasonably prudent person associates his symptoms with a serious or permanent condition and at the same time perceives the role which the defendant has played in inducing that condition. Of course, one's condition may deteriorate to the point where a delay in seeking medical attention is no longer reasonable and to further such delay would be to charge the individual with any knowledge which a medical examination would otherwise have disclosed.

If knowledge of the occupational disease, its symptoms, and its causes is widespread among persons similarly situated to plaintiff, then we hold that plaintiff, as a reasonable person, should have recognized her condition for what it was and brought the action within the applicable period of limitation following the onset of the symptoms. However, defendants have made no showing that there was any prevalent knowledge concerning the dangers of the fumes from polyvinyl chloride. This is an extremely close case, but we believe we cannot say as a matter of law that a reasonably prudent person would have apprehended more than two years prior to the commencement of plaintiff's action that she was being seriously or permanently injured. Many persons would probably have realized the seriousness of their condition and have gone to a doctor, but not everyone goes to a doctor with the same degree of alacrity. We cannot, therefore, say as a matter of law that anyone who is optimistic about his condition's taking a turn for the better is unreasonable....

The trial court's grant of summary judgment is reversed and the case is remanded for trial.

Notes

1. The *Schiele* problem obviously parallels the *Shearin* problem. Some courts made the statute begin to run from the time of the first exposure or first negligent act. Others used a last exposure or termination of employment trigger. Still others have followed the practice in medical malpractice cases and adopted the discovery rule.

2. What discovery ought to count? Is it a discovery that "something is wrong"? That something is wrong and it was caused by defendant? That something is wrong the nature of which the plaintiff can or should identify, and that it was caused by the defendant? That the defendant was or might be negligent? In *United States v. Kubrick*, 444 U.S. 111, 100 S.Ct. 352, 62 L.Ed.2d 259 (1979) the plaintiff had an operation in a VA hospital and thereafter suffered a hearing loss. In 1969 he discovered that this probably resulted from antibiotics administered in the post-operative care, but it was not until much later that someone suggested that the hospital may have been negligent in administering the antibiotics. The Supreme Court held that the statute began to run in 1969 when he was aware of the injury and possible cause of it, even though he was not then aware of possible negligence. In *Renaud v. Sigma–Aldrich Corp.*, 662 A.2d 711 (R.I.1995), plaintiff brought a timely suit against defendant A for an alleged product defect. Discovery eventually showed that B, not A, had produced the product, but by then the statute of limitations had run. The Court held that the claim against B was time-barred, since plaintiff had discovered the injury, though not its author.

3. *Statutes limiting the discovery rule.* After many courts had adopted a discovery rule, the medical profession, claiming a "medical malpractice crisis," prevailed on most legislatures to enact a variety of protective rules. Some of these are summarized in Chapter 11 below. Many states enacted special statutes of limitation for medical malpractice claims. One kind of statute rules out the discovery rule altogether. The statutes may be unconstitutional under state constitutions in some states but they are perfectly constitutional in others. See *Martin v. Richey*, 711 N.E.2d 1273 (Ind.1999) (unconstitutional applied to plaintiff); *Aicher v. Wisconsin Patients Compensation Fund*, 237 Wis.2d 99, 613 N.W.2d 849 (Wis. 2000). Another kind of statute provided that the discovery rule was limited to cases in which a "foreign object" was negligently left in the patient's body. This kind of statute was held unconstitutional as denying equal protection in *Austin v. Litvak*, 682 P.2d 41, 50 A.L.R.4th 225 (Colo. 1984) Contra: *Ross v. Kansas City General Hospital and Medical Center*, 608 S.W.2d 397 (Mo.1980).

4. *Statutes adopting the discovery rule.* The discovery rule is especially appealing for victims of toxic torts, the effects of which may not appear for many, many years or even for generations. A federal statute creates certain liabilities in connection with disposal or release of hazardous substances. The federal statute goes on to add that in cases brought under *state* law for personal injury or property damage, the state must give the plaintiff the benefit of the discovery rule. The state must also toll the statute of limitations for minors until they reach majority, and toll the statute for

incompetents until they become competent or have a guardian appointed. 42 U.S.C.A. § 9658.

NOTE: LATENT POTENTIAL HARM

Partial Injury, Latent Potential

Shearin v. Lloyd turns in part on the notion that a tort occurs when harm is done and the related notion that the statute of limitations begins to run when the tort occurs, not when the plaintiff learns of it. If the plaintiff knows of the tort, one would imagine at first glance that the statute of limitations presents no problem to the plaintiff. But suppose a tort occurs and the plaintiff knows it, yet the plaintiff wishes to postpone suit because he believes damages may become much worse than they are at present. It is perfectly possible to claim and recover damages that will occur in the future, but under traditional rules this can be done only if the proof shows such damages to be more likely than not. If the plaintiff sues now to stay within the statute of limitations, he will avoid that problem; but he will be limited to damages he can presently prove. The *res judicata* rules will prevent a second suit later on. If he waits to see whether damages will become much worse, he will eventually run into the statute of limitations problem.

In *Hagerty v. L. & L. Marine Serv. Inc.*, 788 F.2d 315 (5th Cir.1986), Hagerty was drenched with dripolene, a carcinogen. He had some dizziness and leg cramps, and stinging in the extremities, all of which disappeared after showers. He undergoes regular medical checkups because of the cancer threat, but he does not presently have cancer and cancer is not "more likely than not." But his present fear of future cancer is real. Consider the options for the court:

(1) Adopt a view similar to that in *Wollen*, Chapter 7, § 2. This would allow the plaintiff to recover now for any actual injury, plus all possible future injuries that might result from it, but future injuries would be reduced to reflect their probability. For example, if future cancer appearing in ten years is a 40% probability and would, if it occurs, impose damages of $100,000, the plaintiff would recover $40,000. This is the "enhanced risk" or reduced chance recovery.

(2) Reject the enhanced risk recovery, allow present actual damages only, but with present damages including the mental anguish or suffering resulting from the plaintiff's fear of future cancer.

(3) Reject the enhanced risk and fear claims, allow the plaintiff to recover what he can prove in actual damages and bar any future claims under *res judicata* rules.

(4) Reject enhanced risk recovery but allow present damages and leave open the possibility for a second suit if substantially different kinds of damage occur. This would allow recovery for cancer if it later develops.

The *Hagerty* court adopted the fourth option. This eliminates the dilemma created by the statute of limitations on the one hand and the *res judicata* rules on the other. A growing number of cases support some such view. See *Mauro v. Raymark Industries, Inc.*, 116 N.J. 126, 138, 561 A.2d 257, 264 (1989) ("neither the statute of limitations nor the single-controversy doctrine will bar a toxic tort plaintiff's timely damage claim instituted after discovery of a causally-related disease"); *Sopha v. Owens–Corning Fiberglas Corp.*, 230 Wis.2d 212, 601 N.W.2d 627 (Wis. 1999) (diagnosis of non-malignant asbestos-related injury does not trigger statute of limitations with respect to a claim for distinct, later-diagnosed asbestos-related malignancy; nor does doctrine of claim preclusion apply). Will such a view work for all kinds of cases?

Exposure without Symptoms

Suppose the plaintiff is exposed to a toxin in sufficient quantities to raise the possibility of future harm that could occur in ten, twenty or thirty years. But suppose also that the plaintiff has no present symptoms at all. You might think in this kind of case there is no problem. There is no statute of limitations to confront because the plaintiff merely waits until injury occurs and then sues. However, the plaintiff exposed to chemical poisons in her water or gases in the air she breathes may have two present "injuries" without symptoms. First, the plaintiff may have fear of future harm and that fear may itself poison her life. Second, the plaintiff may have medical expense because continuous medical monitoring is important to minimize future harm by early detection.

Some decisions have treated the non-symptomatic exposure as a tort and have said, with *Hagerty*, that the plaintiff could recover now for the costs of medical monitoring and that an additional suit could be brought later if cancer or other serious disease actually occurs. A major case is *Ayers v. Jackson Tp.*, 106 N.J. 557, 525 A.2d 287, 76 A.L.R.4th 571 (1987).

But are you willing to say that any exposure, even though not accompanied by symptoms, is a tort for which damages can be recovered?

———

McCOLLUM v. D'ARCY, 138 N.H. 285, 638 A.2d 797 (1994). The plaintiff, fifty years old, sued her parents, now in their eighties, alleging childhood sexual abuse ending more than thirty-five years earlier. She alleged that she repressed all memory of the abuse from the time it occurred until recent flashbacks triggered by attending a "therapy workshop on child abuse." *Held*, if these allegations are true, the statute of limitations will be tolled under the discovery rule, so the trial court properly rejected the defendants' motion to dismiss. Defendants can, however, still argue that the plaintiff discovered or should have discovered the facts earlier.

DOE v. MASKELL

Maryland Court of Appeals, 1996.
342 Md. 684, 679 A.2d 1087.

KARWACKI, JUDGE. . . .

Reviewing the record in a light most favorable to the plaintiffs, the facts of the case are as follows: Jane Doe, from 1967 to 1971, and Jane Roe, from 1968 to 1972, were students at Seton Keough High School [hereinafter "Keough"], a parochial school in Baltimore City. During their tenure at Keough, both girls, individually were referred for counseling to the school chaplain, Father A. Joseph Maskell. According to the complaints filed in the cases, Maskell subjected the girls to repeated sexual, physical, and psychological abuse including:

"vaginal intercourse, anal intercourse, cunnilingus, fellatio, vaginal penetration with a vibrator, administration of enemas, . . . hypnosis, threats of physical violence, coerced prostitution and other lewd acts, physically striking Plaintiff, and forcing Plaintiff to perform sexual acts with a police officer." [Some additional acts were alleged by one plaintiff.]

Both girls were allegedly threatened with extreme punishments if they informed anyone of the abuse, which continued until the girls graduated and left Keough in 1971 and 1972 respectively. At some point, both plaintiffs claim that they ceased to recall the abuse suffered at the hands of Father Maskell, due to a process they term "repression." Both plaintiffs began to "recover" memories of this abuse in 1992.

[The plaintiffs sued Father Maskell, various superiors, a doctor, and the school. On the basis of Maryland's three year statute of limitations, the trial judge gave summary judgment for the defendant.]

[From the court's footnote 3:] . . . Repression theory accommodates at least two models: "serial repression" and "collective repression." As one pair of commentators explain:

"In accordance with this robust repression concept, a person could, for example, banish awareness of the experience of having been brutally raped one or a hundred times during childhood. These distressing memories might be repressed serially, immediately following each event. Alternatively, all the memories might be collectively repressed at some time later, after the abuse stopped. If the memory of rapes were serially repressed, a child could go from rape to rape ignorant of the previous assault . . . ."

Richard Ofshe & Ethan Watters, Making Monsters, 30 Soc'y 4, 5 (March/April 1993). Because we are evaluating the grant of summary judgment, all factual inferences must be resolved in the non-moving party's favor. Thus we must accept that the repression occurred in a serial fashion. . . .

Alternatively, however, if the repression happened in a "collective" fashion, after the plaintiffs achieved majority, and the plaintiffs were under no other disability, the statute of limitations immediately begins to run. Under traditional Maryland law, once the statute of limitations begins to run against a plaintiff, ordinarily no subsequent event will arrest it. Therefore, if Doe or Roe had not yet repressed the memories of the sexual assault by the defendants by even the day after their attaining majority, the statute of limitations barred these claims three years after their eighteenth birthdays, for Doe after August 11, 1974, and for Roe, after April 29, 1975. [End of the court's footnote 3.]

We find that the critical question to the determination of the applicability of the discovery rule to lost memory cases is whether there is a difference between forgetting and repression. It is crystal clear that in a suit in which a plaintiff "forgot" and later "remembered" the existence of a cause of action beyond the 3–year limitations period, that suit would be time-barred. Dismissal of such a case reflects our judgment that the potential plaintiff had "slumbered on his rights," should have known of his cause of action, and was blameworthy. To permit a forgetful plaintiff to maintain an action would vitiate the statute of limitations and deny repose for all defendants.

Plaintiffs in this case, however, claim that in order to avoid the pain associated with recalling the abuse they suffered, their memories were "repressed," not merely "forgotten," and later "recovered," rather than "remembered." They argue that this difference renders them "blamelessly ignorant" and excuses their failure to file suit in a timely manner. To aid in an understanding of plaintiffs' argument, we have extracted two implicit assumptions:

> 1.   That there is a qualitative and quantitative difference between "repression" and mere "forgetting;" and

> 2.   that this difference is of a sufficient quality to compel us to find that plaintiff is excused by operation of the discovery rule and had no reason to have known about the existence of her cause of action.

We have reviewed the expert testimony provided at the summary judgment hearing, and reviewed numerous scientific journals submitted by the parties. We begin by attempting to understand what repression is. Even defining the term is not easy; it originated with Sigmund Freud who used the term differently and sometimes contradictorily throughout his career. David S. Holmes, The Evidence for Repression: An Examination of Sixty Years of Research, in REPRESSION AND DISASSOCIATION: IMPLICATIONS FOR PERSONALITY, THEORY, PSYCHOPATHOLOGY AND HEALTH (J. Singer, ed. 1990) [adopts] a definition of repression based on the manner in which the term is conventionally used:

> "It is my belief that in its general use the concept of repression has three elements: (1) repression is the selective forgetting of materials that cause the individual pain; (2) repression is not under voluntary control; and (3) repressed material is not lost but instead stored in

the unconscious and can be returned to consciousness if the anxiety that is associated with the memory is removed. The assertion that repression is not under voluntary control differentiates repression from suppression and denial, with which it is sometimes confused...."

The Evidence for Repression at 86.

[Plaintiffs and defendants offered articles purporting to validate or discredit the concept of repression.]

First, the adversaries of repression stress that there is no empirical, scientific evidence to support the claims that repression exists. The studies purporting to validate repression theory are justly criticized as unscientific, unrepresentative, and biased. See e.g. Harrison G. Pope, Jr. & James I. Hudson, Can memories of childhood sexual abuse be repressed?, 25 PSYCHOL. MED. 121 (1995); The Evidence for Repression at 96–99. The reason for the failure of repression enthusiasts to obtain empirical evidence may be the nature of the process itself. As Dr. Jason Brandt of the Johns Hopkins University School of Medicine testified:

"... I believe that it is virtually impossible to distinguish psychogenic amnesia from faking, from malingering since the distinction between the two hinges on how conscious it is to the person and how willful it is, how intentional it is. And how conscious somebody is and how willful they're being, are things that in spite of what we may say, we really don't have any way of assessing."

Just because there is so far no empirical validation for the theory of repression is not alone sufficient reason to discount the concept, yet it does cast some doubt.

Second, critics of repression theory point out that the scientific, and specifically, the psychological community has not embraced repression theory, and that, in fact, serious disagreement exists....

Finally, critics of repression theory argue that the "refreshing" or "recovery" of "repressed" memories is more complicated than repression proponents would have us believe. This argument takes two forms: (1) that memories refreshed with the assistance of a mental health professional are subject to manipulations reflecting the biases of the treating professional; and (2) that a repressed memory cannot be retrieved whole and intact from the cold storage of repression. [In this case, the plaintiffs' memories have not been "manipulated by one or more mental health professionals acting in the guise of treatment."] Nonetheless, in crafting a rule we must consider the apparently very real dangers of iatrogenic (therapist created) memories of sexual child abuse.

After reviewing the arguments on both sides of the issue, we are unconvinced that repression exists as a phenomenon separate and apart from the normal process of forgetting. Because we find these two processes to be indistinguishable scientifically, it follows that they should be treated the same legally. Therefore we hold that the mental process of repression of memories of past sexual abuse does not activate the discovery rule. The plaintiffs' suits are thus barred by the statute of limitations.... [The court also held that repression does not count as insanity that would toll the statute of limitations.]

Notes

1. *Reality of childhood sexual abuse.* Scientists and psychologists agree that childhood sexual abuse is real. Sometimes it is inflicted upon quite young children by parents, grandparents, or others in positions of trust and authority. It is often extremely harmful to ordinary emotional development.

2. *Disputes about repression.* However, scientists and therapists often stringently differ about the existence of repression and the accuracy of "recovered" memory. Those who approach the problem as scientists seeking data tend to deny or doubt the supposed "repression." Those who approach the problem as therapists, not surprisingly, adhere to the concept of repression and vigorously support claims of childhood sexual abuse. The conflict presents a difficult problem for the law because the emotional stakes are high. Sexual abuse sometimes causes severe problems to the victim, but false claims of sexual abuse have also caused severe problems to those accused. For an observer whose only agenda is to do justice, it is sometimes a chicken and egg problem—did the sexual abuse cause the plaintiff's psychological problems or did the psychological problems cause false allegations of sexual abuse? The problem is aggravated because there is a small industry devoted to convincing those with emotional troubles that their problems result from sexual abuse whether they remember it is not. As a result, some plaintiffs who see therapists may be talked into believing "remembering" abuse that never occurred. Some therapists may even hypnotically induce or "implant" false memories.

3. Was the *Doe v. Maskell* court right to take sides with one group of experts against another group? In *Doe v. Roe,* 191 Ariz. 313, 955 P.2d 951 (1998) the Arizona Court believed the other set of "experts." The court said that repression exists and also that it furnishes a ground for invoking the discovery rule. Is this how it should work–one group of "experts" controls the law in Arizona, while another controls the law in Maryland? What else could be done?

4. If a court accepts the idea of repression in general, should that toll the statute of limitations for the particular plaintiff? The Arizona Court in *Doe v. Roe,* supra, said:

> A victim whose memory is inaccessible lacks conscious awareness of the event and thus cannot know the facts giving rise to the cause. The policy behind the discovery rule is thus served by application to repressed memory cases involving childhood sexual abuse and is, we believe, logically appropriate given that the intentional act of the tortfeasor caused both the damage and the repression of memory. To hold otherwise would be to effectively reward the perpetrator for the egregious nature of his conduct and the severity of the resulting emotional injury.

In order to decide the statute of limitations questions, did the court assume that the defendant was in fact guilty?

5. *Rejecting the discovery rule in "repression" cases.* A few courts, without overtly rejecting the idea of repression, have rejected the discovery rule in childhood sexual abuse claims. See *Lemmerman v. Fealk,* 449 Mich. 56, 534 N.W.2d 695 (1995) (the rule should apply only when the defendant inflicts tangible harm that can be judged by an objective standard); *Dalrymple v. Brown,* 549 Pa. 217, 701 A.2d 164 (1997) (discovery rule uses objective, not subjective standard in determining whether plaintiff was reasonably diligent in discovering harm; discovery rule applies only when the nature of the injury itself is such that no amount of vigilance will permit discovery).

6. *Corroboration.* Is there special need for corroboration? Some courts have permitted use of the discovery rule only if the plaintiff can produce special corroborating evidence that the sexual abuse took place. *Moriarty v. Garden Sanctuary Church of God,* 341 S.C. 320, 534 S.E.2d 672 (2000) (special evidence needed in light of conflict whether repression exists).

7. *Memory intact but other psychological impediments to suit.* Some judicial decisions would apply the discovery rule when the plaintiff is aware of the abuse but not aware of its connection to her emotional injury or the amount of harm done to her. E.g., *McCreary v. Weast,* 971 P.2d 974 (Wyo.1999) (alleging 20 years of sexual abuse). Some statutes appear to provide for the same result. E.g., N.J. STAT. ANN. § 2A:61B–1. But some courts have held that if the victim retained her memory of the abuse, the discovery rule has no application, even though the plaintiff was unable to understand that the abuse caused her emotional problems. E.g., *Clay v. Kuhl,* 189 Ill.2d 603, 727 N.E.2d 217, 244 Ill.Dec. 918 (2000).

8. *Statutes.* Some states have passed statutes liberalizing the statute of limitations in cases of childhood sexual abuse. E.g., CAL. CODE. CIV. PRO. § 340.1; IOWA CODE ANN. § 614.8a; MONT. CODE ANN. § 27–2–216; WASH. REV. CODE 4.16.340. If you were in the legislature, what provisions would you want to see in such a statute?

9. *Threats and equitable estoppel.* If a molester prevented suit by physical force or threats, he might be estopped from pleading the statute of limitations as a defense. See *John R. v. Oakland Unified School Dist.,* 48 Cal.3d 438, 256 Cal.Rptr. 766, 769 P.2d 948 (1989); *Ortega v. Pajaro Valley Unified Sch. Dist.,* 64 Cal.App.4th 1023, 75 Cal.Rptr.2d 777 (1998).

10. *Adult abuse victims.* The problem is not limited to sexual abuse of minors. In *Riley v. Presnell,* 409 Mass. 239, 565 N.E.2d 780 (1991) the plaintiff "was an epileptic who had been experiencing some emotional difficulties, but did not suffer from any major psychopathology at the time he began treatment." His therapist prescribed Valium to which the patient eventually became addicted. The therapist introduced alcohol and marijuana into therapy sessions and eventually persuaded the patient to engage in sexual activity with him. Thereafter the therapist abruptly terminated the relationship. The patient did not recognize for years that his emotional difficulties resulted from the inappropriate "treatment." The court applied the discovery rule, saying a jury could decide whether the patient should have discovered the cause of his injury sooner. See Jorgenson & Randles, *Time Out: The Statute of Limitations and Fiduciary Theory in Psychotherapist Sexual Misconduct Cases,* 44 OKLA. L. REV. 181 (1991).

NOTE: TOLLING FOR DISABILITIES

1. *Tolling for disabilities.* The discovery rule is not the only avenue of relief for the late-suing plaintiff. Statutes of limitation may be tolled so that the clock is not running while the plaintiff is under a disability such as minority or mental incompetence. Thus if the statutory period is two years and the abused child sued within two years after reaching majority, the suit would be timely. In the sexual abuse cases, the plaintiff sometimes claims tolling because he or she was of unsound mind when the tort was committed or at least during the time in which suit could otherwise have been brought.

2. For purposes of commitment to an institution, an individual might be deemed of unsound mind if he is a danger to himself or others. In this context, however, unsound mind usually means that the individual is unable to manage his or her business affairs or estate, or to comprehend his or her legal rights or liabilities. *Doe v. Roe*, 191 Ariz. 313, 955 P.2d 951 (1998). Thus no matter what the psychological impediments to suit, the victim cannot have the benefits of tolling for unsound mind if he can manage his daily affairs by working, buying food, writing checks or the like.

3. *Grace periods.* Tolling is a true time-out, time not counted on the statute or limitations period. A number of legislatures have now replaced time-out tolling with a grace period. A grace period merely extends the statute of limitations; it does not stop the clock. Some statutes provide hardly any grace at all. For example, Michigan provides that if a child under 13 suffers injury to reproductive organs, she must sue before her fifteenth birthday. Mich.Comp.L.Ann. § 600.5851(8).

4. In *Callahan v. State*, 464 N.W.2d 268 (Iowa 1990) a four-year-old child, "deaf and cerebral palsied," was sexually abused for three years in a state school. By the time his mother discovered the facts he had been out of the school for more than two years. The state pleaded the two-year statute of limitations. Instead of tolling the statute for minority, the court held that the cause of action would not begin to run until the mother discovered or should have discovered the facts. Given the familiar repression by victims of childhood sexual abuse, the court thought the trier could find the suit to be timely.

5. Some statutes are aimed only at sexual exploitation by therapists or at incest. Where that is the case, the court may refuse to apply the discovery rule to the victim of a priest's abuse. See *Pritzlaff v. Archdiocese of Milwaukee*, 194 Wis.2d 302, 533 N.W.2d 780 (Wis. 1995). So victims of sexual abuse by a counselor are treated better than victims of sexual abuse by a priest. If that is unequal treatment, is the fault with the court or with the legislature? It is quite typical for legislation to aim very narrowly at a set of facts rather than broadly at a principle.

DASHA v. MAINE MEDICAL CENTER, 665 A.2d 993 (Me.1995). Defendant erroneously diagnosed the plaintiff as having a fatal brain tumor. On that diagnosis, surgery plus radiation to the brain would prolong life for a short time and the plaintiff opted for that treatment. The treatment itself allegedly caused severe brain damage and the plaintiff became incompetent. Two years after the misdiagnosis and treatments, another physician reviewed the diagnosis and discovered that it was erroneous. The plaintiff's original problem had been a relatively benign tumor not calling for such treatments. His guardian sued, but by this time it was more than three years after the original misdiagnosis. Under Maine's legislation, the discovery rule did not apply. Nor did tolling for mental incapacity work because the plaintiff was mentally capable at the time of the misdiagnosis. The plaintiff argued that, nonetheless, the defendant should be equitably estopped from pleading the statute of limitations, since the defendant's own fault had caused the incapacity as well as the injury. *Held,* no equitable estoppel applies. "[E]stoppel may be used to prevent the affirmative defense of the statute of limitations if the elements of estoppel are present.... The gist of an estoppel barring the defendant from invoking the defense of the statute of limitations is that the defendant has conducted himself in a manner which actually induces the plaintiff not to take timely legal action on a claim. The plaintiff thus relies to his detriment on the conduct of the defendant by failing to seek legal redress while the doors to the courthouse remain open to him."

"The stipulated facts of this case do not meet the elements of equitable estoppel. First, MMC made no affirmative misrepresentation, as required to support the application of equitable estoppel. Although a claim of equitable estoppel can be supported by an act of negligence that is the equivalent of fraud, the misdiagnosis by MMC is not the equivalent of fraud sufficient to support the assertion of equitable estoppel. Dasha relied on the misdiagnosis to seek radiation treatments, but he did not rely on a representation of MMC to decide to forego seeking legal redress."

NOTE: LIMITATIONS NOT BASED ON ACCRUAL

1. The traditional rule seen in *Shearin,* though modified by the discovery rule, remained one based on accrual of a cause of action. The shift to the discovery rule was merely a shift in the legal definition of "accrual." There are at least two forms of limitation not based on accrual, both of which are significant.

2. *The notice bar.* In certain instances a statute or ordinance may require that the plaintiff give notice to the defendant of his claim a specified number of days before filing a legal action. This is commonly required in the cases of actions against public entities, such as cities. Similarly, "retraction statutes" in some states require a plaintiff to demand a retraction before suing for libel. Under the notice statutes and to a lesser extent under the retraction statutes, it may be impossible to file a legal action in any effective way until the notice requirement has been met. If notice must be given 30 days before filing the action, the net

effect is that the statute of limitations is shortened by 30 days—that is, the plaintiff who gives the required notice 15 days before the statute of limitations has run cannot file the legal action in time, since it will be necessary to wait 30 days after notice in order to sue, and at that time the statute will have run.

3. *The pre-accrual bar.* In recent years a new kind of statute has been adopted for certain kinds of cases. For instance, the North Carolina legislature, in effect overruling *Shearin*, has provided that claims for personal injury and physical damage to property "shall not accrue until bodily harm to the claimant or physical damage to his property becomes apparent or ought reasonably to have become apparent ... Provided that no cause of action shall accrue more than ten years from the last act or omission of the defendant giving rise to the cause of action." N.C. GEN. STAT. § 1–52(16). The proviso could obviously bar a claim before it accrues. For example, if a doctor negligently administers a drug which causes no harm for 15 years, the cause of action would not accrue until harm was done, but the statute would have run ten years after the doctor's "last act." A number of states have enacted statutes of this kind, usually aimed at providing protection for some special group. Doctors, architects and engineers have been singled out in some instances to receive the benefits of this pre-accrual bar or statute of "ultimate repose."

One line of attack on this sort of statute questions its constitutionality, usually on the basis of state constitutional provisions. Some courts have held such statutes unconstitutional, but others have upheld them. Much may depend on the exact wording of the particular state constitution.

NOTE: POLICY AND SOLUTIONS

Certainty. The statute of limitations as traditionally construed and applied provided one of those benefits one often longs for in law—certainty. After the stated period, a defendant could be sure that no suit would be filed. How important is the certainty? Insurers, concerned over the potential for losses indefinitely into the future under the discovery rule, may be required to escalate premiums, or even cease to provide coverage. Something like this did happen in medical malpractice insurance at one time. The "long tail" on the cause of action provides added protection for the few plaintiffs who need it, but costs to all doctors may be very high and ultimately it may be patients who pay.

Testimonial accuracy. One pillar of the statute of limitations is the idea that testimony will be lost altogether or will cease to be accurate over time. This might be especially true in some cases but not necessarily true at all in others. Do we need a certain rule like the statute to deal with testimonial accuracy? For instance, in some cases the defendant admits the acts in question. Where this occurs or there is good corroboration, and where the defendant cannot show that witnesses on his behalf have become unavailable, do we need the fixed statutory period?

Alternatives. How should these concerns be balanced? Is there any alternative that will help protect injured plaintiffs while preserving a bright-line termination of the claim? Would you favor any of the following?

The statute begins running when injury is first inflicted, but the plaintiff who fails to file within the time limits:

(a) can still recover, but only for limited, pecuniary losses and not for pain and suffering; or can recover only those damages accrued before the statute ran.

(b) can still recover, but only from the government, which will pay him rather than see an injustice done, but which will not demand payment from the defendant.

(c) can still recover and there should be no limitation; defendants should be held liable to defend at any time and, if they are tortfeasors, to pay as well.

(d) cannot recover, but may purchase his own accident, health, or income interruption insurance, and may be provided for in that way.

REFERENCE: DOBBS ON TORTS §§ 216–223 (2000).

§ 10. COMPLIANCE WITH STATUTE

MILLER v. WARREN, 182 W.Va. 560, 390 S.E.2d 207 (1990). The plaintiffs awoke in their motel room to find it filled with smoke. They attempted to get out, but the door was too hot to touch. They suffered serious burns before they were rescued. In a suit against the motel, the plaintiffs asserted that the motel should have had smoke alarms in the rooms. The fire code did not require such alarms, however. The trial judge instructed the jury: "The Court instructs the jury that compliance with the fire codes under the law meets the standard of care and duty required of the defendant as it relates to the installation or lack of installation of safety devices unless other circumstances appear which would require additional care in order to comply with the requirements to use ordinary care in attendant circumstances." The jury, so instructed, found for the defendant. *Held*, reversed and remanded for new trial. "Failure to comply with a fire code or similar regulation constitutes prima facie negligence, if an injury proximately flows from the non-compliance and the injury is of the sort the regulation was intended to prevent. [But] [c]ompliance with a regulation does not constitute due care per se. Compliance with the appropriate regulations is competent evidence of due care, but not conclusive evidence of due care. If the defendants knew or should have known of some risk that would be prevented by reasonable measures not required by the regulation, they were negligent if they did not take such measures. It is settled law that a statute or regulation merely sets a floor of due care. Circumstances may require greater care, if a defendant knows or should know of other risks not contemplated by the regulation."

Notes

1.   Courts traditionally agree that compliance with statute or regulation is not a defense. Statutory requirements usually reflect a minimum standard of care, not a maximum obligation or as a limit on the defendant's general duty of reasonable care under the circumstances. Compliance with statute, like compliance with custom, is some *evidence* of reasonable care, even though it is not conclusive. For example, the builder or utility company may comply with a building or electrical code but may still be negligent in failing to take more precautions than required by the statute. E.g., *Northern Indiana Public Service Co. v. Sell*, 597 N.E.2d 329 (Ind.App.1992).

2.   Some kinds of federal regulation are deemed to "preempt" the field, so that any state regulation of the same field is ineffective. The effect is to displace tort law and leave the plaintiff without a remedy where the defendant has complied with federal regulations. See *Norfolk Southern Ry. v. Shanklin*, 529 U.S. 344, 120 S.Ct. 1467, 146 L.Ed.2d 374 (2000) (where railroad crossing warnings are constructed with federal funds, no state tort action permitted).

3.   The federal government regulates the kind of headlights required on railroad trains. This regulation has been held to preempt the field, so that state regulation is not permitted. The plaintiff is struck by a railroad train, the engine of which complies with headlight regulation. The plaintiff attempts to prove, in his state tort law suit, that better lights were available, that a prudent person would have used them on the engine, and that had they been used the collision could have been avoided. If state tort law permitted this proof, would that be the same as "regulating" the railroad as to a federally preempted matter? The court so held in *Marshall v. Burlington Northern, Inc.*, 720 F.2d 1149 (9th Cir.1983). Is there any practical way in which this is different from saying that compliance is a defense?

4.   Preemption is an important idea in contemporary litigation. It will appear again in Chapter 22 concerning products liability.

Part III

LIMITING OR EXPANDING THE DUTY OF CARE ACCORDING TO CONTEXT OR RELATIONSHIP

"Duty" can be a confusing word in tort cases. Courts often use the term to describe a standard or measure of one's obligation. For instance, the normal duty is the duty to use the care of the reasonable, prudent person under the same or similar circumstances, but other standards or duties can be used. For example, in some cases the actor is under a strict duty to protect the plaintiff, meaning that he is liable even if he is not at fault. At the other end of the spectrum, there are cases in which the defendant owes no duty at all. In between there are several possible duties that demand more or less than ordinary care under the reasonable person standard. In many cases landowners owe people on the land only the duty to avoid wilful or wanton injury. So the term duty usually refers to a *standard* or general principle that measures the defendant's obligations to the plaintiff. A *standard* can have general application beyond the facts of the particular case.

As already observed, however, courts sometimes use the term duty as a way of talking about what particular acts are required by the exercise of ordinary care. For instance, a court might say that defendant had "a duty to stop, look, and listen before crossing a railroad track." When a court uses the term duty in this way it is not setting a *standard* for cases generally; it is reaching a *conclusion* about the particular case or stating a very specific rule that cannot be generalized beyond the facts. You will see courts using the term duty in both ways. The aim of this Part, however, is to talk about duty in the first sense, as a standard. In this sense, duties (or standards) range from the very demanding to the very lenient.

Topic A

LIMITING DUTIES ACCORDING TO CLASS OR STATUS OF THE PARTIES

Chapter 10

CARRIERS, HOST–DRIVERS AND LANDOWNERS

§ 1. CARRIERS AND HOST–DRIVERS

DOSER v. INTERSTATE POWER CO., 173 N.W.2d 556 (Iowa 1970). Defendant's bus was involved in an automobile accident and a bus passenger was injured. The evidence was that the automobile turned left in front of the bus and the defendant argued that the plaintiff had not shown negligence.

" 'A carrier of passengers for hire must exercise more than ordinary diligence for their protection. Its duty stops just short of insuring their safety. It is bound to protect its passengers as far as human care and foresight will go and is liable for slight negligence.' ... [T]he high degree of care must be exercised in *foreseeing*, as well as in *guarding against*, danger. Plaintiff made a prima facie case by showing she was injured while a passenger on the bus by a collision between the bus and the automobile. This cast upon defendants the burden to show their freedom from negligence in causing the collision.... Given the high degree of care demanded of common carriers and the factual situation presented, we hold the court was correct in submitting the various specifications of negligence to the jury."

Note

Some courts have now rejected the traditional higher standard of care reflected in *Doser* in favor of the general negligence standard based upon reasonable care under all the circumstances. E.g., *Bethel v. New York City Transit Authority*, 92 N.Y.2d 348, 703 N.E.2d 1214, 681 N.Y.S.2d 201 (1998).

ALA. CODE § 32–1–2.

The owner, operator or person responsible for the operation of a motor vehicle shall not be liable for loss or damage arising from injuries to or death of a guest while being transported without payment therefor in or upon said motor vehicle, resulting from the operation thereof, unless such injuries or death are caused by the willful or wanton misconduct of such operator, owner or person responsible for the operation of said motor vehicle.

Notes

1. Some guest statutes state the standard as "gross negligence," others as "wilful or wanton misconduct." There are variations of these two basic forms. The wilful, wanton standard may be construed to require not merely extremely negligent conduct, but also a bad state of mind.

2. The most obvious kind of litigation under guest statutes was litigation over the question whether a jury case has been made on the statutory gross negligence or wilful misconduct standard. It is common to see decisions in which courts announce that some particular act of negligence alone is not sufficient to show wilful misconduct. This is often said of speed. The cases turn on good development of factual detail and careful distinctions more than on broad policy considerations. Thus, though speed alone is not sufficient, speed plus a knowledge of a specific danger, such as an upcoming curve or blind spot, is often enough.

3. The guest statutes also raised some less obvious issues, notably those associated with the question, "Who is a guest?" Problems arise if the "guest" is injured in entering or leaving the car, for example, and also if the "guest" is paying a part of the cost of travel, or is providing non-monetary assistance to the driver. Lawyers who dealt with automobile cases in guest statute jurisdictions necessarily became adept in spotting such issues and developing them in proof.

4. Guest statutes were the product of a specific time, the late 1920s and the 1930s. In *Brown v. Merlo*, 8 Cal.3d 855, 106 Cal.Rptr. 388, 506 P.2d 212 (1973) the court held that the California guest statute was unconstitutional as a denial of equal protection under state law, partly because it treated guests and non-guests differently without any rational reason for doing so. The guest statute does not prevent collusion between host and guest because if they wish to collude they can testify that the passenger paid for the ride. The statute is not explicable as a means of encouraging hospitality because hospitality is extended to others who are not barred, and because in any event it is difficult to see why a "hospitable" host should be free to be negligent toward a guest. After *Brown* a good many other courts adopted similar reasoning under their own state constitutions. Legislatures, too, repealed many guest statutes. In 1985, the Texas Supreme Court, offered this count: "of the twenty-nine states which originally enacted guest statutes, only Texas and four other states still have such statutes." It then promptly reduced the number by holding the Texas statute unconstitutional. *Whitworth v. Bynum*, 699 S.W.2d 194 (Tex.1985).

5. *Evaluating guest statutes.* Some legal rules are likely to affect conduct in the future. Other legal rules seem to be justified on the ground that they reflect the community's sense of right or fairness. If a rule worked to shape conduct in socially desirable ways, it might conceivably be justified even if it did not reflect the community's sense of fairness. And if the rule reflected community notions of justice, it might be justified even if it had no

effect on conduct. Would you say that guest statutes neither affected conduct nor reflected justice? What is just about saying that a driver is free to take unreasonable risks with a guest?

6. The era of the guest statute seems to be about over. Why bother to consider them? One reason is that the guest statute sets up a limited legal duty that closely resembles some others we will see in this chapter. Consider as you proceed whether your evaluation of the guest statutes should reflect your evaluation of other limited duty cases. Consider also whether the constitutional considerations would be the same when we come to other cases of limited duties, starting with the landowners rules.

§ 2. LANDOWNERS' DUTIES TO TRESPASSERS, LICENSEES, CHILDREN, AND INVITEES

GLADON v. GREATER CLEVELAND REGIONAL TRANSIT AUTHORITY

Supreme Court of Ohio, 1996.
75 Ohio St.3d 312, 662 N.E.2d 287.

Greater Cleveland Regional Transit Authority ("RTA") appeals from a jury verdict awarding Robert M. Gladon $2,736,915.35 in damages arising from RTA's operation of a rapid transit train.

Gladon purchased a passenger ticket and boarded an RTA rapid transit train at Terminal Tower after attending a Cleveland Indians' night game with friends. During the baseball game, Gladon consumed about five 16–ounce beers. He left his friends at the stadium in search of a restroom, and ended up traveling alone on the RTA trains. [H]e mistakenly exited the train at the West 65th Street Station and, once on the platform, was chased and attacked by two unknown males. Gladon testified that he remembered being "rolled up in a ball" on the tracks but he could not recall if he had jumped onto the tracks or had been pushed onto the tracks. While there, however, he did recall being kicked in the head.

While Gladon lay on the tracks with his legs draped over the rail, an RTA rapid train approached the West 65th Street Station. Mary Bell, the train's operator, had the train in braking mode when she observed first a tennis shoe and then Gladon's leg on the tracks. The operator pulled the cinestar, or control handle, back and hit the "mushroom," or emergency brake. Unfortunately, the train struck Gladon causing him serious and permanent injuries.

Gladon sued RTA and the operator alleging negligence in the security of RTA's premises and in the operation of the train. Specifically, Gladon alleged that the operator was negligent by failing to bring the train to a stop "after the point she perceived or should have perceived the Plaintiff's peril prior to her striking the Plaintiff." The trial court granted RTA summary judgment as to the negligent security claim and the case proceeded to trial on the negligent operation claim.

The trial court overruled RTA's motion for a directed verdict at the close of Gladon's case-in-chief. The court instructed the jury that "as a matter of law that the only evidence produced by either side indicates that the plaintiff was an invitee." The court further informed the jury that "the driver of a rapid transit car with the right of way must use ordinary care. Therefore, to avoid colliding with a person found on the tracks, the defendant is required to use ordinary care to discover and to avoid danger." . . .

COOK, JUSTICE. . . .

In Ohio, the status of the person who enters upon the land of another (i.e. , trespasser, licensee, or invitee) continues to define the scope of the legal duty that the landowner owes the entrant. Invitees are persons who rightfully come upon the premises of another by invitation, express or implied, for some purpose which is beneficial to the owner.

The status of an invitee is not absolute but is limited by the landowner's invitation. "The visitor has the status of an invitee only while he is on part of the land to which his invitation extends—or in other words, the part of the land upon which the possessor gives him reason to believe that his presence is desired for the purpose for which he has come. If the invitee goes outside of the area of his invitation, he becomes a trespasser or a licensee, depending upon whether he goes there without the consent of the possessor, or with such consent."

. . . RTA's invitation to Gladon to use their premises did not extend to the area on or near the tracks. In fact, Gladon acknowledged that RTA did not permit the public in the area on or near the tracks. . . .

Gladon contends that he retained his invitee status because there was no evidence that he "intentionally or purposely entered upon the track area." According to the Restatement, "so far as the liability of the possessor of the land to the intruder is concerned, however, the possessor's duty, and liability, will be the same regardless of the manner of entry, so long as the entry itself is not privileged."

In determining whether the person is a trespasser within the meaning of this section, the question whether his entry has been intentional, negligent or purely accidental is not material, except as it may bear on the existence of a privilege. . . .

The illustration employed by the Restatement to explain the duties owed to a trespasser is remarkably similar to Gladon's situation. "Without any negligence on his part A, standing on the platform of a subway station of the X Company, slips and falls onto the tracks. While there he is run over by the train of X Company, and injured. A is a trespasser, and the liability to him is determined by the rules stated in sections 333 and 336, notwithstanding the accidental character of his intrusion."

Furthermore, whether Gladon was privileged to enter the tracks is immaterial. A person privileged to enter the land is owed the same duties as a licensee. Because the duties owed to a licensee and trespasser are the same, whether Gladon was privileged to enter the land does not change the standard of care RTA owed to him.

. . . Because Gladon then became either a licensee or a trespasser for purposes of determining the duty RTA owed to him, the trial court erred in instructing the jury that he was an invitee as a matter of law.

[A] landowner owes no duty to a licensee or trespasser except to refrain from wilful, wanton or reckless conduct which is likely to injure him. Furthermore, a railroad owes no duty to anticipate or prevent the presence of licensees or trespassers.

When a trespasser or licensee is discovered in a position of peril, a landowner is required to use ordinary care to avoid injuring him. The duty to exercise ordinary care arises after the landowner "knows, or from facts within his knowledge should know or believe," that a trespasser or licensee is on the land.

Having instructed the jury as a matter of law that Gladon was an invitee, the trial court assigned RTA a duty of ordinary care "to discover and to avoid danger." These instructions erred in two respects. First, the instructions imposed upon RTA a duty to use ordinary care to discover Gladon's presence. To the contrary, RTA was under no duty to anticipate trespassers and could only be liable for injuries resulting from willful or wanton conduct. Second, the instructions imposed upon RTA a duty to use ordinary care to avoid injuring Gladon prior to the operator's discovery of him. Rather, RTA's duty to use ordinary care to avoid injuring Gladon did not arise until RTA knew or should have known that Gladon was on the tracks. Whether the operator knew or should have known a person was on the tracks upon observing the tennis shoe remains a question for the jury.

Given that the instructions were erroneous and prejudicial, we reverse the judgment of the court of appeals and remand this cause for a new trial.

RTA owed Gladon no duty except to avoid injuring him by willful or wanton conduct prior to discovering Gladon on the tracks. Willful conduct " 'involves an intent, purpose or design to injure.' " Wanton conduct involves the failure to exercise " 'any care whatsoever toward those to whom he owes a duty of care, and his failure occurs under the circumstances in which there is great probability that harm will result.' "

At trial, Gladon produced evidence that the tracks were wet when the operator traveled eastbound toward the West 65th Street platform. The testimony of the operator indicates that she had the train in braking mode as she traveled through a dark area near the platform with her high beams on at an estimated 20 m. p. h. Generally, the speed limit in that area is 25 m. p. h. , but when a train is going to pass rather than stop at a platform, the permitted speed is 5 m. p. h.

Gladon also presented RTA regulations which require operators to operate the trains on sight, within the range of vision, at all times, and to anticipate changes in the range of vision. . . .

Viewing these facts in the light most favorable to Gladon, we find that in this trial reasonable minds could have reached different conclusions regarding whether the speed of the train at the time the operator approached the West 65th platform meets the wanton standard in light of the operator's duty to adjust the train's speed to her range of vision and to the known track conditions. Therefore, the trial court did not err in overruling RTA's motions for a directed verdict or judgment notwithstanding the verdict.

RTA owed Gladon a duty to use reasonable care to avoid injuring Gladon after the operator discovered Gladon on the tracks. Here, again, the RTA contends that Gladon failed to produce evidence of a breach of that duty.

Viewing these facts presented in this trial in the light most favorable to Gladon, reasonable minds could have reached different conclusions as to whether the operator exercised ordinary care. First, the point at which this duty arose remains a question for the jury. Reasonable minds could have reached different conclusions regarding whether the operator should have known a person was on the tracks when she saw the tennis shoes. Second, when the operator did realize a person was on the tracks, she was not sure whether she pulled the cinestar all the way back to the maximum braking mode before she hit the "mushroom" when she observed Gladon's legs on the tracks. Furthermore, the operator testified that she was not sure whether she hit the "mushroom" before or after the train struck Gladon. . . .

Judgment reversed and cause remanded. [Dissenting and concurring opinions are omitted.]

Notes

1. *Trespassers*. The traditional common law distinguished among trespassers, licensees, and invitees on the land. As *Gladon* shows, a trespasser included any person who entrance was unconsented to and unprivileged.

2. *Invitees*. (a) An invitee, to whom the duty of ordinary care was owed, was a person who was on the premises (1) at least in part for the benefit of the landowner or occupier or (2) who was on premises held open for the public generally. The first kind of invitee is called a business visitor, although her business may be quite minimal. The second kind is called a public invitee.

(b) Strangely enough, this definition excluded social guests in a home from the invitee category. That meant that social guests were licensees only and entitled to a lesser standard of care. This distinction leads to many decisions which must attempt to determine whether a guest's presence confers a benefit of any kind. For example, suppose the plaintiff is in the defendant's home to help conduct a meeting of a scout troop in which children of both the plaintiff and the defendant participate. If the plaintiff is injured by a condition on the premises, should she be considered a social guest and a licensee only?

(c) A few courts have broadened the definition of invitee to include social guests. See *Burrell v. Meads,* 569 N.E.2d 637 (Ind.1991).

(d) A person upon premises that are open to the public generally is today usually accepted as an invitee. How would you classify a person who is at a picnic table in a public park? In a seat at a bus station? In the aisle of a department store?

3. *Licensees.* A licensee is one who is permitted to be on the land by the owner's consent or the licensee's privilege, but who does not qualify as an invitee. As we've seen, a social guest fits that definition. So does someone who is permitted to use private land for his own pleasure or convenience but who confers no benefit or potential benefit upon the landowner. How would you classify a person who is permitted to fish in the defendant's private pond?

4. *Duties to trespassers and licensees.* (a) As *Gladon* indicates, the duty to trespassers and licensees is substantially similar. Courts usually say with *Gladon* that the landowner owes only the duty to avoid intentional, wanton, or wilful injury. That statement, however, is usually applied only when the landowner has not discovered or received notice of imminent danger to the entrant. Besides the protection of the landowner's limited duty, he may enjoy a privilege–a privilege to use reasonable force to expel the trespasser, for example, or to defend his property. A California statute immunizes landowners for injuries to persons committing a felony. See CAL. CIV. CODE § 847. In *Calvillo-Silva v. Home Grocery,* 19 Cal.4th 714, 968 P.2d 65, 80 Cal.Rptr.2d 506 (1998) this was construed to protect the landowner who actively inflicts harm so long as it is not wilful or wanton.

(b) If the landowner discovers both the presence of the entrant *and* the fact that he about to encounter a danger, the situation is different. In that case, some courts might say that the landowner who fails to act reasonably in the face of this known danger to an entrant, is then guilty of wilful or wanton misconduct. Others might say with the *Gladon* court that in such a case the landowner owes a duty of reasonable care. The two ways of addressing this situation appear to come down to the same thing, with liability in either case for failing to act with reasonable care.

5. *Conditions.* Under the rules just stated, the landowner will often be held to a duty of reasonable care in carrying out affirmative acts such as driving on his private roads, once he knows a trespasser is present. In the case of licensees, the landowner is said to owe an affirmative duty of care to all licensees in carrying out activities on the land. Thus the wilful-wanton rule protecting landowners is mainly addressed to *conditions* on the land, such as a dangerous non-obvious excavation, a dangerous electrical connection, a hidden step, or a rotten railing that may give way.

6. *Landowner knows trespassers frequent the area.* Some courts impose a duty of care upon landowners who have not discovered the actual presence of a trespasser, provided the landowner knows trespassers frequently use a

limited area. This rule is most commonly invoked when trespassers use a footpath across, or sometimes alongside, a railroad track.

NOTE: CHILD TRESPASSERS

1. *The turntable doctrine or attractive nuisance doctrine*. A seven-year-old boy enters a railroad switching yard, attracted by the activity and by a large metal turntable, on to which train engines can be driven. The turntable rotates like a merry-go-round so that the engine can be readily turned to a different track. The table is not locked and the boy plays on it, catching his leg between the moving table and the rim. The limb is severed. Is he to be treated as a trespasser, to whom no duty was owed if the railroad did not discover his presence? This kind of case arose in an era of populist sentiment against railroads. Courts held that the attractive turntable was a lure, like meat put out to attract a dog, and that consequently the landowner had, in effect, invited the child. Thus there was a duty of care. The doctrine originating on such facts came to be called the turntable doctrine or the attractive nuisance rule.

2. *Attraction by injury-causing instrumentality*. At one time the landowner's duty extended only to the case of the child who was injured by the very thing that attracted him in the first place. This is no longer the law, and the landowner may be held for negligence when the child is attracted by one instrument but injured by another.

3. *Tender years*. The landowner's duty is limited, however, to children who, because of their tender years, are foreseeably unlikely to appreciate the dangers and to avoid them. Thus the "attractive nuisance" doctrine applies mainly to children of grade school age or younger and only rarely to teenagers.

4. *Common hazards*. Some courts have said that "common hazards," such as fire and pools of water cannot be considered attractive nuisances and the trespassing child who drowns in the stock pond is entitled to no protection from the landowner. The better explanation for many of these cases may be that there is a duty of care owed, but that given the importance of stock ponds and the difficulty of fencing them, the duty is not breached, which is to say the defendant is not negligent. This explanation is supported by the fact that even in states that announce a "common hazard" rule, recovery is sometimes allowed for swimming pool deaths and for injuries by hidden burning embers.

5. *A contemporary view*. The development of the law from the early turntable cases has led to a rule that holds the landowner to a duty of due care to trespassing children when (a) trespass by children is foreseeable, (b) the landowner knows or has reason to know of the danger, and (c) there is reason to think the child, by reason of his age, will not be able to protect himself from the danger. Given these conditions, the landowner owes a duty of reasonable care, nothing more. So the child does not necessarily recover merely because he is injured by a dangerous

condition on the land. He is forgiven his trespasses, but he must go further and prove the landowner's negligence before he can recover.

O'SULLIVAN v. SHAW

Supreme Judicial Court of Massachusetts, 2000.
431 Mass. 201, 726 N.E.2d 951.

LYNCH, J.

The plaintiff seeks to recover for injuries he sustained when he dived, headfirst, into the shallow end of a swimming pool owned by the defendants and located on their residential property. His complaint alleges that the defendants were negligent in allowing visitors to dive into the shallow end of the pool and in failing to warn of the danger associated with this activity. A judge in the Superior Court allowed the defendants' motion for summary judgment, reasoning that diving into the shallow end of a swimming pool is an open and obvious danger which was known to the plaintiff, and that the defendants therefore did not owe the plaintiff a duty of care. . . .

The pool in question is an in-ground type, measuring eighteen feet in width by thirty-six feet in length, with both shallow and deep ends. The bottom of the pool is level in the shallow end, for approximately ten feet of the pool's length, after which it slopes gradually toward the deep end, the sides of which are tapered. When filled to capacity, the pool is four feet deep at its shallowest point and eight feet at its deepest. There are no markers, either in the pool or on its exterior surround, to indicate the pool's depth at various points along its length or to demarcate the separation of its shallow and deep ends. However, a diving board is affixed to the exterior of the pool at its deep end. The pool's interior is covered with a vinyl liner and there is no underwater lighting, so that the bottom of the pool is not visible at night. . . .

[T]he plaintiff suffered injuries to his neck and back when he dived into the shallow end of the pool. At the time, he was attempting, in racing dive fashion, to clear the ten-foot expanse of the shallow end and surface in the deep end, but he entered the water at too steep an angle and struck his head on the pool bottom, resulting in a fracture of his cervical vertebrae. By his own admission, the plaintiff knew that he could be injured if he were to hit his head on the bottom of the pool when diving, and his purpose in trying to clear the shallow end was to avoid the sort of accident that occurred. The plaintiff's injury caused immediate paralysis in his lower extremities and required a two-day stay in the hospital, but the paralysis was not permanent. . . .

. . . [I]t is well established in our law of negligence that a landowner's duty to protect lawful visitors against dangerous conditions on his property ordinarily does not extend to dangers that would be obvious to persons of average intelligence. Landowners are relieved of the duty to warn of open and obvious dangers on their premises because it is not reasonably foreseeable that a visitor exercising (as the law presumes) reasonable care for his own safety would suffer injury from such blatant hazards. Stated otherwise, where a danger would be obvious to a person of ordinary perception and judgment, a landowner may reasonably assume that a visitor has knowledge of it and, therefore, "any further warning would be an empty form" that would not reduce the likelihood of resulting harm.

The plaintiff argues on appeal that the open and obvious danger rule was implicitly abolished by the comparative negligence statute, which expressly abolishes "the defense of assumption of risk," because, he maintains, the former is a corollary of the latter. Accordingly, he argues, the judge erred in concluding that the defendants owed no duty to the plaintiff due to the obvious nature of the risk, for it properly belongs to a jury to decide the issue of the defendants' liability by applying statutorily mandated principles of comparative fault. We reject this argument.

. . . Assumption of risk, along with contributory negligence, was an affirmative defense to negligence for which the defendant bore the burden of proof at trial. A plaintiff assumed the risk of harm when he voluntarily exposed himself to a known danger which had been caused by the defendant's negligence; the focus of the inquiry was thus on the plaintiff's own carelessness or negligence in failing to avoid a hazard which he knew about and appreciated. By contrast, the open and obvious danger doctrine arises in connection with the separate issue of a defendant's duty to protect others from dangerous conditions about which the defendant knows or should know. Rather than evaluating a particular plaintiff's subjective reasonableness or unreasonableness in encountering a known hazard, the inquiry is an objective one that focuses, instead, on the reasonableness of the defendant's conduct: it presumes a plaintiff's exercising reasonable care for his own safety and asks whether the dangerous condition was, objectively speaking, so obvious that the defendant would be reasonable in concluding that an ordinarily intelligent plaintiff would perceive and avoid it and, therefore, that any further warning would be superfluous.

Thus, the superseded common-law defense of assumption of risk goes to a plaintiff's failure to exercise due care for his own safety, whereas the open and obvious danger rule concerns the existence of a defendant's duty of care, which the plaintiff must establish as part of his prima facie case before any comparative analysis of fault may be performed. . . . [W]e conclude that the Legislature's express abolition of "the defense of assumption of risk" does not alter the plaintiff's burden in a negligence action to prove that the defendant owed him a duty of care in the circumstances, and thus leaves intact the open and obvious danger rule, which operates to negate the existence of a duty of care.

. . . The remaining issue concerns whether the judge, in granting summary judgment for the defendants, correctly concluded that the open and obvious danger rule obviated any duty to warn the plaintiff not to dive headfirst into the shallow end of the defendants' swimming pool. Plain common sense, bolstered by the weight of authority in other jurisdictions where this issue has been addressed, convince us that this conclusion is indisputably correct. . . .

Judgment affirmed.

Notes

1. *Open and obvious danger.* At one time, courts routinely held that the landowner was not liable for injuries to an invitee from an open and obvious danger. Some courts still say this. *General Motors Corp. v. Hill,* 752 So.2d 1186 (Ala.1999). The idea was frequently expressed, as in *O'Sullivan,* by saying the landowner owed no duty to protect from obvious dangers.

2. *Contributory negligence/assumed risk.* Some courts interpreted the rule against liability for open and obvious dangers as a rule based upon contributory negligence or assumed risk, imputing fault to the plaintiff in such cases as a matter of law. With the coming of comparative fault, some of these courts now reject the flat rule against recovery. The fact that danger should have been obvious to the plaintiff then figures as fault with reduction in damages. E.g., *Brooks v. K–Mart Corp.,* 125 N.M. 537, 964 P.2d 98 (1998).

3. *No duty–or no negligence?* Under the mainstream theory, adopted in *O'Sullivan,* the obvious danger rule was not a matter of contributory negligence or assumed risk. It was instead a no duty rule, created by judges as a matter of policy. Yet the theory was that if the danger was obvious, the invitee could avoid it and thus protect himself, so that the landowner would foresee no harm. Under that theory, wouldn't it be more accurate to say that the landowner was under a duty of care, but that a duty of care is not breached–the landowner is not negligent–when no harm is foreseeable? See *Shaw v. Petersen,* 169 Ariz. 559, 821 P.2d 220 (Ariz.App.1991) (characterizing as a negligence rather than a duty issue); *Stinnett v. Buchele,* 598 S.W.2d 469 (Ky.App.1980).

4. *Harm foreseeable in spite of obvious danger.* If you see the issue as one of negligence rather than duty, the trier will decide whether harm was in fact foreseeable even if the danger is obvious. Is that possible? Consider two kinds of cases.

   a. A department store has a hole in its floor large enough to fall into. The hole is obvious. Can you imagine any condition in which a shopper might nevertheless fall into it? Or suppose the landowner operates a bar at the top of a long, dangerous flight of steps that furnish the only means of egress. Is a fall foreseeable? *Fulmer v. Timber Inn Restaurant Lounge, Inc.,* 330 Or. 413, 9 P.3d 710 (2000).

   b. A utility customer must cross an obvious patch of ice to pay her utility bill. Unless she does so immediately, power will be cut off in her home in the dead of winter. If the utility is negligent in failing to sand the ice, is it foreseeable that someone exercising her right to enter will be injured?

Look back at *O'Sullivan* and see whether you think it leaves room for liability in such cases. If so, could the plaintiff's damages be reduced for comparative fault?

5. *Natural conditions; snow and ice.* Some courts follow a rule that landowners owe no duty, not even to an invitee, with respect to dangers created by natural accumulations of snow and ice. The rule does not relieve the landowner of liability for dangers created by the landowner's activities that make the ice more dangerous.

6. *Sharing the landowner's status.* Although this casebook refers to the limited duties of "landowners," the same rules apply to protect (1) possessors of land who are not owners, (2) members of the possessor's family acting on the land, and (3) other persons on the land and acting on the possessor's behalf.

7. *Sharing the entrant's status.* If A is a guest in a hotel and thus acquires the status as an invitee, can his own guests acquire the status merely because they are his guests? The answer is generally yes; the guest's invitees are themselves invitees of the hotel as long at they are there "in the right of" the guest. A similar rule applies in the case of landlords and tenants. See *Ellis v. Luxbury Hotels, Inc.*, 716 N.E.2d 359 (Ind.1999). What would you expect a court to hold about the status of an adult trespasser who enters land to rescue a child endangered by an attractive nuisance?

8. *Scope of invitation.* As *Gladon* indicates, you may be an invitee on some parts of the premises, but not on others. You are no doubt an invitee when you enter the grocery store. Suppose a guest in a motel stays up all night with his own guest, then checks out in the morning, leaving his guest asleep in the room. The motel's rules forbid occupancy after checkout. Is the sleeping guest outside the scope of the invitation because the rules are violated? What if, before the checkout, the paying guest and his friends were playing poker for money in violation of the motel's rules and perhaps in violation of law? *Woodty v. Weston's Lamplighter Motels*, 171 Ariz. 265, 830 P.2d 477 (Ct. App. 1992).

NOTE: DUTY TO PERSONS OUTSIDE THE LAND

Persons on the public way or on adjoining property outside the landowner's land are not in any of the three categories. Where a natural condition on the land creates a risk to persons outside the land, the cases may be moving toward a duty of ordinary care. If the landowner has trees likely to fall on passers-by, the landowner may be obliged to exercise ordinary care to discover the danger and deal with it. Where a landslide from an upper tract of land damaged a lower tract, the California Court has said that the upper owner owed a duty of reasonable care to the lower. *Sprecher v. Adamson Companies*, 30 Cal.3d 358, 178 Cal.Rptr. 783, 636 P.2d 1121 (1981). However, courts may decide as a matter of law that reasonable care does not require regular inspection to discover hidden dangers of which the landowner has no notice. This idea may be expressed by saying the landowner has "no duty" to inspect for hidden dangers resulting from natural conditions like trees. See *Meyers v. Delaney*, 529 N.W.2d 288 (Iowa 1995) (rot in tree branch not apparent, landowner not liable when branch hanging over neighbor's property fell on neighbor). Distinguish cases in which a landowner's vegetation obscures the vision of motorists at intersections and thus leads to a collision. In those cases, nothing from the land causes direct physical harm to a person on the public way and courts often say there is no duty on the landowner's part to control the vegetation. E.g., *Driggers v. Locke,* 323 Ark. 63, 913 S.W.2d 269 (1996); contra, insisting that the issue is negligence, not duty, *Coburn v. City of Tucson*, 143 Ariz. 50, 691 P.2d 1078 (1984) and *Donaca v. Curry County*, 303 Or. 30, 734 P.2d 1339 (1987). As to dangers from natural conditions to persons who are actually on the land itself, the landowner ordinarily owes no duty of care except to disclose natural dangers that appear safe.

In *Davis v. Westwood Group,* 420 Mass. 739, 652 N.E.2d 567 (1995) the landowner operated a race track on one side of a major, divided highway. The parking lot for spectators was on the other side. The plaintiff, attempting to cross from the parking lot to the track, was struck by a car. He claimed that the method of entry to the land was unreasonably dangerous and that the track owner should have provided a safer method. The court rejected the claim. "To hold that Westwood owed the plaintiff such a duty would significantly expand the scope of a landowner or possessor's duties with respect to adjacent public roads, and would make the line which cuts off landowner liability nearly impossible to draw." If the landowner is seen as exercising "control" over adjacent property it does not own, could that change the outcome? See, e.g., *Siddons v. Business Properties Dev. Co.*, 191 Ariz. 158, 953 P.2d 902 (Ariz. 1998).

§ 3.   THE FIREFIGHTER'S RULE

PINTER v. AMERICAN FAMILY MUTUAL INS. CO.

Supreme Court of Wisconsin, 2000.
236 Wis.2d 137, 613 N.W.2d 110.

JON P. WILCOX, J. . . .

[These allegations are taken as true for purpose of determining the defendants' motion for summary judgment. Pinter is a firefighter and emergency medical technician for the city of Brookfield. He responded as an EMT when a woman was injured in a collision allegedly caused by the negligence of Jesmok and Otto. The injured woman, still in the automobile, appeared to be suffering from spinal cord injury. Pinter accordingly had to maintain traction from a difficult position over a period of time. As a result he sustained an inguinal hernia, a serious and permanent injury. He sued the drivers who caused the woman's injury and necessitated his response. The trial court granted motions for summary judgment on the basis of an earlier decision, *Hass*, holding that "one who negligently starts a fire is not liable for that negligence when it causes injury to a firefighter who comes to extinguish the blaze."]

Most jurisdictions in the United States limit liability in negligence cases under a theory of law commonly termed the "firefighter's rule." As applied to firefighters, the rule limits a firefighter's ability to recover damages for injuries sustained while performing his or her duties as a firefighter. In many jurisdictions this rule was originally based on the reasoning that a firefighter who enters premises to fight a fire is a licensee to whom the owner or occupier of the premises owes no duty except to refrain from willful or wanton injury. As the categories of "invitee" and "licensee" gradually have been abolished in tort law, some courts turned to the doctrine of assumption of risk to support the rule. These courts reasoned that " 'one who has knowingly and voluntarily confronted a hazard cannot recover for injuries sustained thereby.' "

More recently, most courts adopting or adhering to the firefighter's rule have justified the rule on public policy grounds. Thirty years ago, public policy led this court to recognize a limitation on liability in a firefighter's negligence action in Hass . . . .

The [Hass] court observed that nearly all fires are caused by negligence. The court therefore determined that requiring a person who negligently starts a fire to pay damages to a firefighter would place too great a burden on owners and occupiers of real estate. In addition, liability would " 'enter a field that has no sensible or just stopping point.' The court held that because of these public policy considerations, "one who negligently starts a fire is not liable for that negligence when it causes injury to a firefighter who comes to extinguish the blaze." . . .

[A series of later cases shows that Hass] bars a cause of action only when the sole negligent act is the same negligent act that necessitated rescue and therefore brought the firefighter to the scene of the emergency . . . .

The real issue in this case is whether the public policy analysis in Hass is still valid, and if so, whether it logically extends to Pinter's negligence action.

We first consider whether the public policy analysis in Hass is still valid. Pinter does not explicitly ask this court to overturn Hass. However, Pinter and the amicus curiae point out that some jurisdictions have recently abolished the "firefighter's rule" by judicial decision or by statute. They also note that the rule has been the subject of criticism and dissent.

The concerns that have led other jurisdictions to abandon or reject the so-called "firefighter's rule" do not persuade us that the public policy analysis in Hass should be rejected. Many jurisdictions that have criticized or rejected their version of the "firefighter's rule" have noted that the licensee/invitee distinction that was the original basis for the rule has fallen out of the law. However, this distinction was never the basis of the public policy analysis in Hass.

Similarly, jurisdictions that relied on the assumption of risk doctrine to justify the "firefighter's rule" have abandoned the rule under comparative negligence principles. However, Hass was never premised on the idea that a firefighter's assumption of the risks inherent in his or her profession makes the firefighter's negligence greater than the alleged tortfeasor's as a matter of law. Instead, Hass was based squarely on Wisconsin's traditional public policy analysis in negligence cases....

Fundamentally, the rule recognized in Hass is an expression of public policy because it prohibits a firefighter from " 'complaining about the negligence that creates the very need for his or her employment.' " As stated by the Supreme Court of Hawaii:

> The very purpose of the fire fighting profession is to confront danger. Fire fighters are hired, trained, and compensated to deal with dangerous situations that are often caused by negligent conduct or acts. "[I]t offends public policy to say that a citizen invites private liability merely because he happens to create a need for those public services."

Permitting firefighters to pursue actions like the one in Hass is therefore not consistent with the relationship of the fire fighting profession to the public. It would contravene public policy to permit a firefighter to recover damages from an individual who has already been taxed to provide compensation to injured firefighters.

In sum, we reaffirm the public policy reasoning set forth in Hass. The limitation stated in Hass has been the law of Wisconsin for thirty years, and it is still good law.

The remaining question is whether the public policy reasoning in Hass logically extends to Pinter's cause of action....

Firefighting and emergency medical assistance are closely related professions; like Pinter, some EMTs also serve as firefighters. Members of both professions have special training and experience that prepare them to provide assistance under dangerous emergency conditions. Persons entering either profession know that they will be expected to provide aid and protection to others in these hazardous circumstances. In short, both EMTs and firefighters are professional rescuers who are specially trained and employed to conduct rescue operations in dangerous emergencies....

[P]ermitting an EMT to recover under the circumstances alleged by Pinter would place an unreasonable burden on drivers who negligently cause collisions. The injury that Pinter sustained is simply too remote from the initial acts of negligence that caused the collision. Permitting Pinter's action to proceed would enter a field with no sensible or just stopping point....

The judgment of the circuit court is affirmed.

[The dissent of SHIRLEY S. ABRAHAMSON, CHIEF JUSTICE, is omitted.]

Notes

1. Most courts have concluded that a firefighter who is injured in fighting a fire has no claim against the negligent fire-setter. The early cases were against landowners and courts tried to resolve the issue by struggling with the licensee classification.

2. *Assumed risk/no duty.* As *Pinter* notes, cases today usually explain the exclusion of firefighters from the negligence system by saying that the firefighter assumed the risk. This could hardly be assumed risk in the sense of contributory fault; it is not negligent to fight fires in a professional way. So the firefighters' rule, though explained in terms of assumed risk, is merely another way of saying "it is appropriate to find that the defendant owes no duty of care." *Neighbarger v. Irwin Industries, Inc.,* 8 Cal.4th 532, 34 Cal.Rptr.2d 630, 882 P.2d 347 (1994).

3. *No duty/public policy.* "No duty" in turn reflects judicial notions of appropriate policy. What public policy supports the assumed risk/no duty rule? Can you glean more than one from *Pinter*? Are they sound? What about these arguments?

    a.   The injured firefighter is paid workers' compensation or other benefits by his public employer, therefore the negligent firesetter should not be liable. (That is not the rule for other employees who receive workers' compensation benefits.)

    b.   A builder who agrees with a homeowner to repair a dangerous roof has no claim against the homeowner if he is injured in carrying out the hazardous task, even if the homeowner negligently caused the roof's dilapidation. (How is that to be compared or contrasted with the firefighter's case?) See *Neighbarger v. Irwin Industries, Inc.,* 8 Cal.4th 532, 34 Cal.Rptr.2d 630, 882 P.2d 347 (1994).

4. *Expansions.* As *Pinter* shows, the firefighters' rule has vastly expanded. It is no longer anchored in premises liability law; it applies outside the land as well as on it. Likewise, it is no longer limited to firefighters; it has been applied to police officers, EMTs, and even lifeguards. E.g., *City of Oceanside v. Superior Court,* 81 Cal.App.4th 269, 96 Cal.Rptr.2d 621 (2000) (lifeguard); *Rosa v. Dunkin' Donuts of Passaic,* 122 N.J. 66, 583 A.2d 1129 (1991) (police officer slipped on confectioner's sugar while providing emergency medical assistance in a donut shop). Maybe the category is not firefighters but publicly employed professional risk-takers or public safety officers. What will courts do with public building inspectors injured in buildings they inspect? See DOBBS ON TORTS § 287 (2000).

5. *Private rescuers.* The firefighters' rule has no application to private individuals who may undertake assistance at a fire. On the contrary, private persons are considered heroic and it is said under one branch of the "rescue doctrine" that it is not contributory negligence or assumed risk to render assistance in a physical emergency. "The extent of the risk which the volunteer is justified in assuming under the circumstances increases in proportion to the imminence of the danger...." *Moravec v. Moravec,* 216 Neb. 412, 343 N.W.2d 762 (1984) (plaintiff injured in fighting a fire could recover from homeowner who negligently set it).

6. *Privately employed professional rescuers.* In a leading California case, *Neighbarger v. Irwin Industries, Inc.,* 8 Cal.4th 532, 34 Cal.Rptr.2d 630, 882 P.2d 347 (1994), the court concluded that the firefighters rule had no application to a professional firefighter/safety officer who was privately employed. The plaintiff as a plant safety officer was therefore permitted to pursue his claim against a negligent outsider who caused a fire in the plant.

7. *Wrongdoing not covered by the rule.* Courts agree that the firefighter's rule does not protect all wrongdoers.

(1) It does not foreclose suit against an intentional or wilful wrongdoer. *Mahoney v. Carus Chemical Co.,* 102 N.J. 564, 510 A.2d 4 (1986); contra: *Young v. Sherwin–Williams Co.,* 569 A.2d 1173 (D.C. App. 1990).

(2) At least in some jurisdictions, it does not foreclose suit for injuries arising from violation of a fire-safety statute or ordinance. For instance, New York has held that a landowner who violated a fire safety statute by blocking a door would be liable to a firefighter injured by dropping into the room from the ceiling. *Mullen v. Zoebe, Inc.,* 86 N.Y.2d 135, 654 N.E.2d 90, 630 N.Y.S.2d 269 (1995).

(3) It does not foreclose suit for harms resulting from risks not inherent in the job the officer has undertaken or those the officer was not paid to assume. One specific effect is that the firefighter's rule "has only been applied to prohibit a fireman from recovering for injuries caused by the very misconduct which created the risk which necessitated his presence" See *Lipson v. Superior Court of Orange County,* 31 Cal.3d 362, 182 Cal.Rptr. 629, 644 P.2d 822 (1982).

Example 1. The officer may recover against a defendant who negligently increases a risk to the officer after the officer's presence is known. This specific rule is statutory in California. See CAL. CIV. CODE § 1714.9; but see *Calatayud v. State,* 18 Cal.4th 1057, 959 P.2d 360, 77 Cal.Rptr.2d 202 (1998) (fellow officer's negligence after plaintiff-officer's presence is known is not actionable in spite of the statute).

Example 2. A traffic officer stops A. While the officer is on the roadside issuing a speeding ticket to A, B, driving another car, negligently strikes him. B is not free of all responsibility on the ground that the officer assumes risks inherent in traffic work. Rather, B's negligence, not being conduct that drew the officer to the location in the first place, is not protected by the firefighter's rule. *Harris-Fields v. Syze,* 461 Mich. 188, 600 N.W.2d 611 (1999). The same point can be illustrated by the case of a firefighter injured by the homeowner's attack dogs; dog danger was not part of the reason for the firefighter's presence, hence he may pursue his claim for the dog bites. Cf. *Wiley v. Redd,* 110 Nev. 1310, 885 P.2d 592 (1994) (police officer). Put in broader terms, dog danger was not one of the risks inherent in the job and not one the public officer was paid to face. See DOBBS ON TORTS § 286 (2000).

8. *Premises open to the public.* Should courts also recognize an exception for the case in which an officer is injured by a condition on premises open to the public, as where the owner has left a slippery substance on the floor? What is the argument for such a rule?

9. *Status of the rule.* Although the firefighter's rule is generally accepted, it has prompted discontent that may be growing. Oregon abolished the rule in *Christensen v. Murphy,* 296 Or. 610, 620, 678 P.2d 1210, 1217 (1984). Some courts have never accepted the rule in the first place. See *Mull v. Kerstetter,* 373 Pa.Super. 228, 540 A.2d 951 (1988). The House of Lords firmly rejected it in *Ogwo v. Taylor,* [1988] A. C. 431 (1987). Statutes have sometimes specifically rejected the rule. See, e.g., FLA. STAT. ANN. § 112.182; N.J.S.A. 2A:62A–21.

§ 4. ADOPTING A REASONABLE CARE STANDARD FOR LANDOWNERS

ROWLAND v. CHRISTIAN

Supreme Court of California, 1968.
69 Cal.2d 108, 70 Cal.Rptr. 97, 443 P.2d 561.

PETERS, JUSTICE.

[Plaintiff was a social guest in Miss Christian's apartment. The porcelain handle of a bathroom faucet broke in his hand and severed tendons and nerves. Miss Christian had known the handle was cracked and had in fact reported it to her lessors, but, though she knew plaintiff was going to the bathroom, she gave him no warning. These facts were established by affidavit and the trial judge gave summary judgment for the defendant.]

Section 1714 of the Civil Code provides: "Everyone is responsible, not only for the result of his willful acts, but also for an injury occasioned to another by his want of ordinary care or skill in the management of his property or person, except so far as the latter has, willfully or by want of ordinary care, brought the injury upon himself. . . ." This code section, which has been unchanged in our law since 1872, states a civil law and not a common law principle. . . .

One of the areas where this court and other courts have departed from the fundamental concept that a man is liable for injuries caused by his carelessness is with regard to the liability of a possessor of land for injuries to persons who have entered upon that land. It has been suggested that the special rules regarding liability of the possessor of land are due to historical considerations stemming from the high place which land has traditionally held in English and American thought, the dominance and prestige of the landowning class in England during the formative period of the rules governing the possessor's liability, and the heritage of feudalism. (2 Harper and James, The Law of Torts, supra, p. 1432.)

The departure from the fundamental rule of liability for negligence has been accomplished by classifying the plaintiff either as a trespasser, licensee, or invitee and then adopting special rules as to the duty owed by the possessor to each of the classifications. . . .

[The court here reviewed the trespasser-licensee-invitee rules and a number of cases which it said created exceptions, complexity and confusion.]

Complexity can be borne and confusion remedied where the underlying principles governing liability are based upon proper considerations. Whatever may have been the historical justifications for the common law distinctions, it is clear that those distinctions are not justified in the light of our modern society and the complexity and confusion which has arisen is not due to difficulty in applying the original common law rules—they are all too easy to apply in their original formulation—but is due to the attempts to apply just rules in our modern society within the ancient terminology.

Without attempting to labor all of the rules relating to the possessor's liability, it is apparent that the classifications of trespasser, licensee, and invitee, the immunities from liability predicated upon those circumstances, and the exceptions to those immunities, often do not reflect the major factors which should determine whether immunity should be conferred upon the possessor of land. Some of those factors, including the closeness of the connection between the injury and the defendant's conduct, the moral blame attached to the defendant's conduct, the policy of preventing future harm, and the prevalence and availability of insurance bear little, if any relationship to the classification of trespasser, licensee and invitee and the existing rules conferring immunity.

Although in general there may be a relationship between the remaining factors and the classifications of trespasser, licensee, and invitee, there are many cases in which no such relationship may exist. Thus, although the foreseeability of harm to an invitee would ordinarily seem greater than the foreseeability of harm to a trespasser, in a particular case the opposite may be true. The same may be said of the issue of certainty of injury. The burden to the defendant and consequences to the community of imposing a duty to exercise care with resulting liability for breach may often be greater with respect to trespassers than with respect to invitees, but it by no means follows that this is true in every case. In many situations, the burden will be the same, i.e., the conduct necessary upon the defendant's part to meet the burden of exercising due care as to the invitees will also meet his burden with respect to licensees and trespassers. The last of the major factors, the cost of insurance, will, of course, vary depending upon the rules of liability adopted, but there is no persuasive evidence that applying ordinary principles of negligence law to the land occupier's liability will materially reduce the prevalence of insurance due to increased cost or even substantially increase the cost. . . .

A man's life or limb does not become less worthy of protection by the law nor a loss less worthy of compensation under the law because he has come upon the land of another without permission or with permission but without a business purpose. Reasonable people do not ordinarily vary their conduct depending upon such matters, and to focus upon the status of the injured party as a trespasser, licensee or invitee in order to determine the question whether the landowner has a duty of care, is contrary to our modern social mores and humanitarian values. The common law rules obscure rather than illuminate the proper consideration which should govern determination of the question of duty. . . .

It may be noted that by carving further exceptions out of the traditional rules relating to the liability to licensees or social guests, other jurisdictions reach the same result. . . .

The Judgment is Reversed.

TRAYNOR, C. J., and TOBRINER, MOSK and SULLIVAN, J. J., concur.

BURKE, JUSTICE (dissenting).

I dissent. In determining the liability of the occupier or owner of land for injuries, the distinctions between trespassers, licensees and invitees have been developed and applied by the courts over a period of many years. They supply a reasonable and workable approach to the problems involved, and one which provides the degree of stability and predictability so highly prized in law. The unfortunate alternative, it appears to me, is the route taken by the majority in their opinion in this case; that such issues are to be decided on a case by case basis under the application of the basic law of negligence, bereft of the guiding principles and precedent which the law has heretofore attached by virtue of the relationship of the parties to one another.

Liability for negligence turns upon whether a duty of care is owed, and if so, the extent thereof. Who can doubt that the corner grocery, the large department store, or the financial institution owes a greater duty of care to one whom it has invited to enter its premises as a prospective customer of its wares or services than it owes to a trespasser seeking to enter after the close of business hours and for a nonbusiness or even an antagonistic purpose? I do not think it unreasonable or unfair that a social guest (classified by the law as a licensee, as was plaintiff here) should be obliged to take the premises in the same condition as his host finds them or permits them to be. Surely a homeowner should not be obliged to hover over his guests with warnings of possible dangers to be found in the condition of the home (e.g., waxed floors, slipping rugs, toys in unexpected places, etc., etc.) . . . .

McCOMB, J., concurs.

Notes

1. This is the first decision to abolish the categories and substitute the general duty of reasonable care. California was also the first state to hold guest statutes unconstitutional. *Brown v. Merlo,* 8 Cal.3d 855, 106 Cal.Rptr. 388, 506 P.2d 212 (1973). Is there any logical relation between the two decisions?

2. By 2000, about 25 jurisdictions had either included social guests in the invitee category or had completely or partly abolished the categories, with the result that all or most entrants upon land were entitled to reasonable care under the circumstances. See JOSEPH PAGE, THE LAW OF PREMISES LIABILITY § 6.4 (1988); Annotation, 22 A. L. R. 4th 294 (1983). At least six states joined this group in the 1990s. Perhaps the last case to join this group before 2000 was *Mallet v. Pickens,* 206 W.Va. 145, 522 S.E.2d 436 (1999).

3. Some of these courts retain the limited-duty-to-trespassers rules even though they have dropped the licensee-invitee rules. See *Bennett v. Napolitano,* 746 A.2d 138 (R.I.2000) (citizen in park after it was closed for the night was a trespasser to whom reasonable care was not owed). Some

recent decisions have continued to affirm all the traditional limited duty categories. In fact, Michigan recently went so far as reject public invitee status and to insist that a person at a church for Bible study was merely a licensee in the absence of a commercial purpose. *Stitt v. Holland Abundant Life Fellowship,* 462 Mich. 591, 614 N.W.2d 88 (2000).

SCURTI v. CITY OF NEW YORK, 40 N.Y.2d 433, 387 N.Y.S.2d 55, 354 N.E.2d 794 (1976). A 14–year old boy was electrocuted in a railroad yard after crawling through a hole in the fence. There was evidence that the fence was part of a city park and the city and others were joined as defendants. New York had previously abolished the trespasser-licensee-invitee distinctions and had adopted the standard of reasonable care.

"Under the standard of reasonable care ... the factors which sustained the landowner's immunity and inspired the exceptions under prior law will no longer be considered decisive. But, as indicated, most of them have some probative value.... The fact that the injury occurred on the defendant's property is certainly a relevant circumstance in assessing the reasonableness of defendant's conduct. The defendant has a right to use his property and to develop it for his profit and enjoyment. That often means that he must conduct dangerous activities or permit dangerous instruments and conditions to exist on the premises. However under those circumstances he must take reasonable measures to prevent injury to those whose presence on the property can reasonably be foreseen. Whether the threat is posed by a dangerous condition or a dangerous activity is of little significance in itself. It may have some bearing on the effort required to prevent the injury, but that depends on the facts of the particular case. In this connection it is important to note that the elimination of the immunity conferred by prior law should not pose an unreasonable burden on the use of the property since all that is now required is the exercise of reasonable care under the circumstances. The defendant can always show that it would have been unduly burdensome to have done more.... The fact that the plaintiff entered without permission is also a relevant circumstance. It may well demonstrate that the plaintiff's presence was not foreseeable at the time and place of the injury.... This does not mean that every case involving injury on private property raises a factual question for the jury's consideration. In any negligence case the court must always determine as a threshold matter whether the facts will support an inference of negligence.... However, in this particular case the question of reasonableness of the parties' conduct cannot be resolved as a matter of law."

Notes

1. When the categories have been abolished, the landowner is still not liable unless he is negligent. E.g., *Senkus v. Moore,* 535 S.E.2d 724 (W. Va. 2000). Do you believe there are any situations that cannot be justly resolved by applying the prudent person standard? Can you give an example?

2.   The Kansas Court has now accepted a reasonable care standard for licensees, but back in 1982, in *Britt v. Allen County Community Junior College*, 230 Kan. 502, 638 P.2d 914 (1982), that court was strongly reaffirming its commitment to the old ways. It quoted at length from Hawkins, *Premises Liability After Repudiation of the Status Categories: Allocation of Judge and Jury Functions*, [1981] UTAH L. REV. 15 (1981). Among other points the court made by reference to Professor Hawkins were these:(1) A survey of 80 cases in jurisdictions that abolished the status categories showed that in 30 of them judges ruled for defendants as a matter of law; (2) in most of the cases surveyed, the outcome would be the same under either the *Rowland* rule or the traditional status-of-entrant analysis. (3) Professor Hawkins agreed with an earlier article by Professor James Henderson, arguing in effect that "structure" was needed to fix the limits of liability and that a reasonable prudent person rule would be merely a conduit funneling all cases to the jury room.

3.   If the result is the same whether the status categories are used or not, what considerations would dictate your choice of one approach or the other? Does the conceptual "conduit" argument conflict with the findings that even under the *Rowland* approach a high percentage of plaintiffs still suffered directed verdicts?

4.   Will new problems arise in the jurisdictions abolishing the status categories? What should be done with the "firemen's rule" in jurisdictions that have abolished the status categories and also the assumed risk doctrine?

§ 5.   RECREATIONAL USES: RE–CREATION OF THE STATUS CATEGORIES

1.   *Recreational use statutes.* Most states have now passed statutes dealing with "recreational users" on private land and waters. The gist of these is to retain the landowners' special immunities as to any non-paying recreational user. The Michigan statute, M.C.L.A. § 324.73301 imposes liability only for "gross negligence or willful and wanton misconduct of the owner, tenant or lessee." It applies to "a person who is on the lands of another without paying … a valuable consideration for the purpose of fishing, hunting, trapping, camping, hiking, sightseeing, motorcycling, snowmobiling, or any other outdoor recreational use, with or without permission…." The original statute has been expanded to similarly restrict the redress available to invitees on a farm to buy produce.

California's version provides:

An owner of any estate in real property … owes no duty of care to keep the premises safe for entry or use by others for any recreational purpose or to give any warning of hazardous conditions, uses of, structures, or activities on such premises to persons entering for such purpose except as provided in this section.

CAL. CIV. CODE § 846. A duty of due care is owed under this section to those who have paid to enter and also those who are "expressly invited rather than merely permitted." Otherwise liability is only for "willful or malicious failure to guard or warn against a dangerous condition, use, structure or activity." Recreational purpose is defined to include many of the activities mentioned in the Michigan statute and others, such as sport parachuting, spelunking and even "viewing or enjoying historical . . . scenic . . . or scientific sites."

2. *Theory of the statutes.* Although the motives for the statutes were undoubtedly associated with a desire to protect landowners from suits and judgments, the *theory* erected for these statutes was that they were being enacted to limit liability in order to encourage landowners to make land available for recreation in a world becoming increasingly crowded. The theory has backfired in some states. In *Crawford v. Tilley*, 780 P.2d 1248 (Utah 1989) the court held that the protections of the statute could not be invoked unless the landowner actually made the land available for public recreation; consequently unpermitted users in the defendant's locked cabin were not barred by the statute. In *Ferres v. City of New Rochelle*, 68 N.Y.2d 446, 510 N.Y.S.2d 57, 502 N.E.2d 972 (1986) the backfire was ignited because the premises were in use as a municipal park. "It would be contrary to reason to assume that the Legislature could have intended that the statute apply in circumstances where neither the basic purpose of the statute, nor, indeed, any purposes could be served–as in the case of the supervised park here where the municipality has already held its recreational facility open to the public and needs no encouragement to do so. . . ."

3. *Constitutionality.* Could recreational use statutes be upheld in states that have already ruled guest statutes to be unconstitutional? Remember that one reason given for automobile guest statutes was that they would encourage hospitality. That sounds a great deal like the encouragement supposedly offered by recreational use statutes. We have seen that the California Court found the guest statute to be unconstitutional and that the hospitality purpose did not save it, since not all non-paying persons were treated alike. Interestingly enough, recreational use statutes have been upheld against constitutional attack. *E.g., Lostritto v. Southern Pacific Transp. Co.*, 73 Cal.App.3d 737, 140 Cal.Rptr. 905 (1977) (constitutional as against equal protection challenge, but not discussing the guest statutes or the decision holding them unconstitutional). See JOSEPH PAGE, THE LAW OF PREMISES LIABILITY § 5.23 (2d ed. 1988).

4. *Scope of recreational use statutes.* Many statutes failed to provide solutions for some obvious problems. If a statute says nothing on the point, what should be done about the following?

   a. The plaintiff child is injured by an attractive nuisance on recreational lands. See Comment, *Tort Liability and Recreational Use of Land*, 28 BUFFALO L. REV. 767 (1979).

   b. The plaintiff is injured on public land such as a park or lake. *Monteville v. Terrebonne Parish Consolidated Government*, 567 So.2d 1097 (La.1990) (statute does not cover); *Sega v. State*, 60 N.Y.2d 183, 456 N.E.2d 1174, 469 N.Y.S.2d 51 (1983) (statute covers).

   c.   The plaintiff is injured on a public highway inside a public forest or on a navigable river that runs through recreational lands. Cf. *Bledsoe v. Goodfarb (Salt River Valley Water Users Ass'n)*, 170 Ariz. 256, 823 P.2d 1264 (1991) (under statute applicable only to agricultural, range, mining and forest lands, private roadways in such lands were not within the statute).

   d.   The plaintiff is injured at the defendant's home or business rather than on a rural tract associated with hunting, fishing or other recreational uses. New Jersey courts originally held that the statute only protected large rural and unimproved tracts, but the legislature amended the statute twice to cover unimproved "premises". See N.J.S.A. 2A:42A–3. What about injury on a dam that created a recreational-use lake? *Stone v. York Haven Power Co.*, 561 Pa. 189, 749 A.2d 452 (2000) (statutory immunity covers lake but not dam).

   e.   The plaintiff is injured when she is on hotel lands both for recreational purposes and to eat lunch at the hotel as a business invitee. *Crichfield v. Grand Wailea Company,* 93 Hawai'i 477, 6 P.3d 349 (2000) (statute does not protect hotel where the plaintiff had business as one of her purposes).

   5.   An early and thorough piece on recreational use statutes is Note, 3 WM. MITCH. L. REV. 117 (1977). See also John C. Barrett, *Good Sports and Bad Lands*, 53 WASH. L. REV. 1 (1977); Comment, *Wisconsin's Recreational Use Statute*, 66 MARQ. L. REV. 312 (1983) (collecting law of many states).

§ 6. LESSORS

PAGELSDORF v. SAFECO INSURANCE CO. OF AMERICA

Supreme Court of Wisconsin, 1979.
91 Wis.2d 734, 284 N.W.2d 55.

CALLOW, JUSTICE.

[Mahnke owned a two-story, two-family duplex. The upper unit was rented to the Blattners and had two balconies. The railing on one had been replaced, but the one in question was the original wooden railing, composed of 2 x 4s parallel to the floor and 2 x 2 spacers perpendicular to the floor. This was secured by nails to upright 4 x 4s at each end. Mr. Blattner left his family and thereafter Mrs. Blattner moved her children out and made arrangements for her brothers to remove her furniture. The brothers secured the aid of Pagelsdorf in moving heavier items. Pagelsdorf lowered a box spring down over the side of the balcony. When he placed his hands on the railing to straighten up afterwards, the railing gave way and he fell to the ground. He claims for the injuries he suffered in the fall. Inspection showed that the railing assembly had dry rot and would not hold well, but this had not been apparent to the eye.

There was evidence that the defendant-lessor had contracted to keep the premises in repair, but also evidence, seemingly accepted by the jury, that this was limited to repair of known or reported defects. The trial judge charged the jury that Mahnke owed no duty to discover dangers of which he was unaware, and the jury found for the defendant.]

[W]ith certain exceptions, a landlord is not liable for injuries to his tenants and their visitors resulting from defects in the premises. The general rule of nonliability was based on the concept of a lease as a conveyance of property and the consequent transfer of possession and control of the premises to the tenant.

There are exceptions to this general rule of nonliability. The landlord is liable for injuries to the tenant or his visitor caused by a dangerous condition if he contracts to repair defects, or if, knowing of a defect existing at the time the tenant took possession, he conceals it from a tenant who could not reasonably be expected to discover it. Additionally, the general rule is not applicable where the premises are leased for public use, or are retained in the landlord's control, or where the landlord negligently makes repairs. The rule of nonliability persists despite a decided trend away from application of the general rule and toward expansion of its exceptions.

None of the exceptions to the general rule are applicable to the facts of this case. The premises were not leased for public use, nor was the porch within Mahnke's control, nor did he negligently repair the railing. The plaintiffs argue that Mahnke contracted to repair defects; but according to Mrs. Blattner's testimony, Mahnke's promise extended only to items the Blattners reported as being in disrepair.... Finally, the concealed-defect exception does not apply because there was no evidence that the dry rot existed in 1969 when the Blattners moved in....

Therefore, if we were to follow the traditional rule, Pagelsdorf was not entitled to an instruction that Mahnke owed him a duty of ordinary care. We believe, however, that the better public policy lies in the abandonment of the general rule of nonliability and the adoption of a rule that a landlord is under a duty to exercise ordinary care in the maintenance of the premises."

Notes

1. *Changing concepts of leases*. The traditional view is that a lease is a conveyance of land. The lessee is an "owner" of the land in question for the period of the lease. Thus the lessor has no more responsibility for the upkeep of the land than any other person who conveys land. A corollary rule is that the landlord owes no more to the tenant's guests than he owes to the tenant himself.

Pagelsdorf and several other decisions have departed from the traditional rules by imposing upon the landlord the duty to exercise ordinary care to the tenant or those on the premises by virtue of the tenant's rights. See *e.g., Favreau v. Miller*, 156 Vt. 222, 591 A.2d 68 (1991). In *Antwaun A. v.*

Heritage Mutual Ins. Co., 228 Wis.2d 44, 596 N.W.2d 456 (1999) the Wisconsin court held that a landlord who did not actually know of lead paint used in his buildings but who was notified of peeling paint in a building constructed before lead paint was banned, was under a specific duty to test for lead.

2. The common law limits on duty and the "exceptions" to that rule are highly consistent with the conveyance theory of a lease. The whole topic, as well as a good deal of other material concerning the law of lessor and lessee, is covered in an extensive article on the subject, Jean C. Love, *Landlord's Liability for Defective Premises: Caveat Lessee, Negligence, or Strict Liability?*, 1975 Wis. L. Rev. 19, cited below as Love.

3. *Undisclosed latent defects known to lessor.* Knowing that a floor-board is loose and that someone may trip on it, the lessor leases a house without a warning. The defect is "latent," that is, not readily noticeable. The tenant trips on the board and causes a visitor to fall as well. Both have an action against the lessor for negligence. Some courts would now go further and hold the lessor liable for negligence if he knew facts from which the defect would be directly inferable. Once the tenant learns of the defect, the lessor's potential for liability is at an end, both to the tenant and to third persons. See Love, supra, 50–52.

4. *Premises leased for admission of public.* Lessor leases a building to Tenant for use as a dance hall, warning Tenant that the entrance stair is dangerous. Tenant agrees to repair the entrance, but does not do so. One of Tenant's customers is injured on the dangerous entryway. Courts have held the landlord liable in spite of the tenant's knowledge of the danger and his agreement to repair it, on the ground that the lessor knew the premises were leased for public use. There is some debate about what constitutes "public use" under this exception. See Love, supra, 53–54.

5. *Covenant to repair.* The lessor leases an apartment and covenants in the lease to keep it in repair. The lessor fails to use reasonable care to keep a hot water heater in repair. It deteriorates and eventually explodes, causing injury to a tenant and the tenant's social guest. The lessor is liable for tort damages. Under the earlier view, still followed by many courts, the lessor is liable only to the tenant for breach of the covenant and then only for "contract damages," based on the diminished value of the premises and not on personal injury. See Love, supra, 57–63.

6. *Negligent repairs.* The lessor, though under no contractual or other obligation to do so, undertakes to repair a porch rail and does it negligently. As a result the rail gives way when the tenant's child leans on it. The lessor is liable. The affirmative action is emphasized in imposing this liability. See Love, supra, 63–65.

7. *Premises in common use.* The lessor of an apartment building maintains stairways, hallways, and sidewalks for the use of all tenants. The lessor, not exercising reasonable care, waxes the hallway floors with a dangerously slippery wax and a tenant slips and falls on it. The lessor is liable. This is sometimes referred to as the common passageway rule, but it is not limited to "passageways." It covers any place reserved in the lessor's control but available for the tenants' use. Some jurisdictions limit this rule

by the provision that the lessor is not obliged to provide illumination in common passageways or to remove snow and ice. See Love, supra, 65–68.

8. *Implied warranty of habitability.* The preceding paragraphs summarize the traditional "exceptions" under which lessors could be held liable for negligence. Courts now often recognize a new liability–an implied warranty of habitability. This could conceivably impose strict liability, but courts have reserved the implied warranty theory for breach of contract damages. They insist that personal injury claims are best adjudicated under the law of negligence. See *Antwaun A. v. Heritage Mutual Ins. Co.,* 228 Wis.2d 44, 596 N.W.2d 456 (1999).

9. *Statutory duties.* Statutes must be consulted. Some set standards or impose liability for specific defects such as the knowing use of lead-based paint that poisons a tenant's child. See *Gore v. People's Savings Bank,* 235 Conn. 360, 665 A.2d 1341 (1995).

10. Was the common law scheme of rights and duties unfair to the tenant or others rightfully on the premises in the same way that, arguably, the licensee-trespasser rules were unfair?

Palsgraf taught that negligence toward one person or class was not necessarily negligence toward another. It may well be that many judges had previously assumed the contrary and that the prolonged reign of the licensee-trespasser categories reflected the fear of such judges that liability without the categories would be unduly extended.

Suppose, for example, you leave the children's marbles lying loosely and not too obviously on the front steps. You are negligent because you expect a business visitor. Before the business visitor arrives, however, a burglar makes an appearance, steps on a marble and does a classic fall. Suppose there were no licensee-trespasser rules; and suppose that Cardozo had lost in *Palsgraf,* with the result that negligence toward one person was treated as negligence toward anyone who was actually injured as a result. In that case, the burglar would recover because negligence toward the expected business visitor would be negligence to the burglar as well. If, before Cardozo decided *Palsgraf,* judges had generally assumed that negligence toward X might entail liability to Y, whose injury could not be foreseen, you can see why the judge might want to adopt licensee-trespasser categories. Those categories would exclude recovery by some of the same plaintiffs that *Palsgraf* excludes, and they would exclude recovery by our burglar.

The advent of *Palsgraf,* with its notion that negligence is focused on a particular person or class of persons, may, then, have made the landowner categories somewhat less important. In this way, *Palsgraf* may have been a remote cause of *Rowland*!

Problems

Paton v. Missouri & Atlantic Railway

Paton lived in a small rural house adjacent to a railroad track. A friend of his, Talbot, lived on the other side of the track. The two men sometimes met at or near the track and drank together in the evenings. One evening in July they met at the track and began drinking. Sometime later Talbot awoke and realized that a train was approaching. He did not see Paton in the dark and the train's light was not bright. After the train passed, however, he found Paton near the track. The lower part of his right leg had been severed by the passing train. Paton's lawyer showed: (1) the engineer of the train said he kept a lookout but never saw Paton or anyone on the track, (2) the train was moving slowly and could have stopped within a very short distance, and (3) the headlight was out of repair and fell short of standards prescribed by a regulatory agency. Although all states would recognize a duty on the part of railroads to keep a reasonable lookout at public crossings, only a few states impose a duty of lookout for trespassers along the track. *If Paton's injury did not occur in a state requiring a lookout for trespassers, did the railroad owe him any duty?*

Christie v. Embry Corp.

Christie, a girl of 11 years, entered a garbage dump maintained by the Embry Corporation on its own land. She was looking for any kind of old toys or comic books. Walking on what appeared to be a solid surface, she suddenly sank through and was burned on hot embers below. In her action against Embry Corp., she proved that in past times Embry had had to call the fire department to put out fires that spontaneously flared in the dump. She also proved that other children often went there looking for comics and toys, that there was no fence and that there were many houses nearby. This was all the proof. *Can she get to the jury?*

Paget v. Owen

Paget asked Owen for permission to enter Owen's large farm to fish in one of the ponds. Owen agreed to this. Owen believed from the location involved, that Paget intended to take the north road on Owen's property. The north road had been undermined by flooding of a creek, though Owen did not know this. The south road had also been undermined by flooding of a different creek, and Owen was well aware of this. Paget drove into the farm land to fish the next day. Although the road appeared to be safe, it caved in where it had been undermined by the flooding. Paget's car overturned and he was injured. *Did Owen breach any duty? Does it matter which road Paget took?*

In re Claims of Picklesimer, Patrick and Plangent

The facts our law firm has after an initial interview with our client, Herman Picklesimer, are as follows:

Picklesimer was driving in a generally southerly direction on highway 101 in an area with which he was only vaguely familiar. It was about 7:30 at night and dark. The road bends slightly to the right about a mile south of the town of Roan. The road also is rising slightly at this point, with the result that headlights are aimed slightly upward. At the point where the road bends to the right, a private unpaved road on the property of James P. Dalzell continues straight ahead. There are no markers, signs, reflectors or other indicators of the curve. Mr. Picklesimer says that there was not even any center stripe and that the road was black. The result of all this was that with his lights forced slightly upward by the road grade, he did not appreciate the fact that it bent to the right. He continued straight until he dropped off the highway and headed downhill on the Dalzell private road. At this point he realized his error, and tried to steer back onto the road, but this compounded the problem and he turned his car over.

According to the police report a car driven by James Patrick was proceeding northerly on the same road at the same time and place. Patrick became confused or at least he tried to react when–according to him–Mr. Picklesimer crossed the road in his path as he proceeded straight onto the Dalzell property. Patrick steered to his left, lost control in the gravel on his left side (the west side) of the road and crashed into a tree some distance from the road. His passenger, Blanche Plangent, suffered head wounds when she hit the windshield. Patrick himself was also injured.

Picklesimer was not aware of any of this. He apparently suffered a concussion and certainly he was confused. He wandered away from the highway on Dalzell's land. He has no recollection of this, but the police report and emergency room report indicate that in the dark he fell into an excavation on Dalzell's land. This was not lighted or marked in any way. In this he broke his hip. He is 68 years old and there were complications in hospital when a nurse, misreading the doctor's drug order, gave the wrong drug, which in turn created complications when Mr. Picklesimer was under anesthetic. He has emerged with a slight speech impairment, though at this stage we are not sure whether this is psychological or whether it is a result of the hospital mishap. The doctor is Dr. Daniel Doubs and the nurse is Mr. Paul Hadini. The hospital was the Murphy Medical Center in the town of Roan.

We should outline our basic claims and the probable defenses and prepare to investigate as needed.

GENERAL REFERENCES ON LANDOWNERS, LESSORS: JOSEPH PAGE, THE LAW OF PREMISES LIABILITY (2d ed. 1988); R. SCHOSHINSKI, AMERICAN LAW OF LANDLORD AND TENANT (1980 and Supp.); DOBBS ON TORTS §§ 231–241 (landowners generally); §§ 284–287 (firefighters' rule) (2000).

Chapter 11

DUTIES OF MEDICAL AND OTHER PROFESSIONALS

§ 1. TRADITIONAL DUTIES OF HEALTH CARE PROVIDERS IN TRADITIONAL PRACTICE

WALSKI v. TIESENGA

Supreme Court of Illinois, 1978.
72 Ill.2d 249, 21 Ill.Dec. 201, 381 N.E.2d 279.

KLUCZYNSKI, JUSTICE.

[Defendants operated to remove plaintiff's thyroid. A well-recognized risk of a thyroidectomy is that the recurrent laryngeal nerves, which run through the thyroid, may be damaged, with resulting loss of voice. One solution to the problem is to locate the nerves and segregate them before removal of the thyroid. In this case, however, there was a great deal of scar tissue present as a result of earlier operations and treatments and the defendants, instead of locating the nerve, made a wide cut so as to avoid the area where the nerve was thought to be. In fact they cut the nerve and plaintiff's vocal chords are paralyzed. The trial court directed a verdict for the defendants and the intermediate appellate court affirmed.]

Dr. David M. Berger testified as an expert witness on plaintiff's behalf. . . . His direct testimony concerning acceptable procedures for thyroid surgery was that "in my feeling the standards by which I feel are acceptable practice, one must identify and preserve the recurrent laryngeal nerves on all occasions." On cross-examination Dr. Berger testified that there are always options available in surgery but that in his own mind it was not a proper option to skirt the left recurrent laryngeal nerve. He stated he could not testify generally but only "on the basis of my own opinion as to what I consider a proper option." When asked on cross-examination if there existed a contemporary school of surgeons that will skirt the nerve when they encounter a host of adhesions, Dr. Berger responded that "in the institutions in which I trained that is not the teaching. And I can't speak for other institutions or other areas of training. I can only speak for my own." Defense counsel read a quotation to Dr. Berger from a medical textbook which indicated that there existed a certain amount of controversy in the medical community concerning deliberate exposure of the laryngeal nerve. The quotation concluded with the remark that the situation remained one in which each surgeon will find the approach which suits him best. Dr. Berger indicated that he did not fully agree with that statement, but indicated the decision whether or not to expose the nerve depends on the surgeon and the technique and care he uses. Dr. Berger stated that "[e]verybody who is a certified surgeon doesn't use the same methods, obviously."

One element of a cause of action for medical malpractice is proof of the standard of care by which the defendant physician's conduct is to be measured.... [T]he appellate decisions in this State have held that the plaintiff in a medical malpractice action generally must establish the standard of care through expert testimony. The plaintiff must then prove that, judged in the light of these standards, the doctor was unskillful or negligent and that his want of skill or care caused the injury to the plaintiff. Generally, expert testimony is needed to support a charge of malpractice because jurors are not skilled in the practice of medicine and would find it difficult without the help of medical evidence to determine any lack of necessary scientific skill on the part of the physician. However, in those situations where the physician's conduct is so grossly negligent or the treatment so common that a layman could readily appraise it, the appellate decisions indicate that no expert testimony is necessary.... A requirement that the standard of care be established through expert testimony except where the common knowledge of laymen is sufficient to recognize or infer negligence is broadly recognized throughout the country....

Plaintiff here had the burden of establishing that the defendant doctors were guilty of malpractice. She failed, however, to introduce evidence of the standard of care to which the defendants were bound to adhere. Plaintiff's expert, Dr. Berger, testified only concerning his own personal preference for isolating the laryngeal nerve under the facts presented to him in the hypothetical question. He at no time testified that there was a generally accepted medical standard of care or skill which required the identification of the laryngeal nerve under the circumstances....

The appellate courts have held that the testimony of the defendant doctor may be sufficient to establish the standard of care , but it is apparent that the defendants' testimony here did not indicate a standard at variance with their actual conduct. Dr. Tiesenga testified that because of prior surgery on and treatment of plaintiff's thyroid, it would have been unwise to attempt to isolate her laryngeal nerve. The better practice, according to Dr. Tiesenga's testimony, was to skirt the area where the nerve might possibly be. Dr. Walsh concurred. When confronted with a statement from a recognized treatise that the first step in performing a thyroidectomy is to expose and identify the recurrent laryngeal nerve, Dr. Tiesenga agreed with the statement only as a general proposition. He testified that where there has been prior surgery and treatment, it is not always good practice to follow the procedure indicated in the treatise. . . .

It is insufficient for plaintiff to establish a prima facie case merely to present testimony of another physician that he would have acted differently from the defendant, since medicine is not an exact science. It is rather a profession which involves the exercise of individual judgment within the framework of established procedures. Differences in opinion are consistent with the exercise of due care. . . .

For the above reasons the judgment of the appellate court is affirmed.

Notes

1. *Medical "standards."* The medical standard discussed in the opinions seldom sounds like a "standard" comparable to the standard of the reasonable prudent person. The term standard suggests a measure or benchmark of some generality. Medical "standards" almost always reflect particular customs or procedures used under very particular circumstances, like the "wide-cut" procedure in *Walski*. The medical "standard" is understood as a rule for the very circumstances involved in the plaintiff's case.

2. "Dr. Roland was performing a laparoscopic procedure on Oakden . . . to remove her gall bladder when the electrosurgical irrigating suction probe that he was using became bent and inadvertently fired, causing a small defect in Oakden's common hepatic duct." This in turn caused further injury. The plaintiff sought to introduce evidence that, in the opinion of at least one other surgeon, Dr. Roland was insufficiently experienced to perform the laproscopic procedure. Is this sufficient to get the plaintiff to the jury on the negligence issue? *Oakden v. Roland,* 988 P.2d 1057 (Wyo.1999).

3. *Instructions.* If the proof is sufficient to get the plaintiff to the jury, the instructions must reflect the medical, not the ordinary care, standard. Instructions often state that the physician must possess the learning, skill and ability of other physicians, must exercise reasonable care in the use of this knowledge and skill and must use his or her best judgment in the care of the patient. It is common also to hear the trial judge emphasize the defense side of the case by telling the jury that the physician is not liable for an honest mistake or bona fide error or that the physician is not expected to be infallible or that he does not guarantee results. These instructions have come under attack by plaintiffs' lawyers as unduly emphasizing the defendant's side of the case or as misleading the jury. The "honest mistake" and "no guarantee" instructions have been rejected in a number of cases. See *McKinnis v. Women and Infants Hosp. of Rhode Island,* 749 A.2d 574 (R.I.2000).

4. *Medical testimony.* In a few obvious cases, as where the surgeon amputates the wrong limb, expert testimony is not required. Otherwise, expert medical testimony is usually required to establish the medical standard of care. If the plaintiff furnishes no such testimony, or it is inadequate to show the standard, the judge will direct a verdict for the defendant.

5. *More than one medical "standard" or practice.* Suppose that among doctors in the relevant medical community, the majority believe that human bite wounds should not be closed with stitches. But suppose that some doctors believe to the contrary, that the wound should be stitched and treated with antibiotics. A patient suffers serious infection when his doctor closes the wound. What is the standard? "Where competent medical authority is divided, a physician will not be held responsible if in the exercise of his judgment he followed a course of treatment advocated by a considerable number of recognized and respected professionals in his given area of expertise." *Sinclair v. Block,* 534 Pa. 563, 633 A.2d 1137 (1993).

6. *Rejecting The T.J. Hooper.* Medical standards are not to be found in an authoritative book. For the most part, the medical standard of care is the practice of the relevant medical community. Does the medical standard rule reject the rule about custom in *T.J. Hooper?*

7. *Rejecting reasonable care.* Medical standards will often reflect reasonable care. Notice that under the reasonable person standard, a professional practitioner would be obliged to exercise the skill and use all the knowledge he actually has, even if that is more skill or knowledge than other people have. So the medical care standard is not different from the reasonable person standard in this respect.

But the medical standard might require *less* care than the reasonable person standard. To see why, suppose Dr. Berger had testified that, as a matter of scientific fact, the risk of severing the nerve is doubled when the wide cut procedure is used as compared to the nerve identification procedure and that there are no corresponding advantages to the wide cut procedure. That testimony seems to be important under a *Carroll Towing* or reasonable care standard, because it shows an increase of risk. But it does not seem relevant at all, much less determinative, under the medical standard, because it does not address what doctors actually do or what they profess as the standard.

8. *Accepting reasonable care standards.* A few decisions have indicated that in extreme cases, the reasonable person standard might be used, but these are quite limited. See *United Blood Services, Div. of Blood Systems, Inc. v. Quintana,* 827 P.2d 509 (Colo.1992); *Helling v. Carey,* 83 Wash. 2d 514, 519 P.2d 981, 67 A.L.R.3d 175 (1974) (cheap, efficient test for glaucoma should be given with opthalmic exam even if that was not the practice of the medical community); *Nowatske v. Osterloh,* 198 Wis.2d 419, 543 N.W.2d 265 (Wis. 1996) (stating that Wisconsin uses a reasonable care standard, although this is applied with due regard to the state of medicine at the time).

9. *Non-medical negligence of health care providers.* Suppose that you, as a hospital patient, slip and fall because the hospital left a slippery substance on the floor. Would you be required to prove the standard of care for hospitals by expert testimony? See *Self v. Executive Committee Georgia Baptist Convention,* 245 Ga. 548, 266 S.E.2d 168 (1980) (not a claim of medical malpractice, no requirement of expert testimony). Consider the need for expert testimony in these cases: (a) A doctor knows a patient is dangerous but fails to warn his coworkers. *Powell v. Catholic Medical Ctr.,* 749 A.2d 301 (N.H.2000). (b) A schizophrenic patient simply walks out of a hospital which was obliged to watch her closely because she was dangerous to herself.

She encounters a man in a park she believes to be either Jesus or a prophet, and proceeds to have sexual relations with him. *D.P. v. Wrangell Gen. Hospital*, 5 P.3d 225 (Alaska 2000). (c) The same facts except that the hospital did not know the patient was a danger to herself and the plaintiff contends it should have known.

10. *Misrepresentation or contract breach claims.* Would you be required to prove a medical standard of care if you asserted that your injury resulted from a doctor's misrepresentation or breach of contract? In *Osborn v. Irwin Memorial Blood Bank*, 5 Cal.App.4th 234, 7 Cal.Rptr.2d 101 (1992) the parents attempted to arrange to donate their own blood and that of friends for the benefit of their child who was to have surgery later. The defendant's employee erroneously told them they could donate blood but could NOT reserve it for their child's use. Accordingly, other blood was used in the February, 1983 transfusions. The child contracted the AIDS virus from the blood transfusions that were used. The court said these facts would show negligent misrepresentation which would be actionable if it is a proximate cause of the harm.

VERGARA v. DOAN

Supreme Court of Indiana, 1992.
593 N.E.2d 185.

SHEPARD, CHIEF JUSTICE.

Javier Vergara was born on May 31, 1979, at the Adams Memorial Hospital in Decatur, Indiana. His parents, Jose and Concepcion, claimed that negligence on the part of Dr. John Doan during Javier's delivery caused him severe and permanent injuries. A jury returned a verdict for Dr. Doan and the plaintiffs appealed. The Court of Appeals affirmed. Plaintiffs seek transfer, asking us to abandon Indiana's modified locality rule. We grant transfer to examine the standard of care appropriate for medical malpractice cases.

In most negligence cases, the defendant's conduct is tested against the hypothetical reasonable and prudent person acting under the same or similar circumstances. In medical malpractice cases, however, Indiana has applied a more specific articulation of this standard. It has become known as the modified locality rule: "The standard of care ... is that degree of care, skill, and proficiency which is commonly exercised by ordinarily careful, skillful, and prudent [physicians], at the time of the operation and in similar localities." Appellants have urged us to abandon this standard, arguing that the reasons for the modified locality rule are no longer applicable in today's society. We agree.

The modified locality rule is a less stringent version of the strict locality rule, which measured the defendant's conduct against that of other doctors in the same community. When the strict locality rule originated in the late 19th century, there was great disparity between the medical opportunities, equipment, facilities, and training in rural and urban communities. Travel and communication between rural and urban communities were difficult. The locality rule was intended to prevent the inequity that would result from holding rural doctors to the same standards as doctors in large cities.

With advances in communication, travel, and medical education, the disparity between rural and urban health care diminished and justification for the locality rule waned. The strict locality rule also had two major drawbacks, especially as applied to smaller communities. First, there was a scarcity of local doctors to serve as expert witnesses against other local doctors. Second, there was the possibility that practices among a small group of doctors would establish a local standard of care below that which the law required. In response to these changes and criticisms, many courts adopted a modified locality rule, expanding the area of comparison to similar localities. . . .

Use of a modified locality rule has not quelled the criticism. Many of the common criticisms seem valid. The modified locality rule still permits a lower standard of care to be exercised in smaller communities because other similar communities are likely to have the same care. We also spend time and money on the difficulty of defining what is a similar community. The rule also seems inconsistent with the reality of modern medical practice. The disparity between small town and urban medicine continues to lessen with advances in communication, transportation, and education. In addition, widespread insurance coverage has provided patients with more choice of doctors and hospitals by reducing the financial constraints on the consumer in selecting caregivers. . . . Many states describe the care a physician owes without emphasizing the locality of practice. Today we join these states and adopt the following: a physician must exercise that degree of care, skill, and proficiency exercised by reasonably careful, skillful, and prudent practitioners in the same class to which he belongs, acting under the same or similar circumstances. Rather than focusing on different standards for different communities, this standard uses locality as but one of the factors to be considered in determining whether the doctor acted reasonably. Other relevant considerations would include advances in the profession, availability of facilities, and whether the doctor is a specialist or general practitioner.

. . . Plaintiff was permitted to present his expert witness, Dr. Harlan Giles, even though he was from Pittsburgh, Pennsylvania (not Decatur or a similar locality). Dr. Giles testified regarding his experience and knowledge of the standard of care in communities similar to Decatur and in hospitals similar in size to Adams County Memorial Hospital. He testified that in his opinion, considering all the factors incident to the pregnancy and birth of Javier Vergara, the standard of care required Dr. Doan to have delivered the baby by cesarean section. He stated that this opinion was based on the standard of care as it existed in 1979 in Decatur or similar communities. He also testified that the failure to have either an anesthesiologist or a qualified nurse anesthetist present at the delivery was a breach of the national standard of care for hospitals the size of Adams County Memorial and smaller. Evidently the jury disagreed with Dr. Giles and found Dr. Doan's conduct reasonable under the circumstances.

We regard our new formulation of a doctor's duty as a relatively modest alteration of existing law. It is unlikely to have changed the way this case was tried. We are satisfied that an instruction without the locality language would not lead a new jury to a different conclusion.

Therefore, we hold that giving instruction 23 was harmless and does not require reversal. . . .

Notes

1. *The local medical standard and problems of testimony.* Adoption of a local standard means that only a local physician, or one who knows what the local standard is, can testify against the defendant-doctor. What problems does this raise for the plaintiff? In *Holmes v. Elliott*, 443 So.2d 825 (Miss. 1983) the plaintiff suffered complications resulting from a hysterectomy, allegedly because it was performed too soon after another medical procedure. In her action against the surgeon brought in Mississippi where the surgery had been performed, Dr. Daniel was her medical witness. He was then practicing in Oklahoma City and had performed over five hundred hysterectomies. He had been attached at various times to hospitals in Bethesda, Guam, Oakland, Annapolis and Georgia. Part of his testimony is: "Q. But you know that the standard of medical care and the way treatment is rendered in Lumberton is the same as it is in Oklahoma? A. It should be, yes. Q. Do you know whether it is or not? A. The standard of care, as defined from a medical standpoint, and from my understanding from a legal standpoint also, is the same throughout the country." Under a local or statewide standard of care is Dr. Daniel's testimony that the defendant violated the standard sufficient to get the plaintiff to the jury?

2. *The national medical standard.* It is sometimes argued that adoption a standard like *Vergara's* would be unfair to doctors in small towns, who might not have the latest equipment. Would a national medical standard be likely to require a small-town doctor to own CAT scan technology? What about the reasonable person standard? In *Hall v. Hilbun*, 466 So.2d 856 (Miss.1985) the Mississippi Court adopted a national standard governing the physician's care and skill but not the resources. If you were a small-town doctor without equipment, what would you do about a patient who needed a CAT scan?

NOTE: SPECIALISTS

1. *Specialists.* The medical profession is organized to a large extent (as the legal profession is not) around recognized specialties. Examples include orthopedics, internal medicine, obstetrics and gynecology, and radiology. Medical specialization usually entails several years of study following medical school and success in an examination administered by the "board" which certifies specialists.

2. *The local standard.* Specialists are held to the standard of their specialties; thus an orthopedic surgeon is held to a higher standard in

setting a fracture than a family practitioner. It is often assumed or held that the relevant medical community for them is the community of specialists, not a geographical community. *Wall v. Stout*, 310 N.C. 184, 311 S.E.2d 571 (1984).

3. *Non-specialist expert testimony.* Could a family practitioner testify against an orthopedic surgeon? Could an obstetrician testify against a radiologist? The answer logically ought to be "yes–provided the witness knows the relevant standard and can state it." Some courts exclude such testimony, others admit it, and still others admit it where the two specialities share common standards or procedures. See DOBBS ON TORTS § 246 (2000).

NOTE: NONMEDICAL PRACTITIONERS

1. *Standard.* Non-medical practitioners such as chiropractors and podiatrists, are permitted to practice according to their schools of belief. They are subject to the standards of the school they profess, not to medical standards. What if a naturopath diagnoses tonsillitis in a child and prescribes orange juice, but in fact the child has diphtheria and dies of it? Should a Christian Scientist practitioner, whose religion opposes medical treatment, be liable for treating a child with prayer when known and readily available medical treatment can save the child's life? In *Lundman v. McKown,* 530 N.W.2d 807 (Minn.App.1995), a child whose mother was a Christian Scientist died when the mother called in a Christian Science practitioner instead of a medical doctor. The practitioner would be held to the standard he professes–healing by prayer–in the case of an adult. Would it be different with a child? Is there a limit somewhere short of torture? In *Guerrero v. Smith,* 864 S.W.2d 797 (Tex.App.1993) the plaintiff alleged that a "homeopathic physician" injected the plaintiff's vagina with compounds not approved for human use, used unsterile instruments, and directed the plaintiff to drink her own urine, with horrible consequences. Does he escape responsibility on the ground that all this is within the homeopathic standard?

2. *Referral.* Medical practitioners must refer their patients to specialists when the standard of care so requires. When a *non*medical practitioner recognizes or should recognize that a patient has a medical problem, some courts hold that they must refer the patient to a medical doctor. *Kerkman v. Hintz,* 142 Wis.2d 404, 418 N.W.2d 795 (1988), however, held that referral is not required or even logically permissible. It is enough, the *Kerkman* court said, that the chiropractor cease treating a condition that lies outside his school of work. What about a church counselor who believes that the word of God is the only counseling anyone requires and for that reason does not refer a suicidal young man to different professional help? *Nally v. Grace Community Church of the Valley,* 47 Cal.3d 278, 763 P.2d 948, 253 Cal.Rptr. 97 (1988). What about a medical health care provider who morally opposes a needed abortion–must he advise the patient that an abortion is available and where? Cf. *Brownfield v. Daniel Freeman Marina Hospital*, 208 Cal.

App.3d 405, 256 Cal.Rptr. 240 (1989) (rape victim, duty to refer for pregnancy prevention supported in dictum).

———

HIRPA v. IHC HOSPITALS, INC., 948 P.2d 785 (Utah 1997). A patient in active labor at a hospital became unresponsive and her hands began to spasm. Her physician broadcast a "Code Blue" over the hospital intercom. Dr. Daines responded, entering the delivery room and taking over. Seventeen minutes later, the patient was dead. The surviving spouse sued Daines and others involved in a federal court. Daines moved for summary judgment. He invoked a statute covering medical providers: "No person licensed under this chapter . . . who in good faith renders emergency care at the scene of the emergency, shall be liable for any civil damages as a result of any acts or omissions by such person in rendering the emergency care." The federal court certified questions to the state court. One question asked whether the statute applied. *Held*, the statute applies. This was an emergency. The statute is intended to encourage aid without fear of liability, so the location of the emergency in a hospital instead of a roadside is irrelevant, so long as the physician had no preexisting duty to aid. It has no application, however, when the physician already had a duty to aid the patient, for in that case he needs no encouragement. Whether the doctor was under a preexisting duty to the patient could depend upon the doctor-patient relationship, his contractual duty to respond, hospital rules or other factors.

Notes

1.   All states have enacted some kind of Good Samaritan statute. The Utah statute provides a virtual immunity. Apparently even the grossly negligent doctor would be protected so long as he acted in "good faith."

2.   A slightly milder version of the Good Samaritan statute leaves open the possibility of liability for gross negligence, or for wanton conduct or intentional wrongdoing. E.g., N.C. GEN. STAT. § 20–166(d). The North Carolina statute applies to any person, not merely to health care providers.

3.   Some statutes appear to be based upon the idea that in an emergency, the physician will not have equipment and support needed. Consistent with this approach, some statutes withhold the immunity in hospital emergencies.

4.   One doctor has suggested that the immunity is not justified in hospital emergencies because even under the encouragement rationale of cases like *Hirpa*, hospital doctors are required by medical ethics and hospital rules to respond and hence need no encouragement. See Stewart R. Reuter, *Physicians as Good Samaritans*, 20 J. LEGAL MED. 157 (1999) (surveying many cases and statutes).

NOTE: OTHER PROFESSIONALS

1. *Nurses.* Courts now seem to assume that nurses are held to the standard of nurses in a similar practice. *Fein v. Permanente Medical Group*, 38 Cal.3d 137, 211 Cal.Rptr. 368, 695 P.2d 665 (1985). However, a medical doctor might be allowed to testify what that standard requires. See *Hall v. Sacred Heart Med. Cntr.*, 100 Wash.App. 53, 995 P.2d 621 (2000). Should the reverse be true? See *Sheffield v. Goodwin*, 740 So.2d 854 (Miss.1999)(plaintiff offered nurse practitioner as expert witness against dentist).

2. *Hospitals.* The present view seems to be that, in performing their own duties, hospitals owe a duty of reasonable care under national standards fixed by the Joint Commission on Accreditation of Hospitals. See DOBBS ON TORTS § 254 (2000).

3. *Other callings, occupations or activities.* Courts often state the prudent person standard of care by referring to the care that should be exercised by a reasonable person in the defendant's occupation or status as a shorthand way of referring to the circumstances. A court's reference to a reasonable and prudent dog owner is not meant to establish a different standard of care for dog owners.

4. *Architects, engineers, accountants and lawyers.* When courts refer to the standard for members of learned professions or skilled trades, however, reference to the custom or standard of the profession itself may be more than a way of loosely stating that the professional setting is part of the "circumstances" in a reasonable person standard. The result is that expert testimony may be required, not merely to establish a risk, but to establish that the risk was a violation of professional standards. For instance, in *Rentz v. Brown,* 219 Ga.App. 187, 464 S.E.2d 617 (1995) the court insisted that the standard of care for building contractors was the care and skill employed by other contractors under similar circumstances and that expert testimony was required to show that standard. Similar rules standards apply to accountants and lawyers. E.g., *Simko v. Blake*, 448 Mich. 648, 532 N.W.2d 842 (1995).

5. *Educational malpractice.* Educators may commit intentional torts (for example by an unprivileged spanking) or negligent torts (for example by failure to remove a dangerous condition on the school ground). In such cases the rules of intentional tort and the standard of the prudent person seem to govern. When the alleged educational malpractice is the product of training, testing, promotion, failure, or classification of the student, the courts have not merely provided the protective professional standard. Instead they have said there is little duty or none at all. *Ross v. Creighton University*, 957 F.2d 410 (7th Cir.1992); *Peter W. v. San Francisco Unified School District*, 60 Cal. App.3d 814, 131 Cal.Rptr. 854 (1976); *Hoffman v. Board of Education of New York*, 49 N.Y.2d 121, 424 N.Y.S.2d 376, 400 N.E.2d 317 (1979).

SMITH v. KNOWLES

Supreme Court of Minnesota, 1979.
281 N.W.2d 653.

SCOTT, JUSTICE.

This is an appeal by plaintiff, Clinton E. Smith, as trustee for the heirs of Diane Smith (his wife) and Baby Girl Smith (his stillborn child), from an order of the district court in Blue Earth County dismissing plaintiff's wrongful death actions against defendant, Dr. William David Knowles. The dismissals were granted, upon motion of defendant at the close of plaintiff's case, on the ground that the plaintiff failed to offer sufficient expert evidence for the jury to consider his claims of negligence and causation. We affirm.

The actions giving rise to this appeal arose from the deaths of Diane Smith and her unborn child. Both mother and child died as a result of toxemia of pregnancy, or "eclampsia."[1] These actions were commenced against Diane's attending physician, Dr. Knowles. Essentially, plaintiff claims that Dr. Knowles was negligent in failing to make a timely diagnosis of Diane's pre-eclampsia and that he was further negligent in his treatment of that condition once it was diagnosed.

[Mr. Smith testified that his wife suffered serious symptoms of nausea, blurred vision, headaches, chest pains and swelling in the second half of the pregnancy, with the symptoms becoming much worse in early February. There was evidence that such symptoms had been reported to Dr. Knowles in Mrs. Smith's regular visits. Dr. Knowles, however, testified that through the January visit, there were no danger signals and blood pressure and urine were normal.]

On February 13, 1974, Diane Smith awoke sick, but decided to go to work. After arriving at work, she called Dr. Knowles' office and was told to come in. Dr. Knowles testified that she complained of headache, nausea, vomiting and blurred vision. His examination of her revealed that she had edema, that her blood pressure was significantly elevated and that her urine was thick and brownish and had a plus-three albumin level. He testified that he then diagnosed pre-eclampsia and admitted her to the hospital. Mr. Smith, however, testified that his wife called him at work and asked him to come and pick her up at Dr. Knowles' office. He testified that when he arrived, Diane was crying and Dr. Knowles told him to take her home for "rest and medication." Mr. Smith claims Dr. Knowles admitted Diane to the hospital only after he urged the doctor to do so.

Diane was admitted to the hospital at approximately 11:45 a.m. Prior to her arrival, Dr. Knowles called the hospital and verbally ordered

---

1. Eclampsia is an extremely serious complication of pregnancy. It is the full development of a condition known as pre-eclamptic toxemia or pre-eclampsia. Pre-eclampsia is a complication arising in the latter half of pregnancy; it involves an increase in blood pressure, albumin in the urine, and the retention of fluid in the tissues. When pre-eclamptic patients develop convulsions, they are then designated as having eclampsia. 5B Lawyers Medical Cyclopedia, § 37.51(a).

that, at the nurse's discretion, Diane be given Tylenol with Codeine. That medication was never given. Dr. Knowles next spoke to hospital personnel at 1 p.m. He testified that Diane had not yet begun to convulse and that he ordered that she be given 10 milliliters of magnesium sulphate intramuscularly.[3] Dr. Knowles testified that, either while he was on the phone, or immediately after he hung up, but in either event after he had prescribed the magnesium sulphate, Diane suffered her first convulsion. The nurses' notes reflect only that both Dr. Knowles' second call and the convulsion happened at approximately 1 p.m. It is undisputed, however, that Diane did not receive any magnesium sulphate until after her first convulsion.

Dr. Knowles arrived at the hospital between 1:30 and 2 p.m. and, upon the recommendation of Dr. Eisenbeis (an internist), ordered that Diane receive additional magnesium sulphate intravenously. At 3:20 p.m., again on Dr. Eisenbeis' recommendation, Dr. Knowles ordered more magnesium sulphate for Diane. He assumed that all the magnesium sulphate ordered was administered. Diane was responsive after her first convulsion and complained of a headache, but lost consciousness around 2:30 p.m. At 6:40 p.m., Dr. Knowles called Dr. Howard, an obstetrician, and asked for his assistance. Late that evening, after the doctors could no longer hear fetal heart tones, Dr. Howard performed a Caesarean section and delivered a stillborn baby girl. Diane's condition continued to deteriorate following the operation. On February 19, the doctors administered an encephalogram and determined that Diane's brain had ceased functioning. Mr. Smith gave his permission for the doctors to discontinue artificial means of life support, and Diane expired.

At trial, plaintiff sought to show that Dr. Knowles was negligent in both his diagnosis and treatment of Diane's condition. The trial court concluded that plaintiff failed to present sufficient competent medical testimony to allow the case to go to the jury, and thus granted defendant's motion to dismiss. . . .

Clearly, expert testimony is crucial to plaintiff's claims. To establish a prima facie case in an action such as this, the plaintiff here must introduce expert testimony as to both the standard of care and the defendant doctor's departure from that standard .. Moreover, plaintiff's claims required expert testimony to show that Dr. Knowles' action or inaction was a direct cause of the decedents' deaths.

Here, plaintiff called no independent medical witnesses. Instead, he chose to prove his case through his cross-examination of Dr. Knowles and the introduction of excerpts from several recognized medical treatises.[5] The trial court carefully reviewed this evidence and concluded that it was legally insufficient. We agree.

---

3. Magnesium sulphate is recognized as being effective in the treatment of pre-eclampsia. It lowers blood pressure, increases urinary output and prevents convulsions without otherwise depressing the central nervous system.

5. Since the adoption of Rule 803(18). Minnesota Rules of Evidence, once proper foundation is established, learned treatises may be used as substantive evidence.

At trial, plaintiff called Dr. Knowles for cross-examination and asked him a series of hypothetical questions. Dr. Knowles was most forthright and candid in his answers. For example, he was asked:

"Q. Now, is it the standard of care and was it the standard of care back in late 1973 and '74 that where you have a condition of persistent headaches, blurred vision, fatigue, significant epigastric pain, and developing edema of the feet, that the physician managing the woman with those symptoms should suspect pre-eclampsia as a cause?"

He answered yes. He further testified that, when pre-eclampsia is suspected, it should be treated immediately and that immediate treatment increases the likelihood of a cure without the materialization of any adverse complications. His testimony was corroborated, to a large extent, by excerpts from several learned treatises.[6] Giving this general evidence the benefit of all legitimate inferences, we conclude that it was, at best, minimally sufficient to establish the requisite standard of care. Never was any specific expert testimony presented which tended to show that Dr. Knowles departed from this standard.

Even more troubling, however, is the lack of expert testimony on the causation elements of plaintiff's claims. Here, as in Silver v. Redleaf, supra, plaintiff had the burden to prove, by expert testimony, that, " ... it was more probable that death resulted from some negligence for which defendant was responsible than from something for which he was not responsible." 292 Minn. 465, 194 N.W.2d 273. (Citations omitted.) Such proof is absent from this case. Instead, the record would have compelled the jury to speculate as to whether earlier diagnosis or different treatment would have resulted in a cure. The trial court could not permit this, and thus had no alternative but to grant defendant's motion for a dismissal. In light of our disposition of this case, we need not reach the other issues raised by the briefs.

Affirmed.

Notes

1. *Common law exclusion of treatises as hearsay.* The common law of evidence excluded all hearsay from the trial. This meant that a witness could

---

6. Although it is unclear from the record whether these were admitted into evidence during the trial, the trial court admitted them into evidence for the purpose of ruling upon defendant's motion to dismiss. Thus these treatises are properly before us on appeal. Plaintiff, in his brief, relies heavily upon the following excerpt from Williams on Obstetrics: "Since eclampsia is preceded in most cases by premonitory signs and symptoms, its prophylaxis is in many ways more important than its cure and is identical with the treatment of pre-eclampsia. Indeed, a major aim in treating the pre-eclampsia is to prevent convulsions.

The necessity of regular and frequent blood pressure measurements thus becomes clear, as well as the importance of detection of rapid gain of weight and of proteinuria, and the immediate institution of appropriate dietary and medical treatment as soon as the earliest signs and symptoms appear. By the employment of these precautionary measures and by prompt termination of pregnancy in those cases that do not improve or that become progressively worse under treatment, the frequency of eclampsia will be greatly diminished and many lives will be saved. Prophylaxis, while valuable, is not invariably successful. ..."

not testify to something he heard or read out-of-court. That excluded statements in medical books. The purpose of the rule was to guarantee the right of cross-examination. This rule still applies to exclude evidence from textbooks in some states. See, e.g., *Aldridge v. Edmunds,* 561 Pa. 323, 750 A.2d 292 (Pa. 2000).

2. *Cross-examination from medical treatises.* The hearsay rule did not exclude the use of medical treatises for every purpose, only for the purpose of proving the truth of the hearsay statements. Under this rule a plaintiff's attorney might sometimes cross-examine the defendant doctor or some other doctor with reference to a medical treatise. In effect the examiner would ask, "How can you square your testimony with this treatise, which you admit is a standard work in the field?" This kind of use of treatises, however, merely "impeached" or cast doubt on the doctor's testimony. It was not admissible to establish the plaintiff's case, since it was hearsay.

3. *Under the Federal Rules of Evidence.* The Federal Rules of Evidence, adopted for federal courts in 1975, have also been adopted in a good many states. Rule 803(18) explicitly provides that learned treatises, such as medical books, are not hearsay and may be admitted into evidence when they are first shown to be reliable authorities.

Does this rule solve all the plaintiff's problems in a medical malpractice case? Suppose the treatise states that as a general rule the best technique in thyroidectomies is to locate and isolate the laryngeal nerves. If Illinois had adopted Rule 803(18) in *Walski* as Minnesota had done in *Smith v. Knowles,* would that have taken the plaintiff's case to the jury?

4. *Manufacturer's directions for use of medical supplies.* If the plaintiff seeks to establish negligence by showing that the defendant failed to follow the manufacturer's directions for use of a drug, will the hearsay rule stand in the way? Several cases have appeared to use the manufacturer's directions as a standard in spite of the hearsay rule, but some reject such evidence.

5. *Defendant's admissions.* The defendant might conceivably admit before trial that he violated the appropriate standard of care. If he does so, evidence of this admission can be introduced to show the standard and its breach. Suppose the defendant, after an operation turns out badly, says "I made a mistake, that should not have happened." Would that suffice to show the standard? *Fossett v. Board of Regents of University of Nebraska,* 258 Neb. 703, 605 N.W.2d 465 (2000).

6. *Medical guidelines.* Medical organizations sometimes establish guidelines for good medical practice. Courts have sometimes accepted evidence of these guidelines as showing the standard of care. Conceivably states might by statute actively encourage the development of guidelines. Maine has done so, but only for the purpose of saying that compliance with guidelines is a defense, not for the purpose of saying that a breach is negligence. If a legislature were considering promoting guidelines to be established either by a governmental agency or by a medical group, what pros and cons should it consider? See DOBBS ON TORTS § 247 (2000).

Other Tort Issues and Defenses

7. Most of the preceding materials deal with the standard of care for medical practitioners. But medical malpractice is a species of negligence, so

the other issues of the negligence case arise here, too. Cause in fact is an issue that appeared in *Smith v. Knowles*. Proximate cause issues could also arise in the medical context. Suppose a doctor prescribed a medicine that was dangerous for the particular patient because, for that patient, it ran the risk of causing a bad side effect, tortosis. In fact, however, the medicine caused an entirely different and unforeseeable side effect, contractosis.

8. Negligence-law defenses are also possible. We have already seen the statute of limitations defense in the medical context. We've also brushed assumed risk defenses in that context. Contributory negligence is occasionally asserted as well. How can a patient be contributorily negligent in a medical malpractice case?

> REFERENCES: DOBBS ON TORTS §§ 242–246 (2000); HARPER, JAMES & GRAY, THE LAW OF TORTS § 17.1 (2d 1986).

§ 2. RES IPSA LOQUITUR

KELLY v. HARTFORD CASUALTY INSURANCE CO.

Supreme Court of Wisconsin, 1978.
86 Wis.2d 129, 271 N.W.2d 676.

COFFEY, JUSTICE.

On July 5, 1975 the seventy-five year-old plaintiff entered Community Memorial Hospital in Spooner complaining of lower back pain. On July 16, 1975 Dr. Rudolf Matzke, the plaintiff's attending physician, ordered an intravenous pyelogram. This procedure is commonly known as a lower GI series examination which includes the bowel, a part of the lower intestinal tract. Before the x-ray procedure is performed, it is required that one or more soap suds enemas are used to clear the bowel.

Mrs. Kelly claims that she was injured during the administration of the enema. Mrs. Kelly states that the nurse was in a hurry and that the plaintiff experienced no pain when the enema tube was inserted, but as the liquid began to flow into the rectum it felt like she was being pinched in the rectal region.

The same evening, the duty nurse discovered a sore to the plaintiff's rectal area which resembled a bruise. On July 19th Dr. Matzke examined the plaintiff and concluded the bruise was most likely caused by the enema. Subsequently, a large hematoma developed in the rectum which required surgical removal. Evidence was received at the trial that Mrs. Kelly had a history of anal diseases. In January, 1969 a proctoscopic examination revealed considerable evidence of hemorrhoid problems. In May, 1975 examinations indicated the plaintiff was suffering from inflamed hemorrhoids and anal irritation caused by torn mucus linings. . . .

In Fehrman v. Smirl, 20 Wis.2d 1, 121 N.W.2d 255 (1963), this court authorized the application of *res ipsa loquitur* to medical malpractice cases. . . . Before a *res ipsa loquitur* instruction can be given to a jury, the evidence must conform to these requirements:

"(1) The event in question must be of the kind which does not ordinarily occur in the absence of negligence; and (2) the agency or instrumentality causing the harm must have been within the exclusive control of the defendant." Trogun v. Fruchtman, 58 Wis.2d 569, 590, 207 N.W.2d 297, 308 (1973).

As a general proposition the doctrine of *res ipsa loquitur* may be invoked in medical malpractice actions where a layman is able to say as a matter of common knowledge that the consequences of the professional treatment are not those which ordinarily result if due care is exercised.

Wisconsin has additionally adopted the position that an instruction embodying the principle of *res ipsa loquitur* may be grounded on expert medical testimony in a malpractice case. The *res ipsa loquitur* standards are satisfied if the testimony and the medical records taken as a whole would support the inference of negligence or if direct testimony is introduced that the injury in question was of the nature that does not ordinarily occur if proper skill and care are exercised.

The plaintiff claims that it is within the common knowledge of a layman that rectal hematoma will not ordinarily occur from the administration of an enema except in circumstances where the proper medical skill and care have not been exercised. Reliance is placed on Davis v. Memorial Hospital, 58 Cal.2d 815, 26 Cal. Rptr. 633, 376 P.2d 561 (1962) wherein it was alleged that an enema caused the patient to suffer a perirectal abscess and a resulting fistula. Without reaching a decision on causation, the California Supreme Court concluded that the plaintiff was entitled to a *res ipsa loquitur* instruction, noting:

> "Although there was no expert testimony as to the probability of negligence in such a situation, it is a matter of common knowledge among laymen that the giving of an enema is not ordinarily harmful unless negligently done." *Davis*, supra 26 Cal. Rptr. at 634, 376 P.2d at 562.

We do not find the *Davis* case to be persuasive precedent in support of the plaintiff's position. First, the *Davis* case is factually distinguishable from the case at bar. In *Davis*, the plaintiff had undergone a prostatic massage which had revealed no abnormalities. Mrs. Kelly has a history of hemorrhoid problems dating back to 1969 and confirmed by examination in May, 1975, one month before the alleged act of negligence. Further, in *Davis*, four attempts were made to insert the tube, the plaintiff testifying that with each attempt a "cutting," "scratching" or "tearing" sensation was experienced. Mrs. Kelly testified there was no discomfort during the insertion of the tube. Rather, only after the liquid began to flow did she experience a pinching sensation in the rectal area. . . .

An application of the doctrine based on common knowledge is allowed only when the occurrence clearly "speaks for itself." Burnside v. Evangelical Deaconess Hospital, supra. We have previously held that the occurrence "speaks for itself" and that *res ipsa loquitur* could be applied where a patient had undergone dilation and curettage surgery and returned from the operative procedure with second degree burns on her posterior, an area not involved in the operation. The court held that a layman could conclude as a matter of common knowledge that burns in an area unassociated with the operation ordinarily do not result if due care is exercised. Beaudoin v. Watertown Memorial Hospital, 32 Wis.2d 132, 145 N.W.2d 166 (1966).

[The court concluded that "whether the application of an enema will cause injury in the absence of negligence is not a matter of common knowledge."] A review of the expert testimony also reveals that the *res ipsa loquitur* instruction was not required because there was no direct medical testimony to prove that the injury was of a nature that ordinarily [does not occur] except for the lack of proper skill and care as to the enema procedure in question. . . .

This brings us to a consideration of the second element required for a *res ipsa loquitur* instruction, that being the question of whether the instrumentality causing the harm is within the exclusive control of the defendant. It is unquestionable that the agent of the Spooner Hospital administering the enema had exclusive control over the tube and bulb through which the solution was introduced into plaintiff's rectum. However, the recent decision of Hoven v. Kelble, 79 Wis.2d 444, 256 N.W.2d 379 (1977) maintains that the use of the word "control" is not an accurate statement of the principle sought to be expressed. Quoting from that decision:

> "Restatement of the Law, Torts, 2d sec. 328D, does not speak in terms of control, at all, but requires that 'other responsible causes . . . are sufficiently eliminated by the evidence.' Prosser, Law of Torts, sec. 39, pages 219–221 (4th ed. 1971), discusses the concept of 'exclusive control' as follows:
>
> " ' . . . It would be far better, and much confusion would be avoided, if the idea of 'control' were discarded altogether, and we were to say merely that the apparent cause of the accident must be such that the defendant would be responsible for any negligence connected with it.' " Id. at 452–53, 256 N.W.2d at 383.

The *res ipsa loquitur* concept of control is thus interpreted to preclude the instruction in medical malpractice actions where the injury can reasonably be attributed to a pre-existing condition, an allergic reaction or some other frailty in the plaintiff. . . .

Judgment affirmed.

SALATHIEL v. STATE, 96 Misc. 2d 72, 411 N.Y.S.2d 175 (Ct. Cl. 1978). Plaintiff was a volunteer participant in a bile study program at Upstate Medical Center Hospital, a state facility. The doctor attempted to insert a nasogastric tube into the plaintiff's right nostril as a part of the study. Some difficulty was encountered and he pushed a cotton-tipped probe into the right nostril. Some other equipment failed at this point and the doctor then inserted the tube into the left nostril where it remained for two days collecting bile. When the plaintiff left the hospital, she noted a watery fluid flowing from her nose. This proved to be cerebrospinal fluid discharging from a hole in the "cribriform plate area," and had to be corrected by surgery. This in turn required severance of the olfactory nerve. The plaintiff relied in part on res ipsa loquitur. "The rationale for the doctrine of *res ipsa loquitur* is that the occurrence in question, itself, contains a sufficient basis for the inference of negligence and causation. This necessarily implies that the circumstances of the occurrence can be reasonably appraised by the common knowledge or experience of an ordinary layman. In some instances, additional evidence may be necessary to provide sufficient explanation in order to allow a layman to reach a conclusion based upon his common knowledge. Such evidence was provided here by the medical expert and the claimant." The injury was "remote from the site of an intubation procedure." It is not an ordinary risk of such procedure and the probe used was capable of inflicting the injury. Prior to the procedure the claimant was in good health and during the procedure claimant was under the control of the hospital personnel. The doctor had difficulty in performing the procedure and the fluid was discovered immediately after leaving the hospital. This is sufficient to show negligence.

Notes

1. *Common knowledge.* The normal basis for medical res ipsa loquitur is that, as a matter of common knowledge the plaintiff's injury is more likely than not to have resulted from negligence. The clearest cases are those in which instruments or towels are left in the patient's abdomen after surgery and those in which injury is inflicted upon a part of the body not being treated. "It is within the common knowledge and experience of a layperson to determine that an individual does not enter the hospital for gallbladder surgery and come out of surgery with an ulnar nerve injury to the left arm." *Wick v. Henderson,* 485 N.W.2d 645 (Iowa 1992).

2. *Expert testimony.* Expert testimony can be used in most jurisdictions to fill the role of common knowledge. Thus an expert who cannot pinpoint negligence can nevertheless testify that the injury is one that, in the common knowledge of experts, is likely to occur only because of negligence. See, citing many cases, *Seavers v. Methodist Med. Ctr. of Oak Ridge,* 9 S.W.3d 86 (Tenn.1999).

3. *Inherent risks.* If a medical procedure carries with it the inherent risk of a particular kind of injury or complication, the court cannot use res ipsa loquitur merely because such an injury in fact occurred. *Chism v. Campbell,* 250 Neb. 921, 553 N.W.2d 741 (1996) (damage to teeth was inherent risk of administering anesthesia by an endotracheal tube, no res ipsa loquitur).

4. To reinforce the site of a hernia, a surgeon places a surgical mesh in the body. The mesh will be incorporated into the body as tissues grow into it. But the mesh becomes infected without fault of the surgeon and a second surgery is required. In this second surgery, the surgeon removes the mesh that has not been incorporated into the body but leaves the rest. Further infection occurs and a third surgery is required. One expert testified that the

standard of care was violated by leaving any mesh in the body. Others testified to the contrary, that the standard of care required the surgeon to leave the parts of the mesh that had been incorporated. The trial judge submitted the case to the jury. Right or wrong? *Kenyon v. Miller,* 756 So.2d 133 (Fla.App.2000).

5. *Abandonment.* Courts agree that a patient may terminate the doctor-patient relationship, but that neither a doctor nor a hospital can abandon a patient before treatment is completed. Would expert testimony be required to show breach of duty if the doctor walked out in the middle of an operation? If the doctor leaving town arranged for coverage by another doctor for his hospitalized patient?

YBARRA v. SPANGARD

Supreme Court of California, 1944.
25 Cal.2d 486, 154 P.2d 687.

GIBSON, CHIEF JUSTICE.

This is an action for damages for personal injuries alleged to have been inflicted on plaintiff by defendants during the course of a surgical operation. The trial court entered judgments of nonsuit as to all defendants and plaintiff appealed.

On October 28, 1939, plaintiff consulted from Dr. Tilley, who diagnosed his ailment as appendicitis, and made arrangements for an appendectomy to be performed by defendant Dr. Spangard at a hospital owned and managed by defendant Dr. Swift. Plaintiff entered the hospital, was given a hypodermic injection, slept, and later was awakened by Drs. Tilley and Spangard and wheeled into the operating room by a nurse whom he believed to be defendant Gisler, an employee of Dr. Swift. Defendant Dr. Reser, the anesthetist, also an employee of Dr. Swift, adjusted plaintiff for the operation, pulling his body to the head of the operating table and, according to plaintiff's testimony, laying him back against two hard objects at the top of his shoulders, about an inch below his neck. Dr. Reser then administered the anesthetic and plaintiff lost consciousness. When he awoke early the following morning he was in his hospital room attended by defendant Thompson, the special nurse, and another nurse who was not made a defendant.

Plaintiff testified that prior to the operation he had never had any pain in, or injury to, his right arm or shoulder, but that when he awakened he felt a sharp pain about half way between the neck and the point of the right shoulder. He complained to the nurse, and then to Dr. Tilley, who gave him diathermy treatments while he remained in the hospital. The pain did not cease but spread down to the lower part of his arm, and after his release from the hospital the condition grew worse. He was unable to rotate or lift his arm, and developed paralysis and atrophy of the muscles around the shoulder. He received further treatments from Dr. Tilley until March, 1940, and then returned to work, wearing his arm in a splint on the advice of Dr. Spangard.

[Medical evidence for the plaintiff established that his problem resulted from some trauma, pressure or strain applied between his shoulder and neck.]

Plaintiff's theory is that the foregoing evidence presents a proper case for the application of the doctrine of *res ipsa loquitur*, and that the inference of negligence arising therefrom makes the granting of a nonsuit improper. Defendants take the position that, assuming that plaintiff's condition was in fact the result of an injury, there is no showing that the act of any particular defendant, nor any particular instrumentality, was the cause thereof. . . .

The present case is of a type which comes within the reason and spirit of the doctrine more fully perhaps than any other. The passenger sitting awake in a railroad car at the time of a collision, the pedestrian walking along the street and struck by a falling object or the debris of an explosion, are surely not more entitled to an explanation than the unconscious patient on the operating table. Viewed from this aspect, it is difficult to see how the doctrine can, with any justification, be so restricted in its statement as to become inapplicable to a patient who submits himself to the care and custody of doctors and nurses, is rendered unconscious, and receives some injury from instrumentalities used in his treatment. Without the aid of the doctrine a patient who received permanent injuries of a serious character, obviously the result of someone's negligence, would be entirely unable to recover unless the doctors and nurses in attendance voluntarily chose to disclose the identity of the negligent person and the facts establishing liability. If this were the state of the law of negligence, the courts, to avoid gross injustice, would be forced to invoke the principles of absolute liability, irrespective of negligence, in actions by persons suffering injuries during the course of treatment under anesthesia. But we think this juncture has not yet been reached, and that the doctrine of *res ipsa loquitur* is properly applicable to the case before us. . . .

The argument of defendants is simply that plaintiff has not shown an injury caused by an instrumentality under a defendant's control, because he has not shown which of the several instrumentalities that he came in contact with while in the hospital caused the injury; and he has not shown that any one defendant or his servants had exclusive control over any particular instrumentality. Defendants assert that some of them were not the employees of other defendants, that some did not stand in any permanent relationship from which liability in tort would follow, and that in view of the nature of the injury, the number of defendants and the different functions performed by each, they could not all be liable for the wrong, if any.

We have no doubt that in a modern hospital a patient is likely to come under the care of a number of persons in different types of contractual and other relationships with each other. For example, in the present case it appears that Drs. Swift, Spangard and Tilley were physicians or surgeons commonly placed in the legal category of independent contractors; and Dr. Reser, the anesthetist, and defendant Thompson, the special nurse, were employees of Dr. Swift and not of the other doctors. But we do not believe that either the number or relationship of the defendants alone determines whether the doctrine of *res ipsa loquitur* applies. Every defendant in whose custody the plaintiff was placed for any period was bound to exercise ordinary care to see that no unnecessary harm came to him and each would be liable for failure in this regard. Any defendant who negligently injured him, and any defendant charged with his care who so neglected him as to allow injury to occur, would be liable. The defendant employers would be liable for the neglect of their employees; and the doctor in charge of the operation would be liable for the negligence of those who became his temporary servants for the purpose of assisting in the operation.

In this connection, it should be noted that while the assisting physicians and nurses may be employed by the hospital, or engaged by the patient, they normally become the temporary servants or agents of the surgeon in charge while the operation is in progress, and liability may be imposed upon him for their negligent acts under the doctrine of respondeat superior. Thus a surgeon has been held liable for the negligence of an assisting nurse who leaves a sponge or other object inside a patient, and the fact that the duty of seeing that such mistakes do not occur is delegated to others does not absolve the doctor from responsibility for their negligence.

It may appear at the trial that, consistent with the principles outlined above, one or more defendants will be found liable and others absolved, but this should not preclude the application of the rule of *res ipsa loquitur*. The control at one time or another, of one or more of the various agencies or instrumentalities which might have harmed the plaintiff was in the hands of every defendant or of his employees or temporary servants. This, we think, places upon them the burden of initial explanation. Plaintiff was rendered unconscious for the purpose of undergoing surgical treatment by the defendants; it is manifestly unreasonable for them to insist that he identify any one of them as the person who did the alleged negligent act.

The other aspect of the case which defendants so strongly emphasize is that plaintiff has not identified the instrumentality any more than he has the particular guilty defendant. Here, again, there is a misconception which, if carried to the extreme for which defendants contend, would unreasonably limit the application of the *res ipsa loquitur* rule. It should be enough that the plaintiff can show an injury resulting from an external force applied while he lay unconscious in the hospital; this is as clear a case of identification of the instrumentality as the plaintiff may ever be able to make.

An examination of the recent cases, particularly in this state, discloses that the test of actual exclusive control of an instrumentality has not been strictly followed, but exceptions have been recognized where the purpose of the doctrine of *res ipsa loquitur* would otherwise be defeated. Thus, the test has become one of right of control rather than actual control. In the bursting bottle cases where the bottler has delivered the instrumentality to a retailer and thus has given up actual control, he will nevertheless be subject to the doctrine where it is shown that no change in the condition of the bottle occurred after it left the bottler's possession, and it can accordingly be said that he was in constructive control. Escola v. Coca Cola Bottling Co., 24 Cal.2d [453], 150 P.2d 436. . . .

In the face of these examples of liberalization of the tests for *res ipsa loquitur*, there can be no justification for the rejection of the doctrine in the instant case. . . .

We do not at this time undertake to state the extent to which the reasoning of this case may be applied to other situations in which the doctrine of *res ipsa loquitur* is invoked. We merely hold that where a plaintiff receives unusual injuries while unconscious and in the course of medical treatment, all those defendants who had any control over his body or the instrumentalities which might have caused the injuries may properly be called upon to meet the inference of negligence by giving an explanation of their conduct.

The judgment is reversed.

REFERENCES: Dobbs on Torts § 249 (2000); Harper, James & Gray, the Law of Torts § 19.7 (3d ed. 1995).

§ 3. INFORMED CONSENT

SCHLOENDORFF v. SOCIETY OF NEW YORK HOSPITAL, 211 N.Y. 125, 105 N.E. 92 (1914). Cardozo, J.: "Every human being of adult years and sound mind has a right to determine what shall be done with his own body; and a surgeon who performs an operation without his patient's consent commits an assault, for which he is liable in damages."

HARNISH v. CHILDREN'S HOSPITAL MEDICAL CENTER

Supreme Court of Massachusetts, 1982.
387 Mass. 152, 439 N.E.2d 240.

O'Connor, Justice.

The plaintiff underwent an operation to remove a tumor in her neck. During the procedure, her hypoglossal nerve was severed, allegedly resulting in a permanent and almost total loss of tongue function.

The plaintiff's complaint charges the defendant physicians and hospital with misrepresentation and negligence in failing to inform her before surgery of the risk of loss of tongue function. The complaint alleges that the purpose of the operation was cosmetic, that the loss of tongue function was a material and foreseeable risk of the operation, and that, had the plaintiff been informed of this risk, she would not have consented to the operation. There is no claim that the operation was negligently performed.

[A medical malpractice tribunal, which functions to screen malpractice claims against physicians, held that the plaintiff's proof was inadequate and on this basis the trial judge dismissed the action.]

... "There is implicit recognition in the law of the Commonwealth, as elsewhere, that a person has a strong interest in being free from nonconsensual invasion of his bodily integrity.... In short, the law recognizes the individual interest in preserving 'the inviolability of his person.' One means by which the law has developed in a manner consistent with the protection of this interest is through the development of the doctrine of informed consent." "[I]t is the prerogative of the patient, not the physician, to determine ... the direction in which ... his interest lie." Cobbs v. Grant, supra, 8 Cal.3d at 242, 104 Cal. Rptr. 505, 502 P.2d 1. Canterbury v. Spence, 464 F.2d 772, 781 (D.C.Cir.1972). Every competent adult has a right "to forego treatment, or even cure, if it entails what for him are intolerable consequences or risks however unwise his sense of value may be in the eyes of the medical profession." Wilkinson v. Vesey, 110 R.I. 606, 624, 295 A.2d 676 (1972). Knowing exercise of this right requires knowledge of the available options and the risks attendant on each. We hold, therefore, that a physician's failure to divulge in a reasonable manner to a competent adult patient sufficient information to enable the patient to make an informed judgment whether to give or withhold consent to a medical or surgical procedure constitutes professional misconduct and comes within the ambit of G.L. c. 231, § 60B.

While we recognize that a patient ordinarily cannot make an intelligent decision whether to undergo a medical or surgical procedure without receiving from the physician information significant to the decision, we also recognize that there are limits to what society or an individual can reasonably expect of a physician in this regard. Medical matters are often complex. Recommendations of treatment frequently require the application of considerable medical knowledge gained through extensive training and experience. Communication of scientific information by the trained physician to the untrained patient may be difficult. The remotely possible risks of a proposed treatment may be almost without limit. The patient's right to know must be harmonized with the recognition that an undue burden should not be placed on the physician. These interests are accommodated by the rule that we adopt today, that a physician owes to his patient the duty to disclose in a reasonable manner all significant medical information that the physician possesses or reasonably should possess that is material to an intelligent decision by the patient whether to undergo a proposed procedure. The information a physician reasonably should possess is that information possessed by the average qualified physician or, in the case of a specialty, by the average qualified physician practicing that specialty. What the physician should know involves professional expertise and can ordinarily be proved only through the testimony of experts. However, the extent to which he must share that information with his patient depends upon what information he should reasonably recognize is material to the plaintiff's decision. "Materiality may be said to be the significance a reasonable person, in what the physician knows or should know is his patient's position, would attach to the disclosed risk or risks in deciding whether to submit or not to submit to surgery or treatment." The materiality determination is one that lay persons are qualified to make without the aid of an expert. Appropriate information may include the nature of the patient's condition, the nature and probability of risks involved, the benefits to be reasonably expected, the inability of the physician to predict results, if that is the situation, the irreversibility of the procedure, if that be the case, the likely result of no treatment, and the available alternatives, including their risks and benefits. The obligation to give adequate information does not require the disclosure of all risks of a proposed therapy, or of information the physician reasonably believes the patient already has, such as the risks, like infection, inherent in any operation.

Many jurisdictions have adopted the rule that a physician must disclose to his patient only such information as is customarily disclosed in similar circumstances. We think that the better is the one we adopt today. The customary practice standard overlooks the purpose of requiring disclosure, which is protection of the patient's right to decide for himself.

We recognize that despite the importance of the patient's right to know, there may be situations that call for a privilege of nondisclosure. For instance, sound medical judgment might indicate that disclosure would complicate the patient's medical condition or render him unfit for treatment. Where that it is so, the cases have generally held that the physician is armed with a privilege to keep the information from the patient.... The physician's privilege to withhold information for therapeutic reasons must be carefully circumscribed, however, for otherwise it might devour the disclosure rule itself. The privilege does not accept the paternalistic notion that the physician may remain silent simply because divulgence might prompt the patient to forego therapy the physician feels the patient really needs" (footnotes omitted). *Canterbury v. Spence,* supra at 789. A full discussion of the privilege is neither required nor attempted here, because the burden of proving it must rest with the physician, and thus the question of privilege is inappropriate to the directed verdict standard....

We turn to the question of causation. "An unrevealed risk that should have been made known must materialize, for otherwise the omission, however unpardonable, is legally without consequence." Whether the alleged undisclosed risk materialized is a medical question appropriate to the tribunal's inquiry. At trial, the plaintiff must also show that had the proper information been provided neither he nor a reasonable person in similar circumstances would have undergone the procedure. Such proof, not relating to medical questions, is not appropriate to the tribunal's inquiry.

[The court found that one of the defendants was only an assistant in the operation and had no duty to give the plaintiff information, and that the hospital itself was not liable.]

The judgment as to the defendants Muliken and Holmes is reversed. The judgment as to defendants Gilman and Children's Hospital Medical Center is affirmed.

So Ordered.

WOOLLEY v. HENDERSON, 418 A.2d 1123 (Me.1980). Defendant operated on the plaintiff's back but because of an abnormality in the spine, he got the wrong interspace between the vertebrae. He also inadvertently tore part of the tissue encasing the spinal cord, which resulted in a number of medical problems for the plaintiff. A tear of this kind is a normal risk of this procedure, but the doctor had not informed the plaintiff. The trial court instructed the jury that the plaintiff was entitled only to disclosures of risks that would be made by a reasonable medical practitioner. The jury found in favor of the defendant. *Held*, affirmed. The standard of disclosure is that of the reasonable medical practitioner and this will ordinarily require expert medical testimony. This rule is justified (1) because this is professional malpractice and the professional standard must be used, (2) because there might be therapeutic reasons for withholding information, and (3) because since the plaintiff must produce medical testimony on other issues, this will add very little burden. The plaintiff in informed consent cases must also prove causation by the objective test, that is, that a reasonable person would have refused the treatment had full information been given, and that the plaintiff herself would have refused it.

MONTGOMERY v. BAZAZ–SEHGAL, 742 A.2d 1125 (Pa.Super.1999). The plaintiff underwent an operation to remove plaque from his penis. In fact, the surgeon implanted an inflatable penile prosthesis that can be pumped up to simulate erection. He felt loss of sensation and more like a machine than a man. The emotional quality of lovemaking with his wife suffered. *Held,* this is a claim for a battery–an unpermitted touching–not an informed consent claim. Unlike an informed consent claim, a claim for battery does not require expert testimony. However, so far as the plaintiff claims loss of sensation, expert testimony would be required to establish the causal connection between the implant and that loss.

Notes

1. *Negligence theory.* Courts today recognize a battery claim if the plaintiff has not consented to the operation at all. But they adopt a negligence approach when the plaintiff has consented to the operation and claims that she was uninformed about risks or needs. Use of a negligence approach is important in part because, since battery usually connotes an intentional tort, the defendant doctor's liability insurance might not cover a

battery claim. It is also important because negligence rules seem to make the doctor's duty of disclosure depend upon the disclosure the medical community would make. Many courts, like the *Woolley* court, have so held.

2. *Professional standard or the "patient rule?"* Beginning in the early 1970s a series of major decisions, though retaining the negligence theory, rejected the requirement of medical proof. These cases, including *Cobbs, Canterbury* and *Wilkinson*, all cited in *Harnish*, held that the standard was "materiality" of the information. In the absence of statutory directive, most of the recent major decisions have taken this view. See, e.g., *Carr v. Strode,* 79 Hawai'i 475, 904 P.2d 489 (1995).

3. *Causation.* Most courts have required an "objective" test of causation. This means that the plaintiff cannot recover merely by showing that she herself would have refused the injury-causing operation had she been fully informed. She will have to go further and show that a reasonable person would also have refused it. Why such a requirement? Is it because the courts are reluctant to permit a jury to believe the plaintiff's testimony on this point? If so, what happened to the usual rule that the jury is the sole judge of credibility? Or is the "objective" test of causation intended merely to limit protection to reasonable patients? Is that what autonomy is about– matching other people's expectations of reasonableness? Several courts have sought a compromise, saying that the issue is to be judged by the reasonable person standard in the light of the plaintiff's personal fears and religious beliefs. *Ashe v. Radiation Oncology Assocs.,* 9 S.W.3d 119 (Tenn. 1999).

4. *Damages.* Knowledge about risks and choices is necessary if patients are to participate in decisions about their bodies. Maybe courts should allow some kind of dignitary damages if the patient is deprived of the right to "vote" on the operation with appropriate knowledge, even if the patient would have given consent if she had been fully informed. What do you think? See *Lugenbuhl v. Dowling,* 701 So.2d 447 (La.1997) (permitting damages for deprivation of self-determination); cf. *Provenzano v. Integrated Genetics,* 22 F.Supp.2d 406 (D.N.J.1998) (negligently depriving mother of opportunity to terminate pregnancy because fetus suffered serious disease).

5. *Patient's waiver of information rights.* Suppose your surgeon says an operation is required but that it will be performed only if you sign a consent form. The form states: "I understand that there are risks that have not been described to me. I agree that the doctor/surgeon need not describe any risk to me, and I consent to all surgical, diagnostic and other medical procedures the doctor/surgeon may undertake, whether or not I have been informed of the nature of the operations or procedures or tests and whether or not I have been told of any risks." Would you sign this consent form? Can you rightfully be denied an operation if you refuse to sign? Does the rule in *Woolley* provide the surgeon with substantially less protection than such a waiver would provide?

6. *Incompetent patients and life-saving treatment.* The informed consent rules imply that the patient may refuse treatment. Consider: (1) May a physician treat a competent patient over her objection if the treatment is required to save her life? *Shine v. Vega,* 429 Mass. 456, 709 N.E.2d 58 (1999) (no). (2) Can a dying patient refuse treatment that would save her fetus? "What we distill from the cases ... is that every person has the right, under

the common law and the Constitution, to accept or refuse medical treatment. This right of bodily integrity belongs equally to persons who are competent and persons who are not. Further, it matters not what the quality of a patient's life may be; the right of bodily integrity is not extinguished simply because someone is ill, or even at death's door. To protect that right against intrusion by others–family members, doctors, hospitals, or anyone else, however well-intentioned–we hold that a court must determine the patient's wishes by any means available, and must abide by those wishes unless there are truly extraordinary or compelling reasons to override them. When the patient is incompetent, or when the court is unable to determine competency, the substituted judgment procedure must be followed." *In re A.C.*, 573 A.2d 1235 (D.C.App.1990). (3) Does the right to refuse life-saving treatment mean that the patient would also have a right to assistance in committing suicide? *Krischer v. McIver*, 697 So.2d 97 (Fla.1997) ("Forty-five states that recognize the right to refuse treatment or unwanted life-support have expressed disapproval of assisted suicide.").

The evidence is that many health care providers disrespect the fundamental right of the patient to reject treatment, foisting unwanted and sometimes costly procedures upon anaesthetized or comatose patients who have already rejected them. And some courts have even refused hold the health care providers responsible for their life-prolonging batteries. See Kellen F. Rodriguez, *Suing Health Care Providers for Saving Lives*, 20 J. LEG. MED. 1 (1999); Mark Strasser, *A Jurisprudence in Disarray: On Battery, Wrongful Living, and the Right to Bodily Integrity*, 36 SAN DIEGO L. REV. 997 (1999).

7. *What must be disclosed under the materiality test? Harnish* tells us that "a physician owes to his patient the duty to disclose in a reasonable manner all significant medical information that the physician possesses or reasonably should possess that is material to an intelligent decision by the patient whether to undergo a proposed procedure." Would a doctor be required to disclose the size of the needle he uses in stitching up an incision? Would a doctor be required to disclose to the patient that he might minimize the risk of an AIDS infection from a blood transfusion by donating his own blood in advance of the operation? See *Doe v. Johnston*, 476 N.W.2d 28 (Iowa 1991).

In *Moore v. Regents of the University of California*, 51 Cal.3d 120, 271 Cal.Rptr. 146, 793 P.2d 479 (1990) the patient claimed that the physicians and hospital withdrew blood at least ostensibly in the course of treatment. They developed a "cell line" that could be used efficiently to produce a commercial product of great value. None of this was mentioned to the patient. The court refused to permit the plaintiff to pursue a conversion claim, but it said that the physician was under a fiduciary duty to disclose some of the facts to the patient. Is this an informed consent case or something different?

In *D.A.B. v. Brown*, 570 N.W.2d 168 (Minn.App.1997) a doctor allegedly received illegal kickbacks from a drug manufacturer when he prescribed the drug, which costs patients up to $30,000 each year. The patients sued, but they did not claim harm resulting from the prescriptions. Instead, they claimed the doctor had breached his fiduciary duty to them. What result do you expect?

Suppose a surgeon has little experience with his proposed brain surgery or a record of bad results. Must he inform his patient? *Johnson v. Kokemoor,* 199 Wis.2d 615, 545 N.W.2d 495 (1996) held that the patient was entitled to information from her surgeon that more experienced brain surgeons were available and had substantially better success rates than inexperienced surgeons. See, discussing and supporting a duty to disclose risks about the particular provider, Aaron D. Twerski and Neil B. Cohen, *The Second Revolution in Informed Consent: Comparing Physicians to Each Other,* 94 Nw. U. L. Rev. 1 (1999). If that becomes the general view, will doctors fudge their records? Reject risky patients to establish a better set of statistics? See Lynn M. LoPucki, *Twerski and Cohen's Second Revolution: A Systems/Strategic Perspective,* 94 Nw. U. L. Rev. 55 (1999).

Georgia says that a physician owes no duty to inform a patient of his cocaine use. *Albany Urology Clinic, PC v. Cleveland,* 272 Ga. 296, 528 S.E.2d 777 (2000), so the patient has neither an informed consent claim nor a battery claim. A little authority goes the other way on such matters as chronic alcohol abuse or AIDS infection. See Dobbs on Torts § 251 (2000).

————

ARATO v. AVEDON, 5 Cal.4th 1172, 858 P.2d 598, 23 Cal.Rptr.2d 131 (1993). Mr. Arato was diagnosed with cancer. Doctors performed surgery, but the cancer was a kind that was overwhelmingly likely to cause death in a short time. Although Arato had indicated to his doctor that he wanted to know the truth, his doctor did not tell him that death in a short time was statistically almost certain. Instead, the doctor recommended some post-operative treatments that had been experimentally successful with some other forms of cancer and that the doctors hoped would help Mr. Arato. The treatments were not successful. Mr. Arato's survivors claimed against the doctor. They said he should have told Mr. Arato that his chances were slim to none because that information would have been relevant to his decision to accept the treatments and that, living in a false hope, Mr. Arato had failed to arrange his economic affairs, a failure that led to business and tax losses. The jury found for the defendants. The Court of Appeal reversed for error in instructions. *Held*, the Court of Appeal is reversed. "Patient sovereignty" or autonomy is an extreme. It was not error to leave to the jury the question whether all material information about risks had been given. Furthermore, the doctor had no duty to disclose statistical life expectancy information because it was not information about risks of the procedures. As to relevant information that is not about risks, the standard of disclosure is the "standard of practice within the medical community". Since expert physicians testified that the standard was NOT to reveal this kind of information voluntarily, there could be no liability for failure to give informed consent. As to Mr. Arato's written request to be told the truth, "a patient may validly waive the right to be informed, [but] we do not see how a request to be told the 'truth' in itself heightens the duty of disclosure imposed on physicians as a matter of law."

TRUMAN v. THOMAS, 27 Cal.3d 285, 165 Cal.Rptr. 308, 611 P.2d 902 (1980). Rena Truman consulted Dr. Thomas as her doctor over a six year period. She died of cervical cancer, which could have been discovered and successfully treated by a pap smear given early enough. Dr. Thomas did repeatedly advise her to have the pap smear, but never warned her of the purpose or of the dangers of not having one. In an action for her death, the trial judge refused to instruct the jury on the failure to disclose the dangers of refusing the pap smear and the jury found for the defendant doctor. On appeal, *held*, reversed. "If a patient indicates that he or she is going to *decline* the risk-free test or treatment, then the doctor has the additional duty of advising of all material risks of which a reasonable person would want to be informed. . . . [A] jury could reasonably conclude that Dr. Thomas had a duty to inform Mrs. Truman of the danger of refusing the test because it was not reasonable for Dr. Thomas to assume that Mrs. Truman appreciated the potentially fatal consequences of her conduct."

Note

Notice that *Truman* departs from the battery context in which informed consent cases had their origin. Suppose the doctor for an 81–year-old woman with a broken hip thinks surgery with screws to hold it together is a bad idea because of her age. He never informs her that without surgery she will probably never walk again. He prescribes bed rest only and in fact she is never able to walk thereafter. Did the doctor breach a duty of providing information? *Matthies v. Mastromonaco,* 160 N.J. 26, 733 A.2d 456 (1999).

———

BROWN v. DIBBELL, 227 Wis.2d 28, 595 N.W.2d 358 (Wis. 1999). After conference with the defendant doctors, Mrs. Brown underwent a double mastectomy with some unfortunate results. She sued on an informed consent theory. The jury found that Dr. Dibbell was not negligent in performing surgery but that he was negligent in obtaining Ms. Brown's consent to surgery. The jury also found that a reasonable patient in Ms. Brown's circumstances, if adequately informed, would have refused to undergo the surgery that was performed. Finally, the jury found that Mrs. Brown was chargeable with 50% of the negligence for failing to exercise care for her own health. The plaintiff argued on appeal that it was error for the trial judge to submit the issue of contributory negligence. *Held,* affirming the Court of Appeals, a new trial is required to correct various errors in instruction. As to the plaintiff's comparative fault, the defense may be invoked in an informed consent action. Specifically, a patient may be chargeable with comparative fault for failing to give truthful and complete family history when it is material. But a patient may ordinarily trust the doctor's information and except in a most unusual case could not be charged with fault for failure to ascertain the truth or completeness of the information presented by the doctor or to seek independent advice.

REFERENCES: DOBBS ON TORTS §§ 250–251 (2000); HARPER, JAMES & GRAY, THE LAW OF TORTS § 17.1, pp. 558–564 (2d ed. 1986 & Supps.).

§ 4. CHANGING MEDICINE, CHANGING LAW

a. The Medical Malpractice "Crisis" and Statutory Responses

Medical costs have increased enormously in the last generation. The cost of insurance for doctors has also increased. In some instances and in some years it was once difficult for doctors to procure liability insurance.

Some people have pointed the finger at lawyers: costs go up and insurance becomes expensive or impossible to get because greedy lawyers bring too many malpractice suits (and courts permit judgments against doctors). This kind of talk can be misleading for several reasons:

(1) At least in some locales, plaintiffs are actually more likely to win claims against health care workers who are *not* medical doctors, and against medical doctors win only about one claim in five that is submitted to a jury. See Deborah Jones Merritt and Kathryn Ann Barry, *Is the Tort System in Crisis? New Empirical Evidence,* 60 OHIO ST. L.J. 315, 358 (1999).

(2) As to increases in insurance costs, this has been partly a result of investment cycles. Insurers invest premium monies until they are needed to make payouts under the policy. These investments produce large incomes that help make the payments required by the policy. When investment income is down, premium income must go up if the insurer is to pay. So to some extent, the insurer and the insured are subject to the fluctuations of the market, and increased costs to the doctors reflect this as well as other factors. But premium increases were less than the increase of doctors' incomes, see 1 BARRY R. FURROW, THOMAS L. GREANEY, SANDRA H. JOHNSON, TIMOTHY S. JOST, & ROBERT L. SCHWARTZ, HEALTH LAW 517 (1995), and insurance costs are not high enough to explain the vehement attacks on the law. See Patrick Hubbard, *The Physicians' Point of View Concerning Medical Malpractice: A Sociological Perspective on the Symbolic Importance of "Tort Reform,"* 23 GA. L. REV. 295 (1989).

(3) Costs of medical treatment have gone up for a number of reasons not associated with lawsuits. These include the costs of new equipment and buildings and increased technology, and an increase in the pool of elderly. In addition, an increase in the pool of patients who do not pay for services received may also add to costs, which must be borne by other patients or by public funds.

The medical profession has sought favorable legislation before the insurance crisis–the Good Samaritan statutes, for example–but the insurance problem prompted even more demands for special rules. In at least two different crises, many states passed statutes attempting to relieve the insurance problem for health care providers, either directly or indirectly. The exact package of provisions varies from state to state, but most states have adopted one or more of the kinds of provisions listed below.

(a) SUBSTANTIVE LAW CHANGES.

(1) The plaintiff must prove actual negligence, or, more explicitly, res ipsa loquitur may not be used against a health care provider, or may not be used in traditional cases. In *Larsen v. Zarrett,* 498 N.W.2d 191 (N.D.1993), the court interpreted a statute to forbid the use of res ipsa loquitur against a surgeon when the plaintiff awoke from an operation with an injury to a separate, previously healthy, portion of her body.

(2) The standard of care must be local or statewide, not national.

(3) The statute of limitations has an absolute outside limit, even when the patient cannot discover the negligence for many years.

(4) No malpractice claim may be based on a contract unless the contract is in writing.

(5) Informed consent claims are limited or discouraged.

(b) REMEDIAL CHANGES. Some states have limited damages in various ways, the most important of which is the absolute cap on recovery. Some of these limitations are discussed in Chapter 20.

(c) PROCEDURAL CHANGES. The statutes have imposed various procedural changes. One type of statute excludes testimony of experts who do not meet some arbitrary test. In *Endorf v. Bohlender,* 26 Kan.App.2d 855, 995 P.2d 896 (Kan.App.2000) the court held that a statute required the trial judge to exclude testimony of a qualified expert who was Medical Director of a major hospital and who taught at the University of Arizona because he spent only 25% of his time in actual clinical work, devoting the rest to teaching and administration. Another type of statute may require the plaintiff to submit her claim to arbitration or screening panels before suing or permit contracts between patient and medical provider to require arbitration in lieu of tort claims. In *Engalla v. Permanente Medical Group, Inc.,* 15 Cal.4th 951, 938 P.2d 903, 64 Cal.Rptr.2d 843 (1997) you can read about the terrible delays seemingly intentionally produced by a gigantic HMO. Statutes of limitations have been amended to limit the "discovery" rule by providing a possible pre-accrual bar or "ultimate statute of repose." (Similar statutes have been enacted to protect product manufacturers.)

(d) INSURANCE CHANGES. A fourth group of changes does not directly affect tort law; these attempt to facilitate insurance coverage.

————

What injuries fall under the statutes? Not all claims that occur in a health care setting are medical malpractice claims that garner special statutory protections. A failure to protect the patient from fire is not. Cf.

Taylor v. Vencor, Inc., 136 N.C.App. 528, 525 S.E.2d 201(2000). Some courts refuse to treat a supplier of HIV infected blood as a health care provider; since the blood bank is not engaged in diagnosis, treatment, or care, it does not get the more favorable medical statute of limitations. *Silva v. Southwest Florida Blood Bank, Inc.*, 601 So.2d 1184 (Fla.1992). The issue depends upon statutory wording and the court's own conception of policy. In *Rome v. Flower Memorial Hospital*, 70 Ohio St.3d 14, 635 N.E.2d 1239 (1994) the court found injuries covered by the medical malpractice statute when the plaintiff, allegedly improperly secured to a tilting radiology table, slipped off and injured her head when the table was tipped up. This was medical malpractice because it was "ancillary" to an X-ray procedure that was medical in nature.

b. *The Medical Malpractice Reality*

Whether any kind of crisis justified the limitations on patients' rights or not, the underlying reality of preventable injury remains. The Institute of Medicine recently published a study of preventable medical errors and the "silence" about them. The Institute study concluded that more people died from medical errors than from all motor vehicle accidents or from breast cancer. The Institute wasn't discussing traditional and perhaps debatable cases. It began by mentioning a patient who died of a chemotherapy overdose, another who had the wrong leg amputated, and another, a child who died during minor surgery because of a drug mix-up. See INSTITUTE OF MEDICINE, TO ERR IS HUMAN: BUILDING A SAFER HEALTHY SYSTEM (2000). The committee responsible for the study (composed of health care professionals) concluded that the aim should be "to make errors costly to health care organizations and providers, so they are compelled to take action to improve safety." Id. at 3. Does this sound like *Carroll Towing*?

The committee recognized that individuals are responsible for errors, but emphasized that safety would be best improved by designing the health care system so that errors are prevented or minimized (much as highway and vehicle design has minimized the harms from driver error). For example, equipment can be simplified and standardized and drugs that look or sound alike can be given distinctively different names or packaging.

Unlike those who emphasized "crisis" and costs of insurance, the Institute of Medicine recognizes the overwhelming prevalence of medical malpractice (or preventable errors) and emphasizes the need for patient safety. It also adopts one tort-law goal: making errors costly enough to discourage them. Yet it does not emphasize tort law solutions. It wants design and management solutions. If the Institute of Medicine is on the right track, should tort law wither away, or would it retain an important role?

c. *Medical Costs, Containment Efforts and Tort Standards*

Fee for service system and over-utilization of medical services. Until very recently, people who received services of doctors or hospitals paid a fee for the service rendered. If services were greater, the fee was greater. If the patient could not pay the fee, chances were good that the patient would not get the service needed. Insurance plans first simply provided for payment of the medical costs, whatever they were. This led to over-utilization of medical services, either because patients demanded more extensive services (like testing, or longer hospital stays, for example) or because doctors and hospitals provided more. Neither doctor nor patient had economic incentives to keep costs down. As health concerns increased, governments and private employers added many potential patients through government payments or private insurance. Over-utilization became an even more significant cost.

Managed care strategies. One solution to over-utilization is managed care. A variety of Managed Care Organizations (MCOs) have sprung up, including Health Maintenance Organizations (HMOs) and other systems under which a provider accepts a flat fee or premium and guarantees to provide all needed medical services described in the agreement.

The Medicare form. Another form of managed care is the Medicare DRG system. Hospital admittees covered by Medicare are classified in Diagnostic Related Groups. Depending on the group and some related factors, Medicare will pay the hospital a predetermined amount, no more, no less. What are the economic incentives for the hospital with a Medicare patient? Suppose Medicare pays for a four-day hospital stay. Does the hospital have any economic incentive to discharge the patient one day early? If the doctor believes the Medicare patient needs a fifth day, is there nevertheless an economic incentive to discharge at the end of four days? Incentives are similar for HMOs. In the case of hospitals, is there an incentive to overadmit patients at the same time there is an incentive to provide less than optimum care? See Timothy S. Jost, *Policing Cost Containment: The Medicare Peer Review Organization Program,* 14 Univ. Puget Sound L. Rev. 483 (1991).

Utilization review. Insurance and MCO arrangements provide strategies that work somewhat like DRGs. These are generically called utilization review. In many instances "review" is a misleading word because the review will take place *before* medical service is delivered or concurrently with that service. The pre-certification or concurrent review will tell the health care provider such as a hospital exactly what the insurer will pay for. That might be a four-day hospital stay or none at all. In such cases utilization review sets the economic incentive for the health care provider. If insurance will pay only for a four-day hospital stay, the hospital may discharge the patient at the end of four days.

Liability for denial of coverage. One possibility suggested by these changes in the way medical service is delivered and financed is that an insurer whose utilization review is negligent might be held liable to the patient who gets limited medical care as a result of the insurer's refusal to pay. Several cases have now said that a provider could be held liable for wrongful refusal to authorize payment in advance. See *Wilson v. Blue Cross of Southern California,* 222 Cal.App.3d 660, 271 Cal.Rptr. 876

(1990) (suicide by patient whose hospitalization for depression was terminated); *McEvoy v. Group Health Cooperative of Eau Claire*, 213 Wis.2d 507, 570 N.W.2d 397 (1997) (an HMO's bad faith breach of contract is a common law tort, not a medical malpractice claim subject to the malpractice rule); *Long v. Great West Life & Annuity Ins. Co.*, 957 P.2d 823(Wyo.1998) (Kafkaesque stonewalling by health insurer, tortious breach of contract claim with punitive damages would be authorized).

Other liabilities of MCOs. (a) If an MCO has information about risks of an approved physician or statistics about success rates of its physicians, must it disclose that information to patients? What if an HMO knows that a surgeon has a low success rate and is a drug addict? Aaron D. Twerski and Neil B. Cohen, in *The Second Revolution in Informed Consent: Comparing Physicians to Each Other*, 94 Nw. U. L. Rev. 1 (1999), argue that MCOs should be under a duty to disclose provider risk information they actually have in usable form.

(b) Suppose it is reasonable for an HMO to assign no more than 3,500 patients to a single physician. The HMO assigns more, say 4,000 or 5,000, or knows that the physician has a thousand other patients from his non-HMO practice. Is there a risk that the physician will be forced to rely inappropriately on telephone interviews instead of physical exams or that he will not have time to bring good judgment to bear on the patient's complaint? If so, would the HMO be responsible? *Jones v. Chicago HMO Ltd. of Illinois*, 191 Ill.2d 278, 730 N.E.2d 1119, 246 Ill.Dec. 654 (2000).

d. *Mandatory Emergency Treatment and Screening*

SMITH v. RICHMOND MEM. HOSPITAL

Supreme Court of Virginia, 1992.
243 Va. 445, 416 S.E.2d 689.

LACY, JUSTICE.

In this case we consider whether the trial court properly sustained a demurrer without leave to amend on the ground that the motion for judgment failed to state a cause of action under the [Federal] Emergency Medical Treatment and Women in Active Labor provisions of the Consolidated Omnibus Budget Reconciliation Act (COBRA or the Act), 42 U.S.C. § 1395dd (1988)....

Connie Elizabeth Smith was admitted to Richmond Memorial Hospital (the Hospital) as a patient on July 18, 1988. Ms. Smith was approximately 33 weeks pregnant and had premature rupture of the uterine membranes. Ms. Smith remained at the Hospital until July 23, 1988.

[During the afternoon of July 22, Ms. Smith developed some acute medical problems as well as contractions. After things became worse, the hospital called a physician, who was not Ms. Smith's attending physician. At 1:00 a.m., without examining her, he ordered her transferred to the Medical College of Virginia. After some difficulties in securing ambulance service, the Richmond hospital agreed to pay for it and she was transferred to MCV at 2:30 a.m., July 23. There she signed a consent for caesarian. At 4:20 she was taken "emergently" to the delivery room where Taja Smith was taken by caesarean at 9:48. Both mother and child suffered substantial injuries. Taja has severe brain damage. The trial court sustained a demurrer to the complaint against the Richmond Memorial Hospital.]

Congress enacted COBRA in 1986 in response to the growing number of instances in which hospitals were refusing to treat individuals with emergency medical conditions, a practice generally referred to as "patient dumping." Under the common law, private hospitals have no duty to accept or to provide treatment for patients. While private hospitals traditionally did treat people in emergency situations, they generally were not fully compensated, or were not compensated at all, for treatment of indigent patients. With growing competition among hospitals, shifting this cost to paying patients became more difficult. As the hospitals' economic losses increased, the instances of patient dumping also increased. To counteract patient dumping and the resultant hardship and injury, COBRA established specific standards for the evaluation, treatment, and transfer of patients....

[T]he crux of the issue in this case is one of statutory interpretation: (1) whether COBRA's treatment and transfer requirements are limited solely to an emergency medical condition or active labor which has not been stabilized and which occurs in conjunction with initial admission to an emergency department; or (2) whether those requirements also apply when an emergency medical condition or active labor commences after the admission and initial stabilization of the patient's condition.

To resolve the parties' conflicting interpretations, we begin with an examination of the Act itself. At the time of the alleged violation, 42 U.S.C. § 1395dd stated in relevant part:

> (a) ... In the case of a hospital that has a hospital emergency department, if any individual (whether or not eligible for benefits under this subchapter) comes to the emergency department and a request is made ... for examination or treatment ... the hospital must provide for an appropriate medical screening examination ... to determine whether or not an emergency medical condition ... exists or to determine if the individual is in active labor....

> (b) ... If any individual (whether or not eligible for benefits under this subchapter) comes to a hospital and the hospital determines that the individual has an emergency medical condition or is in active labor, the hospital must provide either—

>> (A) ... such further medical examination and such treatment as may be required to stabilize the medical condition or ... provide for treatment of the labor, or

>> (B) for transfer of the individual to another medical facility in accordance with subsection (c) of this section....

(c) . . . If a patient at a hospital has an emergency medical condition which has not been stabilized . . . or is in active labor, the hospital may not transfer the patient unless—

(A)(i) the patient . . . requests that the transfer be effected, or (ii) a physician . . . or other qualified medical personnel when a physician is not readily available in the emergency department, has signed a certification that . . . the medical benefits reasonably expected from the . . . [transfer] outweigh the increased risks to the individual's medical condition from effectuating the transfer. . . .

The language used in each subsection describes distinct patient circumstances requiring different treatment protocols. If an individual "comes to the emergency department," the hospital must provide an appropriate medical screening examination. Id. at § 1395dd(a). If an individual "comes to a hospital" and the hospital determines that an emergency medical condition or active labor exists, the hospital must stabilize the condition or transfer the person. Id. § 1395dd(b). If a "patient at a hospital" has an emergency condition or is in active labor, the hospital may transfer that patient only under certain conditions. Id. § 1395dd(c).

The statutory language clearly requires a patient to be in an emergency medical condition or to be in active labor before the provisions of subsections (b) and (c) apply. But we find nothing in the language of the Act which limits application of these subsections solely to a patient who initially arrives at the emergency room and who has not been stabilized, as the Hospital argues here. When the words of the statute are plain and unambiguous we need not resort to rules of statutory construction or legislative history.

This interpretation of the Act is consistent with the legislation's purpose. Patient dumping is not limited to a refusal to provide emergency room treatment. It occurs, and is equally reprehensible, at any time a hospital determines that a patient's condition may result in substantial medical costs and the hospital transfers the patient because it fears it will not be paid for those expenses. Dumping a patient in this manner is neither related to, nor dependent upon, the patient arriving through the emergency room and never being stabilized. . . .

[The hospital argued that the suit could not be brought because the plaintiff had not complied with Virginia's statutory prerequisites for a malpractice suit.] The Virginia notice provisions not only require a plaintiff to provide written notice of the claim to the health care provider, they also absolutely prohibit the filing of a medical malpractice claim against the health care provider until 90 days after such notification. . . . The state statute of limitations is tolled during this period. It is this aspect of the notice of claim provision which is in direct conflict with the provisions of COBRA. . . .

. . . Compliance with the notice provisions of the Virginia statute could result in the inability of a litigant to file a claim within the COBRA two-year statute of limitations period. Consequently, we hold that the trial court correctly ruled that the notice of claim provisions of Code § 8.01–581.2 conflict with the requirements of COBRA and, therefore, are inapplicable to COBRA causes of action.

For the reasons discussed above, the judgment of the trial court will be affirmed in part and reversed in part, and the case remanded for further proceedings.

Affirmed in part, reversed in part, and remanded.

Notes

1. The statute involved in *Smith* is now usually called the Emergency Medical Treatment and Active Labor Act, known by its acronym, EMTALA. Although EMTALA is a federal statute, states must follow it, as Virginia did in *Smith*.

2. In accord with *Smith,* that coming to the emergency department is not necessary to invoke the act: *Lopez-Soto v. Hawayek,* 175 F.3d 170 (1st Cir.1999). *James v. Sunrise Hospital,* 86 F.3d 885 (9th Cir.1996) reached the opposite conclusion, holding that the duty to screen, to stabilize, and to continue treatment in subsections (a), (b) and (c) applied only to one who comes to the emergency department.

3. Must the violation of the statute be a cause of the plaintiff's harm? Subsection (d) of the statute provides that "Any individual who suffers personal harm as a direct result of a participating hospital's violation of a requirement of this section may, in a civil action against the participating hospital, obtain those damages available for personal injury under the law of the State in which the hospital is located, and such equitable relief as is appropriate."

4. A boy is seriously injured. By telephone, a hospital agrees to accept him, then calls back to say he will not be accepted without insurance. He had none and is delayed seven hours getting to a hospital that will accept him. The delay causes the boy's condition to worsen. On these allegations is the first hospital that originally accepted and then rejected him liable under EMTALA? What statutory words control? *Miller v. Medical Center of Southwest Louisiana,* 22 F.3d 626 (5th Cir.1994). See also *Johnson v. University of Chicago Hospitals,* 982 F.2d 230 (7th Cir.1992) (hospital operator told ambulance, only five blocks away, not to bring patient to hospital).

5. *What is "appropriate" screening?* The statute requires "appropriate" medical screening. Would negligent screening violate the statute? Federal courts fear that tests based upon negligence would turn the statute into a federal medical malpractice statute. One idea is that disparate screening–providing better screening to some patients than others–would be a violation of the appropriate screening requirement. *Power v. Arlington Hospital Ass'n,* 42 F.3d 851 (4th Cir.1994). If that is right, would it also be right to say that the screening is appropriate whenever it is of the same quality provided all other individuals?

6. In *Roberts v. Galen of Virginia, Inc.,* 525 U.S. 249, 119 S.Ct. 685, 142 L.Ed.2d 648 (1999), the Supreme Court said that liability may be

imposed under the stabilization requirement even if the hospital had no bad motive, such as a motive to dump patients who had no insurance. The Court did not decide whether motive played in part in liability for screening failures.

7. "Baby K" was born anencephalic, that is, with a brain stem that operates autonomic body functions like breathing but without a cerebrum, the part that people usually mean when they refer to the brain. She is permanently unconscious and cannot see, hear, or interact with her environment. She has no awareness of any kind and of course no cognitive ability. In the normal course of events, anencephalics die within a short time. The hospital applied to the court for permission to refuse further treatments when Baby K suffered breathing difficulties. It proposed instead to provide warmth, hydration, and nutrition only. The court held that the EMTALA required continued treatment anytime Baby K suffered a respiratory "emergency." In *Matter of Baby "K"*, 16 F.3d 590 (4th Cir.1994). Is this morally right or morally wrong? The court said the moral question did not matter because (in its opinion) Congress has clearly spoken and what it said was that stabilizing treatment had to be provided in any emergency.

8. In cases like that of *Baby K, Power,* and *Miller,* should the medical standard of care be lowered when patients cannot pay? See James A. Henderson and John A. Siliciano, *Universal Health Care and the Continued Reliance on Custom in Determining Medical Malpractice,* 79 CORNELL L. REV. 1382 (1994).

9. *Coordinating with or trumping state law.* How does EMTALA fit with state law of medical malpractice? EMTALA does not either enhance or limit whatever state-law medical malpractice claim the plaintiff might have. But could state-law limits on health-care claims also limit EMTALA claims? In *Smith*, the court said that the state-law pre-suit notice of claim requirement had no application to suits brought under the federal EMTALA statute. But in *Hardy v. New York City Health & Hospital Corp.,* 164 F.3d 789 (2d Cir.1999) the court asserted that by authorizing damages measured by state law damages rules, EMTALA meant to exclude claims that would be barred altogether under state law because of the plaintiff's failure to give notice of claim within 90 days of the occurrence. Look at the EMTALA damages provision in note 3 above and see if you agree.

Would you distinguish the pre-suit notice requirement in *Hardy* from a state's statutory cap on damages for health care injury? In *Barris v. County of Los Angeles,* 20 Cal.4th 101, 972 P.2d 966, 83 Cal.Rptr.2d 145 (1999) the California Court applied the state's damages cap to an EMTALA claim.

Suppose that, under state law, a hospital is completely immune from all tort liability and therefore liable for zero damages. Would an an EMTALA claim be barred? *Root v. New Liberty Hospital Dist.,* 209 F.3d 1068 (8th Cir.2000).

———

CORREA v. HOSPITAL SAN FRANCISCO, 69 F.3d 1184 (1st Cir. 1995). Mrs. Gonzalez went to the defendant hospital's emergency room complaining of chest pains, chills, and dizziness. The hospital gave her a number—47—and told her to wait until called. An hour and fifteen minutes later, the emergency room had reached number 24. After two hours of waiting, Mrs. Gonzalez left to seek help from Dr. Rojas. She was then vomiting and suffering extremely low blood pressure. Dr. Rojas began treatment, but Mrs. Gonzalez died soon thereafter. Her survivors brought suit in federal court under the Emergency Medical Treatment and Active Labor Act, EMTALA. They recovered $700,000. On appeal, the defendant argued that it had no duty to screen Mrs. Gonzalez because she did not have a medical emergency condition when she arrived and in any event that it did not refuse to screen her because she lacked funds or insurance. *Held,* the judgment is affirmed. (1) "EMTALA requires participating hospitals to provide appropriate screening to all who enter the hospitals' emergency departments, whether or not they are in the throes of a medical emergency when they arrive." (2) "A hospital fulfills its statutory duty to screen patients in its emergency room if it provides for a screening examination reasonably calculated to identify critical medical conditions that may be afflicting symptomatic patients and provides that level of screening uniformly to all those who present substantially similar complaints. The essence of this require-ment is that there be some screening procedure, and that it be adminis-tered even-handedly.... [F]aulty screening, in a particular case, as opposed to disparate screening or refusing to screen at all, does not contravene the statute. In this case, HSF's delay in attending to the patient was so egregious and lacking in justification as to amount to an effective denial of a screening examination." And "a desire to shirk the burden of uncompensated care is not a necessary element of a cause of action under EMTALA."

e. *Strict and Limited Liability Proposals*

A number of scholars have suggested that health care providers should be strictly liable for some kinds of untoward medical events. See Barry Furrow, *Defective Mental Treatment: A Proposal for the Applica-tion of Strict Liability to Psychiatric Services*, 58 B.U.L. REV. 391 (1978); Clark C. Havinghurst, *"Medical Adversity Insurance"–Has Its Time Come?*, [1975] DUKE L.J. 1233. With strict liability, the damages award might be limited; pain and suffering damages might be excluded, for example. For this reason, it might even be cheaper for doctors or hospitals to pay every injured patient than to defend legal actions. See Jeffrey O'Connell, *Offers That Can't Be Refused: Foreclosure of Personal Injury Claims by Defendants' Prompt Tender of Claimants' Net Econom-ic Losses*, 77 NW.U.L.REV. 589 (1982).

The American Law Institute's REPORTER'S STUDY OF ENTERPRISE LIABIL-ITY FOR PERSONAL INJURY (ALI 1991) suggested (1) eliminating individual doctor liability in favor of hospital liability when injury results from the practice of a hospital-affiliated doctor; (2) limiting pain and suffering damages, with some other adjustments in damages awards; (3) awarding attorney fees to the prevailing plaintiff (since pain and suffering recover-ies, from which such fees might have been paid, would be limited or barred). It also supported a strict liability or no-fault plan when the patient and hospital agreed.

A large study of medical incidents causing harm to patients showed that a very high percentage of patients injured by practices that doctors themselves would consider to be below-standard, never sued. Most of did not even make a claim. The study also showed that among those who *did* sue, only a fraction had valid claims, although some of them did win judgments. The authors concluded that the people who *should* recover something most often do not, and those who should not recover sometimes do. See Localio, Lawthers, Brennan, Laird, Hebert, Peterson, Newhouse, Weiler & Hiatt, *Relation between Malpractice Claims and Adverse Events Due to Negligence*, 325 N. ENG. J. MED. 245 (July 25, 1991); PAUL WEILER, MEDICAL MALPRACTICE ON TRIAL (1991). Does this bear on the decision to impose strict liability?

One strict liability plan is actually in use. In Virginia, obstetricians contribute to a fund which pays for the pecuniary needs of infants who suffer brain damage at birth. No pain and suffering award is made. VA. CODE § 38.2–5001. See Note, *Innovative No–Fault Tort Reform for An Endangered Specialty*, 74 VA. L. REV. 1487 (1988).

REFERENCES: BARRY R. FURROW, THOMAS L. GREANEY, SANDRA H. JOHNSON, TIMOTHY S. JOST & ROBERT L. SCHWARTZ, HEALTH LAW (2 vols. 1995).

§ 5. NURSING HOMES, LONG–TERM CARE AND ELDER ABUSE

HORIZON/CMS HEALTHCARE CORP. v. AULD

Texas Court of Appeals, 1999.
985 S.W.2d 216.

DIXON W. HOLMAN, JUSTICE. . . .

In August 1994, Martha Hary, age 76, became a resident at the nursing home. The case was tried upon allegations that beginning in December 1994, the nursing home neglected to provide Martha with medical care and treatment within the acceptable standard of care. . . . At trial, Auld asserted that while a resident at the nursing home between mid-December 1994 and August 1995, and because of substandard nursing care, Martha's body developed pressure sores, some of which deteriorated to a condition described as Stage IV, where the tissue overlying a person's bone rots away and leaves the bone exposed. Auld asserted that Martha suffered contractures in all extremities and that the nursing home did not provide Martha all of the wound care treatments and pressure relieving devices that had been ordered. Auld contended that the care administered for Martha's pressure sores was painful, including surgical excision of foreign matter and all dead and devitalized tissue in the wounds, a procedure known as debridement. On August 6, 1995, Martha was taken from the nursing home to Fort Worth's Osteopathic Hospital where she was treated for 10 days. After her discharge from the hospital, Martha spent the remaining year of her life at a facility that is not a party to this suit. She died August 9, 1996. . . .

. . . The jury found that the nursing home's negligence proximately caused Martha's injury and found $2,371,000 as actual damages [a sum later adjusted by agreement to $2,370,941.71]. That sum includes $1,750,000 for physical pain and mental anguish, $150,000 for disfigurement, $250,000 for impairment, and $221,000 for medical care. The jury did not find that Martha's injuries resulted from malice, but found the nursing home grossly negligent. . . . The jury found $90,000,000 as exemplary damages.

[Much of the courts's opinion on appeal is devoted to the application of statutes capping damages. Actual damages of $2,371,000 were capped to leave the plaintiff $1,541,203.13 including an award for interest. Punitive damages were capped at four times the uncapped actual damages for a total of $9,483,766.92.]

The nursing home does not complain that either the jury finding of $90,000,000 in punitive damages or the court's reduction of that sum to $9,483,766.92 is excessive. . . .

[The nursing home argued that the trial judge erred in admitting into evidence the written investigation reports made by investigators for the Texas Department of Human Services to determine compliance with state licensing requirements and federal and state Medicaid requirements.] The nursing home argues that the survey reports merely measure the extent of the home's compliance with contractual and regulatory standards, not whether it has negligently deviated from the standard of medical care necessary for patients.

After the defense rested its case, a hearing was held out of the jury's presence where Auld offered as rebuttal evidence thirteen state "survey reports" labeled exhibit 22, pages A through M, covering the period from September 1, 1994 to December 31, 1995. For most of that time, Martha resided at the home. Auld's exhibit list identifies exhibit 22 as "certified copies of Texas Department of Human Services, Long Term Care Records, Vendor 498–51, Heritage Western Hills Nursing Home." . . .

Both the opening statement to the jury by the nursing home's attorney, and the eventual testimony of the nursing home's witnesses about a good quality of care given to Martha, opened the door to the admission of exhibit 22 and the use of its contents as impeachment material. The trial court observed:

Well, your witnesses have testified that no patient ever failed to have the basic care. So, if there is an incident [recorded within exhibit 22] showing that a patient failed to have basic care, it is at least impeachment if it goes to the issues that are the basis of this case. . . .

Because exhibit 22 is (and was presented to the trial court as) a certified copy of a record of a public agency, it is not inadmissible hearsay. Moreover, evidence of a defendant's subjective knowledge of the peril his conduct creates is admissible to prove gross negligence, which was an issue at this trial. The information contained in exhibit 22 confirms the nursing home's knowledge of the conditions in the home that adversely affected Martha's care and showed that the state did bring those conditions to the home's knowledge in a timely manner with regard to Martha's stay at the home. . . .

[W]e conclude that the trial court did not abuse its discretion by admitting exhibit 22. . . .

[The nursing home argued that the compensatory damages award was excessive.] Our review of all the evidence reveals that at trial, Auld established that (1) four basic nursing interventions were necessary to prevent Martha from developing pressure sores and contractures on her body; (2) the first intervention required that Martha be turned and repositioned regularly; (3) the second intervention required that Martha receive adequate nutrition; (4) the third intervention required that, as an incontinent patient, Martha's skin be kept clean and dry; (5) the fourth intervention required that to stimulate blood flow to the skin and prevent contractures, Martha's joints should have been treated with a passive range of motion exercises; (6) in the beginning of Martha's stay at the nursing home, she received those types of care which kept pressure sores and contractures from developing on her body; (7) from mid-December 1994 until she was taken from the nursing home on August 6, 1995, Martha did not receive those types of nursing care; (8) during the latter time-period, Martha's body was not turned or repositioned during approximately 210 eight-hour shifts, totaling 1,680 hours; (9) that during the same period of months, Martha was not fed regularly and missed 238 meals; (10) that during the same period of months, Martha was not given incontinent care during approximately 216 eight-hour shifts, totaling 1,728 hours; (11) during that period of months, no range of motion exercises were administered to Martha; (12) the nursing home's current and past employees admitted that its records (flow sheets) for Martha accurately reflected these deficiencies, and they testified that they had no reason to doubt the records' accuracy; (13) that between mid-December 1994 and August 1995, Martha's body developed between nine and 12 pressure sores, at least four of which deteriorated to Stage IV, and she also developed contractures in all of her extremities; (14) after Martha developed the pressure sores, the nursing home did not furnish all of the wound-care treatments and pressure-relieving devices that were ordered for her; (15) those conditions resulted in painful wound care and debridement; (16) when she was taken from the nursing home to the hospital, the hospital personnel considered her condition to be terminal due to the pressure sores, contractures, infection, and malnutrition; (17) that those conditions caused her to have to undergo painful treatments at the hospital; and (18) the injuries she suffered while at the nursing home caused her severe physical pain, mental anguish, physical impairment, and physical disfigurement, which lasted until her death nearly a year after she left the nursing home. Auld carried her burden to prove and secure jury findings that the nursing home proximately caused Martha's injuries.

. . . The evidence is both legally and factually sufficient to support the jury's findings of damages for physical pain and mental anguish, disfigurement, and impairment. We overrule the nursing home's third issue.

. . . Finding no reversible error, we affirm the trial court's judgment. . . .

Notes

1.   This case was affirmed in the Texas Supreme Court except on the issue of prejudgment interest, which that court held was capped by a statute. The punitive damage award was allowed to stand. *Horizon/CMS Healthcare Corp. v. Auld,* ___ S.W.3d ___, 2000 WL 1199263 (Tex. 2000).

2.   *Extent of elder abuse.* A federally funded study indicates that around half a million elders are abused every year in their own homes, usually by their adult children or spouses. *Sieniarecki v. State,* 756 So.2d 68 (Fla.2000), upholding the constitutionality of Florida's criminal punishment, gives a graphic and upsetting description.

3.   *Nursing homes.* Nursing homes range from mom-and-pop outfits with a few beds to giant corporate enterprises, some of which can take in or lose billions in any given year. Horizon/CMS, the defendant in *Auld,* showed total operating revenues of $1,753,084,000 ($1.75 Billion) in its 1996 annual report filed with the Securities and Exchange Commission. Manor Care, Inc., itself a subsidiary of Health Care and Retirement Corp., is another chain. It reported assets of $2,280,866,000 at the end of 1999 and revenue for the year of $2,135,345,000. According to a company profile, the President and CEO has an annual salary of $1,600,000.

4.   *Nursing home finance.* A high percentage of nursing home residents are on Medicaid. Their social security income if any plus Medicaid pays the nursing home. Medicaid pays only to the extent that nursing home care is needed and to the extent that the resident cannot himself pay the costs. Distinguish Medicare. Medicare pays for covered items without regard to the beneficiary's wealth or income, but it does not cover basic custodial care in a nursing home, only some special items. The two programs together, administered by the Health Care Financing Administration (HCFA), directly pay nursing homes for care provided. These programs have thus helped create the big chain nursing home industry.

5.   *Underreporting of abuse.* Abuse and neglect in care facilities ranges from physical and sexual attacks on residents to systematic neglect as seen in the *Auld* case. The amount of abuse is enormous, but it is hard to document its exact extent because residents are often incompetent or too afraid to report it.

6.   *Affordability for the lawyer.* Even when a resident or outsider reports deficiencies in care and injury, a tort action is often impractical. In the *Horizon/Auld* case, actual physical harm was discovered and Horizon's own records helped document its neglect. But in most cases, family members

(if any) may not discover the harm or its cause. The nursing home records may not document the abuse. If a suit is brought, the patient may make a poor witness. Actual damages may be quite limited in many cases: the nursing home may have inflicted pain and misery, but its neglect does not deprive the resident of an active life; if the nursing home hastens death, it does not hasten it by very much. Lawyers can hardly afford to take cases that will require enormous investments of time to recover small damages, so many of these claims may be rejected by lawyers or possibly settled cheaply without suit. See 1 BARRY R. FURROW, THOMAS L. GREANEY, SANDRA H. JOHNSON, TIMOTHY JOST, & ROBERT L. SCHWARTZ, HEALTH LAW §§ 1–2 (1995). These circumstances make punitive damages especially important in nursing home cases–first to provide an appropriate level of deterrence, since ordinary damages may be small, and second to encourage lawyers to bring suits they could not afford to try without a fee based on punitive recoveries.

7. *Standard of care and coverage by medical malpractice statutes.* If a victim's survivors manage to identify abuse and bring suit, does the medical standard of care control and do the medical malpractice reforms statutes apply to present further obstacles to suit? Suppose the nursing home does not provide adequate nutrition, doesn't provide the patient the pain medication prescribed by a doctor, or doesn't wash or clean a helpless patient. Is that really a matter of health care as distinct from ordinary negligence? See *Taylor v. Vencor, Inc.,* 136 N.C.App. 528, 525 S.E.2d 201(N.C.App.2000) (defendant failed to supervise resident properly, with the result the resident caused a fire from which she suffered deadly burns, ordinary negligence). What about unnecessary chemical or physical restraint–could the plaintiff recover without expert professional testimony about the standard of care on the ground that the defendant has committed a battery or false imprisonment? See *Roberson v. Provident House,* 576 So.2d 992 (La.1991) (battery). In *Clites v. State,* 322 N.W.2d 917 (Iowa 1982) the court proceeded on a malpractice theory and upheld a judgment for the restrained plaintiff because actual harm was done and the use of chemical restraints for staff convenience violated the medical standard of care.

8. *Res ipsa loquitur.* Since the nursing home has a large measure of control over the relatively helpless (sometimes totally helpless) resident, would res ipsa loquitur apply to establish negligence when the resident has bedsores? What if the resident suffers injury because she ingests the wrong medicine? *Harder v. F.C. Clinton, Inc.,* 948 P.2d 298 (Okla.1997) (doctrine applied though defendant denied providing the medicine, which was not prescribed for the resident at all).

9. *Using regulations to prove a standard of care and/or breach.* Long-term care facilities like nursing homes are regulated both by state and federal law. HCFA regulations can conceivably be put in evidence as standards to which the facility must conform. For example, one regulation provides that "Each resident must receive and the facility must provide the necessary care and services to attain or maintain the highest practicable physical, mental, and psychosocial well-being, in accordance with the comprehensive assessment and plan of care." Other regulations provide many more specific standards. For example, the facility must ensure that "(1) A resident who enters the facility without pressure sores does not develop pressure sores unless the individual's clinical condition demonstrates that

they were unavoidable; and (2) A resident having pressure sores receives necessary treatment and services to promote healing, prevent infection and prevent new sores from developing." 42 C.F.R. § 483.25. In *Conservatorship of Gregory,* 80 Cal.App.4th 514, 95 Cal.Rptr.2d 336 (2000), understaffing of a nursing home led to injuries. Although suit was brought under state law, the trial court instructed the jury on federal regulatory standards. This was upheld on appeal.

10.   *Inspection or survey reports.* In *Horizon/CMS v. Auld,* the court admitted into evidence the reports of state inspections. These reflect annual surveys made by the states pursuant to federal standards. Failure to meet federal standards (deficiencies) are noted in standardized ways. In the *Auld* case, admission of the survey evidence showed that Horizon knew of its own violations. This might create a basis for punitive damages. Conversely, if the trial judge does not admit such evidence in the case, the plaintiff will have no claim for punitive damages unless she can show the nursing home's malice or recklessness by some other means.

11.   *Elder abuse, residents' rights statutes.* Some states have created statutory tort claims for elders against caregivers under specified circumstances. Protection is sometimes illusory. A Florida court has held that if the patient died, but not as a result of injuries sustained in the nursing home, the statutory claim is lost. *Beverly Enterprises–Florida, Inc. v. Knowles,* 766 So.2d 335 (Fla. 2000). California's statute in effect says that neglect such as failure to provide nourishment or abuse such as sexual assault is actionable, which seems to add very little if anything to ordinary tort law. But the statutes may advance the rights of patients in other ways. The Washington statute permits the prevailing victim to recover attorney fees. REV. CODE WASH. § 74.34.200. The California statute also permits the victim to recover attorney fees, although only if the plaintiff proves oppression, recklessness, or malice by clear and convincing evidence as well as the abuse or neglect itself. See CAL. WELF. & INST.CODE § 15657. Such proof then permits the plaintiff to avoid limitations that would apply to medical malpractice claims. See *Delaney v. Baker,* 20 Cal.4th 23, 971 P.2d 986, 82 Cal.Rptr.2d 610 (1999). The statute also permits suits not only against institutional caregivers but also against anyone violates the statute's terms, including independent doctors. See *Mack v. Soung,* 95 Cal.Rptr.2d 830, 80 Cal.App.4th 966 (2000). In states where pain and suffering damages do not survive the death of the victim, the elder abuse statute may permit the pain claim to survive. *Guardianship of Denton,* 190 Ariz. 152, 945 P.2d 1283 (1997). Such statutes do little or nothing to help identify abuse or neglect.

NOTE: REGULATION OR FINANCIAL PARTNERSHIP?

Nursing homes, like much of the rest of the health care industry, are largely financed through Medicare or Medicaid payments. The Health Care Financing Administration authorizes medicaid payments to certified care providers. Although HCFA indisputably issues regulations, that is more or less incidental to the business to managing medicare/medicaid. In theory, HCFA can enforce its standards by terminating payments, but in practice its aim is to deliver health care or long-term care and in that sense it is in a kind of partnership with nursing facilities. If a nursing home fails to meet standards, you might expect that HCFA would simply terminate the the nursing home as a certified provider. This has occasionally happened. See *Northern Health Facilities, Inc. v. United States,* 39 F.Supp.2d 563 (D.Md.1998). However, elimination of a nursing home at a time when the elderly population is increasing may be unwise in the long term and certainly is likely to disrupt the lives of all the present residents. Given the widespread deficiencies among nursing homes, the dilemma may be like that presented to child protective workers–movement from one bad home may turn out to be movement to another that is just as bad or worse. Besides this, HCFA is not designed as a regulatory agency and not imbued with regulatory zeal. It is a financing agency. In consequence, the regulations may sometimes help lawyers seeking to establish a standard of care, but they may not do the job of preventing abuse in the first place.

NOTE ON THE FALSE CLAIMS ACT AND QUI TAM ACTIONS

False claims. Social control of nursing home abuse may come about in another way. Federal prosecutors, who are in no way connected with HCFA, are charged with prosecuting crimes of all sorts. Under the Federal False Claims Act, anyone who knowingly presents a false claim against the United States is criminally liable and also liable for a civil fine and treble damages. 18 U.S.C.A. § 287 & 31 U.S.C.A. § 729. If a nursing facility presented a claim for medicaid reimbursement for services it did not deliver, this would be a false claim and it could be criminally and civilly liable under the False Claims Act. Could it also be liable if it presented a claim for medicaid or medicare payments when its care did not meet standards? Maybe companies seeking medicaid reimbursement from the government impliedly certify that they have complied with regulatory standards. If they in fact provide the kind of "care" the court found was provided for Martha Hary in the *Auld* case, wouldn't that be a false claim?

Qui tam. The question takes on added importance because of a bounty hunter provision in the False Claims Act. This provision permits private citizens to sue on behalf of the government for False Claims Act violations. The government can then take over the lawsuit or not, but even if it does, the private plaintiff who brought suit in the government's name is paid a percentage of the recovery. These private citizen actions are called qui tam actions, from the first words of a Latin phrase used in common law actions to describe the plaintiff–one who sues for the king as well as for himself. The question here is whether federal prosecutors or a qui tam plaintiff could recover treble damages under the False Claims Act on proof that the facility sought reimbursement for woefully substandard care. A few such cases have been settled in favor of the government. At least one such implied certification claim has received judicial approval. *United States ex rel. Aranda v. Community Psychiatric Centers of Oklahoma, Inc.,* 945 F.Supp. 1485 (W.D.Okla.1996). But another court has denied a similar claim. *United States ex rel. Mikes v. Straus,* 84 F.Supp.2d 427 (S.D.N.Y.1999).

———

Refocusing. One problem about nursing home abuse or neglect is that it may not be discovered at all. Nursing home residents are elderly and expected to die within a short period anyway. Unless the resident has close family members who monitor her condition, neither mistreatment nor neglect is likely to be known. A second problem is affordability of suit. When nursing home abuse and negligence are discovered, suit may not be feasible because expected damages awards will often not pay for the time the lawyer must invest. The result is underdeterrence on one side and under- or no-compensation on the other. This section reflects three ways in which courts or legislatures can deal with the affordability problem. Which is the best? Should all three be available?

§ 6. INTENTIONAL TORTS AND SEXUAL HARASSMENT BY PROFESSIONALS

The focus of this chapter is on negligent, not intentional torts. But some torts that appear to be intentional in some sense, may be treated as negligent torts for one purpose or another. The characterization of the tort as one based upon negligence or one based upon battery often becomes important in determining whether the defendant's liability insurance will cover the case.

a. *Sexual Battery or Exploitation of Patients, Parishioners, or Clients*

When a health care provider is guilty of sexual harassment of a patient, two issues aside from the merits may become dominant: (1) Will his liability insurance policy cover intentional misconduct? (2) Is his conduct covered by medical malpractice statutes so that he gets whatever special benefits those statutes provide in his jurisdiction?

(1) On the first question, you could guess that insurers dislike covering criminal misconduct, but more to the point they are likely to exclude coverage for non-professional conduct. Yet non-professional sexual harassment may arise rather directly from the physician patient relationship. In that case, the court may hold that the policy provides coverage that will pay for the harasser's legal liability. That was the result in *St. Paul Fire and Marine Ins. Co. v. Shernow,* 222 Conn. 823, 610 A.2d 1281 (1992). In that case, a female patient of a dentist alleged that the dentist administered nitrous oxide and that she lost consciousness. Regaining consciousness, she realized that the dentist's tongue was in her mouth and that her breasts felt painful. She resisted and the dentist turned up the nitrous oxide. On regaining consciousness again, she found the dentist on top of her. Again he turned up the gas. Although the insurance policy excluded coverage for battery, the court

held that battery was so mixed with negligent professional treatment–too much gas–that the policy covered all of the dentist's liability.

(2) Does a malpractice statute with its special rules cover a sexual attack or harassment claim against a health care provider? In *Hagan v. Antonio*, 240 Va. 347, 397 S.E.2d 810 (1990) a female plaintiff sued a male doctor alleging that in the course of a medical examination he improperly played with her breasts and made sexual remarks. The doctor defended on the ground that the plaintiff had failed to give the special pre-suit notice required by the statute. The plaintiff argued that the statute only covered claims based on health care or professional services rendered, and that the acts complained of were not such professional services. The court held, however, that the doctor was protected by the notice requirement because the alleged act "stemmed from, arose from, and was 'based on' the performance of a physical examination." The court thought rape would be distinguishable.

b. Exploitation of the Consenting Patient, Parishioner, or Client

Many professionals appear to engage in consensual sexual relationships with patients or clients. The problem is especially common with therapists such as psychologists, psychiatrists, or analysts. A number of states have enacted statutes that permit the patient to recover, at least under some circumstances, for injury suffered as a result of sexual contact with the therapist, regardless of consent. CAL.CIV.CODE § 43.93 (b) (if there is therapeutic deception); ILL. STAT. CH. 70 ¶ 802 § 2 (if the patient was emotionally dependent or the therapist practiced deception); MINN. STAT. § 148A.02 (similar); WIS. STAT. ANN. § 895.70 (regardless of emotional dependence or deception).

Even apart from the statutes, the patient's consent may not be a defense if it is less-than-informed or the therapist manipulates the patient. If consent is no defense, is the claim against the therapist a claim for battery, so that the therapist's liability insurance does not protect the therapist and does not provide a source of funds for the victim? Patients attempt to avoid the battery trap by asserting that the therapist has negligently mishandled the "transference" phenomenon. That is, that the therapist mishandled the well-known tendency of patients to develop sexual, romantic, or dependent relationships with their therapists. Sexual relationships with patients in therapy is regarded as a way of negligently mishandling transference and "[c]ourts have uniformly regarded mishandling of transference as malpractice or gross negligence." *Simmons v. United States*, 805 F.2d 1363 (9th Cir.1986). This reasoning converts a battery into negligence.

Therapist exploitation cases also incidentally call into question the professional standard of care. Although the American Psychiatric Association states that sexual contact with patients is unethical, many therapists of various persuasions do in fact engage in sexual relations with patients. See Linda Jorgenson, Rebecca Randles, and Larry Strasburger,

The Furor over Psychotherapist-patient Sexual Contact: New Solutions to an Old Problem, 32 Wm. & Mary L. Rev. 645 (1991). If the "custom of the industry" is to take advantage of the relationship to engage in sexual relations with patients, can the therapist be held liable after all?

Clergy sexual exploitation. What if a clergy person exploits the pastoral relationship with parishioners to engage in sexual relationships that prove emotionally harmful? A number of these cases hold in favor of the allegedly exploitive clergy, sometimes advancing the view that religious freedom protects the clergy and their churches from liability for sexually exploitive behavior. See *Pritzlaff v. Archdiocese of Milwaukee,* 194 Wis.2d 302, 533 N.W.2d 780 (Wis. 1995); cf. *Byrd v. Faber,* 57 Ohio St.3d 56, 565 N.E.2d 584, 5 A.L.R.5th 1115 (1991) (considerations based in First Amendment impose requirement of more specific pleading when church is sued for negligent hiring). Courts tend to say that there is no such tort as clergy malpractice or clergy breach of fiduciary duty. *Schieffer v. Catholic Archdiocese of Omaha,* 244 Neb. 715, 508 N.W.2d 907 (1993). A similar result may be reached even when the priest or minister is functioning as a counselor to his parishioner. *Bladen v. First Presbyterian Church of Sallisaw, Okla.,* 857 P.2d 789 (Okla.1993). The *Bladen* court thought that the claim would lie against a member of the clergy only upon a showing that he misused the transference mechanism or breached a fiducial duty. A few cases go the other way, holding the clergyman responsible for sexual exploitation of a parishioner. See *F.G. v. MacDonell,* 150 N.J. 550, 696 A.2d 697 (1997). A little authority supports the parishioner when she claims negligence of the religious body itself in hiring or supervising clergy, or breach of a fiducial duty that might occur when the religious body does not seek to prevent or ameliorate the effects of priestly sexual behavior with vulnerable parishioners. See *Moses v. Diocese of Colorado,* 863 P.2d 310 (Colo.1993).

Lawyers. Suppose a lawyer counsels a client about divorce. The lawyer induces the client to engage in sexual activity. How does this compare or contrast with similar scenarios in the case of therapists and clergy? A few states have adopted specific ethical rules prohibiting such behavior by lawyers. See Cal. Rules Prof. Conduct 3–120.

NOTE: IMMUNITIES

The defendants encountered in Chapters 10 and 11—landowners and health care professionals—usually obtained special protections from liability because courts limited the duties they owed to something less than duties of reasonable care. In Chapters 12 and 13, defendants such as family members, charities, and governmental entities obtain similar protections, but the locution is slightly different. Here courts say that these defendants are immune from tort suits or tort liability. The difference between a no-duty rule and an immunity rule, if the difference exists at all, is minuscule. In short, the immunity rules are quite similar to the limited duty rules except that they tended in their original form to be absolute and without exception.

Chapter 12

FAMILY MEMBERS AND CHARITIES

§ 1.   FAMILY MEMBERS

NOTE: THE TRADITIONAL FAMILY IMMUNITIES

Spouses. The common law took the view that upon marriage the wife lost her legal identity, which was merged with that of the husband. The logical result of this conception was, of course, that the spouses could not sue each other. A complete history of the immunity, with analysis of all the other reasons given for it, is found in Carl W. Tobias, *Interspousal Tort Immunity in America*, 23 GA. L. REV. 359 (1989).

Parent and child. There was no such conceptual reason to bar suits between parents and children. The parent-child immunity was introduced rather casually in *Hewellette v. George*, 68 Miss. 703, 9 So. 885 (1891) with the unadorned argument that family harmony would not permit such actions. "[S]o long as the parent is under obligation to care for, guide, and control, and the child is under reciprocal obligation to aid and comfort and obey, no such action as this can be maintained." Other states followed this decision and it became the general law in America.

Scope and exceptions. *(1) Property interests*. Children were allowed, however, to sue parents to protect property, and after the Married Women's Property Acts spouses were also allowed to sue for such property torts as conversion. The parental immunity terminated when the child reached majority and also when the child was emancipated, that is, was recognized as self-supporting or married. The parent-child relationship might also be terminated, some states have held, when the parent dies–with the result that the parent's estate could be sued though the parent could not be; but this rule was not followed everywhere. *(2) Relationship terminated*. Missouri once held that the immunity did not protect the non-custodial parent. *Fugate v. Fugate*, 582 S.W.2d 663 (Mo.1979), but Connecticut held that a divorced father who had visitation rights without physical custody, retained the parental immunity. *Ascuitto v. Farricielli*, 244 Conn. 692, 711 A.2d 708 (1998). *(3) Intention-*

al torts. Some courts were willing to impose liability upon spouses or parents for intentional torts even where they were not willing to do so for negligent torts. A striking case of this is *Lusby v. Lusby*, 283 Md. 334, 390 A.2d 77 (1978), where the wife alleged her husband and two other males forced her off the road, that her husband then raped her at gun point and assisted the two other males in attempted rape. Another example is the sexual abuse of children within the family. See *Hurst v. Capitell*, 539 So.2d 264 (Ala.1989). As we have become aware of the high incidence of spousal abuse, allowance of the tort suit seems almost a necessity, although almost certainly an inadequate response to the problem. See Douglas Scherer, *Tort Remedies for Victims of Domestic Abuse*, 43 S. C. L. Rᴇᴠ. 543 (1992). *(4) Family injury from violation of duty owed to larger class.* In some cases, family members seem to be involved only fortuitously, and injury and the family relationship in no way intersect. If a teenage daughter negligently drives a car and strikes a pedestrian in the cross-walk, the fact that he turns out to be her father will not bar recovery even where the immunity is retained. *Schenk v. Schenk*, 100 Ill.App.2d 199, 241 N.E.2d 12 (1968). Put differently, the immunity may be limited to cases in which the parental conduct involves discretion in discipline or supervision, and does not apply to ordinary negligent accidents. See *Cates v. Cates,* 156 Ill.2d 76, 189 Ill.Dec. 14, 619 N.E.2d 715 (1993).

Rationale. Two reasons predominate as justifications for the family immunities: (1) To permit suits between family members would be to encourage fraud and collusion; and (2) to permit suits of this kind would be to interfere with the family, and disrupt family harmony or unity.

Put baldly, the two main reasons for the immunity seem to have little force. Can these reasons be fleshed out? If liability insurance covers the defendant spouse, there is no doubt a tendency of the insured spouse, with the approval of the other, to assert fault. What may be an ordinary home accident, with no witnesses, may become a case of "negligence" quite readily. And even if it is negligence there is the probability that both spouses will share in some sense in the recovery. This obviously does not square with ordinary notions of accountability, because the faulty party, far from paying, would share in payment by his insurer.

In the case of parent-child actions, there was obviously some notion at one time that these would interfere with "discipline," and that if the child could sue, the parent's appropriate authority would be disrupted by judicial interference. This argument perhaps has little appeal today, especially if, as is often the case, the parent encourages the child's tort action in order to tap insurance funds. If there is no insurance, the danger is not fraud but misallocation of family funds. If a child recovers $100,000 from a parent, the parent may be unable to meet other obligations within the family, so that one child may enjoy relative riches while others are unable to receive any of the ordinary benefits of childhood. As these comments suggest, the two arguments of fraud and harmony can be expanded quite a bit. Is further elaboration of these arguments possible? When the arguments are fully developed, do you find them convincing or not?

Rejection of the immunities. By the end of the 1970s a majority of courts had abolished the spousal immunity, though sometimes only as to motor vehicle collisions. An example of complete abrogation of the immunity is *Waite v. Waite,* 618 So.2d 1360 (Fla.1993).

The courts have been a bit slower in abolishing the parent-child immunity, but it appears that a majority have now done so. Some states have abolished the immunity only for special groups of cases, such as those arising out of intentional torts, sexual abuse, motor vehicle accidents, or the conduct of a family business. E.g., *Henderson v. Woolley,* 230 Conn. 472, 644 A.2d 1303 (1994) (parental immunity does not bar child's claim for sexual abuse). A number, however, have simply abolished the immunity altogether, and applied the ordinary duty of reasonable care. *Broadbent v. Broadbent,* 184 Ariz. 74, 907 P.2d 43 (1995).

Where the immunities have been generally abolished, a whole set of new problems is arising, centered primarily now on the question of duty and negligence.

GOLLER v. WHITE, 20 Wis.2d 402, 122 N.W.2d 193 (1963). Goller was a foster child living in White's home under an arrangement with the Milwaukee County Welfare Department. White permitted Goller, who was 12 years old, to ride on the draw bar of White's tractor without warning him of protruding bolts on the wheels. These caught Goller's trouser leg and caused injury for which he sues. The trial court entered summary judgment for the defendant. *Held* reversed and remanded. Courts generally have held that a foster parent or one who stands *in loco parentis* can claim the parental immunity. The existence of insurance in a particular case offers no ground for an exception to the immunity. But "the wide prevalence of liability insurance in personal injury actions [is] a proper element to be considered in making the policy decision of whether to abrogate parental immunity in negligence actions.... [T]he existence of insurance tends to negate any possible disruption of family harmony and discipline." The immunity should be abrogated "except in these two situations: (1) where the alleged negligent act involves an exercise of parental authority over the child; and (2) where the alleged negligent act involves an exercise of ordinary parental discretion with respect to the provision of food, clothing, housing, medical and dental services, and other care."

COMMERCE BANK v. AUGSBURGER, 288 Ill.App.3d 510, 223 Ill.Dec. 872, 680 N.E.2d 822 (1997). The Illinois Department of Children and Family Services arranged for placement of a three-year old with foster parents, the defendants here. The defendants allegedly confined the child "in an enclosed space described as the 'upper half of a divided shelf of a wooden cabinet inside a bedroom closet at [their] home with the door closed' and did not supervise or monitor her; as a result, she died of asphyxia and hyperthermia. *Held,* dismissal affirmed. The plaintiff did not allege an intentional tort. Illinois has limited the immunity to cases of parental discretion but "parental discretion in the provision of care includes maintenance of the family home, medical treatment, and supervision of the child." The defendant's conduct, though severe, was the very kind to be protected under this standard.

Notes

1. *The reasonable person standard.* The *Goller* formula is a popular one. Are you happy with its application in *Commerce Bank v. Augsburger?* Some courts have gone beyond that formula by saying that parents will be liable under a reasonable person (or "reasonable parent") standard. See *Broadbent v. Broadbent,* 184 Ariz. 74, 907 P.2d 43 (1995); *Gibson v. Gibson,* 3 Cal.3d 914, 92 Cal.Rptr. 288, 479 P.2d 648 (1971); *Anderson v. Stream,* 295 N.W.2d 595 (Minn.1980). Does this demand too much of parents, or fail to recognize their important role in making decisions about care of children? In *Hartman v. Hartman,* 821 S.W.2d 852 (Mo.1991), Judge Covington concluded that the reasonable care standard was better than a classification scheme like that in *Goller.* She said: "The standard of reasonable care under the circumstances is well understood in tort law and does not require parents to meet an idealized standard of a father or mother."

2. *Immunity in negligent supervision cases.* Some courts, like those of New York and Texas, have moved in the other direction from *Goller.* They emphasize that "[e]ach child is different, as is each parent; as to the former, some are to be pampered while some thrive on independence; as to the latter, some trust in their children to use care, others are very cautious. Considering the different economic, educational, cultural, ethnic and religious backgrounds which must prevail, there are so many combinations and permutations of parent-child relationships that may result that the search for a standard would necessarily be in vain–and properly so.... [P]arents have always had the right to determine how much independence, supervision and control a child should have, and to best judge the character and extent of development of their child." *Holodook v. Spencer,* 43 A.D.2d 129, 350 N.Y.S.2d 199 (1973), quoted with approval on appeal, 36 N.Y.2d 35, 364 N.Y.S.2d 859, 324 N.E.2d 338 (1974).

The New York formulation is that the parent owes no duty enforceable in tort to supervise children adequately. See also *Shoemake v. Fogel, Ltd.,* 826 S.W.2d 933 (Tex.1992). Thus in *Holodook* there was no liability when a parent failed to control a small child who ran into the street and was struck by a car. New York has at times carried the "inadequate supervision" category to great lengths. In *Nolechek v. Gesuale,* 46 N.Y.2d 332, 413 N.Y.S.2d 340, 385 N.E.2d 1268 (1978) the Court of Appeals held that when a father provided a motorcycle to his teenage son, who was blind in one eye and had impaired vision in the other, it was only a case of "parental supervision," in the same way that decision to monitor a child's play is. Cf. *Foldi v. Jeffries,* 93 N.J. 533, 461 A.2d 1145 (1983) (liability where failure of parental supervision becomes willful or wanton misconduct).

3. *Applications.* A father leaves his child alone in the swimming pool, although he knows the child cannot swim. The child is found at the bottom

of the pool and rescued, but he suffers irreparable brain damage from lack of oxygen. In a suit by the child's guardian against the father, what results (a) under *Goller*; (b) under the negligence formulation described in note 1 above; (c) under New York's rule?

4. *Expansions*. It is clear that there will be demands for greater liability and expanded duties among family members. In *Burnette v. Wahl*, 284 Or. 705, 588 P.2d 1105 (1978), an action was brought against a parent who had deserted a child, with traumatic emotional results. The court denied liability, but the case suggests extreme possibilities. As to harm suffered by a child because of her mother's ingestion of substances during pregnancy, see Chapter 18 on prenatal harms generally.

5. *Foster parents*. Notice that the defendants in *Goller* and *Augsburger* were foster parents. Courts are somewhat divided as to whether they are entitled to the parental immunity. The Supreme Court of Illinois in *Nichol v. Stass*, 192 Ill.2d 233, 248 Ill.Dec. 931, 735 N.E.2d 582 (2000) concluded foster parents should receive the parental immunity except for acts in violation of regulations, criminal acts, or child neglect. The court concluded, however, that the foster parents were not state employees entitled to any immunity, even though, paradoxically, they were entitled to indemnification from the state if they were held liable.

GENERAL REFERENCE: DOBBS ON TORTS §§ 279–281 (2000).

§ 2. CHARITIES

Traditional rule. Beginning in the mid-nineteenth century, in response to an English decision, most American states adopted the view that charities were not liable in tort. This included virtually all "non-profit" organizations, such as hospitals, the Boy Scouts, the YWCA and many others, of which, however, hospitals were by far the most important. The idea initially was that tort liability would divert the trust funds from their intended purpose.

Exceptions. This rule followed a development that is by now familiar. First a number of exceptions were developed, with varying emphasis and acceptance in each state:

(1) The charity was not exempt from liability as to non-trust funds. Charities would be liable to the extent that insurance or other free funds were available to pay the judgment.

(2) Some jurisdictions had phrased the rule by saying that the charity would not be liable for the negligence of its servants. Thus the hospital would not be liable for the negligence of the orderly who leaves a slippery substance on the floor. However, the view was developed that the charity could somehow act "itself" rather than through agents or servants if it acted through the top administrators. In this view, if the hospital administrator had been negligent in hiring a dangerous orderly who was likely to and did attack patients, the hospital would not enjoy an immunity. This is sometimes called "administrative negligence."

(3) The charity could not claim the immunity as to those who paid for its services. A hospital could not claim an immunity to a paying patient, but could as to a "charity" patient.

(4) The charity could not claim an immunity as to its collateral commercial activities. Thus the YMCA ski trip, for which fees were charged, would not be protected by an immunity.

(5) Intentional or "reckless" torts were not protected by the immunity in some states.

General abolition of immunity. Some states retain the immunity but litigate over exceptions or over factors in a complicated analysis to determine whether the immunity applies in a particular case. E.g., *George v. Jefferson Hospital Ass'n,* 337 Ark. 206, 987 S.W.2d 710 (1999). Most states, however, have very substantially abolished the immunity. In some of these, the abolition has been by statute. The statutes of some states abolish the immunity only as to particular charities such as hospitals. S.C. Code § 44–7–50 abolishes the charitable immunity as it relates "to hospitals and other medical facilities." What issues might this limited abolition of immunity raise in South Carolina? The Restatement Second of Torts § 895E (1979) states the rule that there is no charitable immunity.

Legislative reaction. What is the next predictable step in the light of the materials we have seen before? A New Jersey Statute, N.J.S.A. 2A:53A–7, provides that the immunity is retained for charities "organized exclusively for religious, charitable, educational or hospital purposes" as to any "beneficiary . . . of the works of such non-profit corporation." The immunity does not extend, however, to those who are "unconcerned in and unrelated to and outside of the benefactions of such corporation. . . ." Are there problems in interpreting this kind of statute? Is a paying patient outside the "benefactions" of the hospital? What about constitutional issues here?

In *Schultz v. Roman Catholic Archdiocese of Newark*, 95 N.J. 530, 472 A.2d 531 (1984), the plaintiff alleged that the Archdiocese, through the Franciscan Brothers of the Poor, engaged an instructor in the parish school known as Brother Edmund, and that Brother Edmund forced one of his Boy Scout charges, Christopher Schultz, into certain sexual acts. This in turn led to Christopher's suicide at the age of 12. The court held that under the New Jersey Charitable Immunity Act the Archdiocese was a charity "not liable for negligence." Should the charity be liable for the intentional tort of Brother Edmund?

Individuals engaged in charitable activities. The traditional charitable immunity protected the charity itself in its form as a trust or corporation, but did not protect individuals who were engaged in its activities. A number of contemporary statutes provide some kind of limitation on the duty of various individuals associated with charities or even with individual charitable acts. We have already seen one example–the medical Good Samaritan statutes. Some others are ridiculously specific in identifying the specially privileged or protected group. An Illinois statute lowers the standard of care for volunteers who coach or umpire in nonprofit sports programs. 745 ILL. STATS. § 80/1 (liability only if conduct falls substantially below standard). Although such statutes are highly specific, there are a number of them and various sports programs are singled out for protection.

A much broader protection for individuals and organizations comes with statutes protecting donors of food to non-profit organizations. E.g., CAL. CIVIL CODE § 1714.25. Broader yet, some states have enacted statutes protecting all volunteers who assist non-profit corporations. The federal Congress has also enacted such a statute. The federal statute begins by providing absolute immunity for volunteers who work for non-profit corporations, then recognizes some exceptions. See 42 U.S.C.A. § 14503 (a) (3). An interesting twist on this statute is that it protects volunteers working for any nonprofit organization that escapes income taxes under the Revenue Code, 26 U.S.C.A. § 501(c). That includes a number of organizations you might not think of as charities. The Chamber of Commerce is one example.

GENERAL REFERENCE: DOBBS ON TORTS §§ 282–283 (2000).

Chapter 13

GOVERNMENTAL ENTITIES
AND OFFICERS

§ 1. TRADITIONAL IMMUNITIES AND THEIR PASSING

1. *Governmental tort immunity.* The English common law had it that "The King can do no wrong," an ambiguous statement that ultimately was taken to mean that one could not sue government in tort. This idea was carried over to America and perpetuated even after the American Revolution, with the result that the federal government and the states were immune from tort actions. This immunity extends to all their agencies unless statutes provide otherwise. On rare occasions it may even protect government contractors following government specifications, a point covered in Chapter 23. In addition to this general "sovereign immunity" of the federal and state governments, the 11th Amendment of the United States Constitution is construed to immunize states from federal court suits.

2. *Taking of property.* One important qualification to the governmental immunity is that under the due process clauses of the 5th and 14th Amendments of the United States Constitution, neither state nor federal governments may "take" property without just compensation.

3. *Municipal immunity.* Municipalities are not "sovereigns." They are corporations chartered by the sovereign but not agencies of the government. Nevertheless municipalities are traditionally accorded an immunity from tort liability. Its history and theory are different from the sovereign immunity, but the immunity is substantial nonetheless. However, courts more freely created exceptions to the municipal immunity. Municipalities are of course liable for takings of property, but very often also liable for nuisances such as an unsanitary garbage dump. In addition, they are held liable for torts committed in the course of proprietary activities, as distinct from governmental activities. For example, a city might be liable for negligence in the operation of a city-owned electrical company. Cities are also held liable in many states for negligent failure to maintain streets properly.

4. *Abolishing state and municipal immunity*. New York waived its sovereign immunity in 1929, a waiver that later was interpreted to apply as well to municipal immunities. *Bernardine v. City of New York*, 294 N.Y. 361, 62 N.E.2d 604 (1945). Most states lagged behind for many years. In 1954 no other state had substantially abolished its sovereign immunity. In the 1960s and 1970s, both courts and legislatures acted to abolish or limit the immunity of states and municipalities. Today most states have enacted statutes that abolish the state's immunity to at least some extent. They almost always preserve a degree of immunity or other special privilege, and in some cases a very extensive degree indeed. In a few states, immunity is more or less entirely retained. See *Fuqua v. Flowers,* 20 S.W.3d 388 (Ark.2000). Lawyers must therefore always research local statutes.

5. *Abolishing federal immunity*. Immunity of the federal government became a nuisance to the Congress because citizens denied access to courts would often seek a recovery through the political process. They would ask their congressperson to sponsor a "private bill" awarding compensation. Such bills consumed congressional time. To minimize time-loss, Congress finally passed the Federal Tort Claims Act in 1946, in effect turning over many claims to the judicial process and in the process abolishing some but not all of the tort immunity.

§ 2. THE FEDERAL TORT CLAIMS ACT

a. *The General Structure of the FTCA*

1. *General provisions.* The FTCA is codified mainly in 28 U.S.C.A. §§ 2671–2680. Section 2674 provides: "The United States shall be liable, respecting the provisions of this title relating to tort claims, in the same manner and to the same extent as a private individual under like circumstances, but shall not be liable for interest prior to judgment or for punitive damages." The plaintiff must submit the claim to the government agency involved and suit is not permitted until the agency has refused payment or has delayed over six months in making a decision on it. Liability is determined by state tort law. The case is tried only in federal court. Neither party can have a jury trial; the judge sits as the trier of fact.

2. *Specific statutory exceptions.* The statute itself lays out a number of specific instances in which the government is not liable, that is, in which the immunity is retained. One set of exceptions retains the immunity for specific governmental activities (combatant activities of the military and delivery of mail, for example).

Another group retains the immunity for a number of torts, mostly those of a dignitary or economic kind, including those "arising out of" assault, battery, false imprisonment, malicious prosecution, abuse of process, libel, slander, misrepresentation and interference with contract.

Suppose the government negligently hires a man who has a propensity to commit sexual assaults or to molest children. The man uses his government job to take advantage of a child. The government usually escapes liability in such cases because the claim arises out of assault or battery, even though the legal basis of the claim is that the government is negligent in hiring without adequate investigation. *Johnson v. United States*, 788 F.2d 845 (2d Cir.1986) (letter carrier's child molestation in the course of duty); *Satterfield v. United States*, 788 F.2d 395 (6th Cir.1986) (serviceman, beating).

Two limitations are imposed on the immunity for assault, battery, and the like. First, if an off-duty employee commits a battery, the government might be liable for its negligence in fostering the risk. For example, it might be liable for its negligence in permitting an employee to take a government rifle off-duty. *Sheridan v. United States*, 487 U.S. 392, 108 S.Ct. 2449, 101 L.Ed.2d 352 (1988). But this rationale does not appear to apply to *on*-duty employees. Second, under the statute itself, the government may be liable for the assault, battery, or false imprisonment if it is committed by "investigative or law enforcement officers."

3. *Judicially established exceptions.* The Court has construed the statute to permit liability of the government only for negligent or other "wrongful" acts. Strict liability, even when a private individual would be strictly liable, is not permitted. See *Laird v. Nelms*, 406 U.S. 797, 92 S.Ct. 1899, 32 L.Ed.2d 499 (1972). However, Congress can still appropriate funds directly to compensate for harm without fault. See *Land v. United States*, 29 Fed.Cl. 744 (1993). A second and more important judicially created exception is considered next.

b. The Feres Exception

BROOKS v. UNITED STATES, 337 U.S. 49, 69 S.Ct. 918, 93 L.Ed. 1200 (1949). Two brothers named Brooks were in the armed forces but were on furlough. While they were driving on a public road, their vehicle was struck by a negligently driven army truck. One man was killed, the other injured. The government as defendant argued that it should be immune from liability for its negligence when the injured persons were members of the armed forces. *Held*, the government has no such immunity. "[W]e are dealing with an accident which had nothing to do with the Brooks' army careers, injuries not caused by their service except in the sense that all human events depend upon what has already transpired." Congress authorized a suit for 'any claim.' It created 12 exceptions, but none applies here. The FTCA "excludes claims arising out of combatant activities of the military or naval forces, or the Coast Guard, during time of war.... [S]uch exceptions make it clear to us that Congress knew what it was about when it used the term 'any claim.' It would be absurd to believe that Congress did not have the servicemen in mind in 1946, when this statute was passed. The overseas and combatant activities exceptions make this plain."

FERES v. UNITED STATES, 340 U.S. 135, 71 S.Ct. 153, 95 L.Ed. 152 (1950). Three cases considered together. In *Feres* the decedent was killed in a barracks fire while he was on active duty in the service of the

United States. The claim alleges negligence. In *Jefferson* the plaintiff underwent an abdominal operation while he was in the army. Eight months later, after he was discharged, a doctor removed a towel 30 inches long and 18 inches wide from his abdomen. It was marked "Medical Department U.S. Army." The third case, *Griggs*, claimed that army surgeons were responsible for the death of a soldier on active duty. *Held*, all these claims are barred because injuries received were "incident to service." The FTCA makes no specific exception for service-connected injuries to members of the armed forces but the act as a whole was not intended to impose unprecedented liability upon the government. There are three reasons for this conclusion. (1) Although private persons do practice medicine and cause fires, no private persons operate armies. So government liability would find no private-law analogue. (2) The FTCA invokes the tort law of the state where the injury occurred. This would subject the unique government-to-soldier relationship to the varied laws of the states. (3) The armed forces provide substantial compensation in the form of pensions or otherwise. These can operate, like state workers' compensation laws, as a substitute for tort liability.

Notes

1.   *Feres* has been applied to bar recovery even when the claim was that a military trainer brutally held a recruit under water until he died. *Kitowski v. United States*, 931 F.2d 1526 (11th Cir.1991). It also applies to bar claims brought for violation of Constitutional rights rather than for violation of state tort law. *Chappell v. Wallace*, 462 U.S. 296, 103 S.Ct. 2362, 76 L.Ed.2d 586 (1983).

2.   Long after *Feres* itself was decided, the Court began to emphasize a fourth reason for the immunity, insisting that a suit by a service person would somehow interfere with military discipline. Military discipline is given an extremely broad meaning.

In *United States v. Johnson*, 481 U.S. 681, 107 S.Ct. 2063, 95 L.Ed.2d 648 (1987), a Coast Guard pilot, flying under the control of a civilian FAA controller, was killed in a crash. The surviving spouse asserted that the FAA was negligent in causing the death. The Court applied the *Feres* immunity, partly because "a suit based upon service-related activity necessarily implicates the military judgment and decisions" and "military discipline involves not only obedience to orders, but more generally duty and loyalty to one's service and to one's country. Suits brought by service members against the Government for service-related injuries could undermine the commitment essential to effective service and thus have the potential to disrupt military discipline in the broadest sense of the word."

In *United States v. Stanley*, 483 U.S. 669, 107 S.Ct. 3054, 97 L.Ed.2d 550 (1987), a service person was seriously injured when the government conducted LSD experiments upon him without informing him of risks. Because he was a volunteer for the experiments (although an uninformed one), he argued that injury did not occur in the chain of command and therefore that no military discipline was involved. The Court nevertheless held that *Feres* barred his claim. Even though injury did not occur in the chain of command, it was "incident to service."

3. *Spouses and children. Feres* does not bar a recovery by a spouse or child of a person in the armed forces if the spouse or child is directly injured. Common examples of recovery by spouses or children are those involving medical malpractice in military hospitals. E.g., *Doe v. United States*, 737 F.Supp. 155 (D.R.I.1990).

Suppose, however, that the army subjects a serviceman to inoculations or exposure to radioactive materials that result in birth defects in his or her children? Can the children recover for the harms done to them? *Minns v. United States*, 155 F.3d 445 (4th Cir.1998) (Gulf War inoculation causing birth defects, *Feres* bars children's claim because it had its genesis in injury to service person and would implicate military discipline); *Hinkie v. United States*, 715 F.2d 96 (3d Cir.1983) (exposure of service personnel to radioactive materials, children injured by genetic damage to parent are barred by *Feres*). There are a number of similar cases. But suppose a military doctor is negligent in the prenatal care he gives to a servicewoman. The result is that the servicewoman's child is born with serious birth defects that could have been avoided. Can the child recover against the government, or is he *Feres*-barred because treatment of his mother was incident to her service? Compare *Scales v. United States*, 685 F.2d 970 (5th Cir.1982) (barred) with *Romero v. United States*, 954 F.2d 223 (4th Cir.1992) (not barred).

4. *Incident to service. Feres* formally covers only those injuries that are "incident to service," seemingly on the assumption that the policy reasons advanced for rejecting liability more or less automatically apply when injury is incident to service and do not apply otherwise. Service members injured while on furlough are not injured incident to service. Judge Calabresi has attempted to make the rationale for *Feres* more coherent by emphasizing analysis of "incident to service." If the injury is not incident to service, no military discipline issue arises. Likewise, if it is not incident to service, the fact that military benefits are paid looks like an analogy to a civilian employer's voluntary provision of health benefits rather than an analogy to workers' compensation payments that would protect the employer from a tort suit. Incident to service thus becomes central in determining whether *Feres* bars the claim. See *Taber v. Maine,* 67 F.3d 1029 (2d Cir.1995).

c. *The Discretionary or Basic Policy Immunity*

28 U.S.C.A. § 2680(a)

The provisions of this chapter and section 1346(b) of this title shall not apply to–

(a) Any claim based upon an act or omission of an employee of the Government, exercising due care, in the execution of a statute or regulation, whether or not such statute or regulation be valid, or based upon the exercise or performance or the failure to exercise or perform a discretionary function or duty on the part of a federal agency or an employee of the Government, whether or not the discretion involved be abused.

LOGE v. UNITED STATES

United States Court of Appeals, Eighth Circuit, 1981.
662 F.2d 1268.

HANSON, SENIOR DISTRICT JUDGE. . . .

In June 1963, the Secretary of HEW licensed Lederle Laboratories to manufacture Orimune—a trivalent, live, oral poliovirus vaccine. Orimune is composed of all three Sabin strains of live poliovirus corresponding to the three different types of polio (known as Types 1, 2, and 3), thus the designation "trivalent." A characteristic of live Sabin polio vaccines such as Orimune is that not only is the vaccine's recipient immunized from polio, but unimmunized persons who come into close contact with the recipient also are immunized through a shed virus which spreads from the recipient to the "contact." Because Sabin strains contain the live polio virus, there is a risk that either a recipient or a contact could develop polio. Accordingly, the Secretary has promulgated regulations pertaining to the safety and potency of these strains which serve to protect susceptible persons from contracting the disease. Drug manufacturers must prove their product's conformity to these regulations before the Secretary will issue a license to manufacture.

A risk-free alternative to inoculation with the live Sabin vaccine is the Salk vaccine in which the virus is killed so that the recipient cannot contract polio nor can the recipient shed a live virus to unimmunized contacts. But the Secretary has promoted the use of risk-bearing live vaccines because they are able to effect total immunization of the public through transmission of the shed virus with less than total inoculation. Mrs. Loge was exposed to the shed virus in 1976 after a doctor inoculated her infant son Todd with Orimune. Within one month after her son's inoculation, Mrs. Loge was stricken with a vaccine-associated case of poliomyelitis, Type 2. As a result, she is now a paraplegic. The Loges brought suit in the United States District Court for the Western District of Arkansas against the United States and unknown employees of the Department of HEW.

[The complaint was construed to allege a number of specific items of negligence in two categories: (1) that the government was negligent in not requiring the drug manufacturer to comply with the government's own regulations; (2) that the government was negligent in licensing at all, or in licensing without additional safety regulations.] . . .

The FTCA does not waive sovereign immunity for "[a]ny claim . . . based upon the exercise or performance or the failure to exercise or perform a discretionary function or duty on the part of a federal agency or an employee of the Government, whether or not the discretion involved be abused." 28 U.S.C. § 2680(a). Insofar as the Loges' amended complaint alleged that the government was negligent in promulgating or failing to promulgate regulations that would ensure the safety of live, oral poliovirus vaccines and properly protect susceptible persons such as

Mrs. Loge, the district court correctly found that such actions by the government were discretionary functions and therefore immune from suit under FTCA. Cf. *Dalehite v. United States*, 346 U.S. 15, 27, 73 S. Ct. 956, 963, 97 L. Ed. 1427 (1953) ("It was not 'intended that the constitutionality of legislation, the legality of regulations, or the propriety of a discretionary administrative act, should be tested through the medium of a damage suit for tort.' ") . . . .

The district court did find that two causes of action under the FTCA were not barred by the discretionary function exception: the negligent failure of the government to require the mandatory tests of 21 C.F.R. § 630.10(b) when Lederle was licensed to manufacture Orimune in 1963 and the negligent failure to follow mandatory tests when Lederle's Lot 451–162 was approved. The Secretary has no discretion to disregard the mandatory regulatory commands pertaining to criteria a vaccine must meet before licensing its manufacture or releasing a particular lot of vaccine for distribution to the public.

Nevertheless the district court concluded that the Loges had still failed to state a claim under FTCA because no circumstances were alleged "where the United States, if a private person, would be liable to the claimant in accordance with the law of the place where the act or omission occurred." 28 U.S.C. § 1346(b). This section has been construed to require that the entire law of the place where the act or omission occurred must be applied, including its choice of law principles. Richards v. United States, 369 U.S. 1, 82 S.Ct. 585, 7 L.Ed.2d 492 (1962). Without deciding which venue's law applied, the district court concluded that neither the law of the District of Columbia–the place of the negligent acts and omissions–nor the law of Arkansas–the place of the harmful impact–imposes a duty of due care on a person for activity similar to the government's in this case. . . .

Construing the Loges' allegations in their favor, we find that claims have been stated under any one of the three alternative grounds for liability stated in Restatement Second of Torts § 324A. It can be said that the government increased the risk of harm to the Loges by licensing an allegedly untested product, Orimune, and by releasing to the public an allegedly untested or negligently tested lot of that vaccine: if either the product itself or a particular lot of that product failed to conform to standards established by the regulations, then proper testing or proof of testing would have revealed the nonconformity and the vaccine would never have been disseminated to Todd Loge. Likewise, it can be said that the government undertook a duty owed by the drug manufacturer to the Loges when it required that proof of the drug's safety be demonstrated to the government before releasing it to the public. Finally, the Loges alleged they relied on the government's use of due care in approving for release the particular vaccine lot that was eventually administered to Todd Loge. Therefore, the district court erred in concluding that the Loges had failed to state a claim under the law of Arkansas.

Notes

1. *Private person analogues.* In the earlier days of the FTCA, courts denied liability when government conduct was negligent if that conduct bore no factual similarity to private activities. If this approach is applied to *Loge*, it could be said that since private persons cannot regulate the manufacture of drugs, there is no analogous private liability; hence the government is immune. As *Loge* shows, however, courts have moved away from this position. What they seek today is a *principle* of tort liability applied to private persons, not a factual similarity in their activities. One of the principles in *Loge*, for example, was that a private person may be responsible if he undertakes to make something safe and negligently fails to do so.

2. *Discretionary immunity.* If a court could impose liability when Congress fails to enact safety legislation, courts, not elected members of the political branch, would have ultimate legislative control. This principle seems to be behind the decision in *Loge*. Was the principle correctly applied?

3. *Violation of regulations.* Where there is a professional standard of safety incorporated in federal regulations, the government's violation of that standard is not discretionary and is actionable, according to *Loge* and the authority it cited. This is somewhat anomalous, since the FTCA explicitly invokes *state* law as the basis of tort liability, and since the regulation is a federal one. How does this work?

4. *Planning level vs. operational level decisions.* Courts sometimes suggest that planning level decisions are discretionary, but that operational level decisions are not. For FTCA cases, the Supreme Court seems to have disapproved of this kind of analysis in *United States v. Gaubert*, 499 U.S. 315, 111 S.Ct. 1267, 113 L.Ed.2d 335 (1991). The question, it said, is whether the government is exercising discretion based on public policy, not the level of that policy. State courts, applying their own law, may still treat planning decisions as discretionary and operational decisions as not. See *Crawford v. State*, 57 Ohio St.3d 184, 566 N.E.2d 1233 (1991).

5. *Where the government makes no conscious decision.* In some cases, the government pursues a course of action without having made any conscious decision, either of policy or otherwise. Occasionally courts have said that in such cases the discretionary immunity has no application, since no discretion was exercised. Cf. *Dube v. Pittsburgh Corning*, 870 F.2d 790 (1st Cir.1989). But in *Gaubert*, supra note 4, the Supreme Court used this language: "The focus of the inquiry is not on the agent's subjective intent in exercising the discretion conferred by statute or regulation, but on the nature of the actions taken and on whether they are susceptible to policy analysis." Does this language mean that immunity does not depend on whether the government actually made any conscious decision?

MAAS v. UNITED STATES

United States Court of Appeals, Seventh Circuit, 1996.
94 F.3d 291.

MANION, CIRCUIT JUDGE. . . .

Nearly thirty years ago a United States Air Force airplane carrying nuclear weapons crashed in Greenland. The four plaintiffs in this case were among the servicemen assigned to cleanup the wreckage. Two plaintiffs allege they suffer from cancer and two contend they are sterile as a result of radiation exposure during the cleanup effort. . . .

In January 1968 a United States Air Force Strategic Air Command B–52 bomber armed with four thermonuclear hydrogen bombs crashed into an ice-covered bay in Greenland. The plane was destroyed and the simultaneous explosion of 200,000 tons of jet fuel and the high explosives within the hydrogen bombs blew the warheads into highly radioactive plutonium and tritium fragments which scattered over the ice flows.

Alerted by the nearby Thule Air Base, the U.S. Air Force Command Post at the Pentagon activated its "Broken Arrow" Control Group which handles lost or damaged nuclear weapons. It put into action a clean-up operation known as Project "Crested Ice." The four plaintiffs in this case were among 300 servicemen and Danish civilian workers who worked on this project.

[The cleanup of radioactive debris entailed extreme hardship and workers were exposed to radioactive particles, including radioactive plutonium oxide.] Aware of the possibility of radiation exposure, the government tested the workers, but the extreme weather conditions may have compromised the results. The government also tested some of the plaintiffs for up to three years after Project Crested Ice ended, but did not test them after they left the service.

In its "Bier V" report, issued in the 1980's, the National Academy of Sciences noted an increased risk of cancer connected with low-level doses of ionizing radiation. The plaintiffs allege the government became aware of these effects and thus learned that Project Crested Ice participants were more likely to develop certain cancers as a result of their 1968 Greenland tour of duty. The government did not notify the Crested Ice veterans of this new information.

[Plaintiff Maas was diagnosed with cancer in 1991; plaintiff Bennebose with T-cell lymphoma in 1994. Both assert their cancers developed as a result of participation in Project Crested Ice.]

Project Crested Ice participants may apply for and receive service-connected disability benefits on the same basis as other veterans. Each of the plaintiffs filed claims with the government for damages resulting from radiation exposure. Because the plaintiffs did not receive notices of final disposition of their claims within six months of filing, each exercised his option to consider his claim as finally denied pursuant to 28 U.S.C. § 2675(b) and sued the United States.

[The District Court dismissed the claims. As to the claim of negligence preceding discharge of the plaintiffs, this is affirmed. However, the court held that the *Feres* immunity would not protect the government from liability for its negligence in failing to warn the plaintiffs after their discharge.]

[T]he district court concluded that 28 U.S.C. § 2680(a) barred the post-discharge negligence claims of Maas and Binnebose. This FTCA section excepts from its waiver of sovereign immunity claims based upon the exercise or performance of discretionary functions regardless of "whether or not the discretion involved be abused." This "discretionary function" exception covers acts requiring an element of judgment or choice and is intended to "prevent judicial 'second-guessing' of legislative and administrative decisions grounded in social, economic, and political policy through the medium of an action in tort." . . .

The government [argues] that the decision to inform, warn, or test veterans who participated in Project Crested Ice based on new studies is purely discretionary because it involves judgment and execution. It submits that a warning of the type plaintiffs seek—which would include resource allocation decisions and involve the weighing of evidence, a matter of agency discretion—places it within the discretionary function exception.

This court recently considered the contours of the discretionary function exception in Rothrock v. United States, 62 F.3d 196 (7th Cir.1995). We recognized two factors in determining whether the exception bars suit against the United States: (1) it covers only discretionary acts, that is, which involve an element of judgment or choice; and (2) even assuming the challenged conduct involves an element of judgment, it remains to be decided whether that judgment is of the kind that the exception was designed to shield. Because the purpose of the exception is to prevent judicial second guessing of legislative and administrative decisions grounded in social, economic, and political policy, it protects only governmental actions and decisions based on considerations of public policy.

The circumstances of this case easily satisfy the first of the two elements in Rothrock. No statute or regulation gives the Air Force a precise and optionless directive in handling studies showing a greater incidence of cancer in servicemen involved in past military activities. Without statutes or regulations which would require the military to undertake a program to alert Crested Ice veterans of new cancer statistics, the decision to warn these plaintiffs is the military's. Rather than rote ministerial actions, the path down which Maas and Binnebose would have the military travel is replete with choices: To provide notice would require resources and assignment of employees. How many resources, and who should be assigned? It would also require scientific and administrative determinations. How much radiation was too much? How much exposure is enough to require notice? Which veterans were exposed to how much radiation? And which were exposed to too much? How should such a notice be phrased to avoid panic? To answer these questions requires the exercise of judgment and discretion.

Moreover, these exercises of discretion involve policy considerations. Those things plaintiffs wish were done—warning, further testing, etc.— are susceptible to policy analysis. In ascertaining the need for a warning and its cost, and in determining the group to be alerted, as well as the content and procedure of such notice, the government would balance safety with economic concerns. Deciding whether health risks justify the cost of a notification program, and balancing the cost and the effectiveness of a type of warning, are discretionary decisions covered by § 2680(a). The second Rothrock factor—that the judgments are based on policy considerations—is thus satisfied as well.

. . . The nature of the decisions they claim the government should have made—to inform, warn, or test veterans who participated in Project Crested Ice—would require it to exercise discretion implicating safety, economic, and efficiency concerns. Thus, we can conclude on this record that the discretionary function exception bars plaintiffs' claims. . . .

Notes

1.   A park ranger negligently directs a visitor to drive his snowmobile near a moose. The moose kicks the visitor and breaks his neck. Was the ranger's decision a policy decision? *Tippett v. United States,* 108 F.3d 1194 (10th Cir.1997).

2.   The government allegedly built a bridge with defective materials and then did not maintain it properly. When the plaintiff's car struck the guardrail, it gave way and he fell to the highway below. Is building defective bridges out of substandard material a discretionary decision because it requires an allocation of resources? *Baum v. United States,* 986 F.2d 716 (4th Cir.1993).

3.   Private Roderick R. Woods allegedly raped and sodomized Private X. He was charged with rape. While the case was pending, officers transferred him to a nearby installation and told him he was restricted to the post. However, the officer who restricted him did not live on the post and he told no one on post about the restriction. Woods offered to plead guilty to the rape of Private X. The next day, he left the post unhampered, then allegedly raped and sodomized the plaintiff, a civilian. Did the army have discretion and did it make policy decisions about how to restrict Woods, or is the government liable? *Malone v. United States,* 61 F.Supp.2d 1372 (S.D.Ga. 1999).

4.   Would a negligent professional judgment such as a medical diagnosis ever count as a discretionary act?

§ 3.   IMMUNITIES UNDER STATE LAW

RISS v. CITY OF NEW YORK

Court of Appeals of New York, 1968.
22 N.Y.2d 579, 293 N.Y.S.2d 897, 240 N.E.2d 860.

[Linda Riss was terrorized for months by a rejected suitor, one Pugach. He threatened to kill or maim her if she did not yield to him. She repeatedly sought protection from law enforcement officers. Eventually she became engaged to another man. At a party celebrating the event, she received a phone call warning her that it was her "last chance." She again called police, but nothing seems to have been done. The next day Pugach carried out his threat by having a person hired for the purpose to throw lye in Linda's face. She was blinded in one eye, lost a good portion of her vision in the other and suffered permanent scarring of her face. This is her action against the city for failure to provide police protection. The trial court dismissed the complaint at the end of all the evidence and the Appellate Division affirmed.]

BREITEL, JUDGE.

This appeal presents, in a very sympathetic framework, the issue of the liability of a municipality for failure to provide special protection to a member of the public who was repeatedly threatened with personal harm and eventually suffered dire personal injuries for lack of such protection. . . .

It is necessary immediately to distinguish those liabilities attendant upon governmental activities which have displaced or supplemented traditionally private enterprises, such as are involved in the operation of rapid transit systems, hospitals, and places of public assembly. Once sovereign immunity was abolished by statute the extension of liability on ordinary principles of tort law logically followed. To be equally distinguished are certain activities of government which provide services and facilities for the use of the public, such as highways, public buildings and the like, in the performance of which the municipality or the State may be liable under ordinary principles of tort law. The ground for liability is the provision of the services or facilities for the direct use of members of the public. In contrast, this case involves the provision of a governmental service to protect the public generally from external hazards and particularly to control the activities of criminal wrongdoers.

The amount of protection that may be provided is limited by the resources of the community and by a considered legislative-executive decision as to how those resources may be deployed. For the courts to proclaim a new and general duty of protection in the law of tort, even to those who may be the particular seekers of protection based on specific hazards, could and would inevitably determine how the limited police resources of the community should be allocated and without predictable limits. This is quite different from the predictable allocation of resources and liabilities when public hospitals, rapid transit systems, or even highways are provided.

Before such extension of responsibilities should be dictated by the indirect imposition of tort liabilities, there should be a legislative determination that that should be the scope of public responsibility.

It is notable that the removal of sovereign immunity for tort liability was accomplished after legislative enactment and not by any judicial arrogation of power. It is equally notable that for many years, since as far back as 1909, in this State, there was by statute municipal liability for losses sustained as a result of riot . Yet even this class of liability has for some years been suspended by legislative action, a factor of considerable significance. When one considers the greatly increased amount of crime committed throughout the cities, but especially in certain portions of them, with a repetitive and predictable pattern, it is easy to see the consequences of fixing municipal liability upon a showing of probable need for and request for protection. To be sure these are grave problems at the present time, exciting high priority activity on the part of the national, State and local governments, to which the answers are neither simple, known, or presently within reasonable controls. To foist a presumed cure for these problems by judicial innovation of a new kind of liability in tort would be foolhardy indeed and an assumption of judicial wisdom and power not possessed by the courts.

Nor is the analysis progressed by the analogy to compensation for losses sustained. It is instructive that the Crime Victims Compensation and "Good Samaritan" statutes, compensating limited classes of victims of crime, were enacted only after the most careful study of conditions and the impact of such a scheme upon governmental operations and the public fisc. And then the limitations were particular and narrow.

For all of these reasons, there is no warrant in judicial tradition or in the proper allocation of the powers of government for the courts, in the absence of legislation, to carve out an area of tort liability for police protection to members of the public. Quite distinguishable, of course, is the situation where the police authorities undertake responsibilities to particular members of the public and expose them, without adequate protection, to the risks which then materialize into actual losses (Schuster v. City of New York, 5 N.Y.2d 75, 180 N.Y.S.2d 265, 154 N.E.2d 534).

Accordingly, the order of the Appellate Division affirming the judgment of dismissal should be affirmed.

DeLONG v. COUNTY OF ERIE, 60 N.Y.2d 296, 469 N.Y.S.2d 611, 457 N.E.2d 717 (1983). At 9:29 Mrs. De Long called the 911 emergency number covering all cities and towns in Erie County, New York. She reported that someone was attempting to break in and gave her address. The "complaint writer" assured her someone would come right away. Since her own local police station in the town of Kenmore was only a block and a half away, assistance might have been readily available except for the fact that the complaint writer sent officers to an address in Buffalo instead of Kenmore. When the officers found "no such address," the complaint writer dropped the call as a "fake." In the meantime the burglar gained entrance and at 9:42 Mrs. De Long was seen running from the house bleeding. She collapsed and died of stab wounds. A jury found for the plaintiff in a wrongful death action, returning a verdict for a total of $800,000. *Held*, affirmed. Where police refuse assistance, there is an issue of how to allocate public resources and it should be left to the executive and legislative branches. But in this case "the decision had been made by the municipalities to provide a special emergency service...." There is, as defendants argue, a "familiar rule," that public entities are not liable for "negligence in the performance of a governmental function, including police and fire protection, unless a special relationship existed between the municipality and the injured party...." But here there is a special relationship between the city and the caller. The "victim's plea for assistance was not refused." The special relationship between the defendants and the caller required the defendants "to exercise ordinary care in the performance of a duty it has voluntarily assumed."

BARILLARI v. CITY OF MILWAUKEE, 194 Wis.2d 247, 533 N.W.2d 759 (1995). Charles Estergard sexually assaulted Shannon Barillari at knife point when Shannon attempted to break off their relationship. At the hospital, Shannon was interviewed by police officers who allegedly promised (a) to protect her from further attacks by Estergard and (b) to be at Shannon's home at 3:30 p.m. that day when Estergard was expected to return and to arrest him then. Estergard showed up at Shannon's at 3:30, engaged in an altercation with Shannon's stepfather and fled. The police were not present as promised. They did not apprehend Estergard elsewhere either and they did not notify Shannon that Estergard was still at large. Several days later Estergard went to Shannon's home and killed her and then himself. In a suit against the city based on these facts, *held*, (1) the city is immune for discretionary decisions of the police; (2) the police decisions here are discretionary; (3) the promises did not create any ministerial, non-discretionary duties. "[T]he nature of law enforcement requires moment-to-moment decision making and crises management, which, in turn, requires that the police department have the latitude to decide how to best utilize law enforcement resources."

HARRY STOLLER AND CO., INC.
v. CITY OF LOWELL

Supreme Judicial Court of Massachusetts, 1992.
412 Mass. 139, 587 N.E.2d 780.

[The plaintiff's five brick buildings were destroyed by a fire which started on the sixth floor of one of them. A sprinkler system was in place and had been tested two days earlier. Firefighters, in violation of accepted practice, chose not to use it, fighting the fire with hoses instead. All five buildings and their contents were destroyed. After a jury awarded the plaintiff $785,000, the trial judge granted judgment NOV for the defendant under the state's statutory discretionary immunity. *Held*, reversed.]

WILKINS, J.

This court has declined to apply the discretionary function exception to a variety of governmental acts. A police officer deciding whether to remove from the roadways a motorist, known to be intoxicated, is not making a policy or planning judgment. A physician employed by a city is not engaged in a discretionary function, within the meaning of § 10(b), in her treatment of a patient in a hospital emergency room.... The failure to provide sufficient information to enable a person to protect his property against the conduct of a client of the Department of Mental Health does not involve the exercise of choice regarding public policy and planning but rather the carrying out of previously established policies or plans....

There are aspects of firefighting that can have an obvious planning or policy basis. The number and location of fire stations, the amount of equipment to purchase, the size of the fire department, the number and location of hydrants, and the quantity of the water supply involve policy considerations, especially the allocation of financial resources. In certain situations, firefighting involves determinations of what property to attempt to save because the resources available to combat a conflagration are or seem to be insufficient to save all threatened property. In such cases, policy determinations might be involved, and application of the discretionary function exception would be required.

The case before us is different. The negligent conduct that caused the fire to engulf all the plaintiff's buildings was not founded on planning or policy considerations. The question whether to put higher water pressure in the sprinkler systems involved no policy choice or planning decision. There was a dispute on the evidence whether it was negligent to fail to fight the fire through the buildings' sprinkler systems. The firefighters may have thought that they had a discretionary choice whether to pour water on the buildings through hoses or to put water inside the buildings through their sprinkler systems. They certainly had discretion in the sense that no statute, regulation, or established municipal practice required the firefighters to use the sprinklers (or, for that matter, to use hoses exclusively). But whatever discretion they had was not based on a policy or planning judgment. The jury decided that, in exercising their discretion not to use the buildings' sprinkler systems, the Lowell firefighters were negligent because they failed to conform to generally accepted firefighting practices. When the firefighters exercised that discretion, policy and planning considerations were not involved. Therefore, the discretionary function exception does not shield the city from liability....

Notes

1. In considering *Riss*, remember that New York had abolished the state's immunity. Judge Breitel was obviously concerned about allocation of public resources by way of tort judgments. But *any* tort judgment against the city would allocate resources, including a judgment based on a city bus driver's negligence. Does the distinction between tort suits against the police department and those against the bus authority hold up? Why would there be predictable limits in the bus case but not in the police case? What if plaintiffs asserted that the city was liable for failure to supply bus service as needed?

2. Judge Breitel did not really say why the police in *Riss* refused assistance. Both he and the dissenting judge seemed to assume, however, that there was a professional reason bearing on resource allocation. Suppose that was not the case; suppose the police simply did not follow good police procedure, or that by clerical mistake they failed to record Miss Riss' call. Would the result be different? The *DeLong* court seemed to suggest that a special relationship, some affirmative action, would still be required. But maybe that's the wrong way to look at the facts in *DeLong*. *DeLong* is also a case in which it is clear that no professional judgment was involved, only a clerical or mechanical mistake.

3. With this in mind, consider *Torres v. State*, 119 N.M. 609, 894 P.2d 386 (N.M. 1995). That case involved a murder committed in New Mexico. One police unit obtained an identification of the murderer, but did not promptly communicate the information to the investigating unit. As a result, the murderer escaped to Los Angeles, where he murdered other victims. In a wrongful death action, the New Mexico Court held that the police were subject to liability for the California deaths. Can you plausibly postulate that the protective rule in *Riss* would not apply unless the police really are making a policy decision, or the court assumes that to be the case?

4. Courts are reluctant to second-guess fire and police departments in their decisions not to act. In line with *Riss*, New York has held that the fire department's failure to enforce a fire safety rule was not actionable on behalf of someone who suffered a fire loss that could have been avoided, and this was true even though the city had actual notice of the danger. *Motyka v. City of Amsterdam*, 15 N.Y.2d 134, 256 N.Y.S.2d 595, 204 N.E.2d 635 (1965). How can we explain *Harry Stoller Co.*? Or liability for harm caused by a police officer's negligent driving? *City of Little Rock v. Weber*, 298 Ark. 382, 767 S.W.2d 529 (1989). A few courts have imposed liability for failure to provide enforcement of fire safety laws. *Adams v. State*, 555 P.2d 235 (Alaska 1976). And statutes may impose a duty to enforce criminal law for the protection of potential victims, such as those subject to domestic violence. See *Roy v. City of Everett*, 118 Wash.2d 352, 823 P.2d 1084 (1992).

5. *Where government function is to provide safety.* Can you argue that where the governmental function is to provide safety or exercise care, the government has no discretion to act unsafely? See DOBBS ON TORTS § 270, at 721 (2000). Would the following cases support such an argument? *Brantley v. Dept. of Human Resources*, 271 Ga. 679, 523 S.E.2d 571 (1999): a decision to

leave a two-year old child unattended in a swimming pool was not a policy decision but one of routine child care. No immunity was warranted. *Trujillo v. Utah Dept. of Transport.*, 986 P.2d 752 (Utah Ct.App.1999): dangerous management of traffic control in a construction area was not protected by the discretionary immunity. What about a school that fails to take any steps at all when one student is threatened by another? See *L.W. v. McComb Separate Municipal School Dist.*, 754 So.2d 1136 (Miss.1999).

———

PLETAN v. GAINES, 494 N.W.2d 38 (Minn.1992). Sgt. Barrott, receiving a radio call reporting a snatch and grab nearby, saw a driver matching the criminal's description. He pursued the suspect, one Kevin Gaines, lights flashing. Gaines drove up to 75 mph, weaving and running red lights. Eventually Gaines, seeking to avoid capture, ran a red light and in so doing ran directly into and killed 7–year-old Shawn Pletan, a pedestrian. "Gaines pled guilty to manslaughter and to six counts of theft. Gaines admitted he was a heavy drug user and had used both heroin and cocaine within 24 hours of the car chase. The entire chase took slightly more than 2 minutes." In a suit for Shawn's death brought against both Gaines and the officer, *held,* the officer is immune. "The common law provides that 'a public official charged by law with duties which call for the exercise of his judgment or discretion is not personally liable to an individual for damages unless he is guilty of a willful or malicious wrong.' The discretion involved in official immunity is different from the policymaking type of discretion involved in discretionary function immunity afforded governmental entities. Official immunity involves the kind of discretion which is exercised on an operational rather than a policymaking level, and it requires something more than the performance of 'ministerial' duties.... The decision to engage in a car chase and to continue the chase involves the weighing of many factors. How dangerous is the fleeing suspect and how important is it that he be caught? To what extent may the chase be dangerous to other persons because of weather, time of day, road, and traffic conditions? Are there alternatives to a car chase, such as a road block up ahead? These and other questions must be considered by the police officer in deciding whether or not to engage in a vehicular pursuit. And these questions must be resolved under emergency conditions with little time for reflection and often on the basis of incomplete and confusing information. It is difficult to think of a situation where the exercise of significant, independent judgment and discretion would be more required."

Note

Approaches to the high speed chase injury. What is the best way to handle injuries resulting from high-speed chases? (1) Provide a complete immunity; (2) lower the standard of care so that liability is permitted only when the driver is guilty of reckless misconduct; or (3) judge the case according to ordinary negligence analysis, taking into account the importance of the particular arrest attempt and the degree of risk the chase imposes or does not impose upon others? All three approaches can be found in the cases. See DOBBS ON TORTS § 272, at 730 (2000).

NOTE: THE PUBLIC DUTY DOCTRINE

(1) *The doctrine.* The public duty doctrine is formally different from discretionary immunity. The public duty doctrine holds that public entities and officers are not liable to individuals for failure to carry out a duty, even a statutory duty, owed to the public at large rather than to particular individuals or groups. For example, some courts hold that a public entity is not liable for a police officer's failure to arrest a drunk driver who, left free, drunkenly injures or kills others. *Ezell v. Cockrell,* 902 S.W.2d 394 (Tenn.1995). Perhaps the most important effect of the doctrine is that statutes commanding action by public entities or officers are frequently construed to impose public duties only, so that no private person can recover for a public officer's failure to enforce the statute.

(2) A few courts reject or narrowly limit the doctrine. See DOBBS ON TORTS § 271 (2000).

(3) *Distinguishing discretionary immunity.* The public duty doctrine can differ from the discretionary immunity not only in adopting the language of duty but also in recognizing that the duty may be narrowed and liability imposed if the officer or entity takes affirmative action that endangers the plaintiff or if the duty becomes individualized because of a special relationship with the plaintiff. In other words, the traditional rule about nonaction: the officer is not liable for failure to arrest a drunk, but he is liable if he himself causes injury by driving negligently. See *Hetzel v. United States,* 43 F.3d 1500 (D.C.Cir.1995). This much is essentially a specific application of rules about nonaction we will see in Chapter 14.

(4) *Statutes creating particular duties.* In addition, a statute might create a special duty to a particular group rather than to the public at large. In that case, the court may conclude that the statutory duty is not merely a duty owed to the public at large. For example, a statute creating a specific duty to protect victims of domestic violence may be construed to impose a duty to a special group, so that a failure to provide the protection required will be actionable. See *Calloway v. Kinkelaar,* 168 Ill.2d 312, 213 Ill.Dec. 675, 659 N.E.2d 1322 (1995) (liability for wilful or wanton negligence of the police in failing to protect).

(5) *Public duty doctrine as discretionary immunity.* In spite of what has been said above, a number of courts have verbally identified the public duty doctrine with discretionary immunity. For instance, Rhode Island expresses the doctrine in terms of discretionary immunity by saying that it "shields the state and its political subdivisions from tort liability arising out of discretionary governmental actions that by their nature are not ordinarily performed by private persons." Stated this way, the doctrine sounds like a discretionary immunity that could

protect affirmative action as well as a failure to act. Yet Rhode Island also recognizes that a special relationship between public officer and individual plaintiff may eliminate the immunity. See *Schultz v. Foster–Glocester Regional Sch. Dist.*, 755 A.2d 153 (R.I.2000).

Notes

1. A state agency may be under a statutory duty to inspect child-care facilities and to revoke their licenses if need be. If a child is injured because the agency failed to find an unsafe condition or if the agency found it and did nothing, does the public duty doctrine bar liability to a child injured as a result of the condition that should have been corrected? Consider whether the duty was to the general public or more focused on a special group. See *Andrade v. Ellefson*, 391 N.W.2d 836, 68 A.L.R.4th 245 (Minn. 1986); cf. *C.T. v. Martinez*, 845 P.2d 246 (Utah 1992); *Jamierson v. Dale*, 670 S.W.2d 195 (Mo.App.1984).

2. Do we need a public duty doctrine? If it is a matter of construing the statute, it is not a doctrine at all but merely a matter of construing each statute as it arises. If it is independent of the legislature's intent, why should courts add this additional immunity to the discretionary immunity that already exists?

Problem

Claims of Picklesimer, et al.

[Memo from partner in charge of the case.]

Since the initial memo [p. 335 supra], I have talked with an engineer who says that the highway design at the point of the accident was dangerous. He is quite specific. The highway appears to be a state highway rather than a local road. Can we sue the state for this, assuming the testimony really does support the claim of negligence? Would it matter whether we claimed (1) failure to mark the road, (2) failure to provide warning signs, (3) the design of the curve or the slope? Also, would our claim against Dalzell prejudice a claim against the state or vice versa?

THOMPSON v. COUNTY OF ALAMEDA

Supreme Court of California, 1980.
27 Cal.3d 741, 167 Cal.Rptr. 70, 614 P.2d 728.

RICHARDSON, JUSTICE.

[One James F. was a "juvenile offender" in the custody of defendant county. According to the complaint, the defendant knew he had "latent, extremely dangerous and violent propensities regarding young children and that sexual assaults upon young children and violence connected therewith were a likely result of releasing [him] into the community." In fact, the plaintiffs alleged, James had said that if released he would kill a child in the neighborhood. Nonetheless the county released James F. on temporary leave to his mother's custody, but gave no warning to local police, or to nearby families. Within 24 hours of his release James F. sexually assaulted plaintiff's 5–year-old son and murdered him. This is an action by the parents against the county for wrongful death. The trial court sustained the county's demurrer.]

[The California Code provided a general discretionary immunity in § 820.2. It also provided a number of specific immunities, one of which is § 845.8, providing that there is no liability for "parole or release of a prisoner." The court first held that the decision to release James F. was protected by both these immunities. It then considered the claim that the county was negligent in selecting James' mother as custodian and in failing to supervise her. It concluded that this also was protected by the discretionary immunity, because the choice of a custodian for an antisocial minor involved balancing factors such as concern for the public, the needs of the minor, the suitability of the proposed home environment, and the availability of other resources.]

We now examine the principal and most troublesome contentions of plaintiffs, namely, that County is liable for its failure to warn the local police and the parents of neighborhood children that James was being released or, alternatively, to warn James' mother of his expressed threat. We first inquire whether there would be liability in the absence of immunity and determine initially whether in any event County had a duty to warn for the protection of plaintiffs.

In *Johnson*, the state, acting through a Youth Authority placement officer, placed a minor with "homicidal tendencies and a background of violence and cruelty" in the plaintiff's home. Following his attack on the plaintiff, she sued the state. In sustaining plaintiff's cause of action, we held "[a]t the outset, we can dispose summarily of the contention, not strenuously pressed by defendant, that the judgment should be affirmed because the state owed no duty of care to plaintiff. As the party placing the youth with Mrs. Johnson, the state's relationship to plaintiff was such that its duty extended to warning of latent, dangerous qualities suggested by the parolee's history or character. [Citations.] These cases impose a duty upon those who create a *foreseeable peril*, not readily discoverable by endangered persons, to warn them of such potential peril. Accordingly, the state owed a duty to inform Mrs. Johnson of any matter that its agents knew or should have known that might endanger the Johnson family...." (*Johnson*, supra, 69 Cal. 2d at pp. 785–786, 73 Cal. Rptr. at p. 243, 447 P.2d at p. 355 [emphasis] added.)

In *Johnson* we emphasized the *relationship* between the state and plaintiff-victim, and the fact that the state by its conduct placed the specific plaintiff in a position of clearly foreseeable danger. In contrast with the situation in *Johnson*, in which the risk of danger focused precisely on plaintiff, here County bore no special and continuous relationship with the specific plaintiffs nor did County knowingly place the specific plaintiffs' decedent into a foreseeably dangerous position. Thus the reasoning of our holding in *Johnson* would not sustain the complaint in this action....

In summary, whenever a potentially dangerous offender is released and thereafter commits a crime, the possibility of the commission of that crime is statistically foreseeable. Yet the Legislature has concluded that the benefits to society from rehabilitative release programs mandate their continuance. Within this context and for policy reasons the duty to warn depends upon and arises from the existence of a prior threat to a specific identifiable victim. In those instances in which the released offender poses a predictable threat of harm to a named or readily identifiable victim or group of victims who can be effectively warned of the danger, a releasing agent may well be liable for failure to warn such persons. Despite the tragic events underlying the present complaint, plaintiffs' decedent was not a known, identifiable victim, but rather a member of a large amorphous public group of potential targets. Under these circumstances we hold that County had no affirmative duty to warn plaintiffs, the police, the mother of the juvenile offender, or other local parents.

Because we have concluded that County was either statutorily immunized from liability or, alternatively, bore no affirmative duty that it failed to perform, we need not reach the other contentions raised by County.

The Judgment of Dismissal is Affirmed.

Notes

1. If the allegations of the complaint are taken to be true, could the officer releasing James F. possibly have been considering delicate policy factors suggested in the opinion? Why doesn't the court permit a trial to develop the facts so that we can see whether policy judgment was required?

2. In terms of accountability, is this the kind of case in which the state and its officers should not be accountable for fault? Is that the decision here? Or is the decision really merely a decision on the negligence issue with the court deciding that issue before any proof is in?

3. *Identifiable victims.* Are you satisfied with the justice of a decision that makes liability turn on whether the plaintiff's son was specifically in danger? If James F. had said, "I'll kill the Thompson boy," presumably the case would have gone the other way.

4. *Mini-problem*: A state statute requires the state's child protection agency to investigate day-care centers to protect children and to take appropriate action in the event of a centers' failure to meet standards or its abusive treatment. The agency fails to respond to reports of probable abuse of children by a Mr. Talman. Later, the plaintiff is abused at the center by Mr. Talman. The state has abolished the public duty doctrine or has construed the statute to impose a private duty. Does either *Riss* or *Thompson* nevertheless bar the plaintiff?

5. What victims are identifiable under the *Thompson* rule? In *Division of Corrections v. Neakok*, 721 P.2d 1121 (Alaska 1986), the state paroled a violent criminal. Evaluations represented that he would be violent again if he drank. The state imposed no conditions on his parole, although it could

have done so. Neither did it provide any warnings. As expected, he returned to his home in a small town that had no police. He got drunk and committed terrible acts of violence on several victims. Given the size of the community, the potential victims were not merely "members of a limitless class of unidentifiable victims." So the state was under a duty of reasonable care to them and would be liable if it was negligent.

In *Sorichetti v. City of New York*, 65 N.Y.2d 461, 492 N.Y.S.2d 591, 482 N.E.2d 70 (1985), a wife, victimized by a violent husband, obtained a protective order which authorized police to take into custody any person violating its terms. When her husband did not return her child after a visitation, she sought police help, but they repeatedly refused, on the ground that she should wait a little. The husband in fact attacked the child. The court thought that the class of potential victims was sufficiently limited by the court order to permit liability for negligence if any was proven.

6. *Dangerous persons in custody.* The decision to release a dangerous person in custody, such as a violent mental patient or a violent criminal, is typically regarded as "discretionary," both in state and federal cases. E.g., *Payton v. United States*, 679 F.2d 475 (5th Cir.1982). However, even when release does not violate regulations, a few courts might impose liability for a negligent or reckless release. See *Grimm v. Arizona Board of Pardons and Paroles*, 115 Ariz. 260, 564 P.2d 1227 (1977) (potential liability for gross negligence or recklessness in release).

7. *Protection of persons in custody.* The public entity usually owes a duty of care *to* persons it has in custody. Thus a jailer owes a duty of care to prisoners, schools owe care to school children, and presumably the county owed care to James F. in the principal case, though no duty to innocent citizens.

8. *Thompson* reflects several statutory sections establishing immunity in particular cases or settings. Some states have enacted a number of more or less specific immunities of varying scope. Other states have enacted a general immunity and then created specific exceptions. For example, a statute might enact a broad immunity, then permit tort claims based upon negligent maintenance of a public building or negligent operation of a motor vehicle. Some states create other special privileges for governmental defendants. For instance, comparative negligence may be rejected and contributory negligence may operate as a complete bar when the plaintiff sues governmental entities, or the statute may artificially limit the amount of damages recoverable. In some states the immunities vary with the public entity involved. As you would guess, strict liability is almost always rejected for states and other public entities.

§ 4. OFFICERS

PENTHOUSE, INC. v. SABA

District Court of Appeal of Florida, Second District, 1981.
399 So.2d 456.

OTT, JUDGE.

Appellees, the five commissioners of Sarasota County, were sued as individuals in an action brought by appellant under 42 U.S.C. § 1983.

The complaint alleged that appellees had acted arbitrarily, capriciously, and in violation of the Sarasota County Zoning Ordinances, in withholding approval of appellant's preliminary site plan for a proposed condominium project. The trial court dismissed the action on the ground that "the defendants may not be held individually liable for their official acts based upon the facts alleged in the complaint." We affirm because the dismissal was proper, but the reason why it was correct bears brief exposition.

Government officials no longer enjoy absolute immunity from personal liability for all of their official acts. As the states have gradually withdrawn the sovereign immunity of governmental units, so, too, have Congress and the federal courts narrowed the immunity of individual officials. The degree of immunity varies, depending upon the nature of the act. If an exercise of legislative or judicial power is involved, the immunity is absolute. But the common-law doctrine of "official immunity" no longer acts as an absolute bar to the individual liability of a public officer exercising executive power. When an official, acting under color of local law, has deprived any person of a right or privilege protected by the Federal Constitution or other federal law, he can be held personally liable in damages to the injured party under section 1983 unless he pleads and establishes, as an affirmative defense, that he acted reasonably and in good faith with a bona fide and reasonable belief in the constitutional validity of the local law he was enforcing.

As applied to the facts at bench, the rule is that appellees would have had absolute immunity from suit under section 1983 if, for instance, they had enacted (legislative power) an unconstitutional zoning ordinance, but they (and all other county officials) would have had only qualified immunity for their acts in implementing and enforcing (executive power) such an ordinance. The existence of qualified immunity is a question of fact and, when properly presented, cannot be resolved summarily.

The ruling of the court below was therefore erroneous, or at least premature, insofar as it may have intimated that appellees were immune from liability.

[The court held, however, that although there was no immunity, the plaintiff's constitutional rights had not been violated. The trial court's ruling was affirmed for this reason.]

Notes

State and Federal Judicial Officers

1. *Absolute immunity.* Legislative and judicial officers are traditionally given absolute immunity under the common law, so long as they are acting in their judicial or legislative capacity. The rule applies both to state and federal officers. Thus both state and federal judges are absolutely immune. The immunity also applies whether the claim is based on ordinary state tort law or on federal civil rights claims.

State Executive Branch Officers

2. *Suits against state officers under state law.* Under the common law, state or local officers did not share the sovereign immunity of the states themselves. If their conduct was characterized by the court as ministerial, they were held liable for any tort. If their acts were characterized as discretionary, they were protected by a qualified immunity, that is, by an immunity destructible by improper purpose or "malice." See *Pletan v. Gaines*, supra. These tests left much room for litigation.

In *B.W. v. Meade County*, 534 N.W.2d 595 (S.D.1995) the plaintiff child claimed that if officers had properly investigated her earlier claim of child sexual abuse, they would have discovered that her father was abusing her and thus would have avoided further abuse. The child's mother presented her in person to investigating officers. In violation of standards, the interviews were carried out by officers (1) who were male, (2) who wore uniforms, and (3) who wore side arms. The child had a venereal wart on her lip, but the officers failed to call for a medical exam, either on that ground or any other. A statute expressly provided for an immunity for any person "involved in the investigation and treatment of child abuse." If the common law rule of official immunity applied, would it have protected the officers?

3. *Suits against state and local executive branch officers under federal law.* When state or local officers are sued under federal civil rights laws, federal courts apply a qualified immunity. They characterize it as a good faith immunity, but that is misleading, because the test is objective rather than subjective. That is, the officer can be held liable in spite of his personal good faith if a reasonable officer would have known that the plaintiff's constitutional rights were impaired by the action in question. *Harlow v. Fitzgerald*, 457 U.S. 800, 102 S.Ct. 2727, 73 L.Ed.2d 396 (1982). Conversely, though, the officer is immune if decisions at the time he acted had not established the right the plaintiff now asserts. In *Richardson v. McKnight*, 521 U.S. 399, 117 S.Ct. 2100, 138 L.Ed.2d 540 (1997), the Supreme Court refused to apply the good faith immunity to a private contractor that was operating a state prison.

Federal Executive Branch Officers

4. *Suits against federal executive branch officers under federal law.* Section 1983 has no application to federal officers unless they happen to be acting under color of state law. There is no statute comparable to § 1983 granting a claim against federal officers acting under color of *federal* law. However, in *Bivens v. Six Unknown Named Agents of Federal Bureau of Narcotics*, 403 U.S. 388, 91 S.Ct. 1999, 29 L.Ed.2d 619 (1971), the Court held that federal officers could be sued for constitutional violations directly under the Constitution. There is no general absolute immunity in such cases. The President of the United States is not immune for his purely unofficial acts committed before he took office, *Clinton v. Jones,* 520 U.S. 681, 117 S.Ct. 1636, 137 L.Ed.2d 945 (1997), but is absolutely immune for official acts even when they violate the Constitution. *Nixon v. Fitzgerald*, 457 U.S. 731, 102 S. Ct. 2690, 73 L.Ed.2d 349 (1982).

5. *Suits against federal executive branch officers under state law.* Where the federal officer is sued under *state* law, older authority afforded an

absolute immunity for discretionary decisions, one not destroyed by malice or improper purpose. This was true not only with judicial officers acting within their jurisdiction and with members of Congress doing legislative business, but also with executive officers acting within the "outer perimeter" of the scope of their duties. *Barr v. Matteo*, 360 U.S. 564, 79 S.Ct. 1335, 3 L.Ed.2d 1434 (1959). This may still be the law. The clearest case for the plaintiff against a federal officer is therefore the claim that he violated the federal Constitution rather than state law. This would invoke the rules stated in paragraph 4 above. When you shift to the claim that the federal officer was negligent in a case where no discretion is involved, the officer is given an immunity by the FTCA, so that your sole claim is against the government.

The FTCA Immunity

6. *Creating a new immunity for federal officers and a hiatus in liability.* In a statute known as the Westfall Act, the FTCA was amended to provide that when the plaintiff sues a federal employee, the attorney general may certify that the acts of the employee were within the scope of his federal employment. When such a certificate is presented to the court, the court must dismiss the suit against the allegedly negligent employee. The plaintiff may proceed against the United States alone, subject to all the limitations of the Federal Tort Claims Act. Suppose the plaintiff is injured by a negligent federal agent in Italy or Colombia. The attorney general presents a certificate that the employee was within the scope of employment at the time. Since the United States retains immunity for negligent acts committed outside this country, has Congress deprived the plaintiff of her claim both against the government and the individual tortfeasor? *United States v. Smith*, 499 U.S. 160, 111 S.Ct. 1180, 113 L.Ed.2d 134 (1991) (yes). Any doubts about the justice, policy, or constitutionality of this statute? The Supreme Court has left the plaintiff a tiny possibility: the plaintiff can seek judicial review of the attorney general's determination. *Gutierrez de Martinez v. Lamagno*, 515 U.S. 417, 115 S.Ct. 2227, 132 L.Ed.2d 375 (1995). If the court concludes that the attorney general was wrong and that the federal employee was not after all within the scope of his employment, then the plaintiff could sue the employee because the Westfall Act's immunity would not apply.

K.H. v. MORGAN, 914 F.2d 846 (7th Cir.1990). This is a suit against officers of the Illinois Department of Children and Family Services. The Department, upon discovering that the plaintiff, then 17 months old, had gonorrhea contracted in vaginal intercourse, removed her from her parents, then shuttled her for years among various "foster parents," some of whom further abused her. All defendants allegedly knew the psychological and emotional risk of constantly shuttling the plaintiff to new "parents," and some allegedly knew that some of the foster homes were themselves too likely to be abusive. The defendants asserted an immunity as public officers. Posner, J:

"The defense of public officer immunity in civil rights damages suits is thought in some quarters a second-best solution to the problems created by imposing tort liability on public officers. The defense is not found in the civil rights statutes themselves, but is a judicial addition to the statutes.... The defense has been thought necessary to prevent undue timidity by government employees–faced with enormous personal liabilities if they overstep the bounds of their authority (bounds that may have not been apparent when they acted) and someone is hurt, but denied, by methods of compensating civil servants that may be entailed by the very concept of a civil service, commensurate rewards when their vigor and initiative yield net social benefits. The justification becomes strained, however, when, as is increasingly common, the governmental entity indemnifies its employees for damages and other expenses that they incur in defending against suits that complain about their performance of official duties. The indemnity is not always complete, and some governmental entities provide no indemnity, the federal government being a prominent example. But if the public employer itself, by refusing to indemnify its employees for torts committed in the course of public employment–or the legislature, by refusing to authorize indemnity, out of concern with the public fisc–manifests indifference to the disincentive effects of tort liability, it may be questioned whether the courts should worry about those effects and seek to offset them."

§ 5.   STATE AND MUNICIPAL LIABILITY UNDER § 1983

Although state and municipal immunities have been widely abrogated or limited, considerable immunity remains as cases like *Riss* and *Thompson* show. These immunities lead plaintiffs to assert federal civil rights claims against states and municipalities in hopes of avoiding any immunity.

1. *State liability under § 1983.* The Eleventh Amendment, as construed, provides that citizens cannot subject states to federal court suits against their will. In addition, the Supreme Court has held that states are not "persons" who can be sued under § 1983. *Will v. Michigan Dept. of State Police*, 491 U.S. 58, 109 S.Ct. 2304, 105 L.Ed.2d 45 (1989). Although state officers may be sued for acts done in the course of their official duties, a judgment against the officer cannot serve as a basis for reaching the state's funds. See *Hafer v. Melo*, 502 U.S. 21, 112 S.Ct. 358, 116 L.Ed.2d 301 (1991).

2. *Liability of municipalities under § 1983.* It is now settled that municipalities are "persons" who may be liable under § 1983. There are two peculiarities about this, however. First, the municipality is liable only if the right is violated because of some "policy" or custom of the municipality. *Monell v. Department of Social Services*, 436 U.S. 658, 98 S.Ct. 2018, 56 L.Ed.2d 611 (1978). It is not liable, in other words, for the casual derelictions of the police officer on the beat, but is liable for denial of a due process hearing to accused employees. Second, the municipality, unlike the officer, is not entitled to a good faith defense. *Owen v. City of Independence*, 445 U.S. 622, 100 S.Ct. 1398, 63 L.Ed.2d 673 (1980).

NAVARRO v. BLOCK

United States Court of Appeals, Ninth Circuit, 1995.
72 F.3d 712.

PREGERSON, CIRCUIT JUDGE. . . .

At 10:30 p.m. on August 27, 1989, Maria Navarro was celebrating her birthday with her relatives and friends in her home in East Los Angeles when she received a telephone call from the brother of her estranged husband, Raymond Navarro, warning her that Raymond was on his way to her house to kill her and any others present.

Maria immediately dialed 911 to request emergency assistance. She told the 911 dispatcher that she had just received a warning that her estranged husband was on his way to kill her, that she believed that he was in fact on his way to kill her, and that he was under a restraining order.

When Maria stated that her estranged husband had not yet arrived, but that she believed he would definitely come to her house, the dispatcher responded, "O.K., well, the only thing to do is just call us if he comes over there. . . . I mean, what can we do? We can't have a unit sit there to wait and see if he comes over."

Fifteen minutes after the 911 call, Raymond Navarro entered through the rear of Maria Navarro's house, shot and killed Maria Navarro and four other people, and injured two others.

[The Navarros filed suit against Los Angeles County and the Sheriff, who handled 911 calls. The trial court granted summary judgment for the defendants on all claims.]

Under Monell v. Dept. of Social Services, 436 U.S. 658, 691, 98 S.Ct. 2018, 2035, 56 L.Ed.2d 611 (1978), municipalities may not be held liable under 42 U.S.C. § 1983 "unless action pursuant to official municipal policy of some nature caused a constitutional tort." The Supreme Court made clear that in addition to an official policy, a municipality may be sued for "constitutional deprivations visited pursuant to governmental 'custom' even though such custom has not received formal approval through the [governmental] body's official decisionmaking channels."

Proof of random acts or isolated events is insufficient to establish custom. But a plaintiff may prove "the existence of a custom or informal policy with evidence of repeated constitutional violations for which the errant municipal officials were not discharged or reprimanded." Once such a showing is made, a municipality may be liable for its custom "irrespective of whether official policy-makers had actual knowledge of the practice at issue."

The Navarros claim that the County carried out a policy and practice of not treating 911 requests for assistance relating to domestic violence as "emergency" calls. The Navarros rely primarily on the deposition of Helen Pena, the 911 dispatcher who answered Maria

Navarro's call. In her deposition, Helen Pena testified that it was the practice of the Sheriff's Department not to classify domestic violence 911 calls as Code 2 or "emergency procedure" calls. Ms. Pena also testified that dispatchers were not instructed to treat domestic violence calls as emergencies, that there were no clearly delineated guidelines for responding to domestic violence calls, and that as such, the dispatchers were allowed to exercise unbridled discretion.

The County points out that Helen Pena testified that there was no written policy or procedure that precluded dispatchers from sending a patrol car to the scene of an impending domestic violence crime, nor any policy or procedure that accorded domestic violence 911 calls less priority than non-domestic violence calls. However, this testimony does not contradict Ms. Pena's admission that it was the practice of the Sheriff's Department not to classify domestic violence calls as an "emergency." Because there was no conclusive evidence that the Sheriff's Department has a policy of refusing to send a squad car to non-domestic crimes not yet in progress, or of only treating crimes in progress as emergencies, a practice of not treating domestic crimes as emergencies may have been the cause of the failure to send a squad car to assist Navarro.

. . . [T]he district court erred in concluding that there were no genuine issues of material fact as to whether the County had a policy or custom of not classifying domestic violence calls as an "emergency."

The County argues that even assuming that it had a policy of affording victims of domestic violence less police protection than other crime victims, there was no evidence that discrimination against women was a motivating factor behind the administration of the alleged policy.

The Equal Protection Clause of the Fourteenth Amendment states: "No State shall . . . deny to any person within its jurisdiction the equal protection of the laws." Gender-based classifications must pass the "intermediate scrutiny" test, i.e., the classification "must serve important governmental objectives and must be substantially related to achievement of those objectives."

The Navarros contend that the County's custom of treating domestic violence 911 calls differently from non-domestic violence calls impermissibly discriminates against abused women. The custom of according different treatment to victims of domestic violence is gender-neutral on its face. However, it is well established that discriminatory application of a facially neutral law also offends the Constitution.

Nevertheless, a long line of Supreme Court cases make clear that the Equal Protection Clause requires proof of discriminatory intent or motive.

. . . In the present case . . . aside from the conclusory allegation that the County's custom of not classifying domestic violence calls as an emergency discriminates against abused women, the Navarros have failed to offer any evidence of such invidious intent or motive.

Nevertheless, even absent evidence of gender discrimination, the Navarros' equal protection claim still survives because they could prove that the domestic violence/non-domestic violence classification fails even the rationality test. Unless a statute employs a classification that is inherently invidious (such as race or gender), or that impinges on fundamental rights, we exercise only limited review. At a minimum, however, the Supreme Court "consistently has required that legislation classify the persons it affects in a manner rationally related to legitimate governmental objectives." Although we may not substitute our personal notions of good public policy for those of the legislature, the rational-basis standard is "not a toothless one."

Because the district court did not review the rationality of the County's domestic violence/non-domestic violence classification, we remand for a proper determination.

The Navarros also contend that the Sheriff's failure to train dispatchers on how to handle 911 domestic violence calls, and to instruct dispatchers to treat such calls in the same manner as they treat non-domestic violence calls, amounts to deliberate indifference to the equal protection rights of abused women. However, the Navarros fail to offer any evidence to support these claims.... Accordingly, we affirm the district court's conclusion that the Navarros' deliberate indifference claim fails to survive summary judgment.

For the foregoing reasons, we (1) affirm the district court's conclusion that the Navarros have failed to provide sufficient evidence to defeat summary judgment on their claim of deliberate indifference to constitutional rights arising from a failure to train 911 dispatchers; and (2) reverse the district court's grant of summary judgment on the Navarros' equal protection claim because genuine issues of material fact remain as to whether the County had a custom of not classifying domestic violence 911 calls as "emergencies." On remand, if the Navarros prove the existence of a discriminatory custom against victims of domestic violence, the district court must review the rationality of such a custom.

AFFIRMED in part, and REVERSED and REMANDED in part.

Notes

1. A city's failure to train can constitute a "deliberate indifference to the rights of persons with whom the police come into contact," that amounts to a city policy so that the *Monell* rule is satisfied. *City of Canton, Ohio v. Harris*, 489 U.S. 378, 109 S.Ct. 1197, 103 L.Ed.2d 412 (1989). However, the city is still not liable unless its policy is one that violates an identifiable constitutional right. *Collins v. City of Harker Heights, Tex.*, 503 U.S. 115, 112 S.Ct. 1061, 117 L.Ed.2d 261 (1992).

2. On remand of the *Navarro* case, the trial judge concluded that the sheriff's policy excluded domestic violence cases because they were usually cases of violence-not-in-progress and that it was rational to give not-in-progress cases a lower priority than cases in which violence had already

begun. On second appeal, however, the Ninth Circuit held that, at the pleading stage, domestic violence calls could not be equated with not-in-progress calls because some domestic violence calls could involve violence in progress. "Nothing in the pleadings suggests that victims of domestic violence are less likely to suffer severe injury or death than are victims of other 9–1–1 emergency crimes." The case was remanded again "for a hearing to determine first, whether the city had a policy or custom of giving lower priority to domestic-violence calls than to non-domestic-violence calls, and second, if such a policy or custom exists, whether that policy or custom has a rational basis." *Fajardo v. County of Los Angeles,* 179 F.3d 698 (9th Cir.1999).

3. Other domestic violence claims have not fared so well. In *Soto v. Flores,* 103 F.3d 1056 (1st Cir.1997), an abused wife secretly approached police for protection. The police revealed the wife's plea for help to the husband, although they knew the husband would become enraged at his wife. Neither this fact nor the fact that the police in question disapproved of a law protecting wives from abuse was sufficient to show discriminatory intent required for an equal protection claim when the enraged husband killed the wife's children and himself.

General Reference: Dobbs on Torts §§ 260–278 (2000); Lester S. Jayson and Robert C. Longstreth, Handling Federal Tort Claims (1998).

Topic B

RELATIONSHIPS OR THEIR ABSENCE: NONACTION, CONTRACT AND PROTECTION FROM OTHERS

Chapter 14

NONFEASANCE

§ 1. THE NO DUTY TO ACT RULE

"Dawson was standing at the window of his third-floor apartment when he saw a woman on the sidewalk below. The woman later proved to be Mrs. Perrera. A man approached her, took out a knife, and appeared to demand her purse. She resisted somewhat, and the man grabbed the purse. Dawson's telephone was within reach but he did not use it. The man did not depart after taking the woman's purse, but began some kind of verbal altercation. She tried to run, but he grabbed her and began to beat her. Dawson continued to watch as he beat her to death, perhaps as long a ten minutes. This is a wrongful death action brought by Perrera's family against Dawson. The allegation is that he could have prevented her death without danger to himself by calling 911. Taking this allegation to be true, the trial judge upheld Dawson's motion to dismiss the claim. We must affirm."

The "case" above is fictional but true to life and to legal traditions. Under the general common law rule, one person owes another no duty to take active or affirmative steps for the other's protection. There is liability for misfeasance–negligence in doing something active–but no liability for nonfeasance. See RESTATEMENT SECOND OF TORTS § 314, Ill. (1965); DOBBS ON TORTS § 314 (2000). In this chapter, consider: (1) Is the distinction between misfeasance and nonfeasance meaningful? (2) If the distinction is useful, is it right to say that liability is not imposed for nonfeasance? (3) What are the exceptions to the no liability rule?

NEWTON v. ELLIS, 5 El. & Bl. 115, 119 Eng. Rep. 424 (K.B. 1855). The Local Board of Health contracted with defendant to dig certain wells in the road. Defendant did so, leaving unlighted excavations at night. The plaintiff's carriage was drawn into the unlighted hole and he was injured. Plaintiff sued the contractor, Ellis. Lord Campbell, C.J.: "The action is brought for an improper mode of performing the work. How can that be called a nonfeasance? It is doing unlawfully what might be done lawfully: digging improperly without taking the proper steps for protecting from injury.... Cases where the action has been for a mere nonfeasance are inapplicable: the action here is for doing what was positively wrong."

Note

The reasoning in *Newton* can apply in many situations. Suppose the defendant drives a car. When a bicycle appears in front of him he does nothing. In particular, he does not move his foot to the brake pedal. As a result he strikes the cyclist. Is this nonfeasance? Can we really set a standard for determining what is and what is not mere inaction?

YANIA v. BIGAN

Supreme Court of Pennsylvania, 1959.
397 Pa. 316, 155 A.2d 343.

BENJAMIN R. JONES, JUSTICE....

On September 25, 1957, John E. Bigan was engaged in a coal strip-mining operation in Shade Township, Somerset County. On the property being stripped were large cuts or trenches created by Bigan when he removed the earthen overburden for the purpose of removing the coal underneath. One cut contained water 8 to 10 feet in depth with side walls or embankments 16 to 18 feet in height; at this cut Bigan had installed a pump to remove the water.

At approximately 4 p.m. on that date, Joseph F. Yania, the operator of another coal strip-mining operation and one Boyd M. Ross went upon Bigan's property for the purpose of discussing a business matter with Bigan, and, while there, were asked by Bigan to aid him in starting the pump. Ross and Bigan entered the cut and stood at the point where the pump was located. Yania stood at the top of the cut's side walls and then jumped from the side wall–a height of 16 to 18 feet–into the water and was drowned.

Yania's widow, in her own right and on behalf of her three children, instituted wrongful death and survival actions against Bigan contending Bigan was responsible for Yania's death. [The trial judge sustained preliminary objections in the nature of demurrers.]

... Appellant initially contends that Yania's descent from the high embankment into the water and the resulting death were caused "entirely" by the spoken words and blandishments of Bigan delivered at a distance from Yania. The complaint does not allege that Yania slipped or that he was pushed or that Bigan made any *physical* impact upon Yania. On the contrary, the only inference deductible from the facts alleged in the complaint is that Bigan, by the employment of cajolery and inveiglement, caused such a *mental* impact on Yania that the latter was deprived of his volition and freedom of choice and placed under a compulsion to jump into the water. Had Yania been a child of tender years or a person mentally deficient then it is conceivable that taunting and enticement could constitute actionable negligence if it resulted in harm. However, to contend that such conduct directed to an adult in full possession of all his mental faculties constitutes actionable negligence is not only without precedent but completely without merit.

Lastly, it is urged that Bigan failed to take the necessary steps to rescue Yania from the water. The mere fact that Bigan saw Yania in a position of peril in the water imposed upon him no legal, although a moral, obligation or duty to go to his rescue unless Bigan was legally responsible, in whole or in part, for placing Yania in the perilous position. Restatement, Torts, § 314. Cf. Restatement, Torts, § 322.... The complaint does not aver any facts which impose upon Bigan legal responsibility for placing Yania in the dangerous position in the water and, absent such legal responsibility, the law imposes on Bigan no duty of rescue.

Recognizing that the deceased Yania is entitled to the benefit of the presumption that he was exercising due care and extending to appellant the benefit of every well pleaded fact in this complaint and the fair inferences arising therefrom, yet we can reach but one conclusion: that Yania, a reasonable and prudent adult in full possession of all his mental faculties, undertook to perform an act which he knew or should have known was attended with more or less peril and it was the performance of that act and not any conduct upon Bigan's part which caused his unfortunate death.

Order affirmed.

Notes

1. *Nonfeasance v. misfeasance.* Are *Newton* and *Yania* essentially contrary to one another in the way they characterize conduct? Why is *Yania* not a case of one complex act, a case of enticing-without-aiding?

2. *Is the distinction critical?* Is the nonfeasance/misfeasance distinction itself critical in reaching the right result in these cases? Suppose the Pennsylvania Court had considered that, overall, Bigan's conduct showed affirmative action and that the failure to help Yania was merely one omission in the overall conduct that was, as a whole, affirmative. Would there then be any reasons left to deny liability?

3. How does the rule work in this case: The Rockweit families camped together and used a communal firepit in the ground. Tynan was a friend at a nearby campground with its own firepit. She joined the Rockweits one evening. One of the Rockweits was an 18–month old child, Anthony. Tynan and some others stayed up until 4:00 a.m. playing cards. No one took care to make sure the embers were safe. Hours later Anthony got up, slipped into the pit and was terribly burned. Is Tynan liable? *Rockweit v. Senecal*, 197 Wis.2d 409, 541 N.W.2d 742 (Wis. 1995).

4. How does the rule work in this case: The defendant operates a rapid transit system. At 5:00 a.m., personnel on one of its trains discover a man in the system warming room, either drunk or unconscious, possibly with blood nearby. They notify the company, which notifies security, which is too busy at the moment. On the next two rounds, the same personnel discover the same man, still there, still not conscious. They call again. Only after 10:00 a.m. does someone arrive, and at that time the man speaks briefly and is taken to the hospital where he dies soon thereafter. He had a closed head injury, not caused by the defendant, and could have been saved if he had been helped sooner. He may not have been a ticketed passenger. *Rhodes v. Illinois Central Gulf Railroad,* 172 Ill.2d 213, 216 Ill.Dec. 703, 665 N.E.2d 1260 (1996).

§ 2. EXCEPTIONS, QUALIFICATIONS AND QUESTIONS

SOUTH v. NATIONAL RAILROAD PASSENGER CORP., 290 N.W.2d 819 (N.D.1980). Plaintiff was injured in a collision between his pickup truck and the railroad's train. At trial there was evidence that the engineer did not assist the plaintiff after the collision and some discussion of the engineer's deposition testimony that he did not cover up the plaintiff with his jacket because it was new and he did not want to get it bloody. The plaintiff recovered $948,552 and his wife recovered $126,000. Held, admission of evidence that the engineer refused to provide aid to the plaintiff was not error. "[W]e hold that a person who knows or has reason to know that his conduct, whether tortious or innocent, has caused harm to another has an affirmative duty to render assistance to prevent further harm. One who breaches such duty is subject to liability for damages incurred as a result of the additional harm proximately caused by such breach."

MALDONADO v. SOUTHERN PACIFIC TRANSPORTATION CO., 129 Ariz. 165, 629 P.2d 1001 (Ct. App. 1981). Plaintiff attempted to board defendant's freight train while it was moving. The defendant's employees bumped the train as plaintiff was boarding, causing him to fall under the wheels, which severed his left arm and severely damaged his left leg. He called for help to defendant's employees on the caboose, but, allegedly, they refused to assist him and also yelled at bystanders not to do so. *Held*, this states a valid claim. Under § 322 of the Restatement Second of Torts there is an independent duty to aid when harm is caused by defendant or through its instrumentality, and if defendant's failure to assist aggravates the injury, defendant can be liable, even though its original conduct was not a legal cause of the aggravation and even though the plaintiff was guilty of contributory negligence in causing the original harm. In addition, the plaintiff on these facts can claim intentional infliction of mental distress. If defendant had prevented others from effecting a rescue that would be an independent ground for recovery.

FARWELL v. KEATON

Supreme Court of Michigan, 1976.
396 Mich. 281, 240 N.W.2d 217.

LEVIN, JUSTICE.

[Richard Farwell, 18, and his friend David Siegrist, 16, waiting for a friend to finish work, had a few beers. When teenaged girls walked by, they attempted to engage in conversation without success. The girls complained to friends that they were being followed, and six boys chased Farwell and Siegrist back to a trailer lot. Siegrist escaped but Farwell was severely beaten. Siegrist found him under a car, put ice on his head and then drove around for two hours, stopping at drive-in restaurants. Farwell "went to sleep" in the back of the car and around midnight Siegrist drove him to his grandparents' home, where he left him in the back of the car after an attempt to arouse him. Farwell died three days later from the beating and there was evidence that prompt medical attention could have prevented this. The jury found for the plaintiff in an action for Farwell's death, but the Court of Appeals reversed on the ground that Siegrist had not assumed any duty to aid Farwell.]

Without regard to whether there is a general duty to aid a person in distress, there is a clearly recognized legal duty of every person to avoid any affirmative acts which may make a situation worse. "[I]f the defendant does attempt to aid him, and takes charge and control of the situation, he is regarded as entering voluntarily into a relation which is attended with responsibility. Such a defendant will then be liable for a failure to use reasonable care for the protection of the plaintiff's interests." Prosser, supra, § 56, pp. 343–344. . . .

Courts have been slow to recognize a duty to render aid to a person in peril. Where such a duty has been found, it has been predicated upon the existence of a special relationship between the parties; in such a case, if defendant knew or should have known of the other person's peril, he is required to render reasonable care under all the circumstances. . . .

Farwell and Siegrist were companions on a social venture. Implicit in such a common undertaking is the understanding that one will render assistance to the other when he is in peril if he can do so without endangering himself. Siegrist knew or should have known when he left Farwell, who was badly beaten and unconscious, in the back seat of his car that no one would find him before morning. Under these circumstances, to say that Siegrist had no duty to obtain medical assistance or at least to notify someone of Farwell's condition and whereabouts would be "shocking to humanitarian considerations" and fly in the face of "the commonly accepted code of social conduct." . . .

Farwell and Siegrist were companions engaged in a common undertaking; there was a special relationship between the parties. . . .

The Court of Appeals is reversed and the verdict of the jury reinstated.

KRIEG v. MASSEY, 239 Mont. 469, 781 P.2d 277 (1989). Van Hoose was 77 years old. He moved into the Massey Apartments, managed by Mrs. Young, who was in her seventies. The next day Mrs. Young saw Van Hoose with a pistol, walking around the room. She took it from him and, climbing a chair, put it at the top of his closet. She had arranged to take him to the doctor's later, but after about an hour she heard a noise. Upon investigation she found that Van Hoose had killed himself with the pistol. Van Hoose's nephew brought suit against the apartment house for his death. *Held,* summary judgment for the defendant affirmed. The plaintiff argued that "that because Mrs. Young 'interjected herself into the situation' by taking the gun from Mr. Van Hoose, she imposed a duty upon herself. He contends that she then breached this duty by negligently placing the gun on top of the cabinet rather than removing it. We decline to affirm plaintiff's contention that Mrs. Young's actions created a duty to prevent suicide since, as previously stated, the general rule is that no duty exists in this area absent a custodial relationship or special circumstances. However, even if a duty had arisen, the acts of Mrs. Young placed Mr. Van Hoose in no worse position than before she took the gun from him."

Notes

Defendant "Takes Charge"

1. *Negligent action.* A helicopter rescue crew locates an injured woman stranded in a dangerous ice gorge from which, without such a rescue, she could not escape. The crew lowers a sling, and begins to haul her aboard. It then negligently reverses the ratchet and the sling drops into the gorge again, causing a further injury to the woman. Is the crew under a duty to use reasonable care and liable to the woman for the second injury?

2. *Making matters worse.* Where the defendant discontinues aid, the Restatement imposes liability only if the defendant has left the victim in a "worse position." RESTATEMENT SECOND OF TORTS § 324 (b) (1965). How does this stack up with the *Farwell* case? Could it be said that Farwell would have been better off if Siegrist had shrugged his shoulders, and walked home, leaving Farwell under the car? The Restatement itself seems to have a very special notion about what counts as "worse off." It tells us that if B is lying in a trench filled with poison gas and A lifts him up so that he is free from the poison, A cannot change his mind and lower him back. The result may be right enough but can it really be said that A made B worse off than he would have been without A's intervention? Perhaps the explanation is simpler: once you begin a rescue you must perform it with reasonable care.

Special Relationships as a Basis for a Duty of Affirmative Action

3. "The Restatement recognizes five kinds of formal relationships that require the defendant to use reasonable care for the plaintiff's safety, including reasonable affirmative efforts to rescue. The relationships are those of (1) the carrier-passenger, (2) innkeeper-guest, (3) landowner-invitee,

(4) custodian-ward, and (5) employer-employee." Dobbs on Torts § 317 (2000).

4. What results if a carrier or jailer fails to seek aid for a passenger or prisoner who is ill? A department store fails to call for medical attention when a customer passes out on the floor? Suppose an employer routinely provides medical tests for employees but does not tell one of them that he is suffering from a disease that needs medical attention?

5. *Other determinate relationships.* What other preexisting relationships might generate a duty to act affirmatively when one party is in danger? What if a parent sees a child in danger? What if a town counsel member sees a fire but doesn't report it?

6. *Indeterminate or ad hoc relationships.* In *Farwell* the two boys, Farwell and Siegrist, were not in any preexisting, recognized status with respect to each other. But they did have a relationship that was, for the evening, special in the sense that people in general did not and could not share it. By agreement, they were doing things together. Is this enough to impose upon Siegrist a duty he would not have had if Siegrist had simply glanced out of a second story window and had seen the beating?

7. *Nonfeasance and public entity defendants.* In Chapter 13, § 3, we saw *Riss v. City of New York*, 22 N.Y.2d 579, 293 N.Y.S.2d 897, 240 N.E.2d 860 (1968), where the police department failed to protect Linda Riss from serious threats. The court rejected Linda's claim on grounds that sound like some form of discretionary immunity. Are cases like *Riss* "really" cases of nonfeasance or "really" cases of discretionary immunity?

DeSHANEY v. WINNEBAGO COUNTY DEPT. OF SOCIAL SERVICES*

Supreme Court of the United States, 1989.
489 U.S. 189, 109 S.Ct. 998, 103 L.Ed.2d 249.

Chief Justice Rehnquist delivered the opinion of the Court.

Petitioner is a boy who was beaten and permanently injured by his father, with whom he lived. The respondents are social workers and other local officials who received complaints that petitioner was being abused by his father and had reason to believe that this was the case, but nonetheless did not act to remove petitioner from his father's custody. Petitioner sued respondents claiming that their failure to act deprived him of his liberty in violation of the Due Process Clause of the Fourteenth Amendment to the United States Constitution. We hold that it did not.

The facts of this case are undeniably tragic. Petitioner Joshua DeShaney was born in 1979. In 1980, a Wyoming court granted his parents a divorce and awarded custody of Joshua to his father, Randy DeShaney. The father shortly thereafter moved to Neenah, a city located in Winnebago County, Wisconsin, taking the infant Joshua with him. There he entered into a second marriage, which also ended in divorce.

---

* Headings are inserted by the editors for convenience of reference only.

[The First Two Abuse Reports, State Protective Measures]

The Winnebago County authorities first learned that Joshua DeShaney might be a victim of child abuse in January 1982, when his father's second wife complained to the police, at the time of their divorce, that he had previously "hit the boy causing marks and (was) a prime case for child abuse." Winnebago County Department of Social Services (DSS) interviewed the father, but he denied the accusations, and DSS did not pursue them further. In January 1983, Joshua was admitted to a local hospital with multiple bruises and abrasions. The examining physician suspected child abuse and notified DSS, which immediately obtained an order from a Wisconsin juvenile court placing Joshua in the temporary custody of the hospital. Three days later, the county convened an ad hoc "Child Protection Team"—consisting of a pediatrician, a psychologist, a police detective, the county's lawyer, several DSS caseworkers, and various hospital personnel—to consider Joshua's situation. At this meeting, the Team decided that there was insufficient evidence of child abuse to retain Joshua in the custody of the court. The Team did, however, decide to recommend several measures to protect Joshua, including enrolling him in a preschool program, providing his father with certain counselling services, and encouraging his father's girlfriend to move out of the home. Randy DeShaney entered into a voluntary agreement with DSS in which he promised to cooperate with them in accomplishing these goals.

[Third Abuse Report; Caseworker Observation of Injury]

Based on the recommendation of the Child Protection Team, the juvenile court dismissed the child protection case and returned Joshua to the custody of his father. A month later, emergency room personnel called the DSS caseworker handling Joshua's case to report that he had once again been treated for suspicious injuries. The caseworker concluded that there was no basis for action. For the next six months, the caseworker made monthly visits to the DeShaney home, during which she observed a number of suspicious injuries on Joshua's head; she also noticed that he had not been enrolled in school and that the girlfriend had not moved out. The caseworker dutifully recorded these incidents in her files, along with her continuing suspicions that someone in the DeShaney household was physically abusing Joshua, but she did nothing more. In November 1983, the emergency room notified DSS that Joshua had been treated once again for injuries that they believed to be caused by child abuse. On the caseworker's next two visits to the DeShaney home, she was told that Joshua was too ill to see her. Still DSS took no action.

[Joshua's Last Beating]

In March 1984, Randy DeShaney beat 4–year-old Joshua so severely that he fell into a life-threatening coma. Emergency brain surgery revealed a series of hemorrhages caused by traumatic injuries to the head inflicted over a long period of time. Joshua did not die, but he suffered brain damage so severe that he is expected to spend the rest of his life confined to an institution for the profoundly retarded. Randy DeShaney was subsequently tried and convicted of child abuse.

[THE LEGAL CLAIMS; DUE PROCESS]

[Joshua and his mother filed this action against the county and its social services department, as well as some individual employees involved. They claimed rights under 42 U.S.C.A. § 1983 on the ground that the defendants denied due process to Joshua. The trial court granted summary judgment for the defendants. The Court of Appeals affirmed.]

The Due Process Clause of the Fourteenth Amendment provides that "[n]o State shall ... deprive any person of life, liberty, or property, without due process of law." Petitioners contend that the State deprived Joshua of his liberty interest in "free[dom] from ... unjustified intrusions on personal security," by failing to provide him with adequate protection against his father's violence. The claim is one invoking the substantive rather than procedural component of the Due Process Clause; petitioners do not claim that the State denied Joshua protection without according him appropriate procedural safeguards, but that it was categorically obligated to protect him in these circumstances.[2]

[DUE PROCESS DOES NOT IMPOSE AFFIRMATIVE DUTIES]

But nothing in the language of the Due Process Clause itself requires the State to protect the life, liberty, and property of its citizens against invasion by private actors. The Clause is phrased as a limitation on the State's power to act, not as a guarantee of certain minimal levels of safety and security. It forbids the State itself to deprive individuals of life, liberty, or property without "due process of law," but its language cannot fairly be extended to impose an affirmative obligation on the State to ensure that those interests do not come to harm through other means. Nor does history support such an expansive reading of the constitutional text. Like its counterpart in the Fifth Amendment, the Due Process Clause of the Fourteenth Amendment was intended to prevent government "from abusing [its] power, or employing it as an instrument of oppression," Its purpose was to protect the people from the State, not to ensure that the State protected them from each other. The Framers were content to leave the extent of governmental obligation in the latter area to the democratic political processes.

... If the Due Process Clause does not require the State to provide its citizens with particular protective services, it follows that the State cannot be held liable under the Clause for injuries that could have been averted had it chosen to provide them.[3] As a general matter, then, we

2. Petitioners also argue that the Wisconsin child protection statutes gave Joshua an "entitlement" to receive protective services in accordance with the terms of the statute, an entitlement which would enjoy due process protection against state deprivation.... But this argument is made for the first time in petitioners' brief to this Court: it was not pleaded in the complaint, argued to the Court of Appeals as a ground for reversing the District Court, or raised in the petition for certiorari. We therefore decline to consider it here.

3. The State may not, of course, selectively deny its protective services to certain disfavored minorities without violating the conclude that a State's failure to protect an individual against private violence simply does not constitute a violation of the Due Process Clause.

[THE ROLE OF SPECIAL RELATIONSHIPS]

Petitioners contend, however, that even if the Due Process Clause imposes no affirmative obligation on the State to provide the general public with adequate protective services, such a duty may arise out of certain "special relationships" created or assumed by the State with respect to particular individuals. Petitioners argue that such a "special relationship" existed here because the State knew that Joshua faced a special danger of abuse at his father's hands, and specifically proclaimed, by word and by deed, its intention to protect him against that danger. Having actually undertaken to protect Joshua from this danger–which petitioners concede the State played no part in creating–the State acquired an affirmative "duty," enforceable through the Due Process Clause, to do so in a reasonably competent fashion. Its failure to discharge that duty, so the argument goes, was an abuse of governmental power that so "shocks the conscience," as to constitute a substantive due process violation.

[THE ESTELLE V. GAMBLE CASE]

We reject this argument. It is true that in certain limited circumstances the Constitution imposes upon the State affirmative duties of care and protection with respect to particular individuals. In Estelle v. Gamble, 429 U.S. 97, 97 S.Ct. 285, 50 L.Ed.2d 251 (1976), we recognized that the Eighth Amendment's prohibition against cruel and unusual punishment, made applicable to the States through the Fourteenth Amendment's Due Process Clause, requires the State to provide adequate medical care to incarcerated prisoners. We reasoned that because the prisoner is unable "by reason of the deprivation of his liberty [to] care for himself, it is only just" that the State be required to care for him.

[THE YOUNGBERG V. ROMEO CASE]

In Youngberg v. Romeo, 457 U.S. 307, 102 S.Ct. 2452, 73 L.Ed.2d 28 (1982), we extended this analysis beyond the Eighth Amendment setting, holding that the substantive component of the Fourteenth Amendment's Due Process Clause requires the State to provide involuntarily committed mental patients with such services as are necessary to ensure their "reasonable safety" from themselves and others. As we explained, "[i]f it is cruel and unusual punishment to hold convicted criminals in unsafe conditions, it must be unconstitutional (under the Due Process Clause) to confine the involuntarily committed—who may not be punished at all—in unsafe conditions."

[INTERPRETING THE CASES]

But these cases afford petitioners no help. Taken together, they stand only for the proposition that when the State takes a person into its

Equal Protection Clause. See Yick Wo v. Hopkins, 118 U.S. 356, 6 S.Ct. 1064, 30 L.Ed. 220 (1886). But no such argument has been made here.

custody and holds him there against his will, the Constitution imposes upon it a corresponding duty to assume some responsibility for his safety and general well-being. The rationale for this principle is simple enough: when the State by the affirmative exercise of its power so restrains an individual's liberty that it renders him unable to care for himself, and at the same time fails to provide for his basic human needs—e.g., food, clothing, shelter, medical care, and reasonable safety—it transgresses the substantive limits on state action set by the Eighth Amendment and the Due Process Clause. The affirmative duty to protect arises not from the State's knowledge of the individual's predicament or from its expressions of intent to help him, but from the limitation which it has imposed on his freedom to act on his own behalf. In the substantive due process analysis, it is the State's affirmative act of restraining the individual's freedom to act on his own behalf—through incarceration, institutionalization, or other similar restraint of personal liberty—which is the "deprivation of liberty" triggering the protections of the Due Process Clause, not its failure to act to protect his liberty interests against harms inflicted by other means.[8]

[As Interpreted, the Cases Do Not Assist Joshua's Claim]

The Estelle–Youngberg analysis simply has no applicability in the present case. Petitioners concede that the harms Joshua suffered did not occur while he was in the State's custody, but while he was in the custody of his natural father, who was in no sense a state actor. While the State may have been aware of the dangers that Joshua faced in the free world, it played no part in their creation, nor did it do anything to render him any more vulnerable to them. That the State once took temporary custody of Joshua does not alter the analysis, for when it returned him to his father's custody, it placed him in no worse position than that in which he would have been had it not acted at all; the State does not become the permanent guarantor of an individual's safety by having once offered him shelter. Under these circumstances, the State had no constitutional duty to protect Joshua.

[The Possible Role of State Tort Law]

It may well be that, by voluntarily undertaking to protect Joshua against a danger it concededly played no part in creating, the State acquired a duty under state tort law to provide him with adequate protection against that danger. See Restatement (Second) of Torts § 323 (1965) (one who undertakes to render services to another may in some circumstances be held liable for doing so in a negligent fashion); see generally W. Keeton, D. Dobbs, R. Keeton, & D. Owen, Prosser and Keeton on the Law of Torts § 56 (5th ed. 1984) (discussing "special relationships" which may give rise to affirmative duties to act under the common law of tort). But the claim here is based on the Due Process

---

8. Of course, the protections of the Due Process Clause, both substantive and procedural, may be triggered when the State, by the affirmative acts of its agents, subjects an involuntarily confined individual to deprivations of liberty which are not among those generally authorized by his confinement.

Clause of the Fourteenth Amendment, which, as we have said many times, does not transform every tort committed by a state actor into a constitutional violation. A State may, through its courts and legislatures, impose such affirmative duties of care and protection upon its agents as it wishes. But not "all common-law duties owed by government actors were ... constitutionalized by the Fourteenth Amendment." Because, as explained above, the State had no constitutional duty to protect Joshua against his father's violence, its failure to do so—though calamitous in hindsight—simply does not constitute a violation of the Due Process Clause.[10]

Judges and lawyers, like other humans, are moved by natural sympathy in a case like this to find a way for Joshua and his mother to receive adequate compensation for the grievous harm inflicted upon them. But before yielding to that impulse, it is well to remember once again that the harm was inflicted not by the State of Wisconsin, but by Joshua's father. The most that can be said of the state functionaries in this case is that they stood by and did nothing when suspicious circumstances dictated a more active role for them. In defense of them it must also be said that had they moved too soon to take custody of the son away from the father, they would likely have been met with charges of improperly intruding into the parent-child relationship, charges based on the same Due Process Clause that forms the basis for the present charge of failure to provide adequate protection.

The people of Wisconsin may well prefer a system of liability which would place upon the State and its officials the responsibility for failure to act in situations such as the present one. They may create such a system, if they do not have it already, by changing the tort law of the State in accordance with the regular law-making process. But they should not have it thrust upon them by this Court's expansion of the Due Process Clause of the Fourteenth Amendment.

Affirmed.

JUSTICE BRENNAN, with whom JUSTICE MARSHALL and JUSTICE BLACKMUN join, dissenting. . . .

I would focus first on the action that Wisconsin has taken with respect to Joshua and children like him, rather than on the actions that the State failed to take. . . . [T]he fact of hospitalization was critical in Youngberg not because it rendered Romeo helpless to help himself, but because it separated him from other sources of aid that, we held, the State was obligated to replace. Unlike the Court, therefore, I am unable

---

10. Because we conclude that the Due Process Clause did not require the State to protect Joshua from his father, we need not address respondents' alternative argument that the individual state actors lacked the requisite "state of mind" to make out a due process violation. See Daniels v. Williams, 474 U.S., at 334, n. 3, 106 S.Ct., at 677, n. 3. Similarly, we have no occasion to consider whether the individual respondents might be entitled to a qualified immunity defense, see Anderson v. Creighton, 483 U.S. 635, 107 S.Ct. 3034, 97 L.Ed.2d 523 (1987), or whether the allegations in the complaint are sufficient to support a § 1983 claim against the county and its Department of Social Services under Monell v. New York City Dept. of Social Services, 436 U.S. 658, 98 S.Ct. 2018, 56 L.Ed.2d 611 (1978), and its progeny.

to see in Youngberg a neat and decisive divide between action and inaction.

... I would recognize, as the Court apparently cannot, that "the State's knowledge of [an] individual's predicament [and] its expressions of intent to help him" can amount to a "limitation of his freedom to act on his own behalf" or to obtain help from others. Thus, I would read Youngberg and Estelle to stand for the much more generous proposition that, if a State cuts off private sources of aid and then refuses aid itself, it cannot wash its hands of the harm that results from its inaction....

[JUSTICE BRENNAN argued that Wisconsin's child-welfare system effectively excluded others from helping the child.]

In these circumstances, a private citizen, or even a person working in a government agency other than DSS, would doubtless feel that her job was done as soon as she had reported her suspicions of child abuse to DSS. Through its child-welfare program, in other words, the State of Wisconsin has relieved ordinary citizens and governmental bodies other than the Department of any sense of obligation to do anything more than report their suspicions of child abuse to DSS. If DSS ignores or dismisses these suspicions, no one will step in to fill the gap. Wisconsin's child-protection program thus effectively confined Joshua DeShaney within the walls of Randy DeShaney's violent home until such time as DSS took action to remove him. Conceivably, then, children like Joshua are made worse off by the existence of this program when the persons and entities charged with carrying it out fail to do their jobs.

It simply belies reality, therefore, to contend that the State "stood by and did nothing" with respect to Joshua....

I would allow Joshua and his mother the opportunity to show that respondents' failure to help him arose, not out of the sound exercise of professional judgment ... but from the kind of arbitrariness that we have in the past condemned.

... My disagreement with the Court arises from its failure to see that inaction can be every bit as abusive of power as action, that oppression can result when a State undertakes a vital duty and then ignores it.

JUSTICE BLACKMUN, dissenting.

Today, the Court purports to be the dispassionate oracle of the law, unmoved by "natural sympathy." But, in this pretense, the Court itself retreats into a sterile formalism which prevents it from recognizing either the facts of the case before it or the legal norms that should apply to those facts. As Justice BRENNAN demonstrates, the facts here involve not mere passivity, but active state intervention in the life of Joshua DeShaney–intervention that triggered a fundamental duty to aid the boy once the State learned of the severe danger to which he was exposed....

Notes

1. *Conceptions of nonfeasance.* Was it really nonfeasance in *DeShaney*? Argue pro or con: (a) The officials took affirmative action to manage the case and then managed it in a negligent way. (b) The state "undertook" to provide protection and did not do so, with the result that it would be liable. (c) The officials established a special relationship with Joshua, either by the statutory enactments or otherwise.

2. Are there practical considerations that would make you want to be cautious about imposing liability upon social workers who fail to intervene in family life?

State Tort–Law Protections for Abused Children

3. A number of courts have now held that state child protective statutes requiring investigation and intervention on behalf of children who may have been abused can establish a direct duty to the child or create a special relationship that requires reasonable care by the protective agency. E.g., *Sabia v. State,* 164 Vt. 293, 669 A.2d 1187 (Vt. 1995). Some decisions go the other way, however. See *P.W. and R.W. v. Kansas Dept. of Social and Rehabilitation Services,* 255 Kan. 827, 877 P.2d 430 (1994).

4. In *Jensen v. Anderson County DSS,* 304 S.C. 195, 403 S.E.2d 615 (1991), a teacher reported suspected abuse of Shane. The Child Protection Act required investigation and a determination by social workers whether the report was well founded, with a petition to the court to remove the child if it was. The social worker interviewed Shane, found unexplained bruises and great fear of his mother's boyfriend, Wayne Drawdy. However, the social worker did nothing else and merely closed the file. Thereafter Drawdy beat Shane's brother Michael to death. Because the statute was closely focused on protection of a specific class of persons and directed action by specific public entities, the court concluded that it imposed a duty that was a "special" duty rather than a public duty. The DSS had no discretionary immunity to do nothing.

Custody and Section 1983 Claims

5. *Custody.* The main basis for claiming a constitutional right of protection, *DeShaney* seems to say, is the public entity's custody of the plaintiff. Do the plaintiffs have a constitutional claim in the following cases?

A. A high school student is sexually molested by a teacher; she sues the principal who had ignored many warning signs and failed to provide protection. Cf. *Doe v. Taylor Independent School Dist.,* 975 F.2d 137 (5th Cir.1992) ("custody" under compulsory attendance laws).

B. The defendant, a superintendent in charge of a state school for children with certain disabilities. The plaintiff child was voluntarily admitted there. The defendant allegedly knew that the plaintiff, a developmentally disabled child in the school, had been or was being sexually abused by other students and failed to prevent further abuse. *Stevens v. Umsted,* 131 F.3d 697 (7th Cir.1997).

Distinguish claims authorized by federal anti-discrimination statutes. See *Davis v. Monroe County Bd. of Educ.,* 526 U.S. 629, 119 S.Ct. 1661, 143 L.Ed.2d 839 (1999) (school board's duty to protect against known and severe student-student harassment).

6. *Other forms of special relationship.* Custody is one kind of special relationship. Would the other relationships that would create a duty at common law also create a constitutional duty of state protection? The common law recognizes that employers are in special relationships with employees and owe them a reasonably safe place in which to work. At times this entails protecting them from injury by others. See DOBBS ON TORTS § 328 (2000). The Supreme Court, however, has flatly said that there is no Due Process right to a safe place in which to work. *Collins v. City of Harker Heights, Texas,* 503 U.S. 115, 112 S.Ct. 1061, 117 L.Ed.2d 261 (1992).

K.H. v. MORGAN, 914 F.2d 846 (7th Cir.1990). Posner, J. "The complaint paints an ugly picture of official neglect of human misery. K.H., the plaintiff, is a black girl born in Chicago in 1981. When she was seventeen months old she was discovered to have gonorrhea contracted in vaginal intercourse. The juvenile court of Cook County ordered her removed from the custody of her parents. Pursuant to this order, the Department of Children and Family Services placed her with a foster parent. This was placement number one. Two weeks later the Department transferred her to another foster parent, with whom she remained for four months. At the end of that time she was transferred to a third foster parent, with whom she remained for ten months before being transferred to foster parent number four. She remained for more than a year with that foster parent and then was returned to her natural parents. Three months after that, however, she was again removed from her parents' custody on grounds of parental neglect and placed with her sixth parental custodian (counting her parents as the fifth). She was now three years old. Shortly after this transfer K.H. was shifted to yet another foster parent–who beat her; in addition, a neighbor of this foster parent abused K.H. sexually. The hospital staff that discovered this outrage advised the Department that K.H. needed psychotherapy, but none was administered and instead she was shunted to another foster parent, who, far from having the training or ability to care for what had become an emotionally disturbed child, abused her physically. After this abuse came to light, K.H. was transferred to an institution that provides safe and professional care. But that care is expensive. The complaint seeks $300,000 in damages to help defray the psychiatric treatment needed to alleviate the consequences of the defendants' irresponsible discharge of their duty to provide foster care for K.H. We do not know whether, if the suit fails, there is any source of public or private funds for defraying these expenses.

"In 1987, when at last K.H. was placed in an adequate facility, she was not yet six years old. She had changed homes nine times in four years. The defendants argue from the juvenile court transcript that there were good reasons for each of the moves and–inconsistently–that none of K.H.'s foster parents abused her. As confession and avoidance, this argument leaves more to be desired than consistency. To change an infant's parents nine times in four years not only is suggestive of profound disarray in the state's system of caring for abused and neglected children; more to the point, it may–though this depends on the state of mind with which the authors of this shuttle, the defendants, acted–bespeak violations by these state actors of their constitutional obligations.

"One of the less controversial aspects of the due process clause is its implicit prohibition against a public officer's intentionally killing a person, or seriously impairing the person's health, without any justification. The right to be free from this kind of governmental oppression, although not from lesser oppressions such as defamation and simple assault, is among the "negative liberties" that the due process clause of the Bill of Rights and the Fourteenth Amendment has been held to protect. The extension to the case in which the plaintiff's mental health is seriously impaired by deliberate and unjustified state action is straightforward.

"This is not a 'positive liberties' case, like DeShaney, where the question was whether the Constitution entitles a child to governmental protection against physical abuse by his parents or by other private persons not acting under the direction of the state. The Supreme Court agreed with this court that there is no such entitlement. Here, in contrast, the state removed a child from the custody of her parents; and having done so, it could no more place her in a position of danger, deliberately and without justification, without thereby violating her rights under the due process clause of the Fourteenth Amendment than it could deliberately and without justification place a criminal defendant in a jail or prison in which his health or safety would be endangered, without violating his rights either under the cruel and unusual punishments clause of the Eighth Amendment ... if he was a convicted prisoner, or the due process clause if he was awaiting trial. In either case the state would be a doer of harm rather than merely an inept rescuer, just as the Roman state was a doer of harm when it threw Christians to lions. . . .

"The Roman analogy is sound even if one concedes, as one must in the light of DeShaney, that the State of Illinois has no constitutional obligation to protect children from physical or sexual abuse by their parents. The state could have left K.H. to the tender mercies of her parents without thereby violating her rights under the Constitution. But having removed her from their custody the state assumed at least a limited responsibility for her safety. If the fire department rescues you from a fire that would have killed you, this does not give the department a constitutional license to kill you, on the ground that you will be no worse off than if there were no fire department. The state, having saved a man from a lynch mob, cannot then lynch him, on the ground that he will be no worse off than if he had not been saved. The Illinois

Department of Children and Family Services could not have subjected
K.H. to sexual abuse and then defended on the ground that by doing this
it did not make her any worse off than she would have been had she
been left with her parents. The law does not ask a prisoner complaining
of unsafe and unsanitary prison conditions to prove that he is worse off
than he would be if restored to the criminal milieu from which he had
been taken off to prison. Once the state assumes custody of a person, it
owes him a rudimentary duty of safekeeping no matter how perilous his
circumstances when he was free. The distinction follows the lines of tort
law. There is no duty to rescue a bystander in distress, Yania v. Bigan,
397 Pa. 316, 155 A.2d 343 (1959); but having rescued him from certain
death you are not privileged to kill him. This is not to say that you
assume responsibility for his future welfare. You do not. Our point is
only that the absence of a duty to rescue does not entitle a rescuer to
harm the person whom he has rescued.

"The complaint alleges that the two caseworkers who are defendants knew that the foster parent was incompetent and that the administrator defendants, although they did not know about K.H.'s case
specifically, knew that mindless shuttling of the Department's wards
among incompetent foster parents was rampant, and indeed had, without justification, formulated and approved the departmental policies that
caused such shuttling to occur.... If, as the complaint alleges, the
defendants must have known they were placing K.H. in a sequence of
foster homes that would be destructive of her mental health, the ingredi-
ents of a valid constitutional claim are present."

Notes

1. *Bases for constitutional duties.* DeShaney seemed to recognize a
plaintiff could have a constitutional claim if

> (a) the plaintiff was in custody and officials intentionally failed to
> protect her;

> (b) the plaintiff was a victim of selectively unfavorable treatment of
> disfavored groups;

> (c) the plaintiff had an entitlement created by state law and the
> officials deprived her of that entitlement without due process; or

> (d) officials actively created the danger that resulted in harm to the
> plaintiff.

In each instance, the plaintiff would also be required to establish the
defendant's culpability–an intentional deprivation of constitutional rights or
deliberate indifference or the like.

2. *State-created danger.* A public entity takes custody of an abused
child, then unaccountably returns her to her father's custody in spite of
strong evidence that she will be abused by her father's friend. She is in fact
abused. Is this *DeShaney*, or is this state-created danger? If it is a state-
created danger case, the defendants are under a constitutional duty to the

plaintiff. That leaves the question whether the duty was breached by deliberate indifference or the like.

In *Henderson v. Gunther,* 931 P.2d 1150 (Colo.1997), state prison authorities had custody of a man known to be dangerous, one Sojka. It also employed the plaintiff to work in the prison. The prison-employer placed the plaintiff employee in an office with no guard and gave prisoners access to it; it deprived her of a weapon. Sojka held her as a hostage for more than five hours, during which time he cut her with a shank of a mirror and subjected her to electrical shocks. On the plaintiff's constitutional claim against the prison authorities, is her best argument based upon (1) the defendants' custody of Sojka, (2) the special relationship between the plaintiff and the defendants, or (3) state-created danger?

———

SINTHASOMPHONE v. CITY OF MILWAUKEE, 785 F.Supp. 1343 (E.D.Wis.1992): Two women called for police when they found a young Laotian man "buck naked," seriously hurt and drugged at "25th and State." By the time police arrived, so had Jeffrey Dahmer. The two women resisted Dahmer's attempts to take the young man back to his apartment, but the police escorted the men there and released the young man to Dahmer's custody, even though, according to the complaint, there were grounds for believing he needed protection. Dahmer killed him soon thereafter and has since pleaded guilty to killing a large number of other young men. In a civil rights claim by the young man's family, *Held*, motion to dismiss denied. *DeShaney* does not bar the claim as stated in the complaint. (1) The police here were guilty of affirmative acts, not mere inaction. (2) In addition, the court cannot say that there was no special relationship established when the police took the young man into custody and escorted him into danger. (3) "Finally, the cases uniformly emphasize that if police action—or even police inaction—is a product of intentional discrimination, it violates the equal protection clause. The Sinthasomphone complaint clearly states a claim that the actions of the officers and the policy of the City both are due to intentional discrimination on the "basis of race, color, national origin, or sexual orientation." (4) The complaint sufficiently alleged a city policy of discrimination against racial minorities. The police handling of this event can be viewed as exemplifying that policy. (5) The motion to dismiss was granted as to claims made because of the death of other, later victims of Dahmer. The police had no special relationship with these persons and took no positive action toward them. Police failure to deal with Dahmer in the Sinthasomphone incident may have been a cause in fact but was too remote for liability.

Note

Many thoughtful people have worried about the nonfeasance rules or their appropriate scope. See John M. Adler, *Relying upon the Reasonableness of Strangers: Some Observations about the Current State of Common Law*

Affirmative Duties to Aid or Protect Others, 1991 WIS. L. REV. 867; Thomas Galligan, *Aiding and Altruism: a Mythopsycholegal Analysis,* 27 U. MICH. J. LAW REFORM 439 (1994); Steven J. Heyman, *Foundations of the Duty to Rescue,* 47 VAND. L. REV. 673 (1994); Jean Elting Rowe & Theodore Silver, *The Jurisprudence of Action and Inaction in the Law of Tort: Solving the Puzzle of Nonfeasance and Misfeasance from the Fifteenth Through the Twentieth Centuries,* 33 DUQUESNE L. REV. 807 (1995); Ernest J. Weinrib, *The Case for a Duty to Rescue,* 90 YALE L.J. 247 (1980).

GENERAL REFERENCES: DOBBS ON TORTS §§ 314–319 (2000); HARPER, JAMES & GRAY, THE LAW OF TORTS § 18.6 (2d ed. 1986).

Chapter 15

CONTRACT AND DUTY

§ 1. NONPERFORMANCE OF PROMISES

a. *Unenforceable Promises*

THORNE v. DEAS

4 Johns. (N.Y.) 84 (1809).

[The Thornes owned a one-half interest in a vessel called the Sea Nymph; and Deas, the defendant, owned the other one-half interest. The vessel sailed from New York bound for North Carolina and in two conversations on the subject, Deas assured one of the Thornes that he would procure insurance. He did not do so and the vessel was wrecked off the coast of Carolina. The Thornes brought this action against Deas, "on the case, for nonfeasance in not causing insurance to be made...." There was a verdict for the plaintiffs for one-half the value of the vessel, subject to the opinion of the court on the issue whether a recovery was proper.]

KENT, Ch. J., delivered the opinion of the court:

The chief objection raised to the right of recovery in this case, is the want of a consideration for the promise. The offer on the part of the defendant to cause insurance to be effected, was perfectly voluntary. Will, then, an action lie when one party intrusts the performance of a business to another, who undertakes to do it gratuitously, and wholly omits to do it? If the party who makes this engagement enters upon the execution of the business and does it amiss, through the want of due care, by which damage ensues to the other party, an action will lie for this misfeasance. But the defendant never entered upon the execution of his undertaking, and the action is brought for the nonfeasance....

A short review of the leading cases will show that, by the common law a mandatory, or one who undertakes to do an act for another without reward, is not answerable for omitting to do the act, and is only responsible when he attempts to do it and does it amiss. In other words, he is responsible for a misfeasance but not for a nonfeasance, even though special damages are averred. Those who are conversant with the doctrine of *mandatum* in the civil law, and have perceived the equity which supports it, and the good faith which it enforces, may, perhaps, feel a portion of regret that Sir William Jones was not successful in his attempt to engraft this doctrine in all its extent, into the English law. I have no doubt of the perfect justice of the Roman rule.... But there are many rights of moral obligation which civil laws do not enforce, and are, therefore, left to the conscience of the individual, as rights of imperfect obligation....

Judgment for the defendant.

Notes

The Restatement of Contracts, in its famous § 90, puts forward the notion that a promise by defendant plus a reasonable reliance upon it by the plaintiff might operate as a kind of substitute for consideration in certain cases. Would that section eliminate the problem and permit the plaintiffs in *Thorne v. Deas* to recover?

b. Enforceable Promises

LEAVITT v. TWIN COUNTY RENTAL CO., 222 N.C. 81, 21 S.E.2d 890 (1942). The defendant lessor promised to repair ceiling plaster in the plaintiff's house. It did not do so, and the plaster fell and injured the plaintiff, who sought damages for the personal injury. The trial court on this proof nonsuited the plaintiff. *Held*, affirmed. Damages for personal injury are "too remote" and not "within the contemplation of the parties" to the contract. The plaintiff may recover for the cost of making repairs but not for personal injury.

MOBIL OIL CORP. v. THORN

Supreme Court of Michigan, 1977.
401 Mich. 306, 258 N.W.2d 30.

Fitzgerald, Justice.

[Mobil, the plaintiff, sued its lessee for monies due from the sale of petroleum products. The lessee-defendant counterclaimed for injury on the leased premises, alleging that the roof leaked, but that after Mobil had notice to repair, it failed to do so and that as a result the floor was slippery and the lessee was injured in a fall. A provision of the lease obligated Mobil to make repairs after notice, but the trial court and the Court of Appeals held this could be no basis for liability.]

It is apparent that the trial court correctly found that defendant's claim was unenforceable under existing law, as it has been a well settled rule in this state that

"... an action in tort cannot be predicated, by a tenant, upon a breach by the lessor of an agreement to make repairs."

While this common law rule has been abrogated in its applicability to leases for residential dwellings with the enactment of 1968 P.A. 286, § 136, M.C.L.A. § 125.536; M.S.A. § 5.289(16), the rule has been left unchanged in its applicability to leases for commercial premises. The question before this Court then is whether to retain the rule enunciated … as limited by the Legislature, or to reject the rule in its entirety.

… It appears that at present, 26 states have rejected the rule that a lessor is not liable for personal injuries under such circumstances. See the extensive annotation on this subject, 78 A.L.R. 2d 1238, and later case service. The American Law Institute has adopted the modern rule which is stated in 2 Restatement Torts, 2d § 357, p. 241 as follows:

"A lessor of land is subject to liability for physical harm caused to his lessee and others upon the land with the consent of the lessee or his sublessee by a condition of disrepair existing before or arising after the lessee has taken possession if

"(a) the lessor, as such, has contracted by a covenant in the lease or otherwise to keep the land in repair, and

"(b) the disrepair creates an unreasonable risk to persons upon the land which the performance of the lessor's agreement would have prevented, and

"(c) the lessor fails to exercise reasonable care to perform his contract."

Plaintiff maintains that the "social considerations" which led the American Law Institute to adopt § 357 of Restatement Torts, 2d, that is, the need to protect the tenant renter, "[exclude] its provisions from applicability to the commercial lease." However, there is no distinction made between "residential" and "commercial" leases in § 357. We believe that had the American Law Institute intended to limit § 357 to residential leases, it would have done so with clear language to that effect. Nor do we find convincing plaintiff's argument that parties to a commercial lease are necessarily in a more equal bargaining position than are the parties to a residential lease. To be sure, the parties in the instant case, a major oil corporation and a service station operator, cannot seriously be said to have been in an equal bargaining position.

… We remand the matter to the trial court for further proceedings. . . .

DCR INC. v. PEAK ALARM CO., 663 P.2d 433, 37 A.L.R.4th 35 (Utah 1983). The plaintiff alleged that defendant installed a burglar alarm in the plaintiff's clothing store, pursuant to a contract which limited the defendant's liability to $50. A burglary occurred, resulting in extensive losses. The plaintiff sued defendant, alleging it was negligent in using a system that could be and was rendered inoperative by a simple technique, and was negligent in failing to warn the plaintiff. Defendant pleaded the $50 limitation. Held, the $50 limitation has no application to this claim. The limitation relates solely to claims on the contract.

"[D]efendant's duty to warn plaintiff of the vulnerability of its alarm system does not originate from any promise contained within the service contract itself [but] is derived from defendant's general duty of due care which accompanies its ongoing contractual relationship with plaintiff.... Thus, plaintiff's allegation of failure to warn provides the basis for a cause of action in tort which is entirely separate from any contract-based claims which plaintiff might present."

SOUTHWESTERN BELL TEL. CO. v. DELANNEY, 809 S.W.2d 493 (Tex.1991). "We consider whether a cause of action for negligence is stated by an allegation that a telephone company negligently failed to perform its contract to publish a Yellow Pages advertisement. The court of appeals held that the company's failure to perform its contract was a basis for recovery in tort as well as contract, and that the clause limiting the telephone company's liability could not apply to limit tort damages. We reverse the judgment of the court of appeals and render judgment in favor of Bell." The jury found negligence and the Court of Appeals affirmed an award for the plaintiff's lost profits. Held, reversed, the plaintiff is to take nothing.

" 'Tort obligations are in general obligations that are imposed by law–apart from and independent of promises made and therefore apart from the manifested intention of the parties–to avoid injury to others.' W. KEETON, D. DOBBS, R. KEETON & D. OWEN, PROSSER AND KEETON ON THE LAW OF TORTS § 92 at 655 (5th Ed. 1984). If the defendant's conduct–such as negligently burning down a house–would give rise to liability independent of the fact that a contract exists between the parties, the plaintiff's claim may also sound in tort. Conversely, if the defendant's conduct–such as failing to publish an advertisement–would give rise to liability only because it breaches the parties' agreement, the plaintiff's claim ordinarily sounds only in contract.... We hold that Bell's failure to publish the advertisement was not a tort. [The court's footnote:] Prosser and Keeton suggest seven generalizations as helpful in distinguishing between tort and contract liability. Those which are useful to this case include: (1) obligations imposed by law are tort obligations; (2) misfeasance or negligent affirmative conduct in the performance of a promise generally subjects an actor to tort liability as well as contract liability for physical harm to persons and tangible things; (3) recovery of intangible economic losses is normally determined by contract law; and (4) there is no tort liability for nonfeasance, i.e., for failing to do what one has promised to do in the absence of a duty to act apart from the promise made. PROSSER AND KEETON at 656–57.'

§ 2. PROMISES TO THIRD PERSONS

WINTERBOTTOM v. WRIGHT, 10 M. & W. 109, 152 Eng. Rep. 402 (Exch. Pl. 1842). Defendant was under contract with the Postmaster-General to supply coaches for use in delivering mail. The contract also called for the defendant to keep them in good repair. Plaintiff was the coachman on one of the coaches supplied by the defendant and was allegedly lamed for life when the coach broke down and he was thrown from his seat. He alleged that it broke down because the defendant neglected to perform the repair portion of his contract. *Held*, for the defendant. Lord Abinger, C.B.: "Here the action is brought simply because the defendant was a contractor with a third person; and it is contended that thereupon he became liable to every body who might use the carriage. If there had been any ground for such an action, there certainly would have been some precedent of it; but with the exception of actions against innkeepers, and some few other persons, no case of a similar nature has occurred in practice. That is a strong circumstance, and is of itself a great authority against its maintenance. It is however contended that this contract being made on the behalf of the public by the Postmaster–General, no action could be maintained against him, and therefore the plaintiff must have a remedy against the defendant. But that is by no means a necessary consequence—he may be remediless altogether. There is no privity of contract between these parties; and if the plaintiff can sue, every passenger, or even any person passing along the road, who was injured by the upsetting of the coach, might bring a similar action. Unless we confine the operation of such contracts as this to the parties who entered into them, the most absurd and outrageous consequences, to which I can see no limit, would ensue. Where a party becomes responsible to the public, by undertaking a public duty, he is liable, though the injury may have arisen from the negligence of his servant or agent. So, in cases of public nuisances, whether the act was done by the party as a servant, or in any other capacity, you are liable to an action at the suit of any person who suffers. Those, however, are cases where the real ground of the liability is the public duty, or the commission of the public nuisance. There is also a class of cases in which the law permits a contract to be turned into a tort; but unless there has been some public duty undertaken, or public nuisance committed, they are all cases in which an action might have been maintained upon the contract. Thus, a carrier may be sued either in assumpsit or case; but there is no instance in which a party, who was not privy to the contract entered into with him, can maintain any such action. The plaintiff in this case could not have brought an action on the contract; if he could have done so, what would have been his situation, supposing the Postmaster–General had released the defendant? That would, at all events, have defeated his claim altogether. By permitting this action, we would be working this injustice, that after the defendant had done everything to the satisfaction of his employer, and after all matters between them had been adjusted, and all accounts settled on the footing of their contract, we should subject them to be ripped open by this action of tort being brought against him."

Alderson, B.: "The only safe rule is to confine the right to recover to those who enter into the contract: if we go one step beyond that, there is no reason why we should not go fifty."

Note

It was once thought that *Winterbottom v. Wright* established a rule about privity, not a rule about nonfeasance. The result was that even if the defendant was guilty of affirmative negligence in performance of a contract, he would not be liable to third persons who were not parties to the contract. This was attacked, not only on grounds of injustice, but on the ground that *Winterbottom v. Wright* was really only a nonfeasance case and that its rule should be applied only to cases of nonfeasance in the performance of a contract. Do you agree that it was a nonfeasance case? Compare *Newton v. Ellis*, supra Chapter 14.

H.R. MOCH CO. v. RENSSELAER WATER CO.

Court of Appeals of New York, 1928.
247 N.Y. 160, 159 N.E. 896.

CARDOZO, C.J. The defendant, a waterworks company under the laws of this state, made a contract with the city of Rensselaer for the supply of water during a term of years. Water was to be furnished to the city for sewer flushing and street sprinkling; for service to schools and public buildings; and for service at fire hydrants, the latter service at the rate of $42.50 a year for each hydrant. Water was to be furnished to private takers within the city at their homes and factories and other industries at reasonable rates, not exceeding a stated schedule. While this contract was in force, a building caught fire. The flames, spreading to the plaintiff's warehouse near by, destroyed it and its contents. The defendant, according to the complaint, was promptly notified of the fire, "but omitted and neglected after such notice, to supply or furnish sufficient or adequate quantity of water, with adequate pressure to stay, suppress, or extinguish the fire before it reached the warehouse of the plaintiff, although the pressure and supply which the defendant was equipped to supply and furnish, and had agreed by said contract to supply and furnish, was adequate and sufficient to prevent the spread of the fire to and the destruction of the plaintiff's warehouse and its contents." By reason of failure of the defendant to "fulfill the provisions of the contract between it and the city of Rensselaer," the plaintiff is said to have suffered damage, for which judgment is demanded. A motion, in the nature of a demurrer, to dismiss the complaint, was denied at Special Term. The Appellate Division reversed by a divided court.

Liability in the plaintiff's argument is placed on one or other of three grounds. The complaint, we are told, is to be viewed as stating: (1) A cause of action for breach of contract within Lawrence v. Fox, 20 N.Y. 268; (2) a cause of action for a common-law tort, within MacPherson v. Buick Motor Co., 217 N.Y. 382, 111 N.E. 1050, L.R.A. 1916F, 696, Ann. Cas. 1916C, 440; (3) a cause of action for the breach of a statutory duty. These several grounds of liability will be considered in succession.

(1) We think the action is not maintainable as one for breach of contract.

No legal duty rests upon a city to supply its inhabitants with protection against fire. That being so, a member of the public may not maintain an action under Lawrence v. Fox against one contracting with the city to furnish water at the hydrants, unless an intention appears that the promisor is to be answerable to individual members of the public as well as to the city for any loss ensuing from the failure to fulfill the promise. No such intention is discernible here. . . . In a broad sense it is true that every city contract, not improvident or wasteful, is for the benefit of the public. More than this, however, must be shown to give a right of action to a member of the public not formally a party. The benefit, as it is sometimes said, must be one that is not merely incidental and secondary. It must be primary and immediate in such a sense and to such a degree as to bespeak the assumption of a duty to make reparation duty to the individual members of the public if the benefit is lost. The field of obligation would be expanded beyond reasonable limits if less than this were to be demanded as a condition of liability. A promisor undertakes to supply fuel for heating a public building. He is not liable for breach of contract to a visitor who finds the building without fuel, and thus contracts a cold. . . .

An intention to assume an obligation of indefinite extension to every member of the public is seen to be the more improbable when we recall the crushing burden that the obligation would impose. The consequences invited would bear no reasonable proportion to those attached by law to defaults not greatly different. . . . If the plaintiff is to prevail, one who negligently omits to supply sufficient pressure to extinguish a fire started by another assumes an obligation to pay the ensuing damage, though the whole city is laid low. A promisor will not be deemed to have had in mind the assumption of a risk so overwhelming for any trivial reward. . . .

(2) We think the action is not maintainable as one for a common-law tort.

"It is ancient learning that one who assumes to act, even though gratuitously, may thereby become subject to the duty of acting carefully, if he acts at all." The plaintiff would bring its case within the orbit of that principle. The hand once set to a task may not always be withdrawn with impunity though liability would fall if it had never been applied at all. A time-honored formula often phrases the distinction as one between misfeasance and nonfeasance. Incomplete the formula is, and so at times misleading. Given a relation involving in its existence a duty of care irrespective of a contract, a tort may result as well from acts of omission as of commission in the fulfillment of the duty thus recognized by law. What we need to know is not so much the conduct to be avoided when the relation and its attendant duty are established as existing. What we need to know is the conduct that engenders the relation. It is here that the formula, however incomplete, has its value and significance. If conduct has gone forward to such a stage that inaction would commonly result, not negatively merely in withholding a benefit, but positively or actively in working an injury, there exists a relation out of which arises a duty to go forward. Bohlen, Studies in the Law of Torts, p. 87. So the surgeon who operates without pay is liable, though his negligence is in the omission to sterilize his instruments; the engineer, though his fault is in the failure to shut off steam; the maker of automobiles, at the suit of some one other than the buyer, though his negligence is merely in inadequate inspection The query always is whether the putative wrong-doer has advanced to such a point as to have launched a force or instrument of harm, or has stopped where inaction is at most a refusal to become an instrument for good.

The plaintiff would have us hold that the defendant, when once it entered upon the performance of its contract with the city, was brought into such a relation with everyone who might potentially be benefitted through the supply of water at the hydrants as to give to negligent performance, without reasonable notice of a refusal to continue, the quality of a tort.... We are satisfied that liability would be unduly and indeed indefinitely extended by this enlargement of the zone of duty. The dealer in coal who is to supply fuel for a shop must then answer to the customers if fuel is lacking. The manufacturer of goods, who enters upon the performance of his contract, must answer, in that view, not only to the buyer, but to those who to his knowledge are looking to the buyer for their own sources of supply. Everyone making a promise having the quality of a contract will be under a duty to the promisee by virtue of the promise, but under another duty, apart from contract, to an indefinite number of potential beneficiaries when performance has begun. The assumption of one relation will mean the involuntary assumption of a series of new relations, inescapably hooked together .....

(3) We think the action is not maintainable as one for the breach of a statutory duty....

Notes

1. *Winterbottom v. Wright* reasoned in the language of privity but might be best understood as a nonfeasance case. *Moch* reasoned in part in the language of nonfeasance, but could it be best understood as a privity case?

2. Maybe *Moch* is not a nonfeasance case at all. Did the defendant not operate a water company and operate it badly? How would the case have been handled if the defendant had caused the pressure to fall by (a) failing to read its own instruments? (b) failing to open a valve? (c) opening the wrong valve?

3. If the problem in *Moch* is not nonfeasance, consider this: *Moch* was decided the same year as *Palsgraf*. Is it plausible to treat *Moch* as a scope-of-duty problem rather than a nonfeasance problem? You could ask (a) what persons are within the defendant's promised protection? and (b) what risks are within the promised protection? Such an approach would delineate the duty by asking about the scope of the promise or undertaking rather than by asking about foreseeability, but otherwise it would sound pretty much like a basic proximate cause approach.

4. Another possibility is that the court is simply afraid of potentially unlimited liability and will arbitrarily mark a limit to that liability. In *Strauss v. Belle Realty Co.*, 65 N.Y.2d 399, 492 N.Y.S.2d 555, 482 N.E.2d 34, 54 A.L.R.4th 655 (1985) the defendant, an electrical utility, was grossly negligent in permitting an electrical failure and general blackout over a large urban area for a long period of time. The 77–year-old plaintiff had a contract with the utility for electrical service in his apartment. When the electricity failed, the plaintiff could not get running water, which depended upon electrical pumps. On the second day of the blackout, he went to the basement of the building in an attempt to obtain water, to be carried up to his apartment. He fell in the darkened basement and sustained injury. Although the plaintiff was a utility customer for service in his apartment, he had no contract with the utility for electrical service in the basement; the basement was a common area covered by the landlord's contract for electrical service. The Court held that the utility was not liable even though its negligence was "gross." However, other victims of the blackout who had contracted directly with the utility for electrical services were allowed to recover in similar circumstances. The court did not characterize the defendant's conduct as nonfeasance. Instead it emphasized its fear of unlimited liability and frankly invoked privity as an implement of judicial policy to "limit the legal consequences of wrongs to a controllable degree."

5. One kind of risk covered by contracts is economic. A breach of contract may cause financial loss but not physical injury. Most of Cardozo's examples in *Moch* were like this. But suppose a contract promise is intended to protect against physical injury. Would there by any need to worry about extended liability in the examples Cardozo gives? Did Cardozo overlook the fact that *Moch* was a physical harm case and that his concerns about extensive economic liability were misplaced?

6. Is it possible to interpret the "intent of the parties" without resorting to an automatic rule based on privity? In *Libbey v. Hampton Water Works Co.*, 118 N.H. 500, 389 A.2d 434 (1978) the court in a *Moch*-type case observed: "Water companies are in business to supply water, not to extinguish fires. Their rates reflect this assumption; they are uniform, not varying with the greater or lesser inherent danger in given areas." This kind of reasoning suggests that even one in privity might be denied recovery for some consequential damages if those damages did not represent harms against which the parties were contracting. Compare the contemplation-of-the-parties rule of *Hadley v. Baxendale*, as to which see Dan Dobbs, The Law of Remedies §§ 12.4 (4)–12.4 (7) (1992).

7. In the water cases could the courts be actuated by the feeling that it is simply cheaper for the victim to rely upon fire insurance than to litigate tort cases about responsibility?

––––––

PALKA v. SERVICEMASTER MANAGEMENT SERVICES CORP., 83 N.Y.2d 579, 611 N.Y.S.2d 817, 634 N.E.2d 189 (1994). Palka was a nurse employed by Ellis Hospital. Ellis had contracted with Servicemaster to manage maintenance operations at the hospital. Before that, the hospital had conducted its own safety inspections of such things as fans mounted on walls. After Servicemaster took over, the hospital left all such programs to Servicemaster. Servicemaster did not exercise reasonable care with respect to wall-mounted fans and one of them fell on the plaintiff. She sued Servicemaster. *Held:* (1) safety of such items as wall-mounted fans was within the scope of the contract obligation; and (2) Servicemaster was under a duty to the plaintiff, a non-contracting party. Palka "proved not only that Servicemaster undertook to provide a service to Ellis Hospital and did so negligently, but also that its conduct in undertaking that particular service placed Palka in an unreasonably risky setting greater than that, had Servicemaster never ventured into its hospital servicing role at all." "[U]nlike our decisions in Moch Co. v. Rensselaer Water Co. and Strauss v. Belle Realty Co., the instant case presents this array of factors: reasonably interconnected and anticipated relationships; particularity of assumed responsibility under the contract and evidence adduced at trial; displacement and substitution of a particular safety function designed to protect persons like this plaintiff; and a set of reasonable expectations of all the parties. These factors, taken together, support imposition of liability against this defendant in favor of this plaintiff."

Notes

1. *Some effects of shifting a duty to another.* Notice that if A by contract or other understanding shifts his duty to the plaintiff to B, any one or more of three distinct results might follow: (a) Plaintiff is entitled to the same care to which she was entitled from A; (b) B is subjected to a duty he did not have before; and (c) A may or may not be relieved of the duty A owed to the plaintiff before the contract. The Restatement attempts to deal with some problems in this setting under the doctrines of proximate cause. RESTATEMENT SECOND OF TORTS § 452(2) (1965). Very commonly, when A contractually shifts responsibility to B, the contract also provides that if A is held liable for B's acts, A will be entitled to indemnity from B.

2. *Implied contract–transfer of control.* Duty might be shifted from A to B without a formal or express contract. For example, suppose a landowner hires a contractor to build on the land. While the contractor is at work, it is in control and owes duties of care commensurate with that control, even though no contract articulates such a duty. When the contractor completes the project and returns the improved land back to the landowner, the landowner assumes the duty of care, even as to danger created by the contractor.

3. Are there not some occasions in which a defendant can exercise reasonable care by arranging for someone else to exercise that care? Can the defendant arrange for the plaintiff to provide the care needed?

PAZ v. STATE OF CALIFORNIA

Supreme Court of California, 2000.
22 Cal.4th 550, 93 Cal.Rptr.2d 703, 994 P.2d 975.

CHIN, J. . . .

[Osborne, which runs north and south, dead-ends at Foothill Boulevard. Stoneman Corporation was developing condos and other residential projects near that intersection. As a condition of granting a permit for the development, the city required Stoneman to install traffic signals and road markings. Stoneman hired Jennings for engineering, and in 1989 Jennings hired KOA to design and install the signals. In 1991, the signals still had not been installed, in part due to KOA's delay in seeking permits from the state. The intersection was already dangerous because of road angles and obscured sight lines; a number of accidents had occurred there. In 1991, the signals still not installed, the plaintiff, riding a motorcycle in a westerly direction on Foothill, crashed into a car that had been headed south on Osborne and was in the process of turning left or east onto Foothill. The plaintiff sued a number of defendants, including the state and its transportation department, the city, Stoneman and KOA. He alleged that they were negligent in failing to get the traffic signals installed. The trial court granted summary judgment in favor of KOA and Stoneman. The Court of Appeals reversed.]

In this court, plaintiff reiterates his claim that defendants negligently discharged a contractual obligation to install traffic signals. Plaintiff asserts that timely installation of the signals would have alleviated the allegedly dangerous condition of obstructed sight lines at the intersection, and hence prevented his collision with Trafton's car. Thus, plaintiff's claim necessarily is grounded in the negligent undertaking theory of liability articulated in section 324A.

Section 324A reads:

> One who undertakes, gratuitously or for consideration, to render services to another which he should recognize as necessary for the protection of a third person or his things, is subject to liability to the third person for physical harm resulting from his failure to exercise reasonable care to [perform] his undertaking, if
>
> > (a) his failure to exercise reasonable care increases the risk of such harm, or
> >
> > (b) he has undertaken to perform a duty owed by the other to the third person, or
> >
> > (c) the harm is suffered because of reliance of the other or the third person upon the undertaking.

. . . In assessing the applicability of section 324A here, we assume for the sake of discussion that defendants undertook the tasks they are alleged to have performed negligently. . . . Similarly, we assume that defendants' agreement to install traffic control signals for the City constituted an undertaking "to render services to another which [defendants] should recognize as necessary for the protection of [third persons]...."

However, the negligent undertaking theory of liability requires more than simply establishing defendants' undertaking to another.... In this case, none of these three conditions for section 324A liability are present.

The evidence fails to support an inference that defendants' conduct increased the risk of physical harm to plaintiff beyond that which allegedly existed at the intersection. Plaintiff alleged that the intersection was dangerous because of restricted sight lines. However, nothing in the record suggests that defendants did anything that increased the risk to motorists that allegedly existed because of these sight lines. Instead, defendants simply did not succeed in completing—before plaintiff's collision—a project that might have reduced the preexisting hazard at the intersection. In this instance, where the record shows that nothing changed but the passage of time, a failure to alleviate a risk cannot be regarded as tantamount to increasing that risk....

Neither the record nor the law shows any basis for satisfying the second alternative condition required for section 324A liability. In agreeing to the traffic signal installation condition, Stoneman (and by extension KOA) did not undertake to perform a duty that the City owed to plaintiff. As our cases and statutes establish, cities generally have no affirmative duty to install traffic control signals....

Finally, plaintiff did not submit, and the record does not contain, any evidence that he was harmed because either he or the City relied on defendants' timely installation of traffic control signals. The only reasonable inferences available from the record are to the contrary. The City and Stoneman did not make a contract to install the traffic signals. Instead, the City only made the signals a condition of Stoneman's condominium development project. If Stoneman had abandoned the development project–a decision that real property developers may face if financing becomes uncertain or if litigation entangles a project–Stoneman would not have been obliged to install the traffic signals at all. Thus, imposing the traffic signal installation as a condition of development did not give the City a basis for relying on the installation's being completed at any time before the condominium project's completion.

The fact that the City was not relying on defendants to complete traffic signal installation within any particular time is further demonstrated by the City's own conduct in the matter. [T]he City did not apply for its own encroachment permit, necessary to operate and maintain the signals, for more than two months after Caltrans stopped KOA's work on the project just days before it would have been completed....

[Remanded with instructions to enter judgment for KOA and Stoneman.]

Concurring Opinion by MOSK, J. . . .

This is therefore not a case in which a developer breached an obligation to install traffic improvements before commencing the operation of a commercial or residential development. Under such circumstances, a municipality may be said to rely upon a developer's timely installation of the traffic signal, and the developer could accordingly be held liable for harm resulting from its negligent delay based on that reliance. (Rest.2d Torts, § 324A, subd. (c).) Thus, I do not understand the majority as foreclosing liability for negligent delay when a developer has breached a legal obligation to install a traffic improvement by a certain time or under a certain condition.

Dissenting Opinion by GEORGE, C.J. . . . .

[Chief Justice George first argued that the city could be found to have a duty to make the intersection safer and hence that KOA was undertaking to perform the city's duty.]

Second, . . . I believe the developer owed a duty to the users of the intersection under the third condition of section 324A, because in these circumstances the city (and the neighborhood residents who repeatedly had lobbied the city for the installation of a traffic signal at the intersection) reasonably relied upon the developer's undertaking to install the traffic signal[1]. . . .

Once a developer has made a commitment to install a needed safety measure as a condition of obtaining a development permit and goes ahead with work under the permit . . . the local entity and the public reasonably anticipate that the safety measure in question will be provided by the developer within a reasonable period of time. Thus, under these circumstances the public entity would have no reason to expend its own funds or to seek to impose a similar requirement upon some other entity, absent some indication from the developer that it does not intend to fulfill its responsibility under the permit. . . .

Notes

1. *Increased risk–increase over what?* Consider the increased risk clause in § 324A. Does that clause mean that liability is appropriate if the risk is greater than it would have been had the defendant performed his contract? Or must it be greater than it would have been if there were no contract at all? Can you tell whether Justice Chin has a view about that?

2. *A model for increased risk cases?* In an omitted portion of the opinion, Justice Chin gave an example of increased danger based upon *Thirion v. Fredrickson & Watson Construction Co.,* 193 Cal.App.2d 299, 14 Cal.Rptr. 269 (1961). In that case the plaintiff lost control when his car struck loose gravel on a highway. The jury could find (a) that the defendant contractor had not begun work on the portion of the highway where the

---

1. Although there is no evidence in this case that plaintiff was aware of, or relied upon, the developer's commitment to install a traffic signal, under section 324A the rele-vant reliance may be either by the injured person or by the entity for which the developer undertakes to render the service, here, the city. . . .

plaintiff lost control, but (b) he had conducted his operations on a different part of the road so as to cause loose gravel to be deposited outside the work area. The jury could also find that this gravel was a cause of the plaintiff's injury. Liability was held to be proper. If this case is the only model for increased risk, isn't it clear that there was no increased risk in *Paz*?

3. *Architects or engineers supervising job safety.* Suppose an architect or engineer contracts with a landowner or developer to supervise job safety on a construction project and to order a work stoppage when unsafe conditions are found. He knows of dangerous levels of silica dust but does nothing. Is he liable to injured workers who are not parties to the contract? *Caldwell v. Bechtel, Inc.*, 631 F.2d 989 (D.C.Cir.1980) says he is. *Wilson v. Rebsamen Ins., Inc.*, 330 Ark. 687, 957 S.W.2d 678 (1997) is similar. Would the *Paz* court agree?

4. *Another's duty.* Should clause (b) of § 324A apply to create a duty in *Paz*, or is that case different from *Palka*?

5. *What counts as reliance?* If you say you relied on a contract, don't you have to say that your conduct was different because of the contract or promise? In what way can you say that the city's conduct was different because of the promise?

§ 3. ACTION AS A PROMISE OR UNDERTAKING

FOLSOM v. BURGER KING, 135 Wash.2d 658, 958 P.2d 301 (1998). Pursuant to its contract with the restaurant owner, defendant installed a security system on the premises, including an alarm button in the freezer. Subsequently the restaurant was purchased by a new owner who terminated the contract. However, the security system was never removed because the security company "didn't get around to it." About a year later, two restaurant employees were killed by robbers. Evidence showed that the alarm button in the freezer was pushed during the robbery, and that the security company received the alarm, but disregarded it because it was a "closed account." The workers' estates sued the security company for negligence alleging a "special relationship" between the workers and the company. *Held*, defendant owed no duty to the workers. Defendant was no longer contractually obligated to provide security, and did not assume a continuing duty to the employees when it failed to remove the equipment after the contract had expired.

FLORENCE v. GOLDBERG

Court of Appeals of New York, 1978.
44 N.Y.2d 189, 404 N.Y.S.2d 583, 375 N.E.2d 763.

JASEN, JUDGE.

[A mother took her 6–year-old child to school each day for two weeks, during which time the city police had stationed a guard at a street crossing. The mother, having observed this protection, ceased to take the child to school. On the day in question the crossing guard regularly assigned there called in sick. Departmental regulations called for sending a substitute if possible and, if not, to cover the most dangerous crossings. No substitute was sent and the principal of the school was not notified. The child was struck at the unguarded crossing and suffered severe brain damage. The plaintiffs recovered against the city and those responsible for operation of the car. The city appeals.]

[A] municipality cannot be held liable for failure to furnish adequate police protection. This duty, like the duty to provide protection against fire, flows only to the general public. (Riss v. City of New York, 22 N.Y. 2d 579, 583, 293 N.Y.S.2d 897, 899, 240 N.E.2d 860, 861 . . . .)

[T]here is little question that the police department voluntarily assumed a particular duty to supervise school crossings. . . .

Significantly, the duty assumed by the police department was a limited one: a duty intended to benefit a special class of persons—viz., children crossing designated intersections while traveling to and from school at scheduled times. Thus, the duty assumed constituted more than a general duty to provide police protection to the public at large. Having witnessed the regular performance of this special duty for a two-week period, the plaintiff infant's mother relied upon its continued performance. To borrow once more from Chief Judge Cardozo, "[i]f conduct has gone forward to such a state that inaction would commonly result, not negatively merely in withholding a benefit, but positively or actively in working an injury, there exists a relation out of which arises a duty to go forward." (Moch Co. v. Rensselaer Water Co., 247 N.Y. at p. 167,159 N.E. at p. 898, supra). Application of this principle to the present case leads unmistakably to the conclusion that the police department, having assumed a duty to a special class of persons, and having gone forward with performance of that duty in the past, had an obligation to continue its performance. Had the police department not assumed a duty to supervise school crossings, plaintiff infant's mother would not have permitted her child to travel to and from school alone. The department's failure to perform this duty placed the infant plaintiff in greater danger than he would have been had the duty not been assumed, since the infant's mother would not have had reason to rely on the protection afforded her child and would have been required, in her absence, to arrange for someone to accompany her child to and from school.

[The court found that there was also proof that the city was negligent in failing to provide a guard.]

The order of the Appellate Division should be affirmed, with costs.

KIRCHER v. CITY OF JAMESTOWN, 74 N.Y.2d 251, 544 N.Y.S.2d 995, 543 N.E.2d 443 (1989). The plaintiff was entering her car in a drug store parking lot when a man, Blanco, accosted her. She screamed. Karen Allen and Richard Skinner heard the screams and saw Blanco force her into the car. Allen and Skinner gave chase, but lost sight of the car in heavy traffic. While trying to catch up to the car, they saw a police officer, Carlson. They explained what they had seen and gave him the car's description and license number. He promised to "call in," but in fact Carlson never even reported the incident. Meanwhile, Blanco repeatedly raped and beat the plaintiff, fracturing her larynx and inflicting other brutal injuries. In the Court of Appeals, *held*, the plaintiff cannot recover.

(1) A city is not held liable for negligent exercise of government functions unless it is in a special relationship with the claimant. "Nevertheless, where a municipality voluntarily undertakes to act on behalf of a particular citizen who detrimentally relies on an illusory promise of protection offered by the municipality, we have permitted liability because in such cases the municipality has by its conduct determined how its resources are to be allocated in respect to that circumstance and has thereby created a 'special relationship' with the individual seeking protection."

(2) Liability on this ground requires the municipality to be in "direct contact" with the claimant and requires justifiable reliance by the claimant upon the municipality's affirmative undertaking. Although Allen and Skinner were in direct contact with police, the plaintiff was not, so the direct contact requirement is not fulfilled.

(3) The reliance requirement is not fulfilled, either. "[T]he helpless and isolated plaintiff could not even communicate with the police, much less rely on any promise of protection the police might have offered. Yet, although plaintiff's failure to rely can be directly attributed to her dire circumstances, this does not, as the dissenters urge, provide a justification for ignoring the reliance requirement altogether."

Notes

1. *Action as undertaking.* The issue in many cases is whether the defendant's conduct counted as an undertaking at all. The insurer for a manufacturing plant regularly inspects it for safety. The insurer makes recommendations for increased safety and adjusts its premium charges based on what it finds. It should have discovered a danger that cost the lives to two employees. Could a jury find that by its inspections, the insurer undertook a duty to use care for the benefit of employees? See *Schoenwald v. Farmers Cooperative Ass'n of Marion,* 474 N.W.2d 519 (S.D.1991) (no); *Hodge v. United States Fidelity & Guaranty Co.,* 539 So.2d 229 (Ala.1989) (yes).

In *Florence* is it clear that the city's actions counted as undertakings because they seemed to promise continued protection for the children?

2. *Reliance and discriminatory enforcement.* If *Florence* requires reliance in order to justify recovery, is that desirable? What about a child whose parents never knew of the presence of a guard? Or a child both of whose parents knew there was no guard but neither of whom could take the child to school because they both worked? Is there anything wrong with permitting a recovery for the Florence boy but not for the child of non-relying parents?

3. *Why is reliance necessary?* The requirement of reliance works even more dramatically to deny a recovery in *Kircher.* In addition, that case

reflects New York's more recent additional "direct contact" requirement. Why require either on the facts of *Kircher*? Can you have no special relationship without reliance? Was the city making some careful calculation about its limited resources when the officer failed even to report as he promised?

4. *Why is undertaking relevant?* Turn to a different problem with "undertakings." The idea that "undertaking" may create a duty that did not otherwise exist is generally recognized but profoundly uncertain. First consider why an undertaking might be relevant to the question of the defendant's duty. Would it show: (a) a special relationship, established by the undertaking itself; (b) affirmative action, not mere nonfeasance; (c) the equivalent of a promise from which a tort duty might arise if there is consideration or reliance?

NOTE: CONTENT AND SCOPE OF DUTY DERIVED FROM "UNDERTAKINGS"

1. *Scope of duty imposed by undertaking.* In *Coyle v. Englander's*, 199 N.J.Super. 212, 488 A.2d 1083 (1985) the plaintiff band contracted to play at the defendant's place of business. The defendant contracted to provide helpers to assist with loading and unloading equipment. The defendant breached this provision so that the plaintiff had to load equipment himself. While doing so, he slipped on ice in the street and was injured. The court denied recovery. Its essential point seems to have been that the injury was not within the scope of the contract duty. What is undertaken in the following cases?

    a. A mother, seeing the crossing guards in the afternoon, assumes that the school has undertaken to provide crossing safety before and after school and thus allows her child to walk to school unaccompanied the next morning. There are no crossing guards and the child is struck in a crosswalk by a motorist. The school has never provided guards in the morning. Did it (a) undertake to provide crossing safety and do it negligently? or (b) undertake to provide afternoon guards only? In *Jefferson County School District R–1 v. Gilbert*, 725 P.2d 774 (Colo.1986) the court took the narrower view, that the school had assumed the duty to provide afternoon guards only.

    b. A pharmacist, filling a doctor's prescription for a patient had no duty under existing law to give any warnings to the patient. However, the pharmacist placed a warning in the form of a drowsy eye to indicate that the prescription might cause drowsiness. The pharmacist did not give an appropriate warning that the prescription should not be combined with alcohol. What did the pharmacist undertake by placing a warning label on the prescription? *Frye v. Medicare–Glaser Corp.*, 153 Ill.2d 26, 178 Ill.Dec. 763, 605 N.E.2d 557 (1992).

2. *Scope and breach.* The scope of the duty is important in determining whether it was breached. The defendant contracts with a hospital

to provide "rodent sanitation services." Thereafter, the plaintiff, who was a hospital patient, was injured when a rat ran across her feet, causing her to fall into a bathtub. Did the defendant breach its duty to provide rodent sanitation services? See *Hill v. James Walker Memorial Hospital*, 407 F.2d 1036 (4th Cir.1969).

3. *Content of duty.* Granted that the defendant's undertaking creates a duty and that it is limited to persons and harms within the risk, what is the content or measure of the duty? Is it a general duty of due care? Or is it a specific duty to do whatever the contract or undertaking calls for? If the latter, is it an absolute duty, a case of strict liability, or only a duty to make reasonable effort to perform? Should this be determined by what the promisor promised?

4. *Strict liability.* Ordinary contract duties are often strict. The seller who fails to deliver the wheat when promised is liable for its value when delivery was due, even if he made every effort to perform and was himself the victim of fate. On the other hand, his liability is often quite limited and does not exceed the value of the very thing promised. In *Moch* the plaintiff appeared to claim that breach of contract alone supported liability, since there was no showing (in the Court of Appeals at least) that there was any particular instance of negligence. Thus the *Moch* plaintiff sought to import into a case of physical harm the strict liability rules applied to contracts dealing with economic relationships. At the same time, the plaintiff in *Moch* sought damages of the kind not common in contract cases, that is, damages for consequences of non-performance rather than for the value of the water itself. Might the plaintiff's position in *Moch* have been more acceptable if it had tried to show a failure to use ordinary care to perform the contract?

5. *Privity.* Many contracts have no safety purposes. In others it is sometimes difficult to determine the purposes or to establish the scope of the defendant's obligation. Perhaps in such cases, the promisor should not be held liable except in the contract sense that he must pay the promisee the value of the promised performance. If, on the other hand, it is clear that the promisor undertook to provide protection against risks of physical harm to person or property, and if he is guilty of negligence in failing to perform the contract, why should he not be liable for harms within the risks he agreed to protect against and to persons within the class he agreed to protect? Is it possible that the word "privity" has been only a crude expression of all this? Does it matter to practical lawyers and judges?

Problem

Salmon v. Ungar

Salmon was taken by ambulance to the R.C. Henderson Memorial Hospital in a medical emergency. Ungar was the cardiologist on call. The emergency team quickly determined that a cardiologist was required and called Ungar, but he was out of town. It was an hour before Emelia Jones, a cardiologist from a nearby town, could be located. Salmon died shortly after Jones arrived. Salmon could have been saved by prompt attention of a specialist such as Ungar or any qualified substitute. Ungar and all other staff members of the hospital are subject to its on-call assignments as a condition of staff privileges. Ungar claims he arranged for Dr. Prager, another cardiologist, to take his calls, but Prager denies this and the hospital operators had no record showing that Prager should be called instead of Ungar. You represent Salmon's son. Do you advise bringing suit against Ungar?

GENERAL REFERENCE: DOBBS ON TORTS §§ 319–321 (2000).

Chapter 16

THE DUTY TO PROTECT FROM THIRD PERSONS

Courts routinely say that, with only limited exceptions, the defendant owes no duty to protect the plaintiff from a third person's conduct. E.g., *Williams v. Mayor & City Council of Baltimore*, 359 Md. 101, 753 A.2d 41 (2000). This chapter considers possible exceptions to the no duty rule.

§ 1. DEFENDANT'S RELATIONSHIP WITH THE PLAINTIFF

POSECAI v. WAL–MART STORES, INC.

Supreme Court of Louisiana, 1999.
752 So.2d 762.

MARCUS, JUSTICE. . . .

[On July 20, 1995, Mrs. Posecai shopped at Sam's, then returned to her car in Sam's parking lot. It was not dark, but a man hiding under her car grabbed her ankle and pointed a gun at her. He robbed her of jewels worth about $19,000 and released her. Mrs. Posecai sued Sam's, claiming it was negligent in failing to provide security guards in the parking lot. The courts below assessed almost $30,000 in damages against Sam's. Evidence showed that Sam's was adjacent to but was not in a high-crime area. From 1989 to 1995, there were three robberies on Sam's premises. But during the same period, there were 83 predatory offenses at 13 businesses in the same block at Sam's.]

A threshold issue in any negligence action is whether the defendant owed the plaintiff a duty. Whether a duty is owed is a question of law. In deciding whether to impose a duty in a particular case, the court must make a policy decision in light of the unique facts and circumstances presented. The court may consider various moral, social, and economic factors, including the fairness of imposing liability; the economic impact on the defendant and on similarly situated parties; the need for an incentive to prevent future harm; the nature of defendant's activity; the potential for an unmanageable flow of litigation; the historical development of precedent; and the direction in which society and its institutions are evolving. . . .

Other jurisdictions have resolved the foreseeability issue in a variety of ways, but four basic approaches have emerged. The first approach, although somewhat outdated, is known as the specific harm rule. According to this rule, a landowner does not owe a duty to protect patrons from the violent acts of third parties unless he is aware of specific, imminent harm about to befall them. Courts have generally agreed that this rule is too restrictive in limiting the duty of protection that business owners owe their invitees.

More recently, some courts have adopted a prior similar incidents test. Under this test, foreseeability is established by evidence of previous crimes on or near the premises. The idea is that a past history of criminal conduct will put the landowner on notice of a future risk. Therefore, courts consider the nature and extent of the previous crimes, as well as their recency, frequency, and similarity to the crime in question. This approach can lead to arbitrary results because it is applied with different standards regarding the number of previous crimes and the degree of similarity required to give rise to a duty.

The third and most common approach used in other jurisdictions is known as the totality of the circumstances test. This test takes additional factors into account, such as the nature, condition, and location of the land, as well as any other relevant factual circumstances bearing on foreseeability. As the Indiana Supreme Court explained, "[a] substantial factor in the determination of duty is the number, nature, and location of prior similar incidents, but the lack of prior similar incidents will not preclude a claim where the landowner knew or should have known that the criminal act was foreseeable." The application of this test often focuses on the level of crime in the surrounding area and courts that apply this test are more willing to see property crimes or minor offenses as precursors to more violent crimes. In general, the totality of the circumstances test tends to place a greater duty on business owners to foresee the risk of criminal attacks on their property and has been criticized "as being too broad a standard, effectively imposing an unqualified duty to protect customers in areas experiencing any significant level of criminal activity."

The final standard that has been used to determine foreseeability is a balancing test, an approach which has been adopted in California and Tennessee. This approach was originally formulated by the California Supreme Court in Ann M. v. Pacific Plaza Shopping Center in response to the perceived unfairness of the totality test. The balancing test seeks to address the interests of both business proprietors and their customers by balancing the foreseeability of harm against the burden of imposing a duty to protect against the criminal acts of third persons. The Tennessee Supreme Court formulated the test as follows: "In determining the duty that exists, the foreseeability of harm and the gravity of harm must be balanced against the commensurate burden imposed on the business to protect against that harm. In cases in which there is a high degree of foreseeability of harm and the probable harm is great, the burden imposed upon defendant may be substantial. Alternatively, in cases in which a lesser degree of foreseeability is present or the potential harm is slight, less onerous burdens may be imposed." Under this test, the high degree of foreseeability necessary to impose a duty to provide security, will rarely, if ever, be proven in the absence of prior similar incidents of crime on the property.

We agree that a balancing test is the best method for determining when business owners owe a duty to provide security for their patrons. The economic and social impact of requiring businesses to provide security on their premises is an important factor. Security is a significant monetary expense for any business and further increases the cost of doing business in high crime areas that are already economically depressed. Moreover, businesses are generally not responsible for the endemic crime that plagues our communities, a societal problem that even our law enforcement and other government agencies have been unable to solve. At the same time, business owners are in the best position to appreciate the crime risks that are posed on their premises and to take reasonable precautions to counteract those risks.

. . . The greater the foreseeability and gravity of the harm, the greater the duty of care that will be imposed on the business. A very high degree of foreseeability is required to give rise to a duty to post security guards, but a lower degree of foreseeability may support a duty to implement lesser security measures such as using surveillance cameras, installing improved lighting or fencing, or trimming shrubbery. . . .

In the instant case, there were only three predatory offenses on Sam's premises in the six and a half years prior to the robbery of Mrs. Posecai. The first of these offenses occurred well after store hours, at almost one o'clock in the morning. . . . Two years later, an employee of the store was attacked in the parking lot and her purse was taken, apparently by her husband. . . . It is also relevant that Sam's only operates during daylight hours and must provide an accessible parking lot to the multitude of customers that shop at its store each year. . . .

We conclude that Sam's did not possess the requisite degree of foreseeability for the imposition of a duty to provide security patrols in its parking lot. . . .

Notes

1. *Applying Posecai.* How does the balancing test in *Posecai* work in these cases: (a) The plaintiff is attacked in a mall parking lot and claims the mall owners should have provided better lighting. (b) The plaintiff is attacked in a mall which had security guards but scheduled the guards' rounds negligently so they were not covering the attack area appropriately. (c) The plaintiff leases space in an underground parking garage. She is sexually attacked at her car. The garage's surveillance cameras do not work;

some of the lights are out; the place is deteriorating; there is a smell of urine. No crimes of personal violence have been committed in the garage though plenty of other crimes have been committed nearby. *Sharon P. v. Arman,* 21 Cal.4th 1181, 1203, 91 Cal.Rptr.2d 35, 989 P.2d 121 (1999).

2. *Negligence and causation.* In all these cases, the plaintiff must prove not only a duty but also negligence and causation. Would better lighting avoid nighttime attacks? Always, never, or sometimes?

3. *Business creating or enhancing risks.* Suppose a business creates or enhances risks that third persons will attack customers. Suppose a business sells items or brands that are especially coveted by violent people, so that the business itself attracts violence. What if it merely maintains a large, unguarded parking garage? In *Stewart v. Federated Dep't Stores, Inc.,* 234 Conn. 597, 662 A.2d 753 (1995) the court imposed liability upon a retail store for the murder of a customer in the store's parking garage. The court thought that the unguarded garage, constantly filled with customers laden with packages, was an "invitation" to violence.

4. *Imminent harm known.* Early cases involved landowners who were present when their invitees were subjected to some imminent threat of harm from others. For instance, in *Greco v. Sumner Tavern, Inc.,* 333 Mass. 144, 128 N.E.2d 788 (1955) the defendant knew that a man had been drinking in the defendant's tavern all day and causing "trouble." About 10:00 that night he attacked and seriously injured another customer. The tavern owner was held liable for negligence in failing to deal with the situation.

5. *Risk neither created by business nor imminent.* The Restatement Second of Torts § 344 generalized cases like *Greco* broadly to provide for liability of a possessor of land open to the public if he failed to exercise care to discover that harm by others was likely. This led to decisions that imposed liability when attacks by third persons were foreseeable and the business failed to take reasonable steps to protect those on its premises. The usual basis for finding foreseeability in these cases is that there were previous crimes on the premises or nearby. E.g., *Erichsen v. No–Frills Supermarkets of Omaha, Inc.,* 246 Neb. 238, 518 N.W.2d 116 (1994); *Nallan v. Helmsley–Spear, Inc.,* 50 N.Y.2d 507, 429 N.Y.S.2d 606, 407 N.E.2d 451 (1980).

6. *Prior similar incidents approach.* Predictably, what looks like a simple matter of evidence about foreseeability became something of a rule of law for some judges, so that if no similar incidents had occurred on or near the premises, crime was deemed unforeseeable and the business would not be under any duty to take reasonable steps to protect its visitors. This view leads to litigation over what incidents are sufficiently similar. A more conservative view insists upon similar incidents as the sole basis for a finding of foreseeability, See *Sturbridge Partners, Ltd. v.Walker,* 267 Ga. 785, 482 S.E.2d 339 (1997) (knowledge of burglaries might mean that rape is foreseeable).

7. *Totality of circumstances approach.* Instead of requiring prior similar incidents to show foreseeability, courts more recently have treated foreseeability as a fact question to be determined like other facts from any relevant circumstances. Some courts have labeled this the totality of circumstances rule. Recent major examples of this view can be found in *Delta Tau Delta, Beta Alpha Chapter v. Johnson,* 712 N.E.2d 968 (Ind.1999) and

Clohesy v. Food Circus Supermarkets, Inc., 149 N.J. 496, 694 A.2d 1017 (1997) ("Generally, our tort law, including products liability, does not require the first victim to lose while subsequent victims are permitted to at least submit their cases to a jury.").

8. *"Balancing" approach.* The balancing approach postulates that the defendant may have no duty to deal with even foreseeable harm. The idea got its impetus from *Ann M. v. Pacific Plaza Shopping Center*, 6 Cal.4th 666, 25 Cal.Rptr.2d 137, 863 P.2d 207 (1993). In that case, the plaintiff, working in a store at a strip mall, was accosted by a man in her place of work, held at knife point, and raped. She sued the mall, claiming it should have had security guards. The court said: "Foreseeability, when analyzed to determine the existence or scope of a duty, is a question of law to be decided by the court.... [T]he social costs of imposing a duty on landowners to hire private police forces are also not insignificant. For these reasons, we conclude that a high degree of foreseeability is required in order to find that the scope of a landlord's duty of care includes the hiring of security guards." Given this test, the court held that the shopping mall was not liable in that case for failing to have security guards.

9. *Duty vs. negligence.* As later summarized by the Tennessee Court, the balancing test works this way: "In determining the duty that exists, the foreseeability of harm and the gravity of harm must be balanced against the commensurate burden imposed on the business to protect against that harm." *McClung v. Delta Square Ltd. Partnership,* 937 S.W.2d 891 (Tenn. 1996). This sounds like the risk-utility balance for determining negligence doesn't it? Does it matter that the California and Tennessee Courts have used it in determining duty rather than breach of duty? In *Staples v. CBL & Assocs.,* Inc., 15 S.W.3d 83 (Tenn.2000) Justice Holder concurring argued that unless the question was so clear that reasonable people could not differ, the balancing should be done by the jury as part of its decision on the negligence issue, not by judges. In *Delta Tau Delta, Beta Alpha Chapter v. Johnson,* 712 N.E.2d 968 (Ind. 1999) the court rejected the balancing test on the ground that it put the question or reasonable precautions in the hands of judges. "We believe that this is basically a breach of duty evaluation and is best left for the jury to decide."

10. Suppose a robber appears at Kentucky Fried Chicken while you are ordering. The robber demands money from the cash register, threatening to shoot you if an employee does not provide it immediately. The employee attempts a delaying ploy, whereupon the robber shoots your foot. The robber escapes and you sue Kentucky Fried Chicken. Was the defendant under a duty to you? See *Kentucky Fried Chicken of California, Inc. v. Superior Court*, 14 Cal.4th 814, 59 Cal.Rptr.2d 756, 927 P.2d 1260 (1997).

PARISH v. TRUMAN, 124 Ariz. 228, 603 P.2d 120 (App. 1979). Plaintiff was a social guest in defendant's home, located in a high crime area. When there was a knock on the door about 10:00 p.m., defendant opened the door without ascertaining the identity of the callers. Three men, unknown to either the plaintiff or the defendant, rushed in, apparently in search of drugs or money, and after a brief fight shot the plaintiff three times. The plaintiff sued his host, contending that it was negligent to have opened the door under the circumstances, since defendant was well aware of criminal activities in the area. The trial judge denied defendant's motion for summary judgment. *Held*, the court should grant the motion. "The question ... is whether [defendant's] duty to his social guest includes a duty to protect him from criminal attacks by third persons. The general rule is that in the absence of some special relationship, a private person has no duty to protect another from criminal attacks by third persons. A special relationship giving rise to such duty may ... exist ... between common carrier-passenger, innkeeper-guest, landowner-invitee, custodian-ward. Plaintiff Saunders' relationship with [defendant] is not one of these."

Notes

1. An unknown assailant abducted a ten-year-old girl from a sidewalk adjacent to the Landmark apartments where she lived. He took her diagonally across the street to the Chalmette Apartments and into a vacant apartment. There he raped her and shut her in a closet. The apartment unit was unoccupied and empty except for filthy debris. Its door was off its hinges. Would Chalmette's owner or property manager be liable for the injury to the child? See *Waters v. New York City Housing Authority*, 69 N.Y.2d 225, 513 N.Y.S.2d 356, 505 N.E.2d 922 (1987); *Nixon v. Mr. Property Management Co., Inc.*, 690 S.W.2d 546 (Tex.1985).

2. In *Fiala v. Rains*, 519 N.W.2d 386 (Iowa 1994) a man named Fiala met a woman named Rains in a bar. Rains invited Fiala (and some others) to go to her house. Rains did not warn Fiala that (a) her special male friend was extremely jealous and (b) that he was probably angry because she had stood him up that very evening, going to the bar instead. Rains' special friend, Moeller, was indeed lurking outside. Shortly after Fiala arrived at Rains' house, Moeller entered and kicked Fiala in the head until he was unconscious. In Fiala's suit against Rains, he did not claim that she owed him a duty to control Moeller or protect him but that she did owe him a duty to warn. The Supreme Court of Iowa affirmed a directed verdict for Rains. The court treated the case as one of nonfeasance, so that no duty to protect (or warn) was owed, even though there was evidence that Moeller was known to be especially violent. Rains was not liable as a landowner because Fiala was not an invitee, only a social guest.

3. If a defendant negligently creates an affirmative risk of harm by third persons, liability normally follows. Are *Parish* and *Fiala* contrary to this? Landowners are normally under a duty to use reasonable care (no more) to protect invitees. Why were they not in *Parish* and *Fiala*?

————

HOSEIN v. CHECKER TAXI CO., INC., 95 Ill.App.3d 150, 50 Ill.Dec. 460, 419 N.E.2d 568 (1981). Decedent Hosein leased a cab from Checker, and while operating it was shot by two passengers. Checker had not equipped the cab with a bullet-proof shield as required by statute. The statute, however, was held unconstitutionally vague and the court also held that though some invalid statutes could be used to set a standard of care in a civil case, one that was vague could not. There was no common law duty of care owed, since an affirmative duty would be owed only to persons in a special relationship of the kind listed in the Second Restatement, § 314A. These are: carrier-passenger, innkeeper-guest, business invitor-invitee, and custodian-ward. Therefore, *held*, the motion to dismiss the complaint should be granted.

Note

The Restatement's § 314B recognizes a special duty to employees, but only if the employee "comes into a position of imminent danger" and this is known to the master. If Hosein had been an employee of Checker, would this section have imposed a duty?

MARQUAY v. ENO

Supreme Court of New Hampshire, 1995.
139 N.H. 708, 662 A.2d 272.

HORTON, JUSTICE. . . .

The plaintiffs are three women who were students in the Mascoma Valley Regional School District. In separate complaints filed in the district court, each plaintiff alleges that she was exploited, harassed, assaulted, and sexually abused by one or more employees of the school district. According to the complaints, Lisa Burns was sexually abused by Brian Erskine, a high school teacher, beginning in her sophomore year and continuing beyond graduation. . . . [Other plaintiffs made similar allegations about Michael Eno, a sports coach, and Brian Adams, a teacher.] Each plaintiff also alleges that a host of school employees, including other teachers, coaches, superintendents, principals and secretaries either were aware or should have been aware of the sexual abuse. . . .

[The plaintiffs sued the district and its allegedly abusing employees. The federal district court where the suits were brought certified a number of questions to the Supreme Court of New Hampshire. The opinion that follows is written in answer to those questions.]

I.   RELATIONSHIP OF STATUTORY VIOLATION TO CIVIL LIABILITY

The first certified question asks whether RSA 169–C:29, which, under penalty as a misdemeanor, requires that any person "having reason to suspect that a child has been abused or neglected shall report the same [to the State]," creates a private right of action in favor of abused children against those who have violated the statute's reporting requirement. . . .

At first glance, our cases appear to be inconsistent on this issue. Everett v. Littleton Construction Co., 94 N.H. 43, 46 A.2d 317 (1946), instructs that "the violation of a penal statute is an actionable wrong only when the Legislature expressly so provides ... , or when the purpose and language of the statute compel such inference...." We have also held, however, that ... "[t]he breach of a statutory duty results in liability ... when the plaintiff is in a class the statute is designed to protect and the injury is of the type that the statute is intended to prevent," Island Shores Estates Condo. Assoc. v. City of Concord, 136 N.H. 300, 307, 615 A.2d 629, 633 (1992)....

The apparent inconsistency in our jurisprudence arises from a failure to distinguish two distinct bases of civil liability: (1) statutorily expressed or implied causes of action; and (2) negligence per se. The former, recognized in Everett, is the principle that whether or not the common law recognizes a cause of action, the plaintiff may maintain an action under an applicable statute where the legislature intended violation of that statute to give rise to civil liability. The doctrine of negligence per se, on the other hand, provides that where a cause of action does exist at common law, the standard of conduct to which a defendant will be held may be defined as that required by statute, rather than as the usual reasonable person standard. The doctrine of negligence per se, however, plays no role in the creation of common law causes of action. Thus, in many cases, the common law may fail to recognize liability for failure to perform affirmative duties that are imposed by statute....

We hold that the reporting statute does not support a private right of action for its violation because we find no express or implied legislative intent to create such civil liability. First, we note that where the legislature has intended that civil liability flow from the violation of a statute, it has often so provided. Where, as here, civil liability for a statutory violation would represent an abrupt and sweeping departure from a general common law rule of nonliability, we would expect that if the legislature, which is presumed to recognize the common law, intended to impose civil liability it would expressly so provide. Here there was no expressed intent. Nor can we divine any implied intent.

We now turn to the negligence per se question.... [U]se of a statute to establish the standard of care is limited to situations where a common law cause of action exists, and then, only if the statute is "applicable." Whether a statutory standard is applicable depends, in part, on whether the type of duty to which the statute speaks is similar to the type of duty on which the cause of action is based. Because the duty to which the statute speaks—reporting of abuse—is considerably different from the duty on which the cause of action is based—supervision of students—we hold that a violation of the reporting statute does not constitute negligence per se in an action based on inadequate supervision of a student.

II. COMMON LAW CAUSES OF ACTION

The plaintiffs argue that all school district employees have a common law duty to protect students whom they know or should know are being sexually abused by another school employee. We hold that some employees owe such a duty while others do not. The duty owed by some defendants is based on their relationship to the students; for other defendants the duty derives from their relationship to the alleged abusers.

As a general rule, a person has no affirmative duty to aid or protect another. Such a duty may arise, however, if a special relationship exists. The plaintiffs argue that a special relationship exists between educators and school children, imposing a duty upon educators to protect students whom they know or should know are being sexually abused by another school employee.

"One who is required by law to take or who voluntarily takes the custody of another under circumstances such as to deprive the other of his normal opportunities for protection is under a . . . duty to the other." Restatement (Second) of Torts § 314A at 118 (1965). "[A] child while in school is deprived of the protection of his parents or guardian. Therefore, the actor who takes custody . . . of a child is properly required to give him the protection which the custody or the manner in which it is taken has deprived him." Id. § 320 comment b at 131. We agree with the majority of courts from other jurisdictions that schools share a special relationship with students entrusted to their care, which imposes upon them certain duties of reasonable supervision. The scope of the duty imposed is limited by what risks are reasonably foreseeable. . . .

Major factors influencing our conclusion that a special relationship exists between schools and students include the compulsory character of school attendance, the expectation of parents and students for and their reliance on a safe school environment, and the importance to society of the learning activity which is to take place in public schools, For these reasons, we conclude that "the social importance of protecting the plaintiff[s'] interest outweighs the importance of immunizing the defendant from extended liability."

School attendance impairs both the ability of students to protect themselves and the ability of their parents to protect them. It is this impairment of protection from which the special relationship between school and student arises and from which the duty of supervision flows. We decline, however, to accept the plaintiffs' argument that every school employee shoulders a personal duty simply by virtue of receiving a paycheck from the school district. Instead, the duty falls upon those school employees who have supervisory responsibility over students and who thus have stepped into the role of parental proxy. Those employees who share such a relationship with a student and who acquire actual knowledge of abuse or who learn of facts which would lead a reasonable person to conclude a student is being abused are subject to liability if their level of supervision is unreasonable and is a proximate cause of a student's injury.

While the impairment of protection creates an affirmative duty, it also circumscribes the limits of that duty. Thus the existence of a duty is limited to those periods when parental protection is compromised. That is not to say that employees with a special relationship to a student may not be liable for injuries that occurred off school premises or after school hours, if the student can show that the employee's negligent acts or omissions, within the scope of his or her duty, proximately caused injury to the student. This is a question for the jury.

We note that the principal or superintendent rarely has primary supervisory authority over a student. Because, however, it is the school to which parents turn over custody of their children and from which they expect safety and because the superintendent and principal are charged with overseeing all aspects of the school's operation, we hold that a duty of supervision is owed to each student. Where the principal or superintendent knows or should know that a particular school employee poses a threat to a student, entrustment of the student to the care of that employee will not satisfy the duty of reasonable supervision.

[The court went on to hold that employees with supervisory powers of hiring and firing might be liable for negligent hiring or retention of a person they knew or should have known was an abuser. And "[w]hile we held in section I that the reporting statute is not applicable in an action based on negligent supervision, we hold that it is applicable in a negligent hiring or retention action. Accordingly, under these circumstances, failure to report abuse in accordance with the statute could give rise to liability, provided the plaintiff can show that reporting would have prevented the subsequent abuse."]

Remanded.

————

MIRAND v. CITY OF NEW YORK, 84 N.Y.2d 44, 614 N.Y.S.2d 372, 637 N.E.2d 263 (1994) Virna, a student, "accidentally bumped into Donna Webster, another student with whom Virna had not had any previous encounters. Although Virna apologized, Webster, believing the contact to be intentional, cursed Virna and attempted to kick her. Virna blocked the kick and caught Webster's leg. According to Virna, Webster threatened to kill her. At that point a bystander intervened and prevented anything further from occurring." Virna twice tried to report the encounter to the security office, but it was closed and she could find no security officers. She did report the altercation and apparently the death threat to a teacher in the hall, however. She then met her sister, Vivia, who had just finished her last class. As the two started down the stairs, Webster and some companions approached and struck Virna on the head with a hammer. Virna's sister Vivia had joined her and Vivia tried to seize the hammer, but she was hit in the back by one of the group. One of the males stabbed Vivia through the wrist with a knife. The court held in favor of Virna. "Schools are under a duty to adequately supervise the students in their charge and they will be held liable for foreseeable injuries proximately related to the absence of adequate supervision." The care owed is that which " 'a parent of ordinary prudence would observe in comparable circumstances.' The duty owed derives from the simple fact that a school, in assuming physical custody and control over its students, effectively takes the place of parents and guardians." The school knew of the threat (through the report to the teacher in the hall) and also knew security was needed at dismissal time, yet no security was present and no steps had been taken to deal with the death threat.

FAZZOLARI v. PORTLAND SCHOOL DIST. NO. 1J, 303 Or. 1, 734 P.2d 1326 (1987). The plaintiff was a 15–year-old high school student, dropped off at school at 6:50 a.m. by a mother on her way to work. An unknown person dragged her into bushes, beat her, and raped her. The trial judge directed a verdict for the defendant. The intermediate court reversed and remanded. *Held*, per Linde, J., the directed verdict was error; remanded.

The Restatement's § 344 has little relation to this case; the school's duty is not based on its ownership of property but on its relation to the student. Its duty applies, for example, on field trips off its property. The duty arising from its relationship to the student results from the "relationship between educators and children entrusted to their care apart from any general responsibility not unreasonably to expose people to a foreseeable risk of harm. The compulsory school attendance law virtually mandates that children be so entrusted to a school and, for most families, leaves little choice to which school. The vast majority of students are minors, and school personnel assume a great deal of authority over their conduct during the school day. The scope of this obligation does not exclude precautions against risks of crime or torts merely because a third person inflicts the injury. Another person's crime was once thought to lie beyond a defendant's responsibility on grounds of "proximate cause," but more recent decisions have dealt with the behavior of others, lawful or otherwise, as part of the general analysis of foreseeable risks.

"[D]efendant argues that although schools have such a responsibility toward students, it is limited to the school day. Plaintiff was dropped in front of the school building on her mother's drive to work at 6:50 a.m., more than an hour before classes. This was not exceptional or improper. There was testimony that custodians routinely opened the building before that time and that some teachers and other students were present in the building for preparatory or extracurricular reasons. It cannot be said that the school 'had no duty as a matter of law' to be concerned about the safety of students arriving at that time, when this is translated to mean that no reasonable factfinder could conclude that a sensible school administration would take some precautions, if not to provide supervision, then at least to warn students and their parents about its absence before a designated hour.

There was evidence of other violence on the school ground, so a trier can find that violence was foreseeable to the school. "[F]oresight does not demand the precise mechanical imagination of a Rube Goldberg nor a paranoid view of the universe. [T]he concept of foreseeability refers to generalized risks of the type of incidents and injuries that occurred rather than predictability of the actual sequence of events.''

Notes

1. In *Marquay,* the plaintiffs claimed at-school sexual abuse by employees of the school. The actual abusers are no doubt liable. In fact, if the coach is a public-school employee, his molestation of a student might even count as a violation of § 1983, on the ground that molestation is an infringement of a liberty interest protected by the due process clause, and, so far as it is a sexual harassment, it is also a denial of equal protection. *Doe v. Taylor Independent School Dist.,* 975 F.2d 137 (5th Cir.1992).

2. Employers (including school districts) are normally liable for the torts of their employees, provided the torts are committed within the scope of their employment. When the employee is acting for purely personal reasons, the employer's liability may be doubtful. We consider this topic in Chapter 20.

3. When the school officials know or should know of abuse or harassment by teachers or coaches, the officials seem to be in violation of their duty of care if they do nothing about the abuse. *Marquay* seems to support that rule. In addition, the United States Supreme Court has held that a student has a claim under one of the federal civil rights acts if school officials do nothing about sexual harassment by a sports coach. *Franklin v. Gwinnett County Public Schools,* 503 U.S. 60, 112 S.Ct. 1028, 117 L.Ed.2d 208 (1992). See also *Gebser v. Lago Vista Indep. School Dist.*, 524 U.S. 274, 118 S.Ct. 1989, 141 L.Ed.2d 277 (1998)(setting forth requirements for civil rights claim based on teacher's sexual harassment of student).

4. *Reporting and other kinds of statutes.* Every state has some kind of child abuse statute. There are at least three distinct statutory directives that can arise in tort cases. (1) The statute directs a child protective agency to investigate suspected child abuse and to act for the protection of the child. This was the kind of problem seen in *DeShaney,* supra Chapter 14. (2) The statute directs a public agency to investigate child-care facilities and to refuse or cancel a license if these facilities present dangers to children. (3) The statute directs anyone who reasonably suspects child abuse to report it to the protective agency.

5. *Marquay* involved a reporting statute. Suppose a public school teacher notices that Johnny is bruised one day, has burns on his body another, a broken arm the third. Absent violence at school, the teacher should undoubtedly suspect child abuse at home. If she does suspect such abuse but makes no report as required by the statute, would she have any liability in New Hampshire?

6. Most courts would apparently hold that the reporting requirement does not affect tort law. E.g., *Perry v. S.N.,* 973 S.W.2d 301 (Tex.1998). *Landeros v. Flood,* 17 Cal.3d 399, 131 Cal.Rptr. 69, 551 P.2d 389 (1976), however, appears to support a claim based upon violation of the statute. As a common law matter, any duty to report child abuse would ordinarily be based upon a special relationship, with the child or with the abuser. See *J.A.W. v. Roberts,* 627 N.E.2d 802 (Ind.App.1994).

7. If a medical doctor violates the medical standard of care in failing to report suspected child abuse, would he be liable for abuse that occurs thereafter? If so, is this independent of the statutory reporting requirement? The court appeared to answer both questions yes in *First Commercial Trust Company v. Rank*, 323 Ark. 390, 915 S.W.2d 262 (1996).

Duties of Colleges

8. *College temptations and stress*. Courts have generally refused to impose upon universities any duty to protect or guide new students with respect to the pleasures and dangers of sex, alcohol, drugs, or even overstudy. See *Beach v. University of Utah*, 726 P.2d 413 (Utah 1986); *Hegel v. Langsam*, 29 Ohio Misc. 147, 273 N.E.2d 351, 55 O.O.2d 476 (1971); *Wilson v. Continental Insurance Companies*, 87 Wis.2d 310, 274 N.W.2d 679 (1979).

9. *Risks of attacks*. Consider whether the college owes a duty of care to its students in these cases.

    a. One evening an underage sorority member attended a number of parties hosted by other Greek houses at her college. The college provided employees to supervise at some of the fraternity parties. The young woman became so intoxicated that she fell from a fire escape. *Coghlan v. Beta Theta Fraternity,* 133 Idaho 388, 987 P.2d 300 (1999). Or suppose a college has rules against drinking parties in dorms, but does not enforce them. A college woman is sexually assaulted by several college football players after she and some of the players attend a drinking party in their dorm. *Tanja H. v. Regents of the University of California*, 228 Cal.App.3d 434, 278 Cal.Rptr. 918 (1991).

    b. A prisoner applied for admission to a state university and was admitted upon his release. The university knew he was a prisoner when he applied but not much else. The new student, with a ten-year history of heroin addiction and a string of arrests, made friends with three other students and shared an apartment with them. He then seriously injured one of his roommates, raped another, and murdered the third. *Eiseman v. State*, 70 N.Y.2d 175, 518 N.Y.S.2d 608, 511 N.E.2d 1128 (1987).

    c. A college assigns a student to practicum work at a dangerous location. The college knows the danger but it neither warns the student, arranges a different practicum, nor provides protection. The student–an adult–is abducted from the practicum site, robbed, and sexually assaulted. *Nova Southeastern University, Inc. v. Gross*, 758 So.2d 86 (Fla.2000). What if the student knows of the danger before she is attacked?

Duties of Landlords

10. In a leading case, *Kline v. 1500 Massachusetts Avenue Apartment Corp.*, 141 U.S. App. D.C. 370, 439 F.2d 477, 43 A.L.R.3d 311 (1970), the plaintiff leased one of 585 apartments in the defendant's building. At that time, there were several forms of protection against intrusion, including a doorman. Seven years later, there was no doorman and other forms of protection had also been withdrawn, although assaults, larcenies and robber-

ies against tenants in the common hallways had increased. Plaintiff was attacked and injured by an intruder in the hallway. The court held that the landlord was under a duty to protect tenants against attacks by third persons. Among other things, the court emphasized (a) the control of the landlord over common passageways and the tenant's lack of power to control them or to protect themselves there; (b) the special character of the modern urban multiple-unit lease; (c) the notice of the landlord that the tenants were being subjected to crimes against their persons. The court added: "[T]he applicable standard of care in providing protection for the tenant is that standard which this landlord himself was employing ... when the appellant became a resident. . . ." The court said that the precise protections need not be kept, but that the same relative degree of security had to be maintained.

11.   In *Doe v. Dominion Bank of Washington*, 963 F.2d 1552 (D.C.Cir. 1992) the court extended the *Kline* principle to commercial leases so that office workers, for example, would enjoy the same protection as the residential tenants in *Kline*. But several other decisions reject any general duty on the part of the commercial landlord to protect tenants or their employees from third persons. E.g., *Doe v. Grosvenor Properties (Hawaii) Ltd.*, 73 Haw. 158, 829 P.2d 512 (1992).

12.   If the lessor itself brings in dangerous third persons, as tenants or as visitors to tenants, the case seems a relatively easy one for imposition of a duty. What if the lessor leases an office in a commercial building to a mental health clinic which does a major business in seeing violent criminals on parole and one of these "clients" of the mental health clinic attacks another tenant? *Samson v. Saginaw Professional Building, Inc.*, 393 Mich. 393, 224 N.W.2d 843 (1975).

13.   Suppose the plaintiff is not the tenant but a guest of the tenant. Does the landlord owe the plaintiff a duty of care while he is rightfully in the parking lot provided by the landlord or in other portions of the premises in the possession and control of the landlord? *Martinez v. Woodmar IV Condominiums Homeowners Association, Inc.*, 189 Ariz. 206, 941 P.2d 218 (1997) (duty of care owed to tenant's guest to protect from attacks in common areas).

14.   *Apportionment*. Suppose a landlord negligently creates or enhances a risk that someone will criminally attack the plaintiff. Someone does attack the plaintiff but he cannot be found or has no funds. Recall that in states that have abolished joint and several liability, the rule is that each tortfeasor is liable only for his own proportionate fault share. What do you think the landlord's share would be as compared to the rapist? Should several liability states return to the joint and several liability rule for this kind of case? This point is considered in more detail in Chapter 23, but you may wish to have the problem in mind as you review the preceding cases and examine those that follow.

§ 2.   DEFENDANT'S   RELATIONSHIP   WITH   DANGEROUS PERSONS

ROSALES v. STEWART, 113 Cal.App.3d 130, 169 Cal.Rptr. 660 (1980). Action for the death of a 10–year-old child, Noemi, who, while standing in her own yard, was struck by a bullet fired by Boyer. Boyer was firing from the yard of a dwelling he rented from Stewart, the defendant here. Plaintiffs alleged that Stewart, as lessor, knew that Boyer occasionally discharged a firearm in the backyard and failed to exercise care to prevent this. The trial court sustained a demurrer to the complaint without leave to amend. *Held*, reversed and remanded with direction to permit amendment. If the lessor has control over a danger from the tenant, he is under a duty of care, though he is not liable if there is no control. "In effect ... the landlord is under a duty to third persons to do all that he legally can to get rid of a dangerous condition *on the leased premises*, even if it means getting rid of the tenant." The plaintiff failed to allege here that the lessor could have terminated the tenancy or otherwise controlled the tenant, but the plaintiffs should be permitted so to allege if they can do so.

Notes

1. *Leasing to a dangerous person.* How broad is the new idea introduced in *Rosales*? A closely similar case involves leasing to a person who is known to be dangerous. Suppose a prospective tenant tells a prospective landlord that he has a vicious dog. Should the landlord refuse to lease the premises to him? *Strunk v. Zoltanski*, 62 N.Y.2d 572, 479 N.Y.S.2d 175, 468 N.E.2d 13 (1984) holds that the landlord is under a duty to take reasonable precautions to protect others from injury by the dog. What reasonable precautions? What if the same landlord leases premises to a tenant who carries on drug trafficking activities there and the landlord knows it? *Muniz by Gonzales v. Flohern, Inc.*, 77 N.Y.2d 869, 568 N.Y.S.2d 725, 570 N.E.2d 1074 (1991).

2. *Negligent hiring and supervision.* By extension of the same idea, could an employer be liable for negligently hiring a dangerous person? Or for negligently failing to supervise an employee who might cause harm? Doctors who work in hospitals are often not employees of the hospital at all; they simply enjoy "staff privileges." The hospital, however, could terminate staff privileges if it chose. Should the hospital be under a duty to monitor doctors and to exclude those not deemed to be safe? In *Darling v. Charleston Community Memorial Hospital*, 33 Ill.2d 326, 211 N.E.2d 253 (1965), the plaintiff, an 18 year old, broke his leg in a football game. Dr. Alexander treated him in the emergency room and applied a cast, which was heat-dried. Shortly thereafter the plaintiff was in pain and his foot became dark and swollen, and eventually cold. A few days later, Dr. Alexander cut the cast and in so doing cut the plaintiff's leg on both sides. There was blood and other seepage and a "stench in the room," the worst a witness had smelled since World War II. The leg eventually had to be amputated. The plaintiff, in an action against the hospital, alleged, among other things, that the hospital was negligent in failing to have a sufficient number of trained nurses capable of recognizing the progress of gangrene, and a failure to require that the work done by Dr. Alexander be examined by others or to review his treatment and seek consultation. The plaintiff's recovery was upheld with the comment that the evidence would support these claims.

3. *Negligent hiring or supervision of dangerous clergy.* A little authority supports liability of a church organization for negligent hiring, supervision, or retention dangerous or sexually predatory clergy. But other courts insist that any such claims automatically raise issues of church doctrine that courts are forbidden to consider. Cases are cited in Dobbs on Torts § 258 (2000).

———

DUDLEY v. OFFENDER AID AND RESTORATION OF RICHMOND, INC., 241 Va. 270, 401 S.E.2d 878 (1991). Spencer was a convicted felon with a long, active career in crime. In prison he engaged in vicious beatings of new inmates and set fires; psychologists warned that he was a potential security problem. Because of his violence and for other reasons, he was not eligible to serve any part of his term in a halfway house. Nevertheless, he was permitted to live in one, operated by a private organization. He repeatedly violated rules there, including rules about prompt return from outside work. Security was "practically nonexistent" and Spencer was permitted to leave without much control. He was unaccounted for at 7:00 p.m. During that night he broke into an apartment nearby, bound Davis, beat and raped her, then strangled her to death. In an action against the operator of the halfway house, the trial court sustained the defendant's demurrer. *Held*, reversed and remanded. Under the general rule one owes no duty to control the conduct of a third person for the benefit of the plaintiff. However, if the defendant is in a special relationship to either the plaintiff or the third person, the defendant is under a duty of care. The halfway house, upon receiving Spencer, became a custodian in charge. The defendant's duty ran not only to victims that might be identified in advance but to all those who are "directly and foreseeably exposed to risk of bodily harm" from the defendant's negligence. The decedent was within the area of danger.

Notes

1. *"Custody."* Is strict "custody" required to invoke the duty of care imposed in *Dudley*? Suppose: (a) A parole officer does not warn the parolee's employer that the parolee is a high-risk sexual offender. *Schmidt v. HTG, Inc.,* 265 Kan. 372, 961 P.2d 677 (1998). (b) DSS, a child protection agency of the state, takes custody of JH, then places him in a foster home without revealing to the foster parents that JH might molest children. JH made inappropriate sexual touchings of a neighbor child while JH was in foster care. Would DSS be subject to liability? *E.P. v. Riley,* 604 N.W.2d 7 (S.D.1999). (c) What if an employer knows that her employees lob fire-crackers out the window that may harm passers-by?

2. *A duty to control spouses or family members?* Consider: A wife knows her husband has a history of sexual misconduct with young children and might invite neighborhood girls to go swimming in the family pool while she is away. Has she any duty to warn anyone? What if she told neighbors it would be safe for the girls to swim? On similar facts, see *Pamela L. v.*

Farmer, 112 Cal.App.3d 206, 169 Cal.Rptr. 282 (1980); *J.S. v. R.T.H.*, 155 N.J. 330, 714 A.2d 924 (1998) (duty of care exists). In *Eric J. v. Betty M.*, 76 Cal.App.4th 715, 90 Cal.Rptr.2d 549 (1999) the court held that parents and brothers of a repeat offender, paroled on child molesting charges, had no duty to warn the molester's new woman friend that her son might be in danger even though the boy was taken to the home of some of them and molested here.

3. *A duty to control children?* Parents are not liable for a child's torts merely on the basis of the parental relationship alone, nor even merely because the child is known to be rough. Parents are liable only for failing to control some specific dangerous habit of a child of which the parent knows or should know in the exercise of reasonable care.

Normal children. Are parents responsible if they leave a teen-aged son alone at home while they are out of town and he has irresponsible sex with a teen-aged girl? *McNamee v. A.J.W.*, 238 Ga.App. 534, 519 S.E.2d 298 (1999).

Children known to be violent. In *Dinsmore-Poff v. Alvord*, 972 P.2d 978 (Alaska 1999), plaintiffs' decedent was murdered by defendants' 17 year-old son. The son had a long history of emotional disturbance and violence. In fact, he had been arrested once for shooting a boy. The parents did not impose curfews or search his belongings. The son used a gun to kill his victim. The court absolved the parents. It said: "plaintiff must show more than a parent's general notice of a child's dangerous propensity. A plaintiff must show that the parent had reason to know with some specificity of a present opportunity and need to restrain the child to prevent some imminently foreseeable harm."

Williamson v. Daniels, 748 So.2d 754 (Miss.1999) absolved the mother of a 15–year-old boy who shot the plaintiff in the chest. Since the mother was not aware of this specific kind of misconduct in the past, she was not responsible. It thought liability would "would pose the risk of transforming parents from care givers and disciplinarians into the jailors and insurers of their minor children," and that "this is a role most parents are ill equipped to take on."

In one astonishing case the "child"—a teenager with a history of aggressive, anti-social behavior—began beating a woman with a hammer. He demanded she remove her clothes. A daughter ran for the phone; he began beating her with a hammer, then began to saw off an ear of his original victim. His parents were well aware of a long history of serious behavior. Psychiatrists had recommended that the boy be treated. The parents were not liable. Apparently the theory was that they could not have foreseen the particular type of violence. *Parsons v. Smithey*, 109 Ariz. 49, 504 P.2d 1272, 54 A.L.R.3d 964 (1973); see also *Popple v. Rose*, 254 Neb. 1, 573 N.W.2d 765 (1998) (parents knew teenaged son was violent but did not know it would take the form of a sexual assault upon children he was babysitting; parents under no duty to warn).

What if the parent or the parent's domestic partner knows that a ten-year-old child has a propensity for sexually abusing younger females and knows also that a four-year-old girl is playing in the home? *Gritzner v. Michael R.*, 235 Wis.2d 781, 611 N.W.2d 906 (Wis. 2000).

TARASOFF v. REGENTS OF UNIVERSITY OF CALIFORNIA

Supreme Court of California, 1976.
17 Cal.3d 425, 131 Cal.Rptr. 14, 551 P.2d 334.

TOBRINER, JUSTICE.

On October 27,1969, Prosenjit Poddar killed Tatiana Tarasoff. Plaintiffs, Tatiana's parents, allege that two months earlier Poddar confided his intention to kill Tatiana to Dr. Lawrence Moore, a psychologist employed by the Cowell Memorial Hospital at the University of California at Berkeley. They allege that on Moore's request, the campus police briefly detained Poddar, but released him when he appeared rational. They further claim that Dr. Harvey Powelson, Moore's superior, then directed that no further action be taken to detain Poddar. No one warned plaintiffs of Tatiana's peril.

Concluding that these facts set forth causes of action against neither therapists and police involved, nor against the Regents of the University of California as their employer, the superior court sustained defendant's demurrers to plaintiffs' second amended complaints without leave to amend. This appeal ensued.

Plaintiffs' complaints predicate liability on two grounds: defendants' failure to warn plaintiffs of the impending danger and their failure to bring about Poddar's confinement. . . . Defendants, in turn, assert that they owed no duty of reasonable care to Tatiana and that they are immune from suit. . . .

In analyzing this issue, we bear in mind that legal duties are not discoverable facts of nature, but merely conclusory expressions that, in cases of a particular type, liability should be imposed for damage done. As stated in Dillon v. Legg (1968) 68 Cal. 2d 728, 734, 69 Cal. Rptr. 72, 76, 441 P.2d 912, 916: "The assertion that liability must . . . be denied because defendant bears no 'duty' to plaintiff 'begs the essential question whether the plaintiff's interests are entitled to legal protection against the defendant's conduct. . . . [Duty] is not sacrosanct in itself, but only an expression of the sum total of those considerations of policy which lead the law to say that the particular plaintiff is entitled to protection.' (Prosser, Law of Torts [3d ed. 1964] at pp. 332–333.)"

In the landmark case of Rowland v. Christian (1968) 69 Cal. 2d 108, 70 Cal. Rptr. 97, 443 P.2d 561, Justice Peters recognized that liability should be imposed "for an injury occasioned to another by his want of ordinary care or skill" as expressed in Section 1714 of the Civil Code. Thus, Justice Peters, quoting from Heaven v. Pender (1883) 11 Q.B.D. 503, 509 stated: " 'whenever one person is by circumstances placed in such a position with regard to another . . . that if he did not use ordinary care and skill in his own conduct . . . he would cause danger of injury to the person or property of the other, a duty arises to use ordinary care and skill to avoid such danger.' "

We depart from "this fundamental principle" only upon the "balancing of a number of considerations"; major ones "are the foreseeability of harm to the plaintiff, the degree of certainty that the plaintiff suffered injury, the closeness of the connection between the defendant's conduct and the injury suffered, the moral blame attached to the defendant's conduct, the policy of preventing future harm, the extent of the burden to the defendant and consequences to the community of imposing a duty to exercise care with resulting liability for breach, and the availability, cost and prevalence of insurance for the risk involved."

The most important of these considerations in establishing duty is foreseeability. As a general principle, a "defendant owes a duty of care to all persons who are foreseeably endangered by his conduct, with respect to all risks which make the conduct unreasonably dangerous." As we shall explain, however, when the avoidance of foreseeable harm requires a defendant to control the conduct of another person, or to warn of such conduct, the common law has traditionally imposed liability only if the defendant bears some special relationship to the dangerous person or to the potential victim. Since the relationship between a therapist and his patient satisfies this requirement, we need not here decide whether foreseeability alone is sufficient to create a duty to exercise reasonable care to protect a potential victim of another's conduct....

Although plaintiffs' pleadings assert no special relation between Tatiana and defendant therapists, they establish as between Poddar and defendant therapists the special relation that arises between a patient and his doctor or psychotherapist. Such a relationship may support affirmative duties for the benefit of third persons. Thus, for example, a hospital must exercise reasonable care to control the behavior of a patient which may endanger other persons. A doctor must also warn a patient if the patient's condition of medication renders certain conduct, such as driving a car, dangerous to others....

Defendants contend, however, that imposition of a duty to exercise reasonable care to protect third persons is unworkable because therapists cannot accurately predict whether or not a patient will resort to violence. In support of the argument amicus representing the American Psychiatric Association and other professional societies cites numerous articles which indicate that therapists, in the present state of the art, are unable reliably to predict violent acts; their forecasts, amicus claims, tend consistently to overpredict violence, and indeed are more often wrong than right. Since predictions of violence are often erroneous, amicus concludes, the courts should not render rulings that predicate the liability of therapists upon the validity of such predictions....

We recognize the difficulty that a therapist encounters in attempting to forecast whether a patient presents a serious danger of violence. Obviously we do not require that the therapist in making that determination, render a perfect performance; the therapist need only exercise "that reasonable degree of skill, knowledge, and care ordinarily possessed and exercised by members of [that professional specialty] under similar circumstances." Within the broad range of reasonable practice and treatment in which professional opinion and judgment may differ, the therapist is free to exercise his or her own best judgment without liability; proof, aided by hindsight, that he or she judged wrongly is insufficient to establish negligence....

Amicus contends, however, that even when a therapist does in fact predict that a patient poses a serious danger of violence to others, the therapist should be absolved of any responsibility for failing to act to protect the potential victim. In our view, however, once a therapist does in fact determine, or under applicable professional standards reasonably should have determined, that a patient poses a serious danger of violence to others, he bears a duty to exercise reasonable care to protect the foreseeable victim of that danger. While the discharge of this duty of due care will necessarily vary with the facts of each case, in each instance the adequacy of the therapist's conduct must be measured against the traditional negligence standard of the rendition of reasonable care under the circumstances. As explained in Fleming and Maximov, The Patient or His Victim: The Therapist's Dilemma (1974), 62 Cal. L. Rev. 1025, 1067: " ... the ultimate question of resolving the tension between the conflicting interest of patient and potential victim is one of social policy, not professional expertise.... In sum, the therapist owes a legal duty not only to his patient, but also to his patient's would-be victim and is subject in both respects to scrutiny by judge and jury." ...

The risk that unnecessary warnings may be given is a reasonable price to pay for the lives of possible victims that may be saved. We would hesitate to hold that the therapist who is aware that his patient expects to attempt to assassinate the President of the United States would not be obligated to warn the authorities because the therapist cannot predict with accuracy that his patient will commit the crime.

Defendants further argue that free and open communication is essential to psychotherapy; that "Unless a patient ... is assured that ... information [revealed by him] can and will be held in utmost confidence, he will be reluctant to make the full disclosure upon which diagnosis and treatment ... depends." The giving of a warning, defendants contend, constitutes a breach of trust which entails the revelation of confidential communications.

We recognize the public interest in supporting effective treatment of mental illness and in protecting the rights of patients to privacy, and the consequent public importance of safeguarding the confidential character of psychotherapeutic communication. Against this interest, however, we must weigh the public interest in safety from violent assault. The Legislature has undertaken the difficult task of balancing the countervailing concerns. In Evidence Code section 1014, it established a broad rule of privilege to protect confidential communications between patient and psychotherapist. In Evidence Code section 1024, the Legislature created a specific and limited exception to the psychotherapist-patient privilege: "There is no privilege ... if the psychotherapist has reasonable cause to believe that the patient is in such mental or emotional condition as to be dangerous to himself or to the person or property of another and that disclosure of the communication is necessary to prevent the threatened danger."[13]

We realize that the open and confidential character of psychotherapeutic dialogue encourages patients to express threats of violence, few of which are ever executed. Certainly a therapist should not be encouraged routinely to reveal such threats; such disclosures could seriously disrupt the patient's relationship with his therapist and with the persons threatened. To the contrary, the therapist's obligations to his patient require that he not disclose a confidence unless such disclosure is necessary to avert danger to others, and even then that he do so discreetly, and in a fashion that would preserve the privacy of his patient to the fullest extent compatible with the prevention of the threatened danger. (See Fleming & Maximov, *The Patient or His Victim: The Therapist's Dilemma* (1974), 62 CAL. L. REV. 1025, 1065–1066.)

The revelation of a communication under the above circumstances is not a breach of trust or a violation of professional ethics; as stated in the Principles of Medical Ethics of the American Medical Association (1957), section 9: "A physician may not reveal the confidence entrusted to him in the course of medical attendance . . . *unless he is required to do so by law or unless it becomes necessary in order to protect the welfare of the individual or of the community.*" (Emphasis added.) We conclude that the public policy favoring protection of the confidential character of patient-psychotherapist communications must yield to the extent to which disclosure is essential to avert danger to others. The protective privilege ends where the public peril begins.

Our current crowded and computerized society compels the interdependence of its members. In this risk-infested society we can hardly tolerate the future exposure to danger that would result from a concealed knowledge of the therapist that his patient was lethal. If the exercise of reasonable care to protect the threatened victim requires the therapist to warn the endangered party or those who can reasonably be expected to notify him, we see no sufficient societal interest that would protect and justify concealment. The containment of such risks lies in the public interest. For the foregoing reasons, we find that plaintiffs' complaints can be amended to state a cause of action against defendants

---

13. Fleming and Maximov note that "White [section 1024] supports the therapist's less controversial *right* to make a disclosure, it admittedly does not impose on him a *duty* to do so. But the argument does not have to be pressed that far. For if it is once conceded . . . that a duty in favor of the patient's foreseeable victims would accord with general principles of tort liability, we need no longer look to the statute for a source of duty. It is sufficient if the statute can be relied upon . . . for the purposes of countering the claim that the needs of confidentiality are paramount and must therefore defeat any such hypothetical duty. In this more modest perspective, the Evidence Code's 'dangerous patient' exception may be invoked with some confidence as a clear expression of legislative policy concerning the balance between the confidentiality values of the patient and the safety values of his foreseeable victim." (Emphasis in original.) Fleming & Maximov, *The Patient or His Victim: The Therapist's Dilemma* (1974), 62 CAL. L. REV. 1025, 1063.

Moore, Powelson, Gold, and Yandell and against the Regents as their employer, for breach of a duty to exercise reasonable care to protect Tatiana. . . .

Turning now to the police defendants, we conclude that they do not have any such special relationship to either Tatiana or to Poddar sufficient to impose upon such defendants a duty to warn respecting Poddar's violent intentions. Plaintiffs suggest no theory, and plead no facts that give rise to any duty to warn on the part of the police defendants absent such a special relationship. . . .

[The court held that the decision not to warn was not a basic policy decision and that there was therefore no immunity.]

[Dissenting opinions are omitted.]

Notes

1. *Scope.* Consider whether, given a *Tarasoff* duty, therapists will be liable in every case in which a patient causes harm after making a threat. On what facts would a therapist be counted as reasonably prudent even if he fails to warn after a threat is made?

2. *Tarasoff and Thompson.* After the California Court decided *Tarasoff*, it decided *Thompson v. County of Alameda*, 27 Cal.3d 741, 167 Cal.Rptr. 70, 614 P.2d 728 (1980), supra Chapter 13. In that case, the court refused to impose liability upon a county which had released a dangerous criminal who was threatening to kill some unnamed child. When released on furlough, he did in fact kill a 5–year-old child. Can *Thompson* and *Tarasoff* be squared? The *Thompson* court suggested a possibility: "In those instances in which the released offender poses a predictable threat of harm to a named or readily identifiable victim . . . a releasing agent may well be liable for failure to warn such persons." This suggests, doesn't it, that if Poddar had shown a clear and strong probability that he would kill a number of small children, or old women, the psychiatrist would enjoy an immunity? Is there something dubious, not to say fundamentally wrong, with a legal system that produces these two cases, or do you feel the distinction is a sound one? The Wisconsin Court thought there was "no legitimate policy" for the *Thompson* limitation on the duty of care. *Schuster v. Altenberg*, 144 Wis.2d 223, 424 N.W.2d 159 (1988).

3. *Elaborating or extending the* Tarasoff *duty.* A number of courts have accepted the Tarasoff duty and some have extended it. In *Hedlund v. Superior Court of Orange County*, 34 Cal.3d 695, 194 Cal.Rptr. 805, 669 P.2d 41, 41 A.L.R.4th 1063 (1983) the court extended the duty not only the direct victim of a threatened beating but her son who was emotionally upset at seeing his mother attacked.

In *Eisel v. Board of Education of Montgomery County*, 324 Md. 376, 597 A.2d 447 (1991) some junior high students told school counselors that 13–year-old Nicole was planning to commit suicide. The counselors talked to Nicole, who denied it, but shortly thereafter she in fact died in a murder-suicide pact, seemingly part of her involvement in Satanism. The court held that counselors were under a duty to use reasonable means to attempt to prevent the suicide of a student once they were on notice of suicidal intent and that the risk did not disappear merely because Nicole had denied it. But California refused to recognize a therapist's duty to protect a suicidal patient in *Bellah v. Greenson*, 81 Cal.App.3d 614, 146 Cal.Rptr. 535 (1978).

4. *Authority accepting or rejecting Tarasoff*. Statutes in a number of states have adopted some version of the *Tarasoff* duty. See See Steven Smith, *Mental Health Malpractice in the 1990s*, 28 Hous. L. Rev. 209 (1991). In addition, almost all courts that have considered the question have accepted some kind of *Tarasoff* duty. E.g., *Emerich v. Philadelphia Center for Human Development, Inc.*, 554 Pa. 209, 720 A.2d 1032 (1998). At least two courts have rejected *Tarasoff*. *Thapar v. Zezulka*, 994 S.W.2d 635 (Tex.1999); *Nasser v. Parker,* 249 Va. 172, 455 S.E.2d 502 (1995).

———

DiMARCO v. LYNCH HOMES–CHESTER COUNTY, INC., 525 Pa. 558, 583 A.2d 422 (1990). Janet Viscichini, a blood technician, was taking a blood sample from a resident at Lynch Homes. The patient struck Viscichini, causing the needle to puncture Viscichini's skin. The patient was a hepatitis carrier. Viscichini consulted two doctors, who told her that if she remained symptom free for six weeks, she would not have been infected. She did remain symptom free and after eight weeks she resumed sexual relations with Joseph DiMarco, to whom she was not married. But later she in fact was found to be suffering from hepatitis which had been communicated to DiMarco as well. DiMarco sued, claiming that Viscichini should have been warned to avoid sexual relations for six months. The trial court dismissed DiMarco's claim. The intermediate court reversed. *Held*, affirming the intermediate court, the physicians owed a duty of care to DiMarco. "When a physician treats a patient who has been exposed to or who has contracted a communicable and/or contagious disease, it is imperative that the physician give his or her patient the proper advice about preventing the spread of the disease. . . . Such precautions are taken *not* to protect the health of the patient, whose well-being has already been compromised, rather such precautions are taken to safeguard the health of others. The duty of a physician in such circumstances extends to those 'within the foreseeable orbit of risk of harm.' " The class of persons likely to be injured "includes *any*one who is physically intimate with the patient."

WITTHOEFT v. KISKADDON, 557 Pa. 340, 733 A.2d 623 (1999). The complaint alleged that Dr. Kiskaddon, an opthalmologist, tested Mrs. Myers and found her visual acuity to be 20/80. That fell below the standard set by the state for legally operating a motor vehicle. The statute required Dr. Kiskaddon to report his findings to the state, but he did not do so, nor did he warn his patient of the danger of driving. Because of her inability to see properly, the patient struck and killed a bicyclist. The estate here sues Dr. Kiskaddon, relying on *DiMarco. Held*, Dr. Kiskaddon was under no duty to warn his patient. *DiMarco* does not apply because it involved a contagious disease. Mrs. Myers was in the "best position" to know of her visual deficiency. Injury to others from Mrs. Myers' optical deficiency is unforeseeable. To impose liability would be to impose absolute or strict liability. And the statute requiring a report to the state does not create a tort cause of action.

Notes

1.   Might a person have gradually failing eyesight without realizing that it had become dangerous? If so, would it make sense to distinguish *DiMarco* because it involved contagious disease? Or to say that liability, if imposed, would be strict rather than based upon negligence?

2.   Suppose the doctor prescribes a medication that makes it dangerous to drive but does not warn the patient. If the patient causes harm to others that would have been avoided by a warning to the patient, is there any reason to protect the doctor against liability? Notice that the burden of a warning is small in any event. Warning for the benefit of anyone who may be injured is not an added burden if the doctor should warn the patient for the patient's own benefit anyway. Even so, some cases hold that the doctor cannot be liable to an injured third person. In *Lester v. Hall,* 126 N.M. 404, 970 P.2d 590 (N.M. 1998) the court said that a warning to the patient would be burdensome, that the physician cannot control the patient, and that a duty to third persons would intrude upon the doctor-patient relationship. How is any of that possible if the issue is merely a duty to warn the doctor's own patient? Distinguish claims that the doctor negligently failed to diagnose a disease.

3.   Suppose T has AIDS or is at risk for AIDS because he received a blood transfusion from a contaminated batch and D knows it. D also knows that T is about to marry P or has regular sexual relations with P. Should D advise P? In this case the public health interest in containing the AIDS epidemic as well as P's interest in her own life suggest that the warning must be given. The privacy interest of the AIDS victim points in the other direction. It is also possible that people will refuse to have AIDS tests if information would be passed on to others. Legislatures have enacted strong medicine: doctors, health care providers, blood suppliers may be prohibited from revealing that a person has AIDS or even that he is at risk. See *Santa Rosa Health Care Corp. v. Garcia,* 964 S.W.2d 940 (Tex.1998). A California statute permits the doctor to disclose a positive test for AIDS to anyone reasonably believed to be a spouse, sexual partner or needle sharer, but the doctor is not permitted to disclose any information that will identify the patient. In any event the doctor is not required to make disclosure. CAL. HEALTH AND SAFETY CODE § 199.25.

––––––

WEST AMERICAN INSURANCE CO. v. TURNER, 1990 WL 2322 (Ohio App.1990). Disputed evidence indicated that 18–year-old Turner had been drinking for hours in a bar, ending with a Jack Daniels and that Christerson, knowing this, nevertheless permitted Turner to drive the Christerson car. Turner almost immediately ran the car into a house, causing damages for which the plaintiff sues. The plaintiff's claim against Christerson was based on the negligent entrustment theory. The trial court entered judgment for the plaintiff. *Held*, affirmed. "Liability for negligent entrustment results when an owner, having knowledge of a person's incompetency, inexperience, or recklessness, entrusts his automobile to another with permission to use it. At the time of the entrustment, the owner must have actual or constructive knowledge of the entrustee's incompetency to operate an automobile by reason of some mental or physical disability evidenced by youthful age, mental impairment, physical handicap or intoxication." The evidence was sufficient to show that Turner drove the vehicle with Christerson's permission; Turner was an incompetent driver; and when he allowed Turner to drive, Christerson had actual or constructive knowledge that Turner was an incompetent or unqualified driver.

VINCE v. WILSON, 151 Vt., 425, 561 A.2d 103 (1989). The plaintiff suffered serious injury in an auto accident. He claimed against the great aunt of the allegedly negligent driver. The great aunt had provided funding for purchase of the car when she knew that the driver was incompetent to drive, having failed the driver's test several times, and also knew he abused alcohol and other drugs. The seller of the car knew the same and it was also made a defendant. *Held*, proof of these allegations is sufficient to get the case to the jury. The tort of negligent entrustment arises when one negligently entrusts an automobile or other dangerous item to another who is incompetent to use it safely. Some courts have limited negligent entrustment liability to cases in which the defendant is the owner of the entrusted chattel and has a right to control. But other courts have extended the duty to sellers who know or should know that the buyer is a danger to others. Cases restricting liability to owners, according to "the leading commentators on the law of torts," "look definitely wrong" because it is the negligence in entrusting that creates the unreasonable risk, and this is none the less when goods are sold instead of loaned. The evidence was sufficient here to make out a prima facie case against the great aunt and the seller.

BRIGANCE v. VELVET DOVE RESTAURANT, INC.

Supreme Court of Oklahoma, 1986.
725 P.2d 300.

HODGES, JUDGE.

[The defendant, the Velvet Dove Restaurant, served intoxicating beverages to a group of minors, including one Jeff Johnson. The restaurant company knew Jeff Johnson drove the group to the restaurant. The plaintiffs alleged that alcohol served by the defendant caused Johnson to become intoxicated or increased his earlier intoxication and that this in turn caused a one-car accident in which the plaintiff Shawn was injured. The trial court dismissed the claim.]

At common law a tavern owner who furnishes alcoholic beverages to another is not civilly liable for a third person's injuries that are caused by the acts of an intoxicated patron. Such rule is principally based upon concepts of causation that, as a matter of law, it is not the sale of liquor by the tavern owner, but the voluntary consumption by the intoxicated person, which is the proximate cause of resulting injuries, so that the tavern owner is therefore not liable for negligence in selling the liquor.

In recent years, many states have retreated from the common law rule of nonliability for a liquor vendor regarding it as antiquated and illogical. Several states with dram shop laws have also recognized a new common law right of action against a vendor of liquor. Many of the jurisdictions which now recognize a civil right of action do so on the theory enunciated in Rappaport v. Nichols, 31 N.J. 188, 156 A.2d 1 (1959):

> "When alcoholic beverages are sold by a tavern keeper to a minor or to an intoxicated person, the unreasonable risk of harm ... to members of the traveling public may readily be recognized and foreseen; this is particularly evident in current times when traveling by car to and from the tavern is so commonplace and accidents resulting from drinking are so frequent."

As shown by the modern trend, the old common law rule of nonliability has been changed by judicial opinion: "Inherent in the common law is a dynamic principle which allows it to grow and to tailor itself to meet changing needs...."

... The development of the law of torts is peculiarly a function of the judiciary. Because duty and liability are matters of public policy they are subject to the changing attitudes and needs of society....

Appellees assert that we are not free to change the common law because the Legislature has expressly spoken in this area by its 1959 repeal of Oklahoma's dram shop act and its failure to reenact such provision since that time. We are not persuaded by this argument. The dram shop act was not selectively repealed for it was repealed when intoxicants were legalized in 1959. Because the Legislature has failed to act to impose civil liability, for reasons unknown, does not unequivocally demonstrate legislative intent. To hold otherwise, would be indulging in a type of psychoanalysis of the Legislature. We simply cannot conclude that statutory silence is here indicative of legislative intent to bar the cause of action before us.

We also cannot accede to the view urged by appellees that this area of law is better dealt with by the Legislature. We find that on the basis of the clear trend in this area we are free to establish a civil cause of action by an injured third person against a commercial vendor of liquor for on the premises consumption. In rendering the opinion of Vanderpool v. State, 672 P.2d 1153, 1157 (Okla.1983), which modified the common law doctrine of governmental immunity, this Court stated in response to the oft-expressed view that if the doctrine is to be abrogated such should be done by the Legislature and not the courts of this State: "But having come to the conclusions that the judicially recognized doctrine of governmental immunity in its present state under the case law is no longer supportable in reason, justice or in light of the overwhelming trend against its recognition, our duty is clear. Where the reason for the rule no longer exists, that alone should toll its death knell."

We believe the application of the old common law rule of a tavern owner's nonliability in today's automotive society is unrealistic, inconsistent with modern tort theories and is a complete anachronism within today's society.

The automobile is a constant reminder of a changed and changing America. It has made a tremendous impact on every segment of society, including the field of jurisprudence. In the "horse and buggy" days the common law may not have been significantly affected by the sale of liquor to an intoxicated person. The common law of nonliability was satisfactory. With today's car of steel and speed it becomes a lethal weapon in the hands of a drunken imbiber. The frequency of accidents involving drunk drivers are commonplace. Its affliction of bodily injury to an unsuspecting public is also of common knowledge. Under such circumstances we are compelled to widen the scope of the common law.

We, thus, hold that one who sells intoxicating beverages for on the premises consumption has a duty to exercise reasonable care not to sell liquor to a noticeably intoxicated person. It is not unreasonable to expect a commercial vendor who sells alcoholic beverages for on the premises consumption to a person he knows or should know from the circumstances is already intoxicated, to foresee the unreasonable risk of harm to others who may be injured by such person's impaired ability to operate an automobile.

. . . A commercial vendor for on the premises consumption is under a common law duty to exercise ordinary care under the circumstances. We reach our conclusion in accordance with other courts finding a common law duty, relying on the general rule expressed in Restatement (Second) of Torts § 308 (1965):

> "It is negligence to permit a third person to use a thing or to engage in an activity which is under the control of the actor, if the actor knows or should know that such person intends or is likely to use the thing or to conduct himself in the activity in such a manner as to create an unreasonable risk of harm to others."

And, Restatement (Second) of Torts § 390 (1965):

> "One who supplies . . . a chattel for the use of another whom the supplier knows or has reason to know to be likely because of his youth, inexperience or otherwise to use it in a manner involving unreasonable risk of physical harm to himself and others . . . is subject to liability for physical harm resulting to them."

Even if a commercial vendor for on the premises consumption is found to have breached its duty, a plaintiff must still show the illegal sale of alcohol led to the impairment of the ability of the driver which was the proximate cause of the injury and there was a causal connection between the sale and a foreseeable ensuing injury. . . .

... Ordinarily the question of causation in a negligent tort case is one of fact for the jury and becomes one of law only when there is no evidence from which the jury could reasonably find a causal nexus between the negligent act and the resulting injuries. . . .

In adopting a new rule of liability which creates a civil cause of action, we specifically hold that the law hereby established will be applied prospectively to all causes of action occurring from and after the date the mandate issues herein [except that the rule of liability also applies to the parties in this case. Reversed and remanded.]

Notes

1. *Proximate cause analysis or duty analysis in the traditional rule.* Courts traditionally denied the kind of liability imposed in *Brigance* on the ground that the alcohol provider was not a proximate cause of harm done by the drinker. Some courts or legislatures still say so. See *Wegleitner v. Sattler,* 582 N.W.2d 688 (S.D.1998) (legislative no-liability rule). Would the plaintiff have a better case if the defendant, instead of providing alcohol to a drinker, had left it where it could be stolen by teenagers? See *Dettmann v. Kruckenberg,* 613 N.W.2d 238 (Iowa 2000).

2. Proximate cause is usually decided case by case, often by the jury but in any event on the facts peculiar to the case. In the alcohol provider cases, however, judges made a rule of law for all cases: the provider's fault was *never* a proximate cause. Would it make more sense to say that this was a no-duty rule?

3. Are there any policy bases for exculpating the seller of alcohol? What if the server cannot be sure whether a customer is intoxicated?

4. The common law has expressed in many ways a strong belief that each individual should be responsible for his or her own actions. Not only does this imply, for some judges, that one is not responsible for the acts of others, but it implies that responsibility should not be shared. Thus courts had some difficulty in imposing joint and several liability upon multiple wrongdoers. If the last actor was an intentional wrongdoer, the feeling at one time apparently was that he and only he should be liable. To impose joint liability would lighten his burden and thus diminish his accountability. What arguments can you mount against this kind of outlook? Relatedly, you'll want to remember why the plaintiff is suing the alcohol provider.

5. *Regulatory statutes.* The traditional view is that violation of a statute regulating sales of alcohol–for example, a statute prohibiting sales to minors or intoxicated persons–was not actionable. Some courts still so hold. *Robinson v. Matt Mary Moran, Inc.,* 259 Va. 412, 525 S.E.2d 559 (2000). Others, however, have sometimes relied in part upon the statutes in imposing *Brigance*-type liability.

6. *Dram shop statutes or "civil damage acts."* Although violation of the alcohol regulation statutes was not traditionally actionable, some states had a very different set of statutes on the books. They are called Dram Shop statutes or Civil Damage Acts. These did not merely impose criminal penalties; instead, they expressly imposed civil liability upon the dispenser of

alcohol. Some of these impose liability only for certain kinds of sales, such as sales to a minor or intoxicated person. Others seem to create a kind of strict liability upon the provider of alcohol.

One example is the Illinois statute, 235 ILCS 5/6–21. It provides in part: "Every person who is injured within this State in person or property by any intoxicated person, has a right of action in his own name, severally or jointly, against any person [licensed to sell alcoholic liquor] who by selling or giving alcoholic liquor ... , causes the intoxication of such person.... Any person owning, renting, leasing or permitting the occupation of any building or premises with knowledge that alcoholic liquors are to be sold therein ... shall be liable severally or jointly...."

The Illinois statute limits liability to $30,000 for injury, and where death is caused, to $40,000 for each person who lost support.

7. *Related issues.* Courts imposing liability in *Brigance*-type situations have been quickly confronted with important additional issues.

A. *Duty of care to the drinker?* Does the alcohol provider owe a duty of care to the drinker himself, or only to third persons who may be injured? Some courts have said the duty runs to the drinker as well as to others. Most appear to hold that the adult drinker is responsible for his own injury and the provider owes him nothing.

B. *Effect of the drinker's fault on his own claim.* If a duty of care is owed to the drinker himself, will the drinker's recovery be barred or reduced by his contributory fault? Is this a *Bexiga* situation?

C. *Liability of social hosts.* Not surprisingly, some courts willing to impose liability upon sellers of alcohol are not willing to impose liability upon social hosts who provide alcohol with the same results. See, e.g., *Reynolds v. Hicks*, 134 Wash.2d 491, 951 P.2d 761 (1998). Nevertheless, a few courts have imposed liability upon social hosts. New Hampshire has done so, but only when the social host is reckless is serving alcohol. *Hickingbotham v. Burke,* 140 N.H. 28, 662 A.2d 297 (1995).

D. *Proximate cause.* Granted that there is a *Brigance* type duty, the defendant might still avoid liability in some cases because the injury is outside the scope of the duty–or, if you prefer, is not a proximate result of the breach. Suppose the provider supplies alcohol to an obviously intoxicated person, who drives safely to a friend's house where he falls asleep smoking a cigarette. The cigarette causes a fire and the friend's house burns down. What if the provider supplies alcohol to a minor, who shares it with another minor with disastrous results?

8. *Alternative solutions.* (a) Should we simply require all drivers to carry adequate liability insurance and then hold the driver, not the provider liable? (b) Professor Paul LeBel, after noting the deadly role of alcohol consumption in a high percentage of traffic accidents, described the inadequacies of tort law rules to provide compensation to victims of drinking drivers. He proposed an increased tax on alcoholic beverages to be paid by the industry. The revenues from the increase would be used to fund a victims' compensation system, which would pay for otherwise uncompensated injuries to drinkers' victims. PAUL LEBEL, JOHN BARLEYCORN MUST PAY:

COMPENSATING THE VICTIMS OF DRINKING DRIVERS 211–222 (1992). What effects would you expect if such a tax-based fund were created?

9. *Drug statutes.* Some states have passed statutes imposing broad civil liabilities upon those who "participate" in the drug market. The Oklahoma statute, for instance, provides that: (1) Donors of drugs, at a party, say, could be liable under the statute; (2) Liability covers harms from any use of a "same type" of drug in the "drug market target community" where the defendant lives; liability is not limited to harms resulting from use of the specific drug provided by the defendant. Likewise, liability can be imposed if the defendant participated in the illegal drug market at any time the individual user used the same type of drug; (3) Liability runs to a variety of persons and entities, including a parent, legal guardian, child, spouse, or sibling of the individual drug user, the individual who is exposed in utero; the employer of a user; and a medical facility, insurer, governmental entity, employer, or other entity that funds a drug treatment program or employee assistance program for the individual drug user or that otherwise expended money on behalf of the individual drug user. The individual user himself can sue under some conditions. OKLA STAT. ANN. tit. 63 § 2–422, et seq.

SNYDER v. AMERICAN ASSOCIATION OF BLOOD BANKS

Supreme Court of New Jersey, 1996.
144 N.J. 269, 676 A.2d 1036.

POLLOCK, J. . . . .

On August 23, 1984, Snyder underwent open-heart surgery at St. Joseph's Hospital in Paterson. During the surgery he received transfusions of several units of blood platelets, including unit 29F0784, which BCBC had supplied to St. Joseph's. At the time, no direct test existed to determine whether blood was infected with Human Immunodeficiency Virus (HIV), the cause of AIDS . . . . . [Snyder developed AIDS, and the evidence indicates that the infection was transmitted by blood supplied by BCBC and that could have been screened out by the surrogate testing techniques discussed below. Suit was brought against the various defendants, including the local blood bank that supplied the blood and also against the American Association of Blood Banks (AABB), the trade or professional association of blood banks. Except for AABB, all other defendants have settled or secured dismissals.]

At the conclusion of an eight-week trial, the jury found that the AABB had been negligent in not recommending surrogate testing. Surrogate testing refers to identifying people at risk for a disease by testing for some symptom or characteristic manifested by a majority of people who have contracted or are at risk of contracting the disease. In the early 1980s, one available surrogate test for HIV infected blood was that for the antibody to the hepatitis B core antigen (the HBc antibody). The jury further found that the AABB's negligence was a substantial factor in causing Snyder to contract HIV. [The Appellate Division affirmed.]

Crucial to the assessment of the AABB's alleged duty of care is its role in the blood-banking industry in 1983–84. [The Food and Drug Administration of the Public Health Service in the United States Department of Health and Human Services, inspects and licenses blood banks. AABB is a professional association of blood banks, providing information and setting standards. AABB annually inspects and accredits member institutions, the local blood banks, applying its own standards, which often become the FDA standards. A blood bank that is licensed by the FDA but loses its AABB accreditation will have significant practical problems because hospitals prefer to work with AABB accredited institutions. The FDA also probably relied, some said too heavily, on advice of the AABB. Finally, states would accept the AABB standards in their licensing determination for blood banks.]

. . . Our initial inquiry is whether the BCBC should have known in 1984 that blood and blood products could carry the HIV virus. [The court here extensively reviewed the increasing evidence that HIV was transmitted both sexually and by blood. The evidence before 1984 had become overwhelming that there was at least a serious risk that HIV could be transmitted by blood.]

Alarmed at the prospect of AIDS in the blood supply, the CDC called an emergency workshop in Atlanta for January 4, 1983. The purpose of the meeting was to ascertain how to prevent the transmission of AIDS through blood and blood products. Representatives of government, the AABB, the American Red Cross, the Council for Community Blood Banks, the National Hemophilia Foundation, the National Gay Task Force, and other organizations attended the meeting. The AIDS Task Force was convinced that AIDS was blood-transmissible, and that its epidemiology mirrored that of hepatitis B, "involving the same high-risk groups and in the same proportions."

The Task Force also presented disturbing information about the risk of the transmission of AIDS in the blood supply. By that time, the CDC had reported six cases of transfusion-associated AIDS. . . .

The Task Force recommended three methods to screen out high-risk donors: (1) direct questioning of prospective donors to determine if they belonged to high-risk groups; (2) detailed recording of medical histories of prospective donors to determine any indications of early AIDS symptoms; and (3) institution of surrogate testing of collected blood. Together, these three methods would have prevented blood from high-risk donors from entering the blood supply. . . .

At the January 4, 1983, meeting, the AABB and other blood-banking representatives strenuously disagreed with the CDC. Dr. Joseph Bove, chairman of the AABB Committee on Transfusion Transmitted Disease, stated that he was unconvinced that blood could transmit AIDS. He argued that surrogate testing was unnecessary and that direct questioning was improper.

Dr. Francis rejoined that the AABB's response was "remarkably obstructive." He recognized the response as "basically an attempt to deny that there was a threat." The AABB nonetheless persisted in arguing that surrogate testing and direct questioning would be too costly and would lead to the rejection of too much blood. Dr. Francis described the meeting: "[T]he reluctance and the inertia that we at CDC faced with the blood banks in that meeting was so … ridiculous and so alarming that it got to the point of me literally pounding on the table and shouting to these individuals as to how many deaths it's going to take before you will act. And I was saying, do you need ten, do you need twenty, do you need forty, when we get to that level, then are you going to act? This was a very heated meeting because of this incredible counter balance of those of us investigating the epidemic and seeing the urgency of the situation … to put the responsibility for action onto the blood banks, because presumably, they were the only ones that could act, that there—the imbalance of this urgency from us and the obstruction, the negative response from them was a most disturbing time, one of the most disturbing times in my twenty years in public health."

[AABB continued its hard-line resistance, with the help of the American Red Cross. Both refused to require surrogate testing or any questioning of donors, although in an internal memos, Dr. Bove of the AABB said his current best guess was an infectious agent in blood and called attention to a study by Dr. James W. Curran and other researchers documenting a number of transfusion related AIDS cases.]

The plasma industry, which relies on paid donors, took a much more cautious view. Whenever a plasma donor later developed AIDS, the industry would withdraw all coagulation products made from that donor's blood. . . .

On April 24, 1984, Secretary Margaret Heckler of the DHHS announced that researchers had isolated the AIDS virus and had developed a blood test for AIDS. She believed that the test, now known as the ELISA test, would be available within six months. In fact, the DHHS approved the ELISA test on March 4, 1985, seven months after Snyder received his transfusion.

Against that background, we consider whether the AABB owed Snyder a duty of care. Our analysis begins by recognizing that the AABB did not directly obtain, process, or transfuse the infected platelets that caused Snyder to contract AIDS. Thus, the AABB had no immediate connection with either the donor or with Snyder.

The determination of the existence of a duty ultimately is a question of fairness and policy. An important, although not dispositive consideration, is the foreseeability of injury to others from the defendant's conduct. Also important are the nature of the risk posed by the defendant's conduct, the relationship of the parties, and the impact on the public of the imposition of a duty of care. The absence of a contractual or special relationship is not dispositive.

Blood banks, hospitals, and patients rely on the AABB for the safety of the nation's blood supply. A patient contemplating surgery cannot assure the safety of blood drawn from others. Of necessity, patients rely on others, including the AABB, for that assurance.

Society has not thrust on the AABB its responsibility for the safety of blood and blood products. The AABB has sought and cultivated that responsibility. For years, it has dominated the establishment of standards for the blood-banking industry. To illustrate, the AABB's January 1983 joint statement with the Red Cross and Council of Community Blood Centers endorsed the AABB-recommended screening measures as "prudent and appropriate." In a March 31, 1983, AABB press release, Dr. Bove stated: "We would also like to assure the public that the chance of anyone acquiring AIDS through a blood transfusion is remote. . . . Every precaution is being taken to assure that each unit of blood transfused is the safest possible." By words and conduct, the AABB invited blood banks, hospitals, and patients to rely on the AABB's recommended procedures. The AABB set the standards for voluntary blood banks. At all relevant times, it exerted considerable influence over the practices and procedures over its member banks, including BCBC. On behalf of itself and its member banks, the AABB lobbies legislatures, participates in administrative proceedings, and works with governmental health agencies in setting blood-banking policy. In many respects, the AABB wrote the rules and set the standards for voluntary blood banks.

We next examine the severity and foreseeability of the risk that blood transfusions could spread the AIDS virus. The severity of the risk of transfusion-related AIDS is a function of the mortality rate and the infection rate. In 1984, the overall mortality rate of AIDS was forty percent, but for those who had AIDS for more than three years, the rate approached nearly 100%. The infection rate was increasing exponentially. . . .

The risk also was foreseeable. Epidemiologists at the CDC believed as early as 1982 that the AIDS virus could be transmitted by blood and blood products. In January 1984, Dr. Curran's article in the New England Journal of Medicine confirmed that belief. Thus, before Snyder received his transfusion, the AABB should have foreseen that a blood transfusion could transmit AIDS.

We are unpersuaded by the AABB's argument that because the evidence was inconclusive, it owed no duty to Snyder. The foreseeability, not the conclusiveness, of harm suffices to give rise to a duty of care. By 1983, ample evidence supported the conclusion that blood transmitted the AIDS virus. In early 1984, the AABB knew that AIDS was a rapidly spreading, fatal disease and that apparently healthy donors could infect others. The AABB also knew that blood and blood products probably could transmit AIDS and that each infected blood donor could infect many donees. Thus, the AABB knew, or should have known, in 1984 that the risk of AIDS infection from blood transfusions was devastating. We agree with the lower courts that the record establishes that the AABB owed Snyder a duty of care.

The dissent urges that we accord the AABB the benefit of qualified immunity without imposing on it the burdens of public office. It contends that "[t]he majority seeks to have it both ways: by finding a duty of care and liability because of the governmental authority delegated to the AABB, but then denying immunity because of a perceived lack of governmental authority." Not so. The contrary is true. By defending the AABB's status as a private organization free from public accountability while conferring on the AABB governmental immunity, the dissent seeks to impute to the AABB power without responsibility. . . .

The record reveals that the AABB led the charge against direct questioning of donors and surrogate testing. Viewed most favorably to the AABB, the evidence suggests that it was concerned that such questioning and testing would be of limited effectiveness and could diminish the supply of blood and blood products. A less favorable view suggests that the AABB resisted surrogate testing because it did not want to suffer the added inconvenience and costs of such testing. . . .

On the record, the jury could have concluded that the AABB in 1984 unreasonably resisted recognizing that blood transmits HIV. That resistance led the AABB to sacrifice an uncontaminated supply of blood for one that was contaminated, but more readily available. The jury could have found that if the AABB had not been so intransigent, its members, particularly the BCBC, would have instituted surrogate testing. Further, the jury could have found that if the BCBC had instituted surrogate testing, it would have rejected Unit 29F0784. . . .

The judgment of the Appellate Division is affirmed.

[The dissenting opinion is omitted.]

Notes

1. In *N.N.V. v. American Ass'n of Blood Banks,* 75 Cal.App.4th 1358, 89 Cal.Rptr.2d 885 (1999) the same defendant won on facts similar to *Snyder*. The court there said: "We believe deference should be given to professional associations that are making these sorts of policy decisions based on evolving medical and scientific knowledge."

2. If a good test is now available to determine whether blood is infected with HIV, is *Snyder* of any legal interest?

3. Is it true as one witness thought, that AABB was the only organization that could have done something? How about the American Red Cross, which joined in AABB's "intransigence"? How about the state or federal government–could those governments not have required protection for the blood supply, not to mention for individual human beings who were needlessly killed?

4. Is the standard of care for this kind of case–whatever kind that is–to be the standard of the reasonable and prudent person under the circumstances? Or some kind of standard based on reasonable regulation of medical standards?

Problems

1. A railroad, trying to clear its track after a derailment, works an employee more than 24 hours with no substantial rest. When the employee finally heads home, he falls asleep at the wheel and crashes into the plaintiff's car. Since the employee is not "on the job," the employer is not vicariously liable. Is the employer liable for negligence?

2. The defendant, a physician, prescribed anabolic steroids for a patient. The patient's reaction to the drug or its dosage was to become extremely aggressive and hostile to those around him. After his behavior led his wife to leave the house out of fear, the physician talked to him and concluded he was safe and so advised the wife. The wife then went back to the house to get her clothes, taking a friend with her. The patient shot the friend, causing injury. In prescribing for the patient, did the physician owe any duty to protect third persons? Assume you are in a jurisdiction that recognizes the rule in *Brigance*.

3. Defendant left the keys in the ignition of his car while he went to the bank. The car was parked in a shopping center parking lot. A thief took advantage of the opportunity, took the car, and proceeded to an interstate highway. The vehicle was reported stolen at 11:13 a.m. The thief took an exit when he was spotted by a state trooper. In a high speed chase through a small town, the thief drove 80 miles an hour through a stop light and into a car at 11:33 a.m. The collision killed the driver, a thirty-one-year-old woman who was six to eight months pregnant. The viable fetus was delivered but later died. A four-year-old child in the car also died. Still another child in the car was injured. The surviving husband-father sues the defendant.

4. Defendant owned a pistol, which he left in his bedroom. He had a safe on the premises but did not keep the pistol there. While defendant was out of town, his daughter invited guests to the house. One of them stole the pistol and used it later in a robbery, killing decedent in the process. The estate sues the defendant alleging that he negligently failed to secure the pistol.

5. One Corker, serving a life sentence, escaped from the state penitentiary. He had no wallet, no money, no driver's license and no identification. He entered a hardware store just before closing time and negotiated the purchase of a clothes washer and drier to be delivered (to a fictitious address) the next day, and a used gun which he was allowed to take. He paid with a worthless check. Federal law requires the seller to complete a form, which includes identification, before selling a gun. This was not done. Corker took the pistol, robbed a grocery store, took hostages, and murdered two of them. Should a wrongful death action lie against the seller of the gun? Assume you are in a jurisdiction that follows the traditional common law rule as to alcohol dispensers.

REFERENCES: DOBBS ON TORTS §§ 322–332 (2000); HARPER, JAMES & GRAY, THE LAW OF TORTS § 18.7 (3d Ed. 1995).

Topic C

LIMITING DUTIES TO PROTECT AGAINST SPECIAL TYPES OF HARM

Judicial attitudes about tort liabilities depend in part upon the relationships of the parties, but also in part upon the kind of harm the plaintiff claims.

In the absence of special relationships, courts are most receptive to tort claims when the defendant has risked and the plaintiff has suffered physical harm to person or property. What tort cases do *not* involve physical harms? First, cases of stand-alone economic harm. For instance, defendant negligently provides the plaintiff with information that leads the plaintiff to purchase property. The information proves unreliable and the plaintiff takes a financial loss on the purchase. Second, cases of stand-alone emotional harm or stress. For instance, the defendant negligently provides the plaintiff with information that makes the plaintiff believe her child has been injured. Before the plaintiff discovers that the information is false, she suffers great emotional harm.

Several different torts besides the tort of negligence address emotional interests. Physical torts like battery, assault and false imprisonment obviously have protection of emotional interests as one component. Defamation (libel and slander), malicious prosecution, the right to privacy, and even the tort called nuisance likewise protect emotional interests involved in reputation, seclusion, and the use and enjoyment of land.

The three chapters that follow consider how courts treat the undifferentiated negligence claims for emotional harm or loss generally, in pre-natal injury cases, and in wrongful death cases.

Chapter 17

EMOTIONAL HARM

Special note to the chapter. A plaintiff who establishes a tort claim for personal injury, or a claim based on trespassory torts like battery, assault, or false imprisonment, is always entitled to recover for any pain and suffering proven as well as for any pecuniary damages. Emotional harm, when proven, is recoverable as a species of pain and suffering if not as some separate item of damage. Such recoveries are often called parasitic damages. They represent the damages recoverable for some other tort, not for a stand-alone claim of emotional distress. This chapter is concerned primarily with stand-alone claims for distress.

SUBCHAPTER A. INTENTIONAL AND RECKLESS HARMS

§ 1. INTENTIONAL INFLICTION OF EMOTIONAL DISTRESS

GTE SOUTHWEST, INC. v. BRUCE

Supreme Court of Texas, 1999.
998 S.W.2d 605.

[Plaintiffs are several employees of GTE working under Morris Shields. They alleged that over a period of years, Shields engaged in a pattern of grossly abusive, threatening, and degrading conduct, regularly using the harshest vulgarity, verbally threatening and terrorizing them. He would physically charge at the employees, putting his head down, balling his hands into fists, and walk quickly toward or lunge at the employees, stopping very close to their faces. A number of witnesses testified that Shields frequently yelled and screamed at the top of his voice, and pounded his fists when requesting the employees to do things.... There was testimony that he often called one employee into his office and kept her standing there up to thirty minutes while he simply stared at her. He required employees to vacuum their own offices daily even though regular janitorial services were provided by others. Testimony detailed many abuses of this kind. The trial court entered judgment on the jury's verdict for the plaintiff. The Court of Appeals affirmed.]

To recover damages for intentional infliction of emotional distress, a plaintiff must prove that: (1) the defendant acted intentionally or recklessly; (2) the conduct was extreme and outrageous; (3) the actions of the defendant caused the plaintiff emotional distress; and (4) the resulting emotional distress was severe. In addition, "[a] claim for intentional infliction of emotional distress cannot be maintained when the risk that emotional distress will result is merely incidental to the commission of some other tort." Accordingly, a claim for intentional infliction of emotional distress will not lie if emotional distress is not the intended or primary consequence of the defendant's conduct.

Generally, insensitive or even rude behavior does not constitute extreme and outrageous conduct. Similarly, mere insults, indignities, threats, annoyances, petty oppressions, or other trivialities do not rise to the level of extreme and outrageous conduct.

In determining whether certain conduct is extreme and outrageous, courts consider the context and the relationship between the parties.... In the employment context, some courts have held that a plaintiff's status as an employee should entitle him to a greater degree of protection from insult and outrage by a supervisor with authority over him than if he were a stranger. This approach is based partly on the rationale that, as opposed to most casual and temporary relationships, the workplace environment provides a captive victim and the opportunity for prolonged abuse.

In contrast, several courts, including Texas courts, have adopted a strict approach to intentional infliction of emotional distress claims arising in the workplace. These courts rely on the fact that, to properly manage its business, an employer must be able to supervise, review, criticize, demote, transfer, and discipline employees. We agree with the approach taken by these courts.

... Thus, to establish a cause of action for intentional infliction of emotional distress in the workplace, an employee must prove the existence of some conduct that brings the dispute outside the scope of an ordinary employment dispute and into the realm of extreme and outrageous conduct....

Shields's ongoing acts of harassment, intimidation, and humiliation and his daily obscene and vulgar behavior, which GTE defends as his "management style," went beyond the bounds of tolerable workplace conduct.... Occasional malicious and abusive incidents should not be condoned, but must often be tolerated in our society. But once conduct such as that shown here becomes a regular pattern of behavior and continues despite the victim's objection and attempts to remedy the situation, it can no longer be tolerated. It is the severity and regularity of Shields's abusive and threatening conduct that brings his behavior into the realm of extreme and outrageous conduct.

Affirmed.

TAYLOR v. METZGER, 152 N.J. 490, 706 A.2d 685 (1998). The plaintiff is an African American female officer in the sheriff's office. She alleges that the sheriff referred to her as a "jungle bunny" in the presence of another supervisor and asserts claims both under state anti-discrimination statutes and under the law of emotional distress. The Sheriff offered an apology, but she received harassing phone calls and suffered hostility at work. The trial judge dismissed the claims and the Appellate Division affirmed. *Held,* reversed and remanded. On the common law emotional distress claim, "[t]he conduct must be so outrageous in character, and so extreme in degree, as to go beyond all possible bounds of decency, and to be regarded as atrocious, and utterly intolerable in a civilized community. The liability clearly does not extend to mere insults, indignities, threats, annoyances, petty oppressions, or other trivialities. A racial slur uttered by a sheriff directed against a subordinate officer is not, as a matter of law, a mere insult or triviality.... 'The use of the term "nigger" has no place in the civil treatment of a citizen by a public official.' Likewise, when defendant called plaintiff a 'jungle bunny,' he may have stepped beyond our civilized community's bounds of decency. A jury should determine whether defendant's remark was outrageous or merely an insult. We recognize that many jurisdictions have held that a supervisor's utterance of racial slurs toward his subordinates is not, as a matter of law, extreme and outrageous conduct that would give rise to an intentional infliction of emotional distress cause of action.... In this day and age, in this society and culture, and in this State, an ugly, vicious racial slur uttered by a high-ranking public official, who should know better and is required to do better, cannot, in light of this State's strong and steadfast public policy against invidious discrimination, be viewed as a picayune insult. That view would be blind and impervious to the lessons of history.... 'Racial insults, relying as they do on the unalterable fact of the victim's race and on the history of slavery and race discrimination in this country, have an even greater potential for harm than other insults.' [Richard Delgado, Words That Wound: A Tort Action for Racial Insults, Epithets, and Name–Calling, 17 Harv. C.R.-C.L. L.Rev. 133, 143 (1982)].... We do not hold that a single racial slur spoken by a stranger on the street could amount to extreme and outrageous conduct. But, a jury could reasonably conclude that the power dynamics of the workplace contribute to the extremity and the outrageousness of defendant's conduct."

Notes

1. *The Restatement.* The Restatement first recognized an independent tort based on intentional infliction of distress in the 1948 supplement. See RESTATEMENT SECOND OF TORTS § 46 (1965). The claim is actionable only if (a) the conduct of the defendant was extreme and outrageous, (b) intended to cause severe distress or at least was reckless in risking that distress, and (c) actually caused severe distress. Many lawyers refer to this as the tort of outrage.

2. *Dead bodies.* One early kind of case involved intentional or reckless interference with a dead body. Such cases still arise. In *Travelers Ins. Co. v. Smith,* 338 Ark. 81, 991 S.W.2d 591 (1999) an insurer refused to pay insurance due for the decedent's funeral until an autopsy was performed, then insisted that someone else arrange and pay for the autopsy. The result was that the funeral was so delayed that the body could not be viewed. The court upheld a jury verdict for the plaintiff.

3. *Markers of outrage.* In determining whether the defendant's conduct is sufficiently outrageous, courts have tended to emphasize that the conduct is (a) repeated or carried out over a period of time or (b) an abuse of power on the one hand or abuse of a person known to be especially vulnerable. A single request for sexual contact might be offensive but is usually not sufficiently outrageous. See *Jones v. Clinton,* 990 F.Supp. 657 (E.D.Ark. 1998). On the other hand, repeated and harassing requests for sexual attention can be outrageous. *Samms v. Eccles,* 11 Utah 2d 289, 358 P.2d 344 (1961). Similarly, a creditor is not outrageous in demanding payment of an overdue debt, but numerous demands for payment of a debt not due may be actionable. *George v. Jordan Marsh Co.,* 359 Mass. 244, 268 N.E.2d 915 (1971). Abuse of power by the defendant is another marker for outrage. Could you cite any authority for that proposition?

4. *Public humiliation.* Sometimes unwanted publicity is treated as a separate tort, invasion of privacy. However, in some cases it may fit the emotional distress tort better. What if the owner of a bagel shop, angry with a male customer, loudly and in crude terms asks his female companion about her sex life and discusses her body in front of other customers? See *Meyers v. Hot Bagels Factory, Inc.,* 131 Ohio App.3d 82, 721 N.E.2d 1068 (1999) (affirming judgment for the plaintiff on similar facts).

5. *Insult and outrage.* As indicated in the Restatement, insult is not sufficient; the defendant's acts must be "outrageous," and intended to inflict severe emotional distress. "Insult" is a term used in contrast to indicate conduct falling short of this. A special rule imposed liability upon common carriers (such as railroads), public utilities and innkeepers even for mere insult to patrons, but this liability is under attack. *Adams v. New York City Transit Auth.,* 88 N.Y.2d 116, 643 N.Y.S.2d 511, 666 N.E.2d 216 (1996).

6. *Proof of distress.* Aside from the special liability for insult, severe emotional distress must be intended and caused. How can a jury know this? What if plaintiff is surrounded by a circle of men who threaten him with the most severe bodily reprisals unless he gives up his job or joins the garbage haulers association? Would you be more convinced by expert psychiatric testimony than by a detailed recitation of the threats? See *Miller v. Willbanks*, 8 S.W.3d 607 (Tenn.1999).

7. *Severe distress.* Although severe distress can be proved without showing physical symptoms, courts really insist that the distress must be severe or even debilitating. You give blood at the blood bank, which then sends you a letter saying your blood had tested positive for syphilis and that the test had been confirmed. You are upset, your spouse is upset and worried, you feel your character is on the line, you both go into counseling and get new blood tests (proving the blood bank wrong). Is there anything

here to show severe distress? *Fisher v. American Red Cross Blood Services,* 2000 WL 1132576 (Ohio App. 2000). See DOBBS ON TORTS § 306 (2000).

8. *Discrimination.* Discrimination against individuals on the basis of race, gender, religion, or disability may involve emotional harm. Discrimination is most often redressed under separate statutes, some of which are sketched in Chapter 32.

Some Important Current Issues

9. *Persons under a disability.* Statutes sometimes provide causes of action for discrimination against persons suffering from disability. A federal statute has been held to create a cause of action for a disabled person who was denied an airline flight because of her disability. Most of the $80,000 recovery was for emotional harm. *Tallarico v. Trans World Airlines, Inc.,* 881 F.2d 566 (8th Cir.1989)

10. *First Amendment and public figures.* The First Amendment to the Federal Constitution forbids state or federal interference with free speech. What counts as "speech" is a complicated subject. Sometimes intentional or even merely negligent misstatements of fact might be grounds for recovery on a libel or slander theory, in spite of the First Amendment. (There is more on the First Amendment and libel in Chapter 29.) In general, however, statements not understood to be factual–opinions and satire, for example–are protected. Public figures in particular may be denied tort recovery based on such "speech," since it is especially important to preserve the right of discussion about public affairs.

11. *The First Amendment and religion.* Another clause of the First Amendment protects free exercise of religion and another prevents the government from supporting religion. Can courts uphold emotional distress claims based the defendant's promulgation of "false" or distressing religious doctrine? See *Tilton v. Marshall,* 925 S.W.2d 672 (Tex.1996). Suppose a religious group threatens a member or former member with divine retribution under frightening circumstances. If the member is severely distressed, would she have a claim or would the courts hesitate to interfere this much with religion? In *Molko v. Holy Spirit Ass'n for the Unification of World Christianity,* 46 Cal.3d 1092, 252 Cal.Rptr. 122, 762 P.2d 46 (1988) a threat of divine retribution was not actionable, but the plaintiff's claim that the church fraudulently induced the plaintiffs "into an atmosphere of coercive persuasion," could go to the jury as an intentional infliction of mental distress.

For a complete discussion and analysis of the religious distress cases, see Paul T. Hayden, *Religiously Motivated "Outrageous" Conduct: Intentional Infliction of Emotional Distress as a Weapon against "Other People's Faiths,"* 34 WM. & MARY L. REV. 579 (1993).

———

WINKLER v. ROCKY MOUNTAIN CONFERENCE OF THE UNITED METHODIST CHURCH, 923 P.2d 152 (Colo.App.1995). The plaintiff was a member of a church in which defendant Chambers was the senior pastor. The plaintiff also did volunteer work at the church on the recommendation of her therapist to work in a safe environment as a means of overcoming her fears of the workplace. The defendant on several occasions put his arm around the plaintiff, stroked her thigh or rubbed his body against hers, expressing love for her. The plaintiff sued for intentional infliction of emotional distress and breach of fiduciary duty. The jury awarded $28,675 on each of these two claims. *Held*, these awards are affirmed. (1) A fiduciary duty is based on an undertaking to act primarily for the benefit of another. The jury could find a fiduciary relationship between Chambers and Winkler on the basis of his counseling and a breach of that duty by his conduct. (2) Although Chambers' conduct would be a battery, the same conduct can amount to intentional infliction of distress. That is an independent tort and the plaintiff is not required to sue on a battery theory merely because the facts would have sufficed to show a battery. Where the plaintiff can assert an intentional infliction claim, the fact that the battery claim is barred by the statute of limitations is irrelevant.

Notes

1. *Sexual harassment.* Sometimes sexual harassment can be redressed under federal or state anti-discrimination statutes. If the sexual harassment is not a battery but instead consists of verbal harassment such as repeated demands for sexual conduct, could the victim claim damages on a theory of intentional or reckless infliction of distress? In *Ford v. Revlon, Inc.,* 153 Ariz. 38, 734 P.2d 580 (1987) the plaintiff recovered $10,000 in compensatory and $100,000 in punitive damages from the employer who knew of continuous physical and verbal harassment by the plaintiff's superior, but refused to interfere with it.

2. Federal statutory law of employment discrimination most commonly protects economic rights rather than rights in emotional tranquility. Since the 1991 Civil Rights Act, plaintiffs in some employment discrimination cases can recover limited emotional harm damages. The statutes are usually covered in advanced courses in employment law.

3. On a different note altogether, consider whether courts should permit an intentional infliction claim to proceed if the intentional infliction is accomplished solely by acts that would count as a battery and if the battery claim is barred by the statute of limitations.

HOMER v. LONG

Court of Special Appeal of Maryland, 1992.
90 Md.App. 1, 599 A.2d 1193.

WILNER, CHIEF JUDGE.

[The plaintiff alleged: He and his wife had been married many years when she was hospitalized for depression. While she was hospitalized, her therapist used confidential information and took advantage of her dependent, needy and vulnerable condition to seduce her. His wife's personality changed and he and his wife were ultimately divorced. The plaintiff here sues the therapist, among other things for intentional or reckless infliction of distress.]

To recover in an action for intentional infliction of emotional distress, a plaintiff must show (1) conduct that is intentional or reckless; (2) conduct that is also extreme and outrageous; (3) a causal connection between the wrongful conduct and the emotional distress; and (4) that the emotional distress is severe.

... Mr. Homer alleged that [the conduct alleged] was intentional and reckless, and ... we must accept the premise as pleaded by Mr. Homer. Whether, for purposes of this tort, the conduct is extreme and outrageous depends, at least in part, on the context in which it is viewed. Intrinsically, of course, it is extreme and outrageous; as noted, it violates clear standards set by the medical community itself. But the essence of the requirement is that the conduct must not simply be extreme and outrageous from the perspective of society at large, or from the perspective of someone else, but must be so as to the plaintiff. Outrageous conduct directed at A does not necessarily give B a cause of action.

There is no doubt that Dr. Long's conduct, as alleged, would be extreme and outrageous as to Ms. Homer, who, so far at least, has not chosen to complain of it. And ... had Mr. Homer also been a patient of Dr. Long, it could be regarded as outrageous to him as well.... But that is not the case here.

There are situations in which conduct directed principally at one person has been regarded as extreme and outrageous as to another, but normally the other person must be present to witness the conduct in order to recover. Restatement (Second) of Torts § 46, which defines the tort in question, states, in subsection (2): "Where such conduct is directed at a third person, the actor is subject to liability if he intentionally or recklessly causes severe emotional distress (a) to a member of such person's immediate family who is present at the time, whether or not such distress results in bodily harm, or (b) to any other person who is present at the time, if such distress results in bodily harm."

Comment 1 explains the presence requirement: "Where the extreme and outrageous conduct is directed at a third person, as where, for example, a husband is murdered in the presence of his wife, the actor may know that it is substantially certain, or at least highly probable, that it will cause severe emotional distress to the plaintiff. In such cases the rule of this Section applies...." [Prosser and Keeton note:] "Ordinarily recovery in such cases is limited to plaintiffs who are not only present at the time, but are known by the defendant to be present, so that the mental effect can reasonably be anticipated by the defendant. The distinction between the wife who sees her husband shot down before her eyes, and the one who hears about it five minutes later, may be a highly artificial one; but an argument in justification is the obvious necessity of drawing a line somewhere short of the widow who learns of the decease ten years afterward, when the genuineness and gravity of her distress may very reasonably be doubted."

The requirement of presence has been relaxed by some courts in particularly compelling circumstances, as, for example, where a parent sued the defendant for sexually molesting or kidnaping the plaintiff's child....

We see no reason not to apply the general rule, for the pragmatic reason noted in the Restatement and by Prosser and Keeton. The emotional and economic trauma likely to arise from the seduction of one's spouse is not limited to the case where the seducer is the spouse's therapist. The conduct may be just as outrageous and the harm may be just as great where the seducer is a neighbor, a good friend, a relative, an employee or business associate of the plaintiff, or indeed anyone in whom the plaintiff has imposed trust or for whom he or she has special regard....

———

REID v. PIERCE COUNTY, 136 Wash.2d 195, 961 P.2d 333 (1998). Several consolidated cases. Various plaintiffs assert that employees of the county appropriated autopsy photographs of plaintiffs' deceased relatives for their own purposes. One employee allegedly made a personal scrapbook of such photos; another used them when instructing on road safety. The plaintiffs claimed the "tort of outrage." *Held,* the allegations do not establish such a claim because the plaintiffs were not present at the time the county employees appropriated or used the photographs. "In Schurk, we held a mother could not maintain a tort of outrage action as a result of the molestation of her daughter, in part because 'the mother was not near the scene of the molestations; she did not observe these injuries occurring to her daughter, and learned of the occurrences at a later date from a third person.' "

NOTE: EMOTIONAL HARM IN THE
MARITAL RELATIONSHIP

Claims for emotional harm as well as other tort claims arising out of marriage relationships are now beginning to appear at the time of divorce, either as separate tort suits or as claims asserted in divorce proceedings. This raises a number of problems. Is some outrageous conduct less so in marriage–or, given the trust and intimacy involved, perhaps more so? Are some acts inflicting emotional distress in marriage privileged? Courts have not yet provided many answers. Suppose one spouse says "I don't love you anymore and I want a divorce?" Or repeatedly demeans the other spouse? Or engages in adultery? Should any of this count as outrage? If it does, should the aggrieved spouse be permitted to pursue the claim once a divorce is entered or a property settlement made? See Ira Mark Ellman & Stephen D. Sugarman, *Spousal Emotional Abuse as a Tort?*, 55 MD. L. REV. 1268 (1996); DOBBS ON TORTS § 281 (2000). To what extent, if at all, would a non-marital domestic partnership raise similar issues?

SUBCHAPTER B.   NEGLIGENT INFLICTION OF DISTRESS OR EMOTIONAL HARM

§ 2.   FRIGHT OR SHOCK FROM RISKS OF PHYSICAL HARM

a.   *Development of Liability for Fright*

MITCHELL v. ROCHESTER RY. CO., 151 N.Y. 107, 45 N.E. 354 (1896). In the spring of 1891, in Rochester, New York, the plaintiff was in the street about to board a street railway car when the defendant drove a team of horses at her. By the time the horses were stopped, the plaintiff found herself standing between the team, although never touched by them. The plaintiff suffered shock and a miscarriage as a result. The New York Court of Appeals held (1) there could be no recovery for fright alone and (2) as a corollary there could be no recovery for consequences of fright, even physical consequences like the miscarriage. Without a "physical injury," the negligence of the defendant would not be a proximate cause.

Notes

1. *Parasitic damages.* To interpret the rules in *Mitchell,* recall that if the defendant negligently causes physical injury to the plaintiff, the plaintiff can recover all damages that result, including damages for pain, suffering, and emotional harm. So if horses had actually run into Mitchell, causing some small physical harm, she would ordinarily recover not only for that harm but for any immediately ensuing emotional harm as well. In the light of this understanding, Mitchell seems to be establishing a rule requiring some kind of impact preceding any emotional harm.

2. *The fright or shock pattern.* Notice that *Mitchell* involved a very definite pattern: (a) the defendant's negligent acts put the plaintiff at immediate risk of a personal injury at a very definite time and place and (b) the plaintiff's reaction to that risk was fright and shock. *Mitchell* was not, for example, a case in which the defendant merely used words nor one in which the plaintiff suffered depression or anger, humiliation, or long-term sense of loss.

3. *Duty vs. proximate cause.* Because the *Mitchell* court made a rule for all cases of fright without impact/physical injury, the rule looks like a no duty rule rather than a proximate cause rule. Proximate cause, in today's practice, at least, is usually fact-specific. It requires analysis of the facts and application of general ideas to the particular case. In contrast, no-duty rules specify a lack of liability for a whole class of cases.

4. *Overruling the impact requirement.* In the next stage of development, cases like *Mitchell* were overruled. In *Battalla v. State,* 10 N.Y.2d 237, 219 N.Y.S.2d 34, 176 N.E.2d 729 (1961) the New York Court overruled *Mitchell's* requirement of an impact, observing that although some claims might be fraudulent, that would also be the case if the plaintiff could claim emotional harm after showing a slight impact and that although it would be

possible to imagine a flood of litigation over purely emotional harms, courts are instituted to resolve the rights of parties in individual disputes. Some claims would no doubt be speculative, the court thought, but the solution to that is to deny those claims and not to exclude the entire class. Other courts now usually take the same view, so the impact requirement is seldom a bar to relief. However, some courts continue to state and apply the impact rule. E.g., *R.J. v. Humana of Florida, Inc.,* 652 So.2d 360 (Fla.1995); *Lee v. State Farm Mutual Ins. Co.,* 272 Ga. 583, 533 S.E.2d 82 (2000). An excellent review of these rules and others yet to be mentioned can be found in *Camper v. Minor,* 915 S.W.2d 437 (Tenn.1996).

5. *Physical injury or physical manifestation of objective symptoms still required.* Although impact preceding injury is no longer a general requirement for the emotional harm claim, many courts impose a different limitation. They refuse to permit recovery for fright or shock alone and insist that where there has been no impact, the plaintiff cannot recover unless she produces evidence of physical harm resulting from the shock or some kind of objective physical manifestation of the shock or fright occurring after the events in question. See *Brueckner v. Norwich University,* 169 Vt. 118, 730 A.2d 1086 (Vt. 1999). The physical manifestation or objective symptom rule can easily be confused with the impact rule and sometimes it is not clear whether a court is discussing one or the other.

6. *Diluting the physical injury or physical manifestation rule.* Some courts have modified or diluted the physical injury or physical manifestation requirement. For example, Massachusetts has held that it really only requires "objective corroboration of the emotional distress alleged." Although transient symptoms, or mere upset or dismay will not be enough, the plaintiff's long continued diarrhea was sufficient objective evidence of emotional distress. *Sullivan v. Boston Gas Co.,* 414 Mass. 129, 605 N.E.2d 805 (1993). But perhaps the best evidence there and in many other cases lay in the events themselves. The *Sullivan* plaintiffs had watched in horror as their house was blown up. Since anyone would be seriously distressed by such events, the facts themselves strongly corroborated the claim.

7. *Modifying the physical manifestation rule.* The Courts of North Carolina and Washington have substantially modified the requirement of objective manifestations of harm. They have said that the emotional injury must be medically diagnosable as an emotional disorder, but not necessarily reflected in observable physical manifestations. *Johnson v. Ruark Obstetrics and Gynecology Assocs., P.A.,* 327 N.C. 283, 304, 395 S.E.2d 85, 97 (1990); *Hegel v. McMahon,* 136 Wash.2d 122, 960 P.2d 424 (1998). Does this rule cut both ways?

8. *Abolishing the physical injury or objective manifestation rule.* A number of states have now gone further by abolishing the requirement of physical injury altogether. A leading case on this point is *Molien v. Kaiser Foundation Hospitals,* 27 Cal.3d 916, 167 Cal.Rptr. 831, 616 P.2d 813, 16 A.L.R. 4th 518 (1980). In that case, the court said that the focus on physical injury was "overinclusive" because it permitted recovery for trivial emotional distress resulting from innocuous physical harm and "underinclusive" because it "mechanically denies" claims that might be proved valid if the plaintiff were permitted to introduce evidence. In any event, the court said,

the distinction between physical and emotional injury is "not clearly delineated." Finally, likelihood that an emotional injury is genuine can be found in the facts; we are all likely to feel distress when seriously threatened and that is a good guarantee that the plaintiff herself would feel such distress as well.

9. In a state that has abolished the impact rule but retains the physical manifestation rule, what result in the following cases:

(a) Defendant negligently performed surgery upon the plaintiff in such a way that the plaintiff lost the use or her right hand. She suffers periodic depression and a deep sense of loss, especially on bowling nights, but has no physical symptoms of the depression.

(b) Defendant, angry with a domestic partner, fired a pistol at random in an upscale restaurant. No one was hit, but one shot narrowly missed the plaintiff, breaking the back of his chair. The plaintiff was not touched and suffered no physical injury but wakes up with nightmares every night and has been unable to complete his college courses.

(c) Defendant negligently drove his car into the plaintiff's car, scratching the car but not physically touching or harming the plaintiff. Shortly thereafter, the plaintiff broke out in sweats and rashes, then fainted, all proveably a result of the fright or shock.

MILEY v. LANDRY, 582 So.2d 833 (La.1991). The plaintiff suffered from physical and emotional problems before she was in an automobile collision for which the defendant was responsible. After the collision "she was a grossly different person," suffering paranoia, distress, illogical thinking and other problems. The trial court awarded damages only for physical injury. On appeal, held, award increased to provide damages for mental suffering. "Nelda Miley has a borderline personality, but she was functioning before the accident. There was a dramatic change in Nelda Miley's condition before and after the accident: the most important factor in the change was the accident.... Although Nelda Miley's descent into psychosis might have occurred without the automobile accident, Dr. Ehrlich testified that her illness was precipitated by the accident.... When a defendant's negligent conduct aggravates a pre-existing condition, the victim must be compensated for the full extent of the aggravation."

It has been argued that traditional accounts of the law of emotional harm have been misleading because they see the legal rules as "degendered," that is as rules that are neutral with respect to gender, when in fact the traditional rules especially burden women. Women, it is said, bring more fright-based suits than men. The old law denying all recovery for stand-alone emotional injury was, in this view, a manifestation of a hierarchy of values that made property worth protecting but not emotional security or human relationships. These ideas and others are developed in Martha Chamallas & Linda K. Kerber, *Women, Mothers, and the Law of Fright: A History,* 88 MICH. L. REV. 814 (1990). Can you match these or similar ideas to material we've covered or the material that follows?

b. Emotional Harm or Loss Resulting From Injury to Another

(1) The General Mental Distress Claim

GRUBE v. UNION PACIFIC R.R.

Supreme Court of Kansas, 1994.
256 Kan. 519, 886 P.2d 845.

DAVIS, JUSTICE.

... Ernest A. Grube was employed by Union Pacific Railroad Company (Union Pacific). This case arose when the train he was operating as engineer collided with an automobile trapped upon a railroad crossing outside Lawrence. One of the occupants in the automobile died and two others suffered serious injury as a result of the collision. [Grube claimed against his employer, the railroad,] seeking damages for negligent infliction of emotional injury with accompanying physical manifestations.

Grube saw the trapped car before the collision. He remembers the driver of the vehicle, a young man, looking at the approaching engine with an expression of shock, fright, or fear. Grube sustained no physical injury as a result of the collision, but when the train eventually stopped, he ran back to the accident scene attempting to render aid. He felt the pulse of the driver and touched the deceased, attempting to find a pulse. At the accident scene, Grube exhibited physical manifestations of his emotional distress; he became physically ill and, as he testified, he "threw up ... [and] that's when it started hitting me." Grube further testified that he had no thoughts of fear of personal injury at the time of the accident but was reacting and not thinking at the time and merely doing his job. The other employee in the cab of the engine with Grube, however, ducked down before impact out of fear of possible explosion at the time of impact.

[The jury returned a verdict for Grube in the sum of $121,500.]

Section 1 of FELA provides in pertinent part: "Every common carrier by railroad ... shall be liable in damages to any person suffering injury [or death] while he is employed by such carrier ... for such injury or death resulting in whole or in part from the negligence of any of the officers, agents, or employees of such carrier, or by reason of any defect or insufficiency, due to its negligence, in its cars, engines, appliances, machinery, track, roadbed, works, boats, wharves, or other equipment." 45 U.S.C. § 51.

Kansas law is clear in its requirements that a plaintiff demonstrate some physical impact/injury in order to recover for negligent inflection of emotional distress. The United States Supreme Court has made clear, however, that federal common law governs such claims under FELA....

[In Consolidated Rail Corporation v. Gottshall, 512 U.S. 532, 114 S.Ct. 2396, 129 L.Ed.2d 427 (1994), the Supreme Court discussed] the concern the courts have experienced with the recognition of a cause of action for emotional injury when not related to any physical trauma. One such concern is that these claims "may inundate judicial resources with a flood of relatively trivial claims, many of which may be imagined or falsified, and that liability may be imposed for highly remote consequences of a negligent act."

A more significant concern was that "[e]motional injuries may occur far removed in time and space from the negligent conduct that triggered them." There are no necessary limits on the number of persons who might suffer emotional injury because of the negligent act. Thus, many courts note that recognition of this cause of action raises the real possibility of "nearly infinite and unpredictable liability for defendants."

[The Gottshall Court] concluded that the zone of danger test best harmonized all concerns: "We believe that allowing recovery for negligently inflicted emotional injury as provided for under the zone of danger test best harmonizes these considerations. Under this test, a worker within the zone of danger of physical impact will be able to recover for emotional injury caused by fear of physical injury to himself, whereas a worker outside the zone will not...."

... Grube acknowledges that he expressed no fear at the time of the collision, but argues that the zone of danger test adopted by the Supreme Court does not require a contemporaneous expression of such fear. He points out that many times people react to dangerous situations automatically and only later come to the realization of the danger they were in at the time of the peril. This point is well taken, and we do not believe that the zone of danger test adopted in Gottshall necessarily requires that there be fear for one's personal safety expressed contemporaneously with the collision. However, fear for one's safety is an essential element of the zone of danger test and must be expressed at or near the time of the danger in order for plaintiff to prevail in the action.

The problem with Grube's position is that the record fails to establish that Grube expressed fear for his own personal safety at any time. His fear was for the youth whose face he saw before impact and whose face he touched afterwards. As a result of this fear, Grube became physically ill immediately after the collision. There is ample evidence to establish that Grube experienced his severe emotional problems because of his concern about the lawsuit and his involvement in an accident in which a man died and others were injured. We also agree that the entire damages may include emotional distress resulting from concern or fear for the safety of another person as long as plaintiff establishes that he or she suffered imminent apprehension of physical harm. In both instances, however, essential elements for recovery under the zone of danger test are that plaintiff be within the zone of danger and suffer imminent apprehension of physical harm which causes or contributes to the emotional injury. In this case, Grube failed to establish that he feared for his personal safety at any time. His emotional injury did not result from fear of his personal safety but rather from his experiences relating to others affected by the impact.

Grube nevertheless argues that the physical impact he experienced at the point of collision brings him within the zone of danger test.... As we understand Grube's argument, he contends that he was thrown against the console in the cab of the engine at the time of the collision and sustained physical impact. Thus, according to his contention, he falls within the physical impact test as well as within the zone of danger test because of the physical impact he sustained.

Grube was pushed against the console of the engine because of the emergency braking of the train at the time of the collision. However as Union Pacific points out, there was no evidence that this action caused Grube any physical or emotional injuries. He suffered no bruises or abrasions as a result of the impact....

We therefore reverse the judgment of the trial court and enter judgment for the defendant, Union Pacific.

Notes

1. *Original denial of claims based on another's risk of injury.* The classic case of emotional harm resulting from injury to another was an extension of the fright and shock pattern. A mother watches in horror as a car strikes her child. The mother's fear and shock is much like the fear and shock in *Mitchell*, but it is fear for her child rather than for herself. Courts originally denied these claims altogether. A court that still retains the impact rule might continue to deny such a claim. See *Lee v. State Farm Mutual Ins. Co.*, 272 Ga. 583, 533 S.E.2d 82 (2000) (unless mother is herself impacted at the same time).

2. *Zone of danger "exception."* Courts eventually recognized the zone of danger exception discussed in *Grube*. If the mother were actually within the zone of danger, she could claim a *Mitchell*-type claim, and with the impact requirement discarded, she could recover on that, at least so long as part of her fear was fear for herself. As indicated in *Grube,* the Supreme Court has adopted the zone of danger test for emotional injury claims brought under the Federal Employer's Liability Act. *Consolidated Rail Corp. v. Gottshall,* 512 U.S. 532, 114 S.Ct. 2396, 129 L.Ed.2d 427 (1994).

3. *Close relatives outside the zone of danger.* California long ago recognized a claim for emotional harm by persons who suffered no impact but were in the zone of danger. In 1968, California went a step beyond that with a famous decision in *Dillon v. Legg,* 68 Cal.2d 728, 69 Cal.Rptr. 72, 441 P.2d 912 (1968). *Dillon* permitted recovery for emotional harm by persons who were merely bystanders–not in the zone of danger. In *Dillon,* a mother and sister saw a vehicle strike Erin Lee Dillon as she crossed the road, causing

her death. The court held that a defendant might owe a duty to protect not only the injured person but those who might foreseeably suffer emotional harm because of the injury. The court identified several factors or guidelines to be considered in determining foreseeability:

> (1) Whether plaintiff was located near the scene of the accident as contrasted with one who was a distance away from it. (2) Whether the shock resulted from a direct emotional impact upon the plaintiff from the sensory and contemporaneous observance of the accident, as contrasted with learning of the accident from others after its occurrence. (3) Whether plaintiff and the victim were closely related. . . .

The opinion is too long to set out. The thrust of it is that mental distress injuries can be real and serious, and that real and serious injuries should be compensated by the negligent defendant in the absence of some special reason to relieve him. The only reasons to relieve a defendant of liability were rejected as inadequate to the purpose—the danger of fraudulent claims and the inability to fix sufficient definitions or guidelines. The court did recognize, however, that the mother's claim was derivative and would be barred by the daughter's contributory negligence.

————

THING v. La CHUSA, 48 Cal.3d 644, 257 Cal.Rptr. 865, 771 P.2d 814 (1989). Maria Thing, hearing that her son had been struck by an automobile, rushed to the scene. She found her bloody and unconscious child lying in the road. She believed him to be dead. She neither saw nor heard the accident. She sued for emotional distress. *Held*, she cannot recover. Dillon's foreseeability test, limited only by guidelines rather than by rules, has left too much uncertainty in the law and too much room for unlimited expansion of liability. "We conclude, therefore, that a plaintiff may recover damages for emotional distress caused by observing the negligently inflicted injury of a third person if, but only if, said plaintiff: (1) is closely related to the injury victim; (2) is present at the scene of the injury producing event at the time it occurs and is then aware that it is causing injury to the victim; and (3) as a result suffers serious emotional distress—a reaction beyond that which would be anticipated in a disinterested witness and which is not an abnormal response to the circumstances."

Notes

1. *Sensory perception.* The plaintiff's sensory perception of the accident or injury when it happens or at least shortly thereafter is important as a factor under *Dillon* or as a strict rule under *Thing*. A strict view of perception was advanced in *Fernandez v. Walgreen Hastings Co.*, 126 N.M. 263, 968 P.2d 774 (N.M. 1998) where a grandmother suffered emotional harm watching her 22-month-old grandchild suffocate to death because the defendant had mis-filled a prescription. The court denied recovery because the grandmother was not a witness to a "sudden, traumatic injury-producing event" or its immediate aftermath and not aware of the event as causing injury.

2. *Delayed perception.* The clear case for recovery is one in which the plaintiff actually sees an injury as it occurs. A parent who does not see the event itself but only sees the injured child later, in the hospital, is likely to be denied recovery. *Roitz v. Kidman,* 913 P.2d 431 (Wyo.1996). What about all the times in between? Suppose a family member arrives at the scene of the injury immediately after impact? That would not suffice under the *Thing* rules. Under the more flexible *Dillon* guidelines, however, courts are willing to permit the plaintiff to recover if she arrived at the scene of injury before the victim's location or condition had changed. See *Hegel v. McMahon,* 136 Wash.2d 122, 960 P.2d 424 (1998).

3. *Close relationship.* Whether courts use the rules as guidelines or as bright-line rules, they usually insist upon a close relationship–usually a family relationship–between the plaintiff and the injured person. In *Migliori v. Airborne Freight Corp.*, 426 Mass. 629, 690 N.E.2d 413 (1998), the court held that a stranger who came to the aid of the an accident victim, giving CPR and becoming covered with her blood, had no claim against the tortfeasor when the primary victim died; rescuers and potential rescuers constituted too large a class. The rule was applied to deny recovery in *Michaud v. Great Northern Nekoosa Corp.,* 715 A.2d 955 (Me.1998), where the plaintiff, a diver, attempted to rescue another diver whose leg was trapped deep underwater and who watched as surface chains pulled him up, tearing his body apart. In *Grotts v. Zahner,* 989 P.2d 415 (Nev.1999), the court denied recovery to a fiancee who witnessed the fatal injury of the man she was engaged to marry.

4. *Other formulations.* Courts may accept the basic ideas in *Dillon* or *Thing* but formulate them differently. In *Groves v. Taylor,* 729 N.E.2d 569 (Ind.2000) an eight-year-old plaintiff standing in her driveway watched her six-year-old brother cross the street, then turned away. She heard a pop, turned back, and saw her brother's lifeless body rolling off the highway. The boy had been struck by a police car, which turned around and headed back. The court revised its earlier requirement of impact-and-direct-involvement formula to say that when the plaintiff does not suffer an impact, she may nevertheless recover for emotional harm if (1) harm to the injured person was death or severe injury, (2) the plaintiff witnessed the harm or came on the scene soon after, and (3) the relationship was "analogous to" that of spouse, parent, child, grandparent, or grandchild.

5. *Dillon v. Legg* rejected the zone of danger rule as a limitation upon liability. It expanded liability to include an uncertain group of bystanders. *Thing* then contracted liability by imposing firm rules instead of guidelines about which bystanders could recover. Would a California plaintiff who is within the zone of danger be permitted to recover without meeting the firm rules in *Thing*? Put differently, did *Thing* discard zone of danger liability by allowing a very limited recovery to those outside the zone of danger?

––––––

BURGESS v. SUPERIOR COURT, 2 Cal.4th 1064, 9 Cal.Rptr.2d 615, 831 P.2d 1197 (1992). The plaintiff, Julia Burgess, was given prenatal care by her obstetrician, Gupta, who also delivered her child,

Joseph. During Burgess' labor, Gupta diagnosed a prolapsed cord, which meant that the child would receive insufficient oxygen. Burgess was aware of this and of the urgent comings and goings thereafter. She knew when she was sedated for the cesarean that followed that something was wrong with the child. By the time the child was taken by cesarean, he had been deprived of oxygen for a lengthy period. He suffered permanent brain damage. Joseph brought suit against Gupta and the hospital. Julia asserted a separate claim for her own emotional distress.

Held, the *Thing* rules do not apply. California recognizes two classes of emotional harm cases. In the first, the plaintiff is a bystander, a person who has no preexisting relationship with the defendant. To this class of cases, the *Thing* rules apply. In the second, the plaintiff is a "direct victim." This phrase means that the plaintiff was in some kind of preexisting relationship with the defendant and that her claim is based on a breach of duty "assumed by the defendant or imposed on the defendant as a matter of law, or that arises out of a relationship between the two." As to these claims, the *Thing* rules do not apply. Liability in this class of cases is not unlimited; it is limited by the relationship established by the parties themselves. Both parties here understood that the physician owes a duty to the pregnant woman, not merely to the fetus alone. If the mother were treated as a bystander, the physician would have an incentive to sedate her, so that she would not see or hear injury and thus would be defeated by the *Thing* rules.

Notes

1. The fright and shock cases normally involve strangers, that is, persons who had no particular relationship that might affect duties. Any number of people might be frightened by runaway horses and if you add the possibility of liability to bystanders, even more. *Burgess* is important because it recognizes that some claims are asserted against a defendant who has at least implicitly undertaken to protect the plaintiff and that such cases might call for quite different rules.

2. The *Burgess* perception is that relationships (including implicit agreements between the parties) are important in determining the duties owed. Suppose that a mother, who is a doctor's patient, and a father, who is not, both suffer emotional harm as a result of the doctor's negligent treatment of their child but neither is a witness to the events causing harm? In a jurisdiction applying both *Thing* and *Burgess,* the mother would presumably recover under *Burgess.* But the father, who was not the doctor's patient, would presumably come under the *Thing* rules and would be barred because he was not actually present when the injury occurred. Cf. *Carey v. Lovett,* 132 N.J. 44, 622 A.2d 1279 (1993).

3. Suppose that a driver negligently loses control and crashes into the plaintiff's yard, nearly striking her. She suffers, she says, emotional trauma. Or that the an airline negligently crashes an airplane so close to the plaintiff that she feels the heat and the rush of air but isn't touched. Unless *Thing* reinstated the impact rule or abolished California's traditional liability to

those within the zone of danger, you might expect that both these plaintiffs would get to the jury. But consider whether the *Burgess* test had the effect of abolishing the zone of danger rule or requiring an impact. Some of the cases have tried to work out a result without relying upon the old zone of danger rule. In *Wooden v. Raveling*, 61 Cal.App.4th 1035, 71 Cal.Rptr.2d 891 (1998), the near-miss by a car, the court thought the plaintiff could get to the jury, but relied principally on the idea of direct harm as understood in *Burgess* and similar cases rather than zone of danger. In *Lawson v. Management Activities, Inc.*, 69 Cal.App.4th 652, 81 Cal.Rptr.2d 745 (1999), the airline crash case, the court rejected all liability. It appeared to equate bystander with those in the zone of danger but in any event disregarded categories like direct victim. Instead it analyzed the defendant's duty in terms of broad considerations such as burden to the defendant, moral blame, deterrence and the like. What is the right answer under *Burgess?* Or do you think *Burgess* addresses these two cases at all?

(2) *The Loss of Consortium Claim*

NOTE ON CONSORTIUM

The loss of consortium claim is quite different from the emotional harm claim in its origin. In the earlier common law, the master of an apprentice had a claim against the tortfeasor when the apprentice was injured, since the master would lose the services of the apprentice and might still be bound to provide him with food and housing. The claim had a firm economic basis in such cases. By the 17th century, the idea was carried over to permit a husband to recover from the tortfeasor when the wife was injured, on analogy, then all too true, to the master-servant relationship. Originally the claim was for loss of services, but it gradually expanded to take in non-economic losses such as loss of society and sexual relations.

"The concept of consortium includes not only loss of support or services, it also embraces such elements as love, companionship, affection, society, sexual relations, solace and more." *Millington v. Southeastern Elevator Co., Inc.*, 22 N.Y.2d 498, 293 N.Y.S.2d 305, 239 N.E.2d 897 (1968). After 1950, courts began to permit the wife to recover for loss of consortium when the husband was injured, thus putting the marital partners on an equal footing in this respect. In doing so, they often emphasized the non-financial side of the claim.

Emphasis on the intangible losses inflicted upon one person when another person is injured brings up the latent comparison to the bystander mental distress claim. Is the claim not one for a species of mental distress or emotional losses? The difference may lie in judicial attitudes. In the emotional distress claim, courts traditionally emphasized an acute moment–shock or fright. With the consortium claim, they recognize legal harm in a chronic, ongoing sense of loss. If emotional distress is the emotional equivalent of a stab wound, then loss of consortium is the emotional equivalent of carrying a large pack all day or living all your life in a cramped room. But both involve intangible and real losses in quality of life.

BOUCHER v. DIXIE MEDICAL CENTER

Supreme Court of Utah, 1992.
850 P.2d 1179.

HALL....

Daniel Boucher, the eighteen-year-old son of James and Torla Boucher, was admitted into Dixie Medical Center with a severely injured right hand. He underwent surgery and lapsed into a coma during the post-operative recovery period. He remained in a coma for ten days before awakening as a severely brain-damaged quadriplegic who will need extensive care for the rest of his life. The Bouchers were present at the hospital and observed their son's condition both before and after he awoke from the coma.

[The Boucher parents claimed damages for (1) negligent infliction of mental distress and (2) loss of their child's consortium or society, in addition to the claim of Daniel Boucher himself. The trial court dismissed the complaint. The Supreme Court in this opinion concluded that the Boucher parents could not recover for negligent infliction of mental distress because they were not in the zone of danger. The court then considered the loss of consortium claim as follows.]

The Bouchers' second claim presents an issue of first impression in this court: Should Utah judicially adopt a cause of action that allows the parents of a tortiously injured adult child to recover for loss of the child's consortium?

Loss of consortium claims are based on the recognition of a legally protected interest in personal relationships. Accordingly, if one member of the relationship is tortiously injured the noninjured party has a cause of action to recover for damage to their relational interest, i.e., the loss of the injured party's " 'company, society, co-operation, [and] affection.' " In the instant case, we are asked to recognize a right of recovery based on the relationship between parents and their adult son. For the reasons set forth below, we decline to adopt such an approach.

A review of the case law reveals little support for the adoption of a cause of action for the loss of filial consortium. At common law, the father of a tortiously injured child did have a cause of action to recover the value of the child's loss of services and the medical expenses incurred on the child's behalf. However, this action was based on a father's right to his minor children's services and a father's obligation to pay his minor children's medical expenses. This right of recovery, therefore, did not extend beyond these two elements of damages, nor did it extend to injuries involving adult or emancipated children.

These common law principles have undergone some modification. However, no widely accepted development has occurred that allows recovery in cases involving adult children, nor has any widely accepted development occurred that allows recovery for the loss of a child's society and affection.

Indeed, the majority of jurisdictions that have addressed the issue have declined to recognize a cause of action for loss of filial consortium. . . . Furthermore, our research reveals only one jurisdiction that has expressly recognized the specific right the Bouchers urge this court to adopt: a judicially created right to recover for the loss of an adult child's consortium.

[But Utah's Married Woman's Act had been construed to abolish the claim of spousal consortium.] [A]llowing recovery for the loss of an adult child's consortium and denying recovery for the loss of a spouse's consortium would lead to anomalous results. In many instances, the marital relationship is closer and more involved than the relationship between parents and their adult children and therefore should be granted greater or equal protection. However, . . . we cannot recognize a filial consortium claim and extend the same right of recovery to a plaintiff who suffers a loss of consortium because his or her spouse has been tortiously injured. The adoption of the Bouchers' claim, therefore, would invite inequitable applications of the consortium doctrine. . . .

[C]onsortium claims have the potential for greatly expanding the liability that can flow from one negligent act, and courts that have adopted consortium claims have been unable to develop rational limits on this liability. . . . [T]he recognition of consortium claims may [also impact] the cost and availability of insurance. Finally, given these concerns and the fact that the legislature has previously acted in this area, . . . the legislature is the appropriate body to determine if Utah should recognize consortium claims. . . .

Furthermore, we do not find the Bouchers' arguments persuasive. They claim that because they have reorganized their lives in order to undertake the care of their son, they should be able to recover personally from the parties responsible for their son's condition. However, the expense incurred for Daniel Boucher's nursing care is recoverable as part of the damages in Daniel Bouchers' own suit. Even the jurisdictions that allow recovery for loss of consortium would not allow the Bouchers to recover for the nursing care they have provided, because to do so would be to allow a double recovery.

The Bouchers also contend that because Utah allows recovery for the loss of society and affection in wrongful death cases, it is logical to extend this theory of damages to cases involving nonfatal injuries.

However, we view wrongful death cases as distinguishable from consortium cases. In wrongful death cases, the party that suffers the actual physical injury has no cause of action and the legislature has prescribed the parties who have a right to recover for the loss of the deceased's society and affection. Therefore, there is no danger of expansive liability and no need for the judiciary to attempt to fashion rational limits on relational interests. Indeed, we rejected a similar argument in Hackford. . . .

We decline to adopt a cause of action that allows the parents of a tortiously injured adult child to recover for the loss of consortium. The trial court, therefore, did not err in dismissing the Bouchers' claims of negligent infliction of emotional distress and loss of filial consortium.

Affirmed. [STEWART, JUSTICE, concurred and dissented.]

Notes

1. *Spousal consortium claims.* When one spouse is injured in a way that tends to diminish the ability of the partners to take pleasure in each other's company–in conversation, sports, travel, sexual relations, or any other pleasures of life–the other spouse has a lost consortium claim. "[P]rior to the accident, the Alexanders spent most of their time together, enjoying walking, gardening, and fishing." As a result of injury to one spouse, "they no longer engage in their outdoor activities, and instead spend much of their time watching television." That was evidence of lost consortium. *Wal-Mart Stores, Inc. v. Alexander,* 868 S.W.2d 322 (Tex.1993).

Should the non-injured spouse have a lost consortium claim if the injured spouse suffers no physical harm but does suffer a severe and compensable emotional injury? See *Barnes v. Outlaw,* 192 Ariz. 283, 964 P.2d 484 (1998).

2. *Derivative nature of spousal consortium claims.* Consortium claims are traditionally said to derive from the claim of the physically injured spouse. A derivative claim can rise no higher than the claim from which it is derived. E.g., *Wine-Settergren v. Lamey,* 716 N.E.2d 381 (Ind.1999). For example, the contributory negligence of the injured spouse will bar or reduce the consortium claim just as it will bar or reduce the injured spouse's claim. Some cases, however, hold that the claim is independent and not affected by the fault of the physically injured victim or even by his release. E.g., *Hardy v. St. Clair,* 739 A.2d 368 (Me.1999) (husband's release in advance and indemnity agreement did not bar wife's consortium claim).

3. *The child's claim for loss of parental consortium.* In 1980, Massachusetts permitted a claim by a child for loss of parental consortium following a serious injury to a father. *Ferriter v. Daniel O'Connell's Sons, Inc.,* 381 Mass. 507, 413 N.E.2d 690, 11 A.L.R.4th 518 (1980). A good number of other courts have accepted the idea. E.g., *United States v. Dempsey,* 635 So.2d 961 (Fla.1994). A number of other contemporary cases, however, continue to reject any such extension of liability. E.g., *Mendillo v. Bd. of Educ. of Town of East Haddam,* 246 Conn. 456, 717 A.2d 1177 (1998). The classic article is Jean C. Love, *Tortious Interference with the Parent–Child Relationship: Loss of an Injured Person's Society and Companionship,* 51 IND. L.J. 591 (1976).

4. *The parents' claim for loss of a child's society and companionship.* Earlier common law gave the father a claim for loss of a child's services under some circumstances, but this was usually a reflection of the fact that the father was entitled to a child's earnings and to actual work around the house. Otherwise, parents of an injured child have not generally been allowed a recovery for intangible harm such as loss of society or companionship. E.g., *Elgin v. Bartlett,* 994 P.2d 411 (Colo.1999). A few courts, however,

have allowed the parents' claim. In most of these, the child was severely injured or comatose and some of the courts emphasized that the injury was total and permanent, or even that it was closely similar to death. E.g., *United States v. Dempsey,* 635 So.2d 961 (Fla.1994). There are a few statutes on point as well.

5. *Basis of the general rule.* Grounds for denying a child's recovery for loss of parental consortium have included the points made in *Boucher.* It has also been argued that if children can recover such losses, then there is no principled basis for excluding recovery by siblings, grandparents, and others. In addition, some judges have professed great deference to the legislative branch on this claim. They have also said that damages could readily be magnified by the number of children in a family, with resulting high costs in liability insurance, and that the return for the increased insurance costs would be quite low since a child might become rich on the award, but would remain nonetheless a child deprived of parental guidance. See, discussing these ideas, *Russell v. Salem Transportation Co.,* 61 N.J. 502, 295 A.2d 862 (1972) and *Borer v. American Airlines, Inc.,* 19 Cal.3d 441, 138 Cal.Rptr. 302, 563 P.2d 858 (1977). In *Norwest v. Presbyterian Intercommunity Hospital,* 293 Or. 543, 652 P.2d 318 (1982) Judge Linde rejected the child's consortium claim on a much broader ground–because it involved a claim of harm resulting from the negligent treatment of another person. As to claims resulting from injuries to other human beings, Judge Linde thought more than mere foreseeability would be required.

6. *Unmarried cohabitants.* Up until 1994, courts pretty consistently rejected consortium claims by unmarried consorts. See *Elden v. Sheldon,* 46 Cal.3d 267, 758 P.2d 582, 250 Cal.Rptr. 254 (1988). But in *Dunphy v. Gregor,* 136 N.J. 99, 642 A.2d 372 (1994) the court approved an emotional distress recovery by an unmarried cohabitant who witnessed her fiance's fatal injury. The plaintiff underwent psychiatric and psychological treatment for depression and anxiety. There was no question about a close relationship. They had a joint checking account and a jointly owned car; they had life insurance policies on each other. Michael had introduced her in public as his wife. What about gay or lesbian partnerships? Vermont's civil union statute treats formalized same-sex unions like marriage. See 15 Vᴛ. Sᴛᴀᴛ. §§ 1204(a) & 1204(e) (2). What about a consortium claim by someone who married the injured person after the injury occurred? See *Trombley v. Starr–Wood Cardiac Group, PC,* 3 P.3d 916 (Alaska 2000).

7. *Consortium and the* Dillon–Thing *factors.* Most courts that permit bystander recovery for mental distress do so under either the constraints of the zone of danger rule or those imposed by the *Dillon-Thing* rules. Notice that the consortium claim relies solely upon the relationship of the plaintiff and the injured person and on proof of actual loss of services or society. Why the difference? Could a marital partner ever recover both under the general mental distress claim and consortium?

8. *Animals.* Consider how the rules of this and the preceding section would apply if your cat, dog, or horse is negligently treated. Suppose you see the defendant nearly run over your cat; alternatively, he actually does injure or kill it. Cf. *Fackler v. Genetzky,* 257 Neb. 130, 595 N.W.2d 884 (1999) (vet not liable for emotional distress when he negligently destroyed a race horse).

Courts have generally rejected emotional distress liability based upon either breach of contract or negligent damage to property. See *Erlich v. Menezes,* 21 Cal.4th 543, 87 Cal.Rptr.2d 886, 981 P.2d 978 (1999).

§ 3. DUTIES OF CARE TO PROTECT EMOTIONAL WELL–BE-ING INDEPENDENT OF PHYSICAL RISKS

WASHINGTON v. JOHN T. RHINES CO., 646 A.2d 345 (D.C.App. 1994). "Mrs. Washington contracted with appellee John T. Rhines Company ('Rhines'), a funeral home in the District of Columbia, to prepare, embalm, and dress Mr. Washington's body. Pursuant to the agreement, Rhines also transported the casket containing the body to National Airport. From there it was shipped to a funeral home in El Paso, Texas, for an open-casket memorial service and eventual burial in El Paso National Cemetery." Mrs. Washington alleged that "when the casket arrived in El Paso on June 25, it was discovered that the clothing and the inside of the shipping case were drenched with fluid; there was an offensive odor of embalming and body fluids; there were extreme skin slips, blisters, and discolorations on several parts of the body; the body had begun to turn green and was rapidly decomposing; there was swelling in the face and neck areas; and a catheter tube which had been inserted in the deceased's body during his hospitalization had not been removed." In her claim for emotional distress damages, *held,* the trial court properly dismissed the complaint. Since the plaintiff was not in a zone of danger, she cannot claim negligent infliction of emotional distress.

Notes

1. Good or bad, the zone of danger test was comprehensible when the plaintiff claimed emotional harm based on danger of physical harm to herself or others. Does it make any logical sense at all when the plaintiff's claim is not based on a physical danger to a person?

2. What if a hospital negligently loses the body of a patient who has died there? What if a hospital negligently permits the plaintiff's newborn baby to be abducted from the hospital? New York has allowed the plaintiff's negligent infliction claim in the first case but denied it in the second. *Lando v. State,* 39 N.Y.2d 803, 385 N.Y.S.2d 759, 351 N.E.2d 426 (1976); *Johnson v. Jamaica Hospital,* 62 N.Y.2d 523, 478 N.Y.S.2d 838, 467 N.E.2d 502 (1984). Is this sensible?

3. Reconsider *Burgess v. Superior Court.* Would a court following the idea in that case expect the mortuary to act with reasonable care for the very purpose of protecting the emotional well-being of the family? In *Christensen v. Superior Court,* 54 Cal.3d 868, 2 Cal.Rptr.2d 79, 820 P.2d 181 (1991) the plaintiffs alleged that defendant mortuaries and crematories had contracted to provide dignified burials or cremations, but that they in fact harvested various human organs from the remains of deceased persons and sold them. Saying the context was "unique," the California Supreme Court held the defendants had "assumed a duty to the close relatives . . . for whose benefit

they were to provide funeral and/or related services." So if the plaintiffs were aware that the services were being performed, they could recover damages, even though they learned about the indignities only from news media. See also *Janicki v. Hospital of St. Raphael,* 46 Conn.Supp. 204, 744 A.2d 963 (1999) (hospital's dissection of stillborn 19–week-gestation fetus over the mother's objection was actionable although the mother had no "contemporaneous sensory perception of the event" as required in bystander cases; the mother was the primary victim).

———

HEINER v. MORETUZZO, 73 Ohio St.3d 80, 652 N.E.2d 664 (1995). Defendants tested the plaintiff for AIDS, but, according to allegations accepted as true, negligently and erroneously reported to the plaintiff that she was infected with that disease. They then did a re-test and erroneously confirmed the diagnosis and recommended a specialist in that disease. In fact the plaintiff later discovered that the diagnosis was wrong. She sued for negligent infliction of distress. *Held,* the plaintiff has no claim. "[T]he claimed negligent diagnosis never placed appellant or any other person in real physical peril, since appellant was, in fact, HIV negative. . . . [W]e hold that Ohio does not recognize a claim for negligent infliction of serious emotional distress where the distress is caused by the plaintiff's fear of a nonexistent physical peril."

Notes

1. Florida, a holdout for the old impact rule, also denied recovery in a negligent misdiagnosis-of-AIDS case where there was no impact. *R.J. v. Humana of Florida, Inc.,* 652 So.2d 360 (Fla.1995). Some other courts have upheld a right to recover in misdiagnosis cases. *Chizmar v. Mackie,* 896 P.2d 196 (Alaska 1995) (AIDS misdiagnosis); *Bramer v. Dotson,* 190 W.Va. 200, 437 S.E.2d 773 (1993); cf. *Molien v. Kaiser Foundation Hospitals,* 27 Cal.3d 916, 167 Cal.Rptr. 831, 616 P.2d 813, 16 A.L.R.4th 518 (1980) (wife misdiagnosed as having venereal disease, leading to emotional distress of husband).

2. *Other misinformation cases.* Misinformation–like the misdiagnosis of AIDS–seldom creates a direct risk of physical harm, so it is not surprising that courts steeped in the tradition of the physical risk cases have produced mixed results when the plaintiff suffers emotional harm as the result of receiving erroneous information. If lawyers argue the *Burgess* idea, would this change?

3. *Death messages.* One kind of misinformation is treated as special in some courts. This is the message, usually carried by telegraph, erroneously announcing the death of a close relative. One group of cases has long permitted the plaintiff to recover for emotional harm in such cases. E.g., *Johnson v. State,* 37 N.Y.2d 378, 372 N.Y.S.2d 638, 334 N.E.2d 590, 77 A.L.R.3d 494 (1975).

4. *Information about the plaintiff.* When the plaintiff's emotional distress arises because the defendant has communicated information about the plaintiff rather than because the defendant has communicated information

to the plaintiff, courts have almost never dealt with the claim as one for negligence, but have considered invasion of privacy, libel, slander, or malicious prosecution rules instead.

———

BOYLES v. KERR, 855 S.W.2d 593 (Tex.1993). Dan Boyles, then 17, secretly videotaped his sexual intercourse with 19–year-old Susan Kerr. The tape also included comments made by Boyles' friends. Boyles then showed the tape on several occasions to various friends. Kerr claimed negligent infliction of emotional distress resulting from the tape, its showing, and the gossip that ensued. *Held,* there is no general duty to avoid negligent infliction of distress. Texas will not recognize a cause of action for emotional distress except where the defendant creates a risk of physical harm. Thus bystander recovery is permissible under the rules of *Dillon v. Legg.* Some courts recognize a claim for serious or severe distress, but that standard is inadequate. "It is difficult to imagine how a set of rules could be developed and applied on a case-by-case basis to distinguish severe from nonsevere emotional harm. Severity is not an either/or proposition; it is rather a matter of degree. Thus, any attempt to formulate a general rule would almost inevitably result in a threshold requirement of severity so high that only a handful would meet it, or so low that it would be an ineffective screen. A middle-ground rule would be doomed, for it would call upon courts to distinguish between large numbers of cases factually too similar to warrant different treatment. Such a rule would, of course, be arbitrary in its application." [Quoting Richard N. Pearson, *Liability to Bystanders for Negligently Inflicted Emotional Harm–A Comment on the Nature of Arbitrary Rules,* 34 U.FLA.L.REV. 477, 511 (1982).]

Notes

1. *Relationships.* The *Kerr* majority said it would recognize a duty based upon special relationships of the parties, and cited the telegraphic death message cases and dead body cases as examples. But it went on to say, without much discussion, that there was no such relationship in this case. Is that right? If the phrase "betrayal of confidence" comes to mind, it surely suggests an important relationship was involved. Even if so, however, it does not necessarily suggest that negligence is the proper basis for liability.

2. *Intentional infliction.* (a) While Boyles' acts were intentional as well as reprehensible, it does not look as if he intended to inflict distress unless you think Boyles intended that Kerr would discover the taping. So it is not clear that the plaintiff could succeed on an intentional infliction claim. Sometimes, however, courts confuse the intentional acts with intent to cause distress and hold that an intentional tort is made out in cases similar to *Boyles. Williams v. City of Minneola,* 619 So.2d 983 (Fla.App.1993).

(b) If Kerr had won on an intentional infliction theory, she might have collected little, since the defendants' insurance policies probably covered negligent but not intentional torts.

3. *Privacy*. Mental distress is often part of the harm associated with a number of torts that do not entail physical harms, or even risks of physical harms. For example, invasion of privacy, under some circumstances, can be a tort. Some invasions of privacy produce mental distress damages. *Boyles* might have been brought as a privacy invasion claim in some jurisdictions. See *Fontaine v. Roman Catholic Church of Archdiocese of New Orleans*, 625 So.2d 548 (La.App.1993) (allegation: a priest sexually abused a 17–year old and later published photographs in a magazine and circulated video tapes; a privacy invasion claim is stated). But the privacy claim would be undesirable to the plaintiff if the defendant's liability insurance did not cover privacy claims.

SACCO v. HIGH COUNTRY INDEPENDENT PRESS, INC.

Supreme Court of Montana, 1995.
271 Mont. 209, 896 P.2d 411.

NELSON, JUSTICE. . . .

[The complaint alleged that when the plaintiff, Dianne Poynter Sacco left her employment at the High Country Independent Press newspaper in Belgrade, Montana, the company and its officers and stockholders falsely told police sergeant Dighans that she had stolen photographic negatives and proof sheets. This led Dighans to swear out a criminal complaint. The plaintiff asserted a number of theories against various defendants, including a theory of negligent infliction of distress against Dighans. The trial judge gave summary judgment for defendants.]

After thoroughly reviewing our own case law and the authorities from other jurisdictions, we conclude that it is appropriate that we join a multitude of jurisdictions in recognizing both [negligent and intentional infliction] torts as independent causes of action with recovery for damages based upon satisfaction of the standard we set forth in the instant case. An independent cause of action for the tort of infliction of emotional distress will arise under circumstances where serious or severe emotional distress to the plaintiff was the reasonably foreseeable consequence of the defendant's negligent or intentional act or omission. . . .

Based upon the logic and analysis in [Molien and other cases] and the state of our prior case law, we conclude that it is appropriate to clarify the existing law on negligent infliction of emotional distress and to delineate a better approach to such claims. We recognize that negligent infliction of emotional distress as an independent tort action under the narrow Versland analysis is archaic and does not fully address all plaintiffs who are deserving of relief. Therefore, we adopt the following standard for determining whether a plaintiff has demonstrated a cause of action for the negligent infliction of emotional distress. A cause of action for negligent infliction of emotional distress will arise under circumstances where serious or severe emotional distress to the plaintiff was the reasonably foreseeable consequence of the defendant's negligent act or omission.

Concern over a floodgate of claims for emotional distress, particularly fraudulent claims, is alleviated by the necessity to prove that the emotional distress suffered is severe or serious. Concern over seeming unlimited liability for defendants is alleviated by the necessity of demonstrating that plaintiff's serious or severe emotional distress was the reasonably foreseeable consequence of defendant's negligent act or omission. . . .

The requirement that the emotional distress suffered as a result of the defendant's conduct be "serious" or "severe" ensures that only genuine claims will be compensated. We conclude that a jury is capable of determining whether the emotional distress claimed to have been sustained is "serious" or "severe." As stated in Molien, citing Rodrigues: "In cases other than where proof of mental distress is of a medically significant nature, [citations] the general standard of proof required to support a claim of mental distress is some guarantee of genuineness in the circumstances of the case. This standard is not as difficult to apply as it may seem in the abstract. As Justice Traynor explained in this court's unanimous opinion in State Rubbish [Collectors] Assn. v. Siliznoff, supra, 38 Cal. 2d [330] at page 338, 240 P.2d 282, the jurors are best situated to determine whether and to what extent the defendant's conduct caused emotional distress, by referring to their own experience. In addition, there will doubtless be circumstances in which the alleged emotional injury is susceptible of objective ascertainment by expert medical testimony. . . .

Accordingly, we hold that, the District Court erred in granting Dighans' motion for summary judgment on the issue of negligent infliction of emotional distress, and we remand for further proceedings consistent with the new standard enunciated above. . . .

An independent cause of action for infliction of emotional distress will arise under circumstances where serious or severe emotional distress to the plaintiff was the reasonably foreseeable consequence of the defendant's negligent or intentional act or omission. The difference between the negligent and intentional versions of the cause of action lies, not in the elements of the tort, but in the nature and culpability of the defendant's conduct. That being the case, when a cause of action for intentional infliction of emotional distress is pled, the plaintiff may request relief in the form of punitive damages ... to address the culpability of the defendant's conduct. Serious or severe emotional distress to the plaintiff which was the reasonably foreseeable consequence of defendant's negligent or intentional act or omission will be addressed in both causes of action, as stated above, through a prayer for relief in the form of compensatory damages. . . .

CAMPER v. MINOR, 915 S.W.2d 437 (Tenn.1996). Camper was driving a cement truck. Jennifer Taylor, 16-years-old, had been stopped at a stop sign, but suddenly pulled out in front of the plaintiff. "The vehicles collided, and Ms. Taylor was killed instantly. Camper exited his truck moments after the crash, walked around the front of his vehicle, and viewed Ms. Taylor's body in the wreckage from close range." Camper sued her estate, claiming negligent infliction of emotional distress, in the form of a post-traumatic stress syndrome. *Held:* (1) The physical manifestation or injury rule will no longer be followed; (2) Negligent infliction of emotional distress claims should be analyzed under the general negligence approach, that is, no differently from any other negligence case. "[T]he plaintiff must present material evidence as to each of the five elements of general negligence–duty, breach of duty, injury or loss, causation in fact, and proximate, or legal, cause–in order to avoid summary judgment. [T]o guard against trivial or fraudulent actions, the law ought to provide a recovery only for serious or severe emotional injury. A serious or severe emotional injury occurs where a reasonable person, normally constituted, would be unable to adequately cope with the mental stress engendered by the circumstances of the case. Finally, we conclude that the claimed injury or impairment must be supported by expert medical or scientific proof."

Notes

1.   The *Sacco* and *Camper* courts appear to discard all the constraining rules. Do you forecast that they will always be applied in accord with this appearance?

2.   *Malicious prosecution.* The *Sacco* facts might be expected to generate a claim based on the tort of malicious prosecution rather than one based on a general emotional distress theory. Although emotional distress damages might be recoverable for malicious prosecution, the latter tort is a kind of intentional tort and constrained by special rules. These provide that no defendant is liable for causing the criminal prosecution of a person unless (a) the defendant instigated the prosecution (that is, was a proximate cause of it), (b) the prosecution was initiated or pursued without probable cause, (c) the defendant acted in bad faith, and (d) the prosecution was terminated favorably to the person who is now the plaintiff. See Chapter 29. Can you see at least two effects of treating the claim as one for negligent infliction of mental distress?

3.   *Defamation.* Defamation cases, that is, those based on a claim that the defendant has libeled or slandered the plaintiff and thus adversely affected the plaintiff's reputation, also allow damages for mental distress. But defamation claims are carefully circumscribed by a number of special rules to make sure that the Constitutional guarantee of free speech is fully protected. See Chapter 29.

§ 4.   TOXIC EXPOSURES: FEAR OF FUTURE HARM:
LIMITS ON RECOVERY?

POTTER v. FIRESTONE TIRE AND RUBBER CO.

Supreme Court of California, 1993.
6 Cal.4th 965, 25 Cal.Rptr.2d 550, 863 P.2d 795.

BAXTER, JUSTICE....

[Firestone operated a tire manufacturing plant near Salinas. It contracted with Salinas Disposal Service and another company for disposal of industrial wastes in a class II sanitary landfill operated by the City. Class II landfills prohibit disposal of toxic substances because of the danger that they will leach into the groundwater. In addition, the disposal service prohibited solvents, oils and other substances. Firestone assured the service that no such waste would be sent to the landfill. For a while official plant policy required proper disposal of hazardous wastes in a Class I landfill, but that program was costly. A production manager, sent to California from Firestone's Akron, Ohio office to make the plant more profitable, became angered over the costs of the hazardous waste disposal program. As a consequence, Firestone's hazardous waste materials were once again deposited and these materials included serious toxins.]

[The plaintiffs, including the Potters, lived near the landfill. They discovered that toxic chemicals had contaminated their domestic water wells. At least two of the chemicals, benzene and vinyl chloride, are known human carcinogens and others are strong suspects. The plaintiffs sued Firestone on theories that included negligent infliction of emotional distress. The trial court awarded $269,500 for psychiatric illnesses and the cost of treating them, $142,975 for the cost of medical monitoring of the plaintiffs, and punitive damages of $2.6 million. The court of appeal modified the judgment in some respects, but affirmed the main elements.]

[The Supreme Court of California raised the possibility that if the plaintiffs had suffered harm to their cells or their immune systems, that might constitute physical injury and that if so, emotional distress damages could be recovered as parasitic to a recovery for that harm. But it concluded that there was not enough evidence in the record to pass on that question.]

We next determine whether the absence of a present physical injury precludes recovery for emotional distress engendered by fear of cancer....

Our reasons for discarding the physical injury requirement in Molien remain valid today and are equally applicable in a toxic exposure case. That is, the physical injury requirement is a hopelessly imprecise screening device....

We next consider whether recovery of damages for emotional distress caused by fear of cancer should depend upon a showing that the plaintiff's fears stem from a knowledge that there is a probable likelihood of developing cancer in the future due to the toxic exposure. This is a matter of hot debate among the parties and amici curiae. . . .

A carcinogenic or other toxic ingestion or exposure, without more, does not provide a basis for fearing future physical injury or illness which the law is prepared to recognize as reasonable. The fact that one is aware that he or she has ingested or been otherwise exposed to a carcinogen or other toxin, without any regard to the nature, magnitude and proportion of the exposure or its likely consequences, provides no meaningful basis upon which to evaluate the reasonableness of one's fear. For example, nearly everybody is exposed to carcinogens which appear naturally in all types of foods. . . .

[W]e would be very hard pressed to find that, as a matter of law, a plaintiff faced with a 20 percent or 30 percent chance of developing cancer cannot genuinely, seriously and reasonably fear the prospect of cancer. Nonetheless, we conclude, for the public policy reasons identified below, that emotional distress caused by the fear of a cancer that is not probable should generally not be compensable in a negligence action. . . .

[A]ll of us are potential fear of cancer plaintiffs, provided we are sufficiently aware of and worried about the possibility of developing cancer from exposure to or ingestion of a carcinogenic substance. The enormity of the class of potential plaintiffs cannot be overstated; indeed, a single class action may easily involve hundreds, if not thousands, of fear of cancer claims.

With this consideration in mind, we believe the tremendous societal cost of otherwise allowing emotional distress compensation to a potentially unrestricted plaintiff class demonstrates the necessity of imposing some limit on the class. Proliferation of fear of cancer claims in California in the absence of meaningful restrictions might compromise the availability and affordability of liability insurance for toxic liability risks.

A second policy concern that weighs in favor of a more likely than not threshold is the unduly detrimental impact that unrestricted fear liability would have in the health care field. As amicus curiae California Medical Association points out, access to prescription drugs is likely to be impeded by allowing recovery of fear of cancer damages in negligence cases without the imposition of a heightened threshold. To wit, thousands of drugs having no known harmful effects are currently being prescribed and utilized. New data about potentially harmful effects may not develop for years. If and when negative data are discovered and made public, however, one can expect numerous lawsuits to be filed by patients who currently have no physical injury or illness but who nonetheless fear the risk of adverse effects from the drugs they used. Unless meaningful restrictions are placed on this potential plaintiff class, the threat of numerous large, adverse monetary awards, coupled with the added cost of insuring against such liability (assuming insurance would be available), could diminish the availability of new, beneficial prescription drugs or increase their price beyond the reach of those who need them most. . . .

A third policy concern to consider is that allowing recovery to all victims who have a fear of cancer may work to the detriment of those who sustain actual physical injury and those who ultimately develop cancer as a result of toxic exposure. That is, to allow compensation to all plaintiffs with objectively reasonable cancer fears, even where the threatened cancer is not probable, raises the very significant concern that defendants and their insurers will be unable to ensure adequate compensation for those victims who actually develop cancer or other physical injuries. . . .

A fourth reason supporting the imposition of a more likely than not limitation is to establish a sufficiently definite and predictable threshold for recovery to permit consistent application from case to case. . . .

Finally, while a more likely than not limitation may foreclose compensation to many persons with genuine and objectively reasonable fears, it is sometimes necessary to "limit the class of potential plaintiffs if emotional injury absent physical harm is to continue to be a recoverable item of damages in a negligence action." . . .

Unless an express exception to this general rule is recognized: in the absence of a present physical injury or illness, damages for fear of cancer may be recovered only if the plaintiff pleads and proves that (1) as a result of the defendant's negligent breach of a duty owed to the plaintiff, the plaintiff is exposed to a toxic substance which threatens cancer; and (2) the plaintiff's fear stems from a knowledge, corroborated by reliable medical or scientific opinion, that it is more likely than not that the plaintiff will develop the cancer in the future due to the toxic exposure. Under this rule, a plaintiff must do more than simply establish knowledge of a toxic ingestion or exposure and a significant increased risk of cancer. The plaintiff must further show that based upon reliable medical or scientific opinion, the plaintiff harbors a serious fear that the toxic ingestion or exposure was of such magnitude and proportion as to likely result in the feared cancer.

[But] we hold that a toxic exposure plaintiff need not meet the more likely than not threshold for fear of cancer recovery in a negligence action if the plaintiff pleads and proves that the defendant's conduct in causing the exposure amounts to "oppression, fraud, or malice" as defined in Civil Code section 3294, which authorizes the imposition of punitive damages. Thus, for instance, fear of cancer damages may be recovered without demonstrating that cancer is probable where it is shown that the defendant is guilty of "despicable conduct which is carried on by the defendant with a willful and conscious disregard of the rights or safety of others." . . .

In our view, Firestone's conduct brings this case within the "oppression, fraud or malice" exception for recovery of fear of cancer damages. . . .

[The court held similarly that the more likely than not threshold need not be met in an intentional infliction claim. It remanded for reconsideration but not necessarily denial of punitive damages. It approved the award of medical monitoring costs without regard to whether future cancer was more likely than not. Three judges concurred and dissented.]

Notes

1. Notice that *Potter* is a kind of stranger case, in the sense that the defendant was in no contractual relationship with the plaintiffs. So it would be difficult to treat Firestone like a doctor or other professional who might be viewed as undertaking a special duty to the patient under *Burgess*.

2. Notice also that the court emphasized heavily its concern with mass torts. Given the mass tort element and the stranger element, would the California Court impose a similar more-likely-than-not rule, or any other special limiting rule when (a) the defendant is in a special relationship with the plaintiff and (b) the threat of mass exposure is not present?

3. In *Kerins v. Hartley,* 27 Cal.App.4th 1062, 33 Cal.Rptr.2d 172 (1994) Dr. Gordon performed surgery upon the plaintiff to remove a large uterine tumor at a time when he was infected with HIV, the AIDS virus, and when he allegedly knew of his infection. Since the plaintiff patient had insisted that she wanted no surgery except by a healthy surgeon, the court originally held that she stated a good claim for emotional distress and for a battery based on the prohibited touching. The Supreme Court ordered a reconsideration in the light of *Potter*. On reconsideration, the Court of Appeal held that the plaintiff had no claim for emotional distress, not even during a "window of anxiety" period before testing could confirm that she did not suffer from HIV infection. It thought all the policy reasons given in *Potter* applied to an individual's suit against her doctor. Since AIDS infection was feared, but not more-likely-than-not, she could not recover.

HARTWIG v. OREGON TRAIL EYE CLINIC

Supreme Court of Nebraska, 1998.
254 Neb. 777, 580 N.W.2d 86.

Gerrard, Justice. . . .

[Hartwig worked for a cleaning service, cleaning non-medical trash at a the defendant clinic. When she lifted a trash bag, a needle in the bag penetrated her leg. An employee swabbed the site and applied a bandage. The employee then asked Hartwig to retrieve the needle. In so doing, Hartwig was stuck by yet another needle disposed of in the non-medical trash. A disease control nurse then called Hartwig to discuss the risks of AIDS and hepatitis B, warning her that intercourse with her husband would put him at risk. Hartwig underwent vaccinations and tests for a period of months. Eventually after a negative test three months later, authorities concluded that, to a 95% probability, she was not infected. The clinic was unable to identify the patients upon whom the needles had been used. For reasons not explained at trial, the clinic did not test the needles themselves.]

... Prior to trial, the district court sustained the Clinic's motion in limine to exclude testimony concerning Hartwig's mental anguish occasioned by her fear that she had indeed been infected with HIV. The court concluded that to recover such damages, Hartwig would have to prove actual exposure to HIV.

By way of offers of proof at trial, Hartwig offered the deposition testimony of her husband, Roger Hartwig, who, if allowed to testify, would have stated that during the 6–month period after her accident, Hartwig would disappear into a room and cry for hours on end, was impatient with their children, and showed no affection for him or their children. He would also have testified that Hartwig was shunned by their friends because of the friends' irrational fear of HIV infection....

At the close of the evidence, the trial court sustained Hartwig's motion for a directed verdict as to the Clinic's negligence. However, regarding the issue of damages, the court instructed the jury that it

> may not award any damages to [Hartwig] for anxiety, emotional distress or mental suffering alleged to have been sustained or incurred by her or her husband, Roger Hartwig, as the result of fear of contracting AIDS or fear or anxiety of testing positive for the presence of the HIV virus or other infectious disease.

The jury returned a $3,000 verdict in favor of Hartwig, and judgment was entered accordingly. Hartwig's motion for new trial was overruled, and she timely appealed....

The question presented in this matter is purely one of law: Whether a plaintiff who sustains a minimal physical injury, caused by the defendant's negligence, may recover damages for anxiety and mental suffering occasioned by his or her fear of testing HIV positive and contracting AIDS, absent a showing of actual exposure to blood or body fluid infected with HIV. We note that in her amended petition, Hartwig pled a cause of action in simple negligence resulting from the Clinic's failure to properly dispose of medical waste, not a cause of action for negligent infliction of emotional distress....

[T]he Clinic contends that only a severe injury can reasonably cause anxiety and mental suffering sufficient for compensation. Accordingly, the Clinic asserts that it is only when a plaintiff such as Hartwig is actually exposed to HIV that such plaintiff suffers a severe injury for which it is reasonable to conclude that anxiety and mental anguish are a consequence.

This argument is the basis of the "actual exposure" rule, which the Clinic asserts is the majority rule, having been adopted in 13 jurisdictions. Although the Clinic is correct in claiming that the actual exposure rule is the majority rule, the application of this rule has not been as widespread as the Clinic suggests–particularly when one considers the wide variety of factual contexts in which the "fear-of-AIDS" question has been presented.

The vast majority of the fear-of-AIDS cases have been pled as negligent infliction of emotional distress claims. Only a handful of cases have been tried on the theory presented in the instant appeal–as parasitic damages consequent to a physical injury." . . .

For the most part, those jurisdictions that have required an actual exposure to HIV as a prerequisite to recovery for mental distress damages do so in order to objectively quantify the reasonableness of a plaintiff's fear of contracting AIDS.

In order for one to have an actual exposure to HIV, there is a necessary confluence of two factors. First, there must be an exposure to tissue, blood, or body fluid infected with HIV, and second, the exposure to the infected tissue, blood, or body fluid must be by way of a channel of communication or transmission deemed medically or scientifically sufficient to cause an HIV infection. When both factors are capable of proof or disproof, the actual exposure rule functions as a viable means through which the reasonableness of a plaintiff's fear of AIDS may be objectively tested. . . .

Many of the cases cited by the Clinic in support of the actual exposure rule involve this sort of factual context, that is, cases in which HIV exposure and a medically sufficient channel of transmission were capable of proof or disproof. [The court cited 11 cases requiring exposure and a channel of transmission where those elements were capable of proof one way or another.]

Application of the actual exposure rule in such cases is inapposite to the case at bar for the reason that it is not unreasonable to fear HIV infection or AIDS when one such as Hartwig is exposed via a medically sufficient channel of transmission to the tissue, blood, or body fluid of another and it is impossible or impracticable to ascertain whether that tissue, blood, or body fluid is in fact HIV positive. When this narrower factual issue is examined, the actual exposure rule is neither the majority rule nor is it persuasive in the context of the instant case.

The Clinic cited three cases in which courts have required that a plaintiff must suffer an actual exposure to HIV-infected blood or body fluid as a prerequisite for recovery of emotional damages notwithstanding the fact that it was impossible or impracticable to ascertain whether the suspected infectious agent was contaminated. . . .

The logical flaw running through this line of cases is the failure of these courts to recognize the fact that modern medicine treats a potential exposure to HIV virtually the same as it treats an actual exposure to HIV. When a person such as Hartwig is potentially exposed to HIV through a medically viable channel of transmission, the applicable standard of medical care requires that such person conduct his or her life as if they were actually exposed to HIV-positive tissue, blood, or body fluid until such a time that a blood test reveals, to a certain statistical level of confidence, that such person is HIV negative.

We think it inconsistent to suggest that during the period of time in which such person is required by competent medical advice to conduct his or her life as though he or she were HIV infected, the law would conclude that it is unreasonable, speculative, fanciful, or whimsical for such person to have a real and intense fear that he or she is HIV positive and may suffer a slow, agonizing death from AIDS. The cases requiring an actual exposure when such is incapable of proof fail to give deference to the fact that from the time of exposure until after successive blood tests indicate that such a person is HIV negative, the genuineness of that person's mental anguish resulting from a fear of AIDS is medically beyond dispute. . . .

[A]pplication of the actual exposure rule is antithetical to the goal of objective quantification of the reasonableness and genuineness of one's claimed fear of AIDS in circumstances where (1) the identity of the patient upon whom the contaminated needle or instrument was used is unknown and (2) it is impossible or impracticable to prove or disprove that the suspect tissue, blood, or body fluid was in fact HIV positive, even though the injury occurred via a medically sufficient channel of transmission. . . .

[Remanded for trial on the issue of damages.]

Notes

1. When the plaintiff is actually exposed to HIV, recovery for the resulting distress does not seem to be a problem even if the plaintiff suffers no physical harm. See *John and Jane Roes, 1–100 v. FHP, Inc.,* 91 Hawai'i 470, 985 P.2d 661 (1999). Recovery is limited to harms inflicted in the window of anxiety, that is, to the time before testing indicates to a high probability that HIV infection is unlikely. However, emotional harm in this period might conceivably cause permanent emotional harm for which damages should be assessed.

2. Several state supreme court cases are in accord with the Nebraska Court in permitting recovery in at least some cases even though exposure is not established. See *Chizmar v. Mackie,* 896 P.2d 196 (Alaska 1995) (misdiagnosis of AIDS); *Faya v. Almaraz,* 329 Md. 435, 620 A.2d 327 (1993) (doctor with AIDS infection); *South Central Regional Med. Ctr. v. Pickering,* 749 So.2d 95 (Miss.1999) (unsafe disposal of instruments, rebuttable presumption in favor of the plaintiff); *Williamson v. Waldman,* 150 N.J. 232, 696 A.2d 14 (1997) (reasonable fear standard, imputing to the plaintiff "that level of knowledge of the disease that is then-current, accurate, and generally available to the public"); *Madrid v. Lincoln County Medical Center,* 122 N.M. 269, 923 P.2d 1154 (N.M. 1996) (blood containers leaked onto plaintiff's hand; plaintiff had papercuts, but did not know whether blood was infected); cf. *Howard v. Alexandria Hosp.,* 245 Va. 346, 429 S.E.2d 22 (1993) (unsterile instruments used, actionable without mention of exposure rules; the "plaintiff sustained positive, physical and mental hurt"). Connecticut

cautiously avoided adopting the actual exposure rule but found that fear was unreasonable on the facts in *Barrett v. Danbury Hospital*, 232 Conn. 242, 654 A.2d 748 (1995).

3. A "majority" of courts considering the issue say "actual exposure" is required, meaning that there must be a channel of exposure and also a virus or toxin must be shown to exist. This majority is composed in part of several trial and intermediate court opinions and several of those are from one state, New York. However, there are also decisions of the high courts of several states that also adopt the twin exposure requirements. Some of these involve needle sticks or scalpel cuts in circumstances similar to those in *Hartwig*. E.g., *Majca v. Beekil*, 183 Ill.2d 407, 233 Ill.Dec. 810, 701 N.E.2d 1084 (1998); *Carroll v. Sisters of Saint Francis*, 868 S.W.2d 585 (Tenn.1993). Some of the judges fear that ignorant people would flood the courts with claims based upon unfounded fears unless the exposure rules were adopted. Why not simply require reasonable fear?

4. In *K.A.C. v. Benson*, 527 N.W.2d 553 (Minn.1995), the defendant was a medical doctor who had developed lesions on his hands and forearms and exudative sores. He eventually tested HIV positive. He wore two pairs of gloves while performing gynecological examinations upon the plaintiff, but the Board of Medical Examiners and the Minnesota Department of Health provided a letter from Dr. Benson to 336 patients on whom Dr. Benson performed one or more invasive procedures during his exudative dermatitis period. The letter emphasized that the risk of HIV infection was very small, but recommended AIDS testing. *Brzoska v. Olson*, 668 A.2d 1355 (Del.1995) was somewhat similar except that it involved an AIDS-positive dentist and his patients. In suits by patients upon whom the doctors performed gynecological examinations or did dental work, can you determine (a) how the case would be decided under the pair of "actual exposure" rules? (b) How *Hartwig* would decide the case? (c) How the case *should* be decided?

5. What do you make of the *Hartwig* court's point about parasitic damages? What counts as a physical injury that will invoke this rule? In *Temple-Inland Forest Products Corp. v. Carter*, 993 S.W.2d 88 (Tex.1999) two workers were exposed to extensive asbestos dust for weeks before the defendant told them what it was. The doctor said they had been physically injured by inhalation of the dust, but that injury was producing no present symptoms. On the other hand, the likelihood that they would suffer asbestos related diseases in the future was greatly increased. The court acknowledged the rule that physical injury warrants mental distress recovery, but held that at least in the case of asbestos, where future disease was highly uncertain, recovery for emotional distress would not be allowed. Although the court acknowledged that the fear was both real and reasonable, it also said that claimants would be overcompensated if it turned out no disease eventuated.

REFERENCE: DOBBS ON TORTS §§ 302–16 (2000).

Chapter 18

PRENATAL HARMS

§ 1. PRENATAL AND PRECONCEPTION INJURY

NOTE: PRENATAL INJURY

1. *Traditional rule.* A pregnant woman is injured by defendant's negligence. She herself may have a claim for her injury. If the fetus is also injured is there an additional claim? Suppose, for example, a physician negligently prescribes a drug to the mother and the child is born with serious defects. In *Dietrich v. Northampton*, 138 Mass. 14 (1884), Holmes took the view that there could be no action. The opinion suggested the absence of precedent, "remoteness" and the logical problem of injuring a being "before he became a person," but gave little justice or policy reasoning.

2. *Contemporary rules: child born alive.* The *Dietrich* decision held sway for many years. Judicial reversals began shortly after the end of World War II and today most courts would allow the action when the child was born alive. Some have insisted that the child must also be viable–capable of living independent of the mother–at the time of the injury. But that requirement seems strikingly unrelated to the reality of suffering after a live birth. When the child is born alive, then, courts generally reject any requirement of viability. *Torigian v. Watertown News Co.*, 352 Mass. 446, 225 N.E.2d 926 (1967); *Kalafut v. Gruver*, 239 Va. 278, 389 S.E.2d 681 (1990).

3. *Contemporary rules: not born alive but viable at injury.* (a) Most courts passing on the question now appear to hold that the a wrongful death action is allowable when a fetus is stillborn, at least when the fetus was viable at the time of injury. A Texas court has even held it unconstitutional as a denial of equal protection to exclude liability when a viable fetus is injured and then stillborn. *Parvin v. Dean*, 7 S.W.3d 264 (Tex. App. 1999). (b) But extreme cases refuse to impose any responsibility upon a negligent defendant who injures a fetus if the fetus is stillborn. See *Chatelain v. Kelley*, 322 Ark. 517, 910 S.W.2d 215 (1995) (if doctor negligently caused the "death" of a full-term child just before

Caesarean section, that would not be actionable, since a fetus not born alive is not a person); *Shaw v. Jendzejec,* 717 A.2d 367 (Me.1998).

4. *Contemporary rules: not born alive and not viable at injury or thereafter.* (a) The variables are weakest for the plaintiff when the fetus was not born alive and was never viable at any time. Most courts reject liability here. E.g., *Santana v. Zilog,* Inc., 95 F.3d 780 (9th Cir.1996); *Crosby v. Glasscock Trucking Co.,* Inc., 532 S.E.2d 856 (S.C. 2000). (b) However, a few cases have supported liability under wrongful death statutes for loss of a fetus that was never viable. *Wiersma v. Maple Leaf Farms,* 543 N.W.2d 787 (S.D.1996); *Farley v. Sartin,* 195 W.Va. 671, 466 S.E.2d 522 (1995). *Nealis v. Baird,* 996 P.2d 438 (Okla.1999) holds that liability can be imposed for death of a fetus that was never viable if it was "born alive," that is, had an instant of life outside the womb even though it was incapable of sustaining life apart from the mother.

5. *In summary.* If the child is born alive, most courts recognize that she has an action for tortiously inflicted prenatal injury regardless whether she was viable at the time of injury or not. When the child is stillborn and never lives, a wrongful death recovery is more likely to be permitted if the fetus was viable at some time during gestation. Divergent cases can be found on both points, however.

Notes

1.   Should courts hold a mother liable to her child for ingesting dangerous substances while pregnant? Or for failing to get appropriate pre-natal care? See *Stallman v. Youngquist,* 125 Ill.2d 267, 126 Ill.Dec. 60, 531 N.E.2d 355 (1988); *Chenault v. Huie,* 989 S.W.2d 474 (Tex.App.1999) (child suffering permanent and serious harm because of mother's use of cocaine during pregnancy).

2.   In *Roe v. Wade,* 410 U.S. 113, 93 S.Ct. 705, 35 L.Ed.2d 147 (1973) the Supreme Court held that a woman has a right to decide for herself whether to have an abortion during the first trimester of pregnancy and that the states may not prohibit this. The Court refused to overrule that decision in *Planned Parenthood of Southeastern Pa. v. Casey,* 505 U.S. 833, 112 S.Ct. 2791, 120 L.Ed.2d 674 (1992). Should this bear on tort liability for injury inflicted during that period?

RENSLOW v. MENNONITE HOSPITAL, 67 Ill.2d 348, 10 Ill.Dec. 484, 367 N.E.2d 1250, 91 A.L.R.3d 291 (1977). When plaintiff's mother was 13 years of age, defendants negligently transfused her with Rh-positive blood. This was incompatible with her own blood, though she had no knowledge of this at the time. Years later when she became pregnant she discovered that her blood had become sensitized by this negligent transfusion. As a result of this her child, the plaintiff, was born jaundiced and suffering from hyperbilirubinemia. She has suffered various damages for which she here sues. The trial judge dismissed the claim because plaintiff had not been conceived at the time of the alleged negligence. *Held*, the plaintiff states a claim for relief. Although foreseeability alone does not establish a duty, a duty of care may be owed to one who may be foreseeably harmed, even if the person is unknown or is remote in time or place. The defendants argue a need for an end of liability somewhere and "raise the spector of successive generations of plaintiffs complaining against a single defendant for harm caused by genetic damage done an ancestor," but the judiciary "will effectively exercise its traditional role of drawing rational distinction, consonant with current perceptions of justice, between harms which are compensable and those which are not."

ALBALA v. CITY OF NEW YORK, 54 N.Y.2d 269, 445 N.Y.S.2d 108, 429 N.E.2d 786 (1981). Ruth Albala underwent an abortion at Bellevue Hospital during which her uterus was perforated. The plaintiff Jeffrey Albala was born some four years later. This action on his behalf claims he suffered brain damage as a result of his mother's negligently perforated uterus. *Held*, this does not state a good cause of action. Although harm of this kind was foreseeable, foreseeability alone does not establish a duty to the plaintiff. And although New York recognizes prenatal injury claims, those cases are not controlling here because in those cases "there are two identifiable beings within the zone of danger each of whom is owed a duty independent of the other and each of whom may be directly injured." Were liability established in this case, it would be difficult to preclude liability "where a negligent motorist collides with another vehicle containing a female passenger who sustains a punctured uterus ... and subsequently gives birth to a deformed child," and the "staggering implications are manifest.... [R]ecognition of a cause of action under the circumstances of this case would have the undesirable impact of encouraging the practice of 'defensive medicine.' A physician faced with the alternative of saving a patient's life by administering a treatment involving the possibility of adverse consequences to later conceived off-spring of that patient would, if exposed to liability of the magnitude considered in this case, undoubtedly be inclined to advise against treatment rather than risk the possibility of having to recompense a child born with a handicap." This would place "physicians in a direct conflict between their moral duty to patients and the proposed legal duty to those hypothetical future generations outside the immediate zone of danger."

Notes

1. Suppose that, in 1970, D builds a defective building. At the time there is no other building around, though it is foreseeable that others will be built. In 1992 another building is completed adjacent to D's building. D's building, because of its defect, collapses and causes harm to the new building. Should New York allow a recovery if *Albala* is still recognized authority in that state?

2. *DES grandchildren.* A number of manufacturers once marketed a drug, DES, for use by pregnant women. The drug turned out to cause

cancers and a number of other problems for the daughters of the women who ingested the drug. In several ways, New York has recognized that the manufacturer of the drug would be liable to the DES daughter. E.g., *Hymowitz v. Eli Lilly & Co.*, 73 N.Y.2d 487, 541 N.Y.S.2d 941, 539 N.E.2d 1069 (1989). Is that inconsistent with *Albala*? What if it is a DES granddaughter rather than a DES daughter who suffers? See *Enright v. Eli Lilly & Co.*, 77 N.Y.2d 377, 568 N.Y.S.2d 550, 570 N.E.2d 198 (1991).

3. A number of cases are in accord with *Renslow* on various facts. E.g., *Lynch v. Scheininger,* 162 N.J. 209, 744 A.2d 113 (2000); see DOBBS ON TORTS § 290 (2000). In a state that follows *Renslow*, Defendant negligently injures Christine Taylor in an auto accident. She requires hospitalization and operations twenty-five times as a result and still suffers some deformity of pelvic bones. Seven years later she gives birth to a child, whose head is damaged because during gestation it was shaped by the deformed pelvic bones. If the court would impose liability under *Renslow*, would it also impose liability on these facts? *Taylor v. Cutler,* 306 N.J.Super. 37, 703 A.2d 294 (1997), aff'd, 157 N.J. 525, 724 A.2d 793 (1999).

§ 2. WRONGFUL LIFE, BIRTH, OR CONCEPTION

GRECO v. UNITED STATES

Supreme Court of Nevada, 1995.
111 Nev. 405, 893 P.2d 345.

SPRINGER, JUSTICE. . . .

The Grecos, mother and child, in this case seek to recover damages from the United States arising out of the negligence of physicians who, they claim, negligently failed to make a timely diagnosis of physical defects and anomalies afflicting the child when it was still in the mother's womb. Sundi Greco asserts that the physicians' negligence denied her the opportunity to terminate her pregnancy and thereby caused damages attendant to the avoidable birth of an unwanted and severely deformed child. On Joshua's behalf, Sundi Greco avers that the physicians' negligence and the resultant denial of Joshua's mother's right to terminate her pregnancy caused Joshua to be born into a grossly abnormal life of pain and deprivation.

These kinds of tort claims have been termed "wrongful birth" when brought by a parent and "wrongful life" when brought on behalf of the child for the harm suffered by being born deformed.

We decline to recognize any action by a child for defects claimed to have been caused to the child by negligent diagnosis or treatment of the child's mother. . . . Implicit in [the wrongful life claim] is the assumption that the child would be better off had he never been born. These kinds of judgments are very difficult, if not impossible, to make. Indeed, most courts considering the question have denied this cause of action for precisely this reason. Recognizing this kind of claim on behalf of the child would require us to weigh the harms suffered by virtue of the child's having been born with severe handicaps against "the utter void of nonexistence"; this is a calculation the courts are incapable of performing. Gleitman v. Cosgrove, 49 N.J. 22, 227 A.2d 689, 692 (1967). The New York Court of Appeals framed the problem this way:

> Whether it is better never to have been born at all than to have been born with even gross deficiencies is a mystery more properly to be left to the philosophers and the theologians. Surely the law can assert no competence to resolve the issue, particularly in view of the very nearly uniform high value which the law and mankind has placed on human life, rather than its absence.

Becker v. Schwartz, 46 N.Y.2d 401, 413 N.Y.S.2d 895, 900, 386 N.E.2d 807, 812 (1978). We conclude that Nevada does not recognize a claim by a child for harms the child claims to have suffered by virtue of having been born.

With regard to Sundi Greco's claim against her physician for negligent diagnosis or treatment during pregnancy, we see no reason for compounding or complicating our medical malpractice jurisprudence by according this particular form of professional negligence action some special status apart from presently recognized medical malpractice or by giving it the new name of "wrongful birth." Sundi Greco either does or does not state a claim for medical malpractice; and we conclude that she does.

Medical malpractice, like other forms of negligence, involves a breach of duty which causes injury.... In the case before us, we must accept as fact that Sundi Greco's physicians negligently failed to perform prenatal medical tests or performed or interpreted those tests in a negligent fashion and that they thereby negligently failed to discover and reveal that Sundi Greco was carrying a severely deformed fetus. As a result of such negligence Sundi Greco claims that she was denied the opportunity to terminate her pregnancy and that this denial resulted in her giving birth to a severely deformed child.

It is difficult to formulate any sound reason for denying recovery to Sundi Greco in the case at hand. Sundi Greco is saying, in effect, to her doctors: "If you had done what you were supposed to do, I would have known early in my pregnancy that I was carrying a severely deformed baby. I would have then terminated the pregnancy and would not have had to go through the mental and physical agony of delivering this child, nor would I have had to bear the emotional suffering attendant to the birth and nurture of the child, nor the extraordinary expense necessary to care for a child suffering from such extreme deformity and disability."

The United States advances two reasons for denying Sundi Greco's claim: first, it argues that she has suffered no injury and that, therefore, the damage element of negligent tort liability is not fulfilled; second, the United States argues that even if Sundi Greco has sustained injury and damages, the damages were not caused by her physicians. To support its first argument, the United States points out that in Szekeres v. Robinson, 102 Nev. 93, 715 P.2d 1076 (1986), this court held that the mother of a normal, healthy child could not recover in tort from a physician who negligently performed her sterilization operation because the birth of a normal, healthy child is not a legally cognizable injury. The United States argues that no distinction can be made between a mother who gives birth to a healthy child and a mother who gives birth to a child with severe deformities and that, therefore, Szekeres bars recovery.

Szekeres can be distinguished from the instant case. Unlike the birth of a normal child, the birth of a severely deformed baby of the kind described here is necessarily an unpleasant and aversive event and the cause of inordinate financial burden that would not attend the birth of a normal child. The child in this case will unavoidably and necessarily require the expenditure of extraordinary medical, therapeutic and custodial care expenses by the family, not to mention the additional reserves of physical, mental and emotional strength that will be required of all concerned. Those who do not wish to undertake the many burdens associated with the birth and continued care of such a child have the legal right, under Roe v. Wade and codified by the voters of this state, to terminate their pregnancies. Roe v. Wade, 410 U.S. 113, 93 S.Ct. 705, 35 L.Ed.2d 147 (1973); NRS 442.250 (codifying by referendum the conditions under which abortion is permitted in this state). Sundi Greco has certainly suffered money damages as a result of her physician's malpractice.

We also reject the United States' second argument that Sundi Greco's physicians did not cause any of the injuries that Sundi Greco might have suffered. We note that the mother is not claiming that her child's defects were caused by her physicians' negligence; rather, she claims that her physicians' negligence kept her ignorant of those defects and that it was this negligence which caused her to lose her right to choose whether to carry the child to term. The damage Sundi Greco has sustained is indeed causally related to her physicians' malpractice.

. . . If we were to deny Sundi Greco's claim, we would, in effect, be groundlessly excepting one type of medical malpractice from negligence liability. We see no reason to treat this case any differently from any other medical malpractice case. Sundi Greco has stated a prima facie claim of medical malpractice under Nevada law. . . .

This claim for damages relates to the medical, therapeutic and custodial costs associated with caring for a severely handicapped child. There is nothing exceptional in allowing this item of damage. It is a recognized principle of tort law to "afford compensation for injuries sustained by one person as the result of the conduct of another." W. Page Keeton, et al., Prosser and Keeton on the Law of Torts, § 2 at 6 (5th ed. 1984). Extraordinary care expenses are a foreseeable result of the negligence alleged in this case, and Sundi Greco should be allowed to recover those expenses if she can prove them. This leads us to the question of how to compensate for these kinds of injuries.

Sundi Greco correctly observes that Nevada law requires the parents of a handicapped child to support that child beyond the age of majority if the child cannot support itself. Nevada recognizes the right of a parent to recover from a tortfeasor any expenses the parent was required to pay because of the injury to his or her minor child. Accordingly, Sundi Greco claims the right to recover damages for these extraordinary costs for a period equal to Joshua's life expectancy. Other states which require parents to care for handicapped children past the age of majority allow plaintiffs to recover these types of damages for the lifetime of the child or until such time as the child is no longer dependent on her or his parents. We agree with these authorities and conclude that Sundi Greco may recover extraordinary medical and custodial expenses associated with caring for Joshua for whatever period of time it is established that Joshua will be dependent upon her to provide such care.

The United States contends that if this court allows the mother to recover such extraordinary medical and custodial expenses, then it should require the district court to offset any such award by the amount it would cost to raise a non-handicapped child. To do otherwise, argues the United States, would be to grant the mother a windfall.

The offset rule has its origins in two doctrines: the "avoidable consequences rule," which requires plaintiffs to mitigate their damages in tort cases, and the expectancy rule of damages employed in contract cases, which seeks to place the plaintiff in the position he or she would have been in had the contract been performed. We conclude that neither of these doctrines is applicable to the case at bar. To enforce the "avoidable consequences" rule in the instant case would impose unreasonable burdens upon the mother such as, perhaps, putting Joshua up for adoption or otherwise seeking to terminate her parental obligations.

With regard to the expectancy rule, it would unnecessarily complicate and limit recovery for patients in other malpractice cases if we were to begin intruding contract damage principles upon our malpractice jurisprudence. The rule for compensatory damages in negligence cases is clear and workable, and we decline to depart from it.

The United States contends that Sundi Greco should not be allowed to recover any damages for the services of her child lost due to the child's handicap, because Sundi Greco claims that but for the negligence of her physician she would never have carried her pregnancy to term. It follows then, that if the child had not been born, Sundi Greco would have had far less in terms of service and companionship than what she can currently expect from her handicapped child. . . . [T]he crux of Sundi Greco's claim is that she would have aborted the fetus had she been given the opportunity to do so. In that case, she would have had no services or companionship at all. We thus conclude that Sundi Greco may not recover for lost services or companionship.

Sundi Greco asserts that she is suffering and will continue to suffer tremendous mental and emotional pain as a result of the birth of Joshua. Several jurisdictions allow plaintiffs such as Sundi Greco to recover such damages. In line with these cases, we agree that it is reasonably foreseeable that a mother who is denied her right to abort a severely deformed fetus will suffer emotional distress, not just when the child is delivered, but for the rest of the child's life. Consequently, we conclude that the mother in this case should have the opportunity to prove that she suffered and will continue to suffer emotional distress as a result of the birth of her child.

We reject the United States' argument that this court should follow an "offset" rule with regard to damages for emotional distress. Any emotional benefits are simply too speculative to be considered by a jury in awarding emotional distress damages. As Dean Prosser observes: "In the case of the wrongful birth of a severely impaired child, it would appear that the usual joys of parenthood would often be substantially overshadowed by the emotional trauma of caring for the child in such a condition, so that application of the benefit rule would appear inappropriate in this context." Prosser and Keeton on the Law of Torts, supra, § 55 at 371 n. 48. It is beyond cavil, for example, that "[t]here is no joy in watching a child suffer and die from cystic fibrosis." Schroeder v. Perkel, 87 N.J. 53, 432 A.2d 834, 842 (1981). Moreover, it would unduly complicate the jury's task to require it to weigh one intangible harm against another intangible benefit.

We conclude that a mother may maintain a medical malpractice action under Nevada law based on her physicians' failure properly to perform or interpret prenatal examinations when that failure results in the mother losing the opportunity to abort a severely deformed fetus. Sundi Greco should be given the right to prove that she has suffered and will continue to suffer damages in the form of emotional or mental distress and that she has incurred and will continue to incur extraordinary medical and custodial care expenses associated with raising Joshua. We decline to recognize the tort sometimes called "wrongful life."

[Two justices argued that the child himself should have a cause of action for the extraordinary expenses.]

Notes

1. *Wrongful birth*. A substantial number of courts have now upheld the claim on behalf of the parents for wrongful birth based on the defendant's failure to diagnose or inform the mother that a fetus was in genetic difficulty. E.g., *Lininger v. Eisenbaum*, 764 P.2d 1202 (Colo.1988). A few reject the claim entirely. E.g., *Etkind v. Suarez*, 271 Ga. 352, 519 S.E.2d 210 (1999).

2. *Wrongful conception cases*. A wrongful conception claim is usually a claim that the defendant physician failed to prevent conception because he negligently performed a sterilization procedure such as a vasectomy. The child in such cases is normally a healthy child, but the parents, who had attempted to avoid pregnancy and childbirth, will now face financial costs they would have avoided if the defendant had exercised reasonable care. In addition, if they were emotionally unable to care for children, they will almost certainly have increased emotional difficulties. Some courts have recognized such claims. What if the reason for the failed sterilization procedure was the parent's economic needs rather than a genetic risk, but

the child in fact suffered genetic defects? See *Pitre v. Opelousas General Hospital*, 530 So.2d 1151, 74 A.L.R.4th 777 (La. 1988). Some legislatures have forbidden courts to entertain these claims. See *Thibeault v. Larson*, 666 A.2d 112 (Me.1995).

3. *Wrongful fertilization*. No claim goes by the name of wrongful fertilization, but consider *Harnicher v. University of Utah Med. Cntr.*, 962 P.2d 67 (Utah 1998). The plaintiffs there were husband and wife who agreed to in vitro fertilization to promote the chance of pregnancy. They agreed to a specific sperm donor whose blood type and physical appearance matched the husband's and to a fertilization technique in which the donor's sperm and the husband's were mixed so that the plaintiffs could at least hope that any child born was the husband's and could present the child to others as his child. The defendants did not use sperm of the selected donor but of a different donor. Triplets were born and at least some of them have such a physical appearance that observers would think they are not the husband's. The husband and wife are greatly distressed and have plenty of physical symptoms but no bodily injury or illness. If the jurisdiction recognizes wrongful conception, must it logically also recognize this claim? Utah denied the claim under its rule requiring bodily injury to support an emotional harm claim.

4. *Wrongful life*. There is no support in the cases for a general wrongful life claim, as distinct from a wrongful birth or wrongful conception claim. The child, in other words, cannot recover for being born. However, several courts have permitted the child to recover the cost of extraordinary care in his own name. Notice that this element of damages is one that would otherwise be recoverable by the parents in the wrongful birth claim, so it adds nothing to the defendant's liability.

5. *Damages for emotional harm*. Some courts have been reluctant to award damages for emotional harm in wrongful birth cases. Where such damages are recoverable, would the plaintiff be required to show she was in the zone of danger or that she suffered physical injury from her emotional distress? Or can the plaintiff state an ordinary tort claim with emotional distress as parasitic damage? DAN DOBBS, LAW OF REMEDIES § 8.2 (1992). In *Bader v. Johnson*, 732 N.E.2d 1212 (Ind.2000), the court held that so-called wrongful birth actions were merely medical malpractice actions, that general rules of negligence applied, and that all damages proximately caused by the defendant's negligence would be recoverable.

6. *Damages for child-rearing costs*. "Courts that have recognized the wrongful birth claims have allowed a recovery for some of the expenses of rearing the child. The same rule has been applied to the liability of an adoption agency which misrepresents the adoptive child's health. Recovery is usually limited, however, to the 'extraordinary' expenses, those over and above the ordinary expenses of child rearing." DOBBS, supra note 5.

7. *Damages in wrongful conception cases: the healthy but unwanted child*. In wrongful conception cases, most courts have allowed recovery for the mother's pain in pregnancy, and medical costs of pregnancy, abortion, or birth, as well as any lost wages during this period. However, most courts have denied recovery for the cost of rearing the healthy child. "The parents of a normal, healthy child whom they now love have not suffered any injury

or damage," the Kentucky Court said bluntly. *Schork v. Huber*, 648 S.W.2d 861 (Ky.1983). Other courts have emphasized similar ideas, and have said that the damages are speculative or out of proportion to the defendant's fault, or that the avoidable consequences rule would require the plaintiff-mother to have an abortion or put the child up for adoption. A number of recent decisions, however, have framed rules permitting recovery even in healthy-child cases. E.g., *Zehr v. Haugen,* 318 Or. 647, 871 P.2d 1006 (1994); *Marciniak v. Lundborg*, 153 Wis.2d 59, 450 N.W.2d 243 (1990).

WILSON v. KUENZI, 751 S.W.2d 741 (Mo.1988). A mother of a Downs Syndrome child alleged that the defendant doctor had not advised her that she was of high risk (at age 37) or that amniocentesis was available to test for this genetic disorder. She alleged that as a result of having no information, she was denied an opportunity to make an informed decision whether to have an abortion. A state statute provided that "No person shall maintain a cause of action or receive an award of damages on behalf of himself or herself based on the claim that but for the negligent conduct of another, he or she would have been aborted." A similar provision forbad an action based on a claim that but for another's negligence, "a child would have been aborted." The court interpreted this statute as intended to preclude wrongful life and wrongful birth actions. But the statute was a new one and had no application to the case, which had arisen earlier. The court went on to decide, on common law grounds, that neither the mother nor the child could maintain any suit.

> "All, in our opinion, have either closed their eyes to the requirements of causation; or, have blended causation into social policy reasons for permitting recovery; or have blended causation into the discussion of the types of damage permitted to be recovered. . . . In the wrongful birth action, the right to recovery is based solely on the woman testifying, long after the fact and when it is in her financial interest to do so, that she would have chosen to abort if the physician had but told her of the amniocentesis test. The percentage of women who under pressure refuse to consider abortion, whether for reasons of religious belief, strong motherly instincts, or for other reasons, is sometimes astounding. It would seem that testimony either more verifiable based upon experience or more verifiable by some objective standard should be required as the basis for any action for substantial damages."

Note

Notice that all testimony by plaintiffs is given by one who has a financial interest; so is all testimony by defendants. Notice also that much testimony is given long after the event as well. Finally, notice that although constitutional doctrine is not considered in the case, one effect of declaring that there is no common law suit is to bypass the question whether the statute is constitutional.

REFERENCE: (1) Prenatal injury, DOBBS ON TORTS § 288–289 (2000); HARPER, JAMES & GRAY, THE LAW OF TORTS § 18.3; (2) Preconception negligence, DOBBS ON TORTS § 290; (3) Wrongful life, birth or conception: DOBBS ON TORTS §§ 291–293.

Chapter 19

DEATH

"In a civil Court, the death of a human being could not be complained of as an injury...."

—Lord Ellenborough in *Baker v. Bolton*, 1 Camp. 493, 170 Eng. Rep. 1033 (1808).

Lord Ellenborough's statement meant or came to mean three separate things:

(1) If an injured person died before receiving judgment against the defendant, his cause of action died with him; put differently, the cause of action did not survive the death of the plaintiff.

(2) If an injured person remained alive after injury but the defendant died before a judgment was rendered against him, the plaintiff's cause of action died as well; put differently, the plaintiff's cause of action did not survive the death of the defendant.

(3) There was no separate cause of action on behalf of those who were dependent upon the deceased person.

In most states all of these rules have been changed; in all states one or more have been changed.[1] The first two rules have been changed by statutes generally known as "survival" statutes, because they provide that the cause of action survives the death of the plaintiff or the defendant or both. The third rule has been changed by statutes usually called "wrongful death" statutes, or "Lord Campbell's Acts" after the sponsor of the first such legislation.

Both kinds of claims follow the same substantive law of negligence, cause in fact, and proximate cause we see in other tort actions.

SMITH v. WHITAKER

Supreme Court of New Jersey, 1999.
160 N.J. 221, 734 A.2d 243.

STEIN, J.

[The defendant Whitaker, driving a Coastal oil truck, was unable to stop at an intersection due to maladjusted brakes. The truck struck the

---

1. In addition to state wrongful death statutes, the Federal Employers' Liability Act, 45 U.S.C.A. § 51, permits similar recoveries for employees of interstate railroads; the federal Jones Act does the same for employees at sea. 46 U.S.C.A. § 688.

vehicle of Helen Robbins, a sixty-year old widow and overtopped it. Immediately after the collision, Robbins appeared to be unconscious. She was pronounced dead at the hospital. Coastal's vehicle had failed safety inspections that called for removal from service, but Coastal continued to operate the vehicle in the "out of service" condition. Smith, executor of Robbins' estate, brought claims (1) under the wrongful death act and (2) under the Survivor's Act. The trial court dismissed the claim for pain and suffering (under the Survivor's Act) because there was no evidence that Robbins was conscious. The jury awarded $44,000 under the Wrongful Death Act for pecuniary loss to Robbins' survivors, including funeral expenses. The trial court then permitted evidence on the plaintiff's punitive damages claim. On that, the jury awarded $1,250,000. The Appellate Division affirmed.]

At common law, no civil remedy was available for a personal injury resulting in death, either to the decedent's estate or the decedent's dependents.... The "rigors of this harsh and technical rule were relaxed and ameliorated," first in 1848 by the Wrongful Death Act, now codified as N.J.S.A. 2A:31–1 to–6, and later in 1855 by the Survivor's Act, now codified as N.J.S.A. 2A:15–3.

Although both types of actions arise from the identical occurrence, i.e., the death of the plaintiff, they serve different purposes and are designed to provide a remedy to different parties. "The fundamental purpose of a wrongful death action is to compensate survivors for the pecuniary losses they suffer because of the tortious conduct of others."

An award of damages in a wrongful death action "is not a matter of punishment for an errant defendant or of providing for decedent's next of kin to a greater extent than decedent himself would have been able, but is rather a replacement for that which decedent would likely have provided and no more." The amount of recovery is based upon the contributions, reduced to monetary terms, which the decedent might reasonably have been expected to make to his or her survivors.

Consistent with its remedial purpose, damages under the Act are expressly limited to "the pecuniary injuries resulting from such death, together with the hospital, medical and funeral expenses incurred for the deceased."

Further, courts interpreting the Act have consistently held that it permits recovery only of a survivor's calculable economic loss and that the Act does not support an award of punitive damages....

[T]he critical issue before this Court is whether plaintiff established a valid claim for punitive damages under the Survivor's Act in the absence of an underlying award of compensatory damages for pain and suffering.

Some cases have permitted recoveries for death under the basic federal civil rights statute, 42 U.S.C.A. § 1983.

Survival actions, like wrongful-death actions, were unknown at common law. The death of the plaintiff gave his representative no remedy against the tortfeasor. In 1855, New Jersey passed the Executors and Administrators Act, or Survivor's Act ... allowing a decedent's representatives the right to bring an action for trespass to person or property in the same manner as if the decedent had been living. Unlike a wrongful death action, which is a derivative action arising in favor of beneficiaries named under that act, the Survivor's Act preserves to the decedent's estate any personal cause of action that decedent would have had if he or she had survived....

The Survivor's Act was intended to be supplementary to the Death Act and to "afford[] complete and adequate redress to the estates of those who were injured in person or property by injuries causing death," by allowing the decedent's estate to recover any loss to the decedent that accrued between injury and death....

The Survivor's Act, in contrast to the Wrongful Death Act, contains no express limitation on the types of damages recoverable under the statute. A majority of states have decided that punitive damages are recoverable in a survival action, the typical reasoning being that "[l]ogic dictates that if a wrongdoer may be punished if his victim lives, then surely he should not escape retribution if his wrongful act causes a death,"

As a rule, a claim for punitive damages may lie only where there is a valid underlying cause of action. In a negligence action, the maintenance of a valid claim requires the plaintiff to show a breach of duty and resulting damage. In this case, Coastal stipulated negligence and causation, leaving only the issue of damages for the jury's determination. Coastal argues that because pain and suffering comprise the sole compensable injury in a survival action, no punitive damages may be awarded in the absence of an underlying award of compensatory damages for such pain and suffering.

As Coastal notes, the primary damages recoverable in a survival action sounding in tort are for the decedent's pain and suffering between the time of injury and death. Damages for pain and suffering are permitted only for pain and suffering that is conscious. Many states, including New Jersey, have allowed recovery for conscious pain and suffering whenever it can be shown the injured person survived her injuries, however briefly.

In this case, plaintiff was unable to establish compensable pain and suffering due to the unfortunate circumstance that Robbins apparently was killed immediately upon impact with Coastal's vehicle. The question is whether a plaintiff's inability to establish conscious pain and suffering in a survival action involving instantaneous death bars a claim for punitive damages.

As the Appellate Division observed, the irony of a rule requiring conscious pain and suffering is that it makes the recoverability of punitive damages for egregious conduct resulting in death dependent on whether or not the victim died instantaneously. Nevertheless, some jurisdictions do consider conscious pain and suffering essential to any recovery of punitive damages. . . .

We previously have held that in some cases involving egregious conduct, a punitive damages claim may constitute plaintiff's sole basis for recovery, "at least where some injury, loss, or detriment to the plaintiff has occurred." In Nappe, we observed that the true "loss, injury, and detriment" suffered by plaintiff, in this case her death, is not necessarily coextensive with the "compensatory damages" awarded, which is merely "a monetary amount awarded in court to compensate or indemnify a plaintiff." When the value of a real legal injury cannot be measured in money, a plaintiff who has been substantially harmed may not be able to establish an entitlement to compensatory damages. Under such circumstances, we held in Nappe that a defendant should not be freed of responsibility for aggravated conduct because of the fortuitous circumstance that an injured plaintiff cannot prove compensatory damages. Rather, where a plaintiff suffers substantial legal injury due to a defendant's egregious conduct, nominal damages, supporting a claim of punitive damages, may be awarded to vindicate the invasion of plaintiff's rights. . . .

As Coastal points out, punitive damages awarded on a "free-standing" basis, i.e., without an award of compensatory damages in the underlying action, ordinarily must be premised on a valid judgment for, at a minimum, nominal damages. . . .

In 1995, the Legislature amended the Punitive Damages Act to require an award of compensatory damages as a statutory predicate for an award of punitive damages and disallowing nominal damages as a basis for a punitive damages claim. N.J.S.A. 2A:15–5.13(c). That provision did not take effect until October 27, 1995, and thus does not govern our disposition of this appeal. . . .

We recognize that an award of at least nominal damages ordinarily is required to sustain a punitive damages award. Even where a plaintiff has suffered a harm inestimable in terms of dollars and cents, an award of nominal damages serves to confirm the jury's finding that plaintiff has suffered a harm cognizable at law. That deficiency is not significant in these circumstances, however, where the elements of causation and defendant's negligence were established in the related wrongful death action. Thus, the only additional finding by the jury that was required to support a valid survival claim was a finding that Robbins was harmed. . . .

That a negligently-caused death constitutes a legally cognizable injury is irrefutable. Thus, where the other elements of a survival claim have been established in a related action pursuant to the Wrongful Death Act, we hold that to require an award of funeral expenses, compensatory damages for pain and suffering, or even nominal damages to support a claim for punitive damages under the Survivor's Act would be superfluous. Accordingly, where all of the essential elements of a punitive damages claim are established, such a claim may be sustained without proof of pain and suffering.

Notes

Survival Statutes

1. *Survival of claim after plaintiff's death.* A tort victim might bring a suit to redress a tort, then die before the suit goes to judgment. In that case, the claim is "revived" and continued in the name of the personal representative. Or, the victim might die without having brought suit, so that the claim is brought by the personal representative in the first place. Either way, the claim is a survival action. It is a species of property which passes to the estate of the deceased person in the same way a share of stock or a bank account might pass. The personal representative's recovery becomes an asset of the estate to be disbursed to pay the expenses of its administration, and to pay creditors and heirs or legatees.

2. *Survival of claim after defendant's death.* Survival statutes usually also provide for survival of the victim's claim after the defendant's death. In this setting, the living victim asserts the claim for all damages against the estate of the deceased tortfeasor. The case of the deceased victim is the more common one and it is the one discussed here.

3. *Survival damages.* Since the survival action continues the claim held by the decedent for damages accruing up until his death, it may include any medical expenses, wages lost before death, and pain and suffering resulting from the injury. In some states it may also include funeral expenses. Punitive damages are also appropriate if they would have been appropriate had the decedent lived.

4. *Coverage of survival statutes.* Some survival statutes may be applicable only if there is no wrongful death. More commonly, survival statutes exclude recovery for certain kinds of claims, such as those founded on libel or slander or other dignitary torts, or on intentional torts. Some of these limitations have been held unconstitutional. See *Moyer v. Phillips*, 462 Pa. 395, 341 A.2d 441, 77 A.L.R.3d 1339 (1975) (libel and slander).

Wrongful Death Statutes

5. *Measures of damages for wrongful death.* Wrongful death statutes traditionally aimed to replace pecuniary losses that would be suffered by others because of the decedent's death. "Apart from relatively minor items such as funeral expense, most states measure economic loss by the loss of support to dependents. Some measure it differently, by the loss of projected lifetime savings of the deceased. The first measure is usually called loss-to-survivors or loss-to-dependents measure, while the second is called the loss-to-the estate measure." "With the exception of Kentucky, most of the states which use the loss-to-the estate measure calculate the loss by determining the deceased's probable lifetime earnings and then deducting the expenses the decedent would have had in maintaining himself." DAN B. DOBBS, THE LAW OF REMEDIES §§ 8.3 (3) & 8.3 (4) (1993).

6. *Pecuniary emphasis; loss to survivors' measure.* Wrongful death statutes originally limited the recovery to pecuniary losses suffered by dependents or those who would inherit. For example, under the loss to survivors' measure of damages, children of a decedent might recover for loss of support they received in the form of housing, food, and clothing. If the deceased person would not have contributed to any beneficiary during his lifetime, damages would be small or nonexistent. Notice the relatively small compensatory damages awarded for Mrs. Robbins' death.

7. *Loss to estate measure.* The loss to the estate measure might allow substantial damages even where the decedent was not contributing to the support of others. The loss to the estate measure would allow recovery for whatever sums the decedent would have saved in her normal lifetime, even if she were supporting no one. That measure would be helpful where the decedent had no dependents. However, it could call for a zero award if the decedent were devoting every dollar earned to support of a family and hence would have saved nothing.

8. *Combining measures.* Several courts have now permitted death action plaintiffs to recover both the loss of support and a loss of inheritance. The loss of inheritance is essentially like the loss to the estate. The claimant must show that the decedent would have accumulated an estate (or an increase in his estate) and that the claimant would have inherited a share. When the claimants were receiving no support, as is often the case with adult children of the decedent, in such jurisdictions they could still recover for reasonably provable loss of inheritance. See *Schaefer v. American Family Mutual Ins. Co.,* 192 Wis.2d 768, 531 N.W.2d 585 (1995).

9. *Non-earning decedents.* Children, spouses who do not work in the labor market, retired persons, and others whose earnings are small or nonexistent create still another problem under the wrongful death statutes. It would be difficult to say that wrongful death has reduced their ultimate estate and equally difficult to say that they were supporting other persons. Thus neither measure of wrongful death damages is adequate for non-working decedents. In such cases, non-pecuniary damages become all-important.

10. *Non-pecuniary claims generally.* At least three basic kinds of non-pecuniary loss might be claimed in death actions: (1) punitive damages; (2) damages for the mental anguish or grief of the survivors; and (3) loss of consortium, which might include (a) loss of society or companionship, (b) loss of services, and (c) loss of guidance and care. Claims like these were excluded under most original wrongful death statutes. The first two elements are generally rejected in wrongful death suits, though a few states permit their recovery. The third, loss of consortium is usually recoverable. Courts stress that this does not include emotional distress of the survivors, but that it does include a broad range of mutual benefits of family membership, including love, affection, care, companionship and the like. See *Reiser v. Coburn,* 255 Neb. 655, 587 N.W.2d 336 (1998) (a zero award to parents of a young independent adult was inadequate, new trial required).

11. *Future losses.* Both the loss-to-survivors rule and the loss-to-the-estate rule require the court to estimate the earnings the decedent would have had but for the death. How many years would the decedent have lived

to save money or make contributions to dependents? What would those earnings have been? These are difficult matters of proof and complicated by possible inflation and taxes. A discount must be made after all this to take into account the fact that the plaintiffs will recover all future losses now and can invest the sum at interest. See generally DOBBS, supra note 5, § 8.5 (1993).

12. *Statutes.* Subject to a minor exception in federal maritime law, wrongful death and survival claims are entirely statutory. Statutes are amended from time to time and many have idiosyncratic elements. Lawyers must always consult the governing statute and should expect to find local variations in the general scheme described in this chapter.

13. Other materials on damages appear in Chapter 23.

———

KLOSSNER v. SAN JUAN COUNTY, 93 Wash. 2d 42, 605 P.2d 330 (1980). The wrongful death statute provided for recovery "for the benefit of the wife, husband, child or children of the person whose death" was caused by defendant. The surviving wife, Respondent here, "brought this action on behalf of decedent's children from a prior marriage, the children born to her and the decedent, and her own children who had not been adopted by decedent." *Held*: There can be no recovery for the stepchildren.

"The wrongful death and survival statutes, unlike those statutory provisions cited by respondent, contain no mention of stepchildren. The beneficiaries of a wrongful death action are, among others, a 'child or children'. It is a general rule of construction that words in a statute, unless otherwise defined, must be given their usual and ordinary meaning. While the legislature has defined 'child' in some statutes to include stepchildren, there is no such extension of the definition of the term in RCW 4.2–.020."

Notes

1. Other courts have reached similar conclusions. In *Steed v. Imperial Airlines*, 12 Cal. 3d 115, 115 Cal. Rptr. 329, 524 P. 2d 801 (1974) the court held that a stepchild was not an "heir" under the statute and that the statute was not unconstitutional in discriminating against stepchildren who received support from the decedent. The California legislature responded by amending its Civil Procedure Code § 377 to provide that minors living with the decedent for 6 months or more and receiving more than half their support from decedent could recover for wrongful death. Is this adequate? What other persons ought to recover even if they are not heirs?

2. In *Lawson v. Atwood*, 42 Ohio St.3d 69, 536 N.E.2d 1167 (1989) the plaintiff alleged that the defendant was responsible for the wrongful death of 18–year-old Gina Lawson. Gina's mother was 17 years old at the time Gina was born. From the time Gina was two years old the plaintiff, who was in no way related, took care of her. When Gina was four, her mother agreed that

the plaintiff and his wife could adopt Gina. No adoption took place, possibly because some Ohio courts at that time had a policy against permitting adoption when the mother knew the adoptive parents. However, the plaintiff and his wife reared Gina with their other child and as their own child. After the plaintiff and his wife divorced, the plaintiff was given legal custody of all the children. The Ohio statute provided that the wrongful death action would be brought by the personal representative "for the exclusive benefit of the surviving spouse, the children, and the parents of the decedent," or for the benefit of other next of kin. The plaintiff falls in none of these categories. The court held that the plaintiff qualified to recover under the statute. What line of reasoning could support such a result?

3. *Claims by non-custodial parents for a child's death.* Where parents of a minor child are divorced, and one of them has custody of the child and the other has only "visitation rights," should the non-custodial parent be denied any wrongful death recovery? In *Sindelar v. Leguia,* 750 A.2d 967 (R.I.2000) the decedent was a 29–year-old unmarried son with no children. In such a case, the statute called for distribution of the award according to the rules for intestate succession, in this case to his parents. But the parents had been divorced many years earlier with physical custody to the mother and the father had allegedly had no relationship with the deceased son and no expectation of receiving any pecuniary benefit from him. The court refused to assess the quality of relationships and held that the father would take one-half of the wrongful death recovery. But in *Carter v. Beaver,* 577 So.2d 448 (Ala.1991) the court held that the entire award or settlement for the wrongful death of a child must go to the custodial parent. What if part of the award or settlement is based on contributions the deceased would have made to support the non-custodial parent in later years, or on loss of consortium of the non-custodial parent?

4. *Unmarried cohabitants.* Under statutes that distribute damages to heirs, or to named categories, such as "surviving spouse" or "children," there is obviously no room for compensation to the surviving friend or lover. Vermont has dealt with one such case by permitting civil unions analogous to marriage in the case of same-sex couples. The statute specifically affords such couples the same rights as married couples, specifically including the right to sue for wrongful death. See 15 Vt. Stat. §§ 1204(a) & 1204(e) (2).

5. *Transsexual widows.* In *Littleton v. Prange,* 9 S.W.3d 223 (Tex.App. 1999) the plaintiff had been born a male, but had undergone surgery and counseling for a complete sex reassignment. She married Jonathon Mark Littleton. Seven years later, Littleton died, allegedly as a result of the defendant's medical malpractice. The plaintiff has standing to sue for wrongful death under Texas law only if she is the surviving spouse. The court concluded that she could not sue because her marriage was invalid. Once a male always a male. The court did not discuss the policy of the wrongful death statute.

6. Along with distributional defects in the statutory wrongful death schemes, there are problems in jury awards. Studies show that jurors award much larger sums to the female spouse of a male decedent than to the male spouse of a female decedent, even when their earnings are the same. See Goodman, Loftus, Miller & Green, *Money, Sex, and Death: Gender Bias in*

Wrongful Death Damage Awards, 25 L. & Soc'y Rev. 263 (1991). Female decedents are worth less? Or female survivors need more? Is the disparity justified under either hypothesis?

NOTE: PARTIES AND PROCEDURE

The plaintiff in a survival-type claim is the personal representative, that is, the executor or administrator of the decedent's estate. The claim is a debt owed the estate of the deceased person just as any other claim is, and any recovery is paid to the estate. The estate in turn pays debts of the deceased person and costs of administering the estate. If any funds are left, the estate pays those to heirs or the beneficiaries of the deceased's will.

The death action, as distinct from the survival action, does not involve a claim by the estate. The recovery, if any, does not pass through the estate—it is not subject to the debts of the decedent—but goes directly to the survivors designated by the state. Often the survivors may bring the death action directly, and frequently one of them acts as a kind of informal trustee, suing for all of them. Thus it is common to see cases in which a surviving widow sues on behalf of herself and her children. In some states a different technique is used. There is a court-appointed "trustee"—who may be one of the survivors entitled to recover. This trustee brings the action on behalf of all appropriate beneficiaries. Very often statutes provide that this person is to be the personal representative of the estate. But where this is so, the personal representative is a trustee for the survivors entitled to recover, not the representative of the estate generally. This means that a personal representative, say the surviving husband of a deceased wife, may bring one suit for the estate—the survival action; and that he may also bring a separate death action for the appropriate survivors.

What problems could occur when the personal representative does not fairly represent all persons or when one of the survivors sues and other survivors are not included in the claim?

NOTE: DEFENSES

1. *Decedent's contributory negligence or assumed risk.* The rule under most death statutes is that the action could be brought for wrongful death only if the decedent could have sued had he lived. This language obviously means that the defendant is not liable unless he is guilty of conduct that would be tortious toward some individual.

It is sometimes argued, however, that the wrongful death action, always in theory a "new and independent action" for the protection of survivors, should be permitted in spite of the contributory negligence of the decedent. The survivors, it is argued, were guilty of no misconduct, and the defendant should not escape liability to these innocent victims of his wrongful conduct. Is this a sound argument?

Courts may accept the "new and independent action" argument for some purposes but not others. California in effect treats the wrongful death action as a "new and independent action" by holding that survivors may recover for care and comfort lost at the wrongful death of a motorist while he was driving his uninsured vehicle–even though the same motorist, had he lived, would have been denied recovery of all nonpecuniary damages. On the other hand, California treats the wrongful death claim as "derivative" or based upon the deceased's own claim by holding that recovery is reduced by the deceased's contributory fault. See *Horwich v. Superior Court,* 21 Cal.4th 272, 87 Cal.Rptr.2d 222, 980 P.2d 927 (1999). Courts are generally in accord with California in treating the decedent's contributory fault as a defense. In comparative fault systems, that means the damages in the wrongful death suit will be reduced by the percentage of fault attributable to the decedent. E.g., *Adamy v. Ziriakus,* 92 N.Y.2d 396, 681 N.Y.S.2d 463, 704 N.E.2d 216 (1998).

2. *Beneficiary's contributory negligence or assumed risk.*

(a) *Survival claims.* Under survival statutes, the decedent's own claim is being pursued, not a claim for beneficiaries. This point is emphasized by the form of the claim, which is a suit by the estate of the decedent, with proceeds payable to the estate. The fact that an heir was guilty of contributory negligence will be of no direct relevance, even though the heir will inherit the estate, including the survival action recovery. However, in a joint and several liability system, the defendant may obtain contribution from the negligent heir, thus negating his recovery. The same result may be achieved in a several liability system in which each tortfeasor is responsible only for a percentage of damages equal to his percentage of fault.

(b) *Wrongful death claims.* If there was but one beneficiary, and he was guilty of contributory negligence, the common law rule barred his recovery for wrongful death. Where there were several beneficiaries, some guilty of contributory negligence and some not, a number of courts took the view that contributory negligence should not bar the entire death claim, but should bar only the claim of the negligent beneficiary. The comparative fault system seems to make this an easy case. Either by reducing damages or by contribution, the defendant can eliminate liability for the percentage share attributable to any negligent beneficiary. See DOBBS ON TORTS § 299 (2000).

3. *Statutes of limitations.* Albert Weinberg was exposed to asbestos from 1941 to 1948. In 1975 a mesothelioma, or lung cancer, was discovered. This allegedly resulted from the asbestos exposure. Mr. Weinberg brought no action during his life and he died in 1977. Thereafter an action for his death was brought within two years. The death act prescribes two years from death as the limitation period. Is the claim nevertheless barred on the ground that no action for death can be brought unless the decedent could have maintained an action at the same time had he lived? Some courts have taken this view. See *Russell v.*

Ingersoll–Rand Co., 841 S.W.2d 343 (Tex.1992); *Edwards v. Fogarty,* 962 P.2d 879 (Wyo.1998). But many cases hold that the statute begins running at the time of death and that the death claim is not barred even if the decedent would be barred had he lived. *E.g., Chapman v. Cardiac Pacemakers, Inc.*, 105 Idaho 785, 673 P.2d 385 (1983).

4. *Discovery rule.* Courts are divided and uncertain whether the discovery rule applies in wrongful death actions. See DOBBS ON TORTS § 300. What if the decedent never discovered the defendant's tort and the family reasonably fails to discover it for four years after the decedent's death?

5. Try your hand: given the logic and purpose of the survival claim, how should the statute of limitations work?

6. *Inter vivos recovery.* Decedent recovers a settlement or judgment during his lifetime, then dies as a result of the tort. The judgment or settlement would bind him, had he lived, so that he could not sue. Can survivors nevertheless bring a wrongful death action? Most courts have said not, but a few go the other way. See *Alfone v. Sarno*, Chapter 23 below.

REFERENCE: DOBBS ON TORTS §§ 294–301 (2000).

Part IV

THE EBB AND FLOW OF COMMON LAW STRICT LIABILITY FOR PHYSICAL HARMS

In the materials covered so far, fault has been the keynote concept in liability. We now consider three areas involving complete or partial strict liability.

In the last chapter in this part, Chapter 22, the topic is products liability. Products liability law sometimes (but not always) imposes liability without fault upon manufacturers and distributors of defective products, even when the manufacturer or distributor is not negligent.

In Chapter 21 we will see older forms of strict liability, those associated with certain problems of neighboring landowners and those associated with especially hazardous activities that tend to cause harm even when not carried out negligently.

In the first chapter in this Subpart, Chapter 20, we renew acquaintance with an idea introduced at the very beginning of the course–vicarious liability, which can be perceived as a limited form of strict liability in which one person or entity is held legally responsible for the fault-based torts of another.

Chapter 20

VICARIOUS LIABILITY

§ 1. RESPONDEAT SUPERIOR AND SCOPE OF EMPLOYMENT

We recognized early in the course that employers could be held liable for the torts of certain employees, provided those torts were committed within the scope of employment. This principle of liability is often called vicarious liability or the *respondeat superior* principle.

What is meant by the limitation that torts must be committed within the scope of employment? To a large extent the answer to this question turns on a much larger one—why hold the employer liable at all? The employer is not personally at fault, so that his liability is in a sense a kind of strict liability. One case summarized the goals of vicarious liability succinctly as (a) the prevention of future injuries, (b) the assurance of compensation to victims, and (c) the equitable spreading of losses caused by an enterprise. See *Lisa M. v. Henry Mayo Newhall Memorial Hospital*, 12 Cal.4th 291, 48 Cal.Rptr.2d 510, 907 P.2d 358 (1995).

RIVIELLO v. WALDRON, 47 N.Y.2d 297, 418 N.Y.S.2d 300, 391 N.E.2d 1278 (1979). Waldron, employed as a cook at the Pot Belly Pub, a Bronx bar and grill, was talking to a customer and flipping an open knife. This accidentally struck the customer in the eye, causing a loss of its use. The customer sued the bar owner. *Held*, the bar owner is liable; Waldron was within the scope of employment. The scope of employment was originally defined narrowly "on the theory that the employer could exercise close control over his employees during the period of their service." But "social policy has wrought a measure of relaxation of the traditional confines of the doctrine." Reasons for this are that "the average innocent victim, when relegated to the pursuit of his claim against the employee, most often will face a defendant too impecunious to meet the claim, and that modern economic devices, such as cost accounting and insurance coverage, permit most employers to spread the impact of such costs. So no longer is an employer necessarily excused merely because his employees, acting in furtherance of his interests, exhibit human failings and perform negligently or otherwise than in an authorized manner. Instead, the test has come to be whether the act was done while the servant was doing his master's work, no matter how irregularly, or with what disregard of instructions."

FRUIT v. SCHREINER, 502 P.2d 133 (Alaska 1972). Fruit, a life insurance salesman, was at a convention where his employer required him to be. This involved social as well as business events. After business activities were over one evening, he drove to a bar, hoping to find some colleagues, found none and drove back to the convention center. It was 2:00 a.m. He skidded and struck Schreiner, whose legs were crushed. *Held*, Fruit was within the scope of his employment. "The basis of *respondeat superior* has been correctly stated as the desire to include in the costs of operation inevitable losses to third persons incident to carrying on an enterprise, and thus distribute the burden among those benefitted by the enterprise.... Insurance is readily available for the employer so that the risk may be distributed among many like insured paying premiums and the extra cost of doing business may be reflected in the price of the product."

Notes

1. What reasons can you give for holding an employer liable for the employee's negligence in causing harm to others?

2. If the employer is held liable because of the employee's negligence, the employer has a theoretical right to indemnity from the employee. That right is seldom asserted, partly because the employer's liability insurance is likely to protect both employer and employee. Are the New York and Alaska Courts in *Riviello* and *Fruit* giving the same reasons for expansive liability of an employer? Is either court simply using the theory that the employer represents a "deep pocket"?

3. Is it clear that Fruit's employer got any benefit, actual or expected, in his trip to the bar?

4. *Enterprise liability and accident cost reduction.* As reflected in *Fruit*, the concept of enterprise liability is often close to the surface of any strict liability analysis. In his groundbreaking book, THE COSTS OF ACCIDENTS (1970), Professor (now Judge) Guido Calabresi urged that tort law's principal function is to reduce the costs of accidents and the costs of avoiding them. We will see Calabresi's ideas in some more depth in Chapter 22, but some of his central conceptions are worth thinking about here. One idea is that the price of goods and activities should accurately reflect the accident costs they cause. Holding an enterprise strictly liable for harms it causes facilitates this "internalization of costs," which in turn reduces the costs of accidents. How are accident costs reduced? Consumers are influenced by prices. If the price of a particular product or service actually reflects its total costs, including accident costs, the market will tend to favor the cheaper (safer) product or service. Companies will thus have an incentive to make their products and activities safer to compete in the marketplace. Do these ideas support holding an employer strictly liable for the torts of its employees, committed within the scope of employment?

5.   How well does enterprise liability theory mix with accountability for fault? If there is a good reason to hold an employer strictly liable in these cases, why not hold all employers liable, regardless of employee negligence, when an act within the scope of employment causes harm?

NOTE: SERVING GRATUITOUSLY

1.   We've been referring to employers and employees, or in the old language of the law, masters and servants. The relationship of master and servant can be established without payment or promise of payment. See RESTATEMENT SECOND OF AGENCY § 225 (1958). However, that relationship is not established unless the putative servant submits himself to the control of the employer. A church member might accept unpaid duties of delivering cookies to shut-ins for a church program. If the church expects him to act on its behalf and he submits to the church's directions, he is a servant so that the church is liable when he negligently runs someone down while delivering cookies. *Trinity Lutheran Church, Inc. of Evansville, Indiana v. Miller,* 451 N.E.2d 1099 (Ind. 1983).

2.   What about the person who voluntarily assists another, without such submission? See *Austin v. Kaness,* 950 P.2d 561 (Wyo.1997) (adult son feeding cats while parents were away does not become an agent, servant or employee of parents).

3.   What about an employee who volunteers for an extra task and injures someone while doing it? In *Bishop v. Texas A & M Univ.,* ___ S.W.3d ___, 2000 WL 854300 (Tex. 2000), plaintiff, a university student, was playing Vlad the Impaler in a Drama Club performance of Dracula when a fellow student missed the stab pad on his chest and impaled him with a Bowie knife. The plaintiff sued the university on a vicarious liability theory, claiming that the Club's faculty advisors were negligent in allowing the play's directors to use a real knife in the scene, and that those advisers (professors) were employees of the university. The appeals court said the advisors, since they received no pay for serving in their roles and were under no compulsion to serve, were volunteers and thus not acting as employees. Reversing, the Texas Supreme Court said that the lack of either compulsion or additional remuneration for the particular task was not dispositive, stressing that the advisors were in the university's paid service while advising the Drama Club and received a benefit from their advisory positions, in that such "voluntary" work was taken into account in setting salaries.

4.   In the cases that immediately follow, the master-servant relationship is established and the question is whether the servant is acting outside that relationship when he causes harm.

HINMAN v. WESTINGHOUSE ELECTRIC CO.

Supreme Court of California, 1970.
2 Cal.3d 956, 88 Cal.Rptr. 188, 471 P.2d 988.

PETERS, JUSTICE.

Plaintiff, a Los Angeles policeman, was standing on the center divider of a freeway inspecting a possible road hazard when he was struck by a car driven by Frank Allen Herman, an employee of defendant Westinghouse. As a result of the accident he received permanent injuries. The city paid his medical expenses and disability pension. [In a suit against Westinghouse, the jury found for the defendant.]

At the time of the accident, Herman was employed by Westinghouse as an elevator constructor's helper and was returning home from work from a job site. He had been working for Westinghouse for about four months. His work was assigned from the Westinghouse office. He did not go to the office before or after work but instead went from home directly to the job site and after work returned home from the job site. The particular job on which Herman was working was not completed at the time of the accident, and he would ordinarily return to the job site until the job was completed or he was told not to return.

The union contracts under which Herman worked provided for the payment of "carfare" and travel time in certain circumstances depending on the location of the job site in relation to the Los Angeles City Hall. As to this job, which was 15 to 20 miles from the city hall, Herman received an hour and a half per day as his roundtrip travel time and $1.30 for his travel expense. The employer had no control over the method or route of transportation used by Herman.

The trial judge refused instructions that Herman was acting within the scope of his employment at the time of the accident and instead instructed the jury that whether he was acting within the scope of his employment depended upon a number of factors including among others "whether his conduct was authorized by his employer, either expressly or impliedly; the nature of the employment, its object and the duties imposed thereby; whether the employee was acting in his discharge thereof; whether his conduct occurred during the performance of services for the benefit of the employer, either directly or indirectly, or of himself; whether his conduct, even though not expressly or impliedly authorized, was an incidental event connected with his assigned work. . . . [So instructed, the jury found that Herman was not within the scope of his employment and hence gave a verdict for Westinghouse.]

Although earlier authorities sought to justify the *respondeat superior* doctrine on such theories as "control" by the master of the servant, the master's "privilege" in being permitted to employ another, the third party's innocence in comparison to the master's selection of the servant, or the master's "deep pocket" to pay for the loss, "the modern justification for vicarious liability is a rule of policy, a deliberate allocation of a risk. The losses caused by the torts of employees, which as a practical matter are sure to occur in the conduct of the employer's enterprise, are placed upon that enterprise itself, as a required cost of doing business. They are placed upon the employer because, having engaged in an enterprise which will, on the basis of past experience, involve harm to others through the torts of employees, and sought to profit by it, it is just that he, rather than the innocent injured plaintiff, should bear them; and because he is better able to absorb them, and to distribute them, through prices, rates or liability insurance, to the public, and so to shift them to society, to the community at large." . . .

Another leading authority also points out that the modern and proper basis of vicarious liability of the master is not his control or fault but the risks incident to his enterprise. "We are not here looking for the master's fault but rather for risks that may fairly be regarded as typical of or broadly incidental to the enterprise he has undertaken. . . ."

Liability of the employer may not be avoided on the basis of the "going and coming" rule. Under the "going and coming" rule, an employee going to and from work is ordinarily considered outside the scope of employment so that the employer is not liable for his torts. The "going and coming" rule is sometimes ascribed to the theory that the employment relationship is "suspended" from the time the employee leaves until he returns or that in commuting he is not rendering service to his employer Nevertheless, there are exceptions to the rule.

Thus in Harvey v. D & L Construction Co., the court reversed a nonsuit for the employer where it was shown that because of the remote site of the construction project, the employer had asked the employee to recruit other employees, one such employee was riding at the time of the accident, and the employer was furnishing the gas for the trip to the employee's home. . . .

The above cases indicate that exceptions will be made to the "going and coming" rule where the trip involves an incidental benefit to the employer, not common to commute trips by ordinary members of the work force. The cases also indicate that the fact that the employee receives personal benefits is not determinative when there is also a benefit to the employer.

There is a substantial benefit to an employer in one area to be permitted to reach out to a labor market in another area or to enlarge the available labor market by providing travel expenses and payment for travel time. It cannot be denied that the employer's reaching out to the distant or larger labor market increases the risk of injury in transportation. In other words, the employer, having found it desirable in the interests of his enterprise to pay for travel time and for travel expenses and to go beyond the normal labor market or to have located his enterprise at a place remote from the labor market, should be required to pay for the risks inherent in his decision.

We are satisfied that, where, as here, the employer and employee have made the travel time part of the working day by their contract, the employer should be treated as such during the travel time, and it follows that so long as the employee is using the time for the designated purpose, to return home, the doctrine of *respondeat superior* is applicable. It is unnecessary to determine the appropriate rule to be applied if the employee had used the time for other purposes. We also need not decide now whether the mere payment of travel expenses without additional payment for the travel time of the employee ... reflects a sufficient benefit to the employer so that he should bear responsibility to innocent third parties for the risks inherent in the travel.

The facts relating to the applicability of the doctrine of *respondeat superior* are undisputed in the instant case, and we conclude that as a matter of law the doctrine is applicable and that the trial court erred in its instructions in leaving the issue as one of fact to the jury....

FAUL v. JELCO, INC., 122 Ariz. 490, 595 P.2d 1035 (App. 1979). Employee, a construction worker, lived in Winslow, but for the duration of the construction stayed during the week in a trailer near Oracle Junction. During the week he drove from the trailer to a "show up" location, and was then transported from there to the actual job site. He went home to Winslow one weekend, carrying with him the tools he was required to have on the job. Early on Monday, he drove back toward Oracle Junction and was only three miles away when he crossed the center line and struck the plaintiff's vehicle. He was paid an hourly wage. Because of the remote location of the job site he was "paid zone pay, an increased hourly wage, but no separate compensation for travel time, travel expenses or per diem living expenses...." The trial judge granted summary judgment in favor of the employer. *Held*, affirmed. "As a general rule, an employee is not within the scope of employment while commuting to or from work. One exception to this rule is recognized when travel to and from work involves special hazards.... [But authority] rejects the claim that distance alone constitutes a special hazard. A second exception to the going and coming rule is the dual purpose doctrine.... The dual purpose exception applies when in addition to merely commuting, the employee performs a concurrent service for his employer that would have necessitated a trip by another employee if the commuting employee had not been able to perform it while commuting." But in this case he was carrying tools "solely for personal reasons." The plaintiff attempts to claim a dual purpose based on Hinman v. Westinghouse Electric Co., supra, on the theory that it served the employer's purpose to "reach out" into distant labor markets. "Because *Hinman* adopted a risk justification for respondeat superior, in contrast to the control justification applied in Arizona, we are uncertain whether the *Hinman* rule would apply in Arizona. We need not decide that question, however, because the *Hinman* court restricts its holding to cases where the employer compensates the employee for both travel expenses and travel time. In this case, the employee was not directly compensated for either."

Notes

1.   An employee quits for the day, goes home, sets up the barbecue grill, and negligently allows the fire to get out of hand, causing a burn to the next door neighbor, who was invited to share a hamburger. Is the employer liable? The next morning the employee is driving to work, when he negligently rear-ends the car in front. Is the employer liable? The easiest place to draw the line between one's personal and one's work life is at the employer's premises, isn't it? The going and coming rule seems to embody that notion. Why depart from it in *Hinman*?

2.   Are the theories set out in *Hinman* merely ways of getting to the "deep pocket," or do they suggest something more?

3.   Factual variations on the going and coming rule are numerous. For example, the employee might be on an off-premises lunch break when the tort is committed, a police officer or firefighter who is off duty but "on call," or on his day off but checking on information he will need on the job when he gets into a deadly drag race.

4.   *Frolic and detour.* A special factual category involves the employee who, during working hours, goes to a place not associated with employment for a purpose not associated with employment. The employee is instructed to deliver furniture to a town 30 miles north. After she has driven on the road 15 miles she turns to the east, intending to drive two miles in that direction to have a beer with a friend. She has a collision at a point one mile from the highway where she was supposed to be. Was she outside the employment and on a "frolic of her own," or merely on a "detour"? If the court characterizes the departure as a "mere detour," as in cases of trivial departures from the job, the employer will remain liable.

Suppose the employee sees her friend and starts back to the main highway and has a second collision at the same spot, but this time headed back to work? At what point has the employee reentered employment? "First, the employee must have formulated an intent to act in furtherance of the employer's business; second, the intent must be coupled with a reasonable connection in time and space with the work in which he should be engaged." *Prince* v. *Atchison, Topeka & Santa Fe Railway*, 76 Ill.App.3d 898, 32 Ill.Dec. 362, 395 N.E.2d 592 (1979).

The Restatement Second of Agency § 237 (1958) provides that reentry does not occur until the employee is "reasonably near the authorized space and time limits" and also acting with intent to serve the employer's business. Do these statements assist in a solution? Do they suggest the existence of a principle, albeit one that is difficult to apply?

EDGEWATER MOTELS, INC. v. GATZKE

Supreme Court of Minnesota, 1979.
277 N.W.2d 11.

SCOTT, JUSTICE.

[Gatzke, a district manager for Walgreen's, stayed in plaintiff's motel while he was in Duluth, Minnesota supervising the opening of a

Walgreen-owned restaurant. The motel was damaged by fire, allegedly the result of Gatzke's negligence while in his motel room. The motel's claim here is against both Gatzke and his employer.]

[Gatzke] lived at the Edgewater at the company's expense. While in Duluth, Gatzke normally would arise at 6:00 a.m. and work at the restaurant from about 7:00 a.m. to 12:00 or 1:00 a.m. In addition to working at the restaurant, Gatzke remained on call 24 hours per day to handle problems arising in other Walgreen restaurants located in his district. Gatzke thought of himself as a "24-hour-a-day man." He received calls from other Walgreen restaurants in his district when problems arose. He was allowed to call home at company expense. His laundry, living expenses, and entertainment were items of reimbursement. There were no constraints as to where he would perform his duties or at what time of day they would be performed. . . .

[Around midnight or after, Gatzke left the work with others on the job; some went to their hotel rooms, but Gatzke and Hubbard went to the Bellows restaurant for a drink.]

In about an hour's time Gatzke consumed a total of four brandy Manhattans, three of which were "doubles." While at the Bellows, Gatzke and Hubbard spent part of the time discussing the operation of the newly-opened Walgreen restaurant. Additionally, Gatzke and the Bellows' bartender talked a little about the mixing and pricing of drinks. The testimony showed that Gatzke was interested in learning the bar business because the new Walgreen restaurant served liquor.

Between 1:15 and 1:30 a.m. Gatzke and Hubbard left the Bellows and walked back to the Edgewater. Witnesses testified that Gatzke acted normal and appeared sober. Gatzke went directly to his motel room, and then "probably" sat down at a desk to fill out his expense account because "that was [his] habit from traveling so much." The completion of the expense account had to be done in accordance with detailed instructions, and if the form was not filled out properly it would be returned to the employee unpaid. It took Gatzke no more than five minutes to fill out the expense form.

While Gatzke completed the expense account he "probably" smoked a cigarette. The record indicates Gatzke smoked about two packages of cigarettes per day. A maid testified that the ash trays in Gatzke's room would generally be full of cigarette butts and ashes when she cleaned the room. She also noticed at times that the plastic wastebasket next to the desk contained cigarette butts.

After filling out the expense account Gatzke went to bed, and soon thereafter a fire broke out. Gatzke escaped from the burning room, but the fire spread rapidly and caused extensive damage to the motel. The amount of damages was stipulated by the parties at $330,360.

One of plaintiff's expert witnesses, Dr. Ordean Anderson, a fire reconstruction specialist, testified that the fire started in, or next to, the plastic wastebasket located to the side of the desk in Gatzke's room. He also stated that the fire was caused by a burning cigarette or match. After the fire, the plastic wastebasket was a melted "blob." Dr. Anderson stated that X-ray examination of the remains of the basket disclosed the presence of cigarette filters and paper matches.

[The jury found Gatzke to be guilty of 60% of the negligence and the motel guilty of the remainder. The trial judge concluded, however, that Gatzke was not within the scope of his employment, and rendered judgment N.O.V. for Walgreen's.]

To support a finding that an employee's negligent act occurred within his scope of employment, it must be shown that his conduct was, to some degree, in furtherance of the interests of his employer. This principle is recognized by Restatement, Agency 2d, § 235, which states:

> An act of a servant is not within the scope of employment if it is done with no intention to perform it as a part of or incident to a service on account of which he is employed.

Other factors to be considered in the scope of employment determination are whether the conduct is of the kind that the employee is authorized to perform and whether the act occurs substantially within authorized time and space restrictions. No hard and fast rule can be applied to resolve the "scope of employment" inquiry. Rather, each case must be decided on its own individual facts.

The initial question raised by the instant factual situation is whether an employee's smoking of a cigarette can constitute conduct within his scope of employment. This issue has not been dealt with by this court. The courts which have considered the question have not agreed on its resolution. A number of courts which have dealt with the instant issue have ruled that the act of smoking, even when done simultaneously with work-related activity, is not within the employee's scope of employment because it is a matter personal to the employee which is not done in furtherance of the employer's interest.

Other courts which have considered the question have reasoned that the smoking of a cigarette, if done while engaged in the business of the employer, is within an employee's scope of employment because it is a minor deviation from the employee's work-related activities, and thus merely an act done incidental to general employment.

For example, in Wood v. Saunders, a gas station attendant negligently threw his lighted cigarette across an automobile's fuel tank opening while he was filling the vehicle with gasoline. The court, in finding this act to be within the employee's scope of employment, stated:

> In the case at bar, there was no abandonment by the employee of the master's purposes and business while the employee was smoking and carrying the lighted cigarette. There was merely a combining by the employee, with the carrying out of the master's purposes, of an incidental and contemporaneous carrying out of the employee's private purposes. . . .

The question of whether smoking can be within an employee's scope of employment is a close one, but after careful consideration of the issue we are persuaded by the reasoning of the courts which hold that smoking can be an act within an employee's scope of employment. It seems only logical to conclude that an employee does not abandon his employment as a matter of law while temporarily acting for his personal comfort when such activities involve only slight deviations from work that are reasonable under the circumstances, such as eating, drinking, or smoking....

We ... hereby hold that an employer can be held vicariously liable for his employee's negligent smoking of a cigarette [if] he was otherwise acting in the scope of his employment at the time of the negligent act.... It appears that the district court felt that Gatzke was outside the scope of his employment while he was at the Bellows, and thus was similarly outside his scope of employment when he returned to his room to fill out his expense account. The record, however, contains a reasonable basis from which a jury could find that Gatzke was involved in serving his employer's interests at the time he was at the bar. Gatzke testified that, while at the Bellows, he discussed the operation of the newly-opened Walgreen's restaurant with Hubbard. Also, the bartender stated that on that night "[a] few times we [Gatzke and the bartender] would talk about his business and my business, how to make drinks, prices."

But more importantly, even assuming that Gatzke was outside the scope of his employment while he was at the bar, there is evidence from which a jury could reasonably find that Gatzke resumed his employment activities after he returned to his motel room and filled out his expense account. The expense account was, of course, completed so that Gatzke could be reimbursed by Walgreen's for his work-related expenses. In this sense, Gatzke is performing an act for his own personal benefit. However, the completion of the expense account also furthers the employer's business in that it provides detailed documentation of business expenses so that they are properly deductible for tax purposes. In this light, the filling out of the expense form can be viewed as serving a dual purpose; that of furthering Gatzke's personal interests and promoting his employer's business purposes. Accordingly, it is reasonable for the jury to find that the completion of the expense account is an act done in furtherance of the employer's business purposes.

Additionally, the record indicates that Gatzke was an executive type of employee who had no set working hours. He considered himself a 24-hour-a-day man; his room at the Edgewater Motel was his "office away from home." It was therefore also reasonable for the jury to determine that the filling out of his expense account was done within authorized time and space limits of his employment.

In light of the above, we hold that it was reasonable for the jury to find that Gatzke was acting within the scope of his employment when he completed his expense account. Accordingly, we set aside the trial court's grant of judgment for Walgreen's and reinstate the jury's determination that Gatzke was working within the scope of his employment at the time of his negligent act....

Notes

1.   Once the judges determined that Gatzke was acting within the time and place limits of his employment, was there any other issue? Does the issue resemble the issue of legal cause?

2.   *Punitive damages.* If an employer is liable for wilful, wanton or even intentional torts of the employee, should the employer also be liable for punitive damages? The cases are not in complete agreement. Some hold that the employer is ordinarily not liable for punitive damages unless there is serious fault at managerial levels or serious fault in hiring a dangerous employee. 1 DAN DOBBS, THE LAW OF REMEDIES § 3.11 (6) (2d ed. 1993). But should an employer be liable at all for wanton or intentional wrongs of the employee?

3.   *Prohibited acts.* "The general rule is that an employer may be held accountable for the wrongful act of his employee committed while acting in his employer's business and within the scope of his employment, although his employer had expressly forbidden the act.... The true test ... is whether at the time of the commission of the injury the employee was performing a service in the furtherance of his employer's business, not whether it was done in exact observance of the detail prescribed by the employer." *Ohio Farmers Insurance Co. v. Norman*, 122 Ariz. 330, 594 P.2d 1026 (App. 1979). On this principle the court held the employer liable for the loss of plaintiffs' home through fire when a janitor burned trash against orders.

In *Russell v. Noullet*, 721 So.2d 868 (La.1998), plaintiffs sued off-duty police officers and their employer, the City of New Orleans, for injuries they sustained when a barroom fracas moved outdoors. One plaintiff told a police officer who had been among the drinkers that she was going to give his license number to the police. He grabbed her by the neck and slammed her into the back of his car, yelling, "I am the police!" Another plaintiff was shot when the same policeman fired his service revolver several times into the crowd that had gathered in response to his first outburst. *Held*, the City is not vicariously liable. Even if the officers were acting within the scope of employment when they initially tried to break up the barroom fight, the policeman's subsequent acts of battery were "not in the exercise of the function in which he was employed."

LISA M. v. HENRY MAYO NEWHALL MEMORIAL HOSPITAL

Supreme Court of California, 1995.
12 Cal.4th 291, 48 Cal.Rptr.2d 510, 907 P.2d 358.

WERDEGAR, ASSOCIATE JUSTICE....

[The plaintiff, 19 years old and pregnant, was injured in a fall and sought treatment at Hospital's emergency room. At the direction of the examining physicians, ultrasound technician Bruce Wayne Tripoli performed obstetrical and upper-right-quadrant ultrasonic imaging examinations. Tripoli then, on the pretense that additional testing was appropriate, scanned the plaintiff's pubic area, and inserted the ultra sound wand and then his fingers into her vagina. When the plaintiff discovered from her obstetrician that this procedure was not proper, she sued Tripoli and the hospital. The trial court granted summary judgment to the defendant hospital; the Court of Appeal reversed.]

It is clear, first of all, that California no longer follows the traditional rule that an employee's actions are within the scope of employment only if motivated, in whole or part, by a desire to serve the employer's interests. (See Rest.2d Agency, § 228, subd. 1(c) [conduct must be "actuated, at least in part, by a purpose to serve the master"].)

In Carr, this court held a building contractor liable for injuries caused when an employee, angry at a subcontractor's employee for interfering in his work, threw a hammer at the other worker's head. We rejected the defendant's claim its employee was not acting within the scope of employment because he "could not have intended by his conduct to further" the employer's interests: "It is sufficient, however, if the injury resulted from a dispute arising out of the employment. . . . It is not necessary that the assault should have been made as a means, or for the purpose of performing the work he (the employee) was employed to do." . . .

While the employee thus need not have intended to further the employer's interests, the employer will not be held liable for an assault or other intentional tort that did not have a causal nexus to the employee's work. "If an employee inflicts an injury out of personal malice, not engendered by the employment, the employer is not liable." . . .

Because an intentional tort gives rise to respondeat superior liability only if it was engendered by the employment, our disavowal of motive as a singular test of respondeat superior liability does not mean the employee's motive is irrelevant. An act serving only the employee's personal interest is less likely to arise from or be engendered by the employment than an act that, even if misguided, was intended to serve the employer in some way. . . .

Respondeat superior liability should apply only to the types of injuries that are "as a practical matter are sure to occur in the conduct of the employer's enterprise." The employment, in other words, must be such as predictably to create the risk employees will commit intentional torts of the type for which liability is sought.

In what has proved an influential formulation, the court in Rodgers v. Kemper Constr. Co., supra, 50 Cal.App.3d at page 618, 124 Cal.Rptr. 143, held the tortious occurrence must be "a generally foreseeable consequence of the activity." . . . The Rodgers foreseeability test is useful "because it reflects the central justification for respondeat superior [liability]: that losses fairly attributable to an enterprise—those which foreseeably result from the conduct of the enterprise—should be allocated to the enterprise as a cost of doing business."

Was Tripoli's sexual battery of Lisa M. within the scope of his employment? The injurious events were causally related to Tripoli's employment as an ultrasound technician in the sense they would not have occurred had he not been so employed. Tripoli's employment as an ultrasound technician provided the opportunity for him to meet plaintiff and to be alone with her in circumstances making the assault possible. The employment was thus one necessary cause of the ensuing tort. But, as previously discussed, in addition to such "but for" causation, respondeat superior liability requires that the risk of the tort have been engendered by, "typical of or broadly incidental to," or, viewed from a somewhat different perspective, "a generally foreseeable consequence of," Hospital's enterprise.

At the broadest level, Hospital argues sex crimes are never foreseeable outgrowths of employment because they, unlike instances of nonsexual violence, are not the product of "normal human traits." ... We are not persuaded that the roots of sexual violence and exploitation are in all cases so fundamentally different from those other abhorrent human traits as to allow a conclusion sexual misconduct is per se unforeseeable in the workplace....

[A] sexual tort will not be considered engendered by the employment unless its motivating emotions were fairly attributable to work-related events or conditions. Here the opposite was true: a technician simply took advantage of solitude with a naive patient to commit an assault for reasons unrelated to his work. Tripoli's job was to perform a diagnostic examination and record the results. The task provided no occasion for a work-related dispute or any other work-related emotional involvement with the patient. The technician's decision to engage in conscious exploitation of the patient did not arise out of the performance of the examination, although the circumstances of the examination made it possible. "If ... the assault was not motivated or triggered off by anything in the employment activity but was the result of only propinquity and lust, there should be no liability."

... Tripoli's criminal actions, of course, were unauthorized by Hospital and were not motivated by any desire to serve Hospital's interests. Beyond that, however, his motivating emotions were not causally attributable to his employment. The flaw in plaintiff's case for Hospital's respondeat superior liability is not so much that Tripoli's actions were personally motivated, but that those personal motivations were not generated by or an outgrowth of workplace responsibilities, conditions or events.

Analysis in terms of foreseeability leads to the same conclusion....

In arguing Tripoli's misconduct was generally foreseeable, plaintiff emphasizes the physically intimate nature of the work Tripoli was employed to perform. In our view, that a job involves physical contact is, by itself, an insufficient basis on which to impose vicarious liability for a sexual assault. . . .

Here, there is no evidence of emotional involvement, either mutual or unilateral, arising from the medical relationship. Although the procedure ordered involved physical contact, it was not of a type that would be expected to, or actually did, give rise to intense emotions on either side. We deal here not with a physician or therapist who becomes sexually involved with a patient as a result of mishandling the feelings predictably created by the therapeutic relationship but with an ultrasound technician who simply took advantage of solitude, access and superior knowledge to commit a sexual assault. . . .

Plaintiff contends the battery in this case, like the police officer's rape of a detainee in Mary M. v. City of Los Angeles, supra, 54 Cal.3d 202, 285 Cal.Rptr. 99, 814 P.2d 1341, "arose from an abuse of job-created authority." More accurately, Tripoli abused his position of trust, since he had no legal or coercive authority over plaintiff. Assuming an analogy can be fully maintained between authority and trust, Mary M. still provides less than compelling precedent for liability here. In Mary M., we held a police officer's assault was a generally foreseeable consequence of his position. "In view of the considerable power and authority that police officers possess, it is neither startling nor unexpected that on occasion an officer will misuse that authority by engaging in assaultive conduct." . . .

While a police officer's assault may be foreseeable from the scope of his unique authority over detainees, we are unable to say the same of an ultrasound technician's assault on a patient. Hospital did not give Tripoli any power to exercise general control over plaintiff's liberty. He was not vested with any coercive authority, and the trust plaintiff was asked to place in him was limited to conduct of an ultrasound examination. . . .

In reaching our conclusion we have consulted the three identified policy goals of the respondeat superior doctrine—preventing future injuries, assuring compensation to victims, and spreading the losses caused by an enterprise equitably—for additional guidance as to whether the doctrine should be applied in these circumstances. In this case, however, we have drawn no firm direction from consideration of the first two policy goals. [Hospital liability might induce precautionary measures but the impact might be destructive rather than beneficial. As to compensation for victims, hospital liability might entail consequential costs that are not clear.]

Third and finally, we attempt to assess the propriety of spreading the risk of losses among the beneficiaries of the enterprise upon which liability would be imposed. As Hospital points out, this assessment is another way of asking whether the employee's conduct was "so unusual or startling that it would seem unfair to include the loss resulting from it among other costs of the employer's business." For reasons already discussed, we conclude the connection between Tripoli's employment duties—to conduct a diagnostic examination—and his independent commission of a deliberate sexual assault was too attenuated, without proof of Hospital's negligence, to support allocation of plaintiff's losses to Hospital as a cost of doing business. Consideration of the respondeat superior doctrine's basis in public policy, therefore, does not alter our conviction that an ultrasound technician's sexual assault on a patient is not a risk predictably created by or fairly attributed to the nature of the technician's employment.

[The judgment of the Court of Appeals is reversed and the matter remanded for other proceedings. Concurring and dissenting opinions omitted.]

RODEBUSH v. OKLAHOMA NURSING HOMES, LTD., 867 P.2d 1241 (Okla.1993). A nurses' aide at a long-term care facility slapped an elderly resident suffering from Alzheimer's disease. Investigation led the facility to conclude that the aide was intoxicated (it was before 7:30 in the morning). Further investigation showed he had a criminal record of battery with intent to kill. *Held,* the employer is vicariously liable. The employer is not ordinarily liable for the employee's assault upon others. However, this rule does not apply when "the act is one which is fairly and naturally incident to the business, and is done while the servant was engaged upon the master's business and [arises] from some impulse of emotion which naturally grew out of or was incident to the attempt to perform the master's business."

FAHRENDORFF v. NORTH HOMES, INC., 597 N.W.2d 905 (Minn. 1999). The plaintiff was placed temporarily in a group home. A counselor, Kist, was the only adult on a night shift and made sexual advances to her, touching her and speaking to her inappropriately. She sued the owner of the home. *Held*, vicarious liability is a jury question. Evidence indicated that "inappropriate sexual contact or abuse of power in these situations, although infrequent, is a well known hazard" in this kind of enterprise.

Notes

1. Caretakers–those who have undertaken, at least implicitly, to care for the plaintiff who is relatively helpless–may be subject to some special rules of liability. That was most dramatically illustrated in *Ybarra*, Chapter 11, § 2, but there are other examples in the traditional liability of innkeepers and carriers and in the rule applied in *Burgess*, chapter 17, § 2. Should special obligations of caretakers also affect their vicarious liability? Illinois provides by statute that owners and licensees of nursing homes "are liable to a resident for any intentional or negligent act or omission of their agents or employees which injures the resident." Illinois Statutes, 210 ILCS 45/3–601. Should such statutes be extended to cover all caretakers?

2. In *Lourim v. Swensen*, 328 Or. 380, 977 P.2d 1157 (1999), the plaintiff alleged that when the plaintiff was a minor, his Boy Scout leader

(Swensen) sexually abused him. *Held*, the Boy Scout organization may be held vicariously liable. A jury could reasonably infer that Swensen's acts "were merely the culmination of a progressive series of actions that involved the ordinary and authorized duties of a Boy Scout leader," that Swenson's performance of his duties "was a necessary precursor to the sexual abuse and that the assaults were a direct outgrowth of and were engendered by conduct that was within the scope of Swensen's employment." Further, it could be inferred that "Swensen's contact with plaintiff was the direct result of the relationship sponsored and encouraged by the Boy Scouts, which invested Swensen with authority to decide how to supervise minor boys under his care."

Accord as to vicarious liability for alleged sexual abuse by a priest who gained the confidence of the minor and his family through pastoral attentions and who was initially focused on carrying out his duties: *Fearing v. Bucher,* 328 Or. 367, 977 P.2d 1163 (1999) (as alleged, the priest's dutiful acts then led to the acts that injured the plaintiff).

Would these cases necessarily come out differently under the test articulated in *Lisa M.*? Would the Oregon court that decided these cases decide *Lisa M.* differently, do you think?

3. *Trust and authority and incentive.* As recognized in the cases just discussed, an employee's job may provide a "peculiar opportunity and ... incentive for" misbehavior, which might support vicarious liability. The dissenting justices in *Lisa M.* advanced such a view. Justice Kennard wrote that the job of an ultrasound technician involves "intimate contact, inherent in the job," which put plaintiff in a particularly vulnerable position and "contributed to Tripoli's sexual arousal." Justice Mosk thought that Tripoli's "inspiration arose from the mise-en-scene established by the hospital." Where the employee is placed in a position of trust, such views may have particular force. Should vicarious liability be imposed in any of the following cases?

- A public school teacher arranges special sessions with a student, becoming a tutor and counselor. The teacher then threatens failing grades unless the student engages in sexual acts with the teacher. Should the school district be liable? *John R. v. Oakland Unified School District*, 48 Cal.3d 438, 256 Cal.Rptr. 766, 769 P.2d 948 (1989).

- A police officer arrests a woman who is apparently driving under the influence of intoxicants; he then offers kindness by taking her home. Once there, he rapes her. Is the city liable? *Mary M. v. City of Los Angeles*, 54 Cal.3d 202, 285 Cal.Rptr. 99, 814 P.2d 1341 (1991).

- A church encouraged its priests to engage in marriage counseling. One of the priests engaged in illicit sexual activity with one of the marital partners he was counseling. Is the church itself liable for the harm done? *Destefano v. Grabrian*, 763 P.2d 275 (Colo.1988); *Byrd v. Faber*, 57 Ohio St.3d 56, 565 N.E.2d 584, 5 A.L.R.5th 1115 (1991).

4. *Sexual harassment.* Under federal job discrimination statutes (Title VII), courts recognize that on the job sexual harassment by supervisors constitutes actionable discrimination whether it takes the form of quid pro quo demands or hostile work environment. The Supreme Court has held that

agency principles apply, so that the employer is liable for sexual discrimination or harassment by the plaintiff's supervisor in either case. However, if the harassment does not result in the employee's loss of tangible job benefits, the employer can assert an affirmative defense and can escape liability by showing (1) it used reasonable care to prevent and correct harassment and (2) the plaintiff failed to take advantage of preventive/corrective opportunities. *Burlington Industries, Inc. v. Ellerth*, 524 U.S. 742, 118 S.Ct. 2257, 141 L.Ed.2d 633 (1998); *Faragher v. City of Boca Raton*, 524 U.S. 775, 118 S.Ct. 2275, 141 L.Ed.2d 662 (1998).

§ 2.   EMPLOYERS WHO ARE NOT MASTERS

KASTNER v. TOOMBS

Supreme Court of Alaska, 1980.
611 P.2d 62.

MATTHEWS, JUSTICE.

[Clearwater Drilling, owned by Lefevre, was setting a water line. Kastner was employed by Clearwater to lay the pipe. Toombs and To–Bi–Too leased a backhoe to Clearwater for digging the pipe ditch. The lease arrangement called for Toombs to furnish both the backhoe and its operator. Toombs was paid an hourly rate for both. Clearwater demanded a 6–foot ditch. The backhoe operator warned that this would risk a cave-in if the ditch were not shored up, but Clearwater instructed the operator to proceed anyway. The ditch did cave in and Kastner was injured. He here sues Toombs and To–Bi–Too, claiming it should be held vicariously liable for the operator's negligence in digging. The trial court gave summary judgment for the defendants on the ground that these defendants were not vicariously liable for any negligence of the operator while he was working for Clearwater.]

Under the doctrine of *respondeat superior* a master is liable for the torts of his servants committed while acting in the scope of their employment. Current legal thinking bases this doctrine on the concept that a business should pay for the losses which it causes. Its foundation is " 'the desire to include in the costs of operation inevitable losses to third persons incident to carrying on an enterprise, and thus distribute the burden among those benefitted by the enterprise.' "

> [I]n essence the enterprise may be regarded as a unit for tort ... purposes. Employees' acts sufficiently connected with the enterprise are in effect considered as deeds of the enterprise itself. Where through negligence such acts cause injury to others it is appropriate that the enterprise bear the loss incurred.

The borrowed servant rule carves out an exception to the doctrine of *respondeat superior*. Under the borrowed servant rule a servant who is loaned by one master to another is regarded as acting for the borrowing master, and the loaning master is not held responsible for the servant's negligent acts. This result is reached even though the loaned servant is still employed by his first master and is acting within the scope of his employment. A servant may act for two masters simultaneously. Nevertheless, if the borrowed servant rule applies, only one of them is held vicariously liable for the servant's tort. . . .

The function of the borrowed servant doctrine is to determine which of two potentially liable masters will have to pay for the loss caused by the servant's act. The method we have used in the past for making that selection is to consider the several factors listed in Restatement (Second) of Agency § 220(2). See Reader v. Ghemm Co., 490 P.2d at 1203–04. Those factors are designed to answer the question of whether a master-servant relationship exists. But the ultimate question in borrowed servant cases is not whether such a relationship exists; it is, rather, which among two masters should be liable for the servant's tort. It is therefore not surprising that consideration of the Restatement factors has not yielded entirely satisfactory results. . . . Note, Liability for Torts of Borrowed Servant, 28 Ohio St. L.J. 550 at 553.

The traditional approach to the borrowed servant problem emphasizes the factor of control. The rationale is that the master having the right of control would be the one in the best position to prevent the injury. Here again unsatisfactory results are reached because typically both the general employer and the special employer have significant elements of control:

> The courts, in applying the control test, have failed to define what is meant by control. Are the courts speaking of broad control such as the power to discharge the employee, which is usually retained by the general employer, or of detailed on-the-spot control which is usually exercised by the special employer? The courts which emphasize control in the broad sense make the general employer liable; whereas if detailed on-the-spot control is emphasized the special contractor is held liable. In any case under the control test the result depends almost entirely upon which facts the courts wish to emphasize, because in almost all the cases both the general employer and the special employer exercise some type of control over the servant.

Note, supra 28 Ohio St. L.J. at 552.

Another approach asks whose business is being done, apparently with the intent of placing liability upon the master who benefits from the servant's acts. Unfortunately, the answer almost always is that to a substantial extent the servant's work is furthering the purposes of both masters.

In our opinion the borrowed servant rule as an exception to the doctrine of *respondeat superior* has imparted unnecessary complexity to the law of agency. We see no reason for a rule of exclusive liability in situations in which a servant acting within the scope of his employment for two masters negligently causes injury to another. The question of how the loss so caused should be distributed should be determined in accordance with principles of contribution and indemnity. These principles have been devised to answer questions concerning the allocation of losses among potentially responsible parties. These principles may not be easy to apply in every case, but they are at least directly responsive to the problem, while the various approaches taken under the borrowed servant rule are not.

There is considerable authority supporting the position which we have taken. For example, Professor Mechem has argued that dual liability is the simplest and most practical solution to the borrowed servant problem. F. Mechem, Outline of the Law of Agency, § 458 (4th ed. 1952). In Harper & James, The Law of Torts, dual liability is referred to as a "sensible result." . . .

Reversed and remanded.

Notes

1. Accord, on the basis of a "sentiment that a business enterprise cannot justly disclaim responsibility for accidents which may fairly be said to be characteristic of its activities," *Morgan v. ABC Mfr.*, 710 So.2d 1077 (La.1998).

2. Suppose nurses are employed by a hospital. A surgeon is permitted to use hospital facilities for an operation and nurses are furnished by the hospital. At the end of the operation, the doctor removes the sponges and the nurses count them to be sure all are removed. If the nurses negligently counted and sponges are allowed to remain in the body, is the doctor vicariously liable under the borrowed servant doctrine? A few cases have said that the doctor is the "captain of the ship" or that the nurses have become the doctor's special employees. Others say it is a question of fact whether the doctor was actually giving directions and exercising control over the nurses.

DISTRICT OF COLUMBIA v. HAMPTON

District of Columbia Court of Appeals, 1995.
666 A.2d 30.

TERRY, ASSOCIATE JUDGE:

[The District of Columbia's Department of Human Services (DHS) removed two-year-old Mykeeda Hampton from her mother's care on the ground that the mother was not properly caring for the child. DHS placed the child in the care of a foster parent, Geraldine Stevenson. Stevenson left Mykeeda with her two sons for over ten hours. During that time Mykeeda was beaten to death by the 12–year-old son. Mykeeda's mother brought this survival action asserting (1) that the DHS was negligent in selecting or supervising Stevenson as a foster parent and (2) that Stevenson was an agent of the DHS so that DHS or the District was vicariously liable. The jury found for the plaintiff. On appeal, the court first concluded that the evidence did not support the first argument, then addressed vicarious liability.]

The District also maintains that Geraldine Stevenson was not its agent but an independent contractor, and thus that any negligence on her part cannot be imputed to it under the doctrine of respondeat superior. . . .

As it relates to foster care, this is an issue of first impression for this court, and one that has not been addressed by many other courts. The trend of recent case law, however, seems to be that foster parents are not deemed to be agents or employees of state family service agencies. . . .

Whether a master-servant (or principal-agent) relationship exists in a given situation "depends on the particular facts of each case." The person asserting the relationship–in this case, Mrs. Hampton–has the burden of proof. This court has recognized several factors to be considered in determining whether such a relationship exists:

> (1) the selection and engagement of the servant, (2) the payment of wages, (3) the power to discharge, (4) the power to control the servant's conduct, (5) and whether the work is part of the regular business of the employer.

We have often held, however, that of these five factors "the determinative factor" is usually the fourth: "the right to control an employee in the performance of a task and in its result, and not the actual exercise of control or supervision."

In analyzing the employer's right to control, this court has generally looked to the actual relationship between the parties and, if a written agreement existed between them, to the language of that agreement. For instance, in Safeway Stores, supra, there was evidence of several instances in which Safeway management gave instructions to store security guards, who in turn complied with those instructions. We said that "specific instances of actual control are evidence of the general right of Safeway to control [the security guard] in the performance of his duties." . . .

In this case there was very little testimony about the actual relationship between Mrs. Stevenson and the DHS social workers, and none suggesting that the District had a right to control Stevenson's daily performance of her foster care duties. The testimony of Maria Clark, the DHS social worker assigned to supervise Mykeeda's foster care, did not establish that Mrs. Stevenson took direction from Clark in caring for Mykeeda. For example, on one occasion Stevenson telephoned Clark and said that Mykeeda had developed bruises from being spanked by Stevenson and her son, and from using a plastic potty trainer. Clark testified that she did not go to the Stevenson home to check on Mykeeda, but assumed that Mykeeda "simply . . . bruised easily." . . . In fact, as the District points out, Mrs. Stevenson testified that she controlled many areas of her foster children's lives and that she was responsible for making all the day-to-day decisions about their care: what they would eat, what clothes they would wear, when they needed new clothes, when they would bathe, where they would spend their time, and how they would be disciplined. Without any evidence that DHS actually controlled the manner in which Mrs. Stevenson cared for Mykeeda, no reasonable juror could have found that Mrs. Stevenson was the District's agent.

Mrs. Hampton argues that the many rules and regulations concerning foster homes demonstrate that the District reserved the right to control a foster parent. The list of "basic requirements" for a foster home, implicitly gives the District the right to control such matters as the sleeping arrangements for a foster child, the temperature of the foster home, the diet of the foster child, and certain aspects of the foster parents' health. The District also reserves the right to inspect a foster home at any time. There are rules pertaining to the health care of a foster child, and a foster parent must obtain permission from DHS before taking a foster child on an out-of-town trip. Finally, the District has the right to remove a foster child from the foster home at any time and without prior notice.

These regulations obviously show that the District has the authority to dictate many aspects of a foster child's life in a foster home. But that does not establish that the foster parent is under the actual control of the District to a degree sufficient to make him or her the District's agent. To paraphrase what we said in Giles v. Shell Oil, "the right to inspect" and "the right to set standards by which [a foster parent performs her duties] are not indicia of control. They in no way indicate that [the District] had the right to control the day-to-day operation of the [foster home] or the day-to-day performance of [the foster parent]."

For these reasons we hold that the evidence was insufficient to prove that Mrs. Stevenson was the District's agent, and that the trial court therefore erred in allowing Mrs. Hampton's respondeat superior claim to go to the jury.

[Judgment reversed for entry of judgment NOV.]

Notes

1. Subject to limited exceptions, the rule is that the employer is not vicariously liable for the torts of an independent contractor. The issue arises most commonly in a business setting, in which one person (or business) hires another—the independent contractor—to do some particular work. For example, a sawmill might hire independent contractors who are in the business of cutting and hauling timber to perform those tasks, instead of using its own employees. When an injury is caused by the independent contractor while on the job, the sawmill itself will not be vicariously liable. See *Leaf River Forest Prods., Inc. v. Harrison*, 392 So.2d 1138 (Miss.1981).

2. In determining whether an employee is a servant or an independent contractor, courts have, as in *Hampton,* emphasized the right to control details of the work as a sign that the employee is a servant. If the employer can only determine what is acceptable as the end result, that is a sign that the employee is an independent contractor. But control is only one factor. If the employee runs his own business and works for others as well as for the employer, he is not likely to be a servant. If he provides his own tools or uses special skills, that is also likely to indicate that he is an independent contractor. See RESTATEMENT SECOND OF AGENCY § 220 (1958). In many cases these rules are easy to apply. Consider: the employee is a house painter you

hired to paint your house. After the house is painted he will paint somewhere else.

3. *Retained control.* Employees who are ordinarily independent contractors—general building contractors and their subcontractors, for example—may become "servants" if sufficient control is retained by the employer. Retained control may also show that the employer himself was negligent. If the employer fails to exercise reasonable care to control the independent contractor, the employer may then be liable because it is negligent, whether or not it would also be vicariously liable. See *Hammond v. Bechtel, Inc.*, 606 P.2d 1269 (Alaska 1980).

4. *"Corporate negligence."* We have already seen a very similar idea in Chapter 13. Suppose a hospital permits a physician to admit her patients to the hospital for its care and to utilize its operating room and other resources. The physician is not in any sense employed by the hospital and the hospital is not vicariously liable. However, the hospital may be liable for its own corporate or institutional negligence if it allows incompetent or dangerous physicians to use its facilities. This corporate negligence doctrine is now well accepted. See, e.g., *Darling v. Charleston Community Memorial Hospital*, 33 Ill.2d 326, 211 N.E.2d 253 (1965); *Insinga v. LaBella*, 543 So.2d 209 (Fla.1989) (counting 17 jurisdictions that had approved the doctrine at that time). It has now been applied to an HMO that allegedly assigned an overload of patients to independent contractor physicians. *Jones v. Chicago HMO Ltd. of Illinois,* 191 Ill.2d 278, 730 N.E.2d 1119, 246 Ill.Dec. 654 (2000).

O'BANNER v. McDONALD'S CORP.

Supreme Court of Illinois, 1996.
173 Ill.2d 208, 218 Ill.Dec. 910, 670 N.E.2d 632.

JUSTICE HARRISON delivered the opinion of the court:

Reginald O'Banner brought an action in the circuit court of Cook County to recover damages for personal injuries he allegedly sustained when he slipped and fell in the bathroom of a McDonald's restaurant. In his complaint, O'Banner named as defendants McDonald's Corporation (McDonald's) and certain "unknown owners." McDonald's promptly moved for summary judgment on the grounds that the restaurant was actually owned by one of its franchisees and that it neither owned, operated, maintained, nor controlled the facility....

The circuit court here entered summary judgment in favor of McDonald's based on the company's argument that it was merely the franchisor of the restaurant where O'Banner was injured and, as such, had no responsibility for the conditions that caused his accident. O'Banner challenged this conclusion in the appellate court by theorizing that even though McDonald's was a franchisor, it could nevertheless be held liable for the franchisee's negligence under principles of respondeat superior because there was sufficient evidence in the record to establish that the franchisee served as McDonald's actual agent. In the alternative, O'Banner contended that McDonald's could be vicariously liable for the acts and omissions of the franchisee based on the doctrine of apparent agency.

The appellate court rejected the actual agency theory based on the documentary evidence, but held that there remained genuine issues of material fact with respect to O'Banner's alternative theory of apparent agency. Accordingly, it reversed and remanded for further proceedings. . . .

In the appeal before this court, the issue of actual agency has not been pursued. The sole question before us is whether the appellate court erred in reversing and remanding based on the theory of apparent agency. . . .

Apparent agency, also known in Illinois as apparent authority, . . . is based on principles of estoppel. The idea is that if a principal creates the appearance that someone is his agent, he should not then be permitted to deny the agency if an innocent third party reasonably relies on the apparent agency and is harmed as a result.

Under the doctrine, a principal can be held vicariously liable in tort for injury caused by the negligent acts of his apparent agent if the injury would not have occurred but for the injured party's justifiable reliance on the apparent agency. The fundamental obstacle to O'Banner's recovery in this case concerns this element of reliance. Even if one concedes that McDonald's advertising and other conduct could entice a person to enter a McDonald's restaurant in the belief it was dealing with an agent of the corporation itself, that is not sufficient. In order to recover on an apparent agency theory, O'Banner would have to show that he actually did rely on the apparent agency in going to the restaurant where he was allegedly injured.

No amount of liberal construction can alter the fact that the record before us is devoid of anything remotely suggesting that the necessary reliance was present here. The pleadings and affidavit submitted by O'Banner in the circuit court state only that he slipped and fell in the restroom of a McDonald's restaurant. They give no indication as to why he went to the restaurant in the first place. The fact that this was a McDonald's may have been completely irrelevant to his decision. For all we know, O'Banner went there simply because it provided the closest bathroom when he needed one or because some friend asked to meet him there.

If O'Banner had any basis to support his position, he was obliged to present it to the circuit court. He did not do so, and the time for substantiating any claim of reliance has passed. The appellate court was therefore wrong to reverse the circuit court's entry of summary judgment in McDonald's favor based on the apparent agency doctrine.

For the foregoing reasons, the judgment of the appellate court is reversed, the judgment of the circuit court is affirmed, and the cause is remanded to the circuit court for further proceedings consistent with this opinion. [A dissenting opinion is omitted.]

Notes

1. In evaluating *O'Banner,* consider whether the plaintiff there would have to show that he would not have used the bathroom if he had known that the local operators were not agents of McDonald's.

2. *Managed health care or HMOs.* Health maintenance organizations, usually corporations, are not physicians. Instead they are contractors who manage health care programs. In one type of HMO, the HMO hires its own doctors and they are its employees. In a second type, the HMO contracts with independent physicians to provide the services needed. Suppose you go to work for a law firm which has a health care program through an HMO of the second type. You select a physician from the approved list and he negligently injures you. Is the HMO vicariously liable? In *Petrovich v. Share Health Plan of Illinois, Inc.,* 188 Ill.2d 17, 241 Ill.Dec. 627, 719 N.E.2d 756 (1999), the Illinois court held that the HMO was subject to vicarious liability on the same apparent agency theory it rejected in *O'Banner.* The court said the patient would be relying upon the HMO if the patient is not selecting a specific physician for some reason such as a prior relationship with that physician but merely because some physicians had to be selected from the list furnished.

BOROUGHS v. JOINER

Supreme Court of Alabama, 1976.
337 So.2d 340.

[Boroughs alleged that the defendant, Joiner, employed one Carter to apply pesticide to Joiner's crops by spraying from an aircraft, that Carter did so, using Endrin, which is an intrinsically dangerous substance, many times more toxic than DDT, and that the pesticide could not be contained but contaminated the plaintiff's pond, killing the fish and depreciating the value of the plaintiff's land. The trial judge granted a motion for summary judgment on the ground that Carter was not a servant but an independent contractor.]

SHORES, JUSTICE

The general rule in this state, and in most others, is that:

"... one is not ordinarily responsible for the negligent acts of his independent contractor. But this rule, as most others, has important exceptions. One is that a person is responsible for the manner of the performance of his nondelegable duties, though done by an independent contractor...."

It is also generally recognized that one who employs a contractor to carry on an inherently or intrinsically dangerous activity cannot thereby insulate himself from liability....

The rule is stated in Restatement of the Law, Torts 2d, Vol. 2, § 427 (1965), as follows:

"One who employs an independent contractor to do work involving a special danger to others which the employer knows or has reason to know to be inherent in or normal to the work, or which he contemplates or has reason to contemplate when making the contract, is subject to liability for physical harm caused to such others by the contractor's failure to take reasonable precautions against such danger."

Crop dusting and spraying having [sic] been the subject of much litigation in recent years. Many courts have categorized such activity as inherently or intrinsically dangerous, making inapplicable the rule that a principal is not liable for the torts of his independent contractor. . . .

The Legislature of Alabama has recognized that insecticides and pesticides are intrinsically dangerous and has adopted statutes regulating the sale, distribution and application of those products in this state. . . .

Under the statutory scheme adopted by the legislature, such products must be registered with the Department of Agriculture and Industries. Each must bear a label describing the degree of toxicity, and each must bear warnings of the dangers inherent in the use thereof. One must have a permit to purchase such products. Aviators must be licensed to engage in crop dusting or spraying and must pass an examination satisfactory to the Commissioner of Agriculture demonstrating knowledge of the dangers involved in the application thereof.

We hold that aerial application of insecticides and pesticides falls into the intrinsically or inherently dangerous category and, therefore, the landowner cannot insulate himself from liability simply because he has caused the application of the product to be made on his land by an independent contractor.

In so holding, we do not adopt the view, as some courts have done, that such activity is ultrahazardous thereby rendering one strictly liable, notwithstanding his exercise of the utmost care.

The test of liability on the part of the landowner is one of reasonableness. Liability is not absolute but is imposed on the landowner for his failure to exercise due care in a situation in which the work being performed is sufficiently dangerous that the landowner himself has a duty to third persons who may sustain injury or damage from the work unless proper precautions are taken in the performance thereof.

The judgment appealed from is, therefore, reversed and the cause is remanded.

Reversed and remanded.

Notes

1. *Nondelegable duty.* The employer who obtains an independent contractor to do certain work, like that in *Boroughs*, may be held liable vicariously in spite of the independent contractor relationship. This is often expressed as a result of the rule that some duties are "nondelegable." That is to say, the employer cannot delegate or shift the duty of care to another

person, but must guarantee that care is provided. This phrase is not intended to indicate that the independent contractor is immune, only that the employer is not.

2. *Inherent danger and peculiar risk.* The Restatement applies the nondelegable duty rule to inherently dangerous activities in § 427 cited in *Boroughs,* and also, in § 416, to cases of "peculiar risk." The two classes of cases are similar. Peculiar risk must be different in some way from ordinary risks, but it is difficult to discover what courts think the difference might be. Courts have held the duty nondelegable not only in cases of poisons, explosives or fireworks, and strong acids, where the instrumentality is dangerous by nature, but also in many fairly ordinary cases. A contractor sprays paint; some of it splatters on the plaintiff's property next door; an independent distributor hires door-to-door salesmen to sell the manufacturer's vacuum cleaners; one of them had a criminal record and assaulted a woman once in her home; a worker for an independent contractor turns over a tractor on a grassy slope. All these cases and others have been held to count as inherent danger or peculiar risk. See DOBBS ON TORTS § 337 (2000).

3. *Other nondelegable duties.* The Restatement also recognizes that one who is required by specific statute to provide safety protections for others may not avoid ultimate responsibility for this statutory duty by use of an independent contractor. RESTATEMENT SECOND OF TORTS § 424 (1965). Would this cover ordinary safety statutes that say nothing of independent contractors? In *Maloney v. Rath*, 69 Cal.2d 442, 71 Cal.Rptr. 897, 445 P.2d 513 (1968), a car owner had her brakes overhauled by a competent mechanic. Nevertheless, three months later the brakes failed and the plaintiff was injured in the resulting collision. The court first held that the defendant was not liable on the negligence per se doctrine, since her failure to maintain brakes in the statutory working order was excused by her care. But it went on to hold that the defendant was liable because the duty to maintain brakes in safe working order was a nondelegable one. It relied in part on the Restatement's version of "inherently dangerous" instrumentalities (§ 423) and also on § 424. If this is inherent danger, is every auto repair within the nondelegable duty rule? In *MBank El Paso v. Sanchez*, 836 S.W.2d 151 (Tex.1992) a bank hired an independent contractor to repossess Yvonne Sanchez' car because payments had not been made. The contractor found the car in her drive. Over Sanchez' objections, he hooked it to his tow truck. Sanchez then got in the car and locked the doors. Undeterred, the contractor towed the car at high speed to a fenced lot, padlocked the gate, and left Sanchez locked inside the lot, which was also occupied by a loose Doberman Pinscher. After Sanchez was rescued, she sued the bank. Under the Uniform Commercial Code the bank was entitled to repossess the car if it could do so without breach of the peace. The contractor's actions counted as a breach of the peace. Should the bank be liable under § 424 on the ground that the statute in effect provides for safety by the breach-of-the-peace provision?

A third section of the Restatement, § 425, would impose liability upon one who employs an independent contractor to maintain the safety of land held open to the public as a place of business, or a chattel supplied to others for business uses. One illustration involves a hotel which employs an independent plumber to install a shower. The plumber puts the wrong handles on the faucets with the result that a hotel guest is scalded. The hotel is liable. This rule was applied in *Valenti v. Net Properties Management, Inc.*, 142 N.H. 633, 710 A.2d 399 (1998) to hold a mall owner vicariously liable for the negligence of independent contractors in maintaining the premises and placing safety mats at the entrance. The court emphasized that the owner could contract with independent contractors for indemnity and was in the best position to protect against risks.

4. The employer, engaged in "inherently dangerous" distribution of high-voltage electricity, employs an independent contractor to do work on the lines. The contractor is negligent and P is injured. In determining the employer's liability for the contractor's negligence, does it matter whether P is a bystander or is in fact a servant of the independent contractor? Most courts refuse to hold the employer vicariously responsible to the contractor's employees. See *Privette v. Superior Court,* 5 Cal.4th 689, 21 Cal.Rptr.2d 72, 854 P.2d 721 (1993). The reasons are associated with the requirement that the contractor must provide workers' compensation to his employees and with the rule that the workers' compensation claim is the exclusive remedy against the contractor. The employer of course remains liable for its own negligence to the contractor's employees. Even here, however, the employer may find some relief in that it may reasonably count on the contractor to provide many safety precautions, including safety inspections of the job site in some instances. Cf. *Scindia Steam Navigation Co., Ltd. v. De Los Santos,* 451 U.S. 156, 101 S.Ct. 1614, 68 L.Ed.2d 1 (1981).

5. Suppose that an employee of a home for disabled children sexually abuses a helpless patient. Suppose also that the court concludes that the employee, acting for personal gratification, was not within the scope of his employment. Should the court nevertheless hold the nursing home liable on a nondelegable duty theory? Cf. *Stropes v. Heritage House Childrens Center of Shelbyville, Inc.*, 547 N.E.2d 244 (Ind.1989).

6. "Nondelegable duty" obviously expresses a policy or sense of justice for some particular but not perfectly identified kinds of cases. (A) Would it be good policy to hold an operating surgeon liable for the negligence of nurses furnished by the hospital? If so, might the court state that policy by saying that the surgeon had a nondelegable duty rather than by saying that the nurses were borrowed servants? (B) Similarly, could a court reject the ostensible agency or agency by estoppel theory and still hold that a hospital is liable for the negligence of an independent contractor hired to run the hospital's emergency room? Indeed, could a nondelegable duty be found in any case where the independent contractor rule seems unjust or inappropriate?

OTERO v. JORDON RESTAURANT ENTERPRISES

New Mexico Court of Appeals, 1995.
119 N.M. 721, 895 P.2d 243.

APODACA, CHIEF JUDGE....

Defendant hired an independent contractor to expand the premises of its restaurant and bar. As part of the expansion project, the contractor assembled metal bleachers where patrons of the restaurant and bar could be seated to view a large-screen television. Approximately four months after the bleachers were installed, they collapsed. Plaintiff, a patron, fell and was injured. As a result of the accident, he filed suit against Defendant.

Defendant conceded in the trial court that the cause of the collapse was the contractor's faulty and negligent assembly of the bleachers. [Discussion of the defendant's claims against the contractor and manufacturer and the plaintiff's other claims is omitted.]

Before trial, Plaintiff filed a motion for partial summary judgment, seeking an adjudication that Defendant was vicariously liable, or jointly and severally liable, for the contractor's negligence in assembling the bleachers. The trial court granted Plaintiff's motion, ruling that, as a matter of law, Defendant was liable for the contractor's negligence and that Defendant had a nondelegable duty to maintain safety in areas over which it had control. . . .

Section 422 [of the Restatement], in imposing liability on the owner of premises, states that an owner: who entrusts to an independent contractor construction, repair, or other work on the land, or on a building or other structure upon it, is subject to the same liability as though he had retained the work in his own hands to others on or outside of the land for physical harm caused to them by the unsafe condition of the structure. . . . (b) after he has resumed possession of the land upon its completion. Thus, Section 422(b) "makes it impossible for a possessor of land to escape liability for the non-performance of his duty to maintain his land in safe condition, so long as he is in possession of it, by delegating the task of doing the work necessary to the performance of that duty to an independent contractor." Restatement § 422 cmt. e. Liability is imposed on the owner of the premises despite the fact that the owner was not personally at fault in creating the unsafe condition. . . .

[T]he the owner is in a position to prevent or minimize risks by hiring a financially responsible contractor, by making arrangements for indemnification from the contractor, and by requiring the contractor to follow safety procedures and remedy dangerous conditions.

In adopting Section 422(b) of the Restatement, we necessarily reject Defendant's argument that an owner's liability should be limited to situations in which the owner himself is at fault.

Defendant additionally argues that, despite Section 422(b), it should not be held liable for the contractor's negligence because such negligence was only "collateral negligence." We disagree with Defendant's contention.

The collateral negligence doctrine is an exception to an exception. That is, the general rule is that an employer is not liable for the negligence of an independent contractor. This rule, however, as we have previously noted, is riddled with exceptions, one of which is the one established in this case—that an owner of property is liable for the negligence of an independent contractor in building or making repairs to structures on that property, once the owner resumes possession. In turn, those exceptions are also subject to an exception—that the owner is not liable for collateral negligence of the contractor or the contractor's employees. . . .

The concept of "collateral negligence" is set out in Section 426 of the Restatement. Section 426 states: "[A]n employer of an independent contractor, unless he is himself negligent, is not liable for physical harm caused by any negligence of the contractor if (a) the contractor's negligence consists solely in the improper manner in which he does the work, and (b) it creates a risk of such harm which is not inherent in or normal to the work, and (c) the employer had no reason to contemplate the contractor's negligence when the contract was made." . . .

Cases and commentators discussing the collateral negligence doctrine make clear that the concept is limited to negligence that produces a temporarily unsafe condition while the work is in progress. Negligence that produces a poor result or a defect in the final structure, however, is not considered collateral negligence. Thus, a distinction exists between the negligent manner of ongoing work performed by the contractor, for which the employer of the independent contractor may not be liable under the collateral negligence doctrine, and the condition of the premises that results from the negligence, for which the collateral negligence doctrine does not apply.

Here, Defendant had a nondelegable duty to exercise reasonable care that the bleachers were in a safe condition. The contractor's negligent assembly, therefore, made the completed structure unsafe and affected the result that the owner was under a duty to attain—a result of reasonably safe premises. This was not a situation involving an unsafe condition created only while the work was ongoing.

[Judgment affirmed.]

Notes

1. Suppose you hire a contractor to install a skylight in your ceiling. The contractor does so in a negligent fashion, running the risk that the skylight assembly will fall on a guest in your home. Does *Otero* mean you'd be liable to the guest even if you knew nothing about the negligence or the danger?

2. Notice the *Otero* court's suggestion about how an owner-employer could get protection against liability. Since any employer of an independent contractor can always be protected by hiring a financially strong contractor, or one fully insured, is there any real problem? What if a general contractor hires a subcontractor who has no assets and no insurance? The general contractor gets the work cheaper that way, since the subcontractor is not paying the costs of insurance and of course pays for none of the harm caused by its negligence. Should the general contractor *always* be held liable for failing to hire financially responsible independent contractors? *Becker v. Interstate Properties*, 569 F.2d 1203 (3d Cir.1977) held that under New

Jersey law a general contractor was required to retain subcontractors who were financially responsible or suffer the consequences. New Jersey has since firmly rejected the idea. *Mavrikidis v. Petullo*, 153 N.J. 117, 707 A.2d 977 (1998).

3. Reconsider *Maloney* v. *Rath*, discussed in the notes following *Boroughs*. What could the car owner-defendant do to avoid ultimate liability? Justice Traynor commented on the financial responsibility purposes of the nondelegable duty rule as follows:

> Unlike strict liability, a nondelegable duty operates, not as a substitute for liability based on negligence, but to assure that when a negligently caused harm occurs, the injured party will be compensated by the person whose activity caused the harm and who may therefore properly be held liable for the negligence of his agent, whether his agent was an employee or an independent contractor. To the extent that recognition of nondelegable duties tends to insure that there will be a financially responsible defendant available to compensate for the negligent harms caused by that defendant's activity, it ameliorates the need for strict liability. . . .

If the nondelegable duty rule encourages financial responsibility, why should it be limited to a special group of cases?

NOTE: AGENTS WHO ARE NOT SERVANTS

An employer is one kind of "principal." The principal may employ agents to achieve goals of the enterprise. Some of these are "servants," for whose torts committed within the scope of employment the principal is liable. The employer may use other agents who are definitely not servants. Independent contractors are agents but they are not servants. Some independent contractors do have the power to bind the principal about contractual matters, even though the principal is not liable for their torts. For example, an independent salesperson who travels and sells as she sees fit is not under the principal's control and is thus not ordinarily a servant. But the same salesperson may be authorized to sell the principal's goods and bind the principal by a contract to do so.

§ 3. OTHER FORMS OF VICARIOUS RESPONSIBILITY

1. *Partnership.* L and N form a partnership to sell groceries. It is contemplated that they will acquire and use a truck for delivery of groceries, and in fact they do so. N negligently drives the truck while delivering groceries and Grogan is injured. N is liable personally. Is L also liable? If there were a distinct business entity known as the partnership, the partnership could be viewed as the employer. If that were the case, both N and the partnership would be liable, as in any other master-servant relationship. But a partnership is not a separate entity in the way a corporation is—and both partners are personally liable. Each partner can be seen as a general agent for the other partner or partners. See RESTATEMENT OF AGENCY SECOND § 14A (1958).

2. *Joint enterprise.* D, E and F, three sales persons who are selling for three different companies but who are not servants, discover they all intend to drive from Buffalo to Chicago at the same time. They decide to rent a single car, share expenses and share driving. While one of them, D, is driving, there is a collision with Grogan's car. D may have been negligent. Grogan is injured. If D is negligent, he is personally liable. Are E and F also liable?

Courts have imposed liability upon all members of a joint enterprise when persons outside the enterprise are injured. This is said to exist where there is (1) an agreement, express or implied, (2) there is a common purpose, (3) there is a community of interest and (4) there is equal right of control. These terms are sometimes interpreted liberally. The agreement need not be spelled out in words and it is enough if the parties had a tacit understanding. In some cases, however, courts have held or stated that a social venture will qualify if all the elements are present. Under this view three friends sharing expenses, having a common purpose and equal right to control, might all be liable if one of them drives negligently on a fishing trip. Is this sound or not?

When members of the enterprise itself are injured, the rule is different, and there is no imputation of negligence among the enterprisers themselves. Thus if A, B, and C are on a joint enterprise, and A drives negligently, causing an injury to B, B will have a claim against A for his negligence, but no claim against C based on imputation of A's fault to C.

3. *Concert of action, conspiracy, aiding and abetting.* An early basis for joint and several liability was much like the idea behind liability of one partner or joint enterpriser for the acts of another. Conspirators or those who act in concert to commit a tort or crime are partners, as it were, in an illegal or tortious enterprise. Aiders and abetters are in much the same position. In *Courtney v. Courtney*, 186 W.Va. 597, 413 S.E.2d 418 (W.Va.1991), the complaint alleged Maud supplied her son with alcohol and drugs even though she knew that when he used them he beat his wife. The court held the complaint stated a claim on behalf of the family victims. What if, as A begins to beat the plaintiff, A's uncle B shouts "Kill him, kill him!" *Rael v. Cadena*, 93 N.M. 684, 604 P.2d 822 (1979).

4. *Entrustment of vehicle.* Defendant, owner of a car, permits T to drive it. T is not a servant, partner, or joint enterpriser. If T drives negligently, will defendant be liable? There are at least five distinct situations:

(a) *Negligent entrustment.* Defendant may be liable for his own negligent entrustment of the car to one who is incompetent to drive. This is not vicarious liability but requires proof that defendant knew or should have known of the incompetence and that injury resulted from that incompetence.

(b) *Owner in the car with right of control.* When the defendant permits another to drive, but himself remains in the car, as owner he retains some degree of legal control and he may be liable for failing to exercise that control. Again, this may reflect not vicarious liability but ordinary negligence. In some cases courts have emphasized the legal right of control even if he is not actually negligent. This view is probably on its way out. Thus "the mere presence of the owner in an automobile driven by another does not create any presumption of a master-servant relationship or joint enterprise." *Reed* v. *Hinderland*, 135 Ariz. 213, 660 P.2d 464 (1983).

(c) *Ordinary bailment.* If the owner-defendant simply lends the car to a competent driver, so that there is a bailment, with neither actual nor legal right of control, there is no agency and no liability. This is the common law rule.

(d) *Owner consent statutes.* Statutes of several states make the individual owner liable for the negligence of the driver even in the case of a pure bailment, provided only that the owner consented to the use of the car. This kind of statute may give rise to litigation over whether the defendant actually consented to the use of the car and if so whether the driver went beyond the consent. Commercial lessors of vehicles may be subject to further regulation in many states. In Florida, a judge-made doctrine imposes strict vicarious liability upon the owner who provides a motor vehicle to another. But Florida recognizes an exception if the bailee goes so far beyond the owner's consent that the bailee in effect becomes a thief or converter. *Hertz Corporation v. Jackson,* 617 So.2d 1051 (Fla.1993).

(e) *Family purpose doctrine.* This doctrine, invented by the courts, was that if a car was maintained for general family use, the legal owner would be liable for its negligent use by a member of the family. The effect was that the driver was treated as the servant of the owner. At the time the doctrine originated this typically involved holding the husband or father liable for the negligent driving of a wife or child.

5. *Imputed contributory negligence.*

(a) *The "both ways" rule.* M employs S as his servant. S, in the course and scope of employment, negligently drives M's car, causing a collision with T, who is also driving negligently. M is liable to T under ordinary rules of vicarious liability. In M's own action against T for damages to his car, should S's negligence be imputed to M, reducing or even barring M's recovery? The two issues are distinct and, in one well-known decision, the Minnesota Court held that although M should be vicariously liable to T, there was no justification in barring M's own claim against T. *Weber v. Stokely–Van Camp, Inc.*, 274 Minn. 482, 144 N.W.2d 540 (1966). But most courts have not followed this rule. Instead they follow the rule that responsibility operates "both ways"—if M is liable vicariously for S's negligence, then M's recovery against T is either reduced or barred on the basis of S's negligence (depending on the particular state's approach to contributory negligence). The Restatement of Apportionment adopts this "both ways" rule. RESTATEMENT OF TORTS (THIRD) APPORTIONMENT § 5 (1999).

(b) *Negligence of family members.* H, a husband and father, negligently drives his car. T, driving another car in a negligent way, collides with H. W and C, the wife and child of H, are injured in the collision and sue T. Can T defend on the ground that H's negligence is imputed to his wife and child? Older cases said so, but these decisions have now been condemned everywhere. See *LaBier v. Pelletier*, 665 A.2d 1013 (Me. 1995).

Although it is no longer true that a family member's fault will be imputed to another family member in the absence of an agency relationship, the same result may be achieved on other grounds. Consider for example the *Dillon v. Legg* case: if the child crossing the street is guilty of contributory negligence, will the child's mother be permitted to recover for mental distress? Or suppose a consortium claim by a wife: if her husband was guilty of contributory negligence, will the consortium claim be barred or reduced?

(c) *Bailments.* A car owner bails it to a bailee who drives negligently. As we saw above, the owner is not liable to a third person for the bailee's negligence. Is the owner prevented from a recovery against a negligent third person if the bailee is at fault? Again, courts once so held, and again this rule has largely disappeared. See DOBBS ON TORTS § 340 (2000).

Chapter 21

THE DEVELOPMENT OF COMMON LAW STRICT LIABILITY

§ 1. STRICT LIABILITY FOR TRESPASSORY TORTS AND THE ADVENT OF FAULT THEORY

After the Norman Conquest of England (about 1066), the kings of England gradually began to decide many disputes through their judges. But England was a feudal country with many local barons who also had courts and who wished to decide matters for themselves. Many boroughs or free cities also developed courts; there were even church courts. To the extent that the kings' courts decided disputes, local power was diminished. Local interests naturally resisted this.

Among the earliest disputes the king's ministers or agents decided were those affecting land title or possession. It was easy for the king to assert this power, since he was the tenant-in-chief in a feudal system and it was natural that he would assert the power to make ultimate decisions as to land title and possession. Gradually the "king's peace" became the subject of royal power as well, and the king's judges began to handle all cases of violent crime.

Crime and tort were not readily distinguished in the early Norman period, and out of the king's court's jurisdiction over crime there gradually emerged the closely analogous power to decide cases of violent torts.

The king's power in civil cases was exercised when the Chancellor issued an original writ, the effect of which was to command the sheriff to bring the defendant to answer the plaintiff's claims in the king's courts. These writs reflected the "forms of action." The forms of action—that is to say, the types of cases which the king's courts could hear—were limited in number. The local authorities had exerted sufficient pressure to achieve a general recognition that the king's courts were not to recognize any new forms of action or writs, but were to act only in the kinds of cases represented by the writs that then existed. They made one exception—cases that were "similar" to those covered by the old writs.

Trespass. For a long time, the term "trespass" was sometimes used more or less as the equivalent of "tort," referring to acts of the defendant. See MORRIS ARNOLD, SELECT CASES OF TRESPASS FROM THE KING'S COURTS 1307–1399 (1985). Procedurally, however, the term referred to the main writ or form of action. The plaintiff could begin a claim by obtaining a writ of *Trespass*; many of the incidents of the proceeding, including the substantive rules, were determined by the writ chosen. The writ of *Trespass* could be used in any kind of case in which the plaintiff could show that defendant had directly applied physical force to person or property. It came to cover the torts we now think of as assault, battery, false imprisonment, trespass to land and trespass to chattels. The connection between these torts and crimes of violence is sufficiently obvious, but the writ was not limited to cases of intended violence. By the end of the 12th century trespass was recognized as a tort as well as a crime, so that damages could be recovered for any of the acts of force for which the writ of *Trespass* would lie.

One set of rules that went with the writ of *Trespass* told the plaintiff what he had to prove. He had only to prove (1) force and (2) direct application to person or property. Not only was it unnecessary for the plaintiff to show intent or fault, it was also unnecessary to show damages. In a famous assault case, *I de S et Ux v. W de S*, Y.B. Lib. Ass. f. 99, pl. 60. (1348) the defendant, apparently frustrated to find that the tavern was closed, beat on the door with a hatchet and when the plaintiff put her head out of the window, he "struck with the hatchet but did not hit the woman." The Inquest, an early form of the jury, said it seemed to them there was no harm, but the judge instructed them that "There is harm done and a trespass for which [plaintiff] shall recover damages...." Thus when the writ of *Trespass* could be used—whenever direct physical force was applied—there was not only strict liability, but there was a recovery of damages without proof of harm.

Case. We have said that the local interests were willing to recognize power in the king's courts to hear the old writs, such as *Trespass*, and also such other writs as involved "similar cases." This concession, which appeared as the Statute of Westminster II in 1285, is often said to be the source of the new writ, *Trespass on the (Similar) Case*, a writ developed by analogy to the writ of *Trespass*, but different from it. Whether the statute is the source of the new writ or not is much debated, see CECIL FIFOOT, HISTORY AND SOURCES OF THE COMMON LAW 66 ff. (1949). At any rate, the new writ, called *Trespass on the Case*, or simply *Case*, developed after that time and had a foothold in English jurisprudence by the 14th century.

Case covered instances in which the defendant's acts caused harm to the plaintiff, but in which the harm did not result "directly," or did not result from physical force. The classic examples suggest that if you throw a log and it hits the plaintiff, the proper writ is *Trespass*, since there is both force and direct injury. But if you throw a log and it lands in the road where the plaintiff later trips over it in the dark, the proper writ must be *Case*, the force having dissipated and the injury being indirect.

Primitive law tends to be formal, but the distinction between *Trespass* and *Case* had important practical consequences. In *Case* some quality we would now call fault was required—negligence, for example. As we have seen, no fault was required if the writ of *Trespass* could be used.

Changes in the law. It is apparent from the very first cases in this book that the rules applied in medieval England have little or no place in modern law. How did the change occur?

WEAVER v. WARD

Hob. 134, 80 Eng. Rep. 284 (K.B. 1616).

Weaver brought an action of trespass of assault and battery against Ward. The defendant pleaded, that he was amongst others by the commandment of the Lords of the Council a trained soldier in London, of the band of one Andrews captain; and so was the plaintiff, and that they were skirmishing with their musquets charged with powder for their exercise in re militari, against another captain and his band; and as they were so skirmishing, the defendant casualiter & per infortunium & contra voluntatem suam, in discharging of his piece did hurt and wound the plaintiff, which is the same, & c. absque hoc, that he was guilty aliter sive alio modo. And upon demurrer by the plaintiff, judgment was given for him; for though it were agreed, that if men tilt or turney in the presence of the King, or if two masters of defence playing their prizes kill one another, that this shall be no felony; or if a lunatick kill a man, or the like, because felony must be done animo felonico: yet in trespass, which tends only to give damages according to hurt or loss, it is not so; and therefore if a lunatick hurt a man, he shall be answerable in trespass: and therefore no man shall be excused of a trespass (for this is the nature of an excuse, and not of a justification, prout ei bene licuit) except it may be judged utterly without his fault.

As if a man by force take my hand and strike you, or if here the defendant had said, that the plaintiff ran cross his piece when it was discharging, or had set forth the case with the circumstances, so as it had appeared to the Court that it had been inevitable, and that the defendant had committed no negligence to give occasion to the hurt.

Notes

1. Does the court recognize liability without fault? Under what circumstances, if any, could a defendant escape liability? Do the court's examples suggest that the absence of fault, by itself, would be sufficient to avoid liability?

2. In the next century, the 1700s, a second idea occurred. This idea was that the writ of *Trespass* with its strict liability could be used not only when injury was "direct," but also when the injury was the result of an "unlawful" act, such as an intentional harm. This might be important, because the

plaintiff who chose the wrong writ lost his case. If the plaintiff chose *Trespass* and proved an unlawful harm but not a direct one, he would lose, unless this second idea were accepted. And there was some degree of acceptance of this new idea, one result of which may have been to associate the writ of *Trespass* with unlawfulness or intentional harm, rather than with "direct" harm. Cf. *Vosburg v. Putney*, 80 Wis. 523, 50 N.W. 403 (1891) (unlawfulness of schoolroom misbehavior sufficient for liability.)

3. In the 1800s a third idea occurred. It was that if the plaintiff had damages and could show fault in the defendant, he could "waive the trespass," even where harm was direct. Having waived the trespass, he could use the writ of *Case*, which had certain procedural advantages in some instances. Since he had to prove even more than when he used the writ of *Trespass*, this seemed fair enough, and the effect was to give the plaintiff an option whenever he could make proof of fault and damages and had direct harm. If in fact he could make the required proof there was no need to resort to strict liability in *Trespass*. And there were some advantages to *Case*. One of these was that, having the option to sue in *Case*, he would not lose for technical reasons—it would always be the right writ provided he could make the proof of fault and harm. If he chose *Trespass*, on the other hand, he might find himself out of court if the judges thought the harm to be "indirect" and thus unsuited for the *Trespass* writ. The upshot was that *Case* came to be commonly used and negligence was routinely proven even where the harm was direct.

These seemingly minor changes had a large impact on the practice of law; lawyers routinely used *Case* and proved fault and damages in many instances.

4. The exact details of this history, which is here much simplified, are debated. See E.F.Roberts, *Negligence: Blackstone to Shaw to ?*, 50 CORNELL L.Q. 191 (1965). In fact, our book-learning about earlier practices may be an inaccurate reflection of both the practices and the conceptions of earlier periods. Certainly other descriptions of the history could be given. See FRANK VANDALL, STRICT LIABILITY: LEGAL AND ECONOMIC ANALYSIS 1–6 (1989). Still, by 1850, there had been a considerable change in attitude in the profession, but the law on the books remained pretty much in line with notions held as far back as the 14th century—strict liability would be imposed for trespass, but some kind of fault had to be found if only *Case* would lie.

It is important to understand the conceptual shift in the way lawyers understood the writs. But there are more important questions. One of these is whether the lawyers of the time understood the change that was going on in their professional world, and whether we ourselves do today. Another is whether larger forces were and *are* at work, influencing a shift from strict liability to a fault standard, or possibly vice versa.

BROWN v. KENDALL

Supreme Court of Massachusetts, 1850.
60 Mass. (6 Cush.) 292.

This was an action of trespass for assault and battery, originally commenced against George K. Kendall, the defendant, who died pending the suit, and his executrix was summoned in.

[Defendant Kendall was beating two fighting dogs, attempting to separate them with a four-foot stick. In the movement of dogs and men, he backed towards the plaintiff, raised the stick over his shoulder to strike the dogs and accidentally hit the plaintiff in the eye. The defendant requested the judge to instruct the jury, among other things, that if defendant was using ordinary care and the plaintiff was not, the plaintiff could not recover.]

The judge declined to give the instructions, as above requested, but left the case to the jury under the following instructions: "If the defendant, in beating the dogs, was doing a necessary act, or one which it was his duty under the circumstances of the case to do, and was doing it in a proper way; then he was not responsible in this action, provided he was using ordinary care at the time of the blow. If it was not a necessary act; if he was not in duty bound to attempt to part the dogs, but might with propriety interfere or not as he chose; the defendant was responsible for the consequences of the blow, unless it appeared that he was in the exercise of extraordinary care, so that the accident was inevitable, using the word inevitable not in a strict but a popular sense."

. . .

The jury under these instructions returned a verdict for the plaintiff; whereupon the defendant alleged exceptions.

SHAW, C. J. This is an action of trespass, *vi et armis*,[1] brought by George Brown against George K. Kendall, for an assault and battery. . . .

It appears to us, that some of the confusion in the cases on this subject has grown out of the long-vexed question, under the rule of the common law, whether a party's remedy, where he has one, should be sought in an action of the case, or of trespass. This is very distinguishable from the question, whether in a given case, any action will lie. The result of these cases is, that if the damage complained of is the immediate effect of the act of the defendant, trespass *vi et armis* lies; if consequential only, and not immediate, case is the proper remedy. Leame v. Bray, 3 East, 593; Hugget v. Montgomery, 2 N.R. 446, Day's Ed. and notes.

In these discussions, it is frequently stated by judges, that when one receives injury from the direct act of another, trespass will lie. But we think this is said in reference to the question, whether trespass and not case will lie, assuming that the facts are such, that some action will lie. These dicta are no authority, we think, for holding, that damage received by a direct act of force from another will be sufficient to maintain an action of trespass, whether the act was lawful or unlawful, and neither wilful, intentional, or careless. In the principal case cited, Leame v. Bray, the damage arose from the act of the defendant, in driving on the wrong side of the road, in a dark night, which was clearly negligent if not

---

1. *Vi et armis*: with force and arms, words used in certain trespass writs, originally designed to justify intervention of the   King's Courts in the interest of the King's peace.—eds.

unlawful. In the course of the argument of that case (p. 595), Lawrence, J., said: "There certainly are cases in the books, where, the injury being direct and immediate, trespass has been holden to lie, though the injury was not intentional." The term "injury" implies something more than damage; but, independently of that consideration, the proposition may be true, because though the injury was unintentional, the act may have been unlawful or negligent, and the cases cited by him are perfectly consistent with that supposition. So the same learned judge in the same case says (p. 597), "No doubt trespass lies against one who drives a carriage against another, whether done wilfully or not." But he immediately adds, "Suppose one who is driving a carriage is negligently and heedlessly looking about him, without attending to the road when persons are passing, and thereby runs over a child and kills him, is it not manslaughter? And if so, it must be trespass; for every manslaughter includes trespass"; showing what he understood by a case not wilful.

We think, as the result of all the authorities, the rule is correctly stated by Mr. Greenleaf, that the plaintiff must come prepared with evidence to show either that the intention was unlawful, or that the defendant was in fault; for if the injury was unavoidable, and the conduct of the defendant was free from blame, he will not be liable. 2 Greenl. Ev. §§ 85 to 92; Wakeman v. Robinson, 1 Bing. 213. If, in the prosecution of a lawful act, a casualty purely accidental arises, no action can be supported for an injury arising therefrom. Davis v. Saunders, 2 Chit. R. 639; Com Dig. Battery, A. (Day's Ed.) and notes; Vincent v. Stinehour, 7 Vern. 69. In applying these rules to the present case, we can perceive no reason why the instructions asked for by the defendant ought not to have been given; to this effect, that if both plaintiff and defendant at the time of the blow were using ordinary care, or if at that time the defendant was using ordinary care, and the plaintiff was not, or if at that time, both the plaintiff and defendant were not using ordinary care, then the plaintiff could not recover.

In using this term, ordinary care, it may be proper to state, that what constitutes ordinary care will vary with the circumstances of cases. In general, it means that kind and degree of care, which prudent and cautious men would use, such as is required by the exigency of the case, and such as is necessary to guard against probable danger. A man, who should have occasion to discharge a gun, on an open and extensive marsh, or in a forest, would be required to use less circumspection and care, than if he were to do the same thing in an inhabited town, village, or city....

We are not aware of any circumstances in this case, requiring a distinction between acts which it was lawful and proper to do, and acts of legal duty....

The court instructed the jury, that if it was not a necessary act, and the defendant was not in duty bound to part the dogs, but might with propriety interfere or not as he chose, the defendant was responsible for the consequences of the blow, unless it appeared that he was in exercise of extraordinary care, so that the accident was inevitable, using the word not in a strict but a popular sense. This is to be taken in connection with the charge afterwards given, that if the jury believed, that the act of interference in the fight was unnecessary (that is, as before explained, not a duty incumbent on the defendant), then the burden of proving extraordinary care on the part of the defendant, or want of ordinary care on the part of plaintiff, was on the defendant.

The court are of opinion that these directions were not conformable to law. If the act of hitting the plaintiff was unintentional, on the part of the defendant, and done in the doing of a lawful act, then the defendant was not liable, unless it was done in the want of exercise of due care, adapted to the exigency of the case, and therefore such want of due care became part of the plaintiff's case, and the burden of proof was on the plaintiff to establish it. 2 Greenl. Ev. §§ 85; Powers v. Russell, 13 Pick. 69, 76; Tourtellot v. Rosebrook, 11 Met. 460.

Perhaps the learned judge, by the use of the term extraordinary care, in the above charge, explained as it is by the context, may have intended nothing more than that increased degree of care and diligence, which the exigency of particular circumstances might require, and which men of ordinary care and prudence would use under like circumstances, to guard against danger. If such was the meaning of this part of the charge, then it does not differ from our views, as above explained. But we are of opinion, that the other part of the charge, that the burden of proof was on the defendant, was incorrect. Those facts which are essential to enable the plaintiff to recover, he takes the burden of proving. The evidence may be offered by the plaintiff or by the defendant; the question of due care, or want of care, may be essentially connected with the main facts, and arise from the same proof; but the effect of the rule, as to the burden of proof, is this, that when the proof is all in, and before the jury, from whatever side it comes, and whether directly proved, or inferred from circumstances, if it appears that the defendant was doing a lawful act, and unintentionally hit and hurt the plaintiff, then unless it also appears to the satisfaction of the jury, that the defendant is chargeable with some fault, negligence, carelessness, or want or prudence, the plaintiff fails to sustain the burden of proof, and is not entitled to recover.

New trial is ordered.

Notes

1. Is this clearly a new departure? Professor Gregory pointed out that although Shaw asserted that the rules of substantive tort law were the same for those injured directly and those injured indirectly, the evidence pointed to the contrary. See Charles Gregory, *Trespass to Negligence to Absolute Liability*, 37 VA. L. REV. 359, 366 (1951). Notice how some of the conceptual developments mentioned in the notes preceding this case figure in Chief Justice Shaw's opinion, for example, the question of "lawfulness."

2. It is generally thought that *Brown v. Kendall* marked the first clear articulation of the shift from strict liability for direct, forcible harms to a fault-based liability.

3. *Procedural reform.* One of the larger forces that may have played some part in the shift to a negligence approach was the decay of the writ system and concomitant adoption of the Field Code of procedure in New York. The forms of action as reflected in the writs were not merely procedural devices. The forms of action dictated the scope of the jurisdiction of the king's courts, the procedure to be followed and the substantive rules. For example, as we have seen, *Trespass* embodied a substantive notion that liability was strict where harm was direct and forcible. With the adoption of Code procedure and the decay of the forms of action, was there a blank slate for substantive rules?

4. *Subsidizing industry?* An injury that was forcible and direct in 1350 was often the result of violence. An injury that was forcible and direct after the steam engine and the railroad might be unintended. It might also be the product of a desirable development of economic resources. Would judges have favored a negligence system on the ground that strict liability associated with Trespass might smother infant industry? See Gregory, supra note 1, at 368.

Protective legal rules may have been more significant in 1850 than they could be now. At least two important economic institutions now exist that did not exist in 1850. The first is liability insurance, which allows the industry (or anyone) to spread the costs of injury over a period of time, so that no single large disaster will necessarily wipe out the industry. The second is the development of a system of finance which permits relatively easy aggregations of capital through corporate enterprise, together with a central banking system and a series of money markets which permit the borrowing of capital. Without these devices, infant industry may indeed have needed all the help it could get. The most careful scholarship, however, seems to indicate that on the whole, the courts of the early 1800s were sympathetic to the injured victim and quite willing to use negligence law, or negligence law mixed with forms of older strict liability, to aid the injured. Gary T. Schwartz, *The Character of Early American Tort Law*, 36 U.C.L.A. L. Rev. 641 (1989). If Professor Schwartz is right, negligence became dominant in tort law for reasons that had little to do with a "subsidy" for infant industry.

5. *Universalizing principles.* The action on the *Case* often involved suits between persons who had a kind of special or contractual relationship, such as a suit by a farmer against a vet for failure to treat a horse properly. The special relationship or contract imposed a duty of affirmative action upon the provider-defendant, so he was liable for "neglect," hence our word "negligence" for the vast span of actions that arose from *Case*. The relationship of the parties set the duty to be observed. By his implicit undertaking, the vet agreed to use the care that other vets would use. As long as *Case* was limited to parties in some relationship, like carriers and passengers, or innkeepers and guests, duties of care were generated out of those particular relationships and the expectations that those relationships created. It was a kind of reasonable "consumer expectation" test of the duty owed. When

Case was expanded to cover negligence suits between strangers—that is, a between parties who had no contractual relationship—a universal standard was needed for the first time. That seems to appear in *Brown v. Kendall*.

Is it also possible that the scientific revolution and the new ability to state universal laws of the natural world encouraged legal thinkers to seek similarly universal principles of law. For whatever reason, negligence with its reasonable person standard became "the touchstone . . . of a general theory of civil obligation." G. EDWARD WHITE, TORT LAW IN AMERICA 16 (1980).

REFERENCE: DOBBS ON TORTS §§ 14, 111–13 (2000); HARPER, JAMES & GRAY, LAW OF TORTS § 1.3 (3d ed. 1996).

§ 2. STRICT LIABILITY AFTER BROWN v. KENDALL

a. *Trespassing Animals*

Under the writ of *Trespass*, the plaintiff could redress all direct harms, even if the defendant was not at fault; and under the writ of *Case*, he would redress indirect harms, provided they were the result of fault. But there was a period in which the only writ, or the dominant one, was *Trespass*. As an English legal historian, Professor Milsom, has pointed out, a lawyer writing a book about torts in the late 14th century would have called the book *"Trespass,"* because at the time tort law was embodied in *Trespass; Case* developed later. S. MILSOM, HISTORICAL FOUNDATIONS OF THE COMMON LAW 261 (1969). What was done with claims for indirect injury before the writ of *Case* was developed?

As it happened, some of them were treated as trespass cases and strict liability seems to have been imposed. If the defendant owned cattle and drove them onto the plaintiff's land, the writ of *Trespass* would be proper, or at least it could be argued. Such an entry would be reasonably "direct," and it might also meet the later test of "unlawfulness." However, suppose that the defendant's cattle merely strayed, or broke loose from an enclosure, and that they then entered the plaintiff's land and did harm. In such an instance, there seems to be no "direct" connection between the defendant's conduct and the harm—he did not "act"—and consequently the writ of trespass would be inappropriate. But *Case* had not been developed, so the choice was to dismiss the claim or to entertain it under the writ of *Trespass*. The courts seem to have chosen the latter course, and since *Trespass* carried with it the rule of strict liability, cattle trespass became a strict liability tort. This rule, having gained its foothold in *Trespass*, remained the same even after *Case* was developed. As another English historian has said, if the claims had arisen later in time, *Case* would have been available and would have been used, with the result, presumably, that liability would have been based on negligence. G. WILLIAMS, LIABILITY FOR ANIMALS 133 (1939).

The cattle cases were apparently thought of as a special category of liability. Not only did the rule of strict liability for cattle trespass survive the advent of *Case*, in some degree it also survived *Brown v. Kendall*.

The "universal" fault formula in *Brown v. Kendall* found an exception in the cattle cases.

The rule for cattle included the barnyard beasts in general—cows, horses, sheep and others. It did not include pets, such as dogs, even though dogs might have important functions on a farm. There was also a special exception even as to cattle: if they strayed from a highway on which they were being driven, there was no strict liability for their trespass.

Although strict liability for cattle trespass survived *Brown v. Kendall's* universal rule, conditions in America were not the same as those in England, and a number of states adopted quite different rules, especially where large open grazing was feasible and desirable. Thus the strict liability rule of the English common law was rejected and some other rule imposed in many American states, not because of the universal formula proposed in *Brown v. Kendall* but because of different economic needs. Conflicting land uses and needs generated statutory solutions in many states—some requiring the cattle owner to fence the cattle in, some requiring the garden owner to "fence the cattle out." It is now common to find statutes providing for a local option or a fencing district, so that a given county or other area may provide the rule best suited to its economy and geography.

The special strict liability rule for animals, though sometimes changed by American states, served as a reminder that some forms of strict liability would survive *Brown v. Kendall*. The animal trespass cases are in fact quite similar in some ways to another instance which may involve strict liability—nuisance cases.

b. *Nuisance*

BAMFORD v. TURNLEY
3 B. & S. 67, 122 Eng. Rep. 27 (Exch. Ch. 1862).

[Plaintiff declared that the defendant made certain brick kilns on his own land and that these produced "unwholesome vapours, smokes, fumes, stinks and stenches," which proceeded to "enter in, spread and diffuse themselves over, upon, into, through and about" the plaintiff's house. They were "corrupted, offensive, unwholesome, unhealthy and uncomfortable: and thereby the plaintiff had been greatly annoyed and inconvenienced in the possession and enjoyment" and family and servants had become ill. At trial it appeared that defendant had indeed made bricks on his own land, though this was a temporary matter, intended to use the clay on his land for building his own house, and the kilns themselves were as far removed from the plaintiff's property as possible. The trial judge ruled that if the spot chosen for the kilns was "convenient and proper, and the burning of the bricks was, under the circumstances, a reasonable use by the defendant of his own land, the defendant would be entitled to a verdict," and on this basis judgment was entered for the defendant, which is now under review.]

[The judgment of Erle, C.J. is omitted.]

BRAMWELL B. I am of opinion that this judgment should be reversed. The defendant has done that which, if done wantonly or maliciously, would be actionable as being a nuisance to the plaintiff's habitation by causing a sensible diminution of the comfortable enjoyment of it. This, therefore, calls on the defendant to justify or excuse what he has done. And his justification is this: He says that the nuisance is not to the health of the inhabitants of the plaintiff's house, that it is of a temporary character, and is necessary for the beneficial use of his, the defendant's land, and that the public good requires he should be entitled to do what he claims to do.

The question seems to me to be, Is this a justification in law,—and, in order not to make a verbal mistake, I will say,—a justification for what is done, or a matter which makes what is done no nuisance? ... The defendant has infringed the maxim Sic utere tuo ut alienum non laedas. Then, what principle or rule of law can he rely on to defend himself? It is clear to my mind that there is some exception to the general application of the maxim mentioned. The instances put during the argument, of burning weeds, emptying cess-pools, making noises during repairs, and other instances which would be nuisances if done wantonly or maliciously, nevertheless may be lawfully done. It cannot be said that such acts are not nuisances, because, by the hypothesis, they are; and it cannot be doubted that, if a person maliciously and without cause made close to a dwelling-house the same offensive smells as may be made in emptying a cesspool, an action would lie. Nor can these cases be got rid of as extreme cases, because such cases properly test a principle. Nor can it be said that the jury settle such questions by finding there is no nuisance, though there is. For that is to suppose they violate their duty, and that, if they discharged their duty, such matters would be actionable, which I think they could not and ought not to be. There must be, then, some principle on which such cases must be excepted. It seems to me that the principle may be deduced from the character of these cases, and is this, viz., that those acts necessary for the common and ordinary use and occupation of land and houses may be done, if conveniently done, without subjecting those who do them to an action.... There is an obvious necessity for such a principle as I have mentioned. It is as much for the advantage of one owner as of another; for the very nuisance the one complains of, as the result of the ordinary use of this neighbor's land, he himself will create in the ordinary use of his own, and the reciprocal nuisances are of a comparatively trifling character. The convenience of such a rule may be indicated by calling it a rule of give and take, live and let live.

Then can this principle be extended to, or is there any other principle which will comprehend, the present case? I know of none: it is for the defendant to shew it. None of the above reasoning is applicable to such a cause of nuisance as the present. It had occurred to me, that any not unnatural use of the land, if of a temporary character, might be justified; but I cannot see why it being of a temporary nature should warrant it. What is temporary,—one, five, or twenty years? . . .

But it is said that, temporary or permanent, it is lawful because it is for the public benefit. Now, in the first place, that law to my mind is a bad one which, for the public benefit, inflicts loss on an individual without compensation. But further, with great respect, I think this consideration misapplied in this and in many other cases. The public consists of all the individuals of it, and a thing is only for the public benefit when it is productive of good to those individuals on the balance of loss and gain to all. So that if all the loss and all the gain were borne and received by one individual, he on the whole would be a gainer. But whenever this is the case,—whenever a thing is for the public benefit, properly understood,—the loss to the individuals of the public who lose will bear compensation out of the gains of those who gain. It is for the public benefit there should be railways, but it would not be unless the gain of having the railway was sufficient to compensate the loss occasioned by the use of the land required for its site; and accordingly no one thinks it would be right to take an individual's land without compensation to make a railway. It is for the public benefit that trains should run, but not unless they pay their expenses. If one of those expenses is the burning down of a wood of such value that the railway owners would not run the train and burn down the wood if it were their own, neither is it for the public benefit they should if the wood is not their own. . . . [Likewise] unless the defendant's profits are enough to compensate [plaintiff's loss], I deny that it is for the public benefit he should do what he has done; if they are, he ought to compensate.

The only objection I can see to this reasoning is, that by injunction or by abatement of the nuisance a man who would not accept a pecuniary compensation might put a stop to works of great value, and much more than enough to compensate him. This objection, however, is comparatively of small practical importance. . . .

[The judgment of POLLOCK, C. B., is omitted.]

Notes

1. The *Bamford* case reflects many elements of the typical private nuisance case as well as some of the concerns such cases generate. A private nuisance is said to involve an interference, not with possession, but with use and enjoyment. Nuisance cases thus do not involve entry of large physical forces onto the land, but instead typically involve air pollution, as in *Bamford*, or pollution of water, or "noise pollution," as where the defendant plays loud music in a quiet neighborhood or flies airplanes too low. A few nuisances may be accomplished without any invasion, even of this microcosmic kind. A funeral parlor or a "halfway house" for convicts, if located in residential areas, may constitute a nuisance.

2. *Intent.* Was the nuisance in *Bamford* an intentional tort? Dean Page Keeton once suggested at least four distinct kinds of situations:

(a) Defendant knows that its conduct causes non-trespassory invasions and knows it causes substantial and significant annoyance.

(b) Defendant knows only that her conduct causes a non-trespassory invasion, and does not know or believe the invasion to be serious. E.g., defendant burns leaves in the fall.

(c) Defendant knows only that its conduct risks an invasion of the plaintiff's interests, but does not know that any invasion is certain. E.g., the defendant's polluted water seeps through the ground and fouls the plaintiff's wells some distance away.

(d) Defendant causes no physical invasion at all, even by microscopic particles. For example, defendant erects and operates a funeral establishment or a halfway house for convicts in a residential area.

Is it sufficient that the intent is only of the *Garratt v. Dailey* kind and the defendant has no actual purpose or desire to invade the plaintiff's interests? Is it sufficient that the defendant intends an invasion which will be annoying if he does not believe it will amount to the kind of serious annoyance the law will call a nuisance? What does Baron Bramwell say on these two questions?

3. *Negligence and strict liability.* Most cases of nuisance would fit with an intentional tort analysis, using *Garratt v. Dailey* intent. In a few, negligence might be found; this, too, would serve as a basis for liability. See RESTATEMENT SECOND OF TORTS § 822 (1979). What about strict liability? The same section of the Restatement recognizes that strict liability for nuisance is possible where it would be imposed under other independent rules governing abnormally dangerous activities covered later in this section.

4. Does Baron Bramwell use the risk-utility analysis in the same way that Judge Learned Hand used it in *Carroll Towing*? Does Bramwell use custom the same way that Hand used it in *The T. J. Hooper*?

––––––

NOTE: A SHORT SIDE–TRIP: NUISANCES TODAY

This chapter focuses on strict liability, and particularly with the way law changed to impose strict liability for certain activities. It is convenient here, however, to provide a brief sketch of contemporary nuisance law.

1. *Substantial invasion.* The invasion of the plaintiff's interest in use and enjoyment must be substantial. This is a matter of degree and a plaintiff's success will often turn on effective proof. Suppose the plaintiff in *Bamford* only occasionally got a few whiffs of smoke from the brick kiln. Would this be sufficient?

2. *Unreasonable invasion.* The invasion must be unreasonable, not in the sense that the defendant creates an unreasonable risk, but in the sense that given the time, place, and social expectations of the locale, it is unreasonable to expect the plaintiff to put up with the invasion without compensation. An intentional invasion may thus be permissible:

defendant burns leaves in the fall, or operates a brick kiln that regularly causes odors, but not for long. Other intended invasions may be actionable as nuisances if it is unreasonable to expect the plaintiff to put up with them. But this raises the question: how would you prove something is "unreasonable" if not by proving unreasonably risky conduct? Restatement § 826 (1979) provides the traditional answer that the invasion is a nuisance if the gravity of the harm to the plaintiff "outweighs" the utility of the defendant's conduct. This would require a balancing of harm (not *risk* of harm) and utility of the conduct causing the invasion. But the Restatement adds another alternative test: If the defendant could compensate the plaintiff and all others whose interests are invaded by the defendant's conduct, and could still stay in business, then compensation should be made. The idea is that it would be unreasonable to permit the defendant's activity to continue without paying, and the invasion will be regarded as a nuisance.

3. *Proof bearing on reasonableness.* What proof would you try to find in favor of a plaintiff in an industrial nuisance case? Would you expect to be able to get any of the following types of proof admitted into evidence?

(a) The harm is very great; plaintiffs cannot sleep and the value of their property is diminished by fifty per cent.

(b) The plaintiffs are using their property in accord with the traditional uses in the neighborhood.

(c) Defendant's industrial use is unusual in the neighborhood.

(d) The locality is not especially well adapted to the defendant's use; the industry could move.

(e) Plaintiffs began using the neighborhood for residential housing long before defendants moved the industry into the area.

See DOBBS ON TORTS § 465 (2000).

4. *Sensitive plaintiffs and sensitive land uses.* What if a plaintiff has a unique allergy and nearly dies of pulmonary disorders when defendant's factory begins operating nearby. No one else is troubled. Or the plaintiff uses the land for raising animals called sinks. These valuable animals become crazed by noise and eat each other when they hear children yelling. A neighbor with five children moves in across the street. The sinks kill and eat each other. The rule is that there is no nuisance unless the invasion would substantially and unreasonably affect normal persons and normal land uses. How does this compare with the thin skull rule? Or does it compare at all?

5. *Coming to the nuisance.* The fact that the plaintiff moved in next door to a nuisance is a significant fact in judging unreasonableness and hence in judging whether there is a nuisance at all. But no enterprise is allowed to create a noisome condition on its own land and insist that forever after anyone who comes into the area must be willing to tolerate such a condition. To permit this would be to allow an enterprise to condemn the land of others and to force a stasis on a

dynamic and changing world. The fact that the plaintiff came to the nuisance is therefore only one factor to be considered in determining whether a nuisance exists. If the natural spread of a city brings it to the edge of the defendant's smelly feed lot, the lot, which was no nuisance at all when the area was devoted to farming, may become one when the area becomes suburban. On the other hand, the plaintiff who moves from Palm Springs to Bakersfield cannot complain about oil wells.

Another possibility when the plaintiff comes to the nuisance is that he has already been compensated for it. This is so because, if the nuisance is open and obvious, the plaintiff will probably have paid the former owner a smaller price because of the nuisance.

6. *Injunctions.* In many cases the nuisance claim results in a recovery of damages. In some cases, however, the plaintiff may seek and obtain an injunction against the nuisance. Sometimes an injunction may merely require an industrial polluter to experiment to find a pollution-solution, or to install the best available technology to reduce pollution, or to operate at hours that cause less disturbance. In other cases, the plaintiff may ask the court to enjoin the entire operation on the ground that no matter how it is operated, it will constitute a nuisance. This is occasionally done, but it is obviously more extreme than a remedy that merely makes the industrial polluter pay the costs of its pollution. An injunction, for example, might compel discontinuance of a product or service the public wants and needs; it would certainly throw employees out of work. For these reasons, courts balance public interests and the private interests of the parties, and at times exercise discretion not to grant an injunction even if a nuisance is clearly shown. In such cases, the plaintiff may recover damages instead. See generally 1 DAN DOBBS, THE LAW OF REMEDIES § 5.7 (2d ed. 1993).

7. *Public nuisances.* Suppose the defendant, an industrial enterprise, dumps wastes on its own ground. These percolate through the soil and pollute a river, a lake, and even estuarine waters. All these bodies of water are public property. If the fish are killed or the waters become unusable, does anyone have a claim? Conceivably, landowners adjacent to these waters would have a nuisance claim on the principles stated above if the pollution substantially diminished the use and enjoyment of their land. What about a non-landowner who fishes for sport and can no longer catch fish because they are dead? Or one who fishes commercially and can no longer catch them for the same reason? If the pollution constitutes a public nuisance because it substantially interferes with public health, safety, or convenience, the rule is that any person who has damages different in kind from the public generally may recover damages for the nuisance. The claimant who loses commercial fishing profits may thus have "standing to sue" because the claimant's injury differs from that of the public at large. The plaintiff who merely fishes for sport may be denied recovery, since her damages are not so different from those of other persons. In some states, a concern for environmental protection or enhancement may lead to a wider standing on the part of individuals.

8. *Environmental and zoning laws.* The common law of nuisance leads directly to contemporary legislation and administrative regulations aimed at pollution. It also leads to zoning laws, designed to maximize appropriate land-use. Although it would be theoretically possible to import a great deal of environmental and land-use law into a torts course, those fields have become major specialties of their own. Consequently, the bulk of nuisance law today may be better developed in connection with courses in property, land-use, environmental protection and public health and safety.

———

Reconsider the question of strict liability for nuisance. Did *Brown v. Kendall* succeed in imposing a universal principle that liability was limited to cases of "fault?" Or is *Bamford* a strict liability case? One way of making *Bamford* comport with the fault regime of *Brown v. Kendall* is to find fault by finding intent. To do this, intent must be defined in the broad sense encountered in *Garratt v. Dailey*. But imagine a defendant which operates a useful industry. Imagine that it unavoidably pollutes, and that this causes diminished use and enjoyment to the plaintiff, a nearby landowner, who complains to the defendant in no uncertain terms. The defendant spends a great deal of money to reduce the pollution, but it is simply impossible. There may be *Garratt v. Dailey* intent in such a case, but would anyone besides a lawyer say there is fault? Perhaps "intent" was given some rather special definitions to make the law seem compatible with *Brown v. Kendall's* requirement of fault. Could you say that, realistically, however, pockets of strict liability remained even after *Brown v. Kendall*?

It is even possible that *Brown v. Kendall* merely wiped the slate clean of traditional forms of strict liability, only to permit other cases to write in new forms of strict liability. Consider the materials that follow.

RYLANDS v. FLETCHER

Exchequer: 3 Hurl & C. 774 (1865).
Exchequer Chamber: L.R. 1 Exch. 265 (1866).
House of Lords: L.R. 3 H.L. 330 (1868).

[Plaintiff operated a mine in the county of Lancaster. Defendants operated a mill in the vicinity, and had contractors build a reservoir or pond to supply water. The contractors did build such a pond, though in fact it was located immediately over some vertical shafts once used in mining. The shafts had been filled rather inadequately, but gave the appearance of solid earth. When the pond was filled with water, its weight caused the material in the shafts to give way, and the water flooded down the vertical shafts. From there it flowed through horizontal mine shafts of an intervening mine into the plaintiff's mine. This is an action by the plaintiff for damages caused by this flooding. A procedure was used in which an arbitrator stated a special case or found facts. The case was then considered in the Court of Exchequer, followed by review in the Exchequer Chamber and finally in the House of Lords. The style of the case is that used in the House of Lords.]

[IN THE COURT OF EXCHEQUER]

BRAMWELL, B. . . .

The plaintiff's right then has been infringed; the defendants in causing water to flow to the plaintiff have done that which they had no right to do; what difference in point of law does it make that they have done it unwittingly? I think none, and consequently that the action is maintainable. . . .

It is said there must be a trespass, a nuisance, or negligence. . . . But why is not this a trespass? Wilfulness is not material: Leame v. Bray (3 East, 593). Why is it not a nuisance? The nuisance is not in the reservoir, but in the water escaping. As in Backhouse v. Bonomi the act was lawful, the mischievous consequence is a wrong. . . .

MARTIN, B. . . .

First, I think there was no trespass. . . . I think the true criterion of trespass is laid down in the judgments in the former case, viz., that to constitute trespass the act doing the damage must be immediate, and that if the damage be mediate or consequential (which I think the present was), it is not a trespass. Secondly, I think there was no nuisance in the ordinary and generally understood meaning of that word, that is to say, something hurtful or injurious to the senses. The making a pond for holding water is a nuisance to no one. The digging a reservoir in a man's own land is a lawful act. . . . To hold the defendants liable would therefore make them insurers against the consequence of a lawful act upon their own land when they had no reason to believe or suspect that any damage was likely to ensue. . . .

[POLLOCK, C. B., agreed with MARTIN, B., that the facts found by the arbitrator were not a sufficient basis for relief.]

[IN THE EXCHEQUER CHAMBER]

May 14, 1866. BLACKBURN, J., read the following judgment of the court. . . .

We have come to the conclusion that the opinion of Bramwell, B., was right, and that the answer to the question should be that the plaintiff was entitled to recover damages from the defendants by reason of the matters stated in the Case. . . .

What is the liability which the law casts upon a person who, like the defendants, lawfully brings on his land something which, though harmless while it remains there, will naturally do mischief if it escapes out of his land? It is agreed on all hands that he must take care to keep in that which he has brought on the land, and keep it there in order that it may not escape and damage his neighbor's, but the question arises whether the duty which the law casts upon him under such circumstances is an absolute duty to keep it in at his peril, or is, as the majority of the Court of Exchequer have thought, merely a duty to take all reasonable and prudent precautions in order to keep it in, but no more. . . .

We think that the true rule of law is that the person who, for his own purposes, brings on his land, and collects and keeps there anything likely to do mischief if it escapes, must keep it in at his peril, and, if he does not do so, he is prima facie answerable for all the damage which is the natural consequence of its escape. He can excuse himself by showing that the escape was owing to the plaintiff's default, or, perhaps, that the escape was the consequence of vis major, or the act of God; but, as nothing of this sort exists here, it is unnecessary to inquire what excuse would be sufficient. . . .

The case that has most commonly occurred, and which is most frequently to be found in the books, is as to the obligation of the owner of cattle which he has brought on his land to prevent their escaping and doing mischief. The law as to them seems to be perfectly settled from early times; the owner must keep them in at his peril, or he will be answerable for the natural consequences of their escape, that is, with regard to tame beasts, for the grass they eat and trample upon, although not for any injury to the person of others, for our ancestors have settled that it is not the general nature of horses to kick or bulls to gore, but if the owner knows that the beast has a vicious propensity to attack man he will be answerable for that too. . . . So in May v. Burdett, the court, after an elaborate examination of the old precedents and authorities, came to the conclusion that a person keeping a mischievous animal is bound to keep it secure at his peril. . . .

As has been already said, there does not appear to be any difference in principle between the extent of the duty cast on him who brings cattle on his land to keep them in, and the extent of the duty imposed on him who brings on his land water, filth, or stenches, or any other thing which will, if it escape, naturally do damage, to prevent their escaping and injuring his neighbor. Tenant v. Goldwin [a case decided in 1704 and reported in a number of places, including 1 Salk. 21 and 360, 91 Eng. Rep. 20 and 314, 2 Ld. Raym, 1089, 92 Eng. Rep. 222, and 6 Mod. Rep. 311, 87 Eng. Rep. 1051] is an express authority that the duty is the same, and is to keep them in at his peril. [In that case the defendant had a privy on his land and formerly had it enclosed by a wall. By reason of the defendant's failure to repair the wall, the filth of the privy flowed into the plaintiff's cellar.]

In the report in 6 Mod. Rep. at p. 314, it is stated:

"And at another day per totam curiam the declaration is good, for there is a sufficient cause of action appearing in it, but not upon the word solebat. If the defendant has a house or office enclosed with a wall which is his, he is, of common right, bound to use it so as not to annoy another. . . . The reason here is, that one must use his own so as thereby not to hurt another, and as of common right one is bound to keep his cattle from trespassing on his neighbor, so he is bound to use anything that is his so as not to hurt another by such use....

No case has been found in which the question of the liability for noxious vapours escaping from a man's works by inevitable accident has been discussed, but the following case will illustrate it. Some years ago several actions were brought against the occupiers of some alkali works at Liverpool for the damage alleged to be caused by the chlorine fumes of their works. The defendants proved that they had, at great expense, erected a contrivance by which the fumes of chlorine were condensed, and sold as muriatic acid, and they called a great body of scientific evidence to prove that this apparatus was so perfect that no fumes possible could escape from the defendant's chimneys. On this evidence it was pressed upon the juries that the plaintiff's damage must have been due to some of the numerous other chimneys in the neighborhood. The juries, however, being satisfied that the mischief was occasioned by chlorine, drew the conclusion that it had escaped from the defendant's works somehow, and in each case found for the plaintiff. No attempt was made to disturb these verdicts on the ground that the defendants had taken every precaution which prudence or skill could suggest to keep those fumes in, and that they could not be responsible unless negligence were shown, yet if the law be as laid down by the majority of the Court of Exchequer it would have been a very obvious defense. [T]he uniform course of pleading in actions for such nuisances is to say that the defendant caused the noisome vapours to arise on his premises and suffered them to come on the plaintiff's without stating that there was any want of care or skill on the defendant's part; and that Tenant v. Goldwin showed that this was founded on the general rule of law that he whose stuff it is must keep it so that it may not trespass. There is no difference in this respect between chlorine and water; both will, if they escape, do damage, the one by scorching and the other by drowning, and he who brings them on his land must at his peril see that they do not escape and do that mischief.

... But it was further said by Martin, B., that when damage is done to personal property, or even to the person by collision, either upon land or at sea, there must be negligence in the party doing the damage to render him legally responsible. This is no doubt true.... but we think these cases distinguishable from the present. Traffic on the highways, whether by land or sea, cannot be conducted without exposing those whose persons or property are near it to some inevitable risk; and, that being so, those who go on the highway, or have their property adjacent to it, may well be held to do so subject to their taking upon themselves the risk of injury from that inevitable danger ... and it is believed that all the cases in which inevitable accident has been held an excuse for what prima facie was a trespass can be explained on the same principle, namely that the circumstances were such as to show that the plaintiff had taken the risk upon himself. But there is no ground for saying that the plaintiff here took upon himself any risk arising from the uses to which the defendants should choose to apply their land. He neither knew what there might be, nor could he in any way control the defendants. . . .

The view which we take of the first point renders it unnecessary to consider whether the defendants would or would not be responsible for the want of care and skill in the persons employed by them. We are of opinion that the plaintiff is entitled to recover. . . .

[IN THE HOUSE OF LORDS]

LORD CAIRNS, L.C. . . .

The principles on which this case must be determined appear to me to be extremely simple. The defendants, . . . might lawfully have used that close for any purpose for which it might, in the ordinary course of the enjoyment of land, be used, and if, in what I may term the natural user of that land, there had been any accumulation of water, either on the surface or underground, and if by the operation of the laws of nature that accumulation of water had passed off into the close occupied by the plaintiff, the plaintiff could not have complained that that result had taken place. If he had desired to guard himself against it, it would have lain on him to have done so. . . .

On the other hand, if the defendants, not stopping at the natural use of their close, had desired to use it for any purpose which I may term a non-natural use, for the purpose of introducing into the close that which, in its natural condition, was not in or upon it—for the purpose of introducing water, either above or below ground, in quantities and in a manner not the result of any work or operation on or under the land, and if in consequence of their doing so, or in consequence of any imperfection in the mode of their doing so, the water came to escape and to pass off into the close of the plaintiff, then it appears to me that that which the defendants were doing they were doing at their own peril. . . .

These simple principles, if they are well founded, as it appears to me they are, really dispose of this case. The same result is arrived at on the principles referred to by Blackburn, J., in his judgment in the Court of Exchequer Chamber. . . .

In that opinion, I must say, I entirely concur. Therefore, I have to move your Lordships that the judgment of the Court of Exchequer Chamber be affirmed, and that the present appeal be dismissed with costs.

LORD CRANWORTH.

I concur with my noble and learned friend in thinking that the rule of law was correctly stated by Blackburn, J., in delivering the opinion of the Exchequer chamber. If a person brings or accumulates on his land anything which, if it should escape, may cause damage to his neighbor, he does so at his peril. If it does escape and cause damage, he is responsible, however careful he may have been, and whatever precautions he may have taken to prevent the damage. In considering whether a defendant is liable to a plaintiff for damage which the plaintiff may have sustained, the question in general is, not whether the defendant has acted with due care and caution, but whether his acts have occasioned the damage. This is all well explained in the old case of Lambert and Olliot v. Bessey. The doctrine is founded on good sense, for when one person in managing his own affairs causes, however innocently, damage to another, it is obviously only just that he should be the party to suffer. He is bound sic uti suo ut non laedat alienum. This is the principle of law applicable to cases like the present, and I do not discover in the authorities which were cited anything conflicting with it. . . .

Notes

1. Liability for trespass would not be imposed today unless the defendant or his employees intended to enter the plaintiff's land. Perhaps the English law of the 19th century was stricter. Professor Bohlen, who became the Reporter of the first Restatement of Torts, thought that a trespass theory would not work in *Rylands* because the injury was "indirect," since the water did not escape when it was first poured into the reservoir. He thought that a nuisance theory would not work because there was no continuous seeping or percolation and hence no "continuous injurious condition," which he took to be necessary in a nuisance case. Francis Bohlen, *The Rule in Rylands v. Fletcher*, 59 U. PA. L. REV. 298, 311, 373, 423 (1911).

2. What is the scope of strict liability in *Rylands* and why is it imposed? Is *Rylands* merely a nuisance case? If so does it go beyond the implications of *Bamford*?

3. Does *Rylands* require any special hazard as a prerequisite to liability? Substances like dynamite may represent unusual hazards. Is water like that?

4. In one respect *Rylands* may be easy to understand. Suppose that thousands of acres of land in an agricultural area are devoted to farming of Murg, a kind of grain that requires repeated aerial spraying. Into the midst of this great agricultural area move two new businesses: one is a beekeeper and one is a heavy industry. If, without fault, the aerial spraying of the Murg fields injures the bees or prevents them from finding usable pollen, should the beekeeper have a claim? If, without fault, the heavy industry discharges pollution that contaminates 3,000 acres of Murg growing in the fields, should the Murg owners have a claim?

5. Cases like those just suggested, cases like *Rylands*, and most nuisance cases can be thought of as instances of inconsistent land uses. Though there is nothing "wrong" with moving a factory to the country, if it presents dangers to existing investments through its pollution, perhaps the most economical thing to do is to protect those investments without regard to "fault." Does this describe *Rylands*? After all, coal can be mined and that resource exploited only in places where the coal lies, but one could build a millpond almost anywhere in a pluvial country.

6. To test this idea, imagine that the coal mine in *Rylands* somehow caused damage to the mill owner or to nearby farmers. Would strict liability have been imposed then? Take an actual case: Salt water is used in oil well

drilling, and must be stored in ponds. If the oil well driller's salt water pond collapsed without the driller's fault, would the farmer whose fields were ruined have an action based on strict liability? In *Turner v. Big Lake Oil Co.*, 128 Tex. 155, 96 S.W.2d 221(1936), the court rejected strict liability on such facts. While the court said it repudiated *Rylands,* is the result one *Rylands* might actually support? How?

7.   There are similar ideas in pure nuisance cases. Although one who "comes to the nuisance" is not necessarily barred from recovery, since a number of factors must be weighed in nuisance cases, it seems clear that one who moves a home to a factory district cannot successfully enjoin operation of the factories or even recover damages. Compare the situation of the beekeeper in note 4. If the factory moves into a residential neighborhood, the situation is reversed and it may well be found to be a nuisance.

8.   Most situations are not so simple as all this. Nevertheless, *Rylands* and many similar cases seem to involve inconsistent land uses in which the parties inflict nonreciprocal risks on each other. Although it is not "wrong" for a beekeeper or a factory to move into the Murg field, it may be right to expect them to take the situation as they find it. Is this a moral notion or an economic one?

9.   *Animals.* (a) *Cattle.* We have already seen that there was strict liability for cattle trespasses, but this liability was limited to trespassing cattle and did not include personal injuries except so far as they might occur as part of a trespass.

(b) *Other animals generally.* As to other animals, such as dogs, the owner's liability might be predicated upon negligence, but commonly it has been regarded as a species of strict but limited liability. If, but only if, the owner knows of the dog's vicious propensity (to bite, for example) the owner is strictly liable for injuries resulting from that particular propensity. This rule seems to apply to any kind of animal. Statutes and ordinances often impose additional liabilities on dog owners, through leash laws or otherwise.

(c) *Wild animals.* A third category deals with animals often said to be "wild by nature." These include lions and tigers and bears that people have seen fit to import and exhibit. As to this category, the rule existing at the time of *Rylands* was that strict liability would be imposed for injuries connected with the wild characteristic of the animal, so that the person in charge would be held responsible in spite of all possible care. Is this category consistent with the analysis of *Rylands* suggested in notes 4–8 supra? What if someone living in an apartment building decides to keep a polar bear on the balcony of his apartment? A python in his bathroom? If untoward and unexpected events occur causing harm, should the burden fall upon the python owner or the neighbor? Notice again the lack of reciprocity in the risk.

————

THOMALEN v. MARRIOTT CORP., 845 F.Supp. 33 (D.Mass.1994). A Marriott Hotel in Westborough, Massachusetts, hosted a "Murder Mystery Weekend," in which a troupe of actors staged murder mystery entertainments. One member of the group, attempting to perform a fire-eating act, became engulfed in flames; another member ran to the stage to help but knocked over a can of lighter fluid. This ignited and caused burns to Belmont, a guest close to the stage. *Held*, the Marriott is not strictly liable. Massachusetts has adopted *Rylands v. Fletcher* strict liability, but since there was "no escape of a dangerous instrumentality from Marriott's property," that rule does not apply.

c. *Slouching Toward the Abnormal Danger Conception*

SULLIVAN v. DUNHAM, 161 N.Y. 290, 55 N.E. 923 (1900). In June of 1895, Annie E. Harten, 19 years old, was on a public highway near Irvington, New York. Defendant was blasting to get rid of stumps. A stump thus blasted flew through the air and struck and killed Harten. In an action for her wrongful death, held, verdict for plaintiff was properly affirmed by the Appellate Division. Where blasting throws rocks or trees onto the lands of another, there is liability as a trespasser. Though one has the right to blast, the other has the right to the beneficial use of his property. In this case there is no trespass to property, but the same reasons apply to a trespass to person. If the injury had been indirect, from concussion and shaking of the earth, there would have been no liability, as that would not have been a trespass. Likewise, *semble*, if the injury had been the result of an accidental rather than an intentional explosion, there would be no liability. But where there is a direct and trespassory invasion of another's land or person, there is liability.

Notes

1. Is this merely a rejection of *Brown v. Kendall* and a retention of the early common law rules of liability for "direct" harms?

2. If so, then one would expect that a blaster who causes damage by concussion would not be liable, and, as reflected in *Sullivan*, that in fact was the New York rule at the time.

3. It must be clear from the preceding paragraphs that New York had rejected *Rylands v. Fletcher*, since otherwise concussion damage would have been actionable if it resulted from "non-natural" activities. At this time, a number of other states took positions similar to that of *Sullivan*, and explicitly rejected *Rylands*, at least in name.

4. This left the law in a rather awkward state. There was in the first place a rather general acceptance that negligence, not "directness," had become the basis of liability. In other words, *Brown v. Kendall* was largely accepted by American courts, and *Rylands* largely rejected. Yet there were pockets of strict liability, of which *Sullivan* is one example. And this strict liability was a difficult problem because it seemed to proceed, as in *Sullivan*, on the very grounds that had been rejected in *Brown v. Kendall*. Worse, perhaps, it distinguished between two claims that seemed morally indistinguishable—the injury from debris thrown up by a blaster and injury from the same blast but occurring through the medium of vibrations in the ground. In both cases, the defendant's act was the same and the plaintiff's injury equally real.

5. This puzzle could be resolved either by rejecting *Brown v. Kendall* or by accepting *Rylands*, but neither of these options was palatable. Was there any other solution?

———

EXNER v. SHERMAN POWER CONSTRUCTION CO., 54 F.2d 510, 80 A.L.R. 686 (2d Cir. 1931). Defendant was blasting for a hydroelectric development at Bellows Falls, Vermont, about 935 feet from the plaintiff's dwelling and restaurant. There was a severe explosion which shook the house, throwing Mrs. Exner from her bed and damaging the property. There was a jury verdict for the plaintiff, based on violation of a statute. On appeal, *held*, affirmed. The statute was not intended to protect the class of which the plaintiff was a member, but the judgment for the plaintiff may be affirmed if this is a case of "absolute liability" at common law. "While the rule laid down by Blackburn, J., in *Rylands v. Fletcher*, has not been followed in America to the full extent of all its implications, and, at the outset its authority was impaired by [decisions in New Hampshire, New York and New Jersey], yet in the so-called 'blasting' cases an absolute liability, without regard to fault, has uniformly been imposed by the American courts wherever there has been an actual invasion of property by rocks or debris. . . .

"It is true that some courts have distinguished between liability for a common law trespass, occasioned by blasting, which projects rocks or debris upon the property or the person of the plaintiff, and liability for so-called consequential damages arising from concussion, and have denied liability for the latter where the blasting itself was conducted at a lawful time and place and with due care. Yet in every practical sense there can be no difference between a blasting which projects rocks in such a way as to injure persons or property and a blasting which, by creating a sudden vacuum, shatters buildings or knocks down people. . . .

"[T]he imposition of absolute liability is not out of accord with any general principles of law. . . . [I]n trespass, fault ordinarily remained a matter of no consequence, and even in cases of damage to the person the early decisions prior to Brown v. Kendall, seemed to have imposed liability where there was no negligence.

" . . . The extent to which one man in the lawful conduct of his business is liable for injuries to another involves an adjustment of conflicting interests. The solution of the problem . . . has never been dependent upon any universal criterion of liability (such as 'fault') applicable to all situations. If damage is inflicted, there ordinarily is liability, in the absence of excuse. When, as here, the defendant, though without fault, has engaged in the perilous activity of storing large quantities of a dangerous explosive for use in his business, we think there is no justification for relieving it of liability, and that the owner of the business, rather than a third person who has no relation to the explosion, other than that of injury, should bear the loss."

Notes

1. Would this same decision be reached under *Rylands v. Fletcher?*

2. When *Exner* was decided, *Rylands* was unpopular in the U.S., at least by name. How, then should one express the rule in *Exner?*

3. Professor Bohlen relied in part on *Exner* and on *Sullivan* in formulating the Restatement formula. *Sullivan* was important in emphasizing that this form of strict liability was not limited to property. *Exner* and other cases, Bohlen thought, emphasized that the defendant carried on an activity that introduced an "unescapable danger into the community" and did so for his own profit. The First Restatement accordingly introduced a whole chapter on "Ultrahazardous Activities," which years later became the basis for the Second Restatement's rules.

NOTE: THE RESTATEMENT (SECOND) RULES OF STRICT LIABILITY

1. *The principle.* The Second Restatement's strict liability rules are mainly contained in §§ 519 and 520. Section 519 states the general rule that strict liability is imposed for harms done by "abnormally dangerous" activity, so long as it is the kind of harm that makes the activity abnormally dangerous in the first place. Strict liability of course means that the actor is liable even if he exercised the greatest possible care in his activities.

2. *The factors determining abnormal danger.* What makes an activity abnormally dangerous? In § 520, the Second Restatement drags out a list of factors to be considered by the court in deciding the issue: (1) the existence of a high degree of risk of harm; (2) the likelihood that the harm that results from it will be great; (3) the inability to eliminate the risk by using reasonable care; (4) the extent to which the activity is not a matter of common usage; (5) the activity's inappropriateness to the place where it is carried on; and (6) the extent to which the activity's value to the community is outweighed by its dangerous attributes.

3. Does the Second Restatement reflect anything like the *Rylands* rule, or is it instead more grounded in *Exner?* And how do these factors seem to differ from a negligence analysis, especially if one focuses on the final factor in the list?

4. The Second Restatement's factors never proved popular with commentators or courts, for a number of reasons. Even the Reporter for that Restatement, William Prosser, said he "intensely disliked" lists of factors to be considered since they always raise the question of which ones are of greatest importance. 41 A.L.I Proc. 455 (1964). It is perhaps not surprising that most courts have continued to apply the essential requirements of the First Restatement in deciding the abnormal danger issue, concluding that particular activities are abnormally dangerous only where the activity involves a risk of serious harm that cannot be

eliminated by the exercise of due care, and is not a matter of common usage. See, e.g., *Walker Drug Co. v. La Sal Oil Co.*, 972 P.2d 1238 (Utah 1998)(rejecting strict liability for maintaining underground gasoline storage tanks because of a lack of evidence that the risk could not be eliminated by use of reasonable care); *Bosley v. Central Vermont Public Service Corp.*, 127 Vt. 581, 255 A.2d 671 (1969)(rejecting strict liability on ground that transmitting electric power is "usual and normal practice"). For a complete discussion of courts' rejection of the Second Restatement's approach, see Gerald W. Boston, *Strict Liability for Abnormally Dangerous Activity: The Negligence Barrier*, 36 SAN DIEGO L. REV. 597 (1999).

REFERENCE: DOBBS ON TORTS § 346–47 (2000).

§ 3.　STRICT LIABILITY TODAY

a.　*The Subjects of Strict Liability*

To what kinds of cases do the rules of nuisance, *Rylands v. Fletcher*, and "abnormally dangerous activities" apply? Is there a single rationale or principle that covers them all? Do the rationales for vicarious liability that we saw in Chapter 20 support the imposition of strict liability in these situations?

1. *Impoundments.* On the precise facts of *Rylands*—the sudden escape of ponded water—very few modern courts would impose strict liability. However, in two variants on the *Rylands* facts, strict liability may be imposed. The first is where the defendant impounds noxious substances that suddenly escape. For example, in *Cities Service Co. v. State*, 312 So.2d 799 (Fla.App.1975) a defendant mining phosphates was held strictly liable for the escape of its impounded billions of gallons of phosphate slimes. The court was impressed with the very great danger and also with the idea that the mine should pay its own way, bearing the more or less inevitable costs that its industry would inflict on others. And New Jersey, one of the first states to reject *Rylands*, has now overruled its earlier case law and has said that "a landowner is strictly liable to others for harm caused by toxic wastes" that escape from the property, *State Dept. of Environmental Protection v. Ventron Corp.*, 94 N.J. 473, 468 A.2d 150 (1983) (268 tons of mercury).

The second variation involves impounded liquids that do not escape suddenly, but merely percolate through the soil and contaminate a well or otherwise cause harm. These percolation cases almost always involve noxious impoundments, and may be traced to *Tenant v. Goldwin*, discussed in *Rylands*, supra, where the judges appeared willing to impose strict liability for the escape of filth from a privy. See *Yommer* v. *McKenzie*, 255 Md. 220, 257 A.2d 138 (1969) (gasoline); *Iverson v. Vint*, 243 Iowa 949, 54 N.W.2d 494 (1952) (molasses dumped in ditch, percolation into farmer's well, strict liability). Some of these cases can be explained on other grounds, for example, that there was *Garratt v. Dailey* intent, or that there was a species of fault in carrying on an activity in an inappropriate place. Can there really be any principle, other than a whimsical one, that distinguishes damage caused by sudden escape from damage caused by percolation?

2. *Hazardous wastes.* Beyond the situations mentioned above, activities involving toxic substances are good candidates for strict liability based on abnormal danger. In *T & E Industries, Inc. v. Safety Light Corp.*, 123 N.J. 371, 587 A.2d 1249 (1991) a plant used radium that left its own ground contaminated. Later it sold the property, which eventually passed to the plaintiff. Upon discovery of the contamination in the property it had purchased, the plaintiff sued. The court held that seller would be strictly liable not only to adjoining landowners who suffered harm, but also to purchasers like the plaintiff.

3. *Environmental statutes; the Superfund.* Statutes and regulations are now of central importance in such environmental litigation, both public and private, and they must be studied with care by any practitioner dealing with such material. Some statutes envision that government will shoulder the primary task of cleaning up hazardous substances, but leave some room for private litigation as well. The "Superfund Act" provides a fund, derived in part from taxes on industry, for the government to use to clean up substances released into the environment. Representatives of the fund may sue the responsible industry for reimbursement. Liability is strict and applies not only to one who actually released the substance but also to owners of the contaminated land whether they released the substance or not. See 42 U.S.C.A. § 9607(a). Private persons who are victimized by such a release may sue for actual reasonable costs incurred in clean up. Beyond this, public representatives may recover for harm done to natural resources that do not necessarily have any market value, as in the case of harm done to wildlife by an oil spill. There is a very brief summary in 1 DAN DOBBS, THE LAW OF REMEDIES § 5.2 (5) (2d ed. 1993). In *United States v. M/V Miss Beholden,* 856 F.Supp. 668 (S.D.Fla.1994) a vessel was intentionally grounded on coral reef when it was taking on water and could not make port. It was said to be strictly liable for damage to coral under the National Marine Sanctuaries Act, 16 U.S.C.A. § 1431 et seq.

4. *Lateral support.* "Between adjacent landowners, the general principle . . . is that each has an absolute property right to have his land laterally supported by the soil of his neighbor, and if either in excavating on his own premises so disturbs the lateral support of his neighbor's land as to cause it, in its natural state, by the pressure of its own weight, to fall away or slide from its position, the one so excavating is liable." *Prete v. Cray*, 49 R.I. 209, 141 A. 609, 59 A.L.R. 1241 (1928). Can this form of strict liability be explained on the Restatement's "abnormally dangerous activity" theory? How does it compare, if at all, with other cases, such as those involving percolation, that appear to regulate property rights of near neighbors?

The Restatement is in accord with *Prete*, but states its rule some 300 sections after it states the rule for abnormally dangerous activities, and suggests that the theory behind this form of strict liability is that it represents a kind of property right. RESTATEMENT SECOND OF TORTS § 817 (1979). Does the property right theory explain the strict liability result or merely express that result in different language?

The same rule is applied to "subjacent" support, that is, where an owner of minerals removes them so that the surface subsides. See § 820.

5. *Blasting and explosives.* The Restatement obviously rejected the "trespass" theory of *Sullivan* and permitted strict liability for concussion damage from blasting. This reflects the current view in the courts, including the New York courts, which have rejected their own earlier decisions limiting liability to cases in which there was a physical "trespass." See *Spano v. Perini Corp.*, 25 N.Y.2d 11, 302 N.Y.S.2d 527, 250 N.E.2d 31 (1969). Most courts today apply strict liability to either blasting or storage of explosives, although some courts do not see storage as abnormally dangerous. Compare *Yukon Equipment, Inc. v. Fireman's Fund Ins. Co.*, 585 P.2d 1206 (Alaska 1978) with *Liber v. Flor*, 160 Colo. 7, 415 P.2d 332 (Colo. 1966).

6. *Nuclear energy.* (a) *Governmental liability.* Public entities have generally retained immunity as to strict liability claims. Thus, for example, the United States is not liable under the FTCA for damages resulting from sonic booms caused by its planes. *Laird v. Nelms*, 406 U.S. 797, 92 S.Ct. 1899, 32 L.Ed.2d 499 (1972). In the absence of a specific statute providing for liability in particular cases, then, the United States would not be liable for nuclear accidents.

(b) *Private liability.* Private liability of utilities licensed to operate nuclear power plants is a complex question because the field is heavily but not clearly regulated by federal statutes and rules. In the Price–Anderson Act, 42 U.S.C.A. § 2210, Congress provided for tort liability, limiting the total liability of private industry to about $560 million for any one incident. The government in effect provides an insurance policy to cover much of this liability. Some state law is imported into the federal claim, so long as the state law is not inconsistent with the federal rules provided. Conceivably, strict liability could be imposed in some cases, but perhaps not if the utility was in compliance with governing federal regulations. Cf. *O'Conner v. Commonwealth Edison Co.*, 13 F.3d 1090 (7th Cir.1994) (compliance with federal safety standards is a complete defense in a negligence claim). There is no express provision about the basis of liability, so it seems that the states could impose strict liability if they chose.

7. *Fire.* Strict liability is usually not imposed for the spread of fire. But statutes in some states regulate outdoor burning and may impose special liabilities. In *Koos v. Roth*, 293 Or. 670, 652 P.2d 1255 (1982) the court imposed strict liability for the spread of a field-fire on the ground that it was abnormally dangerous, considering its scale. Judge Linde also pointed out that the same destruction that poses the danger to the user's neighbor is the user's very purpose, and that there was a pattern of heavy statutory regulation.

8. *Other high-energy activities.* The strict liability seen in explosives cases carries over to closely analogous activities where enormous force is involved, including the testing of rockets, *Smith v. Lockheed Propulsion Co.*, 247 Cal.App.2d 774, 56 Cal.Rptr. 128, 29 A.L.R.3d 538 (1967) (ground vibration damaged water well); the use of pile driving equipment, *Caporale v. C. W. Blakeslee & Sons, Inc.*, 149 Conn. 79, 175 A.2d 561 (1961) ("intrinsically dangerous," strict liability for vibration damage); and even a "blow out" of an oil well in a populated area, *Green v. General Petroleum Corp.*, 205 Cal. 328, 270 P. 952, 60 A.L.R. 475 (1928).

9. *Utilities.* Should strict liability apply to the transmission of natural gas or electricity? Should this decision be affected by the fact that public utilities are regulated industries with limited profit margin and also with a high ability to pass costs back to consumers? Courts have refused to apply strict liability to uninsulated power lines. See *Kent v. Gulf States Utilities Co.*, 418 So.2d 493 (La.1982). Remember, too, that according to the Restatement, an activity that is a "common usage" cannot be subject to strict liability. Does "common use" tend to show an activity's social value? See Mark Geistfeld, *Should Enterprise Liability Replace the Rule of Strict Liability for Abnormally Dangerous Activities?*, 45 U.C.L.A. L.Rev. 611 (1998).

10. *Fireworks.* If a person is injured by a Fourth of July fireworks display, should strict liability apply? Are such displays like blasting? Or would you call them a matter of "common usage?" And can the risks of such displays be avoided through the use of reasonable care? Compare *Cadena v. Chicago Fireworks Mfg. Co.*, 297 Ill.App.3d 945, 232 Ill.Dec. 60, 697 N.E.2d 802 (Ill.App.1998) with *Klein v. Pyrodyne Corp.*, 117 Wash.2d 1, 810 P.2d 917 (Wash. 1991).

11. *Poisons.* In *Loe v. Lenhardt,* 227 Or. 242, 362 P.2d 312 (1961) strict liability was applied to crop dusting activities. Might this be justified on a pure *Rylands v. Fletcher* rule, without resort to any "abnormally dangerous activity" rule? Courts have imposed strict liability for abnormally dangerous activity in pest control and fumigation cases. *Luthringer v. Moore*, 31 Cal.2d 489, 190 P.2d 1 (1948); *Old Island Fumigation, Inc. v. Barbee*, 604 So.2d 1246 (Fla.App.1992).

12. *Ground damage from aircraft.* Defendant's airplane, without negligence or intent, crashes into the plaintiff's house. The older cases might readily have found a trespass here, as in *Sullivan.* With the elimination of the trespass theory, should courts continue to impose strict liability? Notice that the pilot does not intentionally enter the land. The Restatement Second of Torts § 520A takes the position that strict liability should be imposed. Is flying an abnormally dangerous activity? Could you use *res ipsa loquitur* against the defendant? If so would it tend to show that flying does *not* fall within the Restatement's definition of abnormally dangerous activity? If it is right to hold the flyer liable for non-negligent and unintended ground damage, is it equally right to hold the driver of a car liable when he crashes into a house? Or

into a pedestrian? What if snow slid off defendant's roof and landed on the plaintiff's house, causing damage? *Cobai v. Young*, 679 P.2d 121 (Colo.App.1984). Are these instances of "non-reciprocal risks," where the defendant exposes the plaintiff to certain risks of harm, but not vice versa?

REFERENCE: DOBBS ON TORTS § 348 (2000).

b. *Legal Cause in Strict Liability Cases*

Under the Restatement Second of Torts § 519, the defendant is not strictly liable for *all* harms caused by his abnormally dangerous activity, but only those "the possibility of which makes the activity abnormally dangerous." This simply builds into the strict liability rule the risk rule version of legal cause, doesn't it?

A well-known kind of case involves a defendant who is engaged in blasting, but the harm that results is neither harm from propelled objects, as in *Sullivan*, nor harm from vibrations as in *Exner*. Instead the loud noises upset mother minks on nearby mink ranches and as a result they killed their kittens, resulting in loss to the breeder. This is not the kind of harm which led courts in the first place to consider blasting as abnormally dangerous, since it involves neither flying debris nor vibrations of the earth, and liability has been denied on facts like these. See *Foster v. Preston Mill Co.*, 44 Wash.2d 440, 268 P.2d 645 (1954). Cf. *Indiana Harbor Belt Railroad Co. v. American Cyanamid Co.*, 916 F.2d 1174 (7th Cir.1990) (toxic material leaked from railroad car, but not as a result of the inherent properties of the toxic material; no strict liability). This of course does not preclude liability for negligence or nuisance if that can be established. See *Summit View, Inc. v. W. W. Clyde & Co.*, 17 Utah 2d 26, 403 P.2d 919 (1965).

According to Restatement § 509, this principle is generally applicable to other forms of strict liability as well. Thus if a dog owner knows that the dog has a vicious propensity to bite people, the owner is liable for such bites, but not liable if the dog suddenly bounds through the door and chases a child on a bike until he crashes. The same rule applies to wild animals.

What about intervening causes? How do they fit in? Restatement § 522 provides that one carrying on an abnormally dangerous activity is strictly liable in spite of acts of a third person, or a force of nature, even though those intervening acts or forces are not foreseeable or "expectable." The same rule is applied to "abnormally dangerous" animals, including domestic animals with a known vicious propensity, in § 510. Is this rule sound?

In *Pecan Shoppe of Springfield, Missouri, Inc. v. Tri–State Motor Transit Co.*, 573 S.W.2d 431 (Mo.App.1978) the defendant was a common carrier engaged in hauling dynamite. Its union went on strike and there were a number of acts of violence aimed at the defendant. One Bobby Shuler fired a 30–30 rifle at one of the defendant's tractor-trailer units. There was a tremendous explosion, killing the driver, destroying the unit and causing heavy damage to the plaintiff's property near the highway. The court noted the Restatement's view in § 522 that liability extends even to cases involving intervening forces, but, pointed out that the Restatement expressly avoided taking any position on the matter where there was an intentional wrongdoer causing the harm. The court held that there would be no liability.

Compare *Yukon Equipment, Inc. v. Fireman's Fund Ins. Co.*, 585 P.2d 1206 (Alaska 1978). The defendant stored explosives on a large tract of land quite some distance from other buildings. Thieves broke in and set a charge, apparently in an effort to cover the fact that they had previously stolen explosives. The charge worked very well: the stored explosives caused damages to property for a radius of two miles, registering 1.8 on a Richter scale measurement 30 miles away. The court first held that it would impose liability in cases involving storage of explosives without regard to any balance of the factors listed in § 520 of the Restatement, supra, saying these factors came close to stating a negligence standard, especially so far as these factors invited a judgment about the appropriateness of the location. The court then turned to consider whether the intervening crime in some way relieved the defendant from strict liability. It concluded that the occurrence was not "highly extraordinary," and emphasized that "the particular kind of result threatened by the defendant's conduct, the storage of explosives, was an explosion at the storage site.... Absolute liability is imposed on those who store or use explosives because they have created an unusual risk to others. As between those who have created the risk for the benefit of their own enterprise and those whose only connection with the enterprise is to have suffered damage because of it, the law places the risk of loss on the former.... [I]nsistence that the precise details of the intervening cause be foreseeable would subvert the purpose of that rule of law."

Suppose A manufactures a toxic chemical and delivers it to a rail car provided by B for shipment over the C railroad. While the car is in C's hands, a leak occurs and contaminates property. C expends $1 million in cleanup costs and sues A, claiming strict liability. The harm would not have been done if the chemical were not toxic; on the other hand, the toxic quality of the chemical did not cause the leak. Should the manufacturer be liable? If you ask, "Whose strict liability activity is this?" the answer depends heavily on how you characterize the activity. In a decision involving similar facts, Judge Posner thought the special danger resulted from transportation, not from the toxic qualities of the substance transported. "The relevant activity is transportation, not manufacturing and shipping." *Indiana Harbor Belt Railroad Co. v. American Cyanamid Co.*, 916 F.2d 1174 (7th Cir.1990). As far as we know, it was not a case of intervening negligence. Would joint and several strict liability make any sense? Notice that the claim here is by one of three entities dealing with the hazardous substance, not by some stranger to the operation.

In *Cambridge Water Co. Ltd. v. Eastern Counties Leather*, [1994] 1 All ER 53 (H.L.) the defendant was a tannery. It used a common solvent, PCE, in its tanning process. Small amounts of this solvent were spilled from time to time and as it turned out, over the years at least 1,000 gallons, perhaps much more, made its way into the ground on the defendant's land. From here it progressed downward through fissures about 50 meters. At that point, it was obstructed by an impermeable rock below and it formed a pool, which in turn percolated down the aquifer 173 miles where it polluted the plaintiff's water well. The water produced was not shown to be dangerous, but it counted as unwholesome under government guidelines derived from World Health Organization standards and those of the European Economic Community. Cambridge stopped using the well and had the expense of constructing another elsewhere.

Official government agencies attempted to trace the pollution which was discovered in 1983. Between 1987 and 1989 scholarly or scientific papers were published and they have become the source material on behavior and characteristics of this type of solvent in groundwater; before that, little was known on the subject. "The only harm that could have been foreseen from a spillage was that somebody might have been overcome by fumes from a spillage of a significant quantity."

The plaintiff's only remaining claim by the time the case reached the House of Lords was based on *Rylands v. Fletcher*. The Law Lords took the occasion to suggest strongly that *Rylands* was merely a specific version of nuisance, one based on an isolated instance rather than repeated behavior or harm. They then concluded that foreseebility was required in nuisance cases even though they were also strict liability cases, saying, "It is not sufficient that the injury suffered by the respondents' vessels was the direct result of the nuisance if that injury was in the relevant sense unforeseeable."

From here Lord Goff of Chieveley went on to say that foreseeability was also required in *Rylands v. Fletcher* cases: "[F]oreseeability of damage of the relevant type should be regarded as a prerequisite of liability in damages under the rule." On these grounds, the House of Lords refused to impose strict liability, because, it said, the damage done was not of the type that was foreseeable.

c. *Affirmative Defenses to Strict Liability Claims*

1. *Traditional rule*. The traditional rule, and the one adopted by the Restatement (Second), is that contributory negligence as such is no defense to a strict liability claim. The defendant, not at fault at all, is held fully liable to a plaintiff who is guilty of negligence causing his own harm. At least a formal reason for this result can be found in the argument that since the defendant's liability is not based on negligence in the first place, that liability is not limited by contributory negligence of the plaintiff. Are you satisfied with this reasoning? The Restatement (Second) also takes the view that the plaintiff's "assumed risk," and also

any contributory negligence in "knowingly" subjecting himself to risks of harm, *is* a defense. See RESTATEMENT SECOND OF TORTS § 524 (1977).

2. *Comparative responsibility and the Restatement (Third).* The advent of comparative negligence (or "comparative responsibility," as the Restatement of Apportionment calls it) appears to call for a change in the traditional analysis. Recall that in Chapter 9, supra, we saw that the defense of assumption of risk is no longer a unified one, and it is not self-evident what the label means without examining its context. Suppose, for example, in a comparative negligence state, that the defendant is blasting near or on a highway. Adequate signs are posted but the plaintiff negligently fails to observe them, drives into the danger area and is hurt by falling rock from a blast. Should the plaintiff recover without any reduction in damages, or should a jury be allowed to compare the plaintiff's contributory negligence with the defendant's non-negligent activity? The Restatement of Apportionment, in § 8, provides that in all cases involving physical injury, the factfinder should assign shares of responsibility to each party, regardless of the legal theory of liability. That is, the new Restatement says that juries can and should assign percentages of responsibility even where one party is strictly liable and the other negligent. Further, the new Restatement does not recognize assumption of risk as a separate defense. Is this a workable system? Are there situations in which a plaintiff impliedly consents to encounter a known risk, and thus should not recover even after the adoption of comparative responsibility?

3. *Non-negligent activity by the plaintiff.* Are some activities by plaintiffs such that the plaintiff should be the sole risk-bearer? Suppose defendant utility operates high voltage lines, and that for some purposes this might be considered a strict liability activity. The plaintiff wears a pacemaker which controls his heartbeat and which is interfered with by substantial electrical activity. If neither plaintiff nor defendant is negligent, but the plaintiff's pacemaker is interfered with by the high voltage lines, should the plaintiff be entitled to recover for injury sustained? Compare the problem of the beekeeper who moves his operation into the Murg fields where spray is regularly used. How should the rule be expressed? See RESTATEMENT SECOND OF TORTS § 524A (1977).

REFERENCE: DOBBS ON TORTS §§ 350, 369 (2000).

Chapter 22

TORT LIABILITY FOR DEFECTIVE PRODUCTS

SUBCHAPTER A. DEVELOPING CORE CONCEPTS

§ 1. EVOLUTION OF LIABILITY THEORIES

Products liability law deals with the liabilities of those who manufacture or distribute harm-causing products. That law has undergone significant and sweeping change in the last several decades. Under today's law, those involved in commercial distribution of products are potentially liable for product-caused harm. The basis and extent of such liability, however, continues to be debated. A plaintiff may claim on a contract theory for breach of warranty, or on tort theories of negligence, strict liability, or even fraud. Tort theories dominate in cases of physical harm to person or property, but they cannot be understood in isolation from the law of contract and warranty.

The "Citadel of Privity" And its Fall

Negligence action—the privity requirement. The oldest products cases were brought on a negligence theory, some arising before negligence was regarded as a general theory or approach to tort liability. In these earlier cases, courts thought that the manufacturer's liability for an injury-causing product was derived from some kind of contractual undertaking to the purchaser. Since the basis for liability was not the general duty of reasonable care but the duty implicitly undertaken in a contract of sale, the manufacturer could be liable only to buyers who were in privity of contract—that is, a manufacturer who did not sell directly to the injured plaintiff could not be sued at all by that person. This rule insulated most manufacturers from liability.

In a leading New York case, *Losee v. Clute*, 51 N.Y. 494 (1873), the defendant Clute allegedly manufactured a boiler in a negligent way and sold it to Saratoga Paper Company. The boiler exploded and damaged, not Saratoga Paper, but the plaintiff's nearby property. The Court of Appeals of New York, following the privity rule, held that the complaint was properly dismissed. Defendants "contracted with the company ... and when the boiler was accepted they ceased to have any further responsibility...." Thus even active negligence was protected by the privity rule.

Courts did recognize exceptions for extreme cases. In *Thomas v. Winchester,* 6 N.Y. 397 (1852), the defendant mislabeled a jar of "belladonna, which is a deadly poison," and as a result the plaintiff, consuming it, became ill. Had the defendant sold the jar to the plaintiff, there would have been no privity problem. But the defendant had sold the jar to Aspinwall, who sold it to Ford, who sold it to the plaintiff. There was thus no privity between plaintiff and the defendant. Nevertheless, the Court concluded that where death or great bodily harm would be "the natural and almost inevitable consequence of the sale" under a false label, privity would not be required.

Finally, in 1916, the New York Court of Appeals decided the landmark case of *MacPherson v. Buick Motor Co.*, 217 N.Y. 382, 111 N.E. 1050 (1916). In *MacPherson* the wheel on an automobile collapsed. The plaintiff, who had purchased the car from a retail dealer, was injured. He sued the manufacturer of the car. Since he had purchased from the retailer, not the manufacturer, there was no privity between plaintiff and defendant. Judge Cardozo, writing for the court, said:

> We hold, then, that the principle of *Thomas v. Winchester* is not limited to poisons, explosives, and things of like nature, to things which in their normal operation are implements of destruction. If the nature of a thing is such that it is reasonably certain to place life and limb in peril when negligently made, it is then a thing of danger.... If [the manufacturer] is negligent where danger is to be foreseen, a liability will follow.

Cardozo in effect substituted foreseeability for contract or undertaking and thus applied general negligence principles to a case involving a defective product. Notice that *MacPherson* was definitely not a strict liability case—it simply permitted the application of negligence law to the products setting.

Misrepresentation. MacPherson's rejection of the privity requirement for a products-liability negligence case, while it came to be accepted everywhere, did not assist every plaintiff. Some plaintiffs were injured by products that were not negligently made, and some simply could not prove negligence. Inventive lawyers attempted other theories to assist injured clients. One result was that it came to be held that a manufacturer would be liable for injuries resulting from conditions of the product that were misrepresented, even without privity. In *Baxter v. Ford Motor Co.*, 168 Wash. 456, 12 P.2d 409 (1932), the plaintiff lost his eye when his windshield broke on impact from a pebble. The manufacturer had described its windshields as shatter proof. This was sufficient for liability, even though the manufacturer had not sold the car directly to the plaintiff.

Warranty. Another theory that plaintiffs could rely on when they could not prove negligence was *express warranty*. To take Baxter's facts as an example, if Ford had sold the car to Baxter directly and had, as part of the contract, promised or guaranteed that the windshield was "shatter-proof," this would be an express warranty, a kind of contract. Contract liability is usually strict liability; that is, proving breach of contract does not require proving that the breaching party is at fault. This contract theory is not often available, however, because manufacturers rarely make express guarantees about their products' safety directly to purchasing consumers.

Thus plaintiffs' lawyers began to argue to courts that the sale of goods gave rise to an *implied warranty*. For example, the act of selling a bottle of milk—whether it is sold by a retailer or by a manufacturer—seems to imply that it is not a bottle of belladonna, and also that it is not contaminated with human toes, dead flies, or unspeakable viruses. In other words, it should meet some kind of normal expectation as to quality and safety. Over the years, courts came to reject the maxim *caveat emptor*—let the buyer beware—and to accept the idea of a warranty implicit in the act of sale. The Uniform Commercial Code § 2–314, which applies to any seller of goods, recognizes an implied warranty that goods are "fit for the ordinary purposes for which such goods are used" and that they are as good as the seller claims they are.

The implied warranty theory carried with it all the advantages and disadvantages of contract law—liability for breach is strict, but privity is required. While some courts created exceptions to the privity rule in cases involving such things as bad food and intimate products such as soaps, hair dyes and the like, these cases seemed to lack any underlying principle and they came to an evolutionary dead-end. About 1960, however, courts started off in an entirely new direction.

A leading case of the period was *Henningsen v. Bloomfield Motors, Inc.*, 32 N.J. 358, 161 A.2d 69 (1960). *Henningsen* involved an automobile purchased by Mr. Henningsen as a present for his wife. The car's steering failed, and the car crashed into a wall. The Henningsens sued the retailer and the manufacturer. The manufacturer and dealer had provided in the purchase contract that there were no warranties except that defective parts would be replaced within certain time limits. Since Mrs. Henningsen was badly injured, this was not helpful. The New Jersey Court held that there was an implied warranty in addition to this express warranty, that it ran to the ultimate purchaser and not merely to the retailer, and that the disclaimer of liability would be ineffective to protect the manufacturer. *Henningsen,* in other words, did for warranty about the same thing that *MacPherson* did for negligence.

Warranty remains a viable theory today in many products cases. However, to a very large extent the warranty theory has been displaced, or at least supplemented, by a theory of strict liability in tort, divorced from any conception of warranty.

The Development of Strict Products Liability

Strict tort liability emerged as a leading theory for products cases in *Greenman v. Yuba Power Products, Inc.*, 59 Cal.2d 57, 27 Cal.Rptr. 697, 377 P.2d 897 (1963). In that case, plaintiff's wife bought him a power tool that caused him serious injuries. Claiming the tool was defective, he sued the retailer and manufacturer on the two grounds then available to him: negligence and warranty. Affirming a jury verdict against the manufacturer, the court reasoned that in the case of defective products, "the liability is not one governed by the law of contract warranties but by the law of strict liability in tort." Justice Traynor wrote that the purpose of strict liability "is to insure that the costs of injuries resulting from defective products are borne by the manufacturers that put such products on the market rather than by the injured persons who are powerless to protect themselves."

Greenman was strongly influential in the drafting of the Restatement Second of Torts § 402A, promulgated in 1964. Section 402A quickly gained wide acceptance in the courts. By the mid–1960s, then, the developing law of strict products liability was freed from the older logic of the warranty theory and thus from the privity limitation. Section 402A became the lodestar of products liability discussion and development for a whole generation or more. Its essential provisions were simple: (a) sellers were strictly liable for physical injuries to persons or property other than the product itself; this meant that the injured consumer could recover without proving fault; (b) privity rules were abolished; this meant that the injured consumer could recovery without privity; (c) strict liability attached to products that were "defective" because they were unreasonably dangerous to the consumer; and (d) the consumer's reasonable expectations defined what counted as a defective product.

REFERENCE: DOBBS ON TORTS § 353 (2000).

§ 2. RATIONALES FOR STRICT PRODUCTS LIABILITY

Strict products liability may be justified on one or more of the rationales discussed below. What do you think of them?

1. *Consumer expectations.* Manufacturers implicitly represent that the products they make are safe and healthy, and consumers are justified in relying that implicit representation. Note that this rationale has been used to support liability in express and implied warranty cases, in which the consumer's expectation of safety in some particular respect was obviously justified because the defendant had represented or warranted the product in that respect, and in negligence cases as well.

2. *Enterprise liability or "loss spreading."* Manufacturers and commercial sellers of goods can more easily spread the costs that result from injuries caused by defective products, by raising prices or purchasing insurance. Compensation is needed and the most practical way to secure it is to have all consumers share the cost by paying more for the product.

It has also been argued that strict liability justly imposes legal responsibility for injuries that are statistically associated with the enterprise of manufacturing and selling, making liability a cost of doing business that should be borne by someone other than injured individuals.

3. *Practicality*. Since a retailer in privity with the plaintiff may be held liable on warranty, and since if so held it could have indemnity from the manufacturer, it would be cheaper to permit the plaintiff to sue the manufacturer directly, and second, since most defective products are that way because of negligence, imposing strict liability saves the legal system the time and expense of proving negligence.

4. *Fairness*. Another set of justifications stresses the basic *fairness* of a strict liability regime. First, because the manufacturer enjoys the advantages of sending its products into commerce, it should also take the disadvantages in the form of injury costs when the risks of such activity come to fruition. (On this argument, compare the reasons for the liability of a master for the torts of a servant.)

A second fairness-based justification is that the manufacturer imposes a special kind of risk—*nonreciprocal risks*—on the consumer. That is, the manufacturer imposes risks on the consumer that are quite different from any risks the consumer imposes on the manufacturer, and this fact justifies strict liability. George P. Fletcher developed the theory of nonreciprocal risks in a very influential article, *Fairness and Utility in Tort Theory*, 85 HARV. L. REV. 537 (1972). One example Fletcher uses of a non-reciprocal risk is the risk an airplane pilot imposes upon those on the ground. He imposes a risk of crashing into them but they impose no comparable risk upon him. To Fletcher, the crashing plane that causes ground damages represents a good case for strict liability in the absence of a defense.

Fletcher's theory attacks the fairness of risk-utility balancing commonly followed in analysis of negligence claims. In part, he does so by pointing to criminal law. No individual human being should suffer criminal sanctions for the sake of the common good. Similarly, no injured person should be required to give up a claim against the defendant merely because the defendant's activities are socially useful. If these activities are socially useful, they need not be prohibited, but they should be "taxed" by tort law to provide compensation for harms they cause. Fletcher recognizes that his theory will not lead inexorably to a predictable result. You would have to ask whether the defendant imposed a risk so excessive that it should be considered non-reciprocal. He doubts, however, whether the risk-utility balancing is any more certain. For some later Fletcherian ideas, see George P. Fletcher, *Corrective Justice for Moderns* (Book Review of Jules Coleman, Risks and Wrongs), 106 HARV. L. REV. 1658 (1993).

5. *Deterrence*. If strict liability is imposed, manufacturers will tend to make products safer in order to avoid the increased costs resulting

from liability. Liability of the manufacturer will drive the manufacturer to increase the price so as to cover the liability costs. As prices rise on unsafe products consumers will seek cheaper substitutes. These substitutes will usually be safer products; they are cheaper because they are not bearing the costs of tort liability. In addition, manufacturers, to avoid this loss of customers and the liability itself, will seek to find ways to make products more safe.

Guido Calabresi, in his 1970 book THE COST OF ACCIDENTS, offered an economic analysis of the accident cost-reduction effects of strict liability. Much of his book is devoted to an idea he calls primary accident cost reduction or primary accident cost avoidance, focusing on reducing accident costs by reducing the number or severity of accidents themselves. This can be done in his view by using some combination of two major devices:

a. *Specific deterrence.* One way to reduce primary accident costs is to prohibit conduct that is excessively risky. This can be done by legislation or administrative regulation, for example. Specific prohibitions might be made because conduct is either "immoral" or because it does more harm than good. However, it is difficult to decide by political processes what risks are more harmful than useful. Calabresi believes that "the market" can make this judgment in a much better way.

b. *General deterrence.* This is a technical term and an economic notion. The idea is that if a given activity, such as driving, causes accidents, that activity could be made to pay the costs. Calabresi believes that if an activity is made to pay all the costs it really causes, this will in fact reduce accidents or the severity of accidents. Here's how. Suppose that convertibles are riskier than sedans, especially in turnover accidents. If manufacturers of convertibles had to pay all the costs of convertible injuries, they would raise the price of convertibles. Potential buyers will know comparative risks if the price of the convertibles reflects their true costs to society. Purchasers would not have to think about relative risks at all when they considered purchasing a convertible; they would have only to look at its price tag. Some people would buy the more expensive convertible even so. But others would reject it as too expensive. Even if they did not think about risks that were included in the price, their decision would be more informed because they would know the true costs of operating the convertible. Because a number of people would reject the more dangerous convertible, convertible-caused injuries would be reduced.

Athens and Sparta examples. Calabresi offered an example. He supposed that in Athens accident costs of an activity (like driving) were always charged to that activity so that insurance costs for an activity like driving would be higher than they would be otherwise. In Sparta, on the other hand, all injuries were compensated from general public funds raised by taxes. Taney is thinking of buying a second car. The costs of owning the second car would be $200 a year for operating plus another $200 for insurance. The alternative would be to take taxis occasionally, a cost of about $250 a year. In Athens he might reject the second car because its total cost, including the insurance which reflected accident costs, would be much greater than the cost of taxis. In Sparta, however, he would have no insurance costs, since injuries would be taken care of by public assistance. So his cost for the second car would be $200 a year as compared to taxis costing $250. He would buy the second car.

The Athens plan reduces accident costs by showing people like Taney the true cost of activities they are considering. The point is not that everyone would forgo the car, but that some people, getting the risk information through the price, would do so. Calabresi thought there was a second and maybe more important way that general deterrence would help reduce accident costs. He thought that it would encourage us to make activities safer if we knew the real costs of risks associated with them. If cars cause an average of $200 a year in accident costs but a new brake costing the equivalent of $50 a year can reduce those costs to $100, then Taney would install the new brake if he lived in Athens.

Cheapest cost avoider. Ideally, the costs of accidents should be borne by acts or activities that could avoid the accident costs most cheaply. A new car manufacturer might be a good choice, for example, if the manufacturer could add the $50 brake when it produces the car. If it is liable for car accidents, it will have the incentive to add the $50 brake.

The (Partial) Decline of Strict Products Liability

All of the arguments for broad strict products liability have been challenged, and as courts worked out the details of strict liability over a thirty-year period many critics asserted that strict liability for defectively-designed products was wrong in principle. Many states passed statutes in the 1980s limiting products liability cases in one respect or another as the criticisms reached critical mass.

A major turning point was the 1998 publication of the Restatement Third of Torts: Products Liability, which essentially retains strict liability only for products flawed in manufacture, and adopts a negligence standard or something very like it for design and warning defects. While the ultimate effect of the Products Restatement is uncertain, it has already proved influential and has sparked heated debate about whether, or to what extent, strict liability should be imposed. The Products Restatement itself does not focus on the various theories of liability, but rather on whether products are proven to be "defective."

REFERENCE: DOBBS ON TORTS § 353 (2000); 1 MADDEN & OWEN ON PRODUCTS LIABILITY § 5:4 (3d ed. 2000).

§ 3. EXCLUDING STAND–ALONE ECONOMIC HARM

MOORMAN MANUFACTURING CO. v. NATIONAL TANK CO.

Supreme Court of Illinois, 1982.
91 Ill.2d 69, 61 Ill.Dec. 746, 435 N.E.2d 443.

THOMAS J. MORAN, JUSTICE.

[Plaintiff purchased from defendant a steel grain storage tank for use in plaintiff's feed processing plant. About ten years later, a crack developed in one of the steel plates on the tank. The plaintiff sued on theories of strict tort liability, misrepresentation, negligent design and express warranty.]

The tort law of products liability stems from the contract cause of action for breach of warranty. In MacPherson v. Buick Motor Co. (1916), 217 N.Y. 382,111 N.E. 1050, liability in negligence was imposed upon a manufacturer to an ultimate consumer without privity of contract. Subsequently, courts began to hold manufacturers liable for personal injuries without negligence; the theory generally utilized to reach the manufacturers was based upon the law of sales warranty. (See Prosser, The Assault Upon The Citadel, 69 Yale L.J. 1099,1126 (1960) (Prosser I).) However, recognition of the difficulties facing consumers with respect to items such as notice and privity led most courts to abandon the privity requirement in implied-warranty actions (see Prosser, The Fall Of The Citadel, 50 Minn. L.Rev. 791(1966) (Prosser II)) and to ultimately abandon the fiction of warranty in favor of strict liability in tort.

This State adopted the tort theory of strict liability in Suvada v. White Motor Co. (1965), 32 Ill.2d 612, 210 N.E.2d 182, to allow a plaintiff to recover from a manufacturer for personal injuries. Suvada, however, did not address the question of whether a consumer could recover under a strict liability in tort theory for solely economic loss. That issue was first addressed in Santor v. A & M Karagheusian, Inc. (1965), 44 N.J. 52, 207 A.2d 305. There, the plaintiff purchased, from a third-party seller, carpeting that had been manufactured by the defendant. After several months, unsightly lines began to appear on the surface of the carpeting. The Supreme Court of New Jersey held that the plaintiff could maintain a breach-of-warranty claim directly against the manufacturer despite the lack of privity between them. In dicta, the court went on to declare that although the strict liability in tort doctrine had been applied principally in connection with personal injuries, the responsibility of the manufacturer should be no different where damage to the article sold or to other property is involved. 44 N.J. 52, 66, 207 A.2d 305, 312. Several months later, in Seely v. White Motor Co. (1965), 63 Cal.2d 9, 403 P.2d 145, 45 Cal.Rptr. 17, the Supreme Court of California rejected the rationale by which the court in Santor imposed strict liability in tort for economic loss. In Seely, plaintiff purchased a truck manufactured by defendant. After he took possession, Seely discovered that the truck bounced violently. Nine months later, the truck overturned after brake failure, causing damage to the truck but no personal injury to Seely. Plaintiff had the damage repaired and subsequently stopped making his installment payments. Defendant repossessed the truck, at which time plaintiff sued on theories of breach of express warranty and strict tort liability, and sought damages for the repair of the truck, for money paid on the purchase price, and for profits lost by virtue of the truck's unsuitability for normal use. The court affirmed the trial court's award to Seely for money paid on the purchase price and for lost profits on the basis of express warranty. The court, however, went on to state that these economic losses are not recoverable under strict liability in tort. The court also declared, in reference to Santor, "Only if someone had been injured because the rug was unsafe for use would there have been any basis for imposing strict liability in tort." Thus, the court refused to expand the scope of its opinion in Greenman v. Yuba Power Products, Inc. (1963), 59 Cal.2d 57, 62, 377 P.2d 897, 900, 27 Cal. Rptr. 697, 700, which declared that a manufacturer is strictly liable in tort for a product that has a defect that causes injury to a person.

Subsequent to these two seminal cases in the area, some courts have held a manufacturer liable under the theory of strict liability in tort for solely economic losses. Most courts, however, have denied recovery under strict liability in tort for solely economic losses.... Contrary to the conclusion reached by the appellate court, we believe the language limiting section 402A to unreasonably dangerous defects resulting in physical harm to the ultimate user or consumer, or to his property, reflects sound policy reasons.

First, the law of sales has been carefully articulated to govern the economic relations between suppliers and consumers of goods. The framework provided by the UCC includes the parol evidence rule, implied warranties, express warranties, rules on disclaimers, notice requirements, limitations on the extent of a manufacturer's liability, and a statute of limitations. Although warranty rules frustrate just compensation for physical injury, they function well in a commercial setting. These rules determine the quality of the product the manufacturer promises and thereby determine the quality he must deliver.

We note, for example, section 2–316 of the UCC, which permits parties to a sales contract to limit warranties in any reasonable manner, or to agree that the buyer possesses no warranty protection at all. The parties may even agree to exclude the implied warranties of merchantability and fitness if they do so in writing, and may modify the implied warranty by clear and conspicuous language. Yet, a manufacturer's strict liability for economic loss cannot be disclaimed because a manufacturer should not be permitted to define the scope of its own responsibility for defective products. Thus, adopting strict liability in tort for economic loss would effectively eviscerate section 2–316 of the UCC.

Further, application of the rules of warranty prevents a manufacturer from being held liable for damages of unknown and unlimited scope. If a defendant were held strictly liable in tort for the commercial loss suffered by a particular purchaser, it would be liable for business losses of other purchasers caused by the failure of the product to meet the specific needs of their business, even though these needs were communicated only to the dealer. Finally, a large purchaser, such as plaintiff in the instant case, can protect itself against the risk of unsatisfactory performance by bargaining for a warranty. Or, it may choose to accept a lower purchase price for the product in lieu of warranty protection. Subsequent purchasers may do likewise in bargaining over the price of the product. We believe it is preferable to relegate the consumer to the comprehensive scheme of remedies fashioned by the UCC, rather than requiring the consuming public to pay more for their products so that a manufacturer can insure against the possibility that some of his products will not meet the business needs of some of his customers. . . .

We do hold, however, that when a product is sold in defective condition that is unreasonably dangerous to the user or consumer or to his property, strict liability in tort is applicable to physical injury to plaintiff's property, as well as to personal injury. When an unreasonably dangerous defect is present, such as the truck's nonfunctioning brakes in Seely, and physical injury does, in fact, result, then "[p]hysical injury to property is so akin to personal injury that there is no reason to distinguish them." This comports with the notion that the essence of a product liability tort case is not that the plaintiff failed to receive the quality of product he expected, but that the plaintiff has been exposed, through a hazardous product, to an unreasonable risk of injury to his person or property. On the other hand, contract law, which protects expectation interests, provides the proper standard when a qualitative defect is involved, i.e., when a product is unfit for its intended uses.

Plaintiff argues that economic loss is not sought in this case. It asserts in its brief that a product defect existed that posed an "extreme threat to life and limb, and to property of plaintiff and others, a defect which resulted in a sudden and violent ripping of plaintiff's tank, and which only fortunately did not extend the full height of the tank." Plaintiff further asserts that, because costs of repairs are not economic losses, consequential damages resulting from the loss of use of the tank during repairs does not constitute economic loss either.

"Economic loss" has been defined as "damages for inadequate value, costs of repair and replacement of the defective product, or consequent loss of profits—without any claim of personal injury or damage to other property . . ." (Note, Economic Loss in Products Liability Jurisprudence, 66 Colum. L. Rev. 917, 918 (1966) (Economic Loss) as well as "the diminution in the value of the product because it is inferior in quality and does not work for the general purposes for which it was manufactured and sold." (Comment, Manufacturers' Liability to Remote Purchasers for "Economic Loss" Damages–Tort or Contract? 114 U.Pa.

L.Rev. 539, 541 (1966).) These definitions are consistent with the policy of warranty law to protect expectations of suitability and quality.

The demarcation between physical harm or property damage on the one hand and economic loss on the other usually depends on the nature of the defect and the manner in which the damage occurred....

We ... hold that, where only the defective product is damaged, economic losses caused by qualitative defects falling under the ambit of a purchaser's disappointed expectations cannot be recovered under a strict liability theory. Here, count I of the complaint alleged that during the last few months of 1976 and the first few months of 1977, "a crack developed in one of the steel plates on the second ring of [the] tank; such crack was not discovered by plaintiff ... until such tank was being emptied on or about August 24, 1977." This was not the type of sudden and dangerous occurrence best served by the policy of tort law that the manufacturer should bear the risk of hazardous products....

Our conclusion that qualitative defects are best handled by contract, rather than tort, law applies whether the tort theory involved is strict liability or negligence. Tort theory is appropriately suited for personal injury or property damage resulting from a sudden or dangerous occurrence of the nature described above. The remedy for economic loss, loss relating to a purchaser's disappointed expectations due to deterioration, internal breakdown or nonaccidental cause, on the other hand, lies in contract....

The policy considerations against allowing recovery for solely economic loss in strict liability cases apply to negligence actions as well. When the defect is of a qualitative nature and the harm relates to the consumer's expectation that a product is of a particular quality so that it is fit for ordinary use, contract, rather than tort, law provides the appropriate set of rules for recovery....

[The Court also held that economic losses, though recoverable for intentional misrepresentations, were not recoverable for innocent representations, and that in this case the statute of limitations had run on the warranty claim.]

Notes

1. Most courts, following Justice Traynor's lead in *Seely v. White Motor Co.*, discussed in the *Moorman* case, have agreed that economic harm standing alone must be recovered on the basis of contract or warranty, or not at all. The effect is to allocate cases of non-physical harms to the law of warranty and cases of physical harms to the law of tort.

2. Suppose that TankCo manufactures tanks for storing toxic chemicals. ChemCo purchases toxic chemicals for use in its factory and stores them in tanks it has purchased from TankCo. One of the tanks is defective and a leak occurs. The leak contaminated ChemCo's property and also adjoining property that belongs to the plaintiff. Is TankCo liable for the costs of cleaning up the contamination (a) incurred by ChemCo on its property? (b) incurred by the plaintiff for cleaning up its adjoining property?

3. *Added equipment.* A defect in a tuna boat's engine caused the boat to catch fire, burning expensive equipment on board that had been added after the boat's sale to its initial user. Can the boat's owner sue in tort for the loss of the added equipment? Yes, said the Court in *Saratoga Fishing Co. v. J.M. Martinac & Co.*, 520 U.S. 875, 117 S.Ct. 1783, 138 L.Ed.2d 76 (1997), since the added equipment was not part of the "product itself." Is such a case founded more in logic or in policy, do you think?

4. It is sometimes hard to draw the line between pure economic harm on the one hand and physical injury on the other. What if the tank in *Moorman* had not gradually developed a crack, but had suddenly exploded, destroying itself? Compare *State Farm Mut. Ins. Co. v. Ford Motor Co.*, 225 Wis.2d 305, 592 N.W.2d 201 (Wis. 1999)(barring tort claim where a car's faulty ignition caused the car to catch fire) with *American Fire & Cas. Co. v. Ford Motor Co.*, 588 N.W.2d 437 (Iowa 1999)(rejecting the economic loss doctrine and allowing a tort claim in a truck-fire case, reasoning that tort actions should be allowed where defects cause safety hazards). What if semen used for artificial insemination of cows produces genetic abnormalities? These problems are difficult and fascinating. They occur, however, only at the borderline, and the principle in *Moorman* is quite easy to apply in many, many cases. Would you have any difficulty, for example, with a case in which a vacuum cleaner quits working and consequently is not worth much?

SUBCHAPTER B.   ESTABLISHING
A PRIMA FACIE CASE

Courts have recognized three types of product defects that may lead to liability: (1) Manufacturing defects (also called production flaws); (2) design defects; and (3) information defects. Perhaps the most crucial questions in products cases–and the focus of the Restatement of Products Liability–concern whether a product is "defective" in the first place, and what a plaintiff has to prove to establish such a defect.

§ 4.   MANUFACTURING DEFECTS

LEE v. CROOKSTON COCA–COLA BOTTLING CO.

Supreme Court of Minnesota, 1971.
290 Minn. 321, 188 N.W.2d 426.

ROGOSHESKE, JUSTICE.

[Plaintiff, a waitress in the Norman Steak House at Ada, Minnesota, was injured when a Coca–Cola bottle exploded in her hand. The trial judge refused to submit a claim based on strict tort liability, and the jury, apparently finding no negligence and no breach of warranty, returned a defendant's verdict. Plaintiff appeals, arguing that the strict liability claim should have been submitted under proper instructions to the jury.]

[Evidence showed the bottle exploded in the plaintiff's hand, that it had not struck anything, that it had not been subjected to temperature extremes or mishandling.]

The rule of strict liability, as revised and adopted by the American Law Institute in 1964, is embodied in Restatement, Torts (2d) § 402A. It imposes liability, without proof of negligence or privity of contract, upon a manufacturer or seller for injury caused by a dangerously defective product. To recover under the rule, the injured party must present evidence, direct or circumstantial, from which the jury can justifiably find that (1) the product was in fact in a defective condition, unreasonably dangerous for its intended use; (2) such defect existed when the product left defendant's control; and (3) the defect was the proximate cause of the injury sustained.

The greatest difficulty in establishing liability under this rule is in proving that the product was defective and that the defect existed when the product left defendant's control. While in conventional tort terms no proof of negligence is necessary, in many cases proof of a defect may simply be a substitute word for negligence. Thus, strict liability does not mean that the defendant is held liable as an insurer of his product regardless of circumstances. As is true in negligence cases with respect to the mere fact of an accident, the mere fact of injury during use of the product usually is insufficient proof to show existence of a defect at the time defendant relinquished control.... Also, liability is not imposed where the injured party has not eliminated the probability that improper handling by intermediate parties might have caused the defect....

The narrow question presented here, however, is whether circumstantial evidence, the core of the res ipsa loquitur doctrine, is sufficient to take the case to the jury on the theory of strict liability as well as on the theory of negligence....

It surely must be conceded that circumstantial evidence of the type present in ... this case justifies submission of the issue of liability on the theory of res ipsa.... As testified to by defendant's expert, there are three fundamental causes of bottle failure: Thermo-shock, internal pressure, and external force. According to the expert's testimony, failure because of thermo-shock could only result from drastic changes in temperature applied to the outside of the bottle, such as would be produced by placing a bottle containing hot liquid in cold water. Failure caused by external force, of course, usually results from an impact, such as striking or dropping the bottle. Failure because of internal pressure due to excessive carbonation is ordinarily unlikely because the bottle is designed to withstand approximately four times the pressure created by the gas introduced, and after the carbonated liquid is added to the syrup mixture, any excessive carbonation is equalized by exposure to atmospheric pressure during the interval between carbonation and capping. The capacity of different bottles to withstand internal pressure varies, however, in part due to bottlers' customary reuse of bottles. Some bottles have been refilled for years and might have been subjected to "rough" handling numerous times, thereby increasing the probability that even though they are designed to withstand such handling, some could develop defects which would escape detection by the most careful bottler. This may be the only plausible explanation for the bottle's failure in this case, since there is uncontradicted evidence dispelling the probability that the failure was attributable to thermo-shock or external force. Absent expert opinion, as in a case of this type, circumstantial evidence may be the only available means of establishing a claim of either negligence or a defective product.

Under the theory of strict liability, the elements of proof as noted above are few and uncomplicated. The significant difference is that under strict liability the jury need not infer from the circumstantial evidence that defendant was negligent in order to impose liability. It is sufficient that the evidence establishes that the manufacturer placed a dangerously defective product on the market, knowing that it is to be used without inspection for defects. . . .

In short, under the theory of strict liability plaintiff should not be required to prove specifically what defect caused the incident, but may rely upon circumstantial evidence from which it can reasonably be inferred that it is more probable than not that the product was defective when it left defendant's control. . . .

The jury could properly have found on the evidence submitted that defendant was not causally negligent. This finding, of course, defeats plaintiffs' claim on the theory of negligence. As has been pointed out above, however, it would not necessarily preclude recovery under the theory of strict liability. Under instructions solely on negligence, a jury might conclude that the bottle was defective when it left defendant's control but that defendant was not liable because the defect did not result from negligence. Under instructions on strict liability, on the other hand, a finding that the bottle was defective when defendant put it on the market would *compel* a verdict *for plaintiffs*, absent the aforementioned defenses and without considering the question of negligence.

Thus, the trial court's refusal to submit plaintiffs' claim upon the theory of strict liability in tort must also be regarded as reversible error. The court's ruling deprived plaintiffs of a legitimate choice of theories on which to submit the case. Plaintiffs are entitled to attempt to prove their case on either or both theories—that defendant was negligent or that it put a dangerously defective product on the market.

It could be argued that the case in effect was submitted to the jury on strict liability, since the jury was instructed on implied warranty. Although strict liability in tort and in warranty are very similar, we cannot view the court's instructions as sufficient to constitute submission of the question of strict liability in tort to the jury. The jury was told that defendant warranted that the bottle of Coca–Cola "was reasonably fit for the ordinary and usual handling as it might reasonably anticipate in the exercise of reasonable care." This language falls short of conveying to the jury that if a defect existed in defendant's product when it left its control, defendant should be found liable for the injuries caused by such defect.

Reversed and new trial granted.

Notes

1. *Manufacturing defects.* A manufacturing defect is "a physical departure from a product's intended design." Restatement of Products Liability § 1, cmt. a. In other words, a manufacturing defect can occur even if there is nothing at all wrong with the product's design. Manufacturing defects typically affect only a small percentage of a manufacturer's products in a particular product line.

2. *Effect on consumer expectation test.* Section 2(a) of the Restatement of Products Liability explains that "a product contains a manufacturing defect when the product departs from its intended design even though all possible care was exercised in the preparation and marketing of the product." How does the new Restatement's standard relate to the Second Restatement's "consumer expectations" standard?

3. *Elements of a strict liability claim.* To prevail on a strict liability claim, the plaintiff must prove not only that the product was defective, and that the defect was an actual and proximate cause of plaintiff's harm, but also that the product was defective when it left the defendant's hands. This may not be easy to prove, and as *Lee* shows, drawing inferences is often necessary.

4. *Inferences of cause and defect.* The Restatement of Products Liability § 3, provides that it may be inferred that a product defect existing at the time of sale or distribution caused plaintiff's harm when the event (a) was of a kind that ordinarily occurs as a result of product defect; and (b) was not solely the result of causes other than product defect. What does this remind you of?

5. *Applications.* In *Kerr v. Corning Glass Works*, 284 Minn. 115, 169 N.W.2d 587 (1969), a Pyrex baking dish "exploded" when the plaintiff removed it from the oven. The Minnesota Court held this was not proof of a defect existing when the dish left the manufacturer's hands, since the explosion might have occurred because of subsequent damage. Does the Minnesota Court have a different attitude in *Lee*?

In a 1964 New Jersey case, the plaintiff, working for Ford, operated a grinding machine with a grinding disc produced by the defendant. The same disc had been on the grinder earlier when the machine was used by another employee. When the plaintiff used the machine, the disc snapped and struck him. The court held this did not suffice to prove that the disc was defective. Although a manufacturing flaw was possible, it was equally possible that mishandling would explain the accident. *Jakubowski v. Minnesota Mining & Manufacturing*, 42 N.J. 177, 199 A.2d 826 (1964). In a later New Jersey decision the plaintiff was driving a six-month-old Lincoln Continental. He heard a "gink" in the front and the steering mechanism locked. The car then collided with a tree. The trial judge refused to charge the jury that it could infer a defect, but this time the New Jersey Court held that proof was sufficient to permit a finding of defect. Although other causes were possible, a defect in the car when it left the manufacturer was deemed sufficiently probable. *Moraca v. Ford Motor Co.*, 66 N.J. 454, 332 A.2d 599 (1975). Although the later cases from New Jersey and Minnesota are probably distinguishable from the earlier cases in those states, it is probably fair to say they represent a more relaxed attitude about the proof problem.

The rule remains, however, that the plaintiff must prove a defect in the product that existed when it left the defendant's hands, and this rule does continue to foreclose recovery if the plaintiff's proof is insufficient. Consider *Mixon v. Chrysler Corp.*, 281 Ark. 202, 663 S.W.2d 713 (1984). The plaintiff, driving a year-old car with 30,000 miles on it, suddenly found he could not control it. The car went over an embankment. The brakes were checked afterward and no defect was found. The wreckage was then disposed of before it occurred to anyone to check the steering. The plaintiff then brought suit, claiming that the steering was defective. Given no further facts, can the defendant have a summary judgment?

6. *Proof of specific defect.* An inference of defect may arise even when the plaintiff fails to prove what aspect of the product was defective. RESTATE-MENT OF PRODUCTS LIABILITY, § 3, com. c. Does that mean a jury could infer a defect when the plaintiff's car burst into flames while unattended in her garage even though the plaintiff cannot show whether the fire was caused by a defective fuel tank, electrical system, or something else?

7. *Defect and negligence.* The use of *res ipsa* analogies, as in *Lee,* suggests a similarity between strict liability and negligence, as does the "unreasonable danger" phrase. One difference, however, is that a negligence claim focuses on the defendant's conduct, while a strict products liability claim focuses on the product itself. Thus, as in *Lee,* a jury might find no negligence and still find a product defective. A defendant which has done the best anyone can do to produce a safe product is still liable for the inevitable defects that cause harm. But in the great bulk of cases, it can be inferred that negligence caused the manufacturing defect. Since this will so often be true, this kind of strict liability might be regarded as a "shortcut" to the same result a negligence rule would ordinarily achieve, but without the necessity of long, detailed trials over the fault issue. See Gary T. Schwartz, *Understanding Products Liability,* 67 CAL. L. REV. 435, 460–461 (1979). Under this view, strict liability differs from negligence because it is cheaper to use. But as to most defendants most of the time, it will add very little liability. What do you think of this analysis?

––––––

MEXICALI ROSE v. SUPERIOR COURT (Clark v. Mexicali Rose), 1 Cal.4th 617, 822 P.2d 1292, 4 Cal.Rptr.2d 145 (1992). Clark ordered a chicken enchilada at the Mexicali Rose restaurant. He swallowed a one-inch chicken bone contained in the enchilada, sustaining a throat injury for which he sues. He claims negligence, breach of implied warranty, and strict tort liability.

Held, demurrer to the warranty and tort strict liability claims should be sustained. "If the injury-producing substance is natural to the preparation of the food served, it can be said that it was reasonably expected by its very nature and the food cannot be determined unfit or defective. A plaintiff in such a case has no cause of action in strict liability or implied warranty." The "defendants owe no duty to provide a perfect enchilada," but under this rule they may still be liable for negligence in preparing the food if that negligence is proved.

JUSTICE MOSK, dissenting: "The majority hold that processed food containing a sharp, concealed bone is fit for consumption, though no reasonable consumer would anticipate finding the bone. They declare in effect that the bone is natural to the dish, therefore the dish is fit for consumption. The majority never explain why this should be the rule, when it is universally held that in the analogous case of a sharp bit of wire in processed food, liability occurs under both the implied warranty of fitness and the theory of strict liability for defective consumer products." JUSTICE ARABIAN also dissented.

JACKSON v. NESTLE–BEICH, INC., 147 Ill.2d 408, 168 Ill.Dec. 147, 589 N.E.2d 547 (1992). The plaintiff allegedly broke a tooth on a hard pecan shell embedded in a chocolate-covered pecan-caramel candy purchased in a sealed can and manufactured by Nestle. Nestle moved for summary judgment on the ground that the substance was natural to pecans, not foreign. *Held*, affirming the intermediate appellate court's decision, "the foreign-natural doctrine is unsound and should be abandoned." Instead, the consumer's reasonable expectation is the test of defectiveness under the Restatement's § 402A, Comment i.

Note

Food products and consumer expectations. The new Restatement provides that a harm-causing ingredient in a food product is a defect "if a reasonable consumer would not expect the food product to contain that ingredient." RESTATEMENT OF PRODUCTS LIABILITY § 7. Is the consumer expectations test particularly apropos in food cases? If the standard was simply whether the food "departs from its intended design," which is the new Restatement's general standard for manufacturing defects, would that mean that if the seller of chicken enchiladas or nut-candies never even tried to remove bones or shells there would be no strict liability, since in that case there would be no departure from "intended design?" As the new Restatement indicates, most courts do not follow the foreign-natural distinction in *Mexicali Rose* but rely on consumer expectations instead.

§ 5. DESIGN DEFECTS

LEICHTAMER v. AMERICAN MOTORS CORP., 67 Ohio St.2d 456, 424 N.E.2d 568, 21 O. O. 3d 285 (1981). Plaintiffs were passengers in a Jeep driven by Paul Vance on an off-road facility. Vance was negotiating hills and terraces when he overturned the Jeep in a back-to-front flip over. The rollbar, attached to relatively thin metal housing, displaced toward the passengers when the housing collapsed. Vance and his wife were killed. The plaintiff Jeanne Leichtamer's legs were twisted through the front seat and she is now a paraplegic. The plaintiffs sued claiming that, though Vance was negligent, their injuries were enhanced because of the roll-bar's displacement. The jury found for the plaintiffs, awarding $1 million in compensatory and $1 million in punitive damages to Jeanne and $100,000 compensatory and $100,000 punitive to Carl Leichtamer. *Held*, affirmed. "Appellees did not claim that there was any defect in the way the vehicle was manufactured in the sense of departure by the manufacturer from design specifications. The vehicle was manufactured precisely in the manner in which it was designed to be manufactured. It reached Paul Vance in that condition and was not changed. . . . [T]he vast weight of authority is in support of allowing an action in strict liability in tort . . . for design defects. . . . Strict liability in tort has been applied to design defect 'second collision' cases. While a manufacturer is under no obligation to design a 'crash proof' vehicle, an instruction may be given on the issue of strict liability in tort if the plaintiff adduces sufficient evidence that an unreasonably dangerous product design proximately caused or enhanced plaintiff's injuries in the course of a foreseeable use. . . . [A] product may be found defective in design if the plaintiff demonstrates that the product failed to perform as safely as an ordinary consumer would expect when used in an intended or reasonably foreseeable manner. . . . A product will be found unreasonably dangerous if it is dangerous to an extent beyond the expectations of an ordinary consumer when used in an intended or reasonably foreseeable manner." Since the roll-bar was designed for a side roll-over only and not a back-to-front roll-over, and since the company knew it had not provided tests for this kind of hazard when it advertised the Jeep for off-the-road use, punitive damages were warranted.

Notes

1. *Design defects*. Notice that the "defect" was the design, not a flaw of production. Design defects are difficult to define and identify. In addition, design defect claims threaten manufacturers in ways that production defect claims do not. If a product is flawed in manufacture, only a few products with flaws will be in circulation; but if a product is mis-designed, every one of the products represents a potential lawsuit against the manufacturer.

2. *Consumer expectations and unreasonable danger*. As noted in § 4 above, the Restatement Second's § 402A provided that a product would be considered defective if it was more dangerous than the ordinary consumer would expect. When applied to design defect cases, this test raises many difficult questions. Cars do not provide roll-bars built into the roof. Does the consumer expectation test help decide whether such cars are defective? Would it be enough to show a defect if you could prove that consumers had a general expectation that cars would be safe? Or would it be necessary to show that consumer experience led to specific design expectations? See *Soule v. General Motors Corp.*, 8 Cal.4th 548, 34 Cal.Rptr.2d 607, 882 P.2d 298 (1994). Further, it is not only purchasers, users, and those who service a product who can recover if injured by its defects; bystanders who have no particular relation to the product or its use can, as well. How can bystanders, who are not consumers at all, have any expectation about the particular product's safety? Is the consumer expectation test useful in bystander cases?

3. *Crashworthiness.* At one time, a defendant in a case like *Leichtamer* could prevail on an argument that if a product was used in an unintended way–like getting involved in a car crash–then that unintended use, not any defect, was the sole cause of the harm. Such a restrictive view is no longer followed; manufacturers are liable for harms caused by defective products that are put to "foreseeable uses," even if unintended by the manufacturer. See §§ 8 & 9, infra.

KNITZ v. MINSTER MACHINE CO.

Supreme Court of Ohio, 1982.
69 Ohio St.2d 460, 432 N.E.2d 814.

[Defendant manufactured a press which delivered 60 tons of force in pressing die halves together. It was originally activated with a two-hand button tripping device, so that the operator's hands were necessarily outside the danger area. This press, with the button tripping device, was sold by defendant to Toledo Die and Manufacturing Company. Toledo, however, also purchased an optional foot pedal tripping device and it was in use at the time of the injury. Plaintiff, the press operator for Toledo, found it necessary to move the foot pedal with her foot; in doing so, she leaned on the bottom portion of the die with her hand. Her foot accidentally activated the foot pedal and the press descended, amputating two fingers. There was another safety device, intended to physically pull back the operator's hands, but it was not attached. The trial judge gave summary judgment for the manufacturer.]

WILLIAM B. BROWN, JUSTICE.

The case presents us with the question of whether a motion for summary judgment pursuant to Civ. R. 56 should have been granted to appellee. . . .

The focus of the inquiry in *Leichtamer* was what constituted a "defective condition unreasonably dangerous" as formulated by Section 402A of the Restatement of Torts. We adopted a variation of the familiar "consumer expectation test" of Comment *i* to Section 402: "A product is in a defective condition unreasonably dangerous to the user or consumer if it is more dangerous than an ordinary consumer would expect when used in an intended or reasonably foreseeable manner." This standard followed as a logical development from commercial warranty origins of strict liability in tort. It reflected "the commercial reality that '[i]mplicit in . . . [a product's] presence on the market . . . [is] a representation that it [will] safely do the jobs for which it was built.'

Unlike the factual setting in *Leichtamer*, there are situations in which "the consumer would not know what to expect, because he would have no idea how safe the product could be made." Such is the case *sub judice*. Difficulty could arise, for example, where the injured party is an innocent bystander who is ignorant of the product and has no expectation of its safety, or where a new product is involved and no expectation of safety has developed. Conversely, liability could be barred hypothetically where industrial workmen "gradually learn of the dangers involved in the machinery they must use to make a living and come to 'expect' the dangers." In such cases, the policy underlying strict liability in tort, requires that "a product may be found defective in design, even if it satisfies ordinary consumer expectations, if through hindsight the jury determines that the product's design embodies 'excessive preventable danger,' or, in other words, if the jury finds that the risk of danger inherent in the challenged design outweighs the benefits of such design."

Accordingly, we hold that a product design is in a defective condition to the user or consumer if (1) it is more dangerous than an ordinary consumer would expect when used in an intended or reasonably foreseeable manner, or (2) if the benefits of the challenged design do not outweigh the risk inherent in such design. Factors relevant to the evaluation of the defectiveness of the product design are the likelihood that the product design will cause injury, the gravity of the danger posed, and the mechanical and economic feasibility of an improved design.... [W]e conclude that appellant has made out genuine issues of fact of whether appellee's press design was defective by allowing accidental tripping of the foot pedal control and in failing to provide a point of operation guard when the foot pedal is operative. Specifically, appellant provided an affidavit of James J. McCarthy, a former safety engineer for General Motors Corporation, involved with analysis of machine accident potential. McCarthy's affidavit states, *inter alia*, that in his opinion the press is defective "because of inadequate guarding at the point of operation caused by failure to attach a barrier or interlock gate guard to prevent entry of the operator's hands into the danger area while the ram is descending ... the press is defective because of inadequate guarding of the foot pedal of the foot switch to prevent inadvertent entry and tripping."

Notes

1. *Risks and utilities balanced.* Risk-utility balancing involves weighing the likelihood of harm, the gravity of the harm if it occurs, and the cost of preventing harm by using a different design. The cost of a different design would include any loss of benefits in the present design as well as any direct costs of the alternative design (such as production and marketing costs). In assessing the risk, the capacity of users to protect themselves would be of importance. These factors are discussed in a frequently cited passage by Dean John Wade in his article, *On the Nature of Strict Tort Liability for Products*, 44 MISS. L.J. 825 (1973). Does this sound like *Carroll Towing* and thus like a negligence analysis?

2. *Restatement of Products Liability.* The Restatement says that a product is defective in design when the seller could have reduced or avoided the product's "foreseeable risks of harm" by "the adoption of a reasonable alternative design, and the omission of the alternative design renders the product not reasonably safe." RESTATEMENT OF PRODUCTS LIABILITY § 2(b). Comment *d* explains that this section "adopts a reasonableness ('risk-utility balancing') test as the standard for judging the defectiveness of product

designs." Comment *g* states that consumer expectations "do not constitute an independent standard for judging" design defects, but that such expectations "may substantially influence or even be ultimately determinative on risk-utility balancing," since they relate to foreseeability and frequency of the risks of harm.

3. The Ohio legislature first codified the *Knitz* court's alternative test for design defects, then eliminated the consumer expectation test entirely. See *Perkins v. Wilkinson Sword, Inc.*, 83 Ohio St.3d 507, 700 N.E.2d 1247 (1998)(discussing statutory history).

BARKER v. LULL ENGINEERING CO., 20 Cal.3d 413, 143 Cal. Rptr. 225, 573 P.2d 443 (1978). Plaintiff, an inexperienced operator of a high-lift industrial loader, lifted a load of lumber 10–18 feet off the ground. The ground was uneven and the loader began to vibrate as if it were about to tip over. Responding to warning shouts of fellow workers, the plaintiff scrambled out of the loader. He was hit and seriously injured by lumber falling from the load. The loader had no protective canopy and no outriggers to steady it. "We hold . . . that a product is defective in design (1) if the plaintiff demonstrates that the product failed to perform as safely as an ordinary consumer would expect when used in an intended or reasonably foreseeable manner or (2) if the plaintiff proves that the product's design proximately caused his injury and the defendant fails to prove . . . that on balance the benefits of the challenged design outweigh the risk of danger inherent in such design."

Notes

1. Notice that *Barker* shifts the burden of proof to the defendant to justify its design by pointing to a suitable risk-utility balance. Only a few courts have embraced the burden-shifting idea in design or failure to warn cases. See *Shanks v. Upjohn Co.*, 835 P.2d 1189 (Alaska 1992). The shift occurs quite easily. All the plaintiff must do is prove that the "design caused" harm. The burden of justifying the product's design then falls on the defendant. How does this differ from the usual negligence case?

2. In *Campbell v. General Motors Corp.*, 32 Cal.3d 112, 649 P.2d 224, 184 Cal.Rptr. 891 (1982), the plaintiff was a 62–year-old woman who was injured when thrown from her seat while riding on a city bus. She was sitting in the forward-most front-facing seat. The seats immediately behind the plaintiff had grab bars on them, so that if she had sat in one of them, she would have had something to hold to. There was also a vertical bar in the aisle in front of the side seat immediately in front of the plaintiff, but she could not reach it from her own seat. After she settled with the city, she sued the manufacturer of the bus. *Held*, it can be fairly inferred that the bus' design "caused" the injury, thus she prevails under the second test in *Barker v. Lull*. Would this proof suffice in an ordinary negligence case, do you think?

WILSON v. PIPER AIRCRAFT CORP.

Supreme Court of Oregon, 1978.
282 Or. 61, 577 P.2d 1322.

HOLMAN, JUSTICE.

[Decedents were killed as the result of an airplane crash. There was evidence that the crash occurred because the plane's carburetor iced up. The plaintiff contends that the plane was defective in using a carburetor rather than fuel injection and in failing to provide a carburetor heat gauge. The jury found for the plaintiff. The court first held that though the FAA had approved the plane's design, compliance with its regulations was not a complete defense. It then turned to consider whether the evidence was sufficient to prove defectiveness.]

We have observed in prior products liability cases that charges of defective design present special problems. One of those special problems is the nature, and necessary proof, of a "defect" in a product which reaches the consumer in precisely the condition intended by the designer/manufacturer.

We have held that when a design feature of a manufactured product creates a risk of injury, the test for strict liability in tort, if that injury results, is whether "a reasonably prudent manufacturer would have so designed and sold the article in question had he known of the risk involved which injured plaintiff." *Phillips v. Kimwood Machine Co.*, we discussed the question of reasonableness further in that opinion as follows:

> "To some it may seem that absolute liability has been imposed upon the manufacturer since it might be argued that no manufacturer could reasonably put into the stream of commerce an article which he realized might result in injury to a user. This is not the case, however. The manner of injury may be so fortuitous and the chances of injury occurring so remote that it is reasonable to sell the product despite the danger. In design cases the utility of the article may be so great, and the change of design necessary to alleviate the danger in question may so impair such utility, that it is reasonable to market the product as it is, even though the possibility of injury exists and was realized at the time of the sale. Again, the cost of the change necessary to alleviate the danger in design may be so great that the article would be priced out of the market and no one would buy it even though it was of high utility. Such an article is not dangerously defective despite its having inflicted injury." 269 Or. at 495–96, 525 P.2d at 1038.

We are mindful of defendant's argument that a lay jury is not qualified to determine technical questions of aeronautical design, and of the forceful argument by Professor Henderson that problems of conscious product design choices are inherently unsuited to determination by courts. Henderson, *Judicial Review of Manufacturers' Conscious*

Design Choices: The Limits of Adjudication, 73 Colum. L. Rev. 1531 (1973); Henderson, *Design Defect Litigation Revisited*, 61 Cornell L.Rev. 541 (1976). We do not underestimate the difficulties involved in this type of litigation. We are, however, committed to the position that members of the public are entitled to compensation for their injuries if they are damaged because of improper product design. Actions for negligence would pose the identical difficulty because the evidence is similar. This is not a problem which is peculiar to products liability cases. In the absence of an ability to recover through courts, persons injured by such designs would be without a remedy.... One of the factors to be weighed in making this determination is the manufacturer's ability to eliminate the unsafe character of the product without impairing its usefulness or making it too expensive to maintain its utility. In other words, the court is to determine, and to weigh in the balance, whether the proposed alternative design has been shown to be practicable. The trial court should not permit an allegation of design defect to go to the jury unless there is sufficient evidence upon which to make this determination. If liability for alleged design defects is to "stop somewhere short of the freakish and the fantastic,"[2] plaintiffs' prima facie case of a defect must show more than the technical possibility of a safer design.

In some cases, because of the relatively uncomplicated nature of the product or the design feature in question, evidence of the dangerous nature of the design in question or of a safer alternative design may be sufficient to permit the court to consider this factor adequately. An extreme example is found in the facts of *Passwaters v. General Motors Corp.*, 454 F.2d 1270 (8th Cir.1972). There a passenger on a motorcycle which was involved in a collision with an automobile was injured by purely ornamental blades on the automobile's hubcap. The evidence that the blades were ornamental only would suffice in such a case; the court and the jury could find from that fact alone that it would have been practicable to supply hubcaps of a safer design....

In other instances, however, the question of practicability cannot be properly weighed solely on the basis of inference and common knowledge. That is the case with the allegations we are considering here. Plaintiffs' allegations amount to a contention that an airplane furnished with a standard aircraft engine is defective because an engine of a different type, or with a different carburetor system, would be safer in one particular. It is not proper to submit such allegations to the jury unless the court is satisfied that there is evidence from which the jury could find the suggested alternatives are not only technically feasible but also practicable in terms of cost and the over-all design and operation of the product. It is part of the required proof that a design feature is a "defect" to present such evidence. In at least some instances in the present case, that requirement has not been met.

We consider, because it well illustrates the problems involved, plaintiffs' contention that defendant's airplane was defective because it was provided with a carbureted engine rather than an engine with a fuel injection system. There was evidence that carbureted airplane engines are characteristically subject to icing of a kind which can result in engine failure and that fuel injected engines are not nearly so subject to dangerous icing. There was also evidence that, at the time this airplane was manufactured, fuel injected engines of appropriate horsepower were available, and expert testimony that FAA approval of an airplane like this one with a fuel injected engine could probably have been obtained.

There is not, however, any evidence about what effect the substitution of a fuel injected engine in this airplane design would have had upon the airplane's cost, economy of operation, maintenance requirements, overall performance, or safety in respects other than susceptibility to icing. Plaintiffs' own expert witnesses testified that a carbureted engine of the type used in this airplane was, except for its susceptibility to icing, a highly satisfactory, dependable engine. There was also undisputed evidence that 80 to 90 per cent of all small airplanes comparable to this one are manufactured with carbureted engines rather than with fuel injected engines. There was no explanation of why this is the case.

We also think it is significant that both in 1966, when this airplane was manufactured, and at the present time the FAA safety standards disclose that the agency was aware of the carburetor icing problems and provided for them in its regulations and yet determined that the use of carbureted engines was not unduly dangerous. Although we have held that compliance with the FAA safety standards does not preclude the possibility of liability for a design defect, we nevertheless believe that in a field as closely regulated as aircraft design and manufacture, it is proper to take into consideration, in determining whether plaintiffs have produced sufficient evidence of defect to go to the jury, the fact that the regulatory agency has approved the very design of which they complain after considering the dangers involved.

Taking into account all of the evidence, including the FAA determination that this aircraft design included adequate protection against carburetor icing, we hold that plaintiffs did not produce sufficient evidence that a reasonably prudent manufacturer who was aware of the risks of carburetor icing would not have designed this model of aircraft with a carbureted engine, or that substitution of a fuel injected engine was practicable. On this ground alone, defendant is entitled to a new trial. . . .

Notes

1. *Burden of proof.* Does *Wilson* put the burden of proof on the plaintiff rather than shifting it to the defendant as *Barker v. Lull* would do? Does it require the plaintiff to adduce evidence of a reasonable alternative design? The Restatement Third rejects *Barker v. Lull's* shift of the burden of proof, affirmatively requiring the plaintiff to prove that the product's risks outweigh its utility.

2. *Reasonable alternative design.* Somewhat distinctly, the Restatement also requires the plaintiff to prove that a reasonable alternative design

was or reasonably could have been available at the time the product was sold or distributed. RESTATEMENT OF PRODUCTS LIABILITY § 2, com. *d*. Requiring a plaintiff to prove reasonable alternative design is controversial, but a number of courts and legislatures are in accord with the requirement. E.g., *Vines v. Beloit Corp.*, 631 So.2d 1003 (Ala.1994); TEX. CIV. PRAC. & REM. CODE ANN. § 82.005.

3. *Consumer expectation test eliminating the reasonable alternative design requirement*. Some courts still permit the plaintiff to prevail on a consumer expectation test and hence necessarily reject the reasonable alternative design requirement. See, e.g., *Delaney v. Deere and Co.*, 268 Kan. 769, 999 P.2d 930 (2000); *Kudlacek v. Fiat S.p.A.*, 244 Neb. 822, 509 N.W.2d 603 (Neb. 1994); *Sumnicht v. Toyota Motor Sales, U.S.A., Inc.*, 121 Wis.2d 338, 360 N.W.2d 2 (Wis. 1984).

4. *Manifestly unreasonable designs*. Even if the consumer expectation test is rejected, the jury might properly infer that safer and reasonably feasible alternative designs were available without explicit evidence. The Restatement Third, in § 2, cmt. e, suggests that the design of some products are so "manifestly unreasonable" because of their negligible utility and high risk of danger, that defectiveness could be found even without proof of an alternative. It uses the dangerous toy gun as an example.

5. *Plaintiff strategy*. Why would a plaintiff fail to adduce evidence of a reasonable alternative design? Even if the court does not require such proof, should a plaintiff who has evidence of a feasible alternative design introduce it? What might such evidence tend to prove? See *Kinser v. Gehl Co.*, 184 F.3d 1259 (10th Cir.1999).

6. *What is an alternative design?* A most intriguing question arises when you try to figure out what counts as an alternative design. Suppose there are three drugs on the market that, by different chemical formulas, help avoid some painful symptom like heartburn or rashes. All do the job, although by different means. The defendant manufactures a fourth drug, based on still a fourth formula. The defendant's drug, however, has serious side effects for a substantial number of people. Should the existing drugs be considered as alternatives, on the ground that they have the same end function? Or should they NOT be considered as alternatives on the ground that, whatever their function, their chemical formulas are widely different?

The Restatement Third poses a different set of facts for this problem. It supposes that the defendant manufactures a toy gun that shoots hard pellets at high velocity, presumably very dangerous to those who might be in close range of a child playing with the toy. The defendant could have manufactured a toy gun that is not harmful, say one that fires soft gelatin pellets or ping pong balls. Would a ping-pong-ball gun be an alternative for the hard-pellet gun? It depends how you characterize the product. If you think the product is "toy guns capable of doing injury," the ping pong gun will not be an alternative. You might think the pellet gun was defective because it should not be marketed at all, but you would not think it defective because it fails to achieve the safety of a ping-pong-ball gun. See RESTATEMENT OF PRODUCTS LIABILITY § 2, cmt. e.

7. *Proof issues*. What proof must the plaintiff adduce to prove reasonable alternative design? In *General Motors Corp. v. Sanchez*, 997 S.W.2d 584

(Tex.1999), the plaintiffs' decedent was killed when a pickup truck slipped out of gear and crushed him. Plaintiffs' expert testified that a safer transmission design would have virtually eliminated the risk of such an occurrence. He testified specifically about alterations in G.M.'s transmission design that would provide a "99% solution" to the "mis-shift problem." *Held*, plaintiff's proof raised a fact question to be resolved by a jury. "[P]laintiffs did not have to build and test an automobile transmission to prove a safer alternative design. A design need only prove 'capable of being developed.'" The expert's testimony about the engineering principles supporting his proposed design backed up his opinion that his design would be safer than G.M.'s actual design. Doesn't the plaintiff have the burden of proving that the design is one that can be adopted with reasonable costs?

McCARTHY v. OLIN CORP.

United States Court of Appeals, Second Circuit, 1997.
119 F.3d 148.

MESKILL, CIRCUIT JUDGE....

On December 7, 1993, Colin Ferguson boarded the Long Island Railroad's 5:33 p.m. commuter train departing from New York City and opened fire on the passengers. Six people, including Dennis McCarthy, were killed and nineteen others, including Kevin McCarthy and Maryanne Phillips, were wounded in the vicious attack. Ferguson was armed with a 9mm semiautomatic handgun, which was loaded with Winchester "Black Talon" bullets (Black Talons). The injuries to Dennis and Kevin McCarthy and Maryanne Phillips were enhanced by the ripping and tearing action of the Black Talons because, unfortunately, the bullets performed as designed. [The plaintiffs sued the manufacturer of the bullets, alleging the negligent manufacture, advertising and marketing of a product that was unreasonably designed and ultrahazardous, the making of an unreasonably dangerous product and strict liability in tort. The trial judge dismissed the complaint, and plaintiffs appealed].

The Black Talon is a hollowpoint bullet designed to bend upon impact into six ninety-degree angle razor-sharp petals or "talons" that increase the wounding power of the bullet by stretching, cutting and tearing tissue and bone as it travels through the victim. The Black Talon bullet was designed and manufactured by Olin Corporation (Olin) through its Winchester division and went on the market in 1992. Although the bullet was originally developed for law enforcement agencies, it was marketed and available to the general public. In November 1993, following public outcry, Olin pulled the Black Talon from the public market and restricted its sales to law enforcement personnel. Colin Ferguson allegedly purchased the ammunition in 1993, before it was withdrawn from the market....

[The Court first rejected plaintiff's request for certification to the New York Court of Appeals, then addressed the merits.]

Appellants' first argument is that Olin should be held strictly liable for their injuries because the Black Talon ammunition was defectively designed and the design and manufacture of the bullets were inherently dangerous.

. . . Appellants argue that the Black Talons were defectively designed because the expansion mechanism of the bullets, which causes ripping and tearing in its victims, results in enhanced injuries beyond ordinary bullets. The district court rejected this argument because the expanding of the bullet was an intentional and functional element of the design of the product. We agree.

To state a cause of action for a design defect, plaintiffs must allege that the bullet was unreasonably dangerous for its intended use. "[A] defectively designed product is one which, at the time it leaves the seller's hands, is in a condition not reasonably contemplated by the ultimate consumer." This rule, however, is tempered by the realization that some products, for example knives, must by their very nature be dangerous in order to be functional. The very purpose of the Black Talon bullet is to kill or cause severe wounding. Here, plaintiffs concede that the Black Talons performed precisely as intended by the manufacturer and Colin Ferguson.

> Sadly it must be acknowledged that: [m]any products, however well-built or well-designed may cause injury or death. Guns may kill; knives may maim; liquor may cause alcoholism; but the mere fact of injury does not entitle the [person injured] to recover . . . there must be something wrong with the product, and if nothing is wrong there will be no liability.

DeRosa v. Remington Arms Co., 509 F.Supp. 762, 769 (E.D.N.Y.1981) (under New York law, shotgun as designed by defendant was not unreasonably dangerous for its foreseeable use).

Appellants have not alleged that the bullets were defective. As a matter of law, a product's defect is related to its condition, not its intrinsic function. The bullets were not in defective condition nor were they unreasonably dangerous for their intended use because the Black Talons were purposely designed to expand on impact and cause severe wounding.

Appellants next argue that under the risk/utility test analysis applied by New York courts, appellee should be held strictly liable because the risk of harm posed by the Black Talons outweighs the ammunition's utility. The district court properly held that the risk/utility test is inapplicable "because the risks arise from the function of the product, not any defect in the product." There must be 'something wrong' with a product before the risk/utility analysis may be applied in determining whether the product is unreasonably dangerous or defective.

The purpose of risk/utility analysis is to determine whether the risk of injury might have been reduced or avoided if the manufacturer had used a feasible alternative design. However, the risk of injury to be balanced with the utility is a risk not intended as the primary function of the product. Here, the primary function of the Black Talon bullets was to kill or cause serious injury. There is no reason to search for an alternative safer design where the product's sole utility is to kill and maim. Accordingly, we hold that appellants have failed to state a cause of action under New York strict products liability law.

Appellants also argue that Olin should be held strictly liable because the Black Talon ammunition is "unreasonably dangerous per se." According to the appellants' theory, a product is unreasonably dangerous per se if a reasonable person would conclude that the danger of the product, whether foreseeable or not, outweighs its utility. As the district court held, this is essentially a risk/utility analysis, which we have refused to apply. Under New York's strict products liability jurisprudence, there is no cause of action for an unreasonably dangerous per se product. Thus, this claim was properly dismissed.

. . . The crux of appellants' negligence theory is that Olin negligently marketed and placed the Black Talon ammunition for sale to the general public. Appellants argue that because of the severe wounding power of the bullets, Olin should have restricted sales to law enforcement agencies, for whom the bullet was originally designed. They also argue that Olin should have known that their advertising, which highlighted the ripping and tearing characteristics of the bullet, would attract "many types of sadistic, unstable and criminal personalities," such as Ferguson. . . .

New York courts do not impose a legal duty on manufacturers to control the distribution of potentially dangerous products such as ammunition. Accordingly, although it may have been foreseeable by Olin that criminal misuse of the Black Talon bullets could occur, Olin is not legally liable for such misuse. As the district court pointed out, appellants have not alleged that any special relationship existed between Olin and Ferguson. Here, Olin could not control the actions of Ferguson. "[I]t is unreasonable to impose [a] duty where the realities of every day experience show us that, regardless of the measures taken, there is little expectation that the one made responsible could prevent the . . . conduct [of another]."

. . . To impose a duty on ammunition manufacturers to protect against criminal misuse of its product would likely force ammunition products–which legislatures have not proscribed, and which concededly are not defectively designed or manufactured and have some socially valuable uses–off the market due to the threat of limitless liability. Because Olin did not owe a legal duty to plaintiffs to protect against Colin Ferguson's horrible action, appellants' complaint does not state a cause of action for negligence and the claim was properly dismissed. . . .

[Judgment affirmed. Dissenting opinion omitted.]

Notes

1. Does the product in *McCarthy* have more than negligible social utility when marketed to the public? Does it present an extremely high

danger? Why, then, is it not "defective?" If a product's "sole utility is to kill and maim," does it follow that it is not defective when it inflicts as much pain as possible?

2. *Firearms: Design defect theories.* At the dawn of the new millennium, plaintiffs have had only limited success in design defect cases against gun manufacturers, at least where properly-working guns were at issue. Some of the reasons may be gleaned from *McCarthy*—a properly-working gun is designed to be dangerous and is thus not defective simply because it fulfills that purpose. In *Resteiner v. Sturm, Ruger & Co.*, 223 Mich.App. 374, 566 N.W.2d 53 (Mich.App.1997), the court not only rejected the notion that a handgun manufacturer should be liable for selling a product defectively designed because it can be stolen and used in crimes, but also awarded sanctions to defendant for plaintiff's "frivolous" argument.

3. *Firearms: Other theories of liability.* Given the lack of plaintiffs' success with design defect theories against gun manufacturers, other theories have surfaced. An especially noteworthy case is *Hamilton v. Accu–Tek*, 62 F. Supp.2d 802 (E.D.N.Y.1999). After complicated procedural maneuvering and several court rulings, seven shooting victims and their relatives went to trial against 25 gun manufacturers, claiming negligent distribution and marketing. The theory was that defendants marketed guns in a way that made it likely that they would reach illegal users, including teenagers and criminals, and would ultimately be used in violent crimes. (Plaintiffs' design defect claims were dismissed in 1996, prior to trial.) The jury returned a verdict against 15 of the defendants, but awarded damages against only three, based on a finding that their products were the only ones which proximately caused harm to plaintiffs. Defendants appealed, contending that they cannot be liable as a matter of New York law because they have no duty to exercise reasonable care in the marketing and distribution of handguns. The Second Circuit certified this question to the New York Court of Appeals in *Hamilton v. Beretta U.S.A. Corp.*, 222 F.3d 36 (2d Cir.2000). What result would you predict? See also *Merrill v. Navegar, Inc.*, 89 Cal.Rptr.2d 146 (App. 1999), *vacated and review granted*, 991 P.2d 755, 92 Cal.Rptr.2d 256 (2000)(manufacturer of semi-automatic weapons used in an office-building shooting owed a duty to ensure that its manufacturing, marketing and making its weapons available to the public did not "increase the risk inherently presented" by its products).

Might holding gun manufacturers liable for criminal attacks be justified on the grounds that the manufacturer "enables" such occurrences, and that plaintiffs lack an effective legal remedy against the criminals? Do such justifications underlie *respondeat superior*, in part? See Robert L. Rabin, *Enabling Torts*, 49 DePaul L. Rev. 435 (1999).

4. *Tobacco.* The liability of tobacco companies for smoking-related illnesses is a complex and changing subject. In design defect cases, the companies have usually prevailed in the higher courts, for a variety of reasons, although other theories have met with some success. In *American Tobacco Co. v. Grinnell*, 951 S.W.2d 420 (Tex.1997) the court rejected the plaintiff's design defect claim in the absence of a safer alternative design. But it permitted the plaintiff to pursue a strict liability claim for marketing and manufacturing defects based on defendant's knowledge of product's

addictive qualities and the possibility of pesticide residue in their cigarettes. And in *Buckingham v. R.J. Reynolds Tobacco Co.*, 142 N.H. 822, 713 A.2d 381 (N.H. 1998), the court faced a claim by the estate of a woman who died from cancer caused by second-hand smoke. The court affirmed dismissal of the plaintiff's strict liability claim but reversed dismissal of her negligence claim. The court contemplated discovery by the parties to determine the extent to which the defendants know of their products' hazards, the defendants' expectations as to the use of their products and those who might be affected, causation, and any plaintiff contribution to her own injuries.

In November, 1998, several tobacco companies reached an historic settlement agreement with 46 states, agreeing to pay $206 billion over 25 years to compensate the states for the cost of treating Medicaid patients who have smoking-related illnesses. Four other states settled separately for another $40 billion. For a description and analysis of this agreement, see Hanoch Dagan & James J. White, *Governments, Citizens, and Injurious Industries*, 75 N.Y.U. L. REV. 354 (2000). The settlement agreement did not bar later suits by individuals, however. In July, 2000, a Florida jury in a class action case against five tobacco companies awarded $145 billion in punitive damages, the largest jury verdict in U.S. history. *Engle v. R.J. Reynolds Tobacco Co.*, No. 94–08273 (Cir. Ct. Dade Co.). While most pundits predicted reversal, "scores of suits by individual smokers" are pending. Bob Van Voris, *$145 billion to send a message*, NAT'L L.J. A1, A9 (July 31, 2000).

5. *Drugs.* Section 402A of the Restatement (Second), comment k, provided that some products "are quite incapable of being made safe in their intended and ordinary use," saying that this is often true with drugs. The Pasteur rabies vaccine is given as the prime example, a vaccine which "not uncommonly leads to very serious and damaging consequences," but which guards against a disease which "invariably leads to a dreadful death." Thus, according to comment k, such a product is neither defective nor *unreasonably* dangerous. This court in *Cochran v. Brooke*, 243 Or. 89, 409 P.2d 904 (1966), quoted this comment with approval in affirming a directed verdict for the drug manufacturer in a case in which the plaintiff was rendered almost blind as a result of taking a prescription drug for treatment of arthritis. This seems to reflect a risk-utility balance, doesn't it? What if a consumer expectations test were used instead? That was done in *Allison v. Merck and Company, Inc.*, 110 Nev. 762, 878 P.2d 948 (Nev. 1994) where a children's vaccine caused serious permanent harms, including blindness and brain damage, to a child. A majority, for various reasons, permitted the claim to go to the jury. The test of strict liability in one opinion was to ask whether products are "dangerous because they fail to perform in the manner reasonably to be expected in the light of their nature and intended function.... The nature and intended function of this vaccine, of course, is to create an immunity to measles, mumps, and rubella without attendant blindness, deafness, mental retardation and permanent brain damage." And "a vaccine that causes blindness and deafness is a defective product." Does the public interest in development of prescription drugs demand a rule more protective of those making and distributing them? Cf. *Brown v. Superior Court*, 44 Cal.3d 1049, 245 Cal.Rptr. 412, 751 P.2d 470 (1988)(refusing to apply *Barker v. Lull*'s burden shift to prescription drugs).

6. *Unknowable risks.* Should manufacturers ever be liable for harms that were unforeseeable at the time the product was distributed? You could imagine a system of strict liability that weighed all the actual risks of a product against its utilities, even though the risks were not known or knowable at the time the product was distributed. Such "superstrict liability" has some, albeit little, support in case law. See, e.g., *Sternhagen v. Dow Co.*, 282 Mont. 168, 935 P.2d 1139 (1997) (pesticide manufacturers may be strictly liable, despite their lack of knowledge or reason to know at the time of marketing that their pesticides contained carcinogenic components). Also, some cases have supported strict liability when the danger was not actually unknowable but was "unforeseeable" in the sense that a reasonable person would not have recognized it. See *Ayers v. Johnson & Johnson Baby Products Co.*, 117 Wash.2d 747, 818 P.2d 1337 (1991). Does strict liability for unknowable or unforeseeable dangers discourage production of beneficial goods that consumers want? See Victor Schwartz, *The Death of "Super Strict Liability:" Common Sense Returns to Tort Law*, 27 GONZ. L. REV. 179 (1992). The Restatement of Products Liability rejects any liability for unknowable or unforeseeable risks in § 2(b), with respect to prescription drugs in particular in § 6.

AN END NOTE: ADJUDICATION OF DESIGN DEFECTS

The limits of adjudication? Recent years have seen a shift, reflected in the Restatement of Products Liability and in some case law, away from strict liability for design defects. Much of the intellectual impetus for revision in the law of design defects cases originated in an article, *Judicial Review of Manufacturer's Conscious Design Choices: The Limits of Adjudication*, 73 COLUM. L. REV. 1531 (1973), written by Professor James Henderson, who served as one of the Restatement's two Reporters. In the article, he argued that rules of law must be so constructed that lawyers know what arguments can be constructed and what proof to adduce, and that when the issues are "polycentric," this is not possible. A polycentric problem is one in which there are many appropriate solutions, and in which each step in solving the problem involves a decision that affects the decision in later steps. The late professor Lon L. Fuller, in *Adjudication and the Rule of Law*, [1960] PROC. AM. SOC'Y INT. L. 1, gave several examples. In one example, the coach of a football team had to choose how to deploy the players. If one could equally play end or halfback, the decision to place him at end would also affect his decision about who played guard. The decision as to who played guard would affect other positions. Since there is no prescribed sequence for these decisions, and since each decision will affect the others, it would indeed be difficult for a lawyer to attempt to prove, say, that Dubbs should play guard and Henson should play end. Using this idea, Professor Henderson has developed the notion that design choices are polycentric and that they cannot be appropriately litigated in court. What is your own opinion? Can you back it up with argument?

Jury role. Some critics of products liability, like some manufacturers and insurers, view the jury with trepidation. Whether for these reasons or not, some jurists have argued that the judge should enter aggressively into the decision about what constitutes a design defect so that appropriate policy factors can be considered. See David A. Fischer, *Products Liability—Functionally Imposed Strict Liability*, 32 OKLA. L. REV. 93 (1979); Aaron Twerski, *Seizing the Middle Ground Between Rules and Standards in Design Defect Litigation: Advancing Directed Verdict Practice in Law of Torts*, 57 N.Y.U. L. REV. 521 (1982). The judge would not only weigh the evidence to decide whether it is sufficient to get to the jury on the risk-utility balance, but would also consider, for example, the polycentricity issue or the institutional capacity of courts to handle the litigation (Twerski) or the availability of insurance and the effect of increased prices that strict liability would bring (Fischer). Both would involve the judge more directly in policy-making decisions with the result that the jury's role would be diminished.

Social or economic factors. What social factors should be considered in judging a product to be defective? Saying that tobacco smoking is addictive and that it kills 350,000 persons annually, Professor Frank Vandall argues for "absolute" liability. This would have the effect, he says, of raising the price of smoking so that the cost of cigarettes would reflect their true costs to society. Increased price would drive some smokers to quit. He argues that non-smokers presently bear some of the costs of smoking because smoker's insurance pays some medical expenses and this drives up insurance costs for everyone and because if insurance does not pay the costs, welfare may, again with non-smokers sharing in the costs. Based on these and other arguments he develops a proposal for absolute liability with virtually no defenses. See Frank Vandall, *Reallocating the Costs of Smoking: The Application of Absolute Liability to Cigarette Manufacturers*, 52 OHIO ST. L. J. 405 (1991). Would any of his arguments be relevant in determining whether cigarettes were defective under present law?

Is there a products liability "crisis?" Tort reformers often point to products liability cases, especially design defect cases, as evidence of the tort system running amok. Empirical studies, however, tend to undercut this perception. Recently, two scholars published the results of a 12–year study of cases in Franklin County, Ohio (the city of Columbus and its suburbs). Among their findings: products claims accounted for less than four percent of civil jury verdicts in that period; plaintiffs prevailed in only one of five cases; and plaintiffs' verdicts were modest, with one-third falling under $100,000. Further, not a single plaintiff was awarded punitive damages in a products case in Franklin County over the 12–year period between 1985 and 1996. Deborah Jones Merritt & Kathryn Ann Barry, *Is the Tort System in Crisis? New Empirical Evidence,* 60 OHIO ST. L.J. 315 (1999). Does such data call into question the need for more restrictive rules in design cases, if that is what is occurring?

§ 6. WARNING OR INFORMATION DEFECTS

a. Focusing on Point-of-Sale Warnings

LIRIANO v. HOBART CORP.

United States Court of Appeals, Second Circuit, 1999.
170 F.3d 264.

CALABRESI, CIRCUIT JUDGE:

[Luis Liriano was severely injured on the job when his hand was caught in a meat grinder manufactured by Hobart Corporation and owned by his employer, Super Associated. The meat grinder had been sold to Super with a safety guard, but the safety guard was removed while the machine was in Super's possession and was not on the meat grinder at the time of the accident. The machine bore no warning indicating that the grinder should be operated only with a safety guard attached.

[Liriano sued Hobart, who brought a third-party claim against Super. The only claim that went to the jury was Liriano's failure to warn claim. The jury found for Liriano, attributing a degree responsibility to all three parties. Hobart and Super appealed, arguing (1) that there was no duty to warn, and (2) that even if there had been a duty to warn, the evidence presented was not sufficient to allow the failure-to-warn claim to reach the jury. The federal court certified both questions to the New York Court of Appeals, which rejected appellants' first argument but declined to address the second, leaving it for this court.]

More than a hundred years ago, a Boston woman named Maria Wirth profited from an argument about obviousness as a matter of law that is very similar to the one Hobart urges today. See Lorenzo v. Wirth, 170 Mass. 596, 49 N.E. 1010 (1898). Wirth was the owner of a house on whose property there was a coal hole. The hole abutted the street in front of the house, and casual observers would have no way of knowing that the area around the hole was not part of the public thoroughfare. A pedestrian called Lorenzo fell into the coal hole and sued for her injuries. Writing for a majority of the Supreme Judicial Court of Massachusetts, Oliver Wendell Holmes, Jr., held for the defendant. He noted that, at the time of the accident, there had been a heap of coal on the street next to the coal hole, and he argued that such a pile provided sufficient warning to passers-by that they were in the presence of an open hole. "A heap of coal on a sidewalk in Boston is an indication, according to common experience, that there very possibly may be a coal hole to receive it." And that was that.

It was true, Holmes acknowledged, that "blind men, and foreigners unused to our ways, have a right to walk in the streets," and that such people might not benefit from the warning that piles of coal provided to sighted Bostonians. But Holmes wrote that coal-hole cases were simple, common, and likely to be oft repeated, and he believed it would be better to establish a clear rule than to invite fact-specific inquiries in every such case. "In simple cases of this sort," he explained, "courts have felt able to determine what, in every case, however complex, defendants are bound at their peril to know." With the facts so limited, this was an uncomplicated case in which the defendant could, as a matter of law, rely on the plaintiff's responsibility to know what danger she faced.

Justice Knowlton disagreed. His opinion delved farther into the particular circumstances than did Holmes's opinion for the majority. In so doing, he showed that Lorenzo's failure to appreciate her peril might have been foreseen by Wirth and hence that Wirth's failure to warn might constitute negligence. He noted, for example, that the accident occurred after nightfall, when Lorenzo perhaps could not see, or recognize, the heap of coal for what it was. There was "a throng of persons" on the street, such that it would have been difficult even in daylight to see very far ahead of where one was walking. And the plaintiff was, in fact, a foreigner unused to Boston's ways. "[S]he had just come from Spain, and had never seen coal put into a cellar through a coal hole." In sum, the case was not the "simple" one that Holmes had made it out to be. What is more, none of the facts he recited was either unusual or unforeseeable by Wirth. "What kind of conduct is required under complex conditions, to reach the usual standard of due care, namely, the ordinary care of persons of common prudence, is a question of fact.... [and thus] a question for a jury." Even cases involving "obvious" dangers like coal holes, Knowlton believed, might not be resolvable as matters of law when viewed in the fullness of circumstances that rendered the issue less clear than it would be when posed in the abstract.

Holmes commanded the majority of the Supreme Judicial Court in 1898, but Knowlton's position has prevailed in the court of legal history. " '[T]he so-called Holmes view–that standards of conduct ought increasingly to be fixed by the court for the sake of certainty–has been largely rejected.... The tendency has been away from fixed standards and towards enlarging the sphere of the jury.' " Fowler V. Harper, Fleming James, Jr., & Oscar S. Gray, The Law of Torts § 15.3, at 358–59 n. 16 (2d ed.1986).

The courts of New York have several times endorsed Knowlton's approach and ruled that judges should be very wary of taking the issue of liability away from juries, even in situations where the relevant dangers might seem obvious.... [Even so] there have been situations in which New York state courts have deemed dangers to be sufficiently clear so that warnings were, as a matter of law, not necessary. See, e.g.,.... Caris v. Mele, 134 A.D.2d 475, 476, 521 N.Y.S.2d 260, 261 (1987) (holding that there is no duty to warn of the danger of diving headfirst into an above-ground swimming pool only four feet deep).

... Liriano was only seventeen years old at the time of his injury and had only recently immigrated to the United States. He had been on the job at Super for only one week. He had never been given instructions about how to use the meat grinder, and he had used the meat grinder only two or three times. And ... the mechanism that injured Liriano would not have been visible to someone who was operating the grinder. It could be argued that such a combination of facts was not so unlikely that a court should say, as a matter of law, that the defendant could not have foreseen them or, if aware of them, need not have guarded against them by issuing a warning....

Nevertheless, it remains the fact that meat grinders are widely known to be dangerous.... [W]e might well be of two minds as to whether a failure to warn that meat grinders are dangerous would be enough to raise a jury issue.

But to state the issue that way would be to misunderstand the complex functions of warnings. As two distinguished torts scholars have pointed out, a warning can do more than exhort its audience to be careful. It can also affect what activities the people warned choose to engage in. See James A. Henderson, Jr., and Aaron D. Twerski, Doctrinal Collapse in Products Liability: The Empty Shell of Failure to Warn, 65 N.Y.U. L.Rev. 265, 285 (1990). And where the function of a warning is to assist the reader in making choices, the value of the warning can lie as much in making known the existence of alternatives as in communicating the fact that a particular choice is dangerous. It follows that the duty to warn is not necessarily obviated merely because a danger is clear.

To be more concrete, a warning can convey at least two types of messages. One states that a particular place, object, or activity is dangerous. Another explains that people need not risk the danger posed by such a place, object, or activity in order to achieve the purpose for which they might have taken that risk. Thus, a highway sign that says "Danger–Steep Grade" says less than a sign that says "Steep Grade Ahead–Follow Suggested Detour to Avoid Dangerous Areas."

If the hills or mountains responsible for the steep grade are plainly visible, the first sign merely states what a reasonable person would know without having to be warned. The second sign tells drivers what they might not have otherwise known: that there is another road that is flatter and less hazardous. A driver who believes the road through the mountainous area to be the only way to reach her destination might well choose to drive on that road despite the steep grades, but a driver who knows herself to have an alternative might not, even though her understanding of the risks posed by the steep grade is exactly the same as those of the first driver. Accordingly, a certain level of obviousness as to the grade of a road might, in principle, eliminate the reason for posting a sign of the first variety. But no matter how patently steep the road, the second kind of sign might still have a beneficial effect. As a result, the duty to post a sign of the second variety may persist even when the danger of the road is obvious and a sign of the first type would not be warranted.

One who grinds meat, like one who drives on a steep road, can benefit not only from being told that his activity is dangerous but from being told of a safer way.... Given that attaching guards is feasible, does reasonable care require that meat workers be informed that they need not accept the risks of using unguarded grinders? Even if most ordinary users may–as a matter of law–know of the risk of using a guardless meat grinder, it does not follow that a sufficient number of them will–as a matter of law–also know that protective guards are available, that using them is a realistic possibility, and that they may ask that such guards be used. It is precisely these last pieces of information that a reasonable manufacturer may have a duty to convey even if the danger of using a grinder were itself deemed obvious.

... A jury could reasonably find that there exist people who are employed as meat grinders and who do not know (a) that it is feasible to reduce the risk with safety guards, (b) that such guards are made available with the grinders, and (c) that the grinders should be used only with the guards. Moreover, a jury can also reasonably find that there are enough such people, and that warning them is sufficiently inexpensive, that a reasonable manufacturer would inform them that safety guards exist and that the grinder is meant to be used only with such guards. Thus, even if New York would consider the danger of meat grinders to be obvious as a matter of law, that obviousness does not substitute for the warning. . . .

Hobart [also] raises the issue of causation. It maintains that Liriano "failed to present any evidence that Hobart's failure to place a warning [on the machine] was causally related to his injury." Whether or not there had been a warning, Hobart says, Liriano might well have operated the machine as he did and suffered the injuries that he suffered. Liriano introduced no evidence, Hobart notes, suggesting either that he would have refused to grind meat had the machine borne a warning or that a warning would have persuaded Super not to direct its employees to use the grinder without the safety attachment.

[Hobart's argument] assumes that the burden was on Liriano to introduce additional evidence showing that the failure to warn was a but-for cause of his injury. . . . But Liriano does not bear that burden. When a defendant's negligent act is deemed wrongful precisely because it has a strong propensity to cause the type of injury that ensued, that very causal tendency is evidence enough to establish a prima facie case of cause-in-fact. The burden then shifts to the defendant to come forward with evidence that its negligence was not such a but-for cause.

We know, as a general matter, that the kind of negligence that the jury attributed to the defendant tends to cause exactly the kind of injury that the plaintiff suffered. . . . In such situations, rather than requiring the plaintiff to bring in more evidence to demonstrate that his case is of the ordinary kind, the law presumes normality and requires the defendant to adduce evidence that the case is an exception. Accordingly, in a case like this, it is up to the defendant to bring in evidence tending to rebut the strong inference, arising from the accident, that the defendant's negligence was in fact a but-for cause of the plaintiff's injury.

This shifting of the onus procedendi has long been established in New York. Its classic statement was made more than seventy years ago, when the Court of Appeals decided a case in which a car collided with a buggy driving after sundown without lights. See Martin v. Herzog, 228 N.Y. 164, 170, 126 N.E. 814, 816 (1920). The driver of the buggy argued that his negligence in driving without lights had not been shown to be the cause-in-fact of the accident. Writing for the Court, Judge Cardozo reasoned that the legislature deemed driving without lights after sundown to be negligent precisely because not using lights tended to cause accidents of the sort that had occurred in the case. The simple fact of an accident under those conditions, he said, was enough to support the inference of but-for causal connection between the negligence and the particular accident. . . .

The words that Judge Cardozo applied to the buggy's failure to use lights are equally applicable to Hobart's failure to warn: "If nothing else is shown to break the connection, we have a case, prima facie sufficient, of negligence contributing to the result." . . . See Guido Calabresi, Concerning Cause and the Law of Torts: An Essay for Harry Kalven, Jr., 43 U. Chi. L.Rev. 69 (1975).

. . . The district court did not err. We affirm its decision in all respects.

[Concurring opinion omitted.]

Notes

Duty to Provide Information

1. As indicated in *Liriano*, a manufacturer's failure to provide appropriate information about a product may make an otherwise safe product dangerous and defective. Warnings about dangers represent one important kind of information necessary for some products. Thus, a product becomes defective when the product's foreseeable risks of harm could have been reduced or avoided by the provision of a reasonable warning, and the omission of such a warning renders the product "not reasonably safe." RESTATEMENT OF PRODUCTS LIABILITY § 2(c).

2. The New York Court of Appeals had earlier rejected Hobart's argument that it owed no duty to warn as a matter of law, in *Liriano v. Hobart Corp.*, 92 N.Y.2d 232, 677 N.Y.S.2d 764, 700 N.E.2d 303 (N.Y. 1998). How could Hobart have a duty to warn about the dangers of operating its grinder without a guard when Hobart had equipped it with a guard?

3. *Functions of product information.* Necessary information to make a product reasonably safe may include directions for use, warnings, or some combination. Warnings may be needed either to alert users to risks that are not obvious, or to inform users of safer alternatives. All that seems acceptable enough. Should manufacturers be held to a further duty to provide all material information necessary to permit consumers to make an informed choice, on analogy to the duty of physicians in some informed consent cases? See DOBBS ON TORTS § 361 (2000).

4. *The duty to provide a risk-utility balanced warning.* Since the cost of giving a warning is usually rather small, it may be easy to conclude that the risk-utility balance always calls for a warning. Even so, some warnings simply are not needed. Should a manufacturer of safety glasses warn that they will break under the force of a five-pound sledge-hammer dropped from a height of seven feet? *American Optical Co. v. Weidenhamer*, 457 N.E.2d 181 (Ind.1983). Should a pickup truck manufacturer be required to warn of the risks of riding unrestrained in the open cargo bed? *Josue v. Isuzu Motors America, Inc.*, 87 Hawai'i 413, 958 P.2d 535 (1998). Are consumers more likely to read a few important warnings, or a long list including warnings about trivial risks?

5. *Unknowable risks.* Some cases have supported the idea that a manufacturer might be liable for failure to warn of risks that were not only not known, but not knowable. This position (often called "superstrict liability") is firmly rejected in the Restatement of Products Liability, as seen in note 1 above, and by the vast majority of courts. See *Vassallo v. Baxter Healthcare Corp.*, 428 Mass. 1, 696 N.E.2d 909 (1998)("The thin judicial support for a hindsight approach to the duty to warn is easily explained. The goal of the law is to induce conduct that is capable of being performed. This goal is not advanced by imposing liability for failure to warn of risks that were not capable of being known."). Might superstrict liability serve other goals?

Obvious Danger

6. *Obvious dangers and the no duty rule.* As the Restatement Third has it, "no duty exists" to warn of dangers that are obvious or should be obvious. RESTATEMENT OF PRODUCTS LIABILITY § 2, cmt. j; accord, *Caterpillar, Inc. v. Shears*, 911 S.W.2d 379 (Tex.1995). Is this merely the logical result of using a risk-utility balance and even more clearly dictated by a consumer expectation test?

7. *Obvious dangers and comparative fault.* Distinguish the no duty rule from defenses based upon obvious danger. If the plaintiff is or should be actually aware of the specific danger and its magnitude, the defendant might avoid or limit liability under assumed risk or comparative negligence rules. (See § 8.) Courts sometimes conflate the plaintiff fault issue with the defendant duty issue. In addition, courts may throw in proximate cause and "misuse" into the discussion. The straightforward explanation for most obvious danger problems, however, is simply that if the danger is foreseeably obvious in a significant degree, then the product is not defective at all for lack of a warning.

8. *Obvious danger and design defect.* A product that presents an obvious danger and thus provides its own warning may still be defectively designed. Diving into a pool of unknown depth is obviously dangerous, so no warning for that is required. However, if the manufacturer should foresee that harm will befall users in spite of the obvious danger, the manufacturer may be liable for design defect if it could easily mark the depth and failed to do so. See *Camacho v. Honda Motor Co., Ltd.*, 741 P.2d 1240 (Colo.1987) (a product can be unreasonably dangerous under the risk-utility test even if it is not more dangerous than the consumer expected; the consumer expecta-

tion test cannot be used to bar the plaintiff in such a case); *Uloth v.City Tank Corp.*, 376 Mass. 874, 384 N.E.2d 1188 (Mass. 1978)("If a slight change in design would prevent serious, perhaps fatal, injury, the designer may not avoid liability by simply warning of the possible injury.").

9. *Obvious danger and consumer expectations.* If the danger is truly obvious, the product could seldom be defective under the consumer expectation test, since the consumer could not expect safety in the fact of obvious danger. What would the plaintiff's attorney argue in such a case? See also *Tabieros v. Clark Equipment Co.*, 85 Hawai'i 336, 944 P.2d 1279 (1997)(open and obvious danger may prevent liability for failure to warn under consumer expectations test, but not necessarily under a risk-utility test). What if the consumer expectations test had been applied in *Liriano*? Would the facts about the plaintiff's particular background and situation had any relevance at all?

Causation

10. *Causation in warning failure cases.* Suppose the plaintiff proves that the defendant failed to give a warning that was needed to make the product safe and that a safe warning would have been on the label of the product or on instructions accompanying it. Most case law says that unless the plaintiff would have read, understood and heeded the warning, the failure to warn cannot be a cause of the harm. But courts usually "presume" that the plaintiff would have read and heeded the warning, leaving it to the defendant to show otherwise if it can, a phenomenon known as the "heeding presumption." What result if the plaintiff admits that he did not read any of a product's accompanying instructions or warnings? Would he necessarily lose? Does it matter why he did not read them?

11. *Shifting burden of proof on causation.* The *Liriano* court placed the burden on the defendant to prove that its negligent failure to warn was not a cause in fact of the plaintiff's harm, once the plaintiff proved that such failure "greatly increased the likelihood of the harm that occurred." How, if at all, does this approach differ from the "heeding presumption" mentioned above in note 10? Can you compare *Liriano*'s burden-shifting approach to that in *Barker v. Lull*, supra §5?

CARRUTH v. PITTWAY CORP., 643 So.2d 1340 (Ala.1994). Seven family members were killed in a house fire. Their estates sued Pittway, a smoke-detector manufacturer, claiming that the deaths were caused by its negligence in providing insufficient installation ins and warnings. Just two days before the fire, the victims' fathe the smoke detector near a ceiling-wall junction. The device nied by a seven-page pamphlet, set in small type. The pa "Dead air spaces are often . . . in the corners between ceil Dead air may prevent smoke from reaching a detector." statements was captioned by the words "warning," "cau ger," as were other cautionary statements. The "dead a were contained in a portion of the pamphlet that inclu instructions and illustrations that together "could be viewed as confusing at best." A colored and highly visible diagram purported to show effective smoke detector locations, including the area immediately below a wall-ceiling junction. Ultimately, "from the pamphlet's format and print size, and the seemingly sufficient diagram on the box, a fair-minded person could reasonably infer that a user would be induced to only scan the pamphlet and thereby not get from the pamphlet the information about dead-air-space." A jury question was thus presented "as to whether the Pittway pamphlet provided a legally adequate warning about dead-air-space concerns."

Notes

1. *Content or expression.* Warnings must be reasonably clear, and of sufficient force and intensity to convey the nature and extent of the risks to a reasonable person. "A manufacturer's techniques in promoting the product, inconsistencies or undue qualifications in stating the warning or directions, and depictions of uses that run counter to warnings may each nullify or dilute the warnings provided in printed literature.... When possible harm is severe, quite specific information may be required. A drug warning about possible blood clotting may disguise rather than reveal the possibility of a stroke." DOBBS ON TORTS § 364 (2000).

2. *Form and location.* Can a warning be defective because it is in a form or location where it is not likely to be read? The father in *Carruth* admitted that he did not read the instruction pamphlet "in depth." Why wasn't this enough to support a summary judgment for the defense?

3. *Nature and seriousness of harm.* Sometimes the warning must not only alert the user to danger and how to avoid it but also to the extent of harm that can result. In *Pavlik v. Lane Ltd./Tobacco Exporters International*, 135 F.3d 876 (3d Cir.1998), the estate of a man who died from self-administered butane inhalation sued the distributor, claiming that the single warning on the can ("DO NOT BREATHE SPRAY") was inadequate. The court left it to the trier to determine whether a more specific warning would have averted the harm. What might such a warning have said?

4. *Language of the warning.* If the warning must be reasonably clear, should it be presented in any language besides English? Suppose a manufacturer advertises in Spanish to buyers whose main or only language is Spanish. Should it even include symbols to help convey the message to non-readers? If a poison contains verbal warnings but no skull and crossbones or unhappy faces, is that adequate?

NOTE: MULTIPLE PARTIES, LEARNED INTERMEDIARIES AND SOPHISTICATED USERS

1. *Product combinations.* Sidon manufactures multi-piece tire rims, which, allegedly, are inherently dangerous. Tyre manufactures tires that can be used only with multi-piece rims. Has Tyre any duty to warn users that the only use of its tires will entail danger from the rims? See *Rastelli v. Goodyear Tire & Rubber Co.*, 79 N.Y.2d 289, 582 N.Y.S.2d 373, 591 N.E.2d 222 (1992).

2. *Prescription drugs.* What warnings should accompany a prescription drug and to whom should the warnings be given? Courts usually say the warnings should go to the doctor who might prescribe, not directly to the patient. When the manufacturer does in fact give appropriate warning or information to the physician, it is said that the physician is a "learned intermediary" upon whom the manufacturer can properly rely, and the warning can be couched in terms the physician can understand, not necessarily terms the consumer would grasp. *Johnson v. American Cyanamid Co.*, 239 Kan. 279, 718 P.2d 1318 (1986). And no warning at all is required if the physician already knows the danger. *Christopher v. Cutter Laboratories,* 53 F.3d 1184 (11th Cir.1995).

3. *Bulk goods.* Similar rules apply to those who supply goods in bulk and those who supply to sophisticated users: they may be permitted to rely upon their buyers to use the goods properly and to pass on any appropriate warnings. For instance, a supplier of bulk chemicals to a manufacturer ordinarily need not try to warn ultimate users of the manufactured product. These rules seem to mean that the product is not defective for lack of a warning to the ultimate consumer. But it is common to refer to this idea as the learned intermediary or sophisticated user "defense."

4. *Direct marketing of drugs.* If a drug manufacturer advertises its prescription drugs directly to consumers, does the learned intermediary doctrine apply to defeat a consumer's failure-to-warn claim? In *Perez v. Wyeth Labs., Inc.,* 161 N.J. 1, 734 A.2d 1245 (1999), the defendant argued that it does, and that the physician's prescription of the drugs broke any causal link between its failure to warn consumers of harmful side effects and their resulting harm. The court rejected both arguments. Contra, *In re Norplant Contraceptive Products Liability Litigation,* 165 F.3d 374 (5th Cir.1999)(applying Texas law, holding that learned intermediary doctrine precluded manufacturer's duty to warn consumers, despite aggressive marketing to the public).

5. *The Restatement of Products Liability.* Restatement § 6(d) provides that warnings about the health risks of prescription drugs and medical devices must be given directly to consumers only when the manufacturer knows or has reason to know that the learned intermediary "will not be in a position to reduce the risks of harm in accordance with the instructions or warnings." When might this occur? Comment *e* gives as an example the administration of mass inoculation, where health care providers are not in a position to evaluate individualized risks of the vaccine. Patients should be directly warned in that situation, if such warnings are feasible and would be effective.

6. *Unreliable learned intermediaries.* If birth control pills are routinely prescribed by physicians without individualized warnings, should the manufacturer be required to give a warning directly to the user that such drugs present serious risks? Only a few cases have taken any such view. See *MacDonald v. Ortho Pharmaceutical Corp.,* 394 Mass. 131, 475 N.E.2d 65 (1985).

7. *Government as "learned intermediary?"* In *Macias v. State*, 10 Cal.4th 844, 42 Cal.Rptr.2d 592, 897 P.2d 530 (1995), the State of California sprayed the pesticide malathion over a large area in an attempt to control a Mediterranean fruit fly infestation. Federal regulations require certain label warnings on malathion, including warnings to flush with water if it touches the skin or eyes. The EPA required the state to inform the public of the precautions that would have been on a label, but the state did not do so. Fourteen year-old Juan Macias was sprayed and was eventually rendered legally blind. In his suit against the manufacturers, Macias argued that they were aware of the state's failure to warn, and were aware that children were particularly susceptible and that blindness could result, but failed either to provide a warning themselves, or to persuade the state to do so. *Held,* the manufacturers were under no duty to warn the public nor to request the state to give warnings. It was reasonable to rely on the state to convey required warnings. "To judicially impose a private duty to design and disseminate independent warnings in direct conflict with those formulated by the State would represent an unprecedented intrusion on the State's sovereign authority. . . ." Are you convinced?

b. Focusing on Post–Sale Warnings

COMSTOCK v. GENERAL MOTORS CORP., 358 Mich. 163, 99 N.W.2d 627, 78 A.L.R.2d 449 (1959). Friend purchased a 1953 Buick Roadmaster. In 1954 the brakes suddenly failed, but Friend was able to avoid any harm. He took the car into the Ed Lawless Buick Company for repair, following closely behind another car, which he used as a bumper. He explained the problem, which as a matter of fact was not new to the company because General Motors began experiencing brake problems on that model almost immediately after its introduction. However, General Motors did not notify any of the purchasers. Instead it provided dealers with repair kits. When 1953 Buick was brought in for any reason, the repair would be made to the brakes without disclosing the facts to the customer. As one witness said, "It was a hush thing. They didn't want the public to know the brakes were bad and they were very alarmed." After Friend turned his brakeless car over to the dealer, an employee, knowing but forgetting that the car was without brakes, attempted to drive it to a service stall. Comstock was working behind another car. The driver was unable to stop the brakeless Buick and it crushed Comstock's right leg against the other car. In Comstock's action against General Motors as manufacturer of the brakeless car, *held,* "the facts in this case imposed a duty on defendant to take all reasonable means to convey effective warning to those who had purchased '53 Buicks with power brakes when the latent defect was discovered. . . . If [there is] duty to warn of a known danger exists at point of sale, we believe a like duty to give prompt warning exists when a latent defect which makes the product hazardous to life becomes known to the manufacturer shortly after the product has been put on the market."

GREGORY v. CINCINNATI, INC., 450 Mich. 1, 538 N.W.2d 325 (1995). Defendant designed and produced a sheet metal press in 1964. In 1986 the plaintiff was injured in using the press when the ram descended on his thumb, necessitating amputation. The plaintiff claimed a continuing duty to warn or recall and on this basis introduced evidence that in 1971, OSHA required safety devices that would have avoided the injury and evidence that such devices were developed after the press was made in 1964. The jury found for the plaintiff. *Held,* reversed and remanded for a new trial. The postmanufacture evidence was erroneously admitted. "Generally, before there can be any continuing duty— whether it be to warn, repair, or recall—there must be a defect or an actionable problem at the point of manufacture. If there is no defect or actionable problem at this point, then there can be no continuing duty to warn, repair, or recall." ... In Michigan to date, the only postmanufacture duty imposed on a manufacturer has been the duty to warn when the defect existed at the point of manufacture, but for some reason was undiscoverable by both the manufacturer and the consumer at that time. Comstock, supra. However, we have never held that a manufacturer has a postmanufacture duty to repair or recall in this context, and have never held that any postmanufacture duties can arise from subsequently discovered knowledge unattributable to a defect at the time of manufacture." Comstock's duty to warn arose in "the unique context in which the manufacturer acknowledged the existence of a latent manufacturing defect, as evidenced by numerous failures and the offer to repair". In any event, the manufacturer has no duty to recall or repair. A duty to warn or even to recall might be found on the basis of a unique relationship between the parties, but otherwise such a duty will be recognized only if imposed by statute or regulation.

Notes

1. If a post-sale duty to warn arises only when the defendant was negligent in the first place, or when the product was defective from the start, does a post-sale duty to warn become meaningless as a basis for legal action?

2. Courts are divided about post-sale duties and unsure how far to take them or where they could stop. On the one hand there is authority that if the danger is sufficient and the cost is limited, the manufacturer might even be obliged to provide a corrective device or make a repair itself. See *Gracyalny v. Westinghouse Electric Corp.,* 723 F.2d 1311 (7th Cir.1983). In some pharmaceutical cases, courts have even said that the manufacturer was under a duty to keep abreast of scientific developments and to warn the medical profession of newly discovered side effects. See *Schenebeck v. Sterling Drug, Inc.,* 423 F.2d 919 (8th Cir.1970). If, in the course of "keeping abreast," the manufacturer is put on notice of possible dangers, this may require the manufacturer to institute further investigations or tests and studies of its own. *Barson v. E.R. Squibb & Sons, Inc.,* 682 P.2d 832 (Utah 1984).

3. On the other hand, some courts have firmly denied that there is any post-sale duty at all, even to give a warning. See, e.g., *Bragg v. Hi–Ranger,*

Inc., 319 S.C. 531, 462 S.E.2d 321 (S.C.App.1995) (approving instruction that "A manufacturer, ladies and gentlemen, has no duty to notify previous purchasers of its products about later developed safety devices or to retrofit those products if the products were non-defective under standards existing at the time of the manufacture or sale.").

4. *Restatement of Products Liability.* The Restatement provides that a seller or distributor is obliged to give a post-sale warning when a reasonable person would do so. A reasonable person would give such a warning if he knows or should know that the product poses a substantial risk of harm; those to whom a warning might be given can be identified and assumed to be unaware of the risk; a warning can be effectively communicated; and the risk of harm outweighs the burden of giving a warning. RESTATEMENT OF PRODUCTS LIABILITY § 10. The reasonable person standard means that a jury instruction on post-sale duty to warn should tell the jury to consider any factors that make it burdensome for the manufacturer to provide a warning. *Lovick v. Wil–Rich,* 588 N.W.2d 688 (Iowa 1999).

5. *Statutory recall/repair duties.* Statutes or regulations may require post-sale warnings or repairs. Some standards for motor vehicles are set by federal regulation. If a manufacturer fails to comply with standards, the Secretary of Transportation may require the manufacturer to (a) give notice of the defect to purchasers and dealers and (b) to remedy the defect. 49 U.S.C.A. § 30118. The Consumer Products Safety Commission has the power to require a recall of dangerous products or to order their replacement. 15 U.S.C.A. § 2064 (d). The Restatement Third limits liability for failure to recall or repair to cases in which a recall obligation is imposed by statute or regulation or in which the manufacturer voluntarily undertakes a recall and fails to follow through in a reasonable way. RESTATEMENT OF PRODUCTS LIABILITY § 11.

REFERENCE: DOBBS ON TORTS §§ 363–68 (2000).

§ 7. SPECIAL ISSUES OF PROOF

BITTNER v. AMERICAN HONDA MOTOR CO., INC., 194 Wis.2d 122, 533 N.W.2d 476 (Wis.1995). The plaintiff, riding a three-wheeled, all terrain vehicle (ATV), suffered severe injuries when it overturned. The plaintiff sued the manufacturer asserting both negligence and strict product liability claims, in part because of the allegedly dangerous high-center-of-gravity design. The defendant introduced evidence (1) that injury rates associated with use of snowmobiles, mini-bikes and trail bikes were *less* than injury rates associated with ATVs; and (2) that injury rates of many sports, including scuba-diving, and football were much higher that rates associated with ATV use. From the first set of evidence, the defendant argued that because the recreational vehicles in question were similar in purpose to ATVs, the lower rate of injury suggested that ATV accidents were due to operator error. From the second set of evidence, the defendant argued that "if fewer individuals are injured riding ATVs than, for instance, playing football, then the risk of injury associated with ATV riding is reasonable." *Held,* the first set of evidence is admissible as tending to show operator error, but the second set of evidence is not admissible. Evidence of greater risks of activities that are generally acceptable is not relevant. "[T]he comparative risk evidence comparing ATV riding with dissimilar products and activities, such as sky diving, cannot be introduced, as Honda asserts, to demonstrate that ATVs are not unreasonably dangerous."

Notes

1. *Similar accidents.* In design and information defect cases, evidence that a product either has or has not caused similar accidents is usually admissible as tending to show that the product was or was not defective, and that the defendant did or did not have notice of the danger. See, e.g., *Uniroyal Goodrich Tire Co. v. Martinez,* 977 S.W.2d 328 (Tex.1998)(no error in admission of evidence of 34 other lawsuits against defendant involving similar product claims); *Spino v. John S. Tilley Ladder Co.,* 548 Pa. 286, 696 A.2d 1169 (1997)(no abuse of discretion in the admission of testimony of company president that 100,000 of its ladders had been marketed in a 100–year period, without any prior claims against the company). However, when the plaintiff claims only a manufacturing flaw in the particular item, the safety history of the product line generally seems irrelevant. Does any of this sound like a basis for the *Bittner* court's ruling on the first set of evidence?

2. *Comparative risks and risk-utility weighing.* Consider the second set of evidence in *Bittner,* that the risks of injury in, say, football, were greater than the risks of injury in ATVs. If higher risks are acceptable in a variety of life's activities, would *Carroll Towing* or any form of risk-utility analysis suggest that the risk of ATVs would be a reasonable one? Cf. David A. Fischer, *Proportional Liability: Statistical Evidence and the Probability Paradox,* 46 VAND. L. REV. 1201 (1993)(arguing that liability limited to a percentage of the plaintiff's damages, based on proportional causation, is undesirable because whenever the environment generally becomes more dangerous, the liability of individuals would be reduced).

NOTE: SUBSEQUENT REMEDIAL MEASURES

Suppose that a plaintiff is injured by the defendant's product or property. After the defendant learns of the injury, he repairs the property or modifies the product to make it safer. The rule in negligence cases is that evidence of the defendant's subsequent remedial measures is not admissible to show negligence. First, subsequent repairs or other safety measures (like warnings) do not say much if anything about whether the defendant should reasonably have perceived danger before the injury or whether the a reasonable person would have recognized the need for safety measures. Second, coupled with this low relevance is high risk that the jury would treat subsequent repairs as an admission of negligence. Third, courts have speculated that if evidence of subsequent safety measures were admissible, some defendants might refuse to make needed changes lest their efforts be used against them in court.

A 1997 amendment to the Federal Rules of Evidence makes inadmissible evidence of remedial measures "taken after an injury or harm allegedly caused by an event," including such evidence offered to prove "a defect in the product, a defect in the product's design or a need for a warning or instruction." FED. R. EVID. 407. This rule applies only in federal court, and states are free to depart from it.

Some state courts do so, holding that evidence of subsequent safety measures is admissible in strict liability products cases. A leading case is *Ault v. International Harvester Co.*, 13 Cal.3d 113, 117 Cal.Rptr. 812, 528 P.2d 1148, 74 A.L.R.3d 986 (1974); see also *Caprara v. Chrysler Corporation*, 52 N.Y.2d 114, 436 N.Y.S.2d 251, 417 N.E.2d 545 (1981) ("spirit of strict liability" and desire to aid plaintiff in proof make blanket exclusion in strict liability cases inappropriate); *Forma Scientific, Inc. v. BioSera, Inc.*, 960 P.2d 108 (Colo.1998)(such evidence should be admitted in strict liability design-defect cases, since its probative value outweighs any unfair prejudice to the manufacturer). Does the persuasive weight of these cases suffer in a state that adopts the Restatement Third of Products liability with its emphasis on risk-utility analysis and its rejection of strict liability for product defects?

Although in many jurisdictions, evidence of subsequent safety measures cannot be offered to prove negligence (and maybe not a product defect either), those measures could at least indicate that a safer product is feasible. Such evidence has been admitted for that limited purpose. When that is done, won't the jury use the evidence as it thinks fit?

TURPIN v. MERRELL DOW PHARMACEUTICALS, INC.

United States Court of Appeals, Sixth Circuit, 1992.
959 F.2d 1349.

MERRITT, CHIEF JUDGE.

[The plaintiffs claimed injury from the defendant's drug, Bendectin. The trial court judged for itself the validity of the reasoning process by which the plaintiffs' qualified experts reached their opinions. On that basis, the trial judge granted the defense motion for summary judgment.]

We agree with Judge Siler that, although judges should respect scientific opinion and recognize their own limited scientific knowledge, nevertheless courts have a duty to inspect the reasoning of qualified scientific experts to determine whether a case should go to the jury. Based on the record before us, we also agree with Judge Siler that whether Bendectin caused the minor plaintiff's birth defects is not known and is not capable of being proved to the requisite degree of legal probability based on the scientific evidence currently available. . . .

The nausea of morning sickness affects many pregnant women and, although the causes are not completely understood, in extreme cases may cause permanent injury to the sufferer's unborn child. Merrell Dow manufactured and marketed Bendectin as an anti-nauseant prescription for morning sickness from 1956 until 1983 when it took the drug off the market despite continued approval from the Food and Drug Administration. Estimates indicate that Bendectin was prescribed from 1957 until 1982 to over 30 million women worldwide and to more than 17.5 million women in the United States. These women commonly took Bendectin during the first trimester of pregnancy.

Approximately seven weeks after becoming pregnant, Betty Turpin ingested Bendectin to combat morning sickness. The initial development of the fetus's fingers and toes occurs some four to eight weeks after conception. Seven months after Ms. Turpin first took the drug, her child, Brandy Turpin, the infant plaintiff in this case, was born with "limb reduction defects": severely deformed hands and feet, specifically fused joints and shortened or missing fingers and toes. Ms. Turpin took no other drugs during the course of her pregnancy, nor can her child's deformities be traced to any known genetic disorders. . . .

There are two important questions here: How hard should judges look at the reasonableness of scientific theories and inferences before they decide whether there is enough to the case for it to go to the jury? If we apply a "hard look" doctrine, as we are inclined to do in scientific cases based primarily on expert testimony, what exactly are the general scientific experiments and studies capable of showing about whether Bendectin causes birth defects in a particular case?

We believe that close judicial analysis of such technical and specialized matter is necessary not only because of the likelihood of juror misunderstanding, but also because expert witnesses are not necessarily always unbiased scientists. They are paid by one side for their testimony. Although there is no suggestion of unethical scientific conduct in the present case, the potential for exaggeration and fraud on the court is present and may be impossible to discover without close inspection and careful consideration of the record. . . .

Both sides appear to accept the fact that limb defects generally appear in less than one in 1,000 live births. The defendant's proof consists in large measure of the 35 extant studies published in medical and scientific journals on the statistical relationship between the use of Bendectin and the incidence of various forms of birth defects in babies, none of which conclude that a causal connection exists. . . .

The following examples illustrate the nature and findings of these 35 studies, with six studies representative of the group:

1. The San Francisco Study: Two University of California researchers studied effects of six anti-nauseant drugs on 11,481 pregnancies in the San Francisco area over seven years. Bendectin was prescribed in only 628 of these cases. Birth defects were monitored at three ages: one month, one year, and five years (though limb defects in particular were not isolated and reported). The average rate of all types of birth defects for Bendectin cases at the age of one month was 0.8 in every 100 births. This average rate is less than the average rate of the birth defects found in mothers who did not use Bendectin. . . .

2. The Boston and Harvard Study: Six doctors from Boston University and the Harvard School of Public Health evaluated a group study of 50,282 mothers and children for Bendectin's possible effect on birth defects. Of these mothers, 1,169 took Bendectin during their first four months of pregnancy, with 79 births resulting in various birth defects. Limb defects were not specifically reported. The 49,113 mothers who were not exposed to Bendectin gave birth to 3,169 infants who had various birth defects. Overall, 4.7 percent of those mothers exposed to Bendectin gave birth to deformed infants, while 4.5 percent of non-exposed mothers did. Thus, the relative risk of birth defects for Bendectin use was 1.07 at a 95 percent confidence level. . . .

3. The Atlanta Study: . . . Of 1,231 birth defects cases, 117, or 9.5 percent, of the mothers took Bendectin. Of 129 children born with limb defects, 14 (10.9 percent) had mothers who took Bendectin. The study calculated a relative risk of 1.18 at a 95 percent confidence interval between 0.65 and 2.13. However, for one subgroup of limb defects known as the "amniotic band complex," a higher relative risk—3.88—was reported. Therefore, the risk of a Bendectin-exposed mother giving birth to a child with this specific condition was almost four times greater than that which would occur in a population of non-exposed mothers. . . .

6. The National Institute of Health Study: In the most recent Bendectin study, two National Institute of Health researchers evaluated 31,564 births in Northern California. Of those women 2,771 (nine percent) had used Bendectin. For 58 categories of defects studied—limb defects, however, were not specifically monitored—135 defects occurred in cases of Bendectin exposure, while 1,439 defects occurred in non-exposed cases. Relative risks were greatest in three categories: lung defects (4.6), microcephaly, i.e., small head size (3.1), and cataracts (3.7). The 95 percent confidence intervals varied widely for these three categories, ranging between 1.9 to 10.9 for lung defects, 1.8 to 15.6 for microcephaly, and 1.2 to 24.3 for cataracts. . . .

In addition to the 35 epidemiological studies, the defendant also offers as evidence the fact that no one has detected a decrease in the incidence of birth defects after Bendectin was removed from the market in 1983. Dr. Lamm so testified for the defendant based on a number of studies.

The plaintiffs claim that the defendant's 35 studies are based on samples which are too small to prove the absence of causation in light of the infrequency of instances of birth defects in general; that they do not adequately isolate limb reduction defects from other birth defects; that they do not control for many confounding factors such as smoking and the use of other drugs; that they impose a much higher level of scientific certainty of association (95 percent) than required by the preponderance of the evidence standard of proof (i.e., 51 percent); and that some of the studies can be read to show some statistically significant association if a much lower level of certainty is used. In essence the plaintiffs argue that the 35 statistical studies do not prove or disprove anything concerning the relationship between Bendectin and limb reduction defects.

At least two expert witnesses for the plaintiffs attack the persuasive force of the defendant's statistical comparisons of the incidence of Bendectin-related birth defects. Dr. Glasser criticized the defendant's use of studies by Aselton, Jick, Cordero and Eskenazi as not correctly considering other birth defects, such as heart and pyloric valve defects or cleft palates, in assessing Bendectin's capacity for limb birth defects. In his affidavit, Dr. Glasser also criticized the Cordero, Eskenazi and McCredie studies for incorrectly inferring that no association existed between Bendectin use and infant limb reduction. Dr. Swan, similarly, rejected these studies' sole reliance on a relative risk of 1.0 within a 95 percent confidence interval as a basis for concluding that Bendectin does not cause birth defects in humans. Dr. Swan further claimed that several of the studies were conducted using insufficient populations or control groups, so that scientists wrongly calculated exposures to the drug. Dr. Swan viewed these and other factors as confounding the validity and power of such reports; however, both Drs. Glasser and Swan relied on these studies as the basis for their own recalculations, using a lower confidence interval that is claimed to derive a higher relative risk. Both experts concluded from their own reassessments that to a reasonable degree of epidemiological certainty, there is some association between Bendectin and limb reduction defects.

. . . The defendant's claim overstates the persuasive power of these statistical studies. An analysis of this evidence demonstrates that it is possible that Bendectin causes birth defects even though these studies do not detect a significant association.

Limb reduction defects occur in such a small percentage of both Bendectin and non-Bendectin live births—as noted, these occur in less than one in every 1,000—that it would take a carefully controlled comparison of a very large number of births to instill confidence in the predictive power of the outcome. Also, many of the defendant's studies apparently do not control for many factors that may be crucial for scientists to accord great weight to the studies, such as the stage of pregnancy during which the mother took Bendectin, the other drugs the mother may have taken, or other harmful conditions, natural or otherwise, that may have been part of the mother's environment. . . .

The cartilage cells that later become the bones of fingers and toes begin to form in the human embryo during the fourth through eighth weeks of pregnancy. The plaintiffs' theory is that chemical compounds in Bendectin interfere with the formation of these cartilage cells, or chondrogenesis, and that this causal relationship is shown by animal experiments. . . . The plaintiffs' scientific hypothesis based on these studies is this: Because doxyalamine succinate interferes with cartilage cell formation in animal cells and test animals, Bendectin is "capable" of causing similar limb defects in humans. The following examples illustrate the nature and findings of these animal cell studies:

1. In vitro studies: As a developmental biologist, Dr. Newman stated that he performs experiments on embryonic cells in petri dishes to determine how those cells develop and create tissue. Due to their similarities to the human embryo, chicken and mice or rat embryos are most frequently used in these studies. Limb-forming cells are removed from the embryo—for chickens, wing and leg formation cells are used—and are isolated in a dish, where selected cells are treated with a suspected teratogen. Changes in cell differentiation between the control group of untreated cells and the exposed group are observed and recorded.... Other in vitro tests performed by National Institute of Health experts and relied upon by Dr. Newman found that doxyalamine succinate interfered with cartilage development in mice and chicken limb cells. In one experiment, the addition of 10 micrograms of Bendectin to an animal cell culture reduced one of the components of cartilage cells, proteoglycan, by 30 percent. Similarly, 50 micrograms of Bendectin per milliliter of a culture reduced proteoglycan production by 50 percent, thus suggesting a strong teratogenic effect in the animal cells tested.

Like the other scientists who testify concerning animal experiments, Dr. Newman can only testify that these chemical compounds connected with Bendectin are "capable of causing" limb defects in humans, not that they do cause such defects.

2. In vivo studies: Dr. Gross, a pathologist and veterinary medical expert with the Environmental Protection Agency, described the nature of the in vivo studies proffered by the plaintiffs. In these experiments, suspected teratogens are administered to pregnant female animals.... No defects were observed at the two lower [dosage] levels; however, 40 percent of the litters born to females at the highest dosage had some congenital defects observed. As dosages were increased even higher, "outright death" of animal infants occurred. Dr. Gross rejected several of Merrell Dow's other studies as being confounded by the presence of defects in the non-exposed control group.... Dr. Gross gave his opinion that doxyalamine succinate in Bendectin has the "capacity" to interfere with human cell development at normal dosages but could not testify that it does cause such defects....

Immune systems, nervous systems, and metabolisms (i.e., physical processing of chemical compounds) may differ greatly between species. No doubt there may be other animal experiments which, to cite one example, because of the extreme toxicity of the substance tested, would permit a reasonable jury to find that it is more probable than not that the substance causes a similar harm to humans. But Bendectin is not such a case.

The decisive weakness in the plaintiffs' animal studies is that the factual and theoretical bases articulated for the scientific opinions stated will not support a finding that Bendectin more probably than not caused the birth defect here....

Dr. Palmer, a medical doctor, is the only witness who testified in his affidavit that Bendectin caused Brandy Turpin's defects. He stated: It is my opinion ... that [animal in vivo and in vitro studies, and epidemiological and other human data] shows that Bendectin and specifically its component, doxyalamine succinate, has teratogenic properties.... I have also examined the medical records pertaining to Brandy Turpin and it is my opinion ... that Bendectin did cause the limb defects from which she suffers.

We cannot find, however, that this testimony is anything more than a personal belief or opinion. The grounds for his opinion are subject to the same criticism as the animal studies and epidemiological reanalyses submitted by the plaintiffs' other experts: the evidence cited in support of his conclusion is insufficient to meet the plaintiffs' burden of proof. Dr. Palmer does not testify on the basis of the collective view of his scientific discipline, nor does he take issue with his peers and explain the grounds for his differences. Indeed, no understandable scientific basis is stated. Personal opinion, not science, is testifying here.... Upon analysis, we conclude that Dr. Palmer's conclusions go far beyond the known facts that form the premise for the conclusion stated. This conclusion so overstates its predicate that we hold that it cannot legitimately form the basis for a jury verdict. Beyond that Dr. Palmer's opinion testimony, to the extent that it is personal opinion as described above, is inadmissible.

We do not mean to intimate that animal studies lack scientific merit or power when it comes to predicting outcomes in humans. Animal studies often comprise the backbone of evidence indicating biological hazards, and their legal value has been recognized by federal courts and agencies.

Here, the record's explanation of the animal studies is simply inadequate. Although the animal studies themselves may have been scientifically performed, the exact nature of these tests is explained only in general terms. The record fails to make clear why the varying doses of Bendectin or doxyalamine succinate given to the rats, rabbits and in vitro animal cells would permit a jury to conclude that Bendectin more probably than not causes limb defects in children born to mothers who ingested the drug at prescribed doses during pregnancy. The analytical gap between the evidence presented and the inferences to be drawn on the ultimate issue of human birth defects is too wide. Under such circumstances, a jury should not be asked to speculate on the issue of causation.

Accordingly, the judgment of the District Court is AFFIRMED.

Notes

1. *Relative risk* is a numerical way of representing the difference between risks in the non-Bendectin group and risks in the Bendectin group. By convention, the number 1.0 represents the normal risks to the population at large. So the number 1.18 in the Atlanta study indicates that Bendectin babies had about 18% more risk of birth problems than non-Bendectin babies.

2. *Confidence interval* is a *range* of numbers representing the relative risk you would expect to find if you did further random studies. In the Atlanta study, the limited sample in the study showed children of mothers who took Bendectin suffered more birth defects, but the sample was so limited that statisticians would not be willing to predict identical results if other random studies were done. Instead, they would confidently predict only a wide range of results. In the Atlanta study, the range they would predict—the confidence interval—ran from 0.65 to 2.13. That means that they are predicting some studies would show *less*, not more risk from Bendectin, while others would show more than twice as much risk from Bendectin. Such a confidence interval or range does not help solve the problem; it is as if a pollster were to predict that the Democrats would receive between 40 and 60 percent of the votes in an election.

3. *Confidence level* is the probability that you would get the range of results specified in the confidence interval if you conduct future random studies. If, statistically speaking, you would expect to get the range from a 0.65 risk to a 2.13 risk in 95% of future studies, you would say that the confidence level is 95%. Statisticians conventionally adopted the 95% confidence level, but the number is an arbitrary choice, based on the preference of a scientist who was not deciding legal issues at all. See D.H. Kaye, *Is Proof of Statistical Significance Relevant?*, 61 WASH. L. REV. 1333 (1986).

4. *Altering the confidence level.* Since the confidence level is a convention, not an empirical datum or an authoritative command, you could decide to use a confidence level less than 95%. If you required less certainty about your prediction, you could adopt a 90% level or even an 80% level. If you did that, would it narrow the range of the confidence interval? Yes. At an 80% confidence level you'd expect to be in error in 20% of your predictions. At the 20% error-rate you might predict from an 18% risk increased in the present study that future properly conducted studies would always show *some* risk increase, even though you could not make such a prediction at the 95% confidence level.

5. *Is the issue one of causation or defectiveness?* If the product is shown to increase the risk of harm to users as a class and the only doubt is whether it actually caused harm to the particular plaintiff, then the issue would be one of causation. But if the product risks no injury to anyone, then it is not defective at all, is it?

If you approve of *Turpin*, would you be equally demanding about proof when the issue really is only one of causation in the specific case? For instance, suppose a plaintiff is a DES daughter and DES is shown to cause cancers in a relatively high percentage of DES daughters. Would the court's reasoning in *Turpin* require a directed verdict against such a plaintiff?

6. *Fault in the face of uncertainty.* Is it possible that, under a *Carroll Towing* risk-benefit analysis, it would be negligent to market a product like Bendectin, not because it is known to cause harm but simply because there was a chance that it would do so? Suppose the product on the drawing boards could relieve symptoms of the common cold but that scientists recognized a theoretical danger that the viruses used in the inoculation could mutate and cause a rampant and death-dealing disease. No one is sure. Should the product be marketed in spite of the uncertainty? In thinking

about this question, you could consider how *Turpin* might be decided if, given the uncertainty, the defendant were assigned the burden of proof.

7. *The Supreme Court's rulings.* After *Turpin* was decided, the Supreme Court considered admissibility of "scientific" evidence in federal court. *Daubert v. Merrell Dow Pharmaceuticals, Inc.*, 509 U.S. 579, 113 S.Ct. 2786, 125 L.Ed.2d 469 (1993) was similar to *Turpin.* Under the *Daubert* decision, scientific opinion can be admitted as evidence even though it is not generally accepted. However, the trial judge must decide that it will be "helpful" to the jury and that the opinion offered is "derived by the scientific method" that is, based on "good grounds" in the light of what is known and testable in future scientific studies. The trial judge must make "a preliminary assessment of whether the reasoning or methodology underlying the testimony is scientifically valid" and whether it can be applied in the case. The judge should consider (a) whether the expert's theory or technique has been tested; (b) whether it has been subjected to peer review; (c) whether it has a known potential error rate; and (d) whether it is generally accepted. All these matters, however, are only factors; none is dispositive of the decision. The trial judge's wide discretion in admitting expert testimony (or not) was reaffirmed in *General Electric Co. v. Joiner*, 522 U.S. 136, 118 S.Ct. 512, 139 L.Ed.2d 508 (1997)(holding that such rulings were reviewed only for an abuse of discretion). And in *Kumho Tire Co., Ltd. v. Carmichael*, 526 U.S. 137, 119 S.Ct. 1167, 143 L.Ed.2d 238 (1999), the Court extended *Daubert* to all expert testimony, not just "scientific" testimony.

8. *Legal vs. scientific purposes.* The Supreme Court in *Daubert* viewed science as a continuous inquiry, with answers always tentative and open to revision. More research, a better hypothesis, a different interpretation of data could all yield a different scientific picture. Judicial resolution of disputes, however, requires a final decision and a decision now, not after many years of further research. Does this difference between the goals and methods of science on the one hand and law on the other suggest anything about what law should do in toxic tort cases when the exact risk of the chemical in question cannot be determined? See Heidi Li Feldman, *Science and Uncertainty in Mass Exposure Litigation*, 74 TEX. L. REV. 1 (1995).

9. *Statistical evidence and the preponderance rule.* On remand of the *Daubert* case, the Ninth Circuit reaffirmed the summary judgment for the defendant. *Daubert v. Merrell Dow Pharmaceuticals, Inc.*, 43 F.3d 1311 (9th Cir.1995). *Turpin* assessed the evidence and concluded that it was insufficient. The Ninth Circuit's *Daubert* decision did not assess the evidence; it held the evidence altogether inadmissible. The court emphasized the value of research not generated by litigation itself and the value of published, peer-reviewed studies. Studies that were not published or peer-reviewed would have to be stronger to be admitted in evidence. Finally, the court emphasized that the evidence would be excluded unless it was helpful to the jury. In that particular case, the court thought it was not "helpful" because it did not prove causation by a preponderance of the evidence. Here is what it said:

> California tort law requires plaintiffs to show not merely that Bendectin increased the likelihood of injury, but that it more likely than not caused their injuries. In terms of statistical proof, this means that plaintiffs must establish not just that their mothers' ingestion of Bendectin

increased somewhat the likelihood of birth defects, but that it more than doubled it—only then can it be said that Bendectin is more likely than not the source of their injury. Because the background rate of limb reduction defects is one per thousand births, plaintiffs must show that among children of mothers who took Bendectin the incidence of such defects was more than two per thousand.

Accord, *Merrell Dow Pharmaceuticals, Inc. v. Havner*, 953 S.W.2d 706 (Tex.1997)(saying that a "more than doubling of the risk" standard was justified because of the "more likely than not burden of proof," but that even a relative risk of 2.0 would not necessarily prove causation).

> REFERENCE: 1 MADDEN & OWEN ON PRODUCTS LIABILITY §§ 12:4–5 (3d Ed. 2000).

SUBCHAPTER C. DEFENSES AND DEFEATS

§ 8. COMPARATIVE FAULT AND ASSUMPTION OF RISK

BOWLING v. HEIL CO.
Supreme Court of Ohio, 1987.
31 Ohio St.3d 277, 511 N.E.2d 373.

[Heil manufactured a dump hoist system which was installed on a dump truck owned by Rogers. Brashear borrowed the truck for personal use. He and Bowling delivered gravel to Bowling's residence and dumped it, but the truck bed would not return to the down position after the load had been dumped. Bowling leaned underneath over the truck chassis to see what was wrong. This put him underneath the upraised truck bed. In this posture he grabbed the control lever on the pump valve assembly and manipulated it. The truck bed rapidly descended upon him, killing him instantly. This is an action against Heil and various others involved in the hoist assembly and controls. The jury found that Bowling was guilty of contributory negligence but not assumed risk. Damages were assessed at $1.75 million. The trial court and the court of appeals treated Bowling's contributory negligence in different ways. The effect of contributory fault in a products strict liability case is the main issue before the Ohio Supreme Court in the discussion below.]

HERBERT R. BROWN, JUSTICE . . . .

Included in the body of Ohio law governing products liability is an analysis of the defenses available in actions involving allegedly defective products. Currently, two affirmative defenses based upon a plaintiff's misconduct are recognized. First, an otherwise strictly liable defendant has a complete defense if the plaintiff voluntarily and knowingly assumed the risk occasioned by the defect. Second, such a defendant is also provided with a complete defense if the plaintiff misused the product in an unforeseeable manner. The court of appeals below, construing Comment n to Section 402A, attempted to distinguish between negligent "affirmative action" by a plaintiff and negligent passive conduct by him in failing either to discover a defect or to guard against the possibility of its existence. The court held that although a plaintiff's passive contributory negligence provides no defense to a products liability action, his contributorily negligent "affirmative action" does provide a defense, and that such affirmative negligence should be compared by a jury to the fault of a strictly liable manufacturer of a defective product, in a manner similar to the principles of comparative negligence embodied in [the statute].

Comment n to Section 402A provides:

> "Contributory negligence. * * * Contributory negligence of the plaintiff is not a defense when such negligence consists merely in a failure to discover the defect in the product, or to guard against the possibility of its existence. On the other hand the form of contributory negligence which consists in voluntarily and unreasonably proceeding to encounter a known danger, and commonly passes under the name of assumption of risk, is a defense under this Section as in other cases of strict liability. If the user or consumer discovers the defect and is aware of the danger, and nevertheless proceeds unreasonably to make use of the product and is injured by it, he is barred from recovery."

The court of appeals has carved out a middle ground, to wit: contributory negligence consisting of "affirmative action," theoretically located between a plaintiff's failure to discover or guard against a defect and his voluntary assumption of a known risk. There is no such middle ground. Comment n covers the entire spectrum of conduct which can be termed "contributory negligence," as applicable to products liability actions. That spectrum begins with a mere failure to discover a defect in a product, continues with a failure to guard against the existence of a defect, and concludes with an assumption of the risk of a known defect. "Affirmative action" by the plaintiff is not left uncovered. Failure to guard against a defect can be "affirmative action." Indeed such would describe the conduct of David Bowling in this case.

Under Comment n, either a plaintiff's contributory negligence amounts to a voluntary assumption of a known risk, or it does not. If it does, then that conduct provides an otherwise strictly liable defendant with a complete defense. If it does not, the contributory negligence of the plaintiff provides no defense.

In the case sub judice, the jury found that Bowling was contributorily negligent but that he had not assumed a known risk. Therefore, his contributory negligence did not provide Heil with a defense to appellant's strict liability claim. . . .

The definitive statement of the policy and goals underlying the application of strict liability in tort to cases involving defective products is provided in Comment c to Section 402A, at 349–350:

> "On whatever theory, the justification for the strict liability has been said to be that the seller, by marketing his product for use and

consumption, has undertaken and assumed a special responsibility toward any member of the consuming public who may be injured by it; that the public has the right to and does expect, in the case of products which it needs and for which it is forced to rely upon the seller, that reputable sellers will stand behind their goods; that public policy demands that the burden of accidental injuries caused by products intended for consumption be placed upon those who market them, and be treated as a cost of production against which liability insurance can be obtained; and that the consumer of such products is entitled to the maximum of protection at the hands of someone, and the proper persons to afford it are those who market the products."

Dean Prosser has expressed this idea in slightly different terms:

"The costs of damaging events due to defectively dangerous products can best be borne by the enterprisers who make and sell these products. Those who are merchants and especially those engaged in the manufacturing enterprise have the capacity to distribute the losses of the few among the many who purchase the products. It is not a 'deep pocket' theory but rather a 'risk-bearing economic' theory. The assumption is that the manufacturer can shift the costs of accidents to purchasers for use by charging higher prices for the costs of products."

Prosser & Keeton, Law of Torts (5th Ed.1984) 692–693, Section 98.

Under negligence principles, on the other hand, liability is determined (and, under R.C. 2315.19, apportioned) according to fault. In negligence, we seek to make the person or persons responsible for causing a loss pay for it. In other words, we "blame" the loss on the negligent party or parties because it was they who could have avoided the loss by conforming to due care. Conversely, in strict liability in tort we hold the manufacturer or seller of a defective product responsible, not because it is "blameworthy," but because it is more able than the consumers to spread that loss among those who use and thereby benefit from the product.

We recognize that strict liability cannot be absolutely divorced from traditional concepts of fault. In a sense we "blame" the loss on the manufacturer or seller because it introduced the defective product into the marketplace. However, it must be reemphasized that strict liability is at odds with traditional notions of due care. . . .

Comparative negligence or comparative fault has been applied in products liability cases by a number of courts, both in states that have comparative negligence statutes and in states where comparative negligence was judicially adopted. On the other hand, numerous courts have refused to apply comparative negligence principles to products liability cases.

We believe that the better-reasoned decisions are those that decline to inject a plaintiff's negligence into the law of products liability. We agree with the court's holding in Kinard v. Coats Co., Inc. (1976), 37 Colo. App. 555, 557, 553 P.2d 835, 837, which states:

"... Products liability under § 402A does not rest upon negligence principles, but rather is premised on the concept of enterprise liability for casting a defective product into the stream of commerce. * * * Thus, the focus is upon the nature of the product, and the consumer's reasonable expectations with regard to that product, rather than on the conduct either of the manufacturer or the person injured because of the product."

We agree with Justice Mosk of the California Supreme Court, who stated in his dissent in Daly v. General Motors Corp., supra:

"The defective product is comparable to a time bomb ready to explode; it maims its victims indiscriminately, the righteous and the evil, the careful and the careless. Thus when a faulty design or otherwise defective product is involved, the litigation should not be diverted to consideration of the negligence of the plaintiff. The liability issues are simple: was the product or its design faulty, did the defendant inject the defective product into the stream of commerce, and did the defect cause the injury? The conduct of the ultimate consumer-victim who used the product in the contemplated or foreseeable manner is wholly irrelevant to those issues."

Therefore, when we search the decisions from other jurisdictions, we find no rationale which persuades us that comparative negligence or comparative fault principles should be applied to products liability actions.

Based upon the foregoing analysis, we hold that principles of comparative negligence or comparative fault have no application to a products liability case based upon strict liability in tort. Strict liability, in focusing on the product rather than the conduct of its manufacturer or seller, does not seek to apportion a loss among all persons who have caused or contributed to it. Rather, it seeks to spread the loss among all users of the product. The concept of comparative fault is fundamentally inapplicable.

We therefore reverse the judgment of the court of appeals with respect to its reduction of appellant's verdict by the thirty percent found by the jury to be attributable to contributory negligence....

[A majority of the court supported the opinion, but one Justice concurred in the result and only part of the opinion, another wrote a separate concurring opinion, and a third dissented.]

Notes

1. *Comparative fault reductions. Bowling* applies the traditional rule that contributory negligence of the plaintiff is no defense to a strict liability claim. Some courts still hold these views, although most courts no longer do. In *Daly v. General Motors Corp.*, 20 Cal.3d 725, 144 Cal.Rptr. 380, 575 P.2d

1162 (1978) the California Court rejected that view for products strict liability and applied comparative fault rules to reduce the plaintiff's recovery. The Restatement of Products Liability provides that whatever comparative responsibility system is used in a given state should apply to products liability claims as well. RESTATEMENT OF PRODUCTS LIABILITY § 17.

2. *Unreduced recoveries. Bowling* imports into strict products liability cases the traditional view of contributory negligence as applied in abnormal danger cases, discussed in Chapter 21. Many other courts agree. Does the "time bomb" argument has any application in *Bowling* itself or could the plaintiff have protected himself by ordinary care?

3. *Misuse.* In a footnote the *Bowling* court said: " ... In some sense, [product] misuse is an act of contributory negligence. Nonetheless, it remains a defense to a products liability action based upon strict liability in tort." No reason was given. Why should contributory negligence be a defense if it involves product misuse but not even a basis for reducing damages if it takes some other form? Is it because some misuse cases can be viewed as "no defect" cases?

4. *Discovered vs. undiscovered defect.* Many states that do allow a contributory fault defense in products cases restrict that defense at times. In *Hernandez v. Barbo*, 327 Or. 99, 957 P.2d 147 (1998), the plaintiff was a mechanic whose hand was partially amputated when it contacted a saw blade. He sued the saw's sellers and others, claiming that the product was defective because the on/off switch was inconspicuous. Defendants argued that the plaintiff was contributorily negligent. Held, a plaintiff's recovery will not be reduced when his negligence consisted solely of failure to discover or guard against the product's defect. Many courts agree with this rule. Texas has said that "a duty to discover defects, and to take precautions in constant anticipation that a product might have a defect, would defeat the purposes of strict liability." *General Motors Corp. v. Sanchez*, 997 S.W.2d 584 (Tex.1999). Does this distinction between failing to discover or guard against defects and other kinds of negligence make sense? Would it be better to formulate the rule by saying that a plaintiff is not negligent for trusting the defendant's product until there is some reason to distrust it?

5. *Obvious danger.* We have seen that a product is sometimes considered defective even when its danger is obvious and the plaintiff could be safe by taking the product's characteristics into account. In such a case, would a state adopting the Products Restatement's rule of comparative fault reduce the plaintiff's recovery? And would a court applying the *Bowling* rule allow full recovery?

6. *Assumed risk.* Recall that under the Restatement of Apportionment, assumption of risk is subsumed within the comparative responsibility rules, and is not regarded as a separate defense at all. See Chapter 9, § 7. Some states continue to agree with the *Bowling* court's view, however, that assumption of risk is a complete defense to a strict products liability suit, even if contributory negligence is not. Ohio reaffirmed this view in *Carrel v. Allied Products Corp.*, 78 Ohio St.3d 284, 677 N.E.2d 795 (1997). Should courts distinguish between a plaintiff's negligence and "assumption of the risk," or should all forms of plaintiff "misconduct" enter into the comparison?

7. *Bexiga.* If you would apply ordinary comparative negligence in products cases, maybe there are still cases in which you would not want to apply it. How would you feel about applying the comparative fault rule in *Bexiga*, Chapter 9, § 5? Cf. *Carrel*, supra note 6 (assumption of risk defense not available when the plaintiff "is required to encounter the risk while performing normal job duties"). Or an eclectic approach in which you apply comparative fault where you think it would encourage safety by the plaintiff without removing safety incentives of the defendant? See *Cotita v. Pharma–Plast, U.S.A., Inc.*, 974 F.2d 598 (5th Cir.1992) (nurse exposed to AIDS virus as a result of defectively capped needle, but nurse was himself negligent).

8. *Seatbelts.* The plaintiff occupies a vehicle that is defective because it is not reasonably safe in cases of collision. The door pops open and the plaintiff is ejected. Although the vehicle was defective, the plaintiff's injuries are much worse because he failed to wear an available seat belt. What instructions to a jury about the plaintiff's failure to wear the belt in a jurisdiction that follows the *Bowling* rule?

9. *The firefighter's rule.* A firefighter is injured in a fire. The fire was caused by a defective product manufactured by the defendant. Does the firefighter's rule provide a defense to the product manufacturer? If so, what defense would it be? *Mignone v. Fieldcrest Mills*, 556 A.2d 35 (R.I.1989) concluded that the rule was grounded in assumed risk and that the firefighter was completely barred from recovery. But *Hawkins v. Sunmark Industries, Inc.*, 727 S.W.2d 397 (Ky.1986) held the manufacturer liable when its product made a fire worse. What if the product neither caused the fire nor made it worse, but injured the firefighter on the scene? Should that claim be barred? See *Stapper v. GMI Holdings, Inc.*, 73 Cal.App.4th 787, 86 Cal. Rptr.2d 688 (1999)(injury caused by alleged design defect in garage door).

10. *Effect on deterrence.* Does taking a plaintiff's contributory negligence into account in a products liability case remove incentives from manufacturers to make their products safer? Is this a greater problem in those states that follow either modified comparative fault or the old contributory negligence rules, where barring a plaintiff entirely on negligence grounds is a very real possibility? Or is the newer approach of the Products and Apportionment Restatements a sound way to account for a plaintiff's own responsibility for causing injury?

REFERENCE: DOBBS ON TORTS § 369 (2000).

§ 9. DISTINGUISHING DEFENSES FROM FAILURE TO PROVE DEFECT: PROXIMATE CAUSE AND MISUSE

a. *Misuse, Defectiveness, and Comparative Fault/Assumed Risk*

HUGHES v. MAGIC CHEF, INC.
Supreme Court of Iowa, 1980.
288 N.W.2d 542.

UHLENHOPP, JUSTICE....

Plaintiff Vincent E. Hughes was severely burned on March 9, 1976, when a stove manufactured by defendant Magic Chef, Inc., exploded in on March 7, 1976. After the propane tank was refilled that evening, two pilot lights on the top of the stove were re-lit but a third pilot light in the oven broiler cavity was not re-ignited. Experts testified that a resultant buildup of propane gas in the stove produced an explosion and fire when Hughes attempted to use the stove on the evening of March 9th. . . .

Hughes and his wife Eileen brought this strict liability action against Magic Chef, alleging the stove was unreasonably dangerous in several respects. Magic Chef raised affirmative defenses of assumption of risk and misuse of product. The jury found for Magic Chef and the trial court overruled the Hugheses' motion for new trial. Hugheses then appealed. . . .

A.   As to Hughes' first argument, this court held in *Rosenau* that in an ordinary negligence case in which the defendant raises the issue of the plaintiff's own negligence, assumption of risk is not to be pled and submitted as a separate defense. Instead, the essential elements of assumed risk, if supported by substantial evidence, are to be included in the contributory negligence instruction. Separate instructions on those defenses might result in the jury's rendering inconsistent verdicts and in the trial court's over-emphasizing a particular aspect of a case.

Hughes' argument that the *Rosenau* reasoning applies equally to the products liability defenses of misuse of product and assumption of risk does not recognize the differing natures of those two issues. Misuse precludes recovery when the plaintiff uses this product "in a manner which defendant could not reasonably foresee." Assumption of risk is a defense to a strict liability action when the plaintiff has "voluntarily and unreasonably proceed[ed] to encounter a known danger. . . ." The misuse of product doctrine has to do with the producer's responsibility in the first place; he has no liability at the outset if the product is misused. The assumption of risk doctrine has to do with the user's culpability; he bars himself from recovering if he voluntarily proceeds in the face of known danger. Although we recognize that in certain cases a plaintiff might have *both* used the product in a manner which the defendant could not reasonably foresee and voluntarily and unreasonably proceeded to encounter a known risk, we reject the idea that a plaintiff cannot do one without doing the other.

Despite our rejection of Hughes' attempt to apply *Rosenau* by analogy to this case, we agree with his basic contention that the trial court should not have given an instruction on misuse as a *defense* in this strict liability action. Misuse is not an affirmative defense but rather has to do with *an element of the plaintiff's own case*.

This conclusion departs somewhat from language in some of our prior products cases. Under that language the misuse issue may arise twice: first in connection with the plaintiff's prima facie case and again in connection with the defendant's affirmative defense. . . . [A]s part of his prima facie case, the plaintiff must establish that the product was unreasonably dangerous in a reasonably foreseeable use.

We have also said, however, that a defendant may defend a section 402A action by pleading and proving that the injured person misused the product, that is, he used it in a manner not reasonably foreseeable. The result of this prior language is that precisely the same issue—whether the product was used in a reasonably foreseeable manner—may be decisive both as to whether the plaintiff made a prima facie case and as to whether the defendant established an affirmative defense.

If we continued to treat misuse as an affirmative defense distinct and additional to the plaintiff's burden of proving that the product was used in reasonably foreseeable manner, we would create the potential for inconsistent jury findings in the same case. In addition we would create the possibility of a shifting burden of proof on the issue. The burden of proof regarding the use made of the product should not shift depending on the subtle distinction of whether the defendant offers evidence of misuse to rebut the plaintiff's evidence or instead offers it "to support an affirmative defense he is attempting to raise." . . .

Misuse of product is no longer to be considered an affirmative defense in products liability actions but is rather to be treated in connection with the plaintiff's burden of proving an unreasonably dangerous condition and legal cause. Regardless of whether a defendant does or does not plead misuse of the product the burden is on the plaintiff to prove that the legal cause of the injury was a product defect which rendered the product unreasonably dangerous in a reasonably foreseeable use. . . .

B. Hughes' second challenge to the misuse instruction is that it erroneously held him to a "reasonableness" standard in the use of the product. The instruction directed the jury as follows:

The Defendant asserts the affirmative defense that the Plaintiff Vincent Hughes misused the stove. The burden of proof is on the Defendant.

The Defendant claims that this Plaintiff knew, or ought reasonably to have known, of the existence of the pilot light in the oven area and that it was not lit after the service call by the Thermogas service man. The Defendant claims further that the Plaintiff took no action to relieve against this situation but instead attempted to utilize the oven or broiler on the second day thereafter and that such constituted a misuse of the stove by this Plaintiff.

If you find the Defendant has proved the above, that such action or failure to act on the part of the Plaintiff was not reasonably foreseeably [sic] by the Defendant, and further that such action or failure to act by the Plaintiff was the proximate cause of the accident, then the Plaintiff may not recover. . . .

If Hughes is correct that this misuse instruction imposes a "reasonableness" standard on his conduct the instruction is indeed erroneous, for in some situations negligent use of a product by a consumer is reasonably foreseeable by the producer and therefore is not "misuse" for liability purposes. To hold otherwise would interpose contributory negligence as a defense under the guise of misuse.

We find no necessity to resolve this issue, however, because the misuse instruction is objectionable on another ground; it gives undue emphasis, in such an instruction, to what Hughes personally knew or should have known.

If the ordinary user would reasonably be aware that use of a product in a certain way is dangerous, use of the product in that manner is less foreseeable by the producer than a use to which danger is not normally ascribed. But the ordinary user's awareness that use of the product in a certain manner is dangerous does not conclusively establish that such use is not reasonably foreseeable, for the defendant may in a given case reasonably foresee that a given product will be used by persons such as children who do not possess the knowledge of the ordinary user. Hence knowledge which can be reasonably attributed to the ordinary user is to be considered as a factor in determining whether the manner in which the plaintiff used the product was reasonably foreseeable.

The problem with the misuse instruction here is that it specifically directed the jury to consider what Hughes knew or ought reasonably to have known. What Hughes knew or should have known about the pilot light has slight relevance to the issue of whether Magic Chef should reasonably have foreseen the use to which the stove was put. The personal characteristics of users or, in this case, knowledge of users, becomes relevant to foreseeability of use only when the characteristics are attributable to a substantial group of users. By including a specific reference to what Hughes knew or should have known, the misuse instruction invited the jury to consider a matter of little relevance to the issue it had to resolve—whether Magic Chef should reasonably have foreseen that users would attempt to operate the stove after an interruption in gas service without first igniting all the pilot lights.

We thus hold that on retrial misuse is not to be treated in the jury instructions as an affirmative defense. Instead, the instructions with respect to the use to which the stove was put must place the burden of proof on Hughes to establish by a preponderance of the evidence that the use made of the stove was reasonably foreseeable by Magic Chef. Reference to knowledge reasonably attributable to the ordinary user may be made, but the instruction must make clear that such knowledge is one factor to be weighed in determining whether Hughes' manner of using the product was reasonably foreseeable by Magic Chef. If on retrial Hughes proves by a preponderance of the evidence that the use made of the stove was reasonably foreseeable and that the stove was unreasonably dangerous when so used, then he will have established the first element of his case; otherwise the case is over.

Reversed.

Notes

1. *Misuse*. What does the *Hughes* court think about unforeseeable misuse of a product that causes harm? (a) Unforeseeable misuse means the plaintiff is guilty of contributory negligence. (b) Unforeseeable misuse means the plaintiff assumed the risk. (c) Unforeseeable misuse means that, with respect to harms caused by the misuse and that would not have been caused by a properly used product, the product simply is not defective at all.

2. Suppose you are in a jurisdiction that considers plaintiffs' comparative fault in a products liability action to reduce recovery. If you represent the defendant would you rather establish (a) no defect or (b) plaintiff's fault? Why?

3. Given the answer to the preceding question, can you establish firmly in your own mind whether it is accurate to say "misuse is a defense?"

4. *Comparing contributory fault, assumed risk and no-defect.* How can you determine whether the plaintiff's conduct is "misuse" on the one hand or contributory fault or assumed risk on the other? Is it more important to distinguish one kind of act from another, or foreseeable uses from unforeseeable ones?

b. Misuse, Defectiveness, and Proximate Cause

REID v. SPADONE MACHINE CO.

Supreme Court of New Hampshire, 1979.
119 N.H. 457, 404 A.2d 1094.

GRIMES, JUSTICE.

[Defendant manufactures a "guillotine-type" cutting machine for cutting blocks of molded plastic. A blade descends to a strike plate when two buttons are pressed by the operator's hands. Operators in the Davidson Rubber Company would cut blocks of plastic, then turn the block at right angles to cut it in the other direction.]

[There were several safety devices. Originally the machine could be operated only when activated by pressing two buttons simultaneously, thus requiring the operator's hands to be out of the blade area. However, some workers fashioned a bar so that both buttons could be pressed at once while one hand was free to turn the blocks of plastic. To avoid this danger, the defendant moved the switch to one side of the machine so that the operator would be required to walk to the side of the machine. The machine was intended as a one-person cutter, but some workers in Davidson Rubber Company would at times work together on this machine, one pushing the side-button and one turning the blocks of plastic after each cut. Plaintiff, doing this, reached under the blade without using the push-stick available and his co-worker pressed the buttons. Plaintiff lost three fingers and brings this action.]

[Davidson, the employer, knew of the two-person use and its danger, but did not stop it. In fact, the machine was so used ten per cent of the time, and even supervisors used it in that way.]

The trial court, ... ruled over objection that defendant could not use as a defense Davidson's conduct as a superseding cause. [After the court denied various defense motions, the jury returned a general verdict for the plaintiff, and defendant appealed.]

The evidence supports a finding that the machine was defectively designed. Placement of the buttons on the side required the operator to leave the feeding area open while he actuated the blade. This could be found not only to permit, but actually to encourage, two-person operation. This condition, coupled with inadequate warnings against two-person use, could properly be found to have made the machine "unreasonably dangerous." ...

When the buttons were moved to the side of the machine the danger from one-handed operation of the blade was diminished but the danger of two-person operation was increased. There was evidence that the danger created by a bar being placed across the buttons on the front could have been avoided, for example, by placing one button on each side facing out, thus requiring inward pressure in opposite directions. This design would have discouraged two-person use because the operator would have had to occupy the feeding area while pushing the buttons. In comparison, positioning the buttons to one side not only left open the feeding area for a second person, but required extra effort and time on the part of the single operator. The natural tendency being to save unnecessary effort and time, two-person use was facilitated.... At trial, defendant sought to argue that Davidson's conduct, negligence, and misuse of the bail cutter was the sole proximate cause of plaintiff's injury. The position taken is not that plaintiff's damages should be apportioned by Davidson's comparative causation, but that plaintiff is not entitled to a verdict of any sort against the defendant, because Davidson's conduct and not the defendant's product was the sole proximate cause of the injury. Defendant contends that it is entitled to a new trial because the court committed reversible error in preventing the submission of this superseding cause argument to the jury. A careful consideration of the facts in the case, however, convinces us to the contrary.

The manufacturer or seller faced with an allegation of strict liability in tort for a defective design may have several defenses against liability, for example, product misuse or abnormal use, and what was formerly termed contributory negligence or unreasonable assumption of the risk

These defenses relate to the comparative fault of the plaintiff and are now classified as "plaintiff's misconduct." With respect to a nonparty third person's conduct, however, the manufacturer's sole defense is that of total nonliability based upon the third person's conduct as a superseding cause. In the usual case, no reason of the law stands to prevent a defendant in a products liability action from arguing a third person's negligence or misuse of the product as the sole proximate cause of the plaintiff's injury. The availability of this defense depends, however, on the foreseeability of the alleged misuse or negligence and, on the nature of the alleged design defect.

In New Hampshire, the manufacturer is under a general "duty to design his product reasonably safely for the uses which he can foresee." This duty is necessarily limited " 'to foreseeing the probable results of the normal use of the product or a use that can reasonably be anticipated.' " Thus, before a defendant may successfully argue a third person's negligence or misuse as a superseding cause, he must prove that the negligence or misuse was not reasonably foreseeable.

However, by finding the machine defective in design, the jury has found that two-person use was foreseeable. It was the failure to guard against such foreseeable use that made the machine's design defective. This being so, that same use cannot be a superseding cause, even assuming that Davidson was negligent in not preventing that use. See generally Restatement (Second) of Torts §§ 442, 443 (1965)....

Remanded.

Notes

1. *Defectiveness or superseding cause?* What is the most helpful way to think of the problem represented by *Reid?* (A) It is an issue whether the product is defective at all. (B) It is an issue whether there is legal cause or responsibility for a defective product. Are there other courts that treat misuse of a product as bearing on a different issue?

2. *Plaintiff's misuse as superseding cause.* We saw in Chapter 9, § 4 that some courts may regard a plaintiff's unforeseeable negligence as a superseding cause of harm, barring the plaintiff's recovery on proximate cause grounds. In *Hood v. Ryobi America Corp.*, 181 F.3d 608 (4th Cir.1999), the plaintiff was injured when a blade detached from a miter saw he was using. The plaintiff had removed the saw's guards in contravention of unambiguous warnings. In his suit against the manufacturer, *held*, summary judgment for defendant was proper. The plaintiff's act of alteration was the superseding cause of his harm. If the alternation had been foreseeable to the manufacturer, would the analysis and outcome change?

In *Jeld-Wen, Inc. v. Gamble*, 256 Va. 144, 501 S.E.2d 393 (1998), parents sued a window and screen manufacturer for negligence and breach of warranty after their infant pushed on the screen and then fell two stories to the ground when it gave way. Could the child's own "misuse" constitute a complete defense? What do you see as the key arguments?

3. *Foreseeability of misuse.* Some misuse is foreseeable. The manufacturer must design a product reasonably in the light of known or foreseeable misuses. Thus the usual rule is that if a car will collapse when it is in a foreseeable collision, it may be defective, even though the manufacturer never intended it to be crashed. *Turner v. General Motors Corp.*, 584 S.W.2d 844 (Tex.1979); *Slone v. General Motors Corp.*, 249 Va. 520, 457 S.E.2d 51 (1995). Foreseeability has also become the test for bystander injury. When misuse is foreseeable and a reasonable alternative design would have prevented harm from the misuse, the manufacturer cannot avoid liability on the

ground that the product was not defective or that the defect was not a proximate cause. See, e.g., *Perkins v. Wilkinson Sword, Inc.*, 83 Ohio St.3d 507, 700 N.E.2d 1247 (1998)(rejecting argument by cigarette lighter manufacturer that it did not have to make its lighters childproof since children are not the intended users). Bear in mind, however, that in some cases a plaintiff's "misuse" might be regarded as a form of contributory fault or assumed risk, with whatever defensive advantage those doctrines might produce.

4. *Foreseeability of excessive risk.* As always, it looks as if "foreseeability" is a kind of shorthand expression. Many harms can be foreseen but foreseeability probably refers only to those harms that are foreseeable and also unreasonably risky under the circumstances. It is surely possible to foresee almost any harm from a product, but since some foreseeable risks are reasonable, the product is not necessarily defective merely because harm can be foreseen. So, once again, you cannot take the term literally: foreseeability is necessary but not sufficient to establish liability.

5. *Shifting responsibility.* Granted that the machine is defective in *Reid*, should a manufacturer nevertheless be permitted to shift responsibility to the employer, if the employer actually knows of the danger at the time of purchase? In *Robinson v. Reed–Prentice Div. of Package Mach. Co.*, 49 N.Y.2d 471, 426 N.Y.S.2d 717, 403 N.E.2d 440 (1980), the defendant manufactured and sold a plastics molding machine to the employer, who wished to use it to mold plastic beads on a long string. The machine was equipped with a gate so that the operators' hands could not be in the molding area, but the employer cut a hole in it so that the operator could put his hands into the area and move the string or cord for continuous molding. This facilitated production, but it completely destroyed the safety feature. An operator's hands were seriously injured. Evidence showed that the manufacturer knew that the safety gate it had supplied made it impossible for the employer to mold beads on strings. The manufacturer also knew that other like machines had been modified and that in all probability this one would be modified as well. The court held that the manufacturer was not strictly liable. "Substantial modifications of a product from its original condition by a third party . . . are not the responsibility of the manufacturer. . . . Principles of foreseeability . . . are inapposite where a third party affirmatively abuses a product by consciously by-passing built-in safety features." Cf. *Snyder v. LTG Lufttechnische GmbH*, 955 S.W.2d 252 (Tenn.1997)(evidence that plaintiff's employer removed a safety device from its cotton press, resulting in plaintiff's injury, admissible to prove that product was not defective).

6. *Well-known dangers.* If a product's danger is well-known and generally understood, should the manufacturer be liable for foreseeable abuse? Manufacturers of alcohol can certainly foresee that users of that substance will on occasion, or even very often, become intoxicated and harm themselves or others. Is foreseeability of this misuse enough to make the manufacturer prima facie liable? In *Joseph E. Seagram & Sons, Inc. v. McGuire*, 814 S.W.2d 385 (Tex.1991) the plaintiffs were alcoholics suing the manufacturers and distributors of the brands they drank. They claimed that the defendants depicted alcohol as safe when in fact it was not and that the defendants should have warned them of the danger and the addictive quality

of alcohol. The court held that the danger of alcohol in causing alcoholism has been generally known and that no duty was owed the plaintiffs.

7. *Statutory solutions.* In some states, statutes resulting from "tort reform" initiatives by defense groups have addressed the issue just raised. A California statute provides:

(a) In a product liability action, a manufacturer or seller shall not be liable if both of the following apply:

(1) The product is inherently unsafe and the product is known to be unsafe by the ordinary consumer who consumes the product with the ordinary knowledge common to the community.

(2) The product is a common consumer product intended for personal consumption, such as sugar, castor oil, alcohol, and butter, as identified in comment i to Section 402A of the Restatement (Second) of Torts.

CAL. CIV. CODE § 1714.45. Similar provisions have been enacted in other states as well. E.g., N.J. STAT. ANN. § 2A:58C–3(a)(2).

VAUGHN v. NISSAN MOTOR CORPORATION IN U.S.A., INC., 77 F.3d 736 (4th Cir.1996). The defendant manufactured a car called a Nissan Pulsar. Its voltage regulator failed, allegedly because of bad design and construction. This caused excessive current, which caused the battery fluid to boil. The plaintiff-driver claimed that fumes entered the car and caused her to suffer vocal chord dysfunction and reactive airway dysfunction, a severe asthma. The defendant argued that the plaintiff, who had been abused as a child, suffered from "somatization disorder," a psychological tendency to generate illnesses that have no apparent physiological cause and that there was no physical basis for her injury. Governing law adopted the older Restatement's consumer expectation test. On this basis, the trial judge instructed the jury that it could find a causal defect if the plaintiff inhaled the fumes, suffered asthma as a result, and was an ordinary consumer. The jury, so instructed, found for the defendant. *Held,* the instruction was error. The ordinary consumer is the test of a defect. But if a defect exists, the plaintiff need not be an ordinary consumer or suffer only damages that an ordinary consumer would suffer. This is borne out by the allergy cases. If a manufacturer should be aware that an appreciable number of consumers are unusually susceptible to injury from the product, it is under a duty to warn those with such unusual reactions.

c. *Misuse, Defectiveness, Warnings, and Disclaimers*

Warnings and misuse. Misuse is intimately related to questions about warnings, instructions, and obvious or generally known dangers. For instance, in *Hughes v. Magic Chef,* if Magic Chef had given no instructions or warnings about the number or location of pilot lights, it might be quite easy to say that the product was defective for lack of a warning or instructions and by the same token that the plaintiff's failure to light the third pilot was entirely foreseeable. Conversely, if the user is fully shielded by instructions and warnings, his violation of instructions or failure to heed warnings may quite easily count as an unforeseeable misuse. Cf. *Hood, supra* note 2.

Disclaimers. Granted that a manufacturer can exert a degree of control over the misuse issue by providing warnings or instructions about use, can the manufacturer or other supplier of a product simply disclaim liability altogether? Suppose the product were covered with embossed warnings in bright red letters saying "This product is dangerous. Use it at your own risk. The manufacturer is not liable for any injury that may result." Or suppose the manufacturer provided for a limited remedy by saying that it would be liable for any defects in the product, but only for the cost of repair or replacement.

The usual answer is that the manufacturer cannot avoid liability by disclaimers. The UCC expressly so provides as to warranty claims for personal injury, although it allows disclaimers as to claims for pure economic loss. That is also the generally accepted common law view. The Restatement of Products Liability provides in § 18 that disclaimers do not bar or reduce otherwise valid claims for harms to persons, but takes no position about the validity of disclaimers for harm to other property other than the product itself. See RESTATEMENT OF PRODUCTS LIABILITY §§ 18 & 21, cmt. f.

Suppose the manufacturer or supplier sells an automobile that is dangerous if driven but perfectly harmless if used for scrap metal or old parts and tells the buyer, "this is for parts or scrap only, not to be driven." Suppose the buyer is a 16–year-old who actually drives the car and is injured when it cannot be controlled. Is the manufacturer's description and sale for a limited purpose a warning or a disclaimer? If it is a warning, is the buyer's misuse nevertheless foreseeable? And if it is foreseeable, is the risk great enough to justify imposing liability upon the seller?

REFERENCE: DOBBS ON TORTS § 370–71 (2000).

§ 10. COMPLIANCE WITH OVERRIDING STANDARDS—STATUTE, SPECIFICATIONS AND FEDERAL PREEMPTION

a. *Compliance With Statute*

The traditional view is that while violation of a statute may be negligence per se, compliance with the statute does not conclusively demonstrate the absence of negligence. This is sometimes expressed by saying that the statute provides a minimum standard, a floor and not a ceiling on the defendant's duty. Compliance with a statute may be relevant, however, sometimes as one fact among many tending to indicate that the defendant was not negligent. For this reason, evidence of compliance with government regulations or statutes may be admitted, although compliance is not itself a defense. Statutes may make similar provisions. The Restatement Third is in accord, providing that compliance is to be considered but does not preclude a finding, as a matter of law, that the product was defective in particular cases. RESTATEMENT OF PRODUCTS LIABILITY § 4(b) (1998). What problems of justice or policy would you anticipate if compliance with statute were made a complete defense?

RAMIREZ v. PLOUGH, INC., 6 Cal.4th 539, 25 Cal.Rptr.2d 97, 863 P.2d 167 (1993). The defendant manufactured aspirin for children. It gave a warning about the very serious Reye's syndrome that was associated with use of aspirin by children under certain circumstances. Although the defendant used Spanish-language advertisements to reach the Hispanic market, it did not include warnings in Spanish. It is a fact that many Hispanics are not literate in English. Jorge Ramirez' mother was not. Having no warning intelligible to her, she gave him aspirin during a period of illness when he might have been at serious risk for Reye's syndrome. In fact he developed that condition: severe neurological damage, blindness, spastic quadriplegia and mental retardation. FDA regulations require a warning about Reye's syndrome. But, except for Puerto Rico and areas where some other language predominates, the FDA only requires a warning in English. California statutes were similar. In an action against the defendant for Ramirez' injury, *held,* the defendant was under no duty to provide a Spanish-language warning. "Given the existence of a statute expressly requiring that package warnings on nonprescription drugs be in English, we think it reasonable to infer that the Legislature has deliberately chosen not to require that manufacturers also include warnings in foreign languages. The same inference is warranted on the federal level. The FDA's regulations abundantly demonstrate its sensitivity to the issue of foreign-language labeling, and yet the FDA regulations do not require it. Presumably, the FDA has concluded that despite the obvious advantages of multilingual package warnings, the associated problems and costs are such that at present warnings should be mandated only in English." The task of specifying language of warnings is best left to legislators and administrators. This is true even though the duty to warn in a non-English language could be limited to cases in which the defendant advertised in a different language.

TENN. CODE ANN. § 29–28–104

Compliance by a manufacturer or seller with any federal or state statute or administrative regulation existing at the time a product was manufactured and prescribing standards for design, inspection, testing, manufacture, labeling, warning or instructions for use of a product, shall raise a rebuttable presumption that the product is not in an unreasonably dangerous condition in regard to matters covered by these standards.

b. *"Preemption" of Liability Rules by Compliance With Overriding Law: The Cipollone Example*

Federal preemption. Under the United States Constitution, Congress has the power to override state law, as long as it acts within the limits of its own constitutional powers. Congress can effectively forbid the enforcement of state law not only when the state law would conflict directly with federal statutes or regulation, but also when Congress wishes to impose a single scheme of regulation or control. Congress might thus "preempt" state law by (1) occupying the field with heavy regulation so that there is no room left for state law; (2) by passing laws that actually conflict with state laws; or (3) by providing for preemption in particular cases, either expressly or by implication. Even when Congress has expressly provided for preemption, courts must construe the statute to determine what was and what was not preempted. In general, the Supreme Court is reluctant to find preemption of state powers unless the Congress has clearly manifested its purpose. See *Medtronic, Inc. v. Lohr*, 518 U.S. 470, 116 S.Ct. 2240, 135 L.Ed.2d 700 (1996).

Effect in products cases. Preemption can be important in products liability cases. Suppose a federal statute sets a minimum standard for warnings that must be contained on labels of a dangerous product. A state law that required a better warning or additional information would not actually conflict with the federal statute and would therefore not be preempted under the actual conflict rule. Nevertheless, the federal labeling statute might either expressly or impliedly preempt statute law. If it did, the result would be that the manufacturer who complied with the federal statute would not be liable for failing to comply with the state statute.

Preemption is asserted by defendants under many of the important federal statutes and preemption not infrequently operates to bar the plaintiff's claim. For example, in *Geier v. American Honda Motor Co.*, 529 U.S. 1913, 120 S.Ct. 1913, 146 L.Ed.2d 914 (2000), the plaintiff claimed that Honda was negligent in failing to equip its 1987 Accord with a driver's side airbag. The Court decided, 5–4, that plaintiff's state-law claim was impliedly preempted by federal regulations that had sought a "variety and mix of [restraint] devices" in cars in order to "help develop data on comparative effectiveness," give "the industry time to overcome the safety problems and the high production costs associated with airbags," and "facilitate the development of alternative, cheaper, and safer passive restraint systems." To allow the plaintiff to establish that Honda owed a duty under state law to install an airbag in its 1987 Accords would conflict with these federal goals; thus her claim was pre-empted. Federal regulation of medical devices, federal railroad-crossing safety provisions, and federal warning requirements on insecticide or herbicides can all preempt state law and eliminate tort claims, although courts are not all in agreement about particular cases.

The smokers' claim. One important piece of litigation about preemption is the claim that tobacco use causes cancer or is otherwise unhealthy and that it is also addictive. This double-barreled claim makes it somewhat plausible for a cancer victim to argue (1) I didn't know cigarettes could cause cancer when I began smoking; (2) by the time I learned of the danger, I was addicted; (3) the tobacco company should have warned me both of the danger and of the addictive quality of its product.

Federal tobacco warnings. One difficulty for the claimant in such a case is that in 1965 the Congress passed a statute requiring a label on all cigarette packages to the effect that "Smoking May Be Hazardous to Your Health." In 1970 and 1984 the statute was amended to provide a stronger warning. The 1970 statute also provided in so many words:

> No requirement or prohibition based on smoking and health shall be imposed under State law with respect to the advertising or promotion of any cigarettes the packages of which are labeled in conformity with the provisions of this chapter.

The Cipollone holdings. In *Cipollone v. Liggett Group, Inc.*, 505 U.S. 504, 112 S.Ct. 2608, 120 L.Ed.2d 407 (1992) the Supreme Court split three ways about the preemptive effect of the statute. Three of the nine Justices thought NO claims were preempted. The remaining six Justices differed in degree. Two thought ALL cigarette products claims implicating a warning would be preempted, but four others thought that some kinds of claims were preempted and some not. The governing plurality thought if the plaintiff relied upon a legal rule that "constitutes 'a requirement or prohibition based on smoking and health'" then the claim was preempted, otherwise not. This ruling permitted the plaintiff to sue in *Cipollone* for negligent testing of tobacco, but not to sue for advertising that had the effect of undercutting the warning required.

State-law rejection of claims. Recall that the effect of preemption is to eliminate any preempted state law claim. The effect of the Supreme Court's complex and divided rulings in *Cipollone* is to permit some state law claims in tobacco litigation. However, whether state law recognizes any claim that is not preempted is a matter for the states to decide individually.

Plaintiff-favorable preemption. The preemption discussed above may effectively destroy the plaintiff's claim. But some federal preemption works differently. Instead of effectively enacting a federal defense, some federal statutes enact a federal claim by granting the plaintiff a cause of action more favorable than he had under state law. Others may enact an alternative system of liability, with different claims, defenses, and procedures.

c. Compliance With Specification: Government Contractors and Others

BOYLE v. UNITED TECHNOLOGIES CORPORATION[1]

Supreme Court of the United States, 1988.
487 U.S. 500, 108 S.Ct. 2510, 101 L.Ed.2d 442.

JUSTICE SCALIA delivered the opinion of the Court. . . .

I

On April 27, 1983, David A. Boyle, a United States Marine helicopter copilot, was killed when the CH–53D helicopter in which he was flying crashed off the coast of Virginia Beach, Virginia, during a training exercise. Although Boyle survived the impact of the crash, he was unable to escape from the helicopter and drowned. Boyle's father, petitioner here, brought this diversity action in Federal District Court against the Sikorsky Division of United Technologies Corporation (Sikorsky), which built the helicopter for the United States.

At trial, petitioner presented two theories of liability under Virginia tort law that were submitted to the jury. First, petitioner alleged that Sikorsky had defectively repaired a device called the servo in the helicopter's automatic flight control system, which allegedly malfunctioned and caused the crash. Second, petitioner alleged that Sikorsky had defectively designed the copilot's emergency escape system: the escape hatch opened out instead of in (and was therefore ineffective in a submerged craft because of water pressure), and access to the escape hatch handle was obstructed by other equipment. The jury returned a general verdict in favor of petitioner and awarded him $725,000. The District Court denied Sikorsky's motion for judgment notwithstanding the verdict.

[The Court of Appeals reversed and remanded with directions that judgment be entered for Sikorsky, partly because it was protected by what the court called the "military contractor defense."]

II

[PRE-EMPTION OR DISPLACEMENT OF STATE LAW BY
FEDERAL COURT LAW—"FEDERAL INTERESTS"]

Petitioner's broadest contention is that, in the absence of legislation specifically immunizing Government contractors from liability for design defects, there is no basis for judicial recognition of such a defense. We disagree. In most fields of activity, to be sure, this Court has refused to find federal pre-emption of state law in the absence of either a clear statutory prescription. But we have held that a few areas, involving "uniquely federal interests," are so committed by the Constitution and

---

1. Headings in the text are inserted by the editors for convenience of the reader in locating material.

laws of the United States to federal control that state law is pre-empted and replaced, where necessary, by federal law of a content prescribed (absent explicit statutory directive) by the courts—so-called "federal common law." The dispute in the present case borders upon two areas that we have found to involve such "uniquely federal interests." We have held that obligations to and rights of the United States under its contracts are governed exclusively by federal law. The present case does not involve an obligation to the United States under its contract, but rather liability to third persons. That liability may be styled one in tort, but it arises out of performance of the contract. . . .

Another area that we have found to be of peculiarly federal concern, warranting the displacement of state law, is the civil liability of federal officials for actions taken in the course of their duty. We have held in many contexts that the scope of that liability is controlled by federal law. The present case involves an independent contractor performing its obligation under a procurement contract, rather than an official performing his duty as a federal employee, but there is obviously implicated the same interest in getting the Government's work done.

We think the reasons for considering these closely related areas to be of "uniquely federal" interest apply as well to the civil liabilities arising out of the performance of federal procurement contracts. We have come close to holding as much. In Yearsley v. W.A. Ross Construction Co., 309 U.S. 18, 60 S.Ct. 413, 84 L.Ed. 554 (1940), we rejected an attempt by a landowner to hold a construction contractor liable under state law for the erosion of 95 acres caused by the contractor's work in constructing dikes for the Government. We said that "if [the] authority to carry out the project was validly conferred, that is, if what was done was within the constitutional power of Congress, there is no liability on the part of the contractor for executing its will." The federal interest justifying this holding surely exists as much in procurement contracts as in performance contracts; we see no basis for a distinction.

Moreover, it is plain that the Federal Government's interest in the procurement of equipment is implicated by suits such as the present one—even though the dispute is one between private parties. . . . The imposition of liability on Government contractors will directly affect the terms of Government contracts: either the contractor will decline to manufacture the design specified by the Government, or it will raise its price. Either way, the interests of the United States will be directly affected.

[NO FEDERAL DISPLACEMENT OF STATE LAW WITHOUT A CONFLICT—ILLUSTRATIVE CASES]

That the procurement of equipment by the United States is an area of uniquely federal interest does not, however, end the inquiry. That merely establishes a necessary, not a sufficient, condition for the displacement of state law. Displacement will occur only where, as we have variously described, a "significant conflict" exists between an identifiable "federal policy or interest and the [operation] of state law," or the application of state law would "frustrate specific objectives" of federal legislation....

If, for example, the United States contracts for the purchase and installation of an air conditioning unit, specifying the cooling capacity but not the precise manner of construction, a state law imposing upon the manufacturer of such units a duty of care to include a certain safety feature would not be a duty identical to anything promised the Government, but neither would it be contrary. The contractor could comply with both its contractual obligations and the state-prescribed duty of care. No one suggests that state law would generally be pre-empted in this context.

[In the] present case, however, ... the state-imposed duty of care that is the asserted basis of the contractor's liability (specifically, the duty to equip helicopters with the sort of escape-hatch mechanism petitioner claims was necessary) is precisely contrary to the duty imposed by the Government contract (the duty to manufacture and deliver helicopters with the sort of escape-hatch mechanism shown by the specifications). Even in this sort of situation, it would be unreasonable to say that there is always a "significant conflict" between the state law and a federal policy or interest. If, for example, a federal procurement officer orders, by model number, a quantity of stock helicopters that happen to be equipped with escape hatches opening outward, it is impossible to say that the Government has a significant interest in that particular feature. That would be scarcely more reasonable than saying that a private individual who orders such a craft by model number cannot sue for the manufacturer's negligence because he got precisely what he ordered.

[Principles for Determining Existence of Significant Conflict— Why Feres Does Not Provide the Principle]

In its search for the limiting principle to identify those situations in which a "significant conflict" with federal policy or interests does arise, the Court of Appeals, in the lead case upon which its opinion here relied, identified as the source of the conflict the Feres doctrine, under which the Federal Tort Claims Act does not cover injuries to armed service personnel in the course of military service. See Feres v. United States, 340 U.S. 135, 71 S.Ct. 153, 95 L.Ed. 152 (1950). Military contractor liability would conflict with this doctrine, the Fourth Circuit reasoned, since the increased cost of the contractor's tort liability would be added to the price of the contract, and "[s]uch pass-through costs would ... defeat the purpose of the immunity for military accidents conferred upon the government itself." Other courts upholding the defense have embraced similar reasoning.

We do not adopt this analysis because it seems to us that the Feres doctrine, in its application to the present problem, logically produces results that are in some respects too broad and in some respects too narrow. Too broad, because if the Government contractor defense is to prohibit suit against the manufacturer whenever Feres would prevent suit against the Government, then even injuries caused to military personnel by a helicopter purchased from stock (in our example above), or by any standard equipment purchased by the Government, would be covered. Since Feres prohibits all service-related tort claims against the Government, a contractor defense that rests upon it should prohibit all service-related tort claims against the manufacturer—making inexplicable the three limiting criteria for contractor immunity (which we will discuss presently) that the Court of Appeals adopted.

On the other hand, reliance on Feres produces (or logically should produce) results that are in another respect too narrow. Since that doctrine covers only service-related injuries, and not injuries caused by the military to civilians, it could not be invoked to prevent, for example, a civilian's suit against the manufacturer of fighter planes, based on a state tort theory, claiming harm from what is alleged to be needlessly high levels of noise produced by the jet engines. Yet we think that the character of the jet engines the Government orders for its fighter planes cannot be regulated by state tort law, no more in suits by civilians than in suits by members of the armed services.

[DISCRETIONARY FUNCTION IMMUNITY AS THE GOVERNING PRINCIPLE]

There is, however, a statutory provision that demonstrates the potential for, and suggests the outlines of, "significant conflict" between federal interests and state law in the context of government procurement. In the Federal Tort Claims Act (FTCA), Congress authorized damages to be recovered against the United States for harm caused by the negligent or wrongful conduct of Government employees, to the extent that a private person would be liable under the law of the place where the conduct occurred. 28 U.S.C. 1346(b). It excepted from this consent to suit, however,

> "[a]ny claim . . . based upon the exercise or performance or the failure to exercise or perform a discretionary function or duty on the part of a federal agency or an employee of the Government, whether or not the discretion involved be abused."

We think that the selection of the appropriate design for military equipment to be used by our Armed Forces is assuredly a discretionary function within the meaning of this provision. It often involves not merely engineering analysis but judgment as to the balancing of many technical, military, and even social considerations, including specifically the trade-off between greater safety and greater combat effectiveness. And we are further of the view that permitting "second-guessing" of these judgments, through state tort suits against contractors would produce the same effect sought to be avoided by the FTCA exemption. The financial burden of judgments against the contractors would ultimately be passed through, substantially if not totally, to the United

States itself, since defense contractors will predictably raise their prices to cover, or to insure against, contingent liability for the Government-ordered designs. To put the point differently: It makes little sense to insulate the Government against financial liability for the judgment that a particular feature of military equipment is necessary when the Government produces the equipment itself, but not when it contracts for the production. In sum, we are of the view that state law which holds Government contractors liable for design defects in military equipment does in some circumstances present a "significant conflict" with federal policy and must be displaced.

[Formulating the Defense]

. . . Liability for design defects in military equipment cannot be imposed, pursuant to state law, when (1) the United States approved reasonably precise specifications; (2) the equipment conformed to those specifications; and (3) the supplier warned the United States about the dangers in the use of the equipment that were known to the supplier but not to the United States. The first two of these conditions assure that the suit is within the area where the policy of the "discretionary function" would be frustrated—i.e., they assure that the design feature in question was considered by a Government officer, and not merely by the contractor itself. The third condition is necessary because, in its absence, the displacement of state tort law would create some incentive for the manufacturer to withhold knowledge of risks, since conveying that knowledge might disrupt the contract but withholding it would produce no liability. We adopt this provision lest our effort to protect discretionary functions perversely impede them by cutting off information highly relevant to the discretionary decision.

We have considered the alternative formulation of the Government contractor defense, urged upon us by petitioner, which was adopted by the Eleventh Circuit in *Shaw v. Grumman Aerospace Corp.*, 778 F.2d 736, 746 (1985). That would preclude suit only if (1) the contractor did not participate, or participated only minimally, in the design of the defective equipment; or (2) the contractor timely warned the Government of the risks of the design and notified it of alternative designs reasonably known by it, and the Government, although forewarned, clearly authorized the contractor to proceed with the dangerous design. While this formulation may represent a perfectly reasonable tort rule, it is not a rule designed to protect the federal interest embodied in the "discretionary function" exemption. The design ultimately selected may well reflect a significant policy judgment by Government officials whether or not the contractor rather than those officials developed the design. In addition, it does not seem to us sound policy to penalize, and thus deter, active contractor participation in the design process, placing the contractor at risk unless it identifies all design defects.

[Although the Court agreed with the Court of Appeals' statement of the defense, it remanded to permit the Court of Appeals to state its assessment of the evidence more clearly.]

So ordered.

[Dissenting opinion omitted.]

Notes

1. *Manufacturing defects.* What if the plaintiff is injured by a product made for the government and to government specification, but the injury results because of a manufacturing rather than a design defect? What if the plaintiff claims that the contractor could have supplied a warning to make the product safer?

2. *Boyle as a compliance case. Boyle* turns on the defendant's compliance with overriding law affecting product design. If the plaintiff's injury results from the contractor's non-compliance rather than its compliance with specifications, the *Boyle* defense would not apply. Notice that the compliance required to trigger the *Boyle* defense, however, is not a compliance with a legislative enactment, but with specifications used by the government in making a private contract.

3. *The rationale in Boyle.* The government contractor or government specification defense established in *Boyle* does not seem to cover all contractor cases. The defense is not merely a tort defense; it is a "preemption" or "displacement" of state law by overriding federal law. That displacement occurs, according to Justice Scalia, only when (a) there is a significant federal interest at stake and (b) the state law demands would significantly conflict with it. The test for determining whether there is such a conflict is found in the discretionary immunity we first saw in connection with the Federal Tort Claims Act. Is Justice Scalia saying, then, that the contractor's compliance with specifications will provide it a defense only when the government itself would be immune under the discretionary immunity?

4. *Which controls—the formula or the rationale?* In the end Justice Scalia's opinion approves a formula previously used by some courts of appeal. This provides that the contractor is immune "when (1) the United States approved reasonably precise specifications; (2) the equipment conformed to those specifications; and (3) the supplier warned the United States about the dangers in the use of the equipment that were known to the supplier but not to the United States." Is this formula the same as or narrower than the rationale? Does it require that the government's decisions about contract specifications be within the discretionary immunity?

5. In *Richardson v. McKnight,* 521 U.S. 399, 117 S.Ct. 2100, 138 L.Ed.2d 540 (1997), the Court held that the qualified immunity accorded to government employees in § 1983 actions does not extend to prison guards who are employees of private prison management firm. The Court stressed that the private firm had "limited direct supervision by the government." Is this consistent with *Boyle?*

6. *Is Boyle limited to military contractors or product manufacturers?* Up until *Boyle,* some of the courts of appeal had been much taken with the military aspects in government contractor cases and some had even referred to the "military contractor" defense. These cases emphasized the impropriety of judicial interference with military decisions and they grounded the

defense partly in those concerns. Does the *Boyle* rationale make it clear that the defense is much broader than that?

7. *State (not federal) contractors. Boyle* was distinguished in *Conner v. Quality Coach, Inc.*, 561 Pa. 397, 750 A.2d 823 (Pa. 2000). In that case, a private company had contracted with a state agency to provide modifications on the vehicles of disabled persons. The plaintiff alleged that the defendant contractor utilized a defective design for its brake/throttle control, resulting in an injury-causing accident. The defendant argued that it was immune under *Boyle,* but the state court disagreed. *Boyle* is limited to federal contractors. In Pennsylvania, the courts have abolished common law immunity, leaving only immunities established by the legislature, which has established none here. Contractors are protected when they reasonably rely upon specifications, but only because in that case they are not negligent at all. When they participate in the design decision, as here, they are liable for their negligence. Any general policy to lower government procurement costs by protecting government contractors is "lacking in empirical support," and is "ill-suited to serve as a counterweight to the policies favoring just compensation underlying our tort system."

8. *What counts as "approval."* What counts as government "approval" of specifications? The Court in *Boyle* specifically rejects the *Shaw* formula, which denied the contractor any defense if the contractor itself substantially participated in the design. The Supreme Court thought this not sufficiently protective of government interests, because the government might make "significant policy judgment" even if the contractor itself designed the equipment and the government only "approved" that design.

The result, however, is that the contractor may defectively design equipment which is dangerous to many citizens, and escape the normal state-law liability merely because the government then approves the design and adopts it as a specification for its procurement contract. Most government agencies do not consider themselves to be in charge of public safety and probably do not invest heavily in designing products with that safety in mind. So it may be that the Court has created a substantial hiatus in the web of safety incentives for products. In contrast, state tort law would probably ordinarily impose liability upon the drafter of specifications (like the contractor). E.g., ILL. ST. ANN. ch. 110 ¶ 2–621 (c) (1). In the light of this, would you expect a government "rubber stamp" acceptance of contractor-drawn specifications to count as approval? See DOBBS ON TORTS § 274 (2000).

9. *Private contractors providing products to private customers.* Suppose the local bus company orders a fleet of buses, specifying a gas tank in a dangerous location and in fact the gas tank blows up when the bus is rammed by a car. Would an injured bus passenger have a products liability claim against the manufacturer?

§ 11. STATUTES OF LIMITATION

1. *Choice of statute.* If a plaintiff sues on a negligence or strict tort liability theory, most statutes will expressly cover the claim under provisions for tort cases or personal injury cases, and there will be little problem in choosing which statute applies. If the plaintiff sues on a warranty theory, or includes a warranty theory among others, the

statute of limitations intended to govern "contract" or warranty claims may apply. The UCC in fact specifies in § 2–725(1):

> An action for breach of any contract for sale must be commenced within four years after the cause of action has accrued.

A number of courts have held that this provision governs a warranty claim, even where the damage claimed is for personal injury. This is important in a state–Alabama, for instance–in which strict tort liability is not accepted as such and in which most strict liability may be based on a warranty theory.

Other courts, however, seem more interested in determining whether the underlying claim is the kind tort law has sought to protect, and in these courts the fact that "warranty" is the theory might not be determinative if the underlying claim is a claim for physical harm to person or property of the same kind a products tort liability case might cover. The New York Court of Appeals said something like this in *Victorson v. Bock Laundry Machine Co.*, 37 N.Y.2d 395, 373 N.Y.S.2d 39, 335 N.E.2d 275, 91 A.L.R.3d 445 (1975). Quoting Prosser on Torts, the court said that "The fundamental difference between tort and contract lies in the nature of the interests protected." Even if warranty is part of the verbiage used to state the claim, if physical harm is the damage claimed, the warranty statute of limitations is inappropriate, and whatever statute governs torts or personal injury claims would be chosen instead. This view is consistent with the distinction drawn in Section 3, supra, between economic harm, for which warranty is especially suited, and physical harm, for which tort doctrine seems to work better.

2. *Accrual of the claim.* (A) *Sales or later date.* If the claim is for personal injury and based solely on tort doctrine, the tort statute, however that may be phrased in a particular state, will govern. When will the statute begin to run? In tort law this ordinarily occurs when injury is inflicted, subject to the discovery rule. Certainly, it does *not* begin to run on the date of sale. If the claim is based on a warranty theory, however, and if the UCC statute is applied, it is quite possible that the statute begins to run from the time the product is sold by the defendant. This is, in fact, the express provision of UCC § 2–725(2): "A breach of warranty occurs when tender of delivery is made...." Although the UCC statute is for four years, and although this is longer than most tort statutes, it begins running before injury. In *Waldrop v. Peabody Galion Corp.*, 423 So.2d 145 (Ala.1982), the defendants sold (or "tendered delivery" of) a garbage truck in 1974. The plaintiff, a city employee working on the truck was injured, allegedly by a defect, in 1976. At that time the statute had already been running two years. When his suit was actually brought in 1979 it was barred by the four year statute. If he had been able to sue on a tort theory and a three-year tort statute had applied, his suit would have been timely.

(B) *Injury or later date.* Most states will not force an injured plaintiff to use warranty theory to pursue a products liability claim, but will permit or even require use of a tort theory instead. Under the general statutes of limitation applied to tort claims, the claim does not accrue until injury; and the statute cannot start running before injury. Under the discovery rule seen in Chapter 9, the statute does not begin to run until the harm is or should have been discovered.

3. *Statutes of repose.* (A) *The problem.* The typical statute of limitations in tort cases has run from the time of injury or some later date. After the initial explosive expansion of product liability, manufacturers and others in the commercial world exerted considerable effort to restrict liability. One special problem was the "long tail" of possible liabilities that could occur. A product sold in 1959 might not cause harm until 1999. If the victim sued immediately, he would not be barred by an ordinary statute of limitations, which does not begin to run until injury occurs, or later. But this would mean that a manufacturer would have to plan for potential liabilities 20, 30, 40 years into the future, or even more.

(B) *Statutory response.* With ideas like these in mind, many legislatures have passed statutes of "ultimate repose," under which products claims are barred if injury occurs more than, say, 12 years after the product was initially sold or delivered.

Similar statutes of repose have been passed in some states to protect architects, engineers, real estate developers and doctors. All these are structured like the products statute: the statutory period is a long one, but it begins to run from the time the product was sold, or the work or service completed.

(C) *Constitutionality.* Some of these statutes have been held unconstitutional under the provisions of state constitutions. New Hampshire also held its statute to be in violation of its State constitution partly because it denied equal protection to products plaintiffs and partly because it denied reasonable access to courts. The Court commented:

> The unreasonableness inherent in a statute which eliminates a plaintiff's cause of action before the wrong may reasonably be discovered was noted by Judge Frank [who] condemned the Alice in Wonderland' effect of such a result:
>
> > 'Except in topsy-turvy land, you can't die before you are conceived, or be divorced before you marry, or harvest a crop never planted, or burn down a house never built, or miss a train running on a non-existent railroad. For substantially similar reasons, it has always heretofore been accepted, as a sort of logical "axiom," that a statute of limitations does not begin to run against a cause of action before that cause of action exists, i.e., before a judicial remedy is available to a plaintiff.'

Heath v. Sears, Roebuck & Co., 123 N.H. 512, 464 A.2d 288 (1983).

The quotation from Judge Frank is a beautiful example of effective rhetoric. Is there, however, any rule of state constitutions that requires the legislature to accept logical axioms? Given the difficult problem, can you be sure that the solution of the legislature is not only unjust but a violation of the constitution? Local constitutional provisions are most important in these cases.

(D) *Continuing duty to warn.* Whatever the constitutionally of the statutes of repose in the ordinary case, can they apply at all to the case in which the defendant's liability is based, not upon defect at the time of sale, but upon failure to warn of the defect it discovers after sale? Five years after a car is marketed, the manufacturer discovers a steering defect and does nothing. Unwarned, the plaintiff has a horrible wreck six years after that. Should the statute of repose apply to such a case? See, e.g., *Watkins v. Ford Motor Co.*, 190 F.3d 1213 (11th Cir.1999). What if liability is based on failure to warn of an unknown defect?

REFERENCE: DOBBS ON TORTS § 374 (2000).

SUBCHAPTER D. EXTENDING THE SCOPE OF PRODUCTS LIABILITY

§ 12. BEYOND THE MANUFACTURER OF NEW GOODS

In the earlier days of products liability expansion, there was uncertainty about a good many details. Did this liability extend to all goods, or only to foods or to intimate products? Did it extend to containers, or only the goods themselves? These questions have long since been answered favorably to the consumer, provided only that a defect is proven. This section considers whether strict liability is imposed upon persons besides manufacturers and whether it is imposed for defects besides those in "goods."

a. *Tangible Goods and Property*

1. *Distributors and only distributors.* Persons who count as distributors and only such persons are subject to the products liability rules. All commercial providers of products are distributors. Noncommercial providers generally are not distributors. See RESTATEMENT OF PRODUCTS LIABILITY § 1, cmt. c. For instance, if you are not in the car business, you are not a distributor when you sell your car. The commercial-noncommercial distinction may not fully capture the idea, however. Suppose a non-profit organization devoted to health has a massive continuing program for providing, free, a drug to help respiratory patients and the drug proves to be defective, causing injuries. Could its systematic provision of the drug make it a distributor?

What about a business that sells a product outside its usual line, in a "casual sale?" In *Griffin Industries, Inc. v. Jones*, 975 S.W.2d 100 (Ky.1998), plaintiff brought a products liability case against defendant, which had manufactured and sold to plaintiff's employer a conveyor belt system that caused the injury. The defendant's main business was rendering animal waste. It manufactured the belts for its own use, did not market them, and sold the belts to plaintiff's employer in an isolated transaction. Held, defendant is an "occasional seller," thus not liable in a products suit. See RESTATEMENT OF PRODUCTS LIABILITY § 1, cmt. c.

2. *Retailers, wholesalers, component manufacturers.* Distributors subject to the products rules include manufacturers, wholesalers, and retailers. Under some circumstances, even an endorser, or a franchisor/trademark licensor might be strictly liable for the product that bears the franchise name. See *Torres v. Goodyear Tire & Rubber Co., Inc.*, 163 Ariz. 88, 786 P.2d 939 (1990). The Restatement of Products Liability provides in § 14 that one who "distributes as its own a product manufactured by another" is liable as if it were the manufacturer. A retailer or wholesaler who is held liable usually has an indemnity claim in its favor against the manufacturer.

3. *The former requirement of a sale; lessors.* At one time it was supposed that products liability could be triggered only when there was a "sale" of goods. It now seems well accepted that a technical sale is not required, and a plaintiff injured by the explosion of a defective soft drink bottle in the grocery store recovers whether the explosion occurred after he paid for it or before. And suppliers who do not sell are also liable for defects, provided they are in the business of supplying goods. This covers lessors of goods, for example. What if a retailer gives away chewing gum to shoppers as part of a promotion and the gum proves to be deleterious?

4. *Used goods.* An individual who sells her car is not in the business of selling cars and is thus not liable as a distributor. What about a dealer in used cars? The dealer in used goods may be held liable for negligence, misrepresentation, or breach of any express warranty. The UCC § 2–316 (a) permits exclusion of warranty when selling goods "as is" with all faults. For personal injury cases, strict tort liability represents the most interesting possibility. The cases are somewhat divided. What about letting the commercial seller of used goods use an "as is" disclaimer, even for strict products liability? Do you expect to have more difficulty in judging defectiveness of a used product? What about a used product sold for a limited purpose, as where an old car is sold for scrap metal?

5. *Builders and sellers of real property.* The common law rule was that a contractor who negligently built or repaired real property (including buildings) could not be liable for injuries caused by his negligence once the property was turned over to the owner and accepted by him. This rule no longer holds, and contractors and builders are liable for their negligence.

The law of warranty developed in chattel cases did not historically apply to real property sales. The deed was thought to express the whole obligation of the parties. Since the deed did not express any warranty of safety, there could be no implied warranty at odds with the deed. However, in 1965 New Jersey applied an implied warranty of habitability to the sale of mass production homes by a builder whose failure to install a valve permitted scalding water to flow from a faucet and to burn a child. *Schipper v. Levitt & Sons, Inc.*, 44 N.J. 70, 207 A.2d 314 (1965).

Although the vendor might be liable without privity in such cases, it would seem that only vendors in the business of selling (and perhaps only those in the business of building) houses would be held. Strict liability has also been applied to home builders in some cases. See, e.g., *Hyman v. Gordon*, 35 Cal. App. 3d 769, 111 Cal. Rptr. 262 (1973) (builder-designer of a house could be strictly liable for a design defect because of the dangerous location of a heater). Cf. RESTATEMENT OF PRODUCTS LIABILITY § 19, cmt. e (contractor who sells a building with appliances or other manufactured equipment in it is considered a product seller of that equipment, and builders of pre-fabricated buildings may be considered product sellers with respect to the building itself).

There are, however, decisions refusing to apply strict liability in real property cases, and the issue is not resolved yet in most jurisdictions. If you were suing or defending such an action in a state with no decisions on point, what arguments would you invoke for strict liability? Against it?

6. *Lessors of real property*. Landlords are traditionally not strictly liable for defects in premises; indeed, even their liability for negligence was traditionally limited along the lines seen in Chapter 10. A few states have imposed an implied warranty of habitability on lessors, but most of these cases involve only economic harm, that is, the lessened value of the leased premises because of the defects, or else cases in which the lessor had notice of a defect and did not correct it. If lessors are held strictly liable, should this include any lessor, or only lessors of multiple unit dwellings? Would it matter whether the premises were furnished or unfurnished? Whether the lease was a short-term, month-to-month, or long-term, for years, lease?

In *Becker v. IRM Corp.*, 38 Cal.3d 454, 698 P.2d 116, 213 Cal.Rptr. 213 (1985) the California Court imposed strict liability upon landlords for premises defects. Ten years later, however, it repudiated that decision in *Peterson v. Superior Court*, 10 Cal.4th 1185, 43 Cal.Rptr.2d 836, 899 P.2d 905 (1995). The court reasoned that the landlord was not in a stream of commerce in the defective goods and not in a good position to urge the manufacturer of the defective item to make it safer. It said the landlord is more in the position of a seller of used goods and consumers cannot expect the same safety. The court also feared economic ruin for landlords. Thus it thought the law of negligence was quite adequate. It did not mention nondelegable duties.

Lead-based paint has poisoned children for many years. When the paint peels, small children pull the peelings off the wall and put them in their mouths. Should landlords be strictly liable for using or failing to remove such paint, or should the debilitated child hope that someone will sue his parents for the permanent injuries? Compare *Ankiewicz v. Kinder*, 408 Mass. 792, 563 N.E.2d 684 (1990) with *Gore v. People's Savings Bank*, 235 Conn. 360, 665 A.2d 1341 (1995).

b. *Intangibles—Services and Endorsements*

NEWMARK v. GIMBEL'S INC.

Supreme Court of New Jersey, 1969.
54 N.J. 585, 258 A.2d 697.

FRANCIS, J.

[The plaintiff, Mrs. Newmark, went to one of defendant's beauty shops where she had a standing appointment. Her regular operator, Valante, made a recommendation about a permanent and she accepted it. During the treatment she felt a "burning" on more than one occasion, and Valante took steps to diminish it. However her forehead later blistered and her hair fell out. A dermatologist concluded she had contact dermatitis resulting from the application of the permanent solution. The trial court dismissed Mrs. Newmark's claim in warranty on the ground that the defendant was rendering a service, not making a sale. The Appellate Division reversed this, holding that there might be an implied warranty as to the lotion applied.]

Valante identified the permanent wave solution as "Candle Glow," a product of Helene Curtis. He said the liquid was mild but could damage a scalp which had scratches on it or could cause a sting if the solution were rubbed into the scalp. He applied the solution as it came from the original package or container, and his experience had shown that a tingling or burning sensation, the degree varying with different persons, was fairly common. The label on the package contained a caveat for the beauty operator. It said:

> "Always wear rubber gloves when giving a wave. Make sure patrons hair and scalp are in condition to receive a cold wave. Never brush or rub the scalp vigorously either before or after shampooing. If the scalp is excessively tender or shows evidence of sores or abrasions, the wave should not be given. Ask the patron her previous experience with cold waves to be sure she does not have a sensitivity to waving lotion."

Mrs. Newmark did not see this label, and there is nothing in the record to indicate Valante asked her about any previous experience with cold waves. It does appear, however, that she had four permanent waves without ill effects after the incident involved here and before trial of this case. . . .

If the permanent wave lotion were sold to Mrs. Newmark by defendants for home consumption or application or to enable her to give herself the permanent wave, unquestionably an implied warranty of fitness for that purpose would have been an integral incident of the sale. Basically defendants argue that if, in addition to recommending the use of a lotion or other product and supplying it for use, they applied it, such fact (the application) would have the effect of lessening their liability to the patron by eliminating warranty and by limiting their responsibility to the issue of negligence. There is no just reason why it should. On the contrary by taking on the administration of the product in addition to recommending and supplying it, they might increase the scope of their liability, if the method of administration were improper (a result not suggested on this appeal because the jury found no negligence).

The transaction, in our judgment, is a hybrid partaking of incidents of a sale and a service. It is really partly the rendering of service, and partly the supplying of goods for a consideration. Accordingly, we agree with the Appellate division that an implied warranty of fitness of the products used in giving the permanent wave exists with no less force than it would have in the case of a simple sale. Obviously in permanent wave operations the product is taken into consideration in fixing the price of the service. The no-separate-charge argument puts excessive emphasis on form and downgrades the overall substance of the transaction. If the beauty parlor operator bought and applied the permanent wave solution to her own hair and suffered injury thereby, her action in warranty or strict liability in tort . . . against the manufacturer-seller of the product clearly would be maintainable because the basic transaction would have arisen from a conventional type of sale. It does not accord with logic to deny a similar right to a patron against the beauty parlor operator or the manufacturer when the purchase and sale were made in anticipation of and for the purpose of use of the product on the patron who would be charged for its use. Common sense demands that such patron be deemed a consumer as to both manufacturer and beauty parlor operator.

A beauty parlor operator in soliciting patronage assures the public that he or she possesses adequate knowledge and skill to do the things and to apply the solution necessary to produce the permanent wave in the hair of the customer. When a patron responds to the solicitation she does so confident that any product used in the shop has come from a reliable origin and can be trusted not to injure her. She places herself in the hands of the operator relying upon his or her expertise both in the selection of the products to be used on her and in the method of using them. The ministrations and the products employed on her are under the control and selection of the operator; the patron is a mere passive recipient. . . .

It seems to us that the policy reasons for imposing warranty liability in the case of ordinary sales are equally applicable to a commercial transaction such as that existing in this case between a beauty parlor operator and a patron.

Defendants claim that to hold them to strict liability would be contrary to Magrine v. Krasnica, 94 N.J. Super. 228, 227 A.2d 539 (Cty. Ct. 1967), aff'd sub nom. Magrine v. Spector, 100 N.J. Super. 223, 241 A.2d 637 (App.Div.1968), aff'd 53 N.J. 259, 250 A.2d 129 (1969). We cannot agree. Magrine, a patient of the defendant-dentist, was injured when a hypodermic needle being used, concededly with due care, to administer a local anesthetic broke off in his gum or jaw. The parties agreed that the break resulted from a latent defect in the needle. It was held that the strict liability in tort doctrine was not applicable to the professional man, such as a dentist, because the essence of the relationship with his patient was the furnishing of professional skill and services. We accepted the view that a dentist's bill for services should be considered as representing pay for that alone. The use of instruments, or the administration of medicines or the providing of medicines for the patient's home consumption cannot give the ministrations the cast of a commercial transaction. Accordingly the liability of the dentist in cases involving the ordinary relationship of doctor and patient must be tested by principles of negligence, i.e., lack of due care and not by application of the doctrine of strict liability in tort.

Defendants suggest that there is no doctrinal basis for distinguishing the services rendered by a beauty parlor operator from those rendered by a dentist or a doctor, and that consequently the liability of all three should be tested by the same principles. On the contrary there is a vast difference in the relationships. The beautician is engaged in a commercial enterprise; the dentist and doctor in a profession. The former caters publicly not to a need but to a form of aesthetic convenience or luxury, involving the rendition of non-professional services and the application of products for which a charge is made. The dentist or doctor does not and cannot advertise for patients; the demand for his services stems from a felt necessity of the patient. In response to such a call the doctor, and to a somewhat lesser degree the dentist, exercises his best judgment in diagnosing the patient's ailment or disability, prescribing and sometimes furnishing medicines or other methods of treatment which he believes, and in some measure hopes, will relieve or cure the condition. His performance is not mechanical or routine because each patient requires individual study and formulation of an informed judgment as to the physical or mental disability or condition presented, and the course of treatment needed. Neither medicine nor dentistry is an exact science; there is no implied warranty of cure or relief. There is no representation of infallibility and such professional men should not be held to such a degree of perfection. There is no guaranty that the diagnosis is correct. Such men are not producers or sellers of property in any reasonably acceptable sense of the term. In a primary sense they furnish services in the form of an opinion of the patient's condition based upon their experienced analysis of the objective and subjective complaints, and in the form of recommended and, at times, personally administered medicines and treatment. . . .

Thus their paramount function—the essence of their function—ought to be regarded as the furnishing of opinions and services. Their unique status and the rendition of these *sui generis* services bear such a necessary and intimate relationship to public health and welfare that their obligation ought to be grounded and expressed in a duty to exercise reasonable competence and care toward their patients. In our judgment, the nature of the services, the utility of and the need for them, involving as they do, the health and even survival of many people, are so important to the general welfare as to outweigh in the policy scale any need for the imposition on dentists and doctors of the rules of strict liability in tort. . . .

Strict liability to the injured consumer does not leave the dealer without remedy. He has an action over against the manufacturer who should bear the primary responsibility for putting defective products in the stream of trade. . . .

The judgment of the Appellate Division is affirmed for the reasons stated, and the cause is remanded for a new trial.

Notes

1. *The "sale" and tangible products.* The traditional requirement was that there be a "sale." Sale implied that tangible chattels be passed. The sale requirement itself has now been bypassed by decisions that permit recovery in the case of leases. And the requirement that goods or chattels be involved has been bypassed by decisions in some states affecting real property. Nevertheless, as a rule, only tangible things can count as products that can be defective. See RESTATEMENT OF PRODUCTS LIABILITY § 19.

2. *Hybrid transactions.* Many transactions involve both the transfer of tangible items and also the delivery of a service. *Newmark* is the leading decision dealing with such transactions. Does it mark a satisfactory line between cases of strict liability and cases that will require proof of negligence? What if a doctor selects a medical prosthesis, then surgically implants it. The prosthesis proves to be defective and its manufacturer is bankrupt. Should the doctor be strictly liable as a seller or distributor? *Cafazzo v. Central Medical Health Services, Inc.*, 542 Pa. 526, 668 A.2d 521 (1995) held not, arguing that first and most simply there was no sale, but that in any event the policy basis of strict products liability had no application. Doctors could not get better safety for products approved by the Food and Drug Administration. The health care system should not bear and spread the costs of bad medical prostheses because that would "further endanger the already beleaguered health care system." Accord, *In re Breast Implant Product Liability Litigation*, 331 S.C. 540, 503 S.E.2d 445 (S.C. 1998)(health care providers who implanted breast implants were not "sellers" of medical devices and thus could not be held strictly liable).

Yet a contractor who builds a house and sells it with a defective water heater may be strictly liable. *State Stove Manufacturing Co. v. Hodges,* 189 So.2d 113 (Miss.1966). So is a contractor who remodels a house and provides defective parts in the process. *Worrell v. Barnes*, 87 Nev. 204, 484 P.2d 573 (1971). Why the difference?

3. *Professional services.* If strict liability is extended to the architect for defective plans, should it also be extended to doctors? Or even to lawyers? Cases have uniformly rejected this notion. See RESTATEMENT OF PRODUCTS LIABILITY § 19 (b) ("Services, even when provided commercially, are not products.").

4. *Dangerous media communications.* What about television shows or movies that show (a) dangerous activities that might be emulated by children or (b) violent and antisocial activities that might stimulate some people

to commit crimes? In *Walt Disney Productions, Inc. v. Shannon,* 247 Ga. 402, 276 S.E.2d 580, 20 A.L.R.4th 321(1981), a television show demonstrated a BB pellet inside a balloon. A child attempted to repeat this himself, but his balloon burst, impelling the lead into his eye. Should his claim be entertained? Would strict liability make sense if the television show created a danger reasonable producers would not recognize? The Restatement Third takes the view that books might themselves be tangible products, but not the information contained in them. RESTATEMENT OF PRODUCTS LIABILITY § 19, cmt. d.

5. *Blood and other body products.* Statutes typically provide, directly or indirectly, that suppliers of blood and related products such as body organs or tissues are not strictly liable. Some statutes attempt to prohibit strict tort liability by providing that the provision of blood is the provision of a service, not the sale of a product. Others directly state that the supplier of blood is not to be held strictly liable. The Restatement Third imports the statutory rules, treating them as a common law rule by providing that human blood is not subject to the rules of the Restatement. RESTATEMENT OF PRODUCTS LIABILITY § 19(c).

UNITED BLOOD SERVICES, DIVISION OF BLOOD SYSTEMS, INC. v. QUINTANA

Supreme Court of Colorado, 1992.
827 P.2d 509.

QUINN. . . .

UBS is a non-profit blood banking division of Blood Systems, Inc., and operates blood centers throughout the western United States. In procuring whole blood, UBS relies strictly on volunteer donors and then processes the blood in the form of whole blood or blood components, such as red blood cells, platelets, and fresh frozen plasma, and supplies the blood or blood components to hospitals. In April 1983 UBS received blood from a donor and then processed the blood for use in medical treatment. The blood was transferred to Southwest Memorial Hospital in Cortez, Colorado.

Approximately one month later, May 27, 1983, Mrs. Quintana suffered a gunshot wound and was taken to Southwest Memorial Hospital, where she underwent emergency surgery. During the surgery she received several units of whole blood and fresh frozen plasma which had been collected and processed by UBS. [Mrs. Quintana thereafter experienced symptoms consistent with the presence of the AIDS virus, later tested positive for the virus, then developed the ARC or AIDS–Related Complex, and finally was diagnosed as having AIDS.] It was later determined that the donor of the unit of blood collected in April 1983 and given to Mrs. Quintana tested positive for the AIDS virus. UBS learned from the donor's physician that the donor [was in a high risk group for AIDS].

[T]he Quintanas predicated their negligence claim on UBS's failure to properly screen the blood donor for potential infection with the AIDS virus through the use of questioning and physical examination and in failing to properly screen the donated blood through surrogate testing. . . .

Prior to trial, UBS filed a motion to preclude one of plaintiff's expert witnesses, Doctor Marcus Conant, a dermatologist, from rendering an expert opinion on the standard of care applicable to UBS's blood banking operations. Doctor Conant had extensive experience in AIDS research and had treated between 3,000 and 5,000 patients who either had the AIDS virus, had AIDS–Related Complex, or had full blown AIDS. . . . Doctor Conant filed an affidavit stating that he was prepared to testify at trial to the following matters: as of January 1983 there was ample evidence available to the medical community and to national blood banks that the AIDS virus was transmissible in blood and blood products and that transfusion recipients were at risk of contracting AIDS if adequate precautions were not taken by blood banks in screening donors and performing surrogate tests on donated blood; that as of January 1983 there was ample evidence that the highest risk groups for AIDS were homosexual males, intravenous drug users, Haitians, and hemophiliacs and that these groups were known at that time to present the highest risk for transmitting the AIDS virus and thus needed to be more carefully screened and tested before being allowed to donate blood or, at the very least, before their donated blood was released for transfusion; that in early 1983 blood banks ignored the warnings and advice of AIDS experts and were negligent in not implementing more stringent screening and testing procedures then available, such as direct questioning of potential donors and surrogate laboratory testing of donated blood; that as of April 18, 1983, the date the contaminated blood in issue was donated, various segments of the blood banking community failed to take adequate steps and precautions to screen donors and test blood in order to protect the nation's blood supply from contamination with the AIDS virus; and that as of April 18, 1983, blood banks had inappropriately placed the privacy of blood donors over the safety of the nation's blood supply and the safety of transfusion recipients.

The trial court ruled that, pursuant to section 13–22–104(2), 6A C.R.S. (1987), the acquisition, preparation, and transfer of blood and its components for purposes of medical treatment is "the performance of a medical service" and that, consequently, the procedures utilized by UBS in 1983 to protect the blood supply against the risk of AIDS contamination must be evaluated according to the professional standard of the blood banking community rather than the general standard of reasonable care. Because Doctor Conant was not directly practicing in the blood banking industry, the court ruled that he would not be permitted to testify that the screening and testing procedures of the blood banking community were substandard and unreasonably deficient in safeguarding transfusion recipients from AIDS contamination. . . .

[The court here discusses recommendations of many groups that blood banks screen donors in a number of ways to minimize the risk of transmitting the virus. Groups making recommendations included the

American Red Cross, the National Gay Task Force, the National Hemophilia Foundation and others.]

The evidence at trial indicated that in April 1983, when the blood donation in question was given, UBS had revised its donor screening process in response to the Food and Drug Administration's recommendations.... The screening procedures utilized at this time by UBS, however, did not include the aggressive questioning and physical examination of blood donors as recommended by the National Hemophilia Foundation. Nor did UBS at this time employ surrogate testing of donated blood, as had been instituted by source plasma centers in early 1983.

It was established at trial that the donor of the blood used in the treatment of Mrs. Quintana was served with the following written interrogatory under oath prior to trial: Assume that the following questions had been read to you on April 18, 1983: a. Have you ever had sexual contact with someone who had received a blood transfusion? b. Have you ever had sexual contact with someone who is in a group at high risk of AIDS or exposure to AIDS? c. Have you ever visited Haiti? d. Have you ever injected drugs into your vein(s)? e. Have you ever had sex with a man since 1978? f. Are you a hemophiliac? If these questions had been read to you, would your answer to any of these questions have been "yes"? (you do not need to specify which question, if any, you would have answered in the affirmative.) The donor, whose identity remained confidential, responded "yes" to the interrogatory.

Based on the trial court's pretrial ruling, the Quintanas were not permitted to present testimony from Doctor Conant as to the allegedly substandard character of the screening and testing procedures utilized by the blood banking industry at the time the donation in question was obtained by UBS. [The trial court made the same rulings about other witnesses who would have testified much like Doctor Conant. The trial court's instructions to the jury were in accord with its evidentiary rulings. The judge told the jury that the industry standard of care governed the case. So instructed, the jury returned a verdict for the defendant.]

While a defendant practicing a profession is entitled to be judged by the standard of care applicable to the professional school to which the defendant belongs, W. Keeton, et al., Prosser and Keeton on Torts § 32, at 187, that standard is not always conclusive proof of due care. We have held, in a somewhat different context, that compliance with administrative safety regulations is a circumstance to be considered on the issue of due care but is not conclusive proof of that issue. [The court quoted Judge Learned Hand's opinion in *The T.J. Hooper*, 60 F.2d 737, 740 (2d Cir.1932).] If the standard adopted by a practicing profession were to be deemed conclusive proof of due care, the profession itself would be permitted to set the measure of its own legal liability, even though that measure might be far below a level of care readily attainable through the adoption of practices and procedures substantially more effective in protecting others against harm than the self-decreed standard of the profession. . . .

To be sure, there is a presumption that adherence to the applicable standard of care adopted by a profession constitutes due care for those practicing that profession. The presumption, however, is a rebuttable one, and the burden is on the one challenging the standard of care to rebut the presumption by competent evidence. In a professional negligence case, therefore, a plaintiff should be permitted to present expert opinion testimony that the standard of care adopted by the school of practice to which the defendant adheres is unreasonably deficient by not incorporating readily available practices and procedures substantially more protective against the harm caused to the plaintiff than the standard of care adopted by the defendant's school of practice. A plaintiff may establish that proposition by the opinion testimony of a qualified expert practicing in the same school or by the opinion testimony of an expert practicing in another school if the expert is sufficiently familiar with the standard of care applicable to the school in question as to render the witness's testimony as well-informed on the applicable standard of care as would be the opinion of an expert witness practicing the same profession as the defendant, or if the standard of care at issue is substantially identical to both schools of practice.

If the plaintiff offers competent and credible evidence that the professional standard of care adopted by the school of practice to which the defendant adheres is unreasonably lacking in available safeguards offering substantially more protection against the harm caused to the plaintiff, the issue of whether the standard of care adopted by the defendants constitutes due care is a question for the jury to resolve under appropriate instructions.

We turn now to whether . . . UBS's conduct should be measured by the general negligence standard of ordinary reasonable care or whether, as the trial court ruled, UBS's conduct should be measured by a professional standard of care applicable to the blood banking community to which UBS belongs. [S]ection 13–22–104, 6A C.R.S. (1987), which states in pertinent part as follows:

(1) The availability of scientific knowledge, skills, and materials for the . . . transfusion . . . of human . . . blood, or components thereof[,] is important to the health and welfare of the people of this state. . . . The imposition of legal liability without fault upon the persons and organizations engaged in such scientific procedures may inhibit the exercise of sound medical judgment and restrict the availability of important scientific knowledge, skills, and materials. It is, therefore, the public policy of this state to promote the health and welfare of the people by emphasizing the importance of exercising due care, and by limiting the legal liability arising out of such scientific procedures to instances of negligence or willful misconduct.

(2) The donation, whether for or without valuable consideration, the acquisition, preparation . . . or transfusion of any human

... blood, or component thereof[,] for or to a human being is the performance of a medical service and does not, in any way, constitute a sale. No ... blood bank ... shall be liable for any damages of any kind or description directly or indirectly caused by or resulting from [transfusions and related] activity; except that each such person or entity remains liable for his or its own negligence or willful misconduct.

... Because section 13–22–104(2) expressly categorizes the acquisition, preparation, and transfer of human blood or its components for medical transfusion as "the performance of a medical service," the statutory scheme clearly contemplates that a blood bank's conduct in procuring or processing blood is to be measured by a professional standard of care.... The acquisition and preparation of human blood for use in medical transfusion and the safeguarding of donated blood against contamination require the exercise of medical and scientific expertise by health care professionals in both the donor screening and the blood testing stages of the process. Any alleged negligence of a blood bank in performing those operations can occur only by reason of the action or inaction of its officers and employees functioning as health care professionals.

We thus hold that UBS's conduct in acquiring and testing the blood subsequently used in treating Mrs. Quintana must be judged by a professional standard of care established by expert testimony.... The court of appeals, therefore, erred by concluding that UBS's conduct should be measured against the general nonprofessional standard of reasonable care rather than the national professional standard of care applicable to the blood banking community of which UBS was a member.

The fact that the court of appeals erred in its adoption of a general standard of reasonable care does not mean that it also erred in ordering a new trial. We are satisfied that the trial court, after having correctly ruled that a professional standard of care applied to UBS's conduct, erroneously applied that standard in a manner that effectively precluded the Quintanas from establishing that the national blood banking community's standard of care was itself unreasonably deficient in not incorporating available safeguards designed to provide substantially more protection against the risk of infecting a transfusion recipient with AIDS.

... The Quintanas' expert opinion evidence was calculated to show that the national blood banking community's screening and testing procedures on which UBS relied were unreasonably deficient in guarding against the transmission of the AIDS virus through blood and blood components and that those procedures, in that respect, were not in accordance with the then "available and proven scientific safeguards" designed to minimize the risk of transmitting AIDS through contaminated blood.

The trial court's ruling prohibiting the Quintanas from offering expert opinion evidence on the unreasonably deficient character of the blood banking community's screening and testing procedures was tantamount to permitting the blood banking community to establish its own standard of legal liability despite the existence of expert opinion evidence tending to show that the blood banking community had adopted unreasonably deficient practices and procedures in place of substantially more protective and readily available safeguards. We hold, therefore, that the trial court's exclusion of the Quintanas' proffered expert opinion evidence was error.

... If the jury had determined that the national blood banking community's standard was itself unreasonably deficient, it would have been required to resolve the issue of UBS's negligence on the basis of all the evidence bearing on UBS's conduct in procuring and processing the blood donation in question, including the data generated by the Centers for Disease Control, the Food and Drug Administration's recommendations for whole blood centers and source plasma centers, the data and recommendations generated by various groups within the national blood banking community, and the practices employed by particular entities in attempting to minimize the risk of transmitting AIDS through blood and plasma transfusion. . . .

[Remanded for a new trial.]

Notes

1. Does the statute really mandate a professional standard, or even address negligence standards at all?

2. Consider the court's idea that although the defendant is held only to the professional standard of care, nevertheless the plaintiff can prove that the standard itself is unreasonable. Suppose a medical doctor has complied with the medical standard of care but that the plaintiff can show by opinion testimony of other doctors that the medical procedure used by the doctor was dangerous in fact, that there was an alternative procedure that cost no more and that was safer. Will such proof allow the plaintiff to get to the jury by the *Quintana* route? If the answer is yes, is that the same in all cases as saying that the professional standard is NOT the standard after all?

REFERENCE: DOBBS ON TORTS §§ 375–76 (2000).

Part V

PRACTICALITIES AND VALUES

Chapter 23

SETTLEMENT, APPORTIONMENT, AND DAMAGES

In one way, everything in this chapter is about settlement of tort cases. Settlement entails an estimate of what would happen if the case were tried. That in turn requires lawyers to know the rules of damages and to estimate the probable award. It also requires lawyers to estimate whether the defendant has assets or insurance that would pay the award. And since most torts involve at least two potential defendants, intelligent settlement also requires lawyers on all sides to know how liability can be apportioned among defendants.

Although the next chapter expressly considers some criticisms of tort law, the practical concerns in this chapter–insurance, damages, apportionment–also raise important questions about values and goals.

SUBCHAPTER A. INSURANCE AND SETTLEMENT

§ 1. AN INTRODUCTION TO THE INSTITUTION OF INSURANCE

a. *The Basic Insurance Coverages*

1. *First party insurance—fire and collision.* Two common examples of "first party" insurance are fire insurance, in which one's property is insured against fire, and collision insurance, in which one's car is insured against damage in a collision. There are many variations and additional protections that can be obtained under these policies. These forms of insurance are "first party" insurance in the sense that the insured party is the first and only party besides the insurer. If there is a loss, the insured person reports it to his own insurer and makes a claim. The rights of the insured are governed by the insurance contract. The insured's rights do not depend on any other person.

A second common feature of these policies is that the insured is entitled to recover upon proof of loss covered by the policy and it is not necessary to show fault on the part of anyone. Indeed, even the insured's own fault, short of intentional damage to his own property, is irrelevant. You recover on your contract, not in tort.

2. *Subrogation.* A feature of much first party insurance is subrogation. You insure your house against fire loss by obtaining a policy with the Kentuckasee Insurance Company. Durfee Construction Company negligently excavates, cutting a gas line and causing an explosion and fire, which burns your house down. You could ignore the fire policy and sue Durfee in tort, but if the policy is adequate to protect your loss, you might simply make a claim against your insurer. Subrogation permits the insurer to "stand in the shoes" of its insured, and take over any claim the insured had against the tortfeasor. Having paid for your loss, Kentuckasee will thus pursue its subrogation right against Durfee Construction. If it proves Durfee's negligence toward you and the other elements of a tort claim you yourself could have made, it will be entitled to recover. The same principle applies in the case of collision insurance on your car, although usually with a "deductible" under which you pay the first portion of the loss in a sum you and the insurer agree upon–say $100 or $250.

Subrogation does not apply in *all* first party insurance. It has no application, for example, in life insurance. The survivors of one who is negligently killed have *both* a claim against the life insurance company which insured his life *and* a claim against the tortfeasor.

3. *Liability insurance.* The idea of first party insurance is the idea of "indemnity"—that is, a recompense or paying back for a loss suffered. In the latter part of the 19th century, this indemnity idea was expanded to cover a new kind of loss, namely, loss through legal liability. If an industry's factory burned down, it would need first party fire insurance to protect against loss. If the industry negligently injured a worker and were required to pay a judgment in his favor, it would need liability insurance to protect against loss. Since liability could arise from many kinds of risks, not merely risks associated with factories, this form of insurance expanded further, and it became quite common for owners of vehicles to purchase liability policies covering risks from their operation. Liability insurance has played an important part in providing indemnity for many other unintended torts as well.

The liability insurance policy as originally conceived had two important characteristics. The first was that it covered only the legal liability of the insured. If the insured caused harm, but was not legally liable for it, the insured would not be liable and neither would the insurer. The insurer, in other words, could take advantage of any rule of law and any fact that favored the insured.

The other characteristic of the liability policy as originally conceived was that it could be invoked only by the insured himself, not by his victim. If the insured tortiously injured a plaintiff, and was legally liable to pay him, the injured plaintiff had no claim against the insurance funds. He would be obliged to collect directly against the insured tortfeasor or not at all. If he did collect, the tortfeasor could in turn obtain the indemnity promised by his insurer. But if the tortfeasor was insolvent or for any other reason avoided payment to the injured person, the tortfeasor's liability insurer had no responsibility. This was true even if the insured tortfeasor was legally liable, so long as he had not actually paid the victim.

As liability insurance became more common, the public began to regard it as a source of recompense for injury rather than as an indemnity for the tortfeasor's loss. As a result of these changing ideas, statutes or policies themselves now permit the injured person to reach the insurance funds (up to the limits of the policy) once legal liability is shown. It is no longer possible for an insurer to escape liability merely because its insured is insolvent. See ROBERT KEETON & ALAN WIDISS, INSURANCE LAW § 4.8 (b) (1988). This reflects an increased "socialization" of insurance, in which liability insurance is now considered in part as a tool for financing injury loss rather than as a tool for indemnity of the tortfeasor, though both goals may be accomplished at the same time. However, this social use of liability insurance to spread the costs of injury loss is incomplete, since "legal liability" of the insured person is still the first prerequisite to recovery. In other words, the liability policy is still not an accident or health policy.

4. *Liability insurance as second party insurance.* The shift from the view of liability insurance as an indemnity arrangement between the insured and insurer to a more "social" view of insurance as a device for assisting the injured has consequences in practice. One consequence is that the insurer takes charge of investigating and defending the claim. The injured person who makes the claim, then, must deal, not with his or her own insurer, but with the insurer for the alleged tortfeasor, the named defendant. In this respect liability insurance is now quite distinct from the first party insurance coverage in, say, collision insurance. It also differs, of course, in that liability turns, not on loss to the injured person, but on legal liability of the insured.

5. *Other forms of insurance.* Since you might be injured by the fault of a driver who had no liability insurance, the protections afforded by liability insurance are incomplete. Many drivers now purchase additional insurance in the form of medical payments insurance, which will pay certain limited medical expenses resulting from auto accidents, without regard to fault. And many have also purchased *uninsured motorist insurance*. No-fault self-insurance plans are more complex and are covered separately in Chapter 27.

6. *The impact of liability insurance.* One important effect of liability insurance is that it provides a fund available to pay judgments for injured persons, without which legal liability might be meaningless. But the existence of liability insurance could at times encourage excessive damages awards, and maybe even the expansion of tort liability itself. Whether that is true or not, does the protection you have under your liability policy undercut the whole idea of individual accountability?

b. *The Liability Insurer's Duties*

The liability insurer's exact duties depend primarily on the contract between it and the insured, that is, upon the policy terms. Lawyers for both the insured defendant and for the plaintiff must be aware of the terms and limits of the policy. For example, a term of the policy might exclude all coverage in a particular case. In cases of this sort, the insurer is said to have a "policy defense" or a "coverage defense," and if that defense is sound, the policy is not operative at all.

In most cases, the insurer's defense to a claim against its insured is not a policy defense but a defense on the merits. The insurer asserts that the insured defendant was not negligent, or that the injured plaintiff was guilty of contributory negligence, or that the insured's behavior was not a proximate cause or that damages are insignificant. This kind of defense, unlike the policy defense, does not deprive the insured of coverage under the policy. If the defense is successful the insured will be protected, but if it is not, the insurer will still be obliged to pay the injured plaintiff up to its policy limits.

Most policies today provide that the insurer has two main obligations, if there is coverage at all. One is to pay any judgment against the insured based on risks covered by the policy and up to the limits of the policy. The other is to defend the insured. The obligation to defend the insured, like the obligation to pay, applies only if the policy is actually in force. The obligation to defend is not limited to cases in which the plaintiff sues the insured defendant in good faith, but extends to any case "even if such suit is groundless, false or fraudulent."

The duty to defend carries with it the insurer's right to be involved in, if not to control, the investigation, negotiation and settlement of the case. It imposes upon the insurer the obligation to retain an attorney to make the defense once the case has reached court. The result of all this is that to a very large extent the insurer is the defendant, though in most states the named defendant in court is the insured, not the insurer. The named defendant's insurer, its attorneys or adjusters, are usually the persons with whom the plaintiff or his attorneys must deal.

The insurer's right and duty to influence or control the process of negotiation, settlement and trial affect lawyers involved on both sides. Suppose an insured defendant has, perhaps negligently, run over a spouse or best friend. If the defendant is fully covered by insurance, will he have an interest in defeating the plaintiff's claim or assisting it? What can the insurer do in such a case except to insist upon its policy right to the cooperation of its insured? If the insurer is vulnerable in such a case, what is its position when dealing with an injured person who has no lawyer? Does the fact that the adjusters are experienced and knowledgeable have any practical effects on the rights of the injured person? How exactly does the defendant's insurer deal with negotiation and settlement? Many of the nuances of this problem must be left to specialized courses in insurance and professional responsibility. But the predominant role of insurance is worth keeping in mind in considering the problems of settlement raised in the next section.

§ 2. SETTLEMENT AND NEGOTIATION

a. *Settlement*

Importance of settlement. The great majority of tort cases are settled by negotiation. The plaintiff accepts a sum of money and gives the defendant a document, usually a "release," the effect of which is to absolve the defendant of further liability. Settlement is economically important to the public and to the parties. If all cases had to be tried, the legal system could not bear the weight of the work and the parties probably could not bear the weight of the delay. The tort system works, then, partly because settlement is the usual method of dealing with claims.

Protecting the effort to settle. The process of settlement negotiation is important enough to deserve some protection. Suppose D offers to settle for $100,000 and P rejects the offer. Can P show in court that D made the offer and therefore that he must have been admitting negligence? The usual answer is no. If negotiation terms could be admitted in court, the parties might be afraid to negotiate and their negotiation and settlement are very much needed to keep the system running.

Statutes in about a dozen states contain a provision of great tactical significance in settlement negotiations. These statutes, with some variation, provide that a defendant may make a written offer to settle a claim for a certain amount (called an "offer of judgment"). If the plaintiff rejects this offer and then fails to obtain a more favorable judgment at trial, the plaintiff must pay all of the defendant's costs, including attorney fees, from the time of the offer. See, e.g., N.Y. MCKINNEY'S CIV. PRAC. LAW § 3221; CAL. CODE CIV. PROC. § 998 (also applying, in a limited way, to plaintiffs' offers). What impact do such provisions have on settlement strategy? What goals are served by such laws?

The lawyers' obligations. Parties in personal injury litigation often negotiate a settlement without lawyers; the insurance adjuster pays the injured person an agreed sum and takes a release. Once the claim has reached lawyers on both sides, negotiation is still overwhelmingly likely and indeed it usually produces settlement. The client has the ultimate authority to accept or reject settlement of a matter, and the lawyer is obligated to explain the ramifications of settlement offers with sufficient clarity to allow the client to reach such a decision. This is both an ethical and a legal obligation. ABA MODEL RULES OF PROFESSIONAL CONDUCT 1.2(a) & 1.4; ABA MODEL CODE OF PROFESSIONAL RESPONSIBILITY EC 7–7 & 7–8. The lawyer who fails fully to inform his client about acceptance of a settlement is subject to liability for malpractice. *Wood v. McGrath, North, Mullin & Kratz, P.C.,* 256 Neb. 109, 589 N.W.2d 103 (1999).

Factors in settlement. Styles of negotiation differ a great deal, often embodying personal preferences of the lawyers, sometimes, too, embodying local traditions or practices. However, all negotiation in legitimate cases must proceed from the lawyers' estimates of what would happen if the case were tried. The lawyer can negotiate competently and effectively only when investigation is complete and when all legal points have been thoroughly researched and understood. For example, if the plaintiff's lawyer negotiates a settlement without seeing that the client has had a good medical examination, the client may wind up with a settlement that falls far short of compensating for his real injuries. The lawyer must estimate the evidence and its effect on the judge. (Is a directed verdict a distinct possibility?) It also requires the lawyer to estimate the effect of evidence on the jury. (Will the jury find for the defendant or bring in a low verdict even though the judge has refused to direct a verdict?) These estimates in turn can be made only when the lawyer has formed an opinion about the judge, the jury and the opposing counsel in the case.

None of these estimates can be made with certainty, and when they are finally made the lawyer may be able to say only that the case has a small probability of coming in at $1 million and a high probability of coming in at $100,000. Every variable in the case will have an impact on the final figure each side will be willing to settle for. If the plaintiff is an unattractive personality the case may settle for $90,000, whereas it would go for $100,000 if the plaintiff were an ordinary person. The same is true with counsel. If the plaintiff's counsel is a poor lawyer, or makes a bad impression on juries, or usually settles instead of trying a case, the defense lawyer will recommend a smaller settlement than if plaintiff's counsel is an excellent lawyer, effective with juries and quite willing to try cases that cannot be fairly settled. It is obviously impossible to detail every kind of fact that will go into deciding the value of a case, but it will not be an overemphasis to say that the lawyer's evaluation of both law and the rational import of the evidence are as critical as the lawyer's evaluation of personalities involved in the trial.

b. *Improvident Settlement*

GLEASON v. GUZMAN

Supreme Court of Colorado, 1981.
623 P.2d 378.

QUINN, J.

On September 29, 1970, Darlene Benavidez, then a fourteen-year-old minor, was struck on the head by a vending machine that fell from a truck operated by Irwin Gleason in the course of his employment with Coin Fresh, Inc. (defendants). Darlene Benavidez has since married and is now known as Darlene Guzman (plaintiff). Immediately after the accident she was taken to Denver General Hospital for examination. She complained of headache, vomiting and some disorientation and, after two days of observation and testing, her injury was diagnosed as a left temporal lobe contusion and she was released as improved. On October 13, 1970, the plaintiff was readmitted to the hospital with complaints similar to those previously experienced. Further testing resulted in a diagnosis of left intratemporal lobe hematoma and the plaintiff was discharged as improved on October 20, 1970. Shortly thereafter plaintiff returned to high school and a normal routine. She and her parents, Mr. and Mrs. Benavidez, believed that plaintiff had fully recovered from the injury.

In November 1970 the plaintiff's parents retained an attorney in connection with their daughter's claim. Approximately two years later this attorney initiated settlement negotiations with the defendants' insurance carrier. It was mutually agreed that the case be settled for $6,114.35. The insurance carrier hired an attorney to prepare a petition for the probate court's approval of settlement and the appointment of the plaintiff's father, Mr. Benavidez, as guardian of his minor daughter's estate. The probate court approved the settlement and Mr. Benavidez, as duly appointed guardian, executed a general release of his daughter's claim against the defendant.

In May 1974, approximately forty-four months after the accident, the plaintiff experienced her first epileptic seizure during her senior year in high school. Other seizures followed. Having become emancipated through marriage, she retained her present attorneys and a complaint was filed in November 1975. The complaint sought money damages against the defendants for negligently causing personal injuries to the plaintiff in the accident of September 29, 1970. The defendants in their answer raised as an affirmative defense the release executed by the guardian and endorsed on their answer a demand for a jury trial. Thereafter, the defendants filed a motion for summary judgment on the basis of the guardian's release. The plaintiff countered with a motion to set aside the release on the ground that it was executed under a mistake as to the nature of the injury actually sustained. The court heard both motions in a consolidated hearing on November 14, 1977.

[The trial judge granted the defendant's motion for summary judgment and denied the plaintiff's motion to set aside the release. In the Supreme Court of Colorado, the defendant attempted first to support the trial judge's action by arguing that a motion to set aside a release is essentially a suit in equity to rescind, that an equity court tries cases without a jury and that the trial judge's decision is therefore to be upheld as if it were a jury verdict. The Supreme Court rejected this argument on the ground that the case remained "legal," in spite of the motion, and that the plaintiff therefore had a right to have a jury trial unless there were grounds for summary judgment. It then addressed that question as follows.]

The defendants urge two reasons why the court of appeals erred in reversing the trial court's entry of summary judgment. First, they argue that the mistake related to a future complication of a known injury, as distinct from a mistake about the nature of the injury actually suffered in the accident. Next, they contend that the release was a general release encompassing both known and unknown injuries and it thereby precluded rescission even for a mistake as to an unknown injury.

Since these arguments are presented to us in the context of a summary judgment review, the determinative considerations are whether the record shows a genuine issue as to any material fact and whether the defendants are entitled to judgment as a matter of law ...

Cases addressing the problem of mistake in the settlement of personal injury claims reflect a tension stemming, on the one hand, from the general need for finality in the contractual settlements of actual or potential lawsuits and, on the other hand, from a recognized need to alleviate the distorting and unintended effects which human error can impose on a transaction. See, e.g., II G. Palmer, The Law of Restitution § 11.2,12.22 (1978); Dobbs, Conclusiveness of Personal Injury Settlements: Basic Problems, 41 N.C.L. Rev. 665 (1963); Note, Avoidance of Tort Releases, 13 W. Res. L. Rev. 768 (1962); Havighurst, Problems Concerning Settlement Agreements, 53 Nw. U.L. Rev. 283 (1958). Although the approaches are not totally discrete, they do lean in different directions. One approach denies rescission even though the injuries were not known or suspected at the time of the settlement. Under this view the releasor assumes the risk that the nature and extent of known injuries might be more severe than was believed at settlement. Another approach allows rescission based on any mistake as to the condition of the injured claimant, whether the mistake relates to the nature of the injuries or to their further consequences. Midway between these approaches is the view that rescission is available for mistakes relating to the nature of known injuries but not for mistakes as to the future course and effects of those injuries. E.g., Casey v. Proctor, 59 Cal. 2d 97, 378 P.2d 579, 28 Cal. Rptr. 307 (1963). The assumption here is that rescission must be based on mistake, and mistake for legal purposes must relate to a past or present fact rather than an opinion or prophecy about the future.

This latter approach represents the rule in this jurisdiction. [In McCarthy v. Eddings] the plaintiff suffered a broken arm but, based on his doctor's representation, believed that the injury was temporary in duration and executed a release. Thereafter, he discovered that the broken bones in the arm had not united and the resulting disability was permanent. We affirmed the jury verdict for the plaintiff and held that a release obtained as the result of a mutual basic mistake could be set aside as ineffective.

The *McCarthy* rule was further refined in Davis v. Flatiron Materials Co., 182 Colo. 65, 511 P.2d 28 (1973), which upheld the validity of a release.... Noting that the injury was correctly diagnosed and that the plaintiff was fully informed about the nature of her condition, we held that to justify rescission the mistake "must relate to a present existing fact or a past fact," rather than as there present, a mistake concerning the future course of recovery from the known injury.

We again addressed this problem in Scotton v. Landers, 190 Colo. 27, 543 P.2d 64 (1975), where the plaintiff, believing that he suffered a fractured rib and bruises in an automobile accident, executed a general release only to discover shortly thereafter that his spleen had been ruptured and had to be surgically removed. We concluded that the mistake was sufficient to avoid the release because it was grounded in the nature of injuries suffered in the accident.

As *McCarthy, Davis* and *Scotton* demonstrate, the distinction between unknown injuries and unknown consequences of known injuries is a useful analytic standard but it does not yield a litmus-type resolution to these problems. The words we use, "though they have a central core of meaning that is relatively fixed, are of doubtful application to a considerable number of marginal cases." Indeed, this is such a marginal case. With respect to post-traumatic epilepsy, the margin of difference between a mistake in diagnosis and a mistake in prognosis, or the difference between that condition as an injury and as a consequence, cannot easily be fitted into predetermined categories of exclusivity.

Judge Learned Hand pointed up the difficulty of conceptual differentiation in these matters:

> "There is indeed no absolute line to be drawn between mistakes as to future, and as to present facts. To tell a layman who has been injured that he will be about again in a short time is to do more than prophesy about his recovery. No doubt it is a forecast, but it is ordinarily more than forecast; it is an assurance as to his present condition, and so understood."

Scheer v. Rockne Motors Corp., 68 F.2d 942, (2d Cir.1934). . . .

Knowledge of the nature of an injury requires an awareness and some appreciation of its extent, severity and likely duration. Admittedly, line-drawing here is difficult and its direction may well vary with the thrust of evidence. These basic components of knowledge, however, relate primarily to a comprehension of the basic character of the injury as distinct from a prediction or opinion about the future course of recovery when its basic nature is otherwise known. . . .

The record before us provides an adequate basis from which one may reasonably infer the existence of mistake in the execution of the release by the guardian. He had little formal education and was not adept or articulate in the English language. According to the deposition testimony of the attorney who originally represented the plaintiff, the most sophisticated concept used by the guardian in connection with the injury was "concussion."

As noted by the court of appeals, from the date of the accident through the settlement the plaintiff experienced only minor symptoms. It may reasonably be inferred that when the release was executed the guardian believed the injury was minor, that it posed no risk of complication, that it was temporary in duration, and that his daughter had fully recovered. There is no evidence that anyone, including physicians and the original attorney, disabused the guardian of these beliefs. In fact, the attorney's legal preparation and his settlement correspondence to the defendants' insurance carrier belie any awareness that the injury posed any risk of brain dysfunction, much less post-traumatic epilepsy. This attorney's belief that the plaintiff had fully recovered from her injury is clearly discernible in his representations to the probate judge at the settlement hearing. . . .

When the record is examined in its entirety, it is apparent that there exists a genuine factual issue on whether the guardian was mistaken about the nature of his daughter's injury when he executed the release.[6] Under these circumstances, summary judgment was inappropriate. . . .

The defendants argue that the guardian's release constitutes a bar to the plaintiff's claim as a matter of law because its terms are all inclusive and encompass unknown injuries that may later develop or be discovered as well as their effects and consequences.

Although some jurisdictions give effect to the language of a release so as to preclude avoidance even as to unknown injuries, the tendency of the law is to the contrary. Most courts provide for avoidance in appropriate circumstances, such as mistake or lack of intent, despite the presence of language in the release broad enough to cover the claim in question. . . .

Resolution of the intent issue necessarily means going behind the language of the release. If unknown injuries were not within the contemplation of the parties, the release will be set aside. . . .

[Judgment of the Court of Appeals, which reversed the trial court's judgment, is affirmed. Concurring and dissenting opinions are omitted.]

BERNSTEIN v. KAPNECK, 290 Md. 452, 430 A.2d 602 (1981). Irene Schulman, a five-year-old child, was injured in a two-car collision with defendants. Medical opinion was that she had an extensive laceration of the forehead, chip fractures of the nasal bones, a non-displaced fracture of the right shoulder and a "moderately severe traumatic neurosis." Her mother, Bernstein, on advice of competent counsel accepted settlement of $7500, and by agreement of all parties a consent judgment was entered by the court in this sum. The release specified that Bernstein "individually and as parent and natural guardian of Irene Schulman," accepted the money and in return released and discharged the defendants from all claims and demands on account of "bodily injuries, known and unknown, and which have resulted or may in the future develop. . . ." Irene later developed epileptic symptoms diagnosed to be a "post-traumatic psychomotor seizure disorder resulting from a brain injury she sustained in the 1975 accident." Bernstein then ap-

---

6. The probate court's approval of the settlement has no effect on the underlying issue of mistake.

"We find no persuasive reason why a minor, whose claims cannot satisfactorily be compromised and released except through court approval, should be more rigorously denied relief than an adult from mutual mistake, simply because the court was laboring under the same mistake."

peared in the original action and moved to vacate the consent judgment and avoid the release on the ground of mistake. *Held*, affirming the trial court and Court of Special Appeals, the release may not be set aside. Although most courts will set aside some releases on one theory or another, there are two policy considerations to be considered. On the one hand, it is important to the individual and to society to redress injury, but on the other hand the law favors compromises. To permit vacation of settlements except for the most compelling reasons would create chaos and confusion, and would undermine compromise settlements which are essential to the working of the system in this era of "burgeoning litigation." "Given the fact that a release of unknown injuries is almost universally permissible, it seems to us that the real issue, as is often the case involving contractual disputes, boils down to a question of the intent of the contracting parties.... [T]he liberal stance casts aside the centuries old methodology utilized for the interpretation of contracts in favor of an approach which rejects the objective theory of contracts.... This approach often overlooks or avoids the words used by the parties to express their agreement and in its place substitutes undefined conjecture as to what the releasor would have intended if the full extent of the injuries had been known.... If hardship is the criterion, then the line of enforceability should not be drawn in accordance with the nature of the claim, but rather the extent of the hardship suffered. If, on the other hand, the issue is (as we think) whether there has been a mutually intended release of unknown injuries then the nature and extent of the misfortune is beside the point...."

Notes

1.   Is it clear how you can apply the rule in *Gleason*? In *Nevue v. Close*, 123 Wash.2d 253, 867 P.2d 635 (1994) the plaintiff thought she had a neck sprain and settled for $150, then discovered a back injury. The court said its rule was that "where there are known injuries, here the neck sprain, the release is binding as to those injuries and as to the unknown consequences of the known injury. However, as to an injury unknown to the plaintiff, and not within the contemplation of the parties to the release, the release should not be binding per se. The plaintiff should bear the burden of proving that the injury was reasonably unknown and not within the contemplation of the parties." This rule seems to be about the same as the rule in *Gleason*. Given that rule, how would the court decide the case?

2.   If you buy a painting you believe to be a Georgione, but you realize you cannot be sure, are you mistaken? What if you believe you know the nature or extent of your injuries, but you realize, as you must, that you cannot be sure; are you mistaken? Conscious ignorance—an awareness that you do not know—may negate any idea that you are mistaken. See 2 DAN DOBBS, LAW OF REMEDIES § 11.2 (1993). Should the release case be treated like an ordinary commercial contract case?

3.   If the release itself provides that the injured person assumes the risk of unknown injuries, should that prevent a recovery later if the plaintiff can show that she never had any intent to assume the risk? See *Williams v.*

Glash, 789 S.W.2d 261 (Tex.1990); 2 DAN DOBBS, LAW OF REMEDIES § 11.9 (1993). What if the release itself provides that the plaintiff is releasing claims for unknown injuries? *Smothers v. Richland Mem. Hospital*, 328 S.C. 566, 493 S.E.2d 107 (1997).

4. Consider what you would do as a lawyer to fulfill your special responsibility to ascertain the client's condition before advising a settlement.

5. Notice that if the release is set aside, the plaintiff must still prove her case. Suppose that the jury ultimately finds for the defendant. The defendant is out the money paid for the release and didn't get the peace that settlement was supposed to bring either. Would the alternative be to require the plaintiff to restore the consideration paid for the release as a prerequisite to a suit on the merits?

6. *Grounds other than mistake.* Fraud, coercion, and incapacity are also grounds for avoiding a release. Incapacity represents a serious problem if the injured person is approached for settlement in the hospital, or is under sedation. Some states have enacted statutes designed to provide safeguards. New York makes it unlawful to enter a hospital to negotiate a settlement or obtain a release in most instances. N.Y. JUDIC. L. § 480. Maryland provides that any personal injury release signed within five days of the injury is voidable for the next sixty days. MD. CTS. & JUD. PROC. CODE § 5–401.1.

———

ALFONE v. SARNO, 87 N.J. 99, 432 A.2d 857 (1981). Concetta Alfone sued Dr. Sarno in 1968, alleging medical malpractice. She recovered a general verdict of $100,000. Thereafter she died and the present action was brought by her father as administrator of her estate, alleging that Sarno's malpractice had caused her death and seeking damages, including losses to Concetta's mother, himself and her daughter. The trial judge granted summary judgment for the defendant on the ground that the personal injury action barred any recovery. The intermediate court reversed. *Held*, the personal injury recovery does not necessarily bar a second recovery for death; remanded for further development of facts. In some respects death actions are derivative. Thus there can be no claim unless there was a tort to the decedent. However, once it is established that the defendant's act was tortious, the fact that there is some personal defense that would have barred the decedent's own claim is not necessarily a bar to the dependent's claims, which are partly independent. Here the prior judgment for Concetta would bar her, were she alive and suing, but it should not necessarily bar dependents who have losses from her death. However, certain issues may not be relitigated. If the defendant wins in the first action, no new action may be brought when death occurs. Likewise, determinations as to percentages of negligence will be binding. And plaintiff may not assert new theories. Where the first action is terminated by settlement, whether these issues can be litigated "may depend upon the terms of such settlement or release." In any event, it will be necessary in the death action to prove what elements of damages were recovered in the first suit or in the settlement to avoid duplication of damages, and to preclude all recoveries that could have been made in the first action.

Notes

1. What exactly is the danger of duplicated damages? Recall the measures of damages awarded in death actions. Suppose Concetta had proved she was permanently injured and would never work again. Is there any way to know that the $100,000 awarded by the jury covered that item? If it did, would any substantial recovery in the wrongful death action duplicate the earlier award?

2. Suppose Concetta had not died, but had received an inadequate award or accepted an improvidently low settlement. If she could not attack the award or settlement, neither could her dependents. Why should they be better off when she has died? Or, alternatively, would you want to say that although the injured victim is bound by a release, her dependents are not?

3. If you were an insurance attorney in New Jersey and you wanted to settle a routine injury case, what could you do to protect your client against a second suit? The problem might be the same even after trial. Is there anything you can do to bring this dispute to an end when the trial is over?

4. The traditional statement is that a settlement in the injured person's lifetime, or a judgment for either party, will bar the death action. See *Varelis v. Northwestern Mem. Hospital*, 167 Ill.2d 449, 212 Ill.Dec. 652, 657 N.E.2d 997 (1995). A few courts take the *Alfone* position, including the Supreme Court for one narrow band of admiralty cases based on judge-made law. *Sea-Land Services v. Gaudet*, 414 U.S. 573, 94 S.Ct. 806, 39 L.Ed.2d 9 (1974).

c.   *Clients' Rights Against Their Own Lawyers*

OHIO CODE OF PROFESSIONAL RESPONSIBILITY
Rule DR–5–106.

A lawyer who represents two or more clients shall not make or participate in the making of an aggregate settlement of the claims of or against his clients, unless each client has consented to the settlement after being advised of the existence and nature of all the claims involved in the proposed settlement, of the total amount of the settlement, and of the participation of each person in the settlement.

Notes

1. Lawyers are governed by rules of ethics and discipline adopted by states through their courts, legislatures, or bar associations. The Ohio rule above is adopted from the Model Code of Professional Responsibility, first promulgated by the American Bar Association in 1969. The ABA has since promulgated a the Model Rules of Professional Conduct, which contains the same rule, now designated as Model Rule 1.8(g). Most states have adopted

these Model Rules in some form. The ABA works more or less constantly on rule revisions; a comprehensive revision of the Model Rules, called "Ethics 2000" is underway.

2. What is the problem to which the rule is addressed? Suppose a lawyer has ten clients with claims against various defendants but all the defendants are insured by the same liability insurance company. Try to imagine how a negotiation between the lawyer and the insurance company's lawyer might proceed and how a single client's interest might be hurt.

3. In *Lloyd v. Fishinger*, 380 Pa.Super. 507, 552 A.2d 303, aff'd per curiam and remanded, 529 Pa. 513, 605 A.2d 1193 (1992), Fishinger was seriously injured and in the hospital recovering from surgery and sedation when Lloyd obtained his signature on a contingent fee agreement. Fishinger could not remember signing the contract. He informed Lloyd he did not want Lloyd's representation and Fisinger's new attorney formally terminated Lloyd's employment. At this point Fishinger had not reached a settlement, but Lloyd had been offered $100,000 by the tortfeasor's insurer almost immediately. Lloyd claims his contingent fee, 37.5% of the $100,000. How do you think this claim might (a) impede ultimate settlement or solution of the case and/or (b) prevent appropriate recompense to the plaintiff?

4. Would clients have any right to be informed on all settlement negotiations? Suppose the lawyer for the plaintiff receives an offer to settle for $100,000, but that the lawyer believes the offer is too low and does not inform the client. If the plaintiff ultimately loses, has she any informed consent claim?

SUBCHAPTER B.   SETTLEMENT AND TRIAL WITH MULTIPLE DEFENDANTS

§ 3.   THE TRADITIONAL ALLOCATION OF RESPONSIBILITY AMONG MULTIPLE DEFENDANTS

NOTE: REVIEWING JOINT AND SEVERAL LIABILITY

We have already seen that several defendants might be held liable together, jointly and severally, so that the plaintiff might enforce a judgment entirely against any one of them. Recall that under the rule of joint and several liability, if one defendant pays more than his share, he could obtain contribution from the other tortfeasors. Recall also that the plaintiff could enforce her judgment in part against one and in part against another, but that in no event could she recover a total of more than the total amount of her judgment. Finally, recall that this system helps assures the plaintiff of compensation when one or more tortfeasors have insufficient funds to pay the judgment.

The rule of joint and several liability applies in four distinct situations.

(1) **Concerted action**. Joint and several liability applies to true joint torts, those in which A and B act in concert to commit an

unlawful act. This includes intentional torts pursued jointly, as where A and B agree, tacitly or formally, to beat the plaintiff. It also includes intended law violations, as where A and B agree to race on the public highway and in the course of the race A collides with the plaintiff.

(2) **Indivisible injury**. The rule of joint and several liability applies in cases of concurrent torts where there is no concert or agreement, but where the acts of A and B produce a single indivisible injury. In one kind of case in this category, A's act standing alone and B's act standing alone would have been sufficient to cause the same harm. In a distinct kind of case, A's act would not suffice to cause all of the harm done, but it is still impossible to determine how much of the harm was caused by A and how much by B.

(3) **A creates a risk of harm by B**. The rule of joint and several liability applies in part when A's negligence not only creates a harm to the plaintiff, but also creates a risk of further harm by reason of B's negligence. A negligently runs the plaintiff down and leaves him concussed and unconscious, but otherwise unharmed, in the street. B later negligently runs over and breaks the plaintiff's leg. Although B can only be held liable for the separate injury he caused, A is jointly and severally liable for the entire harm under the rules of "proximate cause, since he created a foreseeable risk of harm from B." Thus if B proved to be uninsured and insolvent, the plaintiff would be entitled to recover his entire damages from A. This is the import of the proximate cause rules. Similarly, if A does not directly harm the plaintiff but creates a risk that B will do so, joint and several liability is no doubt proper. For instance, in *Nallan v. Helmsley–Spear, Inc.*, 50 N.Y.2d 507, 429 N.Y.S.2d 606, 407 N.E.2d 451 (1980), a building owner failed to protect an invitee from a gunman. The building owner was held subject to liability, not merely its comparative fault share.

(4) **A defendant is vicariously liable**. An employer is liable for the torts of an employee committed in the scope of employment. The employee is also liable for his own torts. The result is that they are jointly and severally liable.

NOTE: REVIEWING CAUSAL APPORTIONMENT

Plaintiff drives to work and on her way is struck from behind by a car driven by A. Her neck is sore, but she goes on to work. On her way home in the evening she is struck by a car driven by B, aggravating her neck condition, which becomes serious. This looks very much like a case in which joint liability could be imposed upon A and B on the basis of the second rule, because a single indivisible injury has resulted. But none of the other grounds for joint liability appear sufficient. Now suppose that the plaintiff's neck is injured in the collision with A, but that the collision with B is not a rear end collision but a T-bone collision and that

B's collision causes the plaintiff a broken arm without aggravating her neck condition at all. In this instance, the harms flow from two injuries, not one. Since the other grounds for joint liability are also lacking, A and B are severally liable for the injury each has produced, but not jointly liable at all.

Many cases of injury are not so clear. How can one be sure, for example, that the collision with B did not in fact aggravate the neck injury that occurred a few hours earlier? This kind of question presents serious problems of proof. Should the burden of proving that damages are divisible fall upon the party who seeks to avoidable responsibility for the whole? See RESTATEMENT OF APPORTIONMENT § 26, cmt. h. (yes). In the case of the rear-end and the T-bone collision, what is the practical effect of this rule?

Is causal apportionment inherently desirable? Should juries be given a lot of freedom to estimate how much injury was caused by each tortfeasor? The Restatement Second calls for apportionment not only where there are "distinct harms," but also where there is a "reasonable basis for determining the contribution" of each tortfeasor to a "single harm." RESTATEMENT SECOND OF TORTS § 433A (1965). Perhaps if apportionment is really desirable, many ways of apportioning each defendant's causal contribution could be found. See Gerald W. Boston, *Toxic Apportionment: A Causation and Risk Contribution Model*, 25 ENVIRONMENTAL L. 549 (1995).

NOTE: TRADITIONAL FORMS OF SETTLEMENT WITH ONE OF SEVERAL TORTFEASORS

And now for something entirely different. Suppose that instead of getting a judgment against all tortfeasors, the plaintiff settles with one of them. Imagine that the plaintiff has damages of $200,000 and A offers to settle his share for $100,000. Can the plaintiff accept this settlement and then pursue B for the remainder?

1. *Plaintiff's claim is fully satisfied.* If the plaintiff sues A separately, and recovers a judgment that is then paid by A, he has no claim against B. The reason lies in the rule that the plaintiff may recover only one compensation. Her claim is said to be satisfied and extinguished because it is paid and she is compensated. The same kind of consideration governs settlements. If A has fully paid the plaintiff's claim in a settlement, the plaintiff has no just claim against B. But since a settlement may not always represent full payment, it is obviously more difficult for B to take advantage of this rule in such cases.

2. *Releases under common law rule.* A very different rule at common law was that release of one tortfeasor was a release of all those who were jointly and severally liable. This rule was independent of the rule about satisfaction of the claim. Thus if the plaintiff settled with A for $10,000, when his total damages were $100,000, he would not be barred by the satisfaction rule from a recovery against B. But if he gave a

release to A upon payment of the settlement monies, he would then be prevented from any recovery against B under the release rule. The idea was that a release extinguished the cause of action itself, so that there was no ground left on which to sue B.

3. *Covenants not to sue.* In the situation just described, settlement would be unlikely. The plaintiff would not give a release, since that would end his claim against B. A would not make a payment unless he could be assured by a release that he would not be held liable a second time. To effect a settlement in this situation, lawyers came up with a new kind of settlement document–a "covenant not to sue." This was not a release of the claim at all, but merely a contract or covenant by the plaintiff not to sue A and in fact to indemnify A if he were held liable. Thus if a plaintiff wished to settle with one tortfeasor and still sue the other, this was the settlement paper he would use.

4. *Modern developments.* In some states statutes or court decisions have changed all this. The UNIFORM CONTRIBUTION AMONG TORTFEASORS ACT (1955) § 4 provides expressly that a release of one tortfeasor "does not discharge any of the other tortfeasors from liability ... unless its terms so provide.... " Lawyers effecting a settlement with one tortfeasor will obviously have to be alert to local law provisions, but in one way or another it is now practical to attain a settlement with less than all tortfeasors.

NOTE: CONTRIBUTION AND INDEMNITY

1. *Contribution. (a) General availability.* In Chapter 6, we saw that if one tortfeasor, A, paid more than his fair share of the plaintiff's damages, he could recover contribution from the other tortfeasors to rectify their respective liabilities. The common law rule was opposed to contribution and perhaps contribution would still be denied among intentional tortfeasors. Otherwise, however, the states generally permit contribution when A pays more than his share of a judgment for the plaintiff.

(b) Payment in settlement. In some states A can obtain contribution from B only when A has paid a judgment for the plaintiff. That rule would deny contribution if A paid the plaintiff's claim in a settlement rather than by paying off a final judgment. Such an approach is now outdated. If A settles with P for full compensation, A is now usually entitled to contribution from B.

(c) Traditional amount of contribution. The amount of the appropriate share to be paid in contribution may not be obvious, as we will see. However, the traditional rule is quite clear: if there is a single indivisible injury caused by two tortfeasors, each should pay one-half. Thus if A pays the entire $200,000, B would be liable to make contribution to A of $100,000. This rule is known as the pro rata share rule.

The leading article is Robert A. Leflar, *Contribution and Indemnity Between Tortfeasors*, 81 U. PA. L. REV. 130 (1932). See generally DOBBS ON TORTS § 386 (2000).

2. *Indemnity.* In a few situations, A may be technically liable to the plaintiff, but it may be that B is the only person really at fault. If A, because of a technical liability, pays the entire amount of the plaintiff's damages, A may recover, not merely a share from B, but the entire sum. This is known, traditionally, as indemnity. Thus while contribution involves a sharing of liability between the tortfeasors, indemnity involves a shifting of that liability.

There are not many occasions for indemnity in this sense. The chief example involves the negligence of the employee. Though the employer is liable to the plaintiff, it has a right of indemnity against the negligent employee, though it is not a right often exercised in practice. There is also a right of indemnity in some products cases, as where the retailer is held strictly liable for a defective product supplied by the manufacturer: the retailer will be entitled to recover indemnity from the manufacturer. At one time, some courts permitted indemnity in favor of a tortfeasor who was only passively negligently and against a tortfeasor who was actively at fault. This ground for indemnity has become largely irrelevant with the adoption of comparative fault systems almost everywhere, since the comparative fault share of the passive tortfeasor can measure the extent of his contribution right.

ASCHEMAN v. VILLAGE OF HANCOCK

Supreme Court of Minnesota, 1977.
254 N.W.2d 382.

TODD, JUSTICE.

The village of Hancock appeals from the dismissal of its third-party complaint against Floyd Ascheman for contribution. We affirm.

Floyd Ascheman (Floyd) consumed intoxicating beverages at a municipal bar in the village of Hancock. Shortly after Floyd departed from the bar he suffered injuries when the automobile he was operating was involved in a one-car accident. Floyd's wife and daughter commenced an action against the village of Hancock asking to recover damages for the loss of their means of support under the Civil Damage Act, Minn. St. § 340.95. In support of their complaint, it is alleged that the municipal bar continued to serve Floyd liquor despite the fact that he was obviously intoxicated. The village of Hancock thereafter initiated third-party proceedings seeking contribution from Floyd on the grounds that any damages incurred by the plaintiffs were caused jointly by Floyd and the village.

At a pretrial hearing the trial court granted Floyd's motion for summary judgment dismissing the third-party action. . . .

1. It is contended that common liability exists between the village and Floyd. The village premises this contention upon the assumption that Floyd breached his duty to support his family as a result of injuries he sustained while negligently operating a motor vehicle in an inebriated condition.

It is the rule in Minnesota that a husband is legally responsible for the support of his wife while they are married. This court has also stated, in the context of divorce proceedings, that a father has the primary responsibility for the support of his minor children. However, each of these cases which recognized a duty of support relied upon a statute which specifically provided for the obligation.

The underlying premise of the village's contention that common liability exists in this case is that Floyd's wife and daughter could bring a direct action against him for damages because his negligent conduct operated to diminish their means of support. Thus, if the village's argument is accepted, Floyd's liability to his family would lie in negligence rather than a violation of statutory duty of support. We are unaware of any decisions which recognize such a direct action in negligence for loss of a family's means of support.

The village cites several recent decisions by this court which modified the defenses of the intrafamilial immunities in tort in support of its proposition that a direct action does exist in favor of a family against the father-husband for loss of support. While the absolute defenses of interspousal and child-parent immunity have been largely abrogated in this state, a parent nevertheless remains immune from suit by his child when the alleged negligent act involves an exercise of ordinary parental discretion involving the provision of food, clothing, and other necessities.

It should also be noted that the judicial abrogation of the intrafamilial immunity defenses did not create a new cause of action or a new tort but merely abolished the use of a particular defense to a preexisting tort claim. A determination of whether common liability exists is to be made at the instant the tort is committed. This is precisely the requirement which has not been satisfied in the present case. Since Floyd's wife and daughter could never bring a direct action against him in negligence for the loss of their means of support, common liability does not exist between Floyd and the village. Thus, we conclude that the action of the trial court in dismissing the third party complaint was proper insofar as the dismissal was based upon an absence of common liability.

2.   As its second argument, the village urges this court to relax the requirement of common liability to allow contribution between a liquor vendor and vendee even though the plaintiffs are members of the vendee's family. . . . We decline to abolish the requirement of common liability in situations where the liability of the party seeking contribution is founded upon an alleged violation of the Civil Damage Act.

In adopting this position, we have given due consideration to the legislative purpose behind the adoption of the Civil Damage Act. The Civil Damage Act has been characterized as both penal and remedial in nature, its intent being to suppress the illegal furnishing of liquor and to provide a remedy.

The village contends that a failure to relax the rule of common liability in this and other similar factual situations creates a grave injustice. This inequity is readily apparent, argues the village, when one considers that Floyd, as a member of the Ascheman household, will share in the proceeds of any award to his family. The village's argument continues by stating that it is inequitable to assess 100 percent of any damage award for loss of support against the liquor vendor merely because of the fortuity that the vendee and plaintiffs are in the same family. However, the reverse of the village's position is that to allow contribution from the husband-vendee would diminish his ability to support his wife and family and thereby frustrate the remedial purpose of the Civil Damage Act.

Given the class of persons to be protected by the act and its legislative purpose, as well as the social impact on the family of the injured party if contribution is allowed, we decline to overrule or limit our previous decisions to permit contribution in this case. AFFIRMED.

Notes

1. *General rule.* The general rule is that contribution is available only when there is common liability and when the tortfeasor seeking contribution has paid more than his equitable share.

2. *Spousal or parental immunity.* The common liability is a formal way of stating the result in family immunity cases. Suppose a child is injured by the concurrent negligence of her father and another tortfeasor. When the child sues the tortfeasor, he seeks contribution from the negligent father. If the father is not liable directly to the child because the state retains parental immunity, he is not liable to the tortfeasor for contribution, either. See *Crotta v. Home Depot, Inc.*, 249 Conn. 634, 732 A.2d 767 (1999). Instead of stating this result by stating the formal rule, could courts state a policy that produces this result?

3. *Pro rata shares.* Common liability, and hence a potential for contribution, is readily found in routine concurrent negligence cases. The traditional measure of contribution was a pro rata share, that is, a share proportionate to the number of tortfeasors. If there were two tortfeasors and B paid the entire loss, B would be entitled to contribution of one-half from A. If there were three and C paid the entire loss, C would be entitled to contribution of one-third each from B and A. In the end, each tortfeasor paid the same amount of the plaintiff's loss unless there was some special equitable reason to ignore the share of one, as where one of them is insolvent. Should the pro rata sharing of liabilities through contribution continue today or might courts adopt other solutions?

DUNN v. PRAISS, 139 N.J. 564, 656 A.2d 413 (1995). Dunn was a member of a Health Maintenance Organization called HCP. When he complained of inflammation and swelling in his scrotum, his primary care physician under the HMO plan sent him to Dr. Praiss, whose tests revealed a mass in the scrotum. Another physician, Marmar, told him to notice any change in the mass, but scheduled no further tests or evaluations. Neither the test results nor the evaluations reached the primary care physician. Months later, after other complaints, physicians discovered that Dunn had testicular cancer and that it had spread to his liver. He underwent extensive chemotherapy, then died. Dunn's widow settled her wrongful death action against Marmar and Marmar sought contribution from HCP, the Health Maintenance Organization, on the ground that its breach of contract in supplying care to Dunn was a cause of his injury. *Held*: if contribution rights are procedurally preserved, then on facts like those here, one whose negligence is a cause of injury can recover contribution from one whose breach of contract is a cause of the same injury. Cases that permit contribution between a negligent actor and a strictly liable actor suggest the pragmatic and equitable basis for this rule.

§ 4. NEW FORMS OF APPORTIONMENT AMONG TORTFEASORS

AMERICAN MOTORCYCLE ASS'N v. SUPERIOR COURT, 20 Cal.3d 578, 146 Cal.Rptr. 182, 578 P.2d 899 (1978). Glen Gregos, a teen-aged boy, was seriously injured in a motorcycle race sponsored by American Motorcycle Association (AMA). He brings this action against AMA for negligence, and AMA seeks to bring in the parents on a claim that they were also negligent and should share in liability. AMA also argued that it should not be jointly and severally liable with the parents or any other tortfeasors, but should, after the adoption of comparative negligence, be held only for its own percentage share of negligence. *Held*: (1) Adoption of comparative negligence does not abolish joint and several liability. In some cases each defendant's act alone would be sufficient to cause the whole harm, and in others it is impossible to tell how much would have been caused by each defendant. It is no answer to limit such defendants' liability in proportion to their negligence when that negligence may have caused the entire harm. Joint and several liability continues to help guarantee adequate compensation in cases where individual tortfeasors may be unable to pay their share. (2) Although the state has a contribution statute limiting contribution to cases involving a joint judgment and in such cases providing for pro rata contribution, this is not intended to prevent judicial development of equitable sharing arrangements. In the past this has been done under the all-or-nothing concept of "indemnity" but that concept will now be adapted to permit tortfeasors to share liability in proportion to fault. Thus if a tortfeasor guilty of 10% of the fault is made to pay all of the plaintiff's damages, that tortfeasor will be entitled to "equitable indemnity" for the 90%.

Notes

1. *Effect of comparative negligence on joint and several liability.* In § 6 below, we'll consider how the facts in *American Motorcycle* might play out in a proportionate fault jurisdiction. For now, can we say that under the rule in *American Motorcycle,* the comparative negligence system does *not* do away with joint and several liability?

2. *Effect of comparative negligence on contribution.* Can we say that under the rule in *American Motorcycle,* the comparative negligence system *does* change the way contribution is calculated? Remember that before the adoption of comparative negligence, contribution among tortfeasors was usually based on equal ("pro rata") shares. If there were two tortfeasors each should pay one-half; if one paid the whole judgment for the plaintiff, that one would be entitled to recover one-half from the other. This did not apportion according to fault but according to the number of tortfeasors. Exactly how is that changed under the *American Motorcycle* rule?

3. *"Indemnity." American Motorcycle* spoke of "indemnity." The term indemnity does not track traditional usage because the claim looks like an ordinary contribution claim. Perhaps the courts used the indemnity terminology because contribution statute did not permit contribution based on settlement, as distinct from judgment.

4. *Fault apportionment.* With the advent of comparative fault, the all or nothing system was abandoned. Juries might apportion some responsibility to the plaintiff, some to A and some to B. If the plaintiff suffers an indivisible injury, then under *American Motorcycle* and the general rules of comparative fault, each party is ultimately responsible for a share of the losses proportioned to his fault.

SAFEWAY STORES, INC. v. NEST–KART

Supreme Court of California, 1978.
21 Cal.3d 322, 146 Cal.Rptr. 550, 579 P.2d 441.

TOBRINER, JUSTICE.

In January 1972, plaintiff Rita Elliot was injured in a Safeway supermarket when the shopping cart she was using broke and fell on her foot, causing serious injuries requiring surgery. Plaintiff brought suit against Safeway (the owner of the shopping cart who had made it available for customers' use), Nest–Kart, a division of Folding Carrier Corporation (the manufacturer of the cart), and Technibilt Corporation (a company that, on occasion, had repaired some of Safeway's shopping carts), alleging that the various defendants were liable for her injuries under both strict product liability and negligence principles; defendants, in response, claimed that the plaintiff's own negligence was a proximate cause of the accident. At trial, the jury absolved both plaintiff and Technibilt of any responsibility for the accident, and returned a verdict for plaintiff of $25,000 against both Safeway and Nest–Kart.

[The jury made "special findings," that Safeway was liable both on negligence and strict liability grounds and that Nest–Kart was liable solely on strict liability grounds. The jury found that the "comparative fault" was 80% for Safeway and 20% for Nest–Kart.]

Thereafter, the trial court entered a judgment of $25,000 in favor of plaintiff and against Safeway and Nest–Kart. After the judgment had initially been satisfied by Safeway and Nest–Kart on an 80 percent–20 percent basis, Safeway moved in the trial court for a judgment of contribution to require Nest–Kart to pay an additional 30 percent of the judgment to Safeway, so as to achieve an equal 50–50 apportionment between the two tortfeasors.... [T]he trial court granted Safeway's motion and ordered each defendant to bear 50 percent of the judgment. It is from this order that Nest–Kart appeals....

American Motorcycle has now explicitly held that, contrary to the trial court's conclusion, the existing contribution statutes do not in themselves necessarily prohibit apportionment of liability among multiple tortfeasors on a comparative fault basis.

The question remains, however, whether the comparative indemnity doctrine, recognized in *American Motorcycle* as a permissible basis for apportioning liability among multiple negligent tortfeasors, may also be applied to apportion liability when, as in the instant case, the liability of one or more defendants derives from principles of strict liability....

First, and most significantly, we believe that the basic equitable considerations that led our court to adopt a rule permitting comparative apportionment of liability among multiple tortfeasors apply equally in the instant setting....

Nothing in the rationale of strict product liability conflicts with a rule which apportions liability between a strictly liable defendant and other responsible tortfeasors. Although one of the principal social policies served by product liability doctrine is to assign liability to a party who possesses the ability to distribute losses over an appropriate segment of society (see Greenman v. Yuba Power Products, Inc....), this policy has never been viewed as so absolute as to require, or indeed as to permit negligent tortfeasors who have also contributed to the injury to escape all liability whatsoever....

It is sometimes suggested, however, that while apportionment between strictly liable and negligent defendants may be a desirable goal, we encounter a fundamental doctrinal obstacle to any such apportionment in that no logical basis can be found for comparing the relative "fault" of a negligent defendant with that of a defendant whose liability rests on the "no fault" concept of strict product liability.... As our recent decision in Daly v. General Motors Corp., supra, explains, however, the suggested difficulties are more theoretical than practical, and experience in other jurisdictions demonstrates that juries are fully competent to apply comparative fault principles between negligent and strictly liable defendants....

Finally, we note that a contrary conclusion, which confined the operation of the comparative indemnity doctrine to cases involving solely negligent defendants, would lead to bizarre, and indeed irrational, consequences. Thus, if we were to hold that the comparative indemnity doctrine could only be invoked by a negligent defendant but not a strictly liable defendant, a manufacturer who was actually negligent in producing a product could frequently be placed in a better position than a manufacturer who was free from negligence but who happened to produce a defective product, for the negligent manufacturer would be permitted to shift the bulk of liability to more negligent cotortfeasors, while the strictly liable defendant would be denied the benefit of such apportionment. Because we can discern no policy considerations that demand or justify such a result, we hold that in a case such as the instant one, the comparative indemnity doctrine may be utilized to allocate liability between a negligent and a strictly liable defendant ...

[Concurring and dissenting opinions are omitted.]

Notes

1. *Apportioning contributory negligence and strict liability.* The principle that comparative fault can operate to reduce recovery from a person who is strictly liable is applied in *Safeway* on the contribution issue. If it is a valid principle there, then presumably it is equally valid to reduce the recovery of a faulty plaintiff under contributory negligence/comparative fault rules. See *Daly v. General Motors Corp.*, 20 Cal.3d 725, 144 Cal.Rptr. 380, 575 P.2d 1162 (1978).

2. *Apportioning tortfeasor fault and strict liability.* On its facts, *Safeway* operates to deny a negligent party any contribution from a non-negligent party who has paid its "comparative fault" share. But is this the legal significance of the case? Suppose Nest–Kart had paid the entire judgment in favor of the plaintiff and had sought contribution. Does the principle adopted in the case limit Nest–Kart's recovery from Safeway to 80%? If so, is this justified, given the fact that Nest–Kart is not shown to be guilty of any fault and Safeway is?

3. The same problem may arise if Safeway had paid the entire sum and sought contribution (or "equitable indemnity"). Is it clear that the case would allow Safeway, though negligent, to recover 20% from Nest–Kart? This view was adopted in *Cartel Capital Corp. v. Fireco of New Jersey*, 81 N.J. 548, 410 A.2d 674, 19 A.L.R.4th 310 (1980). Why not hold that as between a faulty and a non-faulty party, the burden should fall entirely upon the party guilty of fault?

4. *Apportionment methods.* Consider how apportionment of liability can be accomplished. We first saw a but-for cause kind of apportionment: where harm was divisible, each defendant was liable for the harm he caused, no more and no less. We have now seen the possibility of a fault-based apportionment (under comparative negligence rules), an equal shares apportionment (in contribution claims) and whatever kind of apportionment is accomplished in the *Safeway* case. What is it exactly that is being apportioned there? Is it possible to apportion something other than separable injuries or fault?

5. *Comparative causation.* A number of courts and some of the comparative fault statutes say that we must be apportioning responsibility by comparative causation. That is, we must be deciding the relative importance of two or more causes of the plaintiff's harm. E.g., *Duncan v. Cessna Aircraft Co.*, 665 S.W.2d 414 (Tex.1984); Robert N. Strassfeld, *Causal Comparisons*, 60 FORDHAM L. REV. 913 (1992).

6. *Comparing causation by the leap of intuition.* Is it feasible to base apportionment on the relative importance of causation? One way to do this

might be to make a rough or intuitive judgment. This sounds much like what the trier must do in deciding proximate cause issues. The trier might conclude, for example, that the defendant was negligent and also a but-for cause of harm, but that the defendant's causal connection was too insignificant to warrant liability. Could the trier go beyond that and decide that the causal significance of one cause should be rated at 20% and another at 80%? Remember that the trier should be excluding judgments about fault.

7. *Comparing causation by comparing causal potency.* Another way to rate the significance of two causes would be to estimate their respective capacities for harm. Suppose that the plaintiff suffers cancer as a result of exposure to two different products and that the two manufacturers are wholly without fault but are strictly liable. Valid epidemiological studies show that exposure to the first product increases the probability of cancer by .40 and that exposure to the second increases the probability of cancer by .80. Finally, suppose the combination of the two adds nothing to the risk. Could you apportion liability between the two manufacturers if the plaintiff's total recovery was $1,200,000? See Mario J. Rizzo & Frank S. Arnold, *Causal Apportionment in the Law of Torts: An Economic Theory*, 80 COLUM. L. REV. 1399 (1980). Notice that the apportionment formula suggested by this example is not based on "how much" harm was caused by each product in this particular case.

8. Professor Strassfeld criticizes all the approaches to comparative causation, including that suggested by the preceding paragraph. He thinks judgments about comparative causation are possible even though they are largely unquantifiable, but they can be "cumbersome, unpredictable and subjective." Consequently, he favors using causal apportionment only when comparing fault is not possible. See Strassfeld, supra note 5. In the practical world of trials and settlements would it be better to use a rule of thumb, such as pro rata apportionment when comparative fault is impossible? Or go back to liability for fault with true comparative negligence apportionment?

9. *Restatement of Apportionment.* Recognizing that comparing negligence, intentional wrongdoing, and activities that warrant strict liability requires the trier to compare incommensurable qualities, the Restatement of Apportionment rejects the terms comparative negligence and comparative fault altogether in favor of comparative responsibility. See RESTATEMENT OF APPORTIONMENT § 8, cmt. a. Under this section, the trier considers various factors in assigning responsibility. "The nature of each person's risk-creating conduct includes such things as how unreasonable the conduct was under the circumstances, the extent to which the conduct failed to meet the applicable legal standard, the circumstances surrounding the conduct, each person's abilities and disabilities, and each person's awareness, intent, or indifference with respect to the risks." Id., cmt. c.

Is this merely one way of saying the trier considers the *Carroll Towing* factors? If not, then does this approach invite the triers to exercise their biases? How can an appellate court review the sufficiency of evidence for any particular assignment of "responsibility?"

HYMOWITZ v. ELI LILLY AND COMPANY

Court of Appeals of New York, 1989.
73 N.Y.2d 487, 541 N.Y.S.2d 941, 539 N.E.2d 1069.

WACHTLER, CHIEF JUDGE.

[In 1941, the Food and Drug Administration (FDA) approved marketing of a drug known generically as diethylstilbestrol or DES. Over the years the drug was marketed for use by pregnant women. One of its purposes was to prevent miscarriages. The drug was a generic drug, that is, not the patented property of any one company. New companies would market the drug, others would drop out. Some 300 companies in all sold the drug for varying lengths of time to varying numbers of consumers.

[Although the drug first appeared to be safe, it later appeared that female children of mothers who used the drug were at risk for vaginal cancers and terrible complications when they reached adult years. It was often impossible for mothers to know or recall the name of the manufacturer of a drug she had taken twenty years earlier. For this reason, a DES daughter might be unable to show which of the manufacturers produced the particular specimen ingested by her mother.

[The cases before the Court here are suits by DES daughters against one or more DES manufacturers. In the trial court, the defendants moved for summary judgment on the ground, among others, that the defendant which had produced the particular chemical ingested by the plaintiffs' mothers could not be identified. These motions were denied. The Appellate Division affirmed.]

The paradigm of alternative liability is found in the case of Summers v. Tice, (33 Cal.2d 80, 199 P.2d 1). In Summers (supra), plaintiff and the two defendants were hunting, and defendants carried identical shotguns and ammunition. During the hunt, defendants shot simultaneously at the same bird, and plaintiff was struck by bird shot from one of the defendants' guns. The court held that where two defendants breach a duty to the plaintiff, but there is uncertainty regarding which one caused the injury, "the burden is upon each such actor to prove that he has not caused the harm" The central rationale for shifting the burden of proof in such a situation is that without this device both defendants will be silent, and plaintiff will not recover; with alternative liability, however, defendants will be forced to speak, and reveal the culpable party, or else be held jointly and severally liable themselves. Consequently, use of the alternative liability doctrine generally requires that the defendants have better access to information than does the plaintiff, and that all possible tort-feasors be before the court It is also recognized that alternative liability rests on the notion that where there is a small number of possible wrongdoers, all of whom breached a duty to the plaintiff, the likelihood that any one of them injured the plaintiff is relatively high, so that forcing them to exonerate themselves, or be held liable, is not unfair.

In DES cases, however, there is a great number of possible wrong-doers, who entered and left the market at different times, and some of whom no longer exist. Additionally, in DES cases many years elapse between the ingestion of the drug and injury. Consequently, DES defendants are not in any better position than are plaintiffs to identify the manufacturer of the DES ingested in any given case, nor is there any real prospect of having all the possible producers before the court. Finally, while it may be fair to employ alternative liability in cases involving only a small number of potential wrongdoers, that fairness disappears with the decreasing probability that any one of the defendants actually caused the injury. . . .

Nor does the theory of concerted action, in its pure form, supply a basis for recovery. This doctrine, seen in drag racing cases, provides for joint and several liability on the part of all defendants having an understanding, express or tacit, to participate in "a common plan or design to commit a tortious act" (Prosser and Keeton, Torts § 46, at 323 [5th ed.];) As . . . the present record reflects, drug companies were engaged in extensive parallel conduct in developing and marketing DES. There is nothing in the record, however, beyond this similar conduct to show any agreement, tacit or otherwise, to market DES for pregnancy use without taking proper steps to ensure the drug's safety. Parallel activity, without more, is insufficient to establish the agreement element necessary to maintain a concerted action claim. Thus this theory also fails in supporting an action by DES plaintiffs.

In short, extant common-law doctrines, unmodified, provide no relief for the DES plaintiff unable to identify the manufacturer of the drug that injured her. This is not a novel conclusion; in the last decade a number of courts in other jurisdictions also have concluded that present theories do not support a cause of action in DES cases. Some courts, upon reaching this conclusion, have declined to find any judicial remedy for the DES plaintiffs who cannot identify the particular manufacturer of the DES ingested by their mothers. Other courts, however, have found that some modification of existing doctrine is appropriate to allow for relief for those injured by DES of unknown manufacture

We conclude that the present circumstances call for recognition of a realistic avenue of relief for plaintiffs injured by DES. . . .

Indeed, it would be inconsistent with the reasonable expectations of a modern society to say to these plaintiffs that because of the insidious nature of an injury that long remains dormant, and because so many manufacturers, each behind a curtain, contributed to the devastation, the cost of injury should be borne by the innocent and not the wrong-doers. This is particularly so where the Legislature consciously created these expectations by reviving hundreds of DES cases. Consequently, the ever-evolving dictates of justice and fairness, which are the heart of our common-law system, require formation of a remedy for injuries caused by DES

We stress, however, that the DES situation is a singular case, with manufacturers acting in a parallel manner to produce an identical, generically marketed product, which causes injury many years later, and which has evoked a legislative response reviving previously barred actions. Given this unusual scenario, it is more appropriate that the loss be borne by those that produced the drug for use during pregnancy, rather than by those who were injured by the use, even where the precise manufacturer of the drug cannot be identified in a particular action. We turn then to the question of how to fairly and equitably apportion the loss occasioned by DES, in a case where the exact manufacturer of the drug that caused the injury is unknown. . . .

In Sindell v. Abbott Labs., [26 Cal. 3d 588, 163 Cal. Rptr. 132, 607 P.2d 924 (1980)], the court synthesized the market share concept by modifying the Summers v. Tice alternative liability rationale in two ways. It first loosened the requirement that all possible wrongdoers be before the court, and instead made a "substantial share" sufficient. The court then held that each defendant who could not prove that it did not actually injure plaintiff would be liable according to that manufacturer's market share. The court's central justification for adopting this approach was its belief that limiting a defendant's liability to its market share will result, over the run of cases, in liability on the part of a defendant roughly equal to the injuries the defendant actually caused.

In the recent case of Brown v. Superior Ct., 44 Cal.3d 1049, 245 Cal.Rptr. 412, 751 P.2d 470, the California Supreme Court resolved some apparent ambiguity in Sindell v. Abbott Labs., and held that a manufacturer's liability is several only, and, in cases in which all manufacturers in the market are not joined for any reason, liability will still be limited to market share, resulting in a less than 100% recovery for a plaintiff. Finally, it is noteworthy that determining market shares under Sindell v. Abbott Labs. proved difficult and engendered years of litigation. After attempts at using smaller geographical units, it was eventually determined that the national market provided the most feasible and fair solution, and this national market information was compiled (see In re Complex DES Litig., No. 830/109, Cal.Super.Ct.).

Four years after Sindell v. Abbott Labs., the Wisconsin Supreme Court followed with Collins v. Lilly & Co., 116 Wis.2d 166, 342 N.W.2d 37, supra. Deciding the identification issue without the benefit of the extensive California litigation over market shares, the Wisconsin court held that it was prevented from following Sindell due to "the practical difficulty of defining and proving market share" (id., at 189, 342 N.W.2d, at 48). Instead of focusing on tying liability closely to the odds of actual causation, as the Sindell court attempted, the Collins court took a broader perspective, and held that each defendant is liable in proportion to the amount of risk it created that the plaintiff would be injured by DES. Under the Collins structure, the "risk" each defendant is liable for is a question of fact in each case, with market shares being relevant to this determination (id., at 191, 200, 342 N.W.2d 37). Defendants are allowed, however, to exculpate themselves by showing that their product could not have caused the injury to the particular plaintiff (id., at 198, 342 N.W.2d 37).

The Washington Supreme Court, writing soon after Collins v. Lilly & Co., took yet another approach (see, Martin v. Abbott Labs., 102 Wash.2d 581, 689 P.2d 368, supra). . . .

Under the Washington scheme, defendants are first allowed to exculpate themselves by proving by the preponderance of the evidence that they were not the manufacturer of the DES that injured plaintiff. Unexculpated defendants are presumed to have equal market shares, totaling 100%. Each defendant then has the opportunity to rebut this presumption by showing that its actual market share was less than presumed. If any defendants succeed in rebutting this presumption, the liability shares of the remaining defendants who could not prove their actual market share are inflated, so that the plaintiff received a 100% recovery (id., at 605–606, 689 P.2d 368).[7] The market shares of defendants is a question of fact in each case, and the relevant market can be a particular pharmacy, or county, or State, or even the country, depending upon the circumstances the case presents (George v. Parke–Davis, 107 Wash.2d 584, 733 P.2d 507).

[W]e are led to the conclusion that a market share theory, based upon a national market, provides the best solution. As California discovered, the reliable determination of any market smaller than the national one likely is not practicable. Moreover, even if it were possible, of the hundreds of cases in the New York courts, without a doubt there are many in which the DES that allegedly caused injury was ingested in another State. Among the thorny issues this could present, perhaps the most daunting is the spectre that the particular case could require the establishment of a separate market share matrix. We feel that this is an unfair, and perhaps impossible burden to routinely place upon the litigants in individual cases.

Nor do we believe that the Wisconsin approach of assessing the "risk" each defendant caused a particular plaintiff, to be litigated anew as a question of fact in each case, is the best solution for this State. Applied on a limited scale this theory may be feasible, and certainly is the most refined approach by allowing a more thorough consideration of how each defendant's actions threatened the plaintiff. We are wary,

---

7. The actual operation of this theory proved more mathematically complex when the court was presented with the question of what to do about unavailable defendants. Recognizing that the possibility of abuse existed when defendants implead unavailable defendants, who would then be assumed to have had an equal share of the market, the court placed the burden upon appearing defendants to prove the market share of the absent ones (George v. Parke–Davis, 107 Wash.2d 584, 733 P.2d 507). If this can be proved, the plaintiff simply cannot recover the amount attributable to the absent defendant, and thus recovery in the case is less than 100%. If the market share of the absent defendant cannot be shown, the remaining defendants who cannot prove their market shares have their shares inflated to provide plaintiff with full recovery. Finally, if all appearing defendants can prove their market shares, their shares are never inflated, regardless of whether the market share of a nonappearing defendant can be proved or not; thus, in this situation, the plaintiff again will not recover her full damages (id.).

however, of setting loose, for application in the hundreds of cases pending in this State, a theory which requires the fact finder's individualized and open-ended assessment of the relative liabilities of scores of defendants in every case. Instead, it is our perception that the injustices arising from delayed recoveries and inconsistent results which this theory may produce in this State outweigh arguments calling for its adoption.

Consequently, for essentially practical reasons, we adopt a market share theory using a national market. We are aware that the adoption of a national market will likely result in a disproportion between the liability of individual manufacturers and the actual injuries each manufacturer caused in this State. Thus our market share theory cannot be founded upon the belief that, over the run of cases, liability will approximate causation in this State. Nor does the use of a national market provide a reasonable link between liability and the risk created by a defendant to a particular plaintiff. Instead, we choose to apportion liability so as to correspond to the over-all culpability of each defendant, measured by the amount of risk of injury each defendant created to the public-at-large. Use of a national market is a fair method, we believe, of apportioning defendants' liabilities according to their total culpability in marketing DES for use during pregnancy. Under the circumstances, this is an equitable way to provide plaintiffs with the relief they deserve, while also rationally distributing the responsibility for plaintiffs' injuries among defendants.

To be sure, a defendant cannot be held liable if it did not participate in the marketing of DES for pregnancy use; if a DES producer satisfies its burden of proof of showing that it was not a member of the market of DES sold for pregnancy use, disallowing exculpation would be unfair and unjust. Nevertheless, because liability here is based on the over-all risk produced, and not causation in a single case, there should be no exculpation of a defendant who, although a member of the market producing DES for pregnancy use, appears not to have caused a particular plaintiff's injury. It is merely a windfall for a producer to escape liability solely because it manufactured a more identifiable pill, or sold only to certain drugstores. These fortuities in no way diminish the culpability of a defendant for marketing the product, which is the basis of liability here.

Finally, we hold that the liability of DES producers is several only, and should not be inflated when all participants in the market are not before the court in a particular case. We understand that, as a practical matter, this will prevent some plaintiffs from recovering 100% of their damages. However, we eschewed exculpation to prevent the fortuitous avoidance of liability, and thus, equitably, we decline to unleash the same forces to increase a defendant's liability beyond its fair share of responsibility.

[The court also upheld the constitutionality of the statutory renewal of causes of action theretofore barred by the statute of limitations.]

MOLLEN, JUDGE [concurring in part and dissenting in part].

. . . I respectfully disagree with the majority's conclusion that there should be no exculpation of those defendants who produced and marketed DES for pregnancy purposes, but who can prove, by a preponderance of the evidence, that they did not produce or market the particular pill ingested by the plaintiff's mother. Moreover, in order to ensure that these plaintiffs receive full recovery of their damages, as they are properly entitled to by any fair standard, I would retain the principle of imposing joint and several liability upon those defendants which cannot exculpate themselves. . . .

Notes

1. *The Sindell adoption of market-share.* Market-share apportionment is one of those rules that has a specific beginning point. Building on the suggestion of a law review writer, Comment, *DES and a Proposed Theory of Enterprise Liability*, 46 FORDHAM L. REV. 963 (1978), the California Supreme Court initiated market-share liability in *Sindell v. Abbott Laboratories*, 26 Cal.3d 588, 163 Cal.Rptr. 132, 607 P.2d 924 (1980).

2. *Several, not joint liability.* The idea was so new that the California Court itself may initially have had some kind of idea that it involved joint and several liability. The California Court later made it clear that the market-share idea is not one of joint and several liability. It is several liability apportioned according to the defendant's relative share of the market in the drug that caused injury. Thus it is not (a) liability apportioned according to fault; (b) it is not liability apportioned on the basis of relative causation; and (c) it is not joint and several liability. See *Brown v. Superior Court*, 44 Cal.3d 1049, 245 Cal.Rptr. 412, 751 P.2d 470 (1988).

3. *Market-share and probabilistic causation.* Is market-share similar to the idea we first saw in *Wollen* (Chapter 7)? *Wollen* and some similar cases have seemingly approved a recovery for the lost *chance* of good health, even if that chance was not a very large one; and, correspondingly, such cases seem to contemplate that damages would be proportional to the chance, which would be only a fraction of the damage caused by the injury itself. Professor Farber has described "proportional" recovery as one that "spreads compensation over all possible victims, fully compensating no one but paying something even on the weakest claim." Daniel A. Farber, *Toxic Causation*, 71 MINN. L. REV. 1219 (1987). In a sense, market-share, if it works, merely spreads compensation over all possible victims *and* all possible injurers. Notice, however, that the market-share solution addresses only the defendants' causal responsibility for *exposure* to the drug. The connection between exposure and subsequent injury remains an issue of fact.

4. *Acceptance of market-share theories.* As indicated in the Court of Appeals' opinion in *Hymowitz*, several courts have accepted the central thrust of the market-share idea but have modified some details. In *Smith v. Cutter Biological, Inc.*, 72 Hawai'i 416, 823 P.2d 717 (1991), the court said: "[W]e feel that equity and fairness calls for using the market share approach." But the approach has been controversial and several states have expressly rejected it. Illinois, for instance, rejected market-share on the

ground that the plaintiff's burden of proving causation was a fundamental principle of tort law. *Smith v. Eli Lilly & Co.*, 137 Ill.2d 222, 148 Ill.Dec. 22, 560 N.E.2d 324 (1990). Ohio took a similar line in *Sutowski v. Eli Lilly & Co.*, 82 Ohio St.3d 347, 696 N.E.2d 187 (1998). Rhode Island rejected the whole thing in two conclusory sentences, without giving a single reason pro or con. *Gorman v. Abbott Laboratories*, 599 A.2d 1364 (R.I.1991).

5. *Alternative causation.* Michigan rejected market share in favor of a *Summers v. Tice* approach, but then it hampered practical use of that approach by requiring the plaintiff to bring in all the actors and to prove negligence rather than strict liability. *Abel v. Eli Lilly and Co.*, 418 Mich. 311, 343 N.W.2d 164 (1984).

6. *Concert of action, enterprise liability.* A theory often raised in these cases but almost never accepted is that all of the manufacturers should be held jointly and severally liable because they acted in concert. The conscious parallel actions in the way they produced or warned of the product might be interpreted as an implicit agreement, just as two drag racers who take off together from a stop light might be regarded as having agreed to race even if no one spoke a word. The concert of action theory appeals to the oldest form of joint and several liability, and it works in the drag racing case. But in the products liability cases it has not been accepted on the basis of parallel business practices alone. A variation on the idea of concerted action is sometimes called "enterprise liability." It is based on common adherence to an industry wide standard, which only seems to be a different form of proof. Most decisions have refused to apply these theories to products liability cases.

Two unusual cases that found enough on the particular facts to justify potential liability on an "enterprise liability" or concerted action theory are *Hall v. E.I. Du Pont De Nemours & Co.*, 345 F.Supp. 353 (E.D.N.Y.1972) (six manufacturers produced all the dynamite caps, none labeled, followed practices of trade association); *Nicolet, Inc. v. Nutt*, 525 A.2d 146 (Del.1987) (actual conspiracy to fraudulently conceal dangers of asbestos alleged).

7. *Cases for excluding market-share liability?* Should market-share liability, if appropriate in DES cases, be used in any of the following: (a) The strict liability claim is not based on the claim of a design defect but only a manufacturing flaw. (b) The defendant's product is one of many using the dangerous substance, but the various products use the substance in different amounts. For example, shipyard workers were once exposed heavily to asbestos in working around insulating materials but they might also be exposed if they had used hair dryers in the same period of time. (c) Only a small number of people are exposed to the dangerous substance in quantities that create a risk of harm.

8. *Blood products.* People whose blood does not readily coagulate (hemophiliacs) sometimes require administration of a blood protein called a "factor" in order to control bleeding. The factor is derived from donated blood and can carry the AIDS virus or HIV. Plaintiff has tested positive for AIDS. The virus was apparently communicated through the Factor VIII administered to the plaintiff. It was produced by one of several manufacturers, but no one can say which one. The blood shield law provided against liability except that each entity "shall remain liable for . . . its own negli-

gence or wilful misconduct." Does "its own negligence" mean that no entity supplying blood can be liable on market-share theories? In any event, notice that the blood factor provided is not uniform, because not all units will contain HIV. Should the producers nevertheless be held on a market share theory? *Smith v. Cutter Biological, Inc.*, 72 Hawai'i 416, 823 P.2d 717 (1991).

9. *Useful drugs.* When a plaintiff attempted to apply market-share theories to an injury from a childhood vaccine (DPT), the New Jersey Court drew back. Although the court did not reject market-share generally, it did reject that theory as applied to the vaccine involved. Because the vaccine was "essential to public welfare," and because some manufacturers had withdrawn from the market due to threats of products liability, the court feared market-share liability would either diminish manufacture of the drug or diminish safety research. It might also prevent development of other important drugs, such as a vaccine against AIDS. In addition, the court was persuaded that the right of vaccine-injured plaintiffs to recover compensation under the new National Childhood Vaccine Injury Act provided an adequate, non-tort remedy. *Shackil v. Lederle Laboratories*, 116 N.J. 155, 561 A.2d 511 (1989). The Vaccine Injury Act creates a fund for payment of specified vaccine injuries by levying a tax on the vaccines. The fund is then liable for individual injuries covered by the statute's terms. Doesn't this work out to be a form of market-share liability?

10. If market-share liability works in practice as its theory predicts, would it impose any liabilities greater than the liability that would be imposed if we knew all the facts about causation? If the concern is that liability may drive manufacturers from the market or from desirable research, is that concern limited to market-share claims, or does it apply to *any* liability? And why do we ordinarily argue that liability will encourage more safety research but think that it would prevent such research in the drug or vaccine case? These or similar ideas are discussed by Justice O'Hern in dissenting to *Shackil.* Is it possible to think of the *Shackil* rule as an exemption from liability which amounts to a subsidy paid by the injured persons?

11. *Firearms.* In *Hamilton v. Accu–Tek,* 62 F.Supp.2d 802 (E.D.N.Y. 1999), *question certified by Hamilton v. Beretta U.S.A. Corp.*, 222 F.3d 36 (2d Cir. 2000), the court held that manufacturers of handguns might be subjected to market share liability. The plaintiff Fox was a victim of a shooting with an illegal handgun which could not be located. It was a .25 mm gun. A number of defendants manufactured .25 mm. handguns and marketed them negligently so as to increased the risk that they would become part of the gun underground and used criminally. Gun makers who did not manufacture .25 mm. guns could be excluded, the remainder held liable in proportion to market share.

12. *Evaluating market-share.* How would you evaluate the market-share rule? Consider whether you think it could be designed so that any given DES manufacturer would be ultimately liable for a pretty good approximation of its correct liability. Would this tend to happen if all DES cases were decided on a *national* market share of the kind adopted in *Hymowitz*? If so, principles of fairness to the defendant would presumably be met. What about plaintiffs? In fact many producers of DES are no longer in

business. Compare how that fact would affect plaintiffs under (a) market share liability and (b) traditional joint and several liability.

§ 5.   MULTIPLE DEFENDANTS: SETTLEMENT AND SUIT IN A JOINT AND SEVERAL LIABILITY SYSTEM

Problem

Perkins v. Alter and Bain

Alter and Bain, each driving a vehicle, collided when Alter made a left turn and Bain, who was attempting to pass, drove into the left front of the Alter car. This collision caused both drivers to lose control and the two cars went off the highway. One or both struck Perkins, who was seriously injured. You represent Bain, having been hired by her liability insurance company for this purpose. Perkins has brought an action against your client and Alter, claiming joint and several liability. Investigation and discovery are complete. You estimate that Perkins will recover against both Alter and Bain, though each defendant contends the other was guilty of the only causal negligence. You also estimate that Perkins will recover a sum between $100,000 and $150,000, but you believe it will be closer to the low end of that estimate. At the same time, you recognize there is some chance that the jury would return a very large verdict, in excess of $200,000. Perkins has made some settlement overtures and you believe you could reach a settlement with his attorney for about $100,000. Your company would be willing to pay $50,000 if Alter's is willing to pay the other half. Alter's attorney, however, has been adamant. She believes that Alter was not at fault and further believes that liability would not exceed about $50,000 in any event. The liability insurer for Alter, according to his attorney, would be willing to contribute no more than $10,000 to a settlement. Perkins' attorney has made it clear that there is no point in discussing any offers of less than $100,000. Consider whether you want to recommend to Bain's insurer that it pay $100,000 in settlement. What issues will you need to research? What document would you use?

Note

Assume that a joint judgment is not required and that contribution is available to a tortfeasor who settles the plaintiff's claim in full and who has paid more than his share of common liability. In such a case would you recommend that B pay the entire sum? What factors will you take into account?

Problem

Parrott v. Amlyn and Bumgartner

Parrott was injured severely when Amlyn, driving a car rented to him by Bumgartner, ran over him in a cross walk. Parrott alleged that Amlyn was intoxicated, driving at a high speed and not keeping a proper lookout. He alleged that Bumgartner knew or should have known of Amlyn's intoxication and should not have rented a car to him under those circumstances; and that, in addition, the brakes on the car supplied were wholly inadequate. Parrott joined both and claimed against them jointly and severally.

Parrott's injuries were quite serious and permanent. Bumgartner took the position that if Amlyn was intoxicated his servants neither knew nor had reason to know it, and also disputed the evidence that the brakes were defective. In any event, Bumgartner has said in negotiations that it is unlikely that better brakes could have made anything different if Amlyn was as drunk as Parrott claimed. Bumgartner has refused to pay more than a modest sum in settlement, and Parrott has refused to accept this offer.

Amlyn, through his liability insurer and lawyer, has taken a different position. Amlyn believes damages may well exceed $500,000. Amlyn's liability insurance policy is for only $300,000. The insurer, following recommendations by the attorney it retained on Amlyn's behalf, has told Parrott they are interested in settling at the policy limit if it can be worked out. Parrott is willing to settle for this sum if he can pursue his claim against Bumgartner, since he believes Bumgartner will be found liable.

If you represent Amlyn at this stage, do you settle or not? What documents would you propose? What concerns must you deal with and reveal to your client and to the liability insurer? After you have made some preliminary notes about the problems you foresee, consult the materials that follow.

Notes

1. As counsel for Amlyn, would you consider the possibility that Bumgartner might be held liable for a large sum of money, say, $900,000? If that happened, what would Bumgartner then consider doing?

2. Some states, once said to be a majority, have indicated that if A settles with the plaintiff, B may still have contribution from A if B later settles for a greater sum or is forced to pay a larger judgment. See *Skaja v. Andrews Hotel Co.*, 281 Minn. 417, 161 N.W.2d 657 (1968).

3. If the Minnesota rule is followed in your jurisdiction, would you advise Amlyn to settle? What advantage would you get?

4. Both your client and the plaintiff want to settle. The sum is agreed upon. The only difficulty is your client's potential liability for contribution to Bumgartner if Parrott recovers a large judgment against him. You, your client and the insurer are all unwilling to settle so long as that potential exists. Can you draft some form of settlement that will protect Amlyn from potential contribution claims by Bumgartner? Assume that your jurisdiction follows the common law pro rata rule of contribution and that you expect Parrott to get a judgment from Bumgartner of any amount up to $900,000. Your insurer will pay and Parrott will accept $300,000. What agreement can you devise to protect Amlyn and the insurer from contribution if this scenario is played out?

5. If you can't devise an agreement that suits you, research will reveal helpful cases like *Pierringer v. Hoger*, 21 Wis.2d 182, 124 N.W.2d 106 (1963), where the parties had similar problems. In that case plaintiff settled with A,

accepting payment of settlement sums and giving an agreement that the plaintiff would reduce his claim against B to B's proportionate liability, whatever that turned out to be. In addition the plaintiff agreed to guarantee that if for any reason B was allowed contribution against A, the plaintiff would indemnify A to that extent.

6. Is it clear how this protects Amlyn? Suppose Amlyn pays $300,000 in settlement and Parrott proceeds with the claim against Bumgartner. In that action the jury finds the total damages were $900,000. If the plaintiff is not permitted to recover more than his total loss, his judgment against Bumgartner must be reduced to $600,000, since $300,000 has already been paid. But even so, this would leave Bumgartner paying twice as much as Amlyn, clearly more than his pro rata share. He might be permitted, then, under the rule in states permitting contribution against a settling tortfeasor, contribution from Amlyn in the sum of $150,000. This would equalize the payments of the two tortfeasors at $450,000 each, but it would deprive Amlyn of the benefit of the settlement. However, under the *Pierringer* type agreement, Amlyn could then claim indemnity from Parrott and thus recoup the $150,000 and have the benefit of his settlement agreement. There is a simpler way to achieve all this, isn't there? The plaintiff simply reduces his judgment against Bumgartner to achieve this equalization. Bumgartner then has no claim for contribution because he will not have paid more than his share. And plaintiff will not be forced to pay indemnity since Amlyn will not have paid contribution. The same principle can be applied under a comparative fault apportionment rule.

CAL. CODE CIV. PROC. § 877

Where a release, dismissal with or without prejudice, or a covenant not to sue or not to enforce judgment is given in good faith before verdict or judgment to one or more of a number of tortfeasors claimed to be liable for the same tort . . . it shall have the following effect:

(a) It shall not discharge any other such party from liability unless its terms so provide, but it shall reduce the claims against the others in the amount stipulated by the release, the dismissal or the covenant, or in the amount of the consideration paid for it whichever is the greater.

(b) It shall discharge the party to whom it is given from all liability for any contribution to any other parties. . . .

CARDIO SYSTEMS, INC. v. SUPERIOR COURT, 122 Cal.App.3d 880, 176 Cal.Rptr. 254 (1981). Manoocher Kafai died in the defendant Hospital while he was undergoing open heart surgery, apparently because a hospital employee connected a heart-lung machine incorrectly and caused air to reach his heart. The machine arguably should have been designed to prevent such a misconnection. It was manufactured by CINCO and distributed by Cardio. Kafai's survivors sued Hospital, Cardio and others. Plaintiff's trial counsel concluded that the presence of Cardio would only complicate a case of clear liability against the hospital, although he also believed he had a good tort claim against Cardio. As a matter of tactics he agreed to settle with Cardio in exchange for Cardio's waiver of any claim for costs. After this settlement, the plaintiffs accepted a settlement with Hospital for $1 million. Hospital now seeks contribution from Cardio. *Held*, the settlement with Cardio was in good faith and Cardio is thus protected under § 877, which applies to equitable indemnity claims under *American Motorcycle* as well as to contribution claims.

Notes

1. *Cardio* and similar decisions on "good faith" were disapproved by name in *Tech-Bilt, Inc. v. Woodward–Clyde & Assoc.*, 38 Cal.3d 488, 213 Cal.Rptr. 256, 698 P.2d 159 (1985). The court held that the statutory good faith rule required a judicial review of the settlement to assure that appropriate settlements would be encouraged and that one defendant would not be held for an unfair share of the costs. The effect of this was to inject the court into a determination of the settlor's fair proportionate share of the liability. The court appeared to think that a settlement like that in *Cardio* was, as a matter of law, not a good faith settlement. What costs and benefits are added by a court hearing on the good faith issue?

2. In *Baker v. ACandS*, 755 A.2d 664 (Pa.2000), an asbestos cancer case, three defendants settled with the plaintiff, taking a release that specified a pro rata credit. The fourth defendant, the trust for bankrupt Manville, settled for a relatively small amount, $30,000, taking a release that specified a pro tanto credit. The fifth defendant went to trial. The judge as trier found that the defendants were jointly and severally liable and that each defendant's share of the $2,200,000 damages was $440,000. Under provisions similar to California's, what must the fifth defendant pay?

CARTEL CAPITAL CORP. v. FIRECO OF NEW JERSEY

Supreme Court of New Jersey, 1980.
81 N.J. 548, 410 A.2d 674, 19 A.L.R. 4th 310.

SCHREIBER, J.

[Plaintiff, Country Burger, operated a place of business equipped with a fire extinguishing system manufactured by Ansul. Fireco distributed and serviced the equipment. Plaintiff suffered a fire, perhaps partly because of grease buildup and the stacking of paper plates near the grill. The fire equipment failed, as a result of which the fire did considerable damage. Fireco, the servicer, was found to be negligent and Ansul's equipment was found to be defective. The "fault" was allocated by the jury as follows: Country Burger, 41%, Ansul, 29% and Fireco, 30%. The total damages were found to be $113,400. However, Ansul, the manufacturer, had settled with the plaintiff for $50,000. Plaintiff's claim against Ansul, and Fireco's cross claim for contribution or indemnity, were dismissed. Both plaintiff and Fireco appealed. The court first held that the plaintiff's conduct in creating risks of fire was not to be considered at all, since it did not constitute an unreasonable and voluntary exposure to a known risk. It then turned to the claim for contribution by Fireco against Ansul.]

We have previously held that the Contribution Law does not require that joint tortfeasors be liable on the same theory of recovery, so that a defendant whose responsibility arises out of strict liability and another defendant whose responsibility is due to negligence may be joint tortfeasors under that law. . . .

As indicated previously a joint tortfeasor's recovery is limited under the Contribution Law to any excess paid over "his pro rata share." N.J.S.A. 2A:53A–3. In this respect it is important to note the effect on the Joint Tortfeasors Contribution Law of the Comparative Negligence Act, N.J.S.A. 2A:15–5.1 et seq. Under the act the percentage of each party's fault must be found and "[a]ny party who is so compelled to pay more than such party's percentage share may seek contribution from the other joint tortfeasors." N.J.S.A. 2A:15–5.3.[7] Thus the Legislature has seen fit to redefine the "pro rata" allocation to be a party's "percentage share" in the contribution scheme between and among joint tortfeasors. . . .

Under the joint tortfeasors law we had held that a settlement with a joint tortfeasor, even though for less than a pro rata share of the total claim, reduced the plaintiff's total claim against the nonsettling codefendant or codefendants by the pro rata share and thus barred contribution from the settling tortfeasor. Theobald v. Angelos, 44 N.J. 228, 208 A.2d 129 (1965); . Now the effect on the plaintiff of a joint tortfeasor's settlement will depend upon the percentage of fault found against him. When one defendant settles, the remaining codefendant or codefendants are chargeable with the total verdict less that attributable to the settling defendant's percentage share. . . .

Applying the foregoing principles, we find that the total relevant fault is that of Ansul and Fireco, there being no contributory negligence as a matter of law. Ansul's 29% and Fireco's 30%, or 59%, constitute the total fault in the case. In a sense, the 59% is 100%. Thus, Fireco's responsibility is 30/59ths or 50.8% and Ansul's is 29/59ths or 49.2%. It follows that Fireco's proportionate share of the entire damages of $113,400 is $57,661.01 and Ansul's proportionate share is $55,738.99. Ansul, however, had settled its obligation to the plaintiff for $50,000. Fireco remains liable for its share, namely $57,661.01.

Notes

1. *Solving the contribution problem.* Accord, that the judgment against a tortfeasor who goes to trial is reduced by the comparative fault share

---

7. We have previously held that the Comparative Negligence Act pertains to fault emanating from strict product liability. Suter v. San Angelo Foundry & Machine Co., 81 N.J. at 162–163, 406 A.2d 140.

attributable to the settling tortfeasor, RESTATEMENT OF APPORTIONMENT § 16. Does this solution resolve all the problems? The non-settling tortfeasor would never need to seek contribution from the settling tortfeasor, since it would be liable only for its relative fault share.

2. *Solving the Cardio/good faith problem.* Are there any other advantages to New Jersey's solution? If California applied this rule, would the plaintiff have risked a settlement with *Cardio Systems* in that case? If not, is that a problem, since the plaintiff did not want to complicate the trial with the *Cardio Systems* defendants?

3. *Potential windfalls.* In *Duncan v. Cessna Aircraft Co.*, 665 S.W.2d 414 (Tex.1984), a products liability case, the Texas Court had this to say against the pro tanto or "dollar credit" rule:

> "A dollar credit reduces the liability of non-settling defendants, pro tanto, by the dollar amount of any settlement. The defendant's liability may thus fluctuate depending on the amount of a settlement to which he was not a party. This fluctuation cannot be reconciled with the policy of apportioning liability in relation to each party's responsibility, the conceptual basis of comparative causation. A dollar credit also encourages collusion by shielding plaintiffs from the effect of bad settlements while denying them the benefit of good settlements."

The court accordingly adopted what it called a "percent credit" under which the settlement with A reduces B's liability by A's percentage share of causal responsibility. If A's percentage share was only 10%, but A paid 50% of the plaintiff's damages, the plaintiff could still recover 90% of his damages from B. The plaintiff in such a case would obtain a 140% recovery, but the Texas Court thought the plaintiff was entitled to the advantage of a good settlement if he was going to be held to the disadvantages of a bad one.

4. *Windfalls and accountability.* Conceivably, the policy of accountability for fault would require use of a comparative fault or comparative causation rule of contribution. In *Dobson v. Camden*, 705 F.2d 759 (5th Cir.1983) a restaurant asked police for assistance in dealing with a customer who was thought to be spending too much time in the rest room. The police beat him. The customer filed an action against the restaurant and the police officer under § 1983. The restaurant settled for $30,000 and the jury then brought in a verdict against the officer for $25,000. The pro tanto rule would relieve the officer of any direct liability to the plaintiff. Would this violate the policy thrust of § 1983?

5. *The problem of settlement with an underinsured tortfeasor.* What would be done under the New Jersey rule if the plaintiff had settled with Ansul for only $10,000 because that was the limit of Ansul's resources? Is there any way to combine the New Jersey rule with the joint liability rule of *American Motorcycle*? Or would a settlement like this mean that the plaintiff in the principal case would only recover the $10,000 of its Ansul settlement plus the $57,000 from its award against Fireco? This would leave the plaintiff almost $60,000 short of a full recovery.

Alternatively, Fireco could be held jointly and severally liable for the entire damages, with a credit only for what Ansul had actually paid. This would impose liability beyond the relative fault of Fireco, but this might be justified, even in a relative fault jurisdiction, if the settling tortfeasor's resources were exhausted by the settlement. How should the rule be written?

6. *Trial: what should the jury know about previous settlements?* A problem of tactics, quite distinct from the calculation of contribution, arises for both lawyers in these cases. Put yourself in the shoes of counsel for one side or another. Plaintiff has settled with one tortfeasor and is ready to go to trial against defendant. Does either party want the jury to know about the settlement?

§ 6. MULTIPLE DEFENDANTS: SETTLEMENT AND SUIT (MOSTLY) IN A PROPORTIONATE SHARE SYSTEM

a. Abolishing or Limiting Joint and Several Liability

CAL. CIV. CODE § 1431.2

(a) In any action for personal injury, property damage, or wrongful death, based upon principles of comparative fault, the liability of each defendant for non-economic damages shall be several only and shall not be joint. Each defendant shall be liable only for the amount of non-economic damages allocated to that defendant in direct proportion to that defendant's percentage of fault, and a separate judgment shall be rendered against that defendant for that amount.

(b) (1) For purposes of this section, the term "economic damages" means objectively verifiable monetary losses including medical expenses, loss of earnings, burial costs, loss of use of property, costs of repair or replacement, cost of obtaining substitute domestic services, loss of employment and loss of business or employment opportunities.

(2) For the purposes of this section, the term "non-economic damages" means subjective, non-monetary losses including, but not limited to, pain, suffering, inconvenience, mental suffering, emotional distress, loss of society and companionship, loss of consortium, injury to reputation and humiliation."

Notes

1. *Effects.* The most obvious effect of abolishing joint and several liability is that the plaintiff, not the tortfeasor, will bear the risk of a second tortfeasor's inability to pay. If A's share is 60% and B's is 40% but B is insolvent, the plaintiff will recover only 60% of her loss from A and none from B, even though A is a proximate cause of the entire harm.

2. *Successive tortfeasors.* A negligently causes injury. B, a health care practitioner, negligently aggravates the injury. Under traditional proximate cause rules, A is jointly and severally liable with B for the aggravation as well as severally liable for the initial harm. Where joint and several liability is abolished, is the proximate cause rule for medical aggravation changed so that A is no longer liable for the aggravation? See *Haff v. Hettich,* 593

N.W.2d 383 (N.D.1999) (A is not liable for aggravation). Suppose that in the same situation the plaintiff sues B for the damages caused by B, not including those caused before B took any action. The traditional rule is that the tortfeasor takes the plaintiff as he finds her. Does the abolition of joint and several liability affect that, or is B still liable for all the damages he separately causes by negligent medical treatment? *Kitzig v. Nordquist,* 81 Cal.App.4th 1384, 97 Cal.Rptr.2d 762 (2000) (B is still liable). Another way to state the rule in *Kitzig* might be to say that abolition of joint and several liability does not affect causal, as distinct from fault apportionment.

3. *Adoption of several liability statutes.* By 1990 the tort reform lobbies had obtained statutory change in the traditional joint and several liability rules in about half the states, relieving defendants of joint liability and limiting their liability to their comparative fault share under some or all circumstances.

4. *Constitutionality.* So far, courts have generally upheld statutes of this kind. E.g., *Jimenez v. Sears, Roebuck and Company,* 183 Ariz. 399, 904 P.2d 861 (1995); *Evangelatos v. Superior Court,* 44 Cal.3d 1188, 246 Cal. Rptr. 629, 753 P.2d 585 (1988). However, there are some striking and recent decisions condemning the statutes as violations of various state constitutional provisions. *Best v. Taylor Machine Works,* 179 Ill.2d 367, 228 Ill.Dec. 636, 689 N.E.2d 1057 (1997); *State v. Sheward,* 86 Ohio St.3d 451, 715 N.E.2d 1062 (1999).

5. *Federal statutes.* Some federal statutes impose joint and several liability for matters within their scope. This is the rule under CERCLA, a statute imposing liabilities for hazardous substances. See *United States v. Stringfellow,* 661 F.Supp. 1053 (C.D.Cal.1987). Presumably the federal statutory liability is unaffected by the state rules. Even states that generally abolish joint and several liability have retained it in some instances.

6. *The economic/non-economic distinction.* The California statute is one of a group which *retains* joint and several liability for actual pecuniary ("economic") losses. New York is another such state. See NEW YORK CIV. PRAC. L. & R. § 1601.

7. *The relative fault distinction.* Another kind of statute retains some joint and several liability when the plaintiff's fault is small or the defendant's is great. New York's statute, for example, limits a defendant's liability to his comparative fault share but only when his liability is "fifty percent or less of the total liability assigned to all persons liable." N.Y. CIV. PRAC. L. & R. § 1601. Illinois offered similar protection to defendants whose fault is less than 25% of the total relevant fault. 735 ILCS 5/2–1117. But that statute was held unconstitutional in *Best v. Taylor Machine Works,* 179 Ill.2d 367, 228 Ill.Dec. 636, 689 N.E.2d 1057 (1997).

8. *Combination systems.* A number of statutes combine the non-economic loss distinction with the relative fault distinction in some way. For instance, Florida prescribes:

> "(3) In cases to which this section applies, the court shall enter judgment against each party liable on the basis of such party's percentage of fault and not on the basis of the doctrine of joint and several liability; provided that with respect to any party whose percentage of fault equals

or exceeds that of a particular claimant, the court shall enter judgment with respect to economic damages against that party on the basis of the doctrine of joint and several liability."

Fla. Stat. Ann. § 768.81

9. *The more severe statutes.* Another group of statutes is more severe, abolishing joint and several liability as to all the plaintiff's damages, both pecuniary and non-pecuniary, and regardless of the plaintiff's lack of fault. E.g., Ariz. Rev. Stats. § 12–2506. As with most other statutes, some of these exempt particular torts, such as those based on hazardous wastes or pollution.

10. *Judicial adoption of several liability.* Several states have judicially rejected the traditional joint and several liability rule, setting up a judicially created several liability system, seemingly along the lines of the more severe statutes. See, e.g., *Volz v. Ledes,* 895 S.W.2d 677 (Tenn.1995).

b. Comparative Fault Effects and Adjustments

PRICE v. KITSAP TRANSIT, 125 Wash.2d 456, 886 P.2d 556 (1994). The plaintiff, already suffering from a whiplash in an earlier bus accident, was riding the defendant's bus. A four-year old boy, walking in the aisle and holding his father's hand, suddenly reached into the driver's area and engaged an emergency stop switch, bringing the bus to a sudden halt and causing serious injury to the plaintiff. The jury found that the boy was guilty of 80% of the negligence, his father 10% and the bus company 10%. Tort reform legislation required the jury to apportion fault among "every entity which caused the claimant's damages, including the claimant or person suffering personal injury or incurring property damage, defendants, third-party defendants, entities released by the claimant, entities immune from liability to the claimant and entities with any other individual defense against the claimant...." *Held,* no fault can be apportioned to the boy. Children under six years of age are incapable of negligence. Although fault of an immune entity is to be considered, the boy is not immune; rather, he is not at fault. "This interpretation agrees with the fundamental practice of not assigning fault to animals, inanimate objects, and forces of nature which are not considered "entities" under the statute.

Notes

1. *Effects of eliminating tortfeasors from the calculus.* As *Price* suggests, the effects of abolishing joint and several liability may be mitigated if the negligence of some persons is disregarded in calculating comparative fault. Notice that the result in *Price* does not quite mimic the result of a joint and several liability system. The bus company is not liable for 90% but presumably only 50%.

2. *Eliminating remote causes.* What other fault should be disregarded besides that of minors too young to be guilty of legal fault at all? Presumably courts should disregard any fault that is not a proximate cause of the

plaintiffs harm. This could lead plaintiffs to argue that the fault of insolvent parties is too remote to count. This might, however, be an uncongenial argument for lawyers who regularly represent plaintiffs, because a narrow view of proximate cause in today's case might cut off liability of the only solvent party in tomorrow's case.

3. *Phantom tortfeasors.* Plaintiffs have sometimes argued that the fault of any person who is not joined as a party in the suit should be ignored, so that only the fault of the plaintiff and the actual defendants should be compared. The plaintiff would not join an insolvent tortfeasor and could not join an unknown tortfeasor like a hit and run driver. Courts usually hold, however, that the fault of everyone, joined or not joined, is to be considered. E.g., *Fabre v. Marin*, 623 So.2d 1182 (Fla.1993).

4. *Immune tortfeasors.* The same idea has been applied to count the negligence of tortfeasors who are immune from liability, inevitably reducing the amount of comparative fault attributable to the solvent and non-immune defendant. Sometimes statutes so provides. See LA. CIV. CODE § 2324 B. To see how this works, suppose the plaintiff is injured by A and B, and that B is the plaintiff's employer. As an employer, B is immune to tort claims and is liable only for workers' compensation payments. If the plaintiff's fault is 10%, A's 10%, and B's 80%, A would have been liable for 90% of plaintiff's damages under the joint and several liability system. If B's fault is disregarded because he is immune, A would presumably be liable for 50% of the plaintiff's damages (because A and the plaintiff were found to be equally at fault). But under the rule that considers all tortfeasors regardless of joinder or immunity, A is liable for only 10%.

5. *Settlement effects.* Suppose the plaintiff suffers $100,000 damages as a result of the combined negligence of A and B. A settles for $50,000. The plaintiff goes to trial against B and the jury finds her total damages to be $100,000 and B's negligence is 70%, while P's negligence is 10% of the total. If joint and several liability is abolished, isn't it clear that the plaintiff should recover $70,000 from B, even though that gives her a recovery in excess of the total damage? See *Wells v. Tallahassee Memorial Regional Medical Center, Inc.*, 659 So.2d 249 (Fla.1995).

c. Comparing Negligence With Intentional and Strict Liability Wrongs

BOARD OF COUNTY COMMISSIONERS OF TETON COUNTY v. BASSETT

Supreme Court of Wyoming, 2000.
8 P. 3d 1079.

GRANT, DISTRICT JUDGE. . . .

The Wyoming Highway Patrol pursued Ortega from Dubois at high speeds. [Ortega was wanted in two jurisdictions and considered to be armed and dangerous.] Ortega repeatedly swerved from his own lane toward oncoming traffic, and otherwise presented a menace to the traveling public in an apparent attempt to cause a crash which would divert the pursuing officers or involve them in a crash. These efforts failed, but the officers were unable to stop Ortega making the roadblock necessary.

[Sheriff's deputies decided to establish the roadblock] beyond the intersection of U.S. Highway 89 and Antelope Flats Road. At that location, they placed improvised road spikes in the hope that Ortega would turn off of the highway onto the road and be stopped when the spikes disabled his vehicle. Ortega did not turn off of the highway, and continued on until he was stopped by the crash just on the Jackson side of the roadblock.

As these events were unfolding, appellees, Michael Coziah (Coziah) and Rayce Bassett (Bassett), were enroute home from fishing at Coulter Bay. As they approached Moran Junction, where they would turn south toward Jackson, they passed several officers who were at the right of the road. These were Sergeant Wilson of the Wyoming Highway Patrol and park police whom he was briefing. None of these officers made any effort to warn appellees of the hazardous situation developing on U.S. Highway 89 onto which appellees' vehicle turned.

As appellees approached the roadblock, surprised officers began frantically gesturing for them to go through as a deputy sheriff moved his car for their passage. Ortega, approaching at 100 miles per hour or more, went through the same opening, smashing into Coziah's car which was going approximately thirty miles per hour. Coziah and Bassett were injured, and Ortega was arrested.

. . . [Bassett and Coziah sued.] The jury allocated 0% fault to Coziah, 40% fault to the Wyoming Highway Patrol, 20% fault to the Sheriff's officers, and 40% fault to the National Park Service. . . .

Since it is dispositive, we turn first to the question of whether Ortega, whose conduct was willful and wanton or intentional, should have been included among the actors whose fault would be determined and compared with that of the other actors by the jury in apportioning fault among the actors as required by Wyo. Stat. Ann § 1–1–109. Appellees contend, and the district court held, that Ortega's willful and wanton or intentional conduct could not be compared with the conduct of appellants. . . .

Unlike the version before the 1994 amendment to Wyo. Stat. Ann. 1–1–109, which used "negligence," its present iteration introduces the more inclusive term "fault" and defines it as including conduct that is "in any measure negligent" eliminating degrees or varieties of negligence consistent with one of the purposes of the statute, that is to ameliorate the harshness of the doctrine of contributory negligence. The comparative negligence statute remedied the injustice of the doctrine of contributory negligence by stating that a plaintiff's negligence prevents recovery only in proportion as it causes plaintiff's damages.

The use of the word "includes" is significant because "includes" generally signifies an intent to enlarge a statute's application, rather than limit it, and it implies the conclusion that there are other items includable, though not specifically enumerated.

Appellees insist this is not so because the words "reckless," "wanton," "culpable" or "intentional" were stricken from the definition of "fault" in Senate File No. 35 evincing clear intent that they were not included in the definition of "fault" as conduct "in any measure negligent." This argument reads more into the deletion than we think justified. It leaves unexplained the legislature's expansion of "negligence" to "fault" which includes conduct "in any measure negligent." It may be as reasonable to attribute the deletions to a belief that the deleted words are subsumed in the phrase "in any measure negligent" as it would be to attribute them to other motives....

Application of Wyo. Stat. Ann. § 1–1–109 in this case to include Ortega as an actor is also consistent with the other purpose of the statute, the elimination of joint and several liability. Subsection (e) provides that "[e]ach defendant is liable only to the extent of that defendant's proportion of the total fault * * *." To leave an actor such as Ortega out of the apportionment calculation exposes the remaining appellants to the possibility that they will be held to answer for his misconduct. Such a result does act as an incentive to those with a duty to protect against intentional harm, and "[a] number of courts therefore have concluded that persons who negligently fail to protect against the specific risk of an intentional tort should bear the risk that the intentional tortfeasor is insolvent." Restatement (Third) of Torts § 24 cmt. b at 164 (Proposed Final Draft (Revised) 3/22/99). The statutory elimination of joint and several liability, however, forecloses our consideration of the merits of such a policy....

The exclusion of Ortega from the verdict form frustrates the legislature's expressed intent, and the defendants were entitled to have the causation rule of DeWald given as an instruction to the jury. We reverse and remand for a new trial.

Notes

1. The proposition in *Bassett* is clear–negligence of one party can be compared with intentional or wilful wrongdoing of another. It is supported in *Slack v. Farmers Ins. Exchange,* 5 P.3d 280 (Colo. 2000) (statute construed to require comparison of intentional wrong and negligence where defendant referred plaintiff to a chiropractor it should have known might sexually assault her). See also *Barth v. Coleman,* 118 N.M. 1, 878 P.2d 319 (1994) (bar owner negligently failed to oust or control a threatening attacker, he attacked plaintiff; fault must be apportioned between bar owner and attacker, bar owner liable only for his own percentage of fault).

2. Such cases raise three distinct questions: (a) Is the comparison sound as a matter of philosophy or jurisprudence? (b) Is it based upon sound statutory construction? (c) What is its practical effect?

TURNER v. JORDAN

Supreme Court of Tennessee, 1997.
957 S.W.2d 815.

ANDERSON, CHIEF JUSTICE. . . .

[The plaintiff was a nurse and the defendant a psychiatrist at the same facility. One of the defendant's patients had a known history of violence, but the psychiatrist took no steps to protect those who might be attacked. He later said he did not know the patient's history of violence, but he himself had been attacked by the patient, and he had referred to that history in suggesting that the patient be encouraged to leave "against medical advice." The patient beat the plaintiff, causing a severe head injury. The jury attributed all the fault to the psychiatrist and awarded the plaintiff $1,186,000. The trial judge, however, thought the allocation of fault unjustified and ordered a new trial. The Supreme Court of Tennessee first held the that the psychiatrist owed the nurse a duty of care and that the duty was breached.]

Having determined that a duty of care exists in this case, we now turn to the issue of whether the defendant psychiatrist's negligence should have been compared with the intentional act of the non-party patient Williams in determining the extent of the defendant's liability to the plaintiffs.

The plaintiffs' argument is twofold: a psychiatrist's liability should not be reduced by the occurrence of a foreseeable act he had the duty to prevent; and as a matter of practice and policy, the negligent act of a tortfeasor should not be compared to the intentional act of another tortfeasor. The defendant maintains that comparison is proper because it limits his liability to his percentage of fault in causing harm to the plaintiff. . . .

[W]e have considered cases in which the negligence of a tortfeasor was compared with the negligence of other tortfeasors. We have also considered the question of comparing the negligence of a defendant with the strict liability of third-party defendants. This case presents our first opportunity to determine whether the negligent act of a defendant should be compared with the intentional act of another in determining comparative fault.

Other jurisdictions have addressed the issue. In Veazey v. Elmwood Plantation Assoc., Ltd., 650 So.2d 712 (La.1994), the plaintiff was sexually assaulted by an intruder and filed a negligence action against her apartment complex for failing to maintain adequate security; the defendant apartment complex, in turn, defended on the basis of the intentional act by the assailant. The Louisiana Supreme Court declined to compare the negligent act of the defendant with the intentional act of the third party primarily because it believed the negligent defendant should not be allowed to reduce its fault by relying on an intentional act it had the duty to prevent. It also expressed several public policy concerns that supported its conclusion: that comparison would reduce the plaintiff's recovery because juries will likely allocate most if not all fault to the intentional actor; that allocating fault to the intentional party may reduce the incentive for the negligent actor to act with due care; and that comparison is impractical because intentional and negligent torts are different "not only in degree but in kind, and the social condemnation attached to it."

In another sexual assault case, Kansas State Bank & Trust Co. v. Specialized Transportation Services, Inc., 249 Kan. 348, 819 P.2d 587 (1991), the parents of a child who was sexually assaulted by a school bus driver filed a negligence suit against the school and the bus company. The Kansas Supreme Court held that a negligent defendant should not be permitted to reduce its liability by intentional acts they had a duty to prevent. . . .

[T]he concern in cases that compare the negligence of a defendant with the intentional act of a third party is not burdening the negligent tortfeasor with liability in excess of his or her fault; conversely, the primary concern in those cases that do not compare is that the plaintiff not be penalized by allowing the negligent party to use the intentional act it had a duty to prevent to reduce its liability.

In our view, the conduct of a negligent defendant should not be compared with the intentional conduct of another in determining comparative fault where the intentional conduct is the foreseeable risk created by the negligent tortfeasor. As other courts have recognized, comparison presents practical difficulties in allocating fault between negligent and intentional acts, because negligent and intentional torts are different in degree, in kind, and in society's view of the relative culpability of each act. Such comparison also reduces the negligent person's incentive to comply with the applicable duty of care. Moreover, while a negligent defendant may, of course, raise a third party's intentional act to refute elements of the plaintiff's negligence claim such as duty and causation, fairness dictates that it should not be permitted to rely upon the foreseeable harm it had a duty to prevent so as to reduce its liability. . . .

Accordingly, we conclude that the lower courts incorrectly determined that the negligence of the defendant should have been compared with the intentional act of the defendant's patient. In this case, however, the error was harmless in that the jury apportioned 100 percent of the fault to the defendant. Thus, we remand the case to the trial court for entry of a judgment consistent with the jury's verdict. . . .

Notes

Negligence and Intent in Plaintiff–Defendant
Apportionment of Responsibility

1. *Comparing intentional wrongs with negligence.* One question is whether you should ever compare intentional wrongdoing with negligence.

This question can arise when the plaintiff is guilty of contributory negligence but the defendant is guilty of an intentional wrong. The old regime in which contributory negligence was a complete bar allowed the negligent plaintiff a full recovery against an intentional wrongdoer. Should courts carry that rule forward and apply it in a comparative fault regime? See DOBBS ON TORTS § 206 (2000).

2. *Intent and Negligence under the Apportionment Restatement.* The Restatement of Apportionment in general favors comparison of all forms of culpability, so that the trier assigns a percentage of responsibility both to the negligent and to the intentional actor. However, when it comes to comparing negligence of a plaintiff with intentional wrong of a defendant, the Restatement appears to draw back with the comment that "[a]lthough some courts have held that a plaintiff's negligence may serve as a comparative defense to an intentional tort, most have not. This Restatement takes no position on that issue." § 1, cmt. c.

Negligence and Intent in Defendant–Defendant Apportionment of Responsibility

3. *Apportionment among intentional and negligent defendants where joint and several liability has been abolished.* The question in *Basset* and *Turner* was whether to reduce the negligent defendant's liability by comparing the misconduct of the intentional wrongdoer. Consider the plaintiff's stake in that issue and the approaches available to resolve it.

    a. *Approach 1.* Assign responsibility by considering all kinds of legal wrongs, including intent, negligence and strict liability activity. This may run the risk that the negligent actor in cases like *Basset* and *Turner* would substantially escape liability on the ground that his fault was necessarily small in comparison to a murderer or rapist.

    b. *Approach 2.* Apportion responsibility by considering all kinds of legal wrongs, but to permit a jury to find that a murderer or rapist was *less* at fault than the defendant whose negligence made the murder or rape all too likely. In *Hutcherson v. City of Phoenix,* 192 Ariz. 51, 961 P.2d 449 (1998) decedent made a 911 call reporting a credible threat that she would be killed in a few minutes. She was, and it could have been prevented if the dispatcher had categorized the call as a priority one call, which would have provided an immediate police response. The jury allocated 75% of the fault to the city based upon the dispatcher's negligence and only 25% to the killer. This was upheld. Would the city be entitled to indemnity against the killer? See *Degener v. Hall Contracting Corp.,* 27 S.W.3d 775 (Ky. 2000).

    c. *Approach 3.* As in *Turner,* refuse to apportion fault among negligent and intentional defendants with the result that the negligent defendant bears 100% of the responsibility to the plaintiff. The plaintiff would also have a right to recover fully from the intentional tortfeasor, but never more than one full recovery. The negligent defendant would have a theoretical right of contribution or indemnity from the intentional tortfeasor. Statutes may actually define comparative negligence or "fault" in such a way to require this result. See

Whitehead v. Food Max of Mississippi, Inc., 163 F.3d 265 (5th Cir.1998); *Welch v. Southland Corp.,* 134 Wash.2d 629, 952 P.2d 162 (1998). The effect is to retain joint and several liability when one tortfeasor is negligent and one is intentional.

d.   *Approach 4.* Institute or maintain the general principle of apportionment among negligent and intentional tortfeasors but refuse the apportionment when the negligent defendant breaches a duty to protect against the specific risk of harms by the intentional tortfeasor, as in *Basset* and *Turner.* This is the solution preferred by the RESTATEMENT OF APPORTIONMENT § 14.

How would you evaluate the solutions? Could you mount principled arguments to (as distinct from political pressure on) the legislative committee considering them?

4. *Intent and concert of action.* The Restatement of Apportionment provides that intentional tortfeasors are always jointly and severally liable for their torts, even though their negligent co-tortfeasors are not. RESTATEMENT OF APPORTIONMENT § 12. Beyond that, the court in *Woods v. Cole,* 181 Ill.2d 512, 230 Ill.Dec. 204, 693 N.E.2d 333 (1998) held that a statute abolishing joint and several liability was not intended to apply when such liability was based upon concert of action. It distinguished the common case of tortfeasors who act independently. In that case, joint liability was imposed under common law rules only because apportionment was not feasible. In the case of defendants who act in concert, however, the tortfeasor is fully liable because he entered into a legal relationship with the others, creating a kind of joint enterprise: the act of one is the act of all. In such cases joint liability is retained even if the statute abolishes joint liability for independent tortfeasors.

Evaluating Joint and Several Liability

5. *Single, indivisible injury; either defendant's act is sufficient to cause harm.* Suppose two defendants negligently set separate fires. Each fire is blown by winds towards the plaintiff's farm. Either would suffice to burn the house down, but by happenstance of the winds, the two fires "combine" before they reach the plaintiff's farm. It is then burned down by the combined fire. Defendant A is fully insured but B has no insurance and no assets. Should A be liable for only one-half the damages? Notice that (a) his negligence is exactly the same as if B did not exist, and (b) the damage is exactly the same as if B did not exist.

6. *A's negligence creates B's opportunity for harm.* In the second kind of traditional joint and several liability case, the first tortfeasor's negligence makes the second tortfeasor's fault possible. In *Hines v. Garrett,* 131 Va. 125, 108 S.E. 690 (1921) the railroad was responsible for putting the plaintiff at risk of rape by unknown persons. She was in fact raped and the railroad was held liable. The railroad's fault is significant but obviously not in the category with that of the rapists. Does it really make any sense to apportion fault at all in this kind of case, and if so to limit the railroad's liability?

REFERENCES. There are a number of articles besides those already cited. Among them, see Richard Wright, *Allocating Liability Among Multiple*

Responsible Causes: A Principled Defense of Joint and Several Liability for Actual Harm and Risk Exposure, 21 U. C. DAVIS L. REV. 1141 (1988); Richard Wright, *Throwing Out the Baby with the Bathwater: A Reply to Professor Twerski*, 22 U.C. DAVIS. L. REV. 1147 (1989); Aaron Twerski, *The Baby Swallowed the Bathwater: A Rejoinder to Professor Wright*, 22 U.C. DAVIS L. REV. 1161 (1989).

SUBCHAPTER C. MULTIPLE CLAIMANTS

§ 7. SETTLEMENT AND TRIAL WITH MULTIPLE CLAIMANTS

In many instances the nominal defendants are also injured victims and they, too, have claims for injury. These claims may be asserted as counterclaims against the plaintiff and as cross-claims against each other. Thus if P sues both A and B for injury, the final configuration after all pleadings are in will quite often involve two claims by each party against each other party for the injury suffered by the pleader and a claim for contribution in the event the pleader is held liable.

Before the advent of comparative negligence there was ordinarily only one winner. It is now quite possible for all three parties (or more in some cases) to be "winners." What problems arise when two or more parties are called to recover against each other?

JESS v. HERRMANN

Supreme Court of California, 1979.
26 Cal.3d 131, 161 Cal.Rptr. 87, 604 P.2d 208.

TOBRINER, JUSTICE.

[Plaintiff, Jess, and the defendant, Herrmann, both asserted injuries resulting from an auto collision, each claiming against the other.]

At the conclusion of the trial, the jury, in its special findings on comparative negligence (BAJI No. 14.94), determined that both parties were partially responsible for the accident, allocating 40 percent of the fault to plaintiff Jess and 60 percent to defendant Herrmann. The jury additionally found that Jess had suffered $100,000 in overall damages and that Herrmann had sustained $14,000 in damages. Reducing each of the parties' total damages by the amount of the party's respective fault, the jury determined that Jess was entitled to recover $60,000 ($100,000 less (40 percent of $100,000)) and that Herrmann was entitled to recover $5,600 ($14,000 less (60 percent of $14,000)).

The trial court, however, did not enter separate judgments in favor of each party in the amount of the recoverable damages ascertained by the jury. Instead, over the objection of both parties, the court offset the two awards and entered a single judgment in favor of Jess for $54,400, the difference between the awards. Under the trial court judgment, Herrmann obtained no recovery whatsoever.

Both Jess and Herrmann have appealed from the trial court judgment, each arguing that the trial court should not have set off the respective awards but instead should have entered separate judgments corresponding to the jury verdicts, i.e., a judgment in favor of Jess for $60,000 and a judgment in favor of Herrmann for $5,600. . . .

In cases in which neither party in a comparative fault action is covered by liability insurance, no conflict arises between ordinary setoff rules and the maintenance of a fair comparative fault system, since in such circumstances a setoff procedure simply eliminates a superfluous exchange of money between the parties. Thus, for example, if neither Jess nor Herrmann carried any automobile liability insurance and both were financially able to pay the judgment against them, the setoff procedure applied by the trial court in the present case would not affect either party's net recovery, but would simply operate as an accounting mechanism to avoid a payment and repayment of the same funds from one party to another. . . .

Moreover, in an uninsured setting a setoff rule may operate to preclude an unfair distribution of loss if one of the parties is totally insolvent or is unable to pay a portion of the judgment against him. For example, if in the instant case, Herrmann is uninsured and insolvent, the traditional setoff rule would prevent Herrmann from first recovering $5,600 against Jess and thereafter defaulting on her larger $60,000 debt to Jess. . . .

In cases in which the opposing claimants in a comparative fault action carry adequate liability insurance, however, the effect of a mandatory set-off rule differs completely, and the inequities which give rise to the present plaintiff's and defendant's objection to the trial court's action become readily apparent.

The facts of the instant case illustrate the problem. If both Jess and Herrmann carry adequate automobile insurance, in the absence of a mandatory setoff rule Jess would receive $60,000 from defendant Herrmann's insurer to partially compensate her for the serious injuries caused by Herrmann's negligence, and Herrmann would receive $5,600 from Jess' insurer to partially compensate her for the injuries suffered as a result of Jess' negligence. Under the setoff rule applied by the trial court, however—despite the fact that both Jess' and Herrmann's injuries, financial losses and insurance coverage remain in fact unchanged— Jess' recovery from Herrmann's insurer is reduced to $54,400 and Herrmann is denied any recovery whatsoever from Jess' insurer.

As these facts demonstrate, a mandatory setoff rule in the typical setting of insured tortfeasors does not serve as an innocuous accounting mechanism or as a beneficial safeguard against an adversary's insolvency but rather operates radically to alter the parties' ultimate financial positions. Such a mandatory rule diminishes both injured parties' actual recovery and accords both insurance companies a corresponding fortuitous windfall at their insureds' expense. Indeed, in this context, application of a mandatory setoff rule produces the anomalous situation in which a liability insurer's responsibility under its policy depends as much on the extent of the injury suffered by its own insured as on the amount of damages sustained by the person its insured has negligently injured.

Such a result runs directly contrary to the main objective of this state's financial responsibility law (see Veh. Code, § 16000 et seq.), which is to assure "monetary protection to that ever changing and tragically large group of persons who . . . suffer grave injury through the negligent use of [the] highways by others." As Professor Fleming has recently explained, "The purpose of liability insurance is not only to protect the insured against the adverse impact of liability but to assure that the victim be actually compensated for his tort loss instead of having merely an empty claim against a judgment-proof defendant . . . [T]o allow setoff between A's and B's liability insurers would thwart the latter function and confer an undeserved windfall on the insurers." . . .

For these reasons, virtually all of the commentators who have analyzed this issue concur in Professor Fleming's conclusion that "[t]he only sensible solution from the point of view of compensation and loss spreading is . . . to proscribe setoff under 'pure' comparative negligence law whenever the participants are insured." (Fleming, Foreward: Comparative Negligence at Last—By Judicial Choice (1976) 64 Cal. L. Rev. 239, 247. . . .

In Stuyvesant Ins. Co. v. Bournazian (Fla.1977) 342 So. 2d 471, the court concluded that while a setoff rule could properly be applied "between injured parties liable to each other in order to avoid an unnecessary exchange of checks and the possibility of inequitable judgment executions," the setoff concept "should have no effect on the contractual obligation of liability insurance carriers to pay the amounts for which their insureds are legally responsible."

Various amici in the instant case proffer a number of criticisms of the general rule adopted in the *Stuyvesant* case, asserting that at least under some circumstances the rule may afford an unfair advantage to uninsured motorists over insured motorists.[5] We need not decide at this juncture, however, whether the "*Stuyvesant* rule" should necessarily be applied under all circumstances in California comparative fault cases. At

---

5. Amici contend that when one party is insured and the other party is uninsured, a no-setoff rule operates unfairly because it permits the uninsured party to recover from the insured party's insurer, while the insured party may be unable to collect if the uninsured party is insolvent. Under the mandatory setoff rule advocated by amici, however, an insured party certainly has no greater ability to recover for his injuries if his adversary is uninsured and insolvent. We have some question whether a no-setoff rule is necessarily "unfair" simply because it permits an uninsured and insolvent party, who has in fact suffered real injury as a result of another party's negligence, to recover from an insurance company which has in fact been paid premiums to provide insurance for *just such a situation*. Moreover, in many cases an insured party will benefit from a no-setoff, as opposed to a setoff, rule even if the other negligent party is uninsured and insolvent. In that situation the insured will frequently be able to obtain at least some recovery by levy and execution on the sums which its insurer pays to the uninsured party. In addition, if, like most insured drivers in California, the insured party has not deleted uninsured motorist coverage from his automobile insurance policy (see Ins. Code, § 11580.2, subd. (a), an insured driver may frequently benefit from a no-setoff rule because his recovery under the uninsured motorist provision will not be reduced by setoff principles. ·

least in cases in which both parties to a lawsuit carry adequate insurance to cover the damages found to be payable to an injured party, both the public policy of California's financial responsibility law and considerations of fairness clearly support a rule barring a setoff of one party's recovery against the other. Because the trial court in the instant case set off the parties' respective judgments without considering the status of the parties' insurance coverage, we conclude that equitable considerations would best be served by remanding the matter to the trial court so that it may ascertain the parties' actual insurance coverage and thereafter resolve the setoff issue with full knowledge of such coverage .....

BIRD, C.J., and MOSK and NEWMAN, JJ., concur.

MANUEL, JUSTICE, dissenting....

The basic obligation undertaken by an insurer in an automobile liability policy is to pay on behalf of the insured all sums, up to the stated policy limit, which the insured becomes legally liable to pay as damages arising out of an automobile accident. "This means that the insurer must discharge the liability of the insured, within the policy limits, even though the claim could not have been collected from the insured by reason of his insolvency."

The indicated "liability," of course, is that which, following a determination pursuant to applicable legal principles, the insured would himself be obliged to discharge if he were not protected by insurance....

The majority, however, would essentially convert what is protection against liability to *third parties* into protection against injury to the *insured himself*—i.e., would essentially convert liability coverage into first party coverage—to the extent of any possible setoff[10]....

The legislative body is peculiarly fitted not only to assess the equity and wisdom of present law as compared with all alternative approaches, but also to include in its consideration the effects, both immediate and long range, which the adoption of any such alternative might have on such matters as insurance rates and costs; such efforts, it appears, are presently ongoing. This court, on the other hand—limited in its proper institutional function to the consideration of individual cases brought before it—is denied such breadth of vision and its concomitant range of available solutions. As the opinion of the majority so eloquently demonstrates, to stray beyond your proper sphere is to invite confusion and uncertainty into the law.

I would affirm the judgment.

10. Thus, if no setoff is ordered, Herrmann's insurer (assuming full coverage) will pay Jess $60,000—rather than the $54,400 for which Herrmann herself would be responsible in an action between her and Jess in which each was uninsured but solvent. Jess's insurer will pay $5,600–even though its insured would be wholly without liability if she were uninsured. The out-of-pocket payment of each insurer, then is precisely equal to the sum of (1) the amount of liability which would otherwise attach to its insured, *plus* (2) the amount by which its insured's own damages would be uncompensated due to the application of setoff in the determination of such liability.

CLARK AND RICHARDSON, JJ., concur.

Note

Accord: *Pham v. Welter*, 542 So.2d 884 (Miss.1989) (adding a stern warning to attorneys for the liability insurance company to the effect that in raising the setoff argument they appear to have a conflict of interest because that argument is not for the benefit of the insured, who is entitled to their representation). The Uniform Comparative Fault Act provides for a setoff of claim and counterclaim, with a proviso that if the claims are covered by liability insurance, the insurance carrier must pay to its own insured any savings it makes in liability by reason of the reduction. (§ 3). The net result seems in accord with *Jess*. See HENRY WOODS & BETH DEERE, COMPARATIVE FAULT § 17.3 (3d ed. 1996).

GRACI v. DAMON

Appeals Court of Massachusetts, 1978.
6 Mass.App.Ct. 160, 374 N.E.2d 311.

[Plaintiff, Gerald Graci, owned a dry cleaning establishment in a shopping center. Air conditioning and electrical work was being done in the center which required contractors to have access to a large electrical box 8 x 8 feet in size. This box was protected by locked doors, to which Graci had the keys. Contractors borrowed the keys from him, but in spite of their repeated promises to lock the doors and to return the keys, the doors were left open. Graci, who had repeatedly expressed concern that children might be injured if the doors were not locked, was never able to get the keys back. He did, however, nail the doors shut on more than one occasion after the contractors had left them open. On a final occasion he was nailing the doors shut when he slipped. His hammer came into contact with hot wires and he was severely burned and shocked. This is his action against the owner of the shopping center, McCauley, and contractors Lind and Damon. The jury found negligence of the parties as follows:

Plaintiff Graci	15%
Lind	40%
McCauley	40%
Damon	5%

The 1969 comparative negligence statute applied to the case. It provided that the plaintiff could recover in spite of contributory negligence on his part "if such negligence was not as great as the negligence of the person against whom recovery is sought...." The trial judge entered a judgment against all defendants.]

Damon argues that he is absolved from liability because the jury found his negligence to be less than Graci's and that Graci could recover from him only if his "negligence was not as great as the negligence of the person against whom recovery is sought"–otherwise "the court shall enter judgment for the defendant." Damon points out that the wording of the 1969 statute is the same as that of the Wisconsin statute (Wis. Stat. Ann. § 895.045 [West 1966]) in effect when the 1969 statute was passed.... Damon contends that we should adopt the Wisconsin case law which has consistently refused to compare a plaintiff's negligence with the total negligence of multiple defendants but has rather compared a plaintiffs' negligence with that of each defendant, denying recovery against any defendant whose negligence was less than the plaintiff's. Walker v. Kroger Grocery & Baking Co., 214 Wis. 519, 536, 252 N.W. 721 (1934) (first establishing the rule)....

However, the Wisconsin rule has been rejected in Arkansas in Walton v. Tull, 234 Ark. 882, 891–895, 356 S.W.2d 20 (1962), decided under a statute similar to the Wisconsin statute and containing the same ambiguity. The court in the *Walton* case characterized the result under the Wisconsin rule as "demonstrably unjust" in denying recovery to a plaintiff whose negligence is less than the total negligence of all the defendants....

In view of the *Walton* case and the split in the Wisconsin court, we cannot assume (as we ordinarily do) that the Massachusetts Legislature intended to import the entire Wisconsin case law relating to the Wisconsin statute.

Any assumption that our Legislature intended to adopt the Wisconsin rule is further vitiated by the 1973 statute.... [T]he 1973 statute changes the phrase "negligence of the person against whom recovery is sought" to read "the total amount of negligence attributable to the person or persons against whom recovery is sought." It thus makes clear that the negligence of a plaintiff is to be compared with the total negligence of all the defendants, all of whom are liable to the plaintiff, with contribution among the joint tortfeasors on a pro rata basis in accordance with G.L. c. 231B, which remains unchanged.

This is an appropriate occasion to use G.L.c. 4, § 6, fourth, which provides, among other things, that "words importing the singular number may extend and be applied to several persons or things." This interpretation has the added advantage that it allows all plaintiffs in actions arising from and after January 1, 1971, the effective date of the 1969 statute, to be treated more nearly equally. Also, this interpretation makes it unnecessary for the courts to deal with two sets of complexities, one of which would be applicable only to actions arising in the three year period between January 1, 1971, and January 1, 1974, the effective dates of the 1969 statute and the 1973 statute, respectively.

Judgments affirmed.

Notes

1. The Supreme Judicial Court of Massachusetts affirmed this decision in a brief statement that it agreed "with the reasoning and the result," *Graci* v. *Damon*, 376 Mass. 931, 383 N.E. 842 (1978).

2. The problem in *Graci* obviously arises only with the "modified" form of comparative negligence and not with the pure form.

3. Only one person was injured in *Graci*. Is it, however, clear that the rule announced makes it possible for several injured persons to recover even in modified comparative negligence states?

4. As *Graci* recognized, when a legislature adopts a statute from another state, it is often "presumed" that the legislature also intended to adopt the judicial construction placed on that statute in the originating state. Yet *Graci* did not follow this rule. Why not? Idaho followed this principle of statutory construction and applied the case law of Wisconsin on this point in *Odenwalt v. Zaring*, 102 Idaho, 1, 624 P.2d 383 (1980). Oklahoma followed the same principle, but its statute was derived from the Arkansas case law interpretation, which, as *Graci* reflects, is quite different from Wisconsin's. *Laubach v. Morgan*, 588 P.2d 1071 (Okla.1978). If this leaves you feeling unsatisfied, is there any principle to support either the Arkansas or the Wisconsin rule?

5. Is it arguable that under traditional rules aggregation is required as a logical concomitant of joint and several liability? This would support the Arkansas rule.

6. Even if there is some logic in aggregating the fault of all defendants where they are jointly and severally liable, does this logic fly in the face of the legislative rule that forbids a plaintiff to recover when his negligence is equal to or greater than a defendant's? If so, is this an argument, not for aggregation, but for adoption of a pure comparative negligence system?

7. For anyone who believes that the pure comparative negligence system is a better one, the Arkansas rule has some obvious attractions, since it partly evades the limits imposed by the modified system. But might it create some new additional issues? Suppose the plaintiff is guilty of 20% of all the negligence, that A is guilty of 35% and that B is guilty of 45%. Plaintiff can clearly recover against B. If he does so, can B have contribution from A? Notice that B's negligence is greater than A's but less than that of A and the plaintiff's taken together. Should the answer for contribution claims be the same as the answer for claims by an injured plaintiff? In *Sitzes* v. *Anchor Motor Freight*, 169 W.Va. 698, 289 S.E.2d 679 (1982) the court followed an Arkansas-type rule as to the plaintiff's claim, but held that contribution would be available even to a defendant guilty of 70% of the negligence. If this is right can the modified form of comparative negligence by justified?

8. See generally HENRY WOODS & BETH DEERE, COMPARATIVE FAULT § 17.3 (3d ed. 1996); VICTOR SCHWARTZ, COMPARATIVE NEGLIGENCE § 16.6 (3d ed. 1994).

FELTCH v. GENERAL RENTAL CO., 383 Mass. 603, 421 N.E.2d 67, 25 A.L.R.4th 107 (1981). Donald Feltch was injured when a truck snagged a large cable Feltch was holding. Feltch was flipped 30 feet into the air and thrown to the ground. He suffered disabling injuries, became depressed, irritable and sexually impotent. This is an action by Donald and his wife Anne. The jury found defendants negligent but found Donald to be guilty of 37.5% of the negligence. *Held*, Anne Feltch's claim for loss of consortium is independent, not derivative, and Feltch's negligence cannot be the basis for reducing her claim. To reduce her claim would be to impute the husband's fault to the wife. The defendant's argument that Anne Feltch's claim could be asserted in part against her own husband is rejected as being only another way of imputing his negligence to her, and to permit a wife to claim against her own husband for his negligence in causing loss of consortium would invade privileged aspects of married life. In addition, the present language of the comparative negligence statute is that "the negligence of each plaintiff shall be compared to the total negligence of all persons against whom recovery is sought." This language indicates that Ann Feltch's personal negligence is to be compared against all others, and she is not personally negligent. Hence there should be no reduction in her consortium recovery.

Notes

1.   This case represents a different kind of situation for multiple claimants. Might it become complex? Imagine three married couples injured in a three-car collision.

2.   One view is that claims for loss of consortium are derivative, that is, derived from the injured person's claim. In this view, the consortium claim is barred if the injury claim is barred and reduced if the injury claim is reduced. E.g., *Jacoby v. Brinckerhoff*, 250 Conn. 86, 735 A.2d 347 (1999) (if injured spouse refused to sue, the other has no consortium claim). The other view is the one seen in *Feltch*–that the consortium claim is independent and stands even if the injury claim is barred or reduced.

3.   In holding that Donald is *not* liable for contribution, is the court merely following the principle of *Ascheman v. Village of Hancock*, supra § 3? Is it fair that Donald, though found to be substantially at fault, should bear no part of Anne's loss, which in turn is not reduced by Donald's negligence? Courts have sometimes seemed to feel that to permit contribution against the negligent spouse would tend to reduce the family treasury and ultimately harm the innocent spouse. This reasoning seems predicated upon the notion that some form of practical "unity" of the spouses remains even after immunities are abolished. If it is correct, would it not be equally correct that a full recovery by Anne would tend to increase the family treasury and thus ultimately benefit the negligent spouse? If so, the negligent spouse not only does not pay his share of the loss, but actually recovers, indirectly, a benefit.

SUBCHAPTER D. DAMAGES

§ 8. COMPENSATORY DAMAGES GENERALLY

Factors affecting settlement are largely factors that affect the trial and ultimate award. As a plaintiff you don't accept an offer of $100 if you think the jury will award you $100,000. As a defendant you don't offer $100,000 if you think the jury will award nothing at all. Estimating probable jury awards is no easy matter. Lawyers must consider matters having little to do with legal rules–the probable evidence that the jury will hear and the jurors' probable reaction to that evidence for example. However, lawyers must also know the legal rules that guide, counsel, and constrain jurors–rules that may be enforced by the judge's instructions, directed verdict, or reduction in awards for excessiveness.

a. Proving and Computing Basic Damages

The topic of tort damages is a small part of two larger fields. One field might be called "trial practice," which concerns itself with strategy, tactics, and rules of procedure and evidence governing trials. This is not only a field in itself, but is one that can be best appreciated in the circumstances of particular cases in practice rather than through the medium of appellate opinions. Accordingly, the trial tactics side of damages appears here only incidentally. The other field is that of "remedies," which includes not only the damages remedy but also the remedies of injunction and restitution. All three remedies are available in many tort cases. The field of remedies, however, is a broad one, summarized most recently in three volumes. See DAN DOBBS, THE LAW OF REMEDIES (2d ed. 1993), hereafter cited as DOBBS, REMEDIES. Consequently, coverage of all remedies and remedial rules pertaining to torts is impractical in any torts course. This section sketches a limited number of damages problems.

Constitutional torts. We have seen that the plaintiff might have a personal injury or property damage claim under § 1983 based on the defendant's violation of his constitutional rights. In such cases, courts apply the damages rules they apply in any personal injury or property damage case. Some constitutional violations, however, cause no obvious physical injury, either to person or property. For instance, suppose you are denied the right to vote, or your right to free speech is infringed in violation of the Constitution. In these cases the Supreme Court has so far insisted that you must prove actual damages, such as pecuniary loss or at least actual mental distress, in order to recover anything more than nominal ($1) damages. This problem is discussed in Jean C. Love, *Presumed General Compensatory Damages in Constitutional Tort Litigation: A Corrective Justice Perspective*, 49 WASH. & LEE L. REV. 67 (1992); 2 DOBBS, REMEDIES § 7.4.

Property torts. Quite a few torts involve physical injury to, or dispossession of, tangible property, real or personal. We have already seen that for total dispossession of personalty there is a conversion action, in which damages are measured by the full market value of the thing converted. When there is similar dispossession of real property, there is no analogous damages claim. Instead the plaintiff recovers the rental value of the property during the time of dispossession. When physical harm is done to tangible property, the measure of damages is very often the diminished value of the property. Thus if A trespasses on Blackacre and damages a house, the owner or possessor will be entitled to recover a sum equal to the difference between the value immediately before and the value immediately after the damage.

The same diminished value rule, based on the market value, is applied in cases of damage to chattels, such as automobiles. However, for a number of reasons, the cost of repair may be substituted as a measure of damages in certain cases, especially where the repair is not likely to enhance the damaged property and make it more valuable than before.

The injunctive remedy is also important in certain tort cases. If the defendant repeatedly trespasses on the plaintiff's land, or threatens to trespass in some way that will cause irreparable harm, as by cutting down old oak trees, the plaintiff may be entitled to an injunction prohibiting such a tort. Injunction is also important in many cases involving intangible property, such as a trademark, and in other business tort cases, such as those involving interference with contracts. See generally, 1 DOBBS, REMEDIES, Chapter 5 (2d ed. 1993).

Personal injury torts. Personal injuries may occur through intentional torts, through negligence or through strict liability torts. The damages, however, are the same for any given broken jaw, without regard to whether the jaw was broken through intent, negligence or wholly without fault. Punitive damages may be warranted in some cases, where the defendant's conduct is "malicious" or wanton. Those damages aside, the main elements of damages in personal injury cases can be stated quite easily.

(1) Damages for reasonably incurred medical expenses resulting from the tort.

(2) Damages for lost earning capacity or wage loss resulting from the tort.

(3) Damages for pain and suffering resulting from the tort, including mental pain and suffering.

(4) In a limited number of cases, an award to pay for the cost of medical monitoring of the plaintiff's condition to intercept a prospective disease, such as cancer, that may develop in the future.

(5) Any other specifically identifiable harm that has resulted from the tort, such as special expenses necessary to travel for medical attention.

In each category, the plaintiff is entitled also to recover for future damages if they are reasonably certain to occur. How difficult is it to calculate these elements of damage?

MARTIN v. UNITED STATES

United States District Court, District of Arizona, 1979.
471 F.Supp. 6.

JAMES M. BURNS, DISTRICT JUDGE.

[Federal Tort Claims case tried to the judge. The plaintiffs, two school boys, riding a motorbike, struck a sagging power line negligently maintained by the government. Each "suffered tragically severe and permanent injuries" from the burns.]

As to the plaintiff Melvin Burrows II, the court first noted that he sustained severe burns to his face, head, back, buttocks, arms and legs. Before considering loss of earning capacity, the court found that medical expenses to Burrows to the time of trial came to $48,130.97, and that future medical expenses would come to about $49,000 additional. Finally, the court awarded $5,000 for psychological treatments.

Clarence Martin is principal of the Florence middle school, owner of a roofing business that employs Melvin Burrows' father, and uncle of the other plaintiff in this case. He testified upon the basis of his observation of Melvin during the seven years he has known him and the month and a half that Melvin had attended the middle school prior to the accident. He believed that Melvin was average or above average in intelligence and probably would have become a skilled worker, perhaps a mechanic or a carpenter. Dr. Glenn Wilt, an associate professor of finance at Arizona State University and an investment counselor stated:

[I]t can be reasonably presumed that, but for their injuries, both Melvin and Jeffrey would have gravitated into positions in one of the construction trades. Clearly, that is exactly what most of their uninjured classmates will do, and considering the general demand in this territory, due to the growth of population and need for attendant services in the construction field, a strong demand can be forecast for these jobs.

Dr. David Yandell, a clinical psychologist and vocational rehabilitation counselor called by the defendant, testified that the intelligence and aptitude tests administered by Dr. Donald Guinoud show that Melvin could not have pursued a career in the skilled crafts but instead probably would have become a laborer. Defendant's other witness, Dr. John Buehler, chairman of the department of economics at the University of Arizona, expressed his opinion that neither plaintiff probably would have become a worker in the skilled trades, but rather each would have earned average wages.

Based upon my evaluation of the testimony and the expertise and credibility of the witnesses, I conclude that Melvin Burrows probably would have become a skilled worker. Dr. Wilt stated that a carpenter would, at 1978 wage rates, earn about $9,450 per year during a four-year apprenticeship and during a subsequent 42–year career as a journeyman carpenter would earn about $18,900 annually in wages and $3,900 annually in fringe benefits. I accept these figures as reasonable approximations of Melvin's lifetime earnings had he not experienced this accident.

Dr. Guinourd testified that Melvin might be employable as a night watchman or night diesel mechanic not involved with the public interaction aspect of either business. Dr. Wilt concluded that, because of Melvin's disfigurement and intolerance to sunlight and perspiration, he would probably be unable to find a job suited to his handicap. Dr. Canter testified that Melvin would benefit psychologically from working even at a lowly position.

Based upon the testimony and my own observation of Melvin Burrows, I conclude that he probably will be able to work at an entry-level position for at least half of his normal working life. According to Dr. Wilt, such work would generate an annual income of $3,120 in 1978 dollars. Thus, Melvin is entitled to recover in 1978 dollars $6,330 per year for four years (apprenticeship period), then $19,680 per year for the following 42 years (journeyman period)....

I find that the award can presently be invested at very little risk and return 7.5% compounded annually. I find that 5.5% is a reasonable annual rate of wage inflation to be expected during Melvin's working lifetime.

I award an amount for the loss of Melvin's earning capacity sufficient when invested at a 7.5% annual rate of return to generate in 1978 dollars $6,330 per year for the four years 1983–1986 (hypothetical apprenticeship period) and $19,680 per year for the following 42 years 1987–2028 (hypothetical journeyman period). These amounts in 1978 dollars are to be converted to current dollars for each year by application of a 5.5% expected annual rate of wage inflation, then discounted at 7.5% per year back to 1979. By this method of calculation, the award for loss of Melvin's earning capacity amounts to $548,029.

The power line struck Melvin on the face, head and perhaps also on the back, causing severe and extensive burns on those areas and on "blowout holes" on his buttocks, legs, left arm and right hand, where the electric current left his body seeking the ground. More than 80% of his head and face was burned, 70% to the third degree or worse. He also suffered third degree burns on 40% of his back, on his entire left buttocks and on at least six blowout ulcers. Melvin regained consciousness soon after the accident and was found wandering in the desert near the scene. Dr. Williams Clemans, a general practitioner in Florence, treated Melvin briefly in the back of a pickup truck outside the local hospital before having him sent to the burn treatment unit at the Maricopa County Hospital in Phoenix. Dr. Clemans testified that Melvin appeared to be in critical condition. He doubted whether Melvin would survive long enough to reach the burn unit.

At the Maricopa County Hospital where Melvin remained for four months, the surgeons removed the charred layers of skin and tissue from Melvin's face, head, buttocks and other areas of his body. They performed numerous skin grafts and attempted to fashion a functioning right eyelid, which Melvin still cannot close. Melvin lost his right ear entirely and the top third of his left ear. To graft skin onto his left temple, which had been burned down to the skull, the doctors ground the skull down to granulation tissue that would accept a graft. Restoring hair growth to this area would require an additional series of scalp rotation operations. The operations have left Melvin's face and scalp severely scarred, his mouth permanently contorted into a sneer. Because his facial nerves and muscles have been burned away, even additional surgery will never restore to him the ability to smile.

Of the expected eleven future operations, Melvin will undergo eight additional operations to his face. Skin grafts not infrequently dry out, crack, become infected and ulcerated and must be replaced by new grafts. Sunlight darkens grafted skin permanently, highlighting the injured area. Grafted areas are also more susceptible to skin cancer than normal tissue. Melvin testified that the grafted areas hurt and itch constantly. Dr. Sacks testified that additional plastic surgeries and skin grafts will not restore a normal appearance to Melvin.

Melvin has suffered psychologically as well as physically. At the burn unit Dr. Canter treated Melvin by hypnosis to relieve pain, prevent regurgitation of food and restore a will to live. Since emerging from the hospital Melvin has faced teasing and ridicule from his peers and startle reactions and revulsion from strangers.

For several months Melvin wore a mask to protect his healing face from further injury. His schoolmates labeled him "Maskatron." During a school outing children from another school saw him and ran away in horror. Strangers often ask, "What happened to you?" Clarence Martin testified that Melvin has become reclusive, reluctant to attend school. Dr. Canter stated that Melvin has become somewhat detached from life, blames himself for his father's heart trouble and may develop schizophrenic tendencies as a result of his injuries. Nor is it likely that Melvin will have a normal social or sexual life, given the severity of the injuries.

Based upon the testimony and my own observation of Melvin, I award $1,000,000 in compensation for pain and suffering.

[The Court here made a similar analysis of the claims by plaintiff Martin.]

I find that the plaintiffs are entitled to awards as follows:

	BURROWS	MARTIN
Past Medical	$48,130.97	$15,384.38
Future Medical	53,629.00	30,000.00
Loss of Earning Capacity	548,029.00	453,088.00
Pain and Suffering	1,000,000.00	750,000.00
Total	$1,649,788.97	$1,248,472.38

The foregoing shall constitute findings of fact and conclusions pursuant to Rule 52, Fed. R. Civ. P., together with earlier findings and conclusions set out in my oral opinion on February 14, 1979.

Notes

1. *Inflation and reduction to present value.* Notice that the judge had to make an upward adjustment in the award for future loss in order to account for expected inflation. The inflation adjustment usually requires expert testimony to show the expected changes in the value of the dollar over the

entire loss period. The judge also made a downward adjustment to account for the fact that although the loss will take place over many years in the future, all of the money to compensate the plaintiff will be paid now and can be invested. This reduction to present value requires the judge or the trier to determine the amount the plaintiff can earn in safe investments of the award. The reduction may also require expert testimony. These adjustments, and some others, are considered in 1 DOBBS, REMEDIES §§ 3.7 & 8.5. Still other adjustments are considered in *subsection b* below.

2. *Periodic payments.* These adjustments would not be necessary if, instead of a lump sum award, future loss were compensated in periodic payments that could be varied as inflation occurred. Some states now authorize such payments in a limited class of cases. See Roger Henderson, *Designing a Responsible Periodic Payment System for Tort Awards*, 32 ARIZ. L. REV. 21 (1990). At least two courts have held periodic payment statutes unconstitutional under state constitutional provisions against denial of due process or against limitation of damages.

3. *The scope of pain and suffering.* The pain and suffering recovery includes all forms of pain, including mental or emotional distress. As this implies, the recovery includes the negative emotional reactions to pain as well as the pain itself. For example, a disfiguring injury, no longer physically painful, may cause a plaintiff to become self-conscious or even to withdraw from social contact. If so, such reactions count as part of the pain for which damages may be assessed. See 2 DOBBS, REMEDIES § 8.1 (4) (2d ed. 1993). Pain or suffering in this broad sense might also include fear or anxiety about future harms, as where the plaintiff is exposed to a toxic substance and fears that she will later suffer cancer as a result. On that score, some courts have imposed special limiting rules covered in Chapter 17.

4. *Dollarizing pain.* Pain is notoriously difficult to measure or even to talk about meaningfully. In *District of Columbia v. Howell*, 607 A.2d 501 (D.C.App.1992) a nine-year-old boy was badly burned in a chemical explosion in school. "The chemicals burned at 5000 degrees Fahrenheit, and Dedrick was burned over 25% of his body including his hands, arms, chest, and face." The jury awarded $8 million in pain and suffering damages. If this award and Martin's had been made in the same year, could you say that one was wrong or even that one was closer to the mark than the other?

5. *Argumentation.* Lawyers have developed some effective jury arguments, one of which is called the per diem or unit-of-time argument. It asks the jury to consider the value of pain by the minute or hour and then to multiply by the number of hours the plaintiff will continue to suffer pain over his lifetime. Evaluating the jury's conversion of proof and argument into dollar amounts is more difficult. Many commentators have expressed concern that our measurements are too crude and that results are not even-handed.

6. *Reinforcing pain.* Another and distinct problem with pain awards is that the award itself may conceivably reinforce some kinds of pain, that is, operate as a psychological factor that helps cause the pain to continue. See Ellen Smith Pryor, *Compensation and the Ineradicable Problems of Pain*, 59 GEO. WASH. L. REV. 239, 280 (1991)

7. *Pain and suffering pays attorney fees.* One important thing to bear in mind when you judge pain and suffering awards is the American Rule that each side pays its own attorney. See 1 DOBBS, REMEDIES § 3.10. That rule explains why the contingent percentage fee is so important in personal injury cases. Lawyers for injured people must recover their fee from the damages award, since hardly any individual would be able to pay a guaranteed hourly fee for the lawyer's services. If there were no substantial pain and suffering award, lawyers would often be unable to pursue the claim with the vigor it requires, simply because damages equal to the plaintiff's pecuniary loss would not bring enough money to justify the time invested.

McDOUGALD v. GARBER

New York Court of Appeals, 1989.
73 N.Y.2d 246, 538 N.Y.S.2d 937, 536 N.E.2d 372.

WACHTLER, CHIEF JUDGE.

This appeal raises fundamental questions about the nature and role of nonpecuniary damages in personal injury litigation. By nonpecuniary damages, we mean those damages awarded to compensate an injured person for the physical and emotional consequences of the injury, such as pain and suffering and the loss of the ability to engage in certain activities. Pecuniary damages, on the other hand, compensate the victim for the economic consequences of the injury, such as medical expenses, lost earnings and the cost of custodial care....

On September 7, 1978, plaintiff Emma McDougald, then 31 years old, underwent a Caesarean section and tubal ligation at New York Infirmary. Defendant Garber performed the surgery; defendants Armengol and Kulkarni provided anesthesia. During the surgery, Mrs. McDougald suffered oxygen deprivation which resulted in severe brain damage and left her in a permanent comatose condition. This action was brought by Mrs. McDougald and her husband, suing derivatively, alleging that the injuries were caused by the defendants' acts of malpractice.

[The trial court charged the jury that if Emma McDougald was so neurologically impaired that she was incapable of experiencing painful sensation or any emotional reaction to it, then there could be no recovery for pain and suffering. But the court went on to instruct the jury that the plaintiff could recover for loss of the pleasures and pursuits of life even if she was unaware of any loss.]

A jury found all defendants liable and awarded Emma McDougald a total of $9,650,102 in damages, including $1,000,000 for conscious pain and suffering and a separate award of $3,500,000 for loss of the pleasures and pursuits of life. The balance of the damages awarded to her were for pecuniary damages—lost earnings and the cost of custodial and nursing care. Her husband was awarded $1,500,000 on his derivative claim for the loss of his wife's services. On defendants' posttrial motions, the Trial Judge reduced the total award to Emma McDougald to $4,796,728 by striking the entire award for future nursing care ($2,353,-374) and by reducing the separate awards for conscious pain and suffering and loss of the pleasures and pursuits of life to a single award of $2,000,000. Her husband's award was left intact. [The Appellate Division affirmed.] . . .

We conclude that the court erred, both in instructing the jury that Mrs. McDougald's awareness was irrelevant to their consideration of damages for loss of enjoyment of life and in directing the jury to consider that aspect of damages separately from pain and suffering.

We begin with the familiar proposition that an award of damages to a person injured by the negligence of another is to compensate the victim, not to punish the wrongdoer. The goal is to restore the injured party, to the extent possible, to the position that would have been occupied had the wrong not occurred. To be sure, placing the burden of compensation on the negligent party also serves as a deterrent, but purely punitive damages—that is, those which have no compensatory purpose—are prohibited unless the harmful conduct is intentional, malicious, outrageous, or otherwise aggravated beyond mere negligence.

Damages for nonpecuniary losses are, of course, among those that can be awarded as compensation to the victim. This aspect of damages, however, stands on less certain ground than does an award for pecuniary damages. An economic loss can be compensated in kind by an economic gain; but recovery for noneconomic losses such as pain and suffering and loss of enjoyment of life rests on "the legal fiction that money damages can compensate for a victim's injury". We accept this fiction, knowing that although money will neither ease the pain nor restore the victim's abilities, this device is as close as the law can come in its effort to right the wrong. We have no hope of evaluating what has been lost, but a monetary award may provide a measure of solace for the condition created .

Our willingness to indulge this fiction comes to an end, however, when it ceases to serve the compensatory goals of tort recovery. When that limit is met, further indulgence can only result in assessing damages that are punitive. The question posed by this case, then, is whether an award of damages for loss of enjoyment of life to a person whose injuries preclude any awareness of the loss serves a compensatory purpose. We conclude that it does not.

Simply put, an award of money damages in such circumstances has no meaning or utility to the injured person. An award for the loss of enjoyment of life "cannot provide (such a victim) with any consolation or ease any burden resting on him * * * He cannot spend it upon necessities or pleasures. He cannot experience the pleasure of giving it away".

We recognize that, as the trial court noted, requiring some cognitive awareness as a prerequisite to recovery for loss of enjoyment of life will result in some cases "in the paradoxical situation that the greater the degree of brain injury inflicted by a negligent defendant, the smaller the award the plaintiff can recover in general damages" (McDougald v. Garber, 132 Misc. 2d 457, 460, 504 N.Y.S.2d 383, supra). The force of this argument, however—the temptation to achieve a balance between injury and damages—has nothing to do with meaningful compensation for the victim. Instead, the temptation is rooted in a desire to punish the defendant in proportion to the harm inflicted. However relevant such retributive symmetry may be in the criminal law, it has no place in the law of civil damages, at least in the absence of culpability beyond mere negligence.

Accordingly, we conclude that cognitive awareness is a prerequisite to recovery for loss of enjoyment of life. We do not go so far, however, as to require the fact finder to sort out varying degrees of cognition and determine at what level a particular deprivation can be fully appreciated. With respect to pain and suffering, the trial court charged simply that there must be "some level of awareness" in order for plaintiff to recover. We think that this is an appropriate standard for all aspects of nonpecuniary loss. No doubt the standard ignores analytically relevant levels of cognition, but we resist the desire for analytical purity in favor of simplicity. . . .

We turn next to the question whether loss of enjoyment of life should be considered a category of damages separate from pain and suffering.

There is no dispute here that the fact finder may, in assessing nonpecuniary damages, consider the effect of the injuries on the plaintiff's capacity to lead a normal life. Traditionally, in this State and elsewhere, this aspect of suffering has not been treated as a separate category of damages; instead, the plaintiff's inability to enjoy life to its fullest has been considered one type of suffering to be factored into a general award for nonpecuniary damages, commonly known as pain and suffering.

Recently, however, there has been an attempt to segregate the suffering associated with physical pain from the mental anguish that stems from the inability to engage in certain activities, and to have juries provide a separate award for each.

Some courts have resisted the effort, primarily on the ground that duplicative and therefore excessive awards would result. Other courts have allowed separate awards, noting that the types of suffering involved are analytically distinguishable. . . .

We do not dispute that distinctions can be found or created between the concepts of pain and suffering and loss of enjoyment of life. If the term "suffering" is limited to the emotional response to the sensation of pain, then the emotional response caused by the limitation of life's activities may be considered qualitatively different. But suffering need not be so limited—it can easily encompass the frustration and anguish caused by the inability to participate in activities that once brought pleasure. Traditionally, by treating loss of enjoyment of life as a permissible factor in assessing pain and suffering, courts have given the term this broad meaning.

If we are to depart from this traditional approach and approve a separate award for loss of enjoyment of life, it must be on the basis that such an approach will yield a more accurate evaluation of the compensation due to the plaintiff. We have no doubt that, in general, the total award for nonpecuniary damages would increase if we adopted the rule. That separate awards are advocated by plaintiffs and resisted by defendants is sufficient evidence that larger awards are at stake here. But a larger award does not by itself indicate that the goal of compensation has been better served.

The advocates of separate awards contend that because pain and suffering and loss of enjoyment of life can be distinguished, they must be treated separately if the plaintiff is to be compensated fully for each distinct injury suffered. We disagree. Such an analytical approach may have its place when the subject is pecuniary damages, which can be calculated with some precision. But the estimation of nonpecuniary damages is not amenable to such analytical precision and may, in fact, suffer from its application. Translating human suffering into dollars and cents involves no mathematical formula; it rests, as we have said, on a legal fiction. The figure that emerges is unavoidably distorted by the translation. Application of this murky process to the component parts of nonpecuniary injuries (however analytically distinguishable they may be) cannot make it more accurate. If anything, the distortion will be amplified by repetition.

Thus, we are not persuaded that any salutary purpose would be served by having the jury make separate awards for pain and suffering and loss of enjoyment of life. We are confident, furthermore, that the trial advocate's art is a sufficient guarantee that none of the plaintiff's losses will be ignored by the jury.

The errors in the instructions given to the jury require a new trial on the issue of nonpecuniary damages . . . . .

TITONE, JUDGE (dissenting).

The majority's holding represents a compromise position that neither comports with the fundamental principles of tort compensation nor furnishes a satisfactory, logically consistent framework for compensating nonpecuniary loss. Because I conclude that loss of enjoyment of life is an objective damage item, conceptually distinct from conscious pain and suffering, I can find no fault with the trial court's instruction authorizing separate awards and permitting an award for "loss of enjoyment of life" even in the absence of any awareness of that loss on the part of the injured plaintiff. Accordingly, I dissent. . . .

The capacity to enjoy life—by watching one's children grow, participating in recreational activities, and drinking in the many other pleasures that life has to offer—is unquestionably an attribute of an ordinary healthy individual. . . .

As in the case of a lost limb, an essential characteristic of a healthy human life has been wrongfully taken, and, consequently, the injured party is entitled to a monetary award as a substitute, if, as the majority asserts, the goal of tort compensation is "to restore the injured party, to the extent possible, to the position that would have been occupied had the wrong not occurred." . . .

Significantly, this equation does not suggest a need to establish the injured's awareness of the loss. The victim's ability to comprehend the degree to which his or her life has been impaired is irrelevant, since, unlike "conscious pain and suffering," the impairment exists independent of the victim's ability to apprehend it . . . .

Moreover, the compensatory nature of a monetary award for loss of enjoyment of life is not altered or rendered punitive by the fact that the unaware injured plaintiff cannot experience the pleasure of having it. The fundamental distinction between punitive and compensatory damages is that the former exceed the amount necessary to replace what the plaintiff lost . . . .

Simons, Kaye, Hancock and Bellacosa, JJ., concur with Wachtler, C.J.

Titone, J., dissents and votes to affirm in a separate opinion in which Alexander, J., concurs.

Notes

1. *Hedonic damages: the terminology.* In the 1980s, plaintiffs' lawyers and some judges began to use the term hedonic damages from the Greek word referring to pleasure or happiness. The term has acquired ambiguity because those who use it sometimes seem to suggest (a) a right of recovery for the plaintiff's awareness of lost pleasures, sometimes (b) a right of recovery for lost pleasures even when the plaintiff is not aware of the loss or in fact has died, and sometimes (c) a certain type of economic evidence. To avoid misunderstanding, the term is avoided here.

2. *Plaintiff aware of loss.* When the plaintiff has lost the ability to pursue life's pleasures and knows it, that knowledge or awareness is itself a source of unpleasant feelings, a sense of loss, and even anguish. Recovery is allowed in most courts nowadays without hesitation. See *Leiker v. Gafford*, 245 Kan. 325, 778 P.2d 823 (1989); *Kenton v. Hyatt Hotels Corp.*, 693 S.W.2d 83 (Mo.1985) (emphasizing plaintiff's loss of ability to play tennis, ski, jog, and carry on other athletic activities).

3. *Instructions for the plaintiff aware of loss.* Granted that recovery is appropriate for the sense of loss of life's pleasures, how is this to be expressed to the jury? Should the court instruct the jury that the plaintiff can recover (a) for pain and suffering and also (b) an additional award for loss of enjoyment of life? Some courts have approved this idea. *E.g., Kirk v. Washington State University*, 109 Wash. 2d 448, 746 P.2d 285 (1987). Would it be less confusing to the jury to instruct broadly on pain and suffering and to make it clear that consciousness of lost enjoyment is a part of that pain and suffering? See *Gregory v. Carey*, 246 Kan. 504, 791 P.2d 1329 (1990).

4. *Plaintiff unaware of loss.* When the plaintiff is unaware of her loss, as in *McDougald*, there is no tradition of awarding damages for that "loss", but when the issue has arisen recently, cases have gone both ways. A number of cases, directly or indirectly, are aligned with New York's decision in *McDougald*. E.g., *Dillingham v. IBP, Inc.*, 219 F.3d 797 (8th Cir.2000); *Bulala v. Boyd*, 239 Va. 218, 389 S.E.2d 670 (1990). Several others have strongly argued for allowing the recovery for loss of enjoyment of which the plaintiff will never be aware. See *Flannery v. United States*, 171 W.Va. 27, 297 S.E.2d 433, 34 A.L.R.4th 281 (1982). *Holston v. Sisters of Third Order of St. Francis*, 165 Ill.2d 150, 209 Ill.Dec. 12, 650 N.E.2d 985 (1995) may have accomplished the same thing by permitting recovery for the "disability" of a comatose patient who died after a week.

5. *In wrongful death/survival cases.* The claim for lost pleasures of life seems hard to fit into the ordinary wrongful death claim where the measure of damages is based upon loss to survivors or is focused on pecuniary losses. However, the statute may be construed to permit recovery for "loss of life" in addition to whatever pecuniary measure it permits. See *Marcotte v. Timberlane/Hampstead Sch. Dist.*, 143 N.H. 331, 733 A.2d 394 (N.H. 1999).

MERCADO v. AHMED

United States Court of Appeals, Seventh Circuit, 1992.
974 F.2d 863.

COFFEY, CIRCUIT JUDGE.

[Six-year old Brian Mercado was struck by a taxi driven by the defendant. His problems after the accident were severe and he is institutionalized and will remain so for the rest of his life. However, he had a wide range of problems before the accident. The jury awarded $50,000 for Brian's pain and suffering and $29,000 for medical expenses. The plaintiff, aggrieved that the verdict did not include substantial amounts for lost pleasures of life, appealed in part because testimony as to the value of life's pleasures was excluded.]

The first alleged evidentiary error centers on the district court's refusal to allow the receipt in evidence of the testimony of Stanley Smith. Smith was offered by the plaintiff as an expert on the disability damages owed Brian Mercado because of the "pleasure of living" the boy will be denied as a result of the injuries he received in the taxi accident. Smith, a professional economist who holds a Masters degree in Business Administration from the University of Chicago, would have testified as to the monetary value of "the reduction of Brian's ability to engage in and experience the ordinary value of life that he was experiencing prior to the injury." These damages are sometimes referred to as "hedonic damages."[3]

The district court conducted an extensive voir dire to determine the method Smith employs in calculating the monetary value of the "lost

3. Defendants do not argue that damages for the lost pleasure of living are unavailable under Illinois law. Thus, we, like the district court, will assume their availability in our consideration of the admissibility of Smith's testimony.

pleasure of living" an individual such as Brian suffers due to an injury. Smith testified that in his computation he first assumes a "percentage range" representing the degree an injured individual's capacity to experience life has been diminished. This method measures an individual's impairment in four areas: occupational, practical functioning, emotional, and social functioning. Smith does not compute this figure himself, but instead consults with a medical expert to arrive at the appropriate range. In this case the expert was Dr. Kathleen Pueschel, a clinical neuropsychologist. According to the plaintiff, Dr. Pueschel concluded that Brian's disabilities were "severe", and that the boy's capacity to experience life was diminished 66% to 83%.

Smith then applies his own analysis to the diminished capacity figure.... Smith focuses on how much Americans are willing to pay for reductions in health and safety risks, and how much they are compensated for assuming extra risk. This method, according to Smith's economic theory, reveals the value we actually place on living.... He relies on three types of willingness-to-pay studies: studies of how much consumers, through the purchase of devices such as smoke detectors and seat belts, pay for increased personal safety; studies of how much more people who assume extra risk (e.g., policemen) are paid because their jobs are dangerous; and studies of cost-benefit analyses conducted in the evaluation of government safety regulation. Smith testified that he relied on some 75 such studies in his valuation.

Through this analysis, Smith concluded that the value of the enjoyment of a statistically average person's life was $2.3 million in 1988 dollars. (The statistically average person is 31 years old with a 45 year additional life expectancy.) This averages out to approximately a $60,000–per-year value on the enjoyment of life. Smith took this figure and multiplied it by the percentage range of Brian's loss of the full experience of life, 66% to 83% (drawn from Dr. Pueschel's calculations). Adjusting for Brian's young age, the plaintiff informs us that Smith concluded the value of Brian's lost pleasure of living due to the injuries he suffered in the taxi accident was $2,207,827 to $2,762,227....

[The trial judge excluded Smith's testimony on the ground that Smith offered no expertise], because (1) no consensus among experts supported Smith's method of valuing life and (2) Smith's research was no more than a compilation of the opinions, expressed through spending decisions, of a large number of Americans as to the value of life. The first criticism is irrefutable: the plaintiff could point to no expert consensus supporting Smith's methodology. The second criticism is also on the mark, since Smith concedes that his method relies on arriving at a valuation of life based on analyzing the behavior of non-experts.

However, even accepting Smith's premise that his method of determining the value of life is different in an important way from submitting the question to a jury because it focuses on observable behavior and not opinion, we have serious doubts about his assertion that the studies he relies upon actually measure how much Americans value life. For example, spending on items like air bags and smoke detectors is probably influenced as much by advertising and marketing decisions made by profit-seeking manufacturers and by government-mandated safety requirements as it is by any consideration by consumers of how much life is worth. Also, many people may be interested in a whole range of safety devices and believe they are worthwhile, but are unable to afford them. More fundamentally, spending on safety items reflects a consumer's willingness to pay to reduce risk, perhaps more a measure of how cautious a person is than how much he or she values life. Few of us, when confronted with the threat, "Your money or your life!" would, like Jack Benny, pause and respond, "I'm thinking, I'm thinking." Most of us would empty our wallets. Why that decision reflects less the value we place on life than whether we buy an airbag is not immediately obvious.

The two other kinds of studies Smith relies upon are open to valid and logical criticism as well. To say that the salary paid to those who hold risky jobs tells us something significant about how much we value life ignores the fact that humans are moved by more than monetary incentives. For example, someone who believes police officers working in an extremely dangerous city are grossly undercompensated for the risks they assume might nevertheless take up the badge out of a sense of civic duty to their hometown. Finally, government calculations about how much to spend (or force others to spend) on health and safety regulations are motivated by a host of considerations other than the value of life: is it an election year? how large is the budget deficit? on which constituents will the burden of the regulations fall? what influence and pressure have lobbyists brought to bear? what is the view of interested constituents? And so on.

... Smith has taken up a daunting task: to develop a methodology capable of producing specialized knowledge to assist jurors in determining the monetary value of being alive. The district court ruled that, despite Smith's training, extensive research and countless calculations, his testimony would not aid the jury in evaluating the evidence and arriving at its verdict (the true test of expert testimony under Fed. R.Evid. 702) because Smith was no more expert in valuing life than the average person. This conclusion may be less a reflection of the flaws in Smith's methodology than on the impossibility of any person achieving unique knowledge of the value of life.

[Affirmed.]

Notes

1.   Before the decision in *Mercado*, one district court in the same circuit had admitted Smith's testimony. See *Sherrod v. Berry*, 629 F.Supp. 159 (N.D.Ill.1985). Other courts have rejected the testimony. *Loth v. Truck–A–Way Corp.*, 60 Cal.App.4th 757, 70 Cal.Rptr.2d 571 (1998) held Smith's testimony inadmissible partly for reasons similar to those in *Mercado*, and partly because to recognize loss of enjoyment of life as a separate category of damages runs risks of duplication with permanent disability and pain

damages. *Montalvo v. Lapez,* 77 Hawai'i 282, 884 P.2d 345 (1994) commented that valuing the joy of life is "a uniquely human endeavor ... requiring the trier of fact to draw upon the virtually unlimited factors unique to us as human beings."

2.   Everyone knows what it is like to lose the pleasure of some enjoyable activity, so the jury can undoubtedly make its own estimate about the value of losing life's pleasures when the plaintiff is aware of the loss. But how can the jury value the loss of pleasures unrelated to actual human sense of loss? If the plaintiff is unaware of the loss, wouldn't it be logical either to (a) deny the claim for lost pleasure altogether or (b) admit the Smith-type evidence?

b.   Capping and Limiting Damages

CAL. CIV. CODE § 3333.2

(a) In any action for injury against a health care provider based on professional negligence, the injured plaintiff shall be entitled to recover noneconomic losses to compensate for pain, suffering, inconvenience, physical impairment, disfigurement and other nonpecuniary damage.

(b) In no action shall the amount of damages for noneconomic losses exceed two hundred fifty thousand dollars ($250,000).

MD. ANN. CODE, CT. & JUD. PROC. § 11–108

(a) In this section: (1) "noneconomic damages" means pain, suffering, inconvenience, physical impairment, disfigurement, loss of consortium, or other nonpecuniary injury; and (2) "Noneconomic damages" does not include punitive damages.

(b) In any action for damages for personal injury in which the cause of action arises on or after July 1, 1986, an award for noneconomic damages may not exceed $350,000....

(d) (1) In a jury trial, the jury may not be informed of the limitation established under subsection (b) of this section. (2) If the jury awards an amount for noneconomic damages that exceeds the limitation established under subsection (b) of this section, the court shall reduce the amount to conform to the limitation.

Notes

1.   *Caps on pain and suffering awards.* In theory, damages are compensatory. For this reason, tort damages have been limited only by the evidence, not by any arbitrary dollar amount or by any formula.

2.   *Two statutory waves.* Two waves of statutes have been passed changing this common law tradition. The first resulted from the supposed medical malpractice insurance "crisis" of the 1970s. The second resulted

from a supposed "crisis" in the 1980s. This second wave, however, was the product of long and persistent efforts by a much wider group of defendants and insurers who felt threatened by tort law. None of the statutory limits or caps on damages was based on the kind of arguments raised above. Rather they were based on a perception that there was a crisis in the affordability and availability of insurance, especially for target groups like health care providers and public entities, or sometimes simply on the claim that juries had gone wild. Whether this perception is justified is considered further in Chapter 24.

3. *Line-up of the states.* Some kind of cap or limit has been enacted in well over half of the states. As indicated below, however, some have been held unconstitutional, some are applied to only one particular kind of claim, and some are overridden by statutes such as California's Elder Abuse statute, which allows recovery for reckless neglect of the elderly without a cap. As to this last, see *Delaney v. Baker,* 20 Cal.4th 23, 82 Cal.Rptr.2d 610, 971 P.2d 986 (1999).

4. *Types of statute: which defendants covered. (a) All injury defendants vs. medical defendants.* Notice that the Maryland statute applies by its terms to "any action for damages for personal injury." The California statute, on the other hand, applies only to claims against health care providers and then only for professional negligence—in other words, to medical malpractice claims. Most of the statutes follow one of these two patterns, applying either generally or to some special group.

(b) Caps partially restoring lost immunities of favored defendants or limiting new statutory claims. In some states the special defendant to which the cap applies reflects traditional protective attitudes that the common law itself shared. For instance, the common law provided immunities to governmental entities and charities. It is not surprising to see that, when liability is imposed on these defendants, legislative caps put a ceiling on that liability. See, e.g., ME. REV. STAT. ANN. tit. 14 § 8105 ($300,000 cap on all claims against government entity or employees). The common law's protective attitude toward purveyors of alcohol, like the traditional attitude toward immunities, has been much modified, but again, it is no surprise to see legislative caps on dram shop recoveries. E.g., UTAH CODE ANN. § 32A–14–101(5) ($100,000 cap). Similarly, some new statutory claims may be subjected to a dollar limit, as where parents are subjected to liability for the torts of their children. E.g., W. VA. CODE § 57–7A02 ($2500). Finally caps may be indirectly imposed when a new compensation system is substituted for traditional tort law, as with the National Childhood Vaccine Injury Act, summarized in Chapter 26.

5. *Types of statute: which damages covered.* Most of the statutes so far enacted cap nonpecuniary damages but do not cap the recovery for actual pecuniary loss. The cap on nonpecuniary damages, however, is serious to plaintiffs, since it is the nonpecuniary recovery that furnishes a basis for the attorney fee, without which attorneys often cannot afford to pursue complex and time-consuming claims. A few statutes go beyond the cap on nonpecuniary damages and place a cap that limits damages of any kind. E.g., COLO. REV. STAT. § 13–64–302.

6. *Capping plaintiffs vs. capping defendants.* Suppose the cap is $250,000 but the plaintiff has damages of $500,000. If two defendants are

liable, could the plaintiff recover up to $250,000 from each? *General Electric Co. v. Niemet,* 866 P.2d 1361 (Colo.1994) (yes, as a matter of statutory construction, Colorado's cap applies to individual defendants, not to plaintiffs). A somewhat similar question arises when the spouse of an injured person claims lost consortium. Does the cap apply to both claims as a unit, or could each spouse recover a sum up to the cap's limit? *In re Certification of Questions in Knowles v. United States*, 544 N.W.2d 183 (S.D.1996) (one action for liability purposes, but two actions with separate caps on damages).

7. *Caps and comparative fault.* Suppose the plaintiff has $300,000 in nonpecuniary damages as well as pecuniary loss that can be separately calculated. The state has a cap on nonpecuniary damages of $250,000 and a pure comparative fault statute. The jury finds the plaintiff to be chargeable with 20% of the negligence. What should the plaintiff recover? Consider:

(A) $300,000 reduced to the cap of $250,000, minus 20% of the $300,000 or $60,000 = a net of $190,000 for nonpecuniary damages.

(B) $300,000 reduced to the cap of $250,000, minus 20% of the damages as capped, or $50,000 = a net recovery of $200,000.

(C) $300,000 minus 20% = $240,000; since this falls below the cap, no further reduction is required.

See *McAdory v. Rogers,* 215 Cal.App.3d 1273, 264 Cal.Rptr. 71 (1989) ("There is no legitimate or logical reason for reducing that award to the $250,000 cap prescribed by section 3333.2 before reducing it further due to Ms. McAdory's 22 percent comparative fault.")

8. *Caps unconstitutional.* Several courts have found the capping statutes to be unconstitutional under various provisions of their respective state constitutions. E.g., *Best v. Taylor Machine Works,* 179 Ill.2d 367, 228 Ill.Dec. 636, 689 N.E.2d 1057 (1997) (special legislation); *Trujillo v. City of Albuquerque,* 125 N.M. 721, 965 P.2d 305 (1998) (no rational basis); *State v. Sheward,* 86 Ohio St.3d 451, 715 N.E.2d 1062 (1999) (in part because caps were unreasonable and arbitrary in imposing "the cost of the intended benefit to the general public solely upon a class consisting of those most severely injured by tortious conduct"); *Lakin v. Senco Products, Inc.,* 329 Or. 62, 987 P.2d 463 (1999), clarified as to running of interest, *Lakin v. Senco Products, Inc.,* 329 Or. 369, 987 P.2d 476 (1999) (denial of jury trial on factual issue of compensation).

9. *Constitutional themes.* The capping statutes, the state constitutional provisions, and the cases are varied. Some statutes have been condemned as special legislation or violation of right to trial by jury. Broad themes discussed, however, include some version of these ideas:

(a) the injured plaintiff cannot be made to bear the burden of reducing insurance costs for others or for society as a whole;

(b) it is arbitrary to select the particular group of defendants for special attention;

(c) no alternative redress or even assistance is provided for the injured plaintiff; the plaintiff shoulders the burden others are feeling without a quid pro quo;

(d) caps are in themselves arbitrary, especially when injuries may be quite different among those affected;

(e) no showing is made that the caps will actually resolve the supposed insurance crisis.

10. *Caps constitutional*. The California statute set out above was upheld in *Fein v. Permanente Medical Group*, 38 Cal.3d 137, 164, 211 Cal.Rptr. 368, 385, 695 P.2d 665, 682 (1985). A number of other recent decisions have upheld caps against claims that they violated jury trial rights, due process, equal protection, or various somewhat analogous state constitutional provisions, or that they contravened the Americans with Disability Act. *Patton v. TIC United Corp.*, 77 F.3d 1235 (10th Cir.1996); *Kirkland v. Blaine County Med. Ctr.*, 4 P.3d 1115 (Idaho 2000); *Murphy v. Edmonds*, 325 Md. 342, 601 A.2d 102 (Md. 1992); *Adams v. Children's Mercy Hospital*, 832 S.W.2d 898 (Mo.1992).

11. *Attorney fees*. One function of the pain and suffering award is to provide a fund from which to pay the plaintiff's attorney the usual percentage fee. Without this fee, attorneys cannot afford to take difficult cases. Is there any way to cap damages without removing just claims from the judicial system?

12. *Reform as discrimination?* Certain kinds of cases produce noneconomic (but real) harms. Some sexual abuse, for example, may be so harmful that the victim is actually unable to work effectively, but very often the main component of damages is noneconomic. Not all sexual abuse victims are women, but most are. Does this mean that if tort reformers cap pain and suffering damages, they discriminating against women? See Thomas Koenig & Michael Rustad, *His and Her Tort Reform: Gender Injustice in Disguise*, 70 Wash. L. Rev. 1 (1995).

NOTE ON ABOLISHING OR LIMITING
PAIN AND SUFFERING DAMAGES

(A) Abolishing Pain and Suffering Awards

Pain and suffering awards have long been questioned for various reasons, some of which are suggested below in connection with the difficulty of proving or measuring such damages. In recent years economic arguments have been advanced against pain and suffering awards. A simplified version of what is sometimes elaborate economic theory might go something like this: When pain and suffering damages are awarded, the defendant must add these liabilities to its cost of doing business and will normally pass along the costs to consumers in the form of higher prices. For example, a product manufacturer, held liable for an injury, will probably raise the costs of its goods. Consumers in the future will then be forced to pay an increased cost or premium for the goods–a premium that reflects costs of paying pain and suffering damages. Since the purchaser of goods or services cannot get them at a cheaper price by renouncing any intention of suing for pain and suffering damages, this amounts to a kind of compulsory insurance. If everyone wanted to purchase such insurance, that might be all right, but most consumers would be better off to take goods at a cheaper price than to enjoy the fruits of a large pain and suffering recovery if they are injured.

In addition, even if one wanted to be sure to recover for pain, recovery through liability insurance is, as will be seen in Chapter 24, an expensive way to do it. A direct purchase of pain and suffering insurance or ordinary accident insurance would be cheaper than a recovery through the elaborate mechanisms of the tort system.

Such arguments suggest that pain and suffering recoveries should be abolished or limited. Would abolition affect safety incentives of toxic tortfeasors or product producers?

Among the economically oriented materials discussing the "compulsory insurance" idea and related problems, see STEVEN SHAVELL, AN ECONOMIC ANALYSIS OF ACCIDENT LAW (1987); Alan Schwartz, *Proposals for Products Liability Reform: A Theoretical Synthesis*, 97 YALE L. J. 353 (1988). A good, succinct and non-technical exposition can be found in Richard B. Stewart, *Crisis in Tort Law? The Institutional Perspective*, 54 U. CHI. L. REV. 184 (1987).

(B) The Reporters' Study

1. *Requiring a minimum or threshold injury.* In 1990 the much-respected American Law Institute published what it called a Reporters' Study entitled *Enterprise Responsibility for Personal Injury*. That study, never voted on by the membership of the ALI, recommends that pain and suffering damages be retained but limited to cases in which injury itself is significant. Whether this would eliminate recovery for negligent infliction of mental distress along the lines of *Dillon* and *Thing* is perhaps not clear. If you agree, how would you set the threshold or minimum injury necessary to trigger pain and suffering damages?

2. *Rejecting caps, embracing guidelines or scales.* The study rejects caps on damages because cumulative inflation erodes nominal-dollar caps and because they are discriminatory in limiting recoveries only of the most seriously injured. (Vol. II, pp. 219–220). However, damages would be controlled by "guidelines," with limits (adjusted for inflation) attached to a number of "disability profiles" accompanied by "authoritative illustrations" to which the jury could refer in "idiosyncratic" cases. Guidelines based on illustrative cases are to be distinguished from schedules of amounts based on particular injuries. A scale might start with the most extreme injury imaginable and state a proper damage award for that injury. At the other extreme, the scale would reflect a minimum injury and state the damage award for that injury. The jury would be told to scale down from the most severe injury to fit the facts of the case before it. But the guidelines would not be limited to the extreme cases; they could illustrate as many in-between cases as the drafters thought feasible. The jury could pick the illustrations they thought most like the plaintiff's case and raise or lower the award on their perception of the scale. (Vol. II, p. 222). See Bovbjerg, Sloan & Blumstein, *Valuing Life and Limb in Tort: Scheduling "Pain and Suffering,"* 83 NW. U. L.

REV. 908 (1988); cf. Robinson and Abraham, *Collective Justice in Tort Law*, 78 VA. L. REV. 1481 (1992) (aggregative valuation based on statistical claims profiles).

3. *An experimental study.* Punitive damages are like pain and suffering damages in that neither can be reliably measured. But an experimental study has concluded that jurors in personal injury cases almost totally agree with one another on underlying values implicated in punitive awards when they are asked to apply a scale. If asked to scale the wrongdoing on a scale of one to six, male, female, black, Hispanic, white, educated, uneducated, wealthy and poor come up with almost identical numbers on the scale. On the other hand, when they are asked to come up with dollar judgments, they differ enormously. The researchers believed that the "unbounded scale" of dollars is the problem, and using a calibrated set of scenarios similar to that proposed by Bovbjerg, Sloan and Blumstein would produce highly predictable awards. See Cass R. Sunstein, Daniel Kahneman & David Schkade, *Assessing Punitive Damages (With Notes on Cognition and Valuation in Law)*, 107 YALE L.J. 2071 (1998).

4. *Awarding plaintiff attorney fees.* Guidelines plus a threshold of significant injury might limit pain and suffering damages, but something is to be added back in the form of attorney fees. The American Rule excuses losing parties from any liability for the prevailing party's attorney fees. Pain and suffering damages awarded in large sums probably serve in part as a surrogate for an attorney fee award. The ALI study (note 1) proposes to award the prevailing plaintiff a reasonable attorney fee as damages. It supports a contingent attorney fee at prevailing market rates. (Vol. II, p. 316).

§ 9. ADJUSTMENTS IN DAMAGES

KEANS v. BOTTIARELLI

Connecticut Court of Appeals, 1994.
35 Conn.App. 239, 645 A.2d 1029.

SCHALLER, JUDGE.

The defendant in this dental malpractice action appeals from the judgment of the trial court in favor of the plaintiff. The trial court awarded the plaintiff damages of $20,000, but reduced the award by $5034.46 after finding that the plaintiff had failed to mitigate her damages. . . .

The trial court could reasonably have found the following facts. On July 19, 1990, the plaintiff consulted the defendant, an oral surgeon, to have a tooth extracted. On the initial visit to the defendant, the plaintiff informed the defendant that she suffered from myelofibrosis, a rare blood disorder that inhibits production of red blood cells and platelets, thereby affecting the blood clotting ability of afflicted individuals. The plaintiff's condition requires her to receive frequent blood and platelet transfusions and to self-administer interferon injections. The plaintiff further informed the defendant that her platelet count was 39,000. The defendant performed the extraction without first consulting the plaintiff's hematologist, concluding that the plaintiff "looked good" and would not require a platelet transfusion. The plaintiff remained in the defendant's recovery room until the area around the extraction site stopped bleeding and was sent home with a prescription for penicillin and a pamphlet detailing postoperative instructions. After returning home, the extraction site began to bleed. The plaintiff's son called the defendant, who advised him that the plaintiff should bite down on a tea bag to release tannic acid to facilitate blood clotting. The plaintiff made no further effort to contact the defendant that day, despite worsening of her condition.

The next morning, the plaintiff contacted Richard Hellman, her hematologist, who admitted her to the hospital. The plaintiff, diagnosed with neutropenia, severe thrombocytopenia, severe anemia and myelofibrosis, was hospitalized for three days and was discharged on July 23, 1990, with no permanent injuries.

The trial court, finding the plaintiff's expert to be more credible than the defendant's experts, concluded that the plaintiff had sustained her burden of proof regarding her claim of malpractice. The plaintiff's expert testified that the defendant deviated from prudent and standard dental practice by failing to consult the plaintiff's hematologist prior to proceeding with the extraction.

In reliance on Preston v. Keith, 217 Conn. 12, 584 A.2d 439 (1991), the trial court concluded that the plaintiff's failure to follow the defendant's postoperative instructions led to the hospitalization, and determined that damages should be mitigated to the extent of the plaintiff's hospitalization expense. . . .

The trial court applied the doctrine of mitigation of damages and reduced the award by the amount of the plaintiff's hospitalization expense. Our Supreme Court has stated that "[w]e have long adhered to the rule that one who is injured by the negligence of another must use reasonable care to promote recovery and prevent any aggravation or increase of the injuries." "When there are facts in evidence that indicate that a plaintiff may have failed to promote his recovery and do what a reasonably prudent person would be expected to do under the same circumstances, the court, when requested to do so, is obliged to charge on the duty to mitigate damages."

The trial court concluded that the three requirements to establish a failure to mitigate damages. . . . The trial court found that the plaintiff's conduct exacerbated her initial injury. The trial court found that the plaintiff failed to take reasonable action to lessen the damages by neglecting to fill the prescription for penicillin and by not following the defendant's postoperative instructions. The trial court further found that this failure on the part of the plaintiff caused the need for her hospitalization. We conclude that the trial court's reduction of the damage award for this reason was not clearly erroneous. We, therefore, also reject the plaintiff's contention on cross appeal that the trial court improperly reduced her award. . . .

The judgment is affirmed.

Notes

1. *Avoidable consequences.* The avoidable consequences or "mitigation" rule requires the plaintiff to exercise reasonable care to minimize damages and denies a recovery to the extent that damages should have been but were not reasonably minimized or avoided. See generally 1 DOBBS, REMEDIES §§ 3.9, 8.7. The common law rules of avoidable consequences worked quite differently from comparative fault rules. Comparative fault rules reduce damages in proportion to the plaintiff's fault. Avoidable consequences rules reduce damages for discrete identifiable items of loss caused by the plaintiff's fault. For example, if the plaintiff, after injury, unreasonably refuses to accept medical attention for a foot injury, and as a result ultimately suffers amputation of the foot which otherwise would have healed, then the avoidable consequences rule would deny recovery for loss of the foot, but would not affect any other damages. In other words, comparative negligence rules are fault apportionment rules while avoidable consequences rules are "causal" apportionment rules.

2. *Why the distinction is important.* Because avoidable consequences rules have never operated as a defense to the plaintiff's cause of action but only to eliminate identifiable items of damage, courts thought that any fault that would count as avoidable consequences should not count as comparative fault. E.g., *Cipollone v. Liggett Group, Inc.*, 893 F.2d 541 (3d Cir.1990), *rev'd on other grounds*, 505 U.S. 504, 112 S.Ct. 2608, 120 L.Ed.2d 407 (1992). Such a view is important because if the plaintiff's fault in failing to avoid injury is counted as comparative fault in a modified comparative fault jurisdiction like New Jersey, it might add up to more than 50% and might bar the plaintiff. If it is not counted as comparative fault, then it would only bar damages that could be traced to that particular conduct.

3. *Distinguishing comparative fault and avoidable consequences.* Courts and writers have often emphasized that avoidable consequences rules come into play after the plaintiff's injury, while contributory or comparative fault comes into play before injury. But doesn't the real difference lie elsewhere, namely in the fact that one rule bases apportionment of responsibility on fault and one on "cause?" One of the advantages of fault apportionment is that fault can be estimated even when evidence cannot separate out items of damages. Fault apportionment works, for example, even when there is only one inseparable item of damage.

4. *Which applies, comparative fault or avoidable consequences?* As indicated in Chapter 9, the RESTATEMENT OF APPORTIONMENT § 3, cmt. b, uses a comparative responsibility approach to avoidable consequences cases. However, it is comparative fault only as to the separate injury caused by failure to minimize. Thus on the facts of *Keans* the Restatement's rule does not call for the *Keans* result; rather, the plaintiff's recovery in *Keans* for the hospital expenses would be reduced for the plaintiff's comparative fault. See ID. § 3,

ill. 4. The Restatement view is that the doctor was alone in culpably causing the initial injury and is fully liable for that, but that he and the plaintiff together culpably cause the indivisible component of hospital expense. Since causal apportionment of the hospital expense is not possible–they both caused it–comparative fault apportionment for that item rather than causal apportionment is required.

NOTE ON OTHER DAMAGES ADJUSTMENTS:
THE COLLATERAL SOURCE RULE AND
ITS COUSINS

1. *The collateral source rule.* Suppose the injured plaintiff, as a result of his injury, collects medical insurance, continues to receive full pay from his job while he is in the hospital, and is a recipient of a donation from sympathetic neighbors. The general rule is that in figuring the defendant's liability, all these "collateral benefits" to the plaintiff must be ignored. See 1 Dobbs, Remedies §§ 3.8, 8.6. The defendant pays the full medical expenses of the plaintiff even though they may have been paid already by the medical insurance. The defendant pays full lost earnings or lost earning capacity even though the plaintiff collected full pay as a gift from his employer or as part of his job benefits.

2. *The windfall effect.* The collateral source rule sometimes gives the plaintiff a kind of windfall; in effect he may collect twice for the medical expenses and the "lost" wages.

3. *The subrogation protection effect.* At other times, however, this rule merely preserves the subrogation right of the insurer who paid the plaintiff to recover back its loss from the tortfeasor. For instance, suppose that the plaintiff's car is damaged by defendant's negligence. The plaintiff's own collision insurer pays for repairs. In the ordinary case, the collision insurer is subrogated to the plaintiff's claim against the defendant to the extent that it has paid for the car damage. In such a case the plaintiff would be entitled to recover against the defendant for the plaintiff's personal injuries and also for the car damage, but the recovery for car damage goes, by way of subrogation, to the plaintiff's collision insurance company. This can be done only because the collateral source rule allows the plaintiff to recover in spite of the fact that he has been paid. If the plaintiff had no right to recover for car damages because his collision insurer had paid those damages, then the collision insurer could not recover by standing in the plaintiff's shoes. In this situation the collateral source rule does not give the plaintiff "double damages" for the car repair; it merely operates to say which insurer— the plaintiff's collision insurer or the defendant's liability insurer—will ultimately bear the loss.

4. *The direct source or direct benefits rule.* The collateral source rule does not apply to payments made by the defendant itself or by a source identified with the defendant, such as the defendant's insurer. For instance, suppose the defendant has "medical pay" insurance—a

kind of accident insurance that protects occupants of the defendant's car even when the defendant is not at fault. If the medical payment insurance makes a payment to the injured occupant and that occupant later sues the defendant in tort, the defendant will be entitled to a credit for the payment. The difference between this situation and the collateral source situation is that here the payment comes from the defendant himself or from his insurer. What counts as a collateral and a direct source is sometimes an issue in the cases, but the principle that damages are reduced for benefits provided directly by the defendant on his behalf is generally accepted.

5. *Criticizing the collateral source rule. (a) Eliminating subrogation to eliminate transaction costs.* The collateral source rule has many critics. In the best case it protects an insurer's subrogation recovery. But even in this best case, it merely sets up a system where one insurer recovers from another. Since this shift of the loss entails costs, it might be better to abolish the collateral source rule. This would mean that the collision insurer would bear the loss instead of the liability insurer for the negligent defendant. In some sense this might be unfair, but perhaps in the next case the roles of the two insurers would be reversed, so that the losses might more or less average out. If so, the costs of shifting the loss could be avoided. Even if this were not the case, abolishing the collateral source rule might be a good idea because it would mean that the loss would be paid by collision insurers which operate more efficiently than liability insurers, and hence that the loss would be handled more cheaply.

(b) *Eliminating windfalls to eliminate windfall costs.* When the collateral source rule does not merely protect a subrogation right, it may be seen as a windfall to the plaintiff. This is not entirely so, because, in the case of insurance at least, the plaintiff has paid for the right to the insurance proceeds. Still, if the plaintiff is to recover twice for some elements of damages, the total cost is excessive. The excess is charged against insurers who must reflect it sooner or later in premiums. Eventually, all insurance purchasers would pay more for insurance or goods in order to give random claimants a windfall. Bear in mind the compulsory insurance arguments sketched above. Putting the compulsory insurance aspects of tort recoveries together with the collateral source rule, we find that citizens who would prefer lower premiums on their liability insurance must nevertheless pay the higher price entailed to provide the windfalls of double recovery.

The criticisms seem sound in theory. Whether elimination of the collateral source rule and the windfalls it may produce would actually reduce overall costs of liability insurance is not clear as a matter of fact.

6. *Abolishing the collateral source rule.* The tort reform movement of the 1980s sought to limit defendants' liabilities in a number of ways, one of them by abolishing or substantially altering the collateral source rule in selective cases, usually medical malpractice claims, or those against public entities. There are technical sides to these statutes in the

collateral benefits and kinds of torts covered, and also in the way the issue is presented to the jury. The main idea here, however, is that the collateral source rule has been significantly changed by statute in at least half the states. E.g., ARIZ. REV. STATS. § 12–565; CAL. CIV. CODE § 3333.1; N.Y. CIV. PRAC. L. & R. § 4545 (c). When the defendant's liability is reduced to account for the collateral source insurance payments to the plaintiff, the reduction is limited to reflect premiums the plaintiff has paid to obtain the insurance.

7. *Constitutional attacks.* As with other tort reform statutes, these collateral source acts will undergo constitutional scrutiny. Again, there have been successful constitutional attacks. Kansas held its statute unconstitutional as discriminating against malpractice victims. See *Farley v. Engelken*, 241 Kan. 663, 740 P.2d 1058, 74 A.L.R.4th 1 (1987). But the statutes have been upheld in other cases. E.g., *Eastin v. Broomfield*, 116 Ariz. 576, 570 P.2d 744 (1977).

8. *Must the benefit be matched to a specific damage element?* Will the defendant be entitled to a deduction for all collateral benefits received by the plaintiff, or only those that match some element of the defendant's liability? For example, suppose the plaintiff received benefits from an accident policy more than sufficient to pay her medical bills. Can the defendant deduct the benefits entirely, or only that portion of the benefits that went to pay off the medical?

9. *Reduced tax liabilities.* Federal tax laws provide that compensatory recoveries for personal injury and death are not taxable, even if those recoveries replace earnings which would have been taxable. The tax windfall to the plaintiff is normally treated in the same way as collateral benefits are treated. That is, the defendant gets no credit for it and pays full damages even though the plaintiff will be better off financially than he would have been with no injury at all. The Supreme Court has altered this rule for torts governed by federal law under the Federal Employers Liability Act (FELA). See *Norfolk & Western Railway v. Liepelt*, 444 U.S. 490, 100 S.Ct. 755, 62 L.Ed.2d 689 (1980). Most states have not changed their traditional view that the windfall was desirable. *Johnson v. Manhattan & Bronx Surface Transit Operating Auth.*, 71 N.Y.2d 198, 524 N.Y.S.2d 415, 519 N.E.2d 326 (1988). In fact, states usually refuse even to let the jury know that the award is not taxed, with the result that the jury may intentionally increase the award because of its mistaken belief that it will be subject to taxes.

§ 10. PUNITIVE DAMAGES

DAN DOBBS, THE LAW OF REMEDIES
Copyright © 1973, 1993 by West Publishing Co.
§ 3.11(1), pp. 453–455 (2d Ed. 1993).

INTRODUCTION AND SUMMARY

1. Punitive damages are awarded only for ... misconduct coupled with a bad state of mind involving malice or at least a reckless disregard for the rights of others.

2. The stated purposes of punitive damages almost always include (a) punishment or retribution and (b) deterrence. Sometimes the purpose also encompasses (c) the desire to assist in financing useful litigation by providing a source from which fees and costs can be paid. The purposes are somewhat conflicting in that they do not necessarily call for the same amount of punitive recovery.

3. If the judge decides that the facts warrant submission of the case to the jury on the punitive damages issue, the jury's discretion determines (a) whether to make the award at all and (b) the amount of the award, as limited by its purposes, subject only to review as other awards are reviewed.

4. Punitive damages are not per se unconstitutional under the double jeopardy, excessive fines, or due process provisions of the United States Constitution. However, extreme awards, given without appropriate guidance to the jury and without adequate review by judges, may violate due process.

5. Statutes in some states now limit the amount of punitive damages that can be awarded, or, alternatively, direct a portion of the award to some public entity. In addition, some double and treble damages statutes may have the effect of precluding ordinary punitive damages.

6. Punitive damages were traditionally proven by the ordinary civil standard of proof, a preponderance of the evidence. Some courts now demand clear and convincing evidence.

7. The jury is normally allowed to hear evidence about the defendant's wealth, income, or profits as a basis for determining an appropriate amount of punitive damages.

8. Under one rule, punitive awards may be levied against defendants who are only vicariously responsible. Under another rule, employers and others can be responsible for punitive damages for torts of agents or servants only if the employer participated in, encouraged, or ratified the tort.

9. Under one view, probably the majority, liability insurers whose policies do not eliminate coverage for punitive damages are liable for punitive damages judgments against the insured. Under another view, the "punishment" will not be effective if the wrongdoer can insure, so insurance coverage for such awards is against public policy.

10. A defendant whose wrongs have caused many harms to different people may be subjected to more than one punitive liability.

11. Courts sometimes say that punitive damages cannot be awarded unless the plaintiff suffers actual harm or recovers actual damages. Some courts now read this rule to mean only that the plaintiff cannot recover punitive damages unless she first establishes a cause of action.

12. Courts sometimes say that the amount of punitive damages must be in some reasonable proportion to actual damages, but normally

this statement is no more than a rough guideline. It may conflict with some other rules.

Notes

1. *Serious misconduct.* Punitive damages are typically awarded only when the defendant's conduct and state of mind both depart seriously from ordinary expectations in a civil society. However, part of what makes us regard conduct as particularly wrong is the state of mind. For this reason, the Supreme Court has held that no separate test of egregious misconduct is required in a federal job discrimination suit under Title VII beyond the defendant's discrimination itself and his awareness that his conduct may violate the federal law. *Kolstad v. American Dental Ass'n,* 527 U.S. 526, 119 S.Ct. 2118, 144 L.Ed.2d 494 (1999).

2. *State of mind.* Punitive or exemplary damages are given partly to punish. They thus share a criminal law purpose. What is the bad state of mind required to trigger punitive damages? It is usually said that the defendant must act with malice or at least wanton or reckless disregard of the rights of others. The latter phrase includes conscious indifference to the risk. Although the wantonness standard is less demanding than the malice standard, both require some kind of bad state of mind, not merely extremely negligent conduct.

3. *Some settings for punitive damages.* Courts often talk as if the punitive award was created to punish the bully who deliberately beats or sexually abuses the plaintiff, and there are indeed cases like that. Cf. *Mrozka v. Archdiocese of St. Paul and Minneapolis,* 482 N.W.2d 806 (Minn.App. 1992) (bishops and archbishop knew of priest's long continued sexual molestation of young boys, refused to do anything significant about it; punitive award justified in spite of First Amendment). But punitive damages in contemporary law have been applied to a wide variety of defendants and in a wide variety of circumstances. Very commonly today, punitive damages are imposed upon defendants who are reaping financial profit from tortious activity and are likely to continue to seek profit unless deterred by punitive awards.

———

OWENS–CORNING FIBERGLAS CORP. v. BALLARD, 749 So.2d 483 (Fla.1999). Ballard proved that he had developed mesothelioma, a cancer of the chest lining, due to thirty years of exposure to asbestos in the defendant's product, Kaylo. Evidence showed that "for more than thirty (30) years Owens–Corning concealed what it knew about the dangers of asbestos. In fact, Owens–Corning's conduct was even worse than concealment, it also included intentional and knowing misrepresentations concerning the danger of its asbestos containing product, Kaylo. For instance, in 1956, Owens–Corning, after having been told by the Saranac Laboratory that Kaylo dust was 'toxic,' and that asbestos was a carcinogen, advertised Kaylo as being 'non-toxic.' In 1972, after Owens–Corning developed an asbestos free version of the Kaylo product, Owens–

Corning knowingly and intentionally contaminated the new product with asbestos containing debris from its old Kaylo, and then intentionally and knowingly claimed falsely that the new Kaylo product was asbestos free." The jury awarded compensatory damages of $1.8 million and punitive damages of $31 million. *Held,* affirmed.

Notes

1. *Deterrence function.* This case represents the tort-for-profit punitive damage case in contrast to the bully or excess testosterone case. The defendant in such cases has a motive to continue its tortious activity unless the total expected damages liability will be greater than the profit. Although the courts always focus on the defendant's bad state of mind as a justification for awarding punitive damages, deterrence seems to be the major goal in many cases.

2. *Illustration.* Suppose the defendant is making so much money from the sale of the product that compensatory damages awards will never induce the defendant to take it off the market. That might be because, although damages are high, some victims do not discover that the defendant caused their harm. A national products manufacturer which deliberately markets a dangerous product like the Dalkon Shield after its dangers are known may continue to do so (as the Robins company did) unless punitive damages are enough to deny it any profit. See the shocking behavior of the manufacturer as described in *Tetuan v. A.H. Robins Co.,* 241 Kan. 441, 738 P.2d 1210 (1987). See also *Gonzales v. Surgidev Corp.,* 120 N.M. 133, 899 P.2d 576 (1995); Dan Dobbs, *Ending Punishment in "Punitive" Damages: Deterrence-Measured Remedies,* 40 Ala. L. Rev. 831 (1989); Thomas Galligan, *Augmented Awards: The Efficient Evolution of Punitive Damages,* 51 La. L. Rev. 3 (1990). Or perhaps the right amount of punitive damages would be to bring the manufacturer's total liability up to the level it would have paid in ordinary compensatory damages if all victims had appropriately recovered. See A. Mitchell Polinsky & Steven Shavell, *Punitive Damages: an Economic Analysis,* 111 Harv. L. Rev. 869 (1998).

3. *Strict liability cases.* Defendants used to argue that punitive awards could not be made in strict liability claims, even if the underlying conduct involved the kind of knowing wrong seen in cases like *Owens-Corning Fiberglas Corp. v. Ballard.* This has now changed and punitive damages are understood to be warranted by conduct and state of mind, not by the name of the legal theory used. The classic article is David G. Owen, *Punitive Damages in Products Liability Litigation,* 74 Mich. L. Rev. 1256 (1976).

4. *Litigation finance function.* Punitive damages, besides providing deterrence, may also encourage lawyers to invest the large amounts of time necessary to prevail in major cases that require extensive technical investigation and evidence. While the lawyer works on the plaintiff's case, she is not earning money in other cases. The lawyer will not pursue the difficult case unless there is reason to hope for a large award sufficient to pay her a reasonable fee. In some cases the lawyer's investment is so large that she must expect a punitive award to cover her fee and expenses, else give up the case. Can you think of any contemporary cases in which this might be a

problem? If so, you can see why a punitive award is a part of the practical financing of litigation in a system where the loser does not pay the winner's attorney fees. In this view, punitive damages may NOT be a windfall at all.

———

CLARK v. CANTRELL, 339 S.C. 369, 529 S.E.2d 528 (2000). Shortly after dark, Cantrell drove at a high speed on a four-lane highway flanked with restaurants, gas stations, and other businesses nearly striking at least one car. The speed limit was 35 mph. Witnesses estimated her speed as ranging from 60 to 100 mph. The plaintiff turned her vehicle into a service station but before the car was entirely off the highway, Cantrell struck its rear. The plaintiff was injured and a passenger was thrown from the car and killed. "When Cantrell emerged from her car, she was upset and screaming about the condition of her car, demanding that bystanders look at what had happened to it. She laughed as a trooper talked to her a short while later, although her laughter ended when she was informed someone had died in the accident. Cantrell told a trooper the next day that she was speeding because her car was low on gas and she was in a hurry to reach a station." The jury awarded the plaintiff $75,000 in compensatory damages and $25,000 in punitive damages. The trial judge reduced compensatory but not punitive damages to reflect the plaintiff's comparative fault. *Held,* affirmed. (1) The trial judge correctly held that punitive damages are not reduced by comparative fault. To shift a portion of the cost of the punitive award back to the plaintiff would be to undermine the deterrent function of the award. (2) The trier could properly find that Cantrell was guilty of "reckless, willful, wanton, or malicious conduct.... Cantrell's excessive speed, her disregard for the commercial nature of the highway, her lack of remorse, and her frivolous reason for speeding amply support the award of punitive damages."

BARDONARO v. GENERAL MOTORS CORP., 2000 WL 1062188 (Ohio App. 2000). Weller, employed by General Motors, was operating a front end loader, clearing snow at a GM plant. He backed the loader into the roadway, forcing Bardonaro to swerve. Bardonaro had words with Weller, then followed him to discover the name of his superior. "Weller ... opened the door of the Bobcat and shouted to Bardonaro that, among other things, his supervisor's name was none of Bardonaro's 'fucking business.' At that, Bardonaro took a couple of steps toward Weller, inadvertently stepping into the bucket of the Bobcat.... Weller's response was to hoist the Bobcat bucket up several inches off the ground while Bardonaro was inside. After Bardonaro lost his balance in the bucket and did not jump out of it, Weller raised the bucket five to seven feet off the ground and began to shake the bucket back and forth. Finally, Weller drove the Bobcat to a nearby snow bank and dumped Bardonaro out of the bucket onto the snow." Weller had never been involved in similar incidents, but GM reprimanded him and apologized to Bardonaro. Weller was convicted of a misdemeanor in municipal court. GM paid Weller $1500 toward the defense of his criminal case under a union grievance procedure. The jury awarded $100,000 in punitive damages against GM. *Held,* affirmed. The jury could properly find that GM ratified Weller's misconduct by contributing to his defense. "[T]he question is not whether ratification itself is a reprehensible act, but whether the conduct ratified was reprehensible. Here, it was."

NOTE: TRADITIONAL FACTORS IN MEASURING PUNITIVE DAMAGES

1. *Reprehensibility of the defendant's misconduct.* If punitive damages are warranted by the defendant's serious misconduct, the law must then identify an appropriate sum. You might think that the most important consideration would be to identify the amount necessary to ensure that the defendant does not repeat the wrong. However, courts have often said that the seriousness of the wrongdoing is the most important single consideration. At the same time, they identify other factors not necessarily consistent.

2. *Wealth.* Courts have traditionally admitted evidence of the defendant's wealth as bearing on punitive damages, on the theory that a person of great wealth might not be deterred by a small award. If the tort itself is profitable, profits from the wrongdoing would also be highly relevant. *Must* the plaintiff introduce wealth evidence to warrant punitive damages? The California Court said so in *Adams v. Murakami,* 54 Cal.3d 105, 284 Cal.Rptr. 318, 813 P.2d 1348 (1991). Judge Posner incisively criticized this view in *Kemezy v. Peters,* 79 F.3d 33 (7th Cir.1996). The introduction of wealth evidence risks prejudice to the wealthy defendant. Consequently it is now common to bifurcate the trial so that the punitive damages evidence is excluded until the jury has already found fault.

3. *Ratio rules.* Courts have long said that punitive damages should bear some kind of reasonable comparison to the compensatory damages, or to actual or potential harm done. In its crudest form, this ratio rule suggests limits incompatible with the purposes of punitive damages in the first place. Suppose the defendant malevolently and repeatedly fires his rifle at the plaintiff, but has so far only chipped the plaintiff's $10 sunglasses. If the jury awards $10 compensatory damages, the ratio rule suggests that punitive awards should be some modest multiple of that sum. It is apparent that this cannot be right under either a punitive or deterrence rationale and it is even less right if the defendant's conduct is profitable even after he pays compensatory damages. The more sophisticated form of the rule does not compare punitive awards to compensatory awards. It compares punitive awards to the potential actual harm that could have resulted from the defendant's conduct. This form of the ratio rule is in fact merely a way of measuring the seriousness of the defendant's misconduct.

4. Some other factors are sketched in discussing the constitutional decisions in the next Note.

NOTE: LIMITING PUNITIVE AWARDS

1. *Moves to limit punitive awards.* Because punitive damages are not reliably measurable, the trier of fact is free to vent any bias or anger it may feel by inflicting an award that cannot be evaluated against any effective standard. As punitive damages have been sought more frequently, and as amounts have sometimes run into the millions of dollars, defendant-oriented lobbies have tried to find ways to limit those awards, both in statutes and by more restrictive judicial decisions.

2. *Two types of limitations.* Although several means have been used to limit punitive awards, they fall mainly into two large categories. Since the main problem with punitive damages is to find a suitable measure or standard for guiding the award and evaluating it afterward, some legal changes attempt to enhance the methods for measuring the awards. A second and much broader way to limit total damages awarded is not to limit the amount of the award but to limit the number of cases in which punitive damages may be awarded. Some courts and statutes have attempted this approach, too.

Filters: Limiting The Number Of Punitive Damages Cases

3. *Increased proof standards.* One way to filter out potential punitive damages claims is to increase the plaintiff's burden of proof. A number of courts and legislatures have done this, usually requiring the plaintiff to prove grounds for punitive damages by clear and convincing evidence rather than by a mere preponderance.

4. *Single liability statute.* Georgia enacted a statute that immunized a product liability defendant from all punitive liability for a given product, once the defendant had been vaccinated by a single punitive award. So the first plaintiff to recover was the only one to do so.

5. *Specific malice requirement.* Another effort to cut punitive damages off at the pass requires the plaintiff to prove some specific malice or oppressive intent toward the plaintiff, eliminating wanton and reckless misconduct as a basis. See KY. REV. STATS. ANN. § 411.184.

6. *Redirection of awards and the problem of financing tort suits.* A fourth line of legislative attack that is intended to cut down the number of claims rather than the amount of the award is the statute that redirects a portion of any punitive award so that it does not go to the plaintiff (or the plaintiff's attorney) but to the state or some designated beneficiary. E.g., KAN. STAT. ANN. § 60–3402. These statutes retain the full capacity for deterring the defendant once the award is made because they do not reduce the award. In *Kirk v. Denver Pub. Co.*, 818 P.2d 262 (Colo.1991), the court held one such statute unconstitutional as a taking of property without just compensation. Can you formulate a policy argument against this kind of statute? Can you see how the statute might limit the number of punitive damages claims?

7. *Assessing the filters.* What is your assessment of these efforts? One trouble with them is that they do nothing at all about the problem of measurement. Once a case gets past these filters, the problem of standardless punitive awards remains. Another problem is that the filters may be too fine. Is there a good chance, in your view, that the deterrence function or the litigation finance function of punitive awards will be needed in some of the cases filtered out by these rules?

Affecting the Measurement or Standards Problem

8. *Statutory ratios, multiples or caps.* With the push for tort reform, some statutes have enacted ratio cap statutes. For instance, Colorado limited punitive awards to no more than actual damages, with the added possibility of punitive damages up to three times actual damages if the defendant's misbehavior continued during the trial. WEST'S COLO. REV. STAT. ANN. § 13–21–102. Utah, by court decision, has produced a kind of sliding scale ratio rule that varies according to whether the compensatory damages awarded were low or high. *Crookston v. Fire Ins. Exchange*, 817 P.2d 789 (Utah 1991) (3–1 ratio for punitive awards under $100,000, much closer ratio for higher awards). Georgia enacted a flat cap limiting punitive damages in some cases to $250,000. GA. CODE § 51–12–5.1.

9. *Due process limits.* Due process of law requires courts to consider the amount awarded with care, both by giving appropriate jury instructions and by post-trial review. In *BMW of North America v. Gore*, 517 U.S. 559, 116 S.Ct. 1589, 134 L.Ed.2d 809 (1996) the Court concluded that an award of $2 million in punitive damages was grossly excessive and violated the constitutional rights of due process, where the defendant's tort was an economic tort only and caused no more than $4,000 in actual damages. The Court emphasized three factors to be considered: (1) The "reprehensibility" of the defendant's conduct; (2) the ratio between the amount awarded and the harm actually inflicted; (3) the comparison between criminal penalties and the punitive award with the idea that punitive awards should not grossly exceed criminal penalties.

The *BMW* Court was also very much concerned with a kind of federalism issue. It wanted to be sure that the courts in one state did not level a punitive damage award to deter the defendant's misconduct in other states. That would impose "undue burdens on interstate commerce," and no state has the power to impose its regulatory policies upon the whole nation.

Earlier decisions of the Supreme Court recognized some of the traditional common law factors besides those listed above. These are (4) The profitability of the defendant's misconduct; and (5) the financial wealth of the defendant. The wealthier the defendant, the more justified a high punitive award. See *Pacific Mutual Life Ins. Co. v. Haslip*, 499 U.S. 1, 111 S.Ct. 1032, 113 L.Ed.2d 1 (1991).

10. *Profit or attorney fee as a limit.* If neither caps nor redirected recoveries furnish good limits on punitive damages, there remains a

strong desire to find some kind of limit on such open-ended liability that can be fueled by the jury's anger rather than by any measurable need. To achieve a more rational limit, it has been proposed that punitive damages should be limited to the amount of the defendant's profit resulting from the tort, or, where that limit is not practical, then to the amount of a reasonable attorney fee for the plaintiff. The point would be to retain full deterrence by eliminating the profits and to retain the capacity of the punitive award to provide appropriate incentives to sue. See Dan Dobbs, *Ending Punishment in "Punitive" Damages: Deterrence–Measured Remedies*, 40 ALA. L. REV.831 (1989).

Problem

O'Brien v. Spring Department Store, Inc.

James O'Brien was 16 years of age. He was an African–American employed at the Spring Department Store. The store's "security" agents accused him of theft. They imprisoned him for hours in a small windowless room and refused to let him leave or call his parents. During this period, they coerced a confession. They now concede that the confession was false and a product of coercion.

After the security agents obtained a confession, they permitted O'Brien to leave. He discussed the events with his parents, who then took him back to the store to discuss these events with the manager. The manager, Bob Hurley, said in this discussion: "You people–you nigger boys make me sick, but you're going to burn for this, you sucker."

James was charged criminally for the supposed theft. However, there was no evidence that he stole anything or indeed that anything at all had been stolen. He then sued for false imprisonment and some other torts. The jury found in his favor in the first trial and besides compensatory damages awarded $350,000 in punitive damages. The highest state court reversed because some of the tort theories pursued at trial were invalid and the punitive award might have been generated in part because of multiple tort claims.

On a second trial, the jury awarded compensatory damages and $9 million in punitive awards. The defendant argued that this was excessive and should be reduced as a matter of law. You are the trial judge. Do you reduce the award? If so, what sum of punitive damages would you permit? Because substantial sums are involved no matter what you decide, your decision on this point is likely to be reviewed by the state's highest court. Consequently, you want to give persuasive reasons for your decision.

Chapter 24

EVALUATING TORT LAW

There are at least two distinct tort systems–one based on "fault" and the other on strict liability. How good are these systems at coping with the problem of injury in modern American life? Any system used to deal with the injury problem will be severely strained. In round numbers, Americans suffer

- about 19 million disabling injuries per year, and more than 2 million from motor vehicle accidents alone.

- 92,000 accidental deaths a year; as of 1998 about 42,000 from motor vehicle accidents alone.

- almost 4 million work-related injuries.

- total costs of unintended injury as of 1998, including loss of wages and productivity, medical expenses, and property damage, was more than $480 *billion*.

§ 1. RULES, PRACTICES AND THEORIES OF TORT LAW

Looking back over the rules of torts, would you have any major criticisms? The rule of contributory negligence and the rules of assumed risk and fellow-servant were often the butt of serious criticisms until the recent past. These rules no longer automatically bar recovery. What, in the fault system of torts, would you find that warrants substantial change?

In the strict liability system, the current confusion is obvious. Is this any more, however, than the problem the law will always have in making changes of great magnitude? An astute and careful observer has argued that the expansion of tort liability that occurred in the latter half of the 20th century was accomplished largely through negligence law, not strict liability, and that in any event tort law had become stabilized by the late 1980s. Gary T. Schwartz, *The Beginning and the Possible End of the Rise of Modern American Tort Law*, 26 GA. L. REV. 601 (1992).

The practical application of tort law seen in Chapter 23 may give some a little more ground for concern. Are there practices that cause serious problems? Are some of them irremediable, or can they simply be changed by a serious legal profession? What about the theoretical problems in tort law? Is there any need to move from a theory based predominantly on fault to a theory based on, say, general deterrence? Reciprocity? Would these changes, if they occurred, resolve any of the practical problems in administering tort law on a massive scale?

§ 2. TORT WARS

The New Tort Reform

Major Criticisms Advanced by the Tort Reformers

According to a common complaint of critics, a litigation explosion occurred in the 1980s; suddenly, everyone was suing everyone else. Critics say the tort system is running amok; liability is everywhere; the American public wants to sue whenever anything goes wrong; and lawyers' greed has brought the country to the brink of disaster.[1] Some of these charges led to long battles over the question whether litigation really had increased.

More soberly, tort reformers say that the tort system as presently administered has caused specific problems because of the costs it imposes on defendants and insurers:

(1) liability insurance costs too much, especially for certain defendants like malpractice defendants (the affordability crisis);

(2) insurance has or may become unavailable for some defendants (the availability crisis);

(3) some goods or services of vast importance may become unavailable because the threat of tort liability is driving some producers out of the market, as perhaps the diminished availability of certain vaccines suggests.

Evaluating the Criticisms

Availability of actual data is limited. However, existing data suggest that injured people actually should be claiming redress more often than they do and that juries, far from running amok, award recoveries less often than judges do. Here are some major items of information.

- The number of personal injury claims made, adjusted for population growth, seems to be pretty stable. Deborah Jones Merritt and Kathryn Ann Barry, *Is the Tort System in Crisis? New Empirical Evidence,* 60 Ohio St. L.J. 315 (1999). Only about 10% of injured

---

1. The Congressional Record provides many examples of such claims, as well as many pages of the accompanying rhetoric. For example:

Mr. McConnell: Mr. President, I am introducing legislation today that will put the brakes on the lawsuit crisis that is running amok in this country. My bill is called the Lawsuit Reform Act of 1989, because its purpose is to reform the "sue-

for-a-million" mentality that has gripped our civil justice system.

135 Cong.Rec. S5989–02 (June 1, 1989). See also P. Huber, Liability: The Legal Revolution and Its Consequences (1988) (claiming that the "tort tax" adds to the cost of almost everything we buy or use, accounting for 30 per cent of the price of stepladders and 95 percent of the price of certain vaccines).

people make any claim at all; probably many more could justly assert claims. See Marc Galanter, *Real World Torts: An Antidote to Anecdote,* 55 MD. L. REV. 1093 (1996).

- The total of loss payments may have risen.[2] But: (1) Settlements, which constitute the great majority of tort dispositions, on the average probably undercompensate. (2) A Bureau of Justice Statistics study showed that the median total award in a sample of tort cases was only $33,000, although the National Safety Council estimates that the average economic cost (apart from human cost) of incapacitating injury is about $44,000. See BUREAU OF JUSTICE STATISTICS BULLETIN 1 (September 1999) and NATIONAL SAFETY COUNCIL, INJURY FACTS 83 (1999).

- Juries have not run amok; in the Bureau of Justice Statistics sample, juries found for the plaintiff in less than half the cases. Judges found for the plaintiff only a little more often.

- Some torts, with disastrous consequences to human beings, really are being committed. This is suggested by the fact that almost one-half the amounts paid by Florida medical malpractice insurers were paid on behalf of health care providers for whom insurers had already paid one or more previous claims. Nye, Gifford, Webb, & Dewar, *The Causes of the Medical Malpractice Crisis: An Analysis of Claims Data and Insurance Company Finances,* 76 GEO. L. J. 1495 (1988).

- Insurance premium costs depend in part on the amounts insurers must pay out. But costs also depend on the insurers' investments of premium income. The premiums paid are invested until they are needed to pay insured losses or other expenses. The investment returns help pay the insurer's total costs, including the insured losses. When the economy is in trouble and dividends or investment interest is low, the insurer's returns on invested premium funds are lower. That means premiums must be raised to pay the costs when the economy is bad. See, e.g., Glen Robinson, *The Medical Malpractice Crisis of the 1970's: A Retrospective,* 49 L. & CONTEMP. PROBS. 5 (1986). This reason for premium increases is unrelated to tort suits. Costs for insurance also depend on the appropriate estimate of a proper premium for a risk, and some of the increase in premiums is due to the fact that insurers underestimated and undercharged in some earlier years. See Nye, Gifford, Webb and Dewar, supra.

- The impression of increased litigation is partly the result of the raw fact that the numbers of tort suits filed in some courts has increased. However, when the increase in population is taken into account, the increase is quite moderate. In addition, the perception of increased filings may be misleading: in some courts, filings on other kinds of claims have increased far more, so that the

---

2. David J. Nye & Donald G. Gifford, *The Myth of Liability Insurance Claims Ex-* *plosion: An Empirical Rebuttal,* 41 VAND. L. REV. 909 (1988).

percentage of tort cases in some courts is actually less than it was a few years earlier. These and many other data are discussed in Michael J. Saks, *Do We Really Know Anything About the Behavior of the Tort Litigation System—And Why Not?*, 140 U. Pa. L. Rev. 1147 (1992) (one of the most complete, most helpful, and most accessible sources); Sanders and Joyce, *"Off to the Races": The 1980s Tort Crisis and the Law Reform Process*, 27 Hous. L. Rev. 207 (1990) (good clear discussion of some of the data and its defects, as well as the political process of tort reform).

- Increased litigation should be perceived as a problem only if litigation outruns actionable injury. Striking studies show that in fact many more tortious injuries are caused than are sued for. See Saks, supra; Localio, Lawthers, Brennan, Laird, Hebert, Peterson, Newhouse, Weiler & Hiatt, *Relation between Malpractice Claims and Adverse Events Due to Negligence*, 325 N. Eng. J. Med. 245 (July 25, 1991). The question perhaps should be, not whether the amount of litigation has increased in any given time period, but whether it is too extensive or not enough and whether there are better alternatives. See Dan Dobbs, *Can You Care for People and Still Count the Costs?*, 46 Md. L. Rev. 49 (1986) (commenting on Marc Galanter, *The Day After the Litigation Explosion*, 46 Md. L. Rev. 3 (1986)).

In the light of the data, why have some people claimed that the courts are giving money away in ridiculous cases? For some legislators, this may reflect bias against courts–which, after all, are independent and on the whole not subject to political pressure or legislative control. In other cases opinion has been molded by anecdotes that shamefully distort the cases they purport to report. For example: (1) The story was that a burglar recovered when he fell through a skylight of a building he was trying to burglarize; the fact was that it was a student who fell when he was on the roof of a school to fix a floodlight. (2) The story was that a man who was struck by a car while he was in a telephone booth recovered from the phone company; the fact was that he tried desperately to get out of the booth when he saw the car coming, but the door jammed and he was trapped. Even if anecdotes were correct, they would tell us little about the system as a whole. When they are so terribly misleading, they generate conflict but not information. On the anecdotes, see Joseph Page, *Deforming Tort Reform*, Book Review of Peter W. Huber, Liability: The Legal Revolution and Its Consequences (1988), 78 Geo. L. J. 649 (1990); Saks, supra.

Were the legislatures right to enact tort reforms by capping damages and eliminating joint and several liability? See, describing part of one legislative process, Sanders and Joyce, supra.

§ 3. THE IMPACT OF TORT LAW ON THE INJURY PROBLEM

The Old Tort Reform

The tort reform movement discussed above was and is fueled mainly by industries, insurers and others who wish to see greater protection for defendants. The first tort reformers approached tort law with different questions and a different orientation. They did not concern themselves with the alleged greed of lawyers and litigants, but asked in part: How well does the tort system work in the real world? Does it cope adequately with the problem of massive injury? Does it adequately deter wrongdoing? Compensate the injured? Encourage rehabilitation and otherwise minimize economic loss?

People can bring many viewpoints to the problem of injury. Here are two that may account in part for some of the criticisms we see of injury systems:

(1) Insurance funds, created by premiums to which many of us contribute, might be regarded as community funds, to be used in the interest of those whose contributions make them up. They are, in a sense, a bit like public funds created by tax contributions. The taxpayer or premium payer should have something to say about how they are used. In other words, the premium payer might like to "buy" more or less liability insurance, but what in fact is bought must depend largely on what the law says about the extent of liability. The premium payer might want the law to contract or expand liability so that the insurance funds are distributed differently. Not only might the premium payer be interested in how the insurance pie is cut, one might also be interested in how efficiently it is cut. The premium payer might want to find ways to reduce overhead costs and hence to minimize the premium paid. Since liability insurance is the fuel of the torts system, these concerns, however, cannot be dealt with directly by the insurance market, because the market must reflect the legal liability. If anyone is interested in changing the distribution or efficiency of liability insurance, then, that person must first change the law of torts.

(2) Injury on the massive scale we know it in contemporary American society is a social problem. Injury that causes economic loss, at least, has radiating effects that impose losses on others—family members, employers, and society as a whole. The effects are not necessarily only economic in nature, and society also has an interest in seeing to it that uncompensated economic harm to a worker, for example, does not lead to a spiraling disintegration of the family structure itself. This view might result in the feeling that some minimal compensation would be more important than a careful determination of fault.

Nine points involving some of these criticisms are set out below for discussion. To what extent are these points predicated upon one or both of the viewpoints stated above?

Problems With the Tort System—?

1. *Undercompensation.* Studies have repeatedly shown that many claimants are not fully compensated. This point has three parts: (a) undercompensation is itself a failure of the tort system to achieve its own goals; (b) undercompensation has social consequences–the hardships on the injured and their families may be translated into welfare claims

on society, or into crime and juvenile delinquency; (c) undercompensation of some groups of claimants is part of a larger picture in which some other groups are–according to many thinkers–overcompensated, with the result that the system not only fails its goals, but also provides a "maldistribution" of the insurance pie and fails to treat people equally.

How does undercompensation come about under the tort systems? Consider these possibilities: (1) The cost of going to court is such that settlement is imperative; in many ranges of injury, lawyers will encourage settlement and, with or without encouragement, plaintiffs will be compelled to accept a fraction of their actual losses. (2) Delay in trial may force the claimant to accept a settlement now. (3) Other factors would encourage a settlement for less-than-loss. These include estimates of liability, and estimates about problems in proof, effectiveness of witnesses and the bias of juries. (4) In spite of compulsory insurance laws, one in five or six drivers are uninsured and often insolvent, so that their victims have little chance of collecting any compensation, much less adequate compensation. This is a very serious problem the states have not dealt with adequately. A recent California statute provides that a vehicle owner cannot recover pain and suffering damages for injuries he sustains in an accident with his vehicle if that vehicle is uninsured. CAL. CIV. CODE §§ 3333.4. Do you think this would adequately address the problem of the underinsured motorist?

One of the earliest studies was CONARD, MORGAN, PRATT, VOLZ & BOMBAUGH, AUTOMOBILE ACCIDENT COSTS AND PAYMENTS (1964), hereafter cited as CONARD. Of 86,000 persons who suffered economic loss, some 20,000 received no compensation from any source. Of those who were compensated, the majority received compensation from their own insurance, workers' compensation or the like–not from the tort system. More recent figures suggest that more than two-thirds of those injured in vehicle accidents receive at least some compensation, although because of the problem of uninsured motorists, that compensation may be from their own uninsured motorist coverage. See Gary T. Schwartz, *Auto No-fault and First-party Insurance: Advantages and Problems,* 73 S. CAL. L. REV. 611, 624 (2000).

Are the individual and social consequences of these facts significant enough to warrant changing the tort system if this is the only objection?

2. *Overcompensation.* Students of accident compensation have repeatedly found that some claimants are grossly overcompensated. Although one expects that many claimants will recover more than their financial losses–because of pain and suffering recoveries–this does not seem to explain the enormous overcompensation at the lower end of the scale. The Department of Transportation completed an extensive study of the auto accident problem in the early 1970s. This showed, in line with some other studies, that where the economic loss was low, the average recovery might more than double the loss. For instance, if the average economic loss was $330, the average recovery was $829. WESTAT RESEARCH CORP., ECONOMIC CONSEQUENCES OF AUTOMOBILE ACCIDENT INJURIES

38 (Department of Transportation Automobile Ins. and Compensation Study, 1970) (hereafter cited as Economic Consequences). At the upper end of the scale, where pain and suffering would be likely to be more, the reverse was true, and undercompensation was common.

Knowing what you do about the tort system and how it works, what is your best guess as to the reason for this overcompensation feature?

What impact does this overcompensation have? Is it, standing alone, sufficient to warrant changing the tort system?

3. *Misuse of limited resources.* The DOT study concluded that the personal economic losses from auto accidents in the year 1967 were between $5 and $9 billion. See Economic Consequences at 40. Whatever the figure, it will continue to be extremely large, year in and year out. And the figure does not include either pain and suffering or social losses, such as lost production. The same study concluded that the tort-insurance system paid net compensation of about .8 billion dollars or less than 20% of the actual economic losses. See Economic Consequences at 146.

Do figures like these reflect any misuse of resources? Some of the division of the "insurance pie" goes for pain and suffering claims. Every dollar paid for pain and suffering is a dollar that cannot be used to pay basic economic loss. The result is that while some claimants recover for pain, other claimants don't even get their medical bills or lost wages paid. There simply is not enough in the premium fund to go around.

Is this, as some critics argue, a misuse of the limited resources available? If it is, would this be ground, standing alone, for changing the tort system in any substantial way? Would you, instead, favor multiplying liability insurance premiums several fold in order to cover all economic losses?

Notice that the misuse of resources argument as it is cast here could be resolved in part by eliminating the pain and suffering recovery in tort. Would that be desirable, neutral or undesirable?

4. *Inefficiency of the tort-liability insurance system.* Without liability insurance there would be no tort system as we know it in auto accident cases. The liability insurance system is, however, a three-party system, in which you buy insurance from the company, who will pay a third person–the plaintiff. This builds in certain costs and the tort system itself builds in more. The insurer must investigate fault, cause, damage, and, sometimes, complex legal issues as well. Given fault as a costly trigger of liability, the premium dollar itself must be devoted largely to administration costs. At one time, only about 44 cents of each premium dollar actually went to paying compensation–the rest was cost. (Even that was not necessarily efficient, because it paid for losses that were compensated from other sources.) In contrast, health insurance, workers' compensation and other forms of insurance return 70 to 90 cents on the premium dollar. Still, the best figures available today seem to indicate that when you consider claims that are settled rather than tried, the return on the premium dollar is much higher.

The inefficiencies indicated by these figures do not reflect the inefficiency that results from the fact that the tort system imposes costs on the public because it entails the cost of judges, courthouses, juries, clerks and the other paraphernalia of the judicial system. Spectacular inefficiencies, as well as delay and other problems, appear in mass tort cases. Agent Orange, Dalkon Shield, and asbestos cases, pursued mostly in class actions, have literally involved hundreds of thousands of claims.

A rather different inefficiency comes from the fact that in mixing a liability insurance system with other kinds of insurance, there will be double coverage on some items. Double coverage means more premium charges. If you and your brother each drove a car and each had hospital insurance, you might agree between yourselves that if one of you negligently injured the other, the injured person would not hold the other liable for hospital costs, and the injured person would collect from the hospital insurance instead. (This would utilize the more efficient premium dollar.) The two of you might then approach your insurance agent and ask to have your liability policy amended accordingly and your premium reduced. "I'll never be liable to pay for the hospital costs," you might say, "because my brother will guarantee to rely on his own hospital insurance. So reduce my premium." If you could agree with all persons who might be hurt by your driving to rely on their hospital insurance, this plan might work and the liability insurer might indeed reduce the premium because it would have reduced its risks of liability. But you cannot agree with the whole world, so the scheme won't work. The result is that for practical purposes the law forces you to purchase the same insurance twice.

Would the inefficiencies suggested in these paragraphs be enough, standing alone, to warrant any attempt to find substitutes for the tort system in auto accident cases?

5. *Delay in payment under the tort system.* If a claimant is entitled to recover but cannot be paid for months or even years, a number of harmful consequences come about. This is not a problem peculiar to torts. All law attempts to make a careful investigation into the facts and to give full opportunity to debate the legal issues. These good points of law, however, carry a heavy price in forcing delay. In tort cases, the substantive rules requiring proof of fault, cause and damage, along with the ambiguities of many rules, require especially intensive investigation and especially intensive trials. Delay seems unavoidable.

Delay is also due to the fact that the claimant must assert all claims for the future in one legal action. This may require a period of waiting to better estimate future losses and it certainly requires extensive proof about the future.

Delay may also be used strategically by defendants. The procedural system, aimed at supporting the law's aim of full investigation and complete opportunity to be heard, is readily manipulated to delay trial. Defendants can, within the ethics of the system, often delay trial and hence delay settlement or payment. This is useful from the defendant's point of view, since the plaintiff, deprived of wages, will feel more and more pressure to accept smaller and smaller settlements as time goes by.

Would these problems of delay warrant making a substantial change in the tort system if they stood alone? Could you eliminate some of the problems of delay without eliminating the tort system?

6. *The failure to deter or compensate.* The tort system begins with a determination to fix fault. It assumes that fault can be determined rationally, and that when it is determined, the imposition of liability in accord with fault will accomplish two purposes: (a) it will administer justice by imposing liability upon faulty persons, and (b) it will deter similar faulty conduct in others. To some, the justice argument itself fails. We have all been faulty in driving at one time or another, quite probably very often by today's standards of negligence in auto cases. Since we are all at fault, according to this view, it is largely a matter of fortuity that some of us get involved in an accident because of fault and some escape an accident. It is even more a matter of fortuity that some of us may cause large damages and some may cause quite small damages. Cf. Marc Franklin, *Replacing the Negligence Lottery*, 53 VA. L. REV. 774 (1967). Under these circumstances, it is less than clear that imposing liability in accord with fault is truly "just."

Whatever may be said about the justice side of the argument, the deterrent effect of tort liability is undercut by the presence of liability insurance. When a defendant is held liable, that defendant does not ordinarily make payments to the injured plaintiff in the tort system. The liability insurer does so. In many states, punitive as well as compensatory damages are covered by insurance, so that insurance may protect even a reckless defendant from any personal accountability in money. In addition, the court's desire to compensate the plaintiff has led to many cases in which "fault" is found in a defendant who has behaved in a way that, but for insurance, most people would not find faulty at all. In this view, then, the tort system fails to accomplish one of its main purposes—deterrence.

Is it true that the tort system does not accomplish any of its main goals—justice, deterrence, compensation? If it is true, would this criticism standing alone lead you to seek a substitute system?

7. *Participation in the insurance fund—lack of reciprocity.* Although the tort system is fueled on liability insurance, not everyone purchases such insurance. Among those who do purchase it, many have procured only low-limit policies, inadequate to protect a seriously injured plaintiff. A person who purchases only minimal insurance protection or none at all may nevertheless be the beneficiary of a high-limits policy purchased by someone else. Suppose X buys no insurance, but, while driving recklessly, causes serious harm to C. Unless X has extraordinary personal resources, the result will be that C will recover little or nothing from X and will rely instead on public resources or on his own private resources. But X, having failed to provide even minimal compensation for his own negligence, is in no way limited in his own recovery. If X is injured by

D's negligence, and D has provided himself with adequate insurance, X will receive full compensation. He can, in short, draw on the insurance others have provided, without providing his share of the protection for others. This is only one of several peculiarities of using liability insurance in which the protection of one rests in the hands of others. Is this justified on the ground that, after all, X may be relatively poor and may find it possible to drive only because he does not purchase liability insurance?

A second problem of reciprocity in the participation in insurance funds can be seen if one imagines that poor people as a class will draw less of the insurance pie than others because for any given injury they will have less wage loss. Yet they will pay the same premiums paid by wealthier persons. Again, this is a result of the fact that injury is compensated through the insurance of others, not through one's own insurance.

Do these observations amount to a criticism of the tort system? If so, would this criticism standing alone warrant an effort to change the tort system?

8. *Is the tort system a lottery?* Some lawyers think so. There are at least three senses in which this may be so.

(a) There is a large element of fortuity from the injured person's point of view. If a woman is injured in an ordinary car collision, she will have to prove negligence to recover. If the collision occurs while she is in the course of employment, she will not be required to prove negligence, though her workers' compensation recovery will be limited to economic losses. If the collision occurs because of a defective steering apparatus, she will be entitled to recover from the manufacturer without proving negligence and she will not be limited to economic losses. From her point of view, her legal rights depend almost wholly on the luck of the case— whether she was working or not, whether her injury was caused by the manufacturer or by another driver. There are a number of these fortuitous elements in the negligence case. Consider: The defendant is negligent, but by luck he causes no harm at all; or the defendant is negligent, but by luck the plaintiff was also guilty of substantial negligence, though the defendant would have caused the same harm to a non-negligent plaintiff. See Franklin, supra.

(b) The tort system may be viewed as a lottery for more quotidian reasons. Consider: the plaintiff is injured, but as luck would have it, the plaintiff herself is not very attractive and does not capture the jury's sympathy; or the only witness is quite truthful, but has an abrasive personality and makes a bad impression; or there is no witness at all; or defendant's witnesses have been packaged and stage-managed to create the best impression; or the defendant is a sympathetic local person and the plaintiff is an outsider. Similarly, lawyers' abilities to deal with complex issues vary greatly; some plaintiffs lose because their lawyers were not up to the demands of the particular case, not because the case itself was unworthy.

(c) A final sense in which the tort system may be considered a lottery is rather different. Tort damages range from quite trivial sums to many millions. Suppose a defense attorney, defending a case in which the plaintiff is seriously injured but the defendant does not appear to be at fault, makes a small offer of settlement. The plaintiff's attorney might believe that the plaintiff will in fact lose the case on a directed verdict and that, therefore, a small offer should be accepted. But the lawyer might also believe that there is one chance in a thousand that the trial judge will let the case go to the jury and that there is one chance in ten that the jury, if it gets the case, will bring in a very large judgment indeed. If so, the lawyer may press on to trial. He may have to try 1,000 such cases to realize his hopes of a million dollar verdict, just as he might have to buy a large number of lottery tickets to win a new car. But the temptation will be strong for many lawyers and their clients. The result is that many weak cases that probably should not win under the tort rules may go to trial in the same spirit that one buys a lottery ticket–the chances are not very good, but the payoff is still highly tempting. This is not necessarily unethical, but it costs the legal system a lot.

Are any of these "lottery" reasons ground for reconsidering the tort system?

9. *Are the lump-sum award and pain and suffering compensation justifiable?* The instinctive answer of almost everyone is that something should be paid for pain and suffering, at least when that pain is caused by wrongdoing of others. Yet the pain and suffering award does not compensate in the ordinary sense. If wages are lost, money can repay that loss. If one is in pain, the money award cannot relieve the pain. (Pain relievers are covered under medical expense awards.) To the extent these awards are used to pay lawyer's fees, they are explicable in practical terms; but lawyers are needed in the first place chiefly because the tort system requires detailed analysis of fault, cause and damage. If the system were changed, the role of lawyers would be very different, as it is in workers' compensation systems. Perhaps pain awards are symbolically important and important in deterrence. What do you think?

A related question turns on the fact that many people who recover under the tort system have no experience in managing money. Many lawyers have had the experience of seeing a large recovery, meant to provide for twenty years of future wage loss, mismanaged by the plaintiff, or bled off by unscrupulous friends and advisors. Both the lump-sum award and the pain award are implicated in this problem.

If you think there is something wrong with pain awards, do you also think that is ground standing alone to reconsider the whole tort system?

New Directions

If either the old or the new tort reformers are right or partly right in their central perceptions, would it be a good idea to find alternatives to some or all parts of the tort system?

Many of the criticisms summarized above are reviewed by Professor Sugarman, who insists that tort law fails in the goal of inducing safety, providing compensation, or doing justice if you look at the system as a whole and consider alternatives. STEPHEN SUGARMAN, DOING AWAY WITH PERSONAL INJURY LAW (1989). Sugarman proposes a comprehensive welfare program that would take care of injuries as well as any other misfortune. Employers would cover short term needs, government the rest. Safety incentives would be provided by regulation, not by threat of liability. Professor Alfred Conard gives a short, careful, and sympathetic review in *Coup de Grace for Personal Injury Torts?*, 88 MICH. L. REV. 1557 (1990). But regulation does not always work or work efficiently and we do not know a great deal about how to make it effective as a substitute for liability. See JERRY MASHAW & DAVID HARFST, THE STRUGGLE FOR AUTO SAFETY (1990); Michael J. Trebilcock, *Requiem for Regulators: The Passing of a Counter–Culture?*, 8 YALE J. REG. 497 (1991).

Others among the newer critics have suggested that society should allocate certain kinds of injury problems to some institutions other than tort law, but that tort law should be retained for at least some kinds of cases. E.g., Richard B. Stewart, *Crisis in Tort Law? The Institutional Perspective*, 54 U. CHI. L. REV. 184 (1987); W. Kip Viscusi, *Toward a Diminished Role for Tort Liability: Social Insurance, Government Regulation, and Contemporary Risks to Health and Safety*, 6 YALE J. REG. 65 (1989). See also the good short discussion as to toxic torts in Robert Rabin, *Book Review*, 98 YALE L. J. 813 (1989) (reviewing P. SCHUCK, TORT SYSTEM ON TRIAL: THE BURDEN OF MASS TOXICS LITIGATION (1987).

One alternative "institution" for dealing with injury might be specific regulation, such as regulation requiring air bags or seat belts. Another institution might be the free market, leaving people to contractual arrangements. Finally, some form of social or private insurance might provide the best institution for dealing with certain injuries not suited to the tort system. In evaluating the tort reform movement, and tort law itself, some of these alternatives must be considered. Some of the major ones other than regulation or contract are considered next.

Part VI

ALTERNATIVES TO TORT LAW

For many, including many legislatures, the disadvantages of the tort system have outweighed the advantages, at least in particular settings. In consequence, legal thinkers and state and federal legislatures have provided several non-tort alternatives to the tort system. All of these, however, have limited application, for example, to employment injuries or automobile injuries.

This subpart introduces some of those alternatives. In many ways they are enormously different from tort systems. But this should not obscure the similarities. In considering these alternatives, consider whether the same issues must be resolved and whether, in new language, similar problems arise for the judiciary. More importantly, consider whether any of these alternative systems is better than the tort system. If they are not to wholly supplant the tort system, can they be satisfactorily meshed with tort law?

Chapter 25

WORKERS' COMPENSATION

§ 1. INTRODUCTION

a. *The Employer's Tort Liability at Common Law*

In the pre-industrial period in England, servants injured in the service of a master were often living in the household as apprentices or indentured servants. At least at some times and places, the practice and legal obligation of masters was to take care of the injured servant by furnishing him room and board during the period of the indenture or contract. A similar practice developed in the maritime law, and seamen injured in the service of the ship were entitled to "maintenance and cure"—basic support and medical attention. The assistance received by the servant or seaman in such cases was no doubt minimal compared to a tort remedy, but was available without respect to the employer's fault. In addition, the seaman injured by an "unseaworthy" condition on a ship had a strict liability claim against the owner. See Thomas Schoen-baum, Admiralty and Maritime Law §§ 4–28–4–35 (1994); 5 U.S.C.A. § 8102.

With the development of industrial plants, the picture was very different. The force of machinery was multiplied through levers, pulleys and gears, then through water and steam power. The injuries caused by massive forces in the factory or on the rails were both numerous and horrible. At the very time injury was becoming the formidable problem it remains today, the system of apprentices and indentured servants was becoming obsolete. An injured plant worker could not expect that the employer would provide for him when injury made work impossible.

The common law tort system might have provided a very handsome remedy for the injured worker had it retained or developed the notion that an actor was liable for *trespassory* torts to the person, even without intent or negligence. But as we saw in Chapter 21, that notion largely went underground with the decision in *Brown v. Kendall*. The result was that the injured employee was required to prove employer negligence in all injury cases.

This might not have been an intolerable burden in many instances, but the defenses erected against the employee were effective barriers to many claims. The absolute common law defenses of contributory negligence, assumed risk and fellow servant barred a great many claims. The fellow servant rule in particular was often a hardship. That rule, supposedly grounded in assumed risk, held that the worker could not recover against the employer for negligence of the worker's fellow servant. Even though the master would be liable for the torts of a servant, he would not be liable for the torts of one servant to another.

Injured industrial workers in the 19th century were in difficult straits. They were without insurance or health benefits, without modern social services, and very often without a tort remedy. Piecemeal efforts were made in legislatures to ameliorate this situation. Factory acts sometimes attempted to provide safer working conditions. One example of safety legislation was the Federal Safety Appliance Act, 45 U.S.C.A. § 1 et seq., enacted in 1893 and requiring railroads to use such safety devices as automatic couplers and brakes operable by the engineer. In 1908, the Federal Employers' Liability Act (FELA), 45 U.S.C.A. § 51 et seq. was passed. This attacked some major sources of the problem by abolishing the defenses of fellow servant and assumed risk and by adopting a comparative negligence scheme. The statute applied to railroad workers in interstate commerce, and as it stands today it applies to virtually all railroad workers.

The FELA did not address the problems of factory or other workers. Nor did it address the fundamental problem of delay. The worker who was injured by an employer's negligence could indeed recover once the defenses were abolished. But recovery might take years if litigated in the court system. Since urban workers had little if any support if they were unable to work, even a good tort remedy might in practice be illusory.

This was the situation when workers' compensation provisions were first considered.

b. *The Adoption of Workers' Compensation*

The first workers' compensation scheme was adopted in Germany in 1884. Although German philosophers had laid down the foundations of the idea in their conception of the state as a protector of the citizens, there were more immediate reasons for the adoption of the scheme, the foundation of which is compulsory insurance. One reason may have been that the German state, united under Prussian leadership in 1870, was a convenient means through which to organize the capital necessary to manage a widespread insurance scheme. An even more immediate reason was Bismarck's fear that, without some such plan, radical Marxist movements would be successful. With Bismarck's support, workers' compensation was adopted to provide a sufficient level of support to undermine Marxism. See generally ARTHUR LARSON, WORKERS' COMPENSATION (1992).

American states began enacting workers' compensation statutes, some quite limited, just after the turn of the century. The first comprehensive act was the 1910 New York statute. It was quickly declared unconstitutional in *Ives v. South Buffalo Ry. Co.*, 201 N.Y. 271, 94 N.E. 431 (1911) on the ground that in imposing liability without fault of the employer, the statute was a taking of property without due process of law. "When our Constitutions were adopted, it was the law of the land that no man who was without fault or negligence could be held liable in damages for injuries sustained by another." The liability of the employer to pay workers' compensation under a compulsory insurance scheme "is a liability unknown to the common law, and we think it plainly constitutes a deprivation of liberty and property. . . ."

New York amended its constitution, however, and a new statute was passed in 1913. Other states began enacting workers' compensation statutes, sometimes avoiding constitutional challenge by making the provisions elective. Most states had enacted a statute by 1920, and all states eventually did so. There is a separate federal statute for federal employees and another for longshoremen and harbor workers.

c. *Characteristics of the Statutes*

Although the statutes are varied in detail, they are alike in these characteristic provisions:

1. *Strict liability.* Employers are made strictly liable for on-the-job injury of employees. Thus a worker injured on the job is entitled to compensation even if the employer is not negligent.

2. *Defenses are abolished.* Contributory negligence, assumed risk and fellow servant defenses are abolished completely. This is not a rule of comparative negligence. Even the employee who is guilty of contributory negligence recovers full compensation.

3. *Limited liability.* The employer's liability is limited. The compensation provided is not common law damages, but relatively fixed amounts, expressed as specific sums for certain injuries like the loss of a thumb, or as a percentage of average wages where there is total disability. Liability includes compensation for medical needs and wage loss, but nothing for pain and suffering. This limited liability is a trade-off for strict liability and sometimes is much emphasized as a constitutional justification for the strict liability.

4. *Immediate and periodic payment.* An injured worker is entitled, after a short waiting period, to immediate periodic payments. This is in contrast to the common law lump-sum method. Payments continue as long as the disability exists, subject to any statutory maximum amounts.

5. *Enforcement and administration.* Where there is no dispute, the employer (or its insurer) pays directly to the worker on a periodic basis. If there is a dispute, the worker reports the claim to an administrative agency, called the Industrial Commission, Workers' Compensation Commission or something similar. The agency usually sends a hearing officer

or referee to the locality to hold an informal hearing and settle the dispute. The statutes contemplated that there would be no need for lawyers, but today lawyers do in fact appear in many of these hearings. However, the procedure is relaxed and informal, and there are no rules of evidence, so it remains true at least in theory that lawyers are not required.

6. *Financing.* The scheme is essentially a compulsory insurance scheme, though in some states the "insurance" fund is managed by the state rather than by private insurers. The employer is required by statute to purchase insurance. The insurance must provide coverage as outlined by the statute.

7. *Courts.* Courts have a most limited role in workers' compensation. They do, however, decide the meaning of the statute and whether evidence is sufficient to warrant the decisions of the administrators who decide disputes under the statute. In other words, one may appeal from an award of the compensation tribunal, but the courts will not overturn the award if there is evidence to support it and it is based on a correct interpretation of the law. There is no jury trial in either the initial hearing or in the appeal to the courts.

8. *Exclusive remedy and third-party claims.* Most statutes provide that the injured employee's remedy against the employer is workers' compensation, and that this remedy is exclusive of any other remedy. In other words, with few exceptions, there is no tort action against the employer. The exclusive remedy provision, however, is aimed only at preventing suits against the employer. The employee injured by a third person, such as a manufacturer of a machine used on the job, still has a tort suit against that third person.

d. Coverage

No state has enacted workers' compensation benefits for every single worker within the state. Several devices in the statutes operate to limit coverage of workers.

1. *Election of coverage.* At one time many of the statutes provided that workers' compensation coverage was not compulsory, but was elective only. The employer could elect not to be covered, but if this happened, the employer would be liable in tort and would be deprived of the common law defenses. The employer was thus encouraged to elect workers' compensation. The employee also had an election, but was presumed to elect in favor of compensation in the absence of some active rejection of it. This system has met with much disapproval, and many states now use a fully compulsory system. In states where an election is possible, an election by either employer or employee may eliminate workers' compensation coverage in particular cases.

2. *Definition of employer.* Several of the critical determinants of compensation are hidden in definitional sections of the statutes. The statute may define "employer" or "employee" or both, and the statutory definitions will necessarily exclude certain persons from coverage. Many

statutes exclude from coverage the following groups of workers, usually by definition of terms like "employee":

(A) *"Casual workers."* Example: someone who trims your hedge for you on one occasion. Obviously this category can present line-drawing problems, but it is not a major problem.

(B) *Domestic workers.* Example: a home cleaning person. Notice this is not the same as "janitorial."

(C) *Agricultural workers.*

(D) *Non-business employees.* This seems broader in some ways than "domestic workers."

(E) *Small employers.* Several states exempt employers whose employees are not numerous. The cut-off varies from two to six employees.

Since the definition of employee may take several pages of statutory print, there are a good many details to be assessed under particular statutes. Although many states do not cover agricultural employees, public employees and corporate executives are often covered. Even prisoners may be covered. Obviously the governing statute must be consulted.

3. *Expanding coverage.* In some situations an enterprise that would not normally be considered an employer will be defined as an employer under the compensation statute. Material on "statutory employers" and "loaned employees" is considered in § 3.

e. Benefits

If an entire section could be devoted to a study of the benefits payable under workers' compensation, quite a few major issues would emerge. Some of the decisions and some of the statutes would be subject to various criticisms. In some cases, benefits are woefully inadequate. In others, courts seem to have moved to a more tort-like assessment of liability. However, the mainstream cases and the principles of workers' compensation benefits are fairly straightforward. In general they look something like this:

1. *Death benefits.* If the worker dies from an on-the-job injury, death benefits based on his or her earnings are paid to certain survivors. Often, these are dependents rather than heirs. In this respect, some workers' compensation statutes differ from many of the wrongful death statutes governing tort liability.

2. *Medical benefits.* Statutes now provide more or less unlimited medical benefits, including all forms of needed care, prosthetic devices, and the like. For the most part, issues over medical care have been extremely narrow and minor.

3. *Disability benefits.* In principle, workers' compensation statutes sought to replace or avoid economic loss suffered from injury. There was no award for pain and suffering. The award was intended instead to

replace wages lost due to disability. Thus if a worker was injured and disabled for six months, during which time he or she could earn no wages, the ideal benefit would be equal to six months' wages. And if the worker regains part of her earning capacity, benefits would be reduced accordingly. See *Metropolitan Stevedore Co. v. Rambo*, 515 U.S. 291, 115 S.Ct. 2144, 132 L.Ed.2d 226 (1995).

Limits on benefits. No statute affords 100% wage replacement in providing disability benefits. If a worker collected 100% of wages during disability, there would be an incentive to feign injury or disability. Even if that did not happen, there might be an unconscious tendency to prolong disability. In addition, federal law makes payments for personal injury tax-exempt. Workers' compensation benefits, since they are not taxable, are "worth more" than the wages themselves. For these and similar reasons, compensation is limited to a percentage of average wages. This percentage is often fixed at two-thirds of the average wage, and it is, ordinarily, paid on a weekly or monthly schedule. There are, in some instances, also limits on the total amount in any given week. This might be expressed in terms of a dollar amount, such as $200 per week. Or it might be expressed as a percentage of the average wage for the entire state. In either event, very high-earning employees might be entitled to considerably less than their actual wage loss. Finally, there may be limits on the total number of weeks for which compensation is payable.

Classifications of disability. Disability is typically classified as temporary or permanent on the one hand, and as either partial or total on the other. Most industrial injuries cause some temporary total disability, as where an employee is injured and cannot work at all for two months. Such an employee would ordinarily be entitled to two months' compensation. If the disability is permanent, compensation may run for life, but in some states it may be limited to a specified period, such as 500 weeks or 600 weeks. In the case of partial disability there may be compensation due, but at a reduced level.

Scheduled injuries. Injuries that were painful but caused no wage loss were not originally compensable at all, since there was no claim for pain and suffering. A worker who lost testicles or was sexually disfigured might, therefore, recover medical benefits and wage loss during any healing period, but since these injuries would not prevent work, there would be no compensation after the healing period. Some statutes have now added a small compensatory sum in the case of "disfigurement." More importantly, virtually all states have a "schedule" of benefits for certain injuries. For example, if a worker loses the sight in one eye in an industrial injury, the schedule specifies a fixed amount of compensation. Such a worker might receive 66 2/3% of the average monthly wage for 30 months. This would be awarded even if there was no demonstrable "disability," as reflected in wage loss. An unscheduled injury, in comparison, would be compensable only if it resulted in a disability.

Functional or industrial disability. The principle of computing benefits by schedule and the principle of computing by actual wage loss are obviously at odds. The original idea was to replace wages, or at least a reasonable percentage of wages. Over the years, the principle behind the schedules has moved courts and legislatures toward a "functional" assessment of disability and away from the wage-loss or "industrial" assessment of disability. This may permit courts to say that, though the claimant has not lost work time except for a healing period, nevertheless the body as a whole is impaired in function, and a disability should be found accordingly. Different statutes and different courts may thus get quite different results when a worker is injured in a way that impairs bodily function but does not seriously affect earning capacity. This particular problem is treated by Professor Larson in a section entitled "Disability: Wage Loss Versus Medical Incapacity." This section and the next, which deals with scheduled benefits, runs over 300 pages. ARTHUR LARSON, WORKMEN'S COMPENSATION §§ 57–58.

These notes suggest that problems arise in computing benefits. In addition, benefits may tend to under-compensate, as where there is a 500–week limit on compensation for total and permanent disability. And benefits may over-compensate where the principle of the schedule is carried out. All of these problems and others, that could be identified in computing benefits, are problems worthy of attention by those who could improve the law. But, especially for the purpose of comparisons to tort law, the central features of benefits payable under workers' compensation statutes are quite simple. In the great majority of cases, benefits will be paid regularly and without dispute as long as disability continues, but in most cases, benefits will reflect something less than actual wage loss.

————

On the theoretical side, workers' compensation was justified on grounds much like those that were advanced later for vicarious liability and strict products liability. The ideas was that enterprise ought to bear responsibility for the costs it typically or recurrently imposed and pass those costs along to consumers. As workers were routinely injured, the costs of their injuries should be treated as a cost of doing business and internalized by the business. See George L. Priest, *The Invention of Enterprise Liability: A Critical History of the Intellectual Foundations of Modern Tort Law,* 14 J. LEG. STUD. 461, 465–67 (1985).

Pragmatic justifications were different. Workers' compensation statutes attempted to provide for some minimum well-being for injured workers. But they also attempted to provide a quick, efficient remedy, one that would not bog down in litigation, one that would provide payments quickly and with relative certainty. They thus attempted to provide a system that allowed for a minimum of dispute. Benefits, for example, were relatively fixed and certain; there were no long trials devoted to proving extensive pain and suffering. Likewise, by eliminating investigations into fault, grounds for dispute were minimized.

With fault out of the picture and little ground for litigating over benefit levels, did they provide for that Utopia, long sought by citizens the world over, a system that worked without lawyers? That was, quite clearly, the drafters' goal. To achieve it, they would have to provide what is missing in some of the torts cases—an efficient trigger for liability. In the workers' compensation statutes, the trigger for liability is only job relatedness; that is, the injury must be one "arising out of and in the course of employment." The next section explores how efficient this trigger is.

§ 2. JOB RELATED INJURY

a. *Arising Out of and in the Course of Employment*

"Every employer subject to this chapter shall ... secure compensation to his employees and pay or provide compensation for their disability or death from injury arising out of and in the course of employment without regard to fault as a cause of the injury...."

—N.Y. Workers' Compensation Law § 10.

JAEGER BAKING CO. v. KRETSCHMANN

Supreme Court of Wisconsin, 1980.
96 Wis.2d 590, 292 N.W.2d 622.

... The facts are undisputed. Heinrich Kretschmann was injured while walking to work shortly before 2:00 a.m. the morning of January 27, 1974, when two unknown persons attacked him on a public sidewalk in the City of Milwaukee. Kretschmann was on his way to work the 2:00 a.m. shift at the Jaeger Baking Company. On the night of the injury, he took a city bus to work. Upon alighting at the bus stop, at a location undisclosed by the record, Kretschmann walked directly toward the bakery's employee entrance. Kretschmann was walking on the public sidewalk adjacent to the bakery building and was about 50 feet from the employee entrance when attacked.

The place where the attack occurred was on the direct route which an employee using the parking lot would have taken in travelling from the lot to the employee entrance. Had Kretschmann used the parking lot and then walked to the employee entrance, his route would have taken him to the point where he was attacked....

The general rule prior to the amendment was that employees going to or coming from work were ordinarily not performing services incidental to their employment and thus were not covered unless actually on the employer's premises when injured. In accordance with this general rule, we have held that the statute covered employees injured while in a parking lot owned or maintained by the employer for the convenience of its employees, but did not cover employees injured while walking from the employer's parking lot to the work premises. [The court's footnote 3 noted: "In contrast to the vast majority of other jurisdictions, Wisconsin has steadfastly denied compensation to employees injured while traveling between any two portions of an employer's business premises. . . ."]

The legislature subsequently enacted the parking lot coverage extension . . . to cover employees "going between an employer's designated parking lot and the employer's work premises." . . . . When the statutory language is unambiguous, as we conclude it is in this case, the intention of the legislature must be arrived at by giving the language its ordinary and accepted meaning. Given the factual context of *Halama* and *Frisbie*, the cases prompting the statutory amendment, and the plain meaning of the phrase, "going between an employer's designated parking lot and the employer's work premises," it is apparent that the legislative intent in amending the statute was to cover employees injured while going directly from the one portion of the employer's premises to the other. The legislative intent is expressly stated and is apparent when the pertinent portions of the statute are read in their entirety. The clause immediately following the one quoted provides, "while on a direct route and in the ordinary and usual way." The plain and simple meaning is that coverage may be allowed when an employee is traveling from the parking lot to the work premises, or vice versa, on a direct route. . . .

The court of appeals reasoned, and the department argues on appeal, that following the plain meaning of the statute will produce absurd results by distinguishing between employees injured in the same manner and place on the basis of how they got to work. Although the argument has superficial merit, the construction of the statute urged by the department would produce even more arbitrary results.

The department's construction would differentiate between two employees proceeding to work from the same bus stop if one happened to be injured at a location on the direct route between the employer's parking lot and work premises and the other, following the same route to work, was injured several inches, yards, or blocks off the "route between." It was fortuitous that Kretschmann was injured at a point on the direct route from the employee parking lot to the bakery. . . .

We find Professor Larson's discussion of the problem presented by this case persuasive. Professor Larson is generally critical of judicial attempts to broaden the time tested premises rule. He notes that:

> "It is a familiar problem of law, when a sharp, objective, and perhaps somewhat arbitrary line has been drawn, producing the kind of distinctions just cited, to encounter demands that the line be blurred a little to take care of the closest cases. For example, one writer says that there is no reason in principle why states should not protect employees 'for a reasonable distance' before reaching or after leaving the employer's premises. This, however, only raises a new problem without solving the first. It raises a new problem because it provides no standard by which the reasonableness of the distance can be judged. It substitutes the widely-varying subjective interpretation of 'reasonable distance' by different administrators and judges for the physical fact of a boundary line. At the same time,

it does not solve the original problem, because each time the premises are extended a 'reasonable distance,' there will inevitably arise new cases only slightly beyond that point and the cry of unfairness of drawing distinctions based on only a few feet of distance will once more be heard." 1 Larson, *Worker's Compensation Law*, sec. 15.12 at 4–6 (1978). . . .

We agree with Professor Larson's analysis. . . .

Note

Traditional analysis distinguishes the course of employment issue from the arising out of employment issue. Course of employment emphasizes time and place–injury must occur "at work" and during working hours. Arising out of employment emphasizes the qualitative connection with work–injury must be work related to risks of work as opposed to personal risks. Look at the typical statute quoted above. Must the claim show both these elements?

————

McCANN v. HATCHETT, 19 S.W.3d 218 (Tenn.2000). "Donald Eugene King was employed by Glen Hatchett Carpet Services, a Memphis-based business. King, with other employees, had been sent to Rutland, Vermont, by their employer to lay carpet at a Rutland motel. While in Rutland, King and the other employees were lodged at the Days Inn at the employer's expense. While off-duty, at approximately 10 p.m. on June 23, 1996, King drowned in the Days Inn pool." Relying on 2 Arthur Larson & Lex K. Larson, Arthur Larson's Workers' Compensation Laws, § 25.00 (1998), "we now adopt the majority rule and hold that a traveling employee is generally considered to be in the course of his or her employment continuously during the duration of the entire trip, except when there is a distinct departure on a personal errand. Thus, . . . the injury or death of a traveling employee occurring while reasonably engaged in a reasonable recreational or social activity arises out of and in the course of the employment."

KOLSON v. DISTRICT OF COLUMBIA DEPT. OF EMPLOYMENT SERVICES, 699 A.2d 357 (D.C.App.1997). The claimant completed a 12–hour shift driving a bus for Greyhound. When he turned the bus in at the Washington, D.C. terminal about 4:30 a.m, he was given a voucher for a hotel provided by the company. Walking to the hotel from the terminal, he was attacked by an assailant with a pipe. He remained unable to work for about four months. *Held*, the injury was compensable. "Although the concepts 'arising in the course of the employment' and 'arising out of the employment' have distinct meanings, 'the two are not totally independent; frequently proof of one will incidentally tend to establish the other.' " Here, "injury also grew out of his employment because it resulted from a risk created by his employment–his arrival at odd hours in places away from his home and the necessity of using the public streets to seek lodging."

UNION COLLIERY CO. v. INDUSTRIAL COMMISSION, 298 Ill. 561, 132 N.E. 200 (1921). This is a claim for compensation by a widow and children of a deceased worker. The deceased was employed in the employer's coal mine, working at the top of the "cage" or elevator on which coal was hoisted. He was to dump the coal when the cage arrived at the top, but he also had underground duties. On the night of his death, he rode up on the cage with a load of coal. Circumstantial evidence suggested he was crushed between the cage and a beam. To ride up in a loaded cage or hoist was a violation of the state statutes on mining safety. The Industrial Commission made an award of compensation, but the trial court, reviewing this, set it aside. *Held*, compensation should be awarded. The employer argues that violation of the statute, like violation of an employer's instruction, would show that the injury and death "did not arise out of and in the course of employment." However, violation of the statute would at most show negligence. Nor does violation of an employer's rules automatically place the employee outside the sphere of his employment. In this case, injury arose out of employment.

Notes

1. Conceivably, some violations of statute or employer rules would show more than negligence. What would have to be shown?

2. Early cases sometimes took a narrow view about what injuries arose in employment. On facts similar to those in *Union Colliery*, the Pennsylvania Court barred recovery in *Pokis v. Buck Run Coal Co.*, 286 Pa. 52, 132 A. 795 (1926). In so doing it relied in part on an earlier decision in which a worker entered a portion of the mine known to contain gas. This was prohibited by law. The court said that "as to this danger zone, he had no employment," and that the injury was not therefore one arising out of employment. *Walcofski v. Lehigh Valley Coal Co.*, 278 Pa. 84, 122 A. 238 (1923).

3. Narrow decisions of this kind no longer represent the courts' approach to the issue of "arising out of employment," although an employee's wilful misconduct may in some instances be a defense. The modern approach is and long has been to give a very liberal interpretation to coverage under workers' compensation statutes and to resolve doubts in favor of the employee's coverage.

4. Traumatic injury in "dark, satanic mills," in factories, mines or on railroads or heavy construction projects represents the core of typical claims, about which there is now little litigation. These claims easily "arise out of employment." And this remains true even if the employee is negligent. What kinds of injuries would *not* arise out of employment?

STATE INDUSTRIAL COMMISSIONER v. LEFF

Supreme Court of New York, 1934.
265 N.Y. 533, 193 N.E. 307.

Appeal from an order of the Appellate Division of the Supreme Court in the Third Judicial Department (241 App. Div. 898, 271 N.Y.S.

1025), entered May 24, 1934, affirming an award of the State Industrial Board made under the Workmen's Compensation Law. The deceased was employed as a press feeder by the appellants Herman and Lillian Leff who were engaged in the printing business. The injury causing his death was the result of an explosion in an adjoining building which caused the wall of the latter building which extended up four stories above the roof of the employer's premises to fall over onto and through the roof of these premises crushing the employee beneath the falling material. The Industrial Board found that the injuries were accidental injuries arising out of and in the course of his employment. The Appellate Division affirmed the award on the authority of Matter of Filitti v. Lerode Homes Corporation, 244 N. Y. 291,155 N. E. 579.

PER CURIAM. Order Affirmed, with costs.

Notes

1. *Risk classification.* Some risks are particularly associated with a given employment or with employment in general. At the opposite extreme, some risks are not risks of employment at all, but personal risks that happen to erupt in injury while the employee is on the job. In between are neutral risks, not especially associated with the work and not especially associated with the employment either. When an employee is injured by a risk especially associated with the work, the claim for benefits arises out of employment. When the injury results from a personal risk, it does not. The process of classifying risks, explicitly or implicitly, is central in determining whether an injury arises out of employment.

2. *Increased risk.* Courts no longer insist that the employment risk be "peculiar" to the employment in the sense that it is different in its nature from risks people in general face. They very commonly do, however, insist that employment must somehow increase these risks. Thus if employment requires a worker to drive a van delivering flowers, injury in a collision on the street will be one arising out of employment, even though everyone is subjected to "street risks." The worker in such a case has increased exposure, though the nature of the risk is the same. Some courts would impose liability for compensation in such a case even if the employment only occasionally puts the employee on the streets, so long as it in fact does so. The street risk cases are well covered in ARTHUR LARSON, WORKMEN'S COMPENSATION § 9.00 et seq.

3. *Positional risks.* The increased risk test is commonly used, but some courts have adopted and used a "positional risk" test for risks that are not purely personal. This is basically a rule that liability for compensation is triggered if the employment is a but-for cause of injury. A well-known decision is *Industrial Indemnity Co. v. Industrial Accident Commission*, 95 Cal.App.2d 804, 214 P.2d 41 (1950). In that case, an angry wife entered a bar and fired a shot at her husband. The shot ricocheted off the bar and struck a waitress, who had nothing to do with the quarrel but who died as a result. Conceivably, one could say that risk of injury of bar employees as a result of angry customers (or spouses) is somewhat increased by their employment. The court took a much broader line, however, emphasizing that "her

employment required her to be in what turned out to be a place of danger."
It would be sufficient for liability, the court said, that "injury results from a
danger to which [the employee] was exposed as an employee." What if an
employee simply falls down while working, but not from either a risk special
to employment or any risk personal to the employee? *Circle K Store #1131 v.
Industrial Com'n of Arizona*, 165 Ariz. 91, 796 P.2d 893 (1990).

4. *Acts of God—the positional test.* What result under the positional
test if the employee while in the course of employment in a factory is killed
in a tornado or is struck by lightning? In *Whetro v. Awkerman*, 383 Mich.
235, 174 N.W.2d 783 (1970), two cases involving tornado deaths were
consolidated. One employee, Whetro, was injured when a tornado destroyed
the building in which he was working. The other employee, Emery, was
killed when a motel in which he was staying on a business trip was
destroyed. The employers asserted that the tornados were acts of God and
did not arise out of employment. A divided court thought that "it is no
longer necessary to establish a relationship of proximate causality between
employment and an injury in order to establish compensability." The act of
God defense "retains too much of the idea that an employer should not pay
compensation unless he is somehow at fault."

5. *Acts of God—increased risk test.* How would the increased risk test
work in cases involving acts of God such as tornados or lightning? In
Nebraska a social caseworker, en route to a call on a client, is injured when a
severe rainstorm occurs and a tree falls on his car. What if he had been
selling tickets at a drive-in theatre when a windstorm blew over the
somewhat flimsy booth?

6.   How do these tests work where the employee's injury results in part
from personal activities? Consider the materials that follow.

CARVALHO v. DECORATIVE FABRICS CO.

Supreme Court of Rhode Island, 1976.
117 R.I. 231, 366 A.2d 157.

BEVILACQUA, CHIEF JUSTICE.

[The employee worked in a factory handling yarn. At the end of the
shift fellow employees customarily assisted removing lint from each
other's clothes by using an air hose. On this occasion a fellow worker
placed the air hose "in the vicinity of petitioner's rectum," and the
petitioner felt his stomach blow up. He was unable to work the next day
and later went to the emergency room in pain. He was found to have a
perforated rectum. The commission denied compensation on the ground
that this involved horseplay and assault and was therefore not arising
out of employment.]

In the early workmen's compensation cases involving "horseplay"
(sometimes referred to as "sportive assault," "larking" or "skylarking")
courts were reluctant to award compensation, even to the innocent, non-
participating victim. Reasoning that employees were hired to work and
not to play, courts concluded that injuries resulting from "horseplay"
did not arise out of and in the course of employment. In addition, courts

denied compensation sustaining the defense that the claimant was a "participant" in or "instigator" of "horseplay." However, these decisions are contrary to the scope and intent of the Workmen's Compensation Acts. These Acts were designed to provide compensation to victims of work-connected injuries and to eliminate the tort defenses of negligence and fault. In effect, these early decisions judicially reinstituted common law defenses which had been abolished by statute.

Later courts recognized that the primary purpose of workmen's compensation is to provide economic assistance to an employee who is injured and thereby suffers a loss of earnings; such legislation ... was intended to impose upon the employer the burden of taking care of the casualties occurring in his employment, thus preventing the injured employee from becoming a public charge." Moreover, the worker need no longer be free from fault to receive compensation....

In the case of the victim who does not participate in the "horseplay" and is innocent of any wrongful conduct, we need no extended justification to hold that the injuries received are compensable. In *In re Leonbruno v. Champlain Silk Mills*, supra, the late Mr. Justice Cardozo stated:

> "The claimant was injured, not merely while he was in a factory, but because he was in a factory, in touch with associations and conditions inseparable from factory life. The risks of such associations and conditions were risks of the employment." Id. at 472,128 N.E. at 711.

When people are placed together and are in close association with one another in performing their work there is a natural instinct to fool around and play pranks on one another. Such activity is part of the work environment, an incident of the employment. The claimant need only establish that the injury arose out of and in the course of employment: a nexus or causal connection between the injury and the employment must be shown....

The injured claimant should not be denied compensation merely because of his participation in "horseplay." As the court in *Maltais v. Equitable Life Assur. Soc'y of United States*, 93 N.H. 237, 40 A.2d 837 (1944) stated:

> "... to hold that an injury arises out of the employment if it is inflicted on a workman attentive to duty by the sportive conduct of a fellow-employee, but that it does not so arise if the injured workman participates, however slightly, in the sport is to draw a distinction based on the injured workman's fault, when the only faults specifically named in the statute as precluding recovery are intoxication, violation of law, and serious or wilful misconduct."[1] Id. at 242, 40 A.2d at 840.

---

1. In *Maltais v. Equitable Life Assur. Soc'y of United States*, 93 N.H. 237, 40 A.2d 837 (1944), two workers, while cleaning each others' clothes off with an air hose, began fooling around with it, causing claimant's death. Although claimant participated in the "horseplay," compensation was awarded.

Clearly, where horseplay has become customary, a participant can recover since his act is an incident of the work environment. However, where there is no evidence that "horseplay" is customary, the issue is whether the "horseplay" constituted a substantial deviation from the employment. The substantiality of the deviation should be determined not by the seriousness of the resulting injuries but solely by the extent to which the "horseplay" constitutes a departure from the course of the employment. 1 Arthur Larson, Workmen's Compensation Law, § 23.63 (1972).

Where the use of an air hose to clean off clothes is a daily practice, play with the hose is a risk of the employment and part and parcel of the working environment. Such activity should be regarded as part of the course of employment, particularly where, as in the instant case, the employer places in the hands of the employee the instrumentality which was used in the "horseplay" and caused the injury. . . .

Notes

1. *Instigators.* Even the instigator of horseplay may claim compensation for horseplay injury, provided that the horseplay is not a substantial deviation from the job. See *Prows v. Industrial Com'n of Utah,* 610 P.2d 1362 (Utah 1980).

2. *Intended battery.* Even an intended battery, distinct from a playful injury, could be considered to be within the scope of employment if it arises from a job related dispute. In *Ford Motor Co. v. Industrial Commission,* 78 Ill.2d 260, 35 Ill.Dec. 752, 399 N.E.2d 1280 (1980), the claimant and a co-worker named Simmons had some bad feeling because claimant had reported Simmons as the welder who had performed an unsatisfactory job. Simmons was thereafter repeatedly critical of the claimant's work on the job, and after several weeks of this bad feeling there was a scuffle between the two men. The claimant was injured and required surgery to insert a plate in his skull. The injury was held to arise out of employment because the conflict itself derived from employment issues.

3. *Company-sponsored recreation.* Sometimes unintended injuries occur during company social or recreational events. Courts often scrutinize the facts of these cases very carefully. If the employer actually sponsors the event, expects employee attendance, and pays the costs, injury during the event is likely to be one that arises from employment. If any of these elements is missing, courts may hold that injury is unrelated to employment.

———

KERR–McGEE CORP. v. HUTTO, 401 So.2d 1277 (Miss.1981). Mr. and Mrs. Scruggs each managed separate gas stations in Pascagoula, with Mr. Scruggs as general supervisor of both. Mr. and Mrs. Scruggs were not living together. Instead, Mrs. Scruggs was living with one Tommy Hutto, a 21–year-old single man who worked at her gas station. Mr. Scruggs was well aware of this arrangement. One day he drove to the station where Tommy worked and called his wife to the car. After she refused to move back in with him, he asked her to send Tommy Hutto out. At the time, Tommy was in the station stocking shelves with cigarettes. In response to Scruggs' request, he went out to the car. Scruggs shot him, and he died from the wound. *Held*, the death was compensable. It "occurred as a result of [Hutto's] being about his business at his place of employment.... Tommy Hutto was injured while responding to a directive from his immediate superior, Mrs. Scruggs, that her husband, also his superior, wanted to speak to him.... In our opinion, the employee's death was so strongly connected to the directive of his superior that it cannot be completely disassociated from his employment."

Notes

1. If the motive for the assault is personal to the employee and not job related, courts deny compensation. How do you explain *Hutto,* then?

2. Are the following injuries compensable?

    A. An employee is subject to seizures. He has a seizure during his work in a factory and falls to the floor, suffering a fracture. The employment circumstances do not make the harm worse than it would have been elsewhere nor do they make the seizure itself more likely.

    B. An employee, whose work provides no occasion for use of firearms and who is not in any kind of danger, takes a pistol to work with the intent of shooting at rats in a nearby field during his lunch hour. He drops it in his clothes locker at work and it goes off, causing him serious injury.

    C. Two employees in the supermarket are working in close proximity in the stock room. A storm arises, the lights flicker out and they find themselves comforting one another. One thing leads to another, and they find themselves in a sexual encounter. One employee suffers back injury as a result; the other becomes pregnant. Is either due compensation?

b. Accident, Injury and Disease

Most states initially provided for compensation only when the worker was injured by accident, or suffered an "accidental injury." In addition, workers might be compensated when disabled by certain occupational diseases. The two categories—accidental injury and occupational disease—did not, however, cover all disabilities a worker might suffer in the course of employment.

VIRGINIA ELECTRIC & POWER CO. v. COGBILL

Supreme Court of Virginia, 1982.
223 Va. 354, 288 S.E.2d 485.

THOMPSON, JUSTICE.

In this appeal of an Industrial Commission (Commission) award, the sole question for decision is whether the Commission erred in holding that Sarah L. Cogbill suffered an injury by industrial accident. Cogbill filed an application with the Commission on May 5, 1980, seeking compensation and medical benefits for a back injury, and on December 8, 1980, the Commission awarded her compensation.

The Virginia Electric and Power Company (Vepco) employed Cogbill as an operations clerk. This position required her to work seated at a desk in a cushioned office chair. Cogbill testified that she could "move around" when she wished.

On Saturday, April 19, 1980, Cogbill worked at a public auction of Vepco's surplus motor vehicles. She sat in a straight, hard-back chair on a truck bed while recording bids on a clipboard resting on her lap. She worked bent over for three and one-half to four hours without interruption. During the auction her back "began to bother her," and grew painful that evening. Cogbill worked at her regular job the following Monday, Tuesday, and Wednesday. On Thursday, at her supervisor's suggestion, she went to the company doctor. He referred her to an orthopedic doctor who diagnosed her backache as lumbar strain resulting from her prolonged sitting at the April 19 auction.

The record further establishes that Cogbill had had previous trouble with her back. Between 1969 and June 23, 1975, she took 111 days of sick leave. Of this, a portion was for back-related complaints. From October, 1977, to March 7, 1978, she was absent 20 days for back problems resulting from a fall. Since March, 1978, she had not taken sick leave and had not received medical treatment for backaches or injury.

The hearing commissioner ruled that Cogbill had suffered an injury by accident and awarded compensation. Vepco sought a review before the full Commission. Affirming, the Commission referred to the broad definition of "accident" found in *Reserve Life Ins. Co. v. Hosey*, 208 Va. 568, 159 S.E.2d 633 (1968).

A year ago we addressed the interpretation of "injury by accident" in *Badische Corp. v. Starks*, 221 Va. 910, 275 S.E.2d 605 (1981). The claimant, a creeler, regularly lifted weights exceeding 40 pounds. She testified she did nothing unusual at work on the day her back "began to bother her." The pain increased that evening and during the next day at work. She did not work on the third day, but saw a physician who diagnosed her ailment as back sprain. The evidence also revealed that she had suffered similar, but less intense, pains for two years prior to this complaint.

After examining prior case law, we reaffirmed the rule ... which requires "an obvious sudden mechanical or structural change in the body" for accidents resulting from ordinary exertion to be compensable. We also noted that the claimant must prove that the injury by accident arose "from an identified incident that occurs at some reasonably definite time." Starks' normal activities caused her injuries, but those injuries did not produce a sudden, obvious physical change. We denied recovery because Starks merely had a worsening, but preexisting, condition which she could not attribute to any identifiable incident.

Cogbill's situation is analogous to that of the claimant in *Badische*. First, her injury resulted from an activity similar in nature to her regular job, requiring no different or unusual exertion. Cogbill argues that her bent position, the hard-back chair, and the enforced prolonged sitting combine to make this activity significantly different from her regular job. We disagree. Her required actions and the level of exertion in no way distinguish the two activities. Both jobs were sedentary, requiring Cogbill to write. During the auction, she was at liberty to stand, but chose not to do so because it was more convenient to sit. Finally, the difference between a hard-back and cushioned chair is immaterial.

Second, Cogbill suffered no sudden, obvious mechanical or structural change. Her back, like the claimant's in *Badische*, "bothered" her, growing more painful later. Cogbill could not pinpoint when her back began aching or what caused the ache, but she urges this court to accept her argument that prolonged sitting in a bent-over posture caused the injury. She relies on *Hosey*, supra, for the definition of accident as an unusual and unexpected event. We reject this argument.

In *Rust Engineering Co. v. Ramsey*, 194 Va. 975, 980, 76 S.E.2d 195, 199 (1953), we held that The Workmen's Compensation Act was adopted for the benefit of the employees and their dependents and that it should be liberally construed in order to accomplish this humane purpose. But liberal construction does not mean that the Act should be converted into a form of health insurance." With this principle in mind, we find *Hosey*, supra, factually distinguishable from the case before us. In *Hosey*, the claimant injured her knee while climbing steps. The evidence revealed that the step where the injury occurred was higher than normal steps, requiring unusual exertion, and her injury was sudden and severe. Cogbill's exertions fell within the scope of her normal activities; we do not consider her exertion unusual in any significant particular. Her injury developed slowly, not suddenly. We hold this injury stemming from mere sitting is not an accidental injury.

We will reverse the award entered against Vepco and enter final judgment dismissing Cogbill's application.

Reversed and final judgment.

Notes

1. The statutory phrase, "injury by accident," or the more liberal "accidental injury," has been made to bear the weight of a multitude of legal issues. The requirement of accident might mean:

(a) the injury must not have been intentional; or

(b) the injury must have occurred on some definite occasion, or "event;" or

(c) the injury must have proceeded from external causes, as distinct from a degenerative breakdown within the body, or some combination of these three ideas. Actually, analysis reveals even further ambiguities. If the word "accident" refers to something that is not expected, is it the cause, or is it the result? If it refers to a definite occasion or event, is it the cause or the result?

2. *Accident and self-inflicted injury; suicide.* Statutes frequently exclude from coverage the self-inflicted injury, including suicide and injuries resulting from intoxication. The requirement of "accident" would perhaps have sufficiently covered the self-inflicted injury. When the self-inflicted injury is suicide, complications occur. If injury on the job causes insanity, which in turn leads to suicide, the resulting death may still be considered part of the "accident," and, on reasoning like that used in the tort cases, not the product of a "moral being." The death in such cases is compensable. Thus the legal cause reasoning is imported into the workers' compensation area. The exact kind of insanity—or "depression"—sufficient to permit this causal analysis in favor of the workers' dependents had been subject to debate and vacillation. It is perhaps fair to say that nothing like "insanity" is really required in many of the cases, and that pain and depression will be sufficient instead. See ARTHUR LARSON, WORKMEN'S COMPENSATION § 36.

The term "accident" may exclude cases that "self-inflicted injury" would not exclude. A worker has an unsatisfactory conversation with his superior and vents his rage on various objects with no apparent ill effects upon himself until he slams his fist into a locked metal door, causing a displaced fracture. Is this a self-inflicted injury? Is it an accident? *Glodo v. Industrial Com'n of Arizona,* 191 Ariz. 259, 955 P.2d 15 (1997).

3. *The definite occasion aspect.* In an old case from Minnesota, the statute actually defined "accident" to mean a sudden, unforeseen event. A worker worked for years at a machine which vibrated. Her nerves were gradually killed and the muscles atrophied, so that use of the arms was no longer possible. This was held to be no "accident," since there was no sudden event. *Young v. Melrose Granite Co.,* 152 Minn. 512, 189 N.W. 426 (1922).

4. *External events—the "heart attack" problem.* Since the human body is "a dying animal," continuously in the process of degenerating in one way or another, the mere fact that something goes wrong during work hours should not in itself indicate that the enterprise is responsible. Perhaps, even without the requirement of "accident," one would think that some ailments are personal rather than job related. The requirement of accident, however, can be taken to reinforce this idea.

Suppose a worker, in the ordinary course of work, suffers:

(a) a coronary thrombosis when some fatty deposit in a blood vessel breaks off and is swept along until it blocks the blood supply to the heart itself, which in turn results in death of the heart from insufficient oxygen.

(b) a stroke, in which a somewhat similar thing happens to blood vessels in the brain.

(c) a hernia, in which a weak muscle gives way and can no longer contain internal organs, resulting in a ballooning out of these organs or viscera, with possible constriction of them, inadequate blood supply to them and resulting complications.

(d) back pain, either from muscles or from collapse of intervertebral discs, which, when collapsed, press on the spinal cord.

5. *Unusual exertion; sudden event.* Where there is a sudden internal event, a rupture, breaking, herniation or the like, most courts now seem willing to permit compensation even where there is no unusual exertion, in the absence of a specific statutory requirement to the contrary. See ARTHUR LARSON, WORKMEN'S COMPENSATION § 38.20. Even in heart attack cases, many courts may reach this same result. Many others, however, require, as in *Cogbill*, some unusual strain or exertion preceding the heart attack, stroke or general backache.

6. *Pre-existing conditions and amount of award.* Should it be a necessary and a sufficient basis for compensation that the work, whether usual or unusual, precipitated the heart attack? In tort cases, it is at least theoretically possible that, though the defendant takes the plaintiff as he finds him, the plaintiff's damages will be calculated with the fact in mind that his pre-existing conditions would sooner or later have caused the same kind of harm. Cf. *Dillon v. Twin States Electric Co.*, Chapter 7, § 2. Is there room in the workers' compensation statutes for any adjustment of the award to accomplish the same end if the job triggers a heart attack, but the plaintiff would have suffered such an attack sooner or later even without working?

7. *Mental and emotional disorders.* Would the unusual strain rule help resolve the issue if an employee claimed disability because of stress and emotional breakdown? In some cases, the answer is relatively easy. Stress may trigger some kinds of heart problems or even stroke. When a physical injury results from emotional strain, compensation is permitted. The reverse of this case is one in which physical injury causes mental or emotional harm. Injury (or the pain from it) can cause many forms of emotional harm which itself is disabling. When the disability is real, many cases have permitted recovery.

But these cases are not very close precedent for compensation where there is no physical injury, either causing emotional harm or resulting from it. Suppose a worker becomes emotionally disabled because of an on-the-job accusation by a superior that she had committed a theft. Or that a worker voluntarily commits himself for intensive psychiatric care after months of job stress working on an important project. Is this case an "accident?" Is either case a better case for compensation than the other?

In *Carter v. General Motors Corp.*, 361 Mich. 577, 106 N.W.2d 105 (1960), the claimant worked on an assembly line. If he handled his job as required by instructions, he made the assembly correctly, but he was too slow and workers down the line would revile him. If he speeded up, he would mix up parts, with even worse results. Caught in this dilemma, he found escape in an emotional collapse described as "paranoid schizophrenia" of "schizophrenic reaction residual type." The court held this compensable.

But in *Seitz v. L. & R. Industries, Inc.*, 437 A.2d 1345 (R.I.1981), a secretary and office manager was given responsibility for supervising a company's move to a new location. At the new location nothing went right, and in addition employees at the new location did not accept her authority as office manager. There was a great deal of stress over a period of several weeks, and she ultimately terminated her employment. A psychiatrist who treated her described her problem as "depressive neurosis," and said she had an "obsessive compulsive personality disorder" aggravated by the job. The court denied compensation. "A number of the states that have approved compensation for psychic injuries produced by mental stimulus have done so on the basis of dramatic psychological trauma." Since there was no unusual stress or dramatic event, there was no "injury." What if the employee is subjected to intense harassment by coworkers because he would not join in their work slowdown and suffered drastic weight loss and psychic injury? *Martin v. Rhode Island Pub. Transit Auth.*, 506 A.2d 1365 (R.I.1986).

Is there any solution to these cases other than to adopt either *Carter* or *Seitz*? What about provision of medical benefits and a scheduled disability benefit limited to a specific number of weeks?

8. Is there either injury or accident if the worker develops cancer or arthritis while employed as a high school teacher? What if a hospital worker with access to drugs becomes a drug addict?

9. Questions about liability for strokes, heart attacks, cancer or drug addiction represent, perhaps, points on a long spectrum of cases shading toward disease. Even though many heart attack cases are compensable, disease itself is not an injury by accident.

10. *Occupational Disease.* Statutes now provide for some degree of coverage for occupational diseases. Coverage is usually more restrictive than for "injury by accident."

First, the disability must count as a "disease." in *Stenrich Group v. Jemmott*, 251 Va. 186, 467 S.E.2d 795 (Va. 1996), several claimants suffered repetitive stress injuries from use of their hands and fingers in constant small movements like those in typing or constantly pulling a water-gun's trigger all day. The disability (and pain) is real, but the court concluded that cumulative stress injuries did not count as injury by accident, so it was not compensable as "injury." On the other hand, the injury was not a "disease" so it couldn't be an occupational disease, either. If this is not an injury by accident for lack of a definite occasion, and not a disease because it is injury (though not one occasioned by an "accident"), then can the worker sue the employer for negligence in failing to provide suitable braces or an otherwise safe place in which to work? Perhaps not. The workers' compensation statute is the exclusive remedy, sometimes even when it is no remedy at all. Cf. *Murphy v. American Enka Corp.*, 213 N.C. 218, 195 S.E. 536 (1938).

Second, courts sometimes insist that a disease is not compensable unless it is somehow especially related to the job. What about someone who suffers serious respiratory disability from second hand smoke on the job? Since one might be subjected to smoke in many places, does that mean the disability is not compensable as a disease? See *Palmer v. Del Webb's High Sierra,* 108 Nev. 673, 838 P.2d 435 (Nev. 1992) (environmental smoke in casino where claimant worked was not uniquely incident to employment, bronchitis not compensable). However, in *Johannesen v. New York City Dept. of Housing Etc.*, 84 N.Y.2d 129, 615 N.Y.S.2d 336, 638 N.E.2d 981 (1994), the court held that injury from second hand smoke is compensable as accidental injury rather than as an occupational disease.

JACKSON TOWNSHIP VOLUNTEER FIRE CO. v. W.C.A.B. (WALLET)

Pennsylvania Commonwealth Court, 1991.
140 Pa.Cmwlth. 620, 594 A.2d 826.

KELLEY, JUDGE. . . .

Wallet was a volunteer of the Ambulance Association, a division of the fire company, when he responded to a call involving a fatal auto accident on July 7, 1988. The victim was pronounced dead at the scene of the accident. In the process of assisting at the scene, helping other volunteers remove the victim from his car and transporting the victim's bodily remains to a nearby funeral home, Wallet got some of the victim's blood and body fluids on his hands and shirt.

The victim was found to have had AIDS and was actively infected with the hepatitis B virus. Wallet testified that after leaving the funeral home, he and several other members of the ambulance crew cleaned the blood and other fluids from the stretcher and the back of the ambulance and scrubbed them both with bleach. They then responded to a brush fire. While on that call, Wallet was informed that Coroner John Barron wanted to see him at the hospital.

When Wallet arrived at the hospital, Barron and an unidentified physician at Conemaugh Valley Memorial Hospital informed him that arrangements had been made for him to receive tests for AIDS and hepatitis. Blood was drawn and as a precaution, Wallet received a series of injections to kill the hepatitis virus, had he contracted it. All tests came back negative.

The fire company and its insurer refused to pay for these medical services. Wallet then filed a petition under the Act seeking only reimbursement for medical costs incurred. [T]he referee found that Wallet's exposure to AIDS and hepatitis constituted an injury under the Act and directed the fire company and/or its insurer to pay for Wallet's tests and immunizations. The fire company appealed to the Board which affirmed the referee. This appeal followed.

. . . Section 306(c)(1) of the Act provides: "the employer shall provide payment for reasonable surgical and medical services . . . when needed." 77 P.S. § 531. Section 306(f)(4) limits compensation for medical services to situations where an "injury" has occurred. The fire company contends that Wallet was not injured and that if he was, he has not established that his injury was causally related to his work.

The term "injury" has been broadly defined to encompass all work-related harm including "any hurtful or damaging effect which may be suffered by anyone." Wallet claims that his injury was the risk of infection. We agree.

It is uncontroverted that Wallet was exposed to the blood and bodily fluids of an individual with AIDS and hepatitis B. His exposure prompted both the coroner and a physician at the hospital to arrange for testing and precautionary measures to be taken in the form of tests and shots. It is also clear that Wallet, who was only sixteen years old at the time of this incident, has not pursued his claim for medical expenses in bad faith. He reasonably relied on the advice/directive of the coroner and a physician who recommended and arranged for diagnostic testing and a series of preventative inoculations for hepatitis B. Wallet has not claimed an ongoing disability, nor does he seek compensation for mental anguish or distress; he simply seeks reimbursement for the necessary medical expenses incurred for his work-related exposure to two highly contagious and deadly diseases.

As we have often stated, the Act is remedial in nature and intended to benefit the worker, and its provisions should be liberally construed to effectuate its humanitarian objectives. This purpose would surely be thwarted should benefits be denied here, particularly considering that Wallet was injured while performing the humanitarian services of an ambulance crew volunteer.

Therefore, we hold that persons exposed to a serious risk of contracting a disease which is commonly known to be highly contagious/infectious and potentially deadly, have been "injured" for the purpose of receiving compensation under the Act. This conclusion is based on careful consideration of factors, such as the seriousness and immediacy of the risk created by exposure, as well as the reasonableness of the services sought and rendered. In this case, the actions and advice of the coroner and a physician clearly indicate that Wallet's exposure created a real, immediate, and serious risk of infection. The seriousness of Wallet's exposure is also evidenced by the urgency with which the recommended testing and precautionary treatment was pursued. These medical directives are consistent with a strong public policy in favor of restricting the spread of such serious and deadly contagious/infectious diseases as AIDS and hepatitis.

The fire company analogizes this case to a coal miner's pneumoconiosis case to imply that by granting compensation in this case, we will open the flood gates to litigation of claims involving employees who incur unwarranted and unreasonable medical expenses. The fire company hypothesizes that because exposure to coal dust may cause debilitating occupational lung diseases and even death, an employee might report to a doctor for diagnostic testing after each shift, then seek compensation for such expenses. However, this case is clearly distinguishable from a coal miner's pneumoconiosis case, and our holding is not nearly so broad.

We know of no cases in which a single incidence of exposure to coal dust has resulted in pneumoconiosis or death. The same cannot be said for AIDS and hepatitis, diseases so contagious and deadly that a person may contract them after being exposed only once. In addition, Wallet's expenses were not unwarranted nor unreasonable and, in fact, were incurred pursuant to the directives of health care professionals. Furthermore, as discussed above, only those persons exposed to a real and serious risk of contracting highly contagious/infectious and potentially deadly diseases are entitled to compensation. . . .

Accordingly, we affirm the order of the Board.

c. *Multiple Exposure or Injury*

UNION CARBIDE CORP. v. INDUSTRIAL COMMISSION, 196 Colo. 56, 581 P.2d 734 (1978). Benally worked as a uranium miner from 1955 to 1970 and died of lung cancer. He worked for Climax Uranium for four years before he was hired on April 28, 1970 by Union Carbide. The Union Carbide hiring was based upon a proviso that he pass a physical examination, but he began work before the test results were in. He worked eight days for Union Carbide before the tests came back and showed lung cancer. He was dismissed under the original proviso of his hiring. He was exposed to radiation during his short tenure at Union Carbide as well as at his earlier employment. *Held*, Union Carbide is liable for the worker's compensation death benefits since Benally's last injurious exposure was there. "[T]his rule makes good sense. . . . If the employee has worked for many different employers, it may well be that no single exposure with any one employer was in fact sufficient, in itself, to cause the disease. . . . [A] test for liability based upon the employee's actual length of exposure with each employer could well deny the employee any recovery for the disease. In contrast, the 'last injurious exposure' rule looks at the concentration of radiation received during the last employment to determine whether the employee was exposed to a harmful quantity. . . . If the rule were otherwise, the employee would be burdened with the almost impossible task of apportioning liability among his several employers."

BRACKE v. BAZA'R, INC., 293 Or. 239, 646 P.2d 1330 (1982). Bracke worked as a meat wrapper from 1974 until early 1977 for Baza'r. In early 1977, she also worked part time for Albertson's and Thriftway food markets. Her last employment with Baza'r ended March 30, with Albertson's on May 9, and with Thriftway on May 13. Claiming "meat wrapper's asthma," she applied for compensation with all three, and all denied her claim. She did not seek a hearing as to Thriftway's denial within the required 60–day limit. The Worker's Compensation Board found she suffered an occupational disease and that Thriftway would have been responsible because of the last injurious exposure rule, except that no hearing had been requested. Since Thriftway was the last injurious exposure, neither other employer was responsible. The Court of Appeals reversed this order of the board. In the Supreme Court of Oregon, *held*, the Court of Appeals judgment is affirmed. Testimony showed that with this disease there is no problem until one becomes sensitized by exposure to the fumes involved in cutting plastic wrap with a hot wire and dealing with price labels. But once one is sensitized, there will always be an allergic reaction thereafter. Sensitization occurred while the plaintiff was working for Baza'r, and later work does not make this "sensitization" any worse. Justification for the several variants of the last injurious exposure rules may be found "not in their achievement of individualized justice, but rather in their utility in spreading liability fairly among employers by the law of averages and in reducing litigation.... It is fair to employers only if it is applied consistently so that liability is spread proportionately among employers by operation of the law of averages." Hence the employer may assert the rule as a defense, as Baza'r does here, since this will "assure that they are not assigned disproportionate share of liability relative to other employers...." But in this case Baza'r was properly held liable, because subsequent employment "did not cause or aggravate the underlying disease. Had that occurred, a later employer would be liable.... Rather, claimant's subsequent employment only activated the symptoms of a pre-existing disease."

Notes

1. Several problems must be distinguished. One problem is whether any employer is responsible for injury or disease. In the case of a disease, it must not be merely a disease to which everyone is more or less equally at risk. What is the test of liability for compensation where both work and non-work exposures contribute to the disease? Is there any comparable problem in cases of injury by accident?

2. A separate problem is to allocate responsibility among employers where several have, or may have, contributed to disease or injury. The last injurious exposure rule deals with this problem. What is the test of liability under that rule?

3. *Second injury funds.* In addition to the two problems just identified, there are two other broad problem areas. The first involves the worker who comes to the job with an existing injury or disability. If he is injured on the job, his pre-existing condition may mean that the job injury will be much more serious than otherwise it would have been. For example, if he comes to the job with one eye, an injury to his good eye may mean total blindness, not merely the partial loss of vision. Total blindness in turn might mean that the employer would be liable for a great deal more compensation than if a worker merely lost one of two good eyes. Given this situation, an employer might discriminate heavily against workers with an existing disability. To avoid this employer discrimination, most states created a second-injury fund which would pay any added compensation needed in such situations. The result is that the employer in the example given pays for the loss of one eye, not for total blindness; the additional compensation is paid from the fund. The fund itself is created in various ways, sometimes by what amounts to a special tax levied against compensation insurance carriers.

4. *Compensable injury causing further injury.* The employer may be held liable for compensation not only for the original injury, but for medical aggravation.

In *Shoemaker v. Workmen's Compensation Appeal Bd.*, 145 Pa.Cmwlth. 667, 604 A.2d 1145 (Pa.Cmwlth.1992) the claimant suffered an on-the-job-injury that required surgery in 1980 and again in 1982. He received a blood transfusion of 26 units in the first operation and 40 units in the second. He developed AIDS and died as a result of that disease in 1987. Evidence pointed to the transfusions as the source of the AIDS virus. The court upheld the claim for compensation for disability resulting from AIDS.

§ 3. WORKERS' COMPENSATION AS THE EXCLUSIVE REMEDY

> The liability of an employer under this act shall be exclusive and in place of any and all other liability to such employees, their legal representative, husband or wife, parents, dependents, next of kin or anyone otherwise entitled to damages in any action at law or otherwise on account of any injury or death or occupational disease as defined in this Act.

In one form or another, workers' compensation statutes contain such an exclusive remedy provision, in effect forbidding the employee's tort recovery against the employer. Seamen, interstate railroad workers, and job discrimination victims all have tort claims under federal statutes. These are not barred by the workers' compensation claim. Otherwise, the exclusive remedy provision has broad impact to immunize both employers and co-workers from liability to victims of on-the-job injury. Co-workers share the employer's immunity on the ground that the statute intended to put the burden on the enterprise as a whole, and most definitely not upon individual workers. Employers enjoy the tort immunity on the ground that it represents the price workers paid to get workers' compensation rights.

SNYDER v. MICHAEL'S STORES, INC., 16 Cal.4th 991, 68 Cal. Rptr.2d 476, 945 P.2d 781 (1997). The plaintiff, Mikayla Snyder, sued her mother's employer in tort, claiming that she had been exposed in utero to a gas at her mother's workplace and suffered injury as a result. The trial court sustained the employer's demurrer on the ground that the claim was derived from her mother's exposure and that it was barred because her mother's tort claim would be barred by the exclusive remedy provision. The court of appeals reversed. *Held,* the court of appeals is affirmed. Mikayla's action is for her own injuries, not her mother's. The trial court therefore should have overruled Michael's Stores' demurrer.

MARTIN v. LANCASTER BATTERY CO., INC.

Supreme Court of Pennsylvania, 1992.
530 Pa. 11, 606 A.2d 444.

LARSEN, JUSTICE. . . .

[A]ppellant Stuart C. Manix (Mr. Manix) was a part owner and manager of the Lancaster Battery Company, Inc. Appellant Lancaster Battery Company, Inc. (LBC) manufactured automotive/truck wet storage batteries. The manufacturing process involved extensive employee exposure to lead dust and fumes. Federal safety regulations require that employees in such working environments be tested on a regular basis for lead content in their blood. Appellee Joseph H. Martin, Sr. (Mr. Martin) was employed by LBC, and his blood was tested along with the other employees of LBC who were exposed to lead. Mr. Manix, who oversaw and administered the blood testing at LBC, willfully and intentionally withheld from Mr. Martin the results of Mr. Martin's blood tests between January 1, 1982, and July, 1985. In addition, Mr. Manix intentionally altered blood test results before forwarding the results to Mr. Martin. Subsequently, Mr. Martin was diagnosed with chronic lead toxicity, lead neuropathy, hypertension, gout, and renal insufficiency. The severity of his condition would have been substantially reduced if his employer had not perpetrated a delay by failing to accurately report the elevated levels of lead in Mr. Martin's blood.

[Martin and his wife sued LBC and Manix in tort, alleging intentional and willful misconduct of Manix. The trial court sustained the defendant's objections in the nature of a demurrer. The appellate court reversed, holding that the tort claim could proceed in spite of the exclusive remedy provision.]

We agree with the Superior Court that the cases cited by the trial court regarding the exclusivity issue are not applicable to the instant action. In sustaining LBC's preliminary objections, the trial court cited this Court's decision in Poyser v. Newman & Co., 514 Pa. 32, 522 A.2d 548 (1987). In that case, we held that the exclusivity provision of the Workmen's Compensation Act precluded an employee from bringing an action against his or her employer for a work-related injury caused by the employer's willful and wanton disregard for employee safety as manifested by the employer's fraudulent misrepresentation of factory safety conditions to federal safety inspectors. Poyser is distinguishable from the case presently before the Court in that the fraudulent misrepresentation in Poyser was made to a third party and was not made to the injured employee. In the case sub judice, it has been alleged that the fraudulent misrepresentation was made directly to the employee. Moreover, Poyser did not involve a claim for the aggravation of a work-related injury as is the case herein. . . .

Courts in [some] other jurisdictions have considered the exclusivity issue presently before this Court and some have determined that the applicable workmen's compensation statute is not the exclusive remedy for the aggravation of an employee's work-related injury where the employer's fraudulent misrepresentation has been alleged. The reasons advanced to support recovery for such injuries in a common law action include the following: 1) "[a] hazard of employment does not include the risk that the employer will deprive an employee of his workers' compensation rights to medical treatment and compensation," 2) there is a strong state interest in deterring an employer from deliberately concealing the nature and extent of the danger following an initial injury, and 3) "[a]n employer's fraudulent concealment of diseases already developed is not one of the risks an employee should have to assume. Such intentionally-deceitful action goes beyond the bargain struck by the Compensation Act.''

In [still other] jurisdictions, the courts have determined that such injuries are exclusively compensable under the applicable workmen's compensation statute. The courts refusing to permit common law actions where employees allege fraudulent misrepresentation are generally concerned with employees receiving duplicate monetary awards for single injuries.

We do not find the reasoning of the courts refusing to permit common law actions under these circumstances to be persuasive. The employee herein has alleged fraudulent misrepresentation on the part of his employer as causing the delay which aggravated a work-related injury. He is not seeking compensation for the work-related injury itself in this action. Clearly, when the Legislature enacted the Workmen's Compensation Act in this Commonwealth, it could not have intended to insulate employers from liability for the type of flagrant misconduct at issue herein by limiting liability to the coverage provided by the Workmen's Compensation Act. There is a difference between employers who tolerate workplace conditions that will result in a certain number of injuries or illnesses and those who actively mislead employees already suffering as the victims of workplace hazards, thereby precluding such employees from limiting their contact with the hazard and from receiving prompt medical attention and care. The aggravation of the injury arises from and is related to the fraudulent misrepresentation of the employer. Thus, the appellees are not limited to their remedies under the Workmen's Compensation Act and are not precluded from bringing a common law action against LBC. . . .

With these standards in mind, and reviewing appellees' complaint in light of all reasonable inferences deducible therefrom, we find that the appellees have pleaded facts sufficient to support a cause of action for fraudulent misrepresentation. A cause of action for fraudulent misrepresentation is comprised of the following elements: ''(1) a misrepresentation, (2) a fraudulent utterance thereof, (3) an intention by the maker that the recipient will thereby be induced to act, (4) justifiable reliance by the recipient upon the misrepresentation, and (5) damage to the recipient as the proximate result.''

Notes

1. *General rule.* When the employee suffers physical injury, the workers' compensation statute routinely applies and limits recovery to that provided in the statute. This will ordinarily include not only the original injury but subsequent aggravations.

2. *Dual capacity.* One exception applied in some states is the dual capacity doctrine derived from *Duprey v. Shane,* 39 Cal.2d 781, 249 P.2d 8 (1952), where the claimant, a practical nurse employed by a chiropractor,

was injured on-the-job, then treated for that injury by the employer. She claimed compensation and received an award, then sued for malpractice. The court there thought that where the original injury is "aggravated by the negligence of the attending physician" provided by the employer, the compensation claim is exclusive, but that where the attending physician causes a new injury to the worker, the employee may claim both compensation and tort damages. The employer contended that even though such a tort claim might lie against an independent doctor treating an industrial injury, it would not lie against the employer himself. This argument was rejected. Here the doctor "bore towards his employee two relationships of employer and that of a doctor...." As employer he was liable for compensation, and as doctor he was liable for malpractice if he caused a new injury by negligence. However, a California statute has severely limited the dual capacity doctrine in that state. See CAL.LABOR CODE § 3602.

Where the employer furnishes medical attention for on the job injuries but is not itself in the business of providing medical care, a number of courts, including New York's, have rejected tort liability. *Garcia v. Iserson*, 33 N.Y.2d 421, 353 N.Y.S.2d 955, 309 N.E.2d 420 (1974). This is not necessarily a rejection of the dual capacity doctrine as it might apply in other situations.

3. *Intentional torts of the employer.* One way to deal with intentional torts of the employer is to retain the exclusive remedy provision but to raise the workers' compensation benefits substantially. Another is to permit recovery in tort in lieu of compensation where the employer is guilty of a "deliberate intention" to injure or kill the employee, or even to permit both compensation and tort recovery. See Jean C. Love, *Actions for Nonphysical Harm: The Relationship Between the Tort System and No–Fault Compensation (With an Emphasis on Workers' Compensation)*, 73 CALIF. L. REV. 857 (1985). California merely increases compensation for ordinary intentional torts, but when the intentional tortious conduct takes the case "beyond the boundaries of the compensation bargain," the tort recovery is permitted. This occurs if the conduct goes beyond the normal risk of employment. See the summary of California's system in *Vuillemainroy v. American Rock & Asphalt, Inc.*, 70 Cal.App.4th 1280, 83 Cal.Rptr.2d 269 (1999). What if the employer knowingly fails to maintain brakes on a heavily loaded truck and the employee is killed when brakes fail on a steep hill?

4. *Intentional torts of coworker.* As we've seen, coworkers are ordinarily immunized by the exclusive remedy provision. What if, in the course and scope of employment, the coworker intentionally shoots the plaintiff? See, e.g., *Mayberry v. Dukes*, 742 A.2d 448 (D.C.App.1999) (coworker liable in tort).

———

BERCAW v. DOMINO'S PIZZA, INC., 258 Ill.App.3d 211, 196 Ill.Dec. 469, 630 N.E.2d 166 (1994). A pizza delivery driver was attacked and killed while making a delivery to a suspicious address in response to a pay-phone order. Survivors sued the pizza business, claiming negligence in the business' training about dangers and in its acceptance of suspicious orders to be delivered in dangerous circumstances. *Held,* the exclusive remedy provision is a bar to the suit. "Plaintiffs argue that Bercaw's death was 'not accidental' in that Shipman knew with substantial certainty that sending the untrained Bercaw out to deliver an order placed on a pay phone would result in an assault on Bercaw. Shipman claims that Bercaw's death was accidental because Shipman did not specifically intend to injure Bercaw.... We believe ... that use of the substantial certainty standard would be unduly difficult to employ in distinguishing between accidental and nonaccidental injuries and that adoption of the substantial certainty test would upset the Act's balance of interests.... Specifically, use of the substantial certainty test could well lead to a proliferation of suits against employers whose employees' jobs entail a high risk of injury. It would be open to argument and speculation at what point an employer's knowledge that a certain task presented a risk of employee injury became knowledge on the part of the employer that injury was substantially certain to occur. Here ... plaintiffs have not alleged a specific intent by Shipman to harm Bercaw, and we believe they could not credibly do so on the facts alleged. While an employer that requires employees to work day after day in an asbestos-contaminated workplace easily could be said to have intended to harm its employees, the same conclusion does not follow from an employer's sending a pizza deliveryman out to deliver an order made from a pay phone."

Notes

1.   Some courts have invoked what they said was the substantial certainty test of intent, and, finding intent on that ground, concluded that the exclusive remedy provision was not bar. But some of the cases seem to apply "substantial certainty" for what is no more than a substantial *risk* of harm. In *Bercaw,* would a straight application of substantial certainty rules lead you to honestly conclude that the employer was guilty of an intentional tort? In *Birklid v. Boeing Co.,* 127 Wash.2d 853, 904 P.2d 278 (1995), the court rejected substantial certainty definitions of intent and insisted that the exclusive remedy provision would be avoided only in the case of a deliberate intention to injure.

2.   In *Blankenship v. Cincinnati Milacron Chemicals, Inc.,* 69 Ohio St.2d 608, 433 N.E.2d 572 (1982), employees alleged that noxious fumes in the employer's plant caused them harm, and that the defendant-employer knew that these dangerous fumes existed and that certain occupational diseases "were being contracted," presumably as a result of these fumes. The employees claimed tort damages. The Ohio Court held that intentional torts by an employer did not arise out of employment, and hence that as to such torts there was no immunity under exclusive remedy provisions. The court remanded for a determination of fact "whether an intentional tort occurred." Do the plaintiffs' allegations support the idea that there was an intentional tort? The Ohio legislature responded to the possibility of tort liability based upon substantial certainty intent by abolishing the tort claim

unless the employer "deliberately and intentionally" injures or causes disease. OHIO. REV. CODE § 2745.01.

3. The exclusive remedy clause may require construction. In Indiana the clause for injury cases made workers' compensation exclusive for all claims based on "personal injury or death by accident." Since "accident" excluded intentional torts, the employee could still proceed against the employer for intentional injuries. But the exclusive remedy clause in the occupational disease provisions was broader. It provided that occupational disease rights under the statute were exclusive of "all other rights and remedies of such employee ... on account of such disablement or death." Doesn't the occupational disease clause mean that the employer who intentionally causes an occupational disease is protected from tort liability? *Baker v. Westinghouse Electric Corp.*, 637 N.E.2d 1271 (Ind.1994).

Intentional Torts without Physical Injury

4. Workers' compensation statutes were intended to deal with injury or death. They envisioned compensating for an injured worker's loss of wages and for medical expenses. What is to be done when an employer, either directly or through an agent, commits an intentional tort that does not actually cause physical harm or inability to work? In *Fermino v. Fedco*, 7 Cal.4th 701, 30 Cal.Rptr.2d 18, 872 P.2d 559 (1994), the California Court held that an employer's false imprisonment of an employee, committed by way of excessive interrogation in a closed room, was actionable as a tort and not barred by the exclusive remedy provision because false imprisonment, at least on its facts, was outside the compensation bargain in which the employer accepted strict liability in exchange for limited liability. Similarly, fraud by the employer that causes economic harm without physical injury, might be outside the bargain and thus actionable. What else?

KERANS v. PORTER PAINT CO.

Supreme Court of Ohio, 1991.
61 Ohio St.3d 486, 575 N.E.2d 428.

This case arose from the alleged sexual harassment of appellant, Sally Kerans, a decorator for appellee, Porter Paint Company ("Porter Paint"), by Al Levine, who was a store manager for the company at the time. In her deposition, Kerans claimed that she was sexually molested by Levine on five separate occasions on September 5, 1985. According to Kerans, while she was working with Levine at Porter Paint's Kenwood store, he touched her breasts without her consent, put his hand up her dress against her will, forced her to touch his genitalia, exposed himself to her in a back room, and finally appeared naked before her and requested that she watch him masturbate. Some time after Kerans reported the incidents to the Porter Paint management, Levine resigned from the company.

In response to these incidents, Kerans and her husband, Lewis Kerans, filed the instant case in Hamilton County, Ohio, on September 5, 1986, naming both Levine and Porter Paint as defendants. Subsequently, they settled their claims against Levine but expressly reserved their right to pursue their claims against Porter Paint. Appellants' complaint against the appellee contains five separate counts. In their first count, the appellants allege that the appellee intentionally or negligently maintained a policy of encouraging, permitting, or condoning sexual harassment by Levine. In their second count, the appellants charge the appellee with assault and battery. In their third count, they charge the appellee with negligent or intentional infliction of emotional distress. In their fourth count, the appellants claim that the appellee negligently or intentionally failed to provide Sally Kerans with a safe work environment. In that count, they also charge the appellee with the negligent hiring and/or retention of Al Levine. The fifth count of the complaint is a claim by Lewis Kerans for loss of consortium.

[The lower courts held that the claim was barred by the exclusive remedy provisions of the workers' compensation statute.]

ALICE ROBIE RESNICK, JUSTICE . . . .

R.C. 4123.74 provided, in pertinent part, "Employers who comply with section 4123.35 of the Revised Code shall not be liable to respond in damages at common law or by statute for any injury, or occupational disease, or bodily condition, received or contracted by any employee in the course of or arising out of his employment * * *." . . .

There are several difficulties with appellee's argument. First, it assumes that appellant's injury is an injury within the meaning of R.C. 4123.74, that is, within the definition of "injury" in R.C. 4123.01. We are not prepared to so hold at this time. The injury alleged by the appellant in this case is a non-physical injury with purely psychological consequences. In Ryan v. Connor (1986), 28 Ohio St.3d 406, 28 OBR 462, 503 N.E.2d 1379, we held that a physical injury occasioned solely by mental or emotional stress received in the course of employment is an "injury" within the definition found in R.C. 4123.01(C). In that case, the plaintiff suffered a heart attack and died after being pressured into an early retirement by company officials. While the harm suffered by appellant in the case at bar was also occasioned by emotional stress, the alleged consequence, the development of post-traumatic stress disorder, is purely psychological.

Since this court's ruling in Ryan, supra, the legislature has not amended the definition of "injury" in R.C. 4123.01(C) to include psychiatric ailments resulting solely from stressful workplace conditions. In fact, R.C. 4123.01(C) now specifically states that "injury does not include * * * psychiatric conditions except where the conditions have arisen from an injury or occupational disease." In light of this limitation, we are not prepared to assume that psychological disturbances arising solely from emotional stress in the workplace fit within the definition of "injury" in R.C. 4123.01.

If the workers' compensation scheme were adjudged to be the exclusive remedy for claims based upon sexual harassment in the workplace, as appellee urges, victims of sexual harassment would often be left without a remedy . . . .

The mismatch between the workers' compensation laws and claims arising out of sexual harassment in the workplace was recently recognized by the Florida Supreme Court in Byrd v. Richardson–Greenshields Securities, Inc. (Fla.1989), 552 So.2d 1099. In that case, the court specifically held that Florida's workers' compensation statute does not provide the exclusive remedy for claims based on sexual harassment in the workplace. In justifying its holding, the court stated: " * * * workers' compensation is directed essentially at compensating a worker for lost resources and earnings. This is a vastly different concern than is addressed by the sexual harassment laws. While workplace injuries rob a person of resources, sexual harassment robs the person of dignity and self esteem. Workers' compensation addresses purely economic injury; sexual harassment laws are concerned with a much more intangible injury to personal rights. * * * "Id. at 1104.

[W]e reject appellee's argument that the appellants' claims are barred by R.C. 4123.74.

Appellee argues that even if appellants' claims are not barred by R.C. 4123.74, appellee cannot be held liable for its employee's intentional acts since the activities which form the basis of the complaint took place outside the scope of the perpetrator's employment. Appellee contends that because it did not hire Levine to sexually harass female employees, and because Levine's actions in no way facilitated appellee's business, it may not be held liable for the harm which resulted from his egregious behavior....

Our response to this argument is twofold. First, we find that there is a genuine issue of material fact as to whether Levine's actions took place within the scope of his employment with the Porter Paint Company. In determining whether to impose liability based on respondeat superior on an employer for the sexually harassing acts of one of its employees, federal courts have employed traditional agency principles. Specifically, they have held that where an employee is able to sexually harass another employee because of the authority or apparent authority vested in him by the employer, it may be said that the harasser's actions took place within the scope of his employment....

In the case at bar, there is a genuine issue of material fact regarding the extent of Levine's authority. While appellee contends that Levine was not Kerans's supervisor, there is evidence in the record which suggests that he did hold that position vis-a-vis both Kerans and some of those who preceded her as decorator at the Kenwood store. Moreover, there is evidence in the record which suggests that Levine had the authority to control Kerans's work hours and time of departure from the Kenwood store. If he did have this authority, and if he used this authority to cause Kerans to feel that she had to endure his advances in order to keep her job, then a jury could reasonably find that he acted within the scope of his employment....

Moreover, even if Levine's activities took place outside the scope of his employment, summary judgment against appellants' claims would not be proper. 2 Restatement of the Law 2d, Torts (1965) 125, Section 317, provides as follows:

> "A master is under a duty to exercise reasonable care so to control his servant while acting outside the scope of his employment as to prevent him from intentionally harming others or from so conducting himself as to create an unreasonable risk of bodily harm to them, if
>
>> "(a) the servant
>>
>>> "(i) is upon the premises in possession of the master or upon which the servant is privileged to enter only as his servant, or
>>>
>>> "(ii) is using a chattel of the master, and
>>
>> "(b) the master
>>
>>> "(i) knows or has reason to know that he has the ability to control his servant, and
>>>
>>> "(ii) knows or should know of the necessity and opportunity for exercising such control."

On the basis of this principle, both state and federal courts have held that an employer may be liable for failing to take appropriate action where that employer knows or has reason to know that one of its employees poses an unreasonable risk of harm to other employees. In Ford v. Revlon, Inc. (1987), 153 Ariz. 38, 734 P.2d 580, the plaintiff brought suit against her employer for intentional infliction of emotional distress after the company failed to respond to her repeated complaints regarding offensive sexual advances by her supervisor. The jury found the company liable for intentional infliction of emotional distress, despite its finding that the supervisor was liable only for assault and battery. In upholding the jury verdict, the Arizona Supreme Court held that a company's failure to investigate a complaint of abusive treatment is independent of the abusive treatment itself and a company may be liable for failing to stop the abusive treatment regardless of whether the treatment itself rises to the level of an actionable tort....

Following the reasoning put forth in the aforementioned cases, we hold that where a plaintiff brings a claim against an employer predicated upon allegations of workplace sexual harassment by a company employee, and where there is evidence in the record suggesting that the employee has a past history of sexually harassing behavior about which the employer knew or should have known, summary judgment may not be granted in favor of the employer, even where the employee's actions in no way further or promote the employer's business. An employer has a duty to provide its employees with a safe work environment and, thus, may be independently liable for failing to take corrective action against an employee who poses a threat of harm to fellow employees, even where the employee's actions do not serve or advance the employer's business goals. Whether the employer has acted appropriately in a particular situation is a factual matter to be determined on a case by case basis.

However, where an employer knows or has reason to know that one of his employees is sexually harassing other employees, he may not sit idly by and do nothing. The appropriate response, which may range in severity from a verbal warning, to a transfer, to a temporary suspension, to a firing, will depend on the facts of the particular case, including the frequency and severity of the employee's actions.

In the case at bar, there is an abundance of evidence indicating that Porter Paint knew or should have known of Levine's perverse sexual proclivities and the danger he posed toward female employees. [Details, which were ample, are omitted.]

The evidence further suggests that Porter Paint management trivialized these reports and was entirely unconcerned with the threat which Levine posed to the safety of female employees. Finally, there is nothing in the record which suggests that the management ever fired, demoted, transferred, or even meaningfully disciplined Levine in response to these reports. Consequently, we hold that the trial court erred in granting summary judgment on appellants' second, third, fourth and fifth claims for relief.

[The dissent of Justice Holmes is omitted]

DRISCOLL v. GENERAL NUTRITION CORP., 252 Conn. 215, 752 A.2d 1069 (2000). The plaintiff, a sales clerk for the defendant, was at work when Gregory Popielarczyk entered, forced her into a back room, and forced her to perform fellatio. In this tort action against her employer, the plaintiff claims only for emotional harm. *Held,* in an opinion per Peters, J., the exclusive remedy provision bars this tort claim. Workers' compensation is payable for personal injury. The legislature has defined personal injury to exclude emotional harm when that harm does not arise from personal injury, but in this case the emotional harm was a direct result of physical injury–the sexual assault perpetrated by Popielarczyk. Hence the harm is a personal injury covered by workers' compensation statute and the exclusive remedy provision applies to bar this tort suit.

Notes

1. *Where injury is compensable under workers' compensation.* If the employee's emotional distress arising from sexual harassment is compensable under the state's workers' compensation statutes, the exclusive remedy provision applies to bar a common law claim for the distress or the sexual harassment that gives rise to it. So far as the common law claim is based upon sexual harassment, it might also be barred by the exclusive remedy provision of the state's civil rights or sexual harassment statute. On both points, see *Green v. Wyman–Gordon Company,* 422 Mass. 551, 664 N.E.2d 808 (1996).

2. *Where injury is not compensable under workers' compensation.* If the employee's emotional harm claim–from sexual harassment, stranger assault,

or otherwise–is not compensable under the statute, courts have been permitting the plaintiff to sue the employer in tort, either for its own negligence in permitting such attacks or vicariously because the attack was carried out by the employer's servant. See *Onstad v. Payless Shoesource,* 9 P.3d 38 (Mont. 2000) (stranger attack, employer negligence); *Coates v. Wal–Mart Stores, Inc.,* 127 N.M. 47, 976 P.2d 999 (1999) (tort action may proceed if injuries are not compensable, or if they do not arise out of employment, or if the employer intended injury); *GTE Southwest, Inc. v. Bruce,* 998 S.W.2d 605 (Tex.1999) (supervisor's harassment did not give rise to compensation claim because it was not rooted in particular event, tort claim is actionable).

3.   In *Byrd v. Richardson–Greenshields Securities, Inc.,* 552 So.2d 1099 (Fla.1989), the court reasoned that "workers' compensation generally is the sole tort remedy available to a worker injured in a manner that falls within the broad scope and policies of the workers' compensation statute," but that this was true only when there was something that counted as an "injury." As suggested by the quotation in *Kerans,* the Florida Court apparently felt that sexual harassment was never covered by workers' compensation at all because it did not involve the kind of economic injury addressed by workers' compensation statutes. However, the *Byrd* Court also emphasized a rationale that could prove to be quite different. Its obligation to honor the other enactments of the state and federal governments led it to consider many statutes dealing with and the broad policy against sexual discrimination and harassment generally. It suggested that the exclusive remedy provision, if applied in sexual harassment cases, would conflict with the policies expressed in other statutes.

4.   Distinguish two questions: (a) Did the employer commit a tort, either vicariously or directly? and (b) Is there ground for holding a tortious employer liable in spite of the exclusive remedy clause?

5.   *Catch–22. A. Personal attacks.* In some cases, workers' compensation might be denied because the rape or harassment does not "arise out of employment." Why not? Because if it is "personal" to the attacker, not job-related. *Anderson v. Save–A–Lot, Ltd.,* 989 S.W.2d 277 (Tenn.1999) (so holding). Some statutes codify this idea.

B.   If compensation is denied, could the victim then recover in tort? Maybe not. If the attacker's motives were "personal," the exclusive remedy provision would not apply, but the employer might escape tort liability on the ground that the attacker was not acting within the scope of employment on the ground that the employer was not independently negligent in making the attack possible.

C.   *Work related attacks.* Finally, suppose the employer is at fault, say in letting security lapse. In that case the employer may assert that the attack was work related after all, so that he is immune to tort liability and pays workers' compensation only. See *Holland v. Commonwealth,* 136 Pa. Cmwlth. 655, 584 A.2d 1056 (1990) (rapist's lack of personal animosity toward the plaintiff showed the attack was work-related, so plaintiff was limited to compensation claim); cf. *Melo v. Jewish Bd. of Family and Children's Services, Inc.,* 183 Misc.2d 776, 706 N.Y.S.2d 569 (1999) (employee attacked on employer's premises by unidentified assailant; work environment increased risk of attack, so it was work related and exclusive remedy provision limited employer's liability to workers' compensation).

6. Do you think that the *Kerans* court would allow a recovery in tort against the employer if an employee was raped by another employee or by a supervisor?

7. *Case A*: The plaintiff is sexually harassed but suffers no physical harm and incurs neither medical bills nor wage loss. *Case B*: The plaintiff is physically harmed by a sexual assault, incurs medical bills and suffers wage loss during a period of healing. If the employer is not guilty of any negligent or intentional wrongdoing, no tort action would lie even if the exclusive remedy clause were repealed. Should there be a workers' compensation claim in either case? Could you possibly write a statute to give the plaintiff a workers' compensation claim where it is needed and still permit a tort claim where the employer was at fault? See the excellent discussion in Jean C. Love, *Actions for Nonphysical Harm: The Relationship Between the Tort System and No–Fault Compensation (With an Emphasis on Workers' Compensation)*, 73 Calif. L. Rev. 857 (1985).

8. *Workers' compensation's interaction with federal statutes.* Several federal statutes provide rights to workers that can potentially overlap or conflict with workers' compensation rights. These include:

(1) *Title VII*. Title VII forbids discrimination against workers on the basis of gender or race, for example, and under some circumstances permits a federal suit if the employer violates the statute. 42 U.S.C.A. § 2000e.

(2) *ADA*. The Americans with Disabilities Act (ADA) and some similar federal legislation forbids employer discrimination against employees with disabilities and provides that employers must make reasonable accommodations to permit the employee to work. This may require adjustments in work schedules, temporary leave, or addition of special features to the worksite. This statute, too, permits a suit by an employee whose rights under the statute are violated.

(3) *FMLA*. The Family and Medical Leave Act requires employers to grant up to twelve weeks unpaid leave to an employee who becomes a parent, adopts a child or becomes a foster parent, or when the employee suffers "a serious health condition that makes the employee unable to perform the functions of the position of such employee." 29 U.S.C. § 2612.

(4) *Social Security Disability*. The disability provisions of the social security statutes permit totally disabled persons to receive monthly benefits equivalent to early retirement. If the disability results from injury compensable under workers' compensation, adjustment is made, either in the in the compensation benefits or in the social security benefits. Social security disability is considered in the next chapter.

Many problems arise when two or more of these statutes could apply in the same case. The interaction of these statutes must be left to courses in employment law. However, it is important to notice here that since state law cannot control federal rights, the exclusive remedy provision of the states' workers' compensation statutes does not prevent a worker from claiming her rights under any of these federal statutes. See, e.g., *Worthington v. City of New Haven,* 1999 WL 958627 (D. Conn. 1999).

9. *State anti-discrimination statutes.* State statutes may also give the plaintiff rights against an employer who engages in forbidden discrimination. As a matter of construing the statutes, the court may conclude that the exclusive remedy provision does not bar either the discrimination claim or a claim for emotional harm that grows out of the discrimination. See *Murray v. Oceanside Unified Sch. Dist.,* 79 Cal.App.4th 1338, 95 Cal.Rptr.2d 28 (2000).

§ 4. TORT CLAIMS AGAINST THIRD PARTIES

Virtually all states permit the injured worker to sue a third party or outsider who tortiously causes an on-the-job injury. In such a case, the worker may have both a tort claim against the outsider and a compensation claim against the employer, subject only to certain adjustments to prevent "double recovery." This raises a number of questions of practice, procedure and principle.

a. Who Is a "Third Party?"

MAKAROVA v. UNITED STATES, 201 F.3d 110 (2d Cir.2000). Makarova was one of the great classical ballet dancers. While performing at the Kennedy Center in a production of "On Your Toes," Makarova was struck on the shoulder by a piece of falling scenery. Kennedy Center is part of the Smithsonian, which is owned by the federal government. She sued the government claiming negligence under the Federal Tort Claims Act. The government argued that workers' compensation was her exclusive remedy. "Under New York law ... the typical test of whether one is an independent contractor lies in the control exercised by the employer, and in who has the right to direct what will be done and when and how it will be done. Applying these principles, Makarova was an 'employee' rather than an independent contractor." She was contractually required to meet many specific obligations and to give her services exclusively to the Kennedy Center. In addition, "the director and the Kennedy Center maintained artistic control over the show, including Makarova's performance." If District of Columbia law applied, it would reach the same result.

Notes

1. *Co-employees in the scope of employment.* In most states a co-employee who negligently causes injury to the worker is not regarded as a third party who can be sued in tort. Instead, the co-employee shares the employer's immunity under the exclusive remedy rule. The chief reason for this is that the compensation scheme is intended to put the burden of industrial injuries upon the enterprise and to shift them away from the employees. The enterprise itself is thought to be the source of injury, and the products should, in this view, reflect the costs that are inevitable parts of that enterprise. This protection applies so long as the negligent co-employee's acts arise out of employment.

2. *Co-employees not in the scope of employment.* If the injuring co-employee deviates sufficiently from employment, engaging in a personally motivated, intentional tort, he loses the immunity. Cf. *West Bend Mutual Ins. Co. v. Berger*, 192 Wis.2d 743, 531 N.W.2d 636 (1995) (coworker liable for sexual harassment only if he intends to produce bodily harm). Likewise when the co-employee responsible for injury acts in another capacity–as a landlord of the building where the employees work, for example–then he may be liable for injuries arising from that other capacity, as where the landlord/co-employee maintains a defective stair. *Sauve v. Winfree*, 907 P.2d 7 (Alaska 1995).

3. *Doctors treating on-the-job injury.* An employee is injured on the job and is sent to an infirmary maintained by the employer. A doctor hired as a staff doctor in the infirmary negligently treats the employee, causing a new injury. In states rejecting the dual capacity doctrine, the employer will be immune here and will owe only compensation, not tort damages. Should the same rule apply to the doctor? In *Wright v. District Court*, 661 P.2d 1167 (Colo.1983), the court held the doctor was not immune, even though co-employees generally would be. The court's conclusion was expressed by saying the doctor was in a dual capacity–as a co-employee and as a doctor. As a doctor, he did not share the workplace dangers that the injured worker faced. In addition, most workplace injuries occur without fault or occur in ways making assessment of fault quite difficult. According to the court, this is not so with medical malpractice. For these and somewhat similar reasons, the court felt the doctor should be held liable.

A nurse suffers on-the-job injury at a hospital. She's given a prescription which is filled by the hospital's pharmacy, which fills prescriptions only for hospital patients and for employees injured on the job. The pharmacy was negligent and as a result the nurse is now totally disabled and will be in a wheel chair the rest of her life. Tort action against the employer? What if the state has already held that further injury resulting from drugs prescribed to treat an on-the-job injury is compensable? *Payne v. Galen Hospital Corp.*, 28 S.W.3d 15 (Tex. 2000).

4. *Workers' compensation insurance carriers.* The insurance carrier may provide safety inspections of the insured working situation, and may offer more attractive rates if its safety demands are met. Suppose such an insurer makes a negligent inspection, failing to recommend a safety device that clearly is needed. Again distinguish the two questions: (a) Did the insurer commit a tort? and (b) Is the insurer a third party or is it merely acting in the stead of the employer? In *Pratt v. Liberty Mutual Ins. Co.*, 952 F.2d 667 (2d Cir.1992), the employer's insurance carrier had advertised extensively about its loss prevention program to make the insureds' operations safe. It had in fact inspected the employer's workplace and had concluded that the work done by the plaintiff needed to be safer, but it had failed to recommend appropriate changes. As a result, the plaintiff was injured. The court held that the advertising materials should have been admitted in evidence, even though the plaintiff did not show she relied upon them. To what issue would the advertising be relevant?

b. ***The Statutory Employer and Borrowed Servants***

PINTER CONSTRUCTION COMPANY v. FRISBY

Supreme Court of Utah, 1984.
678 P.2d 305.

STEWART, JUSTICE. . . .

In April, 1979, Pinter Construction agreed to build a maintenance building for Heber Light and Power. The proposal was written on a Pinter Construction Company form which contained the following typed provision:

"... Owner to carry fire, tornado and other necessary insurance. Our workers are fully covered by Workmen's Compensation insurance."

After receiving a bid from Frisby, Pinter hired Frisby to perform the metal erection portion of the job since Pinter had little experience with metal buildings. Frisby and Pinter entered into an oral agreement which provided that Pinter would pay 10 percent of the total price prior to commencement of the work in order for Frisby to purchase the needed materials. The remainder of the total $25,000 was paid in two lump sums. Pinter and Frisby made no agreements regarding the hiring or paying of any of Frisby's employees and there is no evidence of any agreement on a completion date, although Pinter estimated the total job would take forty days.

While installing metal siding, Frisby fell from a twelve-foot scaffold, severely injuring himself. He is now a quadriplegic. After the accident, Frisby applied to the Industrial Commission for a hearing to determine his entitlement to worker's compensation benefits. The Industrial Commission held that Frisby was entitled to benefits because he was an employee of Pinter. We affirm. . . .

The question on appeal is whether Frisby was a statutory "employee" as that term is used in § 35–1–42(2), which states in relevant part:

Where any employer procures any work to be done wholly or in part for him by a contractor over whose work he retains supervision or control, and such work is a part or process in the trade or business of the employer, such contractor, and all persons employed by him, and all subcontractors under him, and all persons *employed by any such subcontractors, shall be deemed, within the meaning of this section, employees of such original employer.* [Emphasis supplied.]

Thus, if an employer hires a contractor, that contractor, his employees, and all subcontractors under him are "employees" if (1) the employer controls or supervises the contractor's work, and (2) such work is a part or process in the employer's trade or business.

The above-quoted language from § 35–1–42 is used in a class of statutes known as "statutory employer" or "contractor under" statutes. Most states have such statutes, the purpose of which is

> to protect employees of irresponsible and uninsured subcontractors by imposing ultimate liability on the presumably responsible principal contractor, who has it within his power, in choosing subcontractors, to pass upon their responsibility and insist upon appropriate compensation protection for their workers.

1C A. Larson, *Workmen's Compensation Law*, § 49.11 at 9–12 (1982).

An additional purpose of the statutory provision is to prevent an unscrupulous principal contractor who contracts out all or most of his work from avoiding responsibility for insuring his subcontractors....

Other courts in states with similar provisions have indicated that the provisions are intended to expand liability to those who may not qualify as a common law employee. The Arizona Supreme Court, in interpreting provisions almost identical to Utah's, has stated:

> [This section] is a legislatively created scheme by which conceded non-employees are deliberately brought within the coverage of the [Workmen's Compensation] Act....

A number of facts support the Commission's determination that Pinter exercised "sufficient control" for the purposes of § 35–1–42. Pinter and Frisby did not enter into a written contract; and their agreement was oral and informal, without specifications for the details involved in the work. The informality of the arrangement suggests that Pinter expected to have sufficient control over the work to make certain that the work was performed to his satisfaction. Customarily, general contractors obtain written contracts with independent contractors in order to clarify payment, duties, and other details since a general contractor does not have control over an independent contractor.

Pinter's control over Frisby was evidenced on at least four occasions when Pinter directed Frisby to get on with the work and expressed concern about the deadline for finishing the job. Pinter's assertion of some control over Frisby's activities indicates that Pinter in fact had the right to control and could have done so frequently. It is not the *actual* exercise of control that determines whether an employer-employee relationship exists; it is the *right* to control that is determinative....

The evidence also demonstrates that the task Frisby agreed to complete was a "part or process in [Pinter's] trade or business," § 35–1–42(2). That phrase includes "those operations which entered directly into the successful performance of the commercial function of the principal employer", and covers "all situations in which the subcontracted work is such a part of the constructive employer's regular business operation as he would ordinarily accomplish with his own employees."

In addition, Pinter's contract with Heber Power & Light obligated Pinter to provide workers' compensation to all its "workers." That agreement is consistent with Pinter's being a "statutory employer," who is responsible for providing insurance coverage for his subcontractors. Although the Commission does not directly address the contract in its findings, it does state that *"no* contractual evidence was presented that would indicate that [*Frisby*] was held responsible for securing his own compensation coverage."

The instant case is somewhat unusual, because Frisby was both the owner and employee of the subcontracting company. Even so, the purpose of the statute includes Pinter, who as the principal contractor was in a position to insist that Frisby's company provide workmen's compensation insurance on all its employees. Based on the contractual language referred to, it appears that Pinter did in fact undertake that responsibility.

GARCIA v. CITY OF SOUTH TUCSON

Court of Appeals of Arizona, 1981.
131 Ariz. 315, 640 P.2d 1117.

Howard, Judge.

On October 11, 1978, a team of officers from the City of South Tucson and the City of Tucson surrounded a house in South Tucson which was being occupied by a lone gunman who had been firing random shots from the residence. During an attempt to flush the gunman out, appellee Roy Garcia, a policeman for the City of Tucson, was shot in the back by a member of the South Tucson Police Department and, as a result, is now a paraplegic. Other facts will be set forth as they apply to the issues under discussion.

The jury found appellant negligent and awarded appellees damages in the sum of $3,592,213. The issues on appeal are: (1) Whether Garcia's sole remedy was workmen's compensation. (2) whether the "fireman's rule" prevents appellees from recovering damages; (3) whether "assumption of risk" and "sudden emergency" jury instructions should have been allowed; and (4) whether they jury verdict was excessive. We affirm.

At the time of the incident, the City of Tucson police were rendering aid to the South Tucson police by virtue of an "Intergovernmental Agreement for Mutual Aid in Law Enforcement" which had been entered by all the various law enforcement agencies in the area pursuant to A.R.S. §§ 13–1362 (renumbered as § 13–3872 in 1978) and 11–952.

Section Two of the agreement states:

"The purpose of this agreement is to obtain maximum efficiency in cooperative law enforcement operations through mutual aid and assistance within each Party's jurisdiction pursuant to the prior consent herein given by the Chief Law Enforcement Officer and Governing Body of that Party."

Section Five of the agreement covers control in assistance operations and states:

"A Requesting Party shall have and exercise general control directing any assisting Party to places where they are needed; *however, the commanding officer for any assisting Party shall be responsible for exercising exclusive control over his forces in response to the general directions of the Requesting Party.*" (Emphasis added.)

The requesting party in this instance was the South Tucson police which called for help when it perceived that it could not handle the situation by itself.

Appellant contends that Garcia's sole remedy is workmen's compensation because (1) the City of South Tucson and the City of Tucson were engaged in a joint venture and (2) the City of South Tucson is a statutory employer of Garcia. We do not agree.

In Conner v. El Paso Natural Gas Company, 123 Ariz. 291, 599 P.2d 247 (App. 1979), we held that for the purposes of workmen's compensation, each individual joint venturer is the employer of all employees doing work on behalf of the joint venture and each employer is protected by the exclusive remedy provisions of the workmen's compensation laws.

Elements of a joint venture ... are as follows: (1) a contract; (2) a common purpose; (3) a community of interest; and (4) an equal right of control. The element which is missing here is the last one. As provision five of the agreement clearly shows, there was no equal right of control. The control of the requesting party is limited to directing the assisting party to a place where it is needed. Neither the requesting party nor the assisting party has the right to control the forces of the other in any other respect. There was no joint venture.

A.R.S. § 23–902(B) states:

"When an employer procures work to be done for him by a contractor over whose work he retains supervision or control, and such work is part or process in the trade or business of the employer, then such contractors and persons employed by him ... are, within the meaning of this section, employees of the original employer."

Appellant argues that the City of South Tucson, by virtue of the mutual aid agreement, became the statutory employer of Garcia, thus limiting his remedy to workmen's compensation. We do not agree. The test to determine whether one doing work for another is an "independent contractor" or "employee" within the Workmen's Compensation Act is whether the alleged employer retains control over the method of reaching the required result or whether his control is limited to the result reached, leaving the method to the other party. Appellant had no control over the method used by the City of Tucson police to accomplish the desired result and was therefore not a statutory employer. Additionally, Section Five of the agreement provides that "[E]ach party shall be responsible and liable for damages caused by its personnel during the course of rendering mutual law enforcement assistance ..." further contradicting a joint venture, where joint liability could be expected to follow.

. . . The fireman cannot complain of negligence in the creation of the very occasion for his engagement. *Krauth v. GelCer*, 31 N.J. 270,157 A.2d 129 (1960). . . . The pertinent inquiry is whether or not the negligently created risk which resulted in plaintiff's injury was the reason for his being at the scene in his professional capacity. The fireman's rule also applies to police officers. . . .

The negligence which caused Garcia's injury was the negligence of the sergeant in control of the South Tucson police in ordering an assault without warning. The act which occasioned the summoning of the police in the first instance was the random shooting by the gunman. Since Garcia's injuries were caused by the independent negligence of a third person, the fireman's rule is inapplicable.

Notes

1. If General Construction negligently injures an employee of a subcontractor, would General Construction be liable to pay compensation as a statutory employer? If so, would General Construction be immune from a negligence claim? The assumption in *Garcia* seems clear on this point.

2. What if the statute provided that the general contractor was liable "secondarily," only if the subcontractor failed to secure compensation? Could the subcontractor's employee then sue the negligent general contractor?

Borrowed Servants

3. A supplies temporary employees to B, who controls the details of their work in B's business. Suppose such an employee is injured by B's negligence. Does the exclusive remedy provision bar a tort claim against B? *Kaiser v. Millard Lumber, Inc.* 255 Neb. 943, 587 N.W.2d 875 (1999) (when labor broker who employs worker provides worker to business that controls his work, the worker is the employee of both and workers' compensation is his only remedy).

4. Suppose Papadoc Corp. owns two other corporations, Brodoc and Sisdoc companies. Papadoc leases a truck to Brodoc. Brodoc hires drivers and leases truck with driver to Sisdoc. The driver of such a truck, while hauling Sisdoc goods, is injured. In part, the injury results because brakes were defectively maintained. Under the borrowed servant doctrine we first saw in *Kastner v. Toombs*, Chapter 20, would both Brodoc and Sisdoc have immunity from tort suit? What about Papadoc as the parent corporation? Cf. *Smith v. CRST International, Inc.*, 553 N.W.2d 890 (Iowa 1996) (analogous facts, truck owner cannot claim immunity of the exclusive remedy provision).

5. The borrowed servant rules are very similar to one form of the statutory employer provisions–the kind quoted in *Garcia*, for example. But notice that the borrowed servant doctrine is resolved partly by the "control test." Control is not necessarily the conclusive test in all statutory employer

provisions: under some statutes one is a statutory employer only if the subcontractor has failed to secure workers' compensation insurance.

c. Adjustments Among the Parties

(1) The Employer's Subrogation Claim (or Lien) Against Tortious Third Parties

SOURBIER v. STATE

Supreme Court of Iowa, 1993.
498 N.W.2d 720.

ANDREASEN, JUSTICE. . . .

Steve Sourbier was injured on February 3, 1989, in the course of his employment as a highway patrol officer when his parked patrol car was struck from behind by another vehicle. The State of Iowa as employer paid workers' compensation benefits to Sourbier. Sourbier brought an action against Robert Everett Miller and Betty L. Miller for the personal injuries he suffered. The State filed a lien for workers' compensation benefits paid and to be paid as permitted by Iowa Code section 85.22.

[S]ection 85.22(1) . . . states in part:

> If compensation is paid the employee . . . under this chapter, the employer by whom the same was paid, or the employer's insurer which paid it, shall be indemnified out of the recovery of damages to the extent of the payment so made, with legal interest, except for such attorney fees as may be allowed, by the district court, to the injured employee's attorney . . . and shall have a lien on the claim for such recovery and the judgment thereon for the compensation for which the employer or insurer is liable.

If the employee fails to bring a third-party action to recover for injuries within ninety days, then the employer or the employer's insurer is subrogated to the rights of the employee. Under our statute, this subrogation right allows the employer "to maintain the action against such third party, and may recover damages for the injury to the same extent that the employee might." The statute further provides for distribution of the proceeds to repay the employer for the amount of compensation actually paid by the employer and a sum to pay the present worth of future payments of compensation for which the employer is liable. The balance, if any, is then paid to the employee.[2]

[The state paid a total of $13,289.92 in workers' compensation.]While the workers' compensation claim was pending, the tort action against the Millers was tried to a jury. The jury awarded damages of $22,226, of which $6,500 represented pain and suffering.]

2. This paragraph and the preceding one are taken from a later portion of the court's opinion.

The jury found Sourbier twenty percent at fault. On September 18, 1990, after reducing the damage award in proportion to the fault attributed to Sourbier, the court entered judgment for $17,780.80 plus costs and interest. [Later, Sourbier was awarded additional workers' compensation benefits, bringing the total to $17,305.]

Sourbier then filed a petition for declaratory judgment in district court to determine the State's rights in his third-party award. He conceded the State had an interest in the portion of his third-party award for lost earnings, reduction of future earning capacity, loss of function of the body, and medical expenses awarded by the jury. Sourbier, however, believes the State has no right to the portion of his third-party award for pain and suffering. . . .

When determining the employer's rights we look at the language of the statute and the context in which it is used. We have previously held the language of section 85.22(1) providing that "the employer ... shall be indemnified out of the recovery of damages" is ambiguous, because it does not specify the type of damages to which the employer is entitled. Where the statutory language is ambiguous, the manifest intent of the legislature will prevail over the literal import of the words used. . . .

Construing section 85.22 to permit the employer to recoup monies from third-party payments received by the employee for pain and suffering furthers the section's primary purpose. Such a construction was recognized in United States v. Lorenzetti, 467 U.S. 167, 178, 104 S.Ct. 2284, 2291, 81 L.Ed.2d 134, 145 (1984), where the Court recognized:

> the prevailing rule under state workman's compensation statutes is that an employer is fully entitled to be reimbursed from third-party recoveries for pain and suffering, even when the portion of an award attributable to pain and suffering is clearly separable from the portion attributable to economic losses.

This continues to be the prevailing rule in the United States. . . . Because the employer has a subrogation right under section 85.22(2) to bring an action to recover damages to the same extent the employee might, it is reasonable to construe the indemnification provision of section 85.22(1) to impose a lien on the amount recovered by the employee for pain and suffering. The district court erred in finding the State did not have a lien on the portion of the judgment for pain and suffering. . . .

The district court determined the State's lien should be reduced by Sourbier's comparative fault as determined by the jury. We have recently decided this issue. In Fisher, we were faced with whether an insurer's lien is to be reduced by the percentage of fault allocated to the employee. We held:

> The insurer's right of indemnity under [section 85.22(1)] is against the worker's entire recovery, which has already been reduced because of the worker's comparative fault. That reduction is not to be factored into the indemnity calculation because there is no correla-

tion between the liability of the third party and the obligation of the insurer to the worker.

. . . The district court erred in reducing the State's lien by twenty percent for Sourbier's comparative fault.

Notes

1. The employer-carrier's lien or subrogation right often makes sense in principle. It shifts the burden of the injury which fell upon the employer or carrier in a strict liability system so that the burden must be borne by a tortfeasor who is guilty of fault. It thus accords with the idea of accountability for wrongdoing. The subrogation rule also prevents "double recovery" by the worker, since, when the compensation benefits are returned through subrogation, the worker will have recovered full damages through the tort judgment.

2. Recall that the employer is not liable in tort. What if the employer and the third party were negligent in causing the employee's injury. Is there any reason then to allow the employer to claim against the third party or to share in the recovery? How would this work in joint and several liability states? In states that have abolished joint and several liability?

(2) The Third Party's Claim Against the Negligent Employer

LAMBERTSON v. CINCINNATI CORP.

Supreme Court of Minnesota, 1977.
312 Minn. 114, 257 N.W.2d 679, 100 A.L.R.3d 335.

SHERAN, CHIEF JUSTICE.

Cincinnati Corporation, defendant and third-party plaintiff in a personal injury/product liability action, appeals from a judgment of the district court which awarded a worker $34,000 in damages but denied defendant manufacturer contribution from an employer which was partly at fault for the accident. We reverse in part and remand with instructions.

Cincinnati is the manufacturer of a press brake, a large machine used for bending metal. The brake has a large vertical ram which moves up and down. Dies are placed on the ram and on the bed of the machine, and metal to be bent is placed between the ram and the bed. When the ram comes down onto the metal, a bend, or brake, is made in the metal at the point where the die on the ram matches the die in the bed. The movement of the ram is controlled by the operator by means of a single foot pedal at the base of the machine.

Cincinnati sold a press brake to Hutchinson Manufacturing and Sales, Inc., plaintiff's employer. On April 25, 1972, plaintiff was assisting a coemployee in the operation of the press brake. The coemployee was controlling the foot pedal, and plaintiff was placing long metal strips between the ram and the bed and removing them after they had been bent. As the ram was being raised after one cycle, a piece of metal which had been bent fell to the side of the bed opposite to the side where plaintiff was working. Plaintiff reached through the jaws of the machine to retrieve the piece of metal, but his coemployee had kept his foot on the pedal, thus permitting the ram to descend again, crushing plaintiff's arm between the ram and the bed.

After recovering workers' compensation from Hutchinson, plaintiff brought his action against Cincinnati. Plaintiff testified that he had never operated the press brake before and did not know it was capable of double cycling, i.e., continuing through another cycle without the ram's stopping at the top. He testified that he knew he should not have put his arm between the jaws, but that he did not know that his coemployee still had his foot on the pedal or that the ram would descend again before he could retrieve the piece of metal. . . .

The case was submitted to the jury on special verdict on a theory of negligence. The jury found all parties causally negligent and apportioned their comparative negligence as follows: Plaintiff—15 percent; Cincinnati—25 percent; Hutchinson—60 percent. The jury found damages of $40,000. The trial court ordered judgment against Cincinnati for $34,-000, the full amount of the verdict less 15 percent for plaintiff's negligence, and denied Cincinnati's claim for contribution or indemnity from Hutchinson. . . . The essence of the controversy is this: If contribution or indemnity is allowed, the employer may be forced to pay his employee—though the conduit of the third-party tortfeasor—an amount in excess of his statutory workers' compensation liability. This arguably thwarts the central concept behind workers' compensation, i.e., that the employer and employee receive the benefits of a guaranteed, fixed-schedule, non-fault recovery system, which then constitute the exclusive liability of the employer to his employee. If contribution or indemnity is not allowed, a third-party stranger to the workers' compensation system if made to bear the burden of a full common-law judgment despite possibly greater fault on the part of the employer. This obvious inequity is further exacerbated by the right of the employer to recover directly or indirectly from the third party the amount he has paid in compensation regardless of the employer's own negligence. Thus, the third party is forced to subsidize a workers' compensation system in a proportion greater than his own fault and at a financial level far in excess of the workers' compensation schedule. . . .

Cincinnati's claim for contribution, however, confronts two further problems: (1) Our holding in *Hendrickson v. Minnesota Power & Light Co.*, 258 Minn. 368, 104 N.W.2d 843 (1960), that contribution is not available because of the absence of a common liability; and (2) the policy interest of the employer in paying no more than his workers' compensation liability because of an employee injury and the other conflicting policies and statutes discussed earlier in this opinion.

Considering the first of these problems, we cannot find any continuing persuasive force in the reasoning of the court in Hendrickson. . . . While there is no common liability to the employee in tort, both the employer and the third party are nonetheless liable to the employee for his injuries; the employer through the fixed no-fault workers' compensation system and the third party through the variable recovery available in a common law tort action. Contribution is a flexible, equitable remedy designed to accomplish a fair allocation of loss among parties. Such a remedy should be utilized to achieve fairness on particular facts, unfettered by outworn technical concepts like common liability.

The second problem confronting Cincinnati's claim is a more formidable one. The equitable merit in Cincinnati's claim is plain: It has been forced to bear the entire burden of plaintiff's recovery despite the fact that it was only 25–percent negligent and has a 60–percent-negligent employer joined in the action and available for contribution. In contrast, granting contribution would result in substantial employer participation in its employee's common-law recovery despite the exclusive-remedy clause. This problem is, in large part, a legislative one which demands a comprehensive solution in statutory form....

While the opinions of other jurisdictions must be read with caution on this issue because of different statutes and concepts of recovery in negligence cases, we have found direction in the approach taken by the Pennsylvania Supreme Court. That court has allowed contribution from the employer up to the amount of the workers' compensation benefits. This approach allows the third party to obtain limited contribution, but substantially preserves the employer's interest in not paying more than workers' compensation liability. While this approach may not allow full contribution recovery to the third party in all cases, it is the solution we consider most consistent with fairness and the various statutory schemes before us. If further reform is to be accomplished, it must be effected by legislative changes in workers'-compensation-third-party law.

For the reasons expressed above, the judgment is reversed and the case is remanded with instructions....

Notes

1. *General rule.* As reflected in the Annotation to *Lambertson* and in Larson § 76, most courts have denied contribution altogether on the ground that there was no common liability. This follows the general rule applied in other kinds of contribution claims.

2. In *Kotecki v. Cyclops Welding Corp.*, 146 Ill.2d 155, 166 Ill.Dec. 1, 585 N.E.2d 1023 (1991), the court found the Minnesota rule to be the "fairest and most equitable balance between the competing interests," and adopted it for Illinois cases, noting that the vast majority of courts simply permitted no contribution at all.

3. In a jurisdiction that has abolished joint and several liability and has made each tortfeasor liable only for its comparative fault share, is the third-party tort claim substantially reduced? Suppose an employer permits or encourages misuse of a machine, as perhaps was the case in *Reid v. Spadone Machine Co.*, supra Chapter 22. If the jury allocates fault or equities between

the employer and the machine's manufacturer at 90% to the employer, will the injured plaintiff recover only 10% of his damages from the machine's manufacturer? Compare *DaFonte v. Up–Right, Inc.*, 2 Cal.4th 593, 7 Cal. Rptr.2d 238, 828 P.2d 140 (1992) (third party pays only its comparative fault "share" of noneconomic damages; it pays none of the immune employer's share) with *Ridings v. Ralph M. Parsons Co.*, 914 S.W.2d 79 (Tenn.1996) (third party tortfeasors may not assert as an affirmative defense that the plaintiff's employer's actions partially caused plaintiff's injuries; third parties' liability is thus not decreased by a percentage of employer's fault).

Chapter 26

PUBLIC COMPENSATION SYSTEMS, INCLUDING SOCIAL SECURITY

§ 1. TAXING INDUSTRY AND ELIMINATING ITS TORT LIABILITY

Is some kind of public system for compensating injury a good idea, either to supplement or to replace the tort and workers' compensation systems? One approach might be to add a tax upon industries that cause harm and use the fund so created to pay for the harms done.

Something like this has been done in the National Childhood Vaccine Injury Act, 42 U.S.C.A. § 300aa–1. Compulsory vaccination is an overall health benefit, but vaccines cause devastating side effects with permanent brain damage to particular infants. A child who is entirely normal at birth may be so damaged by a vaccine that he cannot move, talk, or feed himself. Such a child will require a lifetime of care and may suffer other medical problem such as repeated seizures. The Vaccine Act addresses this problem and is an important experiment in alternatives to tort law. Judge Breyer (now Justice Breyer) summarized the vaccine act this way in *Schafer v. American Cyanamid Co.,* 20 F.3d 1 (1st Cir.1994):

"The National Childhood Vaccine Injury Act provides a special procedure to compensate those who are injured by certain vaccines. The Act bars those who accept an award under that procedure from later bringing a tort suit to obtain additional compensation. The question before us in this appeal ... is whether the Act also bars the family of such a person from bringing a tort suit to obtain compensation for their own, related, injuries, in particular, for loss of companionship or consortium. . . .

"The National Childhood Vaccine Injury Act represents an effort to provide compensation to those harmed by childhood vaccines outside the framework of traditional tort law. Congress passed the law after hearing testimony 1) describing the critical need for vaccines to protect children from disease, 2) pointing out that vaccines inevitably harm a very small number of the many millions of people who are vaccinated, and 3) expressing dissatisfaction with traditional tort law as a way of compensating those few victims. Injured persons (potential tort plaintiffs) complained about the tort law system's uncertain recoveries, the high cost of litigation, and delays in obtaining compensation. They argued that government had, for all practical purposes, made vaccination obligatory, and thus it had a responsibility to ensure that those injured by vaccines were compensated. Vaccine manufacturers (potential tort defendants) complained about litigation expenses and occasional large recoveries, which caused insurance premiums and vaccine prices to rise, and which ultimately threatened the stability of the vaccine supply. . . .

"The Vaccine Act responds to these complaints by creating a remedial system that tries more quickly to deliver compensation to victims, while also reducing insurance and litigation costs for manufacturers. The Act establishes a special claims procedure involving the Court of Federal Claims and special masters (a system that we shall call the "Vaccine Court"). 42 U.S.C. § 300aa–12. A person injured by a vaccine may file a petition with the Vaccine Court to obtain compensation (from a fund financed by a tax on vaccines). He need not prove fault. Nor, to prove causation, need he show more than that he received the vaccine and then suffered certain symptoms within a defined period of time. The Act specifies amounts of compensation for certain kinds of harm (e.g., $250,000 for death, up to $250,000 for pain and suffering). And, it specifies other types of harm for which compensation may be awarded (e.g., medical expenses, loss of earnings).

"At the same time, the Act modifies, but does not eliminate, the traditional tort system, which Congress understood to provide important incentives for the safe manufacture and distribution of vaccines. The Act requires that a person injured directly by a vaccine first bring a Vaccine Court proceeding. Then, it gives that person the choice either to accept the Court's award and abandon his tort rights (which the Act transfers to the federal government) or to reject the judgment and retain his tort rights. (He can also keep his tort rights by withdrawing his Vaccine Court petition if the Court moves too slowly.)

"The Act additionally helps manufacturers by providing certain federal modifications of state tort law. For example, it forbids the award of compensation for injuries that flow from 'unavoidable side effects'; it frees the manufacturer from liability for not providing direct warnings to an injured person (or his representative); it imposes a presumption that compliance with Food and Drug Administration requirements means the manufacturer provided proper directions and warnings; it limits punitive damage awards; and it requires that the trial of any tort suit take place in three phases (liability; general damages; punitive damages)."

———

Figures on awards are of course constantly changing. By early 2000, some 1532 awards had been made under the Act with compensation totaling over $1.1 billion–an average of a little more than $700,000. But

3581 claims had been denied. Critics of the Act's actual operation have pointed out that causation in fact is still an issue. More than two-thirds of the claims are dismissed and most of those who find no compensation under the Vaccine Act find none in the tort system either. See Elizabeth A. Breen, *A One Shot Deal: the National Childhood Vaccine Injury Act,* 41 WM. & MARY L. REV. 309 (1999). The claims are handled by a handful of special masters who have wide decision-making authority. Claimants have a markedly better chance with some special masters than others. See Derry Ridgway, *No-fault Vaccine Insurance: Lessons From The National Vaccine Injury Compensation Program,* 24 J. HEALTH POL. POL'Y & L. 59 (1999).

If the problems raised by critics are fixable, the statute still raises many issues of policy and justice. It uses public powers for the direct benefit of one class of manufacturers. Among the many questions you might consider are these: (1) What happens to safety incentives under the statute and how would you compare it on that point with workers' compensation? (2) Do you think it is harmful to the interests of vaccine-injured plaintiffs as a whole? (3) How do you rate the Act as a solution to the problem of compensation for injury–is it a good model for developing broader solutions?

§ 2. SOCIAL SECURITY DISABILITY BENEFITS

The Social Security Act was first passed in 1935. That Act and its amendments were aimed at increasing economic security by providing, among other things, unemployment compensation, retirement benefits, and survivor's benefits. Long after the original Act was passed, important new additions were made, including Medicare and Medicaid provisions. This chapter introduces another feature–benefits paid for serious disabilities that prevent work.

The program's public importance is enormous. Although the figures vary from month to month, millions of disabled workers are receiving benefits. The annual payout in benefits to the disabled and their families approximates $21 billion. Over one million claims are made annually.

At the most immediate professional level, lawyers must be aware of the possibility that a client will be entitled to social security benefits and they may need to represent the client in seeking to obtain them. In some cases, the existence of those benefits will figure in a large way in pursuit or defense of a tort claim. Social security benefits may keep the plaintiff going while the tort claim is developed. Or lawyers may find they can reach a settlement only because the total package of benefits, including those under social security legislation, is high enough to provide adequate care. Tort settlements must also be structured with trusts or otherwise to protect the client's rights to such public assistance programs as Medicaid. More broadly, does the disability benefit system suggest an alternative to, or improvement in tort law?

42 U.S.C.A. § 423

(a) Disability insurance benefits

(1) Every individual who—

(A) is insured for disability insurance benefits (as determined under subsection (c)(1) of this section),

(B) has not attained retirement age . . .

(C) has filed application for disability insurance benefits, and

(D) is under a disability (as defined in subsection (d) of this section), shall be entitled to a disability insurance benefit. . . .

(d) "Disability" defined

(1) The term "disability" means—

(A) inability to engage in any substantial gainful activity by reason of any medically determinable physical or mental impairment which can be expected to result in death or which has lasted or can be expected to last for a continuous period of not less than 12 months; or

(B) in the case of an individual who has attained the age of 55 and is blind . . . inability by reason of such blindness to engage in substantial gainful activity requiring skills or abilities comparable to those of any gainful activity in which he has previously engaged with some regularity and over a substantial period of time.

(2) For purposes of paragraph (1)(A)—

(A) An individual shall be determined to be under a disability only if his physical or mental impairment or impairments are of such severity that he is not only unable to do his previous work but cannot, considering his age, education, and work experience, engage in any other kind of substantial gainful work which exists in the national economy, regardless of whether such work exists in the immediate area in which he lives, or whether a specific job vacancy exists for him, or whether he would be hired if he applied for work. For purposes of the preceding sentence (with respect to any individual), "work which exists in the national economy" means work which exists in significant numbers either in the region where such individual lives or in several regions of the country.

(B) In determining whether an individual's physical or mental impairment or impairments are of a sufficient medical severity that such impairment or impairments could be the basis of eligibility under this section, the Commissioner of Social Security shall consider the combined effect of all of the individual's impairments without regard to whether any such impairment, if considered separately, would be of such severity. If the Commissioner of Social Security does find a medically severe combination of impairments, the combined impact of the impairments shall be considered throughout the disability determination process.

(3) For purposes of this subsection, a "physical or mental impairment" is an impairment that results from anatomical, physiological, or psychological abnormalities which are demonstrable by medically acceptable clinical and laboratory diagnostic techniques....

(5)(A) ... An individual's statement as to pain or other symptoms shall not alone be conclusive evidence of disability as defined in this section; there must be medical signs and findings, established by medically acceptable clinical or laboratory diagnostic techniques, which show the existence of a medical impairment that results from anatomical, physiological, or psychological abnormalities which could reasonably be expected to produce [disabling] pain....

Notes

1. *Procedures for claim.* The claim for disability is initially an administrative rather than a judicial matter. The claimant files a claim in the social security office, but it is initially determined by a state agency. The claimant may appeal to a federal Administrative Law Judge (ALJ), who holds a hearing. After administrative appeals from his decision have been exhausted, the claimant can seek review in the United States District Court. The District Judge reviews the record made in the ALJ's hearing and must affirm his factual findings if they are supported by substantial evidence, but may reverse or remand for errors in law and may reject findings of fact not supported by substantial evidence. See 2 HARVEY MCCORMICK, SOCIAL SECURITY CLAIMS AND PROCEDURES 3 (4th ed. 1991 and 1996 Supp.) (available electronically on Westlaw) (flow chart).

2. *Insured status.* The claimant under § 423 must show four elements listed, including insured status as defined in subsection (c)(1). The claimant recovers benefits only because she has worked and paid "premiums" in the form of payroll tax deductions. However, a welfare component of the social security laws provides similar benefits for similar disabilities to persons who have made no contributions or insufficient contributions to the system. This is known as Supplemental Security Income or SSI. The SSI claimant must meet a "needs" test and cannot recover benefits if he or she has assets or income beyond certain levels.

3. *Benefits.* Disability may be viewed as a form of involuntary early retirement, and indeed the benefits provided are calculated as if the claimant were 62 when disability struck. The actual computation is complex, because it takes into account the claimant's monthly wages over a lifetime of employment and also "indexes" the wages so that inflation can be factored out and all wages can be on the same scale. In general you can say that

benefits are not generous but that they matter greatly to anyone unable to work and lacking independent income.

4. *Disability*. Subsection (d) defines disability. The statute defines this in terms of a medical impairment which prevents or is likely to prevent substantial work for at least a year. It then specifies some proof requirements. The disability, for example, must be "medically determinable" by "clinical and laboratory diagnostic techniques." Under subsection (d)(5), there must be "impairment" and if disability is claimed to result from pain, then objective evidence of pain must be considered. Under these rules there is a medical component, impairment. But there is also a work component–we must know that given the medical condition, the claimant cannot engage in any substantial gainful employment in the national economy.

Suppose a claimant is uneducated and over fifty years of age. Suppose she suffers a disability which prevents her carrying out the work she has always done, but that, if she were educated better, or younger, she might be able to get sedentary work, which she is capable of doing. Does the statute take the plaintiff as it finds her, or must she be denied benefits because workers with an average education would not be "disabled?" See § 423(d)(2)(A).

McLAIN v. SCHWEIKER*

United States Court of Appeals, Fourth Circuit, 1983.
715 F.2d 866.

[McLain is 49 years old, has completed high school and two years of college. He has in the past been employed as a traveling sales representative for a cheesecake company and later as a security guard. His testimony is that he can no longer work in these stressful environments, as he cannot tolerate noise, including telephones, and typewriters. Doctors and psychiatrists report a 20 year history of nervous disorders and "inadequate personality." Dr. Katherine Kemp, a psychiatrist, reported a paranoid-like trend in his thoughts and stated he could not "interrelate" with others and would be unable to withstand the pressures of the employment world. The ALJ found an impairment, but concluded that McLain would be able to perform his previous work in "nonstressful environments," noting that this might include telephone sales work and sedentary security guard positions. He therefore denied benefits. The Secretary then denied benefits and the district court affirmed. McLain appeals.]

On appeal, McLain contends that he presented a prima facie case of disability by showing that he was unable to perform his previous work. McLain further contends that the Secretary failed to show by particularized proof that McLain could perform an alternative job existing in significant numbers in the national economy. We agree with McLain with respect to both of these contentions.

* Until 1995, the Secretary of Health and Human Services was the nominal defendant in suits to establish disability benefits that had been denied by the ALJ and the Appeals Council. The nominal defendant is now the Commissioner of Social Security.

The well-established procedure for arriving at a determination of disability under the Social Security Act places the initial burden of proof on the claimant to show that, because of his impairment, he is unable to perform his previous work. Once this prima facie showing of disability has been made by the claimant, then the burden of going forward shifts to the Secretary. To overcome a prima facie case of disability, the Secretary must establish that the claimant has sufficient residual functional capacity to engage in an alternative job existing in the national economy.

In this case we first must determine whether McLain has met his initial burden of establishing a prima facie case of disability. In addition to his own testimony confirming a history of nervous problems, the record reveals that McLain was being treated with medication for a nervous disorder by his personal physician. He was also examined by three other doctors, including two psychiatrists, who all agreed McLain had a psychiatric problem. One psychiatrist, Dr. Kemp, stated that he was border-line psychotic.

Objective medical facts and the opinions and diagnoses of the treating and examining doctors constitute a major part of the proof to be considered in a disability case and may not be discounted by the ALJ.

In the present case the medical findings and opinions unanimously support the conclusion that McLain has a serious psychiatric disorder. It is clear that McLain's impairment prevents him from performing the demands of his previous jobs as a salesman and security guard. Both of those jobs by their very nature involved stress and required interaction with others, which, as the evidence overwhelmingly shows, McLain is unable to tolerate. A return to either of those particular jobs is unquestionably foreclosed.

In order to establish a prima facie case of disability, all that a claimant must ordinarily show is his inability to perform his past specific relevant jobs. We conclude that under the circumstances present in this case McLain has met this initial burden of proof.

Because McLain established his prima facie case, the burden then shifted to the Secretary to come forward with proof of McLain's capacity to perform alternate work. In this case the Secretary came forward with no evidence showing that, considering McLain's age, education, work experience and impairment, there are jobs which he could perform. The reliance by the Secretary and the district court on McLain's testimony that he would be willing and possibly able to try certain jobs is misplaced. This in no way satisfies the requirement of producing evidence of McLain's skills and abilities and says nothing of the availability of work to match those abilities. The ALJ's administrative notice of sales positions and sedentary security guard positions, which would not involve stress or crowds, is totally insufficient in this case to establish, as the Secretary must, McLain's specific vocational ability.

Previous decisions of this Court have held that the testimony of a vocational expert is ordinarily required in order for the Secretary to meet his burden. . . . The case must be remanded to allow the Secretary to adduce appropriate proof to counter the claimant's prima facie case. Of course, the claimant may also submit additional evidence to rebut the Secretary's evidence or to supplement his own.

Notes

1. Suppose the claimant could do limited work sorting potatoes into bins. The only place where such employment is possible is 1,000 miles from the claimant's life-long residence. Is the claimant disabled? What does the statute say?

2. What if the claimant could do limited work sorting potatoes into bins, and such employment actually exists, but there is no job open and long lines of people are on the waiting list? What does the statute say?

3. *The five-step analysis.* The regulations provide for a five-step process or decision tree that goes something like this: (1) Is the claimant currently engaged in substantial gainful activity? If yes, the claimant is not disabled. If no, then (2) does the claimant have a severe impairment that limits her ability to work? If no, she is not disabled, but if yes, then (3) is the impairment in the listings? If yes, disability is proved and benefits computed. If no, then (4) in spite of impairment, can the claimant perform her past work? If yes, she is not disabled. If not, (5) she is presumptively disabled and the burden falls upon the Commissioner to show that there is a job in the national economy that she would be able to perform.

4. *Burden-shifting and older workers.* Although disability is determined by the claimant's ability to perform jobs rather than on her ability to obtain them, the burden shifting in the five-step analysis can greatly assist the claimant. In addition, claimants over 60 get a break. If they suffer a severe impairment, the burden not only shifts to the Commissioner under the five-step analysis, but the burden becomes qualitatively more difficult. The Commissioner must show not only that the over–60 claimant has transferrable skills but also that they are "highly marketable." See, e.g., *Kerns v. Apfel,* 160 F.3d 464 (8th Cir.1998).

5. *The Listings.* At one time each case was decided on the proof adduced in the hearing before the ALJ. This often led to vocational testimony about kinds of jobs the claimant might or might not do. This could be repetitious and wasteful. In some instances, disability was a very likely finding, as in the case of blindness or severe visual impairment. Although some individuals might be able to work with such impairments, most would not. What would you propose? How about a schedule of impairments that would automatically qualify as "disability?" This is what the Secretary provided in the governing administrative regulations, which, like other federal regulations, are codified in the Code of Federal Regulations or CFR. In this case the regulations are known as the "listings" and are found in 20 CFR part 404, Subpart P, Appendix I. Although the listings can be used to provide automatic awards, they cannot be used the other way around, to foreclose awards for disabilities that are not listed. Each claimant is entitled to proceed on the evidence if he fails to succeed under the listings. See *Sullivan v. Zebley,* 493 U.S. 521, 110 S.Ct. 885, 107 L.Ed.2d 967 (1990).

CLEVELAND v. POLICY MANAGEMENT SYSTEMS CORP., 526 U.S. 795, 119 S.Ct. 1597, 143 L.Ed.2d 966 (1999). Cleveland suffered a disabling stroke and lost her job. She applied for social security benefits. These were initially denied but ultimately granted. Before they were finally granted, she sued her former employer for violating the Americans with Disabilities Act by discharging her when it was under a statutory obligation to make reasonable accommodations to her disability. The courts below held that because Cleveland had asserted total disability in claiming social security benefits, she was estopped from claiming in the ADA suit that she could work with reasonable accommodation. *Held,* judgment vacated and case remanded. Cleveland's statements are not in conflict "about purely factual matters, such as 'The light was red/green,' or 'I can/cannot raise my arm above my head.' An SSA representation of total disability differs from a purely factual statement in that it often implies a context-related legal conclusion, namely 'I am disabled for purposes of the Social Security Act.' " The ADA standard for determining ability to perform does so in the light of reasonable job restructuring. The social security standard for total disability, in contrast, does not take reasonable accommodation into account. An individual might qualify for social security benefits because she has a condition named in the Listings, yet might still be able to work with reasonable accommodation. The social security listings "grow out of the need to administer a large benefits system efficiently. But they inevitably simplify, eliminating consideration of many differences potentially relevant to an individual's ability to perform a particular job. Hence, an individual might qualify for SSDI under the SSA's administrative rules and yet, due to special individual circumstances, remain capable of 'perform[ing] the essential functions' of her job." This and other examples show that the two claims asserted by Cleveland are not necessarily in conflict, although they sometimes are. She should therefore be entitled to explain the seeming discrepancy.

NOTE ON THE MEDICAL–VOCATIONAL
GUIDELINES–THE GRIDS

Federal regulations referred to as "the grids" come into play when there is no automatic disability found in the Listings of Appendix I. The grids provide a disability profile of the claimant by setting up a table of several factors: (1) Degree of medical impairment or Residual Functional Capacity; (2) Age; (3) Education; (4) Previous work experience. These four factors are in turn broken down into subcategories. One might have an RFC that permits only sedentary work, or an RFC that permits "limited to light work", or "limited to medium work." Age might be "advanced," "approaching advanced," "younger," and so on. Similarly, education and work experience are categorized.

The Code of Federal Regulations reduces these factors to a set of tables or grids. The ALJ may simply determine the RFC, age, education and experience and then automatically come up with a decision. It is, in short, a simple mechanical version of what a computer might do. Reading the combination of factors on the appropriate grid leads the ALJ to a definite conclusion–disability or no disability.

Here is a sample of two of the grids based upon the Code of Federal Regulations, the compiled regulations of federal administrative agencies, 20 C.F.R. Pt. 404, Subpt. P, App. 2. (They look a little different in CFR.) Note that the title of each table sets one of the conditions that determines the outcome and that when you have the right grid, you can immediately determine the outcome of the claim.

TABLE No. 3—Residual Functional Capacity: Maximum Sustained Work Capability Limited to Medium Work as a Result of Severe
Medically Determinable Impairment(s)

Rule	Age	Education/ Experience	Previous Work	Decision
203.01	closely approaching retirement	marginal	unskilled or none	disabled
203.02	same	limited or less	none	disabled
203.03	same	limited	unskilled	not disabled

TABLE NO. 1—Residual Functional Capacity: Maximum Sustained Work Capability Limited To Sedentary Work As A Result Of Severe Medically Determinable Impairment(S)

Rule	Age	Education/ Experience	Previous Work	Decision
203.01	advanced	limited or less	unskilled or none	disabled
203.02	same	same	skilled or semi-skilled, skills not transferrable	same
203.03	same	same	Skilled or semi-skilled, skills transferable	not disabled

The grids channel decision-making in a very firm way and probably provide a uniformity and simplicity of decision-making that would not otherwise exist. Are they nevertheless unfair?

HECKLER v. CAMPBELL

Supreme Court of the United States, 1983.
461 U.S. 458, 103 S.Ct. 1952, 76 L.Ed.2d 66.

JUSTICE POWELL delivered the opinion of the Court.

The issue is whether the Secretary of Health and Human Services may rely on published medical-vocational guidelines to determine a claimant's right to Social Security disability benefits.

The Social Security Act defines "disability" in terms of the effect a physical or mental impairment has on a person's ability to function in the work place. It provides disability benefits only to persons who are unable "to engage in any substantial gainful activity by reason of any medically determinable physical or mental impairment." And it specifies that a person must "not only [be] unable to do his previous work but [must be unable], considering his age, education, and work experience, [to] engage in any other kind of substantial gainful work which exists in the national economy, regardless of whether such work exists in the immediate area in which he lives, or whether a specific job vacancy exists for him, or whether he would be hired if he applied for work."

Prior to 1978, the Secretary relied on vocational experts to establish the existence of suitable jobs in the national economy. After a claimant's limitations and abilities had been determined at a hearing, a vocational expert ordinarily would testify whether work existed that the claimant could perform. Although this testimony often was based on standardized guides, vocational experts frequently were criticized for their inconsistent treatment of similarly situated claimants.

To improve both the uniformity and efficiency of this determination, the Secretary promulgated medical-vocational guidelines as part of the 1978 regulations. See 20 CFR pt. 404, subpt. P, app. 2 (1982).

These guidelines relieve the Secretary of the need to rely on vocational experts by establishing through rulemaking the types and numbers of jobs that exist in the national economy. They consist of a matrix of the four factors identified by Congress—physical ability, age, education, and work experience—set forth rules that identify whether jobs requiring specific combinations of these factors exist in significant numbers in the national economy. Where a claimant's qualifications correspond to the job requirements identified by a rule, the guidelines direct a conclusion as to whether work exists that the claimant could perform. If such work exists, the claimant is not considered disabled.

In 1979, Carmen Campbell applied for disability benefits because a back condition and hypertension prevented her from continuing her work as a hotel maid. After her application was denied, she requested a hearing *de novo* before an Administrative Law Judge. He determined that her back problem was not severe enough to find her disabled without further inquiry, and accordingly considered whether she retained the ability to perform either her past work or some less strenuous job.

He concluded that even though Campbell's back condition prevented her from returning to her work as a maid, she retained the physical capacity to do light work.... Relying on the medical-vocational guidelines, the Administrative Law Judge found that a significant number of jobs existed that a person of Campbell's qualifications could perform. Accordingly, he concluded that she was not disabled....

The Court of Appeals held that "[i]n failing to show suitable available alternative jobs for Ms. Campbell, the Secretary's findings of 'not disabled' is not supported by substantial evidence." It thus rejected the proposition that "the guidelines provide adequate evidence of a claimant's ability to perform a specific alternative occupation," and remanded for the Secretary to put into evidence "particular types of jobs suitable to the capabilities of Ms. Campbell." The court's requirement that additional evidence be introduced on this issue prevents the Secretary from putting the guidelines to their intended use and implicitly calls their validity into question. Accordingly, we think the decision below requires us to consider whether the Secretary may rely on medical-vocational guidelines in appropriate cases.

The Social Security Act directs the Secretary to "adopt reasonable and proper rules and regulations to regulate and provide for the nature and extent of the proofs and evidence and the method of taking and furnishing the same" in disability cases.

We do not think that the Secretary's reliance on medical-vocational guidelines is inconsistent with the Social Security Act. It is true that the statutory scheme contemplates that disability hearings will be individualized determinations based on evidence adduced at a hearing. But this does not bar the Secretary from relying on rulemaking to resolve certain classes of issues. The Court has recognized that even where an agency's enabling statute expressly requires it to hold a hearing, the agency may rely on its rulemaking authority to determine issues that do not require case-by-case consideration. A contrary holding would require the agency continually to relitigate issues that may be established fairly and efficiently in a single rulemaking proceeding.

... As noted above, in determining whether a claimant can perform less strenuous work, the Secretary must make two determinations. She must assess each claimant's individual abilities and then determine whether jobs exist that a person having the claimant's qualifications could perform. The first inquiry involves a determination of historic facts, and the regulations properly require the Secretary to make these findings on the basis of evidence adduced at a hearing. We note that the regulations afford claimants ample opportunity both to present evidence relating to their own abilities and to offer evidence that the guidelines do not apply to them. The second inquiry requires the Secretary to determine an issue that is not unique to each claimant—the types and numbers of jobs that exist in the national economy. This type of general factual issue may be resolved as fairly through rulemaking as by introducing the testimony of vocational experts at each disability hearing.

As the Secretary has argued, the use of published guidelines brings with it a uniformity that previously had been perceived as lacking. To require the Secretary to relitigate the existence of jobs in the national economy at each hearing would hinder needlessly an already overburdened agency. We conclude that the Secretary's use of medical-vocational guidelines does not conflict with the statute, nor can we say on the record before us that they are arbitrary and capricious.

We now consider Campbell's argument that the Court of Appeals properly required the Secretary to specify alternative available jobs.... Rather the court's reference to notice and an opportunity to respond appears to be based on a principle of administrative law—that when an agency takes official or administrative notice of facts, a litigant must be given an adequate opportunity to respond.

This principle is inapplicable, however, when the agency has promulgated valid regulations. Its purpose is to provide a procedural safeguard: to ensure the accuracy of the facts of which an agency takes notice. But when the accuracy of those facts already has been tested fairly during rulemaking, the rulemaking proceeding itself provides sufficient procedural protection.

The Court of Appeals' decision would require the Secretary to introduce evidence of specific available jobs that respondent could perform. It would limit severely her ability to rely on the medical-vocational guidelines. We think the Secretary reasonably could choose to rely on these guidelines in appropriate cases rather than on the testimony of a vocational expert in each case. Accordingly, the judgment of the Court of Appeals is

Reversed.

[Concurring and dissenting opinions omitted.]

Notes

1. Is Campbell's position a reasonable one? Suppose Campbell has diligently searched for work that fits her skills, education and capacity. She, or her attorney, consults the grids and determines that they will require the ALJ to deny disability. Can she prove there is really *not* a job she can do? Can she effectively dispute the "hidden" premises of the grids—that somewhere there is some undefined job she can somehow find? Just how can the Secretary determine, once and for all, what jobs are available for persons of given impairments?

2. The grid system does not apply to nonexertional limitations. E.g., *Reddick v. Chater*, 157 F.3d 715 (9th Cir.1998). For example, limited

intellectual capacity is a nonexertional impairment, meaning one that does not vary with exertion. Hence a claimant who is found to have a significant mental impairment must be given benefits unless the ALJ hears a vocational expert to show that there are jobs he can perform. *Foreman v. Callahan,* 122 F.3d 24 (8th Cir.1997).

3. Can pain itself count as an impairment and if so is it nonexertional so as to escape the grid?

MARBURY v. SULLIVAN

United States Court of Appeals, Eleventh Circuit, 1992.
957 F.2d 837.

Per Curiam:

In this Social Security case the administrative law judge denied benefits, and the Appeals Council affirmed. A magistrate judge recommended affirmance, and the district court found that the decision was supported by substantial evidence and affirmed. We reverse.

... The ALJ also erred in evaluating Marbury's testimony concerning his pain. Pain alone can be disabling, even when its existence is unsupported by objective evidence. Walker v. Bowen, 826 F.2d 996, 1003 (11th Cir.1987). The Secretary must consider a claimant's subjective testimony of pain if he finds evidence of an underlying medical condition, and either (1) objective medical evidence to confirm the severity of the alleged pain arising from that condition, or (2) that the objectively determined medical condition is of a severity that can reasonably be expected to give rise to the alleged pain. After considering a claimant's complaints of pain, the ALJ may reject them as not creditable, and that determination will be reviewed for substantial evidence. If the ALJ refused to credit subjective pain testimony where such testimony is critical, he must articulate specific reasons for questioning the claimant's credibility. The medical evidence indicates that claimant did have a medical condition that could reasonably be expected to cause pain. Medical evidence includes reports of abdominal pain beginning in March 1983. In July 1983 Marbury was admitted for treatment after two days of worsening abdominal pain with nausea and vomiting. His treating physician noted that he had "severe abdominal pain with well documented history of peptic ulcer disease." In January 1985 he was again hospitalized after complaining of severe abdominal pain. An upper GI series showed two active ulcers, and the diagnosis was peptic ulcer disease. In November 1985 he was hospitalized because of recurrent, progressive seizures. An upper GI series revealed a lesion suggesting a chronic ulcer. At the hearing Marbury testified that his ulcer had become worse in the last three or four years, that his stomach hurts a lot, and that he has stomach pain when bending. After the hearing Marbury was hospitalized at a VA hospital due to abdominal pain, nausea and vomiting, with a diagnosis of acute pancreatitis and peptic ulcer disease with a large gastric ulcer. Evidence in the record thus indicates that the Secretary has not correctly considered claimant's complaints of pain. . . .

Additionally, the ALJ's evaluation of Marbury's reported seizure disorder was flawed. He characterized the seizure disorder as "questionable." But Marbury had been diagnosed with a "persistent and progressive frequent seizure disorder, etiology undetermined (probable psychogenic)." Although no organic cause for seizures has been determined, no physician has characterized the disorder as questionable. A seizure was observed by hospital nursing personnel in 1983. Marbury was hospitalized in 1986 after having a seizure in his physician's office. Relatives and friends have observed the seizures over several years and have described them to medical personnel.

Reversed and remanded.

Notes

1. *Pain.* Both pain and psychological impairments can count as, or cause, disability. What if the claimant merely testifies to pain, but neither he nor anyone else can find a medical source of the pain? See the definition of disability in § 423 (d).

2. *The Pryor proposals.* Professor Ellen Smith Pryor, examining a substantial body of medical work on the subject of pain, believes that the statutory standards are misdirected. She thinks that pain professionals can usually detect malingering. A better standard would require a certificate of a trained clinician that the pain is not feigned, followed by a functional assessment of the claimant's ability to work rather than an assessment of the pain itself. She believes available tests could rate the effects of pain on the claimant's ability to function and that better tests could be developed with experience. Ellen Smith Pryor, *Compensation and the Ineradicable Problems of Pain*, 59 Geo. Wash. L. Rev. 239 (1991).

3. *Sparta vs. Athens.* When disability results from injury would it be better from a public point of view if the loss were borne by the activity that caused the harm rather than from public revenues? Reconsider Calabresi's Sparta and Athens example, supra, Chapter 22.

4. *Expanding welfare programs to eliminate tort law?* Professor Sugarman proposes a system of comprehensive coverage for people in need, without regard to whether their need derives from injury or something else. His program would substantially expand the social program we have just glanced at and do away with tort law altogether. The welfare program would provide compensation, and safety and deterrence would be achieved through regulation. See Stephen Sugarman, Doing Away with Personal Injury Law (1989). This program would significantly reduce costs now borne by the tort system, he thinks, and could be financed in part by that reduction. What do you think?

Chapter 27

PRIVATE INSURANCE SOLUTIONS

Can private insurance solve the injury problem? If it is to improve on the tort system, workers' compensation and social security benefits, it would have to provide at least a large portion of the following:

(1) Basic coverage for most injuries causing medical loss or work-disability; (2) efficient return on premiums; (3) coverage for most if not all persons who may be injured; (4) a limit on any public subsidy; (5) a system of safety incentives. Is it possible that this could be done by private insurance?

NOTE: INSURANCE INSIDE AND OUTSIDE THE TORT SYSTEM

Within the tort system. The principal insurance schemes that work strictly within the confines of the tort system have been directed at one narrow but severe problem of those systems–the negligent driver who has insufficient liability insurance or none at all. Legislatures have enacted financial responsibility laws, under which, after an auto accident, the driver is required to show that he has insurance or the ability to pay damages; but these laws did not require the driver to purchase insurance before an accident occurred and they seldom worked to assure compensation. A few states added a provision for unsatisfied judgment funds, created by assessing an extra fee in licensing. These funds were used to help satisfy claims of injured victims when the defendant could not do so. This might secure a degree of compensation, not by putting responsibility upon negligent drivers but upon drivers as a class, "distributing" the costs of driving in much the way that products liability rules might "distribute" the cost of products to users. A third system simply permits drivers to buy their own insurance against the possibility of injury by uninsured, or underinsured, motorists.

In the last generation, most states have dealt with the uninsured motorist problem by mandating liability insurance for all vehicles. That has proved to be surprisingly ineffective because some drivers leave cars unregistered to avoid insurance, or purchase insurance to register, then cancel it. If you are injured by a negligent driver, chances are about one in five that he won't be insured even under compulsory insurance laws.

Outside the tort system. Uninsured motorists are not the only problem with the tort way of handling vehicle accidents. The time and expense of shifting loss through adjudication and the consequent premium cost for insurance also represent serious problems. Several kinds of insurance that do not require adjudication of fault are available to help protect against losses from injury. You can buy for yourself collision insurance (to pay for damages to your own car), accident insurance (to pay predetermined sums for specified injuries to yourself), or medical payment insurance (to pay limited sums for medical costs resulting to you or occupants of your car in a collision). These methods of covering costs of injury are limited, but they have some advantages. For instance, you yourself decide whether collision insurance is worth buying, how much coverage to buy, and what deductible to use. If you do buy such insurance, you can be assured that your car will be repaired whether or not you can prove that someone else was at fault, and you can handle the matter more or less expeditiously, without going to court. Could these advantages be generalized to supplant tort law for all cases of relatively small injuries, and thus to guarantee compensation without resort to the courts?

NOTE: NO–FAULT AUTO INSURANCE

No-fault auto insurance plans were first proposed by Professor (now Judge) Robert Keeton and Professor Jeffrey O'Connell in a now-classic book, Basic Protection for the Traffic Victim (1965). Their proposal, which they provided in detail and complete with a detailed statute, contained several new ideas for reform. It envisioned a two-tier system of injury law. Tort law would be retained for larger claims, but smaller claims would be handled by insurance similar to medical and disability insurance. The insurer's liability is not based on fault, but on the fact of an auto injury. Yet it is not strict liability in the ordinary sense, because the injured victim merely claims against her own insurer for benefits paid for by her premiums. Benefits include only a percentage of wage loss and all medical expenses up to a maximum with nothing for pain and suffering. If injury is more serious, the victim may then move to the second tier and "re-enter" the tort system.

Principal features of the Keeton–O'Connell plan are as follows:

1. *Insurance is compulsory.* The no-fault insurance is compulsory. The person registering a car must show proof that such insurance covers the car for injury arising from ownership, maintenance or use.

2. *Insurance is "first-party."* The no-fault insurance covering the car provides, by the insurance contract, benefits for auto injury to driver and all occupants, and in addition, to any injured pedestrian. This

contemplates that the injured person claims against her own insurer, not against another's insurer. Even the pedestrian is a kind of third party beneficiary of the insurance purchased by the owner of the car. In other words, the claim is like a claim for medical or disability insurance, not a liability insurance claim.

3. *Tort claims abolished*. In all small claims covered by no-fault, an injured person is deprived of the tort claim altogether and must rely exclusively on no-fault insurance (and any other added insurance that may cover the victim). Correlatively, even a negligent defendant is protected from liability as to these small claims.

4. *Re-entering the tort system*. If injury is severe, the victim will be permitted to sue in tort for injury not compensated by no-fault insurance. The Keeton–O'Connell plan, published in 1965, provided that one could sue in tort if pain and suffering would exceed $5,000 or economic loss would exceed $10,000. In such a case, the victim would first collect no-fault benefits and then sue in tort. If the damages exceeded these sums, the defendant would be liable, but liability would be reduced by $5,000 for pain and suffering and $10,000 for other damages. In other words, no-fault insurance superseded tort liability as to the first $10,000 of economic loss and the first $5,000 of pain and suffering.

Since there is potential tort liability for larger injuries, liability insurance is a part of the no-fault insurance package. But since that portion of the insurance is not responsible for the smaller injuries, the premium would be less in no-fault states.

5. *Benefits*. The Keeton–O'Connell benefits excluded all recoveries for pain and suffering. This is an essential characteristic of all no-fault laws. However, the Keeton–O'Connell plan provided that one could purchase added protection for greater benefits (at a higher premium). Added benefits could include pain and suffering insurance, for instance. The limits on benefits might vary from state to state. The Keeton–O'Connell plan used a maximum limit (in 1965) of $10,000 and also imposed a deductible provision under which the injured person paid the first $100 of work loss. Wage losses were also subject to a monthly maximum. Property damage was not covered at all.

The Keeton–O'Connell plan also adopted a coordination of benefits approach in many respects, in effect rejecting the collateral source rule. This was done by providing that all benefits received or receivable because of injury, from sources other than basic or added no-fault insurance, would be "subtractable." No subtraction would be made, however, for benefits from family members, life insurance, or inheritance.

All the existing no-fault plans follow the Keeton–O'Connell Plan by providing for periodic payments of benefits as the losses accrue. It is interesting to notice that periodic payment—rather than a lump sum payment—is characteristic also of workers' compensation, social security benefits and "structured settlements" of tort claims.

NEW YORK INSURANCE LAW

§ 5103. Entitlement to first party benefits; additional financial security required

(a) Every owner's policy of liability insurance [for automobiles and any other device intended to comply with the compulsory insurance requirements] shall also provide for ... the payment of first party benefits to:

(1) Persons, other than occupants of another motor vehicle or a motorcycle, for loss arising out of the use or operation in this state of such motor vehicle....

(2) The named insured and members of his household, other than occupants of a motorcycle, for loss arising out of the use or operation of (i) an uninsured motor vehicle or motorcycle, within the United States, its territories or possessions, or Canada; and (ii) an insured motor vehicle or motorcycle outside of this state and within the United States, its territories or possessions, or Canada....

(4) The estate of any covered person, other than an occupant of another motor vehicle or a motorcycle, a death benefit in the amount of two thousand dollars for the death of such person arising out of the use or operation of such motor vehicle which is in addition to any first party benefits for basic economic loss.

(b) An insurer may exclude from coverage required by subsection (a) hereof a person who:

(1) Intentionally causes his own injury.

(2) Is injured as a result of operating a motor vehicle while in an intoxicated condition or while his ability to operate such vehicle is impaired by the use of a drug within the meaning of section eleven hundred ninety-two of the vehicle and traffic law.

(3) Is injured while he is: (i) committing an act which would constitute a felony, or seeking to avoid lawful apprehension or arrest by a law enforcement officer, or (ii) operating a motor vehicle in a race or speed test [or carrying out certain other acts].

Notes

1. "First party benefits" required by § 5103, "means payments to reimburse a person for basic economic loss on account of personal injury arising out of the use or operation of a motor vehicle, less: (1) Twenty percent of lost earnings.... (2) Amounts recovered or recoverable on account of such injury under state or federal laws providing social security disability benefits, or workers' compensation benefits, [and certain other benefits]." § 5102(b).

2. "Basic economic loss" for which the first party benefits are to compensate is capped at $50,000, but, subject to that cap, covers all necessary medical or "remedial" expenses, loss of earnings from work that the injured person otherwise would have performed, substitute services expense,

and "all other reasonable and necessary expenses incurred, up to twenty-five dollars per day for not more than one year from the date of the accident causing the injury." § 5102(a).

§ 5104. Causes of action for personal injury

(a) Notwithstanding any other law, in any action by or on behalf of a covered person against another covered person for personal injuries arising out of negligence in the use or operation of a motor vehicle in this state, there shall be no right of recovery for non-economic loss, except in the case of a serious injury, or for basic economic loss....

(b) In any action by or on behalf of a covered person, against a non-covered person, where damages for personal injuries arising out of the use or operation of a motor vehicle or a motorcycle may be recovered, an insurer which paid or is liable for first party benefits on account of such injuries has a lien against any recovery to the extent of benefits paid or payable by it to the covered person....

Notes

1. *Economic losses.* This section creates the tort exemption and sets the threshold for reentry into the tort system. There is no right of recovery for "non-economic loss" unless it is "serious," and no right of recovery for economic losses except so far as they exceed "basic economic loss." Thus the first $50,000 of economic loss must come from the no-fault or PIP benefits, not from the tort claim.

2. *Non-economic losses.* Non-economic loss such as pain and suffering is limited to cases involving "serious injury." Serious injury is defined in § 5102 (d) to mean "a personal injury which results in death; dismemberment; significant disfigurement; a fracture; loss of a fetus; permanent loss of use of a body organ, member, function or system; permanent consequential limitation of use of a body organ or member; significant limitation of use of a body function or system; or a medically determined injury or impairment of a non-permanent nature which prevents the injured person from performing substantially all of the material acts which constitute such person's usual and customary daily activities for not less than ninety days during the one hundred eighty days immediately following the occurrence of the injury or impairment."

Is this a better "threshold" than the dollar amount envisioned in the original Keeton–O'Connell proposal?

Statutes, of course, differ in many such details. It will be helpful, however, to apply the statute to a concrete case:

Problem
In re Claims of Picklesimer, et al.

Since obtaining the basic facts, Mr. Picklesimer has furnished us the following information about damages to date:

Dr. Doubs	$1,250.00
Murphey Med. Center	3,500.00

Dr. Doubs' bill does not include any charge for treatment following the complications. Mr. Picklesimer says that his medical insurance paid $2800 of the hospital and doctor's bill. Dr. Doubs and our own consulting physician, Dr. Newton, say that there will be further treatments over Picklesimer's lifetime, probably calling for $7500 in future medical expenses (for drugs, perhaps prosthetics, and for examination and treatment). They also say that he will have limited motion the rest of his life, though he is mobile.

Please give me a brief memo on the following problems:

(1) Under the no-fault law, do we have any tort suit at all?

(2) Are our no-fault claims likely to be prejudiced by claims of Patrick or Plangent? Specifically, might their claims use up the no-fault coverage?

Notes

1. Should Picklesimer be permitted to sue the landowner, car manufacturer, medical defendants and the state responsible for the road design, even if his damages do not reach the tort threshold? Suppose, for example, his pain and suffering is less than $5,000 and his total economic damages are less than $10,000. The Keeton–O'Connell plan provides the tort exemption for any person who is a no-fault insured, but only "with respect to" the injury in question. If the state, for example, is a no-fault insured because it has a fleet of cars, can it be said that the state is a no-fault insured with respect to this injury? In *Grof v. State*, 126 Mich.App. 427, 337 N.W.2d 345 (1983), two cars collided at a highway intersection that was inadequately marked by the state. The plaintiff recovered no-fault benefits and then sued the state. The court held that the plaintiff could recover from the state without any reduction for no-fault benefits already received. Does the logic of this holding mean that Picklesimer could recover even if his damages were less than $5,000?

2. Could Dalzell claim against Picklesimer's policy for damage to his land if any was done?

3. If Picklesimer's injuries result partly from injury on Dalzell's land after the car came to a stop, and partly from medical negligence, are these injuries covered at all by no-fault? What phrase in the New York statute would be most relevant to resolution of this question? Is there any similar problem in tort law?

4. Suppose Picklesimer recovers several thousand dollars in PIP benefits under his no-fault policy and then recovers in tort from Dalzell, the state agency responsible for road design, the doctor, or the car manufacturer. Should he be compelled to share the tort recovery with his insurer, much as the injured worker must share the tort recovery with the workers' compensation insurer? Does § 5103 cover this situation?

5. *The "threshold" for re-entering the tort system.* Legislatures have had difficulty in defining the cut-off point or the "threshold" for reentering the tort system. Keeton and O'Connell used pain and suffering as one of the doorways back into tort, and relatively high economic loss as the other. The

New York statute does not use pain and suffering as such, but rather lists a number of injury qualities that might suggest pain. See the note following § 5104 above. Economic loss in excess of $50,000 is also a threshold. How serious a problem is this matter of defining the threshold?

LICARI v. ELLIOTT

Court of Appeals of New York, 1982.
57 N.Y.2d 230, 455 N.Y.S.2d 570, 441 N.E.2d 1088.

JASEN, JUDGE.

The issue raised on this appeal is whether the plaintiff in this negligence action brought to recover damages for personal injuries has established a prima facie case that he sustained a "serious injury" within the meaning of subdivision 4 of section 671 of the Insurance Law, commonly referred to as the "No–Fault" Law.

On February 13, 1979, plaintiff was injured in a motor vehicle accident. After being examined at the hospital, plaintiff was diagnosed as having a concussion, acute cervical sprain, acute dorsal lumbar sprain and a contusion of the chest. He was released two hours later and went home. Later that day, plaintiff consulted his family physician and, after relating the events of the day, was told to rest in bed. On February 15, 1979, plaintiff again consulted his physician and complained that he was coughing up reddish phlegm. Concerned about possible rib damage, his physician had plaintiff admitted to the hospital for tests. The test results showed no rib damage and that plaintiff's lungs were clear. The hospital physician examined plaintiff upon his admission and testified at trial that plaintiff's lungs were clear, reflexes normal, and that he suffered only a "very mild limitation" of movement in the back and neck areas. No further medical testimony was elicited with respect to the extent of plaintiff's limitation of movement. On February 17, 1979, plaintiff stated that he felt better and requested his release from the hospital. He was discharged and returned home. On March 9, 1979, 24 days after the accident, plaintiff returned to his job as a taxi driver. Immediately upon returning to work, plaintiff resumed driving a taxicab 12 hours per day, 6 days a week, as he had prior to the accident. The only proof of limitation with respect to his work performance was plaintiff's own testimony that he was unable to help some of his fares with their luggage "if they happened to have luggage." Plaintiff also testified that he could not help his wife with various household chores as much as he had before the accident. Finally, plaintiff stated he had occasional transitory headaches and dizzy spells which were relieved by aspirin.

After the close of evidence, defendant moved to dismiss the complaint on the ground that plaintiff failed to establish that his injury met any of the threshold requirements of a serious injury as defined in subdivision 4 of section 671 of the Insurance Law. The court reserved decision on the motion and submitted the case to the jury on the theories that, in order to recover, plaintiff had to establish, by a preponderance of the evidence, that he had suffered either a medically determined injury of a nonpermanent nature which prevented him from performing substantially all his daily activities for not less than 90 days during the 180 days immediately following the accident or that as a result of the accident he sustained a significant limitation of use of a body function or system. The jury returned a verdict in favor of plaintiff, finding that plaintiff had proven a serious injury under both definitions. Defendant moved to set aside the verdict on the same ground as his prior motion to dismiss the complaint. The court denied the motion.

On appeal, the Appellate Division reversed and dismissed the complaint, holding that the plaintiff had failed, as a matter of law to prove a serious injury under either definition.

We agree and affirm.

In construing the statutory definition of serious injury, it is necessary to examine the policies and purposes underlying this State's no-fault legislation. The so-called No–Fault Law was adopted by the Legislature to correct certain infirmities recognized to exist under the common-law tort system of compensating automobile accident claimants.

The Legislature provided that "there shall be no right of recovery for non-economic loss [i.e., pain and suffering] except in the case of a serious injury, or for basic economic loss." The No–Fault Law, as originally enacted, contained a two-part definition of the term "serious injury" keyed to the nature of the injuries and the amount of the medical expenses. The monetary part provided that if reasonable medical costs exceeded $500, a serious injury would be established. This section was repealed in 1977 when experience demonstrated to the Legislature that the $500 threshold provided a target for plaintiffs which was too easily met and that the standard was unsuitable to fulfill the purpose of the No–Fault Law. It was replaced with the present definition of serious injury. . . .

Although the statute sets forth eight specific categories which constitute serious injury, we are only concerned on this appeal with construing two of them, to wit: whether the plaintiff suffered a serious injury which resulted in either (1) a "significant limitation of use of a body function or system"; or (2) "a medically determined injury or impairment of a nonpermanent nature" which endured for 90 days or more and substantially limited the performance of his daily activities. . . .

There can be little doubt that the purpose of enacting an objective verbal definition of serious injury was to "significantly reduce the number of automobile personal injury accident cases litigated in the courts, and thereby help contain the no-fault premium." "The verbal definition provided in the [legislation placed] a reasonable restriction and further limitation on the right to sue, in order to preserve the valuable benefits of no-fault, at an affordable cost." The Governor voiced his support of these policies when he signed the legislation into law. While it is clear that the Legislature intended to allow plaintiffs to recover for noneconomic injuries in appropriate cases, it had also intended that the court first determine whether or not a prima facie case of serious injury has been established which would permit a plaintiff to maintain a common-law cause of action in tort.

In light of this mandate, plaintiff's argument that the question of whether he suffered a serious injury is always a fact question for the jury is without merit. It is incumbent upon the court to decide in the first instance whether plaintiff has a cause of action to assert within the meaning of the statute. By enacting the No–Fault Law, the Legislature modified the common-law rights of persons injured in automobile accidents, to the extent that plaintiffs in automobile accident cases no longer have an unfettered right to sue for injuries sustained. Thus, to the extent that the Legislature has abrogated a cause of action, the issue is one for the court, in the first instance where it is properly raised, to determine whether the plaintiff has established a prima facie case of sustaining serious injury. Since the purpose of the No–Fault Law is to assure prompt and full compensation for economic loss by curtailing costly and time-consuming court trials requiring that every case, regardless of the extent of the injuries, be decided by a jury would subvert the intent of the Legislature and destroy the effectiveness of the statute. The result of requiring a jury trial where the injury is clearly a minor one would perpetuate a system of unnecessary litigation. "[I]f the procedural system cannot find a way to keep cases that belong in no-fault out of the courthouse, the system is not going to work." (Schwartz, No–Fault Insurance: Litigation of Threshold Questions under the New York Statute—The Neglected Procedural Dimension, 41 Brooklyn L.Rev. 37, 53.) Thus, we believe the Legislature intended that the court should decide the threshold question of whether the evidence would warrant a jury finding that the injury falls within the class of injuries that, under no-fault, should be excluded from judicial remedy. If it can be said, as a matter of law, that plaintiff suffered no serious injury within the meaning of subdivision 4 of section 671 of the Insurance Law, then plaintiff has no claim to assert and there is nothing for the jury to decide.

. . . Since plaintiff was able to maintain his daily routine for most of each day after returning to work, it should be abundantly clear that plaintiff was not prevented from performing substantially all of his daily activities during anything close to 90 days following the occurrence of the injury. Thus, the Appellate Division correctly held, as a matter of law, that plaintiff did not meet the statutory standard of serious injury. . . .

It requires little discussion that plaintiff's subjective complaints of occasional, transitory headaches hardly fulfill the definition of serious injury. Plaintiff offered no proof that his headaches in any way incapacitated him or interfered with his ability to work or engage in activities at home. In fact, plaintiff testified that such headaches occurred only once every two or three weeks and were relieved by aspirin. . . .

To hold that this type of ailment constitutes a serious injury would render the statute meaningless and frustrate the legislative intent in enacting no-fault legislation.

As to plaintiff's contention that he suffered a "significant limitation of use of a body function or system", taken in its most favorable light, the evidence at trial established only that plaintiff suffered a painful sprain which limited the movement of his neck and back. Plaintiff offered no evidence as to the extent of the limitation of movement. . . .

Accordingly, the order of the Appellate Division should be affirmed, with costs.

NOTE: ADOPTING OR EXTENDING NO–FAULT

Existing no-fault plans in the United States are varied in detail. Some major differences in the no-fault statutes are indicated in this classification of existing laws summarized from Roger C. Henderson, *No-Fault Insurance for Automobile Accidents: Status and Effect in the United States*, 56 ORE. L. REV. 287 (1977). About 15 states have enacted a no-fault system. (Another ten permit the driver to buy extra no-fault insurance but these are added-cost systems.)

All of the statutes are so-called modified or "hybrid" rather than pure statutes–meaning that they envision no-fault only for one tier of accidents, not as a complete replacement of the tort system. A pure system would guarantee very high or unlimited payments for actual economic losses, and no access to the tort system at any time. In a few of those states, notably New York and Michigan, the caps on benefits are fairly high. No-fault in those states comes closer to a pure no-fault system.

Outside the vehicle accident setting. The no-fault idea has generated a second-generation of smaller no-fault plans with different mechanisms for other kinds of injury. We have seen one form in the Childhood Vaccine Injury Act, 42 U.S.C.A. §§ 300aa–1, providing limited but certain compensation in lieu of tort liability for injuries resulting from childhood immunization programs. Professor Weiler has proposed a no-fault medical injury idea, and the American Law Institute's leadership has at least suggested that such an idea should be considered as an elective option for patients. See PAUL WEILER, MEDICAL MALPRACTICE ON TRIAL (1991); AMERICAN LAW INSTITUTE, II THE REPORTERS' STUDY (1991).

Is federal no-fault coming? Some members of Congress have long railed at common law tort rights. (See Chapter 24.) Instead of seeing liability of wrongdoers as a matter of responsibility or accountability, they tend to see claimants a fraudulent. Senate Bill 837, pending in the fall of 2000, begins by asserting that the "system" "encourages costly fraudulent claims and unnecessarily contentious behavior by both claimants and defendants," and hence, the bill suggests, federal no-fault is required. The desire of some to protect defendants from responsibility is matched by the desire of others of a different stripe to see that all injuries are compensated without regard to fault. Thus SB 837 goes on to reiterate the criticisms listed in Chapter 24, asserting, for example, that

30% of injured persons receive no compensation. These arguments are presented as "findings."

SB 837 almost totally eliminates any recovery for pain and suffering damages–pretty much the ultimate cap on pain and suffering damages. Consumers could choose a no-fault system much like the one we've seen above. With one exception, however, the insured could never recover pain and suffering damages in any amount from other parties involved in the accident. The exception allows pain and suffering damages from intentional and alcohol impaired drivers.

If you didn't like that system, you could choose to buy tort mainte-nance insurance. That would pay you for your own injuries much as no-fault insurance would, but you could also sue your own insurer for pain and suffering damages if you were injured by the fault of a no-fault insured. You could also buy uninsured motorist coverage that would allow you to recover pain and suffering damages from your uninsured motorist insurer, based upon the fault of the uninsured motorist.

EVALUATING NO–FAULT

One of the most recent discussions of no-fault can be found in Gary T. Schwartz, *Auto No-fault and First-party Insurance: Advantages and Problems,* 73 S. Cal. L. Rev. 611 (2000). Professor Schwartz considers whether no-fault is fair, whether it preserves appropriate deterrence for wrongdoing, whether it can be administered fairly in light of the fact that heavy vehicles inflict more harm upon others than light vehicles, and whether it would help resolve the uninsured motorist problem. Below are a few of the problems it discusses.

1. *Deterrence and market based premiums.* Schwartz concludes that if no-fault insurance premiums are left to the market, insurers will tend to raise premiums for bad no-fault drivers (and also for good drivers who are members of a dangerous group like teenagers). That will have about the same deterrence effect that tort law has, since tort law's deterrence is also based largely on the possibility of insurance costs. (Uninsured drivers may have no assets to protect and may not be deterred under either system.)

2. *Should premiums be regulated?* However, there may be pressure to regulate rates rather than leave them to market forces. Israel's no-fault law mandates an equal rate regardless of accident experience, for instance. In that case, the deterrence if any would presumably be lost. What should be done about this?

3. *Light vs. heavy vehicles.* In a no-fault system, what is to be done about setting premiums for light vehicles? In a light-heavy vehicle collision, light vehicle occupants suffer disproportionately high death rate. That means that insurers allowed to do so might set premiums much higher for light vehicles. Would this be unfair and bad policy, too, in light of the fact that heavy vehicles would get a premium windfall, but

are socially less desirable because they use more gas, cause more pollution, and put greater demand upon the highway system?

4. *Uninsured motorists.* What about the problem of uninsured motorists–is it likely to be better under a thoroughgoing no-fault plan?

5. *Pure vs. hybrid no-fault.* Finally, Professor Schwartz believes that hybrid no-fault systems, though not losers, are definitely not winners. On the other hand, a pure no-fault systems–one that excludes tort law altogether–is a clear winner. Recall that this would eliminate all pain and suffering damages. On the other hand, it would take care of the most serious injuries as well as minor ones. And it would entail much more efficient use of premium dollars, returning as much as 93% of the premium dollar in compensation to the injured. What do you think? Would you favor pure over hybrid no-fault? Over the tort system?

6. *Pain.* If you think pain and suffering represents real loss for which, in justice, the defendant should compensate the plaintiff, it will be hard for you to approve a pure no-fault system. But there is evidence suggesting that awards may actually reinforce some kinds of pain. See Ellen Smith Pryor, *Compensation and the Ineradicable Problems of Pain*, 59 Geo. Wash. L. Rev. 239 (1991). If it is true that awards not only don't help get over pain but actually encourage it, are you willing to eliminate all claims for pain?

Chapter 28

EVALUATING INJURY SYSTEMS: A DISCUSSION AGENDA

This book has explored many facets of tort law. In the last three chapters it has also looked at some prominent alternative systems for dealing with torts that cause physical harm. This chapter poses a few of the many questions that can promote evaluation of the different ways we as a society could deal with accidental injuries.

1. *Judicial Process.*

One thing you might notice about some critics of tort law is their distrust of the judicial system–of judges, juries, and lawyers. Some of them, for example, believe that many fraudulent claims succeed in the "tort system"–meaning in courtrooms where judges and juries actually see and hear each claimant and defendant. What is your guess–that critics know that persons they've never seen are fraudulent while judges and juries somehow systematically miss this fact?

The question is important not because it deals with fraud but because it deals with the judicial process. One salient characteristic of tort law and the judicial process generally is that each claim is judged on its own merits. Judges decide nothing about whether humans are generally fraudulent or whether plaintiffs lie more than defendants. Instead judges and juries look at the particular plaintiff and the particular defendant asserting claims and defenses about their individual facts. Neither is a token in a board game or an icon who stands for a group. To the extent that rules of law eliminate individual characteristics and particular facts from consideration this essential idea of justice is lost.

How do you think alternative systems stack up in this regard? Are any important individual facts–fault or extent of injury, for example–discarded under workers' compensation, social security disability, or no-fault? If so is that good or bad?

2. *Personal accountability and social responsibility–fairness or justice.*

If personal responsibility for wrongs done is an ideal, does tort law actually enforce that accountability? If so, is something lost in moving to workers' compensation, social security, or no-fault? If not, should we rate the systems as equal on this score?

3. *Safety and deterrence*

(a) Some risks are desirable, otherwise nothing is accomplished; but too many risks are not. Does tort law promote optimal risk-taking? Does it appropriately deter undesirable risks? Indeed, does it deter any conduct at all? See Daniel Shuman, *The Psychology of Deterrence in Tort Law*, 42 U. KAN. L. REV. 115 (1993), and Daniel Shuman, *The Psychology of Compensation in Tort Law*, 43 U. KAN. L. REV. 39 (1994). If your answer is that tort law (perhaps along with cultural constraints) does provide some deterrence, would that be lost in any of the other systems considered here?

(b) Even if, by and large, tort theories do not encourage safety in most instances, might some other injury systems have an adverse effect on safety? In a no-fault system, could that depend in part on whether the driver's no-fault insurance premiums are raised when he shows a propensity for numerous accidents? See Gary T. Schwartz, *Auto No-fault and First-party Insurance: Advantages and Problems,* 73 S. CAL. L. REV. 611 (2000), discussed in Chapter 27.

(c) Before making a final decision, consider whether non-tort systems might have some non-obvious deterrence or safety effects. Maybe workers' compensation insurers inspect factories and encourage safer practices. Maybe no-fault insurers would reduce premiums for insureds who have airbags or other safety devices. Could such devices actually create better conditions for safety? If so, would that judgment apply only to vehicle accidents or would it apply equally to, say, toxic tort cases or medical malpractice cases?

4. *Costs*

Pure (not hybrid) no-fault might lead to a highly efficient use of the premium dollar–returning 90% or more in benefits, compared to something around 50% return of the liability insurance dollar. What is the trade off for this great efficiency? Is it worth it? What do you think about the probable cost comparisons of a welfare system for injury modeled on social security disability or workers' compensation? Should we as a society seek to get highly reliable data?

5. *Delay in payment*

One criticism of the courts is that they can take a very long time to produce a decision. Due process is expensive and perhaps not every dispute should be subjected to its rigors. An early study indicated that under Massachusetts' no-fault system, medical expenses were paid in about seven days from the time the insurer received the necessary documentation. See Roger C. Henderson, *No-Fault Insurance for Automobile Accidents: Status and Effect in the United States*, 56 Ore. L. Rev.

287, 308 (1977). Are medical expenses becoming less important as more people are covered by medical insurance?

6. *The most important question*

Questions about fairness, efficiency and deterrence are endless. The editors of this book believe that the most important questions readers should consider are those that trouble them most. What is the most important issue about injury law to you?

Part VII

ECONOMIC AND DIGNITARY TORTS

Chapter 29

COMMUNICATION OF PERSONALLY HARMFUL IMPRESSIONS TO OTHERS

§ 1. DEFAMATION—LIBEL AND SLANDER

a. *The Common Law Defamation Rules*

CASSIDY v. DAILY MIRROR NEWSPAPERS, LTD., [1929] 2 K.B. 331, 69 A.L.R. 720. "Scrutton, L.J. The facts in this case are simple. A man named Cassidy, who for some reason also called himself Corrigan and described himself as a General in the Mexican Army, was married to a lady who also called herself Mrs. Cassidy or Mrs. Corrigan. Her husband occasionally came and stayed with her at her flat, and her acquaintances met him. Cassidy achieved some notoriety in racing circles and in indiscriminate relations with women, and at a race meeting he posed, in company with a lady, to a racing photographer, to whom he said he was engaged to marry the lady and the photographer might announce it. The photographer, without any further inquiry, sent the photograph to the Daily Mirror with an inscription: 'Mr. Corrigan, the race horse owner, and Miss X.'—I omit the name—'whose engagement has been announced,' and the Daily Mirror published the photograph and inscription. This paper was read by the female acquaintances of Mrs. Cassidy or Mrs. Corrigan, who gave evidence that they understood from it that the lady was not married to Mr. M. Corrigan and had no legal right to take his name, and that they formed a bad opinion of her in consequence. Mrs. Cassidy accordingly brought an action for libel against the newspaper setting out these words with an innuendo, meaning thereby that the plaintiff was an immoral woman who had cohabited with Corrigan without being married to him." *Held*: the plaintiff has an action for damages. The words were capable of defamatory meaning by suggesting that Mrs. Cassidy was not married to the man who stayed at her flat. And the fact that the newspaper did not know the facts that would permit some persons to draw the defamatory conclusion is no defense. The publisher must take the consequences even if it has no intent to speak about the plaintiff at all.

Notes

1. *Strict liability at common law.* As *Cassidy* indicates, the common law of defamation was to a large extent a law of strict liability. The fact that the defendant was honest in its belief was no defense. Neither was the fact that the defendant exercised due care to ascertain the truth. In either case, liability would be imposed if there was a "publication" and if the content was "defamatory."

2. *Publication.* This is a term of art. It does not necessarily mean a media publication. Any communication to a third person is sufficient. Defendant tells his neighbor that the minister at the church is having an affair with the choir mistress. This is a publication of the kind called slander, since it is oral. Or defendant writes his cousin that a city councilwoman has taken a bribe. This is also a publication, and since it is in writing it is called libel. Publication must be made intentionally or negligently to support a defamation claim. Defendant writes in his secret diary: "Peggy is having an affair with a married man." This is not a publication. A thief steals the diary and shows it to Peggy's husband. It is still not a publication by defendant. Defendant negligently leaves the diary where her best friend will see it and her best friend reads it. This is a publication.

Single Publication rule. The common law treated each communication as a separate publication which would support a separate cause of action. This became quite important in the case of media publications: a book publisher might subject itself to a separate suit for each book published. And if, after the main sales were over, a few isolated copies were later sold, the statute of limitations would begin anew as to them. This rule has been changed by statute in many states and, where the issue has arisen in the absence of a statute, by court decision. The current rule is the "single publication rule" in which each edition or issue of a book, newspaper or magazine is treated as giving rise to a single cause of action.

3. *Reference to the plaintiff.* Few issues arose as to publication as such. The published material, however, had to be material "of and concerning" the plaintiff—that is, had to refer to the plaintiff in some recognizable way. As *Cassidy* shows, this rule did not require reference to the plaintiff by name, if in fact some readers would reasonably understand that the plaintiff was referred to. It was the readers' reasonable understanding, not necessarily, the intent of the author, that controlled. Thus, reasonable inferences from the published material, or even from outside facts, might lead a reader to believe the defamatory material referred to the plaintiff. In addition, if the publication referred to a small group of which the plaintiff was a member, it was possible that all members of the group would have a claim, since all might feel the sting of the defamation. Suppose defendant publishes: "Is it true that a town cop and a female officer got themselves locked into the back seat of a police car in the gravel pit and had to radio out for help?" If there are only 10 officers on the town force do they all have a claim? What if there are only two female officers?

4. *Defamatory meaning.* Publications were actionable as defamation only if they carried some negative implication, known as defamatory content. A publication that engendered "hatred, ridicule or contempt" for the plaintiff would qualify, but so would publications that merely lowered esteem for the plaintiff among some substantial segment of the community. This hypothetical segment of the public was hypothetically allowed, as in *Cassidy*, to draw a string of quite uncharitable inferences. And defamatory content could be found not only in factual statements, but also in opinion, witticisms and satirical jabs. "In my opinion, his best friends are all members of the Mob," probably easily qualifies as defamatory. On the other hand, mere name calling is not enough. "He's a jerk" with nothing more is not actionable.

Many cases turn on the question whether statements or actions have the effect of asserting defamatory matters. Does it sufficiently affect the plaintiff's reputation to say that she is a racist? *Ward v. Zelikovsky,* 136 N.J. 516, 643 A.2d 972 (1994)(no); *Herlihy v. Metropolitan Museum of Art,* 160 Misc.2d 279, 608 N.Y.S.2d 770 (Sup. Ct. 1994) (yes), *aff'd as modified,* 214 A.2d 250, 633 N.Y.S.2d 106 (1995). That she is a lesbian? *Nazeri v. Missouri Valley College,* 860 S.W.2d 303 (Mo.1993) (attitudes change unevenly and many people still regard homosexuality with disfavor, so a false statement attributing homosexuality is defamatory). That her friends include convicted criminals? *Romaine v. Kallinger,* 109 N.J. 282, 537 A.2d 284 (1988) (no). Suppose the defendant privately discharges the plaintiff from employment and then escorts her to the door without comment. If others see the escort, is the plaintiff defamed? *Bolton v. Department of Human Services,* 540 N.W.2d 523 (Minn.1995).

5. *Judge and Jury.* If there is room for difference, the jury usually determines whether the publication has defamatory meaning. However, courts insist that a degree of rationality must be attributed to the recipient of the publication. So even if some irrational or careless readers would understand the publication to accuse the plaintiff of serious misconduct, the publication is not actionable unless such an understanding is a reasonable one. See *Greenbelt Cooperative Publishing Ass'n v. Bresler,* 398 U.S. 6, 90 S.Ct. 1537, 26 L.Ed.2d 6 (1970) (in context "blackmailer" could only mean that plaintiff was driving a hard bargain); *Charleston v. News Group Newspapers, Ltd.,* [1995] 2 AC 65, [1995] 2 All ER 313, [1995] 2 WLR 450 (H.L. 1995) (photographs of plaintiffs' faces, obviously pasted on photographs of porn stars engaged in sexual activity; no one reading text would think that plaintiffs themselves were pictured or had posed for the pictures).

6. *Damages.* In many cases, including all cases of libel, damages were presumed. This meant that in most cases the plaintiff could recover without proving any actual losses at all. Recovery might be augmented by proof of pecuniary loss, as where the plaintiff lost a job because of the libel. But the derogatory words would be sufficient to warrant a recovery. The damages thus recovered were not merely nominal but were quite substantial. Mrs. Cassidy recovered, in 1929, 500 pounds. Libel verdicts in the millions are brought in today.

7. *Libel and slander.* The common law carefully distinguished libel from slander and made different rules of damages for the two forms of

defamation. Libel was originally thought of as written material; slander as oral. Human vice was more imaginatively carried out than these categories allowed for, and the law had to deal with defamation communicated by effigy and later with communications carried on through electronic media television, films and so on. In general it is probably a good guess that media publications will all be treated as libel if the distinction continues to matter, though there may be close cases, such as the use of a loudspeaker system without broadcast or recording.

8. *Slander per se.* The common law generally treated all libel as libel per se, meaning that damages would be presumed. Slander, however, required that the plaintiff prove pecuniary loss, meaning the loss of money or money's worth. This might happen, for example, if the plaintiff were to lose her job because of slanderous statements. Three or four kinds of slander, however, were regarded as being especially serious and to warrant a presumption of damages. In such cases it was said that the slander was per se and it was not necessary for the plaintiff to prove pecuniary loss to sustain a claim. These were:

A. *An imputation of a serious crime.* Sometimes this is expressed as "felony," or "infamous" crime. An accusation of a crime of moral turpitude would ordinarily suffice.

B. *An imputation of a loathsome disease.* This is the actual formula used, but it referred only to venereal diseases and leprosy. The hand of history obviously weighs heavily in defamation cases.

C. *Imputation of traits or conduct incompatible with the plaintiff's business, trade or profession.* This does not include general derogatory statements; the statements must be related more or less specifically to qualities involved in the plaintiff's vocation. Thus to say of a bank clerk that she is a drunk when off duty is not slander per se, but to say the same thing of a minister might be.

D. *Imputation of serious sexual misconduct.* This is usually stated in a narrow form—as imputation of unchastity to a woman. Conceivably this will be expanded to include any serious sexual misconduct without regard to the plaintiff's gender. Alternatively, the law might drop this category altogether on the ground that damages are no longer very likely to result from a mere oral charge of this kind. Which way is the law likely to go on this?

9. *The truth defense.* If defamatory content was shown, it was then presumed that the statement was untrue. This left the defendant with the entire burden of proving the truth of the statements made. The rule made the defendant liable for the sting of his statement, even where it was literally true. If in *Cassidy* the newspaper had quoted Cassidy as announcing his marriage, the report of an accurate quotation would have been a literally true statement; but it would not have protected the newspaper from Mrs. Cassidy's suit. The sting of the libel—the inference that Mrs. Cassidy slept with a man not her husband—would have remained and would have been actionable.

10. *Privileges.* It is thus clear that under the common law rules a publisher might be held in damages—not only in cases in which he was not at fault but also in cases in which what he published was strictly accurate.

To his defense were mustered a series of privileges—affirmative defenses that could in special cases provide protection, provided the defendant was able to shoulder the burden of proving them. The chief privileges included these:

A. *Official privilege.* Judicial and legislative officers, and sometimes certain others associated in judicial and legislative work, were absolutely protected within the scope of their official duties for utterances reasonably connected thereto. Executive officers have mostly enjoyed only a qualified privilege, one destroyed if there is actual malice, although there are still some cases in which federal executives still enjoy an absolute privilege as to utterances in the scope of their duties.

B. *The privilege to communicate in one's own interest, the interest of third persons, or in common interest of publisher and recipient.* These vaguely worded privileges permitted defendants in some cases to indulge in self defense ("I didn't do it, he did"), protection of loved ones ("Don't trust him, daughter, he's no good") and sharing of important information ("I fired him because I suspected him of theft"). The privilege is destroyed if abused, as where the speaker has an improper purpose or malice, or publishes excessively.

C. *The privilege to report information pertaining to crime or the like to appropriate officers.* Again, the privilege may be lost if there is malice and perhaps if there is negligence.

D. *The privilege to report a public document, meeting or activity.* Example: a report of a trial. This privilege is lost only if the report is biased or inaccurate.

E. *Fair comment.* This is the privilege to comment about accurately stated facts concerning some matter of public concern, including political and social and artistic matters. It is limited to comment about facts that are accurately stated.

11. *Statutory privileges or immunities.* Statutes may create additional privileges. The advent of the internet has made it possible for almost anyone to post defamatory material on web bulletin boards, in chat rooms, or other sites controlled by a provider. Is the internet provider liable for defamation for failing to remove or prohibit a defamatory message posted by others? Some authority imposes a duty upon the owner of business premises open to the public to remove defamation posted on the premises. *Hellar v. Bianco,* 111 Cal.App.2d 424, 244 P.2d 757, 28 A.L.R.2d 1451(1952). Should the internet provider be treated differently? "No provider or user of an interactive computer service shall be treated as the publisher or speaker of any information provided by another information content provider." 47 U.S.C.A. § 230(c)(1).

12. *Free speech.* These common law rules had the effect of putting a great deal of expression, both written and oral, at legal risk. Once defamatory content was shown, it was presumed that the statements were untrue and that damages flowed from them. Furthermore, truth would be a defense only if the sting of the statement were true; an accurate statement of a quotation or of an opinion would not count as "truth" for this purpose. And opinion itself was actionable as libel or slander. All this could be seen as necessary to

protect reputation, or as desirable for keeping publishers honest. It could also be seen as a threat to free speech, especially in the sphere of public affairs. Does the First Amendment, which applies to the states through the Fourteenth, have any effect on the torts of libel and slander in providing that "no law" shall be made "abridging the freedom of speech, or of the press"?

----

b.   *The Constitutional Constraints of Free Speech*

NEW YORK TIMES CO. v. SULLIVAN

Supreme Court of the United States, 1964.
376 U.S. 254, 84 S.Ct. 710, 11 L.Ed.2d 686.

[The New York Times published an advertisement signed by a committee of distinguished persons and asking for donations to help defend Dr. Martin Luther King, Jr. in a perjury indictment against him and for other civil purposes. It said that efforts to enforce civil rights had been met with a "wave of terror," and that "Southern violators" had "bombed his home," and had "arrested him seven times" on various charges. The advertisement referred to the police "ringing" the campus at Alabama State College, and said that "authorities" had padlocked the campus dining hall in an effort to starve the student body into submission.

[The plaintiff in this case is L.B. Sullivan, elected Commissioner of the City of Montgomery, Alabama. In that capacity he is in charge of the Police Department. He was not named in the advertisement, but he contends that references to the police must be read as implicating him; and similarly that references to "arrests" must be read as accusing him of intimidation and violence. The trial judge charged the jury that the statements were libelous per se, that falsity, malice and damages were presumed. The jury awarded $500,000 and the Supreme Court of Alabama affirmed.]

[BRENNAN, J., delivered the opinion of the Court.]

We reverse the judgment. We hold that the rule of law applied by the Alabama courts is constitutionally deficient for failure to provide the safeguards for freedom of speech and of the press that are required by the First and Fourteenth Amendments in a libel action brought by a public official against critics of his official conduct. We further hold that under the proper safeguards the evidence presented in this case is constitutionally insufficient to support the judgment for respondent....

Under Alabama law as applied in this case, a publication is "libelous per se" if the words "tend to injure a person in his reputation" or to "bring [him] into public contempt"; the trial court stated that the standard was met if the words are such as to "injure him in his public office, or impute misconduct to him in his office, or want of official integrity, or want of fidelity to a public trust." The jury must find that the words were published "of and concerning" the plaintiff, but where the plaintiff is a public official his place in the governmental hierarchy is sufficient evidence to support a finding that his reputation has been affected by statements that reflect upon the agency of which he is in charge. Once "libel per se" has been established, the defendant has no defense as to stated facts unless he can persuade the jury that they were true in all their particulars.

His privilege of "fair comment" for expressions of opinion depends on the truth of the facts upon which the comment is based. Unless he can discharge the burden of proving truth, general damages are presumed, and may be awarded without proof of pecuniary injury....

The general proposition that freedom of expression upon public questions is secured by the First Amendment has long been settled by our decisions. The constitutional safeguard, we have said, "was fashioned to assure unfettered interchange of ideas for the bringing about of political and social changes desired by the people."

> "The maintenance of the opportunity for free political discussion to the end that government may be responsive to the will of the people and that changes may be obtained by lawful means, an opportunity essential to the security of the Republic, is a fundamental principle of our constitutional system." "[I]t is a prized American privilege to speak one's mind, although not always with perfect good taste, on all public institutions," and this opportunity is to be afforded for "vigorous advocacy" no less than "abstract discussion."

The First Amendment, said Judge Learned Hand, "presupposes that right conclusions are more likely to be gathered out of a multitude of tongues, than through any kind of authoritative selection. To many this is, and always will be, folly; but we have staked upon it our all."

Mr. Justice Brandeis, in his concurring opinion in Whitney v. California, 274 U.S. 357, 375–376, 47 S.Ct. 641, 648, 71 L.Ed. 1095, gave the principle its classic formulation:

> "Those who won our independence believed ... that public discussion is a political duty; and that this should be a fundamental principle of the American government. They recognized the risks to which all human institutions are subject. But they knew that order cannot be secured merely through fear of punishment for its infraction; that it is hazardous to discourage thought, hope and imagination; that fear breeds repression; that repression breeds hate; that hate menaces stable government; that the path of safety lies in the opportunity to discuss freely supposed grievances and proposed remedies; and that the fitting remedy for evil counsels is good ones. Believing in the power of reason as applied through public discussion, they eschewed silence coerced by law—the argument of force in its worst form. Recognizing the occasional tyrannies of governing majorities, they amended the Constitution so that free speech and assembly should be guaranteed."

Thus we consider this case against the background of a profound national commitment to the principle that debate on public issues should be uninhibited, robust, and wide-open, and that it may well include vehement, caustic, and sometimes unpleasantly sharp attacks on government and public officials.

The present advertisement, as an expression of grievance and protest on one of the major public issues of our time, would seem clearly to qualify for the constitutional protection. The question is whether it forfeits that protection by the falsity of some of its factual statements and by its alleged defamation of respondent.

Authoritative interpretations of the First Amendment guarantees have consistently refused to recognize an exception for any test of truth—whether administered by judges, juries, or administrative officials—and especially one that puts the burden of proving truth on the speaker.... That erroneous statement is inevitable in free debate, and that it must be protected if the freedoms of expression are to have the "breathing space" that they "need ... to survive," was also recognized by the Court of Appeals for the District of Columbia Circuit in Sweeney v. Patterson....

If neither factual error nor defamatory content suffices to remove the constitutional shield from criticism of official conduct, the combination of the two elements is no less inadequate. This is the lesson to be drawn from the great controversy over the Sedition Act of 1798....

[The Court here discussed the Sedition Act, which made it a crime to publish "false, scandalous and malicious writing" against the government or its main officers. The act was attacked by many of the Founders and eventually repealed on a consensus that it was inconsistent with the First Amendment.]

What a State may not constitutionally bring about by means of a criminal statute is likewise beyond the reach of its civil law of libel. The fear of damage awards under a rule such as that invoked by the Alabama courts here may be markedly more inhibiting than the fear of prosecution under a criminal statute....

The state rule of law is not saved by its allowance of the defense of truth. A defense for erroneous statements honestly made is no less essential here than was the requirement of proof of guilty knowledge which, in Smith v. California, 361 U.S. 147, 80 S.Ct. 215, 4 L.Ed.2d 205, we held indispensable to a valid conviction of a bookseller for possessing obscene writings for sale.... A rule compelling the critic of official conduct to guarantee the truth of all his factual assertions—and to do so on pain of libel judgments virtually unlimited in amount—leads to a comparable "self-censorship." Allowance of the defense of truth, with the burden of proving it on the defendant, does not mean that only false speech will be deterred.... Under such a rule, would-be critics of official conduct may be deterred from voicing their criticism, even though it is believed to be true and even though it is in fact true, because of doubt whether it can be proved in court or fear of the expense of having to do so. They tend to make only statements which "steer far wider of the unlawful zone." The rule thus dampens the vigor and limits the variety of public debate. It is inconsistent with the First and Fourteenth Amendments. The constitutional guarantees require, we think, a federal rule that prohibits a public official from recovering damages for a defamatory falsehood relating to his official conduct unless he proves that the statement was made with "actual malice"—that is, with knowledge that it was false or with reckless disregard of whether it was false or not. . . . Since respondent may seek a new trial, we deem that considerations of effective judicial administration require us to review the evidence in the present record to determine whether it could constitutionally support a judgment for respondent. This Court's duty is not limited to the elaboration of constitutional principles; we must also in proper cases review the evidence to make certain that those principles have been constitutionally applied. . . .

[W]e consider that the proof presented to show actual malice lacks the convincing clarity which the constitutional standard demands, and hence that it would not constitutionally sustain the judgment for respondent under the proper rule of law. . . .

[The Court rejected the argument that "actual malice" could be found because the Times did not retract and because it did not check the accuracy against news stories in its own files. The imputed knowledge from its own files was not sufficient to show an actual state of mind necessary to support a finding of knowing or reckless falsehood. The Court also thought the evidence was constitutionally deficient because criticisms did not clearly refer to the plaintiff. This was thought too much like permitting an action for criticism of government itself.]

[JUSTICES BLACK and DOUGLAS and GOLDBERG, in two concurring opinions, argued for an absolute right to speak, with no liability even for knowing falsehoods.]

Notes

1. *Actual malice.* The *Times-Sullivan* Court drew on familiar words in holding that "actual malice" was required as a condition of liability, but the words proved confusing in the end because the court was not referring to spite or ill-will. The proof required to recover for criticism of official conduct was that the defendant knew the publication was false or, just short of this, that the defendant published "recklessly." It is now established that recklessness in this sense requires a "high degree of awareness of probable falsity," or that the publisher "in fact entertained serious doubts as to the truth of his publication." *St. Amant v. Thompson*, 390 U.S. 727, 88 S.Ct. 1323, 20 L.Ed.2d 262 (1968). Clearly enough, negligence, as in a failure to investigate, is not sufficient.

2. *Fair comment.* The common law recognized a privilege to make "fair comment" on officials, and other public figures, such as artists, writers and actors. The fair comment privilege only permitted "comment" or opinion, and there was liability if the publisher misstated any "fact." In addition,

most courts required the publisher to state the facts on which the opinion was based in order to claim the privilege. How does *Times-Sullivan* differ?

3. *Truth.* In the early years after *Times-Sullivan*, libel lawyers continued to think in common law terms and often spoke of the case as erecting a "Constitutional privilege." But common law privileges were affirmative defenses, and it gradually became clear that *Times-Sullivan* rewrote the elements of the plaintiff's prima facie case in all claims brought by public officials. Thus the plaintiff must prove that the published statements are false; the burden is no longer on the defendant to prove truth if it can. When the plaintiff is a public figure, the elements of the prima facie case now seem to be: (1) a false statement; (2) known by the defendant to be false or published in reckless disregard of its falsity; (3) and having defamatory content; (4) referring to the plaintiff. The common law rule that left it for the defendant to prove truth is thus now reversed; the plaintiff must prove falsity. *Philadelphia Newspapers, Inc. v. Hepps*, 475 U.S. 767, 106 S.Ct. 1558, 89 L.Ed.2d 783 (1986).

4. *Public officials and public figures.* The rules in *Times-Sullivan* were applied to appointed as well as to elected public officials. It seemed obvious that the rationale of the opinion required extension to candidates for public office, and the Court so held. Then, in 1967, a much-divided Court extended the same rules to cover "public figures," who were neither candidates for office nor actual public employees. *Curtis Publishing Co. v. Butts*, 388 U.S. 130, 87 S.Ct. 1975, 18 L.Ed.2d 1094 (1967). One reason given for this was that many private citizens have an important role in influencing social policy and in "ordering society."

5. *Private citizens.* Does the rationale of *Times-Sullivan*—an emphasis on vigorous debate of public issues, a desire to avoid self-censorship—also extend to suits by private citizens who are not in any sense public figures? What if a publisher libels a private citizen in discussing a wholly private matter? What if the publisher does so in discussing a public issue? Consider the next case.

GERTZ v. ROBERT WELCH, INC.

Supreme Court of the United States, 1974.
418 U.S. 323, 94 S.Ct. 2997, 41 L.Ed.2d 789.

[The plaintiff, Elmer Gertz, is a lawyer. A police officer named Nuccio shot and killed a youth named Nelson and was convicted of second degree murder. Gertz represented the Nelson family in civil claims against Nuccio. The defendant publishes an organ known as American Opinion, representing the views of the John Birch Society. This organ, arguing that the prosecution of Nuccio was a part of the Communist campaign against police, portrayed Gertz as an architect of the "frame-up" of Nuccio, and went on to identify him as a Leninist and Communist-fronter. In fact Gertz had nothing to do with the criminal prosecution and there was no basis for claiming him to be a Leninist or Communist fronter. Gertz sued. The trial court concluded that Gertz was not a public official or a public figure, but that the *Times-Sullivan* rules applied anyway. Accordingly, it entered a judgment for the defendant. The Court of Appeals concluded that there was no clear and convincing evidence of "actual malice," and it affirmed.]

[JUSTICE POWELL delivered the Court's opinion.]

The principal issue in this case is whether a newspaper or broadcaster that publishes defamatory falsehoods about an individual who is neither a public official nor a public figure may claim a constitutional privilege against liability for the injury inflicted by those statements. The Court considered this question on the rather different set of facts presented in Rosenbloom v. Metromedia, Inc., 403 U.S. 29, 91 S.Ct. 1811, 29 L. Ed.2d 296 (1971). Rosenbloom, a distributor of nudist magazines, was arrested for selling allegedly obscene material while making a delivery to a retail dealer. The police obtained a warrant and seized his entire inventory of 3,000 books and magazines. He sought and obtained an injunction prohibiting further police interference with his business. He then sued a local radio station for failing to note in two of its newscasts that the 3,000 items seized were only "reportedly" or "allegedly" obscene and for broadcasting references to "the smut literature racket" and to "girlie-book peddlers" in its coverage of the court proceeding for injunctive relief. He obtained a judgment against the radio station, but the Court of Appeals for the Third Circuit held the New York Times privilege applicable to the broadcast and reversed. 415 F.2d 892 (1969).

This Court affirmed the decision below, but no majority could agree on a controlling rationale. The eight Justices who participated in Rosenbloom announced their views in five separate opinions, none of which commanded more than three votes.... We begin with the common ground. Under the First Amendment there is no such thing as a false idea. However pernicious an opinion may seem, we depend for its correction not on the conscience of judges and juries but on the competition of other ideas. But there is no constitutional value in false statements of fact. Neither the intentional lie nor the careless error materially advances society's interest in "uninhibited, robust, and wide-open" debate on public issues....

Although the erroneous statement of fact is not worthy of constitutional protection, it is nevertheless inevitable in free debate.... The First Amendment requires that we protect some falsehood in order to protect speech that matters.

The need to avoid self-censorship by the news media is, however, not the only societal value at issue. If it were, this Court would have embraced long ago the view that publishers and broadcasters enjoy an unconditional and indefeasible immunity from liability for defamation....

The legitimate state interest underlying the law of libel is the compensation of individuals for the harm inflicted on them by defamatory falsehood....

The New York Times standard defines the level of constitutional protection appropriate to the context of defamation of a public person. Those who, by reason of the notoriety of their achievements or the vigor and success with which they seek the public's attention, are properly classed as public figures and those who hold governmental office may recover for injury to reputation only on clear and convincing proof that the defamatory falsehood was made with knowledge of its falsity or with reckless disregard for the truth.... We think that these decisions are correct, but we do not find their holdings justified solely by reference to the interest of the press and broadcast media in immunity from liability. Rather, we believe that the New York Times rule states an accommodation between this concern and the limited state interest present in the context of libel actions brought by public persons.... Because an *ad hoc* resolution of the competing interests at stake in each particular case is not feasible, we must lay down broad rules of general application. Such rules necessarily treat alike various cases involving differences as well as similarities. Thus it is often true that not all of the considerations which justify adoption of a given rule will obtain in each particular case decided under its authority.

With that caveat we have no difficulty in distinguishing among defamation plaintiffs. The first remedy of any victim of defamation is self-help—using available opportunities to contradict the lie or correct the error and thereby to minimize its adverse impact on reputation. Public officials and public figures usually enjoy significantly greater access to the channels of effective communication and hence have a more realistic opportunity to counteract false statements than private individuals normally enjoy. Private individuals are therefore more vulnerable to injury, and the state interest in protecting them is correspondingly greater.

More important than the likelihood that private individuals will lack effective opportunities for rebuttal, there is a compelling normative consideration underlying the distinction between public and private defamation plaintiffs. An individual who decides to seek governmental office must accept certain necessary consequences of that involvement in public affairs. He runs the risk of closer public scrutiny than might otherwise be the case. And society's interest in the officers of government is not strictly limited to the formal discharge of official duties. As the Court pointed out in Garrison v. Louisiana, 379 U.S. at 77, 85 S.Ct., at 217, the public's interest extends to "anything which might touch on an official's fitness for office.... Few personal attributes are more germane to fitness for office than dishonesty, malfeasance, or improper motivation, even though these characteristics may also affect the official's private character."

Those classed as public figures stand in a similar position. Hypothetically, it may be possible for someone to become a public figure through no purposeful action of his own, but the instances of truly involuntary public figures must be exceedingly rare. For the most part those who attain this status have assumed roles of especial prominence in the affairs of society. Some occupy positions of such persuasive power and influence that they are deemed public figures for all purposes. More commonly, those classed as public figures have thrust themselves to the forefront of particular public controversies in order to influence the resolution of the issues involved. In either event, they invite attention and comment.

Even if the foregoing generalities do not obtain in every instance, the communications media are entitled to act on the assumption that public officials and public figures have voluntarily exposed themselves to increased risk of injury from defamatory falsehood concerning them. No such assumption is justified with respect to a private individual. He has not accepted public office or assumed an "influential role in ordering society." ...

Thus, private individuals are not only more vulnerable to injury than public officials and public figures; they are also more deserving of recovery....

We hold that, so long as they do not impose liability without fault, the States may define for themselves the appropriate standard of liability for a publisher or broadcaster of defamatory falsehood injurious to a private individual. This approach provides a more equitable boundary between the competing concerns involved here. It recognizes the strength of the legitimate state interest in compensating private individuals for wrongful injury to reputation, yet shields the press and broadcast media from the rigors of liability for defamation. At least this conclusion obtains where, as here, the substance of the defamatory statement "makes substantial danger to reputation apparent." This phrase places in perspective the conclusion we announce today. Our inquiry would involve consideration somewhat different from those discussed above if a State purported to condition civil liability on a factual misstatement whose content did not warn a reasonably prudent editor or broadcaster of its defamatory potential....

Our accommodation of the competing values at stake in defamation suits by private individuals allows the States to impose liability on the publisher or broadcaster of defamatory falsehood on a less demanding showing than that required by New York Times.... But this countervailing state interest extends no further than compensation for injury. For the reasons stated below, we hold that the States may not permit recovery of presumed or punitive damages, at least when liability is not based on a showing of knowledge of falsity or reckless disregard for the truth.

... Under the traditional rules pertaining to actions for libel, the existence of injury is presumed from the fact of publication. Juries may award substantial sums as compensation for supposed damage to reputation without any proof that such harm actually occurred. The largely uncontrolled discretion of juries to award damages where there is no loss unnecessarily compounds the potential of any system of liability for defamatory falsehood to inhibit the vigorous exercise of First Amendment freedoms. Additionally, the doctrine of presumed damages invites juries to punish unpopular opinion rather than to compensate individuals for injury sustained by the publication of a false fact. More to the point, the States have no substantial interest in securing for plaintiffs such as this petitioner gratuitous awards of money damages far in excess of any actual injury. . . .

We also find no justification for allowing awards of punitive damages against publishers and broadcasters held liable under state-defined standards of liability for defamation. . . . Notwithstanding our refusal to extend the New York Times privilege to defamation of private individuals, respondent contends that we should affirm the judgment below on the ground that petitioner is either a public official or a public figure. . . .

Respondent's characterization of petitioner as a public figure raises a different question. That designation may rest on either of two alternative bases. In some instances an individual may achieve such pervasive fame or notoriety that he becomes a public figure for all purposes, and in all contexts. More commonly, an individual voluntarily injects himself or is drawn into a particular public controversy and thereby becomes a public figure for a limited range of issues. In either case such persons assume special prominence in the resolution of public questions.

Petitioner has long been active in community and professional affairs. He has served as an officer of local civic groups and of various professional organizations, and he has published several books and articles on legal subjects. Although petitioner was consequently well known in some circles, he had achieved no general fame or notoriety in the community. None of the prospective jurors called at the trial had ever heard of petitioner prior to this litigation, and respondent offered no proof that this response was atypical of the local population. We would not lightly assume that a citizen's participation in community and professional affairs rendered him a public figure for all purposes. Absent clear evidence of general fame or notoriety in the community, and pervasive involvement in the affairs of society, an individual should not be deemed a public personality for all aspects of his life. It is preferable to reduce the public-figure question to a more meaningful context by looking to the nature and extent of an individual's participation in the particular controversy giving rise to the defamation.

In this context it is plain that petitioner was a not a public figure. . . .

[Remanded for further proceedings. Concurring and dissenting opinions are omitted.]

Notes

1. *The Gertz fault standard.* For public officials and public figures, the *Times-Sullivan* standard remains applicable after *Gertz.* For plaintiffs who are private persons, the *Gertz* Court held that there was no need to prove

knowing or reckless falsehood. The Court did, however, put a Constitutional surcharge on the common law rules for private persons: they can only recover if they prove (a) some kind of fault, to be specified by the states under state tort law, and (b) actual damages.

2. *The states' fault standard.* Most states, accepting *Gertz'* invitation to apply any fault standard they chose, fell back on the most familiar word— negligence. Thus liability would be imposed in most states on *Gertz*-type claims if the jury found defendant published "negligently." A few states have decided on a tougher standard and have kept the *Times-Sullivan* standard even for private-person cases, or have adopted some other variation, such as "grossly irresponsible," or the professional standards of journalists.

3. *Types of fault.* Is it really possible to carry over the negligence standard to these cases? What kind of conduct and what kind of risks are entailed in the fault required here? The *Gertz* Court almost certainly had in mind fault as to the truth or falsity of the defamatory statements, as for example, fault in failure to investigate unsubstantiated charges. Would a negligence analysis work just as well when the fault, if any, lies in a reporter's perception of fast-moving events? Suppose a reporter writes that the plaintiff was leading demonstrating trespassers at a nuclear power plant, but plaintiff says he was merely out in front watching? What about fault that does not bear on the truth or falsity at all, for example, spite or ill-will? What about fault in writing an ambiguous sentence, in which one meaning is defamatory but the meaning intended is not?

4. *Actual damages.* Suppose, however, the private-person plaintiff proves the defendant was guilty of a knowing or reckless falsehood, so that the test laid down in *Times-Sullivan* is met. Would both presumed and punitive damages then be available?

5. *Public figures under Gertz.* After the decisions in *Times-Sullivan* and *Gertz,* one of the central issues has been whether the plaintiff in a libel action is a public official or figure or whether he is a private person, since this determines the kind of proof required. The common law notion of public figures was rather broad, although not necessarily well defined. *Gertz* limited the concept of public figures quite stringently. Justice Powell seemed to concede that a plaintiff might be "drawn into a particular public controversy and thereby [become] a public figure." But his main emphasis seems to be on the case in which the plaintiff "voluntarily injects himself" into a public issue or has "thrust" himself "to the forefront of particular public controversies." Later cases have emphasized this "thrusting" and also the idea that true public figures have a greater access "to the channels of effective communication."

6. *Development of public figures.* Some of the later cases have taken these stringent tests of public figurehood to extremes. The Court has held a party to a lawsuit, at least if it is a divorce, is not a public figure for that reason alone, with the result that a publisher who inaccurately states the court's opinion may be denied the *Times-Sullivan* protections. *Time, Inc. v. Firestone,* 424 U.S. 448, 96 S.Ct. 958, 47 L.Ed.2d 154 (1976). In *Wolston v. Reader's Digest Ass'n, Inc.,* 443 U.S. 157, 99 S.Ct. 2701, 61 L.Ed.2d 450 (1979) the Court held that one who is charged with and convicted of a crime is not a public figure merely for that reason. One responding to criminal

charges, it was said, did not "voluntarily thrust" himself into a public controversy.

7. *Public officials.* The decision that some public employees are not public figures puts renewed emphasis on the idea of a public official. The Court has long recognized that not every public employee is a public official for *Times-Sullivan* purposes. It has so far not clearly delineated its ideas on this subject, but it has said that an employee is not a public official unless "[t]he employee's position [is] one which would invite public scrutiny and discussion of the person holding it, entirely apart from the scrutiny and discussion occasioned by the particular charges in controversy." *Rosenblatt v. Baer*, 383 U.S. 75, 86 S.Ct. 669,15 L.Ed.2d 597 (1966). What if there is evidence that a janitor at the local high school is selling heavy drugs to students? Presumably he would not be an "official" under the *Rosenblatt* test. Presumably also he did not thrust himself into a controversy. Is this a case in which the Court might find he is a public figure because he is "drawn into" a public controversy?

8. *Publishers and broadcasters.* The common law of defamation used the term "publication" and "publisher" to refer to any communication to someone other than the plaintiff. Justice Powell in *Gertz* repeatedly refers, however, to "publishers and broadcasters," and even to "news media." Does he have in mind limiting *Gertz* to cases in which a private citizen sues a media publisher? Suppose an employer or the dean of a college writes a letter about an employee or a college student. If there is reason to require both fault and actual damages in media cases does it apply equally to private publications as well? There are a few cases saying that it does not and that the common law rules apply in full force to the private letter writer. What will the Supreme Court say?

9. *Libel per se and per quod.* The common law rule was that all libel was libel per se. This meant that damages and falsity would be presumed if the published material was defamatory. In the latter 19th century, cases arose in which the defamatory content of a publication might be rather unclear. It might be ambiguous, for example, or it might seem to apply to the plaintiff only if one knew some outside facts that related it to the plaintiff, as in *Cassidy*. Or the material might not seem defamatory of anyone at all until some outside facts, not contained in the publication, were added. "Mrs. Jones gave birth to twins yesterday at Memorial Hospital," is a classic example. The editor who publishes this would have no notice that anyone at all is defamed. If Mrs. Jones had been married only the week before, however, the publication has defamatory meaning. In some of these cases some courts invented a new rule. This rule held that where the defamatory content was not apparent on the face of the publication, the publisher would only be liable for pecuniary damages. This required a showing of pecuniary loss. In this respect it is a more stringent rule than the "actual" damages requirement in *Gertz*. The general rule in *Gertz* requiring fault of the publisher may have made the dispute over libel per quod obsolete, since fault may serve as a better basis of liability than "pecuniary loss." Could a plaintiff ever meet the *Gertz* standards in a case like the "twins" example?

10. *"[T]here is no such thing as a false idea."* This statement in *Gertz* seemed to create a new limitation on recovery for defamation. The common

law denied recovery for mere name calling, but at least on occasion seemed willing to impose liability for statements of opinion and even for unkind satire. *Gertz* seemed to commit the Court to the proposition that the defamation must involve a factual misstatement and that it must be reasonably understood as such. Later, in *Hustler Magazine v. Falwell*, 485 U.S. 46, 108 S.Ct. 876, 99 L.Ed.2d 41 (1988) the defendant published a nasty parody of an ad that used "first time" as its theme. The parody presented Falwell, a famous evangelist, as having his "first time" with his own mother. No one believed that the publisher intended this parody to be taken as a fact and no one did take it as a fact. Because liability depended upon proof that the defendant knowingly or recklessly published a "fact," the defendant could not be held. Later still, the Court said there was no separate constitutional protection for "opinion," but reiterated its holdings that liability depended upon statements or at least implications of fact. *Milkovich v. Lorain Journal*, 497 U.S. 1, 110 S.Ct. 2695, 111 L.Ed.2d 1 (1990). What if protestors at an abortion clinic carry signs saying "This clinic kills babies"?

DUN & BRADSTREET, INC. v. GREENMOSS BUILDERS, INC., 472 U.S. 749, 105 S.Ct. 2939, 86 L.Ed.2d 593 (1985). The defendant, Dun & Bradstreet, supplied a confidential credit rating report about the plaintiff to five subscribers. The report was negligently compiled by a reporter who misinterpreted or mis-transcribed some court documents. It erroneously stated that plaintiff, which was a business operation, had filed a petition for bankruptcy. The plaintiff feared the report would seriously affect credit or other business affairs. He asked for correction and for the names of the subscribers who had received the report. The defendant gave a correction, but the plaintiff regarded it as inadequate. The defendant refused altogether to give him the names of subscribers. In the trial court, the plaintiff recovered $50,000 actual and $300,000 punitive damages, which the Vermont Supreme Court upheld, saying that *Times-Sullivan* had no application to non-media defendants. In the Supreme Court of the United States, *held*, actual and punitive damages are recoverable in this case without proof of *Times-Sullivan* malice. *Gertz* held that a private individual could obtain only restricted damages from a publisher of a libel that involved a matter of public concern, but did not address the case of a private person libeled on a matter of private concern. In the private-figure/private-concern case, the state's interest in compensation is just as strong as elsewhere, but the First Amendment interest is weak. The speech here is not on a matter of public concern, as determined by "content, form, and context." The interest is of the individual speaker and its specific business audience; no free flow of information is involved, since Dun & Bradstreet prohibited subscribers from passing the information on. The speech is also hardy and unlikely to be deterred by "incidental state regulation," because profit motive is involved.

Notes

1.   *Gertz* seemed to make a deliberate choice to focus on the character of the plaintiff rather than the nature of the issue under discussion as the basis for invoking *Times-Sullivan* or avoiding it. For this reason, *Dun & Bradstreet* was a surprise to many observers.

2.   Under *Dun & Bradstreet*, the rules to be applied with respect to proof and damages for libel appear to be a function of at least two variables: First, is the plaintiff a public figure? And second, is the issue under discussion or the communication involved a matter of public interest? *Dun & Bradstreet* addressed the case in which the answer to both questions was "no," and in that case allowed the plaintiff to recover presumed damages without proof of the knowing or reckless falsehood required by *Times-Sullivan*.

3.   *Dun & Bradstreet* involved only the question whether the plaintiff could recover common law "presumed" damages. This means that one of the two main rules in *Gertz* has no application in cases of private-person plaintiffs and private concern issues. What is your prediction about the other rule in *Gertz*?

4.   The Supreme Court's decisions on defamation are constitutional rules which govern the states. But they only prescribe minimum protections for free speech. The states are free to make their own tort rules which provide more protection for speakers and less for victims of defamation. See, rejecting the new liabilities permitted by *Dun & Bradstreet, Newberry v. Allied Stores, Inc.*, 108 N.M. 424, 773 P.2d 1231 (1989).

REFERENCE: DOBBS ON TORTS §§ 400–23 (2000).

§ 2.   MALICIOUS PROSECUTION AND OTHER ABUSES OF THE LEGAL SYSTEM

a.   *Malicious Prosecution*

Illustration 1

Max Parrillo owned a socket wrench purchased from Lambert's Hardware. He wished to replace a socket used on the wrench, so he took the wrench and socket to Lambert's store. He went directly to the wrench display where he took his own wrench out of his pocket and made some comparisons. Not finding the right size, he put his wrench in his pocket and walked out of the store. Right outside the store, a store detective employed by Lambert's stopped him and accused him of stealing the wrench. The detective called the police and told the officer that Parrillo had stolen the wrench. Up until this time, the detective had refused to listen to Parrillo's side of the story. The detective told the officer that he had watched Parrillo the whole time and that he had stolen the wrench. Parrillo was prosecuted on the basis of this information, but was found not guilty. He then sued Lambert's Hardware. These facts will justify a recovery of any special damages, such as cost of defending the criminal trial, plus "general" damages, plus punitive damages.

Illustration 2

Penny Pfennig saw an officer in the act of arresting a friend of Pfennig's, Shirley Schilling. Schilling, it appeared, had been driving while intoxicated. Pfennig stopped her car and walked back to the scene of the arrest. She said: "I don't want to interfere, but this is a friend of mine. Can I help her in any way?" At this point another officer, Rex Stebbins, pulled up and strode aggressively over to the scene. Apparently he assumed that Pfennig was also under arrest; he pushed her back and told her to get on the sidewalk. Pfennig's husband, Thaler, then arrived and protested Stebbins' actions, whereupon Stebbins arrested Pfennig and Thaler for obstructing justice and interfering with an arrest. After they were found not guilty, they sued Stebbins and the city for (a) false arrest and (b) malicious prosecution. They are entitled to recover for false arrest for damages from the time of detention until formal prosecution was begun, and for malicious prosecution for damages arising after prosecution was begun.

The malicious prosecution claim is often compared to a *false imprisonment*, and there is much resemblance. But false imprisonment is a trespassory tort, involving direct physical detention of the person. Prosecution is indirect interference. In the case of false imprisonment, the plaintiff makes a prima facie case by showing an intended detention of which the plaintiff was aware. Any privilege based on the existence of a warrant or probable cause for arrest must be shown affirmatively by the defendant. In the malicious prosecution case, on the other hand, the plaintiff cannot recover unless he affirmatively shows that the accuser lacked probable cause and was also motivated by malice. Damages in the two torts are different, too. The false arrest or imprisonment damages include any damages from the time of detention to the time of prosecution, but no more. Damages for malicious prosecution include any damages occurring after prosecution has begun. Thus in many cases the plaintiff may have both claims and may need to assert both to collect full damages.

Defamation and malicious prosecution. In some ways, malicious prosecution more closely resembles a claim for libel or slander. All malicious prosecution claims necessarily involve a defamatory communication—an accusation of crime. Under the law of defamation, there is a privilege to report a crime and other facts to responsible officials, so that under the ordinary law of libel there could be no recovery for a good faith report which resulted in prosecution. The law of malicious prosecution is, in a sense, a special case of defamation with special rules. What the common law sought in these rules was a system that would redress genuine grievances of the prosecuted plaintiff without discouraging defendants from reporting crimes or suspected crimes. In a very real way, this parallels the *Times-Sullivan* concern to redress injury while avoiding self-censorship.

The common law rule. The common law solution, like that of *Times-Sullivan*, is something of a compromise, and one intended to protect similar values. But the common law solution is structured quite differently from that in *Times-Sullivan*. The common law rule denies the plaintiff any claim unless:

(1) *There is a prosecution.* This is a requirement that the only kind of damage recognized is prosecution itself, and mere report of a crime to an officer is not itself sufficient.

(2) *The defendant in the malicious prosecution suit instigated the prosecution.* Either a private citizen or an officer might instigate the prosecution; indeed, there may be several instigators. The idea is to locate one or more persons who played a significant role in causing prosecution. An honest factual report to an officer, not accompanied by any pressure to prosecute, will ordinarily not be sufficient. On the other hand, it is clear that the store detective in Illustration 1 and the officer in Illustration 2 both are instigators.

(3) *The defendant acted maliciously.* Malice is a specialized term in tort law. It may at times mean spite or ill-will, but is seldom limited to that meaning. Many of the results of cases suggest that any improper purpose will do, and so will abuse of position or authority or denial of ordinary decencies to the accused. Thus in both Illustrations, the defendants refused to hear the plaintiff's side of the story, and considering they acted from positions of power or authority, this may have justified a finding of malice.

(4) *The defendant acted without probable cause.* The false report of a crime is not by itself enough, even if the defendant acts maliciously. The defendant must also have acted without probable cause, that is, without reasonable cause for believing that the plaintiff has committed the crime charged. Where facts are capable of dispute, the accuser may be under some obligation to check the facts where this is reasonably possible. This is one of the grounds on which the store detective could be found to lack probable cause in Illustration 1.

(5) *The criminal action is terminated in favor of the present plaintiff.* The plaintiff cannot recover for malicious prosecution unless the criminal action against him has terminated and terminated in his favor. Thus he cannot sue for the tort while the criminal action is pending. And he cannot sue after it has terminated if he was convicted. In a third group of cases, the criminal action is terminated by compromise or some other procedure that does not determine guilt or innocence. In many courts this is not a termination favorable to the accused; therefore, he may not sue for malicious prosecution.

Defenses. The "judicial" immunities sketched in connection with defamation claims also apply to malicious prosecution and other torts. Thus the judge and the prosecutor are absolutely immune from malicious prosecution claims, so long as they are acting in their judicial and prosecutorial capacities respectively. The prosecutor who takes on police work, however, risks a loss of the absolute immunity. A second defense is "guilt-in-fact." Even if the accuser lacked probable cause for the accusation and acted with malice, even if the accused is found not guilty in the criminal trial, the accuser may offer it as a defense in the malicious prosecution action that the plaintiff there was in fact guilty. This is obviously analogous to the truth "defense" in libel cases.

Judge and jury. For the most part, factual issues about which reasonable people could differ are left to the jury in malicious prosecution as elsewhere. The judge on the other hand decides issues of law, including those that involve facts so clear that dispute is not reasonably possible. But the issue of probable cause is somewhat peculiar. This issue involves a determination of the reasonableness of the defendant's accusation, that is, whether the facts and reasonable inferences would warrant a strong suspicion. This sounds like many evaluative issues ordinarily left to the jury—like the negligence issue in fact. But this issue is *not* left to the jury; it is for the judge to decide. This rule creates a complicated situation. The judge is to decide whether the defendant had probable cause for the accusation; but the jury is to decide the facts on which this conclusion is based. This leads to a difficult procedural question. Should the judge get the facts from the jury by special verdict? Or should the judge instruct the jury that if the facts found are X, Y and Z, there would be probable cause, but otherwise not? Imagine the possibilities.

Malicious prosecution after Times–Sullivan. Since malicious prosecution involves communication, and invariably reputation as well, it may be regarded as merely a special case of defamation. Would *Times-Sullivan* and *Gertz* apply, then, to restrict liability in these cases? In *City of Long Beach v. Bozek*, 31 Cal.3d 527, 183 Cal.Rptr. 86, 645 P.2d 137 (1982), reiterated 33 Cal.3d 727, 190 Cal.Rptr. 918, 661 P.2d 1072 (1983), a citizen sued the city and lost. The city then sued for malicious civil prosecution. The intermediate appellate court applied rules similar to those used in *Times-Sullivan*. The California Supreme Court, however, provided even more protection. It held that when a citizen petitions a governmental entity for redress of grievances, the citizens' protection is absolute and the governmental entity may not sue him at all. Does this suggest that malicious prosecution suits by public figures must meet the rule of *Times-Sullivan*? And that those by private figures must meet the *Gertz* rules?

Look back at the common law rule. Does it effectively provide the same protections provided by *Times-Sullivan* and *Gertz*? One element that may give trouble is the "presumed" damages in malicious prosecution cases. These were forbidden under the *Gertz* test.

b. *Improper Civil Litigation*

The defendant in malicious prosecution cases has accused the plaintiff of a crime and instigated criminal prosecution. But in "malicious civil prosecution" the defendant has brought a civil action against the person who is now the plaintiff. If it was brought without probable cause, was malicious, and was terminated in favor of the person who is now plaintiff, there may be a cause of action for malicious civil prosecution under that name or under some other descriptive term. The rules in the two actions are much the same, but obviously, in a litigious nation, it requires much less reason to bring a civil suit than to accuse of crime, and consequently the want of probable cause must be "very palpable" or otherwise clearly shown. In one or two respects some courts have fashioned special limitations on the claim for improper civil litigation.

FRIEDMAN v. DOZORC

Supreme Court of Michigan, 1981.
412 Mich. 1, 312 N.W.2d 585.

LEVIN, JUSTICE.

[In the course of Dr. Friedman's surgery on Mrs. Serafin, she began to ooze blood uncontrollably and she died five days later. Autopsy showed this was due to a rare blood disease. Acting on behalf of Anthony Serafin, Jr., attorneys Dozorc and Golden brought a death action against Friedman and others. There was no evidence introduced showing a violation of any professional standard by Dr. Friedman and the trial judge directed a verdict in his favor. Friedman then commenced this action against the attorneys for negligence and malicious civil prosecution and also on other theories. The trial court in this action granted the attorneys' motions for summary judgment and the Court of Appeals affirmed in part and reversed in part.]

[The plaintiff argued that the attorneys for Serafin owed them a duty of reasonable investigation and examination of the facts and law so that the attorney would have a basis for a good faith belief that the client had a tenable claim.]

Assuming that an attorney has an obligation to his client to conduct a reasonable investigation prior to bringing an action, that obligation is not the functional equivalent of a duty of care owed to the client's adversary. We decline to so transform the attorney's obligation because we view such a duty as inconsistent with basic precepts of the adversary system.

. . . A decision to proceed with a future course of action that involves litigation will necessarily adversely affect a legal opponent. If an attorney were held to owe a duty of due care to both the client and the client's adversary, the obligation owing to the adversary would extend beyond undertaking an investigation and would permeate all facets of the litigation. The attorney's decision-making and future conduct on behalf of both parties would be shaped by the attorney's obligation to exercise due care as to both parties. Under such a rule an attorney is likely to be faced with a situation in which it would be in the client's best interest to proceed in one fashion and in the adversary's best interest to proceed contrariwise. However he chooses to proceed, the attorneys could be accused of failing to exercise due care for the benefit of one of the parties.

In short, creation of a duty in favor of an adversary of the attorney's client would create an unacceptable conflict of interest which would seriously hamper an attorney's effectiveness as counsel for his client. Not only would the adversary's interests interfere with the client's interests, the attorney's justifiable concern with being sued for negligence would detrimentally interfere with the attorney-client relationship. . . .

Plaintiff argues that concern for the chilling effect on free access to the courts which might result from declaring the existence of an attorney's duty in favor of an adverse party is misplaced. Instead, plaintiff urges that recognition of a cause of action in negligence would facilitate free access to the courts. Plaintiff asserts that the historical check on free access to the courts through independent assessment of the case by the attorney has broken down. Instead of acting as an effective screen against groundless suits, the attorney has become a mere conduit for such suits, particularly in medical malpractice actions where the attorney acquires a contingent fee interest in the outcome of the litigation. . . .

There is, however a public policy of encouraging free access to the courts. Because we are of the opinion that recognition of a cause of action for negligence in favor of client's adversary might unduly inhibit attorneys from bringing close cases or advancing innovative theories, or taking action against defendants who can be expected to retaliate, we decline to recognize a duty of due care of the adverse party. . . .

Plaintiff relies upon the same allegations respecting defendants' conduct and their failure to meet professional standards which assertedly constitute negligence in contending that he has pled a cause of action for malicious prosecution. . . .

A substantial number of American jurisdictions today follow some form of "English rule" to the effect that "in the absence of an arrest, seizure, or special damage, the successful civil defendant has no remedy, despite the fact that his antagonist proceeded against him maliciously and without probable cause." A larger number of jurisdictions, some say a majority, follow an "American rule" permitting actions for malicious prosecution of civil proceedings without requiring the plaintiff to show special injury.

The plaintiff's complaint does not allege special injury. We are satisfied that Michigan has not significantly departed from the English rule and we decline to do so today. . . .

Most commentators appear to favor abrogation of the special injury requirement to make the action more available and less difficult to maintain. Their counsel should, however, be evaluated skeptically. The lawyer's remedy for a grievance is a lawsuit, and a law student or tort professor may be particularly predisposed by experience and training to see the preferred remedy for a wrongful tort action as another tort action. In seeking a remedy for the excessive litigiousness of our society, we would do well to cast off the limitations of a perspective which ascribes curative power only to lawsuits. . . .

The lawyer who "acts primarily for the purpose of aiding his client in obtaining a proper adjudication of his claim," albeit with knowledge that the claim is not tenable, should not be subject to liability on the thesis that an inference of an improper purpose may be drawn from the lawyer's continuing to advance a claim which he knew to be untenable.

[The Court held that the trial court was correct in dismissing all claims by Dr. Friedman.]

Notes

1. *The special injury rule.* The special injury requirement was satisfied only if there were seizure of property, as where property is attached or subjected to an injunction; or there was seizure of the person, as where one is civilly committed; or, in some cases, where there was repeated re-litigation of the same claim. The injury that may arise to a doctor's reputation from a malpractice claim was not sufficient.

2. *State of authority on special injury.* It is often said that most American courts passing on the question reject the special injury requirement. This is perhaps less than clear. Some of the cases that reject it are in fact cases in which special injury could be found. There is, in short, substantial authority both accepting and rejecting the special injury rule.

3. *Physician countersuits.* The *Friedman* case represents a topic of considerable debate. One way to resolve it against the physician is to rely on the special injury rule. As Justice Linde commented in *O'Toole v. Franklin*, 279 Or. 513, 569 P.2d 561 (1977), the special injury rule is not really addressed to the misgivings courts have had in the physician countersuit cases. But he was prepared to retain the rule so that those claims could be excluded, even if it was not a rule he might have adopted in the first place. His concern, in part, was unchilled access to courts. Most courts, even where the special injury rule has been rejected, have found ways of excluding liability in the suits against lawyers like those in *Friedman* and *O'Toole*. Rules of professional responsibility for lawyers provide that it is a disciplinary infraction for a lawyer to bring frivolous claims or make frivolous contentions in litigation. See MODEL RULE OF PROFESSIONAL CONDUCT 3.1; MODEL CODE OF PROFESSIONAL RESPONSIBILITY DR 7–102(A). These provisions have generally not been accepted as furnishing any basis for a claim, either. Liability has been imposed, however, in a few cases in which the attorney has made little or no investigation. *Raine v. Drasin*, 621 S.W.2d 895 (Ky.1981); *Nelson v. Miller*, 227 Kan. 271, 607 P.2d 438 (1980).

c. *Abuse of Process*

Illustration 3

Purtle broke into Dominic's house with felonious intent. Dominic caught him and turned him over to the police, having probable cause to believe he was guilty, which in fact he was. While Purtle was in jail, Dominic visited him. Dominic said "I will drop charges if you will work for one year in my guano factory at minimum wage." Dominic is guilty of an abuse of process.

Illustration 4

Cline, a patient of Dr. Tellman, suffered injury in the course of surgery. Cline consulted a lawyer, Dalmar, who brought suit against Tellman. Dalmar concluded that Dr. Puccinni had nothing to do with the injury suffered by Cline, but that, if sued, Puccinni would testify against Tellman in order to protect himself. For this reason, Dalmar made Puccinni a defendant as well. The jury in the malpractice case brought in a verdict for Puccinni. Dalmar is not guilty of an abuse of process.

Elements of abuse of process. Abuse of process involves misuse of legal process for an ulterior or improper purpose. The defendant may be held liable even if he rightly invoked the process and even if the person against whom it is invoked is in fact guilty of a crime as charged or liable civilly. The reason for this is that the gist of the tort is misuse of the legal system for some personal end. Thus Illustration 3 reflects a typical case in which legal process is properly issued, but the instigator attempts to use it for extortionate purposes. The instigator is thus liable for abuse of process. However, courts have often said that some act, threat or demand must be made *after* process has issued in order to support recovery. Thus the tort is not made out in Illustration 4, since the lawyer there made no demand for favorable testimony from Dr. Puccinni after process was issued. Perhaps not all courts would require this, but a number have done so. Some courts have added a requirement akin to the special injury rule in malicious civil prosecution cases, to the effect that there must be an interference with the plaintiff's person or property. See *Hertz Corp. v. Paloni*, 95 N.M. 212, 619 P.2d 1256 (1980).

Physician counterattack cases and lawyer liability. The physician counterattack cases have not fared well on an abuse of process theory. Sometimes relief has been denied because the lawyer has not threatened the doctor or made any demand after process has issued, as in Illustration 4. See *Drago v. Buonagurio*, 61 A.D.2d 282, 402 N.Y.S.2d 250 (1978) affirmed as to this point 46 N.Y.2d 778, 413 N.Y.S.2d 910, 386 N.E.2d 821 (1978). See generally, Birnbaum, *Physicians Counterattack: Liability of Lawyers for Instituting Unjustified Medical Malpractice Actions*, 45 FORDHAM L. REV. 1003 (1977). However, in *Bull v. McCuskey*, 96 Nev. 706, 615 P.2d 957 (1980) the court found an abuse of process when a lawyer accepted a medical malpractice client, never investigated, never sought a consultation with a medical witness, offered to settle for $750 and presented his case in court without medical witnesses.

In *Friedman*, the Michigan Court emphasized the need to protect the lawyer's adversary role and the need to avoid any chill on access to courts. Do these policies apply where the lawyer uses legal process for some collateral leverage?

Settlement. Does the abuse of process claim chill the prospects of settling a lawsuit? In the criminal case it is arguable that no one should make any kind of bargain whatever with one charged with crime. But consider civil cases. A brings an action against B, attaching B's car. While the car is attached, so that B has no means of transport, A offers to settle all claims between the parties, including some that have no bearing on the attached car. He offers to release the car if settlement is accepted. Does this offer run a risk that B will sue for abuse of process?

SLAPP suits. In recent years some environmentally concerned citizens have argued that some developers, whose projects might be opposed by environmentalists and others, have used lawsuits to discourage their opponents. These suits are said to be Stragetic Lawsuits Against Public Participation (SLAPP suits). The developers do not intend to win, according to this view, only to discourage citizens from taking appropriate part in the process of legislation, zoning, or administrative action involved when large developments are proposed. The SLAPP legislation is intended to immunize public participants from suits that might otherwise be brought for, say, interference with economic opportunity, defamation, or trade libel. The statute may, for instance, require the developer plaintiff to prove before trial or discovery that he will probably win. In effect, it represents a kind of defensive use of the abuse of process idea, but it may have the effect of excluding legitimate claims where the developer-plaintiff's suit is dismissed without opportunity for discovery or a chance to show in court that the citizen-opponents acted wrongly. See *Dixon v. Superior Court (Scientific Resource Surveys, Inc.)*, 30 Cal.App.4th 733, 36 Cal.Rptr.2d 687 (1994); *Briggs v. Eden Council for Hope and Opportunity*, 19 Cal.4th 1106, 81 Cal.Rptr.2d 471, 969 P.2d 564 (1999) (describing requirements). In *Opinion of the Justices (SLAPP Suit Procedure)*, 138 N.H. 445, 641 A.2d 1012 (1994), the New Hampshire Court concluded that a proposed statute was unconstitutional as defeating a jury trial right.

§ 3. PRIVACY

For many years, courts recognized certain rights that might today be labeled rights of privacy but which were originally protected under some other name. And there are still cases today in which interests in privacy are protected under other theories. For instance, if someone enters your apartment without permission, the law will protect your rights of privacy by imposing liability under a trespass theory. If someone publishes your private papers, the law may offer redress under a theory of copyright or conversion. Recognizing this, "two young Boston lawyers, Samuel Warren and Louis Brandeis" argued that the law court recognizes a separate tort for any invasion of privacy. In part they were offended by gossip columnists. But they also saw law as a source of protection for the core of human dignity and they wanted a law of privacy to support the individual's self-development and self-conception by guaranteeing privacy. Long before the term "self-image" came into popular use, they wanted to protect the individual's "estimate of himself." Warren and Brandeis, *The Right to Privacy*, 4 HARV. L. REV. 193

(1890). Gradually the courts accepted the idea and today privacy claims are recognized in some form everywhere.

A wide variety of claims have been brought as privacy claims, although some of them involve privacy only in the most attenuated sense. For instance, non-physical sexual harassment, obnoxious and harassing debt collection methods, even stalking and threats have been characterized as privacy claims. E.g., *Rumbauskas v. Cantor,* 138 N.J. 173, 649 A.2d 853 (1994). Prosser, attempting to make sense out of the mass of cases, came up with the proposition that modern cases really involved four distinct torts, all using the name "privacy." William Prosser, *Privacy,* 48 CAL. L. REV. 383 (1960). Perhaps not all "privacy" cases fit comfortably within these categories, but they remain as the chief modes of privacy analysis. They are:

1. *Intrusive invasions.* Short of trespass, one might still intrude in unpermitted ways on solitude, as by using electronic listening devices.

2. *Commercial appropriation.* One might publish the plaintiff's name, face or figure in a commercial advertisement without the plaintiff's permission. This might not libel the plaintiff, but the plaintiff should still have control over how his or her face or name is used for commercial purposes.

3. *False light.* The plaintiff might be presented in a false light, again without libel. For example, it might be reported that the plaintiff had emotions which were perfectly commendable, but which the plaintiff did not feel or did not wish revealed; or associated with a political cause that was perfectly uplifting but which the plaintiff did not support.

4. *Public revelation of private facts.* The defendant might publish true statements about the plaintiff on matters utterly private. This would not be libelous even if the facts were derogatory since truth could be shown; but it might still be an invasion of privacy.

The intrusive invasion does not necessarily involve publication to third persons, and accordingly it is reserved for consideration elsewhere. The commercial appropriation does involve publication and at least in some sense it may be harmful to personal dignity. The emphasis has been on commercial use, however, and accordingly that category of privacy is left to be considered with certain similar commercial torts. This leaves for consideration here the false light cases and the public revelation cases. Both these involve publication to third persons and in that respect resemble cases of libel.

————

TAYLOR v. K.T.V.B., INC., 96 Idaho 202, 525 P.2d 984 (1974). Taylor threatened his housekeeper's sister with a shotgun. When an officer was dispatched to Taylor's house, Taylor threatened him. Reinforcements were called; the television station heard the call and a cameraman filmed Taylor's arrest as Taylor was brought outside his house. The film showed Taylor in the nude. His "buttocks and genitals were visible to television viewers for a time period of approximately eight-to nine-tenths of one second." Taylor later explained he had been resting in the nude. He had not troubled to dress when he threatened the housekeeper's sister or the police officer. He was still nude when the sheriff ordered him out of the house. *Held*, liability may be imposed for disclosure of embarrassing private facts if there is "malice" in the *Times-Sullivan* sense, that is, if there is purpose to embarrass or if there is reckless disregard whether the disclosure will embarrass.

CAPE PUBLICATIONS, INC. v. BRIDGES

District Court of Appeal of Florida, Fifth District, 1982.
423 So.2d 426, review denied 431 So.2d 988 (Fla.1983).

DAUKSCH, JUDGE.

Appellee Bridges brought suit against appellants on the theories of invasion of privacy, intentional infliction of emotional distress, and trespass, alleging that appellant's conduct in publishing a photograph of appellee was actionable. The news story reported the abduction of appellee by her estranged husband who came to her workplace and at gunpoint forced her to go with him to their former apartment. The police were alerted and after surrounding the apartment began efforts to free appellee. Her husband forced her to disrobe in an effort to prevent her escape. Her life was obviously in danger. This is a typical exciting emotion-packed drama to which newspeople, and others, are attracted. It is a newsworthy story. Upon hearing a gunshot, the police stormed the apartment and rushed appellee outside to safety. Appellee was clutching a dish towel to her body in order to conceal her nudity as she was escorted to the police car in full public view. The photograph revealed little more than could be seen had appellee been wearing a bikini and somewhat less than some bathing suits seen on the beaches. There were other more revealing photographs taken which were not published. The published photograph is more a depiction of grief, fright, emotional tension and flight than it is an appeal to other sensual appetites. The jury awarded appellee $1,000.00 in compensatory damages and $9,000.00 in punitive damages.

It is settled law in Florida that the right of privacy does not necessarily protect a person against the publication of his name or photograph in connection with the dissemination of legitimate news items or other matters of public interest. At some point the public interest in obtaining information becomes dominant over the individual's right of privacy. "It has been said that the truth may be spoken, written or printed about all matters of a private nature in which the public has a legitimate interest." Within the scope of legitimate public concern are matters customarily regarded as "news."[2]

2. Authorized publicity, customarily regarded as "news," includes publications   concerning crimes, arrests, police raids, suicides, marriages, divorces, accidents, fires,

In determining the extent of the right of privacy, the standard by which the right is measured is based upon a concept of the person of reasonable sensibility; the hypersensitive individual will not be protected.

An invasion of the right of privacy occurs not with the mere publication of a photograph, but occurs when a photograph is published where the publisher should have known that its publication would offend the sensibilities of a normal person, and whether there has been such an offense of invasion of privacy is to some extent a question of law.

Although publication of the photograph, which won industry awards, could be considered by some to be in bad taste, the law in Florida seems settled that where one becomes an actor in an occurrence of public interest, it is not an invasion of her right to privacy to publish her photograph with an account of such occurrence.

Just because the story and the photograph may be embarrassing or distressful to the plaintiff does not mean the newspaper cannot publish what is otherwise newsworthy.

Likewise, the publication of the story and photograph does not meet the test of outrageousness as required for the independent tort of intentional infliction of emotional distress.

Courts should be reluctant to interfere with a newspaper's privilege to publish news in the public interest. The trial court erred in denying appellant's Motions for Directed Verdict and Judgment Notwithstanding the Verdict, so we must reverse the judgment.

Reversed.

Notes

1. Analysis in privacy cases is notably loose. Is this case one in which the plaintiff loses because the defendant enjoys a privilege to publish? Or one in which the plaintiff has no privacy right in the first place? There is no false light, is there? What about public disclosure of private facts? If this is not such a case, what could be? Suppose plaintiff, not a public figure, becomes drunk in public. Defendant, making a documentary on alcohol abuse, films the plaintiff's public behavior. Plaintiff presents a totally disgusting spectacle. Can the plaintiff recover when the film is shown?

2. *Fault required*. Both public disclosure of private facts and false light cases involve publicity of some kind. For this reason they resemble libel cases. Do the constitutional rules apply to require fault? The *Times-Sullivan* rules were applied in an early false light privacy case, *Time, Inc. v. Hill*, 385 U.S. 374, 87 S.Ct. 534, 17 L.Ed.2d 456 (1967). the Court has later implied that the *Gertz* rules might be applied to these privacy claims where the

catastrophes of nature, narcotics related deaths, rare diseases, etc. and many other matters of genuine popular appeal. Restatement of (Second) Torts, § 652D Comment G (1977).

plaintiff was not a public figure. See *Cantrell v. Forest City Publishing Co.*, 419 U.S. 245, 95 S.Ct. 465, 42 L.Ed.2d 419 (1974). The Restatement requires knowing or reckless disregard in false light cases, but does not specifically address fault as to public disclosure of private facts. RESTATEMENT SECOND OF TORTS §§ 652D and 652E (1977).

3. *Triviality and Motives.* Are false light claims that do not amount to libel necessarily trivial? Warren and Brandeis and others have emphasized the importance of human dignity in these cases, but many others have noticed that the plaintiff's recovery necessarily gives even more publicity to the claimed private matter. What exactly is accomplished by bringing or winning a privacy claim? Should a lawyer for the plaintiff be ethically obliged to caution the plaintiff?

4. *Truth.* If *Bridges* had been brought on a libel theory, the defense would undoubtedly have argued that the news story and picture were "true." In the light of *Times-Sullivan* and *Gertz* can any publisher *ever* be held liable for publishing the truth? Those cases appeared to require both fault and untruth. Is this changed if the claim is called "privacy?"

In *Cox Broadcasting Corp. v. Cohn*, 420 U.S. 469, 95 S.Ct. 1029, 43 L.Ed.2d 328 (1975) a state statute provided that the names of rape victims were not to be published. The defendant obtained the names from public documents available at the trial and published them. The Supreme Court held the defendant could not be liable for publishing material that was generally available to the public through public documents. It declined to decide whether one could ever be held liable for publishing true statements. The Court has applied the general idea in *Cox* to somewhat variant fact situations. See *Smith v. Daily Mail Publishing Co.*, 443 U.S. 97, 99 S.Ct. 2667, 61 L.Ed.2d 399 (1979); *The Florida Star v. B.J.F.*, 491 U.S. 524, 109 S.Ct. 2603, 105 L.Ed.2d 443 (1989). Could a state constitutionally seal public records so that public business is censored?

Distinguish: A psychiatrist, who gains information about a patient in confidence, then publishes this in a book in a way that permits some people to identify the plaintiff as the person referred to. Or a newspaper interviewer, pretending friendship, gains private information from a public figure and then publishes it in a feature article. Cf. *Humphers v. First Interstate Bank of Oregon*, 298 Or. 706, 696 P.2d 527 (1985).

5. There is a sustained attack on the private-facts privacy claim by Professor Diane L. Zimmerman in *Requiem for a Heavyweight: A Farewell to Warren and Brandeis's Privacy Tort*, 68 CORNELL L. REV. 291 (1983). Would criticism of the private-fact claim apply equally to the false light claim? The Supreme Court of North Carolina has remarked that false light claims could often be pursued under the law of libel, subject to the rules of *Times-Sullivan* and *Gertz*, but that where the claim did not qualify as a good libel claim, it was "constitutionally suspect." Accordingly, the court rejected the false light privacy claim altogether. *Renwick v. News and Observer Publishing Co.*, 310 N.C. 312, 312 S.E.2d 405 (1984). Ten years later, the Texas Court did the same. *Cain v. Hearst Corporation*, 878 S.W.2d 577 (Tex.1994). Even more recently, the Minnesota Court first recognized the common law right to privacy, including intrusion upon seclusion, appropriation, and publication of private facts, but rejected the adoption of a false light publicity

tort, citing "tension between this tort and the First Amendment." *Lake v. Wal–Mart Stores, Inc.*, 582 N.W.2d 231 (Minn.1998). For an analysis of the false light claim's lack of support in current case law, see J. Clark Kelso, *False Light Privacy: A Requiem*, 32 SANTA CLARA L. REV. 783 (1992).

6. *Current issues.* Privacy values are invoked in a number of situations of current importance. Congress passed a statute to prohibit employers from using polygraph machines or lie detector tests, either on employees or prospective employees. 29 U. S. C. § 2001. Would this be justified if the tests were reliable?

Privacy values have likewise been invoked in employment drug testing. The testing usually involves urinalysis and sometimes the employee must be observed as he produces the specimen. This is intrusive enough. What about consent and the employer's interests?

A third current area for important privacy issues concerns AIDS victims. Should a physician engaged in surgery be expected to advise the patient that he suffers from AIDS? *Estate of Behringer v. Medical Center at Princeton*, 249 N.J.Super. 597, 592 A.2d 1251 (1991) (hospital could be liable for public dissemination of the facts, but could require disclosure to an actual patient).

REFERENCE: DOBBS ON TORTS §§ 424–28 (2000).

§ 4.   INTERFERENCE WITH FAMILY RELATIONSHIPS

The Torts

In an early period of the common law, the master could have a real interest in his servant's health. If the servant were injured, the master might be obliged to continue support of the servant, but without getting the work he expected in return. It is not surprising, then, that the common law gave the master a tort action against one who beat and injured the servant. It later came to be thought that the husband stood in a similar relationship to his wife. Consequently, anyone who tortiously injured the wife was subject to tort liability to the husband, and it is true even today that either spouse may have a consortium claim for the injury to the other.

The earlier lines of cases were expanded to permit three other recoveries by the husband, and then later by the wife:

1. *Abduction.* Defendant carried one spouse away from the other, or "harbored" a spouse who wished to escape the marital bonds.

2. *Criminal conversation.* Defendant had sexual relations ("conversation") with the plaintiff's spouse. Even if this did not disrupt the marriage or cause other harm, it was regarded as a dishonor to the non-participating spouse. Consent of the participating spouse was no defense.

3. *Alienation of affections.* The defendant secured the affections of the plaintiff's spouse, or at least alienated those affections from the plaintiff. This might or might not be accompanied by sexual attentions; sometimes friends or relations simply persuaded one spouse to leave the other.

All of these torts required some affirmative action by the defendant, and the defendant's act must have caused harm, though not necessarily financial harm. Negligently alienating affections would not be ground for liability, but the only fault required was an intent to interfere in the prohibited way. For example, this meant that, given an intent to persuade the wife to leave her husband, the defendant would be liable if he succeeded, unless he could affirmatively establish a privilege as a defense. The main privilege was a good faith effort by a relative or disinterested party to persuade the wife for her own good. In some cases this privilege also protected religious advisors. Love and affection were not entitled to any similar protection, however, and the woman who persuaded a man to leave his wife, or the man who induced a woman to leave her husband, would be liable for alienation, or criminal conversation, or both.

If parents sued for interference with their relationships with their children, the rights were substantially constricted. One would be liable for enticement of a child, or abduction, or seduction of a minor, but there is almost no authority for permitting a claim for alienating the child's affections. Similarly, children have been given almost no rights when an outsider interferes with parental relationships. If one parent is induced to leave the home and run off with a "home-wrecker," the children may have claims in only a couple of states.

Abolition of the Actions

Since the 1930s, about half the states have abolished or severely limited the action for alienation of affections or that for criminal conversation or both. Sometimes this is accompanied by abolishing the action for breach of a promise to marry as well. Abolition has been accompanied in many instances through legislation, but in some cases courts themselves have abolished the action, and some jurisdictions have never recognized it. Some of the reasons have been that the action leads to blackmail, that interference without violence or other tortious activity probably has little effect on a healthy family relationship, and that recovery in these actions does not accomplish any real good. In addition, it has been suggested that the criminal conversation and alienation of affections actions imply that one spouse has ownership rights in another, and that they interfere with personal autonomy. See Dan Dobbs, *Tortious Interference with Contractual Relationships,* 34 ARK. L. REV. 335, 358–59 (1980).

What about the argument that free speech permits an outsider to persuade and otherwise establish relationships with a family member, as long as that member does not object and as long as there is no fraud, duress, defamation, violence or other tort? Suppose defendant says, "I love you; leave your wife and come live with me." Given *Times-Sullivan* and *Gertz*, are the states free to make this a tort?

Even after abolition of the alienation of affections tort, some kind of tort claims may still be viable in extreme cases, as where the marriage counselor takes advantage of the therapeutic relationship to alienate the affections of one spouse. One distressing kind of case arises when a divorced parent prevents the non-custodial parent from seeing the child, sometimes with the aid of grandparents or others. Is this a case that should be resolved by tort liability? See *Weirich v. Weirich*, 833 S.W.2d 942 (Tex.1992); *Stone v. Wall*, 734 So.2d 1038 (Fla.1999). What if a childless couple took in a run-away teenager and provided for him. Would the couple be liable to the parents? Cf. *Mackintosh v. Carter*, 451 N.W.2d 285 (S.D.1990).

REFERENCE: DOBBS ON TORTS §§ 441–44 (2000).

Chapter 30

COMMUNICATION OF COMMER-CIALLY HARMFUL IMPRES-SIONS TO OTHERS

In Chapter 29, all of the torts involved communication of facts or impressions about the plaintiff to some other person or persons. In each of these cases, the harm caused might have been partly economic. One who is libeled or maliciously prosecuted, for example, might lose a job. However, the torts involved in that chapter have also involved intensely personal elements, mainly reputation and privacy. No matter how much economic harm is done in those cases, the tort cannot fail to reach a highly personal level. They are, preeminently, dignitary torts.

In the present chapter the torts involved also turn on communication to third persons, but in contrast they are preeminently commercial. Some of them at times touch highly personal or dignitary interests as well; but by and large they are important as means of gaining or preserving some commercial value. They also at times raise questions about political and social values. Since they are communicative torts, there is at least the possibility that First Amendment values will be implicated.

§ 1. INJURIOUS FALSEHOOD

Illustration 1

Dalzell, a consumer advocate, publishes a statement that Parsons' Paint contains chemicals that would rot wood where the paint is used. These statements are false in fact and Dalzell made them either knowing they were false or in reckless disregard of their falsity. As a result of these statements, Parsons has lost a number of major sales, losing net profits of $100,000. Parsons may recover for injurious falsehood.

Illustration 2

O'Dell obtained a judgment against Paton in the State of A. As O'Dell knew, the State of A had no jurisdiction over Paton and Paton had not appeared in the case. Nevertheless, O'Dell took the void judg-

934

ment to the State of B, where Paton lived, and recorded it as a judgment. By the law of State B, this gave O'Dell a judgment lien on Paton's land. Paton lost a sale of his land as a result and later had to sell it at a reduced price. O'Dell is liable for the injurious falsehood.

––––––––

Injurious falsehood is sometimes thought of as a commercial version of defamation, in which the quality of a business, or its product, or some important attribute, is "defamed." It often goes under the name of commercial disparagement, or "trade libel," or, in one fact-pattern, under the name of "slander of title." Illustration 1 typifies the commercial disparagement fact-pattern, while Illustration 2 typifies the "slander of title" fact-pattern. There is obviously poetic license in calling this "slander," as the case bears no resemblance to slander whatever.

The earlier cases did not recognize a separate tort called injurious falsehood. Instead, the cases were tried, appealed and digested under the name of libel, and indeed they will still be found in the digest under that rubric. Before around 1800 libel cases required proof of "malice," to establish a claim. About that time, however, courts began to presume malice from the fact that the plaintiff had communicated defamatory words. Thus in personal libel cases, malice effectively dropped out as an element of the case. In certain cases, however, courts retained or resurrected the malice requirement. In the later l9th century it was possible to look back at the cases and say that, roughly at least, it appeared that malice was required when the "libel" was impersonal and only disparaged a commercial interest. From this the idea gradually caught on that there were in fact two separate torts with separate elements. This history is of considerable practical importance today, if for no other reason than to warn the reader that many discussions in the cases, including some of the contemporary ones, still discuss this tort in terms of "libel."

But the injurious falsehood tort did in fact develop separate elements, the effect of which was to require a heavier burden on the plaintiff than the personal libel cases did.

Elements of the tort. The common law elements of the injurious falsehood tort were as follows:

(1) *Falsity in fact.* The statement had to be false in the sense that falsity was not presumed as in cases of libel. There may have been some understanding, however, that "opinions" could be false and liability might be properly imposed for "false" opinions.

(2) *Malice.* The common law word "malice" was repeatedly used in describing this tort, and if the defendant had no "malice" he was not liable. Malice came to mean a variety of things in this context—spite or ill-will, or improper purpose. There was a long period of confusion in which some writers suggested that there was strict liability so that neither malice nor any other form of fault was required. The orthodox

view now, however, is that some form of fault is required. As to whether "malice" adequately expresses the fault required, see the discussion of *Times-Sullivan* and *Gertz*.

(3) *Special Damages*. The plaintiff had to suffer special damages, meaning pecuniary loss. In general, this requires more than a "paper loss"—the loss must have been actually realized, or there must be quite good proof that the loss would be realized in the future. The losses in Illustrations 1 and 2 are both special in this sense. However, if in Illustration 2, Paton's land had gone down in value while the judgment was recorded, but then had gone back up in value after the judgment was cancelled, and if Paton had not lost a sale, the temporary "paper loss" on his land would not be special damages. Notice that the requirement of special damages is contrary to the presumed damages at common law.

Privilege. The common law rules recognized that in some cases the defendant might be privileged to publish disparaging statements. For instance, statements made in judicial proceedings, if generally relevant, are absolutely privileged whether the tort is libel or injurious falsehood. And it was said that certain "comparative statements," usually opinion statements, were privileged, so that the consumer could be told that A's product is better than B's. The exact role of privilege today is perhaps unclear in the light of the developing law based on *Times-Sullivan* and *Gertz*.

Times-Sullivan and Gertz. Injurious falsehood has an obvious kinship with defamation. Although the interests involved in injurious falsehood cases are primarily commercial, that fact does not eliminate the relevance of free speech under the First Amendment. Do *Times-Sullivan* and *Gertz* apply to injurious falsehood claims? Should they? See Paul T. Hayden, *A Goodly Apple Rotten at the Heart: Commercial Disparagement in Comparative Advertising as Common–Law Tortious Unfair Competition,* 67 Iowa L. Rev. 76 (1990).

In some of the cases the corporate plaintiff in injurious falsehood claims has been a public figure because it has actively presented its product to the public and sought public approval of it. Where that is the case, *Times-Sullivan* law has been applied. A leading case is *Bose Corp. v. Consumers Union of the United States, Inc.* 692 F.2d 189 (1st Cir. 1982). This was affirmed in the Supreme Court. 466 U.S. 485, 104 S.Ct. 1949, 80 L.Ed.2d 502 (1984). The Court assumed but did not decide that the *Times-Sullivan* rule would apply to commercial disparagement cases, and on that assumption held that malice was not shown in a *Consumer Reports* review of a loudspeaker. If *Times-Sullivan* does apply to these cases, does that logically mean that *Gertz* will also apply in any case in which the plaintiff is not a public figure?

Does it even matter? The common law rules to a large extent anticipated the current constitutional rulings. They were more demanding than *Gertz* in requiring special damages, not merely "actual" damages. And they required falsity in fact, as both *Times-Sullivan* and *Gertz* appear to require. Two things, however, may be different. First, the common law may have permitted injurious falsehood actions for mere opinion. This could run afoul of the principle that there is no such thing as a false idea, see *Gertz*, and also afoul of the idea that statements must be "false" to be actionable. Second, the common law may have permitted liability on the basis of "malice" in the sense of spite or ill-will rather than on the basis of knowing, reckless or negligent falsehood. This would run afoul of either *Times-Sullivan* or *Gertz*, whichever applied.

REFERENCE: DOBBS ON TORTS § 407 (2000).

§ 2. TRADEMARK INFRINGEMENT

Illustration 1

Plangent, Inc. produces chocolate candies marketed as ALZAK CHOCOLATES. Delbert, Inc., which has long marketed a number of food items, then begins marketing cookies under the name of ALZAK COOKIES. Both manufacturers use red, green and yellow stripes on their packages. There is a likelihood that customers will believe Plangent manufactures both items. Delbert is infringing Plangent's mark and is subject to an injunction forbidding continued infringement; it is also liable for restitution of profits it made from use of the mark or for any actual damages suffered by Plangent.

Illustration 2

Powell's Bakery, in the city of Fort Smith, manufactures cookies known as "Fort Smith Cookies." A few days after these go on sale, Dingle's Chocolate Company begins selling chocolate under the name "Fort Smith Chocolate." Powell does not have a claim for trademark infringement in the absence of additional proof.

––––––––

A trademark or service mark permits a business to identify its product or service respectively; a trade name permits a business to identify itself. All this is enormously important in modern business practice, since customers tend to recognize favored trademarks and to buy accordingly. For this reason a business may be quite zealous in protecting its trademarks from use by others. When there is a risk that one trademark looks or sounds like another, trademark protection is also a protection for the consumer, who might otherwise be misled. This, in general, is what the law seeks to avoid by protecting trademarks. Since the same policies apply to a large extent whether the identifying mark is a trademark, a service mark or a trade name, the single term trademark will be used here for simplicity.

Federal and state law. The law of trademark is partly the common law of the states. It may be referred to as a form of unfair competition in that setting. A federal statute permits registration of trademarks in federal trademark registers. This is the Lanham Act, 15 U.S.C.A. §§ 1051 et seq. When a registered trademark is the subject of litigation, this permits federal jurisdiction over the case. Registration is prima facie evidence of the mark's ownership. The result of these and other statutory provisions is that the federal law adds jurisdictional and procedural rules to the common law trademark. Through the prima facie rule, it also adds substantive protection as well. On the other hand, the federal law has not preempted the field and it is intended to add to the common law trademark ideas rather than to convert trademark into a wholly federal concept. The result is that in cases where the mark is federally registered, the cases reflect both historic common law ideas about what marks are protectible, and federal statutory provisions. In 1988 Congress amended the trademark statutes to provide federal protection for unregistered trademarks by expanding the statute's rules about false advertising. A more recent amendment covers "cyberpiracy" of domain names. See 15 U.S.C.A. § 1125.

Acquiring trademark rights. Trademark rights are normally acquired by using the mark to identify a product, service, or business. Subject to a limited exception, registration of the mark takes place after the mark is actually used, not before.

What counts as a trademark. Any kind of identifying mark, letter, word, or symbol, including special combinations of color or design may work as a mark if it serves to identify the product, service or business. Are there any businesses who identify themselves by the special shape or color of their buildings or decorations? Could a uniform worn by employees be a protected mark? Cf. *Wal-Mart Stores, Inc. v. Samara Bros., Inc.*, 529 U.S. 205, 120 S.Ct. 1339, 146 L.Ed.2d 182 (2000) (clothing designs themselves not protectible as unregistered trademark unless the primary significance of the designs in the minds of the public is to identify the source of the product); *Qualitex Co. v. Jacobson Products Co., Inc.*, 514 U.S. 159, 115 S.Ct. 1300, 131 L.Ed.2d 248 (1995) (even a single color could count as a trademark provided it has come to identify the source of the product to consumers).

Likelihood of confusion; palming off. The earlier common law cases involved "palming off," an intentional tort in which a seller, being asked by a customer for X product is given Y product instead. A more sophisticated version of this behavior does not actually substitute one product for another, but packages the product to resemble another, so that the customer is misled. The more sophisticated versions of palming off thus became trademark infringements. While palming off was intentional, intent is not required to establish liability for trademark infringement. The test of trademark infringement is whether customers are likely to be confused. In Illustration 1, it is clear that customers will not mistake cookies for chocolate candy, but this is not the point. Rather, it is enough if the customer is confused about the "source," that is, the manufacturer, of the item. The customer may believe that ALZAK cookies are produced by the (trusted) manufacturer of ALZAK chocolates. To some extent cookies and chocolates are interchangeable—many people might satisfy a craving for sweets by choosing either product. If the customer is confused about the source, the result may be a choice to buy the cookies instead of the chocolates and if so, the chocolate manufacturer will have lost a sale due to the trademark infringement.

Fanciful and arbitrary marks contrasted with others. The greatest potential for confusion arises when the plaintiff owns an utterly fanciful or arbitrary mark. ALZAK is such a mark. It has no public use until adopted by the seller, and no meaning except what the seller gives it. It does not describe chocolates or anything else. It does not even carry the hint or suggestion of chocolate that a name like "Chocolate" might carry. This kind of mark is often referred to as a strong mark and is most readily protected against any interference. At the other extreme are marks that are merely descriptive. These might describe the product, or might attribute high quality to it, as with "BEST FLOUR" or "BLUE RIBBON BEAN CURD." Although both geographical names and personal names might be a part of a protected mark, these, too, may in effect be merely descriptive.

Secondary meaning. The plaintiff's ownership of an arbitrary mark is readily recognized and quickly protected against infringement. But the plaintiff who has a descriptive mark may not have any rights in it at all. A descriptive mark is protected if, but only if, it has acquired secondary meaning in the minds of the consuming public. In Illustration 2, "Fort Smith" is geographically descriptive and any seller in that area would be within its rights in calling its product "Fort Smith" products. But here as with other descriptive marks, the public might come to identify the term with one particular producer, manufacturer or seller over a period of time. If that happens, that manufacturer will have a valid trademark even if it is descriptive. But the mark may be "weak" and entitled only to limited protection. "BLUE RIBBON" or "GOLD MEDAL" may have acquired a secondary meaning for beer and flour respectively, and perhaps no competing manufacturer of beer or similar products could use "Blue Ribbon." But the protection might not extend to a manufacturer of jams and jellies who also called its products "BLUE RIBBON" or "GOLD MEDAL."

Generic names. No one can acquire a right in the general or "generic" name for a thing. The seller of lumber could not register LUMBER as a trademark. This problem is obviously similar to the descriptive mark problem, but with a difference. If a mark is considered generic, it cannot be protected, even by acquiring secondary meaning. In many cases it is not so easy to decide which is which. What would you do with ESCALATOR? One special rule applies in these cases. Marks that once were protected because they did in fact identify the manufacturer of the product, may lose protection because the public uses the word to describe the whole class of such products. The word "THERMOS" was once a trademark, but it came to be used for all vacuum bottles and lost its protection. Something similar happened to ASPIRIN. Can you think of any products today that might be in danger?

Confusion of sponsorship; dilution. The original idea of trademark protection was that the consumer could identify the product with its source, the particular seller or manufacturer. This in turn permits the consumer to get the very product she wants—Pepsi rather than Coca-Cola or vice-versa. But suppose one party sells magazines named "Seventeen" and the other sells girdles named "Miss Seventeen." The two parties are not competitors and it is highly unlikely that anyone will buy a girdle believing it to be a magazine, or that anyone will buy a girdle because she believes it is manufactured by the publisher of *Seventeen* magazine. *First*, notice how this might be dealt with if the marks were purely descriptive, like "Blue Ribbon." *Second*, consider how it should be dealt with if the marks are purely arbitrary. There is no customer confusion as to source, but arguably customers *might* believe that *Seventeen* magazine in some way sponsored or approved the girdles by the same name. *Third*, in some cases use of the same name might create a series of associations in the consumers' minds that "dilute" the good associations with the plaintiff's product. Tiffany's—the store—would undoubtedly be unhappy to hear that there was a "TIFFANY'S CAT CHOW" on the market or a "TIFFANY'S PLASTIC STAINED GLASS." To what extent does the next case provide satisfactory answers?

DALLAS COWBOYS CHEERLEADERS, INC. v. PUSSYCAT CINEMA, LTD.

United States Court of Appeals, Second Circuit, 1979.
604 F.2d 200.

Van Graafeiland, Circuit Judge.

[The plaintiff employs a number of women who perform routines at Dallas Cowboys football games. Plaintiff licenses others to manufacture and distribute posters, calendars, T-shirts and other items depicting these cheerleaders in their uniforms. The uniforms themselves consist of white vinyl boots, white shorts, white belt with blue stars, a blue bolero blouse and a white fringed vest. Defendant owns a movie theater which was showing a "gross and revolting sex film" known as "Debbie Does Dallas." In the film, Debbie wishes to become a "Dallas Cowgirl," and she and her friends perform a number of sex acts to gain the money necessary for the trip. Debbie herself spends twelve minutes clad or partially clad in a uniform "strikingly similar" to the official version. Advertisements referred to her as an "X Dallas Cheerleader," though she had never been employed by the plaintiff. The plaintiff alleges Lanham Act trademark violation and also a violation of New York's anti-dilution statute. The trial judge granted a preliminary injunction.]

A preliminary issue raised by defendants is whether plaintiff has a valid trademark in its cheerleader uniform. Defendants argue that the uniform is a purely functional item necessary for the performance of cheerleading routines and that therefore is not capable of becoming a trademark. We do not quarrel with defendants' assertion that a purely functional item may not become a trademark. However, we do not agree that all of the characteristics of plaintiff's uniform serve only a functional purpose or that, because an item is in part incidentally functional, it is necessarily precluded from being designated as a trademark. Plaintiff does not claim a trademark in all clothing designed and fitted to allow free movement while performing cheerleading routines, but claims a trademark in the particular combination of colors and collocation of decorations that distinguish plaintiff's uniform from those of other squads. It is well established that, if the design of an item is nonfunctional and has acquired secondary meaning, the design may become a trademark even if the item itself is functional. Moreover, when a feature of the construction of the item is arbitrary, the feature may become a trademark even though it serves a useful purpose. Thus, the fact that an item serves or performs a function does not mean that it may not at the same time be capable of indicating sponsorship or origin, particularly where the decorative aspects of the item are nonfunctional. In the instant case the combination of the white boots, white shorts, blue blouse, and white star-studded vest and belt is an arbitrary design which makes the otherwise functional uniform trademarkable....

Defendants assert that the Lanham Act requires confusion as to the origin of the film, and they contend that no reasonable person would believe that the film originated with plaintiff. Appellants read the confusion requirement too narrowly. In order to be confused, a consumer need not believe that the owner of the mark actually produced the item and placed it on the market. The public's belief that the mark's owner sponsored or otherwise approved the use of the trademark satisfies the confusion requirement. In the instant case, the uniform depicted in "Debbie Does Dallas" unquestionably brings to mind the Dallas Cowboys Cheerleaders. Indeed, it is hard to believe that anyone who had seen defendants' sexually depraved film could even thereafter disassociate it from plaintiff's cheerleaders. This association results in confusion which has "a tendency to impugn [plaintiff's services] and injure plaintiff's business reputation...." In the *Coca-Cola* case the defendant had manufactured a poster showing the familiar red and white Coca–Cola design with the word "Cocaine" substituted for "Coca–Cola". As in this case, the defendant there argued that no reasonable purchaser would be confused by the poster; however the court held that a person of average intelligence could believe "that defendant's poster was just another effort ... by plaintiff to publicize its product," although in a distasteful way. In another case, a similarity between the plaintiff's and the defendant's trade slogans was held to confuse the public and "[threaten] injury to the good name of the first user." ...

Plaintiff expects to establish on trial that the public may associate it with defendants' movie and be confused into believing that plaintiff sponsored the movie, provided some of the actors, licensed defendants to use the uniform, or was in some other way connected with the production. The trademark laws are designed not only to prevent consumer confusion but also to protect "the synonymous right of a trade-mark owner to control his product's reputation." The district court did not err in holding that plaintiff had established a likelihood of confusion within the meaning of the Lanham Act sufficient to entitle it to a preliminary injunction and that plaintiff had a right to preliminary relief on its claims of unfair competition and dilution. . . .

[Affirmed.]

Notes

1. *Functional features.* Functional features—those having utility to the user or contributing to the economy of manufacture—cannot be given trademark protection as such. Functional features might obtain the protection of patent law, but patent law requires a real invention and in any event provides the patent for only a few years, after which the patented invention is in the public domain. See *Bonito Boats, Inc. v. Thunder Craft Boats, Inc.*, 489 U.S. 141, 109 S.Ct. 971, 103 L.Ed.2d 118 (1989).

Did *Dallas Cowboys Cheerleaders* violate this rule, since clothing is functional? What if a functional feature acquired a secondary meaning? Suppose a manufacturer of a backpacker's stove includes a windscreen with the stove. The buying public comes to associate windscreens with the particular stove. Are other manufacturers forever barred from including windscreens? Would this tend to create monopolies or serious anticompetitive aspects in business?

2. *Dilution.* Is confusion of sponsorship just a special case—and perhaps a weak one—of dilution? A number of states have passed anti-dilution statutes to add to the protection trademarks had at common law. A mark might be diluted by a competing mark simply because it loses its capacity to identify a single product line. In some of the cases discussed in *Dallas Cowboys Cheerleaders,* the competing mark caused dilution in another sense—it associated the plaintiff's product with negative associations. Should dilution be actionable, either for an injunction or for damages? Are all marks alike in this respect? Consider: (a) "Kodak pianos" and "Kodak film." (b) "National Food Service," and "National Warehouses." What about a rule that treats such cases as merely cases of injurious falsehood, for which there would have to be some form of fault in the defendant?

3. *Free speech: copyright.* Could *Times-Sullivan* and *Gertz* apply to protect a publication that would otherwise amount to a trademark infringement? This issue has not been decided. There are some analogous questions in copyright law. Copyright law protects "original" works, such as writings, television shows, and sculptures. This requires a modicum of independent effort by the author, see *Feist Publications, Inc. v. Rural Tel. Service Co., Inc.*, 499 U.S. 340, 111 S.Ct. 1282, 113 L.Ed.2d 358 (1991), but not the "novelty" or "inventiveness" required by patent law for patent protection of inventions. Copyright law protects only the precise form of expression, not the ideas presented. Thus anyone would be free to summarize the ideas in these notes, which are copyrighted, but would not be free to appropriate the notes themselves or to accomplish the same thing by extensive paraphrase. These rules build into copyright law a very considerable respect for free speech. In addition, there is a vague defense to copyright infringement suits known as the "fair use" defense. This permits limited copying for limited

purposes, as where you copy part of these notes for your own study materials. On fair use, see *Harper & Row, Publishers, Inc. v. Nation Enterprises*, 471 U.S. 539, 105 S.Ct. 2218, 85 L.Ed.2d 588 (1985); *Hustler Magazine, Inc. v. Moral Majority, Inc.*, 796 F.2d 1148 (9th Cir.1986). Parody or satire is sometimes protected under fair use doctrine. See *Campbell v. Acuff–Rose Music, Inc.*, 510 U.S. 569, 114 S.Ct. 1164, 127 L.Ed.2d 500 (1994) (a rap music group called 2 Live Crew performed a parody of a copyrighted "rock ballad" called "Pretty Woman;" this was not automatically excluded from the fair use defense merely because it was commercial).

4. *Free speech: trademark cases.* To repeat, is there any free speech interest in infringing a trademark, so that some kind of fault would be required? Might even intentional infringement be protected in some cases? Suppose a group of nutritionists tries to persuade members of Congress that the cold cereal industry should be regulated by federal law. To do this, the group publishes: (1) a booklet reproducing cereal ads in an effort to show that these ads are misleading consumers about the nutritional content of cereals, and (2) posters on which pictures of actual cereal boxes are reproduced, with a stamp across them saying "Dangerous to Your Health." Suppose in each case the reproductions include reproductions of trademarks or trade names. Is there a free speech issue?

> REFERENCE: RESTATEMENT THIRD OF TORTS, UNFAIR COMPETITION, §§ 9–17 (1995); J. THOMAS MCCARTHY, TRADEMARKS AND UNFAIR COMPETITION (4th Ed. 1998); DOBBS ON TORTS §§ 457–58 (2000).

§ 3. MISAPPROPRIATION OF COMMERCIAL VALUE

CARSON v. HERE'S JOHNNY PORTABLE TOILETS, INC., 698 F.2d 831 (6th Cir.1983). Plaintiff John W. Carson is a famous entertainer, whose "Tonight Show" on television is introduced with the phrase "Here's Johnny." The phrase is generally associated with Carson and the show by a substantial segment of the television viewing public. Carson has authorized use of the phrase by others, who have used it to identify restaurants, men's clothing and men's toiletries. The defendant is a corporation which rents and sells portable toilets under the name "Here's Johnny." The founder was aware of the television significance of the phrase when he adopted it for the toilets. Carson sued. The trial court dismissed the claim. *Held,* vacated and remanded for further proceedings. (1) The "Here's Johnny" mark is a relatively "weak" mark, so that its use on other goods should not be entirely foreclosed, and there is insufficient evidence to establish a likelihood of confusion. Consequently the trademark claim fails. (2) Prosser delineated four types of the right of privacy, including intrusion upon solitude, public disclosure of embarrassing private facts, publicity that places one in a false light, and commercial appropriation of one's name for the defendant's advantage. The first three involve the right to be let alone, but the fourth is best referred to, not as a privacy claim, but as a right of publicity. In this case there is no violation of any real right to privacy, even though Carson may be embarrassed to be associated with the defendant's product. However, there is an invasion of the right of publicity, since the plaintiff's identity is valuable in the promotion of products and he has an interest in preventing unauthorized commercial exploitation of that identity.

Notes

1. *Privacy*. Prosser's insights in identifying the four kinds of "privacy" have been generally recognized, but, as in *Carson*, courts and writers now believe that it would be more accurate in this "commercial appropriation" version of privacy to label the right as one of "publicity." The right is well recognized and accepted, though there are problems in describing it. Publication in connection with news or feature stories has generally not been regarded as an invasion of the right of publicity.

2. *Privacy and trademark*. Does it make sense for the law to deny that there is a trademark interest but to create a new interest called "publicity" with none of the restrictions imposed on trademark claims? What about a dilution claim in *Carson*?

3. *Free speech*. Judge Cornelia Kennedy, dissenting in *Carson*, argued that "concern for the First Amendment" should lead to a denial of protection for a phrase like "Here's Johnny." She drew an analogy to copyright law: copyright law escapes condemnation under the First Amendment because its protection is limited in time and because it protects only tangible expressions, not the ideas behind those expressions. The phrase "Here's Johnny" seemed to her "more akin to an idea or concept of introducing an individual" and thus the kind of thing that copyright law could not protect; hence she thought the first amendment concern was evident.

4. *Noncommercial aspects*. Some cases have involved celebrities who, if given the protection invoked in *Carson*, would be able to sell their names, faces, or endorsements for a price. But private individuals, whose face or endorsement would sell for little or nothing, also have a protectible interest. The fact that a citizen is unknown does not permit an advertiser to use her picture to accompany its advertising. If the picture or name is used to advertise a product the plaintiff finds offensive or demeaning, there is undoubtedly a very personal interest involved and not merely a commercial one. Is there also such an interest in *Carson*? Should the court have recognized a privacy right and not a publicity right? Would there be a First Amendment difference?

INTERNATIONAL NEWS SERVICE v. ASSOCIATED PRESS, 248 U.S. 215, 39 S.Ct. 68, 63 L.Ed. 211 (1918). Associated Press (AP) and INS were competitors, each collecting news at its source and supplying accounts to subscriber or member newspapers, who then published the news in their columns. During World War I, AP was able to get news from Europe, but INS was prohibited by foreign governments from doing so. It is alleged that INS provided the news to its subscribers by copying the AP news bulletins on public view in eastern newspaper offices, or copying the AP news as printed in eastern papers. This was then sent to

INS' western subscribers, where it was still fresh news because of the time difference between the east and west coasts. AP brought this suit to enjoin the copying and republication, although the material enjoyed no copyright protection. *Held*: the injunction should be granted. The news is not copyrighted and the Copyright Act does not confer upon anyone the exclusive right to report a historic event, and news of current events may be regarded as common property. But although AP has no property interest in the news as against the general public, it has certain interests as against competitors. It has utilized its enterprise, organization, skill, labor and money to get the news and as against competitors, this gives AP a "quasi property" in it. The defendant INS, "in appropriating it and selling it as its own is endeavoring to reap where it has not sown...."

Notes

1.   The case produced a pair of distinguished dissents by Holmes and Brandeis. Holmes thought that the defendant's conduct might lead some readers to believe that the defendant gathered the news, thus denying credit to AP; and that by extension of this, some readers might think AP was falsely claiming credit for news it had stolen from INS. This misapprehension could be provided for, Holmes thought, but nothing more. Brandeis emphasized the interest of readers in getting the news and the public interest in not foreclosing channels of communication.

2.   The Court in *International News Service* referred to the tort here as "unfair competition." The term was used at one time mostly in connection with palming off cases, but the term is now used in connection with any competitive tort. The tort in *International News Service* is now commonly referred to as "misappropriation."

3.   How would you compare this tort to the "privacy" or "publicity" claim in *Carson*?

4.   Communication was involved in *International News Service*, and it is an extremely common factual element in the cases. Frequently the communication misleads as well. But is it necessary to mislead in order to establish this tort? Are there even cases in which a defendant might be liable for a "misappropriation" without communicating the misappropriated material to anyone? What if an expert on the sewing machine saw the latest fashion design for a swimsuit and concocted one at home for personal use?

5.   *Trade secrets and tortious acquisition.* In *INS* the acquisition of the AP news was not tortious; there was no trespass or conversion. Had there been, those torts would undoubtedly have sufficed to provide at least some relief. Likewise, if anyone tortiously acquires a trade secret, or does so in violation of his duty as an employee, or in violation of a confidence, he will be liable for that. These are cases in which some wrong can be identified in the means by which the information is obtained. *INS*, in imposing liability for copying and publication by means not in themselves tortious, obviously extends liability. Suppose an employee of a drug manufacturer passes along the drug's formula to a competitor, who knows where it came from. There would be liability under trade secret law. Suppose a drug manufacturer buys a competitor's drug over the counter, analyzes it, and on this basis, makes a

drug having identical chemical components. There would be no liability for violation of a trade secret, since there was no tortious means used. Would there be liability under *INS*?

SEARS, ROEBUCK & CO. v. STIFFEL CO.

Supreme Court of the United States, 1964.
376 U.S. 225, 84 S.Ct. 784, 11 L.Ed.2d 661.

MR. JUSTICE BLACK delivered the opinion of the court.

The question in this case is whether a State's unfair competition law can, consistently with the federal patent laws, impose liability for or prohibit the copying of an article which is protected by neither a federal patent nor a copyright. The respondent, Stiffel Company, secured design and mechanical patents on a "pole lamp"—a vertical tube having lamp fixtures along the outside, the tube being made so that it will stand upright between the floor and ceiling of a room. Pole lamps proved a decided commercial success, and soon after Stiffel brought them on the market Sears, Roebuck & Company put on the market a substantially identical lamp, which it sold more cheaply, Sears' retail price being about the same as Stiffel's wholesale price. Stiffel then brought this action against Sears in the United States District Court for the Northern District of Illinois, claiming in its first count that by copying its design Sears had infringed Stiffel's patents and in its second count that by selling copies of Stiffel's lamp Sears had caused confusion in the trade as to the source of the lamps and had thereby engaged in unfair competition under Illinois law. There was evidence that identifying tags were not attached to the Sears lamps although labels appeared on the cartons in which they were delivered to customers, that customers had asked Stiffel whether its lamps differed from Sears', and that in two cases customers who had bought Stiffel lamps had complained to Stiffel on learning that Sears was selling substantially identical lamps at a much lower price.

The District Court, after holding the patents invalid for want of invention, went on to find as a fact that Sears' lamp was "a substantially exact copy" of Stiffel's and that the two lamps were so much alike, both in appearance and in functional details, "that confusion between them is likely, and some confusion has already occurred." On these findings the court held Sears guilty of unfair competition, enjoined Sears "from unfairly competing with [Stiffel] by selling or attempting to sell pole lamps identical to or confusingly similar to" Stiffel's lamp, and ordered an accounting to fix profits and damages resulting from Sears' "unfair competition."

The Court of Appeals affirmed. 313 F.2d 115. That court held that, to make out a case of unfair competition under Illinois law, there was no need to show that Sears had been "palming off" its lamps as Stiffel lamps; Stiffel had only to prove that there was a "likelihood of confusion as to the source of products"—that the two articles were sufficiently identical that customers could not tell who had made a particular one.

Impressed by the "remarkable sameness of appearance" of the lamps, the Court of Appeals upheld the trial court's findings of likelihood of confusion and some actual confusion, findings which the appellate court construed to mean confusion "as to the source of the lamps." The Court of Appeals thought this enough under Illinois law to sustain the trial court's holding of unfair competition, and thus held Sears liable under Illinois law for doing no more than copying and marketing an unpatented article. We granted certiorari to consider whether this use of a State's law of unfair competition is compatible with the federal patent law....

The grant of a patent is the grant of a statutory monopoly;.... Patents ... are meant to encourage invention by rewarding the inventor with the right, limited to a term of years fixed by the patent, to exclude others from the use of his invention. During that period of time no one may make, use, or sell the patented product without the patentee's authority. 35 U.S.C. § 271. But in rewarding useful invention, the "rights and welfare of the community must be fairly dealt with and effectually guarded." To that end the prerequisites to obtaining a patent are strictly observed, and when the patent has issued the limitations on its exercise are equally strictly enforced. To begin with, a genuine "invention" or "discovery" must be demonstrated "lest in the constant demand for new appliances the heavy hand of tribute be laid on each slight technological advance in an art." Once the patent issues, it is strictly construed.... Finally, and especially relevant here, when the patent expires the monopoly created by it expires, too, and the right to make the article—including the right to make it in precisely the shape it carried when patented—passes to the public.

Thus the patent system is one in which uniform federal standards are carefully used to promote invention while at the same time preserving free competition. Obviously a State could not, consistently with the Supremacy Clause of the Constitution, extend the life of a patent beyond its expiration date or give a patent on an article which lacked the level of invention required for federal patents. To do either would run counter to the policy of Congress of granting patents only to true inventions, and then only for a limited time. Just as a State cannot encroach upon the federal patent laws directly, it cannot, under some other law, such as that forbidding unfair competition, give protection of a kind that clashes with the objectives of the federal patent laws.

In the present case the "pole lamp" sold by Stiffel has been held not to be entitled to the protection of either a mechanical or a design patent. An unpatentable article, like an article on which the patent has expired, is in the public domain and may be made and sold by whoever chooses to do so. What Sears did was to copy Stiffel's design and sell lamps almost identical to those sold by Stiffel. This it had every right to do under the federal patent laws. That Stiffel originated the pole lamp and made it popular is immaterial. "Sharing in the goodwill of an article unprotected by patent or trade-mark is the exercise of a right possessed by all—and in the free exercise of which the consuming public is deeply interested." To allow a State by use of its law of unfair competition to prevent the copying of an article which represents too slight an advance to be patented would be to permit the State to block off from the public something which federal law has said belongs to the public. The result would be that while federal law grants only 14 or 17 years' protection to genuine inventions, see 35 U.S.C. §§ 154, 173, States could allow perpetual protection to articles too lacking in novelty to merit any patent at all under federal constitutional standards. This would be too great an encroachment on the federal patent system to be tolerated.

Sears has been held liable here for unfair competition because of a finding of likelihood of confusion based only on the fact that Sears' lamp was copied from Stiffel's unpatented lamp and that consequently the two looked exactly alike. Of course there could be "confusion" as to who had manufactured these nearly identical articles. But mere inability of the public to tell two identical articles apart is not enough to support an injunction against copying or an award of damages for copying that which the federal patent laws permit to be copied. Doubtless a State may, in appropriate circumstances, require that goods, whether patented or unpatented, be labeled or that other precautionary steps be taken to prevent customers from being misled as to the source, just as it may protect businesses in the use of their trademarks, labels, or distinctive dress in the packaging of goods so as to prevent others, by imitating such markings, from misleading purchasers as to the source of the goods. But because of the federal patent laws a State may not, when the article is unpatented and uncopyrighted, prohibit the copying of the article itself or award damages for such copying. The judgment below did both and in so doing gave Stiffel the equivalent of a patent monopoly on its unpatented lamp. That was error, and Sears is entitled to a judgment in its favor.

Reversed.

Notes

1. *Bonito Boats*. Bonito developed a new kind of boat hull. Fiberglass allegedly copied the hull exactly, perhaps by making a direct mold. A state statute prohibited direct molding and selling the copied hulls. In *Bonito Boats, Inc. v. Thunder Craft Boats, Inc.*, 489 U.S. 141, 109 S.Ct. 971, 103 L.Ed.2d 118 (1989), the Court held that the statute was preempted by patent law. Justice O'Connor emphasized that the "bargain" set up by patent laws must be attractive to inventors, so that states must not be free to offer a better protection. Put differently, competitors must be free to compete freely with all unpatented ideas. "State law protection for techniques and designs whose disclosure has already been induced by market rewards may conflict with the very purpose of the patent laws by decreasing the range of ideas available as the building blocks of further innovation." At the same time the Court made it clear that states would be free to give trademark-like protection to "trade dress." If a product's packaging or design itself works like a trademark, identifying the maker of the product by a design that is not "functional," the design could be protected like any other trademark.

2. What is the status of *International News Service v. Associated Press*? The *INS* case was actually a diversity case, decided before *Erie*. In other words it was decided under a belief that there was some general federal law. That being so, it has never been overtly overruled and seems to twist and turn in an uncertain limbo. Perhaps the question should be: Can a state be permitted under *Sears* and *Bonito* to follow the rule announced in *INS*?

———

ZACCHINI v. SCRIPPS–HOWARD BROADCASTING CO., 433 U.S. 562, 97 S.Ct. 2849, 53 L.Ed.2d 965 (1977). Zacchini performed an act as a human cannonball. He was one of the acts shown in the Geauga County Fair in Ohio. The act consists of being shot from a cannon into a net 200 feet away. It takes 15 seconds for the entire performance. This took place in an area open to all those who had properly entered the fair grounds. There was no separate charge. Defendant filmed the entire act, against Zacchini's express wishes. The film was shown on the defendant's television news. The "entire act" was shown. Television commentary was favorable and recommended seeing the act in person. Zacchini sued. The Ohio Court concluded that, under Ohio law, the defendant was guilty of the kind of privacy invasion Prosser had identified as commercial appropriation and which is sometimes called a right of publicity. It thought, however, that recovery was barred by the First Amendment and that the publisher was "privileged" to provide an accurate report. In the Supreme Court of the United States, *held*, reversed. Ohio may apply any state law privilege, but the Constitution does not provide one here. Ohio's preference for enforcing property interest in this act does not offend the decisions in *Times-Sullivan and Gertz*. Those decisions did not deal with the appropriation of an entire act. "The Constitution no more prevents a State from requiring [a defendant] to compensate [a plaintiff] for broadcasting his act on television than it would privilege [a defendant] to film and broadcast a copyrighted dramatic work...." The policy of recognizing a property interest here is partly to compensate for efforts already made, but more significantly to provide economic incentive to do further work of interest to the public. These are indeed the policies behind the copyright and patent statutes. Thus Ohio is free to impose liability if it so chooses, and the federal Constitution does not require otherwise.

Notes

1. The Court also implied that *Gertz* fault could be found in the fact that Zacchini had expressly forbidden any pictures and that the defendant published them anyway. Is this convincing? Defendant was in a place where it had a right to be and no contractual provision in its admission to the grounds limited pictures. In any event, why not require a falsehood, which is required if you say something defamatory about someone?

2. All the discussion in *Zacchini* was about the requirements of the First Amendment. But, First Amendment aside, why don't *Sears* and *Comp-*

co protect the defendant? The policy in imposing liability is, as the Court noted, the same as in patent and copyright statutes; yet, as in *Sears* and *Compco*, this act is not protected by any valid copyright or patent. Should the result not be the same—anyone is free to copy material that is not protected by a valid copyright or patent? Or is the personal element a distinguishing feature?

3. A performer puts on a large costume as a chicken, which is a trademark owned by his employer. In this outfit he performs at local baseball games, where he becomes (inside his costume) something of a celebrity. He later leaves his employment. Can the employer continue the chicken act, imitating the personality of the previous chicken? Or should we say that ownership of the chicken suit as a trademark is in the employer and ownership of the personality traits—the "act"—the employee?

4. A growing number of cases have recognized a "property" interest in one's personality, face, figure, voice or performance characteristics. There are obvious difficulties and will continue to be. Suppose an adoring fan crafts a sculpture in the likeness of Woody Allen. Would Allen have a right to require destruction? To prohibit any mass reproduction and sale? Could a performer adopt mannerisms of other performers—a mustache, cigar, leer and rolled eyes, say? Or a shabby suit, baggy pants, bowler hat, a toothbrush mustache and peculiar gait?

5. If states exercise the freedom given them in *Zacchini* they will have recognized something like a property right in personal traits, including performances, as indeed a number of courts have done. Should this property right be transferable, say, by contract or assignment? Should it pass to heirs or legatees?

REFERENCE: RESTATEMENT THIRD OF TORTS, UNFAIR COMPETITION § 38 (1995); J. THOMAS MCCARTHY, THE RIGHTS OF PUBLICITY AND PRIVACY (1998); DOBBS ON TORTS § 460 (2000).

§ 4. INTERFERENCE WITH CONTRACT AND OTHER ECONOMIC VALUES

Illustration 1

Pergolesi entered into a contract to sell Thrip all the flour Thrip required for his bakery for the next five years, at specified prices. Dillard, knowing of this contract, persuaded Thrip to repudiate it and to buy from Dillard instead. Thrip notified Pergolesi that he was not going to perform and he began purchasing from Dillard. Pergolesi brought an action against Dillard. Dillard was not guilty of any fraud, defamation, or breach of contract. He is liable to Pergolesi for inducing breach of contract.

Illustration 2

Pergolesi had supplied all the required flour for Thompson's Donut Company for many years, but there was no contract. Thompson's was merely a regular customer. Dillard, aggressively seeking new customers, convinced Thompson's to purchase from Dillard. Thompson's switched its business to Dillard. Pergolesi sued for interfering with a business relation or "prospective advantage." Dillard is not liable.

————

Scope of the tort. Although the law has long protected against interference with property, general protection against interference with contract is relatively recent. Very old cases provided protection against interferences that were themselves tortious as where a servant, whom the master was obliged to support, was beaten and injured by the defendant. This was extended around 1600 to permit a husband, who at that time was entitled to the services of his wife, to recover if the defendant beat her, thus depriving the husband-master of her work. One line of cases took off from this to permit the husband to recover also if the wife was seduced, or enticed to leave the husband. This line developed the torts of alienation of affections and criminal conversation.

In the meantime, a severe medieval plague had left a terrible labor shortage and the Parliament had passed an extreme statute, virtually condemning laborers to slavery. Laborers were required to accept only such wages as had been customary in the past, and no other employer was permitted to hire them away. This led to common law recognition of an action by the master, not only against those who beat the servant, but against those who hired him away. This in turn was expanded to provide liability for those who induced the servant not to work at all—as in the case of labor unions promoting a strike.

By the beginning of the 20th century it was recognized that a defendant might be held for inducing breach of any contract, not merely a labor contract. And liability might be imposed also for interference in a contractual relationship that was injurious to the plaintiff even if actual breach did not occur. Finally, it became clear that the interference claim was not limited to interference with existing contracts, but that the defendant might be held for interfering with business relationships or economic prospects even where there was no contract.

Negligent interference with contract. Negligence in the interference with a contract is ordinarily not enough. As stated below, some form of intent is usually required. However, there are certain cases in which negligence will suffice. For example, suppose that A contracts with B to keep B's private road in good repair. T negligently crashes an oil truck into a tree nearby, there is an explosion and the road is heavily damaged. As a result, A must spend additional money in keeping her contract to repair. A has a claim against T. This pattern of cases is equivalent to the subrogation pattern in which A insures B's car. When T negligently damages B's car, A pays and is then "subrogated" to B's rights against T. The damages claimed are the same damages that could have been claimed by someone even if there was no contract at all. In these cases, then, to permit A's claim is merely to say that A, rather than B, is the plaintiff. Hence if negligence would warrant a claim by B, it would equally warrant substituting A as the plaintiff. One or two cases have talked of extending liability to cases that do not fit in these patterns. See *J'Aire Corp. v. Gregory*, 24 Cal.3d 799, 157 Cal.Rptr. 407, 598 P.2d 60 (1979).

Strict liability and intent. One kind of intent is ordinarily required in all these cases. The defendant must know or have reason to know of the contract or other relationship between the plaintiff and others. Once the defendant knows of the contract, however, any intended interference creates a prima facie case against him. The idea of the prima facie tort is that anyone who intends to cause harm is "prima facie" liable for it. Since intent in the sense of *Garratt v. Dailey*—a substantial certainty that harm would result—would be present in any case of interference, a very wide liability was possible. This led to the elaboration of "privileges" or defenses, much as in the case of libel suits.

Privileges. The law of contract interference, using the prima facie tort idea, put the burden on the defendant to show a privilege or to negate the "malice" presumed from his intentional interference. The exact scope of privileges has never been precisely determined, and the Restatement Second of Torts § 767 (1979) merely advises courts to consider the defendant's conduct and motive, the interests of the parties, and the social interests in protecting the defendant's actions. The implication is that a consumer advocate who interferes with a consumer's contract to purchase a refrigerator for an outrageous price, if he acts with a disinterested motive, might not be liable to the seller who is deprived of his unfair sale, and that other "good" but undescribed motives might similarly be protected.

One privilege is well defined, however. This is the privilege to compete. Any competition, if successful, will cause "harm" to competitors, and hence without a privilege, competition would be grounds for liability. But one is free to compete for business by any lawful means. When there is a known, existing contract between A and B, however, T is not privileged to interfere, even for competitive purposes. Thus the defendant is liable in Illustration 1, since there is an existing contract, but not in Illustration 2, since there is not.

ALYESKA PIPELINE SERVICE
v. AURORA AIR SERVICE

Supreme Court of Alaska, 1979.
604 P.2d 1090.

CONNOR, JUSTICE.

[Alyeska, involved in the Alaska oil pipeline, contracted with RCA to provide a communications system along the line. RCA was required to use an aircraft as part of its bargain. RCA contracted with Aurora to provide a plane, pilot, parts and services along part of the pipeline, and provided that this could be terminated at RCA's option. RCA's contract with Alyeska could, in turn, also be terminated at Alyeska's option. Services began under the RCA–Alyeska contract and Aurora began providing flight services as prescribed under the RCA–Aurora contract. However, Alyeska and Aurora had a dispute about payment under an earlier arrangement, and Alyeska then exercised its option under the RCA contract to take over the flight services itself. This resulted in RCA's termination of Aurora under the RCA–Aurora contract. Aurora then brought this action against Alyeska, alleging that Alyeska induced breach of contract by terminating RCA. The trial court denied Alyeska's motion for summary judgment, holding that although Alyeska was entitled under its contract with RCA to terminate RCA (and hence, indirectly to terminate Aurora), it would be liable if it did so in bad faith. It submitted this question to the jury which found for Aurora in the sum of $362,901.]

The unilateral right to modify the Alyeska–RCA contract, accepting the superior court's ruling that there was no ambiguity in regard to the interpretation of "work," was vested in Alyeska, but it had to be exercised in good faith. We reject Alyeska's contention that a privilege arising from a contractual right is absolute and may be exercised regardless of motive. It is a recognized principle that a party to a contract has a cause of action against a third party who intentionally procured the breach of that contract by the other party without justification or privilege. The weight of recent authority holds that even though a contract is terminable at will, a claim of unjustifiable interference can still be made, for "[t]he wrong for which the courts may give redress includes also the procurement of the termination of a contract which otherwise would have [been] continued in effect." . . .

Alternatively, Alyeska asserts that its overriding economic and safety interests constituted a sufficient privilege to require dismissal of Aurora's action as a matter of law. One is privileged to invade the contractual interest of himself, others, or the public, if the interest advanced by him is superior in social importance to the interest invaded. However, if one does not act in a good faith attempt to protect his own interest or that of another but, rather, is motivated by a desire to injure the contract party, he forfeits the immunity afforded by the privilege.

The question of justification for invading the contractual interest of another is normally one for the trier of fact, particularly when the evidence is in conflict.

In the case at bar, the central factual issue, as to which there was evidentiary conflict, was whether Alyeska was genuinely furthering its own economic and safety interests or was using them as a facade for inflicting injury upon Aurora. There was sufficient evidence upon which the jury could properly find that Alyeska was acting out of ill will towards Aurora, rather than to protect a legitimate business interest.[5] The trial judge correctly denied Alyeska's motion for summary judgment and submitted this issue to the jury. . . .

---

5. Alyeska maintains that its primary consideration in taking over the air transportation was safety. Aurora presented evidence that its safety record was far better than that of the Alyeska contracted aircraft that replaced it.

Alyeska next claims that it was error not to give its proposed Instruction No. 10, which stated:

"[P]laintiff has the burden of proving by a preponderance of the evidence that defendants' actions were malicious and committed with the sole intent of injuring plaintiff."

Alyeska argues that Aurora's evidence of the termination of its contract, intentionally procured, made out a prima facie case, that the burden of proof shifted to Alyeska to show justification, and that Alyeska satisfied that requirement by producing evidence of its contract with RCA and its primary interest in the performance of the RCA contract. It is urged that if, in spite of such evidence, the good faith of Alyeska was still a valid issue, the burden of proving Alyeska's lack of good faith should have shifted back to Aurora.

Alyeska supports this argument by reference to the commentary accompanying a recent redraft of the Restatement of Torts (Second) § 767 Comment k at 37–38, in which the drafters note that the rule on allocating the burden of proof is in an unsettled state. The drafters of the commentary leave that question open. However, in *Long v. Newby*, 488 P.2d 719, 722 (Alaska 1971), we laid down the general rule that when a prima facie case is made out by showing that a breach was intentionally procured, it is incumbent upon the defendant to show justification.

Alyeska argues that the case at bar presents a special fact pattern, that Alyeska had the right to change the Alyeska–RCA contract, and that the burden of showing further that Alyeska acted in bad faith or with malice should be part of plaintiff's case. We are not persuaded. The issue presented here was whether Alyeska really did exercise its rights in good faith or whether it acted from an ulterior motive. We think that such proof goes to the question of justification, and that it was not part of Aurora's prima facie case, which only requires a showing that a breach was intentionally procured. Nor do we think that Alyeska has submitted sufficient proof of justification to trigger another shifting of the burden of proof and to require Aurora to rebut such evidence. There may be exceptional situations in which such a treble shifting of burdens should occur, but we do not view this case as one of them. On this point there was no error.

[The court found an error in computing damages and reversed as to permit a correction. Otherwise the case was affirmed.]

Notes

1. *Damages.* Damages in *Alyeska* were calculated on the basis of economic losses to Aurora, comparing what it would have made on the contract if Alyeska had not interfered. Should there have been some kind of reduction for the fact that RCA, at a later date, might have terminated the Aurora contract on its own, for other reasons? Cf. *Dillon v. Twin State Gas & Electric Co.*, 85 N.H. 449, 163 A. 111 (1932).

Aurora could not have recovered against RCA at all, since RCA, having a privilege to terminate, was not in breach. In most interference cases, the contract-promissor, however, has itself breached the contract. The plaintiff may recover either on contract or in tort. Should the damages be the same? There are cases permitting recovery in the tort claim that would not be permitted in the contract claim—punitive damages and mental distress damages, for example. See, e.g., *Mooney v. Johnson Cattle Co., Inc.*, 291 Or. 709, 634 P.2d 1333 (1981) (Linde, J.). Most courts award damages using tort principles; that is, plaintiffs can usually recover damages, such as lost profits, on a theory that such damages were proximately caused by the contract breach, even if not within the contemplation of the parties as contract law would require.

2. *Motive.* The interference torts are among the very few that turn on motive for an intentional act rather than upon an intent to act in a described way. Is this desirable?

3. *Mixed motives.* What should the jury be told to do if they found that Alyeska had mixed motives—one of which was to provide more safety and one of which was to retaliate against Aurora? Dean Prosser proposed a "predominant motive" test. See W. PROSSER, TORTS § 129 (4th ed. 1971). If Alyeska had both motives, and the safety motive was strong enough standing alone to induce its termination, should it be liable merely because it was even more motivated by malice? See *Mt. Healthy City School District Board of Education v. Doyle*, 429 U.S. 274, 97 S.Ct. 568, 50 L.Ed.2d 471 (1977). Notice: Alyeska's conduct, by itself, was perfectly legal and appropriate; if safety was a reasonable concern, Alyeska's action was also socially desirable. See Harvey Perlman, *Interference with Contract and Other Economic Expectancies: A Clash of Tort and Contract Doctrine*, 49 U. CHI. L. REV. 61 (1982) and Dan Dobbs, *Tortious Interference with Contractual Relationships*, 34 ARK. L. REV. 335 (1980).

4. *Burden of proof.* The prima facie tort idea first recognized harmful intent as itself the basis for the claim, then permitted the defendant to offer unspecified justifications. The burden to show good faith or other justification was thus left upon the defendant, as in *Alyeska.* The Second Restatement, in comments to sections 766 and 767, reformulated the rule to say that a defendant is subject to liability for a knowing or purposeful interference only when the defendant's action is "improper," either as to means or as to purpose. This sounds as if the burden may have been placed upon the plaintiff to show some impropriety. While courts have split on who has the burden, a number of recent cases require the plaintiff to prove that the defendant's interference was wrongful. See, e.g., *Mason v. Wal–Mart Stores, Inc.*, 333 Ark. 3, 969 S.W.2d 160 (1998); *Della Penna v. Toyota Motor Sales, U.S.A., Inc.*, 11 Cal.4th 376, 45 Cal.Rptr.2d 436, 902 P.2d 740 (1995).

5. What if another air service company, competing with Aurora, had approached RCA and persuaded RCA to exercise its contractual option to terminate Aurora in the hope of getting RCA's business for itself? If there were no improper means, such as bribery, false statements, or economic pressure, would the competitor be liable? One narrow issue in this kind of case is whether an at-will contract, terminable at RCA's option, should be

treated as a contract and governed by Illustration 1, or as a mere prospect, and governed by Illustration 2. The latter is the rule.

A broader issue, however, is whether the First Amendment, which is invoked under *Times-Sullivan* and *Gertz* to protect even some false statements, equally permits the use of persuasion that does not involve falsity or illegal means. Under *Zacchini*, a plaintiff may own a property interest in his performance as a cannonball or a chicken to such an extent that even truthful publications cannot be made of this performance. Can one own a property interest in a contract, or even in business relationships or prospects? If so, will that exclude the First Amendment from these claims?

CARUSO v. LOCAL UNION NUMBER 690, INTERNATIONAL BROTHERHOOD OF TEAMSTERS

Supreme Court of Washington, 1983.
100 Wn.2d 343, 670 P.2d 240.

DIMMICK, JUSTICE. . . .

Caruso was the sole proprietor of "Linoleum & Carpet City" in Spokane, Washington. He also owned a parking lot approximately a quarter of a mile from his business, where he rented spaces on a monthly basis to members of the general public. Periodically, delivery trucks blocked access to the lot.

On October 26, 1973, Caruso found a beer truck and another smaller van blocking the entrance to his parking lot. After unsuccessfully trying to locate the drivers, respondent, noticing the beer truck was unlocked and the keys were in the ignition, removed the keys, secured the truck, and returned to his place of business. He telephoned the owner, whose name and address were on the side of the truck, and told him to pick up the keys and remove the truck.

Caruso soon received a belligerent telephone call from Mr. Contos, the driver of the beer truck. Caruso then called a tow truck to have both vehicles removed and proceeded back to the lot. Mr. Contos and the driver of the van were at the lot. The driver of the van settled his share of the tow truck costs with the tow truck driver, but the representative of the beer truck's owner and Contos refused to pay. Contos proceeded to curse Caruso and threaten him. He also told Caruso that he would report him to the teamsters union and the union would "break" him. The tow truck driver refused to tow the beer truck until the police arrived. Finally, at the direction of the police, the truck was towed into an adjacent alley.

On November 9, 1973, the following article was published in the Washington Teamster, a weekly paper mailed primarily to union members, active and retired. It was also distributed to several universities and libraries.

Don't [P]atronize Carpet City in Spokane

This is to notify all members of Teamsters Union, Local 690 and all other Teamsters and Laboring people in the State of Washington that when traveling to and from the Expo City—"please do not patronize *Carpet City Carpet & Linoleum Shop* at West 518 Main Avenue"—Spokane, Washington," [sic] (Expo City). The reasons for this request are: This Company is continuously harassing the Teamsters and other laboring people who may at some time use the parking facility at this place of business to make a delivery because of the congested traffic problems in Expo City since construction is going on mainly in that area. Someone from this Company removes the keys of such vehicles, have [sic] the equipment impounded and create [sic] many problems for these employees and their employers including the cost of impoundment to those effected. [sic]

This company will not cooperate with these drivers when told that they will move their equipment and apologize for parking in this area—their equipment is still impounded!

We request that all Laboring people—Teamsters or otherwise— *do not [p]atronize Carpet City Carpet & Linoleum Shop.*

Thanks kindly for your *Support.*

Teamsters Union, Local 690

This article was printed once on the front page of the teamster paper, and twice more in substantially the same form on page 5. The article was again printed in a later edition distinguishing Caruso's business from a store with a similar name.

Soon after the publication of the first three articles, unidentified persons began calling Linoleum & Carpet City and stating that they would not shop at Carpet City. Some characterized the store as a "scab" outfit. Other callers referred to Caruso by various derogatory and profane terms. Sales dropped dramatically, for whatever reason, and in May 1974, he relocated his business hoping to minimize his losses.

On December 17, 1974, Caruso filed the present action seeking damages for business interference. His original attorney died and he thereafter hired another attorney. Trial was eventually set for April 28, 1980. In early April, Local 690 moved for summary judgment to dismiss respondent's claim for business interference. At that time Caruso moved to amend his complaint to allege damages under a defamation cause of action arising from the articles. The trial court denied the motion for summary judgment and granted the motion for leave to amend. Thereupon, at Local 690's request, the trial was continued until January 1981.

Petitioner's only contention before this court is that the publication of the articles is constitutionally protected and cannot give rise to liability for the tort of business interference under *NAACP v. Claiborne Hardware Co.*, 458 U.S. 886, 102 S.Ct. 3409, 73 L.Ed.2d 1215 (1982). We agree.

In *Claiborne*, merchants sued the NAACP and its members for economic losses sustained during a 7–year boycott of their businesses.

During the boycott there were speeches, marches, picketing, threats, and several acts of violence. The United States Supreme Court held that the First and Fourteenth Amendments preclude imposition of liability for tortious interference with business on boycott participants or the NAACP, even though some boycott participants were violent. The opportunity to persuade others to action is clearly protected. The Claiborne Court quoted *Organization for a Better Austin v. Keefe,* 402 U.S. 415, 419, 91 S. Ct. 1575, 1577, 29 L.Ed.2d 1 (1971), where the Court held in a case involving the peaceful distribution of leaflets:

> Petitioners plainly intended to influence respondent's conduct by their activities; this is not fundamentally different from the function of a newspaper. Petitioners were engaged openly and vigorously in making the public aware of respondent's real estate practices. Those practices were offensive to them, as the views and practices of petitioners are no doubt offensive to others. But so long as the means are peaceful, the communication need not meet standards of acceptability.

(Citations omitted.)

The reasoning of the *Claiborne* Court is applicable here. Local 690, perceiving a grievance between one of its members and Caruso, asked its members and other "laboring people" to boycott his business. Though perhaps coercive, petitioner's activity was speech in its purest form and thus is entitled to at least the same degree of protection the NAACP's "speech plus conduct" activities were afforded against imposition of damages for business interference.

We have previously held that "damage to the business of persons subject to a primary boycott, lawfully conducted, is one of the inconveniences for which the law does not afford a remedy." *Wright v. Teamsters' Local 690,* 33 Wash. 2d 905, 913, 207 P.2d 662 (1949). Although petitioner in the instant case was not boycotting in its usual realm (i.e., organizing workers or informing the public of a dispute with an employer), its "do not patronize" message was protected. Protecting the speech here does not affect the statutory prohibition against secondary boycotts which has been upheld. *Claiborne,* supra 102 S. Ct. at 3425–26.

Caruso's only response to the *Claiborne* analysis is that the information upon which the "do not patronize" request was based is false and thus not protected. His claim of falsity, however, properly goes to the defamation cause of action. . . .

[Dismissed as to the business interference claim, remanded for trial on the defamation claim.]

Notes

1. *Boycotts.* One form of interference with contract or prospective advantages is the boycott, which is a refusal to deal. Apart from statutes, such as anti-discrimination statutes, any one individual may refuse to deal with any other for any reason whatever. When the individual organizes

others or calls upon them to join in this refusal, it is a boycott and analysis becomes more complicated. However, boycotts are all examples of interference with contract or business and the rules are largely the same as to both interference and boycott.

2. *Anti-competitive boycotts.* Some boycotts are illegal because of serious anti-competitive elements in them. Suppose T, who controls the entire supply of a rock star's new recording, agrees with retailers A, B, and C that the recording will not be sold to retailer D. D, unable to obtain this popular recording, may be unable to compete, not only in this item, but on others. This kind of boycott, which usually involves a combination of several actors, will very likely be found to violate federal and state antitrust laws. Frequently a complaint in cases of this kind may contain both a claim for antitrust violations and also a common law claim for interference with contract.

3. *Secondary boycotts.* Suppose T has a dispute with B. T, seeking to induce B to discharge certain employees of B, tells B "I won't buy your products until you fire those people." If B agrees, the discharged employees might have a claim for interference with contract on prospects. Suppose, however, T goes further and tells A: "You must also pressure B to discharge the employees, and if you do not do so, I will also quit buying *your* product." This is called secondary boycott. It draws A into a dispute in which he has no part and holds him hostage for B's good behavior. These boycotts are almost always condemned for this reason. If B loses business because of this kind of boycott, B would have a claim. Conceivably A might also have a claim.

4. *Labor boycotts.* Strikes by labor organizations were once considered illegal because they were interferences with contract or with business relations. The union calling a strike was inducing employees not to continue work and it was liable in tort. Over a very long period of time this has been changed by federal statute. Although certain strikes involving secondary boycotts are impermissible under federal law, most others are entirely legal. And to a very large extent federal law has preempted the field of labor organizations. This topic is thus a part of advanced courses in labor law.

5. *Free speech and interference with business claims.* As *Caruso* reflects, the Supreme Court has given free speech protection to political and social boycotts. *Caruso* gave expansive expression to this idea in saying that "persuasion" is protected speech. Is there any room after this for the tort of interference with contract or prospects at all? After all, if a boycott is neither secondary nor anti-competitive, it is only a special instance of the general tort of interference with contract or prospects. If free speech does not permit a tort claim, would the First Amendment nevertheless put some limits on it, as by putting the burden of proof on the plaintiff or by making liability turn on something other than bad motive?

REFERENCE: DOBBS ON TORTS §§ 445–55 (2000).

Chapter 31

MISREPRESENTATION AND
OTHER MISDEALINGS

---

§ 1. THEORIES OF LIABILITY AND THEIR CONSEQUENCES

Illustration 1

DuBois was negotiating to sell his house to Pace. DuBois told Pace that the roof was in good condition and never gave any problems. In fact, as DuBois knew, a tree had fallen on the roof and caused serious damage. This had happened over a year ago and deterioration was now substantial. Pace, relying upon DuBois' statement, purchased the house for $100,000. This would have been its value if the roof had been in good condition, but because of the condition of the roof, the house was worth no more than $90,000. When Pace discovered this, she sued DuBois for fraud. Pace is entitled to recover $10,000.

This illustration typifies many fraud or misrepresentation claims for money damages at common law. The case differs from the kinds of cases involved in the two preceding chapters in that while there is a communication by the defendant, it is made directly to the plaintiff, not to third persons. The fraud claim usually arises in a bargaining situation. The claim is frequently asserted against the seller, or someone representing the seller. Finally, the claim is very often found in real property cases or the sale of securities, such as corporate stocks or bonds. The reason for this is that the law of warranty, with its strict liability, is likely to govern the liability of chattel sellers, so it is only in other cases that the plaintiff will fall back on the law of tort, attempting to prove "fraud."

Misrepresentation is a factual element in many kinds of tort claims. You might intentionally or recklessly inflict emotional distress by a misrepresentation or you might risk physical harm to a person by misrepresenting the safety of a scaffold. Although a misrepresentation is important in such cases, they are not cases we think of when we speak of fraud or deceit. The traditional fraud or deceit claims—or today, the negligent misrepresentation claim—is about economic loss in a bargaining transaction.

———

DERRY v. PEEK, 14 App. Cas. 337 (H.L. 1889). Defendants, selling shares of stock in a Tramways company, represented that they had the right under an act of Parliament, to use steam or mechanical power as well as horses. In fact, they could use steam power only if the Board of Trade consented, though defendants believed that such consent would be given as a matter of course. They were wrong; the consent was never given, and the corporation failed. In the meantime, relying on the statement that the company was authorized to use steam power, the plaintiff had purchased shares of stock. When the corporation failed, he lost his investment and he sued for fraud. The Court of Appeals held that defendants honestly believed their statements to be true, but that they were nonetheless liable to the plaintiff. In the House of Lords, *held*, reversed. (a) A rescission of the contract may be had where there is an innocent misrepresentation, but (b) damages for fraud may not be recovered unless the defendant made a false representation "(1) knowingly or (2) without belief in its truth, or (3) recklessly, careless whether it be true or false."

Notes

1. *Scienter.* The requirement of an intent to deceive—a knowing or reckless falsehood—was called scienter and taken as the common law rule until recent years. It still remains the favored ground for recovery. Does the language sound familiar?

2. *Negligence.* It is now generally accepted that negligence can also form a basis of liability for misrepresentations. However, the conditions for imposing liability are more stringent, and the scope and amount of liability are also limited.

The rule of the Restatement Second of Torts § 552 (1965) would impose liability for negligent misrepresentation only when the defendant makes a representation in the course of business or employment, or in a case in which he has a pecuniary interest. In *Onita Pacific Corp. v. Bronson Trustees*, 315 Or. 149, 843 P.2d 890 (1992) the court held that a negligent misrepresentation would be actionable only if the defendant was in the business of supplying information and would not be actionable as against an adversarial bargainer. As in other cases, the plaintiff must justifiably rely on the representation in order to have a claim.

3. *Representations creating physical risks.* The limitations of the Restatement do not apply to communications that create a physical risk. D tells P that his brakes are safe when D should have known better. In reliance, P drives the car and is injured when the brakes don't work. P has a good claim. What if an employer writes a positive letter of recommendation that fails to disclose that the employee had been subject to complaints about sexual improprieties with students? The employee accepts the new job, working

with middle school students, one of whom he allegedly molests. Would the former employer be liable for those physical harms? See *Randi W. v. Muroc Joint Unified School Dist.*, 14 Cal.4th 1066, 60 Cal.Rptr.2d 263, 929 P.2d 582 (1997). What if a prospective employer makes misrepresentations in a job interview with the plaintiff about the company's growth prospects. The plaintiff suffers no physical harm, but does allege emotional harm. Liability? See *Brogan v. Mitchell International, Inc.*, 181 Ill.2d 178, 229 Ill.Dec. 503, 692 N.E.2d 276 (Ill. 1998).

4. *Representations by non-parties.* Most representations are made by parties to a negotiation which is followed by a contract or sale. However, outsiders could also be held liable for misrepresentations if they were fraudulent. If, in Illustration 1, DuBois' representation is repeated to the plaintiff by a neighbor, who also knows its falsity, the neighbor would also be liable. This rule applies only to fraud; warranty claims require privity.

Suppose in Illustration 1 DuBois had represented to A that his roof was sound and that A repeated it later to B, who then bought the house for $100,000 from DuBois. Should B, to whom no representation was made, have a fraud action? Some older cases took a tough line about this, denying liability to plaintiffs who were merely foreseeable. But according to the Restatement Second § 533, the defendant is liable not only to the person to whom the representation is made, but also to third persons if he "intends or has reason to expect that its terms will be repeated...." This raises the problem seen in the next case.

ULTRAMARES CORP. v. TOUCHE, NIVEN & CO.

Court of Appeals of New York, 1931.
255 N.Y. 170, 174 N.E. 441.

Cardozo, C.J.

[Defendants were public accountants. Pursuant to a contract with Stern they undertook to prepare an independent audit of the business, showing its net worth. As defendants knew, this was to be used by potential lenders, who, relying upon defendants' independent assessment of Stern's financial situation, would lend money to Stern. The audit showed a net worth of over a million dollars, and defendants certified this as accurate and prepared 32 originals for Stern to show potential lenders. In fact, relying on the audit and balance sheet furnished by defendants, the plaintiff loaned $165,000 to Stern. When Stern collapsed, the plaintiff was unable to obtain repayment of the loan. The plaintiff brought this action against the defendants for the damages thus suffered, claiming both scienter fraud and negligent misrepresentation. There was evidence that the defendants did not examine Stern's books with appropriate care, and that had they done so, discrepancies would have been revealed which would have led to a more accurate audit. The trial judge set aside jury's verdict for the plaintiff. The Appellate Division thought that the fraud action should be dismissed, but not the negligence claim.]

We are brought to the question of duty, its origin and measure.

The defendants owed to their employer a duty imposed by law to make their certificate without fraud, and a duty growing out of contract to make it with the care and caution proper to their calling. Fraud includes the pretense of knowledge when there is none. To creditors and investors to whom the employer exhibited the certificate, the defendants owed a like duty to make it without fraud, since there was notice in the circumstances of its making that the employer did not intend to keep it to himself. A different question develops when we ask whether they owed a duty to these to make it without negligence. If liability for negligence exists, a thoughtless slip or blunder, the failure to detect a theft or forgery beneath the cover of deceptive entries, may expose accountants to a liability in an indeterminate amount for an indeterminate time to an indeterminate class. The hazards of a business conducted on these terms are so extreme as to enkindle doubt whether a flaw may not exist in the implications of a duty that exposes to these consequences. We put aside for the moment any statement in the certificate which involves the representation of a fact as true to the knowledge of the auditors. If such a statement was made, whether believed to be true or not, the defendants are liable for deceit in the event that it was false. The plaintiff does not need the invention of novel doctrine to help it out in such conditions. . . .

The assault upon the citadel of privity is proceeding in these days apace. How far the inroads shall extend is now a favorite subject of juridical discussion. In the field of the law of contract there has been a gradual widening of the doctrine of *Lawrence v. Fox*, 20 N. Y. 268, until today the beneficiary of a promise, clearly designated as such, is seldom left without a remedy. Even in that field, however, the remedy is narrower where the beneficiaries of the promise are indeterminate or general. Something more must then appear than an intention that the promise shall redound to the benefit of the public or to that of a class of indefinite extension. The promise must be such as to "bespeak the assumption of a duty to make reparation directly to the individual members of the public if the benefit is lost." *Moch Co. v. Rensselaer Water Co.*, 247 N.Y. 160, 164, 159 N.E. 896, 897, 62 A.L.R. 1199; American Law Institute, Restatement of the Law of Contracts, § 145. In the field of the law of torts a manufacturer who is negligent in the manufacture of a chattel in circumstances pointing to an unreasonable risk of serious bodily harm to those using it thereafter may be liable for negligence though privity is lacking between manufacturer and user. *MacPherson v. Buick Motor Co.*, 217 N.Y. 382, 111 N.E. 1050, L.R.A. 1916F, 696, Ann. Cas. 1916C, 440; American Law Institute, Restatement of the Law of Torts, § 262. . . .

Liability for negligence if adjudged in this case will extend to many callings other than an auditor's. Lawyers who certify their opinions as to the validity of municipal or corporate bonds, with knowledge that the opinion will be brought to the notice of the public, will become liable to the investors, if they have overlooked a statute or a decision, to the same extent as if the controversy were one between client and adviser. Title companies insuring titles to a tract of land, with knowledge that at an approaching auction the fact that they have insured will be stated to the bidders, will become liable to purchasers who may wish the benefit of a policy without payment of a premium. These illustrations may seem to be extreme, but they go little, if any, farther than we are invited to go now. Negligence, moreover, will have one standard when viewed in relation to the employer, and another and at times a stricter standard when viewed in relation to the public. Explanations that might seem plausible, omissions that might be reasonable, if the duty is confined to the employer, conducting a business that presumably at least is not a fraud upon his creditors, might wear another aspect if an independent duty to be suspicious even of one's principal is owing to investors. "Every one making a promise having the quality of a contract will be under a duty to the promisee by virtue of the promise, but under another duty, apart from contract, to an indefinite number of potential beneficiaries when performance has begun. The assumption of one relation will mean the involuntary assumption of a series of new relations, inescapably hooked together." *Moch Co. v. Rensselaer Water Co.*, supra, at page 168 of 247 N.Y., 159 N.E. 896, 899. "The law does not spread its protection so far." *Robins Dry Dock & Repair Co. v. Flint*, supra, at page 309 of 275 U.S., 48 S. Ct. 134, 135.

Our holding does not emancipate accountants from the consequences of fraud. It does not relieve them if their audit has been so negligent as to justify a finding that they had no genuine belief in its adequacy, for this again is fraud. It does no more than say that, if less than this is proved, if there has been neither reckless misstatement nor insincere profession of an opinion, but only honest blunder, the ensuing liability for negligence is one that is bounded by the contract, and is to be enforced between the parties by whom the contract has been made. We doubt whether the average business man receiving a certificate without paying for it, and receiving it merely as one among a multitude of possible investors, would look for anything more. . . .

[The case was sent back for trial as to the fraud action and dismissed as to the negligence claim.]

Notes

1. Suppose Stern had told the accountants to send one copy directly to the plaintiff as quickly as possible, because the plaintiff might make a loan. Would the defendant then be liable for negligence?

2. Suppose the defendant, a jeweler, certifies that a diamond owned by S is genuine. Defendant knows that S will distribute numerous copies of this certificate in an attempt to sell the diamond. S does so and one reader of the certificate buys the diamond in reliance. If the defendant was merely negligent, does *Ultramares* bar recovery against the defendant?

3. Does *Ultramares* make sense to you? Consider another Cardozo decision, *H.R. Moch Co. v. Rensselaer Water Co.* Presumably the water sold

there was priced by the unit of water, not according to the value of houses served by the fire hydrants. Presumably the services of the accountant are priced by the hour or unit of work, not according to the amount of loans that might be made in reliance on the statement. The implication of the price seems to be that indeterminate liabilities to third persons are not part of the bargain. Would it even be possible for a prudent insurer to calculate a premium to insure for accountant's liabilities? After all, we do not know whether any sum will be loaned or how much it will be.

4. Whatever sense *Ultramares* might have made, the Restatement's § 552 took a more liberal position, extending liability to all those in a "limited group of persons for whose benefit and guidance" the information is supplied, if the transaction is similar to the one he expected to influence. New York has also extended liability for negligent misrepresentation, but only when the defendant has a close "bond" with the plaintiff, as by some direct contact or representation. See *Credit Alliance Corp. v. Arthur Andersen & Co.*, 65 N.Y.2d 536, 493 N.Y.S.2d 435, 483 N.E.2d 110 (1985). During the expansive early eighties, several courts went far beyond this, imposing liability for negligent representations for all proximately caused economic harms. *H. Rosenblum, Inc. v. Adler*, 93 N.J. 324, 461 A.2d 138 (1983); *Citizens State Bank v. Timm, Schmidt & Co.*, 113 Wis.2d 376, 335 N.W.2d 361 (1983). In the latter case the court added, however, that public policy might preclude liability on the facts of particular cases, emphasizing factors such as highly extraordinary harm, remoteness, and disproportion between negligence and harm. The expansion to all foreseeable plaintiffs may be at an end. In 1992, California adopted a rule similar to the Restatement's rule, allowing a recovery only by rather specifically identifiable plaintiffs. *Bily v. Arthur Young & Co.*, 3 Cal.4th 370, 11 Cal. Rptr.2d 51, 834 P.2d 745 (1992).

5. Suppose the plaintiff is foreseeable, and even within a limited class for whose guidance the information is purchased, but the plaintiff relies on the information in a wholly unsuspected way: instead of lending money to the business that has been audited, the plaintiff buys its stock. What kind of issue does this raise?

Illustration 2

Durham sells a bull to Bynum, who purchases in reliance on a knowingly false representation by Durham that the bull is a pedigreed Guernsey. If this had been true the bull would have been worth $90,000. It was not true and the bull was worth only $5,000. Bynum paid $80,000 for the bull. He is entitled to recover a sum sufficient to give him the benefit of his bargain. Since, if the bull had been as represented, he would have made a gain of $10,000, he is entitled to recover a sum sufficient to put him in that position. This will require $85,000 in damage. This, added to the value of the bull which he has, will give him $90,000—the benefit of his bargain, for which he paid $80,000.

Illustration 3

Danton, an art dealer, negligently inspected a painting and concluded it was a genuine Giaccomo Jones. He represented this to be the case and relying on this representation Pierre bought it for $200,000, expecting to resell it for $250,000. He would have been able to do so if it had been a genuine Jones, but it was not. It was worth only $175,000. Pierre's loss of bargain is $50,000, but he can only recover his "out-of-pocket," $25,000.

Illustration 4

The facts are the same as in Illustration 3, except that Pierre incurred $10,000 in brokerage fees to sell the painting, and would have incurred no brokerage fee to sell it if it had been a Jones. He is entitled to recover his out-of-pocket damages of $25,000 plus his consequential or special damages of $10,000.

Notes

1. *Scienter fraud: benefit of the bargain measure.* If the defendant is guilty of a scienter fraud, the plaintiff may recover the benefit of his bargain in most jurisdictions. This is a sum sufficient to give him the gain in asset value he would have made had the representation been true. See RESTATEMENT SECOND OF TORTS § 549 (1977); 2 DAN DOBBS, THE LAW OF REMEDIES § 9.2 (1) (2d ed. 1993). Even in the case of scienter fraud, New York limits recovery to the out-of-pocket measure described below and does not permit the usual loss of bargain damages.

2. *Scienter fraud: optional out-of-pocket measure.* The plaintiff who proves scienter fraud also has an option to claim a different measure, the out-of-pocket damages, plus any consequential damages. The out-of-pocket measure can be seen in Illustration 2. This represents the difference between what the plaintiff paid and what he got. In Illustration 2 it is obviously less than the loss of bargain measure, which would have given the plaintiff a recovery of $50,000. The out-of-pocket measure simply puts him in the financial position he would have been in had there been no transaction at all. This stands in contrast to the loss of bargain measure, which puts the plaintiff in the position he would have been in had the representation been true. Why would a plaintiff ever choose this measure of damages if he could claim the loss of bargain?

3. *Consequential damages.* If the plaintiff recovers the out-of-pocket measure, he can also recover appropriate consequential or special damages. This would include any special expenses he incurred because of the fraud. See Illustration 4. These might be denied in New York in order to make its out-of-pocket rule effective.

4. *Negligent misrepresentation.* When the defendant is guilty of negligence, but not scienter fraud, the damages are limited to the out-of-pocket plus the consequential damages. *Danca v. Taunton Savings Bank*, 385 Mass. 1, 429 N.E.2d 1129 (1982); RESTATEMENT SECOND OF TORTS § 552B (1977). Thus in Illustration 2 above, the plaintiff cannot recover the $50,000 loss of bargain.

5. *Negligent representation vs. negligent service; the case of the Federal Tort Claims Act.* In some of the negligent misrepresentation cases there is an

implication that the defendant is held responsible only because he negligent-ly performed some *service* which then led to a misrepresentation. For example, one might negligently weigh beans, then misrepresent their weight. It may be doubted whether this distinction is important in determining common law tort liability today. Might it be important on other issues, however? The Federal Tort Claims Act retains sovereign immunity for claims arising out of "misrepresentation." This has been held to bar a claim by a home buyer who relied on an appraisal by the FHA, which in turn was based on the appraiser's failure to notice defects. The government was held immune in *United States v. Neustadt,* 366 U.S. 696, 81 S.Ct. 1294, 6 L.Ed.2d 614 (1961). But in *Block v. Neal,* 460 U.S. 289, 103 S.Ct. 1089, 75 L.Ed.2d 67 (1983), there was no immunity when the government agency negligently inspected the work being done on a new home and therefore failed to require correction of defective work. The difference was that there was no communi-cation of information as there had been in *Neustadt.* If this distinction is important for the purpose of federal immunity, has it any potential for affecting damages as well? If the plaintiff can recover in *Block* could she recover the benefit of her bargain?

GAUERKE v. ROZGA

Supreme Court of Wisconsin, 1983.
112 Wis.2d 271, 332 N.W.2d 804.

CECI, JUSTICE.

[The Rozgas owned a hotel property, which they listed for sale with the Gudim Realty. They told Gudim that, according to former owners, the property was five and one-half acres. Gudim seems to have put this information in a specification sheet. In the meantime, the Gauerkes were looking for hotel property and asked Robert Frost Realty, Inc. to act for them. A Frost agent contacted Gudim, obtained the specification sheet, put a Frost card at the top, and submitted it to the Gauerkes. The Gauerkes eventually purchased the property, but two years later they discovered that the property contained less than three acres. They brought this action against the Rozgas, Robert Frost Realty, and Gudim. Gudim settled and the case was submitted to a jury against Robert Frost and its agent. A jury found for the plaintiff and Frost was held liable on a "theory of strict responsibility for the misrepresentations."]

Frost argues that the theory of strict responsibility should not have been submitted to the jury, because that theory is only applicable where the defendant could normally be expected to know the facts represented to be true without investigation. . . . The court of appeals reasoned that "in strict liability the loss is to fall on the innocent defendant rather than the innocent plaintiff. . . ."

[Wisconsin requires] (1) a representation made as of defendant's own knowledge, concerning a matter about which he purports to have knowledge, so that he may be taken to have assumed responsibility as in the case of warranty, and (2) a defendant with an economic interest in the transaction into which the plaintiff enters so that defendant expects to gain some economic benefit. In other words, strict responsibility applies in those circumstances which 'indicate that the speaker either had particular means of ascertaining the pertinent facts, or his position made possible complete knowledge and the statements fairly implied that he had it.' Therefore, the speaker ought to have known or else ought not to have spoken."

We agree with the court of appeals that the applicability of the doctrine of strict responsibility does not depend upon the actual source of the speaker's knowledge; rather, this element is satisfied if the speaker professes or implies personal knowledge. The other key element is the buyer's justifiable reliance on the statement. If the fact represented is something that one would not expect the speaker to know without an investigation, this might be a factor in determining there was justifiable reliance on the part of the buyer.... [Money award to the plaintiff affirmed.]

Notes

1.   When should there be strict liability for misrepresentations? A seller of staples honestly and reasonably represents them as safe for use in the buyer's staple gun. In fact they are not safe, a small piece breaks off and puts out the plaintiff's eye. Is there any doubt about strict liability? See RESTATEMENT OF PRODUCTS LIABILITY § 9 (1998).

2.   A homeowner has her roof repaired in May. In June she tells a would-be buyer, "The roof is in excellent shape." She is honest and reasonable, but in fact the roofer has done a poor job and the roof is already developing hidden cracks. Is there to be strict liability?

3.   In some instances a speaker may be guilty of a scienter fraud if he states facts as if he had knowledge of them when in truth he knows that he does not know the facts. Seller says: "The well on this farm will pump enough to water 500 head of cattle." The seller has never tried to pump that much, though he honestly and reasonably believes it is so based on pump specifications. However, it is not in fact the case. If he is consciously aware of his own ignorance is he not guilty of a scienter fraud?

4.   If the seller is *not* consciously aware of his own ignorance, and liability is imposed in these cases, liability is truly strict, isn't it? Should this be limited to cases of people in the business of dealing with the kind of property involved as in the case of strict products liability?

5.   One basis for strict liability is that the buyer may reasonably believe the seller is warranting the statement to be true. But if the theory is warranty or an analogy to warranty, should the claim then be defeated if there is a disclaimer or a merger clause in the deed? The disclaimer or merger clause would often not suffice to defeat an actual scienter fraud claim.

Other Bases for Strict Liability

6.   *Rescission.* Under contract doctrine it is sometimes the case that a mutual mistake of basic fact may be sufficient to avoid a contract and justify

rescission, sometimes on the theory that, given such a mistake, there was no contract at all. The case of an honest misstatement by one party and belief by the other is obviously a special instance of mutual mistake and just as good a ground for rescission. Thus, as recognized in *Derry v. Peek*, neither negligence nor scienter is required when the plaintiff seeks rescission. Should rescission be granted also for misrepresentation of any material fact? Rescission would be granted for misrepresentation that "this is a Guernsey," when in fact it was a polled Hereford. Should rescission also be granted for a misrepresentation that "this cow won first prize at the fair" when in fact it won second?

7. *Fiduciaries.* Fiduciaries, such as trustees in relationship to the beneficiaries of their trusts and lawyers in relationship to their clients, are obliged to exercise the utmost good faith, and to act in each transaction for the best interest of the beneficiary. For failure to do this they may be held for constructive fraud. The effect is strict liability. A similar idea may extend to persons who are not classic fiduciaries, but who have led the plaintiff to place special trust and confidence in them.

8. *Statutory strict liability.* A number of fields are heavily regulated by federal and state statutes. One such field involves the securities industry, in which stocks and bonds are marketed. Another involves certain massive sales of real property, usually in developments or resort properties. In both cases, federal statutes impose regulations, enforced by federal agencies. These require extensive filing of documents. The material given the buyer is likewise heavily regulated. In both cases, certain misstatements may result in strict liability, but the situations in which this is so are limited. It appears more frequently that these statutes require scienter. Both fields are the subject for more specialized study. As to securities, see 15 U.S.C.A. §§ 77a et seq.; as to land sales, see §§ 1701 et seq. State statutes often contain parallel provisions.

Scope of Strict Liability and Damages

9. *The Ultramares problem.* Reconsider the *Ultramares* problem. To what group of potential plaintiffs should strict liability extend? Only to the very person to whom the representation was made? This is the provision of the Restatement Second of Torts § 552C, cmt. d (1977).

10. *The damages problems.* What damages should be available when strict liability is imposed? The Restatement would limit damages to out-of-pocket measure. This eliminates recovery of the benefit of the bargain damages and also consequential damages. See § 552C(2) and cmt. f.

§ 2. RELIANCE AND RELATED DOCTRINES

1. *Reliance in fact.* If the plaintiff pays no attention to the defendant's misrepresentation, or does not care, or relies on his own investigation instead, then the defendant's representations have in fact caused no harm. That is, the normal requirement of actual cause is met in this context by the rule that the plaintiff must have relied in fact on the false statement (or a false implication of silence). If not, then the plaintiff cannot recover under any of the misrepresentation theories.

In rare cases, the plaintiff may be permitted to show that she relied indirectly upon the defendant's representation by relying upon market values that were themselves influenced by the misrepresentation. This is the "fraud on the market" theory, presently available only under federal securities laws. See *Mirkin v. Wasserman*, 5 Cal.4th 1082, 23 Cal.Rptr.2d 101, 858 P.2d 568 (1993) (rejecting the fraud on the market theory for state-law claims); *Kaufman v. i-Stat Corp.*, 165 N.J. 94, 754 A.2d 1188 (2000)(same).

2. *Contributory negligence.* At a time when all actionable misrepresentations were scienter frauds under *Derry v. Peek*, the tort was necessarily an intentional one. As a result, contributory negligence could not furnish any defense. This remains the rule today as to scienter frauds. As to negligent misrepresentations, however, contributory negligence is usually taken into account to either bar or reduce a plaintiff's damages. See, e.g., *Williams Ford, Inc. v. Hartford Courant Co.*, 232 Conn. 559, 657 A.2d 212 (1995); RESTATEMENT SECOND OF TORTS § 552A (1977).

3. *Justified reliance.* Somewhat strangely, the law has required that the plaintiff not only rely, but that the reliance must be "justified." This rule applies not only to negligent misrepresentations, but also to actual fraud. Is the rule distinguishable from a rule of contributory negligence? The Restatement suggests that justified reliance is more subjective and personal to the particular plaintiff and does not impose a community standard of care. See RESTATEMENT SECOND OF TORTS § 545A, cmt. b (1977). Thus perfect fools have been allowed to recover for representations that would not take in the ordinary prudent person. Courts have held that a plaintiff "justifiably relied" on a misrepresentation, but was negligent in doing so, resulting in a reduction of damages rather than none at all. See, e.g., *ESCA Corp. v. KPMG Peat Marwick*, 135 Wash.2d 820, 959 P.2d 651 (1998). On the other hand, the law has developed out of the "justified reliance" requirement a series of rather formalized rules about cases that do not ordinarily justify reliance. These include representations that are not material and representations that are not factual. The latter includes representations of opinion and law and representations about the future. Perhaps the justified reliance requirement is an indirect way to determine whether the plaintiff actually relied, and whether the defendant really made the representation and intended to induce reliance.

4. *Legal cause.* The Restatement Second of Torts § 548A provides that a fraudulent misrepresentation is a legal cause of loss only if the loss might reasonably be expected to result from reliance on that representation. Is this congruent with the rules of proximate cause that we saw in Chapter 8? Should liability for a negligent misrepresentation be more constricted?

5. *Materiality.* The representation must be material and reliance on an immaterial statement is not justified. Example: Defendant, attempting to sell a car, says to the plaintiff, "Oh, are you a member of the

Elks Club? Me, too." Defendant is not a member and has no reason to think that the plaintiff's decision would hinge on the representation, though he does expect to win the plaintiff's good will by this lie.

6. *Opinion*. Abstract opinions furnish little basis for reliance. "This is a great car," is not an actionable misrepresentation. This particular opinion is usually called "puffing" or "dealer's talk." At one time cases labeled some statements as opinion that today we might call factual statements. There are cases in which a seller's statement that he owns 10 acres are treated as "opinion" and hence not actionable. Today this would usually be treated as a statement of fact. How would you treat these statements: "This painting is a steal; it is worth at least $100,000, and you'll be getting it for $50,000." "This painting sold at auction last year for $100,000." Could some opinion statements imply facts? An expert's opinion within the subject of expertise would almost always imply that there was a factual basis for it, wouldn't it? Opinions by neutral parties might have an obviously different impact from opinions of the person trying to sell you something, don't you think?

7. *Representations of law*. The traditional rule was that a pure representation of law would furnish no ground for reliance or an action for fraud. This proposition is now dubious. If the statement is a pure statement of fact—"the legislature repealed the dram shop statute"—the representation seems actionable as one of fact. If the statement is one of opinion, it should permit justifiable reliance to the same extent as any other opinion. This is the view expressed in the Restatement, § 545.

PINNACLE PEAK DEVELOPERS v. TRW INVESTMENT CORP.

Arizona Court of Appeals, 1980.
129 Ariz. 385, 631 P.2d 540.

SANDRA DAY O'CONNOR, JUDGE.

[TRW purchased 40 acres from Pinnacle Peak for a residential subdivision. The purchase agreement required TRW to make certain off-site improvements, such as roads, and electrical, telephone, and water distribution systems. TRW had an option to purchase additional acreage, but only if a certain portion of the off-site improvements had not been completed by the option deadline. When the option deadline was reached, the improvements had been made and the seller took the position that the option had therefore expired. TRW took the position that the seller had fraudulently induced TRW to forego the improvements and that for this reason the option should be treated as extant. TRW's claim is that it was induced to enter into the purchase and option agreement by reliance on Pinnacle Peak's representation that the off-site improvements would be no obstacle to the exercise of the option so long as there was reasonable progress on those improvements. TRW argued that this was a representation false when made. The trial court granted summary judgment for the seller.]

Appellees argue that evidence of the alleged oral representation made prior to execution of the option agreement would be barred by the parol evidence rule.

The appellant urges the admissibility of evidence of an oral promissory representation by appellee, which was made prior to the execution of the written option agreement and which is contrary to an express provision of the written agreement. Appellant offers the evidence and alleges that appellee's promissory representation was false when made, was made with an intention not to honor it, and that appellant relied upon it. . . .

A promise, when made with a present intention not to perform it, is a misrepresentation which can give rise to an action of fraud. *Restatement of Contracts* § 473 (1932)' *Restatement of Torts* § 530 (1938). As stated in *Waddell v. White*, 56 Ariz. 420, 428, 108 P.2d 565, 569 (1940):

> Representations which give rise to an action of fraud must, of course, be of matters of fact which exist in the present, and not merely an agreement or promise to do something in the future, or an expression of opinion or judgment as to something which has happened or is expected to happen. To this there is one exception, that when a promise to perform a future act is made with the present intention on the part of the promisor that he will not perform it, it is such a representation as will give rise to an action of fraud.

A good statement of the parol evidence rule is found in Childres and Spitz, *Status in the Law of Contract*, 47 N.Y.U.L. Rev. 1, at 6–7 (1972):

> "The parol evidence rule, as traditionally stated, renders inadmissible any evidence of prior or contemporaneous oral understandings and of prior written understandings, which would contradict, vary or add to a written contract which was intended as the final and complete statement or integration of the parties' agreement." . . .

A summary of the problem raised in a case such as this one is succinctly stated in James and Gray, *Misrepresentation* (pt. II), 37 Md. Law Rev. 488, at 507–08 (1978):

> Although the notion of promissory fraud is well recognized, it may seriously collide with the policies underlying certain prophylactic legal rules like the Statute of Frauds and the parol evidence rule. Both these rules are designed to prevent fraudulent claims (or defenses) through excluding a type of evidence (viz., evidence of oral agreement) which is too easy to fabricate and too hard to meet. It could go without saying that these rules are not meant to shield fraud, but they may well have just that effect if they prevent a party from showing that he has been deceived by an oral promise, made to induce reliance and action but without the slightest intention of keeping it. Many courts allow oral proof of fraud in such a case and this seems sound because the affirmative burden of proving fraud (i.e., present intent not to keep the promise when it was made, or

even the absence of an intent to keep it) would seem to be a substantial safeguard against trumped-up contracts. Moreover, the safeguard is enhanced by the prevailing procedural rules requiring clear and convincing evidence of fraud and holding that the mere nonperformance of a contract does not warrant an inference of the requisite fraudulent intent. [Footnotes omitted].

The cases from other states are split widely on whether to permit parol evidence which contradicts a writing when fraud in the inducement is alleged. A number of courts appear to follow the *Restatement of Contracts* § 238 (1932), and allow evidence of promissory fraud, notwithstanding the parol evidence rule.

Other courts exclude evidence of promissory fraud which contradicts the terms of the written agreement on the basis of the parol evidence rule.... A case by case study of a large number of cases nationwide dealing with the application of the parol evidence rule has been reported in Childres and Spitz, *Status in the Law of Contract*, 47 N.Y.U.L. Rev. 1 (1972). The results indicate that, in practice, courts generally apply the parol evidence rule to exclude allegations of prior or contemporaneous oral promises which contradict the written agreement in cases involving "formal contracts" which were the result of negotiation between parties with some expertise and business sophistication. *Id*. at 8, 9. There is a much greater tendency in the reported cases to allow such evidence in "informal contracts" between people who lack sophistication in business. *Id*. at 17–24. In cases involving abuse of the bargaining process, such as unconscionable contracts or contracts involving duress, the courts almost always disregard the parol evidence rule and allow evidence of the oral promises or representations.

The pleadings and affidavits in this case reflect that the parties each had experience in business transactions and that the written option agreement was prepared as the result of negotiations between the parties, who were represented by counsel. It involved a relatively substantial and sophisticated real estate transaction. The written option agreement was a "formal contract." The contradiction of the written agreement and the oral representation is clear. Appellant is asking the court to substitute the prior statement by appellee's agent to the effect that completion of the offsite improvements by the June 15 deadline would not be necessary if reasonable progress had been made for the express provision in the written agreement requiring completion of the improvements by June 15. The facts are such that courts in most jurisdictions would exclude the evidence of the prior oral statement on the basis of a strict application of the parol evidence rule. It is our opinion on rehearing that the trial court correctly granted summary judgment to appellee on Count II quieting title to the property covered by the option agreement in appellee.

The application of the parol evidence rule moves along a continuum based on the extent of the contradiction and the relative strength and sophistication of the parties and their negotiations.... There are circumstances under which evidence of a prior or contemporaneous contradictory oral representation or promise would be admissible notwithstanding the subsequent integrated written agreement of the parties. . . .

The judgment is affirmed.

Notes

1. *Rule*. It is generally agreed that one's present intention to do some future act is a fact about one's state of mind, and that a misrepresentation about that state of mind is actionable as fraud.

2. *Proof*. What proof would suffice to show that the speaker did not have the intention at the time the statement was made? Since nonperformance of the stated intention might simply result from a change of heart, the plaintiff's proof can be difficult; mere proof that the statement was made and not performed would not suffice. See *Milwaukee Auction Galleries, Limited v. Chalk*, 13 F.3d 1107 (7th Cir.1994). What if a defendant represents an intention to build a swimming pool for the benefit of those who buy a condominium, but he does not have the money to do so and no prospects of getting any?

3. *Statute of frauds*. Disclaimers or merger clauses in deeds, the parol evidence rule, and the statute of frauds might each prevent a recovery in the case of oral representation. The view of most courts has been that the statute of frauds does not prevent a recovery for a fraudulent misrepresentation, though it would bar enforcement of a promise. The "promissory fraud" cases thus provide a means of circumventing the normal application of the statute of frauds, but only where there is proof that the speaker had no intent to perform when the statement was made.

4. *Parol evidence*. Judge O'Connor in *Pinnacle Peak* said the parol evidence rule "moves along a continuum based on the extent of the contradiction and relative strength and sophistication of the parties. . . . " What did she mean? Consider: *Case 1*: Seller orally promises to deliver a 1985 car; the written contract specifically says the car is to be a 1984 car. *Case 2*: A vendor of land orally represents that the property is not subject to any zoning restrictions. The written contract provides that title is to be subject to all restrictions and encumbrances appearing in the instruments constituting the chain of title. Zoning restrictions appear in some of these instruments. *Case 3*: A lessor orally states that the building will have air conditioning on nights and weekends. The contract and lease contain no reference to this topic at all.

5. *Disclaimers*. Disclaimers may appear in several forms. One is the merger clause, which provides that all promises and agreements are contained in the written documents. This is a contractual form of the parol evidence rule. Disclaimers may also state that the vendor has made no representations, or that the buyer does not rely on representations. If the plaintiff is induced to enter the contract, including the disclaimer, by fraud, then the disclaimer may not protect the defendant from liability. But a statement in the written documents that no representations have been made, or that the buyer does not rely upon them, will at least raise the

question whether the buyer's reliance was reasonable in the light of the notice these documents gave that reliance was not expected. See *Wittenberg v. Robinov*, 9 N.Y.2d 261, 213 N.Y.S.2d 430, 173 N.E.2d 868 (1961).

§ 3.   DUTY TO DISCLOSE

OLLERMAN v. O'ROURKE CO., INC.

Supreme Court of Wisconsin, 1980.
94 Wis.2d 17, 288 N.W.2d 95.

ABRAHAMSON, JUSTICE.

[Ollerman purchased a lot from O'Rourke Co. When he excavated to build a house, an underground well was uncovered and uncapped, and water was released. Ollerman alleged he had spent over $2700 to cap the well and that building changes costing over $10,500 were necessitated by its presence. He alleged that O'Rourke Co. knew of the underground well but did not disclose it. The trial court overruled the defendant's motion to dismiss.]

[The court first held that silence where there is a duty to disclose is equivalent to a misrepresentation of fact and that a seller obliged to disclose could be held liable for an "intentional" misrepresentation.]

We recognize that the traditional rule in Wisconsin is that in an action for intentional misrepresentation the seller of real estate, dealing at arm's length with the buyer, has no duty to disclose information to the buyer and therefore has no liability in an action for intentional misrepresentation for failure to disclose. . . .

Under the doctrine of caveat emptor no person was required to tell all that he or she knew in a business transaction, for in a free market the diligent should not be deprived of the fruits of superior skill and knowledge lawfully acquired. The business world, and the law reflecting business mores and morals, required the parties to a transaction to use their faculties and exercise ordinary business sense, and not to call on the law to stand *in loco parentis* to protect them in their ordinary dealings with other business people.

Over the years society's attitudes toward good faith and fair dealing in business transactions have undergone significant change, and this change has been reflected in the law. Courts have departed from or relaxed the "no duty to disclose" rule by carving out exceptions to the rule and by refusing to adhere to the rule when it works an injustice. Thus courts have held that the rule does not apply where the seller actively conceals a defect or where he prevents investigation; where the seller has told a half-truth or has made an ambiguous statement if the seller's intent is to create a false impression and he does so; where there is a fiduciary relationship between the parties; or where the facts are peculiarly and exclusively within the knowledge of one party to the transaction and the other party is not in a position to discover the facts for himself.

On the basis of the complaint, the case at bar does not appear to fall into one of these well-recognized exceptions to the "no duty to disclose" rule. However, Dean Prosser has found a "rather amorphous tendency on the part of most courts toward finding a duty of disclosure in cases where the defendant has special knowledge or means of knowledge not open to the plaintiff and is aware that the plaintiff is acting under a misapprehension as to facts which could be of importance to him, and would probably affect his decision."

Dean Keeton described these cases abandoning the "no duty to disclose" rule as follows:

> "In the present stage of the law, the decisions show a drawing away from this idea (that nondisclosure is not actionable), and there can be seen an attempt by many courts to reach a just result in so far as possible, but yet maintaining the degree of certainty which the law must have. The statement may often be found that if either party to a contract of sale conceals or suppresses a material fact which he is in good faith bound to disclose then his silence is fraudulent.

> "The attitude of the courts toward nondisclosure is undergoing a change and ... it would seem that the object of the law in these cases should be to impose on parties to the transaction a duty to speak whenever justice, equity, and fair dealing demand it. This statement is made only with reference to instances where the party to be charged is an actor in the transaction. This duty to speak does not result from an implied representation by silence, but exists because a refusal to speak constitutes unfair conduct." *Fraud—Concealment and Nondisclosure*, 15 Tex. L. Rev. 1, 31 (1936).

The test Dean Keeton derives from the cases to determine when the rule of nondisclosure should be abandoned—"whenever justice, equity and fair dealing demand it"—present, as one writer states, "a somewhat nebulous standard, praiseworthy as looking toward more stringent business ethics, but possibly difficult of practical application." Case Note, *Silence as Fraudulent Concealment—Vendor & Purchaser—Duty to Disclose*, 36 Wash. L. Rev. 202, 204 (1961)....

The draftsmen of the most recent Restatement of Torts (Second) (1977) have attempted to formulate a rule embodying this trend in the cases toward a more frequent recognition of a duty to disclose. Sec. 551(1) of the Restatement sets forth the traditional rule that one who fails to disclose a fact that he knows may induce reliance in a business transaction is subject to the same liability as if he had represented the nonexistence of the matter that he failed to disclose if, and only if, he is under a duty to exercise reasonable care to disclose the matter in question.... Sec. 551(2) (e) is the "catch-all" provision setting forth conditions under which a duty to disclose exists; it states that a party to a transaction is under a duty to exercise reasonable care to disclose to the other "facts basic to the transaction, if he knows that the other is about to enter into it under a mistake as to them, and that the other, because of the relationship between them, the customs of the trade or other objective circumstances, would reasonably expect a disclosure of those facts...."

Section 551(2) (e) of the Restatement (Second) of Torts limits the duty to disclose to disclosure of those "facts basic" to the transaction. Comment *j* to sec. 551 differentiates between basic facts and material facts as follows:

> "A basic fact is a fact that is assumed by the parties as a basis for the transaction itself. It is a fact that goes to the basis, or essence, of the transaction, and is an important part of the substance of what is bargained for or dealt with. Other facts may serve as important and persuasive inducements to enter into the transaction, but not go to its essence. These facts may be material, but they are not basic."

However, the draftsmen of the Restatement recognized that the law was developing to expand the duty to disclosure beyond the duty described in sec. 551.... The seller contends, in its brief, that if this court affirms the circuit court's order overruling the motion to dismiss and allows the buyer to proceed to trial, the court is adopting "what really amounts to a strict policy of 'let the seller beware.' " The seller goes on to state, "Woe indeed to anyone who sells a home, a vacant lot or other piece of real estate and fails to itemize with particularity or give written notice to each prospective buyer of every conceivable condition in and around the property, regardless of whether such a condition is dangerous, defective or could become so by the negligence or recklessness of others. A seller of real estate is not and should not be made an insurer or guarantor of the competence of those with whom the purchaser may later contract." ...

The seller's arguments are not persuasive in light of the facts alleged in the complaint and our narrow holding in this case.

Where the vendor is in the real estate business and is skilled and knowledgeable and the purchaser is not, the purchaser is in a poor position to discover a condition which is not readily discernible, and the purchaser may justifiably rely on the knowledge and skill of the vendor. Thus, in this instant case a strong argument for imposing a duty on the seller to disclose material facts is this "reliance factor." The buyer portrayed in this complaint had a reasonable expectation of honesty in the marketplace, that is, that the vendor would disclose material facts which it knew and which were not readily discernible. Under these circumstances the law should impose a duty of honesty on the seller.

... [W]e hold that a subdivider-vendor of a residential lot has a duty to a "non-commercial" purchaser to disclose facts which are known to the vendor, which are material to the transaction, and which are not readily discernible to the purchaser. A fact is known to the vendor if the vendor has actual knowledge of the fact or if the vendor acted in reckless disregard as to the existence of the fact. This usage of the word "know" is the same as in an action for intentional misrepresentation based on a false statement. A fact is material if a reasonable purchaser would attach importance to its existence or nonexistence in determining the choice of action in the transaction in question; or if the vendor knows or has reason to know that the purchaser regards or is likely to regard the matter as important in determining the choice of action, although a reasonable purchaser would not so regard it.

Notes

1. In *Nei v. Burley,* 388 Mass. 307, 446 N.E.2d 674 (1983) a seller knew that the water table on his property was high and that there was a seasonal stream which was not apparent in dry season. He revealed neither. The buyer was required to spend more to install a septic tank because of these unrevealed features of the land. The court followed the traditional rule that there was no duty to disclose. Would the Wisconsin Court, on the basis of *Ollerman*, get a different result in *Nei*? Notice that the limitation of the duty is to "basic" facts. In *Maybee v. Jacobs Motor Co., Inc.*, 519 N.W.2d 341 (S.D.1994) the seller of a used vehicle did not tell the buyer that the engine had been rebuilt and that it used a gas not now generally available. The court held that if these were basic facts, the seller was under a duty to disclose and that it was up to the jury to determine whether the facts were basic.

2. V, attempting to sell a vacant lot, tells P: "I want to warn you— there is an easement across the edge of this property." P finds this acceptable and purchases the property. She then discovers that there is another easement in the middle and she cannot use the property for her purposes. The cases are agreed that P can recover. What is the principle? What if V honestly and reasonably believes there is only the one easement but later, before any contract for sale is signed, discovers the second one?

3. S, attempting to sell a car, moves its odometer back from 65,000 miles to 30,000 miles. He says nothing whatever about the mileage and P does not ask. If P buys in reliance on the odometer, has he a claim? On the basis of what rule?

4. L, a lawyer who represents C, offers to sell C shares of stock in a corporation. He says nothing about the fact that the corporation has manufactured, among other things, asbestos, and may be subject to catastrophic liabilities for injuries. C purchases, then the corporation goes bankrupt over asbestos liabilities. Has C a claim against her lawyer? On the basis of what rule?

5. *Statutes.* The securities laws, the Interstate Land Sales Act, and other statutes, including some state statutes, frequently impose affirmative duties to disclose material. In some states, consumer protection acts have been passed which may also require disclosure. A claim for nondisclosure therefore requires a careful study of the statutes.

REFERENCES: DOBBS ON TORTS §§ 469–483 (2000); Fleming James, Jr. and Oscar S. Gray, *Misrepresentation*, 37 MD. L. REV. 286, 488 (Parts I & II, 1978); 2 HARPER, JAMES & GRAY, THE LAW OF TORTS, Chapter 7 (2d ed. 1986); DAN DOBBS, THE LAW OF REMEDIES § 9.2 (6) (2d ed. 1993).

Chapter 32

TORT ACTIONS TO PROTECT CIVIL RIGHTS

Using the term "civil rights" in an expansive way, this chapter sketches some civil rights claims, not necessarily limited to constitutional rights. Although we have already encountered some civil rights cases, those touched in this chapter are limited to civil rights that protect intangible or economic interests rather than interests in physical security or freedom. This sketch should be regarded as a prelude to one or more advanced courses in such topics as constitutional law, civil rights, employment law, disability law, and others.

§ 1. PRIVACY

The Fourth Amendment to the Constitution protects one narrow kind of privacy: "The right of the people to be secure in their persons, houses, papers, and effects, against unreasonable searches and seizures...." Other provisions of the Constitution may be held to imply a right to privacy; free speech implies free association of persons, and equally a freedom not to associate. Prosser identified the kind of privacy involved here as a right to seclusion or solitude, the invasion of which was actionable under state tort law. It might also be actionable under federal law if the invasion violates the Fourth Amendment and is carried out under color of law.

BIRNBAUM v. UNITED STATES
United States Court of Appeals, Second Circuit, 1978.
588 F.2d 319.

GURFEIN, CIRCUIT JUDGE.

[The CIA and the FBI covertly opened mail of some American citizens, including that of the plaintiffs, who have brought this action under the FTCA. The trial judge, sitting without a jury, found for the plaintiff's and awarded $1,000 to each.]

The manifold nature of what is loosely termed "the right to privacy" is well established. Both Dean W. Prosser, *The Law of Torts*, § 117 (4th ed. 1971), and the advisers of 3 *Restatement (Second) of Torts* § 652A (1977), agree that the right to privacy comprehends four *distinct* rights, "which are tied together by the common name, but otherwise have almost nothing in common except that each represents an interference with the right of the plaintiff 'to be let alone.'" Prosser at 804.

The four privacy rights listed in the Restatement are:

a) unreasonable intrusion upon the seclusion of another . . . or

b) appropriation of the other's name or likeness . . . or

c) unreasonable publicity given to the other's private life . . . or

d) publicity that unreasonably places the other in a false light before the public.

§ 652 (1977).

These cases all concern infringements of a single right—to seclusion free from unreasonable intrusion by another. The activities of the Government in opening and reproducing plaintiff's mail constituted such an intrusion. . . .

Appellant United States contends, however, that New York does not recognize a common law right to privacy. Appellant places its reliance principally on the famous 1902 case of *Roberson v. Rochester Folding Box Company*, 171 N.Y. 538, 64 N.E. 442. There, in commenting upon the seminal article by Warren and Brandeis, *The Right to Privacy*, 4 Harv. L. Rev. 193 (1890), a 4 to 3 majority of the New York Court of Appeals observed that "the so-called 'right of privacy' has not as yet found an abiding place in our jurisprudence," 171 N.Y. at 556, 64 N.E. at 447 and denied a remedy for the appropriation and commercial exploitation of plaintiff's likeness.

Whatever the sweep of some of the language in the case, *Roberson* does not bar a cause of action for *intrusion*. As indicated, the "right to privacy" includes several discrete torts within its ambit, of which appropriation is only one. As Holmes observed, "[w]e do not get a new and single principle by simply giving a single name to all the cases to be accounted for," *The Common Law* at 204 (1945 ed.). That the *Roberson* court rejected a privacy right in the context of an appropriation does not imply a rejection of a remedy for intrusion.

Moreover, the court in *Roberson* rested its decision on the lack of precedent in English law for enjoining the appropriation and publication of a photograph which did not actually defame the plaintiff or injure her reputation. The court was not asked to consider the right to be secure in one's papers as the foundation for an actionable wrong. Had there been occasion to address the intrusion question, the court might well have upheld a cause of action because, unlike appropriation, intrusion had been previously acknowledged as a species of tort.

Such a right had been recognized before the American Revolution. In *Entick v. Carrington,* 95 Eng.Rep. 807, 19 How.St.Tr. 1029 (C.P. 1765), the British Secretary of State issued a non-judicial search warrant to procure evidence of seditious libel. His messengers entered the plaintiff's house under the authority of the purported warrant and seized and perused private papers. Though the action was technically a trespass to the home, Lord Camden read the protections of privacy more broadly. The court commented:

> [W]e can safely say there is no law in this country to justify the defendants in what they have done; if there was, it would destroy all the comforts of society; for papers are often the dearest property a man can have. . . .

[W]e affirm the money judgments . . .

Notes

1. Is this a common law trespass?

2. Why did the plaintiff not sue the United States under the Constitution rather than under state law? Individual federal officers may be held liable for constitutional violations, but the government itself is liable only under the terms set out in the Federal Torts Claims Act. One of these terms is that state law applies.

3. Besides opening letters, what kinds of non-trespassory intrusions would qualify? Consider:

    (a) Eavesdropping, with or without electronic bugging.

    (b) Telephone tapping. This may be actionable under a federal statute, 18 U.S.C.A. §§ 2510 et seq. or under state statutes. See *Burgess v. Burgess,* 447 So.2d 220 (Fla.1984).

    (c) Spying, as peeping through a window.

    (d) Intensive surveillance.

    (e) Harassing telephone calls.

All of these have been recognized as potentially actionable claims in cases where privacy can ordinarily be expected and where there is no special justification.

4. Intensive surveillance and harassing calls might equally give rise to a claim for intentional infliction of mental distress. Sometimes cases in which creditors are particularly obnoxious are called privacy cases; at other times the mental distress theory is used. The similarity has led some to think that an intrusive privacy tort should not be recognized where the elements of intentional infliction of mental distress are not proved. This would require proof of "outrageous" conduct and extreme mental distress. Could you turn this upside down and say that privacy law intends to specify some cases in which the individual is protected even in the absence of outrage and extreme distress?

YORK v. STORY, 324 F.2d 450 (9th Cir.1963). The complaint alleged: plaintiff went to the police station to file charges in connection with an assault upon her. Story, one of the officers there, directed her to undress for photographs. She was told these were necessary to show bruises. She objected, but nude photos were made. A policewoman was in the station, but Story was the only person in the room when the photographs were made. He later circulated the photos to persons in the department. Another defendant, Moreno, allegedly took part in the circulation of the photographs. The plaintiff sued under § 1983. The trial judge concluded that no violation of federal law was shown, and as there was no other basis for federal jurisdiction, dismissed the claim. *Held*, reversed. (1) Conceivably the plaintiff's claim against Story could be sustained on the theory that his acts of photographing her were unreasonable searches and violated the Fourth Amendment. (2) But such a holding would not resolve the claim against Moreno, who only circulated the pictures. Accordingly the court must consider whether all the acts involved "constituted such invasions of [plaintiff's] privacy as to amount to deprivations of liberty without due process of law, guaranteed to her by the Due Process Clause of the Fourteenth Amendment.... We cannot conceive of a more basic subject of privacy than the naked body.... We do not see how it can be argued that the searching of one's home deprives him of privacy, but the photographing of one's nude body, and the distribution of such photographs to strangers does not.... We therefore conclude that, under the allegations ... appellant has laid a foundation for proving, if she can, not only that appellees were acting under color of local authority at the times in question, but that such acts constituted an arbitrary intrusion upon the security of her privacy, as guaranteed to her by the Due Process Clause of the Fourteenth Amendment." Reversed and remanded.

Notes

1. In *Rushing v. Wayne County*, 436 Mich. 247, 462 N.W.2d 23 (1990) the plaintiff was a female held in the defendant's jail. Jail officials required her to strip except for her underpants and kept her in that semi-naked condition where custodians, deputies, other inmates and visitors could see her, ostensibly to prevent suicide. No provision was made to protect her from being on view to all. The jail psychologist, Mr. Kim, testified that he had experienced thousands of people stripped in jail and that in most cases it is good for a person to be stripped and exposed because in that case she will think about the consequences of her actions. The majority of the court held that this evidence, if believed, would suffice to show a violation of rights that could be redressed by § 1983.

2. According to the Restatement Second of Torts § 652B the intrusion must be intentional and must be such as would be "highly offensive to a reasonable person." Is this also a good guide to actions based on constitutional violations?

3. Notice that unlike *Birnbaum, York* is *not* based on state law. It is based on § 1983. It is also possible to sue federal officials "directly" under the Constitution for the federal officer's violation of federal constitutional law.

4. In *Paul v. Davis*, 424 U.S. 693, 96 S.Ct. 1155, 47 L.Ed.2d 405 (1976) Davis was once arrested for shoplifting. The charge was "filed away" with leave to reinstate it. The defendant, a police chief attempting to deal with Christmas shoplifting, sent a flyer to merchants containing mug shots and names of "active shoplifters." Davis' name and photo were included. He had never been convicted and in fact the charges against him were finally dismissed shortly after the flyer was sent. He sued the police officer under § 1983, claiming his due process rights had been violated. The court first held that defamation by a state official does not give rise to any claim based on due process. It then considered whether a privacy claim could be recognized. It recognized that the Constitution implicitly protects certain "zones of privacy," but said the "personal rights found in this guarantee of personal privacy must be limited to those which are 'fundamental' or 'implicit in the concept of ordered liberty' … matters relating to marriage, procreation contraception, family relationships, and child rearing and education." The Court concluded that the plaintiff had failed to state the violation of any constitutional rights. Can *York* survive *Paul*?

§ 2. DUE PROCESS

WILKINSON v. SKINNER, 34 N.Y.2d 53, 356 N.Y.S.2d 15, 312 N.E.2d 158 (1974). This is a suit against a sheriff for placing the plaintiff, a prisoner, in an isolation cell for a supposed infraction of jail discipline without a hearing. The trial judge dismissed the complaint. On appeal, *held*, the plaintiff states a claim. "[T]he punishment meted out in this case must carry with it at least the minimal safeguards afforded by the due process of law. Confining someone in a segregation cell is not a minor punishment…. The requirements of due process are not static; they vary with the elements of the ambience in which they arise…. [O]n the fact pattern alleged in this case, appellant was entitled to a rudimentary administrative hearing…. If it becomes appropriate to award damages in this case, the court should keep in mind that the wrongs if any, were committed by officials performing the most dangerous of jobs…. In a case such as this, courts should be careful to limit monetary damages to those that are closely and directly related to the wrong perpetrated—speculative damages should not be allowed."

CAREY v. PIPHUS

Supreme Court of the United States, 1978.
435 U.S. 247, 98 S.Ct. 1042, 55 L.Ed.2d 252.

MR. JUSTICE POWELL delivered the opinion of the court.

[Plaintiffs were boys in Chicago schools. Piphus was suspended after he was seen smoking "an irregularly shaped cigarette." The principal smelled what he believed was the odor of burning marijuana and ordered suspension without a hearing. A companion case involved a sixth grader who wore an earring in violation of school rules. He was also suspended without a hearing. Both plaintiffs seek damages under § 1983. The trial judge found a denial of due process but awarded no damages, since none were proven. The Seventh Circuit held that the plaintiffs were entitled to substantial damages for the denial of due process.]

[The Court of Appeals held that if defendants proved on remand that the plaintiffs would have been suspended even had a proper hearing been given, damages could not be given for any injuries caused by the suspension itself. The failure to accord due process in such a case would not have caused harm, since, even with a due process hearing, the same suspension would have occurred. The parties do not disagree with this. Nor does the Supreme Court.]

The parties do disagree as to the further holding of the Court of Appeals that respondents are entitled to recover substantial—although unspecified—damages to compensate them for "the injury which is 'inherent in the nature of the wrong,'" even if their suspension were justified and even if they fail to prove that the denial of procedural due process actually caused them some real, if intangible, injury. Respondents, elaborating on this theme, submit that the holding is correct because injury fairly may be "presumed" to flow from every denial of procedural due process. Their argument is that in addition to protecting against unjustified deprivations, the Due Process Clause also guarantees the "feeling of just treatment" by the government. They contend that the deprivation of protected interests without procedural due process, even where the premise for the deprivation is not erroneous, inevitably arouses strong feelings of mental and emotional distress in the individual who is denied this "feeling of just treatment." They analogize their case to that of defamation *per se*, in which "the plaintiff is relieved from the necessity of producing any proof whatsoever that he has been injured" in order to recover substantial compensatory damages. Petitioners do not deny that a purpose of procedural due process is to convey to the individual a feeling that the government has dealt with him fairly, as well as to minimize the risk of mistaken deprivations of protected interests. They go so far as to concede that, in a proper case, persons in respondents' positions might well recover damages for mental and emotional distress caused by the denial of procedural due process. Petitioners' argument is the more limited one that such injury cannot be presumed to occur, and that plaintiffs at least should be put to their proof on the issue, as plaintiffs are in most tort actions.

We agree with petitioners in this respect. As we have observed in another context, the doctrine of presumed damages in the common law of defamation per se "is an oddity of tort law, for it allows recovery of purportedly compensatory damages without evidence of actual loss." *Gertz v. Robert Welch, Inc.*, 418 U.S. 323, 349, 94 S.Ct. 2997, 3011–3012, 41 L.Ed.2d 789 (1974). The doctrine has been defended on the grounds that those forms of defamation that are actionable *per se* are virtually certain to cause serious injury to reputation, and that this kind of injury is extremely difficult to prove. See id., at 373, 376, 94 S.Ct., at 3023, 3025 (White, J., dissenting). Moreover, statements that are defamatory *per se* by their very nature are likely to cause mental and emotional distress, as well as injury to reputation, so there arguably is little reason to require proof of this kind of injury either. But these considerations do not support respondents' contention that damages should be presumed to flow from every deprivation of procedural due process.

First, it is not reasonable to assume that every departure from procedural due process, no matter what the circumstances or how minor, inherently is as likely to cause distress as the publication of defamation *per se* is to cause injury to reputation and distress. Where the deprivation of a protected interest is substantively justified but procedures are deficient in some respect, there may well be those who suffer no distress over the procedural irregularities. Indeed, in contrast to the immediately distressing effect of defamation *per se*, a person may not even know that procedures were deficient until he enlists the aid of counsel to challenge a perceived substantive deprivation.

Moreover, where a deprivation is justified but procedures are deficient, whatever distress a person feels may be attributable to the justified deprivation rather than to deficiencies in procedure. But as the Court of Appeals held, the injury caused by a justified deprivation, including distress, is not properly compensable under § 1983. This ambiguity in causation, which is absent in the case of defamation *per se*, provides additional need for requiring the plaintiff to convince the trier of fact that he actually suffered distress because of the denial of procedural due process.

Finally, we foresee no particular difficulty in producing evidence that mental and emotional distress actually was caused by the denial of procedural due process itself. Distress is a personal injury familiar to the law, customarily proved by showing the nature and circumstances of the wrong and its effect on the plaintiff. In sum, then, although mental and emotional distress caused by the denial of procedural due process itself is compensable under § 1983, we hold that neither the likelihood of such injury nor the difficulty of proving it is so great as to justify awarding compensatory damages without proof that such injury actually was caused . . .

Even if respondents' suspensions were justified, and even if they did not suffer any other actual injury, the fact remains that they were deprived of their right to procedural due process. . . .

Common-law courts traditionally have vindicated deprivations of certain "absolute" rights that are not shown to have caused actual injury through the award of a nominal sum of money. By making the deprivation of such rights actionable for nominal damages without proof of actual injury, the law recognizes the importance to organized society that those rights be scrupulously observed; but at the same time, it remains true to the principle that substantial damages should be awarded only to compensate actual injury or, in the case of exemplary or punitive damages, to deter or punish malicious deprivations of rights.

Because the right to procedural due process is "absolute" in the sense that it does not depend upon the merits of a claimant's substantive assertions and because of the importance to organized society that procedural due process be observed, we believe that the denial of procedural due process should be actionable for nominal damages without proof of actual injury. We therefore hold that if, upon remand, the District Court determines that respondents' suspensions were justified, respondents nevertheless will be entitled to recover nominal damages not to exceed one dollar from petitioners. . . .

Notes

1. The trespassory torts at common law seem to have generated recoveries for substantial, nonpunitive damages, that is, damages greater than the nominal damages recognized in *Carey*. In many of these cases substantial damages may have reflected a recovery for mental distress, but if so, the damages were allowed without any actual proof of such distress.

2. Did Justice Powell reject the idea that constitutional rights of due process were inherently valuable? It might be plausible to say that due process is only a means to an end and hence not a right that has value to the plaintiff apart from the good that due process could produce. So you might think that *Carey* does not necessarily limit damages for violation of a *substantive* constitutional right. What if the plaintiff's home is unconstitutionally searched?

3. After *Carey* the Court decided *Memphis Community School Dist. v. Stachura*, 477 U.S. 299, 106 S.Ct. 2537, 91 L.Ed.2d 249 (1986) where the plaintiff sued for violation of his substantive rights of free speech. The Court once again limited the damages recovery. However, *Stachura* may not be so broad a holding as it seems. The trial judge in that case told the jury in essence to value the plaintiff's free speech rights according to the jury's "subjective perception of the importance of constitutional rights as an abstract matter." Perhaps the Court in disapproving that instruction left room for permitting general damages for violation of a substantive right under a more carefully crafted standard.

4. On these ideas and others about the damages limitation, see Jean C. Love, *Presumed General Compensatory Damages in a Constitutional Tort Litigation: A Corrective Justice Perspective*, 49 WASH. & LEE L. REV. 67 (1992); 2 DAN DOBBS, THE LAW OF REMEDIES § 7.4 (2d ed. 1993).

5. *Limits on procedural due process.* To determine what process is constitutionally due, the Court typically balances three factors: (1) the private interest that will be affected by the official action; (2) the risk of an erroneous deprivation of that interest and the probable value of additional procedural safeguards; and (3) the government's interest. See *Mathews v. Eldridge*, 424 U.S. 319, 96 S.Ct. 893, 47 L.Ed.2d 18 (1976). Applying these principles, the Court in *Gilbert v. Homar*, 520 U.S. 924, 117 S.Ct. 1807, 138 L.Ed.2d 120 (1997), held that a state university policeman who was arrested in a drug raid and charged with a felony was not entitled to notice or a hearing before being suspended without pay. However, the Court thought that not granting him a post-suspension hearing for two weeks after the charges had been dropped may have violated his due process rights, and remanded for consideration of that issue.

6. Are there common law process rights? It has been suggested that in some common law claims, notions analogous to due process have some weight, even when government officials are not the defendants. The store detective who refuses to listen to the customer's side of the story but insists upon an immediate arrest for suspected shoplifting may be held liable for malicious prosecution partly because of the court's feeling that the denial of even a rudimentary chance to explain is, like denial of formal due process in more formal settings, fundamentally unfair.

§ 3. DISCRIMINATION

Discrimination is an inherently difficult subject. Some discrimination—that is, distinctions between persons—is permissible, as where an employer discriminates between a skilled employee and one who is not by promoting the former. Some discrimination is not permissible, as where states provide inferior educational opportunities for minorities. In clear cases like these, we hardly need legal rules to assist us in reaching a decision. In the difficult cases we may find ourselves at a loss to know what the rules are, or what kind of proof may be adduced to show discrimination. What is to be done about an employer's rule that automatically fires anyone who misses more than two days of work? On its face, the rule does not discriminate against anyone; in practice, it works more harshly against pregnant single mothers than anyone else. Is this an unacceptable discrimination?

The inherent difficulties of formulating clear ideas about discrimination and of proving it are complicated by the structure of laws on the subject. The Congress has acted at various times in history, chiefly in the Reconstruction period following the Civil War and again in 1964, with several additional statutes since that time. The statutes have never been correlated, either as to principle, subject matter, procedure, or remedy. The result is that they overlap and invite numerous disputes and strategic moves by lawyers. For instance, under some statutes there is a jury trial, but not under others. In some cases, enforcement is left to public authorities, or is limited to injunctive relief. In others private plaintiffs may recover damages. Damages may include punitive damages or pain and suffering under some statutes, but not under others. Attorneys' fees often may be awarded to the prevailing plaintiff, but this is not always so. In addition to this confusion, the Congress has often omitted to provide even the most elementary guidance, as for example whether intent to discriminate is an element of the plaintiff's claim.

It is not even easy to list the major federal statutes, but some of the important ones include these topics:

(1) *Employment discrimination.* Title VII of the 1964 civil rights act, 42 U.S.C.A. § 2000e, prohibits discrimination in employment based on gender, race, religion or national origin. Employers may not discriminate in hiring, discharging, or in job benefits. Other employment discrimination statutes include statutes against age discrimination, those protecting civil service employees, and those forbidding discrimination against whistleblowers. Under Title VII, the would-be plaintiff must first submit

the claim to a government agency, the Equal Employment Opportunity Commission. The EEOC may pursue the claim, but more likely will simply allow the plaintiff to do so in a private suit. Until the 1991 Civil Rights Act was passed, the remedies were the remedies for an economic tort and were designed to give victims a right of full economic participation. So victims of job discrimination could force the employer to hire or retain them, or to give appropriate promotions, together with appropriate back pay. But they could not have emotional distress or punitive damages. In the 1991 Civil Rights Act, a limited recovery for distress and a limited recovery for punitive damages was permitted for the first time. The prevailing plaintiff can recover a reasonable attorney fee in addition to remedies on the merits.

(2) *Denial of equal protection or discrimination under color of law.* We saw early in the course that constitutional and other federal rights are protected under 42 U.S.C.A. § 1983. Since the Constitution does not in itself forbid discrimination as such by purely private actors, § 1983 is used mainly in suits against officers or local governments. But that use includes the possibility of suing for a denial of equal protection of the laws, as where, for example, a municipality discriminates against African Americans in employment.

(3) *Discrimination against the disabled; the Americans with Disabilities Act.* The Americans with Disabilities Act prohibits job discrimination against those with disabilities as defined in the act. It also requires public accommodations for the disabled. It incorporates the procedures and remedies of Title VII. In the main, the statute provides that "No covered entity shall discriminate against a qualified individual with a disability because of the disability of such individual in regard to job application procedures, the hiring, advancement, or discharge of employees, employee compensation, job training, and other terms, conditions, and privileges of employment." A qualified individual with a disability is "an individual with a disability who, with or without reasonable accommodation, can perform the essential functions of the employment position that such individual holds or desires."

A few other statutes affecting discrimination of one kind or another are listed in a footnote.[1] The topic of discrimination is so large that even

---

1. (1) *Equal rights to contract and sue,* 42 U.S.C.A. § 1981. This statute may at times supplement other statutes in rather surprising ways.

(2) *Property rights.* All citizens shall have the same right to own, buy and sell property. 42 U.S.C.A § 1982. This statute, too, may affect private parties.

(3) *Voting rights.* These are protected by a number of provisions. See 42 U.S.C.A. §§ 19–71 et seq.

(4) *Public accommodations.* Places of public accommodation (such as restaurants, hotels, theaters) are prohibited from dis-

crimination. Public facilities are similarly covered in 42 U.S.C.A. § 2000–a.

(5) *Education and federally assisted programs.* Discrimination in education is forbidden under 42 U.S.C.A. § 2000–c. Similarly, discrimination is forbidden in any program that receives federal financial assistance. 42 U.S.C.A. § 2000–d.

(6) *Fair housing.* This is covered principally by 42 U.S.C.A. §§ 3601 et seq., but again older statutes may be important. See 42 U.S.C.A. § 1982.

(7) *Handicapped persons.* In addition to the Americans with Disabilities Act, a variety of statutes have attacked the problems

specialized courses such as employment law usually deal with only fragments of it. What follows is an illustration of a discrimination problem, but by no means an adequate sample of the range of cases.

INTERNATIONAL UNION, UNITED AUTOMOBILE, AEROSPACE AND AGRICULTURAL IMPLEMENT WORKERS OF AMERICA, UAW v. JOHNSON CONTROLS, INC.

United States Supreme Court, 1991.
499 U.S. 187, 111 S.Ct. 1196, 113 L.Ed.2d 158.

JUSTICE BLACKMUN delivered the opinion of the Court.

In this case we are concerned with an employer's gender-based fetal-protection policy. May an employer exclude a fertile female employee from certain jobs because of its concern for the health of the fetus the woman might conceive?

Respondent Johnson Controls, Inc., manufactures batteries. In the manufacturing process, the element lead is a primary ingredient. Occupational exposure to lead entails health risks, including the risk of harm to any fetus carried by a female employee.

... Between 1979 and 1983, eight employees became pregnant while maintaining blood lead levels in excess of 30 micrograms per deciliter. This appeared to be the critical level noted by the Occupational Health and Safety Administration (OSHA) for a worker who was planning to have a family. The company responded by announcing a broad exclusion of women from jobs that exposed them to lead: " ... [I]t is [Johnson Controls'] policy that women who are pregnant or who are capable of bearing children will not be placed into jobs involving lead exposure or which could expose them to lead through the exercise of job bidding, bumping, transfer or promotion rights." The policy defined "women.... capable of bearing children" as "[a]ll women except those whose inability to bear children is medically documented." It further stated that an unacceptable work station was one where, "over the past year," an employee had recorded a blood lead level of more than 30 micrograms per deciliter or the work site had yielded an air sample containing a lead level in excess of 30 micrograms per cubic meter.

In April 1984, petitioners filed in the United States District Court for the Eastern District of Wisconsin a class action challenging Johnson Controls' fetal-protection policy as sex discrimination that violated Title VII of the Civil Rights Act of 1964, as amended, 42 U.S.C. § 2000e et seq. Among the individual plaintiffs were petitioners Mary Craig, who had chosen to be sterilized in order to avoid losing her job, Elsie Nason, a 50–year-old divorcee, who had suffered a loss in compensation when

of the handicapped. As in other cases, the statutes may make financial provisions and offer a variety of non-tort remedies. One statute of special interest, though it is only one of several affecting handicapped, is the Education for All Handicapped Children Act, 20 U.S.C.A. §§ 1401 et seq. Another is the Rehabilitation Act, which prohibits discrimination by federal employers and federal contractors. 29 U.S.C.A. § 701.

she was transferred out of a job where she was exposed to lead, and Donald Penney, who had been denied a request for a leave of absence for the purpose of lowering his lead level because he intended to become a father. Upon stipulation of the parties, the District Court certified a class consisting of "all past, present and future production and maintenance employees" in United Auto Workers bargaining units at nine of Johnson Controls' plants "who have been and continue to be affected by [the employer's] Fetal Protection Policy implemented in 1982."

The District Court granted summary judgment for defendant-respondent Johnson Controls.

The Court of Appeals for the Seventh Circuit, sitting en banc, affirmed the summary judgment by a 7–to–4 vote. The majority held that the proper standard for evaluating the fetal-protection policy was the defense of business necessity; that Johnson Controls was entitled to summary judgment under that defense; and that even if the proper standard was a BFOQ [Bona Fide Occupational Qualification], Johnson Controls still was entitled to summary judgment. . . .

Applying this business necessity defense, the Court of Appeals ruled that Johnson Controls should prevail. Specifically, the court concluded that there was no genuine issue of material fact about the substantial health-risk factor because the parties agreed that there was a substantial risk to a fetus from lead exposure. The Court of Appeals also concluded that, unlike the evidence of risk to the fetus from the mother's exposure, the evidence of risk from the father's exposure, which petitioners presented, "is, at best, speculative and unconvincing." Finally, the court found that petitioners had waived the issue of less discriminatory alternatives by not adequately presenting it. It said that, in any event, petitioners had not produced evidence of less discriminatory alternatives in the District Court.

Having concluded that the business necessity defense was the appropriate framework and that Johnson Controls satisfied that standard, the court proceeded to discuss the BFOQ defense and concluded that Johnson Controls met that test, too. . . .

The bias in Johnson Controls' policy is obvious. Fertile men, but not fertile women, are given a choice as to whether they wish to risk their reproductive health for a particular job. Section 703(a) of the Civil Rights Act of 1964, 78 Stat. 255, as amended, 42 U.S.C. § 2000e–2(a), prohibits sex-based classifications in terms and conditions of employment, in hiring and discharging decisions, and in other employment decisions that adversely affect an employee's status. Respondent's fetal-protection policy explicitly discriminates against women on the basis of their sex. The policy excludes women with childbearing capacity from lead-exposed jobs and so creates a facial classification based on gender. Respondent assumes as much in its brief before this Court.

[The Court held that this was not a case of a neutral standard which merely happened to have discriminatory effects. If it had been neutral, the defendant could have raised the business necessity defense, which is more favorable to the defendant than the BFOQ defense. The discriminatory policy here was not neutral even if it was arguably benign. "Whether an employment practice involves disparate treatment through explicit facial discrimination does not depend on why the employer discriminates but rather on the explicit terms of the discrimination." Johnson Controls' policy "does not pass the simple test of whether the evidence shows treatment of a person in a manner which but for that person's sex would be different." This conclusion led the Court to disregard the business necessity defense and to consider the BFOQ defense instead.]

Under § 703(e)(1) of Title VII, an employer may discriminate on the basis of "religion, sex, or national origin in those certain instances where religion, sex, or national origin is a bona fide occupational qualification reasonably necessary to the normal operation of that particular business or enterprise." 42 U.S.C. § 2000e–2(e)(1). We therefore turn to the question whether Johnson Controls' fetal-protection policy is one of those "certain instances" that come within the BFOQ exception.

The BFOQ defense is written narrowly, and this Court has read it narrowly. . . .

The wording of the BFOQ defense contains several terms of restriction that indicate that the exception reaches only special situations. The statute thus limits the situations in which discrimination is permissible to "certain instances" where sex discrimination is "reasonably necessary" to the "normal operation" of the "particular" business. Each one of these terms—certain, normal, particular—prevents the use of general subjective standards and favors an objective, verifiable requirement. But the most telling term is "occupational"; this indicates that these objective, verifiable requirements must concern job-related skills and aptitudes. . . .

Johnson Controls argues that its fetal-protection policy falls within the so-called safety exception to the BFOQ. Our cases have stressed that discrimination on the basis of sex because of safety concerns is allowed only in narrow circumstances. . . . [A]lthough we considered the safety of third parties in Dothard and Criswell, those third parties were indispensable to the particular business at issue. We stressed that in order to qualify as a BFOQ, a job qualification must relate to the "essence," . . . or to the "central mission of the employer's business."

Our case law, therefore, makes clear that the safety exception is limited to instances in which sex or pregnancy actually interferes with the employee's ability to perform the job. This approach is consistent with the language of the BFOQ provision itself, for it suggests that permissible distinctions based on sex must relate to ability to perform the duties of the job. Johnson Controls suggests, however, that we expand the exception to allow fetal-protection policies that mandate particular standards for pregnant or fertile women. We decline to do so. Such an expansion contradicts not only the language of the BFOQ and the narrowness of its exception but the plain language and history of the Pregnancy Discrimination Act. . . .

With the PDA, Congress made clear that the decision to become pregnant or to work while being either pregnant or capable of becoming pregnant was reserved for each individual woman to make for herself.

We conclude that the language of both the BFOQ provision and the PDA which amended it, as well as the legislative history and the case law, prohibit an employer from discriminating against a woman because of her capacity to become pregnant unless her reproductive potential prevents her from performing the duties of her job. We reiterate our holdings in Criswell and Dothard that an employer must direct its concerns about a woman's ability to perform her job safely and efficiently to those aspects of the woman's job-related activities that fall within the "essence" of the particular business.

We have no difficulty concluding that Johnson Controls cannot establish a BFOQ. Fertile women, as far as appears in the record, participate in the manufacture of batteries as efficiently as anyone else. Johnson Controls' professed moral and ethical concerns about the welfare of the next generation do not suffice to establish a BFOQ of female sterility. Decisions about the welfare of future children must be left to the parents who conceive, bear, support, and raise them rather than to the employers who hire those parents. Congress has mandated this choice through Title VII, as amended by the Pregnancy Discrimination Act. Johnson Controls has attempted to exclude women because of their reproductive capacity. Title VII and the PDA simply do not allow a woman's dismissal because of her failure to submit to sterilization. . . .

A word about tort liability and the increased cost of fertile women in the workplace is perhaps necessary. One of the dissenting judges in this case expressed concern about an employer's tort liability and concluded that liability for a potential injury to a fetus is a social cost that Title VII does not require a company to ignore. It is correct to say that Title VII does not prevent the employer from having a conscience. The statute, however, does prevent sex-specific fetal-protection policies. These two aspects of Title VII do not conflict.

More than 40 states currently recognize a right to recover for a prenatal injury based either on negligence or on wrongful death. According to Johnson Controls, however, the company complies with the lead standard developed by OSHA and warns its female employees about the damaging effects of lead. It is worth noting that OSHA gave the problem of lead lengthy consideration and concluded that "there is no basis whatsoever for the claim that women of childbearing age should be excluded from the workplace in order to protect the fetus or the course of pregnancy." Instead, OSHA established a series of mandatory protections which, taken together, "should effectively minimize any risk to the fetus and newborn child." Without negligence, it would be difficult for a court to find liability on the part of the employer. If, under general tort principles, Title VII bans sex-specific fetal-protection policies, the employer fully informs the woman of the risk, and the employer has not acted negligently, the basis for holding an employer liable seems remote at best.

Although the issue is not before us, the concurrence observes that "it is far from clear that compliance with Title VII will preempt state tort liability." The cases relied upon by the concurrence to support its prediction, however, are inapposite. . . .

If state tort law furthers discrimination in the workplace and prevents employers from hiring women who are capable of manufacturing the product as efficiently as men, then it will impede the accomplishment of Congress' goals in enacting Title VII. Because Johnson Controls has not argued that it faces any costs from tort liability, not to mention crippling ones, the pre-emption question is not before us. We therefore say no more than that the concurrence's speculation appears unfounded as well as premature.

The tort-liability argument reduces to two equally unpersuasive propositions. First, Johnson Controls attempts to solve the problem of reproductive health hazards by resorting to an exclusionary policy. Title VII plainly forbids illegal sex discrimination as a method of diverting attention from an employer's obligation to police the workplace. Second, the spectre of an award of damages reflects a fear that hiring fertile women will cost more. The extra cost of employing members of one sex, however, does not provide an affirmative Title VII defense for a discriminatory refusal to hire members of that gender. . . .

We, of course, are not presented with, nor do we decide, a case in which costs would be so prohibitive as to threaten the survival of the employer's business. We merely reiterate our prior holdings that the incremental cost of hiring women cannot justify discriminating against them. . . .

The judgment of the Court of Appeals is reversed and the case is remanded for further proceedings consistent with this opinion.

It is so ordered.

[JUSTICE WHITE, with whom the CHIEF JUSTICE and JUSTICE KENNEDY join, concurred in part and concurred in the judgment.]

Notes

1. Does this case render employers powerless to exclude pregnant women from dangerous jobs? Does it give employers a basis to argue that because they lack such power, they cannot be sued for in utero harm to the unborn caused by toxic on-the-job exposures? Cf. *Snyder v. Michael's Stores, Inc.*, 16 Cal.4th 991, 68 Cal.Rptr.2d 476, 945 P.2d 781 (1997) (allowing child's recovery against employer for in utero harm caused by mother's exposure to carbon monoxide on the job site). How can an employer avoid liability?

2. As *Johnson Controls* indicates, workplace discrimination based on gender is not limited to sexual harassment. Sexual harassment is itself a

form of discrimination, however, and statutes forbid such discrimination both in the workplace and elsewhere. Title IX, 20 U.S.C.A. § 1681, provides in part that "[n]o person in the United States shall, on the basis of sex, be excluded from participation in, be denied the benefits of, or be subjected to discrimination under any education program or activity receiving Federal financial assistance...." This statute has been understood by the Supreme Court to create an implied right of action.

3. In *Franklin v. Gwinnett County Public Schools*, 503 U.S. 60, 112 S.Ct. 1028, 117 L.Ed.2d 208 (1992) the complaint alleged in detail that a young woman in high school was repeatedly harassed by a "sports coach," that the school officials knew of it and not only did not put a stop to it but discouraged the student from doing anything about it. The trial court thought that even though the Supreme Court had recognized, a private right of action, the remedies did not include a suit for damages. The Supreme Court held otherwise. *Franklin* was construed in *Gebser v. Lago Vista Indep. School Dist.*, 524 U.S. 274, 118 S.Ct. 1989, 141 L.Ed.2d 277 (1998), a case in which a school district was sued for a teacher's sexual harassment of a student. The Court held, 5–4, that a private right of action for damages under Title IX is not available unless the school district had "actual notice" of the abuse and showed "deliberate indifference" to it. The Court carried forward this analysis in *Davis v. Monroe County Bd. of Educ.*, 526 U.S. 629, 119 S.Ct. 1661, 143 L.Ed.2d 839 (1999), holding that a private damages action under Title IX may lie against a school board for student-on-student harassment, but only where the board acts with deliberate indifference to known harassment that is so severe and pervasive that it effectively bars the victim's access to an educational benefit.

4. Gender differences in educational opportunities in public institutions represent another face of discrimination. See *United States v. Virginia*, 518 U.S. 515, 116 S.Ct. 2264, 135 L.Ed.2d 735 (1996) (Virginia unconstitutionally discriminated against women in providing an all-male military training institution).

5. *Same-sex harassment.* In *Oncale v. Sundowner Offshore Services*, 523 U.S. 75, 118 S.Ct. 998, 140 L.Ed.2d 201 (1998), a male worker on an oil rig complained of repeated "sex-related humiliating actions" by male co-workers. The Court held that such conduct violates Title VII, and is thus an actionable form of employment discrimination.

6. A very different form of "discrimination" occurs when a public employee in the exercise of free speech rights criticizes the public entity and is then discharged in retaliation. The same kind of discrimination can arise if a public entity refuses to do business with contractors who criticize the entity. In such cases, the entity is liable for interference with free speech rights. E.g., *Board of County Comn'rs, Wabaunsee County, Kansas v. Umbehr*, 518 U.S. 668, 116 S.Ct. 2342, 135 L.Ed.2d 843 (1996).

REFERENCE: DOBBS ON TORTS 275–78 (2000).

Index

References are to pages

The indexed topic may also appear in pages following the page reference

995

†